Women and Children as Victims and Offenders: Background, Prevention, Reintegration

Helmut Kury • Sławomir Redo • Evelyn Shea
Editors

Women and Children as Victims and Offenders: Background, Prevention, Reintegration

Suggestions for Succeeding Generations (Volume 1)

Springer

Editors
Helmut Kury
Heuweiler
Germany

Sławomir Redo
Faculty of Law
University of Vienna
Vienna
Austria

Evelyn Shea
Zürich
Switzerland

ISBN 978-3-319-08397-1 ISBN 978-3-319-08398-8 (eBook)
DOI 10.1007/978-3-319-08398-8

Library of Congress Control Number: 2016940501

Printed on acid-free paper

This Springer imprint is published by Springer Nature
The registered company is Springer International Publishing AG Switzerland

Foreword

This volume on "Women and Children as Victims and Offenders: Background, Prevention, Reintegration. Suggestions for Succeeding Generations" takes an interdisciplinary approach to the situation of women and children involved with the criminal justice system, placing a special emphasis on them as offenders and victims of crime.

Over past decades, the international community has adopted important standards to safeguard the rights of women and children who come into contact with the criminal justice system, including as victims and offenders. These include the right to access justice, to legal aid and assistance, to protection from unlawful or arbitrary detention, to social reintegration as well as to freedom from violence.

Unfortunately, the gap between these critical commitments and reality remains wide, compromising the rights of countless children and women around the world. Children and women involved with the criminal justice system remain surrounded by stigma, and their situation is seldom a priority on the national agenda. Awaiting trial for months or even years, denied access to legal aid, placed in overcrowded and unsuitable facilities and deprived of health services, education and vocational training, children and women are also often exposed to humiliating treatment by staff and at risk of harassment, torture, rape and abuse.

As a result of disturbing reports on serious violations of their rights, including human trafficking, sexual violence and homicide, the plight of women and children has gained increasing visibility on the domestic and international justice and security agenda. The urgency of safeguarding their fundamental rights and the need to identify and address the root causes leading to their exposure to violence have helped to generate increasing attention and action across regions. Yet, implementation on the ground remains a serious challenge.

This publication is designed to overcome this challenge and thus promote the effective realisation of the rights of children and women. Risk diagnoses, trust, fairness, justice and restorative justice approaches, the roles of the family, the education system and the media as well as the impact of urban planning in the life of girls are some of the important questions discussed in depth. Another important dimension considered is the implementation of the right to education from preschool to university level, and the attacks against schools that seriously compromise the opportunity to promote children's education and personal development and have been condemned in significant resolutions by the United Nations Security Council.

Taking into consideration intergenerational, intercultural and socio-economic perspectives, this multidisciplinary volume also discusses a wide range of other topics such as bioethics, the promotion of interfaith dialogue, the reintegration and rehabilitation of young offenders, the abolition of the death penalty, the need to counter online abuse of children and women as well as tackling corruption, in which women and children may have an as-yet unexplored preventive role.

As the Special Representative of the UN Secretary General on Violence against Children, I have urged Member States to spare no efforts in mobilising governmental departments, national institutions, civil society partners, faith-based organisations, communities and families at large to build nations free from violence. Violence against children is never justified and all violence against children can be effectively prevented. Strong political will, strategic alliances, sound knowledge and unshakable action can bring violence to an end. This volume makes a significant contribution to this goal and is a useful reminder of the values of the United Nations and its unwavering resolve to build peaceful societies and strong institutions, guided by human rights, committed to justice and fairness, and respectful of the dignity and worth of every person.

UN Special Representative of the
Secretary General on Violence
against Children
New York, NY, USA

Marta Santos Pais

Women and Children as Victims and Offenders: An Introduction

In criminological and public discussions, women and children are often seen as victims rather than as offenders—a view that has not much changed over time. In times of war and armed conflict, they still are the group that has to bear the most suffering: they are displaced, misused, raped and even killed.

It was the founding purpose of UNICEF in 1946, after the horrors of World War II, to protect children from the effects of war. This task is today as necessary as it was then.

The UNICEF Report 2015 ("Children between the Lines") documents this vividly: "We are currently experiencing one of the worst phases of conflicts since the end of World War II. UNICEF estimates that in 2014 about 230 million children grew up worldwide in war and crisis zones. Their everyday life is marked by violence and hatred – often for years ... Wars and armed conflicts have forced nearly 60 million people to leave their homes. More than half of these refugees and the internally displaced are women and children. They are particularly affected by the consequences of war, characterized by poor supply and lack of educational opportunities. Moreover, cases of serious violence have increased dramatically against boys and girls in the war" (p. 1). According to UNICEF one in ten children grows up in a country or region affected by crises and violent conflicts (UNICEF 2015).

Many children do not have adequate supplies of essentials, including food, water and medical assistance. Most are only able to attend school infrequently, if at all. "In the civil wars raging in Syria, Iraq, South Sudan and the Central African Republic children are also targets of the worst form of abuse" (ibid., p. 2). Groups such as ISIS in Syria and Iraq and Boko Haram in Nigeria blatantly disregard the principles of international humanitarian law. The UN Security Council lists for 2014 a total of 23 conflict situations in which children were exposed to serious human rights violations (UNICEF 2015). They were kidnapped, abused as sex slaves or child soldiers or sent to death as suicide bombers. In the first 7 months of 2015, UN officials reported 27 suicide bombings by Boko Haram. In at least three-quarters of the blast, the bombers were women or children (UNICEF 2015).

Why are young people attracted to terror organisations such as IS, even to the extent to give their lives? UNICEF gives the following answer: "The cynical use and display of children as victims makes them an object of political propaganda ... Ideologies like those propagated by IS promise adventure, social inclusion and the feeling to be able to get past the limitations imposed on young people in their everyday life. They make the youngsters feel important, make them believe that they can influence world events and impose their ideas on the whole world" (UNICEF Report 2015, p. 4).

Phenomena such as IS make it clear "that general humanitarian principles are not automatically part of human traditions. They will never be because in times of war they are contrary to many primary instincts. The only way to entrench humanitarian values in the mind of each person – as a civilian, potential fighter, actual combatant or policy maker – is education" (ibid., p. 5).

According to UNICEF, in 2015 more than 62 million children in conflict areas will urgently need food, clean water, medical aid, the possibility to continue their education and protection from exploitation and violence. The realisation of the post-2015 UN sustainable development goals will depend to a large extent on whether we succeed in caring for and protecting children in such situations.

In its "Core Commitments for Children in Humanitarian Action", UNICEF spelled out its main obligations to children in war situations: providing life-saving measures for pregnant women, newborns and children; facilitating school attendance even in emergency situations; help in searching for dispersed family members; and care for victims (UNICEF Report 2015, p. 6). As far as the creation of a durable peace is concerned, UNICEF gives children and adolescents a major role as "natural agents of change", and mediators between the generations. There shall be no more "lost generations", but instead all children shall have access to education and a better economic future. These are ambitious aims. Their realisation will need a greater commitment of wealthier nations and much work at persuasion. This work wants to make a small contribution.

As far as the situation of women is concerned, their equality in society has improved in many countries, but not to an extent that would allow us to speak of true gender equality (Kury and Obergfell-Fuchs 2005). It is not that long ago that the old legal tradition giving the husband dominion over his wife has been abolished in western countries, and it is still alive in many Muslim countries and other countries with a strong tribal tradition.

Recent research on women as victims presents the following picture (Lundgren et al. 2002; McGee et al. 2002; Medina and Barberet 2003; Müller and Schröttle 2004; Rodriguez Menés and Safranoff 2013): "The key findings include confirmation that violence against women is a universal phenomenon and occurs in every age and economic group although at different rates; there is indication that between 35 and 60 % of women in the surveyed countries have experienced violence by a man during their lifetime and that less than one third of women reported their experience of violence to the police (and where they do report, women are more likely to report stranger violence than intimate partner violence)" (Gelsthorpe and Larrauri 2014, p. 193). A study covering nine countries of the European Union concluded that in roughly 25 % of all sexual aggressions, the offenders were either partners or ex-partners of the victim and that in these cases the level of violence was higher (Burman et al. 2009; see also Gelsthorpe and Larrauri 2014, p. 194; Müller and Schröttle 2004).

Hester (2013, p. 634) demonstrated in her study that women are not only more frequently victims of domestic and partner violence, but that the victimisation is more serious and that if they retaliate, the courts treat them worse than the male offenders: "While cases were very varied, there were significant differences between male and female perpetrators of domestic violence in many respects. Men were the perpetrators in a much greater number of incidents; the violence used by men against female partners was much more severe than that used by women against men; violence by men was most likely to involve fear by and control of female victims; women were more likely to use weapons, often in order to protect themselves; and female perpetrators were more likely to be alcoholic, or mentally ill, although alcohol misuse by men had a greater impact on severity on outcomes. Despite these patterns, however, women were three times as likely to be arrested per incident, indicating gendered injustice in the approach. There was little evidence that cases involving dual perpetration might generally be categorised as 'mutual' and men were in the main the primary aggressors".

Not only women, but also children, become victims of domestic violence. As Levi and Maguire (2002, p. 818) point out, there are many reasons that may lead to child abuse, not the least the incessant crying of a baby. "Situational opportunity variables are also salient to baby battering; modern nuclear families are far more isolated than the extended families found in many Third World Countries, where parents are seldom alone in the house". But more than situational opportunities, it is societal factors such as unemployment, poverty or isolation that lead to problems in a family and may expose children to violent reactions from frustrated parent. The fault in such cases is usually attributed only to the offender and society feels no blame. If anything, it is up to "the politicians" to do something about it. Moser (1972, p. 289) says it clearly: "It is astonishing to what extent society gives these children time to develop into full-fledged delinquents. It hardly cares about them, as long as they are the victims. Only when society itself is victimized or at least can present itself as victim, does it decide to act. And then [they act] like neglected and immature parents that hit blindly when the crying and the pranks of their neglected children exasperated them, when the angry need to have peace becomes the main motive of their intervention".

The social cost of domestic violence is very high. In Finland, for instance, it has been estimated that the annual financial cost amounts to approximately 91 million euro (Heiskanen and Piispa 2002, p. 36; see also Walby 2004; Haller and Dawid 2006; Brzank 2009). Such cost are however difficult to estimate and we should not forget that the financial aspect is only one part of "social costs". Numerous studies have shown that "Children who are physically abused or neglected tend to become offenders later in life" (Farrington 2002, p. 674; see also the chapter by Farrington in volume 1; Widom 1989; Widom and Ames 1994). Already in 1951, Bowlby developed the theory that there is a strong connection between broken homes and delinquency (see also Farrington 2002, p. 675; McCord 1983).

Much of domestic violence remains hidden, as many women are reluctant to denounce their partners. In order to get some more precise figures of actual victimisations, victim studies include now specific questions on domestic violence (see, for instance, the British Crime Survey). Many countries have also introduced special legislation to protect women and children from domestic violence. According to Gelsthorpe and Larrauri (2014, p. 194): "European responses to IPV (Intimate Partner Violence) and domestic violence have revolved around civil or criminal protection orders in each country (http://ec.europa.eu/justice/fundamental-rights/document/index_en.htm as well as the Directive 2011/99/EU of the European Parliament and of the Council of 13 December 2011 on the European protection order); additionally all European countries have created new specific public offences or increased penalties, and domestic violence courts; and all have some form of victim support and protection mechanisms".

There is no doubt that there has been considerable progress, especially in the West, concerning equal rights for women and the protection of children, but much still needs to be done. As Gelsthorpe and Larrauri (2014, p. 198) put it: "There is still a need for wider recognition of violence against women (including attention to sub-cultural gender violence such as 'forced marriages', and to women in different structural positions, immigrant women, women with multiple social needs or disability, drugs or alcohol problems, for example). Additionally we need consistent monitoring and evaluation of changing policies in relation to domestic violence and sexual assault across countries, and attention to the high rates of attrition in regard to the prosecution of violence against women, for instance".

The growing increase of refugees fleeing from wars and persecutions creates new problems concerning their integration. Most come from different cultural backgrounds and bring with them traditions and attitudes that may be at odds with those of their host countries, especially their attitudes towards women and children as well as their perception of what constitutes legitimate violence. Stamatel, in her study of female homicide victimisation rates across Europe from 1985 to 2010, calculated time series over four time periods for 33 countries and came to the following conclusion (2014, p. 596): "Better economic conditions reduce female homicide victimization, as they do for violence more generally. Gender dynamics play a contradictory role: less traditional gender roles increase the risk of victimization, whereas improving the collective status of women in society reduces that risk. Most importantly, controlling for these known predictors of female homicide victimization, the historical legacies and socio-historical contexts of nations matter greatly for explaining variation across Europe".

When women turn to offending, they do so considerable less often than men. In his international comparison of crime rates, Heidensohn (2002, p. 496) underlines that "such differences [in crime rates] seem to be common across a variety of nations and cultures. In surveying material on Europe, I found that crime is still an activity overwhelmingly dominated by men in all European countries" (see also Heidensohn and Farrell 1991). The same is true for countries such as Brasil or India

(Lemgruber 2001; Patkar 2001). The author continues (Heidensohn 2002, p. 496): "This apparently consistent pattern has led some commentators to suggest that women offenders are 'only 10 % of the trouble'. Considering different types of offences and changes over time, a more complex and qualified picture emerges. Women contribute to all types of offending, but their share varies considerably". Austin gives a similar assessment of the situation in the United States (2003, p. 560): "I have calculated that if the males behaved like females, violent crime rates would drop by 2/3 and the 2 million people in the prison and jail population would not exceed 200,000. The associated costs of a 112 billion dollar criminal justice system would shrink to less than 20 billion dollars".

Some authors claim however that the situation is changing: female crime rates are rising faster than those of males, and the gap is narrowing. Adler (1975) commented already in the 1970s on this rise and explained it with a change in female behaviour: women, according to him, have become more aggressive and violent, and therefore their offending resembles increasingly that of their male counterparts. Responsible for this change, in Adler's view, is primarily the strengthening of the women's movement and the greater freedom women enjoy today. But the topic remains controversial. Heidensohn puts it as follows: "Arguments about whether female crime was rising at a faster rate than male, and that thus the female share was going up, have been a highly contended criminological issue since the 1970s. Indeed, this is one of the few topics to do with women and crime to excite widespread attention" (Heidensohn 2002, p. 496).

Gelsthorpe and Larrauri (2014, p. 188) refer to another important aspect: "At the beginning of the twenty-first century new crimes and concerns have emerged: terrorism, cyber-crime, human trafficking and other human rights violations for instance, all of which have produced new ways of women being involved in crime as offenders, or as victims". The authors underline further (p. 188): "Women certainly have a much higher profile than they once did, but it can still be argued that there is a general neglect of women in relation to crime and criminal justice". Even if we have more information about crime than ever before, there are still very few empirical studies on gender-related differences and their causes. Crime is still seen as a "male domain".

The situation of women in prison was also for many years a neglected theme in criminology—their number was too small to be noteworthy. Whereas the number of rehabilitation programmes for male offenders was increasing, it didn't seem "worthwhile" to elaborate such programmes for the small number of female prisoners. Only recently more attention has been paid to the collateral damage of female imprisonment, for instance, on children, and the special victimisation risks women are exposed to in prison.

The percentage of female inmates is relatively low: only 4–5 % of the total number of inmates, with little variations between countries. Most of them fit exactly into the category described by Moser (1972, p. 291) already 40 years ago: "Most misfits, in particular those who are locked up, belong to those minorities, who cannot speak for themselves, who have no public voice, can't organise themselves, and can't defend their interests. They depend on an enlightened public that pit their fate, and not just their actual fate but their whole life against the ideal – so dear to society – of the right of each person to personal development; the public will then have to ponder if the kind of punishment meted out today is a just reward for their deeds or if it is not rather help that should be given greater importance".[1] The role of proper public information in this context cannot be underestimated and is a focal concern of this work.

In the quest to improve the plight of women and children, the United Nations has played a most important role. After the horrors of two world wars in the twentieth century, it has made an invaluable contribution to pave the way for a durable peace. The goal, admittedly difficult to reach, is already clearly set out in the Preamble of its foundational Treaty of 1945[2]: "We the Peoples of the United Nations are determined to save succeeding generations from the scourge of war, which twice in our lifetime has brought untold sorrow to mankind"...and "to unite our strength to maintain international peace and security" (1 UNTS 16). Women and children (girls and boys)—now roughly half of the present world's population—determine any "succeeding generation".

The concept of "generations" was formulated in the beginning of the twentieth century (Nora 1997, p. 2992). Combined with the UN Charter's Preamble term "succeeding", it means parents, children and grandchildren succeed each other at more or less regular intervals (Suleiman 2002, p. 278).[3] It is for the "succeeding generations" that the Charter calls for the promotion of "social progress and better standards of life in larger freedom", including full employment, and conditions of economic and social progress and development (art. 55).

This two-volume book responds to this call by focusing on the intergenerational, international and intercultural transmission of values through learning. Yet the main focus of the book is on justice issues with global commonalities. The work blends academic with UN considerations, findings and recommendations on justice. A common thread is the prevention of crime/delinquency and victimisation of women and children. The most glaring form of crime and delinquency is violence. As repeatedly emphasised by the UN leadership, violence against women and children must be countered effectively. Ban Ki-moon, the present Secretary-General has appealed to "break the silence" concerning violence against women,[4] and also the UN Special Representative of the Secretary-General on Violence against Children has underscored that "violence against children is never justified

[1] Free translation by Evelyn Shea.

[2] The Charter of the United Nations was signed in San Francisco, California, on 26 June 1945, by 50 of the 51 original member countries.

[3] It is this a broader context in which the concept of "1.5 generation" originally emerged: of child survivors of the Holocaust "too young to have had an adult understanding of what was happening to them but old enough to have been there during the Nazi persecution of Jews" (Suleiman 2002, p. 277).

[4] http://www.un.org/en/women/endviolence/about.shtml.

and all violence against children can be effectively prevented. With strong political will, wide mobilization and steady action, it can be brought to an end".[5]

While the emphasis on physical component of violence is understandable, violence against children can also be "mental" (art. 19 of the Convention on the Rights of the Child, 1577 UNTS 3). However improper and detrimental, this or that form of violence may be for the future conduct of a child, let us not forget that child's conduct can also be mishandled in many other forms. From a criminological perspective, subtly manipulating child's sense of trust, disorienting a child about his/her entitlements, mishandling mental anguish or facilitating emotional deprivations is likewise important for crime prevention. This work caters also to this broader crime prevention function and vision.

The UN has joined that vision 45 years after the Second World War (1939–1945), when the concept of "succeeding generations" (up to that point faintly related to war prevention) did receive some more attention. In 1990 "The United Nations Guidelines for the Prevention of Juvenile Delinquency" ("The Riyadh Guidelines", A/RES/45/112) emphasised in paragraph 15 the socialisation function of family in the prevention of delinquency: "Special attention should be given to children of families affected by problems brought about by rapid and uneven economic, social and cultural change, in particular the children of indigenous, migrant and refugee families. As such changes may disrupt the social capacity of the family to secure the traditional rearing and nurturing of children, often as a result of role and culture conflict, innovative and socially constructive modalities, for the socialization of children have to be designed".

Ten years later, in the "Guidelines for the prevention of urban crime", the UN Economic and Social Council (ECOSOC) explicitly recommended Member States to "Consider the relevance to the crime prevention action plan of such factors as . . . relationships in the family, between generations or between social groups etc." (ECOSOC resolution 1995/9). Finally, in 2002, the Council adopted the "Guidelines for the Prevention of Crime" (ECOSOC resolution 2002/13). They emphasise how crime prevention action should be developed, with a focus on local communities, where crime is experienced, as well as those with high needs, and that it be conducted through partnerships across government sectors and with civil society and the participation of communities, that it be sustained and accountable, rather than short term, and be based on sound evidence-based practice.

A set of eight basic principles is involved for pursuing these approaches (articles 7–14 in the Guidelines):

1. *Government leadership*: All levels of government should play a leadership role in developing effective and humane crime prevention strategies and in creating and maintaining institutional frameworks for their implementation and review.
2. *Socio-economic development and inclusion*: Crime prevention considerations should be integrated into all relevant social and economic policies and

---

[5] Political will, 'steady action' can end violence against children, UN envoy tells Indonesia, www.un.org/apps/news/story.asp?NewsID=50207.

programmes, including those addressing employment, education, health, housing and urban planning, poverty, social marginalisation and exclusion. Particular emphasis should be placed on communities, families, children and youth at risk.
3. *Cooperation/partnerships*: Cooperation/partnerships should be an integral part of effective crime prevention, given the wide-ranging nature of the causes of crime and the skills and responsibilities required to address them. This includes partnerships working across ministries and between authorities, community organisations, non-governmental organisations, the business sector and private citizens.
4. *Sustainability/accountability*: Crime prevention requires adequate resources, including funding for structures and activities, in order to be sustained. There should be clear accountability for funding, implementation and evaluation and for the achievement of planned results.
5. *Knowledge base*: Crime prevention strategies, policies, programmes and actions should be based on a broad, multidisciplinary foundation of knowledge about crime problems, their multiple causes and promising and proven practices.
6. *Human rights/rule of law/culture of lawfulness*: The rule of law and those human rights which are recognised in international instruments to which Member States are parties must be respected in all aspects of crime prevention. A culture of lawfulness should be actively promoted in crime prevention.
7. *Interdependency*: National crime prevention diagnoses and strategies should, where appropriate, take account of links between local criminal problems and international organised crime.
8. *Differentiation*: Crime prevention strategies should, when appropriate, pay due regard to the different needs of men and women and consider the special needs of vulnerable members of society.

All these UN guidelines adopted for women and children as one of the vulnerable groups with special crime prevention needs are summarised in the subsequent UN handbook, as follows: "In essence, the principles laid out in the 2002 and the 1995 guidelines, establish the normative basis with the importance of the rule of law and respect for human rights, of the social and economic inclusion of populations, whatever their status and background, and the importance of ensuring that the particular needs of vulnerable minorities, as well as gender differences, are taken into account" (UN Handbook 2010, p. 23).

On balance, in the 70 years since the founding of the United Nations, it has paid more attention to "succeeding generations" in its ideology than in its legal instruments. The specific crime prevention needs of women and children, as the succeeding generation, are only nominally addressed. Generally, so far, the balance of the UN's mandate and functions involving "prevention" and "control" has remained negative, not only regarding the needs of "succeeding generations" pointed out above but also demographically and politically—despite the proclamation of the UN Secretary-General that "prevention is the first imperative of justice" (S/2004/616, para. 4). Notwithstanding this imbalance, academic and UN criminology studies have accumulated and reviewed evidence for diagnosing and countering crime not only for the current but also for the succeeding generation. The goal of this work is to widen this perspective.

Before presenting the individual chapters, it may be helpful to clarify the concept of "succeeding generations": First, on a demographical note, the expected lifespan of the present generation is, globally, over 67 years (over 65 for males and 70 for females). In 1945, at the time of the creation of the UN, the expectancy was five years shorter (ST/ESA/SER.A/313). In years 2045–2050 it should increase to 74 years (Cohen 2003, p. 1173). Of course, between one and the other generation, there are overlapping generations, and within one generation, there are smaller decimal-point generations. They may be differently (sub-)divided and named. However, certainly the division between "Generation-C" ("connect, communicate, change") or "Digitally Native" generation (Palfrey et al. 2009; Matvyshyn 2012, p. 1979) and others is worth mentioning, because of the fundamentally different childhood than that of their parents, hence different attitudes to law and ensuing effects (violation and victimisation).

Second, in this work, "education" is a broad term. It "comprise[s] all deliberate and systematic activities designed to meet learning needs [and] involve[s] organized and sustained communication designed to bring about learning" (UNESCO 1997). It includes formal (preschool, primary, secondary, tertiary) and non-formal, i.e. outside the formal education system[6]—both mutually complimentary and necessary for a socio-economic development and the implementation of the right to education (Hausler et al. 2012, pp. 72–77).

Third, education is negatively correlated with women's fertility—"a uniquely universal negative relation between female education and fertility" (Basu 2002, p. 1779)—and positively correlated with infants' health (Krueger and Lindhal 2001, p. 1107). In turn, girls born into smaller families are more likely to be sent to school and to complete more years of education (Basu 2002, p. 1788). This, coupled with the fact that already more than half of the world population experiences fertility rates below the replacement level of two surviving children per woman (exactly 2.1 by a conventional estimate, Wilson 2004), begs the question of the sustainability of our present culture. In particular, as far as the topic of this work is concerned, it begs the question of the sustainability of a culture of lawfulness. This axiologically Western concept—the culture of lawfulness—(Redo 2014) nominally entered the UN crime prevention agenda through the 2002 Guidelines. Only very recently the Declaration of the Thirteenth UN Congress on Crime Prevention and Criminal Justice (Doha, Qatar, 2015) made it a fully-fledged UN concept (A/CONF.222/L.6) with emphasis on education for all children and youth, including the eradication of illiteracy. Education and the eradication of illiteracy are both fundamental to the prevention of crime and corruption and to the promotion of a culture of lawfulness that supports the rule of law and human rights

[6] Education provided through nursing, kindergarten care, human rights training sessions, workshops, seminars and webinars is a non-formal education. Informal education is acquired through other life and work experience.

while respecting cultural identities. Finally, the Declaration stressed the fundamental role of youth participation in crime prevention efforts.

In 1992, in paragraph 21 of the Rio Declaration, Member States of the UN urged that "The creativity, ideals and courage of the youth of the world should be mobilized to forge a global partnership in order to achieve sustainable development and ensure a better future for all" (A/CONF.151/26: Vol. I). But only now, with the forthcoming Rio+20 post-2015 UN sustainable development goals, particularly "Goal 4. Ensure inclusive and equitable quality education and promote lifelong learning opportunities for all" (A/68/970), the organisation took a comprehensive and incisive look into the role of culture in sustainable development. We read there, that by 2030, Member States and other stakeholders should "ensure that all learners acquire the knowledge and skills needed to promote sustainable development, including, among others, through education for sustainable development and sustainable lifestyles, human rights, gender equality, promotion of a culture of peace and non-violence, global citizenship and appreciation of cultural diversity and of culture's contribution to sustainable development" (ibid., p. 13/24).[7]

Fourth, it follows that non-violence is a recognised element of any legal culture. And so is anti-corruption about which the framers of the UN post-2015 sustainable development agenda speak as a part of the envisioned goal 16—the promotion of peaceful and inclusive societies for sustainable development, the provision of access to justice for all and building effective, accountable and inclusive institutions at all levels. A global culture of lawfulness for the succeeding generation will have on its agenda such moral universals.

Interculturally universalising morality by dignifying our partners, children and others is not automatic. Bringing up children in the spirit of universal moral values starts in our bedrooms and homes, becomes public in the nurseries, kindergartens, schools and then goes into the streets, businesses and other governance. Universal morality rather than once and for all "given", every now and then, needs to be revived to keep humanity on the track of progress. Franklin D. Roosevelt, one of the fathers of the UN Charter, said that "the test of our progress is not whether we add more to the abundance of those who have much; it is whether we provide enough for those who have too little" (quoted after Grafton 1999, p. 61).

Since the inception of the UN, Roosevelt's ideas have had a considerable impact on it and in the world. The organisation has witnessed a four-fold increase in the world's quality of life, as measured by the GDP per capita. More precisely, in comparison with 1945, there are now respectively 4 rich to 1 poor *vis à vis* 4 poor to 1 rich in terms of average income per capita in the constant purchasing power parity (PPP) (Acemoglu 2012, p. 5). This considerable improvement concurs with the one

[7] As this book goes to print, the United Nations General Assembly finalised its action on the draft sustainable development goals 2016–2030, now reflected in resolution A/69/L. 85 (pending A/RES/70/?), unanimously adopted on 25 September 2015, with unamended wording. Therefore, the references to them or quotations drawn by the contributors to this book from various earlier UN source documents are fully compatible with A/69/L. 85.

hundred year projection to that effect in 1930 by John Maynard Keynes in his *Economic Possibilities for Our Grandchildren* (Keynes 1935).

As comforting as the factual corroboration of Keynes' projection may now be, those economic possibilities have currently been monopolised by 1 % of the adult population in the world. According to Oxfam, as of 2016, 1 % will proportionally own more than 50 % of global wealth (possessions) than the 99 % of the adult population of the world (Oxfam 2015). Is this moral? In many Western industrialised countries like Germany in the last decades, more people got extremely rich and more poor; the difference between both groups is obviously not decreasing but increasing.

This two-volume book originated with the latent premise that excessive socio-economic inequality is immoral. It reduces opportunities in education, especially in quality education. Notwithstanding the different professional backgrounds of the editors of the work, and even more diverse professional backgrounds of its contributors, we believe we all share in the idea that evidence-based, quality crime prevention and education are the prerequisites for a successful Culture of Lawfulness anywhere in the world. We also believe that to achieve this goal, partnerships of all kinds will become ever more important. They should involve government agencies, the private sector, civil society, academia, philanthropic foundations and faith-based organisations. Their collaboration will prove critical to the implementation of the UN's new sustainable development agenda that stresses inclusiveness as the core vehicle for poverty amelioration and peaceful non-violent societies.

We expose this idea to the critical scrutiny of the readers in the academic spirit of "organized criticism" (Robert Merton). We are keenly aware that this interdisciplinary work covers only some criminological and other aspects of a more equitable, effective and humane treatment of women and children as victims and offenders and that much remains to be said. Yet, we still trust that the various chapters will open new visions how to reduce the victimisation of women and children as well as their offending.

The contributions to this work are opened by *Santos Pais*, the United Nations Special Representative of the Secretary-General on Violence against Children, and closed by H.E. Ambassador *Martin Sajdik*, the 70th President of the United Nations Economic and Social Council. We very much appreciate the contributions of these eminent representatives. These contributions both demonstrate that a strong political will, partnerships, sound knowledge and decisive action can help to counter violence, corruption and other crimes and their negative impact on sustainable development and the fortunes of succeeding generations.

As to the contributors, some of them are academics, some of them practitioners and still others are both academics and practitioners. We hope that this diversified authorship adds to the value of this work that aims at providing suggestions for succeeding generations to deal more effectively and humanely with women and children as victims and offenders. Some of these suggestions are explicit, others implicit. Some articles explicitly and some other implicitly invoke the UN values embodied in the UN crime prevention and criminal justice standards and norms. The five questions at the end of each text were added to stimulate discussion about possible solutions for the problems raised. Since the two volumes are written by academics and policy-makers, scholars and practitioners, their action profile involves more often strategic than tactical work of a "manual" kind.

On the understanding of these limits, in the *Post Scriptum* we roughly outline and envision the implementation of the work's suggestions until 2030. However, the floor is open to alternative recommendations, to a more visionary and incisive discourse, to closer fieldwork and follow-up. When the UN ideas about sustainable development and crime prevention interact with those of the academic world, in the next 15 years the academic world will have a unique opportunity to contribute to improve crime prevention for women and children. In this context we thank all the authors for their generous contributions and sincerely hope that their texts will advance "social progress and better standards of life in larger freedom" (art. 55 of the UN Charter) and the "Future We Want for All".

These texts are grouped in six parts. **Part I "UN Principles for Crime Prevention-Treatment of Women and Children"** starts with "International Human Rights Law on Violence Against Women and Children and Its Impact on Domestic Law and Action", examined by *Goldfarb and Goldscheid*, two US scholars. They examine the impact and potential of international human rights law as a component of efforts to prevent and redress violence against women and children. Other components, such as laws, policies and community-driven initiatives, countering violence against women and children has made important inroads internationally and in several countries domestically. The chapter's authors not only document the scope of these various initiatives, but discuss particular legal cases and other actions against parties of the UN and regional treaties, whose residents complained about gender violence and the lack of due diligence by State authorities to protect them or their children from such a form of violence.

Dussich, an international victimologist, notes in his chapter about "Blue Victimology and Femicide: The UN Response to Victims and Female Victims of Gender Killings" that since its beginning the UN championed the rights of women and children. In the face of the fact that across the globe every day female children and adults are being killed by men ("femicide"), usually with impunity just because they are females, one of the UN's central goals is to reaffirm faith in fundamental human rights, in the dignity and worth of the human person, in the equal rights of men. The author gives a detailed account of the enormity of the problem in different parts of the world and puts his main hopes on the UN as the most significant forum to take unified action. It has the obligation, the resources and the will to bring about the necessary changes across the globe.

Mwenifumbo and Fuentes, two UN officers, present a chapter about "In the Pursuit of Justice for Women and Children and the Right to Development: A Review of Concluding Observations of the United Nations Human Rights Treaty Bodies". The authors discuss relevant to the UN treaties human rights regime criminal and preventive aspects of "justice" and "the right to development", as far as women and children are concerned. The article analyses the intergenerational issues from, both, the local and global perceptions of justice. It looks into how the UN human rights treaty bodies advance the global justice standards and norms for the treatment of women and children, particularly with regard to victims. In the light of the concluding observations by the UN treaty bodies and the right to development in general, the article makes recommendations concerning gender mainstreaming in formal and informal education.

The final contribution to Part I is provided by *Wintersteiner*. His "International Strategies for Building a Culture of Peace Through Access to Good Education" connects this part of the book with the subsequent ones. He stresses that education may be the only instrument for creating and maintaining democratic, just and peaceful societies. Moreover, education is the cornerstone of a strategy towards a culture of peace and describes what happens when this cornerstone is undermined and education comes under attack (for a specific case, see *Carapic* and *Dönges* in Part II). Wintersteiner emphasises that whilst education is a fundamental human right and essential for the exercise of all other human rights, other human rights have to be guaranteed to be able to make use of the right to education. Education is a prerequisite for the economically and socially marginalised adults and children to lift themselves out of poverty and participate fully as citizens. The author concludes with a brief note on the preparation of the post-2015 education agenda in the framework of the UN sustainable development goals that marks a new step in integrating the human rights approach.

Part II "Education and Social Learning: Their Impact on the Development of Children and Adolescents" is composed of 11 chapters.

Carapic and Dönges present a chapter about "Attacks on Education in Conflict, Post-conflict and Non-conflict Settings". The authors discuss the need for a more informed implementation of the right to education. They note that not much is known about the actual prevalence of attacks on education, the perpetrators involved, the circumstances under which it takes place, for what purpose it is used and how it is regulated. They suggest that understanding attacks on education requires disaggregating the phenomenon along four dimensions: frequency, targeting, repertoire and purpose. After discussing the four dimensions, the authors then show the utility of the proposed framework by examining attacks on education carried out by the Nigerian militant group Boko Haram. In conclusion, they note that despite a number of initiatives to provide more and better monitoring and reporting, the mechanisms necessary for systematic data collection have been found wanting.

In their chapter "The Role of Early Childhood Education in Social behaviour of Children", *Nores and Barnett* discuss the importance of the first five years in the development of children and consequently the need for public investments into early childhood care and education. A large body of evidence on early childhood interventions has found short- and medium-term effects that extend beyond narrowly academic or cognitive outcomes to improvements in pro-social behaviours and skills such as self-regulation, commitment to schooling, employment and earnings, as well as mental and physical health (see also Farrington in his chapter). Given the importance of the early years in child development, the chapter focuses on summarising the evidence of the impact of early childhood interventions on children's social and emotional behaviour in the United States and globally; it describes which aspects of these interventions are associated with larger short-term and long-term social and emotional effects and identifies which types of programs have been found to affect parenting and households in ways that matter for children's behavioural development.

Kanngiesser, Schmidt and Rossano write on "Young Children's Understanding of Social Norms and Social Institutions" at the early preschool level. The authors remind us that as adults we typically navigate our social world effortlessly and mostly unaware of the intricate web of social norms and institutions shaping our behaviour. Children are born into this web that defines (mis-)behaviour. Social norms also form the basis of more complex social institutions such as ownership that create obligations, rights and duties. The authors use the example of ownership to argue that it is one of the first social institutions that young children understand. The chapter seeks to broaden our crime prevention perspectives by going beyond "mental violence" that victimises children (Art. 19 of the Convention on the Rights of the Child) to the question of children's understanding of ownership—an issue that may be at the core of early anti-corruption education (see also *Redo* in Part V).

Farrington ("Family Influences on Offending and Family-Based Intervention") discusses the aspect of intergenerational transmission. Mindful that "cold, rejecting parents tend to have delinquent children" and that "parental warmth could act as a protective factor against the effects of physical punishment", he reviews the insights obtained by cross-national research on the effectiveness of family-based interventions (about emotions see also *Kury* in Part V). The author concludes that a great deal still has to be learnt about family influences on offending and effective family-based programmes in order to further corroborate the present research. He points out that the time is ripe to establish national agencies in all countries willing to participate to advance our knowledge about family risk factors (from longitudinal studies) and about effective family-based interventions (from randomised experiments and cost-benefit analyses).

In "Women's Substance Abuse and Its Impacts on Children's Early Development and Deviant Behaviors", *Gao and Liu* examine from an international perspective the root causes of women's substance abuse, including women's victimisation. The authors focus on the intergenerational sociolegal consequences and impacts of women's drug abuse on children's early development. Like other authors in this work, they conclude that with the continued global growth of female substance abuse, the research and discussion in the international arena should focus not only on implementing meaningful gender-specific programmes for women, their children and families, but should also test whether programmes that were successful in other countries fit into their specific cultural needs.

The moral development of children is a complex problem, which has rather been neglected in criminology. Little attention has been paid, for example, to the relationship between justice and trust. *Brugman, Out and Gibbs* ("Fairness and Trust in Developmental Psychology") point out the importance of this relationship. They emphasise that fairness or justice is central to moral development, but without relating it to trust, there is little cooperation among people. This interpersonal relationship starts in early childhood and foreshadows the close social relationship individuals develop later in life. These essential developments have not been sufficiently studied. The authors review them from a theoretical and empirical perspective, both of which bring new insights. They conclude that a successful mutual moral understanding, difficult in practice as it always has been, depends to a large extent on sensitive parenting and a long process of education and schooling.

Marshall discusses in her chapter "Results of the Second Round of the International Self Report Delinquency (ISRD2) Study: Importance of Education and Social Learning for 12–15-Year Olds" criminological aspects of education and schooling. She notes that, typically, policymakers tend to be more concerned about those youth who are involved in frequent, repeated delinquent behaviour. Although repeating classes and below-average performance of pupils may be warning signs, other school-related factors (such as truancy and type of school, e.g. egalitarian/quality-focused) appear to be more strongly linked to delinquent behaviour. Like *Bokil and Raghavan* (Part IV), Marshall notes the importance of social learning (SL) in understanding effective prevention of delinquency. Pupils with higher acceptance levels of violence also tend to have significantly higher levels of involvement in delinquency. Finally, she presents recommendations that may counter delinquency through early education, better training and pay for teachers who work in low-income areas and greater flexibility in allowing students to gradually move to higher tracks.

In "The Role of Justice and Fairness as Global Values: Promoting Public International Law at the (Pre-)university Level"), *Clark* looks into the avenues and precepts of inculcating an appreciation for international law and international principles (especially justice and fairness) through education at the university level, particularly at the pre-university level, based on the UN Charter and other international instruments that promote justice and international law as cornerstones of peace and security. The chapter discusses ways in which relevant learning takes place both in the regular curriculum and in such extra-curricular activities as Model United Nations Conferences, which involve both high school and university students. Various efforts by the UN and its specialised agencies to stimulate such education are noted, such as the "United Nations Academic Impact Initiative". The author also points out the dearth both of curricular requirements and of teaching materials suitable for teaching the subject at the pre-university level.

Pływaczewski and Kraśnicka's chapter "Legal Education in Transition: Is the Bologna Process Responding to Europe's Place in the World?" looks into the implications of the Bologna Process (a series of ministerial meetings and agreements between European countries aimed at harmonising the standards and quality of higher education qualifications) for the region and beyond. The authors regret that the Bologna Process is exclusively centred on Europe and has left out from its purview other regions of the world, such as North America. Europe could, for instance, benefit from the US system of legal education, which promotes not only an effective teaching mechanisms but core fundamental principles such as rule of law and human rights. The authors show how the North American approach could be integrated into European legal education, but that also US universities could learn from the Bologna Process.

Stanners ("A Critical Examination of the Contention of the Existence of a Culture Justice Education at the Vienna International School, Austria") deals with international justice education at the secondary level, exemplified by the curriculum choices of the Vienna International School. She explores research on justice and democracy in education in the context of a school which "gives no message of gender differences in any of its approaches or teaching" and asks which of the characteristics identified as being necessary for justice and democracy to be present exist in the school. The author thinks that whilst the curriculum plays a strong part in providing a context in which justice and democracy can be nurtured, this by itself is insufficient to guarantee a culture of justice but that the real key to the presence of such a culture in the school can be found in the relationships that exist between all the stakeholders.

Barberet writes about college-level "Education for Justice: Experiences and Prospects for Further Internationalization". She discusses in her article the internationalisation of criminal justice education in the United States, highlighting the experiences of John Jay College of Criminal Justice (JJC) of the City University of New York (USA), a leader in international criminal justice education. The author reviews the development of the most recent JJC program, the Master of Arts program: its curriculum, faculty, the undergraduate and graduate students it attracts and the prospects of these programs for the future. The chapter then moves on to international curricular initiatives concerning women, crime and criminal justice. It ends with a discussion of why and how nations around the world might encourage similar curricular development and how the work of intergovernmental organisations such as the UN could contribute to such developments as well as benefit from them.

In **Part III "Children/Juveniles and Women as Victims and Offenders"** (18 chapters), *van Dijk* discusses "The Criminal Victimization of Children and Women in International Perspective". The author presents an overview of the results of the national and international victims surveys regarding the distribution of victimisation according to age and gender with a focus on violent crime. The results show a consistent inverse relationship between age and criminal victimisation for all types of crime. The relationship between gender and victimisation is less straightforward. Men are more exposed to various types of non-sexual violence by strangers, including homicide. Cross-national analyses suggest that violence by intimates against females is most prevalent in countries where gender equality is low. However, self-reported victimisation rates of violence against women by intimates are also relatively high in countries where gender equality is the highest, such as in the Scandinavian countries, presumably because of increased sensitivity to acts of lesser violence among female respondents in those countries. The author ends on a practical note, recommending the expansion of special services for female victims of domestic violence and the provision of similar services tailored to the needs of male victims.

Lappi-Seppälä and Lehti analyse "Global Homicide Mortality Trends by Gender 1950–2010". Historical data series show that the higher the level of violence, the smaller the share of female victims and perpetrators. This chapter tests the current differences in male and female homicide mortality levels with the most extensive available data today. In spite of various differences between male and female homicide mortality, the authors find that social control and economic factors have very similar effects on lethal violence regardless of the gender of victims: High male and female homicide mortality rates as well as female/male homicide ratio correlate with the same socio-economic factors and in almost an equal manner. Increasing gender equality seems to increase the *relative* homicide victimisation risk for women. This is due to the fact that gender equality seems to go along with general welfare indicators, which reduce all types of lethal violence in society; male victimisation decreases in this case even faster than female victimisation. The authors conclude that well-governed, legitimate and prosperous democracies are safe—and equal—societies.

Schröttle and Vogt ("Women as Victims and Perpetrators of Violence: Empirical Results from National and International Quantitative Violence Research") discuss empirical findings on the extent, causes and consequences of violence against women from national and international empirical research. These studies show that if women are victims of physical, sexual and/or psychological violence, it is most often a case of domestic violence by intimate partners. The two authors evaluate the value and effectiveness, as well as the limitations, of violence prevalence studies from a methodological and gender-critical perspective. They conclude that there is still a lack of empirically well-founded analyses that focus on the construction and deconstruction of violence, gender, disability, migration and other aspects. In this respect, a targeted expansion of qualitative research, which would also aim at deepening representative quantitative violence prevalence studies, would be a great gain, in order to be able to better portray contexts of occurrence and causality, as well as the significance of violence.

Lysova presents data about "Victims but also Perpetrators: Women's Experience of Partner Violence". The chapter opens with an analysis of major negative health consequences of partner violence (PV) for women around the world: homicide, suicide, injury, antenatal and postnatal mental disorders and HIV/AIDS. The author then reports on studies analysing why women themselves become active participants in PV. The author concludes that because a "one size fits all" approach does not seem to work for addressing such a complex and multidimensional phenomenon as PV, carefully tailored interventions at various levels for different types of violence and violent types/incidents should be considered. Integrating attention to the dynamics of partner violence with elements of the "violence against women" framework would allow global research to recognise and give voice to women's diverse experiences of partner violence, help reveal its intrinsic, interactional nature and, as a result, promote a more effective approach to crime prevention at the international and domestic level.

Alvazzi del Frate in her text "A Reflection on Women, Girls and Armed Violence" discusses aspects of (lethal) violence against women and girls, with special emphasis on firearm violence. The author presents international data on armed violence against women and girls in different settings. Although there is a correlation between high levels of violence and high numbers of females killed, most of the violent deaths of women and girls occur in settings where there is no declared armed conflict. Whether firearms are used in fatal killings very much depends on the ease of access to such weapons. In conclusion, the author express the hope that the UN Sustainable Development Goals and recent developments in the policy and research agendas on ending violence against women may represent a unique opportunity for a more effective prevention and reduction of many forms of violence impacting on women and girls, including firearm violence.

Nikolic-Ristanovic and Stevkovic's chapter "Women and Children as Victims and Offenders: The Impact of Armed Conflict and Post-conflict Period Challenges" assess the role played by the State, civil society and international actors concerning domestic violence and trafficking in persons in the aftermath of armed conflict. The brutalisation effect of war on crime lasts longer than the war itself, as the factors that drive up crime during armed conflicts continue in the post-war period. Once violence has been legitimised by war and the settling of interpersonal differences by force, these attitudes carry over to the period immediately after. After describing in detail the Serbian experience concerning the victimisation of women and children during the war (1991–1999), the authors acknowledge many important changes in post-war Serbia but note that the lack of timely and adequate protection and support of victims during the war has still not been remedied. They recommend therefore shifting the attention of scholars and policymakers from treating victimisation and offending of women and children merely as a legal problem to that of a social problem.

In their chapter "A Biopsychosocial Model of Female Criminality: Implications for Assessment and Evidence-Based Treatment Approaches", *Peper, Krammer and Klecha* present their cross-disciplinary research findings on offending behaviour by women and indicate how the complex factors underlying female criminality could be integrated in a multilevel model. For this purpose, the authors interlink clinical and other criminological information with recent results from the cognitive, social and affective neurosciences. In the opinion of the authors, because of the anthropological and biological antecedents of early criminology, the contemporary way of dealing with a biopsychosocial model of female criminality may be still short of taking their new approach into account, and it is hence unable to contribute to that multilevel model.

Chesney-Lind and Hadi discuss the important topic of "Criminalizing Women: Global Strategies for Denying Female Victimization". Their chapter opens with the staggering statistics that nearly one-third of the world's female population will become victims of violence and not only that, in many cases, they will also be blamed for it. The authors address the problem of victim blaming from four angles: the merging of religion and law to criminalise female sexuality and sexual expression, the demonisation and sexualisation of "enemy" women as a justification for mass rape in wartime, the criminalisation of reproductive rights and the use of courts to punish victims of sexual abuse who run away from their abusers. The authors suggest that the pattern of criminalising women and girls' victimisation requires both research to document and action to challenge the "legal" abuse of women and enforcement of patriarchal privilege. They try to establish that there is a direct interface between women's victimisations globally and systems that both punish the victim and avoid punishing the assailants.

Krahé addresses a related topic, "Societal Responses to Sexual Violence Against Women: Rape Myths and the 'Real Rape' Stereotype", from a socio-psychological perspective. Her chapter examines the role of stereotypes and myths about rape in understanding societal responses to victims of sexual violence. She notes that there is a widely shared stereotype of the "real rape" that is squarely at odds with the reality of the sexual victimisation of women yet serves to inform the social perception of victims and their credibility. After presenting prevalence rates of sexual assault worldwide, the author analyses the attrition process from the initial police investigation to eventual court proceedings and a verdict. She provides strong evidence of the impact of rape myths and stereotypes on the handling of rape complaints and concludes with a review of potential strategies for challenging rape myths and stereotypes and reducing their influence in the criminal justice system.

Pakzad and Alipour write from an Iranian perspective about "Justice and Family Issues in the Shiite: Confronting with the Domestic Violence in Shiite Communities". The authors incisively discuss domestic violence against children and women in Shia communities and point out the great differences that exist across the Muslim world. Looking at the various approaches of Islamic sects makes it clear that religion is not inflexible in the face of social changes, or regional and cultural components. Since family issues in the Shia tradition depend on a dynamic jurisprudence, some jurisprudents have attempted to interpret religious laws in an up-to-date manner and have brought about legal changes improving the status of women, such as giving women preference over men as primary caretakers of children or introducing sanctions for the ill-treatment of women by men. The chapter also deals with women as offenders, in particular with women who consider it their right to use violence themselves and justify such acts in the light of religion and regional cultures.

Asli and Amrollahi Byouki, also Iranian academics, comment on "Forced Marriage in Islamic Countries: The Role of Violence in Family Relationships". In their chapter, the authors make a clear argument for equality of women and men by contending the custom of forced marriage that deprives both sexes of their fundamental rights and in the case of women often leads to their victimisation. The authors point out that forced marriages have been a persistent issue in most societies, not only in Islamic countries, and have more to do with customs and traditions than with religious rules. In order suggest to eradicate this tradition, Islamic countries must insist that the religious ordinances prohibiting this kind of marriage are followed, fulfil their international obligations in terms of proper legislations for proscribing forced marriage and use the mass media and all public and private resources to raise public awareness about its harmful effects.

Bokil and Raghwawan discuss "The Case of De-notified Tribes in India". Their text renews our interest in the fate of "Indian criminal tribes" under the British colonial rule, the study of which provides material for the social learning theory of criminal behaviour through the intergenerational transmission of values. The two authors review the history of British legislation regulating the conduct of those tribes and point out the incorrect colonial understanding of the Indian caste system. This lack of understanding led to the marginalisation and social exclusion of the de-notified tribes (DNTs) and their eventual de-citizenship and criminalisation. Women and children had to bear the brunt of this process, in terms of institutional and structural violence—poor access to food security, education, healthcare, social protection and justice delivery. The authors argue that the vicious circle forcing the DNTs to remain in the criminal nexus can still be broken through concerted efforts by the state, community associations and individual members of DNTs, and civil society.

Klaus, Rzeplińska and Woźniakowska-Fajst describe "Victimization and Delinquency of Minors in Central-European Countries". The authors note that despite the considerable differences among the individual countries, Central Europe still takes a fairly patronising and paternalistic approach to children. Their research takes a closer look at the situation in Hungary, Poland and the Czech Republic—three former post-socialist countries that have a great deal in common, both from a historical and a socio-economic perspective. The Czech Republic has the fewest juvenile issues, whilst Hungary has the highest level of crime in the region. Hungary, Poland and the Czech Republic also differ in their juvenile justice systems and the ideology underpinning their response to juvenile offences. The authors conclude their chapter by emphasising that Poland, Hungary, and the Czech Republic have been continually striving for higher standards of caring for children and protecting their rights at every stage of criminal trials in the 25 years or more that have elapsed since these countries set out on the road to democracy and during their 10 years as EU members.

Selmini's chapter examines "Sexual Abuse of Children in Comparative and International Perspective". Child sexual abuse (CSA) is a chronic problem that can occur in any family or any country. In recent times, it has increasingly become a priority topic of the European Union, the UN and other intergovernmental and non-governmental organisations. Scholars have also given CSA greater attention, even though more at clinical case study than at policy levels. The author analyses national and international quantitative violence studies which show that if women are the victims of physical, sexual and/or psychological violence, it is most often a case of domestic violence by intimate partners—in contrast to men, who are more often victims of violence in public spaces at the hands of persons known or unknown to them. Both women and men are primarily victims of violence by male perpetrators. Women comparatively rarely act as perpetrators of severe violence.

Kangaspunta, Sarrica and Johansen report on "Trafficking in Persons: The Involvement of Women and Children" from the perspective of the UN "Global Report on Trafficking in Persons". The authors analyse the global dynamics and patterns of trafficking in persons, especially of women and children, who are disproportionately involved, both as victims and as offenders. Women comprise a majority of the detected trafficking victims, but women are also prosecuted and convicted of trafficking in persons in a far larger proportion than for nearly any other crime. Children are frequently victims. The authors draw particularly on findings from the 2012 "Global Report on Trafficking in Persons" and examine some of the patterns of trafficking in persons as detected and reported by countries worldwide. They report that the share of women has somewhat declined during the last years. At the same time, the share of detected girl victims has increased which could indicate that the traffickers are turning to the exploitation of younger victims.

Shirwadkar's chapter "Exploring Hidden Spaces: Sexual Abuse of Girl Children in India" describes different aspects of sexual abuse of girls, focusing largely on an Indian context. In spite of progress and new opportunities of education, social and structural divides, traditional cultural practices and gender inequality are some factors that make girl children particularly vulnerable and easy victims for sexual abuse. The measures taken by the state to control this danger as well as the limitations to address the issue are discussed in the context of the changing social situation in India. The author analyses the different factors underlying the sexual abuse of children and stresses the need to strengthen the effort to improve education and awareness and make every possible effort to control the threat.

In "Sexual Abuse Within the Family: The Intergenerational Transmission of Victimhood and Offending", *Bijleveld, Hill and Hendriks* address a related topic in a European context. Their chapter provides an overview of research carried out on 185 juvenile male sex offenders who received treatment in a residential centre in the Netherlands. In their study, the authors examined both the offenders' and their parents' history of sexual abuse. Specifically they tested hypotheses relating to the mechanisms linking offender and victim status in cases of sexual abuse within families, i.e. intra-familial abuse. Their findings offer support for the theory of social learning of sexual abuse. Juvenile sex offenders either from families where intra-familial abuse has occurred or who have a father with a history of sexual abuse against children occurring during their childhood have an increased risk of abusing children themselves. Also juvenile sex offenders who themselves have been the victim of intra-familial abuse, or who have a sibling that has suffered intra-familial abuse, have an increased risk of committing such an offence themselves.

In his chapter "'Violence Against Children Sells Very Well'. Reporting Crime in the Media and Attitudes to Punishment", *Hestermann* critically evaluates the role of the media in crime reporting. In order to reach a wide audience, the media stir up emotions, especially sympathy with the victim and fear of violence. Whilst children generate a lot of attention as victims of violence, whilst older people are ignored. The more dramatic a crime, the more closely associated it is with sexual violence, the greater the chance of its being presented in detail. The media contrasts a dark image of the perpetrator ("real scum") with a bright iconic image of an idealised victim, preferably childlike and female. Against the background of international findings from Brazil, Colombia, India, Spain and USA, the author finds this dichotomy corroborated by the results of his research in Germany. The contrast between the villain and the innocent victim facilitates the calls for tough sentencing. In effect, politicians come under pressure to introduce stiffer penalties—not as a reaction to a real increase in criminality but as a reaction to assumptions about criminality fed by the media.

Part IV "The Role of Crime Prevention: Punishment–Imprisonment–Alternative Sanctions" opens with a chapter by *Hermann and Dölling*, "General Prevention: Does It Work?" To answer this question the authors present the results of a meta-analysis of 700 international empirical studies on negative general prevention with more than 7800 effect estimates. The questions asked were two in particular: whether deterrent effects are dependent on the age of the target group and whether they also depend on the type of offence. The results vary, depending on the econometric or criminological approach taken to measure those effects. If an economic theory of behaviour is used, the deterrence hypothesis is refuted less often than with a recourse to criminological-sociological theories. The deterrent effects are also confirmed relatively rarely for young people, and they vary depending on the offence. In the light of their very comprehensive research, the authors conclude that "A high discovery probability and consistent prosecution of crimes are more important than severe punishment". This conclusion us shared by the UN penal policy recommendations.

Zapatero's chapter deals with "Actors, Factors and Processes on the Road to the Abolition of the Death Penalty". He addresses the degree of compliance with two UN initiatives: the 2000–2015 Millennium Development Goals (MDGs) and the 2007 General Assembly resolution calling for a universal moratorium on the application of the death penalty. The author sees both UN initiatives as the product of political and academic work of people who have a leading role in the life of the organisation as diplomats, staff members, experts and members of non-governmental organisations that construct a cultural and political heritage of humanity. The author vigorously supports the objective of the eventual abolition of death penalty, stipulated in Art. 6 para. 6 of the International Covenant on Civil and Political Rights. Through Zapatero's contribution we learn that in genuinely inclusive societies, someone's exclusion by the death penalty is not an option. His text supports the further expansion and implementation of the right to life.

Huber in her chapter "Women Prisoners: Women in Criminal Justice Systems and the Added Value of the UN Bangkok Rules", ask various questions. For instance, do prosecutors and judges deal more leniently with female offenders? Should prison conditions, treatment in detention and rehabilitation programmes be equal for all prisoners, and aren't they in correctional facilities nowadays anyway? Her answers outline aspects of discrimination faced by female suspects, defendants and prisoners in criminal justice systems, their number, profile and characteristics, and the offences they are typically charged with or convicted for. The chapter covers key conditions in detention as well as programmes in place with regard to rehabilitation and reintegration. In doing so, it draws on data, country examples and findings from a number of research studies. The findings show that there are usually fewer educational and training opportunities for women and those that are available are less varied and of poorer quality than those offered to male detainees. She concludes that women undeniably face discrimination in the criminal justice system, mirroring discrimination in society as a whole.

Beichner and Hagemann write about "Incarcerated Women: Their Situation, Their Needs and Measures for Sustainable Reintegration". Their chapter centres on incarcerated women offenders worldwide, their experiences, specific problems and needs, as well as correctional programmes intended to help them reintegrate back into society. It provides a theoretical understanding of the general marginalisation of women in almost every modern society and an overview of theories that have been developed to explain why women commit offences. Next, the authors provide statistical information on the prevalence of women prisoners in various parts of the world and the ways in which policy changes in the war on drugs and mandatory sentencing have impacted women's incarceration rates. The chapter then explores the gender-specific differences in women's pathways to prison and their distinct problems and needs, including the detrimental effects of mothers' incarceration on children. Based on experiences of several countries, the authors conclude with suggestions for promising approaches that involve sustainable reintegration.

Gelsthorpe and Durnescu discuss "Probation Supervision for Women and Young Offenders". The authors note that ever since the question of probation has entered the international arena through the Eighth International Penitentiary Congress in Washington, DC (1910), the topic of probation supervision for women and young offenders can be located in a number of theoretical and practice contexts. The focus in this chapter is on the risk/need/responsivity model (RNR): the intensity of the intervention should match the level of risk; interventions should target so-called criminogenic needs such as antisocial attitudes, antisocial cognition, antisocial associates, substance abuse, etc. and, finally, the programme delivery has to be in a style and mode that is consistent with the learning and the ability of the offender. The authors recall in this context the United Nations Rules on the Treatment of Women Offenders and Prisoners and conclude that there is emerging evidence that provision for women offenders in the community should be even more gender-oriented, i.e. on women only.

In her chapter "Release Management for Female and Juvenile Prisoners. How Important Is Release Management in Prison for Crime Prevention?" *Pruin,* in looking for answer to this question, first takes a closer look at the recommendations and results from the debate on prisoner "resettlement" that pertain to pre-release preparation, how these recommendations have been put into practice, and whether we can identify good or promising practices in the literature. Among the most important legal instruments the author lists the United Nations Standard Minimum Rules for the Treatment of Prisoners ("The Mandela Rules") and the Convention on the Rights of the Child. Her findings suggest that the use of open institutions and of strategies that allow women and juveniles to leave the prison temporarily has not yet reached satisfactory levels. Also the provision of gender-specific education, vocational training and work opportunities is greatly lacking in Europe. The author concludes that research does not paint a particularly satisfying picture of release management for women and juveniles, but that there are a number of promising approaches worth monitoring.

Allen analyses "The Impact of Sanctions on Child and Female Offenders". The author notes that meeting basic practical needs in prisons remains crucial. Research on young offenders has shown that supervisors in whatever setting are effective if they are clear about their role show positive social values and behaviour themselves and are prepared to challenge the young persons consistently and fairly about their delinquency. Effectiveness is also enhanced if offenders are helped with problems, which they themselves identify, particularly if these are related to their offending. Tackling substance misuse, lack of employment and damaging relationships with family and peers may be particularly important. Similar factors are likely to be significant for women too. The inappropriateness of custodial sentences for juveniles and women is increasingly recognised, but developing the legal framework, policy and practice, which can reduce and ultimately eliminate its use, has proved difficult in a social climate which places a greater value on punishment than is justified by evidence.

A team of NGOs, *Robertson, Christmann, Sharratt, Manby, Ayre, Berman, Foca, Asiminei, Philbrick, Koivumaa and Garvriluta* write about "Children of Prisoners: Their Situation and Role in Long-Term Crime Prevention". They review an innovative EU-funded project that addresses the distress caused by a parent's imprisonment and the reaction of others to it (especially if it is stigmatising—"your dad's a criminal"). Such responses can result in the children becoming isolated, angry and/or scared, and in some cases developing physical or mental health problems. Studies suggest that whilst parental imprisonment can increase a child's likelihood to offend, positive responses to the situation can aid the children's well-being, attitudes and attainment. Drawing on findings from the project, the chapter explores the factors that help a child to cope with parental imprisonment and the actions that different stakeholders can take to strengthen such factors. It identifies some of the mental health impacts at different stages of parental imprisonment, the roles played by non-imprisoned parents/carers and by schools, and suggests options for further clarifying the factors that help and hinder children of prisoners in the short and long term.

Wemmers and Cyr discuss "Gender and Victims' Expectations Regarding Their Role in Criminal Justice System: Towards Victim-Centred Prosecutorial Policies". These policies include therapeutic jurisprudence—an interdisciplinary approach to law that to study the extent to which legal rules, procedures or practice promote the psychological well-being of the people it affects. Law is a tool and people who engage the criminal justice system do so for a reason. Against a historical background depicting the various ways in which victims are involved in pursuing justice, the authors examine the extent to which current legal procedures meet victims' expectations. Following a discussion of recent international policy developments regarding victims of crime and victims of violence against women in particular, the authors consider how victims' relationship with the offender affects their expectations, including the awareness of possible future victimisation.

Kury discusses in his chapter "Mediation, Restorative Justice and the Social Integration of Offenders: The Effects of Alternative Sanctions on Punishment" the background and development of alternatives to "classical" criminal sanctions. Whereas in traditional societies procedures like victim-offender-reconciliation were common, in modern societies criminal justice, and with it the punishment of the offender, has been taken over by the State. Compensation that formerly was given to the victim is now collected by the state in the form of fines, and the victim is left on the sidelines. Criminological research during the last decades has increasingly shown that victims are more interested in restitution than in harsh punishment of the offenders. This has revived in many countries a discussion about alternatives to punishment. Empirical results show that mediation is not only more successful in re-establishing social peace but also much cheaper than the classical handling of crime.

Dandurand's chapter "Alternative Approaches to Preventing Recidivism: Restorative Justice and the Social Reintegration of Offenders" reviews the original promises of the restorative justice approach as an alternative to the conventional criminal justice response to juvenile crime and seeks to recast mediation and restorative justice programmes as a form of reconciliation between the juvenile offender and the community and a frequent prerequisite to the offender's successful social reintegration. The author emphasises that very few restorative justice elements have been integrated systematically into community-based sentences or into post-release programmes and the capacity of existing restorative justice programmes to achieve social reintegration objectives tends to be quite limited. Some good practices have been identified, but they need to be both better understood and more systematically evaluated. Proponents of restorative justice typically deplore the lack of progress in implementing restorative justice within the juvenile justice system and will continue to do so unless new ways are found to develop restorative justice's full potential in contributing to the social reintegration of offenders.

Hamilton and Yarrow write about "Preventing and Addressing Youth Offending: Restorative Justice and Family Focused Programming". They remind us that "the primary purpose of restorative justice is just that – to restore justice", i.e. the purpose stated by the United Nations Special Representative of the Secretary-General on Violence Against Children, who also provided the Foreword to this volume. This purpose is already reflected in the 1989 Convention on the Rights of the Child, which stipulates that children who come into conflict with the law should be treated in a manner which promotes their own dignity and worth as well as their understanding of the rights and freedoms of others. Restorative justice has, however, limitations. The authors point out that restorative mechanisms often prioritise healing and reparation for victims over addressing the root causes of child offending. They conclude that restorative justice mechanisms may be most valuable where they complement, rather than replace the work done by a wide range of social agencies tackling the risk factors associated with child offending.

Ehret, Szego and Dhondt add to the restorative justice paradigm their own expertise in "Peacemaking Circles, Their Restorative and Crime Prevention Capacities for Women and Children: Insights from a European Pilot Study". Peacemaking circles are a restorative justice approach to conflict resolution that is inclusive and non-hierarchical with long historical roots in indigenous cultures going back to their so-called talking circles. Particularly, the circle traditions of First Nation people of Canada have been further developed for dealing with crime and have spread across the border to the Northern USA, Hawaii and as far as Australia. These traditions aim to repair the harm done by crime through focusing on the effects crime has on relationships between victims, offenders, their families and their communities. The authors emphasise that it is this primary focus that requires a substantially different response to crime by moving away from the adversarial "win or lose" logic of the traditional distributive justice system towards a "win-win" approach aimed at restoring societal peace through the means of dialogue, conflict resolution, amends or redress.

In **Part V "Crime Prevention: Proactive Strategies"** (ten chapters), *Walsh* discusses "Justice, Faith and Interfaith: The Relevance of Faith and Interfaith Relations to Crime Prevention". The chapter opens with an estimate: of the seven billion people living on this earth, the majority identify themselves as belonging to a particular religious tradition, such as Christianity, Judaism, Islam, Hinduism, Buddhism, indigenous traditions, and others. With a global resurgence of religion, along with an increase in religious plurality in many societies, the author sees the growing awareness of religion as a significant factor—sometimes positive, sometimes negative—in the lives of individuals, families, societies and nations. Consequently, we also need an increased awareness of religion as it functions in society and its potential impact on justice. In the latter context, this chapter explores the relevance of religion in particular for crime prevention.

Corrado, Peters, Hodgkinson and Mathesius comment on "Crime Reduction, Reduction of Imprisonment and Community Crime Prevention Programs: Risk Factors and Programs Implemented to Reduce Them". The chapter reviews the general research on this subject focussing on three topics: (1) the typical victim profile, (2) factors associated with serious/violent young offending and victimisation and their distinct developmental pathways and (3) key examples of current intervention programmes that have successfully reduced serious/violent youth offending and victimisation. The authors conclude that treatment interventions will accelerate with breakthroughs in brain imaging technology, which will identify more completely the neurological bases for serious offending. Therapeutic interventions will include pharmacological approaches to target aggression/violence. More controversial therapies may regard stem cell breakthroughs concerning neurologically based disorders related to serious violence.

Lee's chapter "Evaluating Children and Adolescents in Contact with the Justice System" focusses on developmentally sensitive, evidence-based instruments and approaches for evaluating child and adolescent offenders and victims. The author first addresses the assessment of adolescent offenders, with the main emphasis on tools designed to measure risks and needs. Secondly, she looks at the evaluation of child victims, with a focus on investigative interviewing. Once developmentally appropriate, evidence-based instruments and approaches have been established; an important next step is to illustrate whether their use contributes to changes in policy and practice. This is arguably the ideal standard for assessing whether science translates meaningfully into practice to encourage the transformation of the juvenile justice system into a system that applies a developmental framework to all decisions.

Alex and Feltes analyse "The Problem of Risk Assessment: Can Better Crime Prognosis Reduce Recidivism?" They note that every society has to face the fact that there is a very small group of people who do not respect elementary rules of human behaviour and who repeatedly commit very serious violent crimes. But how do we know who belongs to this group and who does not? In order to find answer to this question, the authors review recidivism studies and conclude that the task of assessing the probability of serious re-offending is very difficult, and the risk of erring on the side of caution (false negatives) real. Given the fact that it will hardly ever be possible to predict human behaviour with complete certainty, Alex and Feltes recommend that other means than unlimited imprisonment of offenders labelled as very dangerous be used to manage the problem of crime prevention in a way that considers both human rights' aspects as well as public needs.

Redo writes about "Anti-corruption Education as a Form of Early Prevention of Conflict with the Law for Women and Children: Making the United Nations Law Work 2016–2030". He does so from three perspectives (Western, Eastern and UN) by reviewing some recent measures reported by the State Parties to the 2003 United Nations Convention against Corruption. The author argues that the UN anti-corruption education for women and children is a promising path to follow. In his view, against the intercultural background of anti-corruption challenges, two educational issues may decide about the character and effectiveness of an anti-corruption strategy: the prevalence of patriarchal or contractual features in any legal culture and its accommodation of the sustainable development ideology provided that both engage personal responsibility. The implementation of the UN goal of "peaceful and inclusive societies" in which countering bribery and corruption is included will depend on how well in contractual and sustainable development terms the present and succeeding generation will muster anti-corruption ethical education for women and children.

Beier's chapter "Proactive Strategies to Prevent Child Sexual Abuse and the Use of Child Abusive Images: Experiences from the German Dunkelfeld Project" describes proactive strategies used in Germany to protect children from sexual exploitation though online offences and from direct sexual abuse. These strategies include research on individuals at risk to commit first or persistent sexual offences against children, at the same time offering preventive assessment and treatment. As many offenders in this category remain undetected by legal authorities in the "*Dunkelfeld*" (literally "dark field"), this program focusses on those who admit a longstanding sexual interest in prepubescent and/or pubescent children, self-motivated by the distress experienced due to their sexual preference. The author shows that these people are reachable as long as they can rely on the professional pledge of confidentiality. Public Health Services have then a real chance of encouraging the concerned persons to seek professional help before any kind of sexual offences against children are committed.

Wößner's chapter deals with "Women and Children as Victims of Sex Offences: Crime Prevention by Treating the Offenders?" The author provides an overview of the number of sex crimes in comparison to other crimes and discusses how valid these data are given the problem of considerable underreporting. As a measure of victim protection, one of the most important aspects of offender treatment is crime prevention. Given the tremendous traumatising effects sexual victimisation can have on victims, it is undoubtedly justified to do as much as possible to prevent sexual crimes and to respond to sexual violence appropriately. The author discusses in this context treatment programmes for sex offenders and their impact on recidivism. Even if as yet no unambiguous conclusion on the effectiveness of such treatment programmes can be drawn, they should not be abandoned in favour of more punitive solutions. Long-term imprisonment or lifelong detention can only present an alternative for the most dangerous offenders. For less serious offences, a treatment approach may be a better way to protect the victim and at the same time open for the offender a way back into society.

Dobovšek and Slak discuss "Women and Children at the Centre of Preventing Organized Crime". In their chapter, the authors advance the thesis that the emancipation of women is partly responsible for the greater involvement of women in crime (see also *Gao and Liu* in volume 1 in support of this view and for a different assessment *Beichner and Hagemann* in volume 2). But they also acknowledge that in egalitarian societies women are active in business and politics, which opens up new possibilities for their involvement in organised white-collar crime. The authors see education and information as the most important factor for prevention. Yet in the end, it all depends on the integrity of policymakers. The authors recommend that governments should seriously consider imposing that policymakers include criminologists, fraud experts and other social scientists on their staff.

Howell discusses "Systemic Vulnerabilities on the Internet and the Exploitation of Women and Girls: Challenges and Prospects for Global Regulation". The Internet, as a global phenomenon, has increasingly become host to pervasive forms of cybercrime, among them sexual abuse. Women and girls are, often as a result of underlying socio-economic and political disparities, more vulnerable to many of these forms of cybercrime. This is especially true in lower-income countries. The Internet's "new frontier" is the developing world, where its growth has been extraordinary. In this context, the author points out the "uncomfortable truth" that cybercrimes are also committed by women and even children. Using examples drawn from Africa, the author argues that global regulation is both urgent and needed, but that the development of such a framework will continue to be fraught with difficulties and needs to be contextually and strategically specific to the areas and places in which it is applied. As such, these responses, whether domestic or international, will need to draw on the intellectual capital and resources of multiple state and non-state actors, ranging from local police forces to transnational regulatory agencies, including the UN.

Quirchmayr, Buchegger and Gerö write about a related topic: "Protecting Children and Women Against Online Dangers". The authors argue for increasing domestic and international efforts to protect children from online dangers in a rapidly changing technology-driven world. Whilst criminals usually have to make considerable efforts in the real world, the Internet is a prime platform for such activity at comparatively low costs. After briefly describing the current situation and identifying the resulting challenges for education (especially recommending a holistic approach, i.e. involving families, children, schools, crime prevention specialists, and suitable educational material), the authors present a few case studies, introduce one of the leading European-based computer networks dedicated to this task and look at efforts aimed at online protection of female users. The chapter concludes with arguments for a truly international solution, in which the involvement of many partners, local/domestic and interstate (e.g. Council of Europe and the UN), is essential. At the same time, it is essential to empower children and young people to use the Internet safely.

In **Part VI "Final Discussion"** (seven chapters) *Zhang* writes from a Chinese perspective about "The United Nations, Equal and Inclusive Society and Crime Prevention: Chinese Philosophical Contributions to the Idea of Sustainable Development for Women and Children, and the Current Practice in China". Her chapter takes the reader into another legal culture (see also *Reichel and Albanese* below) and points out the great difference between Chinese and Western legal thought in terms of concepts and methods for dealing with the question of crime prevention for women and children. In Western criminology very little is known in this regard. Recalling Lawrence Sherman's saying that for the practitioners of crime prevention it should not only be an art, but also a science, her article highlights the relevant connotations of sustainable development in traditional Chinese philosophy. With a few strokes the author paints the richness of that philosophy in which Confucian thought already anticipated some of the United Nation's ideas on inclusive and equitable education and on gender equality.

Platzer contributes "Some Insights on the Rights to a Safe City of Women and Girls". He shows the need for such rights by giving the example of gang rapes in India, the murder of "streetwalkers" in the Americas or the kidnapping, trafficking and enslavement of girls in Africa and the Middle East. He then puts those examples in the context of a draft UN sustainable development Goal 11.7 that reads: "by 2030, provide universal access to safe, inclusive and accessible, green and public spaces, particularly for women and children, older persons and persons with disabilities" (A/68/970, p. 18/24). Yet so far, the rights of women and girls to safe cities have been painfully slow to be recognised. By bringing the policies of city officials and the urban planning concerns of adolescent girls together, this can create a real opportunity to create sustainable economic and social change that will benefit all. This means the provision of adequate, safe and affordable housing and infrastructure, but more than that, access to good education, health, transport, human development and social and recreational services. But most importantly, it should involve making cities safe.

Shaw's chapter "Women as Actors in Community Safety: Taking Action Worldwide" approaches the topic of safety from a different angle. The author notes that it has been customary to refer to women's involvement in the criminal justice system and in the field of crime prevention as either victims or offenders, or sometimes as professionals, but that it is much less common to think of the role, which women and girls themselves play in actively promoting safer cities or preventing the violence and crime, which affects them because of their gender. Yet an increasing number of women do assume this role, as demonstrated by the author through concrete examples of such "hands-on" women's participatory approaches in crime prevention, and how they are helping to increase the role of women and girls in decision-making, especially at the local level. The importance of this movement is helping to change policies, attitudes and behaviours towards women and girls in both public and private spaces. The final section of the chapter reflects on the ways in which the Doha Declaration of the Thirteenth United Nations Congress on Crime Prevention and Criminal Justice (12–19 April 2015) aims to strengthen and support this work.

Dünkel discusses "Juvenile Justice and Human Rights: European Perspectives". He underlines that international human rights standards and in particular the Convention on the Rights of the Child (CRC) have had a major impact on juvenile justice reforms in Europe during the last 25 years. The general orientation towards the ideal of education has further been developed in Europe. The development of human rights standards has played a major role in this context. The UN 1985 Beijing-Rules on juvenile justice administration and the CRC have been landmarks in the juvenile justice human rights movement. This chapter evaluates youth justice policies and practice in Europe from a comparative perspective. The focus is on tendencies in youth justice legislation and on the sentencing practice of prosecutors and judges in youth courts. The chapter explains why continental European countries generally have succeeded in resisting "penal populism" in youth crime.

Mitrofanenko writes about "Intergenerational Practice: An Approach to Implementing Sustainable Development and Environmental Justice". She observes that "sustainable development" is a concept hardly pursued in criminal justice, even less so when it comes to the respective role of women and children. The concept is also only nascent in crime prevention, but the elaboration of the post-2015 UN sustainable development agenda may fundamentally change this picture. In line with this agenda, the chapter introduces the idea of intergenerational practice (IP) as a way to operationalise sustainable development and environmental justice (EJ) principles on the local level. Mitrofanenko emphasises that younger people living today are the link between the current and the future society. Yet different generations living today do not always enjoy equitable access to resources and opportunities to engage in the development process. IP has been shown to equalise that access, enhance community cohesion, improve understanding among the younger and older population and diminish the fear of crime in communities.

Breczko and Oliwniak write from a Polish perspective about "Biopolitics, Ethics and the Culture of Lawfulness. Implications for the Next Generation?" Europe is ageing faster than any other continent. The regional demographic crisis and the replacement of generations are currently among the problems most frequently discussed on this continent. This chapter describes the process of the formation of pastoral biopower (Foucault's concept of biopolitics) within the framework of the European culture of lawfulness. It shows how the schools of pronatalism, antinatalism and environmental ethics have shaped the policies of European countries with regard to procreation, as well as people's behaviours in that area. It also describes how demographic policy has evolved under the influence of progress in biotechnology. There is a failure of replacement of generations—successive generations are found to be less populous than the preceding ones; hence the interregionally emanating culture of lawfulness will not be sustained in future.

The authors bring to this volume important philosophical considerations broadening the concept of succeeding generations by including in it humankind's natural environment.

Finally, *Reichel and Albanese* write about "Comparing and Delivering Juvenile Justice Across the World". Their chapter offers a brief historical review of the question of recognition of childhood as an innocent life period followed by a discussion of the nature of formal procedures for handling juvenile offenders and specific governmental and multilateral responses to juvenile delinquency. The chapter considers the variation in attitudes and approaches used over time and place when governments respond to misbehaving young people. The similarities and differences among these approaches are evaluated to assess their contribution to fairness, justice, crime control and delinquency prevention. The authors conclude that the promise of justice for juveniles has not yet been met. Despite international consensus codified in important and universally acclaimed international agreements, the implementation of indicators and procedures to ensure justice for juveniles has lagged, largely because of a shortage of resources. The authors stress the importance to keep the attention focussed on the problem to avoid belated reactions to grave incidents, violence and crises in juvenile justice.

The work closes with the editors following up on the closing statement by H.E. Ambassador *Martin Sajdik*, 70th President of the United Nations Economic and Social Council tasked with the elaboration of the 2016–2030 sustainable development goals for the world. We complement his statement with our Post Scriptum that stresses the need for education in order to arrive at a culture of lawfulness that mirror the United Nations crime prevention and criminal justice values emanating from the United Nations Charter.

Given the size of this collective work, it is published in two separate volumes, each containing the preface, introduction, conclusions and the full index of the work. The editors would like to thank first and foremost all the authors for bearing with us through the long editorial process and attending to our many queries on points of detail. Without their fruitful and interesting cooperation, it would have been impossible to edit this collective work on a very important topic. We also thank the publisher, Springer, and especially Ms. Seyfried for their excellent advice and prompt and efficient publication.

Heuweiler, Germany | Helmut Kury
Vienna, Austria | Sławomir Redo
Zürich, Switzerland | Evelyn Shea
August 2015

References

A/CONF.151/26 (Vol. I) Report of the United Nations Conference on Environment and Development (Rio de Janeiro, 3–14 June 1992).

A/CONF.222/L.6 Draft Doha Declaration on integrating crime prevention and criminal justice into the wider United Nations agenda to address social and economic challenges and to promote the rule of law at the national and international levels, and public participation, Therteent United Nations Congress on Crime Prevention and Criminal Justice (Doha, Qatar, 12–19 April 2015).

A/RES/45/112 (Annex) United Nations Guidelines for the Prevention of Juvenile Delinquency (The Riyadh Guidelines), 14 December 1990.

A/68/970 Report of the Open Working Group of the General Assembly on Sustainable Development Goals, 12 August 2014.

Acemoglu, D. (2012). *The world our grandchildren will inherit: the rights revolution and beyond.* NBER Working Paper No. 17994. http://www.nber.org/papers/w17994

Adler, F. (1975). *Sisters in crime*. New York: McGraw Hill.

Annan, K. (2004). *Letter*. Reprinted in Reuterswaärd CF, Stil aär bedraägeri [Style is Deception]. Vaärnamo: Area.

Austin, J. (2003). Why criminology is irrelevant. *Criminology & Public Policy, 2*, 557–565.

Basu, A. M. (2002). Why does education lead to lower fertility? A Critical review of some of the possibilities. *World Development, 30*(10), 1779–1790.

Behringer, W. (Ed.). (1988). *Hexen und Hexenprozesse in Deutschland*. München: Deutscher Taschenbuch Verlag.

Bloom, P. (2013). *Just babies. The origins of good and evil*. New York: Crown Publishers.

Bowlby, J. (1951). *Maternal care and mental health*. Geneva: World Health Organization.

Brzank, P. (2009). (Häusliche) Gewalt gegen Frauen: sozioökonomische Folgen und gesellschafliche Kosten. *Einführung und Überblick, 52*, 330–338.

Buggle, F. (1992). *Denn sie wissen nicht, was sie glauben. Oder warum man redlicherweise nicht mehr Christ sein kann*. Reinbek b. Hamburg: Rowohlt.

Burman, M., Lovett, J., & Kelly, L. (2009). *Different systems, similar outcomes? Tracking attrition in reported rape cases in eleven countries*. London: Child and Woman Abuse Studies Unit, London Metropolitan University.

BusinessDictionary.Com. http://www.businessdictionary.com/definition/handbook.html

Charter of the United Nations, 1 UNTS 16.

Cohen, J. E. (2003). Human population: the next half century. *Science, 302*, 1172–1175.

Coleman, K., Jansson, K., Kaiza, P., & Reed, E. (2007). *Homicides, firearm offences and intimate violence 2005/6: Supplementary volume 1 to crime in England and Wales 2005/6*. London: Home Office Statistical Bulletin 02/07, Office for National Statistics.

Convention on the Rights of the Child, 1577 UNTS 3.

Cressey, D. R. (Ed.). (1961). *The prison*. New York: Holt, Rinehart and Winston.

Daly, K. (2002). Sexual assault and restorative justice. In H. Strang & J. Braithwaite (Eds.), *Restorative justice and family violence* (pp. 62–88). Cambridge: Cambridge University Press.

Daly, K., & Stubbs, J. (2006). Feminist engagement with restorative justice. *Theoretical Criminology, 10*, 9–28.

ECOSOC resolution 1995/9 (Annex) Guidelines for the prevention of urban crime, 24 July 1995.

ECOSOC resolution 2002/13 (Annex) Guidelines for the Prevention of Crime, 24 July 2002.

Farrington, D. (2002). Developmental criminology and risk-focused prevention. In M. Maguire, R. Morgan, & R. Reiner (Eds.), *The Oxford handbook of criminology* (pp. 657–701). Oxford: Oxford University Press.

Gelsthorpe, L., & Larrauri, E. (2014). Gender and crime in Europe. In S. Body-Gendrot, M. Hough, K. Kerezsi, R. Lévy, & S. Snacken (Eds.), *The Routledge handbook of European criminology* (pp. 188–203). London/New York: Reoutledge.

Grafton, J. (Ed.). (1999). *Great speeches by Franklin Delano Roosevelt*. Mineola, NY: Dover Publications.

Haller, B., & Dawid, E. (2006). *Kosten häuslicher Gewalt in Österreich*. Wien: Institut für Konfliktforschung.

Hausler. K., Urban, N., & McCorqodale, R. (2012). *Protecting education in insecurity and armed conflict: an international law handbook*. London/Doha: British Institute of International and Comparative Law/Education Above All.
Heidensohn, F. (2002). Gender and crime. In M. Maguire, R. Morgan, & R. Reiner (Eds.), *The Oxford handbook of criminology* (pp. 491–530). Oxford: Oxford University Press.
Heidensohn, F. M., & Farrell, M. (Eds.). (1991). *Crime in Europe*. London: Routledge.
Heiskanen, M., & Piispa, M. (2002). *The costs of violence in a municipality. A case study of violence against women and its costs in the city of Hämeenlinna 2001, based on estimates provided by authority representatives*. Helsinki: Ministry of Social Affairs and Health.
Heitmeyer, W., & Schröttle, M. (Eds.). (2006). *Gewalt. Beschreibungen, Analysen, Prävention*. Bonn: Bundeszentrale für politische Bildung.
Hester, M. (2013). Who does what to whom? Gender and domestic violence perpetrators in English police records. *European Journal of Criminology, 10*, 623–637.
Hestermann, T. (2010). *Fernsehgewalt und die Einschaltquote. Welches Publikumsbild Fernsehschaffende leitet, wenn sie über Gewaltkriminalität berichten*. Baden-Baden: Nomos.
Hoffman, M. L. (2000). *Empathy and moral development. Implications for caring and justice Cambridge*. Cambridge: University Press.
Keynes, J. M. (1935). Economic possibilities for our grandchildren. In J. M. Keynes (Ed.), *Essays in persuasion*. London: Macmillan.
Hinckeldey, C., & Kriminalmuseum Rothenburg ob der Tauber (Ed.). (1980). *Strafjustiz in alter Zeit*. Mittelalterliches Kriminalmuseum: Rothenburg ob der Tauber.
Krueger, A. B., & Lindhal, M. (2001). Education for growth: why and for whom? *Journal of Economic Literature, 39*, 1101–1136.
Kury, H. (2003). Wie werden Opfer von Straftaten gesehen? Zur Stigmatisierung von Verbrechensopfern. In S. Lamnek & M. Boatca (Eds.), *Geschlecht – Gewalt – Gesellschaft* (pp. 418–443). Opladen: Leske + Budrich.
Kury, H., & Obergfell-Fuchs, J. (2005). *Gewalt in der Familie. Für und Wider den Platzverweis*. Freiburg: Lambertus.
Lahlah, E., Van der Knaap, L. M., & Bogaerts, S. (2013). Dangerous boys or boys in danger? Esamining the relationship between ethnicity, child abuse and violent offending. *European Journal of Criminology, 10*, 641–658.
Leder, K. B. (1986). *Todesstrafe. Ursprung, Geschichte, Opfer*. München: Deutscher Taschenbuch Verlag.
Lemgruber, J. (2001). Women in the criminal justice system. In N. Ollus & S. Nevala (Eds.), *Women in the criminal justice system: International examples and national responses*. Helsinki: HEUNI.
Levi, M., & Maguire, M. (2002). Violent crime. In M. Maguire, R. Morgan, & R. Reiner (Eds.), *The Oxford handbook of criminology* (pp. 795–843). Oxford: Oxford University Press.
Lewis, H. (2005). Justice from the victim's perspective. *Violence Against Women, 11*, 571–602.
Lundgren, E., Heimer, G., Westerstrand, J., & Kalliokoski, A. (2002). *Captured queen: Men's violence against women in ,equal Sweden – a prevalence study*. Umea: Astrom trykeri AB.
Matvyshyn, A. M., & Generation, C. (2012). Childhood, code, and creativity. *Notre Dame Law Review, 87*, 9–49.
McCord, J. (1983). A forty year perspective on effects of child abuse and neglect. *Child Abuse and Neglect, 7*, 265–270.
McGee, H., Garavan, R., de Berra, M., Byrne, J., & Conroy, R. (2002). *The SAVI report: Sexual abuse and violence in Ireland. A national study of Irish experiences, beliefs and attitudes concerning sexual violence*. Dublin: Liffey Press. http://epubs.rcsi.ie/psycholre/10/
Medina, J., & Barberet, R. (2003). Intimate partner violence in Spain. *Violence Against Women, 9*, 302–322.
Morris, A., & Gelsthorpe, L. (2000). Revisioning men's violence against female partners. *Howard Journal of Criminal Justice, 39*, 412–428.

Moser, T. (1972). *Jugendkriminalität und Gesellschaftsstruktur. Zum Verhältnis von soziologischen, psychologischen und psychoanalytischen Theorien des Verbrechens*. Frankfurt/M.: Fischer.

Müller, U., & Schröttle, M. (2004). *Lebenssituation, Sicherheit und Gesundheit von Frauen in Deutschland. Eine repräsentative Untersuchung zu Gewalt gegen Frauen in Deutschland.* Bielefeld: Interdisziplinäres Frauenforschungs-Zentrum der Universität Bielefeld. www.bmfsfj.de/BMFSFJ/Service/Publikationen/publikationen,did=20560.html

Newburn, T. (2002). Young people, crime, and youth justice. In M. Maguire, R. Morgan, & R. Reiner (Eds.), *The Oxford handbook of criminology* (pp. 531–578). Oxford: Oxford University Press.

Nora, P. (1997). La génération [Generation]. In P. Nora (Ed.), *Les Lieux de mémoire [Sites of memory]* (Vol. 2, Quarto edition). Paris: Gallimard.

Oxfam. (2015, January). Wealth: Having it all and wanting more. Issue Briefing.

Packalén, S. (2010). Culture and sustainability. *Corporate Social Responsibility and Environmental Management, 17*, 118–121.

Palfrey, J., & Gasser, U. (2009). *Born digital*. New York: Basic Books.

Patkar, P. (2001). Consolidating protection against ever-escalating violation. In N. Ollus & S. Nevala (Eds.), *Women in the criminal justice system: International examples and national responses*. Helsinki: HEUNI.

Redo. (2014). Education for succeeding generations in culture of lawfulness. In E. W. Pływaczewski (Ed.), *Current problems of the penal law and criminology* (pp. 698–722). Warszawa: Wydawnictwo C. H. Beck.

Rodriguez-Menés, J., & Safranoff, A. (2013). Violence against women in intimate relations: a contrast of five theories. *European Journal of Criminology, 10*, 584–603.

S/2004/616 Rule of Law and Transitional Justice in Conflict and Post-Conflict Societies. Report of the Secretary-General to the Security Council, 3 August 2004.

Schlesinger, S. E. (2004). *Act of creation: the founding of the United Nations: A story of superpowers, secret agents, wartime allies and enemies, and their quest for a peaceful world*. Cambridge, MA: Westview, Perseus Books Group.

Simon, R. J. (1975). *Women and crime*. Toronto: Lexington Books.

Smart, C. (1977). *Women, crime and criminology*. London: Routledge and Kegan Paul.

Stamatel, J. P. (2014). Explaining variations in female homicide victimization rates across Europe. *European Journal of Criminology*, *11*, 578–600.

ST/ESA/SER.A/313 Department of Economic and Social Affairs, Population Division. (2011). *World population prospects: The 2010 revision, Volume I: Comprehensive tables*. New York: United Nations.

Stubbs, J. (2007). Beyond apology? Domestic violence and critical questions for restorative justice. *Criminology and Criminal Justice, 7*, 169–187.

Suleiman, S. R. (2002). The 1.5 generation: thinking about child survivors and the Holocaust. *American Imago*, *59*, 277–295.

Sykes, G. (1956). *Society of captives*. Princeton: Princeton University Press.

UNICEF-Report 2015. (2015). Kinder zwischen den Fronten. Frankfurt/M.: Fischer (http://www.unicef.de/report2015; http://www.unicef.de/presse/2015/unicef-report--jedes-zehnte-kind-waechst-im-krieg-auf/80378; Summary: http://www.unicef.de/blob/80400/54134727140bd27763126edb7360f25f/zusammenfassung-unicef-report-2015-data.pdf)

Walby, S. (2004). *The cost of domestic violence*. London: Women & Equality Unit, National Statistics. www.statistics.gov.uk

Widom, C. S. (1989). The cycle of violence. *Science,* 244, 160–166.

Widom, C. S., & Ames, M. A. (1994). Criminal consequences of childhood sexual victimization. *Child Abuse and Neglect*, *18*, 303–318.

Wilson, C. (2004). Fertility below replacement level. *Science*, *304*(5668), 207–209.

United Nations. (1945). *Charter of the United Nations*. http://www.un.org/en/documents/charter/preamble.shtml

United Nations Scientific and Cultural Organization. (1997). *International standard classification of education*. Paris: UNESCO.

United Nations Office on Drugs and Crime. (2010). *Handbook on the crime prevention guidelines*. New York: Making them Work, United Nations.

Woźniakowska-Fajst, D. (2015). Criminality and the media. In K. Buczkowski, B. Czarnecka-Dzialuk, W. Klaus, A. Kossowska, I. Rzeplinska, P. Wiktorska, D. Woźniakowska-Fajst, & D. Wójcik (Eds.), *Criminality and criminal justice in contemporary Poland: Sociopolitical perspectives* (pp. 159–169).

Yanay, U., & Borowski, A. (2013). From a court orientation to a victim orientation: the paradigm shift in Israel's Juvenile Probation Service. *European Journal of Criminology*, *10*, 675–689.

Contents of Volume 1

Contents of Volume 2

About the Authors

Jay S. Albanese, Professor of Criminology in the Wilder School of Government and Public Affairs at Virginia Commonwealth University (Richmond, VA, USA). Dr. Albanese served as Chief of the International Center at the National Institute of Justice, the research arm of the U.S. Department of Justice. He has written and edited 17 books, 70 articles and book chapters, and has made keynote and invited presentations in 18 countries. He is recipient of the *Elske Smith Distinguished Lecturer Award* from Virginia Commonwealth University, the *Scholar Award in Criminal Justice* from the Virginia Social Science Association, and the *Gerhard Mueller Award* from the International Section of the Academy of Criminal Justice Sciences. He is a past president and fellow of the Academy of Criminal Justice Sciences. He is currently a member of the Executive Board of the American Society of Criminology.

Dr. Michael Alex, Attorney at Law. He studied law and psychology. His main topics of research/publication are criminal policies and preventive detention. He published several essays on social-therapeutic measures in prison and conducted a study on the legal probation of former prisoners who had been released from prison, although they were still assumed to be very dangerous.

Hassan Alipour, Ph.D. in Criminal Law and Criminology (Shahid Beheshti University, Tehran, Iran, 2009); Assistant Professor of Criminal Law and Criminology at Shahrekord University and Visiting Professor at Isfahan University (Isfahan, Iran). His research interests involve cybercrime, corporate criminal law and national security law. His main articles about family and women issues are: *Women Trafficking: A Crime against Women's Dignity* (2009), *Feminism and Criminology* (2006), *Content-Related Crime*; *the Black Content of Information Technology* (2005).

Charles Robert Mason Allen, Co-Director Justice and Prisons (London, UK); Associate in Penal Reform International; former Director of International Centre for Prison Studies. Main areas of research and publication are youth justice, criminal justice policy, prisons and alternatives to custody. He has authored a number of articles about justice reinvestment and also has an interest in public attitudes to sentencing. He has undertaken assessments of prison systems in various countries and independent investigations into life-threatening incidents of self-harm in UK prisons. He writes a regular blog at http://reformingprisons.blogspot.com/.

Dr. Anna Alvazzi del Frate, Research Director of the *Small Arms Survey* (an independent research project located at the Graduate Institute of International and Development Studies in Geneva, Switzerland) which she joined in 2010, after more than twenty years spent with the United Nations, at UNODC (Vienna, Austria), and earlier at UNICRI (Turin, Italy), and in Angola. A social scientist with vast experience in applied research for evidence-based policymaking, she is a specialist in the application of quantitative and qualitative research methods—especially surveys on crime and violence—in developing and post-conflict settings. Her interests include firearm violence, prevention, monitoring and evaluation, with particular attention to gender aspects.

Mojgan Amrollahi Byouki, Ph.D. Candidate in Criminal Law and Criminology (Albert Ludwigs University, Freiburg im Brsg., Germany). Her research centres on the problems of child abuse and domestic violence; she is an attorney at law, Grade I, Bar Association (Tehran, Iran) and member of the Association for Support of Children against Child Labour.

Dr. Romeo Asiminei, Senior Lecturer, Alexandru Ioan Cuza University of Iaşi (Iaşi, Romania). his main research topics are electoral sociology, political communication and sociological methodology. He is the author of *Electoral Sociology. Elections, Voters and Voting Behavior* (2013) and coauthor of the *Electoral Atlas of Romania 1990 – 2009* (2013).

Dr. Elizabeth V. Ayre, Director of Children of Prisoners Europe (formerly Eurochips), an action research network active in 17 countries across Europe; Research Fellow in European Studies, Maastricht University (Maastricht, The Netherlands). Her research is about policy processes for children affected by parental incarceration in EU Member States from a frame-analytical perspective. Her relevant publications include consultation response to *Strengthening Mutual Trust in the European Judicial Area – a Green Paper on the Application of EU Criminal Justice Legislation in the Field of Detention* (2011); and *Children with Imprisoned Parents: European Perspectives on Good Practice* (co-ed., 2006, 2013), Paris: Eurochips.

Prof. Rosemary Barberet, Professor, (John Jay College of Criminal Justice, City University of New York, New York, NY, USA). She is the Editor of *Feminist Criminology*; author of *Women, Crime and Criminal Justice: A Global Enquiry* (2014); 2014 Recipient of the Distinguished Book Award of the Division of International Criminology, American Society of Criminology; and Recipient of the 2015 Outstanding Book Award, International Section, Academy of Criminal Justice Sciences.

W. Steven Barnett, Ph.D., Director, National Institute for early Educational Research, Board of Governors Professor, Graduate School of Education, Rutgers University (New Brunswick, NJ, USA). His research includes studies of the economics of early care and education including costs and benefits, the long-term effects of preschool programmes on children's learning and development, and the distribution of educational opportunities. His best known works include reviews of the research on long-term effects; benefit-cost analyses of the Perry Preschool and Abecedarian programmes; randomised trials comparing alternative approaches to educating children including length of day, monolingual versus dual-language immersion, the Tools of the Mind curriculum; and the series of State Preschool Yearbooks providing annual state-by-state analyses of progress in public pre-K.

Dawn Beichner, Associate Professor in the Criminal Justice Sciences Department at Illinois State University Normal, Ill, USA; she is a core faculty member in Women's and Gender Studies at that university. She is also a co-director of Peace and Conflict Resolution Studies. Her current research centres on incarcerated mothers in jails and prisons and their transitions home to their families and communities. Recent publications on women as victims, offenders and practitioners in the criminal justice system, include the following which she was a co-author: *"I don't want to go back to that town": Incarcerated mothers and their return home to rural communities*; *An analysis of advertisements: A lens to view the social exclusion of women in police imagery*; *Examining charging agreement between police and prosecutors in rape cases*; *A Comparison of Civil and Criminal Orders of Protection as Remedies for Domestic Violence Victims in a Midwestern County*.

Dr. Klaus M. Beier, M.D., Ph.D., Professor of Sexology and Sexual Medicine at the Charité—Universitätsmedizin Berlin (Berlin, Germany). He specialises in sexual medicine. Since 1997 he has been organising official post-graduate training for physicians and psychologists in this field. His main focus in research is forensic sexology, in particular follow-up studies of previously expert evaluated sex offenders. His current research focuses on the prevention of child sexual abuse. The goal is to encourage self-identified undetected pedophiles and hebephiles to seek professional help in order to avoid committing child sexual abuse or the use of child abusive images (www.dont-offend.org). This project has been awarded in Germany several national prizes. Professor Beier is in charge of the Outpatient Clinic of the Institute of Sexology which deals with the full range of sexual disorders and gender dysphoria. His last English co-authored book publication was *Sexual Medicine in Clinical Practice* (Springer: New York 2013).

Dr. Anne H. Berman, Associate Professor of Clinical Psychology at Karolinska Institutet (Stockholm, Sweden); Licensed clinical psychologist and psychotherapist; chief author of a 2010 Swedish-language textbook *Kriminalvården i praktiken: Strategier för att minska återfall i brott och missbruk [Correctional Work in Practice: Strategies for Minimizing Relapse in Crime and Substance Abuse]*. She is involved in e-health interventions for problematic substance use as well as issues related to criminal justice.

Prof. Dr. Catrien C.J.H. Bijleveld, Director of *Het Nederlands Studiecentrum Criminaliteit en Rechtshandhaving*—NSCR Institute for the Study of Crime and Law Enforcement (Amsterdam, Netherlands); Professor of Research Methods in Criminology at the Vrije Universiteit Amsterdam (VU Amsterdam, Netherlands). Main research interests are criminal careers, female offenders, the intergenerational transmission of offenders, genocide and sex offending. She is the author of several textbooks as well as of edited books, on crime and justice in the Netherlands and on the association between employment and offending.

Dr. Milind Bokil, Freelance writer and Sociologist, Marathi (one of 23 official languages of India) writer from Pune, India. He has been associated with civil society organisations for more than 25 years. He has done extensive work with tribal communities in Maharashtra, and his other research interests centre on natural resource management, rural development, education, gender issues, migrant children and disaster management. He has been writing fiction and non-fiction in Marathi and has published more than ten books: short story volumes, novels, travelogues and socio-anthropological studies.

Prof. Dr. Anetta Breczko, (Habil.), Department of Theory of Law and Philosophy of Law, Institute of Philosophy of Law and Ethics of Law, Faculty of Law, University of Białystok (Białystok, Poland). Fields of study: Philosophy of Law, Theory of Law, Bioethics. From this perspective, she recently published articles on the problem of the legal discourse ethics and the axiology of law in the context of universally recognised moral values (2011), and one article on the question of legalisation of torture, in *War and Peace, Philosophical, Political and Legal Aspects,* co-edited by her (Temida 2, 2013).

Prof. Dr. Daniel Brugman, Emeritus; his professional interests cover the meaning, measurement and conditions of sociomoral functioning, in particular in children and adolescents with externalising problem behaviour. His research focuses on sociomoral development, including moral judgement, moral identity, perception of contextual moral atmosphere, and moral disengagement through self-serving cognitive distortions. His applied research concerns interventions to reduce externalising behaviour in schools and residential settings by stimulating sociomoral development.

Barbara Buchegger, M.Ed. is pedagogical manager of the awareness-raising initiative Saferinternet.at (www.saferinternet.at) based in Vienna, Austria. She is currently developing awareness-raising material on the safe and responsible use of the Internet and mobile devices for the target group of children and young people. She is a teacher trainer and educates parents, young people and children, as well as senior citizens on the safe and responsible Internet use. She is an expert on online behaviour of young people, on social media for NPO, cyber-bullying, sexting, cyber-grooming, online-safety, e-learning, new apps and online tools, as well as on organisational development and large group facilitation for all age groups. She is part of the European network insafe (www.saferinternet.org).

Dr. Jovana Carapic, Political Science; Gender Focal Point in *Small Arms Survey*, an independent research project located at the Graduate Institute of International and Development Studies in Geneva, Switzerland. Her research focuses on the conceptualisations of "authority" with respect to various types of armed groups and what this means for how they interact with the state. Since completing her doctorate, she has been increasingly motivated to extend the insights obtained during her studies to gender-based violence, urbanisation and urban violence mainly through various professional and academic engagements.

Prof. Dr. Meda Chesney-Lind, Chair and Professor of Women's Studies at the University of Hawaii at Manoa (Hawaii, USA); She is nationally recognised for her work on women and crime. Her books include *Girls, Delinquency and Juvenile Justice* awarded by the American Society of Criminology's with the *Michael J. Hindelang Award* for the "outstanding contribution to criminology, 1992" and *The Female Offender: Girls, Women and Crime* (1997, Sage). Her most recent book is an edited collection entitled *Female Gangs in America* (2014, Lakeview Press).

Kris Christmann, Research Fellow, Applied Criminology Centre, University of Huddersfield (Huddersfield, UK). His research is about the effects on children's mental health and well-being when a caretaker is imprisoned (the COPING project); children of prisoners worldwide; political and religious violence, specifically youth radicalisation; hate crime; anti-minority mobilisation; policing of gang-involved young people; and the policing of transnational events.

Prof. Roger S. Clark, Board of Governors Professor, Rutgers University School of Law (Camden, NJ, USA). His scholarship is mostly in the areas of International Criminal Law, International Organizations, Human Rights and the Abolition of Nuclear Weapons. Between 1986 and 1990 he was elected by the United Nations Economic and Social Council as a member of the UN Committee on Crime Prevention and Control. In 1995 he represented the Government of Samoa in the International Court of Justice in the Advisory Proceedings on the use and threat of use of nuclear weapons. He represented Samoa between 1995 and 2010 in the negotiations to create the International Criminal Court and to bring the crime of aggression within its effective jurisdiction. He is currently a member of the team representing the Marshall Islands at the ICJ in its cases against the states possessing nuclear weapons.

Raymond R. Corrado, Professor at the School of Criminology at Simon Fraser University (SFU, Burnaby, BC, Canada). He was an associate SFU faculty member in the Psychology Department and the Faculty of Health Sciences. He is a Visiting Professor in the Faculty of Law at the University of Bergen (Bergen, Norway) and a Visiting Fellow at Clare Hall College and the Institute of Criminology, University of Cambridge (Cambridge, UK). He is a Founding Member of the Mental Health, Law, and Policy Institute at SFU. He also was a former Co-director of the BC Centre for Social Responsibility and former Director of the Centre for Addictions Research British Columbia, SFU site. He is on the editorial boards of 6 major criminology and forensic mental health journals. He has co-authored 9 edited books including, *Multi-Problem Violent Youth*; *Issues in Juvenile Justice*; *Evaluation and Criminal Justice Policy*; and *Juvenile Justice in Canada*, as well as having published over 150 articles, book chapters and reports on a wide variety theory and policy issues, including youth/juvenile justice, violent young offenders, mental health, adolescent psychopathy, Aboriginal victimisation, child/adolescent case management strategies, and terrorism. Currently, he is a principal investigator and co-principal investigator of several research projects including three large-scale studies on incarcerated serious and violent young offenders, on comprehensive risk management instrument for violent children and youth and on early childhood aggression.

Katie Cyr, Ph.D. She is a Researcher at the Université du Québec en Outaouais (Gatineau, Québec, Canada) and a Member of the *Groupe de recherche et d'action sur la victimisation des enfants* (GRAVE). She conducted research on victim's empowerment, on their experience with the criminal justice system and restorative justice. She now conducts research in the mechanisms and dynamics involved in repeat victimisation and in child victimisation, including its effects on child trauma symptoms and delinquent behaviour.

Prof. Yvon Dandurand, Fellow, International Centre for Criminal Law Reform & Faculty, School of Criminology and Criminal Justice, University of the Fraser Valley (Abbotsford, BC, Canada). Specialises in comparative criminal law and criminal justice research and has been extensively involved in juvenile justice reform and policy development projects in Canada and abroad. He recently worked as the UNODC lead consultant for the development of the United Nations Model Strategies and Practical Measures on the Elimination of Violence against Children in the Field of Crime Prevention and Criminal Justice.

Davy Dhondt, Professional Mediator at Suggnomè (the umbrella organisation for victim-offender mediation for adults in the Flemish part of Belgium) with years of experience with different models of mediation and different types of conflicts. For the time of that research project (2 years), he also worked at the Katholieke University of Leuven (Leuven, Belgium) as a researcher of the Criminology Department. In 2013 he co-published *Implementing Peacemaking Circles in a European Context: Additional Findings from a European Research Project.*

Bojan Dobovšek, Professor at Faculty of Criminal Justice and Security, University of Maribor (Maribor, Slovenia). He is also a Member of Parliament of the Republic of Slovenia (from 2014 onwards). His main fields of research are organised crime, corruption, State capture, economic crime, art crime, criminal investigations and lately informal economy researched from a criminological stand point.

Prof. Dr. Dieter Dölling, Director of the Institute of Criminology at the University of Heidelberg (Heidelberg, Germany). His main topics of research include juvenile delinquency, corruption, crime prevention, empirical research on criminal proceedings, and criminal sanctions. His main publications include: *Polizeiliche Ermittlungstätigkeit und Legalitätsprinzip* (1987); *Empfehlen sich Änderungen* *des Strafrechts und des Strafprozessrechts, um der Gefahr von Korruption in Staat, Wirtschaft und Gesellschaft wirksam zu begegnen? Gutachten für den 61. Deutschen Juristentag* (1996); Co-editor: *Jugendgerichtsgesetz. Kommentar*, 12. Edition (2011).

Hannah Dönges, she has a Master of Arts in International Relations/Political Science and is a Ph.D. candidate in International Relations/Political Science. She is pursuing a doctorate at the Graduate Institute of International and Development Studies in Geneva, Switzerland. Her dissertation investigates norms and practices of protecting civilians in armed conflict. She has previously worked with the *Small Arms Survey* (an independent research project located at the Graduate Institute of International and Development Studies in Geneva, Switzerland), in the African regional office of the Centre for Humanitarian Dialogue, the Brookings Institution, the European Council on Foreign Relations, among others. During her research and work, she focuses on aspects of armed violence and conflict analysis, particularly in sub-Saharan Africa.

Prof. Dr. Frieder Dünkel is a Professor of Criminology and Head of the Department of Criminology at the University of Greifswald (Greifswald, Germany). He is author of 36 books and about 500 articles which cover a wide range of empirical studies in juvenile criminology, penology, prisons and community sanctions, alcohol and drunk driving, human rights, etc. He and the other staff of the department conducted several empirical international comparative projects on men's prisons in the states of the Baltic Sea, on women's imprisonment in Europe, on long-term imprisonment in ten European countries and on youth violence in the states of the Baltic Sea. His most recent project involved *Restorative Justice in Penal Matters* in 36 European countries (funded by the Criminal Justice—Programme of the EU, 2015).

Dr. Ioan Durnescu is a Senior Lecturer at the University of Bucarest, Bucarest, Romania; he teaches comparative probation, social work in prison and rehabilitation methods of offenders. He also conducts research on probation or prison issues. He is the co-editor of the *European Journal of Probation* and also of the *Probation in Europe* (2008).

Prof. Dr. John Peter Joseph Dussich is a Master's of Science in Criminology and Corrections; Doctor of Philosophy in Criminology and Sociology; and Professor Emeritus of Criminology and Victimology. His main topics of research are criminology, corrections, work release, parole, coping juvenile delinquency, victimology, victim assistance, child abuse victims, elder abuse victims, sexual assault victims, family violence victims, victims' rights, abuse of power victims, disaster victimization and recovery, psycho-social coping theory; and human trafficking victims and femicide victims.

Prof. Dr. Beate Ehret, she is a Professor at the Federal College of Public Administration (Wiesbaden, Germany), a Researcher, sociologist and criminologist. Her career progression reflects her experience in research of more than 15 years on a variety of topics related to juvenile delinquency, its formal and informal control, recidivism, risk assessment and restorative justice. From 2011 to 2013 she was the Research Coordinator of a pilot study funded by the European Commission on the implementation of Peacemaking Circles in the European Union. Currently she teaches criminology and sociology at the Federal College of Public Administration and conducts a research project with the goal of developing a "best practice" model for police investigators dealing with victims of international and war crimes or human rights violations.

David Philip Farrington, Professor Emeritus of Psychological Criminology, Cambridge University (Cambridge, UK) and Leverhulme Trust Emeritus Fellow, Cambridge University. His main research interest is in developmental and life-course criminology and prospective longitudinal studies of offending. He is Director of the Cambridge Study in Delinquent Development, a prospective longitudinal survey of over 400 London males from age 8 to age 56. He is also very interested in experimental evaluations of crime prevention programmes and in cost-benefit analysis.

Prof. Dr. Thomas F. Feltes, M.A., Chair of Criminology and Police Science, Law Faculty, Ruhr-University Bochum (Bochum, Germany). His main fields of research are in all aspects of law enforcement and justice. Since 1998 he is the editor of the *Police Newsletter*, a monthly published E-mail- and Internet-newsletter on police and criminology, in German, English, French and Spanish (www.police-newsletter.com). He published 15 books and over 160 articles on juvenile law, sentencing, alternative sanctions, public prosecution, policing.

Liliana Foca, Project Manager, Mental health of Romanian children of prisoners. She also consults on family relations; problems faced by partners of prisoners; policies aiming for the wellbeing of vulnerable children in general and of children with parents in prison in particular.

Diana Harumi Fuentes Furuya, Human Rights Officer, United Nations Office of the High Commissioner for Human Rights in Geneva, Switzerland. Main topics of research include the United Nations treaty bodies, multiple and intersecting forms of discrimination, and the human rights of migrant workers. Her current focus is the right to education for persons with disabilities.

Huan Gao, Associate Professor of Criminal Justice, California State University, Stanislaus, CA, USA. She received her Ph.D. from the School of Criminal Justice at Rutgers University. Her areas of expertise include substance abuse and crime, gender, crime and justice, and juvenile criminal gangs. She published a book *Women and Heroin Addiction in China's Changing Society* (Routledge, 2011). She also has publications on drug trafficking, drug control policy, criminological theory and organised crime etc.

Cristina Gavriluta, Professor of Sociology at the Alexandru Ioan Cuza University, Faculty of Philosophy and Social Work (Iași, Romania). Main topics of research are prisons; reintegration of prisoners through labour; mental health of children of prisoners. Author of 5 books and more than 50 articles and studies, including: *Human Trafficking. Secularization and Public Policy Intervention* (2013), *The Social Construction of Justice* (2010), *Sacred Rituals, the Body's Religious Symbolism and Human Trafficking* (2013).

Loraine Gelsthorpe, Professor of Criminology and Criminal Justice at the Institute of Criminology, University of Cambridge (Cambridge, UK); President of the British Society of Criminology (2011–2015). She has international expertise in a range of criminological topics, including: Youth justice, gender, crime and justice, and community sanctions. She teaches research methods, ethics, critical criminological theories, and socio-critical perspectives on crime and justice. Her current research includes: Anti Human Trafficking Measures, Migration and Crime, the Arts in Criminal Justice contexts, and the links between Criminal and Social Justice.

Aleksandra Sandra Gerö, M.A., Psychologist in private practice, Trainer for Media Education, Expert Team Member of the Office of Ombudsman for victims of violence and abuse in the Catholic Church, Management Team Member of the Section Psychotraumatology and the Arbitration Board at the Professional Association of Austrian Psychologists (BÖP), former Member of the Expert Commission of the Austrian Ombudsman Board (2012–2015) and the Human Rights Advisory Board of the Ministry of the Interior (2009–2012). For many years she has been working with victims of domestic and/or institutional violence and in the training of professionals in the victim consultation. She has publications in the field of Knowledge Management, Learning and Reflexivity in Teams, Online Counselling, Media Education for Counsellors.

Prof. John C. Gibbs, Ph.D., His work has concerned developmental theory, assessment of social cognition and moral judgement development, and interventions with conduct-disordered individuals. His authored or co-authored books include *Moral Development and Reality: Beyond the Theories of Kohlberg, Hoffman, and Haidt*; *Moral Maturity: Measuring the Development of Sociomoral Reflection*; and *The EQUIP Program: Teaching Youth to Think and Act Responsibly through a Peer Helping Program.*

Sally Goldfarb, Professor of Law at Rutgers University School of Law (Camden, NJ, USA), where she has earned several teaching awards. She has also taught at Harvard Law School, New York University School of Law, and University of Pennsylvania Law School. Before joining the Rutgers faculty, she was a staff attorney at Legal Momentum (formerly NOW Legal Defense and Education Fund). Whilst at NOW LDEF, she was instrumental in the drafting and passage of the federal Violence Against Women Act of 1994. She is the author of many articles and book chapters on violence against women, family law, and other topics. She has served on several boards and commissions, including the New Jersey Supreme Court Committee on Women in the Courts, the Board of Advisers for the American Law Institute's Principles of the Law of Family Dissolution, and three expert groups on violence against women convened by the United Nations Division for the Advancement of Women or UN Women.

Julie Goldscheid, Associate Dean for Academic Affairs and Professor of Law at the City University of New York (CUNY) School of Law (New York, USA), where she teaches subjects including civil procedure, lawyering, and courses on gender and law. Her scholarship focuses on gender equality, with a particular focus on gender-based violence and economic equality. Before joining the CUNY faculty, she held positions including senior staff attorney and acting legal director at Legal Momentum (formerly NOW Legal Defense and Education Fund), where her litigation and policy work included defending the constitutionality of the civil rights remedy of the 1994 Violence Against Women Act in courts nationwide, and before the U.S. Supreme Court in *United States v. Morrison*. She has served on the Board of Directors of the Stonewall Community Foundation and other NGOs, and has been active in bar association committees and task forces. She has taught at Columbia Law School, NYU School of Law, Penn State Law School and Brooklyn Law School. She received her law degree from NYU School of Law, a master's in social work from Hunter College School of Social Work, and her undergraduate degree from Cornell University.

Dr. Syeda Tonima Hadi, Associate Protection Officer, Division of International Protection, United Nations High Commissioner for Refugees (Geneva, Switzerland). Recently published in *The Routledge Handbook of International Crime and Justice Studies* on the criminalisation of women worldwide and the need for an International Feminist Criminology. For her dissertation, she conducted research on people's perceptions about Intimate Partner Violence (IPV) in the context of Bangladesh. Previously, she has written on gender issues such as patriarchal attitudes of Bangladeshi couples regarding domestic violence.

Prof. Dr. Otmar Hagemann, Kiel University of Applied Sciences (Germany). His main research topics are Restorative Justice at various levels, Victimology, Criminology, Peacebuilding and Action Research in Social Work. His publications include: co-edited: *Victimology, Victim Assistance and Criminal Justice. Perspectives Shared by International Experts at the Inter-University Centre of Dubrovnik.* Mönchengladbach: Hochschule Niederrhein (2009). Hagemann, O. (2010) *Restorative Justice – A European and Schleswig-Holsteinian Perspective. Restorative Justice – Aus der europäischen und Schleswig-Holsteinischen Perspektive.* Kiel: SH Verband für Soziale Strafrechtspflege (2011). Other publications are: *Restorative Justice in the Context of Victim Needs and Coping Strategies of Victims.* In: Lummer, R./Nahrwold, M./Süß, B. (eds) (2012). *Restorative Justice - A Victim Perspective and Issues of Co-operation.* Kiel: SH Verband für Soziale Strafrechtspflege, pp. 46–67. *Exploring and Understanding Victim Empathy.* In: Schäfer, Peter and Weitekamp, Elmar (eds.). *Establishing Victimology. Festschrift for Prof. Dr. Gerd Ferdinand Kirchhoff. 30th Anniversary of Dubrovnik Victimology Course.* Mönchengladbach: Hochschule Niederrhein (2014).

Carolyn Hamilton is Professor Emeritus of Law at the University of Essex, a Fellow of the Human Rights Centre and Director of Coram International at Coram Children's Legal Centre UK. She was also the Senior Legal Adviser to the Children's Commissioner and served as the Children and Families Commissioner to the Legal Services Commission. She is an internationally known child rights lawyer who has published widely on issues of children's rights. Her latest research on Legal Protection for Violence: Analysis of Domestic Laws Related to Violence Against Children in ASEAN Member States was shortlisted for the best of UNICEF research award 2015. She has worked with the UN, in over 20 different countries on issues of juvenile justice, child protection and access to justice.

Prof. Dr. Jan Hendriks, Clinical psychologist at the forensic outpatient treatment centre De Waag in The Hague (The Netherlands) as well as Professor in Forensic Psychiatry and Psychology and Professor in Forensic Orthopedagogics at Vrije Universiteit Amsterdam (University of Amsterdam, The Netherlands). He specialises in the treatment of and research on juvenile sex offenders. He also conducts research on (juvenile) female sex offenders and treatment programmes designed for juvenile delinquents.

Prof. Dr. Dieter Hermann, University Lecturer, Adjunct Professor of Sociology (University of Heidelberg, Heidelberg, Germany); Research in sociology of crime, empirical methods and statistics, sociology of culture, ethics. Publications include: *Posttraditionale Ethik. Empirische Analysen und theoretische Reflexionen*. Hamburg 2008; *Werte und Kriminalität. Konzeption einer allgemeinen Kriminalitätstheorie*. Wiesbaden 2003; *Die Abschreckungswirkung der Todesstrafe – ein Artefakt der Forschung?* In: Dölling, D. et al. (Hrsg.): *Verbrechen – Strafe – Resozialisierung. Festschrift für Heinz Schöch*. Berlin, New York 2010.

Prof. Thomas Hestermann, Ph.D., Media School, Macromedia University of Applied Sciences, Hamburg and Berlin (Germany). He researches on the reporting of violence and media effects. His major topics are changes in journalism, new formats on television, online journalism and media ethics. Before, he worked at the Criminological Research Institute of Lower Saxony, Hannover (Germany). He published numerous articles on the situation of crime victims, especially second victimisation, coping strategies and media coverage of crime victims. He researched also on human trafficking. Besides his academic activities, he works as a journalist for German public television stations.

Jessica M. Hill, M.Sc., Ph.D. candidate at *Het Nederlands Studiecentrum Criminaliteit en Rechtshandhaving* - NSCR Institute for the Study of Crime and Law Enforcement (Amsterdam, The Netherlands). Her Ph.D. research focusses on emerging adulthood, looking at young people aged 18–29 years old. She examines how changes in their lives affect their delinquent and antisocial behaviour, testing criminological theories relating to desistance from crime in adulthood.

Tarah Kathleine Hodgkinson, Ph.D. Student in the School of Criminology at Simon Fraser University (Barnaby, BC, Canada). Her research areas include crime prevention, neighbourhood safety and sustainability, victimisation, policing, political protest, and violence. She currently works with community members of high-crime neighbourhoods to improve safety and social cohesion. She is also working with a national research group focused on the sustainability of policing in Canada.

Dr. Simon Peter Howell, Research Fellow at the Centre of Criminology, University of Cape Town (Cape Town, The Republic of South Africa). He has engaged with and published on a diverse selection of topics pertinent to contemporary South Africa. Recent publications include, for instance, critiques of the legislative framework in which illegal substances have been regulated, gangsterism, youth violence, gender issues and racial conflict. All of these topics share a core concern with questions of identity, and the manner in which they intersect with the structural and legislative frameworks that continue to define the country.

Andrea Huber, Policy Director at Penal Reform International (London, UK) since 2011, responsible for advocacy at a regional and international level and the development of policy. A lawyer by training, research of human rights issues and advocacy for the implementation and advancement of international human rights law have been at the core of her work. Starting as a legal counsellor for asylum seekers in 1997, subsequently she headed the department for refugees and migration of Caritas Austria with a focus on advocacy and policy development. After a one-year engagement in the judiciary as a legal assistant to judges of the Regional Higher Court Vienna she joined Amnesty International, tasked with research and advocacy in different functions in the Vienna office, the EU office in Brussels and as Deputy Director for Europe and Central Asia at Amnesty International's headquarters in London. She published two books and contributed to several evaluation reports and comparative analyses in the European context. She participated in field missions to DR Congo, Ukraine, Syria and Georgia and has got varied experience in trainings.

Raggie Johansen, Research Officer, Researcher for the Global Report on Trafficking in Persons, is part of the small team that produces the biennial UNODC Global Report on Trafficking in Persons. She has focused on analysing case briefs of prosecuted cases of trafficking in persons around the world to learn more about the organisation of trafficking in persons and the modus operandi of traffickers. She is also involved in data collection through in-depth interviews with experienced criminal justice system personnel. She has contributed to UNODC research on illicit drug markets and a broad range of transnational organised criminal activities, in its publications such as the annual World Drug Report and the Transnational Organized Crime Threat Assessment.

Kristiina Kangaspunta, Chief, Global Report on Trafficking in Persons Unit, UNODC. She has been involved with international crime prevention and criminal justice work for more than 20 years. For the last 13 years, she has been working with the United Nations. She is currently heading the preparation of the biennial

Global Report on Trafficking in Persons at UNODC (Vienna, Austria). Previously, she was the Deputy Director of UNICRI, leading the Research Programme. Before UNICRI, she worked with UNODC, as the Chief of the Anti-Human Trafficking Unit. She moved to UNODC from the Ministry of Justice of Finland where she worked at the European Institute for Crime Prevention and Control, affiliated with the United Nations (HEUNI). She has participated in the planning and coordination of several research projects on crime trends and victimisation. She has been involved in the development of the International Violence against Women Survey and she was the chair of the research section of the National Project on Eliminating Violence against Women as well as the chair of the working group to develop the first national violence against women survey in Finland.

Patricia Kanngiesser, Ph.D., Marie Curie Research Fellow, Department of Developmental and Comparative Psychology, Max Planck Institute for Evolutionary Anthropology (Leipzig, Germany). She completed a Ph.D. in Psychology at the University of Bristol in 2012 and was a visiting researcher at Harvard University and Kyoto University. Her research is in the area of social cognition and social interactions, focusing on questions relating to social norms. She has conducted research on the development of ownership norms in young children and adults, and on norms of fairness and promise keeping. In her work she combines a developmental and comparative approach, studying non-human primates and human children from Western and non-Western (small-scale) populations. She has published numerous, peer-reviewed articles and regularly participates in international conferences.

Witold Klaus, Assistant Professor at the Department of Criminology, Institute of Law Studies, Polish Academy of Sciences (Warsaw, Poland); President of the Polish Association for Legal Intervention and Secretary of the Board of the Polish Society of Criminology. Graduate of the School of Human Rights at the Helsinki Foundation for Human Rights. Holds a Post-Graduate Diploma in Evaluating Social Programmes at the Institute of Sociology, University of Warsaw. Main academic interests: the problems of criminality and the victimisation of immigrants; issues related to social exclusion and criminality, juvenile delinquency and restorative justice. Works with migration, the rights of foreigners, and the functioning of the principle of non-discrimination and equal treatment. Currently works on problems of violence against immigrant women and criminalisation of immigration (crimmigration).

Dorothee Klecha, Dr. Med., Dipl.-Psych.; Consultant for Psychiatry and Psychotherapy; Forensic Psychiatry Certificate SGFP; Head of Forensic Psychiatric Service (FPD), University of Bern (Bern, Switzerland). Studied medicine and psychology at the University of Göttingen, Germany, training as a clinical psychiatrist at the University Hospital Freiburg (Freiburg im Brsg., Germany). Since 2012 Head of Forensic Psychiatric Service (FPD), University of Bern, Switzerland. Since 2012 board member of the Swiss Society of Forensic Psychiatry (SGFP). Lectures in Forensic Therapy and Milieu Therapy at the Institut für Opfer- und Täterschutz

(IOT Zurich). Publications on general and forensic psychiatry issues including mental health issues in Africa, problem solving, cognitive behavioural and interpersonal psychotherapy, depressive disorder, effectiveness of offender rehabilitation and psychotherapy programmes, schema therapy in forensic settings and women offenders. Special interests in the development of services and the implementation of forensic treatment programmes for offenders with mental disorders.

Barbara Krahé, Professor of Social Psychology, University of Potsdam, Germany. Her research interests lie in the domain of applied social psychology, in particular aggression research (media violence and aggression, sexual aggression) and social cognition research applied to legal decision-making (rape myths and biases in judgments about sexual assault). Her co-authored book *Sexual Assault and the Justice Gap: A Question of Attitude* was published in 2008.

Sandy Krammer, Dr. Phil., Psychologist. He studied psychology at the University of Zurich (Zurich, Switzerland). Research assistant and doctoral student at the Department of Psychopathology and Clinical Intervention at the University of Zurich, Switzerland (2010–2012). He defended Ph.D. thesis on "Studies on classic and complex PTSD and the role of social-interpersonal factors". Since 2012 he has been research assistant at the Forensic-Psychiatric Service (FPD), University of Bern, Switzerland. He completed postgraduate training at the School of Criminology, International Criminal Law and Psychology of Law, University of Bern. Main topics of research include complex PTSD, psychotraumatology, incarcerated women, forensic therapy evaluation, criminal psychology.

Dr. Izabela Anna Kraśnicka, she holds a doctoral degree in law and is an Associate Professor in the Department of Public International Law of the Faculty of Law at the University ofBialystok (Białystok, Poland). Her research and teaching fields include three main areas: international law of aviation, constitutional law of the United States in comparative perspective, as well as modern challenges of legal education. In addition to her academic responsibilities she acts as the Dean's Representative for International Relations who runs exchange programmes at the Faculty, including the Erasmus Plus programme of the European Union. She has been a member of the board of the Polish Legal Clinics Foundation since its establishment and thus has been involved in the development of the clinical educational programmes nationwide and abroad.

Helmut Kury, Prof. h.c. Mult., Dr. Dipl.-Psych. He studied Psychology at the University of Freiburg (Freiburg im Brsg., Germany), Diploma, Dr. in Psychology and Habilitation at the Unviersity of Freiburg. Between 1970 and 1973 Assistant Teacher at the University of Freiburg, Institute for Psychology, between 1973–1980 and from 1989 to 2006 Senior Researcher at the Max-Planck-Institute for Foreign and International Penal Law in Freiburg im Brsg, Department of Criminology, 1980–1988. First and Founding Director of the Criminological Research Institute of Lower Saxony (KFN). Research in offender rehabilitation, crime prevention, attitudes to punishment, fear of crime, punitivity, alternatives to punishment, methodological problems of empirical social science research, international comparison of crime and punishment. Most recent publications: Kury, H., Ferdinand, T.N. (Eds.) (2008). *International Perspectives on Punitivity*. Bochum: Universitätsverlag Dr. Brockmeyer; Kury, H. (Ed.)(2008). *Fear of Crime – Punitivity. New Developments in Theory and Research*. Bochum: Universitätsverlag Dr. Brockmeyer. Kury, H., Shea, E. (Eds.)(2011). *Punitivity – International Developments*. 3 Vols., Bochum: Universitätsverlag Dr. Brockmeyer.

Dr. Tapio Lappi-Seppälä, Director of the Institute of Criminology and Legal Policy, member of the Finnish Academy of Sciences (Helsinki, Finland) with a long career as a researcher and senior legislative advisor in the Ministry of Justice. He has taken actively part in international research co-operation in several international organisations. His publications cover over 250 titles including books, research reports and articles in several languages in the field of criminal law, criminology and penal policy. His recent research activities are focused on comparative criminal justice and penal policy, on which he has lectured widely in Europe and overseas. Selected writings: Tapio Lappi-Seppälä. *Changes in Penal Policy in Finland*. In Punitivity. International Developments. Vol. 1: *Punitiveness - a global Phenomenon?*, In H. Kury and E. Shea (eds), Universitätsverlag Dr. Brockmeyer. Bochum, Germany, 2011; *Explaining imprisonment in Europe*. European Journal of Criminology, 2011; Co-authored and/or co-edited: *Crime and Justice in Scandinavia. Crime and Justice: A Review of Research*, vol. 40, Chicago: University of Chicago Press, 2011; *The development of crime in light of Finnish and Swedish criminal justice statistics, ca. 1750–2010*. European Journal of Criminology, 2013; *Cross-Comparative Perspectives on Global Homicide Trends*. In: *Crime and Justice: A Review of Research*, vol. 43, Chicago: University of Chicago Press, 2015.

Zina Lee, Assistant Professor School of Criminology (University of the Fraser Valley, Abbotsford, BC, Canada). Her primary research interests include the assessment and development of psychopathic personality traits and aggression in youth. Other research interests include deception, false confession, and programme evaluation. Recent publications examine the challenge of assessing aggression in youth and distinct profiles of high-risk youth. Her recent research focuses on risk and protective factors for youth cybercrime and the development of policies and laws to address youth cybercrime.

Martti Lehti, LL.D., Senior Researcher, Institute of Criminology and Legal Policy, University of Helsinki (Helsinki, Finland). Current projects: Finnish Homicide Monitor. Selected publications in English: *Homicide Trends in Estonia in 1971–1996. In Five Centuries of Violence in Finland and the Baltic Area*. History of Crime and Criminal Justice Series. Columbus: Ohio State University Press, 2001; *Homicide Trends in Finland and Estonia in 1880–1940*. Journal of Scandinavian Studies in Criminology and Crime Prevention, 2011. Co-author of: *Trafficking for Sexual Exploitation*. In: *Crime and Justice* (ed. Michael Tonry), Vol. 34. Chicago: The University of Chicago Press, 2006; *Homicide in Finland, the Netherlands and Sweden. A First Study on the European Homicide Monitor Data. The*

Swedish National Council for Crime Prevention Research Report 2011, Stockholm: Brå., 2011; *Homicide in Finland and Sweden*. In: *Crime and Justice in Scandinavia* (eds. Michael Tonry & Tapio Lappi-Seppälä), Volume 40. Chicago: The University of Chicago Press, 2011; *Social Correlates of Intimate Partner Homicide in Finland: Distinct or Shared with Other Homicide Types?. Homicide Studies*, 2012; *The Declining Number of Child Homicides in Finland, 1960–2009. Homicide Studies*, 2012. Author of *Homicide Drop in Finland, 1996–2012. Journal of Scandinavian Studies in Crime Prevention and Criminology*, 2014.

Jianhong Liu, Professor at University of Macau (Taipa, Macau, China), President, Scientific Commission of International Society for Criminology; President, Asian Criminological Society, Editor-in-Chief, Asian Journal of Criminology. His primary interest is in comparative criminology and criminal justice. His major contribution is in the area of Asian Criminology. He is the author, editor, or co-editor of 19 books, and chief editor of a book series on *Criminal Science and Drug Crimes in China*. He has authored, co-authored more than 60 journal articles and book chapters, many appeared in journals such as *Justice Quarterly, Criminology, British Journal of Criminology, Criminology, the Journal of Research in Crime and Delinquency*.

Alexandra V. Lysova, Dr. of Sociology (Russian Academy of Sciences); Ph.D. candidate in Criminology (University of Toronto), Trudeau Scholar at the Centre for Criminology and Sociolegal Studies at the University of Toronto. For over 10 years her main research interests have been in intimate partner violence, homicide, and the intersection of male and female offending and victimisation. The other research interests involve the examination of situational patterns of violence; gender inequality and violence against an intimate partner cross-nationally; corporal punishment of children in the families; and criminalised women in Canada and Russia. Recent publications appeared in the *Aggressive Behavior, Journal of Interpersonal Violence, Nordic Studies on Alcohol and Drugs, and Handbook of European Homicide Research*.

Martin Manby, Ph.D., Affiliate of the University of Huddersfield (Huddersfield, UK). Previously: Director, Nationwide Children's Research Centre, Huddersfield (UK). Main topics of his research are parenting programmes; family support; child protection. His recent articles have included family support provided in a women's prison; and family processes among families of children and prisoners, including re-appraisal of the imprisoned parent and the emergence of family policy for handling parental imprisonment.

Ineke Haen Marshall, Ph.D., Professor of Criminology and Sociology, Northeastern University (Boston, MA, USA). She specialises in comparative and international criminology and crime policy, migration and crime, self-report methodology, juvenile delinquency and criminal careers. Her current research focuses on cross-national surveys of juvenile delinquency and comparative examination of homicide. She is the chair of the Steering Committee of the International Self-Report

Study of Delinquency (ISRD), an international collaborative study with participants from countries all over the globe (www.northeastern.edu/isrd).

Jeff Mathesius, Ph.D. student in the School of Criminology at Simon Fraser University (Burnaby, BC, Canada). His current research interests include the development of violence and sexual aggression, as well as the risk assessment and management of serious violent juvenile offenders.

Tamara Mitrofanenko, Education for Sustainable Development Consultant in the United Nations Environmental Programme (UNEP, United Nations Office at Vienna, Austria); Project manager at Zoi Environment Network. The main topic of her research and practice is involvement of the local population of the rural mountainous regions, especially the younger and the older people, in sustainable development. Currently she focuses on intergenerational practice as a potential approach to engaging the local youth and elderly in protected area management and tourism development. Her research is linked to the UNEP projects, and aims at being transdisciplinary and at facilitating capacity-building of the research partners and local stakeholders. Co-author of: *Potential for Applying Intergenerational Practice to Protected Area Management in Mountainous Regions. Mountain Research and Development*, 2015; *Transferability Tool Kit. Big Foot. Crossing Generations, Crossing Mountains. Project "Big Foot. Crossing Generations, Crossing Mountains*, Vienna, Austria, http://www.bigfoot-project.eu/transferability-tool-kit.html.

Anganile Willie Mwenifumbo, Legal Practitioner, Human Rights Officer, United Nations Office of the High Commissioner for Human Rights (Geneva, Switzerland). She conducted extensive research and has written on biotechnology, biodiversity, climate change, the right to food, ethnicity and the right to development, post-genocide justice mechanisms in Rwanda, the African human rights system and on the United Nations treaty body system. Her main research focus is on the implementation of human rights standards.

Dr. Vesna Nikolić–Ristanović, Professor at Belgrad University (Belgrad, Serbia). Her main fields of experience and research include: violence against women, war victimisation, women's crime, war and crime, domestic violence, trafficking in people, and truth and reconciliation. Among the most important publications are: *Women, violence and war* (ed.), *From victim to prisoner: domestic violence and women's crime, Social Change, Gender and Violence*: *Post-Communist and War-Affected Societies, Surviving Transition: Everyday life and Violence in Post-communist and Post-conflict Societies, Domestic Violence in Serbia* (ed.) *and Domestic Violence in Vojvodina* (ed.).

Milagros Nores, Ph.D., Associate Director of Research, National Institute for Early Education Research (Rutgers University, New Brunswick, NJ, USA). Her research includes early childhood attainment, the economics of education, poverty, and international and comparative education. She currently runs a randomised longitudinal early childhood study in Colombia and another randomised trial on parental-child educational practices for minority children in the U.S. Her best known works include: reviews of the international research on effects of early childhood interventions; benefit-cost analyses of the Perry Preschool, and research on early achievement gaps for Hispanic and bilingual children.

Sławomir Oliwniak, Ph. D., Senior Lecturer at the Department of Law Theory and Philosophy of Law, Faculty of Law, University of Białystok (Białystok, Poland). His main fields of interests are: postmodernism and law, Foucault and Agamben's analysis of law, biopower and biopolitics, surveillance society. He published respective articles on, e.g. *Foucault and Agamben: law as inclusive/exclusive discourse. In: Language, Law, Discourse,* ed. by M. Aleksandrowicz, H. Święczkowska, Studies in Logic, Grammar and Rhetoric, 2011; *Biopolitics and the rule of law.* In: *Axiology of the Modern State Under the Rule of Law. Selected Issues,* ed. by S. Oliwniak, H. Święczkowska, Studies in Logic, Grammar and Rhetoric, 2009.

Christa Out-van Kessel, MSc., Research Assistant, Faculty of Social and Behavioural Sciences, Utrecht University (Utrecht, The Netherlands). As a research assistant her main interest is in applied research on children and adolescents with externalising behaviour and conduct disorder, and in research on moral development. Furthermore, she participated in research on gene x environment interactions, specifically on the concept of differential susceptibility. Alongside her work as research assistant, she also works as a child psychologist in mental health care, with children aged 4–18, with various diagnoses. She is specialised in doing diagnostic research and treating children and their parents by intensive home treatment programmes.

Batoul Pakzad, Ph.D., Assistant Professor in Criminal Law and Criminology at the Islamic Azad University (Tehran, Iran), Head of the Law Department. Dr. Pakzad is also an attorney-at-law and professional and legal adviser in Iran, and is currently serving as a counsellor in the Ministry of Justice. She has been a deputy and the Chair of the Law Commission of the High Council of Provinces in Iran and advisor of women affairs for the local governor in Rafsanjan. Although her primary interest has always been the study of and research in Criminal Law, Criminology, Islamic Law, jurisprudence and comparative law, other topics of her research and publications include cybercrime, cyber-terrorism, family law and criminality and victimisation of women and children in the real world and cyberspace.

Martin Peper, Prof. Dr. rer. medic. Dr. Phil., Clinical Neuropsychologist GNP, Studied psychology at the University of Heidelberg; Dr. phil. at the University of Heidelberg (Heidelberg, Germany), Dr. rer. medic. at the Charité, Medical Faculty of the Humboldt University Berlin (Berlin, Germany); Assistant Professor and Associate Professor (until 2006), Personality Psychology Section, University of Freiburg im Brsg., Germany; Visiting Scholar, Center for Neural Science, New York University, USA (1992). Since 2007 full Professor of Neuropsychology, Faculty of Psychology, University of Marburg (Marburg, Germany). Adjunct Research Associate and forensic psychology expert at the Forensic Psychiatry

Service (FPD), University of Bern (Bern, Switzerland). Associate board member and chairman of the scientific advisory board of the German Neuropsychological Society (GNP). Main topics of research include medical, clinical and experimental neuropsychology, criminology, neurobehavioural toxicology. Publications on emotional and personality disorders in patients with cerebral diseases, emotional and executive dysfunction in offenders with mental disorders, research on forensic psychotherapy effects; psychophysiological assessment in the clinical setting and in everyday life. Co-author of a textbook on emotion psychology (2014); books and articles on neuropsychology, criminology, behavioural toxicology, ambulant psychophysiological monitoring.

Adrienne M.F. Peters, Ph.D., Sessional instructor in the School of Criminology and Criminal Justice and a research assistant for the Centre for Public Safety and Criminal Justice Research at the University of the Fraser Valley (Abbotsford, BC, Canada). She completed her doctoral research at Simon Fraser University, which examined the offending and risk assessment outcomes for severely mentally disordered, serious-violent, and gang-involved young offenders assigned to specialised community supervision programmes. Her research interests include young offenders; serious and violent youth offending; mental health and its association with delinquency; young offender treatment, programming, and rehabilitation; the Youth Criminal Justice Act and young offender policy; best practices in policing; and collaborative crime reduction strategies. She has presented at conferences and co-authored publications in each of these areas. She acts as the research director for the Study on Specialized Community Case Management of Young Offenders and served as a research assistant on a number of other research projects.

Kate Philbrick, OBE, Board member, Children of Prisoners Europe (COPE). She researches on best practices concerning the guidance on how to support and provide for children of prisoners, from the point of arrest through court and sentencing to imprisonment and release. Particular emphasis on provision for children visiting prisons, and training of prison officers in relation to this.

Dr. Michael Platzer, main topics of scientific activities are Human Rights, Rights of Victims, Prisoners Rights, Prison Pastoral Care, Migrant Rights, Juvenile Justice, Death Penalty, Femicide, Social Media, Radicalization of Youth, Development, Climate Change, Sustainable Development Goals. Main Publications are *Jugendliche im Gefängnis? Modelle im Umgang mit straffälligen Jugendlichen, Schriftenreihe des Bundesministeriums für Justiz.* In: *Chancengleichheit für die Jugend; Österreichische und Europäische Initiativen gegen Soziale Ausgrenzung*, Wien, 2009; *Vienna Conference on the Abolition of the Death Penalty: Working Together towards the Universal Abolition of the Death Penalty*, Bundesministerium, ACUNS, 2011; *"Empfehlungen für die Behandlung von Ausländern in Haft", International Commission for Catholic Prison Pastoral Care, "Grundprinzipien: Religion im Gefängnis", International Commission of Catholic Prison Pastoral Care.* In: *Academics Meet UN Practitioners: An Encounter in Vienna*, Favorita Papers, 2010; *UN Agencies Reaching out to Academia and Civil*

Society, Favorita Papers. Diplomatische Akademie, 2013; *Vienna Vision: Peaceful, Inclusive, Prosperous, and Sustainable World,* Academic Council on the United Nations System, 2015. *Femicide: A Global Issue That Demands Action*, Volumes 1–3, Academic Council on the United Nations System, 2013, 2014, 2015.

Emil Walenty Pływaczewski, Prof. Dr. (Habil.) of Penal Law and Criminology; Dean of the Faculty of Law, University of Bialystok (Białystok, Poland); Director, Institute of Criminal Law; Head of the Department of Penal Law and Criminology. His literary output comprises over 370 publications, published in Poland and abroad (70), a dozen of them are monographs. His research interests include organised crime, money laundering, corruption, criminal policy and public security issues. In 1997 he won the Distinguished International Scholar Award of the International Division of the American Society of Criminology. Many times, he was a guest lecturer or visiting professor at the universities in Australia, Austria, Belgium, Brazil, China, the Czech Republic, Germany, Lithuania, Finland, France, Greece, India, Italy, Japan, The Netherlands, New Zealand, The Republic of Korea, Switzerland, Turkey, and in the United States of America. In the years 1994–2012, he had been the representative of Poland in the International Examination Board of the Central European Police Academy. Since 2005 he is Chief Coordinator of the Polish Platform for Homeland Security (PPHS)—a unique initiative in Europe whose activities aim at creating integrated computer tools to support the broadly defined efforts to improve public security.

Dr. Ineke Pruin, Research Associate at the University of Greifswald (Greifswald, Germany). Her main research interests focus on prisoner resettlement, juvenile justice and sentencing practices. Some of her recent publications in English include co-authored *Young Adult Offenders in Europe: Interdisciplinary Research Results and Legal Practices*. Barrow Cadbury Trust, London, 2014, and her own article *Law, Diversion and Community Sanctions in Juvenile Justice*. In: Bruinsma G, Weisburd D (eds), Encyclopedia of Criminology and Criminal Justice. Springer, New York, 2014, and *Conditional release in Germany*. In: Padfield N, van Zyl Smit D, Dünkel F (eds), *Release from Prison: European Policy and Practice*. Willan, Collumpton, 2010; *Recalling conditionally released prisoners in Germany*. European Journal of Probation, 2012, plus the co-edited book: *Juvenile Justice Systems in Europe – current situation, reform developments and good practices*. 2nd edn. Forum Verlag Godesberg, Mönchengladbach, 2011.

Gerald Quirchmayr, Univ.-Prof. DI, Dr. Dr., Faculty of Computer Science, University of Vienna (Vienna, Austria); Adjunct Professor, School of Information Technology & Mathematical Sciences, University of South Australia. His major research focus is on information systems in business and government with a special interest in security, applications, formal representations of decision-making and legal issues. His publication record comprises approximately 150 peer reviewed papers plus several edited books and conference proceedings as well as nationally and internationally published project reports.

Vijay Raghavan, Professor and Chairperson, Centre for Criminology and Justice, School of Social Work, Tata Institute of Social Sciences (Mumbai, India). Primary research interests include custodial justice and prison reforms in post-colonial societies, social work practice in criminal justice regimes, and more recently, youth involvement in organised crime in post-industrial cities.

Mehrdad Rayeijan Asli, Ph.D., in Criminal Law and Criminology, Shahid-Beheshti University (Tehran, Iran); Assistant Professor, Faculty of Law, Tarbiat-Modares University (Tehran, Iran). Research in victimology, criminology, sociology of crime, criminal policy, and criminal law. Experiences in teaching the above topics at several universities in Iran. Over 50 articles published in scientific-research journals. She published: *The Victim in Criminal Justice Process*, Khatte-Sevom Pub., Tehran, 2002; *Assistant-oriented Victimology*, Dadgostar Pub., Tehran, 2002 and 2006; *Design Out Crime* (translated into Persian), Mizan Pub. Tehran, 2009 and 2011; *Victimology*, Vol. I., Shahre-Danesh, Tehran, 2009; *Handbook of Victimology* (translated into Persian), Armane-Hoquq, Tehran, 2012; *Contemporary Critical Criminology* (translated to Persian), Dadgostar, Tehran, 2013; *Victimology*, Vol. II, Shahre-Danesh, Tehran, 2014; Cyber Crime and Victimization of Women, Majd Pub., Tehran, 2014.

Sławomir Redo, Dr. Habil.(Law/Criminology); former UN Senior Crime Prevention and Criminal Justice Expert and staff of the UNODC (ret.); Senior Programme Adviser, Academic Council on the United Nations System (Liaison Office, Austria, Vienna). Now as an independent scholar and lecturer he teaches "The United Nations and Crime Prevention"—a graduate course delivered at the universities in Austria, China and Poland; Member of the editorial boards of: *Asian Journal of Criminology*; *Caribbean Journal of Criminology*, the *Journal of International Organization Studies*. Author of: "*Blue Criminology. The Power of United Nations Ideas to Counter Crime Globally*" (HEUNI, Helsinki, 2012); and three other books; Co-Editor of: *For the Rule of Law: Criminal Justice Teaching and Training @cross the World* (HEUNI, Helsinki, 2008), and of *Global Crime and Justice Report* (Oxford, 1999). About 70 articles and book chapters on various crime and justice issues, mostly covered by United Nations law and practice, including cross-national crime trends, crime prevention, computerisation of criminal justice, cyberspace crime, extradition, policing, principles of prosecution, judicial independence, victim compensation, death penalty, organised crime; international and intercultural crime prevention in education.

Philip Reichel, Ph.D., Emeritus Professor at the University of Northern Colorado (Greeley, CO, USA) and Adjunct Professor at the University of New Hampshire Law School. He is the author of Comparative Criminal Justice Systems (2013): A Topical Approach, co-editor of *Handbook of Transnational Crime and Justice* (2014); and co-editor of *Human Trafficking: Exploring the International Nature, Concerns, and Complexities* (2012). He has authored or co-authored more than 30 articles, book chapters, and encyclopaedia entries. He has lectured at universities in Austria, Germany, and Poland, was a presenter for a United Nations crime prevention webinar, presented papers at side events during the Twelfth United Nations Congress on Crime Prevention and Criminal Justice (Brazil) and the United Nations Commission on Crime Prevention and Criminal Justice (Vienna), and was an invited speaker at Zhejiang Police College in Hangzhou, China.

Oliver Robertson, Project Manager at the Prison Reform International (London, UK) on: death penalty and alternatives, comparative international studies on the rules and realities for children with parents in prison, international human rights related to children of prisoners, children of parents sentenced to death, wider impacts of the death penalty; death penalty.

Federico Rossano, Ph.D. (Linguistics), Radboud University, Nijmegen (Netherlands). Worked at the Max Planck Institute for Psycholinguistics from 2004 to 2008 and as a guest researcher at the Max Planck Institute for Evolutionary Anthropology from 2009 to 2011. Since 2012, he is a post-doctoral researcher in the Department of Developmental and Comparative Psychology at the Max Planck Institute for Evolutionary Anthropology in Leipzig (Germany). His research interests include: social cognition and communication in human infants and non-human primates, ontogeny and phylogeny of property concerns, value perception, distributive and procedural justice, conversation analysis and the role of visible behaviour (gesture and gaze in particular) in face-to-face interaction.

Irena Rzeplińska, Professor of Law and Criminology in the Department of Criminology of the Institute of Law Studies in the Polish Academy of Sciences (Warsaw, Poland); Vice-Director of the Institute of Law Studies; Editor-in-Chief of the oldest Polish criminological journal „Archives of Criminology". Her fields of research are deviance, self-report studies, crime and crime policy—historical and contemporary, foreigners criminality in Poland, youth crime—past and present. Publications (among others) in H. Kury & E. Shea (eds): *Punitivity. International Developments*, Bochum 2011; A. Selih & A. Zavrsnik (eds): *Crime and Transition in Central and Eastern Europe,* Springer 2012; I. Rzeplińska as co-author in: K. Buczkowski and others: *The Sociopolitical Background of Contemporary Criminality in Poland*, Warsaw, ed. SEDNO 2013 in Polish (Ashgate 2015 in English); and author: *An evergreen or forgotten subject: relationship among crime, criminology and criminal policy*—plenary lecture on EUROCRIM 2013, Budapest, published in Proceedings of Criminology, Hungarian Society of Criminology, 2014.

Fabrizio Sarrica, Research Officer for the Global Report on Trafficking in Persons Unit of the UNODC. He holds a Ph.D. in Criminology, a Master degree in Economics and International Relation and a University degree in Economics. Dr. Sarrica has been working as a researcher for UNODC since the year 2002. In this role, he has conducted researches and assessments on corruption, organised crime, smuggling of migrants and trafficking in persons in different parts of the world. He is the co-author of four UNODC *Global Reports on Trafficking in Persons*.

Dr. Marco F.H. Schmidt, Department of Developmental and Comparative Psychology, Max Planck Institute for Evolutionary Anthropology (Leipzig, Germany). He investigates the developmental origins of human normativity and morality, with a particular focus on mechanisms of norm acquisition, norm enforcement, and norm creation. Furthermore, he is interested in interrelations between moral, social-cognitive, and prosocial development.

Dr. Monika Schröttle, Visiting Professor at TU Dortmund (Dortmund, Germany). Since 2013 Project Director at the Institute for Empirical Sociology at the University of Erlangen-Nürnberg (Nürnberg, Germany). Together with Dr. Renate Klein she coordinates the European Network on Gender and Violence (www.engv.org). She was project director for the first large-scale German representative survey on violence against women. The data of the study that was published in 2004 and then was further analysed in relation to questions of risk factors, levels and types of violence, health impact and migration. With a background in political science and interdisciplinary violence research in women's and gender studies, she focuses on the empirical analysis of violence in gender relations. Her newest quantitative study at the University of Bielefeld was concerned with violence against disabled women in Germany and is the first representative survey on violence with disabled women in Europe.

Rossella Selmini, Ph.D., in Social and Political Science of the European University Institute; Associate Professor and Research Associate, Department of Sociology, University of Minnesota (Minneapolis, MN, USA). Her field of work is the analysis of crime phenomena and of criminal public policies. During her career she has directed many research projects, both quantitative and qualitative, on crime, victimisation, crime prevention and violence against women and she is author or co-author of several books and many papers in Italian and international journals and edited books on the same topics. Her recent works focus on trends in rape e in female homicide in a comparative perspective.

Kathryn Sharratt, M.Sc., Lecturer in Criminology (Department of Criminology, Sociology and Politics, University of Huddersfield, Huddersfield, UK). She researches forensic and criminal psychology; offending behaviour and experiences of imprisonment; the role of personality in suicide-related behaviour among prisoners; children's experiences of visiting parents in prison; validation of emotional and behavioural measures among samples of children affected by parental imprisonment; confirmatory factor analysis; latent class analysis; propensity score matching techniques.

Margaret Shaw, Ph.D., sociologist and criminologist. She was Director of Analysis and Exchange at the International Centre for the Prevention of Crime (ICPC, Montreal, Québec, Canada) from 1999 to 2011. She now works as an independent consultant. Before joining ICPC she worked for over 20 years as a research and policy advisor in the Home Office, England. Between 1986 to 1999 she was a lecturer and Associate Professor in the Department of Sociology & Anthropology at Concordia University, Montréal, and undertook research for Federal, Provincial and municipal governments and police organisations in Canada. She has undertaken extensive research internationally including for UNODC, UN-HABITAT, UN WOMEN and WHO and published widely on crime prevention, youth violence, justice and rehabilitation, gender, women's imprisonment and safety, human trafficking, and evaluation. In 2013 she was awarded the *Saltzman Prize for Contributions to Practice* by the Division of Women and Crime, American Society of Criminology, and in 2014 the *G.O.W. Mueller Award for Distinguished Contributions to International Criminal Justice,* from the International Division of the Academy of Criminal Justice Sciences. Recent publications are: 2010 Preparation of *Handbook on the Crime Prevention Guidelines: Making Them Work,* United Nations, New York; 2013 *Building Inclusive Cities*: *Women's Safety and the Right to the City*. (Co-ed.) London: Earthspan; *Too Close to Home: Guns and Intimate Partner Violence*. In: Small Arms Survey Yearbook 2013; *Everyday Dangers*. Geneva and Cambridge: University of Cambridge Press & Small Arms Survey, 2013; *International, national and local government policies to reduce youth violence*. In: Violence: A Global Health Priority. Edited by Donnelly, P.D. and Ward, C. Oxford: Oxford University Press, 2014.

Evelyn Shea, LL.D. (University of Basel), Diploma in Criminology, Institute of Criminology, Cambridge, England, Ph.D. in Law and Criminology (University Robert Schuman, Strasbourg), Her main interest lies in the role of work in prison, and the rehabilitation of prisoners. Her publications include: *Le travail pé nitentiaire: un défi européen* (Paris: L'Harmattan, 2006), *Why Work?* (Berlin: Drucker & Humblot, 2007), *Punitivity, International Developments*, 3 volumes (Bochum: Universitätsverlag Brockmeyer, 2011) co-edited with Helmut Kury, and several articles in academic journals. She is an independent researcher and currently a prison visitor (Zurich, Switzerland).

Prof. Swati Shirwadkar, Ph.D. in Sociology, University of Pune, India, Dr. h.-c. (Tampere University, Finland); Professor & Head, Department of Sociology and Director, Erasmus Mundus Euroculture Program, University of Pune, India. Her research interests and publications are broadly in the field of socio-cultural changes, gender, sexuality and violence, reproductive health, religion, education and development, globalisation, diaspora and identity issues. Engaged in research projects on life-style issues for the IT sector, regional social history, social changes and empowerment of village people, reproductive health challenges for primitive tribe women, international comparisons of dating violence and violence against women.

Boštjan Slak, Researcher and part-time member of the Chair of Criminal Investigation at the Faculty of Criminal Justice and Security, University of Maribor (Maribor, Slovenia). His research interests are issues of integrity, white-collar and organised crime, as well as media portrayal of criminal investigation and its influence on criminal investigation process.

Elisabeth Stanners, Secondary School Principal, Vienna International School (Vienna, Austria). Facilitator of the generation of data for other researchers on topics related to best practice in schools. Research for implementation within a school setting in the areas of language acquisition, additive bilingualism, assessment, character education, educational leadership and service learning.

Ljiljana Stevkovic, M.Sc., Teaching assistant, Faculty of Special Education and Rehabilitation, University of Belgrade (Belgrade, Serbia). Researcher volunteer at the Victimology Society of Serbia, member of the Victimology Society of Serbia, European Society of Criminology (ESC), ESC Working group of young researchers, European Working Group of Researchers on Organized Crime, and the European Working Group on Victimology. She participated in numerous national and international projects on crime victims, victims of domestic violence, victimisation of children, juvenile delinquency, human and victim rights and protection of women victims of violence who are serving prison sentences. In the area of the research interest she published numerous papers dealing with the problem of domestic violence, juvenile delinquency, victimisation of children and the elderly, and trafficking in human organs.

Dora Szego, Researcher, sociologist and Ph.D. student at Corvinus University Budapest (Budapest, Hungary). She is the assistant director of the Central and East-European department of the International Institute for Restorative Practices. She is involved in research projects since 2011 related to Restorative Justice in prisons, in the criminal justice system, and in local communities at Foresee Research Group.

Jan Van Dijk, degree in law from Leiden University (1970) and a Ph.D. in criminology from the University of Nijmegen (1977). He is Emeritus Professor at the International Victimology Institute (INTERVICT) of the University of Tilburg (Tilburg, The Netherlands) and Visiting Professor at Lausanne University, Switzerland. He is a member and vice-president of the *Group of Experts on Action against Trafficking in Human Beings* (GRETA) of the Council of Europe and vice-president of the Dutch State Compensation Fund for Victims of Violent Crime. He published extensively on victims' rights, crime prevention and human trafficking. His latest monograph is *The World of Crime: Breaking the silence on issues of security, justice and development*, Sage, 2008. He co-edited the book *The New Faces of Victimhood; Globalization, Transnational Crimes and Victim Rights* (Springer, 2011) and *The International Drops in Crime* (Palgrave/Mac Millan, 2012). In 2009 he received the Sellin-Glueck Award of the American Society of Criminology and in 2012 the Stockholm Prize in Criminology.

Kathrin Vogt, M.A., Research assistant at the Universities of Bielefeld, Gießen, Nuremberg and Dortmund (Germany). With a background in pedagogics and interdisciplinary violence research in women's and gender studies she was working at the Institute for Interdisciplinary Women's and Gender Studies, University of Bielefeld from 2011–2014. She is currently research assistant for studies on violence against women (with disabilities) at the Gender Studies Unit of the University of Gießen, as well as at the Institute for Empirical Sociology at the University of Nuremberg, Germany. Here she supported different national as well as international projects on women's political issues, as, e.g. the first representative survey on violence against disabled women in Germany and the Daphne Project "Access to specialised victim support services for women with disabilities who experienced violence". Furthermore she assisted in the (re)establishment of a European network on Gender and Violence.

Dr. Thomas Gerald Walsh (Ph.D. in Religion, Vanderbilt University, Nashville, TN); President of the Universal Peace Federation, an international NGO in special consultative status with the United Nations Economic and Social Council. With academic training in the field of Religion and Ethics, he earned his Ph.D. at Vanderbilt University. He has been a teacher, author and editor, with specialisation in areas of interfaith relations, religious studies, religion and peace, philosophy and social theory. He serves on the International Council of the World Association of Non-Governmental Organizations, and on the board of directors of the International Coalition for Religious Freedom and The Washington Times. He serves as Publisher of *UPF Today* magazine and *Dialogue and Alliance*, a scholarly interfaith journal. He has contributed to and edited more than twenty books related to interfaith, peacebuilding and renewal of the United Nations; among these volumes are *Renewing the United Nations and Building a Culture of Peace* and *The Millennium Declaration of the United Nations: A Response from Civil Society.*

Jo-Anne M. Wemmers, Ph.D. (Leiden University, The Netherlands); Professor, School of Criminology, Université de Montréal (Montreal, Quebéc, Canada). Her research interests focus on victims in the criminal justice system in the broadest possible sense. Central themes in my research are victims' justice judgements and therapeutic jurisprudence. She has published widely in the areas of victimology, international criminal law and reparative justice, including: *Reparation for Victims of Crimes against Humanity* (2014), *Therapeutic Jurisprudence and Victim Participation in Justice* (2011); *Introduction to Victimology* (2003).

Prof. Dr. Werner Wintersteiner, Ph.D., Director of Centre for Peace Research and Peace Education, University of Klagenfurt, Austria. Director of the University Master Program (further education) "Global Citizenship Education". His professional interests include development of a complex transdisciplinary peace research with a strong focus on cultural dimensions including post-colonial approaches, development of a comprehensive peace education, linking civic education, conflict resolution, and a culture of remembrance—globalisation, post-colonialism, transculturality and literature (education).

Gunda Wößner, Professor of Psychology at the University of Applied Police Sciences Baden-Wuerttemberg in Villingen-Schwenningen (Germany). From 2006 to 2014 Senior Researcher in the Department of Criminology at the Max Planck Institute for Foreign and International Criminal Law, Freiburg im Brsg., Germany. Her primary research interests include sexual and violent offending, particularly offender treatment and recidivism, evaluation research, effects of electronic monitoring, and restorative justice in cases of sexual violence. Her recent publications focus on correctional treatment outcome in violent and sexual offenders with particular consideration of recidivism, therapeutic change, prison climate, education and employment, on electronic monitoring of offenders in Germany, and on mental health problems in juvenile offenders.

Dagmara Woźniakowska-Fajst, Doctor of Law, Criminologist, Assistant Professor at the Faculty of Criminology, Institute of Law Studies, Polish Academy of Sciences (Warsaw, Poland), and at the Department of Criminology and Criminal Policy at the Institute of Social Prevention and Resocialisation, University of Warsaw. Interests include victimology, harassment issues in an emotional context, deviant behaviour of juveniles and women, crime as presented in the media, and justice system policy. Member of the European Society of Criminology, the Polish Society of Criminology, and the Association for Legal Intervention.

Elizabeth Yarrow, Senior Researcher with the Coram Children's Legal Centre (London, UK). She specialises in conducting applied social and legal research on a range of thematic rights issues, with a particular focus on the nexus between childhood, gender and violence. She has an LLM in International Human Rights Law and MA in Social and Political Sciences from Cambridge University.

Luis Arroyo Zapatero, Professor Dr. h. c. mult., criminal law professor and Director of the Institute of European and International Criminal Law at the University of Castilla-La Mancha, Spain, of which he is Rector Emeritus. Since 2002 he is President of Société Internationale de Défense Sociale with headquarters in Paris and Milan. Scientific Advisory Board member and Vice President thereof from 2009 of the Max-Planck Institute for Foreign and International Criminal Law in Freiburg i. Br. Vice President of the Association Internationale de Droit Pénal (2007), Member of the Board of Directors of the International Society of Criminology (2005) and of International Scientific and Professional Advisory Council of the United Nations Crime Prevention and Criminal Justice Program (ISPAC). His publications have focused mainly on four areas: penal protection of human rights at the workplace, economic criminal law; European criminal law; relations between criminal law and Constitution and death penalty world abolition processes. Last 10 years publications in http://uclm.academia.edu/LuisArroyoZapatero.

Yingjun Zhang, Ph.D., Associate Professor in International Law (Law Faculty, South-Central University for Nationalities, Wuhan, P.R. China), Member of the Chinese Society of International Law (CSIL). In 2011 and 2013 Visiting Scholar at the Max Planck Institute for Foreign and International Criminal Law, Freiburg im Brsg. Germany. Her research focuses on corporate liability under international criminal law. She published *The Legal Issues of International Law on Transnational Corporate Offences (Beijing, 2012), Corporate Criminal Responsibility in China, 2012.*

Abbreviations

ABA	American Bar Association
ACUNS	Academic Council on the United Nations System
ADHD	Attention deficit hyperactivity disorder
APD	Antisocial Personality Disorder
BPD	Borderline Personality Disorder
BWS	Battered Woman Syndrome
CAI	Child abusive images
CAT	Convention against Torture and Other Cruel, Inhuman or Degrading Treatment or Punishment
CAPTA	The Child Abuse Prevention and Treatment Act (US)
CBT	Cognitive-bahavioural therapy
CCPC	Chicago Child–Parent Center
CED	Committee on Enforced Disappearances
CEDAW	Convention on the Elimination of All Forms of Discrimination against Women
CERD	Committee on the Elimination of Racial Discrimination
CESCR	Committee on Economic, Social and Cultural Rights
CIEL	Center for International Environmental Law
CIP	Center for Inergenerational Practice
CIT	Couter Interrogation Tactics
CMW	Committee on the Protection of the Rights of All Migrant Workers and Members of Their Families
ComEDAW	Committee on the Elimination of All Forms of Discrimination against Women
COPING	Children of Prisoners, Interventions and Mitigations to Strengthen Mental Health
CoSA	Circles of Support and Accountability
CRC	Convention on the Rights of the Child
CRPD	Committee on the Rights of Persons with Disabilities
CSA	Child Sexual Abuse

CTA	Criminal Tribes Act
CWS	(US) Child welfare system
DFG	Deutsche Forschungsgemeinschaft (German Research Foundation)
DNA	Deoxyribonucleic acid
DNT	De-notified tribes
DRF	Dynamic risk factors
DSM	Diagnostic and Statistical Manual of Mental Disorders
EC	European Commission
EMIL	European Map of Intergenerational Learning
EPR	European Prison Rules
ECHR	European Court of Human Rights
EMCDDA	European Monitoring Centre for Drugs and Drug Addiction
ENGW	European Network on Gender and Violence
ESCCJ	European Sourcebook of Crime and Criminal Justice
FBI	Federal Bureau of Investigation
FGC	Family Group Conference
FGM	Female genital mutilation
FRA	Agency for Fundamental Rights (EU)
GBAV	Global Burden of Armed Violence
GCPEA	Global Coalition to Protect Education from Attack
GTD	Global Terrorism Data Base
HOA	Habitual Offenders Act
HRC	Human Rights Committee
IACHR	Inter-American Commission on Human Rights
ICC	Iranian Civil Code
ICCPR	International covenant on Civil and Political Rights
ICD	International Classification of Mental and Behavioural Disorders
ICD	International Criminal Law
ICERD	International Convention on the Elimination of All Forms of Racial Discrimination
ICESCR	International Covenant on Economic, Social and Cultural Rights
ICIP	The International Consortium for Intergenerational Programmes
ICMW	International Convention on the Protection of the Rights of All Migrant Workers and Members of Their Families
ICPED	International Convention for the Protection of All Persons from Enforced Disappearance
ICPS	International Centre for Prison Studies
ICRPD	Convention on the Rights of Persons with Disabilities
ICT	Information and Communication Technology
ICVS	International Crime Victims Surveys
IHDP	Infant Health and Development Program (US)
IHL	International Humanitarian Law
IHTL	International Human Rights Law
IL	Intergenerational Learning

ILO	International Labour Organisation
IOM	International Organisation for Migration
IP	Intergenerational Practice
IPJJ	Interagency Panel on Juvenile Justice
IPV	Intimate Partner Violence
ISRD2/3	International Self Report Delinquency Study
JGG	Jugendgerichtsgesetz (Youth Court Law)
MDG	Millennium Development Goals
MST	Multi-systemic therapy
MTCT	Mother to child transmission of HIV/AIDS
NAFTA	North American Free Trade Agreement
NGO	Nongovernmental Organisation
NIC	National Institute of Correction (US)
NICHD	National Institute of Child Health and Human Development (US)
NIDA	National Institute on Drug aBuse (US)
NSCAW (US)	National Survey of Child and Adolescent Well-Being
OECD	Organization for the Economic Cooperation and Development
OBC	Other Backward Classes
OSRSG	United Nations Office of the Special Representative of the Secretary-General on Violence against Children
PAHO	Pan American Health Organization
PFC	Prefrontal Cortex
PPD	Prevention Project Dunkelfeld
PTE	Potentially Traumatic Events
PTSD	Post-traumatic stress disorder
PV	Partner violence
RAD	Reactive attachment disorders
RJ	Restorative justice
RNR	Risk/Need/Responsivity Model
SC	Schedule of Castes
SCR	(UN) Security Council Resolutions
SD	Sustainable Development
SDGs	Sustainable Development Goals
SDQ	Strength and Difficulties Questionnaire
SES	Self Esteem Scale
SPT	Subcommittee on Prevention of Torture
SRH	Sexual and Reproductive Health
ST	Schedules of Tribes
STAC	Strategies Towards Active Citizenship
STD	Sexually Transmitted Disease
STI	Sexually transmitted infections
TFC	Treatment foster Care
TOA	Täter-Opfer-Ausgleich

ToM	Theory of Mind
TWP	Together Women Programme
UN	United Nations
UNEA	United Nations Environmental Assembly
UNECE	United Nations Economic Commission for Europe
UNDAW	United Nations Division for the Advancement of Women
UNICEF	United Nations Children's Fund
UNICTI	Interregional Crime and Justice Research Institute (UNICRI)
UNiTE	UN Secretary-General's Campaign to end violence against women
UNODC	United Nations Office on Drugs and Crime
UNRISD	United Nation's Research Institute for Social Development
US EPA	United States Environmental Protection Agency
VOM	Victim-offender mediation
WAVE	Women Against Violence Europe
WHO	World health Organization
WCED	United Nations World Commission on Environment and Development
YLS/CMI	Youth Level of Service/Case Management Inventory

Part I
UN Principles for Crime Prevention-Treatment of Women and Children

International Human Rights Law on Violence Against Women and Children and Its Impact on Domestic Law and Action

Sally Goldfarb and Julie Goldscheid

Abstract There is a growing momentum for international and domestic legal reforms to confront violence against women and children, as indicated by the Convention to Eliminate All Forms of Discrimination against Women, the Convention on the Rights of the Child, and recent initiatives by the United Nations and others. This chapter examines the impact and potential of international human rights law as a component of efforts to prevent and redress violence against women and children.

1 Introduction

Violence against women and children exists in every country in the world and constitutes a pervasive violation of human rights, a threat to public health and safety, and an obstacle to the achievement of equality, development, and peace.[1] Laws, policies and community-driven initiatives have made important inroads. The problem's persistence reflects its scope and depth, and underscores the importance of multifaceted, ongoing responses.

The rates of violence against women and children reveal the vast scale of the problem. More than one-third of women worldwide have experienced physical or sexual intimate partner violence or non-partner sexual violence (World Health Organization (WHO) 2013, p. 31). According to the United Nations Special Rapporteur on violence against women, "most Member States have acknowledged that violence against women is the most prevalent human rights violation facing countries, with spousal/partner violence as the most common manifestation of such

[1] See United Nations General Assembly (2011), Annex para. 2 (describing violence against women). This chapter provides an overview of the topic and is not intended to be comprehensive.

S. Goldfarb (✉)
Rutgers Law School, Camden, NJ, USA
e-mail: sfg@law.rutgers.edu

J. Goldscheid
City University of New York, School of Law, New York, NY, USA
e-mail: goldscheid@mail.law.cuny.edu

H. Kury et al. (eds.), *Women and Children as Victims and Offenders: Background, Prevention, Reintegration*, DOI 10.1007/978-3-319-08398-8_1

violence" (Manjoo 2013a, para. 43). Other types of violence against women also occur with staggering frequency. "Significant numbers of the world's population are routinely subject to torture, starvation, terrorism, humiliation, mutilation, and even murder simply because they are female" (Bunch 1990, p. 486).

Violence against children is likewise a widespread phenomenon. Between 500 million and 1.5 billion children throughout the world endure some form of violence every year, according to the United Nations Office of the Special Representative of the Secretary-General on Violence against Children (Office of the Special Representative of the Secretary-General on Violence against Children (OSRSG) 2013, p. 1). In a single year, the World Health Organization (WHO) estimated that 53,000 children worldwide died as a result of homicide, and 150 million girls and 73 million boys under the age of 18 experienced forced sexual intercourse or other forms of sexual violence (Pinheiro 2006a, para. 28).

Despite the prevalence and severity of violence directed at women and children, securing effective remedies through international human rights law has been a slow and laborious process. Progress has accelerated in recent years, as the following discussion will show. Nevertheless, challenges remain. In the words of United Nations Secretary-General Ban Ki-moon, "Violence against women and girls continues unabated in every continent, country and culture. . . . Most societies prohibit such violence—yet the reality is that too often, it is covered up or tacitly condoned" (United Nations Department of Public Information (UNDPI) 2008, p. 1). Similarly, in defiance of the principle that all violence against children is preventable and none is justifiable, it persists throughout the world and is often supported by social acceptance, legal approval, and government authorization (Pinheiro 2006b, pp. XI, 3, 10).

2 Factual Background, History, and Recent Initiatives

2.1 Definitions

The World Health Organization has defined violence as "[t]he intentional use of physical force or power, threatened or actual, against oneself, another person, or against a group or community, that either results in or has a high likelihood of resulting in injury, death, psychological harm, mal-development or deprivation" (Krug et al. 2002, p. 5). This definition is intended to broaden the conventional understanding of violence to include acts that are the products of unequal power in relationships. The definition encompasses neglect as well as all types of physical, sexual and psychological abuse. Recognizing that "[m]any forms of violence against women, children and the elderly . . . can result in physical, psychological and social problems that do not necessarily lead to injury, disability or death," the definition is designed to reflect "the full impact of violence on individuals, communities and society at large" (ibid.).

"Violence against women" has been defined as "any act of gender-based violence that results in, or is likely to result in, physical, sexual or psychological harm or suffering to women, including threats of such acts, coercion or arbitrary deprivation of liberty, whether occurring in public or in private life" (United Nations General Assembly 1993, A/RES/48/104, Art.1).[2] "Violence against women" and "gender violence" are umbrella terms that cover the multiple forms of violence committed primarily against women and girls, including battering, sexual assault, rape, sexual harassment, trafficking in women and forced prostitution, and other harmful practices, including forced marriage, female genital mutilation and so-called honor crimes.[3] Women and girls are disproportionately the targets of these acts.[4] At the same time, gay men and transgender individuals also have a heightened risk for these forms of abuse, although their experiences often are not counted or measured in legal and policy responses.[5]

In defining violence against children, the United Nations Study on Violence against Children reiterated key definitions contained in the Convention on the Rights of the Child (CRC, 1577 UNTS 3) (Pinheiro 2006a, para. 8; Pinheiro 2006b, p. 4).[6] According to the CRC, a child is "every human being below the age of 18 years unless, under the law applicable to the child, majority is attained earlier" (Art. 1).[7] The CRC's definition of violence against children encompasses "all forms of physical or mental violence, injury or abuse, neglect or negligent treatment, maltreatment or exploitation, including sexual abuse" (Art. 19). Children suffer from abuse, neglect and exploitation in myriad forms, including physical abuse, psychological abuse, sexual abuse, cruel, inhuman or degrading treatment or punishment, bullying, peer and gang violence, abduction, torture, trafficking, child

---

[2] This chapter generally uses the terms "violence against women" and "gender violence" interchangeably, reflecting the disproportionate impact of the types of violence discussed on women and girls, as well as the recognition that men, particularly gay and transgender men, may be subjected to these forms of violence. It uses the terms "victim" and "survivor" interchangeably, recognizing that some object that the term "victim" obscures an individual's sense of agency, while others object to the term "survivor" on the ground that not all who are subjected to violence survive.

[3] United Nations General Assembly (1993), A/RES/48/104, Art. 2; United Nations Division for the Advancement of Women (2010), pp. 23–24; World Health Organization (2013), pp. 5–6. See generally United Nations Division for the Advancement of Women (2011) (discussing evolving understandings of "harmful practices").

[4] See, e.g., United Nations Office on Drugs and Crime (2013), pp. 49–56 (indicating that females are the vast majority of victims of homicides committed by intimate partners or other family members); World Health Organization (2013), pp. 16–20, 31 (detailing prevalence of intimate partner and non-partner violence experienced by women globally); United Nations Department of Public Information (2011) (summarizing global statistics). See also, e.g., Black et al. (2011), pp. 2–3 (finding that in the United States, nearly one in four women and one in seven men have experienced severe physical violence by a current or former partner and that one in five women and one in 71 men have been raped at some point in their lives).

[5] See, e.g., National Coalition of Anti-Violence Programs (2013), pp. 13–14.

[6] For further discussion of the CRC, see Sect. 3.2.1 below.

[7] United Nations General Assembly (1989), Art. 1 (quoted in Pinheiro 2006a, para. 8; Pinheiro 2006b, p. 4). Some sources indicate that the definition of children includes all persons under the age of 18, regardless of the local age of majority. See, e.g., Committee on the Rights of the Child (2007), paras. 36–37; United Nations General Assembly (2003), Art. 3(d).

prostitution, child pornography, and harmful practices such as female genital mutilation and forced marriage.[8] As former Secretary-General Kofi Annan observed, violence against children "occurs in homes, schools and streets; in places of work and entertainment, and in care and detention centres. Perpetrators include parents, family members, teachers, caretakers, law enforcement authorities and other children" (Annan 2006, p. XI).

2.2 *International and United Nations Initiatives*

2.2.1 Violence Against Women

The last several decades have witnessed a dramatic expansion in law and policy reform, scholarship, activism and public debate invoking international human rights law to address gender violence. Advocacy efforts brought global attention to the prevalence of the problem, its costs, and its connection to gender inequality and historic gender roles and stereotypes (e.g. Bunch 1990; Charlesworth et al. 1991; Copelon 1994; Edwards 2011; Thomas and Beasley 1995). Building on the foundation of early international human rights instruments such as the Universal Declaration of Human Rights, concerted activism led to enactment of instruments such as the Convention on the Elimination of All Forms of Discrimination against Women (CEDAW) and the Declaration on the Elimination of Violence against Women, discussed more fully below. Experts increasingly laud the value of international human rights law as a tool to advance anti-gender violence advocacy (e.g., Bettinger-Lopez 2008; Merry 2006; Schneider 2004).

As experts have argued, the international human rights framework was slow to address women's human rights generally, and violence against women in particular (e.g., Bunch 1990; Charlesworth et al. 1991; Cook 1993; Edwards 2011; Merry 2006). Historic biases have equated human rights violations with acts in the public sphere, while gender violence typically occurs in private. Entrenched and enduring gender stereotypes are root causes both of gender violence itself, and of limitations in governmental and institutional responses.

Nevertheless, important initiatives within the UN system have advanced and complemented advocacy by civil society. The General Assembly has adopted a series of Resolutions reiterating its ongoing deep concern about the persistence of gender violence and its relationship to all forms of discrimination and calling for

[8] See generally Pinheiro (2006b). See also Hodgkin and Newell (2007), pp. 249–276; NGO Group for the Convention on the Rights of the Child (2008), pp. 11–12; Office of the Special Representative of the Secretary-General on Violence against Children (2013), pp. iv–v; Pinheiro (2006a), paras. 28, 38–80. For further discussion of harmful practices, see Office of the Special Representative of the Secretary-General on Violence against Children (2013), pp. 68–70 (discussing harmful practices affecting children); United Nations Division for the Advancement of Women (2011) (discussing harmful practices affecting women and girls).

intensification of State efforts to address the problem.[9] Other General Assembly pronouncements similarly stress States' obligations to promote and protect human rights, including the right to be free from gender violence. For example, a 2010 resolution adopted the Updated Model Strategies and Practical Measures on the Elimination of Violence against Women in the Field of Crime Prevention and Criminal Justice, which was developed by an intergovernmental expert group in Bangkok in 2009.[10]

These resolutions parallel other United Nations-based initiatives and publications, including the Secretary-General's 2006 In-depth Study on All Forms of Violence against Women, which comprehensively reviewed the persistence and unacceptability of gender violence, its root causes, impact on health, and social and economic costs, and which identified promising practices, including legislation, policies, programs and effective remedies (United Nations General Assembly 2006a). The United Nations Division for the Advancement of Women's 2010 Handbook for Legislation on Violence against Women, and its accompanying 2011 Supplement to the Handbook for Legislation on Violence against Women, lay out international and regional legal and policy frameworks, and a model framework for legislation addressing numerous manifestations of the problem. The UN-appointed Special Rapporteurs on violence against women, its causes and consequences have issued key topical reports in addition to their work monitoring individual countries' compliance with international obligations (Coomaraswamy 1996, 1999; Ertürk 2006, 2008; Manjoo 2013a, b).[11] In 2008, the Secretary-General launched the UNiTE to End Violence against Women campaign to raise public awareness and increase political will and resources to address the problem globally (United Nations Department of Public Information (UNDPI) 2013).

2.2.2 Violence Against Children

Just as the human rights response to violence against women has intensified in recent decades, the same is true for violence against children. The Declaration of the Rights of the Child (Declaration of Geneva), adopted by the League of Nations in 1924, was a brief statement of general duties toward children and did not specifically mention child abuse or neglect (League of Nations 1924). When the United Nations General Assembly adopted a new Declaration of the Rights of the Child in 1959, it contained several provisions addressing violence against children, including a statement that "[t]he child shall be protected against all forms of

[9] See, e.g., United Nations General Assembly (2006b); United Nations General Assembly (2007); United Nations General Assembly (2008); United Nations General Assembly (2009); United Nations General Assembly (2010); United Nations General Assembly (2012a).

[10] United Nations General Assembly (2011), para. 4, Annex.

[11] For further discussion of the Special Rapporteurs' work, see Sects. 2.2.3 (with respect to due diligence) and 4.1 (discussing reports and other initiatives) below.

neglect, cruelty and exploitation" (United Nations General Assembly 1959, Principle 9). Although this represented a conceptual advance in the way that children's rights were viewed, the Declaration lacked the status of a binding treaty (Van Bueren 1995, pp. 9–12). It was not until 1989, with the adoption of the Convention on the Rights of the Child, that a child's right to be free from violence became enshrined in a comprehensive global treaty.[12]

2.2.3 Due Diligence

The principle of due diligence outlines one of the parameters of States' obligations concerning violence against women and children and other human rights violations. The principle holds States responsible for private acts of violence if the State fails to act with due diligence to prevent, protect against, prosecute, punish and provide redress for those acts.[13]

Thematic reports by the Special Rapporteurs on violence against women have elaborated on the scope of States' responsibility to respond to gender violence (Coomaraswamy 1999, paras. 23–24; Ertürk 2006, 2008, paras. 69–115; Manjoo 2013a). The principle of due diligence has become a focus of global advocacy.[14] It is particularly pertinent to gender violence, since it reaches private as well as state-sponsored violence. As Special Rapporteur Manjoo has detailed, due diligence requires States to prevent violence committed by particular perpetrators, and to devise systematic responses to prevent future acts from occurring (Manjoo 2013a, paras. 70–76). It contemplates services that are comprehensive and accessible. It calls for a legal system in which allegations are thoroughly investigated, perpetrators are held to account, and survivors are afforded redress. The principle of due diligence calls on States to assess their responses to gender violence in concert with other human rights principles such as equality, dignity and non-discrimination.

The principle of due diligence also applies to violence against children (United Nations Economic and Social Council 2014). The Convention on the Rights of the Child requires States Parties to "undertake all appropriate legislative, administrative, and other measures for the implementation of the rights" recognized in the Convention (Art. 4). The Committee on the Rights of the Child has articulated a series of affirmative steps that States need to take to ensure that children's rights are fully realized (Committee on the Rights of the Child 2003). As part of their obligation to take "immediate and positive steps to prevent and eliminate all forms of violence against children and to respond to it effectively if it occurs," governments have a duty to adopt measures to prevent parents, guardians and other

---

[12] See Sect. 3.2.1 below.

[13] See Committee on the Elimination of Discrimination against Women (1992), para. 9 (Gen. Rec. No. 19); United Nations General Assembly (1993), Art. 4(c).

[14] See, e.g., Due Diligence Project (2014) (proposing framework based on NGO advocates' recommendations for implementation).

private actors from violating children's rights through violence (Pinheiro 2006b, pp. 39, 41).

2.3 *Other Global Initiatives*

Initiatives from other sectors also have focused global attention on violence against women and children. For example, in 2002, the World Health Organization (WHO) issued the World Report on Violence and Health, which depicted the global extent of interpersonal violence, focusing on its impact on public health (Krug et al. 2002). Subsequently, the WHO issued Preventing Violence: A Guide to Implementing the Recommendations of the World Report on Violence and Health, which drew on recommendations from health ministers, non-governmental organizations, foundations and other UN agencies (Butchart et al. 2004). The WHO has continued to track and report global estimates of the prevalence, forms and effects of violence against women (World Health Organization (WHO) 2013). These reports contribute to the growing body of materials reviewing State and NGO responses, and evaluating promising practices for addressing and ending the problem.[15] In recent years, the WHO has identified and promoted strategies to prevent child maltreatment, including programs that help parents develop positive parenting skills (Butchart and Harvey 2006; World Health Organization (WHO) 2009).

3 Treaties and Other Instruments

3.1 *Key Instruments Concerning Violence Against Women*

3.1.1 CEDAW General Recommendation No. 19

The Convention on the Elimination of All Forms of Discrimination against Women (CEDAW), adopted in 1979 and entered into force in 1981, lies at the core of international human rights provisions addressing gender violence (United Nations General Assembly 1981). As of 15 May 2015, 189 countries had become parties to the Convention.[16] CEDAW is one of six UN conventions that have been widely ratified and that are monitored by a committee. Like other committees charged with monitoring UN treaties, the CEDAW Committee has limited power to compel States' compliance. However, the CEDAW Committee reviews States' submissions for periodic review, issues general recommendations, and adjudicates complaints

[15] For another example of a recent global report, see Kiplesund and Morton (2014). For an example from civil society, see International Women's Rights Action Watch (2013).

[16] See United Nations Treaty Collection (2015a).

filed under CEDAW's Optional Protocol.[17] The Convention requires States to condemn discrimination against women in all its forms, and to adopt legislative and other measures to end it (Art. 2). The Convention covers a broad array of social issues that reflect on gender inequality, including political participation (Arts. 7, 8), nationality (Art. 9), education (Art. 10), employment (Art. 11), health care (Art. 12), and economic and social life (Art. 13). The Convention recognizes the particular challenges faced by women who are trafficked (Art. 6) and by rural women (Art. 14). It also recognizes the need for change in both public and private domains, including changes in traditional roles of men and women (Introduction), and social and cultural patterns and prejudices (Art. 5). States that are parties to the Convention must submit regular reports detailing the country's efforts to give effect to CEDAW's provisions (Art. 18).

The CEDAW treaty itself does not mention gender violence. However, General Recommendation No. 12, adopted in 1989, urged consideration of the issue and required States to maintain statistics on gender violence.[18] After reviewing the reports that were subsequently submitted, the Committee determined that the reports did not uniformly or adequately address the connections among discrimination against women, gender-based violence, and violations of human rights and fundamental freedoms. Consequently, the Committee promulgated General Recommendation No. 19, which contained both general comments and specific recommendations about how States can comply with the Convention's anti-discrimination mandate.[19] Although general recommendations are not legally binding, they elaborate on the obligations enumerated in CEDAW.

General Recommendation No. 19 is significant because it spells out the Committee's views on States' obligations to respond to gender violence. It makes clear that gender violence is a form of gender discrimination, linking violence to historic gender roles in which women are subordinated to men (paras. 1, 6, 7). The General Recommendation makes explicit CEDAW's application to both public authorities (para. 8) and private actors (para. 9). This is particularly important for gender violence, most of which is committed by private actors.

General Recommendation No. 19 complements CEDAW by explaining the connections between domestic and sexual violence and discrimination. For example, the General Recommendation's comments on specific articles of CEDAW state that practices such as family violence, forced marriage, and female genital

[17] The Optional Protocol authorizes the Committee on the Elimination of Discrimination against Women to consider "communications" on behalf of individuals or groups of individuals claiming violations of any rights set forth in CEDAW, and requires the Committee to solicit responses from the pertinent State Party, to inform it of any actions it takes in response, and to include a summary of actions it has taken in its annual reports. See United Nations General Assembly (1999), A/RES/54/4, Annex. If the Committee receives reliable information indicating grave or systemic violations, it may authorize an inquiry by one or more of its members, and will transmit resulting findings, comments and recommendations to the State party for its response. Ibid., Arts. 8, 9.

[18] Committee on the Elimination of Discrimination against Women (1989).

[19] Committee on the Elimination of Discrimination against Women (1992).

mutilation serve to keep women in subordinate roles and contribute to low levels of political participation as well as low levels of education, skills, and work opportunities (para. 11). The comments also explain that poverty and unemployment increase the opportunities for trafficking and other forms of exploitation, and are "incompatible" with respect for women's equal rights and dignity (paras. 14, 15). They expressly recognize that gender violence may include sexual harassment in the workplace (paras. 17, 18), that gender violence puts women's health and lives at risk (paras. 19, 20, 22), and that gender violence is connected to a range of circumstances that increase women's vulnerability, such as war, armed conflict and occupation (para. 16), or living in a rural community (para. 21). The comments stress that lack of economic independence forces women to stay in violent relationships and that men's "abrogation of ... family responsibilities" can be a form of violence and coercion (para. 23).

General Recommendation No. 19 enumerates over 20 steps States should take to eliminate violence against women as part of their efforts to eliminate discrimination against women (para. 24(a)–(v)). These include, among others, providing adequate legal protections, appropriate support services, and gender-sensitive training of judicial and law enforcement officers and other public officials (para. 24(b)). The proposed steps seek to advance CEDAW's transformative goals by including measures such as compiling data and promoting research; ensuring media respect for women; overcoming traditional attitudes, customs, and practices that perpetuate violence against women; and initiatives to provide complaint procedures and remedies, including compensation (paras. 24(c), (d), (e), (i)).

Countries that have ratified or acceded to CEDAW are legally bound to implement its provisions and must submit national reports at least every 4 years, detailing the measures they have taken to comply with their treaty obligations. The CEDAW Committee reviews these reports at hearings in which national government representatives and Committee members discuss the State's compliance.[20] NGOs often submit shadow reports to supplement governmental submissions and highlight how governmental reports may be misleading (International Women's Rights Action Watch 2013). The CEDAW Committee issues "concluding observations" which outline positive aspects, principal subjects of concern, and the Committee's recommendations on how to address a State's compliance challenges.[21] This monitoring process creates a vehicle for mobilization and advocacy, and provides global legitimacy for establishing norms of gender equality and State responsibility for addressing gender equality, including gender violence.

[20] See United Nations Women (2007); Office of the United Nations High Commissioner for Human Rights (2014a).

[21] See Office of the United Nations High Commissioner for Human Rights (2014c).

3.1.2 Declaration on the Elimination of Violence Against Women

The Declaration on the Elimination of Violence against Women, adopted by the United Nations General Assembly in 1993, also places efforts to eliminate violence against women in the context of eliminating discrimination against women (United Nations General Assembly 1993, A/RES/48/104). The Declaration states that violence against women is an "obstacle to the achievement of equality," affirms that it "constitutes a violation of the rights and fundamental freedoms of women," and recognizes the "long-standing failure" to address the problem (Introduction).

The Declaration's recommendations echo those of CEDAW's General Recommendation No. 19 by endorsing initiatives that confront the gender inequality that perpetuates domestic and sexual violence. For example, the Declaration urges comprehensive, preventive approaches that protect women against violence and ensure that women are not re-victimized because of "laws insensitive to gender considerations, enforcement practices or other interventions" (Art. 4(f)). It encourages training for law enforcement and other public officials responsible for preventing, investigating, and punishing violence against women, "to sensitize them to the needs of women" (Art. 4(i)). Another recommendation calls for the adoption of "all appropriate measures . . . to modify the social and cultural patterns of conduct of men and women and to eliminate prejudices, customary practices, and all other practices based on the idea of the inferiority or superiority of either of the sexes and on stereotyped roles for men and women" (Art. 4(j)).

3.1.3 Other Global Treaties

Other treaties require States to report on gender violence even though the treaties themselves have a more general focus. For example, the International Covenant on Civil and Political Rights (ICCPR, 999 UNTS 171) has been interpreted to require reporting on States' efforts to eliminate gender violence as part of their obligations to ensure equality.[22] The Rome Statute of the International Criminal Court (2187 UNTS 90) identifies violence against women as a crime against humanity and affords a forum for redress (Rome Statute of the International Criminal Court 1998). The Convention against Torture and Other Cruel, Inhuman or Degrading Treatment or Punishment (Convention against Torture, 1465 UNTS 85) prohibits rape and sexual assault, recognizing them as forms of cruel and inhuman treatment.[23] These more

[22] United Nations General Assembly (1976); Human Rights Committee (2000), para. 8 (protection from gender-based violence during armed conflict), para. 11 (laws prohibiting domestic violence, including rape, forced sterilization and genital mutilation), para. 12 (prohibitions against trafficking), para. 14 (laws or practices condoning confinement of women), para. 16 (restriction of women's movement), para. 24 (supporting marriage as a free choice by, inter alia, proscribing attitudes that marginalize women victims of rape), para. 31 ("honour crimes" violate Convention).

[23] Committee against Torture (2008), para. 18; United Nations General Assembly (1984). See also Copelon (1994).

recent instruments built on the foundation established by the Universal Declaration of Human Rights (Universal Declaration, G.A. Res. 217 A (III)) which was adopted by the UN General Assembly in 1948, following the experience of the Second World War (United Nations General Assembly 1948). The Universal Declaration set forth fundamental principles of equality and dignity, including the right to life, liberty and security of person, the right to be free from slavery, and the right to a remedy, which continue to be drawn on today.

3.1.4 Regional Treaties

Regional treaties also recognize States' obligations to prevent and address gender violence as part of their obligation to ensure sex equality and human rights for all. A number of treaties applicable to the Americas require government accountability for gender violence, either through explicit prohibitions or as part of States' general human rights obligations. The Convention on the Prevention, Punishment, and Eradication of Violence against Women (Convention of Belém do Pará) sets forth States' positive and comprehensive obligations to ensure that "[e]very woman has the right to be free from violence in both the public and private spheres" (Art. 3).[24] It articulates the meaning of that right and describes States' specific obligations to undertake legislative reform, to make services available, and to provide mechanisms for redress. That Convention builds on more generally framed obligations established in the American Convention on Human Rights (American Convention) which encompasses, among other things, the right to life (Art. 4), right to humane treatment (Art. 5), right to personal liberty (Art. 7), rights of the family (Art. 17), rights of the child (Art. 19), and right to equal protection (Art. 24).[25] Those obligations in turn follow those enumerated in 1948 in the American Declaration of the Rights and Duties of Man (American Declaration), which similarly include the right to life, liberty and security of person (Art. I), and the right to equality under the law (Art. II).[26]

The Protocol to the African Charter on Human and Peoples' Rights on the Rights of Women in Africa (African Protocol) requires African States to prevent and respond to gender violence as part of their obligation to eliminate discrimination (Art. 2), as well as the right to dignity (Art. 3), the rights to life, integrity and security of the person (Art. 4), and the obligation to eliminate harmful practices (Art. 5).[27] The African Protocol's provisions addressing family roles, peace, and the protection of women in armed conflicts, also encompass measures to redress gender violence.[28] The Protocol explicitly recognizes the particular vulnerability of certain

---

[24] Organization of American States (1994) (Convention of Belém do Pará).

[25] Organization of American States (1969) (American Convention).

[26] Organization of American States (1948) (American Declaration).

[27] African Commission on Human and Peoples' Rights (2003) (African Protocol).

[28] Other provisions, for example, addressing education, economic and social rights and health and reproductive rights, complement the provisions addressing gender violence more directly. See,

women, for example, elderly women (Art. 22), women with disabilities (Art. 23), and women in distress (Art. 24).

More recently, the Council of Europe promulgated the Convention on preventing and combating violence against women and domestic violence (Istanbul Convention), a convention specifically focused on gender violence.[29] Like the Declaration on the Elimination of Violence against Women and the African Protocol, it characterizes violence against women as a violation of human rights and a form of discrimination (Art. 3(a)). It requires countries to exercise due diligence to prevent violence, to protect victims and to prosecute perpetrators (Art. 5). It requires States to adopt comprehensive and coordinated legislative and other measures to realize victims' rights (Art. 7). This obligation includes allocating "appropriate financial and human resources," recognizing non-governmental organizations' and civil society's roles in advancing the Istanbul Convention's goals (Arts. 8, 9). The Istanbul Convention enumerates specific required initiatives, including data collection and research (Art. 11); prevention programs (Arts. 12–17); programs to protect victims (Arts. 18–28); substantive legal responses (Arts. 29–48); investigation, prosecution and related protective measures (Arts. 49–58); and other provisions addressing issues such as migration and asylum and international cooperation (Arts. 59–65), and mechanisms for monitoring (Art. 66).

3.2 *Key Instruments Concerning Violence Against Children*

3.2.1 Convention on the Rights of the Child

The preeminent international human rights instrument concerning children is the Convention on the Rights of the Child (CRC). Adopted by the General Assembly in 1989, the CRC has 196 parties,[30] making it the most widely ratified of all international human rights treaties. The CRC embodies an unprecedented level of commitment to children's rights (Weiner 2006, p. 70). It was designed as a "comprehensive set of international legal standards for the protection and well-being of children"[31] and covers a broad range of civil, political, economic, social and cultural rights.

The guiding principles of the CRC include non-discrimination (Art. 2), the best interests of the child (Art. 3), the right to life, survival and development (Art. 6), and respect for the views of the child (Art. 12). Several of its provisions apply directly to violence against children. Most prominently, Article 19(1) requires States Parties to take all appropriate legislative, administrative, social and educational measures "to

e.g., ibid., Art. 12 (Right to Education and Training), Art. 13 (Economic and Social Welfare Rights), Art. 14 (Health and Reproductive Rights), Art. 16 (Right to Adequate Housing).

[29] Council of Europe (2011) (Istanbul Convention).

[30] Not ratified by the United States of America. See United Nations Treaty Collection (2015b).

[31] United Nations General Assembly (2002a), A/RES/S-27/2, para. 4.

protect the child from all forms of physical or mental violence, injury or abuse, neglect or negligent treatment, maltreatment or exploitation, including sexual abuse," while the child is in the care of a parent, legal guardian, or any other person.[32] When a child has been victimized, Article 39 obligates States Parties to "take all appropriate measures to promote physical and psychological recovery and social reintegration" of the child victim. The CRC prohibits torture and any other cruel, inhuman or degrading treatment or punishment (Art. 37). In addition, States Parties must protect children from all forms of sexual exploitation and sexual abuse (Art. 34), from economic exploitation and hazardous or harmful work (Art. 32), and from all other forms of exploitation prejudicial to the child's welfare (Art. 36). The CRC also requires States Parties to take measures to prevent abduction, sale, or trafficking of children (Art. 35) and to combat the illicit transfer or retention of children abroad (Art. 11). Other provisions of the CRC establish protections for children affected by armed conflict (Art. 38) and for children subjected to school discipline (Art. 28(2)).

In 2000, the United Nations adopted two Optional Protocols, supplementing the human rights safeguards provided in the CRC. The Optional Protocol to the CRC on the Sale of Children, Child Prostitution and Child Pornography defines and prohibits the sale of children, child prostitution and child pornography and requires the adoption of certain measures to combat those practices and protect victimized children (United Nations General Assembly 2000b, A/RES/54/263). The Optional Protocol to the CRC on the Involvement of Children in Armed Conflict excludes children under the age of 18 from compulsory military recruitment and direct participation in hostilities, and places restrictions on the participation of children under 18 in armed forces (United Nations General Assembly 2000a, A/RES/54/263). The United States of America has ratified both of these Optional Protocols, even though it has not ratified the CRC itself (Revaz and Todres 2006).

The task of monitoring implementation of the CRC and its Optional Protocols rests with the Committee on the Rights of the Child (Committee) (Art. 43). States Parties are under a duty to take "all appropriate legislative, administrative and other measures" to give effect to the rights in the Convention (Art. 4) and must submit an initial report to the Committee followed by periodic reports every 5 years (Art. 44). The Committee reviews each report and presents "concluding observations" expressing its concerns and recommendations to the State Party.[33] Among its other functions, the Committee publishes general comments on thematic issues, which interpret the content of human rights guarantees. Several of the general comments address topics relating to violence against children.[34]

---

[32] Article 19(2) states, "Such protective measures should, as appropriate, include effective procedures for the establishment of social programmes to provide necessary support for the child and for those who have the care of the child, as well as for other forms of prevention and for identification, reporting, referral, investigation, treatment and follow-up of instances of child maltreatment described heretofore, and, as appropriate, for judicial involvement."

[33] Office of the United Nations High Commissioner for Human Rights (2014b).

[34] See, e.g., Committee on the Rights of the Child (2011); Committee on the Rights of the Child (2006).

Until recently, the effectiveness of the CRC was hampered by the lack of a mechanism for the filing of individual complaints or petitions. To remedy this deficiency, the General Assembly in 2011 approved a third optional protocol, entitled the Optional Protocol on a Communications Procedure, to permit individual children and groups of children to submit complaints regarding specific violations of their rights (United Nations General Assembly 2012b, A/RES/66/138). The third Optional Protocol entered into force in April 2014, following its ratification by ten United Nations member States.[35] Under the new procedure, children or their representatives may submit complaints (known as "communications") to the Committee on the Rights of the Child alleging violations of children's rights under the CRC and its first two Optional Protocols. However, a complaint may not be brought against a State unless that State has ratified both the third Optional Protocol and the instrument that it is alleged to have violated (Arts. 1, 5(1)). If the Committee decides to review the case and determines that a violation has occurred, it will issue recommendations for the State to implement.[36] While it is too soon to gauge the effects of the new complaint mechanism, allowing children and their representatives direct access to bring specific complaints before the Committee is a significant advance. The new Optional Protocol also establishes a procedure for the Committee to conduct inquiries into grave or systematic violations of children's rights (Art. 13).

Since its adoption over 25 years ago, the CRC has been praised for establishing the concept that children are rights holders and for changing the way children are viewed and treated.[37] It has also received credit for contributing to advances such as the adoption of national action plans, increased budgetary allocations, improved data collection, training of professionals, and other measures to promote children's rights. The language and ideas of the CRC have been incorporated into national legislation and constitutions, and a growing number of countries have enacted comprehensive legal prohibitions on violence against children. However, progress toward eradicating violence against children is uneven and difficult to measure, and abuses of all kinds remain far too common. Thus, while the CRC has had positive effects, its full potential has not yet been realized.

3.2.2 Other Global Treaties

Although the Convention on the Rights of the Child and its Optional Protocols are unique among global human rights treaties in their focus on children's rights, other

[35] As of 15 May 2015, the third Optional Protocol had been ratified by 17 Member States. See United Nations Treaty Collection (2015c).

[36] Committee on the Rights of the Child (2013), Rule 27.

[37] For discussion of the impact of the CRC, see generally, e.g., Moccia (2009); United Nations General Assembly (2013); Weiner (2006).

international human rights instruments also offer protection from certain types of violence against children.[38] For example, many of the acts condemned by CEDAW General Recommendation No. 19 affect girls as well as adult women.[39] The Convention against Torture (Art. 2) and the International Covenant on Civil and Political Rights (Art. 7) both contain prohibitions on torture that apply to children as well as adults.

3.2.3 Regional Treaties

Human rights protections concerning violence against children can also be found in instruments adopted by regional entities such as the Organization of American States, African Union, European Union, and Council of Europe (Pinheiro 2006b, pp. 38–40). For instance, Article 19 of the American Convention on Human Rights states, "Every minor child has the right to the measures of protection required by his condition as a minor on the part of his family, society, and the state." In interpreting this provision, the Inter-American Commission on Human Rights and the Inter-American Court of Human Rights have incorporated obligations imposed by the CRC.[40] In 2002, the Inter-American Court of Human Rights issued an advisory opinion concluding that States Parties to the American Convention are obligated to adopt all positive measures to ensure protection of children from mistreatment, whether by public authorities, private individuals, or non-governmental entities.[41]

The African Charter on the Rights and Welfare of the Child, the first regional treaty to concentrate on children, expresses a child's right to survival, protection and development (Art. 5) and requires States to take measures "to protect the child from all forms of torture, inhuman or degrading treatment and especially physical or mental injury or abuse, neglect or maltreatment including sexual abuse" (Art. 16).[42] The African Charter also contains protections against harmful social and cultural practices (Art. 21), participation in and effects of armed conflict (Art. 22), sexual exploitation (Art. 27), and sale, trafficking and abduction of children (Art. 29).

---

[38] See Pinheiro (2006b), pp. 31–32; United Nations Children's Fund (2005), pp. 17–20.

[39] See, e.g., Committee on the Elimination of Discrimination against Women (1992), para. 15 (describing women and young girls forced into prostitution), para. 20 (referring to traditional practices that are harmful to women and children), para. 21 (noting risks to rural women and girls), para. 23 (describing family violence against "women of all ages"). See also discussion of CEDAW General Recommendation No. 19 in Sect. 3.1.1 above.

[40] Inter-American Commission on Human Rights (1999); Inter-American Court of Human Rights (1999).

[41] Inter-American Court of Human Rights (2002).

[42] African Commission on Human and Peoples' Rights (1990).

3.3 Key Instruments Concerning Trafficking

Human trafficking has a disproportionate impact on women and children.[43] The main international instrument targeting this problem is the United Nations Protocol to Prevent, Suppress and Punish Trafficking in Persons, Especially Women and Children (Anti-trafficking Protocol, 2237 UNTS 319), part of the United Nations Convention against Transnational Organized Crime (United Nations General Assembly 2003, A/RES/55/25). The Anti-trafficking Protocol obligates States Parties to adopt legislative and other measures to establish and enforce criminal offenses outlawing trafficking (Art. 5). It enumerates a range of services that should be provided to victims, including legal, psychological, and medical assistance, and contemplates victims' needs for assistance with resources such as housing, employment and educational and training opportunities (Art. 6). In addition, it specifies steps States should take to prevent trafficking, including measures to address poverty, underdevelopment and lack of equal opportunity, and efforts achieved through bilateral or multilateral cooperation (Art. 9). CEDAW (Art. 6), the CRC (Art. 35), and the Optional Protocol to the CRC on the Sale of Children, Child Prostitution and Child Pornography also contain measures designed to combat trafficking.

4 Special Rapporteurs and Special Representatives

4.1 Special Rapporteur on Violence Against Women, Its Causes and Consequences

The Special Rapporteurs on violence against women, its causes and consequences, have been instrumental in bringing international attention to the persistence of the problem, and in highlighting trends and themes that apply to policy debates globally. The United Nations determined to appoint a Special Rapporteur on violence against women in 1994, and most recently extended the Special Rapporteur's mandate in 2013.[44] The Special Rapporteur is charged with seeking and receiving information on violence against women from governments, treaty bodies, specialized agencies and other special rapporteurs. Her mandate includes recommending measures to eliminate all forms of violence against women, working closely within the procedures and mechanisms of the UN Human Rights Council, and continuing to adopt a comprehensive and universal approach to the elimination of violence against women, its causes and consequences. The Special

[43] United Nations Office on Drugs and Crime (UNODC) (2009), p. 11.

[44] Office of the United Nations High Commissioner for Human Rights (2014d).

Rapporteur has authority to transmit individual complaints and to undertake country visits.

The Special Rapporteurs' reports have played an important role in shifting debate and advancing policy. Reports deriving from country visits shine a spotlight on the particular challenges a country faces in addressing gender violence.[45] Annual reports summarize the Special Rapporteur's activities, and also provide expert guidance globally on thematic issues of common concern. For example, a 2013 report by Special Rapporteur Rashida Manjoo elaborated general principles for assessing State responsibility for eliminating violence against women (Manjoo 2013a). A 2006 report by then-Special Rapporteur Yakin Ertürk offered valuable synthesis and guidance on the standard of due diligence as a tool for eliminating violence against women (Ertürk 2006). Other reports have focused, among other things, on cultural practices within the family that constitute violence against women, on the connection between the use of violence as a means of conflict resolution and domestic violence, on the relationship between violence and health, and on the ways in which race, gender and violence against women intersect.[46]

4.2 *Independent Expert and Special Representative of the Secretary-General on Violence Against Children*

In 2001, following a recommendation by the Committee on the Rights of the Child, the United Nations General Assembly adopted a resolution requesting that the Secretary-General conduct an in-depth study on violence against children (United Nations General Assembly 2002b, A/RES/56/138). The Secretary-General appointed an independent expert, Paulo Sérgio Pinheiro, to conduct the study. The resulting UN Study on Violence against Children was submitted to the General Assembly in 2006 (Pinheiro 2006a), along with a more extensive publication, the World Report on Violence against Children (Pinheiro 2006b). These two documents represent a groundbreaking effort to describe and analyze the many facets of violence against children throughout the world. The study was the product of 3 years of research and drew on consultations with governments, UN bodies, non-governmental organizations, research centers, and children themselves.

The UN Study and accompanying World Report identified five settings in which violence against children occurs: the home and family, schools and educational settings, in care and justice institutions, places of work, and the community. The study presented 12 overarching recommendations: strengthen national and local commitment and action; prohibit all violence against children; prioritize prevention; promote non-violent values and awareness-raising; enhance the capacity of all

---

[45] As one example, see Manjoo (2013b).

[46] See, e.g., University of Minnesota Human Rights Library (2003) (summarizing and collecting reports).

who work with and for children; provide recovery and social reintegration services; ensure participation of children; create accessible and child-friendly reporting systems and services; ensure accountability and end impunity; address the gender dimension of violence against children; develop and implement systematic national data collection and research; and strengthen international commitment.[47]

To assist in carrying out its recommendations, the study called for the appointment of a Special Representative of the Secretary-General (SRSG) on violence against children (Pinheiro 2006a, paras. 120–123). After the General Assembly affirmed this request, the Secretary-General appointed Marta Santos Pais as Special Representative in 2009.[48] The SRSG is an advocate for the prevention and elimination of all forms of violence against children. In cooperation with a wide range of entities, the SRSG promotes strategies to advance this agenda.

In 2013, the SRSG on violence against children released a major report, Toward a World Free from Violence: Global Survey on Violence against Children (Global Survey).[49] The Global Survey was "the first comprehensive attempt to assess progress in preventing and eliminating violence against children" since the 2006 UN Study on Violence against Children (p. vi). The Global Survey noted a number of encouraging developments but criticized "the slow pace of progress" and concluded that "[s]even years after the landmark UN Study on Violence against Children, the international community has not yet been able to make a genuine breakthrough in the protection of children from violence" (pp. xvii–xviii). In response to persistent challenges, the Global Survey called for an "urgent response" and set out a list of eight imperatives, including the adoption of national strategies to prevent and address violence against children; enactment and enforcement of explicit legal bans on violence against children; overcoming the social acceptance of violence against children; facilitating children's meaningful participation; ensuring the social inclusion of girls and boys who are particularly vulnerable; improving data collection; focusing on factors that influence levels of violence and the resilience of children, their families and communities; and placing the protection of children from violence at the heart of the future global development agenda (pp. xviii–xix, 127–136).

4.3 Other Mandate Holders

Together with the Special Rapporteur on violence against women, its causes and consequences and the Special Representative of the Secretary-General on violence against children, other United Nations mandate holders whose work is particularly

---

[47] Pinheiro (2006a), paras. 96–109; Pinheiro (2006b), pp. 18–24.

[48] See Special Representative of the Secretary-General on Violence against Children (2014).

[49] Office of the Special Representative of the Secretary-General on Violence against Children (OSRSG) (2013).

relevant to violence against women and children include the Special Rapporteur on trafficking in persons, especially women and children; the Special Rapporteur on torture and other cruel, inhuman or degrading treatment or punishment; the Special Rapporteur on the sale of children, child prostitution and child pornography; and the Special Representative of the Secretary-General for Children and Armed Conflict.

5 Judicial and Other Decisions Concerning Violence Against Women and Children

A growing number of decisions, issued by international, regional and national courts and other bodies, have held States accountable for failing to meet their obligations under human rights laws regarding violence against women and children.[50]

5.1 Decisions Concerning Gender Violence

5.1.1 CEDAW Committee Decisions

A number of decisions adjudicating complaints brought under CEDAW's optional protocol have found States responsible in cases involving gender violence. In *Yildirim v. Austria*, the CEDAW Committee considered a claim on behalf of a woman killed by her abusive husband.[51] He had subjected her to escalating acts of violence, including threats and harassment at her workplace, and threats to kill her. This led his wife to make multiple calls to the police and to obtain an injunction issued against him. At various points, the police declined Ms. Yildirim's requests that he be detained, failed to report incidents of harassment, or responded to reports of his threats and harassment by speaking to him or passing the complaint on to other law enforcement officials. After Ms. Yildirim filed a petition for divorce, Mr. Yildirim followed her home from work and fatally stabbed her. The Committee determined that the Austrian authorities knew or should have known that the situation was "extremely dangerous," and accordingly should not have denied the requests to place Mr. Yildirim in detention. It concluded that law enforcement's failure to detain him violated Austria's due diligence obligation to protect Ms. Yildirim.

---

[50] For further discussion of cases addressing gender violence, see, e.g., Farrior (2004); Goldscheid and Liebowitz (2015); Hodson (2013).

[51] Committee on the Elimination of Discrimination against Women (2007b).

The Committee's decision in *Goekce v. Austria* involved a similar history of escalating violence, threats and disputes over a 3-year period, including threats that he would kill Ms. Goekce, calls to the police, injunctions prohibiting Mr. Goekce's return to the home, violations of those injunctions, and denials of requests that he be detained.[52] The police did not check whether a weapons prohibition was in effect against Mr. Goekce, even though they apparently knew he had a handgun and even though Ms. Goekce's father and brother had alerted the police to Mr. Goekce's threats to kill his wife. The prosecutor had stopped a prosecution against Mr. Goekce for causing bodily harm and making a criminal and dangerous threat on the grounds that there was insufficient reason to prosecute him. Two days later, Mr. Goekce shot Ms. Goekce in front of their two daughters. Ms. Goekce had called the emergency call service a few hours before she was killed, yet no patrol car was sent in response. As in *Yildirim v. Austria,* the CEDAW Committee concluded that the police "knew or should have known" that Ms. Goekce was in serious danger, given the long record of disturbances and calls to the police, including the call immediately preceding the shooting.

The CEDAW decision in *A.T. v. Hungary* similarly held the State accountable for law enforcement's failed response to a survivor of domestic violence.[53] That case involved a 4-year history of regular and severe domestic violence and threats by the petitioner's common law husband. The allegations outlined a history of civil and criminal charges, none of which resulted in detention, and none of which were effective in barring her abuser from her apartment. The CEDAW Committee was concerned that no legislation had been enacted to address domestic violence and sexual harassment, that no protection or exclusion orders or adequate shelters existed for survivors' immediate protection, and that domestic violence cases were not prioritized in court proceedings.

The CEDAW Committee also has prescribed relief in at least one case involving sexual assault. In *S.V.P. v. Bulgaria*, the CEDAW Committee found that Bulgaria had violated CEDAW's provisions by failing to provide adequate support and protection to a child victim of rape.[54] The Committee found Bulgaria in violation for failing to ensure that its law, policies and practices adequately addressed sexual violence against women and girls and its consequences. Its recommendations included law reform to ensure effective investigation and prosecution, and adequate monetary compensation, including compensation for pain and suffering.

[52] Committee on the Elimination of Discrimination against Women (2007a).

[53] Committee on the Elimination of Discrimination against Women (2005).

[54] Committee on the Elimination of Discrimination against Women (2012).

5.1.2 Decisions by Regional Bodies

European Court of Human Rights

The European Court of Human Rights (ECHR) has also held States accountable under the European Convention for failed responses to gender violence. In *Opuz v. Turkey*, the ECHR held that Turkey violated provisions of the European Convention, following a tragic history of an abuser's escalating violence, repeated requests for police protection, and ongoing abuse leading to the abuser's shooting and killing of his mother-in-law.[55] The Court found that the Convention's assurance of the right to life rendered States responsible for doing "all that could be reasonably expected of them" when authorities "knew or ought to have known at the time of the existence of a real and immediate risk to the life of an identified individual" (paras. 129, 130, 149). The Court found that the history of serious violence, combined with Ms. Opuz's mother's final call for intervention shortly before the killing, warranted preventive measures and supported the conclusion that local authorities could have foreseen the lethal attack.

The ECHR similarly reviewed the record of law enforcement responses and found that Croatia had violated a victim's and her child's right to life under the European Convention, in *Tomasic v. Croatia*.[56] The Court there considered claims that the State failed to prevent the killings of a woman and her child by Ms. Tomasic's abusive ex-husband, who psychiatrists had deemed dangerous, and who had been detained and subsequently released. The combination of a history of severe violence, multiple threats to kill his child with a bomb, a psychiatric evaluation concluding that he was in need of compulsory psychiatric treatment, and findings that there was a danger that he would repeat acts of violence, established that the authorities knew of the threats and therefore should have taken "all reasonable steps" to protect the woman and her child from future violence (paras. 52–53, 61).

Inter-American Court of Human Rights and Inter-American Commission on Human Rights

Other decisions have been adjudicated under the treaties that apply to the Americas. For example, the Inter-American Court of Human Rights held Mexico accountable in a case brought under the Convention of Belém do Pará, *González* et al. *(Cotton Field) v. Mexico*.[57] That case was brought on behalf of a young woman and two girls (ages 20, 17 and 15), who had disappeared and died, in the context of circumstances in which hundreds of women and girls had been murdered and

[55] European Court of Human Rights (2009b).

[56] European Court of Human Rights (2009a).

[57] Inter-American Court of Human Rights (2009).

disappeared and the State had failed to act. The Court concluded that Mexico violated its obligations to respond with due diligence once it was aware that there was a real and imminent risk that the victims in the case would be sexually abused, subjected to ill-treatment and killed. The Court held that the State should have initiated a serious, impartial and effective investigation, but instead, it engaged in formalities and took statements, which minimized family members' concerns and led to unjustified delays. The Court detailed a pattern of irregularities in the investigations that resulted in gender violence being treated with impunity, in violation of international law. The State's response violated, among other things, the obligation not to discriminate, the duty to protect the right to life, and the rights of girls.

Similarly, the Inter-American Commission on Human Rights (IACHR), in *Lenahan v. United States*, concluded that the United States violated its due diligence obligations under the American Declaration of the Rights and Duties of Man, including the obligation to prevent violations of the right to life and the right to special protection for girl-children.[58] Ms. Lenahan claimed that local law enforcement failed meaningfully to respond to her calls for assistance after her estranged husband abducted her three children, who were later found shot to death in his truck. She complained to the IACHR after the United States Supreme Court rejected her claim that inadequate law enforcement violated her constitutional right to procedural due process.[59] The IACHR found that the police had failed to take adequate steps to protect Ms. Lenahan and her children after they were put on notice, through multiple calls by Ms. Lenahan expressing concern and imploring the police to intervene. It detailed the steps the police reasonably could have taken, and found the local police response "fragmented, uncoordinated and unprepared" (para. 150). It enumerated various State failures, and spelled out recommendations for individual and systemic relief that would promote law enforcement accountability and equality for women and girls.

The IACHR also addressed States' obligations to provide mechanisms for investigating violations after acts of violence have occurred. In the *Maria Da Penha* case, the IACHR found Brazil in violation of several articles of the American Declaration and the American Convention.[60] Ms. Da Penha became paraplegic after her then-husband, who had assaulted her and her daughters throughout their marriage, attempted to kill her by shooting her while she was asleep; he subsequently attempted to electrocute her in the bathtub. The public prosecutor had filed criminal charges but the case languished for 8 years before the defendant was found guilty and sentenced; subsequently his conviction was vacated after the defense filed a time-barred appeal. Mr. Da Penha was found guilty at a second trial, but an appeal was still pending at the time the IACHR issued its decision, which was more than 17 years after the original charges were brought.

---

[58] Inter-American Commission on Human Rights (2011).

[59] United States Supreme Court (2005).

[60] Inter-American Commission on Human Rights (2001).

In addition to the facts of Ms. Da Penha's case, the Commission took into account allegations that her case was an example of a "pattern of impunity" in domestic violence cases (para. 20). It concluded that the judicial delay and long waits for decisions on appeal violated the right to "prompt and effective remedies" provided for in both the American Declaration and the American Convention (para. 41).

5.1.3 International Human Rights and National Law

International human rights obligations can be a powerful tool in national courts as well. According to reports, courts in Tanzania and Uganda cited CEDAW in cases, respectively, upholding a conviction for rape, and striking down a law requiring corroboration for sexual offenses as unconstitutional (Warner 2010, pp. 6–7). International human rights principles of the rights to liberty, freedom from abuse, family integrity, and respect for family life can be effective sources of authority in domestic violence cases adjudicated in local family courts (Brandt-Young 2009). Arguments grounded in international human rights principles can be incorporated into a range of lawsuits seeking redress from gender violence, including protection orders, custody determinations and tort claims.[61]

In addition, decisions by international human rights bodies can prompt reforms under national law. For example, following the Inter-American Commission on Human Rights' decision in the *Maria da Penha* case, Brazil undertook a range of reforms, including a new statute that sought to rectify failures identified in the decision (e.g., Rodriguez de Assis Machado et al. 2014). The law contained a comprehensive package of measures addressing prevention, social assistance, emergency protection, civil provisions, and punitive measures. Although the law has been praised as signaling a serious attempt to respond to gender violence, it also has been subject to debate and critique, both surrounding its constitutionality, and with respect to its criminal justice provisions eliminating the mechanisms previously authorizing "alternate" paths in domestic violence cases (ibid.). This is but one example of the difficulty of meaningful implementation, even when international standards are incorporated into national laws (e.g., Hein de Campos 2011).

5.2 Decisions Concerning Violence Against Children

In addition to cases that address violence against children along with gender violence,[62] there has been a substantial number of decisions from international,

[61] See generally, e.g., Schneider et al. (2012); see also Park (2013) (describing brief filed with the Supreme Court in the state of Washington, U.S., invoking human rights principles in support of law enforcement accountability for serving orders of protection).

[62] See Sect. 5.1 above.

regional, and national courts that analyze, interpret, and apply human rights guarantees concerning violence against children. As the World Report on Violence against Children pointed out, "The existing standards in international law relevant to violence against children are comprehensive and detailed. The challenge is to ensure that all States implement their obligations" (Pinheiro 2006b, p. 41). Judicial and quasi-judicial bodies can play a significant role in that effort.

5.2.1 Decisions by International and Regional Bodies

The Convention on the Rights of the Child has had a global impact on jurisprudence (Geary 2012, p. 28). Before the CRC's third Optional Protocol entered into force in 2014, individual complaints claiming violations of the CRC could not be submitted to the Committee on the Rights of the Child, but cases involving children's human rights could and did make their way into various tribunals around the world. In many of those cases, decision-makers cited the CRC. The Child Rights International Network, a non-governmental organization that surveyed court decisions mentioning the CRC, identified 30 cases in which the CRC was invoked by international or regional judicial or quasi-judicial bodies (ibid., pp. 9–10, 31–38). For example, in a case prosecuting Uganda's recruitment of child soldiers and other human rights abuses during its invasion and occupation of parts of the Democratic Republic of Congo, the International Court of Justice found that Uganda had violated the CRC and the Optional Protocol on the involvement of children in armed conflict, as well as other human rights laws (International Court of Justice 2005).

Regional human rights instruments have also been the subject of noteworthy decisions concerning violence against children. The range of these cases is suggested by the following examples, drawn from the World Report on Violence against Children:

> [T]he European Court of Human Rights has found violations of the European Convention on Human Rights in a number of judgements concerning cases of corporal punishment in the penal system, schools, and the home. Other judgements of the Court have concerned sexual abuse, failures of child protection systems and juvenile justice. The European Committee of Social Rights, which monitors compliance with the European Social Charter and the Revised Social Charter, has held that these instruments require prohibition in legislation of any form of violence against children. . . . In 2003, the African Commission on Human and Peoples' Rights decided that lashing of students constituted cruel, inhuman or degrading punishment and requested that the State concerned amend the law, abolish lashing as a penalty and take appropriate measures to compensate the victims.[63]

Some cases challenging violence against children under regional human rights instruments have resulted in payment of compensation to victims and changes in

[63] Pinheiro (2006b), p. 38 (citations omitted).

government policy.[64] Even if they do not result in compensation or policy changes, favorable decisions can have educational value and encourage NGOs to advocate for needed reforms (Freeman 2010, p. 246).

5.2.2 International Human Rights and National Law

International human rights law can interact with domestic law in many ways.[65] In addition to decisions by international and regional bodies, discussed immediately above, international human rights obligations are often considered in cases decided by national courts. According to the Child Rights International Network, over 100 national court cases have discussed the CRC; many of these cases involved violence against children (Geary 2012, pp. 9, 13–14, 31–71).

C.K. (a child) v. Commissioner of Police is an example of a case in which a national court relied on international and regional human rights instruments in its decision (Republic of Kenya 2013). In this case, 11 children in Meru County, Kenya, alleged that they were victims of child sexual abuse as defined and prohibited by Kenyan law.[66] They also alleged that when the crimes were reported to the police, the police failed to conduct proper investigations and prosecutions, causing them grave harm and creating a climate of impunity for commission of sexual offenses. In 2013, the Kenya High Court at Meru found that the inadequate police response violated the petitioners' rights under the Constitution of Kenya as well as the CRC, Universal Declaration of Human Rights, African Charter on the Rights and Welfare of the Child, and African Charter on Human and Peoples' Rights. The court issued a writ of mandamus requiring the police to conduct appropriate investigations into the crimes committed against the petitioners and to carry out their constitutional duties with respect to the issues raised in the case. Commentators hailed the decision as a landmark victory, while recognizing that effective implementation is not guaranteed (Armstrong 2013; Reini 2013). Supporters of the petitioners have declared their intention to monitor and enforce the court's order, publicize the decision and its significance, and work for reform of other laws concerning sexual violence in Kenya and elsewhere (Armstrong 2013; The Equality Effect 2013).

When international legal instruments are not enforceable under national law, they can still serve as persuasive authority and influence decision-makers.[67] In the United States, which has signed but not ratified the CRC, judges have cited the CRC

---

[64] See Van Bueren (1995), pp. 249–252 (describing cases claiming that corporal punishment in schools violated the European Convention on Human Rights).

[65] See, e.g., Weiner (2004) (discussing Article 20 of the Hague Convention on the Civil Aspects of International Child Abduction).

[66] The twelfth petitioner was Ripples International, a charitable non-governmental organization in Meru specializing in the protection of children.

[67] See Columbia Law School Human Rights Clinic (2010), pp. 1–3; Geary (2012), p. 5; Northeastern University School of Law Program on Human Rights and the Global Economy et al. (2008), p. 3.

in cases involving violence against children. In the case *In re Adoption of Peggy*, the Supreme Judicial Court of Massachusetts stated that the CRC was not binding but nevertheless cited the CRC's provisions concerning the best interests of the child (Art. 3) and the duty to protect children from all forms of abuse (Art. 19) in support of its decision to terminate the parental rights of a father whose daughter had suffered female genital mutilation and other injuries while in his custody.[68] The federal district court in *Nicholson v. Williams* described the CRC, Universal Declaration, and ICCPR as consistent with the right to family integrity under the United States Constitution; the decision granted a preliminary injunction against a government policy of removing children from mothers who were victims of domestic violence.[69]

International human rights tribunals can influence domestic law reform without even issuing a formal decision. In 2012, four organizations in Bolivia and the United States filed a request with the Inter-American Commission on Human Rights for a thematic hearing on sexual violence against adolescent girls in Bolivia.[70] At the hearing held by the IACHR, testimony showed that sexual abuse of adolescents was endemic in Bolivia and that the country had failed to address the problem and to provide justice for victims, in violation of its obligations under the CRC and other global and regional human rights laws (Stephens et al. 2012b). One aspect of the Bolivian legal system that was criticized in the testimony was the rape marriage law, which permitted a rapist to avoid any criminal punishment if he married the victim.[71] Subsequently, the Bolivian rape marriage law was abolished. The IACHR proceedings were a catalyst for this legislative action (Rutgers-Camden Campus News 2013).

6 Other Advocacy

International human rights instruments and the processes of monitoring and ensuring compliance also play a role in policy-based advocacy. NGOs bring perspectives from civil society and the advocacy community to the process through their submission of "shadow reports" and their participation in proceedings such as

---

[68] Massachusetts Supreme Judicial Court (2002), pp. 37–38.

[69] United States District Court (2002), p. 234.

[70] The four organizations were the Rutgers School of Law—Camden's Child and Family Advocacy Clinic, the American University Washington College of Law's International Human Rights Law Clinic, Centro Una Brisa de Esperanza, and La Oficina Jurídica Para La Mujer. The request was filed on behalf of more than one hundred Bolivian non-governmental organizations. Stephens et al. (2012a).

[71] Stephens et al. (2012b), pp. 16–17 (citing Penal Code Art. 317). Rape marriage laws exist in many countries and are opposed by human rights advocates. See United Nations Division for the Advancement of Women (UNDAW) (2010), p. 25.

CEDAW hearings and CRC pre-session working groups.[72] Advocates have worked in concert with government officials to translate CEDAW's principles and promise into local policies and practices.[73] For example, CEDAW reportedly was used in Afghanistan to support the creation of domestic violence shelters and to promote awareness campaigns (Warner 2010, p. 5). Advocates in Ghana, Mexico, Sierra Leone and Turkey reportedly invoked standards established in CEDAW's General Recommendation No. 19 to support passage of domestic violence legislation (ibid., p. 6). Following its 1998 adoption of a local CEDAW ordinance, the city and county of San Francisco in California adopted a gender analysis methodology that, among other reforms, led to the development of programs, policies and tools to address violence against women (Menon 2010). At the same time that scholars and advocates urge broader adoption and implementation of CEDAW, they also note concerns about the challenges of implementation (McPhedran et al. 2000, p. 15).

Thematic hearings provide a valuable forum for international human rights advocacy. For example, Native American women testified before the IACHR in a thematic hearing on violence against Native women in the United States, in order to call attention to the problem and increase pressure on the United States government to improve its response (Indian Law Resource Center 2010).

International human rights principles and practice are also highlighted through documentation of perceived violations. Reports on family courts in the United States have publicized family court practices charged with routinely violating women's and children's human rights during child custody proceedings involving allegations of domestic violence and child abuse. A landmark 2002 report, entitled Battered Mothers Speak Out: A Human Rights Report on Domestic Violence and Child Custody in the Massachusetts Family Courts, detailed the experiences of women who had litigated child custody cases with an abusive ex-partner (Cuthbert et al. 2002). The report identified a number of common problems, including courts' failure to investigate allegations of abuse in custody cases; refusing to consider evidence that supports a mother's claims of abuse; allowing the abuser to continue the abuse through the family courts; and failing to respect the economic rights of women and children. Arizona advocates also published a report on mothers' and children's experiences in family court that detailed similar problems with gender bias and other obstacles to relief (Arizona Coalition against Domestic Violence 2003). Advocates in other communities, including New York City, similarly have used human rights principles to observe and report challenges survivors of abuse face in seeking relief in family court (Voices of Women Organizing Project 2007).

International human rights principles also have influenced local laws through the adoption of local human rights resolutions. Like the CEDAW ordinance adopted by San Francisco, discussed above, localities in the United States, including Baltimore,

[72] Merry (2006), pp. 86–87; Todres (2014), pp. 574–578; see also International Women's Rights Action Watch (2013).

[73] See, e.g., Byrnes and Freeman (2012); Chlala et al. (2006); McPhedran et al. (2000); Warner (2010).

Boston, Cincinnati, Miami-Dade County and Washington, DC, have enacted resolutions declaring freedom from domestic violence to be a fundamental human right.[74]

Moreover, international human rights instruments form the basis for public education campaigns. For example, the United Nations' UNiTE campaign aims to create awareness and increase political will and resources for preventing and ending all forms of violence against women and girls globally (United Nations Department of Public Information (UNDPI) 2013). The same principles underlie initiatives such as the 16 Days of Activism against Gender-Based Violence Campaign, which has become a mobilizing tool for activists around the world shining a spotlight on violence against women and girls as a human rights issue.[75]

7 Issues for Further Consideration

The issues raised by violence against women and children, and by international, regional, and national responses to the problem, are numerous and complex. The following sections discuss a few key concerns.

7.1 Intersectionality and Impact on Marginalized Communities

As Special Rapporteur Manjoo has recognized, multiple and intersecting forms of discrimination contribute to and exacerbate violence against women (Manjoo 2011). Experts concur that survivors' experience of domestic and sexual violence is shaped by the interaction of gender with other forms of subordination, such as race, ethnicity, immigration status, class, disability, religion, sexual orientation and gender identity.[76] Members of marginalized communities may be particularly vulnerable to abuse (e.g., Manjoo 2011, paras. 40–49). Laws, policies and programs should be especially attentive to how interventions may affect those who suffer multiple forms of discrimination, and should take steps to ensure that interventions do not intensify existing disadvantages. In particular, legal and policy responses that focus on criminalization may have an adverse impact on marginalized

[74] Columbia Law School Human Rights Clinic and Miami Law Human Rights Clinic (2014) (listing resolutions).

[75] See Center for Women's Global Leadership (2013) (detailing campaign activities and materials, which were available to participants in over 60 languages).

[76] See, e.g., United Nations Division for the Advancement of Women (2010), pp. 14–15; United Nations General Assembly (2011), Annex para. 10. See generally, e.g., Crenshaw (1991); INCITE! Women of Color Against Violence (2006); Nixon and Humphreys (2010); Richie (2012); Sokoloff (2005).

communities when those communities are negatively targeted and affected by criminal justice responses.[77]

Children are intrinsically vulnerable because of their age and evolving capacity. Some children face a heightened risk of violence because of factors like age, gender, race, disability, ethnicity, sexual orientation, gender identity, membership in minority or indigenous groups, and migrant or refugee status. For instance, girls are more likely than boys to suffer infanticide, sexual abuse, educational and nutritional neglect, and forced prostitution. Experiencing violence makes child victims more susceptible to further victimization.[78]

In addition, economic disadvantage increases vulnerability to abuse at the same time that abuse produces economic disadvantage (True 2012; Weissman 2013). For both women and children, poverty and income inequality are risk factors for violence.[79] Women's lack of access to financial resources within the family, together with other forms of economic discrimination, makes it more difficult for them to avoid and recover from violence (United Nations General Assembly 2006a, paras. 86–87). For all these reasons, effective responses to violence against women and children must include adequate resources to alleviate poverty, reduce economic inequality, and support needed services and programs.[80]

Legal and policy responses should adopt multifaceted strategies and should follow a holistic approach that acknowledges the structural aspects of discrimination. An effective response to violence against women and children must include an awareness of social and economic hierarchies and the role they play in the experience and effects of violence (Manjoo 2011, paras. 99–108; Pinheiro 2006a, paras. 94–114).

7.2 *Domestic Legal Responses*

In order for States to meet their obligations to safeguard women's and children's human rights, they must enact and enforce comprehensive legislation prohibiting violence against women and children.[81] Criminal laws are a fundamental component of the domestic legal response. Criminal sanctions are seen as providing a

---

[77] See, e.g., INCITE! Women of Color Against Violence (2006); Richie (2012).

[78] For discussion of factors contributing to children's vulnerability to violence, see, e.g., Krug et al. (2002), pp. 66–69; Office of the Special Representative of the Secretary-General on Violence against Children (2013), pp. xv, 11–32, 129–30; Pinheiro (2006b), pp. 65–72.

[79] Krug et al. (2002), pp. 67–68, 99, 158–159; Office of the Special Representative of the Secretary-General on Violence against Children (2013), pp. 11–12.

[80] Butchart et al. (2004), p. 51; Office of the Special Representative of the Secretary-General on Violence against Children (2013), p. 59.

[81] Office of the Special Representative of the Secretary-General on Violence against Children (OSRSG) (2013), pp. 60–74, 79–81, 134; United Nations Division for the Advancement of Women (UNDAV) (2010), p. 1.

unique opportunity to deter and punish acts of violence.[82] An efficient and fair criminal justice system can contribute to offender accountability and convey a strong message of disapproval of violence.

However, criminal laws are not sufficient to address violence against women and children, and criminal justice interventions are sometimes counterproductive. Reliance on police and prisons to solve the problem of violence is expensive and can divert resources from needed social programs, including supports and services for victims (Butchart et al. 2004, pp. 6–7). An intrinsic problem of criminal justice is that it generally magnifies the power of the State and State actors, while giving individual victims little or no control over the process.[83] When administered improperly, criminal law carries the risk of re-victimizing the victim. For example, in some countries, women who are victims of intimate partner violence have been arrested along with the abuser, punished for defending themselves from an attack, or penalized for failing to protect their children from the harm of witnessing the abuse.[84] At a minimum, abusive official practices should be eliminated, and criminal interventions should be implemented in a manner that is sensitive to gender issues and to victims' needs.[85]

Civil legal actions offer a valuable addition to or substitute for criminal proceedings (United Nations Division for the Advancement of Women (UNDAW) 2010, p. 54). National legal systems should offer both.[86] Examples of civil cases include civil protection orders, tort actions for personal injury, and lawsuits for violation of the victim's civil or human rights. In comparison to criminal law, civil law typically allows victims more control over the claims that are brought and the types of relief that are obtained, including financial compensation. In many countries, civil cases are governed by a more favorable burden of proof. While they are not a panacea,[87] civil actions represent a significant and often overlooked remedy for acts of violence.

---

[82] See Butchart et al. (2004), p. 39 (suggesting that "interventions that strengthen the efficiency and improve the fairness of the criminal justice system" would help prevent violence); European Court of Human Rights (1985) (finding that a gap in the law that made it impossible to institute criminal proceedings against the alleged rapist of a 16-year-old girl with an intellectual disability violated the victim's rights under Article 8 of the European Convention on Human Rights).

[83] See Goodmark (2012), pp. 118–124; Hein de Campos (2011), pp. 900–901; Rudolf and Eriksson (2007), pp. 524–25.

[84] See Manjoo (2013a), para. 58; United Nations Division for the Advancement of Women (2010), pp. 15, 37–38.

[85] See Butchart et al. (2004), pp. 61–62, 65; Manjoo (2013a), paras. 53–56; United Nations Division for the Advancement of Women (2010), pp. 38–44.

[86] Rudolf and Eriksson (2007), pp. 524–525; United Nations General Assembly (2011), A/RES/65/228, Annex para. 18(h).

[87] See Goldscheid (2007), pp. 768–770 (describing limitations of civil lawsuits against perpetrators of sexual and domestic violence). In particular, civil proceedings in family law matters are often insufficiently responsive to intimate partner violence and child abuse. See Sect. 6 above (describing family court reports); United Nations Division for the Advancement of Women (2010), p. 54; United Nations General Assembly (2011), A/RES/65/228, Annex para. 14(d).

Remedies afforded through formal legal systems, whether criminal or civil, have their limits. Some survivors prefer other approaches to redress, from compensation funds that provide financial relief, to apology and symbolic reparations, to policy responses aimed at addressing systemic concerns (e.g., Goodmark 2012, pp. 178–186; Strang and Braithwaite 2002). Many are eager to explore alternatives to the traditional legal model. Nevertheless, other advocates caution that restorative justice, batterer intervention programs, and other alternatives must be approached with care, since they may not protect victims' interests and risk deemphasizing the wrongfulness of perpetrators' actions.[88]

When designing domestic legislation, it is crucial to remember that many victims suffer from feelings of powerlessness. Therefore, it is important that the legal response be structured to enhance the victim's sense of dignity and control (United Nations General Assembly 2011, A/RES/65/228, Annex para. 7). Human rights analysis of violence against women has repeatedly stressed the need to empower victims.[89] Precisely because gender violence is often intended to undermine women's independence, the legal system should support victims' status as autonomous agents.[90] An additional reason to provide victims with opportunities to exercise their capacity for self-determination is the fact that victims are highly diverse; offering them choices is the only way to ensure that their needs will be met (Hein de Campos 2011, pp. 900–901; Goldfarb 2011, pp. 67–70).

7.3 Connections and Distinctions Between Violence Against Women and Violence Against Children

There are many links between violence against women and violence against children. Women and children are commonly subjected to similar types of violence, such as beatings, sexual assault, and trafficking. These similarities are especially pronounced for girls, whose experiences of rape, forced marriage, forced prostitution, and other forms of violence in many ways resemble those of adult women. Violence against both women and children often takes place in the home, where until recently, it was socially ignored and legally invisible (Office of the Special Representative of the Secretary-General on Violence against Children (OSRSG) 2013, p. 31; Thomas and Beasley 1995, pp. 1122–23). Many legal systems, public

[88] See Goldfarb (2011), pp. 74–75; Ptacek (2010). See also Manjoo (2013a), para. 63 (warning that many programs designed for men have not been proven effective and compete for funds with services for women and children).

[89] United Nations Division for the Advancement of Women (2010), p. 2; United Nations General Assembly (2011), A/RES/65/228, Annex para. 13.

[90] See Goldfarb (2008), pp. 1499–1504. By virtue of their age, children do not enjoy complete autonomy. Nevertheless, the CRC provides that in judicial and administrative proceedings, children's views should be given due weight in accordance with their age and maturity (Art. 12). See Committee on the Rights of the Child (2009).

officials, and professionals continue to lack sufficient awareness and sensitivity to issues affecting women and children who are victims of violence.

Violence against children, like violence against women, is frequently gender-based. Some children are victimized simply because of their gender; others are targeted because they deviate from prescribed gender roles (Office of the Special Representative of the Secretary-General on Violence against Children (OSRSG) 2013, p. 119). Gender-based violence, whether committed against adults or children, expresses and perpetuates women's subordinate status (ibid.). Under traditional patriarchal attitudes, women and children share a disempowered position in the family and society, rendering members of both groups vulnerable to violence (Van Bueren 1995, pp. 52–53). Therefore, eliminating sex discrimination in all its manifestations is a necessary step toward eradicating violence against children as well as violence against women (Office of the Special Representative of the Secretary-General on Violence against Children (OSRSG) 2013, pp. 118–123).

Studies from many countries show a strong correlation at the household level between abuse of adult women and abuse of children (Krug et al. 2002, p. 68). Among families where mothers are abused by a male partner, approximately half of the children are also abused by the mother's abuser (Silverman et al. 2004, pp. 951–52). Indeed, for a child to witness his or her mother being abused is potentially damaging in itself (Krug et al. 2002, p. 103; United Nations General Assembly 2011, A/RES/65/228, Annex para. 18(g)). Exposure to violence in one's family of origin is a major risk factor for perpetrating or suffering violence later in life (Butchart et al. 2004, pp. vi, 4, 63; Krug et al. 2002, pp. 67–68, 98, 160). In short, "violence begets violence" (Office of the Special Representative of the Secretary-General on Violence against Children (OSRSG) 2013 p. 30). Accordingly, one of the benefits of reducing violence against women and children is that it is likely to cause lower rates of violence in future generations.

Despite the commonalities between violence against women and violence against children, there are risks in considering the two issues together. Women's and children's interests can diverge and even conflict. Grouping women with children threatens to essentialize women's role as mothers at the expense of their other identities, and carries echoes of the view that women and children belong in the domestic sphere, separated from the world of men, commerce, government, and law (Goldfarb 2011, pp. 56–57). Throughout much of history, women and children have both been considered to lack capacity, autonomy, and rights (Van Bueren 1995, pp. 52–53). This inferior status has been used to justify inflicting violence on women and children in the name of "discipline."[91] For all these reasons, it is necessary to exercise caution when addressing violence against women in conjunction with violence against children.

[91] See Goldfarb (2008), p. 1495; Ofei-Aboagye (1994); Office of the Special Representative of the Secretary-General on Violence against Children (2013), p. 31.

8 Conclusion

Efforts to assist survivors, hold perpetrators accountable, and end violence against women and children have expanded dramatically over the last 4 decades. Although research is ongoing, empirical evidence about effective interventions is still scarce. While there has been much improvement, including expansion of laws prohibiting violence and increased services for survivors, the obstacles to progress are daunting. Even when laws are enacted, implementation and enforcement pose complex challenges.

Notwithstanding those caveats, common recommendations include measures that prioritize survivors' safety and autonomy, address economic disadvantage and historic gender biases, and ensure that interventions are culturally appropriate.[92] The concept of due diligence provides a useful framework for analyzing governmental responses (e.g., Due Diligence Project 2014). As discussed above, the concept identifies five key principles: prevention, protection, prosecution, punishment and providing redress, which together outline the breadth of actions that are needed to address the problem. Prevention programs, for example, should promote awareness of violence and should also address its root causes in gender and other forms of subordination. States should implement mechanisms for intervention that will prevent repetition of violence in particular instances. Comprehensive data collection that is disaggregated to reflect the impact of abuse on particular communities is also essential. Programs should recognize that violence does not affect everyone equally, and should account for the increased vulnerability of those from marginalized groups. States should ensure that survivors have access to a range of services, such as hotlines, counseling, shelter, medical care and other support services, and should facilitate coordination among service providers through a multi-sectoral approach where possible.

Laws that prohibit violence against women and children are foundational; the United Nations has begun to identify the kinds of laws that comprise a meaningful response, as well as recommendations for implementation, monitoring, and evaluation.[93] Redress and reparation for survivors are central to any comprehensive legal response to violence and can take multiple forms. Legal initiatives should place the issue of violence in the larger context of underlying social and economic inequities.

Eradicating violence against women and children will require more than changes in laws and their enforcement. Cultural change is also essential. However, legal reform can make a significant contribution to cultural shifts. Attitudes that tolerate or support violence against women and children are widespread, but they are not immutable. Law—including international human rights law—is a force that can help shape culture (Merry 2006). Thus, instead of viewing culture as an insuperable

---

[92] See, e.g., Bott et al. (2005), pp. 14–42; Kiplesund and Morton (2014), pp. 2–4; World Health Organization (2013), pp. 35–36.

[93] United Nations Division for the Advancement of Women (UNDAW) (2010); United Nations Economic and Social Council (2014); United Nations General Assembly (2011), A/RES/65/228.

impediment to the effort to eliminate violence, law should be seen as a potential source of new cultural understandings (ibid.). Of course, other mechanisms, such as education, counseling, the media, social marketing and other communication strategies, also have important roles to play in changing cultural norms.

Emerging recommended practices to address violence against women and children are multifaceted and nuanced, and must be implemented in ways that are culturally specific and tailored to local realities. International human rights law can be a valuable part of that process.

Five Questions

1. How does the principle of due diligence apply to violence against women and children?
2. What are the connections between gender inequality and violence against women and children?
3. Are some women and children more vulnerable to violence than others, and if so, what factors contribute to their vulnerability?
4. In what ways has international human rights law contributed to the effort to eradicate violence against women and children?
5. What additional steps should be taken at the global, regional and national levels to address violence against women and children?

Acknowledgements The authors gratefully acknowledge the helpful comments provided by Martha Davis, Cynthia Soohoo, Beth Stephens, and Merle Weiner, and the research assistance provided by Maura Burk, Hope Deutsch, Rebecca Mamone, and Meghan McLoughlin.

References

African Commission on Human and Peoples' Rights (1990). African Charter on the Rights and Welfare of the Child, OAU Doc. CAB.LEG/24.9/49. http://www.achpr.org/files/instruments/child/achpr_instr_charterchild_eng.pdf. Accessed 21 May 2014.

African Commission on Human and Peoples' Rights (2003). Protocol to the African Charter on Human and People's Rights on the Rights of Women. http://www.achpr.org/files/instruments/women-protocol/achpr_instr_proto_women_eng.pdf. Accessed 14 May 2014.

Annan, K. (2006). Preface. In: P. S. Pinheiro (Ed.) *World report on violence against children*, (p. XI). http://www.unicef.org/violencestudy/I.%20World%20Report%20on%20Violence%20against%20Children.pdf. Accessed 22 May 2014.

Arizona Coalition against Domestic Violence (2003). Battered mothers' testimony project: A human rights approach to child custody and domestic violence. Arizona Coalition against Domestic Violence. http://www.ncdsv.org/images/AzCADV_BatteredMothers'TestimonyProjectHumanRightsApproachToChildCustodyAndDV_5-2003.pdf. Accessed 23 May 2014.

Armstrong, S. (2013). In Kenya, a victory for girls and rights. In: *New York Times*. http://www.nytimes.com/2013/06/05/opinion/global/in-kenya-a-victory-for-girls-and-rights.html?_r=1&. Accessed 22 May 2014.

Bettinger-Lopez, C. (2008). Human rights at home: Domestic violence as a human rights violation. *Columbia Human Rights Law Review, 40*, 19–77.

Black, M. C., Basile, K. C., Breiding, M. J., Smith, S. G., Walters, M. L., Merrick, M. T., Chen, J., Stevens, M. R. (2011). *The national intimate partner and sexual violence survey: 2010 summary report*. Georgia: National Center for Injury Prevention and Control. http://www.cdc.gov/violenceprevention/pdf/nisvs_report2010-a.pdf. Accessed 17 May 2014.

Bott, S., Morrison, A., & Ellsberg, M. (2005). Preventing and responding to gender-based violence in middle and low-income countries: A global review and analysis. World Bank Policy Research Working Paper 3618. http://www-wds.worldbank.org/servlet/WDSContentServer/IW3P/IB/2005/06/28/000112742_20050628084339/Rendered/PDF/wps3618.pdf. Accessed 19 May 2014.

Brandt-Young, C. (2009). Five international human rights citations to use in your next New York State domestic violence brief. New York University School of Law Center for Human Rights and Global Justice, Litigating Human Rights Series. http://www.google.com/url?sa=t&rct=j&q=&esrc=s&source=web&cd=1&ved=0CCAQFjAA&url=http%3A%2F%2Fmarylandlegalaid.pbworks.com%2Ff%2FFive%2BDV%2BRigths.doc&ei=ee6VU5-SD4StyATlp4K4AQ&usg=AFQjCNHBt8oFJtQ-g2n7Zo3ohrGpSDKIbg&sig2=CRlugfUAjdQACEH9fda3ew. Accessed 9 June 2014.

Bunch, C. (1990). Women's rights as human rights: Toward a re-vision of human rights. *Human Rights Quarterly, 12*(4), 486–498. doi:10.2307/762496.

Butchart, A. & Harvey, A. (2006). *Preventing child maltreatment: a guide to taking action and generating evidence*. Geneva: World Health Organization. http://whqlibdoc.who.int/publications/2006/9241594365_eng.pdf. Accessed 12 June 2014.

Butchart, A., Phinney, A., Check, P., Villaveces, A. (2004). *Preventing violence: A guide to implementing the recommendations of the world report on violence and health*. Geneva: World Health Organization. http://www.who.int/violence_injury_prevention/media/news/08_09_2004/en/. Accessed 13 May 2014.

Byrnes, A., Freeman, M. (2012). The impact of the CEDAW convention: Paths to equality. UNSW Law Research Paper No. 2012-7. http://siteresources.worldbank.org/INTWDR2012/Resources/7778105-1299699968583/7786210-1322671773271/Byrnes-and-Freeman-FINAL-18-May-2011-with-acknowledgements.pdf. Accessed 19 May 2014.

Center for Women's Global Leadership (2013). 16 days of activism against gender based violence campaign: 2013 analytical summary. http://16dayscwgl.rutgers.edu/. Accessed 17 May 2014.

Charlesworth, H., Chinkin, C., & Wright, S. (1991). Feminist approaches to international law. *American Journal of International Law, 85*, 613–645.

Chlala, Y., Dharmaraj, K., Levi, R., Washbur, K. (2006). *Making rights real: A workbook on the local implementation of human rights*. San Francisco: Women's Institute for Leadership Development for Human Rights. http://sfgov.org/dosw/sites/sfgov.org.dosw/files/wild-booklet-13mar14.pdf. Accessed 19 May 2014.

Columbia Law School Human Rights Clinic, Sexuality & Gender Law Clinic (2010). Human rights and domestic violence: An advocacy manual. http://web.law.columbia.edu/sites/default/files/microsites/clinics/sexuality-gender/images/domesticviolence5.pdf. Accessed 19 May 2014.

Columbia Law School Human Rights Clinic, Miami Law Human Rights Clinic (2014). Recognizing Freedom from Domestic Violence as a Fundamental Human Right. http://www.law.miami.edu/human-rights-clinic/pdf/2014/local-resolutions-2014.pdf. Accessed 6 June 2014.

Committee against Torture (2008). General Comment No. 2: Implementation of article 2 by States parties. U.N. Doc. CAT/C/GC/2. http://tbinternet.ohchr.org/_layouts/treatybodyexternal/TBSearch.aspx?Lang=en&TreatyID=1&DocTypeID=11. Accessed 15 July 2014.

Committee on the Elimination of Discrimination against Women (1989). General Recommendation No. 12: Violence against women. U.N. Doc A/44/38. http://www.un.org/womenwatch/daw/cedaw/recommendations/recomm.htm#recom12. Accessed 13 May 2014.

Committee on the Elimination of Discrimination against Women (1992). General Recommendation No. 19: Violence against women. U.N. Doc. A/47/38. http://www.un.org/womenwatch/daw/cedaw/recommendations/recomm.htm#recom19. Accessed 13 May 2014.

Committee on the Elimination of Discrimination against Women (2005). A.T. v. Hungary, Communication No. 2/2003. U.N. Doc. CEDAW/C/32/D/2/2003. http://www.bayefsky.com/pdf/hungary_t5_cedaw_2_2003.pdf. Accessed 14 May 2014.

Committee on the Elimination of Discrimination against Women (2007a). Goekce v. Austria, Communication No. 5/2005. U.N. Doc. CEDAW/C/39/D/5/2005. http://www.bayefsky.com/pdf/austria_cedaw_t5_5_2005.pdf. Accessed 14 May 2014.

Committee on the Elimination of Discrimination against Women (2007b). Yildirim v. Austria, Communication No. 6/2005. U.N. Doc. CEDAW/C/39/D/6/2005. http://www.bka.gv.at/DocView.axd?CobId = 29081. Accessed 14 May 2014.

Committee on the Elimination of Discrimination against Women (2012). S.V.P. v. Bulgaria, Communication No. 31/2011. U.N. Doc. CEDAW/C/53/D/31/2011. http://www.worldcourts.com/cedaw/eng/decisions/2012.10.12_S.V.P._v_Bulgaria.pdf. Accessed 14 May 2014.

Committee on the Rights of the Child (2003). General Comment No. 5: General measures of implementation of the Convention on the Rights of the Child. U.N. Doc. CRC/GC/2003/5. http://daccess-dds-ny.un.org/doc/UNDOC/GEN/G03/455/14/PDF/G0345514.pdf?OpenElement. Accessed 12 June 2014.

Committee on the Rights of the Child (2006). General Comment No. 8: The right of the child to protection from corporal punishment and other cruel or degrading forms of punishment. U.N. Doc. CRC/C/GC/8. http://daccess-dds-ny.un.org/doc/UNDOC/GEN/G07/407/71/PDF/G0740771.pdf OpenElement. Accessed 22 May 2014.

Committee on the Rights of the Child (2007). General Comment No. 10: Children's rights in juvenile justice. U.N. Doc. CRC/C/GC/10. http://www2.ohchr.org/english/bodies/crc/docs/CRC.C.GC.10.pdf. Accessed 11 July 2014.

Committee on the Rights of the Child (2009). General Comment No. 12: The right of the child to be heard. U.N. Doc. CRC/C/GC/12. http://tbinternet.ohchr.org/_layouts/treatybodyexternal/Download.aspx?symbolno = CRC%2fC%2fGC%2f12&Lang = en. Accessed 9 June 2014.

Committee on the Rights of the Child (2011). General Comment No. 13: The right of the child to freedom from all forms of violence. U.N. Doc. CRC/C/GC/13. http://www2.ohchr.org/english/bodies/crc/docs/CRC.C.GC.13_en.pdf. Accessed 22 May 2014.

Committee on the Rights of the Child (2013). Rules of procedure under the Optional Protocol to the Convention on the Rights of the Child on a communications procedure. U.N. Doc. CRC/C/62/3. http://srsg.violenceagainstchildren.org/sites/default/files/documents/docs/OP3%20Rules%20of%20Procedure.pdf. Accessed 22 May 2014.

Cook, R. (1993). Women's international human rights law: The way forward. *Human Rights Quarterly, 15*, 230–261.

Coomaraswamy, R. (1996). Report of the Special Rapporteur on violence against women, its causes and consequences. U.N. Doc. E/CN.4/1996/53. http://www.awf.or.jp/pdf/h0003.pdf. Accessed 14 May 2014.

Coomaraswamy, R. (1999). Report of the Special Rapporteur on violence against women, its causes and consequences, violence against women in the family. U.N. Doc. E/CN.4/1999/68. http://daccess-dds-ny.un.org/doc/UNDOC/GEN/G99/113/54/PDF/G9911354.pdf?OpenElement. Accessed 13 May 2014.

Copelon, R. (1994). Recognizing the egregious in the everyday: Domestic violence as torture. *Columbia Human Rights Law Review, 25*, 291–367.

Council of Europe (2011). Convention on preventing and combating violence against women and domestic violence. http://www.coe.int/t/dghl/standardsetting/convention-violence/convention/Convention%20210%20English.pdf. Accessed 14 May 2014.

Crenshaw, K. (1991). Mapping the margins: Intersectionality, identity politics, and violence against women of color. *Stanford Law Review, 43*(6), 1241–1299. doi:10.2307/1229039.

Cuthbert, C., Slote, K., Driggers, M. G., Mesh, C. J., Bancroft, L., Silverman, J. (2002). *Battered mothers speak out: A human rights report on domestic violence and child custody in the Massachusetts family courts*. Wellesley: Wellesley Centers for Women.

Due Diligence Project (2014). Due diligence framework, http://www.duediligenceproject.org/About.html. Accessed 17 May 2014.

Edwards, A. (2011). *Violence against women under international human rights law*. New York: Cambridge University Press.

Ertürk, Y. (2006). Report of the Special Rapporteur on violence against women, its causes and consequences, The Due Diligence Standard As a Tool for the Elimination of Violence against Women. U.N. Doc. E/CN.4/2006/61. http://www.refworld.org/pdfid/45377afb0.pdf. Accessed 13 May 2014.

Ertürk, Y. (2008). Report of the Special Rapporteur on violence against women, its causes and consequences, Indicators on violence against women and State response. U.N. Doc. A/HRC/7/6. http://daccess-dds-ny.un.org/doc/UNDOC/GEN/G08/104/47/PDF/G0810447.pdf?OpenElement. Accessed 24 May 2014.

European Court of Human Rights (1985). X and Y v. The Netherlands, no. 8978/80. http://hudoc.echr.coe.int/sites/eng/pages/search.aspx?i=001-57603. Accessed 9 June 2014.

European Court of Human Rights (2009a). Tomasic v. Croatia, no. 46598/06. http://hudoc.echr.coe.int/sites/eng/pages/search.aspx?i=001-90625. Accessed 9 June 2014

European Court of Human Rights (2009b). Opuz v. Turkey, no. 33401/02. http://hudoc.echr.coe.int/sites/eng/pages/search.aspx?i=001-92945. Accessed 14 May 2014

Farrior, S. (2004). The due diligence standard and violence against women. *Interights Bulletin, 14* (4), 150–151.

Freeman, M. (2010). Upholding the dignity and best interests of children: International law and the corporal punishment of children. *Law and Contemporary Problems, 73*, 211–251.

Geary, P. (2012). *CRC in court: The case law of the convention on the rights of the child*. London: Child Rights International Network. https://www.crin.org/docs/CRC_in_Court_Report.pdf. Accessed 23 May 2014.

Goldfarb, S. (2008). Reconceiving civil protection orders for domestic violence: Can law help end the abuse without ending the relationship? *Cardozo Law Review, 29*, 1487–1551.

Goldfarb, S. (2011). A clash of cultures: women, domestic violence, and law in the United States. In D. Hodgson (Ed.), *Gender and culture at the limit of rights* (pp. 55–77). Philadelphia: University of Pennsylvania Press.

Goldscheid, J. (2007). Elusive equality in domestic and sexual violence law reform. *Florida State Law Review, 34*, 731–777.

Goldscheid, J., Liebowitz, D. (2015). Due Diligence and Gender Violence: Parsing its Potential and its Limits. *Cornell International Law Journal, 48*, 301–345.

Goodmark, L. (2012). *A troubled marriage: Domestic violence and the legal system*. New York: New York University Press.

Hein de Campos, C. (2011). Access to justice and the permissive state: The Brazilian experience. *University of Miami Law Review, 65*, 893–902.

Hodgkin, R., Newell, P. (2007). Implementation handbook for the Convention on the Rights of the Child, 3rd edn. United Nations Children's Fund (UNICEF), Geneva. http://www.unicef.org/publications/files/Implementation_Handbook_for_the_Convention_on_the_Rights_of_the_Child_Part_2_of_3.pdf. Accessed 22 May 2014.

Hodson, L. (2013). Women's rights and the periphery: CEDAW's optional protocol. University of Leicester School of Law Legal Studies Research Paper Series, Research Paper No. 13-01.

Human Rights Committee (2000). General Comment No. 28: Article 3 (The equality of rights between men and women). U.N. Doc. CCPR/C/21/Rev.1/Add.10. http://tbinternet.ohchr.org/Treaties/CCPR/Shared%20Documents/1_Global/CCPR_C_21_Rev-1_Add-10_6619_E.pdf. Accessed 13 May 2014.

INCITE! Women of Color against Violence (Ed.) (2006) *Color of violence: The INCITE! anthology*. Cambridge, MA: South End Press.

Indian Law Resource Center (2010). How Can International Advocacy Reduce Violence Against Native Women? http://www.indianlaw.org/node/499. Accessed 29 July 2014.

Inter-American Commission on Human Rights (1999). Minors in Detention v. Honduras, Case 11.491, Report no. 41/99. http://www.cidh.org/annualrep/98eng/Merits/Honduras%2011491.htm. Accessed 21 May 2014.
Inter-American Commission on Human Rights (2001). Maria da Penha v. Brazil, Case 12.051, Report no. 54/01, OEA/Ser.L/V/II.111. http://www1.umn.edu/humanrts/cases/54-01.html. Accessed 14 May 2014.
Inter-American Commission on Human Rights (2011). Jessica Lenahan (Gonzales) et al. v. United States, Case 12.626, Report no. 80/11, OEA/Ser.L./V/II.142. http://www.equalaccessadvocates.com/2011%20August%2008%20Petitioners%20-%20Report%20No%20%2080-11.pdf. Accessed 14 May 2014.
Inter-American Court of Human Rights (1999). 'Street Children' (Villagrán-Morales et al.) v. Guatemala, (ser. C) No. 63. http://www.corteidh.or.cr/docs/casos/articulos/seriec_63_ing.pdf. Accessed 21 May 2014.
Inter-American Court of Human Rights (2002). Juridical Condition and Human Rights of the Child, Advisory Opinion OC-17/2002, (ser. A) No. 17. http://www.corteidh.or.cr/docs/opiniones/seriea_17_ing.pdf. Accessed 21 May 2014.
Inter-American Court of Human Rights (2009). González et al. (Cotton Field) v. Mexico, (ser. C) No. 205. http://www.corteidh.or.cr/docs/casos/articulos/seriec_205_ing.pdf. Accessed 14 May 2014.
International Court of Justice (2005). Case concerning armed activities on the territory of the Congo, Democratic Republic of the Congo v. Uganda. Judgment, I.C.J. Reports 2005. http://www.icj-cij.org/docket/files/116/10455.pdf. Accessed 22 May 2014.
International Women's Rights Action Watch (2013). Shadow reporting to UN treaty bodies. http://www1.umn.edu/humanrts/iwraw/reports.html. Accessed 9 June 2014.
Kiplesund, S., Morton, M. (2014), Gender-Based Violence Prevention: Lessons from World Bank Impact Evaluations. enGender Impact, World Bank. http://www-wds.worldbank.org/external/default/WDSContentServer/WDSP/IB/2014/05/02/000333037_20140502121541/Rendered/PDF/878540BRI0enGE0Box385206B00PUBLIC0.pdf. Accessed 10 June 2014.
Krug, E., Dahlberg, L., Mercy, J., Zwi, A., Lozano, R. (Eds.). (2002). *World report on violence and health*. Geneva: World Health Organization. http://whqlibdoc.who.int/publications/2002/9241545615_eng.pdf. Accessed 13 May 2014.
League of Nations (1924). Geneva Declaration of the Rights of the Child, O.J. Spec Supp. 21, p 66. http://www.un-documents.net/gdrc1924.htm. Accessed 22 May 2014.
Manjoo, R. (2011). Report of the Special Rapporteur on violence against women, its causes and consequences. U.N. Doc. A/HRC/17/26. http://www2.ohchr.org/english/bodies/hrcouncil/docs/17session/A-HRC-17-26.pdf. Accessed 17 May 2014.
Manjoo, R. (2013a). Report of the Special Rapporteur on violence against women, its causes and consequences. U.N. Doc. A/HRC/23/49. http://www.ohchr.org/Documents/HRBodies/HRCouncil/RegularSession/Session23/A_HRC_23_49_English.pdf. Accessed 13 May 2014.
Manjoo, R. (2013b). Report of the Special Rapporteur on violence against women, its causes and consequences: Mission to Croatia. U.N. Doc. A/HRC/23/49/Add.4. http://www.ohchr.org/Documents/HRBodies/HRCouncil/RegularSession/Session23/A-HRC-23-49-Add-4_en.pdf. Accessed 14 May 2014.
Massachusetts Supreme Judicial Court (2002). In re Adoption of Peggy. 767 N.E.2d 29.
McPhedran, M., Bazilli, S., Erickson, M., Byrnes, A. (2000). *The first CEDAW impact study*. Toronto: The International Women's Rights Project. http://iwrp.org/projects/cedaw/. Accessed 17 May 2014.
Menon, A. (2010). *Human rights in action: San Francisco's local implementation of the United Nations' women's treaty (CEDAW)*. California: San Francisco Department on the Status of Women. http://www.sfgov3.org/Modules/ShowDocument.aspx?documentid=314. Accessed 17 May 2014.
Merry, S. E. (2006). *Human rights & gender violence*. Chicago: University of Chicago Press.

Moccia, P. (Ed.) (2009). *The state of the world's children: Special edition: celebrating 20 years of the convention on the rights of the child.* New York: United Nations Children's Fund (UNICEF). http://www.unicef.org/rightsite/sowc/pdfs/SOWC_Spec%20Ed_CRC_Main%20Report_EN_090409.pdf. Accessed 12 June 2014.

National Coalition of Anti-violence Programs (2013). Lesbian, Gay, Bisexual, Transgender, Queer, and HIV-affected Intimate Partner Violence in 2012. http://www.avp.org/storage/documents/ncavp_2012_ipvreport.final.pdf. Accessed 5 June 2014.

NGO Group for the Convention on the Rights of the Child (2008). Reporting on Violence against Children: A thematic guide for non-governmental organizations reporting to the UN Committee on the Rights of the Child. http://www.childrightsconnect.org/wp-content/uploads/2013/10/NGO_Guidelines_reporting_VAC_to_CRC_2008.pdf. Accessed 22 May 2014.

Nixon, J., & Humphreys, C. (2010). Marshalling the evidence: Using intersectionality in the domestic violence frame. *Social Politics, 17*(2), 137–158. doi:10.1093/sp/jxq003.

Northeastern University School of Law Program on Human Rights and the Global Economy, National Economic and Social Rights Initiative, Columbia Law School Human Rights Institute. (2008). *Human rights, social justice and state law: A manual for creative lawyering.* New York: Columbia Law School Human Rights Institute. http://web.law.columbia.edu/sites/default/files/microsites/human-rights-institute/files/hr%20state%20law%20advocacy.pdf. Accessed 23 May 2014.

Ofei-Aboagye, R. O. (1994). Domestic violence in Ghana: Some initial questions. In M. A. Fineman & R. Mykitiuk (Eds.), *The public nature of private violence* (pp. 260–284). New York: Routledge.

Office of the Special Representative of the Secretary-General on Violence against Children (2013). Toward a world free from violence: Global survey on violence against children. http://srsg.violenceagainstchildren.org/sites/default/files/documents/docs/Toward%20a%20World%20Free%20from%20Violence.pdf. Accessed 22 May 2014.

Office of the United Nations High Commissioner for Human Rights (2014a). Committee on the Elimination of Discrimination against Women – Sessions. http://www2.ohchr.org/english/bodies/cedaw/sessions.htm. Accessed 13 May 2014.

Office of the United Nations High Commissioner for Human Rights (2014b). Committee on the Rights of the Child, Introduction – Monitoring children's rights. http://www.ohchr.org/EN/HRBodies/CRC/Pages/CRCIntro.aspx. Accessed 22 May 2014.

Office of the United Nations High Commissioner for Human Rights (2014c). Information note prepared by OHCHR for NGO participation. http://www2.ohchr.org/english/bodies/cedaw/docs/NGO_Participation.final.pdf. Accessed 13 May 2014.

Office of the United Nations High Commissioner for Human Rights (2014d). Special Rapporteur on violence against women, its causes and consequences. http://www.ohchr.org/EN/issues/Women/SRWomen/Pages/SRWomenindex.aspx. Accessed 14 May 2014.

Organization of American States (1948). American Declaration of the Rights and Duties of Man. http://www.cidh.oas.org/Basicos/English/Basic2.american%20Declaration.htm. Accessed 24 May 2014.

Organization of American States (1969). American Convention on Human Rights. S. Exec. Doc.F, 95-2, 1144 U.N.T.S. 123. http://www.oas.org/dil/treaties_B-32_American_Convention_on_Human_Rights.pdf. Accessed 22 May 2014.

Organization of American States (1994). Inter-American Convention on the Prevention, Punishment, and Eradication of Violence against Women (Convention of Belém do Pará). https://www.oas.org/en/mesecvi/convention.asp. Accessed 24 May 2014.

Park, S. (2013). Advancing the human rights of survivors of domestic and sexual violence in the U.S.: Progress report. In: Move to End Violence. http://www.movetoendviolence.org/blog/advancing-human-rights-survivors-domestic-and-sexual-violence-us-progress-report. Accessed 17 May 2014.

Pinheiro, P. S. (2006a). Report of the independent expert for the United Nations study on violence against children. U.N. Doc. A/61/299. http://daccess-dds-ny.un.org/doc/UNDOC/GEN/N06/491/05/PDF/N0649105.pdf?OpenElement. Accessed 21 May 2014.

Pinheiro, P. S. (2006b). World Report on Violence against Children. http://www.unicef.org/violencestudy/I.%20World%20Report%20on%20Violence%20against%20Children.pdf. Accessed 22 May 2014.

Ptacek, J. (Ed.). (2010). *Restorative justice and violence against women*. New York: Oxford University Press.

Reini, J. (2013). Kenyan sex abuse victims await justice. In: Al Jazeera. http://www.aljazeera.com/indepth/features/2013/06/2013623115942808444.html. Accessed 23 May 2014.

Republic of Kenya, High Court at Meru (2013). C.K. (a child) v. Commissioner of Police. Petition 8 of 2012, Kenya Law Reports. http://ww3.lawschool.cornell.edu/AvonResources/CK%20v%20Commissioner%20of%20Police%20-%20Kenya.pdf. Accessed 23 May 2014.

Revaz, C. R., & Todres, J. (2006). The optional protocols to the convention on the rights of the child and the impact of U.S. ratification. In J. Todres, M. Wojcik, & C. R. Revaz (Eds.), *The U.N. convention on the rights of the child: An analysis of treaty provisions and implications of U.S. ratification* (pp. 293–309). Ardsley: Transnational Publishers.

Richie, B. E. (2012). *Arrested justice: Black women, violence, and America's prison nation*. New York: New York University Press.

Rodriguez de Assis Machado, M., Rodriguez, J. R., Marques Prol, F., Justino da Silva, G., Ganzarolli, M. Z., do Vale Elias, R. (2014). Disputing the application of laws: The constitutionality of the Brazilian statute against domestic violence in the courts. Direito GV Research Paper Series No. 90. http://www.surjournal.org/eng/conteudos/getArtigo16.php?artigo=16,artigo_03.htm. Accessed 19 May 2014.

Rome Statute of the International Criminal Court (1998). U.N. doc. A/CONF.183/9*. http://www.un.org/law/icc/. Accessed 6 June 2014.

Rudolf, B., & Eriksson, A. (2007). Women's rights under international human rights treaties: Issues of rape, domestic slavery, abortion, and domestic violence. *International Journal of Constitutional Law, 5*, 507–525.

Rutgers-Camden Campus News (2013). Inspired by alumna, Rutgers Law-Camden team triumphant in abolishing rape-marriage law in Bolivia. In: Rutgers-Camden News Now. http://news.camden.rutgers.edu/2013/07/inspired-by-alumna-rutgers-law-camden-team-triumphant-in-abolishing-rape-marriage-law-in-bolivia/. Accessed 23 May 2014.

Schneider, E. M. (2004). Transnational law as a domestic resource: Thoughts on the case of women's rights. *New England Law Review, 38*, 689–723.

Schneider, E. M., Bettinger-Lopez, C., Goldscheid, J., Park, S. S., Dike, E., Jacobs, L. R., Drew, M., Haviland, M. (2012). Implementing the Inter-American Commission on Human Rights' domestic-violence ruling. *Clearinghouse Review Journal of Poverty Law & Policy, 46*, 113–121.

Silverman, J. G., Mesh, C. M., Cuthbert, C. V., Slote, K., Bancroft, L. (2004). Child custody determinations in cases involving intimate partner violence: A human rights analysis. *American Journal of Public Health, 94*, 951–957.

Sokoloff, N. J. (Ed.). (2005). *Domestic violence at the margins: Readings on race, class, gender, and culture*. New Jersey: Rutgers University Press.

Special Representative of the Secretary-General on Violence against Children (2014). Mandate. http://srsg.violenceagainstchildren.org/srsg/mandate. Accessed 22 May 2014.

Stephens, B., Perez, M., Cusak, M., Keillor, D., Moran, C., Wilson, R., et al. (2012a). Request for thematic hearing on sexual violence against adolescent girls in Bolivia. Sent to Dr. Santiago A. Canton, Executive Secretary, Inter-American Commission on Human Rights, Washington D.C., 18 Jan 2012 (on file with author).

Stephens, B., Cusak, M., Perez, M., De Angulo, B., Palmer, P., Bellott, M. L. O., et al. (2012b). Denouncing sexual violence against adolescent girls in Bolivia. Materials prepared for the thematic hearing, 144th session of hearings, Inter-American Commission on Human Rights,

Washington D.C., 28 Mar 2012. https://www.crin.org/docs/Thematic_Hearing_Submission_DRAFT_03-08-12_3pm.pdf. Accessed 23 May 2014.
Strang, H., & Braithwaite, J. (Eds.). (2002). *Restorative justice and family violence*. Cambridge: Cambridge University Press.
The Equality Effect (2013). "160 Girls" Malawi update – August 2013. In: The Equality Effect. http://theequalityeffect.org/160-girls-update-august-2013/. Accessed 23 May 2014.
Thomas, D. Q., & Beasley, M. E. (1995). Domestic violence as a human rights issue. *Albany Law Review, 58*, 1119–1147.
Todres, J. (2014). A child rights framework for addressing trafficking of children. *Michigan State International Law Review, 22*, 557–593.
True, J. (2012). *The political economy of violence against women*. New York: Oxford University Press.
United Nations Children's Fund (UNICEF) Innocenti Research Centre (2005). U.N. human rights standards and mechanisms to combat violence against children: A contribution to the U.N. Secretary General's study on violence against children. UNICEF Innocenti Research Centre, Florence. http://www.unicef-irc.org/publications/pdf/un_human_rights.pdf. Accessed 22 May 2014.
United Nations Department of Public Information (2008). UNiTE to end violence against women, fact sheet, DPI/2498. http://www.un.org/en/women/endviolence/pdf/VAW.pdf. Accessed 21 May 2014.
United Nations Department of Public Information (2011). UNiTE to end violence against women, Violence against Women, DPI/2546A. http://endviolence.un.org/pdf/pressmaterials/unite_the_situation_en.pdf. Accessed 9 June 2014.
United Nations Department of Public Information (2013). UNiTE to end violence against women. http://endviolence.un.org/about.shtml. Accessed 17 May 2014.
United Nations Division for the Advancement of Women (2010). *Handbook for legislation on violence against women*. New York: United Nations. http://www.un.org/womenwatch/daw/vaw/handbook/Handbook%20for%20legislation%20on%20violence%20against%20women.pdf. Accessed 17 May 2014.
United Nations Division for the Advancement of Women (2011). *Supplement to the handbook for legislation on violence against women: "Harmful practices" against women*. New York: United Nations. http://www.un.org/womenwatch/daw/vaw/handbook/Supplement-to-Handbook-English.pdf. Accessed 22 May 2014.
United Nations Economic and Social Council, Commission on Crime Prevention and Criminal Justice (2014). Use and application of United Nations standards and norms in crime prevention and criminal justice. U.N. Doc. E/CN.15/2014/L.12/Rev. 1. https://www.unodc.org/documents/commissions/CCPCJ/CCPCJ_Sessions/CCPCJ_23/Draft_Resolutions/E-CN15-2014-L12-Rev1/E-CN15-2014-L12-Rev1_E.pdf. Accessed 11 June 2014.
United Nations General Assembly (1948). Universal Declaration of Human Rights. G.A. Res. 217 A (III) /A/RES/217/ (III) A. http://daccess-dds-ny.un.org/doc/RESOLUTION/GEN/NR0/043/88/IMG/NR004388.pdf?OpenElement. Accessed 13 May 2014.
United Nations General Assembly (1959). Declaration of the Rights of the Child. G.A. Res. 1386 (XIV), U.N. Doc. A/RES/1386(XIV). http://www.refworld.org/docid/3ae6b38e3.html. Accessed 22 May 2014.
United Nations General Assembly (1976). International Covenant on Civil and Political Rights. G.A. Res. 2200A (XXI). http://www.ohchr.org/Documents/ProfessionalInterest/ccpr.pdf. Accessed 13 May 2014.
United Nations General Assembly (1981). Convention on the Elimination of All Forms of Discrimination against Women. G.A. Res. 34/180, U.N. Doc A/RES/34/180. http://www.ohchr.org/Documents/ProfessionalInterest/cedaw.pdf. Accessed 13 May 2014.
United Nations General Assembly (1984). Convention against torture and other cruel, inhuman or degrading treatment or punishment. G.A. Res. 39/46, U.N. Doc A/RES/39/46. http://www.un.org/documents/ga/res/39/a39r046.htm. Accessed 6 June 2014.

United Nations General Assembly (1989). Convention on the Rights of the Child, 1577 U.N.T.S. 3. G.A. Res. 44/25. http://www.ohchr.org/Documents/ProfessionalInterest/crc.pdf. Accessed 22 May 2014.

United Nations General Assembly (1993). Declaration on the elimination of violence against women. G.A. Res. 48/104, U.N. Doc. A/RES/48/104. http://www.un.org/documents/ga/res/48/a48r104.htm. Accessed 12 May 2014.

United Nations General Assembly (1999). Optional Protocol to the Convention on the Elimination of All Forms of Discrimination against Women. G.A. Res. 54/4, U.N. Doc. A/RES/54/4. http://www.ohchr.org/Documents/HRBodies/CEDAW/OP_CEDAW_en.pdf. Accessed 13 May 2014.

United Nations General Assembly (2000a). Optional Protocol to the Convention on the Rights of the Child on the involvement of children in armed conflict. G.A. Res. 54/263, U.N. Doc. A/RES/54/263. http://www.ohchr.org/Documents/ProfessionalInterest/crc-conflict.pdf. Accessed 22 May 2014.

United Nations General Assembly (2000b). Optional Protocol to the Convention on the Rights of the Child on the sale of children, child prostitution and child pornography. G.A. Res. 54/263, U.N. Doc. A/RES/54/263. https://treaties.un.org/doc/source/docs/A_Res_54_263-E.pdf. Accessed 22 May 2014.

United Nations General Assembly (2002a). A world fit for children. G.A. Res. S-27/2, U.N. Doc. A/RES/S-27/2. http://www.un.org/en/ga/search/view_doc.asp?symbol=A/RES/S-27/2&referer=http://www.un.org/depts/dhl/resguide/rspec_en.shtml&Lang=E. Accessed 22 May 2014.

United Nations General Assembly (2002b). The rights of the child. G.A. Res. 56/138, U.N. Doc. A/RES/56/138. http://www.un.org/en/ga/search/view_doc.asp?symbol=A/RES/56/138&Lang=E. Accessed 22 May 2014.

United Nations General Assembly (2003). Protocol to Prevent, Suppress and Punish Trafficking in Persons, especially Women and Children. G.A. Res. 55/25. U.N. Doc. A/RES/55/25. http://www.osce.org/odihr/19223?download=true. Accessed 14 May 2014.

United Nations General Assembly (2006a). In-depth study on all forms of violence against women: report of the Secretary-General. U.N. Doc. A/61/122/Add.1 http://www.un.org/womenwatch/daw/vaw/SGstudyvaw.htm. Accessed 9 June 2014.

United Nations General Assembly (2006b). Intensification of efforts to eliminate all forms of violence against women. G.A. Res. 61/143, U.N. Doc. A/RES/61/143. http://www.un.org/womenwatch/daw/documents/ga61.htm. Accessed 9 June 2014.

United Nations General Assembly (2007). Intensification of efforts to eliminate all forms of violence against women. G.A. Res. 62/133, U.N. Doc. A/RES/62/133. http://www.un.org/womenwatch/daw/vaw/v-work-ga.htm#in. Accessed 9 June 2014.

United Nations General Assembly (2008). Intensification of efforts to eliminate all forms of violence against women. G.A. Res. 63/155, U.N. Doc. A/RES/63/155. http://www.un.org/womenwatch/daw/vaw/v-work-ga.htm#in. Accessed 9 June 2014.

United Nations General Assembly (2009). Intensification of efforts to eliminate all forms of violence against women. G.A. Res. 64/137, U.N. Doc. A/RES/64/137. http://www.un.org/womenwatch/daw/vaw/v-work-ga.htm#in. Accessed 9 June 2014.

United Nations General Assembly (2010). Intensification of efforts to eliminate all forms of violence against women. G.A. Res. 65/187, U.N. Doc. A/RES/65/187. http://www.un.org/womenwatch/daw/vaw/v-work-ga.htm#in. Accessed 9 June 2014.

United Nations General Assembly (2011). Strengthening crime prevention and criminal justice responses to violence against women. G.A. Res. 65/228 (adopted on Dec. 21, 2010), U.N. Doc. A/RES/65/228. http://www.un.org/en/ga/search/view_doc.asp?symbol=A/RES/65/228. Accessed 13 May 2014.

United Nations General Assembly (2012a). Intensification of efforts to eliminate all forms of violence against women. G.A. Res. 67/144, U.N. Doc. A/RES/67/144. http://www.un.org/ga/search/view_doc.asp?symbol=A/RES/67/144&Lang=E. Accessed 15 July 2014.

United Nations General Assembly (2012b). Optional protocol to the Convention on the Rights of the Child on a communications procedure. G.A. Res. 66/138, U.N. Doc. A/RES/66/138. https://treaties.un.org/doc/source/signature/2012/a-res-66-138-english.pdf. Accessed 21 May 2014.

United Nations General Assembly (2013). Status of the Convention on the Rights of the Child. U.N. Doc. A/68/257. http://daccess-dds-ny.un.org/doc/UNDOC/GEN/N13/416/88/PDF/N1341688.pdf?OpenElement. Accessed 12 June 2014.

United Nations Office on Drugs and Crime (2009). Global Report on Trafficking in Persons. https://www.unodc.org/documents/Global_Report_on_TIP.pdf. Accessed 12 June 2014.

United Nations Office on Drugs and Crime (2013). Global Study on Homicide 2013. http://www.unodc.org/documents/gsh/pdfs/2014_GLOBAL_HOMICIDE_BOOK_web.pdf. Accessed 22 May 2014.

United Nations Treaty Collection (2015a). Convention on the Elimination of All Forms of Discrimination against Women, Treaty Status. https://treaties.un.org/Pages/ViewDetails.aspx?src=TREATY&mtdsg_no=IV-8&chapter=4&lang=en. Accessed 15 May 2015.

United Nations Treaty Collection (2015b). Convention on the Rights of the Child, Treaty Status. https://treaties.un.org/pages/ViewDetails.aspx?src=TREATY&mtdsg_no=IV-11&chapter=4&lang=en. Accessed 4 October 2015.

United Nations Treaty Collection (2015c). Optional Protocol to the Convention on the Rights of the Child on a communications procedure, Treaty Status. https://treaties.un.org/pages/ViewDetails.aspx?src=TREATY&mtdsg_no=IV-11-d&chapter=4&lang=en. Accessed 15 May 2015.

United Nations Women (2007). Convention on the Elimination of All Forms of Discrimination against Women, Country Reports. http://www.un.org/womenwatch/daw/cedaw/reports.htm. Accessed 13 May 2014.

United States District Court, Eastern District of New York (2002). Nicholson v. Williams. 203 F. Supp. 2d 153.

United States Supreme Court (2005). Castle Rock v. Gonzales. 545 U.S. 748.

University of Minnesota Human Rights Library (2003). Stop Violence against Women. http://www1.umn.edu/humanrts/svaw/domestic/reports/institution.htm. Accessed 6 June 2014.

Van Bueren, G. (1995). *The international law on the rights of the child*. Dordrecht: Martinus Nijhoff Publishers.

Voices of Women Organizing Project (2007). Justice denied: How family courts in NYC endanger battered women and children (on file with author).

Warner, A. (2010). Recognizing rights promoting progress: The global impact of CEDAW. International Center for Research on Women. http://www.icrw.org/publications/recognizing-rights-promoting-progress. Accessed 19 May 2014.Weiner, M. H. (2004). Using Article 20. Family Law Quarterly, 38, 583–622.

Weiner, M. H. (2004). Using article 20. *Family Law Quarterly, 38*, 583–622.

Weiner, M. H. (2006). Beyond other treaties: The U.N. convention on the rights of the child and the value of "a dedicated line". In J. Todres, M. Wojcik, & C. R. Revaz (Eds.), *The U.N. convention on the rights of the child: An analysis of treaty provisions and implications of U.S. ratification* (pp. 65–85). Ardsley: Transnational Publishers.

Weissman, D. M. (2013). Law, social movements, and the political economy of domestic violence. Duke Journal of Gender Law & Policy 20:221-254. http://scholarship.law.duke.edu/cgi/viewcontent.cgi?article=1240&context=djglp. Accessed 19 May 2014.

World Health Organization (2009). *Preventing violence through the development of safe, stable and nurturing relationships between children and their parents and caregivers*. Geneva: World Health Organization. http://whqlibdoc.who.int/publications/2009/9789241597821_eng.pdf?ua=1. Accessed 12 June 2014.

World Health Organization (2013). *Global and regional estimates of violence against women: Prevalence and health effects of intimate partner violence and non-partner sexual violence*. Geneva: World Health Organization. http://www.who.int/reproductivehealth/publications/violence/9789241564625/en/. Accessed 13 May 2014.

Blue Victimology and Femicide: The United Nations' Response to Victims and Female Victims of Gender Killings

John P.J. Dussich

Abstract Every day men are killing female children and adults usually because they are females. Gender killings of females or femicide, is an issue of global significance. The equality of rights for women is a fundamental principle of the United Nations reflected in the 1945 Preamble to its Charter. Also in the 1948 UN Universal Declaration of Human Rights' Preamble equal rights for women are reaffirmed. In 1985 the UN Declaration of Basic Principles of Justice for Victims of Crime and Abuse of Power was crafted to address issues of all types of crime victims. Later two other UN instruments were created especially for women victims: the 1979 Convention on the Elimination of All Forms of Discrimination against Women; and, the 1993 Declaration on the Elimination of Violence against Women. Further broadening the scope of victimization, the Basic Principles and Guidelines on the Rights to a Remedy and Reparations for Victims of Gross Violations of International Human Rights Law and Serious Violations of International Humanitarian Law was adopted in 2005. Recently the UN General Assembly focused specifically on gender killings of females with the adoption on 18 December 2013 of the resolution on Taking action against Gender-Related Killing of Women and Girls. To recognize these key UN victimological instruments and other victim supported activities the term "Blue Victimology" is herein use.

Abbreviations

CNN	Cable New Network
ECOSOC	UN's Economic and Social Council
FGM	Female Genital Mutilation
IACHR	Inter-American Commission on Human Rights
ICVS	International Crime Victim Surveys
INTERVICT	International Victimology Institute Tilbury
NAFTA	North American Free Trade Agreement
OHCR	Office of the High Commissioner for Human Rights

J.P.J. Dussich (✉)
California State University, Fresno, CA, USA
e-mail: jdussich@csufresno.edu

H. Kury et al. (eds.), *Women and Children as Victims and Offenders: Background, Prevention, Reintegration*, DOI 10.1007/978-3-319-08398-8_2

TIVI	Tokiwa International Victimology Institute
UN	United Nations
UNFPA	United Nations Population Fund
UNICEF	United Nations Children's Fund
UNICRI	United Nations Interregional Criminal Justice Research Institute
UNODC	United Nations Office on Drugs and Crime
WHO	World Health Organization
WSV	World Society of Victimology

1 Introduction

Across the globe every day female children and adults are being killed by men, usually with impunity just because they are females. From the unnecessary abortions of female fetuses and infanticides of girl babies due to the preference for sons creating sex-ratio distortions in India, China and Korea; to the deaths that result from intentional neglect of female children (including female genital mutilations), dowry deaths and bride burning of young brides (called *Sati* where recently widowed wives are expected to throw themselves upon the burning funeral pyre of the deceased husbands) mostly practiced in Bangladesh, India, Pakistan, Nepal, Sri Lanka and some regions of Africa; to the pleasure-killings of youthful women in Mexico, El Salvador, and Guatemala and other parts of Central America and the Caribbean islands; and the honor killings of adulterous wives in South Asian and the Middle East. The obvious question that begs to be asked is: Where are these women's rights?

Since its beginning the United Nations has been the premier champion for the rights of women and children reflected in the 1945 Preamble to its basic Charter. It is one of the UN's central goals to reaffirm "faith in fundamental human rights, in the dignity and worth of the human person, in the equal rights of men and women." In the Preamble to the 1948 UN Universal Declaration of Human Rights equal rights for both men and women are reaffirmed. With these founding principles, the United Nations has continuously promoted the struggle to protect women with the measurement of their victimization, the establishment of their rights and with the call for services for female victims. Subsequently, the 1985 Declaration of Basic Principles of Justice for Victims of Crime and Abuse of Power (UN doc. A/RES/40/34, 29 November 1985) came into being and served as the foundation for all types of crime victims. One of the early pioneer efforts in the field of victimology was the measurement of reported victimizations first in Europe and then in other parts of the world in 1989 and 1992 with the International Crime Surveys under the leadership of the Dutch and English governments. These European initiatives were, in part, also supported by the UN through its Interregional Crime and Justice Research Institute (UNICRI) ultimately evolving to the refined International Crime Victims Surveys (ICVS) which conducted four other "sweeps" in 1996, 2000, 2005 and 2009 (van Dijk et al. 2007; van Dijk 2012/2013). After the Declaration of 1985 two other UN instruments were created especially focused on women victims: the 1979 Convention on the Elimination of All Forms of Discrimination against Women (UN doc. A/RES/34/180); and, the 1993 Declaration on the Elimination of Violence against Women (UN doc. A/RES/48/104). Broadening the scope of victimization, in 2005 the Basic Principles and Guidelines on the Rights to a Remedy and Reparations for Victims of Gross Violations of International Human Rights Law and Serious Violations of International Humanitarian Law was adopted (A/60/147). The most recent specific focus on female victims was embodied in the adoption on 18 December 2013 of the Resolution on Taking Action against Gender-Related Killing of Women and Girls.

In the foreword of the recent book *Blue Criminology* by Slawomir Redo, Dr. Thomas Stelzer, the United Nations Assistant Secretary-General for Policy Coordination and Inter-Agency Affairs from the UN's Headquarters in New York, wrote: "The United Nations, in its 65-year history, has brought to light powerful ideas that have often been translated into international norms and laws" (Stelzer 2012, p. 9). It is the intent of this text to highlight the potential of the United Nations resources to bring to bear the awareness, the expertise and the means to eliminate the scourge of femicide throughout the world and to recognize the need to attend to its victims.

This article is a statement about the many ways that women are killed in culturally *acceptable* ways mostly in places where men are controlling the cultural norms and the responses made by the United Nations. Femicide is the ultimate form of violence against females using many different methods. In every country in the world some females are killed, just because they are females. Although history tells us that women have been killed in many different ways since the beginning of time, the term "femicide" was first seen in a British publication as early as 1801 used to describe a unique type of brutal misogynistic killing of women (Corry 1801). It was considered as an alternate way to identify this special form of hate crime against women rather than use the traditional gender neutral term of homicide. With the term femicide the unusual characteristics of these hate crimes against females could be expressed in the following terms: the use of the female gender as the reason for selecting females as the victim, the fact that these killings included the element of oppression and hate, and that there was a certain routineness about these types of killings such that there was a recognizable *modus operandi* that reflected misogynistic motives of the perpetrator. The word "femicide" appeared again when an American writer, Carol Orlock in preparing to write an anthology on the topic of femicide notified her intent among feminist writers in the US and England. A British feminist authoress, Diana Russell heard about the proposed book (which was never published) and liked it as a way to avoid the gender-neutral term of homicide (Kaye 2007). In 1976 Ms Orlock used the word femicide at a public "speak-out" in Brussels, Belgium, at the First International Tribunal on Crimes Against Women, later to be compiled into a book with Belgian feminist Nicole Van de Ven titled: *Crimes Against Women: The Proceedings of the International Tribunal* published that same year. The definition for "femicide" that Russell used at this event was "a hate killing of females perpetrated by males" (Russell

2011, p. 1). Thus, the word "femicide" emerged from the broader feminist dialectic which accentuated domination of the patriarchy and the use of violence against females as a form of social control to perpetuate male dominance. The simple derivation of the term "femicide" is from the Latin *femina*, female, plus *ceadere*, to kill (Kaye 2007). Today the use of the word "femicide" in used in at least two ways: one is to simply identify the killing of women with or without hatred toward all women (which includes random killings of women as opposed to specifically selecting women); the other way is to specifically limit its use to those killings of women that involve only the malevolent intent to kill because of hatred toward women which influenced the selection of the victim. Across the globe every year about 66,000 females are being killed, mostly by men and usually with impunity, just because they are females (Global Burden on Armed Violence 2011).

The problem of "femicide" is increasing and offenders continue to kill females, for the most part without being punished. Their impunity not only aggravates the vulnerability of females because these females are continually exposed to their predators, it also reflects to the society that killing females is "acceptable and inevitable". Femicide usually takes the following forms:

(1). The murder of women as a result of intimate partner violence; (2) the torture and misogynist slaying of women; (3) killing of women and girls in the name of "Disshonor"; (4) targeted killing of women and girls in the context of armed conflict; (5) dowry-related killings of women; (6) killing of women and girls because of their sexual orientation and gender identity; (7) the killing of aboriginal and indigenous women and girls because of their gender; (8) female infanticide and gender-based sex selection foeticide; (9) genital mutilation related femicide; (10) femicide as a punishment for witchcraft, and (11) femicides connected with gangs, organized crime, drug dealers, human trafficking, and the proliferation of small arms (Laurent 2013).

In some countries, reforms are slowly occurring while in others no significant changes have yet been made. In 2010 the country of Chile, was the first in the world to enact a specific federal law against femicide.

2 Extent of the Problem

2.1 Female Foeticide

In simple words, "female foeticide" is the intentional killing of a female fetus. The motives in such cases are that most couples want a male child first or they prefer only sons. This phenomenon is especially problematic in India, and has led to the result that the total population is skewed in favor of males, with a national average of 914 girls born to every 1000 males. The killing of a fetus in India is against the law, yet medical doctors perform the procedure of aborting the unwanted fetus to earn extra money. It is interesting that in India's largest state, Rajasthan, which has the most skewed ratio in favor of males, a 49-year old man, Rajen Choudhary, has launched a personal crusade against the doctors in his state who perform these illegal abortions. His method for uncovering these offenders is to collaborate with a pregnant female colleague, then, pretending to be a married couple, enter a medical clinic and ask for an ultra-sound examination to determine the gender of the fetus. When the result shows it is a female, they ask the doctor if he would perform an abortion. If the doctor agrees, they contact the police and the doctor is arrested. Rajen Choudhary has become famous in India and is called "the friend of the unborn" (Akhtar 2013). It is estimated that in India roughly one million "selective female foetal abortions" occur each year (Manjoo 2012a).

2.2 Female Infanticide

The killing of an infant is "infanticide;" however, if the killing is done within the first 24 hours, it is referred to as "neonaticide" and likely perpetrated by the mother; if the killing occurs after the first 24 hours, it is likely to have been perpetrated by either parent, more often the father (Marks 2009). Female infanticide is the killing of a female infant. This has been a practice seen throughout history on all continents and in many different cultures (Williamson 1978). In terms of data from ancient history, recent evidence indicates that the Romans did not practice female infanticide (Pappas 2014). However, in ancient China in 2000 B.C., female infants were killed, in particular during famines or due to great poverty. The most commonly mentioned forms of female infanticide were: neglect, drowning, suffocation, or exposure to danger (Hom 1992). Han Fei Tzu, a Chinese philosopher and member of the aristocracy in the 3rd century B.C., wrote: *"As to children, a father and mother when they produce a boy congratulate one another, but when they produce a girl they put it to death"* (Yu-Lan 1952, p. 327). In a 1980 study of China's sex ratio between 1900 and 2000, it was measured that there were 35.59 million missing girls from the total population. More recent research comparing data between 2000 and 2005, showed the preference for sons is more prevalent in the rural areas and this preference is the motive for female infanticide; however, this preference is increasing in the large cities (Croll 1980; Li et al. 2006).

The other Asian country with a very large number of missing women is India with 100 million women absent from the total population as measured in 2003 (Sen 2003). While there are no official statistics available on female femicide in India, the death of "girls under 5 years old was 21 % higher than for boys of the same age" (Manjoo 2012a, p. 20). The main causes of deaths perpetrated by the girls' parents were due to nutritional and deliberate medical neglect (Moccia et al. 2007). In India the reason most often mentioned as causing the high figures for female infanticide is the dowry system where the families of females must raise a large amount of money in order to be able to marry off their daughters. In anticipation of this inevitable family debt, poverty stricken rural parents opt to kill the girl fetus or infant as a necessary solution to avoid social ostracism and financial shame (Oberman 2005).

2.3 Deaths Resulting from Female Genital Mutilation

"Female Genital Mutilation (FGM) is the partial or total removal of the female external genitalia" (World Health Organization 1995 p. 9). While FGM is an atypical form of femicide, death occurs indirectly, it is not motivated by hate, it is not perpetrated by men and it is not intended to kill the victims; nonetheless, a very large number of young girls die from the result of this practice. FGM is a practice found across the globe, especially in 26 of 43 African nations (Toubia 1993)—mostly in northern Africa. The countries with the highest prevalence among all women are: Somalia at 98 %, Egypt 97 %, Eritrea 94.5 %, Mali 93.7 %, Sudan 89.2 %, and in the Central African Republic 43.4 % (Toubia 1993; Reymond et al. 1998; Demographic and Health Survey 1995). All these countries have formally published policies against the practice of FGM; however, none of them have passed a specific law prohibiting FGM (UNFPA/UNICEF 2012). Each of these countries is dominated by patriarchal regimes and these highly dangerous practices many of which result in death are condoned by the local ethnic groups that use them. Approximately two million girls are at risk each year to become victims of this practice (WHO 1999; UNICEF 1996).

2.4 Lesbicide

The legal killing of lesbians has a long history in many cultures. There have been numerous legal systems which have allowed the death penalty for lesbianism. In ancient Rome a husband could legally kill his wife if he learned that she was having sexual relations with another woman, especially if she had not borne him any children (Robson 1992). In Medieval Europe both religious and secular doctrines mandated death for lesbians. In 1256, in Spain a lesbian could only be burned at the stake if she engaged in sex with a material object. In France in 1260 the infamous Code of Orleans secularized the punishment of lesbianism so that the law mandated that she could be burned to death if she had engaged in sex with a woman on at least three occasions. In a small town near Venice, Italy in 1574 if a female was over the age of 12 years and had engaged in sexual behavior with another female she could be burned to death outside the city (Robson 1992; Ferber et al. 2009). There are numerous indications of sanctioned killings of women for lesbian acts throughout earlier European history (Crompton 1981). The legal killing of lesbians has included death by: drowning, burning, starving and hanging, and by both religious and secular powers (Robson 1992).

Although today lesbianism is no longer officially punishable by death across the globe, most governments still punish lesbianism in some ways and it is still prohibited by most religions (Radford and Russell 1992). Killings of lesbians today are perpetrated illegally and are expressions of homophobic femicide hate crimes.

2.5 Witch Killings

In the sixteenth and seventeenth centuries, mostly in Europe many thousands of persons who were accused of witchcraft and condemned to death were overwhelmingly women (Hester 1992). The reasons given for the "witch-craze" of this period of history are a confusing mix of religious, anthropological, political, psychological and sociological perspectives by historians trying to piece together one of the most complicated eras of our time (Barry et al. 1996). In England one writer observed that only certain women were directly affected, "usually older, lower-class, poor, single or widowed" (Hester 1992, p. 27). She further noted that "the 'witch-craze' may be seen as an example of femicide where the use of violence against women by men was reliant on a particular construct of female sexuality" (Hester 1992, p. 27). One of the primary medieval guidelines in Europe to be used by inquisitors (both Catholic and Protestant) for defining witchcraft, prosecuting witches, and deciding on their punishments was the infamous publication *Malleus Maleficarum* (Galloway 1995). This book was written in 1486 by a German Catholic cleric, Heinrich Kramer, with the assistance of another clergyman, Jacob Sprenger of the Dominican order of the Catholic priesthood, and first published in Speyer, Germany. This was the book used to teach judges and prosecutors how to interrogate, torture and condemn to death women accused of witchcraft (Ruickbie 2004). The actual number of women killed because of being convicted of witchcraft is not known; however, for Europe, estimates range from 40,000 to 60,000 women (Levack 2006; Hutton 1999). The killing of women for sorcery and witchcraft has also been documented in Africa, Asia and the Pacific Islands (OHCHR 2013). In Africa, especially in Zimbabwe and Ghana the profiles of those killed as witches showed them to be older and poorer women (Galloway 1995; Adinkrah 2004). According to Amnesty International reports, in Papua New Guinea there are instances where killings for sorcery are in fact cover-ups for planned murders unrelated to sorcery but more based on a range of other reasons aimed at women often as a way to take their property and find scapegoats for expressing greed, revenge or envy. This situation is exacerbated by the inability of law enforcement to properly investigate and make arrests for sorcery-related killings in remote communities (Amnesty International 2009, 2011).

2.6 Honor Killings of Females

We speak of honor killing when a member of a family or social group, usually men, intentionally (and with impunity) kill one of its own members, usually women, because they believed that the victim has brought shame upon the family or group. Sometimes men are also killed in the name of honor. Some of the reasons for femicide are: refusal to accept an arranged marriage, having a relationship that is not approved by the family or social group, having sexual relations outside of marriage, allowing herself to become a rape victim, dressing in an inappropriate manner, or engaging in homosexual behavior (BBC 1970; Merriam-Webster Dictionary 2013; dictionary.reference.com 2013; CNN 2011, 2013).

Some of the more common forms of these honor killings of females are: "direct murder; stoning; women and young girls being forced to commit suicide after public denunciations of their behavior; and women being disfigured by acid burns, leading to death" (Manjoo 2012b p. 1). The countries where most honor killings occur are situated between the Sahara and the Himalayas but we find them also in other areas, especially in countries that attract migrants (Baydoun 2011).

In many countries honor killings of females are reported as suicides; rarely are these killings recorded by the police as honor killings (UNICEF 2013). According to the United Nations Population Fund, it is estimated that roughly 5,000 honor killings by family members occur each year across the globe (UN 2006).

2.7 Dowry and Bride Deaths

These killings occur when a bride is murdered or, by continuous harassment and torture by her husband or his family members, driven to commit suicide. Most of these young women commit suicide by poisoning, self-immolation or hanging. The motive for the groom and his family's aggression is greed with the intent to extort an increase in the bride's dowry or to coerce goods from the wife's family. This form of femicide is mainly practiced in the South Asian countries of Bangladesh, India, Nepal, Pakistan, and Sri Lanka, plus in some areas of Africa. However, the largest *reported* number of dowry deaths in the world is practiced in Pakistan with a rate of 2.45 per 100,000 (Subhani et al. 2009). It is highly likely that the number of dowry deaths, wherever practiced, is underreported (Nasrullah and Muazzam 2010; Miller 1984). This practice is a product of deeply rooted cultural customs. In spite of the laws passed to stop the use of dowries in India in 1961, in Pakistan in 1976, in Bangladesh in 1980 and in Nepal in 2009, it is still a basic part of most weddings in these countries (Nasrullah and Muazzam 2010).

2.8 Female Murders in Latin America and the Caribbean

In 2006, a group of women from Latin America arrived in Washington D.C. to attend the International Women's Day of the Inter-American Commission on Human Rights (IACHR) of the celebration with a most alarming message: *the killing of women in Latin America is spreading* (Paterson 2006). One of the key delegates to the IACHR from Mexico, Marimar Monroy, warned: "Femicide is not only present in Ciudad Juarez and most of Mexico, it is a regional problem" (Paterson 2006, p. 1). Ms. Monroy was joined by grassroots delegates from other impacted Latin American countries (especially Colombia, El Salvador, Guatemala,

Jamaica and Peru) to deliver their femicide report as part of a concerted effort to bring a heightened awareness of this problem of widespread violence against women to the rest of the region. This compelling message was based on a series of earlier investigations from the IACHR to the city of Juarez in 2002 and to Guatemala in 2004 (Paterson 2006; Moloney et al. 2013).

2.8.1 Mexico

The year 1993 is identified as being the starting point for femicide awareness in Mexico. It is the year after which the people of the city of Juarez, in the state of Chihuahua, began to realize they were living in a killing field where many of their girls in their late teens and early 20s were found missing or dead on the desert sands of the cotton fields just outside of their city (Chavez-Cano 2005). Juarez is just across the border from El Paso, Texas; the town is strewn with about 400 foreign factories (called *maquilas* or *maquiladoras*) owned by foreign companies (mostly from Spain, Japan, South Korea, USA, and China) where most of the employees are young girls and women (between 14 and 40 years) who work for minimum wages ($ 4/day). These factories operate along the entire Mexico/US border from the north-west to the northeast touching the states of California, Arizona, New Mexico and Texas. Under the protection of the North America Free Trade Agreement (NAFTA) they generate large profits for their owners who capitalize on the poverty conditions with little concern for the dismal social conditions which they have created. Many of the girls who are employed there have left their home villages far away to come to earn money for their families—away from the familiar communities they were born in and away from traditional social control and protection (Chavez-Cano 2005).

Research shows that between 17 % and 20 % of the victims of femicides were *maquila* employees. The actual number of girls killed has not been accurately recorded as many of these girls just disappeared and their corpses have never been found. The estimate today is that between the years 1993 and 2009, 749 mostly poor and illiterate young females have been sexually abused, tortured, killed and their naked bodies discarded in garbage dumps, in gullies, and on the desert wastelands, among those found, their bodies were often mutilated and dismembered (Segato 2004; Montárrez 2009). As a border city with the US, Juarez is vulnerable, due to the large flow of drugs from Mexico to the US, due to the abundance of young girls employed at the *maquilas* (cc. 108,000), due to rampant poverty, and due to a largely lawless society, where impunity exists for the perpetrators and the justice system is mostly corrupt and incompetent. Among those who have cared for these victims and their families it has been reported that the police are also implicated in some of these killings (Chavez-Cano 2005). The sister of one of the femicide victims, Guillermina Gonzalez, speaking of her city, said "I have no security for myself, because if I take one step on the street, I don't know if with the next one I will give my life" (Rodriguez 2007, p. 6).

Last year, it was two decades since the femicides started in May of 1993. These killings also emerged in other cities across Mexico. From 1985 to 2009 34,000 women have been murdered, and for 2010 alone Amnesty International reported 2418 more victims, with 320 coming from Juarez. On 10 December 2009, the Inter-American Commission on Human Rights a branch of the organization of American States, ruled that "the state of Mexico was responsible for the unsolved murders and disappearances of women in Ciudad Juarez" (Kirkpatrick 2013, p. 2). This ruling has become known as "The Cotton Field" ruling of 2009 and while it was an important milestone for human rights in Mexico, unfortunately the femicides have continued unabated and have even tripled in the subsequent 2 years. A new and unfortunate development has been the harassment, attacks and murders of the victim's families, their supporters and the human rights activists who have been working on behalf of the victims of femicide (Kirkpatrick 2013). Since it is rare for arrests to be made, the identities of these murderers are not known. The struggle of the people of Ciudad Juarez continues.

2.8.2 Guatemala

In the decade from 2000 to 2013 it is estimated that roughly 6,500 femicides have occurred in Guatemala. This number of killings makes Guatemala City one of the world's most dangerous cities for women (Prensa Latina 2009; Musalo and Bookey 2013). If we look at the rates per 100,000 population of women, Guatemala has the third highest rate of femicide in the region at an annual average of 9.7 just below El Salvador at 12 and Jamaica at 10.7 (Geneva Declaration 2011). The trademarks of these killings, like in Juarez, involve horrible torture, sexual aggression, mutilation of body parts and "dumping the victims in empty lots" (Paterson 2006, p. 3). Also like in Juarez, some of the perpetrators are suspected to be the police (Paterson 2006).

Of all the femicides committed in Guatemala, 90 % were perpetrated with small firearms (to a lesser degree with knives or through strangulation); and, carried out mostly in the capital, Guatemala City, the southern town of Escuintla and the western city of San Marcos (Segato 2004; Paterson 2006).

As the result of the hard work of women's rights groups, in April 2008 the government passed a law designed to protect the rights of women such that "femicide" is officially identified as a crime punishable with 25–50 years imprisonment. However, more reforms are urgently needed as femicides continue with impunity (Bo 2009; Musalo and Bookey 2013). Although the enactment of the 2008 law has increased the awareness of the government and the agents of the judicial system, full implementation of this law is still significantly lacking. The findings of recent research conclude that, "The government, as a whole, has not responded effectively, and the rates of violence against women have continued to increase" (Musalo and Bookey 2013, pp. 290–291). This same study recommends that, "the government institute a monitoring program to evaluate the performance of public officials in carrying out their obligation to apply the laws on gender violence, and a system to impose disciplinary actions, including ultimate dismissal, of those who fail to apply the laws effectively and without gender bias" (Musalo and Bookey 2013, p. 291).

2.8.3 El Salvador

According to the 2012 Small Arms Survey, a Geneva-based research project, the highest rate of femicide in the world belongs to the small country of El Salvador in Central America (Moloney et al. 2013). The actual rate cited from its 2012 report *Femicide: A Global Problem* based on data collected from 2004–2009 was 12 femicides per 100,000 inhabitants (Ayala 2013); however, when recent years were included in the calculations the rate went slightly down to 10 femicides per 100,000 inhabitants. Compared to the US at just under 2 femicides per 100,000 inhabitants, it is still very high (Witte 2013). Ironically in the year this report was published (2012), the number of femicides had dropped to roughly half (329) compared to the previous year (647).

The difference seems to have been due to three elements:

1. The initiative of El Salvador's new President, Mauricio Funes, who has given women's rights a high priority in his agenda with his successful enactment of the special and comprehensive Law for a Life Free from Violence for Women, also called the "femicide law" passed on November 25, 2010, and which came into force on January 1, 2012 (Zulver 2014);
2. The first lady's initiative to establish a network of six resource centers for women called "Ciudad Mujer" (Women's City);
3. A government brokered truce (*tregua*) in which the two dominant gangs agreed to a "cease-fire," which became effective in March of 2012 (Witte 2013). This has probably had the largest impact on improving the situation.

It is possible that the demonstrated political will by President Funes to impact the femicide problem has been successful in starting a change in the right direction; however, much more is needed, especially from the judicial system which is not standing firmly behind the new law in femicide cases brought before the courts. The important first steps have been taken, but the society and the culture that supports it, still gives men far more rights, more benefits, more privileges and more power than women who are still seriously disenfranchised (Witte 2013); and thus, females in El Salvador continue to be significantly vulnerable to future femicides.

2.8.4 Jamaica

In the year 2005, the British Broadcasting Corporation called Kingston, Jamaica, the "murder capital of the world" because then the rate of killings was 64 per 100,000 inhabitants roughly ten times that of the USA (Lemard 2009a). The Geneva-based Small Arms Survey of 2012, dubbed Jamaica as the country with the second highest femicide rate in the world (Moloney et al. 2013). Based on a study done in 2007, it was determined that the predominant weapons used for these femicides were: guns (70 %), knives (15 %), Machetes (3 %) and others (12 %) (Lemard 2009b, slide 8). With regard to the number of assailants, 41 % involved one, 5 % involved two, 21 % involved three or more, and 33 % were unknown (Lemard 2009b, slide 16). Some of the key indicators associated with these femicides are: gender roles are changing with women becoming more independent, some men are responding with aggression and try to assert their power with violence, love triangles create conflicts, negative issue arise with intimate partners that result in violence, some women have become scapegoats of revenge, indirect and direct links with drugs and gangs, and sometimes females killing females. Very little femicide research has been done in Jamaica (Lemard (2009a).

3 International Attention on Femicide, Especially Recent Actions Taken at the UN

The United Nations has responded to these type problems since the adoption by the UN General Assembly on 10 December 1948 of the Universal Declaration of Human Rights. This is especially the case after other UN instruments were adopted: the 1985 Declaration of Basic Principles of Justice for Victims of Crime and Abuse of Power; the 1993 Declaration on the Elimination of Violence against Women; the Convention on the Elimination of All Forms of Discrimination against Women; and, the recent resolution on Taking action against Gender-Related Killing of Women and Girls has elevated the issue of "Femicide" to the highest level of the United Nations at its sixty-eighth General Assembly on 18 December 2013 when it adopted, without a vote, the following drafts: the "Model strategies and practical measures on the elimination of violence against children in the field of crime prevention and criminal justice" (UN doc. A/68/475); and, the "Taking action against gender-related killing of women and girls" (UN doc. A/68/191). It goes without saying that the United Nations, especially in recent years, has been exercising international leadership in many areas of the femicide issue; however, it has only been recently that the specific focus on the concept of "femicide" has been articulated and used in its instruments. These developments give strength to the importance of addressing the underlying common variables of femicide. By so doing new more meaningful strategies can be recommended with greater promise of having a significant impact on the many causes of this global scourge.

4 Conclusions

It is obvious that gender killing of females is a serious problem that has been finally recognized for its inhumaneness, its magnitude, its unacceptability, and its urgency. It is also obvious that the United Nations is the most significant forum which can take unified action. It has the obligation, the resources and the will to bring about the necessary changes across the globe so that all females in all nations can be protected from the risks of these forms of death.

With regard to the Declaration of Basic Principles of Justice for Victims of Crime and Abuse of Power, the most significant attempt to support its implementation has been efforts to upgrade this declaration to a convention (Groenhuijsen and Letschert 2008). This intent has resulted in the collaboration by the World Society of Victimology and INTERVICT (the Netherlands) to create a draft UN Convention on Justice and Support for Victims of Crime and Abuse of Power.[1] Another event aimed at strengthening the working draft of this Convention was a dedicated symposium hosted by TIVI (Japan) in 2008. This 2-day symposium was devoted to an in-depth critique of the existing draft of the proposed Convention (Dussich and Mundy 2009). The proceedings of this effort were published and from this work a new draft was written and is now posted on the WSV website.[2]

All these collaborations, instruments, publications, events, and guidelines have been the result of the partnerships and synergy with the United Nations (mostly UNODC). It is this existing bond that the UN has with NGOs, specific states, pioneers in victimology, and its own staff of experts which, is herein referred to as Blue Victimology, and which can be brought to bear on the problem of femicide. I applaud all those persons and organizations which have formed partnerships for the future and which represent the optimism for solving our global challenges, especially the victimization of children and women.

Five Questions

1. What is a short comprehensive definition of femicide?
2. Name at least ten countries where femicide is particularly prevalent?
3. Which types of femicide are mostly practiced today?
4. What role does culture play in female gender killings?
5. How has and does the United Nations contributed to the identification, prevention, and treatment of female gender killings?

---

[1] See Implementing the UN Victim Declaration—INTERVICT at: https://www.tilburguniversity.edu/research/institutes-and-research-groups/intervict/research/current/finalized/undeclaration/.

[2] See http://www.worldsocietyofvictimology.org/publications/Draft%20Convention.pdf.

Appendix: Blue Victimology's Chronological Chart for Key UN Victim-Related Activities

Official United Nations name	Year effective	Type persons	Activities
United Nations Charter	1945	Human beings	UN established
UN Universal Declaration of Human Rights, 10 December	1948	Human beings	International law
Declaration on the Protection of all Persons from being Subjected to torture And Other Cruel, Inhuman or Degrading Treatment or Punishment	1975	All persons	International law
Convention on the Elimination of All Forms of Discrimination against Women	1979	Women	International law
Convention against Torture and Other Cruel, Inhuman or Degrading Treatment or Punishment	1984	All persons	International law
International Crime Surveys & International Crime Victim Surveys	1989–2009	Crime victims	Research survey
Basic UN Declaration of Principles Of Justice for Victims of Crime and Abuse of Power	1985	Victims of crime & abuse of power	International law
Changing Victim Policy: The United Nations Victim Declaration and Recent Developments in Europe. Report of the Ad Hoc Expert Meeting Helsinki, Nov. 1988	1989	Crime & abuse of power victims	Publication
Declaration on the Elimination of Violence against Women	1993	Women victims	International law
Rome Statues of the International Court and Final Act of the United Nations Diplomatic Conference of Plenipotentiaries On the Establishment of an International Criminal Court	1998	Crime victims	International law
Handbook on Justice for Victims, On the use and application of the Declaration of Basic Principles of Justice for Victims of Crime and Abuse of Power, UNODCCP	1999	Crime & abuse victims	Joint publication
Guide for Policy Makers, on the Implementation of the Declaration of Basic Principles of Justice for Victims of Crime and Abuse of Power, UNODCCP	1999	Crime & abuse victims	Joint publication
Convention against Transnational Organized Crime	2000	TIH female victims	International law
Basic Principles on the Use of Restorative Justice Programmes in Criminal Matters	2002	Criminals & crime victims	International law

(continued)

Official United Nations name	Year effective	Type persons	Activities
Protocol to Prevent, Suppress & Punish Trafficking in Persons Especially Women & Children, supplementing the UN Convention against Transnational Organized Crime	2003	Women & child victims	International law
Economic and Social Council's Guidelines on Justice in Matters involving Child Victims & Witnesses of Crime	2005	Child victims & witnesses	International guidelines
UN Declaration of the UN Crime Congress in Bangkok "need to protect witnesses and victims of crime and terrorism"	2005	Witnesses & victims of crime & terrorism	Proposed laws
Basic Principles & Guidelines on the Right to a Remedy & Reparation for Victims of Gross Violations of International Human Rights Law & Serious Violations of International Humanitarian Law	2006	Victims of gross violations of IHRL & SVIHL	International law
Handbook on Restorative Justice	2006	Crime victims	Publication
United Nations Declaration on the Rights of Indigenous People	2007	Indigenous victims	International law
Note by the Secretariat on Crime Prevention and Criminal Justice Responses to Urban Crime, Including Gang-related Activities, and Effective Crime Prevention and Criminal Justice Responses to Combat Sexual Exploitation of Children	2007	Sexual exploitation of children	International law
Secretary-General's Symposium on Supporting Victims of Terrorism, 9 September	2008	Terrorism victims	Symposium
United Nations Declaration on the Rights of Indigenous Peoples	2008	Indigenous victims	Publication
Compilation of International Victims' Rights Instruments, Second (Revised) Edition	2008	Victims of crime & abuse of power	Publication INTERVICT
Justice in Matters involving Child Victims and Witnesses of Crime	2009	Child victims & witnesses	Model law publication
Raising the Global Standards for Victims: The Proposed Convention on Justice for Victims of Crime and Abuse of Power	2009	Victims of crime & abuse of power	TIVI publication
World Society of Victimology's Draft UN Convention on Justice and Support for Victims of Crime and Abuse of Power	2010	Victims of crime & abuse of power	Proposed convention
Manual on Victimization Surveys	2010	Crime victims	Publication
Human Trafficking in the Baltic Sea Region: State and Civil Society Cooperation on Victims' Assistance and Protection	2010	Human Trafficking Victims	Publication
The Criminal Justice Response to Support Victims of Acts of Terrorism	2011	Terrorism victims	Publication

(continued)

Official United Nations name	Year effective	Type persons	Activities
UN University Tokyo and Tokiwa International Victimology Institute, "Helping the Victims of Natural Disasters: From Grassroots to Governance," Sixth TIVI Symposium	2011	Disaster victims	Joint symposium
World Society of Victimology—Statement on Indigenous Peoples as Victims of Crime and Abuse of Power on the occasion of the UN's 11th Session of the Permanent Forum indigenous on Indigenous Issues,	2012	Victims	Letter of support
UN University Tokyo and Tokiwa International Victimology Institute, Victims of Human Trafficking in Japan: Seventh Symposium	2012	Human trafficking victims	Joint symposium
Resolution on Taking action against Gender-Related Killing of Women and Girls—ECOSOC	2013	Femicide victims	International law
UNODC proposed publication of the *Revised Handbook on Justice for Victims*	2015	Victims of crime and abuse of power	Guidelines (TBA)

References

Adinkrah, M. (2004). Witchcraft accusation and female homicide victimization in contemporary Ghana. *Violence Against Women, 10*(4), 325–356.

Akhtar, S. (2013). Fighting female foeticide in India, *Aljazeera; America.* Accessed on January 25, 2014 from: http://www.aljazeera.com/indepth/2013/11/fighting-female-foeticide-india-201311111347515312 83.html

Amnesty International. (2009). *Papua New Guinea: Authorities must act now to prevent more witch hunts.* February 10, Retrieved on July 30, 2014, from: http://www.amnesty.org/en/for-media/press-releases/papua-new-guinea-authorities-must-act-now-prevent-more-witch-hunts-2009

Amnesty International. (2011). Document—Papua New Guinea: violence against women, sorcery related killings and forced evictions: Amnesty International Submission to the UN Universal Periodic Review. May 2011

Ayala, E. (2013). Impunity, machismo fuel femicides in El Salvador. *Inter Press Service News Agency*, Retrieved February 2, 2014, from: http://www.ipsnews.net/2013/04/impunity-machismo-fuel-femicides-in-el-salvador/

Barry, J., Hester, M., & Roberts, G. (Eds.). (1996). *Witchcraft in early modern Europe: Studies in culture and belief.* Cambridge, UK: Cambridge University Press.

Baydoun, A. (2011). *Killing of women in the name of honour: An evolving phenomenon in Lebanon.* Paper presented at the Expert Group Meeting on Gender-Motivated Killings of Women. Convened by the special Rapporteur on violence against women, its causes and consequences, Ms Rashida Manjoo, New York, October 12

BBC. (1970). Ethics: honour crimes. *BBC* 1, January, Retrieved December 223 2013, from: http://www.bbc.co.uk/ethics/honourcrimes/

Bo, T. (2009). Guatemala's 'femicide' crisis. *Aljazeera*, 5 August, Retrieved on February 1, 2014, from: http://www.aljazeera.com/focus/2009/08/200984134334229388.html
Chavez-Cano, E. (2005, November 11). *Violence and Death at the Border*. Fresno: Casa Amigo Centro de Crisis, Speech given at California State University.
CNN (2011). Iraqi immigrant convicted in Arizona 'honor killing' awaits sentence. *CNN*, Com Retrieved August 16, 2013, from: http://edition.cnn.com/2011/CRIME/02/23/arizona.iragi.fat Edition.cnn.com
CNN (2013). Shocking gay honor killing inspires movie—CNN.Com, Retrieved August 16, 2013, from: http://editon.cnn.com/2012/01/13/world/europe/turkey-gay-killing
Corry, J. (1801). *Satirical view of London at the commencement of the nineteenth century*. Edinburgh, Scotland: T. Hurst, Paternoster-Row.
Croll, E. (1980). *Feminism and Socialism in China*. New York: Schocken Books.
Crompton, L. (1981). The myth of lesbian impunity. *Journal of Homosexuality*, *6*(11), 11–25.
Dictionary.reference. (2013). *Honor killing definition*. Retrieved December 23, 2013, from http://dictionary.reference.com/browse/honor+killing?s=t.dictionary.reference.com
Dussich, J. P. J., & Mundy, K. G. (2009). *Raising the global standards for victims: The proposed convention on justice for victims of crime and abuse of power*. Proceedings of the 4th Symposium of the Tokiwa International Victimology Institute, February 15 & 16, 2008.
Ferber, A., Holcomb, K., & Wentling, T. (2009). *Sex, gender, and sexuality: An anthology*. New York: Oxford University Press.
Galloway, S. (1995). *Femicide project, OHCHR, Report by country*. Zimbabwe: Women in Law and Development in Africa (WiLDAF).
Geneva Declaration. (2011). When the victim is a woman, Chapter 4, Geneva Declaration on Armed Violence and Development, Global Burden of Armed Violence. Retrieved January 20, 2014, from: http://www.genevadeclaration.org
Groenhuijsen, M., & Letschert, R. (Eds.). (2008). *Compilation of international victims' rights instruments* (Second (revised) ed.). Nijmegen, Netherlands: INTERVICT in cooperation with Wolf Publishers.
Hester, M. (1992). The witch-craze in sixteenth- and seventeenth- century England as social control of women. In J. Radford & D. E. H. Russell (Eds.). *Femicide: the politics of women killing*. New York, NY: Twayne Publishers, Macmillan.
Hom, S. (1992). Female infanticide in China: the spectrum of human rights and reflections towards another vision. In R. Harmes & D. Russell (Eds.), *Femicide in global perspective*. New York: Teachers College Press.
Hutton, R. (1999). *The triumph of the moon*. Oxford: Oxford University Press.
Kaye, J. (2007). *Femicide, online Encyclopedia of Mass Violence*. Published on November 3, 2007. Retrieved January 23, 2014, from: http://www.massviolence.org/Femicide, ISSN 1961-9898
Kirkpatrick, O. (2013). Femicide in Mexico: The cotton field case and its sequels. *Latin American Bureau*. March 27 Retrieved July 30, 2014, from: http://lab.org.uk/femicide-in-mexico-the-cotton-field-case-and-its-sequels
Laurent C. (2013). *FEMICIDE: The killing of women and girls around the world*. Vienna, Austria: Academic Council of the United Nations System (ACUNS).
Lemard, G. (2009a). *Femicide in Jamaica, in strengthening understanding of femicide: Using research to galvanize action and accountability*. Proceedings of the conference held in Washington, DC April 14–16, 2008
Lemard G. (2009b) Femicide in Jamaica. *Power Point Presentation*, Retrieved February 1, 2014, from: http://www.powershow.com/view/4f35-MWNhZ/Femicide_in_Jamaica_powerpoint_ppt_presentation
Levack, B. P. (2006). *The witch hunt in early modern Europe* (3rd ed.). London and New York: Longman.

Li, S., Jian, B., & Feldman, M. W. (2006). *Xingbie Qishi yu Renkou Fazhan (Gender Discrimination and Population Development) (Chapters 3, 10)*. Beijing: Social Science Academic Press.
Marks, M. (2009, January). Infanticide. *Psychiatry, 8*(1), 10–12.
Manjoo, R. (2012a). *Report of the special Rapporteur on violence against women, its causes and consequences*. Twentieth session of the Human Rights Council, United Nations General Assembly, May 23, 2012.
Manjoo R. (2012b). Harmful traditional practices against women and girls' panel: Laws vs practice, rhetoric vs. reality. *UN Human Rights Council*, 20, Retrieved August 20, 2014, from: http://www.wunrn.com/news/2012/07_12/07_09/070912_un2.htm
Merriam-Webster (2013). Honor killing: Definition and more from the free Merriam-Webster Dictionary. August 31, Retrieved December 23, 2013, from http://wwwmerriam-webster.com/dictionary/honor%killing
Miller, B. D. (1984). Daughter neglect, women's work, and marriage: Pakistan and Bangladesh compared. *Medical Anthropology, 8*(2), 109–126.
Moccia P., Anthony, D., & Orlandi, A. (Eds.). (2007). *The State of the World's Children, South Asia Edition. Women and Children*. The Double Dividend for Gender Equality, UNICEF
Moloney, A., Lopez, J. D., & Rodriguez, U. (2013). Struggling with femicide and impunity for crimes against women in Central America. *Thomas Reuters Foundation, News, Information and Connections for Action*, Retrieved January 30, 2014, from: http://www.trust.org/slideshow/?id=59ccc3c0-c719-467e-bf0b-622739b34ef4
Montárrez, J. (2009). *Trauma de una injusticia. Feminicidio sexual sistémico en Ciudad Juárez*. Mexico: Colegio de la Frontera Norte.
Musalo, K., & Bookey, B. (2013). Crimes without punishment: An update on violence against women and impunity in Guatemala. *Hastings Race & Poverty Law Journal, 10*, 265–292.
Nasrullah, M., & Muazzam, S. (2010). Newspaper reports: a source of surveillance for burn among women in Pakistan. *Journal of Public Health, 32*(2), 245–249.
Oberman, M. (2005). A brief history of infanticide and the law. In G. Margaret & Spinelli (Ed.), *Infanticide psychosocial and legal perspectives on mothers who kill* (1st ed.). American Psychiatric Publishing. ISBN 1-58562-097-1
OHCHR (2013). Special Rapporteur on extrajudicial, summary or arbitrary executions. *Handbook on Victim Groups*, Chapter 8, Victim Groups, Office of the High Commissioner on Human Rights, Geneva.
Pappas, S. (2014). Ancient roman infanticide didn't spare either sex, DNA suggests. *Live Science*, Retrieved 1/25/2014 from: http://www.livescience.com/42834-ancient-roman-infanticide.html
Paterson, K. (2006). *Femicide On the Rise in Lain America*. Americas Program Report, Americas Program: A new world of citizen action, analysis, and policy options, March 8, 2006, Retrieved January 24, 2014, from: http://americas.irc-online.org/am/3142
Prensa Latina (2009). First Femicide Trial in Guatemala. *NISGUA*, February 2, Retrieved February 1, 2014, from: http://www.nisgua.org/themes_campaigns/index.asp?id=3302
Radford, J., & Russell, D. E. H. (1992). *Femicide: The politics of woman killing*. New York: Twayne.
Reymond, L., Mohamud, A., & Ali, N. (1998). *Female Genital Mutilation—The Facts, Program for Appropriate Technology in Health (PATH)*. Retrieved January 26, 2014, from: http://www.path.org/files/FGM-The-Facts.ht
Robson, R. (1992). Lesbicide. In J. Radford & D. E. H. Russell (Eds.), *Femicide: The politics of women killing*. New York: Twayne.
Rodriguez, T. (2007). *The daughters of Juarez*. New York, NY: ATRIA.
Ruickbie, L. (2004). *Witchcraft out of the shadows: A complete history*. London, UK: Robert Hale.
Russell, D. E. H. (2011). *The origin and importance of the term femicide*. Retrieved January 22, 2014, from: http://www.dianarussell.com/origin_of_femicide.html
Segato, R. (2004). Territorio, soberanía y crímenes de segundo Estado: la escritura en el cuerpo de las mujeres asesinadas en Ciudad Juárez. *Serie Antropológica*, 362, Brasil

Sen, A. K. (2003). Missing women revisited. *British Medical Journal, 327*, 1297–8.

Stelzer, T. (2012) *Foreword, in Blue criminology: The power of United Nations ideas to counter crime globally; A monographic study*. by Slawomir Marek Redo. Helsinki, Finland: HEUNI Publication Series No. 72.

Subhani, D., Imtiaz, M., & Afza, S. (2009). *To estimate an equation explaining the determinants of Dowry*. Retrieved 4/9/2012, from: http://mpra.ub.uni-muenchen.de/21365/

Toubia, N. (1993). *Female genital mutilation: A call for global action*. New York: Women, Ink.

UN (1979). *United Nations 34th general assembly, resolution, A/RES/34/180, convention on the elimination of all forms of discrimination against women*. Retrieved August 19, 2014, from http://www.un.org/womenwatch/daw/cedaw/cedaw.htm

UN (1985). *United Nations 40th general assembly resolution A/RES/40/34, declaration of basic principles of justice for victims of crime and abuse of power*. Retrieved August 19, 2014, from http://www.un.org/en/ga/search/view_doc.asp?symbol=A/RES/40/34&Lang=E&Area=RESOLUTION

UN (1993). *United Nations 48th general assembly resolution A RES/48/104, declaration on the elimination of violence against women*. Retrieved August 18, 2014, from http://www.un.org/en/ga/search/view_doc.asp?symbol=A/RES/48/104&Lang=E&Area=RESOLUTION

UN (2006). *United Nations* 61st *general assembly, In-depth study on all forms of violence against women*. (Report of the Secretary-General, A/61/122/Add.1). Retrieved August 2, 2014, from http://daccess-dds-ny.un.org/doc/UNDOC/GEN/N06/623/30/PDF/N0662330.pdf?OpenElement

UN (2013). *United Nations 68th general assembly resolution A/68/191, taking action against gender-related killing of women and girls*. Retrieved August 2, 2014, from http://www.un.org/en/ga/68/resolutions.shtml

UNFPA/UNICEF (2012). *Joint program on female genital mutilation cutting: Accelerating change*. Annual Report

UNICEF. (1996). *The progress of nations 1996 - women*. Retrieved February 24, 2016 from http://www.unicef.org/pon96/womfgm.htm.

UNICEF (2013). *UNICEF Turkey: Protective environment for children; honour crimes and forced suicides*. Retrieved December 23, 2013, from: http://www.unicef.org.tr/en/content/detail/74/honour-crimes-and-forced-suicides-2.html

Yu-Lan, F. (1952). *A history of Chinese philosophy*. Princeton: Princeton University Press.

van Dijk, J. (2012/2013). The international crime victims survey: Latest results and prospects. *Criminology in Europe—Newsletter of the European Society of Criminology*. Retrieved August 9, 2014, from: http://escnewsletter.org/node/108

van Dijk, J., van Kerteren, J., & Smit, P. (2007). *Criminal victimisation in international perspective: Key findings from the 2004–2005 ICVS and EU ICS*. The Hague, Netherlands: Boom Uitgevers.

World Health Organization. (1995). *Female genital mutilation: Report of a WHO technical working group* (p. 6). Geneva: World Health Organization.

World Health Organization. (1999). *Female genital mutilation programmes to date: what works and what doesn't: A review*. Department of Women's Health Systems and Community Health World Health Organization (1999)

Williamson, L. (1978). An anthropological analysis. In M. Hohl (Ed.), *Infanticide and the value of life*. Buffalo, NY: Prometheus.

Witte, B. (2013). Femicide Numbers Fall in El Salvador. *Benjamin Witte's Web Site: A collection of writings by Benjamin Witte*. September 16, Retrieved January 10, 2014, from: http://benwitte.wordpress.com/2013/09/16/femicide-numbers-fall-in-el-salvador/

Zulver, J. (2014, January 31). El Salvador elections: Putting women's right on the agenda. *Aljazeera*, Retrieved February 1, 2014, from: http://www.aljazeera.com/indepth/opinion/2014/01/el-salvador-election;putting-wo-2011288499915469.html

In the Pursuit of Justice for Women and Children and the Right to Development: A Review of Concluding Observations of the United Nations Human Rights Treaty Bodies

Anganile Willie Mwenifumbo and Harumi Fuentes Furuya

Abstract In the implementation process of the core United Nations (UN) human treaties, its monitoring bodies make recommendations to States parties regarding issues of concern. These include the justice issues involving improvements in education for women and children, women's treatment by men and family at large ("domestic violence"), including femicide, rape, female genital mutilation, polygamy, sexual and labour exploitation, including trafficking in women and children. These issues have recently taken centre stage in the UN gender mainstreaming agenda as its contribution to equalize and advance their life chances as a succeeding generation, in line with the objectives of the UN Charter. This article analyses these intergenerational issues from both the local and global perceptions of justice, and looks into how the UN human rights treaty bodies advance the global justice standards and norms for the treatment of women and children, particularly with regard to victims. The article does this by reviewing concluding observations issued by treaty bodies for the period between 2003 and 2013. Finally, in the light of the reviewed concluding observations by the UN treaty bodies and the right to development in general, the article makes recommendations concerning gender mainstreaming in formal and informal education.

Anganile Mwenifumbo and Harumi Fuentes are Human Rights Officers in the United Nations' Office of the High Commissioner for Human Rights (OHCHR), Human Rights Treaties Division, Geneva, Switzerland. They, however, write in their personal capacity. Therefore, the views expressed in this contribution are entirely those of the authors and do not represent the organisation that they work for except as clearly indicated as such in the publicly available documents referred to in the particular context.

A.W. Mwenifumbo (✉) • H. Fuentes Furuya
United Nations Office of the High Commissioner for Human Rights, Geneva, Switzerland
e-mail: amwenifumbo@ohchr.org; hfuentes@ohchr.org

H. Kury et al. (eds.), *Women and Children as Victims and Offenders: Background, Prevention, Reintegration*, DOI 10.1007/978-3-319-08398-8_3

1 Introduction

The history of the United Nations (UN) in the post-adoption period of the Charter of the UN (UN Charter) is partly inundated by anecdotes of the adoption of a litany of international human rights instruments.[1] These instruments have been designed to complement the primary preservationist objective of the UN to save "succeeding generations from the scourge of war".[2] The Universal Declaration of Human Rights itself, a precursor to the twin covenants on civil and political rights, and social, economic and cultural rights, set the normative framework reflecting mankind's hortatory standards that ought to govern international order.[3] Since then, a plethora of human rights instruments has emerged. Today, human rights treaties adopted under the aegis of the UN establish treaty bodies (treaty bodies/committees) mandated to supervise the implementation of specific human rights obligations.[4] The mandates establish a unique platform that entails an exchange between a State party and a treaty body culminating in the adoption of concluding observations. These provide critical guidance for the implementation of a relevant treaty by States parties.[5] The process seeks to ensure the full application by States parties of the normative standards established by the treaty.[6]

The procedures employed by treaty bodies in the enforcement of human rights standards are multifarious. However, they principally consist of the review of State

[1] One of the greatest achievements of the UN has been the creation of a comprehensive corpus of human rights law. Since 1948, over 60 human rights treaties and declarations have been negotiated at the UN, including, inter alia, International Covenant on Civil and Political Rights 1966 (ICCPR); International Covenant on Economic, Social and Cultural Rights 1966 (ICESCR); International Convention on the Elimination of All Forms of Racial Discrimination 1965 (ICERD); Convention on the Elimination of All Forms of Discrimination against Women 1979 (CEDAW Convention); Convention against Torture and Other Cruel, Inhuman or Degrading Treatment or Punishment 1984 (CAT); Convention on the Rights of the Child 1989 (Convention on the Rights of the Child); International Convention on the Protection of the Rights of All Migrant Workers and Members of Their Families 1990 (ICMW); Convention on the Rights of Persons with Disabilities 2006 (ICRPD); and International Convention for the Protection of All Persons from Enforced Disappearance 2006 (ICPED). [Editors note: In this chapter only the acronym CEDAW stands for the Committee on the Elimination of All Forms of Discrimination against Women, while the Convention on the Elimination of All Forms of Discrimination against Women is hereafter referred as CEDAW Convention].

[2] Ibid.

[3] Universal Declaration of Human Rights adopted in 1948.

[4] Human Rights Committee (HRC); Committee on Economic, Social and Cultural Rights (CESCR); Committee on the Elimination of Racial Discrimination (CERD); Committee on the Elimination of Discrimination against Women (CEDAW); Committee against Torture and Other Cruel, Inhuman, or Degrading Treatment or Punishment (CAT); Subcommittee on Prevention of Torture (SPT); Committee on the Rights of the Child (CRC); Committee on the Protection of the Rights of All Migrant Workers and Members of Their Families (CMW); Committee on the Rights of Persons with Disabilities (CRPD); Committee on Enforced Disappearances (CED).

[5] UN (2012), Fact Sheet No. 30/Rev. 1, p. 21.

[6] Ibid.

party reports, the consideration of individual complaints and the conduct of inquiries.[7] Over the years, treaty bodies have gained a venerated normative legitimacy based on the recommendations issued to States parties focusing on varying human rights issues of concern. In the discharge of their supervisory mandates, treaty bodies constitute factories of authority, which churn out country-tailored recommendations. To this end, treaty bodies have become critical agents of both *de facto* and *de jure* reform and bulwarks of localism of international standards as they require States parties to apply these normative standards.

Although the mandates of treaty bodies are circumscribed by the instruments that establish them, the manifold interrelationships of human rights have compelled them to dedicate considerable attention to certain groups of people and other cross-cutting issues.[8] Women and children have arguably been recipients of colossal attention over the years notwithstanding the existence of instruments specifically focusing on these groups.[9] While treaty bodies exercise caution not to overstep their mandates, they have arguably yielded to other external factors, including the UN gender mainstreaming agenda.[10] These factors have succeeded in highlighting human rights issues affecting women and children and have resulted in the emergence of jurisprudence that jealously guards the rights of women and children.[11] Thus, the focus on the protection of women and children by treaty bodies, albeit largely treaty endorsed, arguably highlights the reality that these groups often find themselves in situations of vulnerability where egregious human rights violations are rife. In this regard, the commitment by treaty bodies to protect women and children through their various procedures not only complies with treaty injunctions but also effectively pursues the longstanding ideal and preservationist objective of the UN to advance their life chances as succeeding generations.

---

[7] Ibid.

[8] The particular groups and cross-cutting issues include, inter alia, children, women and issues of equality and non-discrimination. See arts. 3, 6, 8, 17, 24 and 26 ICCPR; arts. 3, 10, 12(2)(a) & 13 (2) ICESCR; arts. 6, 7, 10, 15, 16, 22, 23, 24, 25, 27, ICPRD; arts. 10, 11, 14, 25, 28, 29, 30, 43, 44, ICMW; arts. 5 & 7 ICERD; art. 16 CAT.

[9] See the UN Human Rights Index available at: http://uhri.ohchr.org/en.

[10] COBs Bosnia and Herzegovina, CEDAW/C/BIH/CO/4-5, para. 17 (CEDAW, 2013); COBs Belize, CCPR/C/BLZ/CO/1, para. 12 (HRC, 2013); COBs Vietnam, CRC/C/VNM/CO/3-4, para. 30(d) (CRC, 2012).

[11] UN Human Rights Index available at: http://uhri.ohchr.org/en.

2 The Concept of Succeeding Generations and Gender Mainstreaming in the United Nations

2.1 The Concept of Succeeding Generations and the Protection of Women and Children

It is clear that the preamble of the UN Charter does not just serve as an introduction.[12] From the preparatory conference of Dumbarton Oaks in 1944 to the founding conference at San Francisco in 1945, Field Marshal Jan Smuts wanted to guarantee that the preambular words in the UN Charter impeccably captured the ideology on which the UN as an organisation should rest.[13] The negotiations during the San Francisco conference clearly showed that delegates sought to craft a preamble "so simple and clear" to "be understood by common man everywhere, and warm their hearts and strengthen them after the long exhaustion and sorrow of war".[14]

The final version of the first part of the preamble of the UN Charter, therefore, abandoned certain terminology of an earlier text and opted for a simpler version,[15] which committed the peoples of the UN to "save succeeding generations from the scourge of war" and discarded Jan Smuts' language of preventing "a recurrence of the fratricidal strife".[16] The preamble further reaffirms faith in "fundamental human rights, in the dignity and worth of the human person, in the equal rights of men and women".[17] With these words, the UN Charter posits a contractarian theory, which not only implicitly recognises the inter-temporal nature of human existence but also integrates the paradigms of rights and responsibilities between the contracting parties themselves as well as between contracting parties and their people. Henceforth, international law has imposed substantial restrictions on the domestic affairs of States to protect persons from violations of human rights by their governments.

Since the adoption of UN Charter, international law continues to foster the preservationist ideal of the UN with regard to women and children as evidenced by an avalanche of instruments and resolutions on conflict prevention and human rights.[18] Today, the UN human rights regime on women and children boasts of two comprehensive and near-universally ratified instruments in CEDAW and the CRC, and a total of four Optional Protocols.[19] Nevertheless, the protection of the rights of

---

[12] Schermers (1997), p. 112.

[13] Ransom (1945), p. 338. See also Simma (1994), pp. 10–12.

[14] United States Representative quoted in Heyns (1995), p. 339.

[15] Ibid.

[16] Ibid.

[17] UN Charter 1945.

[18] See generally Hudson (2010).

[19] Optional Protocol to the CEDAW 1999; Optional Protocol to the Convention on the Rights of the Child on the involvement of children in armed conflict 2000; Optional Protocol to the

women and children is guaranteed in almost all the core international human rights treaties of the UN.[20] This renders credence to the commitment of the international community to advance the life chances of these groups as succeeding generations.

2.2 *The United Nations' Gender Mainstreaming Agenda and Treaty Bodies*

During the fourth UN World Conference on Women in Beijing in 1995, which gave birth to the Beijing Platform for Action, the international community established gender mainstreaming as a major global strategy for the promotion of gender equality.[21] Since then, gender mainstreaming has suffused the work of the UN in areas such as disarmament, poverty reduction, health, and education.[22] The idea is to ensure that gender perspectives are factored into all processes within the UN.

The promulgation of the gender mainstreaming agenda within the UN have also had a major impact in shaping the work of treaty bodies. Under the reporting procedure, treaty bodies often engage in the process of assessing the implications for women and men of any action, including legislation, policies or programmes of States parties.[23] The increasingly glaring inequalities between men and women forestall the effective implementation of treaty obligations, which guarantee respect for human dignity and the equal enjoyment of human rights by all. Treaty bodies often employ gender mainstreaming as a strategy to unearth data on issues which reveal all façades of human rights progress,[24] including those affecting women and children in the field of education.[25]

Convention on the Rights of the Child on the sale of children, child prostitution and child pornography 2000; and the Optional Protocol to the Convention on the Rights of the Child on a communications procedure 2011.

[20] See for example, articles. 3, 6, 8, 17, 24 and 26 ICCPR; arts. 3, 10, 12(2)(a) & 13(2) ICESCR; arts. 6, 7, 10, 15, 16, 22, 23, 24, 25, 27, ICPRD; arts. 10, 11, 14, 25, 28, 29, 30, 43, 44, ICMW; arts. 5 & 7 ICERD; art. 16 CAT.

[21] Freeman et al. (2012), p. 26.

[22] UN (2002), *Gender mainstreaming*.

[23] COBs Qatar, CAT/C/QAT/CO/2, para. 7, (CAT, 2013); COBs Dominican Republic, CERD/C/DOM/CO/13-14, para. 13, (CERD; 2013); COBs Mozambique, CCPR/C/MOZ/CO/1, para. 6, (HRC, 2013); COBs Austria, CRC/C/AUT/CO/3-4, para. 41, (CRC, 2013), COBs Portugal, CEDAW/C/PRT/CO/7, para. 41, (CEDAW, 2008); COBs The Former Yugoslav Republic of Macedonia (FYRM), E/C.12/MKD/CO/1, para. 35, (CESCR, 2008).

[24] Ibid.

[25] COBs The Netherlands, CEDAW/C/NLD/CO/5, para. 35, (CEDAW, 2010); COBs Georgia, CEDAW/C/GEO/CO/3, para. 12, (CEDAW, 2006).

3 The State Party Reporting Procedure Under UN Treaty Bodies

The core human rights treaties of the UN mandate treaty bodies to undertake several functions within the remit of their respective treaties. The State reporting procedure remains the primary function of treaty bodies.[26] Under this procedure, the treaty bodies supervise the implementation of human rights obligations established under the treaties.[27] Over the years, treaty bodies have sought to provide clarity to their practices with regard to reviews of State party reports by harmonising working methods, although certain differences inevitably continue to persist.[28] However, these differences do not affect the reporting cycle, which is largely uniform.

A reporting obligation is triggered upon ratifying a human rights treaty that establishes a reporting obligation.[29] Under such a treaty, States parties commit to submit a report, usually within 1 or 2 years upon entry into force of the respective treaty, on the measures they have undertaken to implement it.[30] The process of report preparation often involves the participation of various stakeholders within a State party to ensure that the report is as representative of the situation in the State party as possible. Treaty bodies have issued reporting guidelines to assist States parties in understanding treaty obligations when preparing reports.[31] The preparation of a State party report is then followed by its submissions to the relevant treaty body.

The working methods of treaty bodies in the conduct of the initial assessment of a State party report vary. Some treaty bodies constitute a task force of its members while others appoint a member as rapporteur. The idea is to subject the State party report to an initial review in order to establish possible information gaps.[32] All treaty bodies develop a set of list of issues (LOIs) with the exception of the CERD, which adopts a list of themes (LOTs).[33] Whereas LOIs are questions requiring an additional written reply by States parties, CERD's LOTs are a shorter version of issues grouped thematically and they do not elicit written replies.[34] Both LOIs and LOTs guide the eventual dialogue between the treaty body and the State party's delegation during the review. Some committees also provide for an optional simplified reporting procedure where they issue list of issues prior to reporting

---

[26] UN (2012), Fact Sheet No. 30/Rev. 1, p. 21.

[27] Ibid.

[28] The General Assembly by resolution A/RES/38/117 (1983) called on the Chair persons of human rights treaty bodies to meet to discuss how to enhance the work of the treaty bodies. See also UN (2012), Fact Sheet No. 30/Rev. 1, p. 21.

[29] UN (2012), Fact Sheet No. 30/Rev. 1, p. 19.

[30] Ibid.

[31] UN, Note by the Secretariat (2013), Meeting of Chairpersons, paras. 6, 14–18.

[32] UN (2012), Fact Sheet No. 30/Rev. 1, p. 26.

[33] UN, Note by the Secretariat (2013), Meeting of Chairpersons, paras. 29, 35, 37 and 42.

[34] General Assembly, Report of CERD, A/66/18, 2011, para. 95.

(LOIPR). The LOIPR is a comprehensive list of issues whose responses by a State party constitute a report.[35]

Upon conducting the initial assessment of the report, the review of the State party is scheduled at a date when the treaty body and the State party engage in a constructive dialogue. This permits the treaty body to undertake a fair and thorough assessment of the measures taken by a State party to implement its obligations under a treaty. The ultimate output of this review is a set of concluding observations, which highlights areas of concern and provides recommendations on the measures a State party should undertake to comply with treaty obligations. The follow-up procedure forms part of this process. It is employed by four treaty bodies to follow up on the implementation of specific recommendations, which require urgent attention.[36]

4 The Pursuit of Justice and the Protection of Women and Children by Treaty Bodies

Treaty bodies have over the years gained laudable recognition as bastions of human rights protection.[37] However, their work has not been without criticism. Some commentators on the treaty body system have extended their field of investigation beyond the procedural incongruences within the system to consider the impact treaty body recommendations have in States parties. The most comprehensive scholarly exercise on the subject matter, albeit dated and limited in scope, found that treaty body mechanisms have had a very limited demonstrable impact.[38] However, treaty bodies have arguably played an outstanding role in holding the human rights fortress together in the pursuit of global justice, if they are to be objectively assessed within the limits of their mandates. Treaty bodies were established to operate within the confines of a very limited mandate, which is largely advisory and devoid of any binding supranational enforcement powers. Therefore, any criticism of the impact of the treaty body system should be considered within the limits of these powers.

A thorough assessment of concluding observations indicates that treaty bodies have carved a venerable niche in advancing global justice standards. Although justice is a fluid concept in that it is often context-dependent, treaty bodies have sought to construe the moral standards set by treaties by analysing the various social relationships in the context of the matrix of States parties' obligations to protect,

[35] UN (2012), Fact Sheet No. 30/Rev. 1, pp. 26–27.

[36] Report of the Inter-Committee Meeting working group on follow-up to concluding observations, decisions on individual complaints and inquiries, HRI/ICM/2011/3-HRI/MC/2011/2, 4 May 2011. See also UN (2012), Fact Sheet No. 30/Rev. 1, pp. 28–29.

[37] See generally, Keller and Ulfstein (2012).

[38] Heyns and Viljoen (2001).

respect, promote and fulfil human rights standards. The moral claims and obligations that human rights treaties establish provide treaty bodies with the tools to be able to assess the extent to which social interactions produce claims, which States parties ought to satisfy by virtue of their undertakings to comply with them. Thus, treaty bodies have in their concluding observations continued to advance various forms of justice when assessing social interactions such as (a) States parties' roles in promoting *de facto* equality (distributive justice); (b) States parties' exercise of political power because of its monopoly over violence and the power to provide a remedy (political and corrective justice); and (c) during transactional relationships emanating from individuals' interactions with themselves or with State party officials (transactional justice).

With respect to the protection of women and children, concluding observations, as is demonstrated below, reveal elements of distributive justice, political justice, corrective justice and the promotion of transactional justice.[39] Furthermore, the preoccupation of treaty bodies with contextual issues on the right to development and the promotion of social justice for women and children have resonated with States parties' aspirations to achieve more egalitarian societies. Thus, concluding observations, through the reporting procedure, have tremendously helped treaty bodies in catapulting global justice standards from their seats in Geneva to the rest of the world.

4.1 Education of Women and Children

Treaty bodies have clearly defined the content of the right to education as provided in the various core human rights treaties. In their interpretations, they have dismissed parochial understandings of the right to education. They have underscored the fact that education as a human right goes beyond mere literacy and numeracy.[40] Their position is that education is a tool for empowerment, which equips women and children with the skills to face life's challenges,[41] skills that not only promote individual development but also provide the capacity to claim the right to development and to fully participate in development processes. The right to development is an inalienable human right by virtue of which everyone is entitled to participate in, contribute to and enjoy economic, social, cultural, and political development in which all human rights and fundamental freedoms can be fully realized. The right to education, therefore, guarantees and facilitates the participation of women and children in the process of economic, social, cultural, and political development. Treaty bodies have drawn linkages between literacy and the

[39] Merle (2005).

[40] COBs Togo CEDAW/C/COM/CO/1-4 para. 30 (CEDAW 2012).

[41] CRC General Comment no. 1 (2001) on Article 29 (1): The Aims of Education CRC/GC/2001/1, para. 9 (2001).

enjoyment of all economic, social and cultural rights.[42] In this context, they have highlighted the correlation between the impact of adult literacy and a child's life and development opportunities, such as those linked to birth registration and its consequent advantages in access to health, nutrition and education.[43] Treaty bodies thus recognize the intergenerational and cross-cutting nature of education and its ability to shape and improve individuals and societies through dialogue and respect for diversity.

The jurisprudence of treaty bodies, particularly CRC and CEDAW, on the education of women and children, has been largely shaped by the Beijing Declaration and Platform for Action, the Millennium Development Goals (MDGs),[44] and the goals set in the Education for All and the World Fit for Children goals.[45] Chiefly, the notion that"[i]nvesting in formal and non-formal education and training for girls and women, with its exceptionally high social and economic return, has proved to be one of the best means of achieving sustainable development..."[46] cuts to the heart of the gender mainstreaming agenda in development.

Treaty bodies have largely highlighted the major challenges that women and children encounter in accessing education.[47] The most cited challenges relate to physical and economic barriers,[48] and harassment and violence, including sexual violence, that children, particularly girls, face on their way to and while in school,[49] and which is often met with impunity.[50] All these barriers negatively affect the attendance of female students as well as community life.[51] Furthermore, society's negative attitudes towards child and adult literacy as well as sexual and reproductive health education, continue to complicate efforts to ensure the full realisation of the right to education and the right to development.

Treaty bodies have also highlighted the social and cultural barriers which negatively impact women's access to formal and informal education, including deep rooted stereotypes on the roles of women and children.[52] Negative stereotypes

---

[42] COBs Bosnia and Herzegovina, CEDAW/C/BIH/CO/3, para. 31 (CEDAW 2006); COBs Malawi, CEDAW/C/MWI/CO/5, para. 27 (CEDAW 2006).

[43] COBs Australia, CRC/C/AUS/CO/4 (CRC, 2012) paras. 35 and 74.

[44] General Assembly Resolution A/55/L.2, UN Millennium Declaration, 2000.

[45] World Education Forum, The Dakar Framework for Action, Senegal, 2000; General Assembly Special Session on Children, A/S-27/19/Rev. 1 (2002).

[46] Fourth World Conference on Women, Beijing Declaration and Platform for Action, (September 1995), para. 69.

[47] COBs Guinea Bissau, CEDAW/C/GNB/CO/6, para. 33 (CEDAW, 2009); COBs Japan CEDAW/C/JPN/CO/6 para. 29 (CEDAW, 2009).

[48] COBs Chad CEDAW/C/TCD/CO/1-4 para. 30 (CEDAW 2011). COBs Guinea Bissau, CEDAW/C/GNB/CO/6, para. 33 (CEDAW, 2009).

[49] COBs Pakistan CEDAW/C/PAK/CO/4 para. 27 (CEDAW 2013). COBs Lesotho, CEDAW/C/LSO/CO/1-4 paras. 28–29 (CEDAW 2011).

[50] COBs Lesotho, CEDAW/C/LSO/CO/1-4 paras. 28–29 (CEDAW 2011).

[51] COBs Jamaica CEDAW/C/JAM/CO/6-7, para. 25 (CEDAW 2012).

[52] COBs Mauritania E/C.12/MRT/CO/1, para. (CESCR, 2012).

manifest themselves in school curricula, textbooks, educational materials, and the codes of conduct which society prescribes for women and girls.[53] Often, due to lack of skills and specific training, teachers, counsellors and school personnel lack the tools to support girls in school.[54]

These glaring inequalities between men and women forestall the effective implementation of the right to education. They constitute both the cause and consequence of the failure to guarantee respect for human dignity and the equal enjoyment of human rights by all. However, the employment of a gender mainstreaming strategy affords States parties the opportunity to address these challenges so that women and children can fully enjoy the right to education and participate in the process of development on the basis of equality with men.

4.1.1 Child Literacy

Literacy and numeracy constitute only one component of education. However, these have long been the focus of treaty bodies because the discrimination faced by girls in this regard is emblematic. It largely affects girls in rural areas, minority groups or those with disabilities.[55] In this regard, treaty bodies have expressed concern that the glaring disparities in access to and quality of literacy and numeracy between girls and boys, along with the high repetition and dropout rates of girls, have negative implications on a wide array of issues for girls. These include negative impacts on their long term health and that of their future children, their decision-making capabilities and their personal and professional development.[56]

---

[53] COBs Pakistan CEDAW/C/PAK/CO/4 para. 28 (CEDAW 2013); COBs Bahamas, CEDAW/C/BHS/CO/1-5 para. 32 (CEDAW 2012), COBs Republic of Congo CEDAW/C/COG/CO/6 para. 32 (CEDAW 2012) ; COBs Jordan CEDAW/C/JOR/CO/5, paras. 24–36 (CEDAW 2012), COBs Guinea Bissau, CEDAW/C/GNB/CO/6, para. 33 (CEDAW, 2009); COBs Niger, CEDAW/C/NER/CO/2, para. 29 (CEDAW 2007), COBs Cambodia, CEDAW/C/KHM/CO/3, para. 18 (CEDAW, 2006).

[54] COBs Guinea Bissau CRC/C/GNB/CO/2-4, para. 62 (CRC 2013), COBs Japan CEDAW/C/JPN/CO/6 para. 29 (CEDAW, 2009).

[55] COBs Togo E/C.12/TGO/CO/1 para. 34 (CESCR 2013), CEDAW/C/PAK/CO/4 para. 27 (CEDAW 2013), COBs Ecuador E/C.12/ECU/CO/3, para. 31 (CESCR 2012), COBs Ethiopia, E/C.12/ETH/CO/1-3 para. 26 (CESCR 2012, COBs Uruguay E/C.12/URY/CO/3-4 para. 28 (CESCR 2010), COBs Uruguay E/C.12/URY/CO/3-4 para. 28 (CESCR 2010), COBs Mauritania CRC/C/MRT/CO/2 para. 65 (CRC 2009), COBs Colombia CERD/C/COL/CO/14 para. 23 (CERD, 2009), COBs Namibia CERD/C/NAM/CO/12 para. 8 (CERD, 2008),COBs Nicaragua, CEDAW/C/NIC/CO/6, para. 26 (CEDAW 2007), COBs Pakistan, CEDAW/C/PAK/CO/3. para. 37 (CEDAW 2007) COBs Eritrea, CEDAW/C/ERI/CO/3, para. 26 (CEDAW 2006); COBs FYRM, CEDAW/C/MKD/CO/3, para. 27 (CEDAW 2006); COBs Togo, CEDAW/C/TGO/CO/5, para. 25 (CEDAW 2006); COBs Cape Verde, CEDAW/C/CPV/CO/6, paras. 18–26 (CEDAW 2006); COBs China, CEDAW/C/CHN/CO/6, para. 27 (CEDAW 2006) COBs Mauritius, CEDAW/C/MAR/CO/5, para. 24 (CEDAW 2006).

[56] COBs Gabon E/C.12/GAB/CO/1 para. 30 (CESCR 2013), COBs Peru, CEDAW/C/PER/CO/6 para. 26 (CEDAW 2007).

The HRC has previously observed with concern that women and girls' illiteracy is an obstacle to their full enjoyment of human rights.[57]

States parties are called on to 'strengthen' the implementation of laws and policies aimed at the desegregation of education, 'take urgent and concrete steps' and 'increase' efforts to reduce illiteracy, especially among the most vulnerable and marginalized communities.[58] They are urged to implement and prioritize literacy plans and programmes,[59] in particular for girls and women,[60] and to establish indicators to measure the impact of existing literacy strategies.[61]

4.1.2 Adult Literacy

Treaty bodies address the disparities in literacy rates between men and women based on the understanding that it is engendered by indirect discrimination. For instance, CEDAW has noted that cultural patterns, opposition from husbands, and lack of programmes in remote areas are among the challenges and barriers that women face when attending adult education and literacy classes.[62] States parties have been called upon to take measures to address the high rate of illiteracy of women and the low percentage of women having education beyond primary school,[63] especially in rural areas.[64] States parties are recommended to 'adopt', 'improve' and 'strengthen', literacy campaigns and programmes at the formal and non-formal levels, and through adult education and training[65] and to take the necessary measures to eliminate the barriers preventing women from attending adult education and literacy classes.[66]

---

[57] COBs Yemen CCPR/C/YEM/CO/5 para. 11 (HRC 2012).

[58] Ibid. para. 12 (HRC 2012).

[59] COBs Equatorial New Guinea, CEDAW/C/GNQ/CO/6 para. 32 (CEDAW 2012).

[60] COBs Ethiopia, E/C.12/ETH/CO/1-3 para. 26 (CESCR 2012).

[61] COBs Algeria CEDAW/C/DZA/CO/3-4 para. 36 (CEDAW 2012).

[62] COBs Bahamas, CEDAW/ C/BHS/CO/1-5 para. 32 (CEDAW 2012).

[63] COBs Chad CEDAW/C/TCD/CO/1-4 para. 30 (CEDAW 2011), COBs Guinea Bissau CEDAW/C/GNB/CO/6 para. 33 (CEDAW, 2009); COBs Ethiopia, CEDAW/C/ETH/CO/1 paras. 240 (CEDAW 2004); COBs Nepal, CEDAW/C/NPL/CO/3 para. 204 (CEDAW, 2004), COBs Nigeria, CEDAW/C/NGA/CO/5 (CEDAW 2004) para. 303;, COBs Angola CEDAW/C/AGO/CO/ para. 158, (CEDAW 2004), COBs Brazil, CEDAW/C/BRA/1-5, paras. 122–123 (CEDAW, 2003); COBs Republic of Congo, CEDAW/C/COG/1-5 paras. 170–171 (CEDAW 2003).

[64] COBs Democratic Republic of Congo (DRC) CEDAW/C/COD/CO/6-7 para. 28 (CEDAW 2013), COBs Mauritania, CEDAW/C/MRT/CO/1, para. 14 (CEDAW, 2007), COBs Mexico, CEDAW/C/MEX/CO/6, para. 34 (CEDAW 2006), COBs Bhutan, CEDAW/C/BTN/CO/3 paras. 117–118 (COBs 2004); COBs Ecuador, CEDAW/C/ECU/4-5 (CEDAW 2003) paras. 319–320; COBs Morocco, CEDAW/C/MOR/2, paras. 170–171 (CEDAW 2003).

[65] COBs Congo CEDAW/C/COD/CO/6-7, para. 28 (CEDAW, 2013), COBs Nepal, CEDAW/C/NPL/CO/4-5, para. 28 (CEDAW 2011), COBs Guinea Bissau CEDAW/C/GNB/CO/6 para. 34 (CEDAW, 2009). COBs Mauritania, CEDAW/C/MRT/CO/1, para. 36 (CEDAW, 2007).

[66] COBs Bahamas, CEDAW/ C/BHS/CO/1-5 para. 32 (CEDAW 2012).

Recommendations also urge States parties to look at adult literacy programmes in tandem with the promotion of income-generating activities.[67] In this regard, treaty bodies encourage the development and implementation of comprehensive rural development strategies that include functional literacy, enterprise development, skills training and microfinance, women's equal access to land as a means of poverty alleviation.[68]

4.2 *Sexual and Reproductive Health*

CEDAW and the CRC, with their clear guarantees on the right to health, remain the principal instruments on the protection of sexual and reproductive rights of women and children.[69] However, other treaty bodies play complementary roles in this area. While treaties such as ICESCR, ICRPD, ICERD and ICMW have specific provisions guaranteeing the right to health or access to medical care,[70] treaty bodies such as the HRC and CAT have largely depended on treaty interpretations of the right to life and the prohibition against torture and ill-treatment to advance the protection for sexual and reproductive rights of women.[71]

The jurisprudence of treaty bodies on sexual and reproductive health (SRH) rights education has largely grown based on treaty specific interpretations. However, it has developed within the historical context of two important conferences on SRH rights. The 1994 UN International Conference on Population and Development Programme of Action and the 1995 UN Fourth World Conference on Women Platform of Action were watershed moments for the SRH rights movement. The prescriptions of the outcome documents of these conferences, coupled with the adoption of the MDGs, which set out specific targets on maternal mortality and universal access to reproductive health, have arguably influenced and shaped the understanding and interpretation of norms by treaty bodies in this area.[72] Now the

[67] COBs Djibouti E/C.12/DJI/CO/1-2 para. 15 (CESCR 2013); COBs Angola CEDAW/C/AGO/CO/6, para. 28 (CEDAW 2013); COBs Paraguay CEDAW/C/PRY/CO/6 para. 33 (CEDAW 2011).

[68] COBs Djibouti E/C.12/DJI/CO/1-2 para. 14 (CECSR 2013), COBs Ethiopia, CEDAW/C/ETH/CO6-7 para. 31 (CEDAW 2011), COBs Sierra Leone, CEDAW/C/SLE/CO/5 para. 31 (CEDAW 2007), COBs Mauritania, para. 36 CEDAW/C/MRT/CO/1 (CEDAW 2007), COBs Nicaragua, CEDAW/C/NIC/CO/6, para. 30 (CEDAW 2007COBs Colombia, CEDAW/C/COL/CO/6, para. 31 (CEDAW 2007), COBs Guatemala, CEDAW/C/GUA/CO/6 para. 34 (CEDAW 2006), COBs DRC, CEDAW/C/COD/CO/5, para. 359 (CEDAW 2006), COBs Vanuatu, CEDAW/C/VUT/CO/3, para. 37 (CEDAW 2007), COBs Brazil, CEDAW/C/BRA/CO/6, para. 32 (CEDAW 2007).

[69] Art. 12 CEDAW and art. 24 CRC.

[70] Art. 12 ICESCR ; art. 25 ICRPD ; art. 5(c)(iv); arts. 28, 43(e); 45(1)(c) ICMW.

[71] COBs Bolivia, CCPR/C/BOL/CO/3, para. 9 (HRC, 2013) ; COBs Peru, CAT/C/PER/CO/5-6, para. 15 (CAT, 2013).

[72] The CEDAW Committee in its remarkable General Recommendation No. 24 on women and health requires States parties to ensure the right to sexual health information and education. In

jurisprudence of treaty bodies is filled with a vortex of injunctions demanding States parties to "intensify", "improve", "reinforce", "expand" or "strengthen" efforts and measures to realise the right to SRH information and education.[73]

Treaty bodies employ a twin track approach when monitoring the implementation of the right to SRH information and education, which entails ensuring that the provision of such information and education is undertaken by States parties at both formal and informal levels.[74] Although the HRC has largely maintained the distinction between recommendations targeting the formal and informal levels of society,[75] the lines of formality and informality are often blurred in most concluding observations, particularly when dealing with general awareness-raising. The lines become clear again when treaty bodies recommend the introduction of SRH rights in the education curricula.

The recommendations of treaty bodies to States parties on SRH information and education are context dependent. However, they often exhibit the important elements of availability, accessibility, acceptability and quality of SRH information and education within the matrix of the duty to protect, respect, promote and fulfil human rights standards.

4.2.1 Availability

Treaty bodies have bemoaned the lack of information and education on SRH in States parties.[76] Since information transmission and education provision constitute the main pillars for promoting the exercise of sexual and reproductive freedom, treaty bodies have sought to ensure that such information and education is available at both the formal and informal levels of the society.[77]

At the formal level, treaty bodies have recommended the inclusion of age-appropriate SRH education in the school curricula.[78] In order to ensure that

paragraph 3 of this General Recommendation (GR), the Committee states that in preparing the GR, it took into account "relevant programmes of action adopted at UN world conferences and, in particular, those of the 1993 World Conference on Human Rights, the 1994 International Conference on Population and Development and the 1995 Fourth World Conference on Women", http://www.un.org/womenwatch/daw/cedaw/recommendations/recomm.htm#recom24.

[73] See http://uhri.ohchr.org/.

[74] Ibid.

[75] COBs Paraguay, CCPR/C/PRY/CO/3 (HRC, 2013).

[76] COBs Niue, CRC/C/NIU/CO/1, para. 55 (CRC, 2013); COBs Angola, CEDAW/C/AGO/CO/6, para. 31(c) (CEDAW, 2013); COBs Turkmenistan, E/C.12/TKM/CO/1, para. 22 (CESCR, 2011).

[77] COBs Peru, CCPR/C/PER/CO/5 (HRC, 2013); COBs Paraguay, CCPR/C/PRY/CO/3 (HRC, 2013).

[78] COBs Serbia, CEDAW/C/SRB/CO/2-3, para. 28(c), (CEDAW, 2013); COBs Cuba, CEDAW/C/CUB/CO/7-8, para. 31(c), (CEDAW, 2013); COBs Bosnia and Herzegovina, CEDAW/C/BIH/CO/4-5, para. 36(c), (CEDAW, 2013); COBs Rwanda, CRC/C/RWA/CO/3-4, para. 47 (e), (CRC, 2013); COBs Slovakia, E/C.12/SVK/CO/2, para.25, (CESCR, 2012); COBs Indonesia, E/C.12/IDN/CO/5, (CESCR, 2008); COBs Guatemala, E/C.12/1/ADD.93 (CESCR, 2003).

such education has a comprehensive reach and impact, some treaty bodies have gone further to recommend that subjects on SRH should be mandatory and not delivered as optional courses.[79] CESCR, for instance, has previously expressed concern over a State party's withdrawal of a special course on SRH rights from the school curriculum, which left public schools without any such course.[80]

Treaty bodies have also focused on increasing awareness on the importance of contraceptive use and on SRH rights.[81] The objective is to promote responsible sexual behaviour with a view to preventing teenage and unwanted pregnancies, sexual transmitted infections (STIs), including HIV/AIDS and reducing the incidence of abortions.[82] In doing so, they have also drawn causal relationships between the lack of information on SRH and the prevalence of certain vices such as clandestine abortions, maternal mortality, unwanted pregnancies and the prevalence of STIs.[83] States parties have been required to revise their laws relating to abortion with a view to removing punitive provisions from legislation and to increase sex education so that women do not resort to unsafe abortion,[84] as well as to provide sex education in order to prevent MTCT.[85] In its concluding observations, the HRC has expressed concern that the "insufficient sex education in the school curriculum and public information on how to gain access to a legal abortion continues to cause loss of life among women who have resorted to unsafe abortions".[86]

In most countries, women and girls have largely been the target for SRH rights information and education at the formal level of society, revealing the gendered perceptions and stereotypes regarding the provision of SRH rights education at the formal level. However, treaty bodies have increasingly sought to combat these perceptions by recommending that education on SRH be provided to both women and men, particularly sexually active boys and girls of the reproductive age, in order to enhance their autonomy and choice.[87] At a general level, formal education on

---

[79] COBs Montenegro, CEDAW/C/MNE/CO/1, para. 30 and 31(c), (CEDAW, 2011); COBs Netherlands, E/C.12/NDL/CO/4-5, (CESCR, 2010); COBs Lithuania, CEDAW/C/LTU/CO/4, (CEDAW, 2008).

[80] COBs Moldova, E/C.12/MDA/CO/2, (CESCR, 2011).

[81] COBs Paraguay CCPR/C/PRY/CO/3 HRC, 2013); COBs Peru CCPR/C/PER/CO/5 (HRC, 2013); COBs FYRM, CEDAW/C/MKD/CO/4-5, para. 34(b) (CEDAW, 2013).

[82] COBs Bosnia and Herzegovina, E/C.12/BIH/CO/2, (CESCR, 2013); COBs Cuba, CEDAW/C/CUB/CO/7-8, para. 31(c), (CEDAW, 2013); COBs Philippines, CRC/C/OPSC/PHL/CO/1, paras. 21(e) and 22(e) (CRC, 2013); COBs Slovakia, CEDAW/C/SVK/CO/4, (CEDAW, 2009); COBs Sweden, CRC/C/SWE/CO/4, (CRC, 20009); COBs Costa Rica, A/58/38/(SUPP), (CEDAW, 2003).

[83] COBs Peru, CEDAW/C/PER/CO/5, (HRC, 2013), COBs Slovakia, CEDAW/C/SVK/CO/4, (CEDAW, 2009); COBs Pakistan, CEDAW/C/PAK/CO/3 (CEDAW, 2007).

[84] COBs Belize, CEDAW/C/BLZ/CO/4, (CEDAW, 2007).

[85] MTCT: mother to child transmission of HIV/AIDS; COBs CRC/C/GNB/CO/2-4, para. 57 (d) (CRC, 2013).

[86] COBs Colombia, CCPR/C/COL/CO/6, (HRC, 2010).

[87] COBs Zimbabwe, CEDAW/C/ZWE/CO/2-5, para. 34(d) (CEDAW, 2012); COBs Greece, CEDAW/C/GRC/CO/6 (CEDAW, 2007).

SRH has largely targeted adolescents (teenagers) irrespective of sex in order to promote responsible sexual behaviour.[88]

Treaty bodies have also recommended that States parties provide training and raise awareness on sexual and reproductive rights by, inter alia, targeting health personnel and teachers.[89] This seeks to ensure that providers of SRH services also have the requisite information and skills so that they can render effective services to individuals. Treaty body recommendations have, for instance, highlighted the need to provide training to medical practitioners on unsafe medical conditions during the practice of male circumcision[90] and how to obtain informed consent before carrying out sterilisation in order to curb illegal and forced sterilisations.[91] The jurisprudence reveals how treaty bodies promote elements of transactional justice by ensuring that parties involved in sterilisation procedures are fully aware of the terms of the procedure to be able to make decisions rationally and free from undue influence.[92]

In their efforts to ensure the availability of information and education material targeting the informal levels of society, most treaty body recommendations have focused on the availability of public education and awareness raising programmes.[93] The predominant concern has been the lack of such programmes thereby affecting sexual and reproductive health issues relating to family planning, the prevention of unwanted pregnancies and the contraction of STIs, including HIV/AIDS.[94] In their analysis of country situations, treaty bodies have also established the nexus between the lack of and access to family planning information and the high rates of abortions, maternal and infant mortality, and MTCT.[95]

Information on sexual and reproductive health is vital in the prevention of recourse to life-threatening abortions, STIs, and maternal and infant mortality.

---

[88] COBs Israel, E/C.12/EST/CO/2, para. 24 (CESCR, 2011); CRC Angola, CRC/C/15/ADD.246 (CRC, 2004).

[89] COBs Serbia, CEDAW/C/SRB/CO/2-3, para. 33(c), (CEDAW, 2013); COBs Cuba, CEDAW/C/CUB/CO/7-8, para. 35(b), (CEDAW, 2013); COBs Maldives, CRC/C/MDV/CO/3 (CRC, 2007).

[90] COBs South Africa, CRC/C/15/ADD.122 (CRC, 2000).

[91] COBs Slovakia, CERD/C/SVK/CO/9-10, para. 13 (CERD, 2013).

[92] COBs Hungary, CEDAW/C/HUN/CO/7-8, para. 33 (b), (CEDAW, 2013).

[93] COBs Bolivia, CCPR/C/BOL/CO/3 (HRC, 2013); COBs Jamaica, E/C.12/JAM/CO/3-4 (CESCR, 2013); COBs Angola, CEDAW/C/AGO/CO/6, para. 31 (c), (CEDAW, 2013); COBs Andorra, CRC/C/AND/CO/2/, para. 41, (CRC; 2012); COBs Panama, CERD/C/PAN/CO/15-20 (CERD, 2010).

[94] COBs Philippines, CRC/C/OPSC/PHL/CO/1, para. 21(e), (CRC, 2013); COBs Greece, CEADW/C/GRC/CO/7, para. 31(d), (CEDAW, 2013); COBs Azerbaijan, E/C.12/1/ADD.104 (CESCR, 2004); COBs Costa Rica, A/58/38/ (SUPP) (CEDAW, 2003).

[95] COBs Serbia, CEDAW/C/SRB/CO/CO/2-3, para. 33(e), (CEDAW, 2013). COBs DRC, CEDAW/C/COD/CO/6-7, para. 31(f), (CEDAW, 2013CEDAW/C/JAM/CO/6-7, para. 29 (CEDAW, 2012); COBs Cameroon, E/C.12/CMR/CO/2-3 (CESCR, 2012); COBs Slovakia, CEDAW/C/SVK/CO/4, (CEDAW, 2009); COBs Latvia, A/59/38 (SUPP) (CEDAW, 2004); COBs Nepal, A/59/38 (SUPP) (CEDAW, 2004); COBs Georgia, CRC/C/15/ADD.222 (CRC, 2003).

Treaty bodies have, therefore, urged States parties to undertake public campaigns aimed at disseminating information and knowledge on sexual and reproductive health through, inter alia, the media.[96] The objective has been to ensure a comprehensive dissemination of messages and knowledge through effective public campaigns, which address issues of concern in the area of sexual and reproductive health. Treaty bodies have also made injunctive recommendations where political views and possible stereotypes hamper the access to reproductive health information and services. For instance, CEDAW recommended that a State party "cease all negative interference with women's sexual and reproductive rights, including by ending campaigns that stigmatise abortion and seek to negatively influence the public view on abortion and contraception"[97] and to raise awareness about legislation on abortion on how to seek safe abortion services.[98] CEDAW has also recommended that States parties raise awareness to curb the use of abortion as a form of birth control.[99]

The provision of public education and the delivery of awareness raising campaigns on SRH have also revealed inequalities in the sharing of benefits and burdens by societies. In seeking to foster equality and to comply with the demands of distributive justice, treaty bodies have observed that the lack of information on SRH experienced by specific groups of women such as asylum seekers and women in rural areas have produced lopsided results with regard to the incidence of infant and maternal mortality.[100] CEDAW has previously observed that the lack of such information has hampered access to health services by undocumented female immigrants, and expressed concern that the maternal mortality risk was higher among asylum seekers than among native women in the host country.[101]

4.2.2 Accessibility

Accessibility denotes that States parties should ensure that women and children do not encounter physical and economic barriers in accessing SRH education and information. Treaty bodies enjoin States parties to take measures to address physical and economic barriers in accessing SRH information by, inter alia, recommending free access to SRH information and increasing the number of health

[96] COBs Peru, CCPR/C/PER/CO/5 (HRC, 2013); COBs Estonia, E/C.12/EST/CO/2, para. 24, (CESCR, 2011).

[97] COBs Hungary, CEDAW/C/HUN/CO/7-8, para. 31(a), (CEDAW, 2013).

[98] COBs Zambia, CEDAW/C/ZMB/CO/5-6, para. 34(c), (CEDAW, 2011); COBs Colombia, CCPR/C/COL/CO/6 (HRC, 2010).

[99] COBs Serbia, CEDAW/C/SRB/CO/2-3, para. 33(d), (CEDAW, 2013); COBs Belarus, A/59/38 (SUPP) (CEDAW, 2004).

[100] COBs Cuba, CEDAW/C/CUB/CO/7-8, para. 34, (CEDAW, 2013); COBs Israel, CEDAW/C/ISR/CO/5, (CEDAW, 2011); COBs Brazil, A/58/ (SUPP) (CEDAW, 2003).

[101] COBs Netherlands, CEDAW/C/NLD/CO/5/ (CEDAW, 2010).

facilities that provide services.[102] This has also included the need to adopt legislation to allow adolescents to actually seek information and services on SRH.[103]

Access to such information needs to be effective and comprehensive.[104] Thus, where SRH information is limited or inadequate, States parties have been required to intensify SRH education and awareness raising campaigns.[105] Effectiveness in accessibility has also included ensuring that SRH information is available in accessible formats to cater for specific groups of people such as women with disabilities.[106] In addressing physical barriers, treaty bodies have observed that geographical, cultural and racial barriers have prevented certain groups of women from having equal access to SRH information such as rural women, minority ethnic women and certain age-groups of girls and boys.[107] Hand in glove with principles of distributive justice, treaty bodies have recommended that States parties address these disparities by demanding equal access to such information.[108]

4.2.3 Acceptability

The jurisprudence of treaty bodies on the issue of the acceptability of SRH education and information has sought to promote the dissemination of information in a fashion that ensures that such information is well received. In addressing the provision of SRH education to boys and girls in schools, recommendations have qualified the need that such information be age-appropriate.[109] It is understandable how most States parties would resist SRH education, which imparts knowledge that would be considered inappropriate for children of a certain age. In addition, States parties have been required to remove barriers on access to culturally and gender-sensitive SRH information and education.[110] In order to facilitate the acceptability of such information and its effective transmission, treaty bodies have in certain instances required that States parties implement youth peer programmes targeting adolescent boys and girls.[111]

---

[102] COBs Liechtenstein, CEDAW/C/LIE/CO/4 (CEDAW, 2011); COBs Ecuador, CRC/C/ECU/CO/4, (CRC, 2010); COBs Mozambique CEDAW/C/MOZ/CO/2 (CEDAW, 2007).

[103] COBs Tajikistan, CRC/C/TJK/CO/2, (CRC, 2010).

[104] COBs Serbia, E/C.12/UNK/CO/1 (CESCR, 2008); COBs Maldives, CRC/C/MDV/CO/3 (CRC, 2007).

[105] COBs Philippines, CRC/C/OPSC/PHL/CO/1, paras. 22(e) (CRC, 2013); COBs Namibia CRC/C/NAM/CO/2-3, para. 58(c), (CRC, 2012).

[106] COBs Liechtenstein, CEDAW/C/LIE/CO/4 (CEDAW, 2011); COBs Costa Rica, CRC/C/CRI/CO/4, para. 72(d), (CRC, 2011).

[107] COBs Guinea-Bissau, CEDAW/C/GNB/CO/6 (CEDAW, 2009), COBs Nicaragua, E/C.12/NIC/CO/4 (CESCR, 2009); COBs United States of America CERD/C/CO/6 (CERD, 2008).

[108] COBs United States of America CERD/C/CO/6 (CERD, 2008).

[109] COBs Mauritius, CEDAW/C/MUS/CO/6-7, para. 33 (e), (CEDAW, 2011); COBs Maldives, CEDAW/C/MDV/CO/3 (CEDAW, 2007).

[110] COBs Ecuador, CRC/C/ECU/CO/4, (CRC, 2010).

[111] COBs Zimbabwe, CEDAW/C/ZWE/CO/5-6, para. 34(g) (CEDAW, 2011).

4.2.4 Quality

The quality of SRH information has largely been raised in the context of the provision of formal education.[112] However, it has also been raised in the context of the provision of sex education programmes generally.[113] Issues of concern relate to the sufficiency in the coverage of the subject matter and the actual contents of sexual and reproductive education curricula.[114] For instance, there has been a consistent demand that the contents of the school curricula on SRH be based on scientific evidence.[115]

Concerns have also been raised where SRH education is under-developed[116] and where, despite its availability as a mandatory course, there seems to be a lack of its systematic and accurate provision.[117] In recommending that States parties address such situations, treaty bodies have spelt out the need for States parties to include "systematic, comprehensive and scientific based education on SRH . . . in regular school curricula" and ensure that adequate resources are allocated to such education.[118] Furthermore, in order to ensure quality of SRH education, treaty bodies often recommend that that such education be provided by properly trained teachers.[119] In other instances, States parties have been required to update contents of the school curricula on SRH.[120] This is because the quality of sexual and reproductive education has a direct impact on both the health women and the execution of programmes aimed at improving sexual behaviour. In this regard, where sex education programmes do not give sufficient attention to the prevention of early pregnancies and the control of STIs, it has been recommended that sex education be widely promoted and targeted to address these specific issues.[121]

---

[112] COBs Mexico, CEDAW/C/MEX/CO/CO/7-8, paras. 26–30 (CEDAW, 2012); COBs Algeria, CRC/C/DZA/CO/3-4, para. 59 (CRC, 2012); COBs Republic of Korea, E/C.12/KOR/CO/3 (CESCR, 2009).

[113] COBs Mexico, CEDAW/C/MEX/CO/CO/7-8, para. 30 (CEDAW, 2012), COBs Kenya, CEDAW/C/KEN/CO/6, para. 37, (CEDAW, 2007).

[114] COBs Kenya, Ibid.; COBs Mexico, CEDAW/C/MEX/CO/CO/7-8, para. 26 (CEDAW, 2012).

[115] COBs Mexico, CEDAW/C/MEX/CO/CO/7-8, para. 27 (CEDAW, 2012); COBs Costa Rica, CRC/C/CRI/CO/4, para. 64(f), (CRC, 2011).

[116] COBs Turkey, CRC/C/TUR/CO/2-3, para. 54, (CRC, 2012); COBs Algeria, CRC/C/DZA/CO/3-4, para. 59 (CRC, 2012).

[117] COBs Republic of Korea, CRC/C/KOR/CO/3-4, para. 58 & 59, (CRC, 2012); COBs Republic of Korea, E/C.12/KOR/CO/3, para. 31 (CESCR, 2009).

[118] COBs Costa Rica, CRC/C/CRI/CO/4, para. 64(f), (CRC, 2011).

[119] COBs Hungary, CEDAW/C/HUN/CO/7-8, para. 33(c), (CEDAW, 2013).

[120] COBs Mexico, CEDAW/C/MEX/CO/CO/7-8, para. 26 (CEDAW, 2012).

[121] COBs Kenya, CEDAW/C/KEN/CO/6, paras. 37-38, (CEDAW, 2007).

4.3 Treatment of Women and Children

4.3.1 Domestic Violence and Femicide

Using the relevant treaty provisions, treaty bodies call on States parties to protect women of all ages against violence in the family context. CEDAW states that all forms of violence against women are a form of discrimination and can even constitute acts of torture, cruel, inhuman or degrading treatment or punishment. It affirms that family violence is "one of the most insidious forms of violence against women [. . .] prevalent in all societies".[122] Family, or domestic violence, is violence of all kinds perpetrated on women of all ages within family relationships. It is a violation of the rights and fundamental freedoms of women with grave social costs for society as a whole. Not only does domestic violence violate women's physical integrity and dignity, it also impacts negatively on their ability to exercise all their rights on the basis of equality with men. The varying forms of violence perpetuated against women of all ages within family relationships are fostered by patriarchal and traditional attitudes, *de facto* inequality between men and women in the public and private spheres,[123] and impunity. With regard to violence against children in the family, CRC has made it clear that States parties have the obligation to protect children from all forms of physical or mental violence, while in the care of their parents or any other person charged with the care of a child.[124]

An analysis of concluding observations on violence perpetrated against women and children in their homes/families reveals that recommendations can be grouped under similar categories. Firstly, recommendations regarding the national legal framework, i.e., those States parties that have legislation criminalizing domestic violence, including marital rape and sexual abuse, and protecting children from violence in their homes/families, and those that still do not.[125] In States parties with legislation, the main concern has been the lack of implementation,[126] with treaty bodies urging that relevant laws and penal code provisions relating to domestic violence be strictly enforced and that offenders be penalized.[127]

In those States parties where domestic violence, including marital rape and sexual abuse, is still not criminalized the position of the treaty bodies has been to encourage its specific inclusion in domestic legislation, and a specific

[122] CEDAW General recommendation No. 19 (1992) on violence against women, para. 23.

[123] COBs Cambodia, E/C.12/KHM/CO/1 para. 20 (CESCR 2009).

[124] CRC, The right of the child to protection from corporal punishment and other cruel or degrading forms of punishment (arts. 19; 28, para. 2; and 37, inter alia) CRC/C/GC/8, para. 18 (CRC, 2007).

[125] COBs Uruguay CCPR/C/URY/CO/5, para. 3(c) (HRC 2013).

[126] COBs Mauritania CEDAW/C/MRT/CO/1, para. 29 (CEDAW, 2007); COBs Mauritania CCPR/C/MRT/CO/1, para. 10 (HRC, 2013); COBs Angola, para. 4, CEDAW/C/AGO/CO/6 (CEDAW, 2013); COBs China, CEDAW/C/CHN/CO/6, para. 21 (CEDAW, 2006).

[127] COBs Cambodia, E/C.12/KHM/CO/1 para. 20 (CESCR 2009).

criminalization.[128] In States parties where criminal proceedings against rapists are terminated if they marry their victims, the treaty bodies have urged for amendments to such legislation.[129] In some cases, a review by one treaty body of one State party may reveal a lack of legislation, and the future review of the same State party by another treaty body reveals that although adoption of specific legislation has taken place, in practice, domestic violence persists.[130] Therefore, as part of the implementation of legislation, treaty bodies call for the development and carrying out of national strategies to combat gender-based violence.[131] They also urge States parties to criminalise all forms of physical and mental violence, including corporal punishment and the sexual abuse of children.[132] While many States parties have adopted specific legislation to protect children and to criminalize ill-treatment, abuse, or cruelty, CRC in particular has noted that such laws do not effectively protect children from all corporal punishment and other cruel or degrading forms of punishment, in the family [. . .].[133] CRC has called for the removal of provisions that allow some degree of violence against children in their homes/families.[134] CAT has noted with concern that corporal punishment of children is not prohibited by law in some States parties and appears to be considered a suitable and effective method of education.[135]

A second vital component relates to access to justice and to the specific and more vulnerable situation of women and children victims of domestic violence belonging

---

[128] COBs Paraguay, CCPR/C/PRY/CO/3, para. 12 (HRC 2013), COBs Japan E/C.12/JPN/CO/3, para. 23 (CESCR 2013); COBs Iran, E/C.12/IRN/CO/2, para. 17 (CESCR, 2013), COBs Kuwait, E/C.12/KWT/CO/2, para. 12 (CESCR 2013), COBs Peru CCPR/C/PER/CO/5, para. 10 (HRC 2013); COBs Egyt E/C.12/EGY/CO/2-4, para. 15 (CESCR, 2013), COBs Belarus E/C.12/BLR/CO/4-6, para. 19, (CESCR, 2013), COBs Djibouti, CCPR/C/DJI/CO/1, para. 10, (HRC 2013), COBs Republic of the Congo CEDAW/C/COD/CO/6-7, para. 22 (CEDAW, 2013), COBs Mauritania E/C.12/MRT/CO/1 para. 21, (CESCR 2012), COBs Chile, paras. 18–19 CEDAW/C/CHL/CO/5-6 (CEDAW 2012), COBs Iran CCPR/C/IRN/CO/3, para. 11 (HRC, 2012); COBs Morocco CAT/C/MAR/CO/4, para. 23 (CAT, 2011); COBs Paraguay, CAT/C/PRY/CO/4-6, para. 21 (CAT, 2011); COBs Angola E/C.12/AGO/CO/3, par. 24 (CESCR, 2009); COBs Morocco E/C.12/MAR/CO/3, para. 23 (CESCR, 2006), COBs Colombia CRC/C/COL/CO/3, para. 10 (CRC, 2006).

[129] COBs Morocco CAT/C/MAR/CO/4, para. 23 (CAT, 2011), COBs Nepal CEDAW/C/NPL/CO/4-5, para. 20 (CEDAW 2011) COBs Morocco CEDAW/C/MAR/CO/4, para. 20 (CEDAW, 2008).

[130] COBs Angola, CCPR/C/AGO/CO/1(2013), para. 10 (HRC 2013).

[131] COBs Rwanda CRC/C/RWA/CO/3-4 para. 34 (CRC 2013); CAT/C/RWA/CO/1, para. 16 (CAT, 2012) CEDAW/C/RWA/CO/6, para. 25 (CEDAW, 2009), COBs Sri Lanka CRC/C/LKA/CO/3-4, para 49 (CRC 2010); COBs Japan CAT/C/JPN/CO/2, para. 20 (CAT 2013); COBs Niue CRC/C/NIU/CO/1, para. 36 (CRC 2013) COBs Bolivia, CEDAW/C/BOL/CO/4, para. 24 (CEDAW, 2008), and COBs Morocco CEDAW/C/MAR/CO/4, para. 20 (CEDAW, 2008). COBs Belize CCPR/C/BLZ/CO/1, para. 15 (HRC 2013) CEDAW/C/BLZ/CO/4 para. 19 (CEDAW, 2007).

[132] COBs Morocco, CRC/C/15/Add.211, para. 43 (CRC, 2003).

[133] CRC, The right of the child to protection from corporal punishment and other cruel or degrading forms of punishment (arts. 19; 28, para. 2; and 37, inter alia) CRC/C/GC/8, para. 31 (CRC, 2007).

[134] Ibid.

[135] COBs Mauritania CAT/C/MRT/CO/1, para. 25 (CAT 2013).

to indigenous groups and/or who live in rural areas.[136] This includes the need to ensure the effective investigation of all acts of domestic violence, prosecution and sanctioning of perpetrators. Treaty bodies have taken a position with regard to mediation, conciliation and settlements for cases of domestic violence. They urge States parties to encourage women to opt for legal action, whenever it is justified, given the negative effects that mediation, conciliation and settlements may have on women's access to justice and available remedies.[137] The establishment of effective and independent monitoring and complaints mechanism for victims of domestic violence is seen as critical. For instance, CAT has urged States parties that all allegations of domestic violence, including sexual violence and violence against children, be registered by the police, that all allegations of violence are promptly, impartially and effectively investigated, and that perpetrators be prosecuted and punished.[138] These systems can only carry out their work effectively if they have the proper human resources. It is, therefore, also imperative that appropriate training be given to professionals dealing with these cases. CRC recommends that cases of domestic violence and ill-treatment and abuse of children, including sexual abuse within the family, be properly investigated within a child-friendly judicial procedure and sanctions applied to perpetrators, with due regard given to protecting the right to privacy of the child.[139] An additional component of handling cases on domestic violence and ill-treatment of children is the need to strengthen support for victims/survivors and ensure their access to adequate services for recovery, counselling and other forms of rehabilitation. It also refers to ensuring means of redress, and access to immediate protection for victims of domestic violence.

Thirdly, recommendations focus on the need to undertake training and awareness-raising campaigns including to law-enforcement officials and judges, parents, teachers, care workers, health professionals, men, and children and women themselves. These public information and education campaigns must not only address the deep rooted gender stereotypes and beliefs regarding women, but also the traditional values and social attitudes which permit the use of violence against children as a permissible method of discipline. They must also address the prevention and identification of domestic violence and promote knowledge on existing and new legislation in this regard.[140] These campaigns and programmes call for the involvement of the general public as well as specific sectors working with and for children. In this regard, CAT has also recommended that States parties undertake

---

[136] COBs Peru E/C.12/PER/CO/2-4 para. 14 (CESCR, 2012)

[137] COBs Angola, CEDAW/C/AGO/CO/6, para. 4, (CEDAW, 2013); COBs Colombia, CEDAW/C/COL/CO/6, para. 18 (CEDAW 2007), COBs Republic of Korea CAT/C/KOR/CO/2 para. 17 (CAT, 2006).

[138] COBs Estonia CAT/C/EST/CO/5 (2013) para. 12 (CAT 2013).

[139] COBs South Africa CRC/C/15/ADD.122 para. 27 (CRC, 2000).

[140] COBs Russian Federation E/C.12/RUS/CO/5 para. 22 (CESCR 2011), COBs Belarus CEDAW/C/BLR/CO/7 para. 20 (CEDAW 2011).

programmes involving children, families, communities and religious leaders to educate and sensitize the general public about the harmful effects of corporal punishment on the physical and psychological development of children.[141]

A fourth component often reflected in recommendations is the need to carry out studies to determine the causes, the prevalence extent, nature, and consequences of domestic violence.[142] In cases where studies have already been undertaken, treaty bodies urge the use of findings of such studies to review and improve existing plans and programmes in order to combat violence against women and children.[143] Finally, attention has also focused on the importance of statistics, disaggregated data, and the need to record trends and the incidence of various forms of domestic violence as a basis for understanding and combating this phenomenon.[144]

Femicide

CEDAW and CRC have paid particular attention to gender-related killings, also known as femicide, feminicide, and so-called honour killings as "the extreme manifestation of existing forms of violence against women" and girls.[145] Femicide has been raised in treaty body jurisprudence in those States parties, particularly in South Asia, where societies have a traditional preference for boys.[146] The various treaty bodies have denounced these attitudes insofar as they devalue women and violate their rights.[147]

Although States parties have been recognised for the adoption of legislative measures to regulate sex-selection and prohibit sex-selective abortions, concerns have been raised with regard to persisting illegal abortions, female infanticide and the non-registration and abandonment of female children at birth.[148] Recommendations call for measures to strengthen the enforcement and monitoring of protective legislation that prohibits sex-selective abortion. Treaty bodies have also recommended that sanctions be imposed in order to accelerate ending the practice of sex-selective abortions. Treaty bodies have also advocated for mandatory

---

141 Ibid.

142 COBs El Salvador CMW/C/SLV/CO/1 para. 47 (CMW, 2009).

143 COBs South Africa CEDAW/C/ZAF/CO/4, para 25 (CEDAW 2011) and CAT/C/ZAF/CO/, para. 7 (CAT, 2006).

144 COBs Republic of Korea CEDAW/C/KOR/CO/7 para. 21 (CEDAW, 2011), COBs Nepal CEDAW/C/NPL/CO/4-5 para. 20 (CEDAW, 2011), COBs Malta CEDAW/C/MLT/CO/4 para. 23 (CEDAW, 2010), COBs China CAT/C/HKG/CO/4 para. 13 (CAT, 2009), COBs Brazil CEDAW/C/BRA/CO/6 para. 22 (CEDAW 2007), COBs Colombia CEDAW/C/COL/CO/6, para. 19 (CEDAW, 2007).

145 Human Rights Council Report of the Special Rapporteur on violence against women, its causes and consequences A/HRC/20/16, para. 15.

146 COBs China, CEDAW/C/CHN/CO/6 para. 17 (CEDAW 2006).

147 Ibid.

148 Ibid, para. 31, and COBs India, CRC/C/15/Add.228, paras. 33–34 (CRC 2004).

gender-sensitive training for family planning officials. Besides gender-sensitive training for government officials, treaty bodies have also expressed the need to "vigorously address the causes of son-preference", leaving it to States parties to decided how to deal with it. Further recommendations have called for States parties to develop comprehensive public education campaigns for society in general, and with the involvement of parents and families, communities and community leaders, and law enforcement officials, among others to prevent and combat gender discrimination and traditional practices and attitudes discriminating against girls. It has also focused on birth registration and on increasing efforts to ensure that all children, in particular girls in rural areas are registered. Moreover, CEDAW has expressed its concern that the sex ratio of 0–6 year old girls to boys has worsened and that this "adverse sex ratio, [...] may contribute to the increase in trafficking in women and girls."[149]

Besides addressing the traditional preference of boys over girls in some societies and the consequent female infanticide, treaty bodies have also expressed concern regarding the increase in the rate of killings of women by their partners or ex-partners, especially in Latin America.[150] This attention reflects the dynamism within the treaty bodies in order to appropriately reflect the evolving societies they are reviewing and their efforts to continue advancing global justice standards.

4.3.2 Female Genital Mutilation

Female genital mutilation (FGM), which is also known as female genital cutting, entails the partial or total removal of the external female genitalia for non-medical reasons.[151] This practice occurs in all parts of the world.[152] However, it is prevalent in the western, eastern and north-eastern regions of Africa, some countries in Asia and the Middle East.[153] FGM continues to affect a huge number of women and girls, some of whom have been subjected to its most extreme form known as infibulation.[154] FGM not only violates the physical integrity of women and girls

---

[149] Ibid.

[150] COBs Bolivia CAT/C/BOL/CO/2 para. 15 (CAT 2013), COBs Russian Federation CAT/C/RUS/CO/5 para. 13 (CAT 2012), COBs Dominican Republic CEDAW/C/DOM/CO/6-7 para. 24 (CEDAW, 2013), COBs Mexico CEDAW/C/MEX/CO/7-8 para. 17 (CEDAW 2012); COBs Chile CEDAW/C/CHL/CO/5-6 para. 20 (CEDAW 2012), COBs Italy CEDAW/C/ITA/CO/6 2011 para. 26 (CEDAW 2011), COBs Argentina, CRC 2010 CRC/C/ARG/CO/3-4, para. 54 (CRC 2010), COBs Panama CEDAW/C/PAN/CO/7 para. 12 (CEDAW 2010), COBs Honduras, CAT/C/HND/CO/1 para 21 (CAT 2009), COBs Guatemala CEDAW/C/GUA/CO/7 para. 21 (CEDAW 2009), COBs El Salvador CAT 2009 CAT/C/SLV/CO/2 para. 10 (CAT 2009).

[151] UN (2014), Fact Sheet No. 23.

[152] Ibid.

[153] Ibid.

[154] COBs Djobouti, CAT/C/DJI/CO/1, para. 21, (CAT, 2011); COBs Chad, CCPR/CTCD/CO/1, (HRC, 2009).

but is also responsible for maternal mortality and obstetric complications such as extended bleeding and vesico-vaginal fistula.[155]

Cultural and religious ideologies coupled with deep-rooted stereotypical roles of men and women in society often provide justifications for FGM and they continue to fuel its perpetration.[156] For instance, in some countries local perceptions abound that FGM is useful as it promotes marriage prospects for girls.[157] In such countries where patriarchal ideologies and deeply rooted stereotypes are rife, the need for parents to, inter alia, secure marriage prospects for their children continue to fuel the commission of FGM.

Treaty bodies have used various provisions under their respective treaties to demand States parties to abolish this practice. The HRC and CAT treat FGM as falling under other forms of cruel and degrading treatment.[158] This consideration of FGM under anti-torture provisions elevates the gravity of this scourge. CEDAW itself has innovatively unleashed an equality paradigm which posits that FGM constitutes gender based discrimination because this violence is specifically targeted at women.[159] This position has developed into a fervent fulcrum for advancing the cause for the abolition of discriminatory laws and practices which perpetuate gender-based forms of violence such as FGM. Now the jurisprudential output of treaty bodies firmly advocates for the eradication of FGM through the use of a multi-pronged approach that involves, inter alia, achieving attitudinal changes in society[160] and abolishing FGM through the enactment of anti-FGM laws.[161] Treaty bodies recognise that since FGM is deeply rooted in cultural and religious beliefs, its eradication requires a spirited fight by States parties to challenge these customs within their jurisdictions notwithstanding the cultural justifications underpinning it. Thus, the HRC expressed regrets at a State party's inertia to eradicate the

---

155 COBs Djibouti, CEDAW/C/DJI/CO/1-3, paras. 18 and 30(a), (CEDAW, 2011); COBs Sierra Leone, CEDAW/C/SLE/CO/5 (CEDAW, 2007); CEDAW, General Recommendation No. 19, Violence against women (1992), paras. 12(b) and 18.

156 COBs Angola, CEDAW/C/AGO/CO/6, para. 17, (CEDAW, 2013); COBs United Republic of Tanzania, E/C.12/TZA/CO/1-3, para. 4 (CESCR, 2012); COBs Côte d'Ivoire, CEDAW/C/CIV/CO/1-3, para. 31(d) (CEDAW, 2011); COBs Djibouti, CEDAW/C/DJI/CO/1-3, paras. 16, (CEDAW, 2011); COBs Kenya, CEDAW/C/KEN/CO/7 (CEDAW, 2011); COBs Guinea, CEDAW/C/GIN/CO/6 (CEDAW, 2007); COBs Togo, CEDAW/C/TGO/CO/5 (CEDAW, 2006).

157 COBs Kenya, E/C.12/KEN/CO/1, (CESCR, 2008).

158 COBs Togo, CCPR/C/TGO/CO/4 (HRC, 2011); COBs CAT/C/DJI/CO/1, (CAT, 2011).

159 CEDAW, General Recommendation No. 19, Violence against women (1992), para. 4; Chinkin in Freeman et al. (2012), p. 450.

160 COBs Angola, CEDAW/C/AGO/CO/6, para. 17, (CEDAW, 2013); COBs Nigeria, CRC/C/NGA/CO/3-4 (CRC, 2010).

161 COBs Mauritania, CAT/C/MRT/CO/1, para 24, (CAT, 2013); COBs Angola, CEDAW/C/AGO/CO/6, para. 18(b), (CEDAW, 2013); COBs Cameroon, E/C.12/CMR/CO/2-3, para 20, (CESCR, 2012); COBs Ireland, CERD/C/IRL/CO/3-4 (CERD, 2011); COBs Sudan, CRC/SDN/CO/3-4 (CRC, 2010).

phenomenon.[162] CESCR expressed concern when a State party sought to invoke traditional values to justify this practice.[163]

Treaty bodies exhibit a strong preference towards the need to prevent the occurrence of FGM through the adoption of laws that criminalise it.[164] The inclination towards criminalisation is understandable considering that FGM constitutes violence which is injurious and violates the physical integrity of women and girls.[165] As such, treaty bodies have raised concerns in instances where States parties have not adopted laws which criminalise FGM and at the failure to effectively enforce the law where such law exists. In exceptional cases, treaty bodies have clearly condemned the 'medicalization' of FGM, where States parties have legalised FGM by allowing medical practitioners to conduct FGM under the pretext of protecting victims from unprofessional practitioners.[166] Furthermore, treaty bodies have expressed their abhorrence towards the permissibility of FGM where a State party issues limited permits to medical practitioners to perform this practice.[167]

In the pursuit of the deterrence approach, treaty bodies have also expressed concern about the failure of States parties to prosecute perpetrators, secure convictions and to impose appropriate deterrent sanctions.[168] It has, therefore, become imperative that States parties conduct training for law enforcement personnel and judges.[169] The objective is to enhance their understanding of the gravity and the adverse effects of the phenomenon to be able to enforce the law and mete out appropriate sanctions.[170] In addition, treaty bodies have also focused on the requirement that States parties create conditions or establish mechanisms which facilitate reporting of these offences with a view to curbing impunity.[171] This is

[162] COBs Yemen, CCPR/C/YEM/CO/5, para. 9, (HRC, 2012).

[163] COBs United Republic of Tanzania, E/C.12/TZA/CO/1-3, para. 4 (CESCR, 2012).

[164] COBs Mauritania, CAT/C/MRT/CO/1, para. 24, (CAT, 2013); COBs Liberia, CRC/C/LBR/CO/2-4 (CRC, 2012); COBs Togo, CEDAW/C/TGO/6-7, para. 23(a), (CEDAW, 2012); COBs Uganda, CCPR/CO/80/UGA, (HRC, 2004); COBs Mali, CCPR/CO/77/MLI, (HRC, 2003).

[165] COBs Chad, E/C.12/TCD/CO/3, (CESCR, 2009); COBs Liberia, CEDAW/C/LBR/CO/6 (CEDAW, 2009); COBs Ethiopia, CERD/C/ETH/CO/7-16 (CERD, 2009).

[166] COBs Indonesia, CCPR/C/IDN/CO/1, para 12, (HRC, 2013); COBs Egypt, CEDAW/C/EGY/CO/7, (CEDAW, 2010).

[167] COBs Liberia, CEDAW/C/LBR/CO/6 (CEDAW, 2009).

[168] COBs United Kingdom of Great Britain and Northern Ireland, CEDAW/C/GBR/CO/7, paras. 36 and 37, (CEDAW, 2013); COBs Ethiopia, CEDAW/C/ETH/CO/6-7, para. 20, (CEDAW, 2011); COBs Burkina Faso, CRC/C/BFA/CO3-4 (CRC, 2010); COBs Chad, E/C.12/TCD/CO/3, (CESCR, 2009); COBs Djibouti, CRC/C/DJI/CO/, (CRC, 2008).

[169] Cobs Togo, CAT/C/TGO/CO/2, para. 15(d), (CAT, 2012); COBs Ethiopia, CEDAW/C/ETH/CO/6-7, para. 21(c), (CEDAW, 2011); COBs Ghana, CAT/C/GHA/CO/1, para. 23(c), (CAT, 2011); COBs Benin, E/C.12/BEN/CO/2, (CESCR, 2008).

[170] Cobs Togo, CAT/C/TGO/CO/2, para. 15(d), (CAT, 2012); COBs Ethiopia, CEDAW/C/ETH/CO/6-7, para. 21(c), (CEDAW, 2011); COBs Ghana, CAT/C/GHA/CO/1, para. 23(c), (CAT, 2011); COBs Benin, E/C.12/BEN/CO/2, (CESCR, 2008).

[171] COBs Djibouti, CEDAW/C/DJI/CO/1-3, para. 6(b), (CEDAW, 2011); COBs Ghana, CAT/C/GHA/CO/1, para. 23(b), (CAT, 20011); COBs Chad, CRC/C/TCD/CO/2, (CRC, 2009).

because the culture of silence and the prevalence of reprisals often forestall the effective combat of FGM.

Treaty bodies have also welcomed the introduction of preventive measures which afford more protection to women and girls against FGM such as the introduction of laws that criminalise the failure to report FGM[172] and providing for the extraterritorial prosecution of FGM.[173] However, treaty bodies have been vigilant in ensuring that such measures affording more protection are not inimical to due process and other legal safeguards. Thus, a State party, which had duly enacted a law prohibiting FGM, was condemned for conferring powers on 'chiefs and children's officers' to enter premises without a warrant.[174]

In response to the need to modify gender stereotypes and deep-rooted cultural attitudes, which contribute to the practice of FGM, treaty bodies have relentlessly urged States parties to undertake awareness-raising campaigns and public education programmes to expose the adverse effects of FGM.[175] Interestingly, some treaty bodies have set specific target dates and required the setting of clear timeframes by States parties to eradicate FGM through awareness raising initiatives.[176] Although the focus of these messages has been the general public at large, treaty bodies also recognise the need to ensure that such programmes target traditional and religious leaders including FGM practitioners.[177] Since most practitioners earn a living out of this practice, treaty bodies recommend that States parties retrain them so that they can find alternative sources of income.[178]

Treaty body recommendations also reveal a strong focus on women and girls as victims of FGM requiring redress and recovery.[179] Treaty bodies have placed emphasis on the need for States parties to provide such women and girls with the requisite legal, medical, psychological and rehabilitative services as well as adequate compensation.[180] The emphasis on access to justice and the protection of

---

[172] COBs Djibouti, CEDAW/C/DJI/CO/1-3, para. 6(b), (CEDAW, 2011).

[173] COBs Spain, CRC/C/ESP/CO/3-4, (CRC, 2010).

[174] COBs Kenya, CAT/C/KEN/CO/2, para. 26, (CAT, 2013).

[175] COBs Djibouti, CCPR/C/DJI/CO/1, para. 8 (HRC, 2013); COBs Côte d'Ivoire, CEDAW/C/CIV/CO/1-3, para. 27(b) & 31 (d), (CEDAW, 2011); COBs Belgium, CRC/C/BEL/CO/3-4 (CRC, 2010); COBs Sweden, CCPR/C/SWE/CO/6, (HRC, 2009).

[176] COBs Sudan, A/HRC/24/31, para. 81 (HRC, 2013); COBs Togo, CEDAW/C/TGO/CO/6-7, para. 21(c), (CEDAW, 2012).

[177] COBs Djibouti, E/C.12/DJI/CO/1-2, para. 13(c), (CESCR, 2013); COBs Guinea, CRC/C/GIN/CO/2-4, para. 44(c), (CRC, 2013); COBs Indonesia, CEDAW/C/IDN/CO/6-7, para. 22(b) & (c), (CEDAW, 2012); COBs Mauritania, CRC/C/MRT/CO/2, (CRC, 2010); COBs Gambia, CCOR/CO/75/GMB/ (HRC, 2004).

[178] CRC/C/MRT/CO/2, (CRC, 2009); COBs United Republic of Tanzania, CEDAW/C/TZA/CO/6 (CEDAW, 2009).

[179] COBs Ethiopia, CEDAW/C/ETH/CO/6-7, para. 21(e), (CEDAW, 2011); COBs Kenya, CCPR/CO/84/YEM, (HRC, 2005).

[180] CAT Ghana, CAT/C/GHA/CO/1, para. 23(b), (CAT, 2011); COBs Indonesia, CEDAW/C/IDN/CO/5 (CEDAW, 2007); COBs Mauritania, CEDAW/C/MRT/CO/1 (CEDAW, 2007).

victims is an epitome of treaty bodies' pursuit of corrective justice even in areas where local perceptions regarding the assailed conduct might seem to be in conflict with global perceptions of justice that flow from international human rights law.

4.3.3 Polygamy

Polygamy, which is harmful to the equal enjoyment of human rights by women, remains deeply rooted in traditional and religious values.[181] In pluralistic legal systems, where customary law forms part of the corpus of applicable domestic law, States parties have had to grapple with such entrenched harmful traditional practices.[182] As such, efforts to ban polygamy have often been met with local resistance particularly from traditional and other leaders who perceive the practice as promoting traditionalism.

Although the practice of polygamy undermines the principle of the universality of human rights, treaty bodies remain steadfast in their position that States parties should not invoke local cultural and religious practices to justify the perpetuation of practices which are an affront to human rights.[183] Treaty bodies have firmly argued that polygamy is a form of discrimination[184]; it violates the dignity of women and hampers their enjoyment of human rights, particularly economic, social and cultural rights.[185] While CRC has expressed concern about the debilitating effects that polygamy has on children generally,[186] it has time and again requested State parities to conduct studies to establish the adverse impacts that polygamy has on the upbringing of children.[187]

Treaty bodies recognise that polygamy is deeply rooted in custom and religion and that its continuation is partly propelled by prevalent stereotypes, which are based on the perceptions of the inferiority and superiority of sexes.[188] Unfortunately, patriarchal societies have often provided the milieu for harmful practices

---

[181] CEDAW, General Recommendation No. 21, Equality in marriage and family relations (1994), para. 14; HR Committee, General comment No. 28, The equality of rights between men and women (2000), para. 24; COBs Philippines, CCPR/C/PHL/CO/4, para. 11 (HRC, 2012); COBs Ghana, CEDAW/C/GHA/CO/5 (CEDAW, 2006).

[182] COBs South Africa, CEDAW/C/ZAF/CO/4, (CEDAW, 2011), COBs Malawi, CEDAW/C/MWI/CO/6 (CEDAW, 2010).

[183] COBs United Republic of Tanzania, E/C.12/TZA/CO/1-3, para. 4 (CESCR, 2012).

[184] COBs Ethiopia, CCPR/C/ETH/CO/1, para. 9 (HRC, 2011).

[185] COBs Lesotho, CEDAW/C/LEO/CO/1-4, para. 20 (CEDAW, 2011); COBs Oman, CEDAW/C/OMN/CO/1, para. 44 (CEDAW, 2011); COBs Botswana, CCPR/C/BWA/CO/1 (HRC, 2008).

[186] COBs Mauritania, CRC/C/MRT/CO/2, para. 44, (CRC, 2009).

[187] COBs Djibouti, CRC/C/DJI/CO/2 (CRC, 2008); COBs Yemen, CRC/C/15/Add.267 (CRC, 2005).

[188] COBs Togo, CEDAW/C/TGO/CO/6-7, paras. 20 & 21 (CEDAW, 2012); COBs Indonesia, CEDAW/C/IDN/CO/6-7, para. 23 (CEDAW, 2012); COBs Kenya, CEDAW/C/KEN/CO/7 (CEDAW, 2011); COBs Indonesia, CEDAW/C/IDN/CO/4 (CEDAW, 2007).

such as polygamy to continue to flourish.[189] In order to address this harmful practice, treaty bodies have over the years embarked on a transformative-equality agenda, which seeks to modify and eliminate this harmful practice and equally the stereotypical attitudes and prejudices which perpetuate it.[190] Treaty bodies understand that the prevalence and entrenchment of this harmful practice varies from one country to the other. They also recognise that eradicating deep rooted stereotypes associated with cultural and religious practices might require gradual efforts on the part of States parties.[191] However, treaty bodies require that such efforts be pursued vigorously.[192] Thus treaty bodies have raised concern about delays in amending legislation[193]; in repealing polygamy laws[194] and the absence of court cases on polygamy in countries where it is prevalent.[195]

Concluding observations reveal that States parties affected by polygamy can be grouped under three main categories. Firstly, States parties where polygamy is illegal (*de jure*) but it is still practiced (*de facto*).[196] Secondly, States parties where polygamy is legal and its practice remains widespread.[197] Thirdly, States parties where polygamy is permissible under limited circumstances often requiring a court order.[198] These categories have elicited different recommendations from treaty bodies. However, treaty bodies have taken a holistic approach by employing a wide array of recommendations considering that the modification and eventual eradication of practices rooted in culture and religion is a long term endeavour. For instance, CEDAW has acknowledged efforts by States parties which have adjusted their laws to require consent of the wife before a man takes in another wife.[199] However, the requirement of consent, albeit a significant step in addressing

[189] COBs Mauritania, CEDAW/C/MRT/CO/1 (CEDAW, 2007).

[190] COBs Guinea, CRC/C/GIN/CO/2-4, para. 55 (CRC, 2013); COBs Yemen, CCPR/C/YEM/CO/5, para. 10 (HRC, 2012); COBs Togo, CRC/C/TGO/CO/3-4, para. 46 (CRC, 2011); COBs Chad, CEDAW/C/TCD/CO/1-4, para. 20 (CEDAW, 2011); COBs Ethiopia, CCPR/C/ETH/CO/1, para. 9 (HRC, 2011).

[191] COBs Libya, CEDAW/C/LBY/CO/5 (CEDAW, 2009). See also Holtmaat in Freeman et al 2012, p. 165.

[192] COBs Uganda, CEDAW/C/UGA/CO/CO/7 (CEDAW, 2010); COBs United Republic of Tanzania, CEDAW/C/TZA/CO/6 (CEDAW, 2009); COBs Kenya, CEDAW/C/KEN/CO/6, (CEDAW, 2007).

[193] COBs Sri Lanka, CEDAW/C/LKA/CO/7, para. 45(a) (CEDAW, 2011).

[194] COBs Indonesia, CEDAW/C/IDN/CO/6-7, para. 47(b) (CEDAW, 2012).

[195] COBs Tajikistan, CEDAW/C/TJK/CO/3 (CEDAW, 2007).

[196] COBs Uzbekistan, CCPR/C/UZB/CO/3 (HRC, 2010); COBs Turkmenistan, CEDAW/C/TKM/CO/2 (CEDAW, 2006).

[197] COBs Philippines, CCPR/C/PHL/CO/4, para. 11 (HRC, 2012); COBs Comoros, CEDAW/C/COM/CO/1-4, paras. 21 & 39 (CEDAW, 2012); COBs Jordan, CEDAW/C/JOR/CO/5, para. 49 (CEDAW, 2012); COBs Egypt, CRC/C/EGY/CO/3-4, para. 51(b), (CRC, 2011).

[198] COBs Pakistan, CEDAW/C/PAK/CO/ para. 37 (CEDAW, 2013); COBs Algeria, CEDAW/C/DZA/CO/3-4, para. 46(b) (CEDAW, 2012); COBs Morocco, CEDAW/C/MAR/CO/4 (CEDAW, 2008); COBs Morocco, CCPR/CO/82/MAR (HRC, 2004).

[199] COBs Libya, CEDAW/C/LBY/CO/5 (CEDAW, 2009).

this harmful practice, States parties should still vigorously undertake efforts to ensure the eradication of polygamy.[200] Treaty bodies have remained resolute in their position even in instances where a State party claims to be incapable of implementing the law prohibiting polygamy.[201]

Treaty bodies acknowledge the power of culture in influencing changes in society which are respectful of women's rights.[202] They have, therefore, recommended that States parties use culture itself as a vehicle to modify stereotypes and eliminate harmful practices.[203] Treaty bodies have also recommended States parties do a number of things in their efforts to protect the dignity of women against the harmful practice of polygamy. Firstly, in those countries where polygamy is legal and permissible under limited circumstances but still prevalent, States parties are required to repeal laws permitting polygamy and adopt laws which prohibit polygamy.[204] Secondly, in countries where polygamy is illegal but remains widespread, treaty bodies have required States parties to ensure the enforcement of laws by prosecuting and punishing perpetrators of this harmful practice.[205] It should be noted that although some countries have adopted administrative and other measures to address polygamy, others have criminalised the practice.[206] It would appear that the preference of treaty bodies has been the use of both legal and administrative measures to effectively deter the practice and ensure its eradication.[207] Thirdly, treaty bodies have urged State partiers to discourage polygamy by embarking on public awareness and education about the adverse effects it has on women.[208] Here, the education of traditional leaders, who are custodians of religious and customary norms, is vital in addition to the elimination of stereotypes on gender roles between men and women which perpetuate polygamy.[209] Furthermore, treaty bodies have

---

[200] COBs Jordan, CRC/C/JOR/CO/5, para. 46 (CRC, 2012); COBs Kuwait, CCPR/C/KWT/CO/2, para. 9 (HRC, 2011); COBs Libya, CEDAW/C/LBY/CO/5 (CEDAW, 2009).

[201] COBs Israel, A/60/38 (SUPP) (CEDAW, 2005).

[202] COBs Antigua and Barbuda, A/52/38, para. 270 (CEDAW, 1994); COBs Guyana, A/49/38, para. 101 (CEDAW, 1994).

[203] Ibid.

[204] COBs Djibouti, CCPR/C/DJI/CO/1, para.7 (HRC, 2013); COBs DRC, CEDAW/C/COD/CO/6-7, para. 20(b), (CEDAW, 2013); COBs Indonesia, CEDAW/C/IDN/CO/6-7, para. 47 (CEDAW, 2012); COBs Algeria, CRC/C/DZA/CO/3-4, para. 12 (CRC, 2012).

[205] COBs Mozambique, CCPR/C/MOZ/CO/1, para. 9 (HRC, 2013); COBs Greece, CEDAW/C/GRC/CO/7, para. 37(b), (CEDAW, 2013); COBs Canada, CRC/C/OPSC/CAN/CO/1, para. 21 (d) (CRC 2012).

[206] COBs Uzbekistan, CEDAW/C/UZB/CO/4 (CEDAW, 2009).

[207] COBs Egypt, CRC/C/EGY/CO/3-4, para. 52(g), (CRC, 2011); COBs Niger, CRC/C/NER/CO/2 (CRC, 2009).

[208] COBs Djibouti, CCPR/C/DJI/CO/1, para.7 (HRC, 2013); COBs DRC, CEDAW/C/COD/CO/6-7, para. 38(c), (CEDAW, 2013); COBs Greece, CEDAW/C/GRC/CO/7, para. 37(b), (CEDAW, 2013); COBs Yemen, CCPR/C/YEM/CO/5, para. 10 (HRC, 2012); COBs Côte d'Ivoire, CEDAW/C/CIV/CO/1-3, para. 27(b), (CEDAW, 2011).

[209] COBs Angola, CEDAW/C/AGO/CO/6, para. 36 (b), (CEDAW, 2013); COBs DRC, CEDAW/C/COD/CO/6-7, para. 38(c), (CEDAW, 2013).

recommended that States parties provide protection to women affected by polygamy.[210]

While treaty bodies could be said to be obliquely promoting monogamous values, it is only CRC which has expressly recommended that States parties promote monogamy.[211] Treaty body entreaties to abolish polygamy and to promote monogamy augur well with the need to promote values which fortify the protection of human rights. It is, therefore, unsurprising that while constituting discrimination, polygamy has not been accompanied with recommendations promoting its social equivalent, namely, polyandry. Arguably, polyandry would equally violate the dignity of women and have adverse effects on the upbringing of children. Therefore, in advocating for the abolition of polygamy, treaty bodies seek to ensure the protection of women and children from the adverse effects that this harmful practice generates for current generations and posterity.

4.3.4 Trafficking and Sexual and Labour Exploitation

Within the framework of the protection of women and children, treaty bodies, in particular the CRC, CESCR and CEDAW have consistently raised their concern at the growing number of women and children in situations of sexual and labour exploitation and its link to human trafficking. States parties have the obligation to engage in the suppression of all forms of traffic in women and exploitation of the prostitution of women,[212] to protect children from all forms of violence and exploitation which would hinder a child's life, survival or development.[213]

Treaty bodies have identified particular situations such as poverty and unemployment as increasing the risk for women to be trafficked.[214] Contemporary forms of sexual exploitation, including sex tourism, forced organized marriages and migrant domestic work, which continue to violate women's rights and dignity, have also been identified.[215] Similarly, treaty bodies' recognition of particular groups that are more vulnerable to exploitation and trafficking has evolved over the years. These groups now include young girls from rural areas,[216] and children belonging to the Roma national minority,[217] as well as larger groups of women and

---

[210] COB New Zealand, CEDAW/C/NZL/CO/7, para. 39(b), (CEDAW, 2012).

[211] COBs Mauritania, CRC/C/MRT/CO/2, para. 45, (CRC, 2009).

[212] CEDAW, article 6.

[213] CRC, General comment No. 13 on the right of the child to freedom from all forms of violence/ C/GC/13 (2011), para. 62.

[214] CEDAW, General Recommendation No. 19, Violence against women (1992), para. 14.

[215] Ibid. COBs Mauritania CAT/C/MRT/CO/1 para. 21 (CAT 2013).

[216] COBs Peru CAT/C/PER/CO/5-6 para. 21 (CAT, 2013), COBs Iran CCPR/C/IRN/CO/3 para. 20 (CCPR, 2012).

[217] COBs Albania E/C.12/ALB/CO/2-3 para. 24 (CESCR 2013), COBs Italy CRC/C/ITA/CO/3-4 para. 73 (CRC, 2011).

children in vulnerable situations such as women belonging to ethnic minorities[218]; children living in poverty; lesbian, gay, bisexual and transgender (LGBT) children[219]; children living in difficult family situations; migrant children and children left behind by their migrating parents.[220] Treaty bodies have also identified girls and women who work domestic workers and those living in servitude in landowners' homes as risk groups.[221]

Treaty bodies have dealt with trafficking and exploitation of prostitution, forced labour, sexual exploitation of children, and the worst forms of child labour in great detail. Their observations exhibit a four-pronged approach stemming from provisions within the treaties, as well as from global commitments adopted by States and focus chiefly on the prevention, protection, and rehabilitation of victims and the prosecution of offenders.[222]

Prevention

Although measures to combat trafficking and sexual and labour exploitation of women and children undertaken by States parties are commended, the treaty bodies continue to churn out the "strengthening", "increase of efforts" "continue to strengthen" and "intensification" of measures.[223] The adoption of comprehensive laws[224] or amendments to existing legislation is often recommended,[225] with CRC often calling for legal amendments to harmonize domestic legislation with its Optional Protocol on the sale of children, child prostitution and child pornography[226] and the Protocol to Prevent, Suppress and Punish Trafficking in Persons, Especially Women and Children,[227] and other relevant international standards.

---

[218] COBs Belarus, CERD/C/BLR/CO/18-19 para. 17 (CERD 2013).

[219] COBs United States of America, CRC/C/OPSC/USA/CO/2 para. 23 (CRC 2013).

[220] COBs El Salvador CRC/C/OPSC/SLV/CO/1 para. 17 (CRC, 2010).

[221] COBs Bolivia CAT/C/BOL/CO/2 para. 24 (2013) and CRC/C/BOL/CO/4 para. 77 (CRC, 2009), COBs Pakistan CEDAW/C/PAK/CO/4 para. 23 (CEDAW 2013).

[222] Universal Declaration of Human Rights (1948), UN CRC (1989), OP-CRC-SC (2000), ILO Convention No. 182 "Worst Forms of Child Labor Convention" (1999), UN "Palermo Trafficking Protocol" (2000), Council of Europe Convention on Action against Trafficking in Human Beings; the Protocol to Prevent, Suppress and Punish Trafficking in Persons, Especially Women and Children, supplementing the UN Convention against Transnational Organized Crime; see also Global Commitments made in the 1st, 2nd and 3rd World Congresses against the Commercial Sexual Exploitation of Children (1996, 2001, 2008).

[223] COBs UK CEDAW/C/GBR/CO/7 para. 39 (CEDAW 2013), COBs Russian Federation E/C.12/RUS/CO/5 para. 23 (CESCR 2011).

[224] COBs DRC, CEDAW/C/COD/CO/6-7 para. 23 (CEDAW 2013), COBs Angola CEDAW/C/AGO/CO/6 para. 21 (CEDAW 2013).

[225] COBs Senegal, CERD/C/SEN/CO/16-18, para. 14 (CERD 2012).

[226] COBs Italy CRC/C/ITA/CO/3-4 para. 75 (CRC, 2011).

[227] COBs Peru CRC/C/PER/CO/3 para. 68 (CRC, 2006).

In parallel, the need to develop a 'comprehensive strategy' and 'holistic national frameworks' within a set timeframe, to combat this scourge, and to allocate sufficient human and financial resources, are also part of the treaty bodies' approach.[228]

The lack of data on trafficking in women and girls, on the exploitation of prostitution and on the measures taken to prevent and combat such activities is a predominant concern.[229] Treaty bodies have highlighted that in order to effectively combat the phenomena, States parties must first acknowledge its existence[230] and then, time and again, recommend the carrying out of studies to understand and assess the causes, nature and extent,[231] including possible links between sexual exploitation and national economic sectors such as tourism.[232] Data reporting systems should also be strengthened and data systematically collected,[233] focusing on women and children as victims and not just from a law enforcement perspective.[234]

Achieving attitudinal changes and awareness-raising among professionals and the general public regarding the problems of trafficking and sexual and labour exploitation calls for education, including media campaigns, and campaigns specifically aimed at the individuals and groups creating demand for sexual exploitation of children.[235] CRC has taken on a transformative strategy, recommending that States parties engage on social norms and perceptions, also among parents and children themselves, regarding child prostitution and child pornography. This strategy also seeks to tackle the demand for commercial sexual exploitation.[236] On one level, the role of the mass media is highlighted, but on another equally crucial level, is the role of community leaders, local teachers, youth and children's groups, to change attitudes.[237]

---

[228] (CEDAW 2013); COBs Tanzania E/C.12/TZA/CO/1-3, para. 17, (CESCR 2013); COBs Peru, CAT/C/PER/CO/5-6, para. 21, (CAT 2013); COBs United Kingdom of Great Britain and Northern Ireland CEDAW/C/GBR/CO/7, paras. 38-39 (CEDAW 2013), CEDAW FYRM, CEDAW/C/MKD/CO/4-5, para. 26 (CEDAW 2013), COBs Turkmenistan, CEDAW/C/TKM/CO/3-4, para. 24 (CEDAW 2012). COBs Russian Federation E/C.12/RUS/CO/5 para. 23 (CESCR 2011), COBs Italy CEDAW/C/ITA/CO/6, para. 28 (CEDAW 2011), COBs India CRC/C/15/Add.228 para. 75 (CRC 2004); COBs Italy E/C.12/1/ADD.43 para. 15 (CESCR, 2000).

[229] COBs Estonia CEDAW/C/EST/CO/4 para. 19 (CEDAW, 2007).

[230] COBs Cuba, CEDAW/C/CUB/CO/7-8 para. 26 (CEDAW 2013).

[231] COBs Uzbekistan, CRC/C/OPSC/UZB/CO/1para.23, (CRC 2013); COBs Slovakia, CRC/C/OPSC/SVK/CO/1 para. 27 (CRC 2013).

[232] COBs Malta, CRC/C/MLT/CO/2 para. 62 (CRC 2013)

[233] COBs Belize CCPR/C/BLZ/CO/1 para. 17 (2013), COBs El Salvador CMW/C/SLV/CO/1 para. 48 (CMW, 2009).

[234] COBs United States of America, CRC/C/OPSC/USA/CO/2 para. 7 (CRC 2013).

[235] COBs El Salvador CRC/C/OPSC/SLV/CO/1 para. 21 (CRC, 2010)

[236] COBs USA, CRC/C/OPSC/USA/CO/2 para. 24 (CRC 2013), COBs Philippines, CRC/C/OPSC/PHL/CO/1 para. 21 (CRC 2013).

[237] COBs Philippines, Ibid.

The treaty bodies seem to pay specific attention to the intergenerational issues around the root causes of trafficking and sexual and labour exploitation, and have highlighted the links between poverty, underdevelopment and cultural attitudes, and the vulnerability of women and children to sale, prostitution, pornography and sex tourism,[238] and to the vulnerability of women to exploitation and trafficking.[239] In addressing the root causes of prostitution, States parties are enjoined to offer economic alternatives to prostitution,[240] whereas with regard to trafficking, sale and exploitation of children, they are urged to expand access to education.[241] In carrying out their preventive efforts, States parties are urged to strengthen cooperation with civil society,[242] also invest in international, regional, and bilateral engagement through information exchange and harmonization of legal procedures.[243]

Protection

CEDAW has lamented that sexually exploited and/or trafficked children and women and women victims of prostitution are not always treated as victims, but, rather, are criminalized or penalized by relevant legislation in some States parties.[244] It also bemoans the limited assistance and shelter afforded to victims who are unable or unwilling to cooperate with the prosecution authorities.[245] Victims of exploitation and trafficking do not usually have access to sufficient protection and assistance, which should inter alia, covers health care, psychological and social assistance, and shelter.[246] Since work the private sphere of life increases the vulnerability of women and children, the involvement of labour inspectors in the monitoring of private employment agencies and the informal sectors is seen as one effective measure to facilitate protection.[247] The HRC calls on States parties to

---

[238] COBs El Salvador CRC/C/OPSC/SLV/CO/1 para. 18 (CRC, 2010).

[239] COBs Bolivia CEDAW/C/BOL/CO/4 para. 28 (CEDAW, 2008).

[240] COBs Equatorial Guinea, CEDAW/C/GNQ/CO/6 para. 28 (CEDAW 2012).

[241] COBs Guinea-Bissau CRC/C/GNB/CO/2-4 para. 67 (CRC 2013).

[242] COBs Serbia, CEDAW/C/SRB/CO/2-3 para. 24 (CEDAW 2013).

[243] COBs Belarus, CERD/C/BLR/CO/18-19 para. 17 (CERD 2013), COBs DRC, (CEDAW 2013), para. 24; COBs Greece CEDAW/C/GRC/CO/7 para. 22 (CEDAW 2013).

[244] COBs Albania E/C.12/ALB/CO/2-3 para. 22 (CESCR 2013), COBs Bosnia and Herzegovina CEDAW/C/BIH/CO/4-5 para. 26 (CEDAW 2013), COBs Burkina Faso CRC/C/OPSC/BFA/CO/1 para. 28 (CRC 2013); COBs Togo CEDAW/C/TGO/6-7, para. 24 (CEDAW 2012); COBs Comoros (CEDAW/C/COM/CO/1-4 para. 26 (CEDAW 2012), COBs India CRC/C/15/Add.228 para. 75 (CRC 2004).

[245] COBs Cyprus CEDAW/C/CYP/CO/6-7 para. 20 (CEDAW 2013).

[246] COBs Greece CEDAW/C/GRC/CO/7 para. 22 (CEDAW 2013); COBs Tanzania E/C.12/TZA/CO/1-3, para. 17, (CESCR 2013); COBs Albania E/C.12/ALB/CO/2-3 para. 22 (CESCR 2013), COBs El Salvador CCPR/C/SLV/CO/6 para. 13 (CCPR, 2010).

[247] COBs Cyprus CEDAW/C/CYP/CO/6-7 para. 20 (CEDAW 2013), and CERD/C/CYP/CO/17-22, para. 21 (CERD 2013); COBs Gabon, E/C.12/GAB/CO/1, para. 23 (CESCR 2013); COBs

ensure that in practice, children are afforded special protection.[248] Given the evolving social media, CRC has also been quick to underscore the need for children to be afforded protection from exploitation over the internet.[249]

Rehabilitation

Treaty bodies have commended laws and regulations establishing the right to recovery, rehabilitation and reintegration of victims.[250] However, they have often noted that programmes for the physical and psychological recovery and social reintegration of victims of abuse and exploitation are insufficient.[251] Treaty bodies have encouraged access for victims to appropriate, child or gender-specific assistance, rehabilitation, reintegration and witness protection programmes. In this regard, treaty bodies often require the allocation of sufficient human, technical and financial resources to this cause.[252]

Prosecution

Treaty bodies bemoan the lack of information on prosecutions and sentences in matters of trafficking, undue delays in proceedings and leniency in sentences.[253] Further, they regret the low rate of prosecutions and convictions of traffickers despite the large number of trafficked women for purposes of sexual exploitation and forced labour.[254] As such, they call for statistical data on the number of arrests and convictions under relevant anti-human trafficking legislation.[255]

Training for law enforcement officials, police officers, social workers, prosecutors and judges on the prevention of trafficking in persons and on the strict application of the criminal provisions punishing it is seen as crucial in combating

Kuwait E/C.12/KWT/CO/2 para. 23 (CESCR 2013); COBs Albania, E/C.12/ALB/CO/2-3, para. 24(CESCR 2013); COBs Guinea-Bissau, CRC/C/GNB/CO/2-4, para. 65, (CRC 2013); COBs United States of America, CRC/CO/OPSC/USA/CO/2, para. 26 (CRC 2013).

[248] COBs Mozambique CCPR/C/MOZ/CO/1 para. 18 (HRC 2013).

[249] COBs Slovakia, CRC/C/OPSC/SVK/CO/1 para. 29 (CRC 2013); COBs Canada, CRC/C/OPSC/CAN/CO/1 para. 13 (CRC 2013).

[250] COBs Philippines, CRC/C/OPSC/PHL/CO/1 para. 39 (CRC 2013).

[251] COBs India CRC/C/15/Add.228 para. 74 (CRC 2004).

[252] COBs Philippines, CRC/C/OPSC/PHL/CO/1 para. 40 (CRC 2013).

[253] COBs Bosnia and Herzegovina CEDAW/C/BIH/CO/4-5 para. 23 (CEDAW 2013), COBs Dominican Republic, CEDAW/C/DOM/CO/6-7 para. 26 (CEDAW 2013). COBs Italy CAT/C/ITA/CO/4 para. 22 (CAT, 2007).

[254] COBs Gabon E/C.12/GAB/CO/1 para.23 (CECSR 2013); COBs Philippines, CRC/C/OPSC/PHL/CO/1 para. 29 (CRC 2013).

[255] COBs Senegal CAT/C/SEN/CO/3, para. 115 (CAT 2013), COBs Iran CCPR/C/IRN/CO/3 para. 20 (CCPR, 2012).

trafficking. This also includes training on how to receive, monitor, promptly investigate and prosecute complaints in a gender and child-sensitive manner and to ensure that sanctions are proportionate to the seriousness of the acts committed.[256] Widespread awareness-raising campaigns and comprehensive training courses in all matters concerning sexual and labour exploitation and trafficking to all officials in direct contact with the victims (law enforcement officers, judges, lawyers, social workers, and health care providers) and for the public at large are also often part of the treaty bodies recommendations.[257]

In order to ensure access to judicial remedies for victims of trafficking or labour and sexual exploitation, treaty bodies call for free legal aid and access to witness protection programmes. CEDAW advocates that trafficked women and girls receive adequate support to be able to testify without fear against their traffickers.[258] CRC has specifically recommended a confidential, accessible and child-sensitive mechanism to receive and effectively address individual complaints of all children.

5 Recommendations on Gender Mainstreaming in Education

The mainstreaming of gender in informal education requires a multi-pronged approach focusing on almost every aspect of life of women and children in society. Women and girls need to be portrayed in a positive and non-stereotypical manner and national awareness-raising campaigns need to be undertaken at all levels targeting both women and men. When efforts are undertaken to combat negative imaging of women and girls by the media through participation of all media practitioners, parallel activities should equally target the local and family levels. The support of community and religious leaders should be sought to begin to achieve attitudinal changes about the negative perceptions of the roles of women and girls in society. Men and women of all ages should also be involved in efforts to challenge and modify prejudices, customary and traditional stereotypes that continue to impede access to informal education by women and girls. These sensitization programmes should seek to transmit norms and values which promote the status of women and girls in society as individuals with equal standing and abilities.

Mass media programmes, policies and strategic plans need to be developed in a manner that ensures that messages not only underscore the value and benefits of educating women and girls but also the benefits that accrue to men when women and girls are educated. Furthermore, informal education and media messages

---

[256] COBs Peru CCPR/C/PER/CO/5 para. 20 (CCPR 2013); COBs Dominican Republic, CEDAW/C/DOM/CO/6-7 para. 27 (CEDAW 2013); COBs Chile, CEDAW/C/CHL/CO/5-6 para. 23 (CEDAW 2013).

[257] COBs El Salvador CAT/C/SLV/CO/2 para. 21 (CAT 2009).

[258] COBs El Salvador CEDAW/C/SLV/CO/7 para. 26 (CEDAW, 2008).

should also promote the introduction of gender studies targeting both men and women, which should promote women's access to education, the equal sharing of family responsibilities and highlighting the corrosive nature of domestic women.

Extensive awareness-raising campaigns on education and development should not only seek to make women aware of their human rights but also how to claim them. In this regard, information should also be made available to girls, women and their families through a variety of context-specific channels. This should include targeted information about the various training and education opportunities available informally to women. Awareness-raising programmes should target all school personnel and families to establish systems which are supportive of the attendance of women and girls upon child delivery before re-entry into the formal system. This should be accompanied by appropriate messages which seek to address bullying of girls who seek to return to school after pregnancy.

Media awareness programmes regarding sexual and reproductive health should also modify traditional gender roles of women and men in family life and empower women with information to make decisions on their health and lifestyle. Public education campaigns should also modify traditional thinking on child marriages and teenage pregnancies, raising awareness on the health risks that girls face with early pregnancies. It is equally important that such messages should also target boys with a view to ensuring that they understand the risks of unsafe sex to their health and education.

The efforts sustained in informal education to address gender-based stereotypes also need to be reinforced in formal education. As such, curricula, textbooks and teaching material should be revised with a view to expunging all references which perpetuate gender-stereotypes. Curricula should include SRH which should be consistently revised in light of objective scientific information and available technologies evidence. In this regard, teachers and other trainers need to receive appropriate refresher training to be able to handle general SRH topics in a gender and child-sensitive manner. Teachers and school personnel, particularly males, should be given opportunities to upgrade their skills, mainly on gender-sensitive training of courses and subjects, to ensure that they are able to support and encourage the education of girls. Furthermore, it is trite that teachers and other persons, especially at the community level, have an influence on children's perceptions regarding women and girls' access to education. Media messages and awareness raising campaigns should, therefore, focus at encouraging and promoting respect for girls by combating misogyny and subjugation.

All restrictions on girls' education, including on their participation in certain education fields, in their school enrolment, and on their continuation in school when pregnant, should be eliminated. For instance, the lack of a birth certificate should in no case prevent children from being enrolled into a school. States parties should, therefore, undertake efforts to facilitate the removal of all social and gender barriers, which impede the education of women and children. This includes the need to revise school calendars in order to avert instances where women and children fail to attend school due to specific seasonal household chores they are called to undertake.

Children who are victims of sexual harassment or any violence in the school context should have access to a gender and child-sensitive accountability mechanism for reporting and seeking redress. It is equally important to ensure that information provided to parents is infused with gender aspects on the need to respect their dignity, particularly with regard to the treatment of women and the disciplining of children in the family. Furthermore, education and literacy programmes for children and adult women should promote a shift in perceptions by both men and women aimed at sharing the burden of responsibilities in income generating activities and household chores performed by women and children.

Budget allocations to education, particularly targeted at girls' education, should ensure that compulsory education is of an appropriate quality and is suffused with concepts of gender neutrality. Financial resources should be, at a minimum, on par with the percentage of GDP recommended to achieve universal education and should be monitored for impact with the help of gender budgeting tools. States parties should also address the gendered impacts of poverty and how they affect the outcomes for women and children in the field of education. It is, therefore, important to ensure that programmes designed to provide incentives for the education of women and children such as the provision of scholarships, school meals, and uniforms, are developed using gender lens in order to address the root causes impeding access to education.

6 Conclusion

In the period following the Second World War, the international community has expressed concern in international legal instruments about the rights of both present and future generations. The UN Charter itself pursues a preservationist objective to save succeeding generations from the scourge of war. In order to complement efforts to attain this objective, the international community has committed to standards set by international instruments on human rights. Treaty bodies established under some of these instruments to monitor their implementation by States parties have under the reporting procedure generated considerable jurisprudence on a wide array of issues on the rights of women and children. A review of this jurisprudence reveals that notwithstanding the existence of specific instruments on women and children, all treaty bodies have had the opportunity to consider issues on women and children. Furthermore, the review shows that the spirit of the preambles of the CEDAW Convention and the Convention of the Rights of the Child regarding the asymmetries in the status of men and women as well as the need to provide special care to children are shared across treaty bodies.

Most importantly, treaty bodies have sought to construe the moral standards set by treaties by analysing the various social relationships in the context of the States parties' obligations to protect, respect, promote and fulfil human rights standards. Treaty bodies have in their concluding observations continued to advance various forms of justice when assessing social interactions. As such, concluding observations are replete with examples on how treaty bodies advance justice standards in, for instance: (a) promoting *de facto* equality (distributive justice) in access to education by ensuring equal access between rural and urban dwellers; (b) the need to exercise political power to curb harmful practices such FGM and provide compensation and rehabilitative services because treaty bodies understand that States parties have a monopoly over violence and the power to provide a remedy (political and corrective justice); and (c) during transactional relationships emanating from individuals' interactions with themselves or with State party officials (transactional justice) where, for instance, the conduct of sterilisation would violate the rights of a women if free and informed consent is incapable of being obtained due to illiteracy. Thus, concluding observations reveal elements of distributive justice, political justice, corrective justice and the promotion of transactional justice. Furthermore, the focus of treaty bodies with contextual issues on the right to development, gender mainstreaming and the promotion of social justice for women and children, continue to advance aspirations to achieve equality for women and children.

However, protection gaps still exist in all States parties, which are aggravated by local perceptions of justice. These are prevalent where local perceptions of justice are influenced by deeply rooted customary and religious practices. These perceptions are often used to justify and foment harmful practices and traditions, which in turn entrench negative social constructions on women and children in society. Furthermore, the general lack of statistical data, including sex-disaggregated data, to track progress on the implementation of treaties renders it difficult to assess the impact of States parties' efforts in embracing global human rights standards. Nevertheless, treaty bodies' concluding observations continue to deliver invaluable guidance in elaborating and transposing global justice standards on human rights to domestic levels with a view to advancing the life chances of women and children as succeeding generations.

Five Questions

1. Is the failure to cooperate with State authorities in the prosecution of trafficking cases a legitimate ground for host States to refuse to grant a resident permit to women and girls who are victims of trafficking?
2. How can FGM, polygamy and other harmful practices be eradicated given that these practices are deeply rooted in by custom and religion?
3. How can States ensure that there is a proper balance between any restrictions on the dissemination of sexual and reproductive health information to the general public and the need to protect children from harmful and age-inappropriate sexual and reproductive health information?
4. Does the prohibition of corporal punishment in the school setting have a bearing on the lack of discipline by children in schools?
5. Does the promotion of co-educational institutions have a correlation with the prevalence of teenage pregnancies?

References

Freeman, M., Chinkin, C., & Rudolf, B. (2012). *The UN convention on the elimination of all forms of discrimination against women: A commentary*. Oxford: Oxford University Press.

Heyns, C., & Viljoen, F. (2001). The impact of the United Nations human rights treaties on the domestic level. *Human Rights Quarterly, 23*, 483–535.

Hudson, N. (2010). *Gender, human security and the United Nations: Security language as a political framework for women*. New York: Routledge.

Keller, H., & Ulfstein, G. (2012). *Human rights treaty bodies: Law and legitimacy*. Cambridge: Cambridge University Press.

Merle, J. (2005). *Spheres of global justice: Fair distribution, global economic, social and intergenerational justice*. Cambridge: Cambridge University Press.

Ransom, W. (1945). Let's look at the charter of the United Nations. *American Bar Association, 31*, 336–343.

Schermers, H. (1997). We the peoples of the United Nations. *Max Planck Yearbook of United Nations Law, 1*, 111–128.

Simma, B. (Ed.). (1994). *The charter of the United Nations: A commentary*. Oxford: Oxford University Press.

United Nations (2002). *Gender mainstreaming: An overview*. United Nations, http://www.un.org/womenwatch/osagi/pdf/e65237.pdf.accessed, 29 May 2014.

United Nations (2012) *The United Nations human rights treaty system* (Fact Sheet No. 30/Rev. 1). http://www.ohchr.org/Documents/Publications/FactSheet30Rev1.pdf.accessed, 29 May 2014.

United Nations (2014). *Harmful traditional practices affecting the health of women and children* (Fact Sheet No. 23). Geneva and New York: United Nations. http://www.ohchr.org/Documents/Publications/FactSheet23en.pdf.accessed, 29 May 2014.

United Nations, Note by the Secretariat (2013). Overview of the human rights treaty body system and working methods related to the review of States parties HRI/MC/2013/2, www.ohchr.org/Documents/HRBodies/TB/HRI.MC.2013.2_en.doc.accessed, 29 May 2014.

International Strategies for Building a Culture of Peace through Access to Good Education

Werner Wintersteiner

Abstract Whilst education is a fundamental human right and essential for the exercise of all other human rights, other human rights have to be guaranteed to be able to make use of the right to education.

Education is a necessary, even if not the only, prerequisite that economically and socially marginalized adults and children lift themselves out of poverty and participate fully as citizens. Education is on the other hand a necessary, even if not the only, instrument for creating and maintaining democratic, just and peaceful societies. Moreover, education is the cornerstone of a strategy towards a culture of peace.

Normative instruments of the United Nations lay down international legal obligations for the right to education. These instruments promote and develop the right of every person to enjoy access to education of good quality, without discrimination or exclusion. On the basis of a discussion of these UN documents, from *Education for All* to *Education for a Culture of Peace*, this chapter discusses contradictions and oppositions in education policies in order to find out how a culture of peace and lawfulness as a new educational standard can be best conceived and projected.

> The transformation of society from a culture of war to a culture of peace is perhaps more radical and far-reaching than any previous change in human history. Every aspect of social relations – having been shaped for millennia by the dominant culture of war – is open to change, from the relations among nations to those between women and men. Everyone, from the centers of power to the most remote villages, may be engaged and transformed in the process. (David Adams)

> The keystone of democracy is education. (Edgar Faure)

> Think peace into reality! (Virginia Woolf)

W. Wintersteiner (✉)
University of Klagenfurt, Klagenfurt, Austria
e-mail: werner.wintersteiner@aau.at

H. Kury et al. (eds.), *Women and Children as Victims and Offenders: Background, Prevention, Reintegration*, DOI 10.1007/978-3-319-08398-8_4

1 Introduction

"On the 9th of October 2012, the Taliban shot me on the left side of my forehead. They shot my friends too. They thought that the bullets would silence us. But they failed. And then, out of that silence came, thousands of voices. The terrorists thought that they would change our aims and stop our ambitions but nothing changed in my life except this: Weakness, fear and hopelessness died. Strength, power and courage was born. I am the same Malala. My ambitions are the same. My hopes are the same. My dreams are the same. [. . .] I am here to speak up for the right of education of every child. I want education for the sons and the daughters of all the extremists especially the Taliban. [. . .] So let us wage a global struggle against illiteracy, poverty and terrorism and let us pick up our books and pens. They are our most powerful weapons" (Yousafzai 2013).

These are the words of Malala Yousafzai, Pakistani teenage activist, who survived a Taliban assassination attempt in 2012. She was almost killed for the "crime" of attending school and encouraging other girls to do so. The aim of the terrorists was to hit a "symbol of Western culture", as Malala had already been, from the age of 9 years, a human rights activist, struggling for the rights of girls in Pakistan and elsewhere.

But the terrorists failed doubly. Not only did she survive, but her will to engage in human rights could not be broken. Called "the most courageous girl of the world", she was chosen to speak at a UN forum of Youth, while secretary general Ban Ki-moon has declared June 12th the "Malala Day" and organised an initiative "I am Malala".

In her speech at the United Nations in 2013, from which the quoted lines are an extract, she demonstrates the power of education which can even overcome feelings of revenge and hatred. As she argues, not only her survival, but even more her new role as an "ambassador" for the rights of girls and women to be educated, and for the right of education in general, is a triumph over all those who deny—under any pretext—elementary human rights to some groups of humans: "thousands of voices". In the long run, her belief that pens are stronger than weapons, may prove to be true: "One child, one teacher, one pen and one book can change the world." In 2014, Malala Yousafzai received the Nobel Peace Prize for her struggle for the right of all children to education, together with Kailash Satyarthi, another children's rights activist, from India. At age 17, Yousafzai is the youngest-ever Nobel Prize laureate.

Thus, Malala became a symbol of hope. It is the old and noble hope of social reformers all over the world, not least of the European Enlightenment, to make the world a better place for all by the means of education. It finds its modern expression in the international human rights provisions and legislation, postulating a "right to education" as a basic right in order to enable the learners to become full citizens, aware of their rights, opportunities and duties. Thus Malala's example does not stand for any education, but for the education of a responsible and enlightened citizen. "Nobody is born as a political creature", states German philosopher Oskar

Negt, "thus citizenship education is a precondition for the existence of any peaceable society. [. . .] *Democracy is the only politically constituted social order that has to be learnt – again and again, every day and up to old age*." (Negt 2010, p. 13, my translation, original emphasis) This is an important lesson to keep in mind when it comes to discussing international programmes to promote education for all.

2 Education—A Disputed Field

2.1 The Right to Education

This right to education Malala was ready to defend with her life is determined in a series of international documents. What is important is its double character as both an individual and a social right: on the one hand, it is understood as an individual (or family) right to choose freely the type of education—especially when it comes to "identity issues" like language, religious belief and cultural options. On the other hand, the "realisation of this right requires an effort on the part of the State to make education available and accessible; it implies positive State obligations. This may be called the social dimension of the right to education" (Coomans 2007, p. 125). These two dimensions can already be found in the oldest and most important text, the *Universal Declaration of Human Rights* (A/RES/217 A(III) 1948[1]) where the right to education is codified in Article 26:

1. Everyone has the right to education. Education shall be free, at least in the elementary and fundamental stages. Elementary education shall be compulsory. Technical and professional education shall be made generally available and higher education shall be equally accessible to all on the basis of merit.
2. Education shall be directed to the full development of the human personality and to the strengthening of respect for human rights and fundamental freedoms. It shall promote understanding, tolerance and friendship among all nations, racial or religious groups, and shall further the activities of the United Nations for the maintenance of peace.
3. Parents have a prior right to choose the kind of education that shall be given to their children.

The short paragraphs are remarkably rich in content:

- They make clear that education is an unconditional right for everybody and thus a universal human right;
- They define as the aim of education "the full development" of any human personality as a *social being*, since education shall promote understanding, tolerance, friendship, and peace;

[1] United Nations, General Assembly resolution 217 A (III), 1948.

- While these principles must not be ignored, the families have the right to choose the concrete form of education of their children. However, this point can come into contradiction with the former determination, if parents have radically different concepts of education;
- Finally, the article is astonishingly concrete (compared to other rights) in clearly addressing the state as responsible for providing education as well as in setting out the steps to be taken by the state in realising the right: It is the duty of the state to provide a compulsory and free education, at least at the elementary level.

Later documents provide a more detailed description of this right, mainly the *International Covenant on Economic, Social and Cultural Rights* (1966, entry into force 1976). In Article 13, para. 1, the right is reaffirmed and its social and political dimension is expressed in an even more explicit way (993 UNTS 3)[2]:

> 1. The States Parties to the present Covenant recognize the right of everyone to education. They agree that education shall be directed to the full development of the human personality and the sense of its dignity, and shall strengthen the respect for human rights and fundamental freedoms. They further agree that education shall enable all persons to participate effectively in a free society, promote understanding, tolerance and friendship among all nations and all racial, ethnic or religious groups, and further the activities of the United Nations for the maintenance of peace.

Thus, it is clear that education is not only a human right, but needs also to include human rights education in order to enable the learners to be active citizens "in a free society". Paragraphs 2–4 define more precisely than the *Universal Declaration* what exactly has to be done at all levels of the education scale to realise the right to education.

Of particular interest is Article 14 which states unmistakably that each state which, "at the time of becoming a Party, has not been able to secure in its metropolitan territory or other territories under its jurisdiction compulsory primary education, free of charge, undertakes, within 2 years, to work out and adopt a detailed plan of action for the progressive implementation, within a reasonable number of years, to be fixed in the plan, of the principle of compulsory education free of charge for all." This is a very clear prescription of the approach to follow in case the Article 13 requirements are not met. This allows for a detailed monitoring and international discussion of the implementation of the right to education.

A third landmark document is the *Convention on the Rights of the Child* (1989, entry into force 1990, 1577 UNTS 3). Article 28 is very similar to the provisions of the Covenant. The fact that paragraph 1 (a) still insists on the necessity to "make primary education compulsory and available free to all" reveals that the problem is still not solved even 40 years after the adoption of the *Universal Declaration*. Article 29, clause 1, in turn, repeats basically the principles of education, namely:

[2] General Assembly resolution 2200A (XXI) of 16 December 1966, entry into force 3 January 1976, in accordance with article 27.

(a) The development of the child's personality, talents and mental and physical abilities to their fullest potential;
(b) The development of respect for human rights and fundamental freedoms, and for the principles enshrined in the Charter of the United Nations;
(c) The preparation of the child for a responsible life in a free society, in the spirit of understanding, peace, tolerance, equality of sexes, and friendship among all peoples, ethnic, national and religious groups and persons of indigenous origin. (p. 9)

As a new aspect "the development of respect for the natural environment" is added, and an accent is put on the rights of minorities and migrants, still in article 29, 1 (c), underlining "the respect for the child's parents, his or her own cultural identity, language and values, for the national values of the country in which the child is living, the country from which he or she may originate, and for civilizations different from his or her own." (p. 9)

The right to education has been reaffirmed in other international documents, including the *Convention against Discrimination in Education* (1960, 429 UNTS 3)[3] the *Convention on the Elimination of All Forms of Discrimination Against Women* (1981, 1249 UNTS 13),[4] and the *Convention on the Rights of Persons with Disabilities* (2006, 2515 UNTS 3).[5]

However, despite all these regulations and recommendations, the right to education is, in practice, far from being implemented everywhere. Rather, it is even often an object of dispute: How should this right be interpreted? What is for whom an adequate education? Which contents does this education include? Which obstacles hinder the implementation of the right to education?

2.2 *Attempts to Implement the Right to Education*

Today, for many people, at least in the Western world, the right to education seems to be taken for granted, a claim which goes without saying, even if this right is not yet implemented everywhere. However, things are not as simple. In Europe, the right to education for the working classes was obtained after long struggles (up to the twentieth century) with the ruling classes who did not see any sense in providing the "masses" with too much knowledge. Gaps in education remain still quite important even in the so-called highest "developed" countries, namely in terms of social class, gender and origin (migrants). Furthermore, we have to take into account that (European) imperialism and colonialism destroyed existing social and educational structures all over the world and replaced them with different

[3] http://unesdoc.unesco.org/images/0011/001145/114583e.pdf#page=118.

[4] General Assembly resolution 34/180, A/RES/34/180, 18 December 1979, http://www.un.org/womenwatch/daw/cedaw/cedaw.htm.

[5] http://www.un.org/disabilities/convention/conventionfull.shtml.

forms of colonial education systems which usually did not provide quality education for all. "Prior to the late twentieth century, Westerners imposed their forms of education as part of a conscious attempt to impose Western culture and languages" (Spring 1998, pp. 8–9). This historical "heritage" still causes problems to the concerned countries (see, as an early critique, Altbach 1971). Harber and Mncube (2012, pp. 103) identify numerous obstacles especially to greater democracy in education in developing countries, including the bureaucratic and authoritarian legacy, a school culture which often still implies corporal punishment, as well as deficiencies in teacher education.

Thus, it is no wonder that despite numerous efforts for free and compulsory elementary education (proclaimed in the *Universal Declaration*), this aim is far from being reached today. Even more than 60 years after the adoption of the Declaration, 58 million children are still out of school worldwide (UNESCO 2013/2014, p. 2).[6] While the main actors to change this situation are still the nation states, the efforts undertaken by international agencies and organisations, such as the UN, UNESCO, but also OECD and others, are considerable as well. In the following paragraphs, the main global activities to protect the right to education and to implement it in practice are discussed.

There have been several approaches to support national efforts for better education by international activities. They got a new kick at the end of the 1980s, when a new phase of *business globalisation* took place, and—according to the neo-liberal paradigm—education was more and more conceived as a main resource for (international) economic competition. In this context, international organisations, in particular the OECD, started new initiatives to promote at least basic education for all. Times of business globalisation are also times of globalisation of the efforts for education (see Spring 1998, chapter 6 and 7). This is especially true for UNESCO, which took the leadership of the *Education for All* initiative, started in 1990, with a conference in Jomtien, Thailand. *Education For All (EFA)* is an ongoing global coalition of governments, development agencies, civil society, and NGOs, led by UNESCO, aiming to provide quality education for all on a worldwide scale by 2015. Its main idea was expressed in the title of the 1990 conference, *Meeting Basic Learning Needs*. Adopting a *World Declaration* as well as the *Framework for Action*, *EFA* made a global assessment of the situation and conceived for the first time a global action plan. It determined "major setbacks in basic education in the 1980s in many of the least-developed countries. In some other countries, economic growth has been available to finance education expansion, but even so, many millions remain in poverty and unschooled or illiterate. In certain industrialized countries, too, cutbacks in government expenditure over the 1980s have led to the deterioration of education" (UNESCO/UNICEF 1990, p. 155).

Since "the basic learning needs of millions of people are not being met fully or well, and will not be *if current conditions and trends persist,*" an "expanded vision"

---

[6] Numbers from 2011.

is seen as necessary to meet the basic learning needs of all (UNESCO/UNICEF 1990, p. 33, original emphasis). From the EFA perspective, meeting the *Basic Learning Needs of Children* (and in an analogue form for youth and adults) means four points: increasing relevance, improving quality, promoting equity, and enhancing efficiency. In order to reach these aims, EFA established a worldwide monitoring mechanism, including national reports and regional conferences.

Ten years later, the next global conference was held. The *World Education Forum* (26–28 April 2000, Dakar) reaffirmed the goals of the *World Declaration on Education for All* from 1990, which were, in spite of some progress, still far from being reached. However, based on "the most extensive evaluation of education ever undertaken, the *Education for All* (EFA) 2000 Assessment", it was possible to describe the problems in concrete numbers and to list the unfulfilled tasks: "In the year 2000 [. . .] more than 113 million children have no access to primary education, 880 million adults are illiterate, gender discrimination continues to permeate education systems, and the quality of learning and the acquisition of human values and skills fall far short of the aspirations and needs of individuals and societies" (UNESCO 2000, p. 8). Of the millions of children worldwide who were not in school, more than half were girls. The *Forum* adopted the *Dakar Framework for Action, Education for All: Meeting our Collective Commitments*. Paragraph 7 (ii) includes the task of "ensuring that by 2015 all children, particularly girls, children in difficult circumstances and those belonging to ethnic minorities, have access to and complete, free and compulsory primary education of good quality" (UNESCO 2000, p. 8). In order to do so, at Dakar, the UN created *The United Nations Girls' Education Initiative* (UNGEI), a partnership of organisations dedicated to promoting girls' education.[7]

These *EFA* goals are also understood to contribute to the eight *Millennium Development Goals* (MDGs), namely MDG 2 on universal primary education and MDG 3 on gender equality in education, by 2015.

It is important to say that universal primary education (UPE) is not the only goal of the international campaign. Rather, the aim is a good balance between primary and secondary education, since the more people attend primary schools the more they are interested in continuing their studies. Furthermore, the quality of education, in particular good teacher training, counts among the goals of *EFA*.

However, a balance of mid-2014 shows that the goal of universal primary education (UPE) will be missed by a wide margin (UNESCO 2014a). By 2014, 58 million children were still out of school. This, though, is almost half of the number of 2000, and, given the rise of world population, definitely a lower rate. Nevertheless, according to this report, girls still make up 54 % of the global population of children out of school, with huge regional differences. The same report shows that 15 million girls and 10 million boys, constituting around 43 % of those out of school, are unlikely to ever get access to primary education if the

[7] http://www.ungei.org/.

current situation does not change. Further data: while access to education has been improving globally, there has been little progress in reducing the rate at which children leave school before reaching the last grade of primary education. The survey concludes that global progress towards universal primary education has halted and in stark contrast to progress at the start of the decade the momentum to reach out-of-school children has slowed considerably in recent years (UNESCO 2014a).

In order to accelerate the progress again towards the *Education for All* goals, UN Secretary-General Ban Ki-moon launched the 5-year *Global Education First Initiative* (GEFI) in 2012 (UN 2012). As the aims of this initiative, we read, inter alia, "Put quality, relevant and transformative education at the heart of the social, political and development agendas" and "Generate additional and sufficient funding for education through sustained global advocacy efforts". This is—as it seems—a new tone, compared to the *EFA* language. The three priorities are to put every child in school and to improve the quality of teaching, as well as to foster global citizenship. Thus not only schooling as such but the content of education is also addressed (see Sect. 4.2).

2.3 Education Under Attack

The international character of the action plans discussed in the previous sections may lead us to think that education for all at all levels of the education system, is a worldwide recognised common value and goal and to believe that the problem is only the lack of personal and financial resources. In fact, education is a disputed field and there is ongoing political debate about which education for whom, both at the national as well as at the international level. Thus, education is not only a problem of good governance, but of a political struggle between competing concepts and programmes.

In fact, not only is the right to education not fully respected and implemented, for various motives, including financial, political and ideological reasons, but education suffers also from wars and other violent conflicts, and more often than not, from deliberate attacks against schools, children, teachers and educational administrators. Regrettably, the case of Malala is far from unique. In many parts of the world, girls and women are persecuted for making use of their right to education. And this sexist refusal of rights is not the only problem.

The Global Coalition to Protect Education from Attack (GCPEA) report *Education Under Attack* (2014) shows how much, between 2009 and 2013, teachers and other education staff have been targeted for assassination or killed, injured, tortured, detained, extorted, and harassed in areas of conflict and instability in at least 30 countries, in which a significant pattern of attacks on education has been found.

This report is already the third respective document, after two reports by UNESCO, in 2007[8] and 2010.[9]

"The study reports in detail on 30 countries where there was a significant pattern of attacks in the 5-year reporting period and lists 40 other countries where isolated attacks took place. It concludes that targeted attacks on education and incidents of military use of schools and universities are occurring in far more countries and far more extensively than previously documented" ... "Many attacks involve bombing or burning schools or universities, or killing, injuring, kidnapping, or illegally arresting, detaining or torturing students, teachers and academics. [...] Hundreds have died as a result and hundreds of thousands more have missed out on the right to an education. In many places, children and young people, and those who teach them, live in fear of attacks" (GCPEA 2014a, p. 8).

The motives for attacks, as diverse and context specific they might be, nevertheless show some similar trends across countries. "The reported motives for targeting schools, students, teachers and other education staff include the desire to:

- destroy symbols of government control or demonstrate control over an area by an anti-government group;
- block the education of girls, or any type of education perceived to teach or impose alien religious or cultural values, biased history or an unfamiliar language of instruction;
- restrict teacher trade union activity and academic freedom;
- abduct children for use as combatants, sex slaves or logistical support in military operations, or abduct students and teachers for ransom; or
- seize schools and universities for use as barracks and bases or firing positions, or attack schools because they are being used for these purposes by opposing forces" (GCPEA 2014a, p. 14).

Beside these immediate damages, we have also to consider the long-term effects of violent attacks:

> In countries where attacks have persisted on a significant scale year after year – many countries experienced attacks on education long before the start of this study's reporting period – lengthy school closure has meant that hundreds of thousands of children have been denied access to education, sometimes for months or sometimes for years. [...] In higher education, attacks may not only endanger lives and disrupt education, but also prove devastating for research and teaching by triggering fear, flight and self-censorship among whole academic communities. They also disrupt training of teachers, education planners and managers. [...] Wider and long-term consequences for society include restricting development and – particularly in the case of attacks on higher education – hindering the

---

[8] http://unesdoc.unesco.org/images/0018/001863/186303e.pdf.

[9] http://unesdoc.unesco.org/images/0018/001868/186809E.pdf, or: http://educationandconflict.org/publications/education-under-attack-2010.

> emergence and strengthening of political plurality, accountable government and open democracy (GCPEA 2014a, p. 23).[10]

The report shows clearly how much the phenomenon of attacks against education is spread across the world, with more than 70 states involved in one way or another. However, direct violence against educational institutions is only the tip of the iceberg of all other violations of the right to education. Among all these violations, the structural violence of the opening gap between rich and poor in many countries as well as between the countries seems to be one and maybe the most "efficient" factor to make the goal of quality education for all an unreachable utopia.

3 Education—A Disputed Concept

As we have seen, the struggle for education is not limited to the case of education itself, but to the question in which general direction a society should move. Denying the right to education for some social groups is an attack on democracy, but reducing education to the instruction and training of the labour force instead of the development of the whole personality is an attack as well. And even within the framework of democratic societies, the struggle or debate about the best way to educate is a struggle among competing concepts of the democratic way. Education is not just a disputed field but the very concepts of education themselves are disputed as well.

The global efforts for education are part of a trend of globalisation of education, mainly promoted by international regimes and agencies, like the OECD. Standards are set of how education is organised, but it turns out that the organisation has consequences for the contents of teaching. It may lead to the (global) standardisation of what is knowledge and what is teachable and worth being taught and what not. This is especially true for international comparative assessments, like PISA,[11] PIRLS[12] or TIMSS.[13] Officially and according to their intention, they simply assess some basic competences of pupils. Their hidden agenda, however, is a standardization of what is seen as basic competences and contents. This seems to lead to a homogenisation of the curricula, in the long run. Is this progress or

[10] GCPEA has also published a parallel report in 2014b, *Protecting Education Personnel from Targeted Attack in Conflict-Affected Countries*, as well as the so called *Draft Lucens Guidelines* to prevent violations of school personnel, students and damages on buildings. (http://www.protectingeducation.org/sites/default/files/documents/draft_lucens_guidelines.pdf).

[11] Programme for International Student Assessment (PISA); a worldwide study of 15-year-old school pupils' scholastic performance on mathematics, science, and reading, since 2000.

[12] Progress in International Reading Literacy Study (PIRLS); measures trends in reading comprehension at the fourth grade, since 2001.

[13] Trends in International Mathematics and Science Study (TIMSS); tests students in the fourth and eighth grades, since 1995.

decline? The answer depends on whether or not global standards and global initiatives are to be understood as an instrument for improving the national situation or not. Or: "How can global goals lead to lasting change at a national level?" as Green and Hale (2013) put it.

Moreover, this development may not only lead to a uniformed global education, but also to *capitalist* education policies on a global scale, as many critics lament, and thus risks miss the aim of serving the basic needs of the poor people who need better education in the first instance. This development raises a set of critical questions and provoked some radical criticism as well. Quickly it becomes clear that education is not only contested in its practice, but the very concept of education is a politically and philosophically disputed field.

Indigenous knowledge, for example, is part of the concern for quality education but it has to be transformed in order to fit in the settings of formal learning. Indigenous cultures are only and insofar preserved as they can be used as a tool for the implementation of liberal educational reforms (cf. Spring 1998, pp. 197–198). Others describe, in more general terms, the danger of a uniform world culture, like US sociologist Benjamin Barber's "Mc World", promoted by global mass media (Barber 1995). If education becomes another instrument for the process of cultural homogenisation, the chance of emancipation via education is missed.

An even more severe criticism is that the global education campaigns promote and reinforce a "near-hegemonic, bureaucratic model of formal, Western-style and state-provided schooling. [...] The essential features of this taken for granted model of modern education are that children learn primarily from adults about high stakes academic subjects, on a fixed schedule, in an indoor setting, that includes particular features [...]." (Harber and Mncube 2012, p. 20). They ask the question whether this is not only a one-sided, Eurocentric model of learning, but is also based on a Eurocentric concept of society and on a uniform model of universal democracy. This excludes all other cultural forms of schooling, of democracy and in consequence, of knowledge.

Thus it is no wonder that there are also critics who do not believe in international efforts for nationwide and worldwide schooling, but who are convinced that this goal is not only non-reachable, but, more importantly, undesirable. If this criticism comes from what has been called "one of the most visionary outlooks in the last fifty years in the history of education" (Zaldívar 2011, p. 618) it has to be taken seriously.

3.1 Education—A State Monopoly Over the Social Imagination? A Dissident Voice

Among the many critical educational initiatives from the 1960s and 1970s, Ivan Illich's plea for the abolition of the school system, *Deschooling Society* (1971), is the most remarkable one. Criticizing not the idea of education, but the idea of school and thus, state control over the education, he states:

> Universal education through schooling is not feasible. It would be no more feasible if it were attempted by means of alternative institutions built on the style of present schools. Neither new attitudes of teachers toward their pupils nor the proliferation of educational hardware or software (in classroom or bedroom), nor finally the attempt to expand the pedagogue's responsibility until it engulfs his pupils' lifetimes will deliver universal education. The current search for new educational funnels must be reversed into the search for their institutional inverse: educational webs which heighten the opportunity for each one to transform each moment of his living into one of learning, sharing, and caring (Illich 1971).

He believes that "the institutionalisation of values leads inevitably to physical pollution, social polarisation, and psychological impotence: three dimensions in a process of global degradation and modernised misery. I will explain how this process of degradation is accelerated when nonmaterial needs are transformed into demands for commodities; when health, education, personal mobility, welfare, or psychological healing are defined as the result of services or 'treatments'" (Illich 1971).

Prophetically, he predicts "that most of the research now going on about the future tends to advocate further increases in the institutionalisation of values and that we must define conditions which would permit precisely the contrary to happen." And this is exactly what happened in the 40 years plus after the publication of his book.

His probably strongest and still topical argument is the following: "Welfare bureaucracies claim a professional, political, and financial monopoly over the social imagination, setting standards of what is valuable and what is feasible. This monopoly is at the root of the modernisation of poverty" (Illich 1971). This is not simply a critique of the school, but rather a critique of a totalising control over the citizens by the state machine executed by the educational system. Illich's observations remind other critical thinkers of the school as an instrument of power, like Michel Foucault (*Discipline and Punish*, 1975, in the same decade as Illich's book) or Michel de Certeau (*La Culture au Pluriel*, 1974) who described school in nineteenth century France as "a weapon of political centralisation" (1974/1993, p. 118).

Illich's analysis is difficult to contest, but his proposals for an alternative are not really convincing. He proposes instead of state schools "Learning Webs" of the organised civil society. Illich's proposals, it is true, have served as inspiration for various new grassroots movements, such as indigenous movements or de-growth anti-capitalism alternatives (cf. Zaldívar 2011, p. 620). However, it is very doubtful how education via learning webs can be done at a quality level. And he overlooks a change in power relationships that de Certeau has analysed in detail: the growing influence of mass media on all parts of the society. Deschooling, in this context, would not lead to more freedom, but to a weakening of the resistance of any influence from big business, exerted via mass media. According to de Certeau, under these new circumstances the state school is no longer simply an instrument of the power but has an ambiguous character: "It remains a state institution, ordered by the government, to diffuse a cultural model defined by the centre. On the other hand, it is in a position both threatened and critical towards the culture propagated by the mass media. This ambivalence can constitute a pole of resistance (which is not necessarily a protest movement)" (de Certeau 1993, p. 119, my translation). Today, with all the consequences of a neo-liberal "reform" of the educational sector, de Certeau's analysis is even more relevant. Thus we have to discuss another criticism of education, maybe less spectacular than Illich's, but definitely no less radical.

3.2 Two Paradigms: The Human Capital Approach Versus the Human Rights Approach

The more neo-liberalism has pervaded all dimensions of the political and social life, the more the resistance has grown. In the 1990s, after the launch of the UNESCO *EFA* initiative, a high ranking UNESCO expert not only expressed scepticism about the envisaged aims, but also challenged the ideological background of the initiative. Jacques Hallak criticised "a dominant ideology of regulation by the market, initially applied to economic and finance exchanges, and gradually proposed to all sectors of human activity, including the social sector (education, health, etc.). The aims of increasing return to capital, added to the possibility of locating the units of production of goods and services almost everywhere, have thus contributed to uniting or globalizing the world" (Hallak 1999, p. 8).

In this perspective, education is understood as a tool for global economic competition, designated to deliver the necessary "human capital". The knowledge and the competence to be acquired through education are focused on the qualification of the labour force, not of the development of the whole personality. Thus education becomes a business and is no longer seen as a political endeavour. "Efficiency" is the new key-word. "Human capital investments are treated as similar to investment in other capital goods" (Spring 1998, p. 163).[14] The human capital concept is on the origin of profound transformations of the complete educational system: international assessments, monitoring, transformation of the curricula, reduction of state allocations and encouragement of private business to invest in education—privatisation of all profitable sectors of education.

The human capital approach also became the official education doctrine of the European Union with the *Lisbon Strategy*, an action plan for the development of the EU economy between 2000 and 2010. The aim was to make the EU, by 2010, "the most competitive and dynamic knowledge-based economy in the world capable of sustainable economic growth with more and better jobs and greater social

[14] As Spring (1998) shows, this concept dates back to post-war Europe and the Marshall Plan which eventually led to the foundation of the OECD.

cohesion" (EU 2000). Even if this strategy failed and the aims could not be reached, its principles are still in vigour, namely the eminent role of education: "The knowledge triangle of research, education and innovation is a core factor in meeting the Lisbon goals. Therefore, it has been emphasised right from the beginning that the Lisbon goals would require not only enhancement in research infrastructure and research funding, but also a fundamental transformation of education and training throughout Europe" (EU-Asia Higher Education Platform).

The human capital approach is the result of the ideological take-over of the neoliberal doctrine, but the reason why this doctrine has prevailed is also due to the fact that at first sight it looks like a plausible answer to globalisation. The idea is that more market economy will solve the problems of poverty and underdevelopment and provide universal wealth in a universal competitive economy. Education is a cornerstone of this strategy: first, by promoting "the development of market economies through human resource development and lifelong learning. Second, education is to remedy problems resulting from globalisation such as unemployment, increasing economic inequality, and fears of social and economic change" (Spring 1998, p. 160). It is in this line that a UNESCO report from 2014 states that "if all children enjoyed equal access to education, per capita income would increase by 23 % over 40 years" and "if all women had a primary education, child marriages and child mortality could fall by a sixth and maternal deaths by two-thirds". (UNESCOPRESS 19.09.2013). Who would be against such noble objectives?

However, the human capital approach affects not only national education policies but also international strategies, like the UNESCO sponsored *Education for All* (*EFA*) initiative, and more generally, UNESCO's overall education strategy. In his book *Education and the Rise of the Global Economy* (1998), Joel Spring critically observes a shift away from a human rights approach of UNESCO towards the human capital approach. Comparing two basic documents, *Learning to be* (Faure et al. 1972) and *Learning: The Treasure Within* (Delors 1996), he shows that the former document, despite many Eurocentric biases, conceives the key function of education in preparing for an active role in a democratic society, while the later document is nothing but "a slightly more humane version of the educational plans of OECD and World Bank" (Spring 1998, p. 208). *Learning to be* introduces two concepts that later played a prominent role in the human capital approach, the *learning society* and *lifelong learning*. But, in 1972, these concepts are still embedded in an approach of education to the universal value of democracy. *Learning to be* is already aware of the global responsibility of democratic citizens, of "global citizenry" in nowadays terms: "The new man [sic] must be capable of understanding the global consequences of individual behaviour, of conceiving of priorities and shouldering his share of the joint responsibility involved in the destiny of the human race" (Faure et al. 1972, p. XXV). In contrast, *Learning: The Treasure Within* does not mention this democratic ideal of the new human being. It sees the information society not simply as a general framework but as a goal and the driving force of education. This is, for Spring, the "rhetoric of human capitalism" (Spring 1998, p. 212).

Similarly, Spring criticises the UNESCO sponsored *Education for All* initiative as too short-sighted and too much in line with the human capital approach of OECD and other international agencies. The conference documents and the World Declaration refer to the human right to education, but they do not include human rights education in their agenda. However, this is, according to Spring, the crucial point. If human rights education is not included in a global education strategy, there is no chance that efforts in enrolling students and in the numbers of formal diplomas benefit society. As Spring shows, "although there is reference to human rights, social justice, and peace, this reference is in the context of supporting and tolerating differing political and religious systems and recognizing that the content of basic education will vary between cultures" (Spring 1998, p. 196). In relativising human rights, the idea of their universal value and validity is weakened.

Remarkably, we find, at the same time, programmatic education documents of a very different character, probably according to different agendas of UNESCO. These include the *Declaration and Integrated Framework of Action on Education for Peace, Human Rights and Democracy* (UNESCO 1995), as well as the documents regarding human rights education (UNICEF/UNESCO 2007), and the programmes for a *Culture of Peace* (UNESCO 1994a, b), which will be discussed in the next section.

It seems that UNESCO has adopted, since the 1990s, a two-way strategy (at least, for a moment): on the one hand, the (new) *EFA* initiative, focussing on educational basics which are supposedly ideologically neutral (in fact: a human capital approach), and, on the other hand, the continuation of UNESCO campaigns for explicitly emancipatory education (let's call it: the human rights approach). In my view, this is a dangerous split between so-called educational basic needs and human rights education. Its message is that human rights education is *not* a basic requirement, no educational priority. This is in contrast to the idea that development and democracy are interlinked, moreover, that democracy is in itself a way of development, as Nobel Prize winner Amartya Sen has argued (Sen 1999, see also Harber and Mncube 2012, chapter 1).

However, UNESCO realised that a human capital approach is not sufficient to reach the goals of *EFA*. After some preparatory consultations, in 2007, UNICEF and UNESCO released a common document, *A Human Rights-Based Approach to Education For All*. This document includes an implicit criticism of a one-sided pedagogical approach: "Most international attention has been focused on helping children get into school. What happens once they are there, and the nature of the education they receive, has been afforded far less emphasis. [...] There has been a failure to acknowledge the complexity of the barriers impeding children's access to school" (UNICEF/UNESCO 2007, 1 and 2). It concludes: Many publications have been produced on the multiple aspects of Education for All, but there has been no comprehensive analysis of the actions necessary to undertake a rights-based approach to achieving its goals. This document is intended to fill that gap." (UNICEF/UNESCO 2007, 3). This rights-based approach consists of three elements: the right of access to education, the right to quality education, as well as the right to respect within the learning environment. This was a big step forward to a more holistic understanding of education.

Nevertheless, it is only the *Global Education First Initiative* (2012) of UN Secretary-General Ban Ki-moon which explicitly states that it is not only necessary to put every child in school and to improve the quality of teaching, but to use education as a tool for democracy and peace by fostering global citizenship: "Education is about more than literacy and numeracy—it is also about citizenry. Education must fully assume its central role in helping people to forge more just, peaceful and tolerant societies" (UN 2012).

This initiative has proven to be able to establish a balance between the human capital approach and the human rights approach as the further development shows (see Sect. 4.4 of this paper). However, there is also a tradition of reconciling the two adversary approaches in the UNESCO policy, as I will argue in the next section.

3.3 Conclusions

The rise of neoliberal concepts in education is leading to a profound transformation not only of the educational system, but also of the educational "contents". Today, this is increasingly organised not simply at a national, but at a global level. Moreover, setting educational standards at a global level is revealed more often than not as a way of imposing neoliberal, market-driven concepts of education.

As a result, education is—on the one hand—highlighted and revalued, it is given much more political and public attention, and moreover, more efforts are made to achieve "good education" for all. As Hallak correctly states, the new educational policy, embodied in *EFA*, "implies de facto the definition—at the international, regional and sub-national/local levels—of a new social responsibility which commits governments, donors, families and NGOs to permit the implementation of EFA policies" (Hallak 1991, p. 1). On the other hand, the scope and the meaning of education are reduced: instead of remaining one of the first responsibilities of a state, in order to prepare for a democratic society and to promote the full development of the personality of the learners, education becomes a business itself, destined to prepare for the "big business society".

This affects also the still very important and noble efforts towards a *universal primary education* and an improvement and enlargement of secondary education (EFA initiative, education related MDGs etc.). A split between two educational strategies, the human capital and the human rights approach, with parallel international campaigns seems to be the result. In recent years, however, we have been able to observe an increasing criticism on market strategies of education. Ban Ki-moon's *Global Education First Initiative* from 2012 seems to propose a combination of both approaches. This is not the first time in the UN/UNESCO tradition.

As already mentioned, in the early 1990s, UNESCO officer Jacques Hallak was sceptical about the possibility of achieving the goals of *EFA*, namely universal basic education by the end of the century (as initially planned) (Hallak 1991). A few years later, he has made a very clear-sighted analysis of market oriented educational policies. He does not openly challenge the liberal argument that education is good for (economic) development in a globalised world, but he underlines its restricted validity. He offers two possible alternatives to assess the situation: "This has led to different scenarios for the future, in particular, to contradictions or support between the trends of globalisation and the challenges facing education and the human rights agenda" (Hallak 1999, p. 12).

According to Hallak, *scenario one* is characterised by "conflicts of objectives": "This scenario may lead to domination of future societies by the logic of the market; weakening of states; economic and cultural globalization; productivist concept of education, ignoring values (social and individual); violation of human rights—in particular their universality and indivisibility" (Hallak 1999, p. 16).

The *second scenario*, however, is more "optimistic" and sees "complementarities" instead of conflict: "The main assumption of this scenario can be formulated as follows: education can contribute to the regulation of globalization, in particular by establishing the conditions for respect of human rights—a prerequisite for a successful evolution of globalization" (Hallak 1999, p. 19). In the following, Hallak proposes "to balance economic, social, cultural and ethical interests" (Hallak 1999, p. 21). He believes that it is possible to reconcile two opposite educational paradigms, a problematic standpoint! In my view, however, posing the problem in the way he does is already a challenge of market ideology in education, since usually negative consequences of this ideology are ignored. At first sight, the first scenario seems to reflect a more critical perspective: it lists the negative effects of globalisation and market ideology for human rights and democracy education. However, this perspective underestimates how much global capitalism needs the "language" of human rights and democratisation for imposing its domination. In contrast, putting it like in scenario two may lead (beyond Hallak's argument) to an enhanced critical awareness of any human rights and democracy discourse.

A genuine human rights approach may find its standpoint beyond both scenarios, in a third position, which is characterised by resistance to business globalisation without ignoring its benefits and by a critical human rights discourse. This third position also rejects Illich's argument of de-schooling, as thought-provoking it may be. The argument is that quality education is always a good thing, even if it is initially limited by a certain ideology or doctrine. In the words of Hallak: "The more educated and well informed a population, the more likely the mobilization for an effective respect of human rights" (Hallak 1999, p. 17). A similar argument, but in a more generalised form, is proposed by German educationalist Heinz-Joachim Heydorn who argues that education is always an initial tool for socialising young people in the existing social system and to learn the acceptance of the ruling order and values. However, by acquiring the knowledge and the competences that education provides, it allows as well the challenge to the existing order and thus opens an avenue to autonomy, to maturity and responsibility in the sense of Kant or Adorno (Heydorn 1970, pp. 12–13).

These considerations are, implicitly or explicitly, the background for *Education for a Culture of Peace*, in my view the most advanced and most ambitious programme UN and UNESCO (or any other international agency) has ever proposed.

4 Education and the Culture of Peace

UNESCO developed its *Culture of Peace* programme in parallel with its *Education for All* programme even if it never intended or succeeded to link these two approaches. The following short overview of the main documents shows that the *Culture of Peace* was given similar attention as to *EFA*: in the UNESCO context, *Culture of Peace* was formulated for the first time a year before the *EFA* initiative, in 1989, at the *International Congress on Peace in the Minds of Men*, held in Côte d'Ivoire. In 1994, the first International Forum on the Culture of Peace was held in San Salvador (El Salvador). One year later, in 1995, the 28th General Conference of UNESCO introduced the concept of "Culture of Peace" in UNESCO's *Medium-Term Strategy* for 1996–2001.[15] In 1997, the United Nations General Assembly established a separate agenda item entitled "Towards a Culture of Peace". In 1998, the year 2000 was proclaimed as the *International Year for the Culture of Peace* and furthermore the UN decided to proclaim the decade of 2001–2010 "International Decade for a Culture of Peace and Non-Violence for the Children of the World", based on a proposal made by Nobel Peace Prize laureates. In 1999, The United Nations General Assembly adopted the *Declaration and Programme of Action on a Culture of Peace*,[16] defining eight action areas to be linked through the concept of a culture of peace and non-violence into a single coherent approach. In this framework, there is an eminent role assigned to education.

While *Culture of Peace* is a newly developed approach, it is deeply rooted, however, in the basic assumptions and core values of the UN and UNESCO: "The culture of peace is the contemporary expression of the Constitutional mandate of UNESCO," states David Adams, one of the founding fathers of UNESCO's culture of peace programme (Adams 1995, p. 36). *Culture of Peace* is probably the most important and most comprehensive programme of UNESCO. Its dimensions are still not sufficiently explored, its full potential not yet tapped. Even if *Culture of Peace* reaches far beyond education, education plays a key role, and thus it has to be put in the tradition of respective UNESCO programmes.

The "Learning to live together" dimension of education (in the Delors terminology, Delors 1996) had a prominent role in UNESCO's preoccupation since its beginnings. Already in its constitutional document (UNESCO 1945, preamble), an educational programme is outlined—"the education of humanity for justice and liberty and peace are indispensable to the dignity of man [sic] and constitute a sacred duty which all the nations must fulfil in a spirit of mutual assistance and

[15] Document 28 C/4, http://unesdoc.unesco.org/images/0010/001025/102501E.pdf.

[16] General Assembly resolution A/RES/53/243 (1998), http://www.un-documents.net/a53r25.htm.

concern." This is followed, in 1974, by the first elaborated global strategy *Education for international understanding, co-operation and peace* (UNESCO 1974). Later follows a more sophisticated and timelier document, the *Declaration and Integrated Framework of Action on Education for Peace, Human Rights and Democracy* (1995), as well as the documents specifically regarding human rights education.[17] The title of these declarations already shows that UNESCO's concern was always to link human rights, democracy and peace to a comprehensive concept of emancipatory education. Seen in this way, *Culture of Peace* is not an absolutely new approach, but a continuation and an enhanced conceptualising of a comprehensive civic education, global in its scope, and with a special focus on human rights and non-violence.

4.1 Culture of Peace: History and Definitions[18]

Culture of Peace was developed in the 1980s, but its very origins derive from the political struggles in Latin America where peace researchers were looking for new ways out of the dead end street of ongoing violence and terror in their countries (see Wintersteiner 2010, Dios Diz 2010). The declaration of the UNESCO Yamoussoukro Conference in 1989, the first UNESCO document referring explicitly to *Culture of Peace* proposes "a new vision of peace by developing a peace culture based on the universal values of respect for life, liberty, justice, solidarity, tolerance, human rights and equality between women and men" (UNESCO 1989; IIa, p. 2).

In the first documents already, some main features of the Culture of Peace appear:

- Peace is understood as a process of permanent non-violent conflict resolution
- In order to become sustainable, this peace process has to be democratised, by involving all people, not just politicians
- Education is identified as a central way to change the mind-sets still affected by a culture of war and to make a culture of peace a daily practice

But what exactly is the new approach *Culture of Peace*? The term gains in shape if it is compared to its opposition—the culture of war. The main thesis is that we—i. e. all human societies—are living, to a greater or lesser extent, in a culture of war, that we are practising a culture of war instead of a culture of peace. It is "the idea that war as an institution is based upon a culture of war that is broader and deeper than the wars themselves. It's like an iceberg: war is the tip which may or may not be visible at any given moment, whereas the culture of war exists continually, supporting particular wars from below and being continually reinforced by the wars

[17] For a critical review of both documents in the framework of peace education, see Wintersteiner 1999.

[18] Section 3.1 draws partially from Wintersteiner 2010.

that have already occurred. [. . .] For this reason, a culture of peace needs more than the absence of war. It requires a profound cultural transformation" (Adams 2003, p. 1).

Thus it is clear that the term *culture of peace* is not in opposition to *politics of peace*, but refers to a deeper layer of the social web, upon which the political sphere is built. The argument is that it is not enough *to make peace* (by ending a war), but the task is *to make the peace sustainable*. This is only possible by replacing, step by step, elements of the deep-rooted culture of war with a culture of peace. This is a very broad concept and necessarily, any definition will be vague and open. In some UNESCO documents, a culture of peace is defined as follows:

> "The Culture of Peace is a set of values, attitudes, modes of behaviour and ways of life that reject violence and prevent conflicts by tackling their root causes to solve problems through dialogue and negotiation among individuals, groups and nations" (UN Resolutions A/RES/52/13: Culture of Peace and A/53/243: Declaration and Programme of Action on a Culture of Peace).[19]

Furthermore, this definition shows that the *Culture of Peace* programme understands by culture not a specific civilisation or nation, in contrast to another civilisation or nation, but rather the cultural practices at large, which are, in one way or another, to be found in every civilisation. This cosmopolitan approach to a *Culture of Peace* is conceived as a transcultural, global project of rejecting violence, but cultivating the best positive experiences of each culture.

What makes *Culture of Peace* such an important and even revolutionary concept? Firstly, *Culture of Peace* is the answer to an old and crucial question, the link between the personal and the political. For too long, the one highlighted exclusively the role of political structures and thus, neglected the subjects, the actors, while the other emphasised the role of consciousness of each single person and as such, ignored the impact of the political structures. Both were right and wrong at the same time. The concept of a *Culture of Peace* is likely to overcome this false opposition. It is the missing link between psychological and political approaches. It integrates both into a comprehensive model of social transformation. It is the point of access for post-structuralist, post-colonial and gender-conscious approaches to violence.

Secondly, the *Culture of Peace* overcomes the unproductive dichotomy between negative peace (absence of war) and positive peace (social justice). It conceptualises violence on a scale from high to low rather than as a simple yes or no. It explains better the connection between all forms of violence and shows more clearly that it is necessary to combat them all at the same time. So it opens up more ways of reducing violence and it includes more actors in this process. The peace process is put on a broader basis, the actors are not just politicians and diplomats, but also ordinary people and civil society. *Culture of Peace* in practice is a democratisation of war and peace issues.

Finally, the *Culture of Peace* concept allows to envisage much deeper social transformations than those on the superficial political level—it helps to transcend

[19] http://www3.unesco.org/iycp/uk/uk_cp.htm.

"deep structures" and "deep cultures" like patriarchalism that are at the origin of war and violent social structures. It makes us aware that we are still living in a culture of war and that we must not continue to accept the rules, paradigms and basic assumptions of such a violent culture.

As a consequence, a *Culture of Peace* is mainly the respect and the full implementation of universal human rights. This includes a culture of lawfulness, but is much more. According to Dieter Senghaas (Senghaas 2004, pp. 4–5), at least in the European tradition, some essential conditions for the civilised—i.e. the non-violent—resolution of unavoidable conflicts have emerged, by and by. "In the light of the European experience six cornerstones can be identified: [. . .] a *legitimate monopoly of force by the state*. Disarming citizens is the only way to force them to conduct their conflicts over identity and interests through argument rather than violence. Secondly, such a monopoly of force also creates a need for *control under the rule of law* that can only be guaranteed by [. . .] the modern constitutional state. [. . .] The rule of law provides 'the rules of the game' for the shaping of opinion and the political will, as well as for the decision-making process and the enforcement of law. [. . .] The third major condition for internal peace is *affect control*, which arises from the range and wealth of many inter-dependences characterising modern societies. [. . .] Fourth, *democratic participation* is essential, precisely due to the indispensability of affect control. Fifth, however, in politicised societies, this approach to conflict management will only have permanence if there are continual efforts to ensure *social justice*. The great majority of modern capitalist societies are run on market lines, and social inequality is ever present. Unless efforts are continually made to counter this dynamic of inequality, such societies will develop deep social fissures. [. . .] By contrast, genuine efforts to achieve social justice and fairness give substance *to constructive conflict management*, and also provide legitimacy to public institutions." The interdependency and the interplay of all these factors is called *civilisational hexagon*. Only when all these six factors exist to a certain extent in a society and are well balanced against each other, the civilisational hexagon is able to function. Examined against the background of the *Culture of Peace* programme, it is maybe appropriate to say that the *civilisational hexagon* is a kind of minimal programme for a contemporary peaceful society.

However, this transformative concept has encountered vehement opposition in both the UN member states as well as inside of UNESCO, as David Adams reports:

> Although the Declaration and Programme of Action were approved by the UN General Assembly as Resolution A/53/243 on September 13, 1999, the analysis of the culture of war and violence was deleted from the final version. This is because the European Union threatened to block its passage, claiming that 'there is no culture of war and violence in the world' (. . .). It is not surprising that diplomats from the Great Powers would not wish the culture of war to be mentioned, since it is very basis of their power (Adams 2007, p. 2).

This opposition is another proof of the accuracy of the concept which is touching the sore spots of Western democracy. It shows that there *is* a need for replacing a culture of war by a culture of peace, even if a phrase like this may pose the task in a too simple way. This replacement is a long process of generations, but it has to start now, even if sometimes only very small steps are possible.

In the *Programme of Action on a Culture of Peace* (UN 1999) eight action areas at the national, regional and international levels are identified. Here is a short summary of the main aspect of the eight areas[20]:

- Education by promoting education for all, focusing especially on girls; revising curricula to promote the qualitative values, attitudes and behaviour inherent in a culture of peace; training for conflict prevention and resolution, dialogue, consensus-building and active non-violence ...
- Promoting sustainable economic and social development by targeting the eradication of poverty; working towards environmental sustainability;
- Promoting respect for all human rights by fully implementing international instruments on human rights ...
- Ensuring equality between women and men by integrating a gender perspective and promoting equality in economic, social and political decision-making; eliminating all forms of discrimination and violence against women
- Fostering democratic participation by educating responsible citizens; reinforcing actions to promote democratic principles and practices; establishing and strengthening national institutions and processes that promote and sustain democracy ...
- Advancing understanding, tolerance and solidarity by promoting a dialogue among civilizations; actions in favour of vulnerable groups, migrants, refugees and displaced persons, indigenous people and traditional groups; respect for difference and cultural diversity ...
- Supporting participatory communication and the free flow of information and knowledge by means of such actions as support for independent media in the promotion of a culture of peace; measures to address the issue of violence in the media ...
- Promoting international peace and security through action such as the promotion of general and complete disarmament; greater involvement of women in prevention and resolution of conflicts and in promoting a culture of peace in post-conflict situations; initiatives in conflict situations; encouraging confidence-building measures and efforts for negotiating peaceful settlements ...

This overview demonstrates the comprehensiveness of the *Culture of Peace* programme. It was definitely not conceived as an alternative to political peace, but rather as deepening any political peace process, as providing a wider perspective for peace and as a tool for mobilising the peoples to take peace in their hands, as the campaign's slogan "Peace is in your hands" puts it.

In our context, the most interesting aspect is the important role of education which is not only mentioned first, before any other field of action, but which is also

[20] This paragraph follows in the wording not UN 1999, but UNESCO 2002, a pamphlet that introduces into the Culture of Peace programme. In fact, many changes of the formulation occurred between the initial concepts of UNESCO and the final adoption by the UN General Assembly, as David Adams reports (http://www.culture-of-peace.info/copoj/definition.html).

mentioned several times (e.g. “Fostering democratic participation by educating responsible citizens”) and which underlies implicitly all fields of action. Also remarkable is the attempt to link *Education for a Culture of Peace* with the *EFA* programme, which was admittedly for a long time a unilateral endeavour, since until recently, in *EFA* documents *Culture of Peace* was rarely mentioned and never understood in its full meaning—despite the mentioned UNICEF/UNESCO document (2007).[21] The change has only begun in 2012 (see Sections 4.3 and 4.4).

4.2 Peace Education—Educating for a Culture of Peace

Obviously, education has a very prominent position in the UN/UNESCO concept of a *Culture of Peace*: “Education is the principle means of promoting a *Culture of Peace*. This includes not only formal education in schools, but also informal and non-formal education in the full range of social institutions, including the family and the media. The very concept of power needs to be transformed—from the logic of force and fear to the force of reason and love” (UN 1999).

In the UNESCO vision, *Culture of Peace* and especially education for a *Culture of Peace*, unlike some other campaigns, such as *EFA*, was not conceived as a programme uniquely to address the governments, but to inspire and mobilise initiatives “from below”. And with success. Among many others it was also an international network of peace educators, founded in 1999, the *Hague Appeal for Peace Global Campaign for Peace Education* (see Wintersteiner 2013) which gave itself the task to promote a *Culture of Peace* via peace education. The campaign statement reads:

> A culture of peace will be achieved when citizens of the world understand global problems; have the skills to resolve conflict constructively; know and live by international standards of human rights, gender and racial equality; appreciate cultural diversity; and respect the integrity of the Earth. Such learning cannot be achieved without intentional, sustained and systematic education for peace (Global Campaign for Peace Education (GCPE)).[22]

The concept of the *Culture of Peace* had—in practice—an incredible mobilising effect, at least in its first years.[23] However, in addition, its importance for developing a rationale and a theory of peace education, and education as such, should not be underestimated. It revaluates the role of education in the process of social progress

[21] In the *Dakar Declaration*, a culture of peace is mentioned two times: Once as a specific task of African governments, as if all other governments did not need it (UNESCO 2000, p. 32), and once as the task not of the whole educational strategies, but of schools: Their educational programmes “should be sensitive to cultural and linguistic identities, and respectful of diversity and reinforce a culture of peace (UNESCO 2000, p. 19). This is a very restricted understanding of the transformative idea of Culture of Peace.

[22] http://www.haguepeace.org/index.php?action=pe.

[23] For more information, see the regular bulletins, edited by David Adams, at http://cpnn-world.org/index.php (2001–2010) and http://cpnn-world.org/bulletin/bulletins.html (from 2011 to date).

towards a more peaceful society. It integrates education into an overall strategy for political change and cultural transformation. Obviously, peace education cannot influence the war system directly, but, when integrated in the whole framework of a *Culture of Peace*, it contributes substantially towards transcending the culture of war. It delegitimises violent solutions and war, raises the awareness for peace, opens a space for action and enables people to act. Thus peace education is a factor for a soft and slow, but sustainable change of society: "No other idea has informed peace education with such profound transformational potential as the concept and vision of a culture of peace" (Reardon 2000, p. 414).

To summarise: *Culture of Peace* is an essential progress both as a rationale of the right to education and as a basis for the very aim and the content of education. It could be an important input for the *EFA* campaign, especially in order to better balance economic and political needs, transcending the human capital paradigm. The fact that this did not happen, despite some initial efforts by the *Culture of Peace* programme, is maybe due to its very clear political agenda, which is in contrast to *EFA*. In fact, *Culture of Peace* is also an important tool to challenge the role of education in the still existing culture of war:

> No peace educators have fully addressed the role of education in the formation of consciousness and socialisation for war. [...] Few challenged any of the fundamental assumptions of education, the organisation of the school and the specific processes of the dominant form of pedagogy. Fewer still probed the role of education in the development of consciousness (Reardon 2000, p. 415).

Thus, education for a *Culture of Peace* seems to be a very appropriate and comprehensive concept of education:

- It determines clearly the role of education in a comprehensive and complex concept of social innovation and transformation towards a more just and peaceful society;
- It opens new avenues to education as a process of gaining more autonomy and freedom;
- It combines an approach from above and an approach from below, thus combining the efforts of all who wish to contribute to these aims.

4.3 Global Citizenship Education as a New Formula for Educating for a Culture of Peace?

Any peace education is an inherently global approach, since peace is only conceivable as world peace. However, as we have seen, in times of globalisation, there are new educational approaches, which are both a result of and a reaction to a globalising world society. This is also true for the *Education for a Culture of Peace*, which proposes a global answer to globalisation, an answer that is not in opposition to the *EFA* goals, but certainly to some of *EFA*'s underlying basic assumptions concerning the aims and rationale of education.

It is not about to conform to a global market economy, but to resist to all its dimensions of social injustice, lack of democracy and belligerent behaviour. The systematic critique of a culture of war proves to be also a powerful tool in analysing business globalisation, including its negative consequences. This leads to new educational strategies, or at least to new accents within the culture of peace approach, mainly to what we call today *Global Citizenship Education.* At the origin, there are two ground-breaking books of two outstanding culture of peace advocates, Elise Boulding's (1988) *Building a global civic culture* and Betty Reardon's *Comprehensive Peace Education* (both published in Reardon 1988). Boulding's book focuses on the structures of the new world order, at a time when terms like globalisation were not yet in use, while Reardon's introduction to peace education, drawing from her familiarity with world order studies, emphasises the awareness and values of a global citizen, as her subtitle shows: *educating for global responsibility.* As we have seen, "fostering democratic participation by educating responsible citizens" as well as promoting "democratic principles and practices" are already anchored in the *Culture of Peace Programme of Action* (UN 1999). *Global Citizenship Education* adds, in a more explicit way, the global dimension of the citizenship approach.

Besides this evolution within *peace education*, new educational approaches emerged, including in particular *global education.* The aim of this educational approach is, in the words of the North-South Centre of the Council of Europe, "to give learners the opportunity and competence to reflect and share their own point of view and role within a global, interconnected society, as well as to understand and discuss complex relationships of common social, ecological, political and economic issues, so as to derive new ways of thinking and acting" (Cabezudo et al. 2012, p. 10). A milestone was the *Maastricht global education declaration* (2002). It states:

> Global education is education that opens people's eyes and minds to the realities of the globalised world and awakens them to bring about a world of greater justice, equity and Human Rights for all. Global education is understood to encompass Development Education, Human Rights Education, Education for Sustainability, Education for Peace and Conflict Prevention and Intercultural Education; being the global dimension of Education for Citizenship (Cabezudo et al. 2012, p. 10).

This is consistent with the curriculum of the above mentioned Global Campaign for Peace Education, *Learning to Abolish War,* which defines itself as a "conceptual framework for peace education for global citizenship," stating that "peace education must become even more action-oriented, educating students for active, responsible global citizenship" (Reardon and Cabezudo 2002, book I, p. 24). It links peace education closely with global citizenship and human rights education.

Global citizenship education, having its roots in global education as well as in peace education, is insofar a new strategy as it emphasises the citizenship dimension. Thus, it is a more explicitly political approach than some tendencies in global education or peace education. According to Vanessa Andreotti, a *critical global citizenship* approach has to address issues of inequality and injustice, aiming at empowering "individuals to reflect critically on the legacies and processes of their cultures, to imagine different futures and to take responsibility for decisions and actions" (Andreotti 2006, p. 48).

In 2013, UNESCO adopted Global Citizenship Education as a main component of its overall strategy, in order to support the UN *Global Education First* initiative. After a series of consultations, in Spring 2014, it published a document *Global Citizenship Education; Preparing learners for the challenges of the 21st century* (UNESCO 2014b). Drawing from the experiences of many different countries and currents all over the world, the paper gives a good overview of concepts and programmes.[24]

While *Global Citizenship Education* may not be a new formula for *Educating for a Culture of Peace*, it is definitely a necessary component of it. It certainly assigns an important task for a culture of peace, as well as, in return, a culture of peace informed approach to global citizenship education is able to resist to neoliberal influences on education. Just as *Global Citizenship Education* supports *Education for a Culture of Peace* to define concrete political short- and middle-term goals, so *Education for a Culture of Peace* provides a general strategy for *Global Citizenship Education*.

4.4 Education Beyond 2015

The preparation of the post-2015 education agenda in the framework of the so called *Sustainable Development Goals* (*SDG*) marks a new step in integrating the human rights approach into the *EFA* agenda. In fact, there are two parallel initiatives to align for the education issues of the *SDG*: the targets of the Open Working Group (OWG) of UN and those of the *EFA* Steering Committee.

For the first time, the documents of both initiatives include a clear commitment to culture of peace and global citizenship as basic values of any education in the future. For *EFA*, the relevant document is especially the *Muskat agreement*, the outcome of the 2014 Global EFA Meeting (*GEM*) organized by UNESCO and hosted by the Sultanate of Oman (Muscat, May 2014). The *Muscat Agreement* outlines the new post-2015 education agenda. It represents the shared vision of key stakeholders for the post-2015 education agenda. In our context, target 5 is especially important:

> By 2030, all learners acquire knowledge, skills, values and attitudes to establish sustainable and peaceful societies, including through global citizenship education and education for sustainable development. (UNESCO 2014c)[25]

---

[24] However, also the authors of this document felt the need to reconcile global solidarity with global competition. They try simultaneously to promote global solidarity and individual competitiveness.

[25] www.unesdoc.unesco.org/images/0022/002281/228122E.pdf.

The Open Working Group on Sustainable Development Goals of the United Nations General Assembly (UN 2014) describes the educational goals and targets even more in detail: The proposed goal 4, "Ensure inclusive and equitable quality education and promote life-long learning opportunities for all", includes a number of targets, namely paragraph 4.7:

> By 2030, ensure that all learners acquire the knowledge and skills needed to promote sustainable development, including, among others, through education for sustainable development and sustainable lifestyles, human rights, gender equality, promotion of a culture of peace and nonviolence, global citizenship and appreciation of cultural diversity and of culture's contribution to sustainable development. (UN 2014, A/68/970)[26]

Culture of peace, and global citizenship, as a concrete way of implementing a culture or peace, herewith are recognised as central educational goals by the UN and UNESCO. Their proposed inclusion into the framework of the MDG is an encouraging step towards a fuller and richer concept of education, which helps to eradicate poverty on a worldwide scale and to promote human rights, democracy and peace.

5 Conclusion: The Ambivalences of Education. Research Questions

Education is an ambiguous endeavour in many ways. While education is necessarily organised in order to stabilise and perpetuate the given existing social order, and thus also existing power relations, democratic education has also to prepare learners for the ability to change given structures and concepts. But even if education is not fully organised in a democratic way and does not sufficiently teach for human rights, democracy and peace as the main principles of a "futurable" humanity, the dialectics of the educational process may lead to individual freedom and empowerment and, in the long run, to social change.

This leads us to a series of oppositions any education has to deal with, but especially educational programmes for democratic education for all. These contradictions are at the same time further likely fields of educational research, although this research will be much more concrete and focused on case studies than was possible in this overview (see the questions at the end of this chapter).

The first opposition is between preservation and renewal of traditions. As Hannah Arendt put it in a classical way:

> Education is the point at which we decide whether we love the world enough to assume responsibility for it and by the same token save it from that ruin which, except for renewal, except for the coming of the new and young, would be inevitable. And education, too, is where we decide whether we love our children enough not to expel them from our world and leave them to their own devices, nor to strike from their hands their chance of

[26] http://undocs.org/A/68/970.

undertaking something new, something unforeseen by us, but to prepare them in advance for the task of renewing a common world (Arendt 1961, p. 196).

This fundamental ambivalence underlies all other more concrete and explicitly political oppositions I have discussed in this paper.

One of the main oppositions was between a focus on basic competencies and skills, like in the *EFA* programme, versus an explicit focus on a "learning to live together" approach, based on education for human rights, democracy and a culture of peace (e.g. *Culture of Peace* programme). This opposition is often overlapped by another and deeper one, namely between the paradigm of emancipatory education and the paradigm of education as human capital. In my view, it is nevertheless important not to confuse these two pairs of oppositions. While the second opposition is clearly a political and ideological struggle over two fundamentally different directions, the first gap is probably easier to overcome. Basic "technical" skills (literacy and numeracy) and citizenship skills do not exclude each other, the focus on the one or the other is not necessarily the consequence of different educational paradigms. On the contrary, any citizenship education relies on a certain level of literacy. In the spirit of the *multiliteracies* approach, one can argue that any literacy is at the same time part of a holistic educational aim, namely of the education of the whole personality as an individual, a worker, and a citizen (see Cazden et al. 1996). However, there will always be an ongoing struggle over the extent of the different literacies to be included into a certain programme.

Another important opposition, especially for global educational campaigns, is the risk that education is not provided at the same level for all on the one side, and the risk that the *same education* is provided to all on the other side. Thus the challenge is both to avoid anti-education and to overcome obstacles (including ideological resistance) to education for all, especially girls, women and marginalised groups, as well as to avoid a uniform, Western-centred education and school system all over the world.

No doubt there is a series of further research questions which could also be described in terms of oppositions, like that one between a local agenda and a global scope, between global campaigns and national efforts, formal and non-formal education etc. In order to deal in a productive way with these oppositions what counts is a common understanding of education as part of a bigger project of emancipation. Thus, the practice of education would be impossible without the hope of a better future, and without the belief that education can make an important contribution: "The role played by education in all political Utopias from ancient times onward shows how natural it seems to start a new world with those who are by birth and nature new" (Arendt 1961, p. 176).

Five Questions

1. How to reconcile the focus on cognitive basic competencies and skills (like in the *EFA* programme) with an explicit focus on a social and political contents, mainly human rights, democracy and a culture of peace (e.g. *Culture of Peace* programme)?

2. How can the two opposite paradigms—emancipatory education (including gender sensitive education) and education as human capital—be brought into *productive* dispute, without blurring their differences?
3. How can global educational strategies meet regional, national or local needs? How can we make use of the strength of global campaigns without neglecting local particularities?
4. How can everyday education, necessarily a local approach, be combined with a global perspective?
5. How can education in developing countries make use of Western achievements without becoming dominated by Western paradigms? In more general terms: How can educational particularism and educational universalism be confronted/combined/reconciled?

References

Adams, D. (Ed.). (1995). *UNESCO and a culture of peace: Promoting a global movement*. Paris: UNESCO. Also available as: http://www.culture-of-peace.info/monograph/page1.html

Adams, D. (2003). *Early history of the culture of peace: A personal memoire*. http://www.culture-of-peace.info/history/introduction.html

Adams, D. (2007). *Letter to my academic friends*. http://www.culture-of-peace.info/letter/Letter_to_Academic_Friends.pdf

Altbach, P. G. (1971). Neocolonialism and education. *Teachers College Record, 72*, 543–558.

Andreotti, V. (2006). Soft versus critical global citizenship education. *Policy and Practice: A Development Education Review, 3*, 40–51.

Arendt, H. (1961). The crisis in education. In H. Arendt (Ed.), *Between past and future: Six exercises in political thought* (pp. 173–196). New York: The Viking Press.

Barber, B. (1995). *Jihad versus McWorld*. New York: Times Books.

Boulding, E. (1988). *Building a global civic culture: Education for an interdependent world*. New York: Teachers College Press.

Cabezudo, A., Christidis, Ch., Carvalho da Silva, M., Demetriadou-Saltet, V., Halbartschlager, F., Mihai, G.-P. (2012) *Global education guidelines: A handbook for educators to understand and implement global education*. Lisbon: North-South Centre of the Council of Europe (updated version). http://www.coe.int/t/dg4/nscentre/GE/GE-Guidelines/GEgs-chap1.pdf

Cazden, C., Cope, B., Fairclough, N., Gee, J., et al. (1996). A pedagogy of multiliteracies: Designing social futures. *Harvard Educational Review, Spring 1996*, 60–92.

Coomans, F. (2007). Identifying violations of the right to education. *SIM Special, 20*, 125–146. http://www.right-to-education.org/sites/right-to-education.org/files/resource-attachments/Coomans_Identifying_Violations_Right_to_Education_2007_0.pdf

De Certeau, M. (1993). La culture et l'école. In M. De Certeau (Ed.), *La culture au pluriel*. Paris: Seuil.

Delors, J. (Ed.). (1996). *Learning: The treasure within, report to UNESCO of the international commission on education for the twenty-first century*. Paris: UNESCO. http://unesdoc.unesco.org/images/0010/001095/109590eo.pdf

EU. (2000). Presidency conclusions. *Lisbon European Council*, 23 and 24 March 2000. http://www.consilium.europa.eu/uedocs/cms_data/docs/pressdata/en/ec/00100-r1.en0.htm

Faure, E., et al. (1972). *Learning to be*. Paris: UNESCO. http://www.unesco.org/education/pdf/15_60.pdf.

Global Campaign for Peace Education (GCPE) http://www.haguepeace.org/index.php?action=pe

Global Coalition to Protect Education from Attack (GCPEA) (2014a). Education Under Attack Report, New York. http://tinarobiollemoul.com/2014/03/01/education-under-attack-2014-report/

Global Coalition to Protect Education from Attack (GCPEA) (2014b). Protecting Education Personnel from Targeted Attack in Conflict-Affected Countries, New York, http://www.ei-ie.org/en/news/news_details/3147#

Green, D., & Hale, St. (2013, May 31) How can global goals lead to lasting change at a national level? *The Guardian*, http://www.theguardian.com/global-development/poverty-matters/2013/may/31/global-goals-lasting-change-national-level

Hallak, J. (1991). *Education for all: High expectations or false hopes*, (IIEP Contributions No. 3). Paris: International Institute for Educational Planning. http://www.unesco.org/education/pdf/11_126.pdf

Hallak, J. (1999). *Globalization, human rights and education*, (IIEP Contributions No. 33). International Institute for Educational Planning/UNESCO. http://unesdoc.unesco.org/images/0011/001184/118400e.pdf

Harber, C., & Mncube, V. (2012). *Education, democracy and development: does education contribute to democratisation in developing countries?* New York: Symposiums Books.

Heydorn, H.-J. (1970). *Über den Widerspruch von Bildung und Herrschaft*. Hamburg: Europäische Verlagsanstalt.

Illich, I. (1971). *Deschooling society*. New York: Harper and Row. Also available at: http://ournature.org/~novembre/illich/1970_deschooling.html (retrieved 15 July, 2014)

Negt, O. (2010). *Der politische Mensch: Demokratie als Lebensform*. Göttingen: Steidl.

Reardon, B. A. (1988). *Comprehensive peace education: Educating for global responsibility*. New York: Teachers College Press.

Reardon, B. A. (2000). Peace education: A review and projection. In B. Moon, S. Brown, & M. B. Perety (Eds.), *International companion to education* (pp. 397–425). New York: Routledge.

Reardon, B. A., & Cabezudo, A. (2002). *Learning to abolish war: Teaching toward a culture of peace*. New York: Hague Appeal for Peace. http://www.haguepeace.org/resources/book2/English1.pdf

Sen, A. (1999). *Development as freedom*. Oxford: Oxford University Press.

Senghaas, D. (2004). *The civilisation of conflict: Constructive pacifism as a guiding notion for conflict transformation*. Berlin: Bergh of Research Center for Constructive Conflict Management. http://www.berghof-handbook.net/documents/publications/senghaas_handbook.pdf

Spring, J. H. (1998). *Education and the rise of the global economy*. Mahwah: Erlbaum.

UN. (1948). *Universal Declaration of Human Rights*. A/Res/217 A (III) 1948 http://www.ohchr.org/EN/UDHR/Pages/Language.aspx?LangID=eng

UN. (1976). *International Covenant on Economic, Social and Cultural Rights*. http://www.ohchr.org/EN/ProfessionalInterest/Pages/CESCR.aspx

UN. (1990). *Convention on the Rights of the Child*. (A/RES/44/25) http://www.ohchr.org/Documents/ProfessionalInterest/crc.pdf resp.http://www.un.org/documents/ga/res/44/a44r025.htm

UN *Report on the Open working Group on Sustainable Development Goals*, 12 August 2014, Document A/68/970, http://undocs.org/A/68/970

UN. (1998). *Resolution A/RES/52/13: Culture of peace*. January 15 1998, http://www3.unesco.org/iycp/kits/res52-13_en.htm

UN. (1999). *Resolution A/53/243: Declaration and programme of action on a culture of peace*. http://www.un-documents.net/a53r243a.htm and http://www.un-documents.net/a53r243b.htm

UN. (2012). *Secretary-General SG/SM/14540 Secretary-general spells out priorities at launch of 'Education First', while stressing collective responsibility for new global initiative*. http://www.un.org/News/Press/docs/2012/sgsm14540.doc.htm

UNESCO. (1945). *Constitution of the United Nations Educational, Scientific, and Cultural Organization*. London, http://www.icomos.org/unesco/unesco_constitution.html

UNESCO. (1974). *Recommendation concerning Education for International Understanding, Co-operation and Peace and Education relating to Human Rights and Fundamental Freedoms*.

http://portal.unesco.org/en/ev.php-URL_ID=13088&URL_DO=DO_TOPIC&URL_SECTION=201.html
UNESCO. (1989). *Yamoussoukro declaration on peace in the minds of men*. http://www.unesco.org/cpp/uk/declarations/yamouss.pdf
UNESCO. (1994a). UNESCO's Transdisciplinary Project "Towards a Culture of Peace", Final Report. First International Forum on the Culture of Peace, San Salvador, El Salvador, 16–18 February 1994, http://www.unesco.org/cpp/uk/projects/firstforum.htm
UNESCO. (1994b). *The UNESCO executive board. The culture of peace programme: From National Programmes to a Project Of Global Scope*. http://unesdoc.unesco.org/images/0009/000988/098861Eo.pdf
UNESCO. (1995). *Declaration and Integrated Framework of Action on Education for Peace, Human Rights and Democracy*. http://www.unesco.org/education/nfsunesco/pdf/REV_74_E.PDF
UNESCO. (2000). *The Dakar Framework for Action. Education for All: Meeting our Collective Commitments*. Adopted by the World Education Forum Dakar, Senegal, April 26–28, 2000 http://unesdoc.unesco.org/images/0012/001211/121147e.pdf
UNESCO. (2002). *Mainstreaming the culture of peace*. Paris, http://unesdoc.unesco.org/images/0012/001263/126398e.pdf
UNESCO. (2013). *Education for all global monitoring report. Teaching and Learning for Development*. http://unesdoc.unesco.org/images/0022/002256/225660e.pdf
UNESCO. (2013/14). *Teaching and learning: Achieving quality for all. EFA Global Monitoring Report*. http://unesdoc.unesco.org/images/0022/002256/225660e.pdf
UNESCO. (2014a). *Policy Paper 14/Fact Sheet 28*, June 2014. http://unesdoc.unesco.org/images/0022/002281/228184e.pdf or http://www.uis.unesco.org/Education/Documents/fs-28-out-of-school-children-en.pdf
UNESCO. (2014b). *Global Citizenship Education: Preparing learners for the challenges of the 21st century*. http://unesdoc.unesco.org/images/0022/002277/227729e.pdf
UNESCO. (2014c). *(ED-14/EFA/ME/31) 2014 GEM final statement the muscat agreement*. www.unesdoc.unesco.org/images/0022/002281/228122E.pdf
UNESCOPRESS. (19.09.2013). http://www.unesco.org/new/en/media-services/in-focus-articles/new-unesco-data-proves-education-transforms-development/
UNESCO/UNICEF. (1990). *Meeting basic learning needs: A vision for the 1990s*. http://www.unesco.org/education/pdf/11_92.pdf
UNICEF/UNESCO. (2007). *A Human Rights-Based Approach to EDUCATION FOR ALL. A framework for the realization of children's right to education and rights within education*, New York. http://www.unicef.org/publications/files/A_Human_Rights_Based_Approach_to_Education_for_All.pdf
Wintersteiner, W. (1999). *Pädagogik des Anderen: Bausteine für eine Friedenspädagogik in der Postmoderne*. Agenda: Münster.
Wintersteiner, W. (2010). Renewing peace research with culture of peace. In V. Ratković & W. Wintersteiner (Eds.), *Culture of peace: A concept and a campaign revisited* (pp. 40–57). Klagenfurt/Celovec: Drava, also available at: http://www.uni-klu.ac.at/frieden/downloads/Friedensjahrbuch_2010.pdf
Wintersteiner, W. (2013). Building a global community for a culture of peace: The Hague appeal for peace global campaign for peace education (1999–2006). *Journal of Peace Education, 10*(2), 138–156.
Yousafzai, M. (2013). *Speech at the Youth Takeover of the United Nations*. https://secure.aworldatschool.org/page/content/the-text-of-malala-yousafzais-speech-at-the-united-nations/
Zaldívar, J. I. (2011). Revisiting the critiques of Ivan Illich's Deschooling Society. *International Journal for Cross-Disciplinary Subjects in Education (IJCDSE), 1*(1), 618–626.

Websites

EU-Asia Higher Education Platform: The Lisbon Process. http://www.eahep.org/europeanhigher-education/background/lisbon-process.html
Global Education First Initiative. http://www.globaleducationfirst.org/about.html

Part II
Education and Social Learning: Their Impact on the Development of Children and Adolescents

Attacks on Education in Conflict, Post-Conflict and Non-Conflict Settings

Jovana Carapic and Hannah Dönges

Abstract Despite growing calls for more accurate measurement and comprehensive reporting, the magnitude of attacks on education is under-researched. In addition, understanding attacks on education is further hindered by the exclusion of non-conflict (albeit often extremely violent) settings from analysis. Relying on available evidence and the authors' own database, *Attacks on Education*, this chapter seeks to provide a concise exploration of the global magnitude of attacks on education. Drawing on the work of Wood (2012) we propose that understanding attacks on education requires disaggregating the phenomenon along four dimensions: frequency, targeting, repertoire, and purpose. Firstly empirically elaborating on the four dimensions, the chapter goes on to show the utility of the proposed framework by examining attacks on education carried out by the Nigerian militant group Boko Haram.

1 Introduction

The "attacks on education" debate is largely framed by the Children and Armed Conflict Mandate. Formulated in eight United Nations Security Council resolutions (SCR),[1] the mandate focuses on the "grave violations" against children, whose

[1] This includes SCR 1261(1999), 1379 (2001), 1539 (2004), 1612 (2005), 1882 (2009), 1998 (2011), 2068 (2012), and 2143 (2014).

J. Carapic (✉)
Small Arms Survey, Geneva, Switzerland
e-mail: jovana.carapic@smallarmssurvey.org

H. Dönges
Graduate Institute of International and Development Studies, Geneva, Switzerland
e-mail: hannah.donges@graduateinstitute.ch

H. Kury et al. (eds.), *Women and Children as Victims and Offenders: Background, Prevention, Reintegration*, DOI 10.1007/978-3-319-08398-8_5

presence triggers the application of international law[2] to those parties involved in their perpetration. The six grave violations committed against children in armed conflict include:

1. the recruitment, re-recruitment and use of children by parties to armed conflict;
2. the killing and maiming of children;
3. rape and other sexual violence;
4. abductions of children;
5. attacks against schools or hospitals, and
6. denial of humanitarian access (S/RES/1998 (2011), §1).

In terms of attacks against schools, the most relevant resolution is SCR 1998 (2011), which defines attacks on education (and hospitals) as a violation of international law in a three-fold manner, to include:

(a) recurrent attacks on schools and/or hospitals;
(b) recurrent attacks against protected persons in relation to schools and/or hospitals, and
(c) threats of attacks against protected persons in relation to schools and/or hospitals.

SCR 1998 also stipulates that all parties to a conflict that are found to be engaged in these violations are to be added to the annex of the annual *Children in Armed Conflict Reports* (See SCR 1998 (2011): 2). In addition, it calls on the Secretary-General "to prepare without delay, concrete time-bound action plans to halt those violations and abuses" (See SCR 1998 (2011): 3). Finally, the resolution stresses the need for monitoring and reporting of the military use of schools and hospitals, and attacks on and kidnapping of teachers and medical personnel. The emphasis on monitoring and reporting has recently been re-affirmed by SCR 2143 (2014), which called on United Nations Country Taskforce teams to enhance the monitoring and reporting of the military use of schools (See SCR 2143 (2014), p. 5).

Despite a number of initiatives taking up the call for more and better monitoring and reporting—especially the three *Education Under Attack* reports (UNESCO 2007, 2010b; GCPEA 2014a)—mechanisms necessary for systematic data collection have been found wanting. While wartime attacks on education are assumed to be occurring in many, if not all armed conflicts, in reality not much is known about its actual prevalence, the perpetrators involved, the circumstances under which it takes place, for what purpose it is used, and how it is regulated.

The aim of this chapter is to contribute to the attacks on education debate (UNESCO 2010, p. 5) by shedding light on the global pattern of attacks on education in conflict, post-conflict (often fragile), and non-conflict settings. Relying on available evidence (international reports, existing databases, and media) and the

[2] Here international law is seen to encompass International Humanitarian Law (IHL), International Human Rights Law (IHRL), international criminal law (ICL), and customary international law.

authors' own database, *Attacks on Education,*[3] this chapter seeks to provide a concise exploration of the global magnitude of attacks on education. To achieve this goal, the chapter proceeds in four parts. First, the chapter briefly introduces key concepts and definitions, including a conceptualization of "attacks on education". The chapter then goes on to discuss the contemporary phenomenon of attacks on education. Drawing on the work of Wood (2012), the chapter proposes that understanding any particular form of violence requires disaggregating the phenomenon along four dimensions: frequency, targeting, repertoire, and purpose. In order to show the utility of the proposed theoretical framework, the chapter moves on to a detailed elaboration of the pattern of attacks on education by the Nigerian militant group Boko Haram, whose name loosely translates to "Western education is sinful."

2 Concepts and Definitions

In accordance with recent international debates, in this chapter we limit our analysis to the formal schooling sector, conceptualized as an educational system that has a well-defined set of features. Specifically, **formal education** refers to the highly institutionalized, chronologically graded and hierarchically structured "education system" ranging from lower primary school to the upper reaches of the university (Coombs and Ahmed 1974, p. 8).[4] Attacks on education take place in various settings and are perpetrated by a number of different actors including armed groups (state and non-state) but also individuals. They can be motivated by personal beliefs aimed at achieving particular goals, as well as group or collective objectives (i.e. motivated by political, military, ideological, sectarian, ethnic, religious or criminal reasons). They have been observed in times of armed conflict, but also in non-conflict situations. Depending on the context, attacks on education can take many forms (O'Malley 2007, pp. 39–40).

For the purpose of this chapter, an **attack on education** is the use of force (or threat of) against the education system, especially students, teachers and other educational personnel (both within schools and governmental ministries), and educational facilities.[5] In our analysis we also include the military occupation or use of schools, as this very act is seen to elicit armed retaliation, which has the potential to result in lethal victimization of individuals inside or near the school.

[3] The *Attacks on Education* Database is a collection of seven datasets: *Attacks on Education Incidents dataset*, by armed conflict and year (2008–2013); *Repertoire Dataset* (2008–2013); *Attacks on Secondary and Tertiary Dataset* (March 2011–December 2014); Attacks on Education—Pakistan Dataset (March 2008–December 2014); *Attacks on Education – Honduras Dataset* (2007–2013); *Attacks on Education – Colombia Dataset* (2007–2013); *Attacks on Education – United States Dataset* (2001–2011).

[4] It must be mentioned that in many parts of the world religious schooling is a key elements of the formal education system, and thus is included in our conceptualization of formal education.

[5] For additional information, also see Save the Children 2013, p. 4 and GCPEA (2014a), p. 43.

This is in line with the most recent empirical findings, which suggest that in the majority of countries with armed conflicts in recent years, armed forces and armed groups have used schools and other education institutions for military purposes" (GCPEA 2012, p. 8).

3 Understanding Attacks on Education

3.1 Frequency

The first step in examining the pattern of a particular type of violence is inquiring about its **frequency**, or the number of occurrences of a particular event in a given period of time (Wood 2012, pp. 392–393). Although on the face of it this appears to be a simple endeavour, assessing the frequency of any type of armed violence is difficult. Arguably, two of the main reasons for this are the lack of reliable data, and coincidently the lack of a baseline, which would allow for a comparison of the change in frequency over time.[6] The situation is no different when talking about attacks on education, with the available data usually compiled from a variety of sources including media, human rights reports, and UN monitoring documents. While informative, and often rich with detail, these methods of data collection are problematic for a number of reasons.

The lack of a coherent definition on what constitutes an "attack on education" is perhaps the biggest challenge. While some media outlets might report all instances in which a student or a teacher is killed, others might only report that a school has been hit by a rocket and provide no information on the number of casualties. Similarly, some human rights reports might highlight what portion of the formal security sector has been directly affected by armed conflict—either in terms of its lethal deaths of teachers and students but also military use of schools—and others focus on the overall number of school closures within a conflict-affected area. While all of these "reports" of attacks on education might highlight a particular aspect of the overall phenomenon of "attacks on education," they tell us little about its actual prevalence and frequency in a particular society. Rather, they speak more about the "reporting" mechanisms put in place and what issue source documents—be they media, human rights reports, or UN documents—are focusing on at any given time.

This is best illustrated by the passing of SCR 1998 (2011). Although the previous Security Council resolutions and Secretary-General's reports included attacks on education, it was only with the passing of Resolution 1998 in 2011 that more detailed information on the scope of the violation was provided. Accessing data in times of conflict is difficult, and records and casualty tracking may rely on armed

---

[6] As mentioned, the GTD database constitutes an exception; and adds to the frequency of attacks also their lethality.

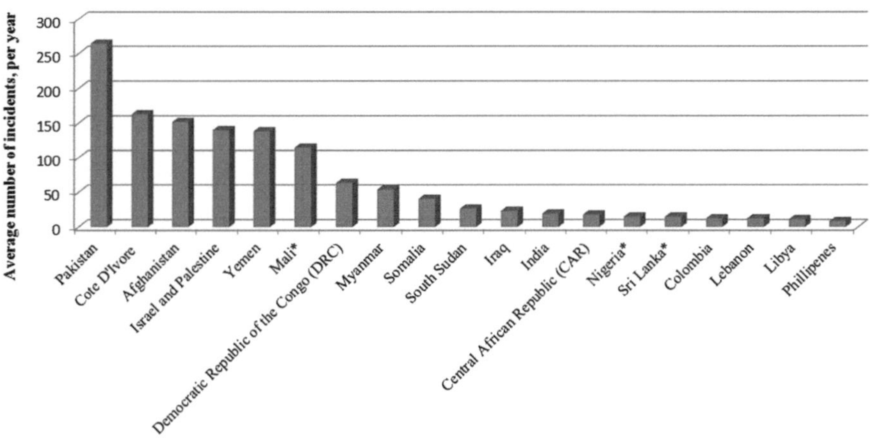

Fig. 1 Average annual number of reported incidents of attacks on schools or military use of schools, 2011–2013. *Source*: Carapic and Dönges (2014); *Data available for one year only: Mali (2012), Nigeria (2013), Sri Lanka (2011)

violence observatories, or policy initiatives that may collect data in a more disaggregated form, identifying victims and targets of attacks. According to the available quantitative data provided in the Secretary-General reports, between 2011 and 2013 there was an average of 1300 incidents of attacks on schools or military use of schools per year (Fig. 1). Although the reports themselves provide more qualitative information on 'attacks on education' and stipulate overall numbers of schools affected by insecurity within each country listed, this data is not reflected in the figure as it is not consistently included in the reports nor across all of the countries.[7]

Although SCR 1998 calls for monitoring of all incidents of attacks on education, not all meet the criteria for listing in the reports on Children and Armed Conflict. Rather, the reports include only those incidents which are found to be in violation of international law. Specifically, incidents are excluded from listing if they include cases in which the school building itself was used to launch military operations, or if students, teachers, or other educational personnel were directly participating in hostilities. In such situations, schools and educational personnel are considered "lawful" targets under international humanitarian law (United Nations 2014a, b, p. 6). Consequently, while SCR 1998 and the monitoring mechanism it triggers leads to more systematic monitoring and collection of data, it underreports the total prevalence of "attacks on education." To get a full picture of the frequency of attacks on education, one much move beyond the parameters of international humanitarian law.

The Global Terrorism Database (GTD), for instance, records all terrorist attacks—including those directed against educational institutions (coded as attacks

[7] "Attacks on Education Incidents Dataset, by armed conflict and year," see Carapic and Dönges (2014).

against school facilities, teachers, students, school guards (GTD 2014a, p. 32)—since 1970. According to the database, between 1970 and 2013 more than 3400 terrorist attacks on educational institutions occurred in 110 countries (GTD 2014b, p. 1). This makes up about 2.7 % of all terrorist attacks that occurred during the time period.[8] Of all the affected countries, Pakistan experienced the most terrorist attacks on educational institutions, with a total of 743 attacks (GTD 2013, 2014b). The majority of these attacks (96 %) took place since 2004. Moreover, between 2004 and 2013, many more attacks on educational targets occurred in Pakistan than in the next three countries combined: Thailand (213), Afghanistan (205), and Iraq (184) (GTD 2014b, p. 2).

Perhaps the most comprehensive collection of information on attacks on education can be found in the Global Coalition to Protect Education from Attack's (GCPEA) *Education Under Attack 2014* report. According to the report, between 2009 and 2010 a significant pattern of attacks on education was observed in 30 countries.[9] Compared to the data obtain from the Secretary-General Reports (Fig. 1; n = 19), the GCPEA data represents a considerable increase in the number of affected countries. This increase is not surprising, however, given that the research of the *Education Under Attack* report aimed to produce a comprehensive picture of the prevalence of "attacks on education" globally. This is evident by the low "threshold" for inclusion of incidents: the report defines a "significant pattern of attacks on education" as "five or more incidents or victims including at least one direct attack on a school or the killing of at least one teacher, student or academic" (GCPEA 2014a, p. 42). According to the report the most heavily affected countries with more than 1000 reported attacks on education or deaths of students, teachers or other education personnel attacked during 2009–2012 were: Afghanistan, Colombia, Pakistan, Somalia, South Sudan and Syria (GCPEA 2014a, p. 42).

Despite the low threshold, the data provided by the *Education Under Attack 2014* report also tends to underrepresent the overall magnitude of attacks on education, mainly because it focuses on targeted attacks on education. The report provides information on schools being used by military forces making them a target in times of war. It does not cover, or even aim to cover, the destruction of schools and death of students and teachers as a result of unintended military combat in the course of an armed conflict generally (Jones and Naylor 2014, p. 46). This is problematic since in situations of high-intensity military operations the damage to physical infrastructure (including roads, bridges, schools and other buildings) can be considerable (Jones and Naylor 2014). Following the withdrawal of Indonesian

[8] According to the GTD, terrorism is defined as "the threatened or actual use of illegal force and violence by a non-state actor to attain a political, economic, religious, or social goal through fear, coercion, or intimidation" (GTD 2014a, p. 8).

[9] Including: Afghanistan, Bahrain, Central African Republic (CAR), Colombia, Côte d'Ivoire, Democratic Republic of the Congo (DRC), Egypt, Ethiopia, India, Indonesia, Iran, Iraq, Israel/Palestine, Kenya, Libya, Mali, Mexico, Myanmar, Nigeria, Pakistan, the Philippines, Russia, Somalia, South Sudan, Sudan, Syria, Thailand, Turkey, Yemen and Zimbabwe. See GCPEA (2014a), p. 42.

forces from Timor-Leste in 1999, for instance, more than 70 % of all infrastructure (including buildings, homes and schools) was destroyed (World Bank 2014). During the Rwandan genocide about 76 % of all schools were damaged or destroyed, and in October 1994 only 648 of 1,836 schools were operational (Obura 2003, p. 47). In the first few months of 2003, the US-led military invasion of Iraq resulted in the damage to 60 % of kindergartens, 89 % of primary schools, and to 69 % of the secondary schools (United Nations General Assembly 2009, p. 2).

The UN Secretary-General reports on Children and Armed Conflict, the Global Terrorism Database (GTD) and the Global Coalition to Protect Education from Attack (GCPEA) report tend to focus on conflict-affected or fragile countries carried out by non-state armed groups. They, thus, often occlude from analysis attacks on education in non-conflict settings that might not fall under the label of terrorism (even if they resemble it, see below) and are committed by individuals not linked to armed groups. However, the focus on armed conflict does not reflect the global changes in the nature and distribution of armed violence, which tends to be concentrated in so-called non-conflict settings such as Central and Latin America and parts of Sub-Saharan Africa (GBAV 2011, GBAV 2015). Arguably, then, the available information on the frequency of attacks on education grossly underestimated the scope of the problem.

Although cross-national data on attacks on education in non-conflict settings is scarce, evidence suggests that students and teachers are often victims. In Honduras—a country that has one of the highest rates of lethal violence in the world (GBAV 2011, p. 53)—it has been suggested that one teacher is violently murdered every month (Telesur 2014). Yet data obtained from the Violence Observatory at the University of Democracy, Peace, and Security (*Instituto Universitario en Democracia Paz y Seguridad*), suggests that this figure is a significant underestimation. According to the available data it appears that from 2007–2013, on average 78 students, 14 teachers, and 50 university professionals are killed each year on school premises.[10]

The case of Honduras highlights that even in (legally defined) non-conflict settings, attacks on education take place regularly and should be taken into account when considering the global frequency of the phenomenon. In the United States, for instance, between 2001 and 2011, on average 59 deaths occurred at school per year.[11] When this number is disaggregated by type of victim, it becomes evident that every year on average 23 teachers and educational staff are killed in primary and secondary schools; there are 19 homicides of youth (5–18 years of age) in primary and secondary schools; and 17 homicides take place in post-secondary educational institutions. Figure 2 shows the 10-year trend in school deaths in the

[10] Attacks on Education—Honduras Dataset (2007–2013); see Carapic and Dönges (2014).

[11] Here "at school" refers to deaths that occur on school property (primary, secondary or tertiary), on the way to or from regular sessions at school, and while attending or traveling to or from a school-sponsored event. Also see BJS (2014), p. 7.

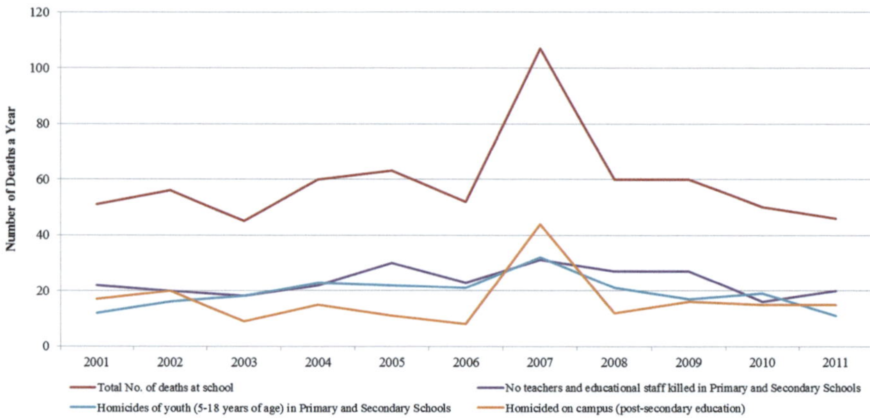

Fig. 2 Number of deaths at school in the United States, 2001–2011. *Source*: Carapic and Dönges (2014)

US, and illustrates that—contrary to common perception—lethal violence at schools is relatively constant. The spike in deaths in 2007 can be largely attributed to the school shooting at Virginia Polytechnic Institute and State University in Blacksburg, Virginia, when on 16 April, 33 individuals (including the perpetrator) were killed.

The examples of Honduras and the United States not only highlight the prevalence of attacks on education in non-conflict settings, but also emphasize the extent to which such attacks occur in secondary and tertiary education. Evidence suggests that although attacks on such educational institutions do occur in times of war, they are more likely to take place in non-conflict situations (GCPEA 2014a, p. 21). According to the *Attacks on Secondary and Tertiary Dataset (March 2011-December 2014)* in conflict and non-conflict settings, there were a minimum of 65 instances of attacks between March 2011 and December 2014, resulting in the death of at least 666 individuals and another 380 injured. Of the total number of instances, 11 occurred in or around secondary schools, while the rest were directed against tertiary educational facilities (colleges and universities). In terms of the type of perpetrator, the majority of instances were committed (in descending order) by identified non-state armed groups[12] (26), unidentified assailants[13] (24), state security forces (mostly police; 14), and civilians (1) (Carapic and Dönges 2014).

[12] "Identified non-state armed groups" refers to instances in which the public authorities have identified the assailants and/or when an armed group has claimed responsibility for an attack.

[13] "Unidentified assailants" refers to instances in which the individual or group of individuals committing the attack was not identified by the public authorities and/or when no non-state armed group has claimed responsibility.

3.2 *Targeting*

The second dimension needed for understanding a particular form of violence is **targeting**. This dimension simultaneously refers to the particular population of victims (*who is the target?*) but also how it is being affected by a particular form of violence (*how are they targeted?*). As such, targeting can take on three forms (Kalyvas 2006, p. 142; Wood 2012, pp. 393–394).

First, targeting can be **selective**, which entails the use of violence against specific individuals due to their personal beliefs or particular behaviours. The second form is **collective targeting,** which overlaps with selective targeting but involves a different level of organization—in the sense that it targets a particular sub-group of the population (ethnic or religious minorities, women and children, the elderly, etc.) or particular sectors of society (depending on socio-economic status, political membership, vocation, and so on). Finally, targeting can be **indiscriminate**, so that anyone regardless of his or her personal beliefs or group membership is at risk of victimization. Indiscriminate violence thus tends to be random (Wood 2012, pp. 393–394).

Available evidence suggests that "attacks on education" tend to be selective targets resulting in few deaths primarily because attackers seem to be more likely to target unoccupied educational facilitates and particular individuals (GTD 2014b, p. 1). Perhaps one of the most notorious examples of selective targeting by armed groups was the attempted killing of Malala Yousafzai. An avid blogger and activists of women's right to education, Malala (along with two classmates) was shot in the head and neck on her ways back from school by Taliban militants who allegedly called out her name before shooting (BBC News Asia 2012). Although Malala's case has drawn a vast amount of international attention, it appears that selective targeting as defined above is more often aimed at teachers, university professors, ministers of education or other educational personnel.

In Pakistan, for instance, selective attacks on teachers, professors, and other educational personnel are more common than collective attacks on students—even though these tend to be more deadly (in the sense that they cause more deaths at once). As mentioned previously, between 1970 and 2013 there were at least 724 attacks on education in Pakistan, with the majority of them (94 %) being non-lethal attacks directed against educational infrastructure; this is evidenced by the fact that attacks were often directed at unoccupied primary, secondary schools and facilities of higher education (GTD 2014b, p. 2). Focusing in on the lethal attacks, between 2008 and 2013 there were at least 38 incidents of lethal attacks on education in Pakistan, out of which about 89 % (34 instances) were targeted killings of teachers, professors, and other educational personnel. Most of the killings took place outside of the school (usually as individuals were on their way to or from work) and were committed with firearms.[14] When focusing in on attacks on

[14] Attacks on Education—Pakistan Dataset (March 2008–December 2014), see Carapic and Dönges (2014).

secondary and tertiary education in Pakistan, the same pattern appears: teachers and professors tend to be targeted on route to or from campus and are often killed with firearms by unidentified assailants.[15]

Selective targeting of teachers and other educational personnel seems to be an especially common occurrence in some countries.[16] Compared to the global average, armed groups in Thailand, for instance, were not only more likely to be deadly but they were also nearly twice as likely to target instructors, professors, teachers and security personnel accompanying them on their commute to the schooling facility (GTD 2014b, p. 3). Colombia also appears to be particularly affected, with the country recently described as being "the most dangerous places in the world to be a teacher:" between 2009 and 2012, more than 140 teachers lost their lives, nearly 1100 received death threats, and about 300 were displaced from their homes due to fear of being targeted (GCPA 2014, p. 43). These findings are confirmed by data compiled by the authors for the purpose of this chapter, which suggest that between 2007 and 2012, on average 25 teachers and 643 students are killed every year in Colombia. In addition, there are at least 16 homicides a year that take place on or near educational centres and facilities.[17]

Collective targeting—attacks on particular sub-groups of society—appears to be more prominent when it is directed against students. In its global overview, the *Education Under Attack* report (2014) provides numerous examples in which "students" as a category of the population itself are targeted with the intention of causing large numbers of casualties. An illustrative example is the October 2011 suicide attack on a Mogadishu governmental compound, housing the Ministry of Higher Education, among others (GCPEA 2014b, p. 14). The attack—which was allegedly carried out by a suicide bomber belonging to Al-Shabaab (Chonghaile 2011)—resulted in between 70 and 100 casualties, most of which were students and parents who were waiting for results of scholarships from the Ministry of Higher Education. This is not the first time students were targeted in Somalia—in 2009 a suicide bomber dressed as a woman detonated his explosives during the graduation ceremony for medical students from Benadir University. The attack resulted in the death of up 30 people, most of whom were students.[18]

The aforementioned example is important for it sheds light on the fact that collective targeting appears to be especially prominent when looking at attacks on secondary and tertiary education. According to the *Attacks on Secondary and Tertiary Dataset (March 2011-December 2014)*, of the 666 deaths that occurred between March 2011 and December 2014 in secondary and tertiary educational

[15] Attacks on Secondary and Tertiary Dataset (March 2011–December 2014), See Carapic and Dönges (2014).

[16] Research has shown that such attacks are prevalent in Afghanistan, Colombia, Iraq, Nepal, Pakistan, Thailand, and Zimbabwe. See GCPEA (2014b), p. 8.

[17] Attacks on Education—Colombia Dataset (2007–2013), see Carapic and Dönges (2014).

[18] Among the dead were also Omar Hashi Aden, Somali security minister, Abdikarim Farah, former Somali ambassador to Ethiopia and the African Union, and a number of other Somali diplomats. See BBC News (2009) and GCPEA (2014a), p. 14.

institution around the globe, at least 486 were students with 96 % of all student casualties (about 469) occurring in just nine instances (Carapic and Dönges 2014).

On 16 December 2014, more than 130 students were killed in Pakistan alone. Members of the Tehreek-e-Taliban group attacked the Army Public School and Degree College in Peshawara province. On 26 September 2014, 43 students went missing in Mexico. Although the circumstances surrounding their disappearance remain controversial (see below), it was subsequently declared that they were killed by a local criminal group (BBC News Latin America 2014). In Syria, about 95 students are thought to have been killed as a result of attacks on universities in 2013. On 15 January 2013 explosions on the campus of the University of Aleppo resulted in 80 individuals being killed (BBC News Middle East 2013). Two months later, on 28 March 2013, a mortar attack on the Damascus University led to the death of 15 students (Holmes 2013). A recent attack on a bus company in Maramag, in the south of the Philippines, killed 11 students as they were going home from school. Although the media has described the attack as extortion against the bus company, the fact that the bomb exploded soon after the students boarded the bus raises questions as to the validity of this statement (Press 2014, Arab News 2014 and AFP 2014).

As will be explored in more detail later on in the chapter, the armed group Boko Haram is recognized for its targeting of students (both male and female) in Nigeria. On two separate attacks occurring in July and September 2013, the militant group attacked pupils at the College of Agriculture, and Mamudo Government Secondary School in Yobe state, killing at least 91 students and one teacher. In both instances, the group stormed the school and killed the occupants with a combination of firearms and explosives. The schools were then burned to the ground. In February 2014, Boko Haram stormed the Federal Government College in Buni Yadi, in Yobe State, killing 43 male students and injuring 11 others (Carapic and Dönges 2014).

On 15 June 2013, a suicide bomber belonging to the Lashkar e Jhangvi, dressed in a burka, detonated his explosives on the campus of Sardar Bahadur Khan Women's University in Quetta, Pakistan. The incident occurred on campus as the female students and teachers were boarding a university bus. The explosion resulted in the killing of 14 female students and teachers. As the injured were taken to hospital, a second attack took place when a separate group of militants opened fire inside the emergency ward, killing three female nurses who were treating the wounded (BBC News Asia 2013). Collective targeting has also been directed against primary schools for girls. In September 2013, the Government Girls' Primary School in Bannu district, in Khyber Pakhtunkhwa Province in Pakistan, was targeted. Allegedly carried out by the local Taliban, the attack occurred when a bomb was detonated injuring 13 female pupils below the age of 10 (United Nations General Assembly 2014, p. 41).

In Afghanistan, female students face significantly higher risks of being attacked than their male counterparts. Although only 19 % of all schools in the country are designated "girls' schools," attacks against them account for up to 40 % of all attacks against education (CARE International 2009, p. 33; Watchlist 2010, p. 25). On 12 November 2008, Taliban militants attacked a group of girls on their way to school by throwing acid on their faces. The militants were allegedly paid 100,000

Pakistani rupees for each girl that was attacked (United Nations General Assembly 2009, p. 4). Attacks on girls' schools have taken place in other armed conflicts as well. On 30 July 2013, Syrian Government forces allegedly shelled the Hamza mosque, recognized as a girls' school, in the Anadan area, north of Aleppo. Nine girls, all younger than 10 years of age, and four female teachers reportedly lost their lives (United Nations General Assembly 2014, p. 31).

Selective and collective targeting of students is not only a feature of armed conflict or fragile situations, but is also found in non-conflict societies. In the literature on non-conflict school shootings, there has been a concerted effort to differentiate between different types of incidents, namely between targeted shootings (i.e. those committed by a single perpetrator and usually involving one specific victim) and random or rampage shootings (defined as "expressive, non-targeted attacks on a school institution") (Muschert 2007, p. 63). Evidence from the US suggests that even though rampage shootings make up a minority of all school shooting incidents, they are nevertheless responsible for the majority of lethal deaths. Of all the rampage school shooting that occurred in the US between 1990 and 2012, three incidents—Columbine High School, Virginia Tech University, and Sandy Hook Elementary School—accounted for more than half of all rampage shooting deaths and nearly 20 % of all school shooting deaths.[19]

Like collective attacks in times of armed conflict, rampage shootings can also be gendered in nature. In fact, 2014 marks 25 years since the deadly attack on female university students at the École Polytechnique at the University of Montreal. On 6 December 1989, Marc Lépine entered the university, separated female and male students, forced the latter to leave, and proceeded to shoot the remaining females, killing 14 women and injuring at least 13. During the attack, he allegedly yelled out "You're all a bunch of feminists. I hate feminists," and in a subsequently published suicide note went on to write that his actions were not for economic reasons but for political ones and he "decided to send the feminists, who have always ruined my life, to their Maker" (Tonso 2009, p. 1271).

3.3 Repertoire

Repertoire is another step in the disaggregation of violence and refers to the circumstances surrounding a violent incident, both before and during its occurrence (Wood 2012, p. 395). Specifically, it demands that a particular form of violence (such as attacks on education) is placed in relation to the other types of violence an armed group engages in (such as lethal violence or sexual violence, compare Wood 2014, p. 3), as well as highlighting the mode or method in which a particular violent

[19] Between 1990 and 2012, there were 215 fatal school shooting incidents, resulting in 363 individuals killed. These were distributed as follows: 25 rampage shooting incidents (135 deaths), 142 targeted shooting incidents (179 deaths), and 48 other shooting incidents in schools (49 deaths); see Shultz et al. (2013).

act is carried out. Not all armed actors have the same repertoire of violence, and a particular actor's repertoire may change (become wider or narrower) as the group grows or as the conflict evolves. In addition, repertoires of violence vary across settings (conflict or non-conflict), and even within a particular setting. Ultimately, this means that in order to truly understand the pattern of attacks on education, we need to take the violent repertoires of armed actors into account.

The *Repertoire Dataset (2008–2013)* uses the 2008–2013 UN Secretary-General's *Children in Armed Conflict Reports* in order to build a systemic dataset of the repertoire of violence against children in armed conflict. Drawing on the Annexes (which list violators of IHL) and the body text of the annual reports (which often provide more detailed information),[20] the dataset features annual data at the level of the armed actors, including 51 non-state actors, 17 state forces, and 5 pro-state militias.[21] At the time of writing, the year 2008 is chosen as the starting point for data collection mainly because previously to this year attacks on education were not systematically reported by the Secretary-General.[22]

Concerning the forms of violence, the dataset focuses on child victimization, disaggregating the information along four types of violence: recruitment and use of child soldiers, killing and maiming of children, rape and other forms of sexual violence against children, and attacks on schools (including military use of schools, collateral damage of schools during fighting, threatening of teachers, and looting of schools). The inclusion of these four forms of violence in one dataset allows us not only to measure their individual occurrence,[23] but provides also insights into the co-occurrence of different forms of violence by particular actors and across actors in a particular conflict.

According to the *Repertoire Database*, between 2008 and 2013 there were at least 33 actors that carried out attacks on education (as defined above), of which 64 % (n = 21) were non-state actors, 24 % (n = 8) state actors, and 12 % (n = 4) were pro-state militias. These findings indicate that attacks on education in times of

[20] Using both the Annexes and the body text of the Children in Armed Conflict Reports means that our dataset includes information on all types of violence a particular armed actor engages in, and not only on the systemic use of a particular form of violence that would put it on the Secretary-General's list and trigger IHL. In addition, it must be mentioned that the dataset aims at describing patterns of violence, which, in turn, means that actors need to be mentioned on at least two occasions (i.e. two consecutive years) in order to be included in the dataset.

[21] In line with current definitions in the field of civil war studies, pro-state militias are defined as groups that are (1) pro-government or sponsored by the government (national or subnational), (2) are not a part of the regular security forces, (3) are armed, and (4) are organized to some degree (Carey et al. 2013, p. 250).

[22] That being said, the authors are working towards expanding the dataset back to 2000, when the first report of the UN Secretary-General on children and armed conflict to the Council was published.

[23] At this point an occurrence of a particular form of violence is recorded (i.e. coded in the dataset) whenever it is made. No distinction between the degree of prevalence (i.e. how frequent it is) is mentioned. In other words, the dataset includes all reported incidents even if they have occurred (or been recorded) just once.

armed conflict are common, but are not always present. In addition, it indicates that in some cases attacks on education do not form part of an armed actor's repertoire of violence—i.e. a particular armed group might not attack students and teachers or use schools as a base, but might commit other forms of violence against children. The Lord's Resistance Army (LRA), an insurgent group of Ugandan origin and active in central Africa, is a case in point: while the LRA has been reported as committing grave violations against children (including recruitment of child soldiers, the killing and maiming of children, and rape and sexual violence), there have been almost no confirmed reports of the group committing attacks on education in the UN Secretary-General's reports (Carapic and Dönges 2014).

The relationship between attacks on education and sexual violence against children is more difficult to discern. While the Secretary-General's reports provide information on the prevalence of sexual violence against children in armed conflict, the information is not systematic. Arguably, one of the main reasons for this is that sexual violence as a phenomenon is extremely hard to verify in times of armed conflict, and when it is reported, key information (relating to the perpetrator, and the location of the attack) is often missing.[24] Indeed, in the *Education Under Attack 2014* report, there were only two verified incidents of sexual violence occurring on school property en route to or from school: one in the Central African Republic and one in India. The report is careful not to suggest that the lack of reporting means that sexual violence and attacks on school are not related; instead it rightly suggests that there is a dearth of data on sexual violence and attacks on school, and on sexual violence in society more generally (GCPEA 2014a, p. 20).

The case of Taliban-affiliated groups in Afghanistan further illustrates this point. The Secretary-General's reports show that between 2008 and 2013, Taliban groups (such as the Tora Bora Front, Jamat Sunat al-Dawa Salafia, and Latif Mansur Network) consistently engaged in attacks on education, the recruitment of child soldiers, and killing and maiming of children (Carapic and Dönges 2014). While cases of sexual violence against children—including rape and sexual exploitation—were documented during the period, they were not attributed to any particular armed actor. The lack of attribution in the Secretary-General's annual reports is surprising given that the use of sexual violence, including that against children, has been recognized as a "widespread phenomenon" in the country (a finding that has been supported by recent qualitative research) (Secretary-General 2010, p. 14; Bloom 2014), and that the Secretary-General has been able to attribute the use of sexual violence to armed groups in other armed conflicts.

The insights obtained from the above paragraphs need to be taken with caution, as the data collection necessary for the contextualizing of attacks on education within a broader repertoire of violence has only just begun. More research needs to be undertaken to determine if and how "attacks on education" relate to other types

[24] It has been recognized that the measurement or sexual violence, including rape and other forms of sexual assault, is one of the most challenging methodological issues in the field of both in times of conflict and non-conflict settings. See Carapic 2014; Fisher 2009.

of victimization of children and other elements of the population. The *Repertoire Dataset* is a first step in this regard, and in the future the data collection will have to be expanded, both in terms of time-period covered, sources analysed, and be placed in relations to other types of targets (including governmental facilities, religious institutions, security personnel, media, journalists).

Understanding an armed actor's repertoire of violence also implies taking into account the mode with which a particular form of violence is carried out. The *Repertoire Dataset (2008–2013)* disaggregates attacks on education along four main categories: threatening[25] and killing of students and teachers, destruction and/or looting of schools, collateral damage during fighting, and military use of schools. While the lack of systematic data makes it difficult to make concrete conclusions, available evidence suggests that the mode of attack on education varies across armed actors and that multiple modes might be used by the same actors over the course of the conflict. Taking Afghanistan as an illustrative example again, attacks on education are often committed by non-state armed groups and take the form of the burning of schools or school equipment, to forced closure of schools, to damage from attacks and fighting or explosions from improvised explosive devices in the vicinity of school buildings, or targeted military attacks and threats made against pupils and educational staff (Carapic and Dönges 2014).

The variety of modes of attack on education makes it extremely difficult to deal with, especially in terms of designing national and international policies. Perhaps for this reason, the international community is increasingly focusing on the military use of schools by parties to a conflict. The debate surrounding the *Lucens Guidelines* is a recent example of this. The guidelines are an attempt to reduce the prevalence of attacks on education in armed conflict by focusing on their most readily observable (and arguably controllable form), the use of schools by armed groups (GCPEA 2014b, p. 2). Norway has taken the lead in finalizing the draft guidelines that "were developed in consultation with experts from the ministries of foreign affairs, defense, education, and armed forces of 12 countries from each region of the world" (HRW 2014c). The *Lucens Guidelines* are timely considering that occupation of schools by armed groups often places students and teachers in danger (GCPA 2014, p. 53), as illustrated by the recent Taliban attacks in Peshwara province (described in more detail below) (Boone and MacAskill 2014a, Aljazeera 2014).

Despite the variety in modes of attacks on education in times of conflict, certain patterns are observable. According to the Global Terrorism Database (GTD), for instance, globally the three main modes of attack are bombings (52 %), firearms (22.7 %), and incendiary (14.4 %) (GTD 2013). Patterns also emerge when looking at lethal attacks against secondary and tertiary education. Of the 64 cases of attacks collated by the authors, nearly 63 % were carried out with firearms, 20 % by bombing (including suicide bombing), while the remaining 17 % were carried out

[25] Threatening actions may be symbolic (i.e. verbal) or physical (i.e. those that cause bodily harm but do not result in death, such as abductions or acid attacks on students/teachers).

by other methods, including: blunt objects, stabbings, beheadings, and unknown weapons (Carapic and Dönges 2014). While there is a need for further research and data collection to confirm the repertoire of violence across different types of armed actors, these findings suggest that the availability of small arms and light weapons in society plays a role in the prevalence of attacks on secondary and tertiary education.

Overt violence as captured by the above two datasets is not the only way armed actors can launch attacks on education. Indeed, in both conflict and non-conflict settings threats levied against students and teachers are a common occurrence, and usually aim to scare pupils and teachers or extort educational personnel for money. In Colombia, for instance, between January and September 2013 more than 350 teachers received death threats (GCPEA 2014a, p. 129). Similarly, in Afghanistan the Taliban have been known to issue threats against teachers (especially of girls' schools). In May 2013, local Taliban members in Nangarhar Province threatened teachers and children at a girls' school with acid attacks if the school continued with its operation (United Nations General Assembly 2014, p. 7). The use of threats also occurs in non-conflict albeit highly violent settings, such as El Salvador and Honduras, where gangs fight over the control of schools which in themselves provide valuable resources—both in terms of potential recruits but also as a source of funding through extortion of teachers. The consequent threat of violence in some schools is extremely high inviting considerable repression from the state (Arce 2014; Bairo 2013).

3.4 Purpose

Purpose is the fourth dimension of disaggregation needed for understanding a particular form of violence. While inherently this dimension inquires about the motivation behind the use of violence, the problem is that motivations are multiple and often combine in contradictory ways. Additionally, motives may change over time, affecting not only the way in which violence is used but also its purpose (Wood 2012, p. 393).

According to the *Education Under Attack 2014* report, the range of motives for attacks on education is large: from undermining of state power and authority, to controlling territory and behaviour of local populations, to threatening particular ethnic groups, to fostering military operations (including occupying schools and recruiting child soldiers), and even extortion (GCPEA 2014a, p. 47). While insightful, the variation in motives makes it extremely difficult to design policies to deal with (or even attempt to prevent) attacks on education. Rather than inquiring about the specific motivations, it is thus perhaps better to step back, take a look at the empirical pattern of violence, and then use this observation as a basis for making inferences about purpose. Such an endeavour would allow for a distinction between "opportunistic violence," "strategic violence," and "violence as practice" (Wood 2012, pp. 393–394).

Opportunistic violence refers to the use of violence for private or personal reasons. While opportunistic violence can re-occur, it is rarely planned in advance and does not take on a distinguishable pattern—rather it occurs when the opportunity presents itself (Wood 2012, pp. 393–394). Arguably, many of the single-perpetrator attacks on education that occur in post-conflict, fragile, and non-conflict settings can be said to be opportunistic attacks on education. Indeed, recent research has found that so-called "lone wolf" terrorist attacks and school shootings are not distinct phenomena, as once thought; rather, both "are spectacular acts of indiscriminate violence perpetrated by a lone actor (or a very small group) that deviate from the usual patterns of violent crime" (Wood 2012, pp. 393–394). While such single-perpetrator attacks on education may have political motivations, the individuals are rarely part of a bigger armed group and instead use attacks on education as a way to achieve their personal political goals (Wood 2012, pp. 393–394).

The opportunistic nature of attacks on education can be glimpsed by taking into account the mode in which high-school teachers and university professors are killed around the globe. Information collated in the *Attacks on Secondary and Tertiary Dataset (March 2011-December 2014)* indicates that in all of the cases where no perpetrator was identified (or no responsibility for an incident was claimed), the attack on education involved a targeted killing of professors or other educational workers on their way to or from campus (Carapic and Dönges 2014). The way in which many of these individuals die is also illustrative of the opportunistic nature of violence, as they were usually ambushed in their cars, homes, or offices and killed through the use of firearms or bombing (including suicide bombing) (Carapic and Dönges 2014).

Many of the school attacks in non-conflict settings—such as the school shootings that have occurred in Canada, Europe, and the US in the past two decades—can also be categorized as opportunistic violence, serving the personal motives of the assailant often to exact revenge on the school or community (Malkki 2014). Rampage school shootings, in particular, are forms of opportunistic violence. Rampage incidents have been defined as "non-targeted attacks on a schools," meaning that they "involve attacks on multiple parties, selected almost at random" (Newman 2004, pp. 14–15). Thus even if the perpetrator may have had a specific target at the outset, in the course of the attack perpetrators tend to get "lost in the moment" and are often unaware of who has been killed until after the fact (Newman 2004, pp. 14–15).

The attention to the motivations behind rampage school shootings has increased since the 1999 Columbine attack, when two high-school students killed 15 pupils at random, and wounded 23 others before committing suicide.[26] Allegedly, the perpetrators were motivated by a combination of personal reasons—including revenge

[26] Part of the reason for this increased focus on motives is that in many incidents since the Columbine shootings, perpetrators have referred to the event explicitly in their communications with media, personal diaries, or suicide notes (Larkin 2009).

on those individuals who had been bullying them in school and as a protest against the school system and society that has allowed such behaviour to proliferate (Larkin 2009; Malkki 2014). Often influenced by the Columbine incidents, perpetrators of rampage shootings tend to act alone but nevertheless frame their actions as being part of a wider socio-political struggle in society: "for them, it was not only about their personal situation, but also about dying for a cause that they felt had wider significance" (Malkki 2014, p. 200).

Strategic violence refers to the pattern of violence which appears to be purposely adopted for achieving a particular goal. While strategic violence can be carried out by individuals, it is more often perpetrated by armed groups (state and non-state). Consequently, when it comes to attacks on education, strategic violence refers to "any violence whose empirical pattern indicates that [an] armed group controls its use: namely, that violence occurs when it is strategically beneficial (in terms of group objectives) and does not occur when it is not" (Wood 2012, p. 394).

The lack of information and systematic data collection makes it difficult to ascertain the strategic nature of attacks on education. That being said, evidence related to the military use of schools and universities does point to its use being strategic. Indeed, of the 30 countries profiled in the *Education Under Attack 2014* report, the military use of schools was recorded in 24 cases, including: Afghanistan, Central African Republic, Colombia, Côte d'Ivoire, the Democratic Republic of the Congo, Egypt, Ethiopia, India, Iraq, Indonesia, Israel/Palestine, Kenya, Libya, Mali, Myanmar, Pakistan, the Philippines, Somalia, South Sudan, Sudan, Syria, Thailand, Yemen and Zimbabwe (GCPEA 2014a, p. 51).

Often being some of the sturdiest buildings in a conflict affected area, schools and universities are thought to be strategically used by armed actors as bases, weapons storehouses, training grounds, and detention centres (GCPEA 2014a, p. 51). While both state and non-state actors have been found to occupy and use schools for military purposes, the evidence also points to another strategic element of schools: they sometimes serve as recruitment grounds. While more research on this issue needs to be conducted, available evidence suggests that in some cases armed groups—such as Al-Shabaab and Boko Haram—rely on schools for the systematic recruitment of male students as soldiers and female students as wives (GCPEA 2014a, p. 47).

Violence as practice refers to situations, in which a particular form of violence is prevalent, but is not necessarily adopted by the leadership of an armed group in order to achieve a specific purpose (regardless of its strategic usefulness in that regard) (Wood 2012, pp. 393–394). Consequently, a particular form of violence (such as attacks on education) can be termed a practice when it is frequently used by group members and which is tolerated by the group's leaders, and takes place when it is strategic as well as when it is not. The development of a particular form of violence as a practice might originate from a number of sources, including diffusion of methods among different armed groups, or from its use as a form of compensation (Wood 2012, p. 394).

Keeping in mind the lack of systemic data, available evidence suggest attacks on education by different types of armed groups should at best be considered practices. That being said, it appears that the practice of attacks on education differs across armed actors, so that certain types of attacks are more likely to be carried out by some groups and less likely by others. State security forces, or armed groups associated with them, for example, are more likely to engage in forms of attacks on education that are aimed at creating order (such as imprisonment, torture, and attack on higher educational facilities) in the face of socio-political discontent (such as quelling union activity or student protests) (GCPEA 2014a, p. 49). This is supported by data obtained from the *Attacks on Secondary and Tertiary Dataset (March 2011-December 2014)* which shows that of the 14 instances in which state security forces were involved in attacks on education, almost all were carried out by police forces and involved shooting of pupils during student protests.[27]

The recent disappearance of 43 students in Mexico is a noteworthy example of the involvement of state officials and security forces in attacks on education.[28] On 23 September 2014, about 100 students from the Raúl Isidro Burgos Rural Teachers College of Ayotzinapa in Tixtla, Guerrero, Mexico, travelled to Iguala, Guerrero, in order to protest against discriminatory hiring and funding practices from the government. On their way to Iguala, the student convoy was allegedly attacked by individuals wearing uniforms. Although the events that led to the disappearance (and potential death) of the students is still unclear, the media has largely reported the involvement of the police and the Iguala mayor, José Luis Abarca Velázquez, in the incident (Gorton 2014; Tuckmann 2014; Piñeda 2014). The attack on the students has gathered international attention and fostered mass protests in Mexico, not least because the event is reminiscent of the 1968 Tlatelolco massacre, when Mexico City police officers and military troops shot into a crowd of unarmed students killing up to 300 individuals (Borden 2005, p. 2). Despite the uncertain circumstances, in 2014 Mexico's attorney general declared that the students were killed by a local criminal group who had mistaken them for members of a rival organization (BBC News Latin America 2014).

Non-state armed groups tend to engage in the recruitment or abduction of students, the targeted killing of teachers, and the collective targeting of pupils. Such attacks on education are often politically motivated. Specifically, the aim is to undermine government control over an area or community (as schools are usually symbols of state presence); controlling who has the "right" to be educated (i.e. preventing the education of certain ethnic groups or sub-groups of the population, such as girls); or reacting to the "substance" of the curriculum (i.e. preventing teachings that revolve around particular social, religious or ethnic subjects) (GCPEA 2014a, p. 49). Apart from the military occupation and use of schools and recruitment of students as soldiers (discussed above), evidence does not

---

[27] In 2 of the 14 cases, students died while in police custody (Carapic and Dönges 2014).

[28] The dataset includes confirmed attacks on education that have resulted in the death of students. With the exception of one, the other missing students have not been identified.

support the claim that attacks on education by non-state armed groups is strategic. Rather, it appears that such acts of violence are more of a "practice" as they are not regular enough and are often not "beneficial" for the group. While attacks on education might bring about considerable (national and international) attention to the armed group and its goals, such actions usually result in swift and heavy-handed retaliation form the state.[29]

The attack on the Army Public School and Degree College in Peshawar, Pakistan, is an example of a politically motivated attack on education. The incident was carried out by the Tehrik-e-Taliban, in retaliation for the Pakistani army's offensive against the Taliban groups in the tribal areas near the Afghan border (Boone and MacAskill 2014b). The army offensive, named Zarb-e-Azb, has been underway in the tribal areas since the summer and has left about 1000 militants dead and tens of thousands of people displaced (Boone 2014). In retaliation for the offensive, seven armed Tehrik-e-Taliban militants (with some wearing suicide vests) entered the Army Public School on 16 December 2014. The siege, which lasted more than eight hours, resulted in the death of more than 140 individuals (of which at least 132 were students) and all seven militants (some of which were killed by state security forces and others by blowing themselves up). Although the Taliban claimed that the militants were only meant to kill older students, reports indicate that once the attack began individuals were shot at random (Boone and MacAskill 2014b). The incident not only gathered substantial international attention and condemnation, but also elicited a fresh counter-insurgency campaign against the Tehrik-e-Taliban (Tribune 2014).

The attack on the Army Public School is not the only case of schools being targeted as a means to achieving political goals. Perhaps one of the most devastating recent attacks occurred in Beslan, a town in the Republic of North Ossetia, Russia. On 1 September 2004, a group of heavily armed separatist-militants, apparently belonging to the Chechen leader Shamil Basayev's Riyadhin al-Salihin group, took about 1200 students, parents, and teachers hostage at School Number One. The 3-day siege resulted in the death of more than 330 hostages (188 of them school children) and about 600 individuals injured, more than half of them children (Tuathail 2009, p. 1). Similarly to the events in Pakistan, the Beslan hostage-taking occurred in retaliation for the aggressive counter-insurgency policies being implemented in Chechnya (Tuathail 2009, p. 8). Although the actual events that transpired during the school siege are contested, the incident nevertheless drew international attention and also paved the way for the passing of stricter counter-terrorism laws in Russia (Banovac and Patterson 2007; Dunlop 2009).

[29] It is for this reason that attacks on schools by some armed actors have been called 'terrorist' acts (Muschert 2007, p. 64).

4 "Western Education is Sinful": A Case Study of Boko Haram

4.1 Background: A Growing Insurgency

Nigeria is party to the International Covenant on Economic, Social and Cultural Rights, and the Convention on the Rights of the Child—both of which guarantee children the right to education. Yet Nigeria's ability to meet the goal of "universal education," as stipulated by the Millennium Development Goals (MDGs), has been criticized largely due to the low amount of attention and funding attributed to the formal education sector by the Nigerian government (Watkins 2014). Particularly in the far north of the country, Nigeria lacks the educational infrastructure to meet the needs of the local population and its international commitments. In the region, the lack of resources and institutional capacity is not limited to the formal education sector but also affects the provision of security, transportation, health, and electricity. The lack of such public goods, especially security, has led to an increase in grievances and violence. Many argue that socioeconomic reasons are the root causes for the violence, but some authors and analysts go further, attributing it to a combination of economic deprivation and corruption in Northern Nigeria (Achebe 2012), and the "failure of nation-building and democratic politics" (Mustapha 2012).

It is in this environment that the armed group Boko Haram emerged in 2009.[30] Although it is not clear if the name "Boko Haram" was given to the group itself, it is nevertheless often referred to as such. A combination of the Hausa word *boko* (meaning book), and the Arabic word *haram* (referring to something forbidden, ungodly, or sinful), the phrase "Boko Haram" is loosely translated as "education is sinful". The group is also often referred to as *Jama'atu Ahlis Sunna Lidda'awati wal-Jihad,* which in Arabic means "people committed to propagating the Prophet's teachings and jihad." Taking the two names into account, "Boko Haram" implies not only that education is sinful, but also that all non-Islamic education is to be prohibited. Specifically, adopting a strict interpretation of the Quran, the group proclaims that secular teachings—in terms of schooling but also Western values—are forbidden. It is this inherent meaning that is reflected in the often simplistic translation of Boko Haram as "Western education is sinful" (Adesoji 2010, p. 99).

Boko Haram claims that false and corrupt Muslims control Northern Nigeria, and thus seeks to impose a harsh form of Sharia in the north of the country (Adesoji 2010; ICG 2014, p. 1; HRW 2014a, p. 1). While the group's leadership criticized Muslims living in North Nigeria for their participation in an illegitimate, un-Islamic state, Boko Haram did not aim to violently overthrow the Nigerian government prior to 2009 (Watchlist 2014, p. 12). Yet increasing religious tensions between the

[30] Although the insurgency emerged in 2009, it is largely believed that the group itself has been around for more than 15 years, albeit under different names (Adesoji 2010, pp. 98–100).

Christian and Muslim communities, combined with repressive police tactics, fostered the radicalization of the group. The tipping point came in the summer of 2009, when after a series of confrontations between Boko Haram and the police the group's leadership proclaimed an all-out insurgency against the state (Adesoji 2010, pp. 98–102; BBC News Africa 2014). Although often portrayed as a radical element in society aiming to change the social and political landscape of a secular state, the Boko Haram insurgency reflects long-standing religious, ethnic and regional fault-lines in Nigeria (Agbiboa 2013, p. 1).

Since the start of the insurgency, the activities of Boko Haram have led to the death of close to 16,000 people. Nevertheless, the group has gained notoriety (at least in the international media) for its attacks on education. Indeed, of all terrorist attacks directed against educational targets in Nigeria, the majority (69 %) were carried out by Boko Haram (GTD 2014b, p. 3). Although historically both Nigerian Christians and Muslims have adopted and invested in modern education, especially the Yoruba (Pérouse de Montclos 2014, p. 266), this did not necessarily translate into the universal provision of education in northeastern Nigeria. In 2008, in areas where the Boko Haram insurgency began (such as in the states of Bauchi, Kano, Yobe and Borno), primary school attendance rates were quite low (37.2, 31.2, and 20.8 %, respectively) (DHS 2011, p. 164).

The attacks on education undertaken by Boko Haram since the start of the insurgency devastated the already weak educational system. The group has not only destroyed and looted schools, but has also carried out targeted killings and abductions of students and teachers. Their actions have also contributed to a climate of fear and insecurity in the northeast, which, in turn, has led to mass school closures. International attention to the existence and fighting of Boko Haram has particularly been raised by the abduction of some 200 school girls in Chibok in the summer of 2014. The teenage girls that were abducted in Borno state were part of a small national minority attending secondary school (Watkins 2014). Boko Haram was added to the annex of the *Children in Armed Conflict Reports* in 2014 because of its "continued, systematic attacks on schools and the killing and maiming of children" (United Nations General Assembly 2014, p. 45).

4.2 Frequency of Boko Haram Attacks on Education

The frequency of Boko Haram attacks on education and the development of the overall uprising are invariably linked to each other (Table 1). Violence perpetrated by Boko Haram escalated in the summer of 2009, after the capture and death of its leader, Mohamed Yusuf, at the hands of the Nigerian police. Following Yusuf's death, the group's second-in-command, Abubakar Shekau, took over leadership and unleashed a series of attacks on symbols of state power. Initially focusing on police stations, military barracks, and government officials, the group soon broadened its violent activities to include attacks on civilian objects, such as places of worship, UN agencies, bars, and schools (ICG 2014, p. ii; Watchlist 2014, p. 13).

Table 1 Number of Boko Haram-perpetrated violent incidents and their lethality in Nigeria, 2011–2014

Year	Number of incidents[a]	Total deaths[a]	Attacks on education[b]	Deaths in attacks on education[b]
2011	114	710	1	1
2012	201	1492	4	18
2013	167	2995	7	115
2014	336	11802	6	129
Total	818	16999	18	285

Source:
[a]Nigeriawatch (2015)
[b]Carapic and Dönges (2014)

The escalating insurgency has led to the deaths of thousands of civilians, including students. Although the exact numbers of victims and the circumstances of their deaths remain unaccounted for, estimates from crime and violence observatories and research institutions, such as Nigeriawatch, put the number of those killed in the tens-of-thousands (NWGAV and AOAV 2013, p. 19). From 1 January 2011 to 31 December 2014, a total of 818 incidents have been recorded by Nigeriawatch, accumulating to a total number of 16,999 deaths in relation to Boko Haram attacks. Although the frequency of Boko Haram attacks has remained relatively constant since the start of the insurgency, the lethality of attacks has increased considerably in recent years. 2013 marks a particularly sharp rise in the lethality of Boko Haram attacks (Fig. 3), and is partly due to the response of the Nigerian police and military forces in an effort to counter Boko Haram (see below for more detail).

While it is already difficult to access the frequency of Boko Haram attacks on an overall scale, the *Attacks on Secondary and Tertiary Dataset* (March 2011–December 2014) makes the first effort to disaggregate attacks on education in particular (Carapic and Dönges 2014). Taking a quick look at the data, it becomes clear that the total number of violent attacks and attacks on education have increased in parallel between 2011 and 2014. Specifically, and reflecting the rise in the number and lethality of overall violent incidents, 2013 is also the year when attacks on education perpetrated by Boko Haram began to occur more readily. Of the 18 Boko Haram perpetrated attacks on education, only 5 occurred prior to 2013 (Table 1). Although the presented data do not capture all attacks of education initiated by Boko Haram—such as kidnappings of students and teachers, and destruction of educational facilities—the figures point to an escalating trend in the use of this form of violence by the armed group.

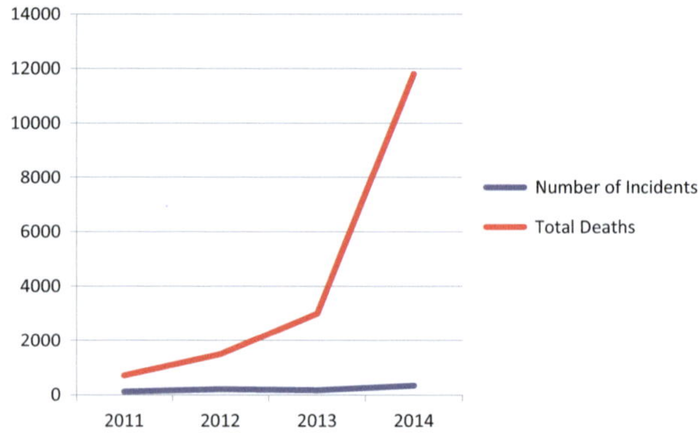

Fig. 3 Number of Boko Haram attacks in Nigeria and total lethality per year, 2011–2014. *Source*: NigeriaWatch (2015)

4.3 Collective Targeting of Students

As mentioned previously, Boko Haram has gained international notoriety for its well-planned, coordinated, and increasingly frequent attacks on educational facilities across northern Nigeria. That being said, evidence suggests that since the start of the insurgency the nature of targeting has shifted from selective attacks on educational facilities to collective attacks on students and teacher. Again, the year 2013 (when Nigerian forces strengthened their counteroffensive against the group) marks a temporal change in targeting strategy. Until early-2013, Boko Haram selectively attacked educational facilities, often at night and with the aim of destroying and looting them in an effort to deter their use (Watchlist 2014, p. 18). Targeted attacks on schools increased since October 2012 and throughout 2013 in Yobe and Borno States, killing at least 100 children and 70 teachers. In March 2013 alone, at least 11 schools in Borno State were attacked, resulting in the killing of at least seven teachers and three children (SCR 2143 (2014), §182).

While the group seemed to predominantly target schools affiliated with the government, its opposition to all forms of education that do not adopt a strict interpretation of the Quran has meant that religious schools are possible targets as well. In 2012, for instance, three of the reported four Boko Haram attacks on educational institutions took place during church assemblies or in Christian residencies or households, highlighting the targeting based on both the provision of "un-Quranic" education and religious cleavages. Christian schools are not the only religious targets, as Boko Haram has also been known to target Quran schools, teachers and Islamic students.[31]

Since early-2013, Boko Haram's attacks appear to be increasingly occurring during the day when schools are occupied. While educational facilities are destroyed in the attacks, it appears that the immediate targets are increasingly

[31] Attacks on Secondary and Tertiary Education (March 2011–December 2014); see Carapic and Dönges (2014).

students.[32] For instance, on 25 February 2014, 59 schoolchildren in the College of Buni Yadi, a secondary school in Yobe State in north-east Nigeria, were reportedly shot or burned alive (SCR 2143 (2014), §184). Although in the past year the militant group has continuously attacked secondary and tertiary institutions, it appears that younger pupils are also being targeted. This is significant as it marks a departure in targeting, especially since during the first few years of the insurgency the group allegedly did not kill children under the age of puberty.[33]

There also seems to be a gendered dimension to the attacks. Available evidence suggests that the majority of students and teachers killed by Boko Haram are male. In the February 2014 attack on the Federal Government College in Buni Yadi, Boko Haram allegedly killed the male school pupils (who were shot in their sleep or rounded up and executed), while the female students were gathered and told to abandon their education and to be married off before they were allowed to leave.[34] This is not to say that female students and teachers are not targeted, however. The Boko Haram attacks on three schools in Maiduguri on 17 March 2013, for instance, led to the death of three female teachers.

That being said, while collective targeting of male students is characterized by lethal violence (often with the use of firearms and bombings), female pupils and teachers tend to be kidnapped. While some kidnappings of women seem to have been arbitrary, most seem to "have been targeted either because of their presumed religious [especially Christian] affiliation or for attending western-styled schools" (HRW 2014b, p. 2). Although it will be discussed in more detail below, it must be already mentioned that the abductions of female students also shows a change in the group's targeting strategy from random and indiscriminate to collective targeting. The kidnapping of 20 female students from a Government Science Secondary School in Konduga village in February 2014, and the abduction of about 200 school-girls from a Girl's Government Secondary School in Chibok, Borno State, in April 2014, illustrate this point (Watchlist 2014, p. 19).

[32] Attacks on Secondary and Tertiary Education (March 2011–December 2014); see Carapic and Dönges (2014); also see AI (2013), p. 6.

[33] The authors would like to thank Dr Adam Higazi Centre for African Studies, University of Cambridge for an interview on 19 August 2014.

[34] Attacks on Secondary and Tertiary Education (March 2011–December 2014), See Carapic and Dönges (2014).

4.4 Boko Haram's Repertoire of Attacks on Education[35]

Recalling that the notion of "repertoire" requires that an armed group's engagement in attacks on education is placed in relation to the other types of violence, such as lethal violence or sexual violence, and to highlight the method used. Access to affected communities for monitoring and verifying incidents has become increasingly difficult since the closure of Maiduguri airport following a Boko Haram attack in December 2013, making it difficult to obtain information necessary for describing the repertoire used (SCR 2143 (2014), §179). That being said, insight into the repertoire of Boko Haram can also be obtained by elaborating further on some of the aspects of frequency and targeting presented above.

Table 1 shows that the overall increasing lethality of attacks on education corresponds with the overall lethality of the Boko Haram uprising (in terms of armed conflict-related deaths). A distinct characteristic of attacks on education in Nigeria is "the prevalence of multi-part, coordinated attacks" (GTD 2014a, p. 3)—almost half (46 %) of all recorded targets on education captured in the GTD database were coordinated with other attacks either targeting education or other types of targets. Although attacks on education only make up about 1.8 % of all lethal deaths related to the Boko Haram insurgency,[36] the increasing trend of collective targeting of students possibly suggests that under some circumstances targeting has become more discriminate over time. The importance of circumstance when understanding repertoires of violence is especially important given the gendered nature of Boko Haram's attacks on education. The higher number of male student deaths during attacks on schools, for instance, is perhaps not surprising given the fact that the majority of the students enrolled in the school system are male, and thus the likelihood of male victimization in attacks on education is disproportionately higher.

Going beyond lethality captured in the *Attacks on Secondary and Tertiary Education (March 2011–December 2014)* dataset, there have been reports of the recruitment and use of children (male and female) as soldiers by Boko Haram. The children (some as young as 12) "are allegedly used for intelligence purposes, tracking movements of the security forces, transporting guns and taking part in attacks, including the burning of schools and churches" (SCR 2143 (2014), §180). Although children seem to be mainly recruited from poor families, there have been instances of recruitment from schools. Specifically, it appears that in some instances children are recruited through Quranic schools in northeastern Nigeria,

[35] The authors would like to thank Hannah Hoechner for providing generous background information on the state of education in Nigeria's northern states. Hannah Hoechner is a Wiener Anspach Postdoctoral Researcher at the Laboratoire d'Anthropologie des Mondes Contemporains at the Université Libre de Bruxelles, Belgium, and a Research Associate at the Oxford Department of International Development, UK.

[36] Attacks on Secondary and Tertiary Education (March 2011–December 2014), see Carapic and Dönges (2014).

where the lack of socio-economic opportunities and extremist teachings are thought to facilitate recruitment. While evidence for recruitment of child soldiers in school is lacking, Nigerian officials had previously accused religious teachers in the area of using their Quranic schools as recruitment and training grounds for new Boko Haram members (HRW 2012). It has even been suggested that Mohamed Yusuf, Boko Haram's founder, taught at a Quranic school (ICG 2014, p. 7; Watchlist 2014, p. 27).

Having lost popular support with the deployment of more violent attacks, Boko Haram now seems to have turned to forced recruitment through the use of kidnapping.[37] Although the group is known for its targeted kidnappings of members belonging to specific communities (such as Christians, traditional leaders, Muslims opposed to its activities, teachers and students, and civil servants and their family members), in the past 2 years Boko Haram has increasingly committed collective abduction of women and girls (Zenn and Pearson 2014a). The year 2013 once again marks a change in recruitment tactics.

While targeted abductions occurred before 2013, Boko Haram's first collective kidnapping—and one that brought international attention to the group and its goals—took place in February 2013, with the abduction of a seven-member French family (including 4 children) in northern Cameroon, which was then brought back to Nigeria (Chrisafis 2013). Between February 2013 and May 2013 kidnapping of women and girls in Nigeria began to occur. Initially the kidnappings were mostly targeted against government officials and their families – a noteworthy example being the May 2013, abduction of 12 Christian women and children from the police barracks in Bama, Borno State. The women were allegedly visiting their relatives at the police station when the attack occurred. As the year progressed, Boko Haram continued kidnapping women and girls, especially from school. As mentioned before, the most notorious example of school kidnapping of girls was the abduction of more than 200 Chibok schoolgirls, who were allegedly married off to Boko Haram fighters.

Although the case of the Chibok school girls has gained international attention, reports indicate that more than 500 women and girls have been kidnapped by Boko Haram and that they experience different forms of victimization, including: psychological and physical abuse, and sexual violence (such as rape, forced marriage, forced labor, and other forms of sexual exploitation) (HRW 2014b, p. 25; Watchlist 2014, p. 24). Women and girls are not only kidnapped to fulfill "personal" needs of Boko Haram members, but also to aid in the organizations fight against state forces. Indeed, with the rise in repressive tactics used by state security forces against Boko Haram, the organization has increasingly forced females into military operations. In June 2013, several women were arrested in the company of suspected Boko Haram militants and found hiding weapons, such as AK–47s and improvised explosive devices (IEDs) (Zenn and Pearson 2014a; HRW 2014), p. 4). GTD data, which

[37] Interview with Dr Adam Higazi, 19 August 2014, Centre for African Studies, University of Cambridge; also see ICG (2014), p. 17.

includes a wider timeframe (1988–2013), finds that "terrorist tactics against educational targets in Nigeria were somewhat varied and primarily included armed assaults (22 %), bombings (27 %), facility/infrastructure attacks (35 %), and kidnappings (12 %)."

4.5 Purpose: Fighting Against the Nigerian State

Although existing since the early 1990s (Adesoji 2010, pp. 98–99)., most political analysts place the emergence of Boko Haram in 2002 in Maiduguri, the capital of the northeastern state of Borno (CFR 2014; ICG 2014, p. 9). Although often portrayed as a counter-state insurgency, the emergence of Boko Haram is rooted in grievances over bad governance and corruption and the resulting stark inequality in Nigerian society (CFR 2014; Watchlist 2014, p. 12). In order to address the ills affecting Nigerian society, Boko Haram's leader, Mohamed Yusuf, advocated for a strict interpretation of the Quran, and thus that a ban (*haram*) be placed on all teachings that are contradictory to the holy book (Watchlist 2014, p. 12).

Although, Yusuf always wanted the creation of a state ruled by Sharia Law, in the first few years he did not want to overthrow the government, but instead preached for a policy of withdrawal from the Nigerian state (CFR 2014; ICG 2014, p. 9). Although Yusuf faced opposition within Boko Haram from more radical members, in the early 2000s the organization did not pose a direct threat to the state (CFR 2014). Rather, it was only with growing inter-religious tensions, and in response to increasing state repression in the summer of 2009 that Boko Haram morphed into a full-blown insurgency. Specifically, it was following the police crackdown on the organization, which saw about 800 Boko Haram members killed (including the death of Yusuf in police custody), that the organization became more "radical"—both in terms of its preaching and lethality of its violent attacks (ICG 2014, p. 9).

Despite the fact that Boko Haram has been portrayed as indiscriminately attacking civilians, the pattern of collective targeting of students and the gender-based repertoire of their attacks suggests that the violence the group employs is strategic—i.e. committed for a particular purpose and is beneficial for achieving the group's overall goals. The strategic nature of violence carried out by Boko Haram is especially evident when attacks on education are taken into account. As mentioned before, all of the 18 attacks on education that the group has carried out since the start of the insurgency have been well-planned and highly coordinated.

Having said that, evidence suggests that attacks on education have only been adopted as a strategy following the state-led counter-attacks against the group in 2010 and 2011, in which Quranic schools in northeastern Nigeria were attacked (Watchlist 2014, p. 12). It was only then that the group's current leader, Abubakar Shekau, stated: "if [Nigerian security forces] are going to places of worship and destroying them, like mosques and Quranic schools, you have primary schools as well, you have secondary schools and universities and we will start bombing them. . .Touch us and see. That is what we will do" (Gambrel 2012). This strategic shift in attacks on education is further reflected in the drastic jump in the number of attacks (and their lethality) since 2013 (Table 1).

The strategic nature of attacks on education by Boko Haram is also evident when the gendered dynamic of such violence is taken into account. Analysts have argued that the strict adherence to the Quran and opposition to Western values has meant that a sense of hyper-masculinity was created within the group. In practice this meant that only adult (Muslim) men were able to take on combat roles. All other individuals—such as "unarmed men, youths, women, cripples and even under age children"—were not only to be exempt from combat, but also constituted illegitimate targets (Zenn and Pearson 2014b). Unlike Christian women, who have been kidnapped, forced to convert to Islam and forced to marry Boko Haram soldiers, it appears that Muslim women are often spared. Even when Muslim men who are perceived of adopting western values or education have been attacked and killed—such as in the 2013 attack on the Yobe college—female students were released (Zenn and Pearson 2014a).

Although there is stronger support for the targeting of Christian females, the group targets women for a number of reasons including opposition to the government and denunciation of western values and education. In particular, as in the case of the strategic attacks on education, it appears that the collective kidnapping of women and girls (regardless of their religion) is a response to the Nigerian government's repressive counterinsurgency tactics implemented in 2012.[38] In fact, an analysis of video messages released by Boko Haram in the beginning of 2013, for instance, suggests three key motives for abductions of women and girls: "to retaliate against the government for its alleged detention of family members, including the wives of the group's leaders; to punish students for attending Western schools; and to forcefully convert Christian women and girls to Islam" (HRW 2014b, p. 4).

5 Final Remarks and Future Research Agendas

This chapter aimed at unpacking the phenomenon of "attacks on education" by proposing an innovative framework which calls for a disaggregation of a particular form of violence according to four dimensions: frequency, targeting, repertoire, and purpose. The authors suggest that given the lack of systematic monitoring and reporting, such a framework allows for a more systematic analysis of the phenomenon across and within contexts (conflict, post-conflict and non-conflict), across

[38] Allegedly, in 2012 the Nigerian government arrested about 100 Boko Haram family members (mostly women and children), including the wives of Abubakar Shekau, the group's leader (HRW 2014b, p. 18; Watchlist 2014, p. 22; Zenn and Pearson 2014a).

different types of armed actors (non-state armed groups, state security forces, and pro-state militias), global regions and even time. In addition, the chapter also points to the necessity of collecting disaggregated data, and furthering of data collection (like the seven datasets put forward in this chapter).

Finally, when it comes to specific instances of attacks on education, such as in the case of Boko Haram, the proposed framework allows for a critical elaboration of the pattern of violence—in particular, it provides mechanism for questioning often simplistic portrayals of victimization. Although Boko Haram attacks students, teachers, and educational facilities, the brutality of such acts (and the media attention attributed to them) often masks the complex pattern of violence—i.e. the emergence and evolution of such attacks. Indeed, despite the fact that Boko Haram proclaims "Western education is sinful"; attacks on education were not always the (main) target. Rather, it was in response to increased state repression that such tactics appear to have been adopted.

Five Questions

1. How do we foster the systematic collection of disaggregated data on attacks on education?
2. What can we learn from the collective targeting of students in secondary and tertiary education?
3. What is the importance of contextualizing attacks on education within a broader repertoire of violence?
4. What does the large variety in modes of attacks on education mean for the development of programming to deal with the problem?
5. What are the policy implications of a comprehensive (conflict and non-conflict) view of attacks on education?

References

Achebe, C. (2012). *There was a country: A personal history of Biafra*. London: Allen Lane.

Adesoji, A. (2010). The Boko Haram uprising and Islamic revivalism in Nigeria. *Africa Spectrum, 45*(2), 95–108.

AFP (2014). Philippines bus bombing 'kills 11'. http://www.dailymail.co.uk/wires/afp/article-2867023/Ten-dead-bus-bombing-southern-Philippines-military.html. Accessed 26 Jan 2015.

Agbiboa, D. (2013). The ongoing campaign of terror in Nigeria: Boko Haram versus the state. *Stability: International Journal of Security & Development*, *2*(3), 52 1–18.

Amnesty International (2013). Keep away from schools or we'll kill you. *Right to Education Under Attack in Nigeria*. http://www.amnesty.org/fr/library/asset/AFR44/019/2013/en/d5ad17da-bfba-419d-8e75-db68cb2b711b/afr440192013en.pdf. Accessed 26 Jan 2015.

Arab News (2014). 11 killed in bus bombing in southern Philippines. http://www.arabnews.com/world/news/672081. Accessed 26 Jan 2015.

Arce, A. (2014). In Honduras, gangs control the schools and what children learn is that crime pays. http://www.abqjournal.com/512185/news/and-what-children-learn-is-that-crime-pays.html. Accessed 26 Jan 2015.

Aljazeera (2014). Children massacred in Pakistan school attack. http://m.aljazeera.com/story/20141216742794184. Accessed 26 Dec 2014.

Bairo, L. (2013). El Salvador: Gangs threaten high school students.' November 22, http://dialogoamericas.com/en_GB/articles/saii/features/main/2013/11/22/feature-01. Accessed 26 Jan 2015.

Banovac, S., & Patterson, C. (2007). Anatomy of a terrorist attack: Terror at Beslan: A chronicle of ongoing tragedy and a Government's failed response. http://www.lesarchivesdebeslan.fr/app/download/5796302108/Beslan+-+Anatomy+of+a+terrorist+attack.pdf. Accessed 26 Jan 2015.

BBC News (2009). Somalia suicide bomb toll rises. http://news.bbc.co.uk/2/hi/africa/8109188.stm. Accessed 26 Jan 2015. Accessed 26 Dec 2014.

BBC News Africa (2014). Nigeria school raid in Yobe state 'leaves dozens dead'. http://www.bbc.com/news/world-africa26338041?Print=true>. Accessed 26 Dec 2015.

BBC News Asia (2012). Malala Yousafzai: Pakistan activist, 14, shot in Swat. http://www.bbc.com/news/world-asia-19882799. Accessed 26 Jan 2015.

BBC News Asia (2013). Pakistan violence: Gunmen storm Quetta hospital. http://www.bbc.com/news/world-asia-22920542. Accessed 26 Jan 2015.

BBC News Latin America (2014). Mexico insists 43 missing students are dead. http://www.bbc.com/news/world-latin-america-31013491

BBC News Middle East (2013). Syria crisis: Dozens killed by Aleppo university blasts. http://www.bbc.com/news/world-middle-east-21029034. Accessed 26 Jan 2015.

Bloom, M. (2014). *Afghanistan's Bacha Bazi: Etiology of child sexual abuse*. Paper Presented at the Workshop on Sexual Violence and Armed Conflict: New Research Frontiers Harvard Kennedy School, 2–3 September 2014.

Boone, J. (2014). Pakistan begins long-awaited offensive to root out militants from border region. http://www.theguardian.com/world/2014/jun/15/pakistan-offensive-militants-north-waziristan. Accessed 26 Jan 2015.

Boone, J., Macaskill, E. (2014a). More than 100 children killed in Taliban attack on Pakistan school. http://www.theguardian.com/world/2014/dec/16/taliban-attack-army-public-school-pakistan-peshawar. Accessed 26 Jan 2015.

Boone, J., Macaskill, E. (2014b). Pakistan responds to Peshawar school massacre with strikes on Taliban. http://www.theguardian.com/world/2014/dec/16/pakistan-taliban-peshawar-massacre-attack. Accessed 26 Jan 2015.

Borden, K. (2005). *Mexico'68: An analysis of the Tlatelolco massacre and its legacy*. Thesis Presented to the Honours College, University of Oregon.

BJS (Bureau of Justice Statistics) (2014). *Indicators of school crime and safety: 2013*. Washington, DC: U.S. Department Of Education and U.S. Department Of Justice Office of Justice Programs.

Carapic, J. (2014). *Beyond armed conflict: sexual violence in a global perspective*. Paper Presented at the Workshop on Sexual Violence and Armed Conflict: New Research Frontiers Harvard Kennedy School, 2–3 September 2014.

Carapic, J., & Dönges, H. (2014). *Database on attacks on education*. Geneva: Small Arms Survey/IHEID.

Carey, S. C., Mitchell, N. J., & Lowe, W. (2013). States, the security sector, and the monopoly of violence: A new database on pro-government militias. *Journal of Peace Research, 50*(2), 249–258.

CARE International (2009). Knowledge on fire: Attacks on education in Afghanistan. *Risks and Measures for Successful Mitigation*. http://www.care.org/sites/default/files/documents/Knowledge_on_Fire_Report.pdf. Accessed 26 Jan 2015.

Chonghaile, C. N. (2011). Mogadishu truck bomb: al-Shabaab insurgents claim responsibility. http://www.theguardian.com/world/2011/oct/04/mogadishu-truck-bomb-al-shabaab. Accessed 26 Jan 2015.

Chrisafis, A. (2013). French family seized in Cameroon by suspected Boko Haram Islamists freed. http://www.theguardian.com/world/2013/apr/19/french-family-kidnapped-cameroon-freed. Accessed 26 Jan 2015.

Coombs, P. H., & Ahmed, M. (1974). *Attacking rural poverty: How nonformal education can help, a research report for the World Bank prepared by the International Council for Educational Development*. Baltimore: Johns Hopkins.

CFR (Council on Foreign Relations) (2014). Backgrounders: Boko Haram, last updated May 5 http://www.cfr.org/nigeria/boko-haram/p25739. Accessed 26 Dec 2014.

DHS (Demographic and Health Survey). (2011). *Nigeria Demographic and Health Survey (DHS) 2010, education data for decision making*. Washington, DC: DHS.

Dunlop, J. B., (2009). The September 2004 Beslan terrorist incident: New findings. *CCDRP Working Papers*, 15 (July 2009). Stanford University: Center on Democracy, Development, and the Rule of Law.

Fisher, B. S. (2009). The effects of survey question wording on rape estimates: Evidence from a quasi-experimental design. *Violence Against Women, 15*(2), 133–147.

Gambrel, J. (2012). Nigeria sect leader threatens new attacks. http://www.sfexaminer.com/sanfrancisco/nigeria-sect-leader-threatens-new-attacks/Content?Oid=2193431. Accessed 26 Jan 2015.

Geneva Declaration Secretariat (2011). *GBAV (Global Burden of Armed Violence) 2011: Lethal encounters*. Cambridge: Cambridge University Press.

GCPEA. (2012). *Lessons in war. Military use of schools and other educational institutions during conflict*. New York: GCPEA.

GCPEA. (2014a). *Education under attack 2014*. New York: GCPEA.

GCPEA. (2014b). *The role of communities in protecting education from attack lessons learned*. New York: GCPEA.

Geneva Declaration Secretariat. (2015). *GBAV (Global Burden of Armed Violence): Every body counts*. Cambridge: Cambridge University Press.

Gorton, T. (2014). Mayor accused as 43 student protesters go missing in Mexico. http://www.dazeddigital.com/artsandculture/article/22277/1/mayor-accused-as-43-student-protesters-go-missing-in-mexico. Accessed 26 Jan 2015.

GTD (Global Terrorism Database) (2014a). Codebook: Inclusion Criteria and Variables. August 2014. National Consortium for the Study of Terrorism and Responses to Terrorism (START). http://www.start.umd.edu/gtd/downloads/Codebook.pdf. Accessed 26 Jan 2015.

GTD (2014b). Background report: terrorist attacks on educational institutions. *START*. https://www.start.umd.edu/pubs/Peshawar%20School%20Background%20Report%20December%202014.pdf. Accessed 26 Jan 2015.

GTD (2013). Global Terrorism Database [Data file]. http://www.start.umd.edu/gtd Accessed 15 Jan 2015.

Holmes, O. (2013). Mortar strike kills 15 in Damascus University: state media. March 28, http://www.reuters.com/article/2013/03/28/us-syria-crisis-students-idusbre92r0e020130328. Accessed 26 Jan 2015.

Human Rights Watch (HRW) (2012). Nigeria: Boko Haram targeting schools: Attacks threaten children, undermine right to education. *HRW News*, 7 March. http://www.hrw.org/news/2012/03/07/nigeria-boko-haram-targeting-schools Accessed 26 Jan 2015.

Human Rights Watch (HRW) (2014a). World Report 2014. Nigeria Country Chapter. http://www.hrw.org/world-report/2014/country-chapters/nigeria. Accessed 26 Jan 2015.

Human Rights Watch (HRW) (2014b). Those terrible weeks in their camp.' Boko Haram violence against women and girls in Northeast Nigeria. http://www.hrw.org/sites/default/files/reports/nigeria1014web.pdf. Accessed 26 Jan 2015.

Human Rights Watch (HRW) (2014c). Norway: Leading way to end military use of schools. http://www.hrw.org/news/2014/06/13/norway-leading-way-end-military-use-schools. Accessed 26 Jan 2015.

International Crisis Group (ICG) (2014). Curbing Violence in Nigeria (II): The Boko Haram Insurgency. *Africa Report* (216). http://www.crisisgroup.org/en/regions/africa/west-africa/nigeria/216-curbing-violence-in-nigeria-ii-the-boko-haram-insurgency.aspx. Accessed 26 Jan 2015.

Jones, A., & Naylor, R. (2014). *The quantitative impact of armed conflict on education: Counting the human and financial costs*. Berkshire: Education Trust.

Kalyvas, S. (2006). *The logic of violence in civil war*. Cambridge: Cambridge University Press.

Larkin, R. W. (2009). The columbine legacy rampage shootings as political acts. *American Behavioral Scientist, 52*(9), 1309–1326.

Malkki, L. (2014). Political elements in post-columbine school shootings in Europe and North America. *Terrorism and Political Violence, 26*(1), 185–210.

Muschert, G. W. (2007). Research in school shootings. *Sociology Compass, 1*(1), 60–80.

Mustapha, A. R. (2012). Boko Haram: Killing in God's Name. *Mail & Guardian*, 5 April. http://mg.co.za/article/2012-04-05-boko-haram-killing-in-gods-name. Accessed 26 Jan 2015.

NWGAV (National Working Group on Armed Violence) and Action on Armed Violence (AOAV) (2013). The violent road. An overview of armed violence in Nigeria. http://aoav.org.uk/wp-content/uploads/2013/12/The-Violent-Road.pdf. Accessed 26 Jan 2015.

Newman, K. S. (2004). *Rampage: The social roots of school shootings*. New York: Basic Books.

Nigeriawatch Database on Violence (2015). http://www.nigeriawatch.org/index.php?Urlaction=evtliste&cherche=1. Last Accessed 1 Feb Dec 2014.

Obura, A. (2003). *Never again: Educational reconstruction in Rwanda*. Paris: UNESCO/International Institute for Educational Planning.

O'Malley, B. (2007). *Education under attack: A global study on targeted political and military violence against education staff, students, teachers, union and government officials, and institutions*. Paris: UNESCO.

Pérouse de Montclos, M.-A. (Ed.). (2014). *Boko Haram: Islamism, politics, security and the State in Nigeria*. Leiden: African Studies Center.

Piñeda, L. (2014). Mexico disarms police in missing students' city. http://www.ticotimes.net/2014/10/07/mexico-disarms-police-in-missing-students-city. Accessed 26 Jan 2015.

Press, T. V. (2014). Explosion kills 11 students in southern Philippine. http://www.presstv.ir/detail/2014/12/09/389495/11-students-killed-in-philippine-blast/. Accessed 26 Jan 2015.

Save the Children (2013). *Attacks on Education: The impact of armed conflict and grave violations on Children's education*. London: Author.

Shultz, J. M., Cohen, A. M., Muschert, G. W., & Flores de Apodaca, R. (2013). Fatal school shootings and the epidemiological context of firearm mortality in the United States. *Disaster Health, 1*(2), 84–101.

Telesur (2014). One Honduran teacher violently murdered, every month. http://www.telesurtv.net/english/news/One-Honduran-Teacher-Violently-Murdered-Every-Month-20140805-0044.html. Accessed 26 Jan 2015.

Tonso, K. L. (2009). Violent masculinities as tropes for school shooters: The Montréal Massacre, the Columbine Attack, and Rethinking Schools. *American Behavioral Scientist, 52*(9), 1266–1285.

Tribune, The Express (2014). Army retaliates to Peshawar attack with strikes in Tirah. http://tribune.com.pk/story/808157/live-nation-mourns-141-lives-lost-in-peshawar-school-attack/. Accessed 26 Jan 2015.

Tuathail, G. O. (2009). Placing blame: Making sense of Beslan. *Political Geography, 28*(1), 4–15.

Tuckmann, J. (2014). Mexican students: first murder victim identified amid continued protests. http://www.theguardian.com/world/2014/dec/07/mexican-students-first-victim-identified-amid-continued-protests. Accessed 26 Jan 2015.

UNESCO. (2010a). *Protecting education from attack: A State-of-the-Art Review*. Paris: Author.

UNESCO. (2010b). *Education under attack 2010*. Paris: Author.

UNESCO. (2007). *Education under attack 2007*. Paris: Author.

United Nations (2014). Goal 2: Achieve Universal Primary Education. http://www.un.org/millenniumgoals/education.shtml. Accessed 26 Jan 2015.

United Nations (2014). *Protect schools and hospitals: Guidance note on security council resolution 1998*. New York: United Nations.

United Nations General Assembly, Human Rights Council (2009). Promotion and protection of all human rights, civil political, economic social and cultural rights, including the right to development. http://www.ecoi.net/file_upload/1227_1245590635_iraq.pdf. Accessed 26 Jan 2015.

United Nations General Assembly. (2009). *Children and armed conflict: Report of the Secretary-General.* A/63/785–S/2009/158.

United Nations General Assembly. (2014). *Children and armed conflict: Report of the Secretary-General.* A/68/878– S/2014/339.

Watchlist (2010). Setting the right priorities: Protecting children affected by armed conflict in Afghanistan. New York: Watchlist.

Watchlist (2014). 'Who Will Care for Us?' Grave violations against children in Northeastern Nigeria. New York: Watchlist.

Watkins, K. (2014). Boko Haram is a vicious sideshow—Nigeria's self-serving elite is the real culprit. http://www.independent.co.uk/voices/comment/boko-haram-is-a-vicious-sideshow--nigerias-selfserving-elite-is-the-real-culprit-9623707.html. Accessed 26 Jan 2015.

Wood, E. J. (2014). *The policy implications of recent research on wartime sexual violence.* Paper Presented at the Workshop on Sexual Violence and Armed Conflict: New Research Frontiers Harvard Kennedy School, September 2 and 3, 2014.

Wood, E. J. (2012). Rape in War is not Inevitable: Variation in war time sexual violence. In M. Bergsmo, A. B. Skre, & E. J. Wood (Eds.), *Understanding and proving international sex crimes* (pp. 389–419). Oslo: Torkel Opsahl Academic Epublisher.

World Bank (2014). Country Brief: Timor-Leste. Timor-Leste, Building resilience, building hope. http://web.worldbank.org/WBSITE/EXTERNAL/NEWS/0,,contentmdk:23174850~menupk:141310~pagepk:34370~pipk:34424~thesitepk:4607,00.html. Accessed 26 Jan 2015.

Zenn, J., & Pearson, E. (2014a). Women, gender and the evolving tactics of Boko Haram. *Journal of Terrorism Research, North America,* 5(1). http://ojs.st-andrews.ac.uk/index.php/jtr/article/view/828/707. Accessed 22 Dec 2014.

Zenn, J., & Pearson, E. (2014b). Boko Haram and the kidnapping of Women: A troubled tactic. *War on the Rocks.* March 11, http://warontherocks.com/2014/03/boko-haram-and-the-kidnapping-of-women. Accessed 22 Dec 2014.

The Role of Early Childhood Education in Social Behaviour of Children

Milagros Nores and W. Steven Barnett

Abstract Public investments in Early Childhood Care and Education have grown and continue to grow considerably, in part based on rigorous research establishing the importance of investing in the first 5 years of life. A large body of evidence on early childhood interventions has found short- and medium-term effects that extend beyond narrowly academic or cognitive outcomes to improvements in pro-social and anti-social behaviours, skills such as self-regulation, commitment to schooling, risky adolescent behaviours, aggression, delinquency, crime, employment and earnings, and both mental and physical health. The potential of high quality early childhood programs to affect a broad range of children's social behaviours, attitudes and skills has strong implications for the development of programs and policies that can prevent antisocial behaviours, delinquency and risky behaviours while improving productivity in the workforce. Given the importance of the early years in child development, this chapter focuses on summarizing the evidence of the impact of early childhood interventions on children's social and emotional behaviour in the United States and globally, describes which aspects of these interventions are associated with larger short-term and long-term social and emotional effects, and identifies which types of programs have been found to affect parenting and households in ways that matter for children's behavioural development. These programs demonstrate remarkable consistency. Implications for international educational policy in the areas of justice and equality are discussed.

1 Introduction

The last decades have seen growing global interest in public investments in early child care and education (ECCE) as a means to improve the development of young children, especially those from socially disadvantaged groups (Choi 2004; Kirp 2007; OECD 2006). This interest is based on strong evidence of the importance of

M. Nores (✉) • W.S. Barnett
Rutgers University, New Brunswick, NJ, USA
e-mail: mnores@nieer.org; sbarnett@nieer.org

H. Kury et al. (eds.), *Women and Children as Victims and Offenders: Background, Prevention, Reintegration*, DOI 10.1007/978-3-319-08398-8_6

environmental influences on early development, the human and economic costs of poor developmental trajectories for children in poverty, and the potential for early interventions to alter such developmental trajectories (Barnett 2008a, 2011; Behrman and Urzua 2013; Cunha et al. 2006; Engle et al. 2007, 2011; Herrod 2007). In the last decade, public investments in ECCE have grown considerably, at least in part based on rigorous research establishing the importance of investing in the first 5 years of life (Choi 2004; Engle et al. 2011; Kirp 2007; Nores and Barnett 2010; OECD 2006).

Overall, research on ECCE interventions has found that strong interventions can have long-lasting effects on a wide spectrum of cognitive and "non-cognitive" outcomes. Cognitive development includes not only literacy and numeracy, but also executive functions such as attention, memory (short and long-term), processing speed and problem solving. The term "non-cognitive" is commonly used to encompass outcomes in all of the other domains of development including dispositions and habits that relate to motivation, persistence, and self-regulation as well as a wide range of social and emotional outcomes including pro-social and adaptive behaviours and anti-social and maladaptive behaviours. We have put "non-cognitive" in quotation marks because even though this term is commonly used, especially in economics, to refer to all of the outcomes in these domains, it encompasses social cognition and other cognitive abilities relating to emotional intelligence, social skills, and behaviour.

A large body of evidence on early childhood interventions has found short- and medium-term effects that extend beyond the narrowly academic or cognitive outcomes of intelligence, vocabulary, and achievement test scores. This wider set of effects includes improvements in school outcomes such as grade repetition and high-school graduation and benefits across an even broader spectrum of pro-social and anti-social behaviours, skills such as self-regulation, commitment to schooling, risky adolescent behaviours (teen pregnancy, smoking and drugs), aggression, delinquency, crime, employment and earnings, and both mental and physical health. The long-term benefits found with respect to reductions in crime, increases in employment and earnings, and improvements in health owe at least as much if not more to improvements in social behaviour and skills than to gains in achievement (Friedman-Krauss and Barnett 2013; Heckman et al. 2006; Heckman and Kautz 2013).

The potential of ECCE to affect a broad range of children's social behaviours, attitudes and skills has strong implications for the development of programs and policies that can prevent antisocial behaviours, delinquency and risky behaviours by fostering rich developmental experiences. In the very long run, such programs may even deter child abuse and the reproduction of violence and delinquency across generations, as the children who receive ECCE eventually become parents. While not all of these types of outcomes have been seen for each and every program evaluated, a common theme emerges: quality early childhood programs have long-term sustained effects on children's social and emotional development and resulting behaviours, and when these include programs include interventions for parents, they can have important effects on families, reducing environmental risks for children in their homes as well as enhancing out-of-home experiences.

Given the importance of the early years in child development, this chapter focuses on summarizing the evidence of the impact of early childhood interventions on children's social and emotional behaviour in the United States and globally, describes which aspects of these interventions are more closely related to short-term and long-term social and emotional outcomes, and discusses which types of programs have shown effects on parenting and households in ways that matter for children's behavioural development. Implications for international educational policy with respect to justice and equality are discussed.

2 Early Childhood Social Development: Why Does It Matter?

Socio-emotional development involves the acquisition of a set of skills including the abilities to: identify and understand one's own feelings and the feelings of others, deal with emotions and their expression constructively, empathize with others, and establish and maintain healthy relationships (National Scientific Council on the Developing Child 2005). These skills interact and build upon one another, becoming more complex as children grow older (Goleman 1994). Healthy socio-emotional development also includes inclinations and dispositions to use these skills in positive ways. Social cognition, for example, can be used to build friendships and comfort others in distress or to bully and intimidate others (Boyd et al. 2005). Children with higher emotional competence are more likely to be engaged in the classroom, more likely to be perceived by teachers as more socially competent, more likely to engage in positive interactions with teachers and peers that promote their development, and more likely to be committed to schooling (Ursache et al. 2012). Likewise, children having difficulty with emotion regulation are more likely to experience peer rejection, disengagement from school and do poorly academically (Ursache et al. 2012).

Consequently, social development in the early childhood years has important implications for subsequent development. Yoshikawa (1995) reviews various longitudinal studies that focus on early childhood programs and concludes that the following are strong early risk factors for later chronic delinquency: a history of antisocial behaviour in childhood, conduct disorder, or troublesomeness, the child's low cognitive ability (especially poor verbal ability), low socioeconomic status, having parents who have been convicted of crimes, and poor parental child rearing (Farrington 1987, 1989; Werner 1987; Yoshikawa 1994). In particular, frequently encountered antisocial behaviours in childhood including hostility, aggression, hitting, stealing, destroying or vandalizing property, lying, refusing to follow the rules in a situation or actively defying the authority of a parent or teacher, are the strongest predictors of chronic delinquency among youths and adults (Farrington

1985). Persistent physical aggression and antisocial behaviour in adolescence can be traced back to early childhood conduct problems (Nagin and Tremblay 2001; LaCourse et al. 2002). Children that have not learned to regulate aggression in the preschool years and who exhibit high levels of physical aggression in elementary school are most likely to engage in violent behaviour as adolescents (Tremblay 2002).

Reynolds et al. (2004) test five different mechanisms that might explain the large effects of ECCE interventions on delinquency and crime among youths and adults. In particular, (1) improved cognitive ability, language and literacy skills, and school readiness, (2) enhancement in parenting practices, attitudes and expectations, and involvement in children's education, (3) transition to high quality primary schools, (4) changes in children's task persistence, self-efficacy, perceived competence, or other self-system attributes and (5) motivational boost due to observed changes in cognitive and intelligence test scores. They found that all five channels significantly contributed to crime reduction and high school completion, but that cognitive improvement and family support accounted for most of the crime reduction. As a consequence, for understanding the long-term impacts of ECCE interventions on children's behaviour, it is important to keep in mind a global sense of the impact of these programs on children's overall development (see Nores and Barnett 2010) and not just on specific behavioural dimensions.

3 Summarizing the Evidence on ECCE and Behavioural Development

ECCE includes various forms of delivery such as centre-based care and/or education, home-visitation, and parenting and stimulation interventions, among others. Similarly, there are various links between the growth and development of programs within the ECCE field and their potential to impact behavioural problems, risky adolescent behaviour and even within-household violence. Pathways, for long-term behavioural outcomes, include short-term effects on both children's cognitive and behavioural dimensions.

The behavioural domain has been more strongly studied in evaluations of centre-based care than in evaluations of other forms of ECCE programming. Research in the United States suggests that intensive, high quality early childhood interventions have direct and persistent effects on cognitive and non-cognitive development (Barnett 2008b; Blau and Currie 2005; Camilli et al. 2010; Nores and Barnett 2010). Randomized trials find short- and long-term effects on intelligence, subject matter knowledge and skills, grade repetition, special education services, delinquency and crime, and depression. Behavioural outcomes include self-regulation, motivation, self-efficacy, educational aspirations, sociability, and aggressive or anti-social behaviours (Borghans et al. 2008). In the behavioural domain estimated effects have been somewhat smaller than in the cognitive domain with effects averaging about 0.33 standard deviations (Camilli et al. 2010; White and Casto 1985), which is equivalent to 33 % of children's achievement gap at Kindergarten entry in the United States.

One explanation for such smaller average effects may be that many of the studied programs were not expressly designed to enhance social and emotional development but primarily focused on cognitive outcomes. Another is that this domain is typically measured by teacher and parental ratings, which have greater measurement error than cognitive measures, and this tends to attenuate estimated effects.

Randomized trials of centre-based care interventions that have included outcomes measures on social and emotional development have found that alternative curricula for ECCE can have similar effects on cognitive development while having very different effects on social and emotional development (Schweinhart and Weikart 1997; Barnett et al. 2008). No trade-off between these two domains is required as balanced approaches can succeed in enhancing development in both broad domains (Diamond et al. 2007).

In addition, the link between ECCE and social-emotional behaviour is also affected by the link between the quality of care and child development (Krzewina 2012), with quality being high for the programs exemplified below. Peisner-Feinberg et al. (2001) found a modest long-term link between child care quality and children's cognitive and social-emotional development through kindergarten, in particular teacher-child relationships. Mashburn et al. (2008) found that teachers' emotional interactions predicted children's teacher-reported social skills. However, this relationship has sometimes appeared to be absent even within high quality programs (Weiland et al. 2013).

4 What Can We Learn From Research in the United States?

Although various programs in the United States have been successfully evaluated, with a few of them having followed children into adulthood, examples can be drawn to exemplify the potential of preschool in modifying the social and behavioural development of children. The following set of programs is widely known for having high quality model programs that have shown long-lasting effects on participants.

The Perry Preschool Study is very well known in the United States and abroad, and quite likely the most cited study of an early childhood program. This study examines the lifetime experiences of 123 children born in poverty in Ypsilanti, Michigan. Between 1962–1967, 3- and 4-year-olds were randomly assigned to "treatment" and "control" groups. The study was designed to evaluate the High Scope Curriculum which uses active participatory learning, a process through which teachers help children plan, carry out, and review their own educational activities. The treatment group received half-day high quality preschool and home visitation for 2 years. The study followed 123 children through age 40, interviewing individuals and collecting information from schools and social services, as well as arrest records (Schweinhart et al. 2005). The program consisted of half-day classes held 5 days a week and weekly home visits; all teachers held bachelor's degrees and certification, and teacher-child ratios were of 1 to 6-or-7. The study found substantial long-term effects including higher secondary school completion rates, higher employment rates, and significantly higher median annual earnings. Preschool participation increased commitment to schooling, reduced antisocial behaviours and substantially reduced arrest rates and had a strong impact on crime, and also provided indications of reductions in smoking and similar risky behaviours (Barnett 1996; Heckman et al. 2010; Nores et al. 2005; Schweinhart 2013). Figure 1 shows various behavioural outcomes for the treated versus the non-treated children several at various ages.

Less well known, a curriculum comparison study followed the original trial. For this second randomized trial, three different curriculum models were compared. In a comparison of direct instruction versus the High Scope curriculum, which was at the core of the Perry Preschool Program, authors (Schweinhart and Weikart 1997) found that children who participated in the High Scope Curriculum reported lower levels of emotional impairment, lower levels of teen misconduct, and only about 10 % had been arrested for a felony by age 23 (versus 43 % of the children that had participated in a direct instruction program). Such findings provided an important indication of the importance of content and form in the program delivery, with a higher potential for behavioural outcomes with the greater scope for child initiated activities and plan-do-review emphasized in the High Scope curriculum.

Another important study of the Chicago Child-Parent Centers (CCPCs) operated by Chicago Public Schools used matched neighbourhoods and statistical controls to estimate program effects (Reynolds et al. 2011). The CCPC longitudinal study followed 989 children enrolled between 1983 and 1986 in 24 preschools in low-income areas. These children who completed preschool and kindergarten in

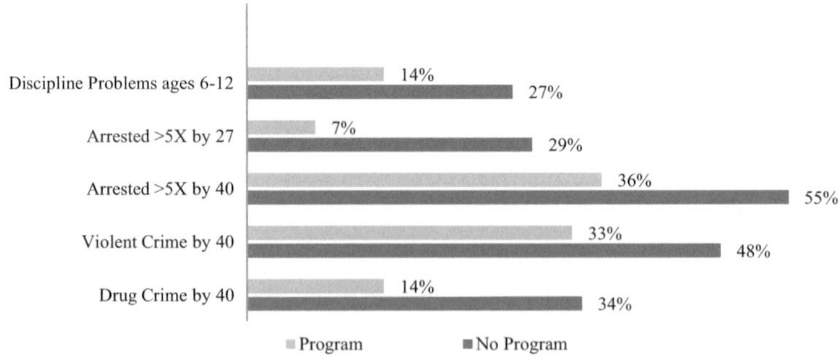

Fig. 1 Perry Preschool Crime Effects. Comparison of incidence in the program and no-program group for the incidence of discipline problems between the ages of 6 and 12, the incidence of five or more arrests by age 27, the incidence of five or more arrests by age 40, and the incidence of a violent crime or a drug crime having been committed by age 40 (Schweinhart et al. 2005)

the CCPCs were compared to 550 children in similar neighbourhoods who did not attend the preschool program. Centre-based half-day preschooling for 3- and 4-year-olds, a ratio of 17:2, teachers with early childhood certification, regular staff development activities, health and social services, as well as free meals were provided by the CCPC. The program had a strong parental involvement component that included classroom volunteering, parent room activities, educational workshops/training and home visits. The CCPC study found a significant increase in high school completion and reductions in crime. Both of these were the result of pre-K impacts on cognitive and social-emotional development. Children and families that were part of the program evidenced lower incidences of child abuse or neglect, adult arrests, and incarceration (Reynolds et al. 2011; Reynolds and Ou 2011). In addition, Arteaga et al. (2014) found that relative to children who attended CCPC 1 year, the 2-year group was significantly less likely to receive special education, to be abused or neglected and even to commit crimes.

A third important longitudinal study of the Abecedarian program followed 111 at-risk children born between 1972 and 1977 in North Carolina through age 30 (Campbell et al. 2012). Unlike the previous two, children were randomly assigned to treatment at birth, rather than in the preschool years (Masse and Barnett 2002; Barnett and Masse 2007). Treatment was composed of intensive, high-quality centre-based childcare for a length of 8 hours a day through the age of five. The program used a child-centric and individualized approach with learning games. Program participants were more likely to graduate high school by age 19, enroll in higher education, and hold a skilled job at age 21. Effects on health behaviours (Muennig et al. 2011) included treated children being significantly older when they first became regular smokers of cigarettes (5.5 years) and marijuana (3.7 years), and having a lower tendency to smoke marijuana.

5 Programs with a Special Focus on Social-Emotional Development

As the importance of social-emotional skills for school readiness and school success has become increasingly more salient, several interventions have been implemented within the context of broader early childhood programs that aim to improve children's social-emotional skills and executive functions (Friedman-Krauss and Barnett 2013). Executive functions, such as playing mentally with ideas, considered rather than impulsive responses, and focusing on task have been found to be central for creativity, flexibility, self-control and discipline.

Tools of the Mind is a preschool curriculum that is designed to improve children's executive function skills. Indeed, a randomized trial of the Tools of the Mind curriculum found significant impacts on children's executive function skills, especially on the most difficult executive function tasks (Diamond et al. 2007). The leading activity in the Tools curriculum is socio-dramatic (pretend/role) play, and it contains many other activities designed to promote executive functions. These include, for example, telling oneself out loud what to do, games similar to "Simon Says," and partner reading in which turn taking is guided by physical props with one child holding a picture of ears and the other a picture of lips. A 2008 randomized trial of Tools found substantial reductions in classroom behavior problems, but a subsequent randomized trial in 2012 did not (Barnett et al. 2008; Wilson and Farran 2012). Differences in outcomes could have been due to differences in maturity of implementation, differences in the counterfactual between the two studies, or differences in the populations served and context. A more recent study of Tools (Blair and Raver 2014) found that children in classrooms implementing Tools of the Mind did significantly better on various measures of executive functions such as working memory, inhibitory control and rule switching than children in the control classrooms.

The Promoting Alternative Thinking Strategies (PATHS) program is another program focusing on children's behaviours and self-regulation (Domitrovich et al. 2007). The program is a social-emotional curriculum designed to improve children's social competence and reduce behavioural problems that was originally developed for elementary school children. A randomized study of an adaptation of the PATHS for preschool children showed that intervention children had higher emotion knowledge skills, and were rated by teachers as more socially competent and less socially withdrawn after a year. PATH places central importance on the integration of affect, behavior, and cognitive understanding. It emphasizes teaching of skills, but also promoting meaningful opportunities to generalize and internalize such skills.

The Chicago School Readiness Project is a cluster-randomized trial of a classroom-based intervention aimed at reducing behaviour problems among preschoolers in Head Start. The program consists of supports for Head Start classroom teachers and classroom assistants, which include a mental health consultant that coaches teachers and classroom assistants on behavior management strategies and stress reduction techniques, workshops for teachers on approaches for reducing children's challenging behaviors, and targeted intervention services to specific children. At the end of the school year children in intervention classrooms had significant reductions in both externalizing and internalizing behaviours (Raver et al. 2009) and improvements in self-regulation skills (Raver et al. 2011). These included such effects as decreases in sadness, withdrawal, aggression and defiance. The importance of these impacts is highlighted by recent findings from a large-scale longitudinal study in which self-regulation during childhood was associated with smoking, substance abuse, dropping out of school, becoming a teen parent, criminal activities, and poor health (Moffitt et al. 2011). Such longitudinal evidence is lacking for most of the other focused programs.

A review of intervention programs with a focus on social and emotional development (McCabe and Altamura 2011) included the previous two programs together with a few others such as the Teaching Pyramid (to promote socio-emotional development), FunFRIENDS (with a focus on social skills, coping skills and resilience), REDI (Research Based, Developmentally Informed; which used

PATHS), and the Incredible Years Curriculum and Parenting Programs. All of these were found to have positive effects on social-emotional development, but the authors acknowledge the need for additional research evaluating outcomes into later childhood and adolescence.

Moreover, a review of diverse activities across different programs or interventions (Diamond and Lee 2011) defines a series of activities related to improved child executive functions: computerized training, noncomputerized games, aerobics, martial arts, yoga, mindfulness, and school curricula. The review states that children with worse executive functions benefit most from these activities but that focusing narrowly on them may not be as effective as also addressing emotional and social development.

6 What Have We Learnt More Globally?

Outside of the United States, studies in countries spanning the entire range of economic development have also substantiated the contributions of ECCE to children's learning development. Substantial positive effects have been found for both, cognitive development and social behaviour (Engle et al. 2011; Nores and Barnett 2010). There is a substantial global research base including rigorous randomized trials, some with long-term follow-ups that have looked at social and cognitive impacts of ECCE (Kagitcibasi et al. 2009; Nahar et al. 2012; Raine et al. 2003; Walker et al. 2006). The evidence of positive effects from high quality ECCE is remarkably consistent around the globe, taking into account that the quality of ECCE must be judged relative to conditions in the home (Barnett 2008b; Burger 2010; Engle et al. 2007; Schady 2006; Vargas-Barón 2009; Vegas and Santibañez 2010). These impacts are long-term as well as short-term and demonstrate remarkable consistency with each other and with the evidence from the United States summarized above. Such consistency across very different social and policy contexts is remarkable and indicates high rates of return from ECCE that are not limited to the more advanced economies.

There is some evidence that policies resulting in the direct provision of ECCE (often with nutritional supplements in lower income countries) are more effective for improving cognition and socio-emotional outcomes than those that solely focus on health or providing families with cash transfers. In a meta-analysis of non-U.S. studies, Nores and Barnett (2010) found average effects of comparable size to those just discussed across multiple domains for conditional cash transfers, nutritional supplementation, and cognitive stimulation or educational programs. Average effect sizes are 0.31sd (standard deviations) for cognition, 0.27sd for social development, 0.30sd for health and 0.27sd for schooling outcomes. Standard deviations is a common measurement used to make findings across studies comparable. These effects are equivalent to about a third of the Kindergarten achievement gap, on average, across countries. Studies with a focus on stimulation or education components (ECCE) had average effect sizes of 0.35sd for cognition, 0.27sd for social development, 0.23sd for health and 0.41sd for schooling outcomes. The authors concluded that programs that encompassed nutrition and stimulation or education seemed to more consistently impact all dimensions of children's development. Based on the dataset from this study in Fig. 2 we calculated average effect sizes for social-emotional outcomes across various program and study characteristics, regardless of intervention type. On average, effects are sustained over time, they are higher for programs that lasted over a year, higher for programs that target either preschoolers (3–5) or infants/toddlers (0–3) separately, higher in higher quality study designs (randomized trials) and only slightly higher in countries with higher economic development levels.

Similarly, Engle et al. (2011) reviewed research on parenting education and support programs and centre based ECCE in lower income countries and concluded that both have significant impacts on children's cognitive and socio-emotional development. Baker-Henningham and Lopez-Boo (2010) reviewed studies of ECCE and other early childhood development interventions in lower income countries. They found positive program impacts for cognitive, socio-emotional, and nutritional development, as well as for schooling outcomes.

Two proof of concept studies in lower income countries stand out that assessed the impacts of ECCE, among other outcomes. A small-scale randomized trial compared a high-quality ECCE program in Mauritius that provided nutrition,

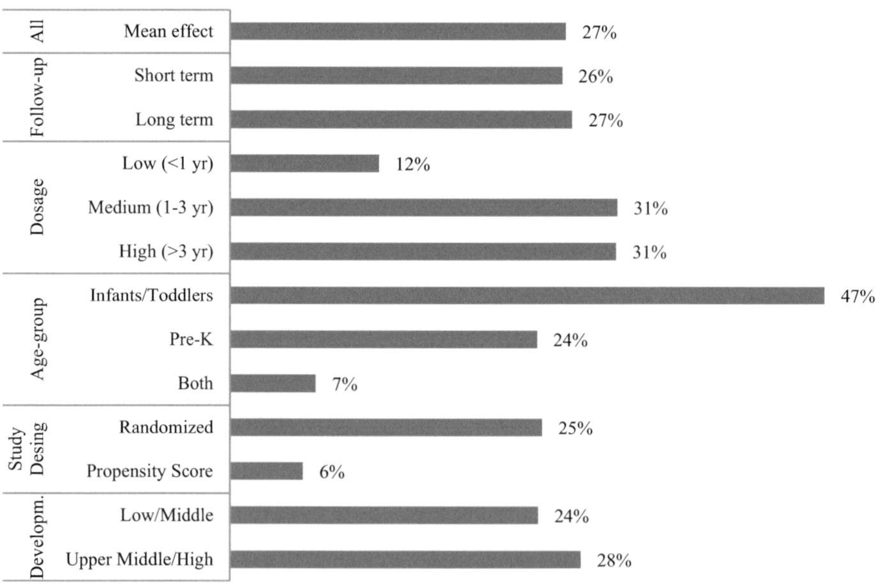

Fig. 2 Average global social-emotional/behavioural effects across a variety of program and study characteristics. We summarize average effect sizes across 65 social and emotional effects (as defined in Nores and Barnett 2010, p. 274) measured between 13 contrast groups across a variety of characteristics. These are author calculations based on the dataset used in the referenced meta-analyses

exercise, and education to 100 children from ages 3 to 5 with typical ECCE of minimal quality and found reductions in later conduct disorders (Raine et al. 2003). A randomized trial of cognitive stimulation and nutritional supplements with 129 disadvantaged infants (ages 9–24 months) in Jamaica found decreased rates of depression and violent behaviour (Walker et al. 2011). These long-term effects in Jamaica were attributable to stimulation only and not to nutritional supplementation. While neither of these interventions were developed with a socio-emotional focus, impacts on the socio-emotional domain were significant.

Recent studies of large-scale ECCE policy implementation further strengthen the evidence on the potential impact on the cognitive and also the socio-emotional domain. In Argentina, the expansion of preschool education increased self-control (e.g., attention and behaviour) and maternal labour market participation (mothers being more likely to work and work more hours on average when their youngest child attended preschool) through third grade (Berlinski and Galiani 2007; Berlinski et al. 2008). Studies in high income countries also find positive long-term effects from large scale ECCE, and that effects vary with quality. The U.K. EPPE study followed over 3000 children from preschool into secondary school and found that higher quality ECCE was associated with larger gains in social behaviour at age 11 (Sylva et al. 2011). A study of universal child care of minimal quality in Quebec found strong effects on maternal labour supply but negative consequences for child development including social behaviour (Baker et al. 2008).

In contrast to the Jamaican study, other rigorous studies find positive effects of nutrition either alone or in combination with ECCE. In Bolivia, the PIDI (Proyecto Integral de Desarrollo Infantil) program provided full-time care in homes of women and targeted low-income areas (with women receiving training and loans or grants to upgrade their homes). The program significantly increased psychosocial test scores, particularly for children who participated at least 7 months (Behrman et al. 2004). This is consistent with the importance of dosage shown in Fig. 2 above.

7 What Do We Know About Interventions Before the Age of Three?

Less of the research has focused on the effects of early education and childcare before age three. However, several randomized trials exist for this age group other than the Abecedarian study described earlier that included infants, toddlers and preschoolers. The Infant Health and Development Program in the United States (IHDP) provides a large multi-site randomized trial of a home visitation program provided for a child's first year and followed by educational child care modelled on the Abecedarian program from ages one to three (Ramey et al. 1992; McCormick et al. 2006). The IHDP study enrolled 985 low birth weight (less than 2500 g), premature infants (less than 37 weeks gestation) children. At age three, the treatment group had fewer behaviour problems. Although no effects persisted beyond age three for the sample as a whole, long-term gains were found for the heavier group of the low birth weight children. They showed cognitive advantages at ages five and eight, and less risky behaviour. No significant effects were found on grade retention, special education, high school graduation, or arrest rates. It is noteworthy that effects were less robust in this study where intervention did not continue beyond age three, unlike Abecedarian. However, caution is warranted in comparing results from this study to theirs, as it did not serve a highly disadvantaged population.

A large-scale multi-site randomized trial of Early Head Start (programs birth to three delivering centre-based and home visitation services) found small effects on children's behavioural problems, parenting, and maternal depression (Zill 2010). These effects did not persist beyond age three to age five. These findings are consistent with the weaker findings of the IHDP study compared to Abecedarian. Again, continuity in the quality and intent of care and education beyond age three may be important for producing lasting gains.

Home visitation models are increasingly used as a means of impacting child and parental outcomes before the age of three. A review of home visitation programs and their effectiveness in preventing violence carried out by the United States' Task Force on Community Preventing Services at the Center for Disease Control and Prevention (Bilukha et al. 2005) found substantial positive effects of prevention of child maltreatment, but found insufficient evidence to determine their effectiveness on violence by children, by parents and intimate partner violence. In particular, and somewhat in contrast to other models emphasizing home visitation that often fail to produce gains, substantial success has been found for the Nurse Family Partnership (Olds and Kitzman 1990; Olds 2010) which targets first-time mothers and their children. Women were recruited for study prior to their 30th week of pregnancy and participated in several randomized trials of the home visitation program. The program provides parent education through home visits by nurses, social support, and referrals to social services until children reach the age of two. The program has been found to reduce the number of pregnancies and births, increase intervals between births, produce a variety of positive outcomes for the mothers and improve their care of children. A key benefit is reduction in child maltreatment or accidental injury. Nurse-visited children demonstrated fewer behaviour problems (Olds et al. 2004). It is yet unclear how broadly beneficial the program is with some research suggesting greater benefits for the subset of the low-income population with low maternal psychological resources.

8 Which Factors Matter in ECCE Interventions?

One of the clearest findings from the research is that programs are more successful if they have an intentional focus on the specific aspects of development and skills in which improvements are desired (Camilli et al. 2010). It is possible to improve some outcomes, academic skills for example, while having no positive impacts, or even negative impacts, on social and emotional development. In addition, intensity and breadth contribute to impact (Camilli et al. 2010; Nores and Barnett 2010). Studies find that ECCE interventions that impact more than one dimension of child development (Wachs and Rahman 2013) have stronger and more sustained impacts on children's development (Engle et al. 2007; Nores and Barnett 2010) and are more likely to impact the socio-emotional domain and, consequently, precursors of aggressive or risky behaviours. Multidimensional interventions address not only individual children's characteristics but also bioecological or contextual dimensions (i.e. in the family and community) thus remediating individual but also bioecological risks, which is fundamental for the formulation of cost-effective ECD interventions (Wachs and Rahman 2013). The review of the literature by Yoshikawa (1995) concluded that ECCE interventions that demonstrated long-term effects on crime and antisocial behaviour tend to combine two main components: (1) early childhood education with elements that foster cognitive and socio-emotional development and (2) family support services that enhance parents' social support and foster positive parenting and family interactions. However, there are clear exceptions among the programs we reviewed above.

It should be recognized that absolute measures of program quality or intensity are not necessarily the most relevant factor, but the extent to which additional support for child development is provided compared to what is available to the child without the program. The resources available to disadvantaged children vary from country to country and within countries. In very high poverty countries or localities, the family's resources may be so limited that even very modest ECCE programs might provide advantages (e.g. Rao et al. 2012). However, there is considerable uncertainty regarding possible thresholds for substantive impact, and care must be taken to ensure that ECCE is of sufficient quality to produce the desired long-term outcomes even in low-income contexts (Raine et al. 2003).

9 Conclusions

Research on a broad range of early childhood interventions including early education and care have found that these have the potential for substantially impacting children's social development and behaviour in the short- and long-term. These impacts go beyond children's school related behaviours, executive functions, and educational attainment and have included their social-emotional and behavioural development. High quality, intensive programs have been found to have long-lasting effects on such outcomes as antisocial and prosocial behaviours, specifically including aggression, hostility, conduct disorder, delinquency and crime. Other positive outcomes include decreases in youth and adult risky behaviour including smoking and drug use, as well as improvements in health related behaviours. Although negative effects when found tend to be quite modest, it appears that ECCE programs of low quality (relative to the experiences children would have if not in the program) may have negative consequences for social development. Studies with long-term follow-ups find substantial impacts for teenagers, young adults and even through middle age. Early childhood programs are the only types of interventions that have shown such depth and breadth in the type and amount of short-term outcomes, which is why cost-benefit analyses for these interventions largely surpass cost-benefit analyses for most social interventions. Findings are strikingly consistent globally and in the United States.

As noted, research on early childhood education has found that the intensity, strength, and breadth of impacts is largely dependent on quality of the intervention. Programs are further strengthened in their effects on social skills and behaviour when they include an intentional focus on addressing social and emotional development and skills. Programs that are multidimensional and include a focus on intentional, individualized teaching are likely to be more effective whether they are focused on children, adults or both. However, when policies or programs strive for breadth and to take advantage of the multiple pathways through which social and development may be enhanced caution is warranted to ensure that sufficient resources are made available to implement all aspects of the strategy well. Trying to do too much with too little is a recipe for failure. Regardless, the large amount of evidence in the early childhood arena makes it clear that there is a strong and unquestionable role for early childhood education in promoting and strengthening children's social and emotional development in ways that can have profound consequences for children and society, including the amelioration of such major social problems as child maltreatment, violence, and crime.

Five Questions

1. What combination of policies relating to parent supports and ECCE might best contribute to improvements in executive functions and social and emotional development including dispositions so as to reduce aggression and violence in young adults?
2. Are there essential ingredients of curricula and a necessary balance of activities for the education of children ages 3 to 5 to optimize both cognitive and social-emotional development?
3. What is the role of nutrition in supporting social and emotional development and influencing later social behavior? To what extent is its contribution contingent on the child's nutritional status, other aspects of the environment (e.g. access to clean water), and the child's health (e.g. being free of parasites)?
4. To what extent are their synergies between educational, nutritional, and public health strategies for supporting social and emotional development?
5. In actual practice are disadvantaged populations most effectively and efficiently reached by targeted or universal ECCE services?

References

Arteaga, I., Humpage, S., Reynolds, A. J., et al. (2014). One year of preschool or two: Is it important for adult outcomes? *Economics of Education Review, 40*, 221–237.

Baker, M., Gruber, J., & Milligan, K. (2008). Universal child care, maternal labor supply, and family well-being. *Journal of Political Economy, 116*(4), 709–745.

Baker-Henningham, H., & Lopez-Boo, F. (2010). *Early childhood stimulation interventions in developing countries: A comprehensive literature review*. Washington, DC: Inter-American Development Bank.

Barnett, W. S. (1996). *Lives in the balance: Age-27 benefit-cost analysis of the High/Scope Perry Preschool Program*. Ypsilanti, MI: Monographs of the High/Scope Educational Research Foundation, Number Eleven. Monograph Series, High/Scope Foundation, 600 North River Street.

Barnett, W. S. (2008a). Why governments should invest in early education. *Journal for Institutional Comparisons Early Childhood Education, 6*(2), 9–14.

Barnett, W. S. (2008b). *Preschool Education and its lasting effects: Research and policy implications*. Colorado: Education and Public Interest Center and Education Policy Research Unit.

Barnett, W. S. (2011). Effectiveness of early educational intervention. *Science, 333*(6045), 975–978.

Barnett, W. S., Jung, K., Yarosz, D. J., et al. (2008). Educational effectiveness of the tools of the mind curriculum: A randomized trial. *Early Childhood Research Quarterly, 23*, 299–313.

Barnett, W. S., & Masse, L. N. (2007). Comparative benefit–cost analysis of the Abecedarian program and its policy implications. *Economics of Education Review, 26*(1), 113–125.

Behrman, J. R., Cheng, Y., & Todd, P. E. (2004). Evaluating preschool programs when length of exposure to the program varies: A nonparametric approach. *Review of Economics and Statistics, 86*(1), 108–132.

Behrman, I.R., Urzua, S.S. (2013). Economic perspectives on some important dimensions of early childhood development in developing countries. *Handbook of early childhood development research and its impact on global policy* (p. 123). Oxford: Oxford University Press.

Berlinski, S., & Galiani, S. (2007). The effect of a large expansion of pre-primary school facilities on preschool attendance and maternal employment. *Labour Economics, 14*(3), 665–680.

Berlinski, S., Galiani, S., & Gertler, P. (2008). The effect of preprimary education on primary school performance. *Journal of Public Economics, 93*, 219–234.

Bilukha, O., Hahn, R. A., Crosby, A., et al. (2005). The effectiveness of early childhood home visitation in preventing violence: A systematic review. *American Journal of Preventive Medicine, 28*(2), 11–39.

Blair, C., & Raver, C. C. (2014). Closing the achievement gap through modification of neurocognitive and neuroendocrine function: Results from a cluster randomized controlled trial of an innovative approach to the education of children in kindergarten. *PloS One, 9*(11), e112393.

Blau, D. M., & Currie, J. (2005). Preschool, day care, and afterschool care: who's minding the kids? In F. Welch & E. A. Hanushek (Eds.), *The handbook of economics of education* (pp. 1163–1267). New York: North Holland.

Borghans, L., Duckworth, A. L., Heckman, J. J., et al. (2008). The economics and psychology of personality traits. *Journal of Human Resources, 43*(4), 972–1059.

Boyd, J., Barnett, W. S., Bodrova, E., et al. (2005). *Promoting children's social and emotional development through preschool education*. New Brunswick, NJ: National Institute for Early Education Research.

Burger, K. (2010). How does early childhood care and education affect cognitive development? An international review of the effects of early interventions for children from different social backgrounds. *Early Childhood Research Quarterly, 25*, 140–165.

Camilli, G., Vargas, S., Ryan, S., et al. (2010). Meta-analysis of the effects of early education interventions on cognitive and social development. *Teachers College Record, 112*(3).

Campbell, F. A., Pungello, E. P., Burchinal, M., et al. (2012). Adult outcomes as a function of an early childhood educational program: An Abecedarian Project follow-up. *Developmental Psychology, 48*(4), 1033.
Choi, S. (2004). *Access, public investment, and equity in ECCE: The nexus in nine high-population countries* (UNESCO, Policy Brief on Early Childhood No. 19). Paris: UNESCO. Available via http://unesdoc.unesco.org/images/0013/001374/137408e.pdf. Accessed January 13, 2015
Cunha, F., Heckman, J. J., Lochner, L., et al. (2006). Interpreting the evidence on life cycle skill formation. *Handbook of the Economics of Education, 1*, 697–812.
Diamond, A., Barnett, W. S., Thomas, J., et al. (2007). Preschool program improves cognitive control. *Science, 318*, 1387–1388.
Diamond, A., & Lee, K. (2011). Interventions shown to aid executive function development in children 4 to 12 years old. *Science, 333*(6045), 959–964.
Domitrovich, C. E., Cortes, R. C., & Greenberg, M. T. (2007). Improving young children's social and emotional competence: A randomized trial of the preschool "PATHS" curriculum. *Journal of Primary Prevention, 28*(2), 67–91.
Engle, P. L., Black, M. M., Behrman, J. R., et al. (2007). Strategies to avoid the loss of developmental potential in more than 200 million children in the developing world. *Lancet, 369*(9557), 229–242.
Engle, P. L., Fernald, L. C. H., Alderman, H., et al. (2011). Strategies for reducing inequalities and improving developmental outcomes for young children in low-income and middle-income countries. *Lancet, 37*, 1339–1353.
Farrington, D. P. (1985). Predicting self-reported and official delinquency. *Prediction in criminology, 8*, 150–173.
Farrington, D.P. (1987). Early precursors of frequent offending. In *Families, schools, and delinquency prevention* (pp. 27–50). New York: Springer.
Farrington, D. P. (1989). Early predictors of adolescent aggression and adult violence. *Violence and Victims, 4*(2), 79–100.
Friedman-Krauss, A., & Barnett, W. S. (2013). *Early childhood education: Pathways to better health*. New Brunswick, NJ: National Institute for Early Education Research.
Goleman, D. (1994). *Emotional intelligence: Why it can matter more than IQ*. New York: Bantam Books.
Heckman, J.J., Kautz, T. (2013). *Fostering and measuring skills: Interventions that improve character and cognition* (No. w19656). Cambridge, MA: National Bureau of Economic Research.
Heckman, J., Moon, S. H., Pinto, R., et al. (2010). Analyzing social experiments as implemented: A reexamination of the evidence from the HighScope Perry Preschool Program. *Quant Economics, 1*(1), 1–46.
Heckman, J.J., Stixrud, J., Urzua, S. (2006). *The effects of cognitive and noncognitive abilities on labor market outcomes and social behavior* (No. w12006). Cambridge, MA: National Bureau of Economic Research.
Herrod, H. G. (2007). Do first years really last a lifetime? *Clinical Pediatrics, 46*(3), 199.
Kagitcibasi, C., Sunar, D., Bekman, S., et al. (2009). Continuing effects of early enrichment in adult life: The Turkish Early Enrichment Project 22 years later. *Journal of Applied Developmental Psychology, 30*, 764–779.
Kirp, D. L. (2007). *The sandbox investment: The preschool movement and kids-first politics*. Boston, MA: Harvard University Press.
Krzewina, J. M. (2012). *Effect of preschool classroom quality on social and language development*. Theses and dissertations, Paper 60, University of Wisconsin Madison, Wisconsin.
LaCourse, E., Cote, S., Nagin, D. S., et al. (2002). A longitudinal-experimental approach to testing theories of antisocial behavior development. *Development and Psychopathology, 14*(4), 909–924.

Mashburn, A. J., Pianta, R. C., Hamre, B. K., et al. (2008). Measures of classroom quality in prekindergarten and children's development of academic, language, and social skills. *Child Development, 79*(3), 732–749.

Masse, L. N., & Barnett, W. S. (2002). *A benefit cost analysis of the Abecedarian early childhood intervention*. New Brunswick, NJ: National Institute for Early Education Research.

McCabe, P. C., & Altamura, M. (2011). Empirically valid strategies to improve social and emotional competence of preschool children. *Psychology in the Schools, 48*(5), 513–540.

McCormick, M. C., Brooks-Gunn, J., Buka, S. L., et al. (2006). Early intervention in low birth weight premature infants: Results at 18 years of age for the Infant Health and Development Program. *Pediatrics, 117*(3), 771–780.

Moffitt, T. E., Arseneault, L., Belsky, D., et al. (2011). A gradient of childhood self-control predicts health, wealth, and public safety. *Proceedings of the National Academy of Sciences, United States of America, 108*, 2693–2698.

Muennig, P., Robertson, D., Johnson, G., et al. (2011). The effect of an early education program on adult health: The Carolina Abecedarian Project randomized con-trolled trial. *American Journal of Public Health, 101*(3), 512.

Nagin, D. S., & Tremblay, R. E. (2001). Parental and early childhood predictors of persistent physical aggression in boys from kindergarten to high school. *Archives of General Psychology, 58*, 389–394.

Nahar, B., Hossain, M., Hamadani, J., et al. (2012). Effects of a community-based approach of food and psychosocial stimulation on growth and development of severely malnourished children in Bangladesh: A randomised trial. *European Journal of Clinical Nutrition, 66*, 701–709.

National Scientific Council on the Developing Child. (2005). *Children's emotional development is built in to the architecture of their brains*. Working Paper II. Available via http://www.developingchild.net/papers/workingpaperII.pdf. Accessed March 15, 2005

Nores, M., & Barnett, W. S. (2010). Benefits of early childhood interventions across the world: (Under) Investing in the very young. *Economics of Education Review, 29*(2), 271–282.

Nores, M., Belfield, C. R., Barnett, W. S., et al. (2005). Updating the economic impacts of the High/Scope Perry Preschool program. *Educational Evaluation and Policy Analysis, 27*(3), 245–261.

OECD. (2006). *Starting Strong II: Early childhood education and care—Final report of the thematic review of early childhood education and care*. Paris: Author.

Olds, D. L. (2010). The nurse family partnership. In R. Haskins & W. S. Barnett (Eds.), *Investing in young children—New directions in federal preschool and early childhood policy* (pp. 69–78). Washington, DC/New Brunswick, NJ: Center on Children and Families at Brookings/National Institute for Early Education Research.

Olds, D. L., & Kitzman, H. (1990). Can home visitation improve the health of women and children at environmental risk? *Pediatrics, 86*(1), 108–116.

Olds, D. L., Kitzman, H., Cole, R., et al. (2004). Effects of nurse home-visiting on maternal life course and child development: Age 6 follow-up results of a randomized trial. *Pediatrics, 114* (6), 1550–1559.

Peisner-Feinberg, E. S., Burchinal, M. R., Clifford, R. M., et al. (2001). The relation of preschool child-care quality to children's cognitive and social developmental trajectories through second grade. *Child Development, 72*(5), 1534–1553.

Raine, A., Mellingen, K., Liu, J., et al. (2003). Effects of environmental enrichment at ages 3–5 years on schizotypal personality and antisocial behavior at ages 17 and 23 years. *The American Journal of Psychiatry, 160*(9), 1627–1635.

Ramey, C. T., Bryant, D. M., Wasik, B. H., et al. (1992). Infant Health and Development Program for low birth weight, premature infants: Program elements, family participation, and child intelligence. *Pediatrics, 89*(3), 454–465.

Rao, N., Sun, J., Pearson, V., et al. (2012). Is something better than nothing? An evaluation of early childhood programs in Cambodia. *Child Development, 83*(3), 864–876.

Raver, C. C., Jones, S. M., Li-Grining, C. P., et al. (2009). Targeting children's behavior problems in preschool classrooms: A cluster-randomized controlled trial. *Journal of Consulting and Clinical Psychology, 77*, 302–316.

Raver, C. C., Jones, S. M., Li-Grining, C. P., et al. (2011). CSRP's impact on low-income preschoolers' pre-academic skills: Self-regulation and teacher-student relationships as two mediating mechanisms. *Child Development, 82*(1), 362–378.

Reynolds, A. J., & Ou, S. R. (2011). Paths of effects from preschool to adult well-being: A confirmatory analysis of the Child-Parent Center Program. *Child Development, 82*(2), 555–582.

Reynolds, A. J., Ou, S. R., & Topitzes, J. W. (2004). Paths of effects of early childhood intervention on educational attainment and delinquency: A confirmatory analysis of the Chicago Child-Parent Centers. *Child Development, 75*(5), 1299–1328.

Reynolds, A. J., Temple, J. A., White, B. A., et al. (2011). Age 26 cost–benefit analysis of the Child-Parent Center Early Education Program. *Child Development, 82*(1), 379–404.

Schady, N. R. (2006). Early childhood development in Latin America and the Caribbean. *Economia, 6*(2), 185–225.

Schweinhart, L. J. (2013). Long-term follow-up of a preschool experiment. *Journal of Experimental Criminology, 9*(4), 389–409.

Schweinhart, L. J., Montie, J., Xiang, Z., et al. (2005). *Lifetime effects: the High/Scope Perry Preschool study through age 40*. Ypsilanti, MI: HighScope Edifcational Research Foundation.

Schweinhart, L. J., & Weikart, D. P. (1997). The high/scope preschool curriculum comparison study through age 23. *Early Childhood Research Quarterly, 12*(2), 117–143.

Sylva, K., Melhuish, E., Sammons, P., et al. (2011). Pre-school quality and educational outcomes at age 11: Low quality has little benefit. *Journal of Early Childhood Research, 9*, 109–124.

Tremblay, R. E. (2002). Development of physical aggression from early childhood to adulthood. In R.E. Tremblay, R.G. Barr, R.De.V. Peters (Eds.), *Encyclopedia on early childhood development, centre of excellence for early childhood development* (pp. 1–6). Montreal, Quebec, 2002. Available via http://www.excellence-earlychildhood.ca/documents/TremblayANGxp.pdf. Accessed December 21, 2006.

Ursache, A., Blair, C., & Raver, C. C. (2012). The promotion of self-regulation as a means of enhancing school readiness and early achievement in children at risk for school failure. *Child Development Perspectives, 6*(2), 122–128.

Vargas-Barón, E. (2009). *Going to scale: Early childhood development in Latin America. Designing successful and sustainable ECD Programs with National-Level Coverage*. Washington, DC: The RISE Institute.

Vegas, E., & Santibáñez, L. (2010). *The promise of early childhood development in Latin America and the Caribbean*. Washington, DC: World Bank Publications.

Wachs, T. D., & Rahman, A. (2013). The nature and impact of risk and protective influences on children's development in low-income countries. In P. R. Britto & C. M. Super (Eds.), *Handbook of early childhood development research and its impact on global policy*. New York: Oxford University Press.

Walker, S. P., Chang, S. M., Powell, C. A., et al. (2006). Effects of psychosocial stimulation and dietary supplementation in early childhood on psychosocial functioning in late adolescence: Follow-up of randomised controlled trial. *British Medical Journal, 333*(7566), 472.

Walker, S. P., Chang, S. M., Vera-Hernandez, M., et al. (2011). Early childhood stimulation benefits adult competence and reduces violent behavior. *Pediatrics, 127*, 849–857.

Weiland, C., Ulvestad, K., Sachs, J., et al. (2013). Associations between classroom quality and children's vocabulary and executive function skills in an urban public prekindergarten program. *Early Childhood Research Quarterly, 28*(2), 199–209.

Werner, E. E. (1987). Vulnerability and resiliency in children at risk for delinquency: A longitudinal study from birth to adulthood. In J. D. Burchard & S. N. Burchard (Eds.), *Primary prevention of psychopathology: Vol. 10. Prevention of delinquent behavior* (pp. 16–43). Newbury Park, CA: Sage.

White, K., & Casto, G. (1985). An integrative review of early intervention efficacy studies with at-risk children: Implications for the handicapped. *Research in Developmental Disabilities, 5*, 7–31.

Wilson, S. J., & Farran, D. C. (2012). *Experimental evaluation of the tools of the mind preschool curriculum*. Society for Research on Educational Effectiveness.

Yoshikawa, H. (1994). Prevention as cumulative protection: effects of early family support and education on chronic delinquency and its risks. *Psychological Bulletin, 115*(1), 28.

Yoshikawa, H. (1995). Long-term effects of early childhood programs on social outcomes and delinquency. *Future of Children, 5*(3), 51–75.

Zill, N. (2010). Ten ideas for improving early head start. In Haskins, R., Barnett, W.S. (Eds.), *Investing in young children—New directions in federal preschool and early childhood policy* (pp. 39–48). New Brunswick, NJ: Center on Children and Families at Brookings and the National Institute for Early Education Research.

Young Children's Understanding of Social Norms and Social Institutions

Patricia Kanngiesser, Marco F.H. Schmidt, and Federico Rossano

Abstract Children are born into a world abundant with social norms that prescribe how one should and should not behave. Social norms also form the basis of more complex social institutions such as ownership that create obligations, rights and duties. As adults we typically navigate our social world effortlessly and mostly unaware of the intricate web of social norms and institutions shaping our behaviour. But when and how do young children first become aware of the norms and institutions of their socio-cultural group? In this chapter, we will first provide a definition of social norms and institutions and explain their most important characteristics. We will then present empirical evidence that children as young as 3 years of age already understand some crucial aspects of social norms. We will further use the example of ownership to argue that it is one of the first social institutions that young children understand.

1 Introduction

We are born into a world full of norms that prescribe how we should and should not behave. Imagine going to a business meeting anywhere in Europe and instead of offering your business partner your hand for a formal handshake, you take her head and press your nose and forehead together. Under most circumstances this would be considered inappropriate behaviour. As a Maori in New Zealand, however, greeting a fellow Maori with this traditional hongi would convey your highest appreciation.

P. Kanngiesser (✉)
Department of Education and Psychology, Freie Universität Berlin, Berlin, Germany
e-mail: patricia.kanngiesser@fu-berlin.de

M.F.H. Schmidt
Department of Psychology, LMU München, Munich, Germany
e-mail: marco.schmidt@psy.lmu.de

F. Rossano
Department of Cognitive Science, University of California, San Diego, CA, USA
e-mail: frossano@ucsd.edu

H. Kury et al. (eds.), *Women and Children as Victims and Offenders: Background, Prevention, Reintegration*, DOI 10.1007/978-3-319-08398-8_7

This example is just one of many that can be used to illustrate how social norms pervade our everyday lives and regulate how we greet each other, eat our food, or talk to our children, parents, friends, and colleagues. Beyond shaping our daily social interactions, social norms also form the basis of more complex social arrangements such as money, marriage, or ownership (we call them "social institutions", see Sect. 2).

As adults, we usually navigate our social world effortlessly and mostly unaware of the intricate web of norms that govern our behaviour. However, parents and educators may have experienced the need to hold back young children from crossing the street on a red light or from hugging and kissing strangers in the street. Also, parents may remember the time when they picked up their child from a friend's house and discovered later that their child had helped herself to (or "stolen") some of her friend's toys. Despite these rough beginnings most of us adults will intuitively stop at a red traffic light, greet strangers respectfully, and only take what is ours or what we have paid for. When and how do children come to understand this intricate fabric of invisible social norms and become experts at navigating their social environment?

In this chapter, we will show that young children are already able to recognize, learn and apply the social norms of their environment. We will begin with a definition of social norms and sketch some of their most relevant characteristics (Sect. 2). Then, we will present empirical evidence that young children learn social norms quickly, understand that different norms apply in different contexts, and even (jointly) create their own norms (Sect. 3). Furthermore, we will use the example of ownership and demonstrate that it is one of the first more complex social institutions that children understand (Sect. 4). While children are equipped with the capacity to learn social norms just as they possess the capacity to learn a language, we recognize that the socio-cultural environment children grow up in plays a crucial role in shaping which social behaviour they will learn to view as correct (take our opening example of Western and Maori greetings). The majority of empirical studies to date have been conducted with children growing up in Western societies, but whenever possible, we will include cross-cultural findings.

2 Social Norms and Social Institutions

Social norms pervade our lives across environments and situations—in our homes, at work, and in public. They are rules that coordinate and constrain behaviour in a group and are based on agreements and expectations about how members of one's group ought to behave (Bicchieri and Muldoon 2014). They are thus not just statements of personal preferences (e.g., people in this group like to wear red t-shirts) or descriptions of behavioural regularities (e.g., today most people in this group wear read t-shirts), but entail obligations and duties to conform to certain rules (e.g., people in this group ought to wear red t-shirts). Crucially, what distinguishes norms from other sets of rules or regularities is that group members can be held accountable and sanctioned by others for violating norms, whereas there are usually no grounds for sanctioning people on the basis of their personal taste. That is, we may dislike it if someone wears a red t-shirt, but we have no right to demand of them to stop wearing read t-shirts (unless there are strict norms against wearing red t-shirts, for instance, at funerals). Norm violations may be sanctioned by bad looks or shunning or by more direct forms of punishment (e.g. fines).

A typical and much used example of a social norm is the norm to drive on the right (or left) side of the road. Members of a group with this norm will expect everyone to drive on the right side of the road, will adjust their own behaviour accordingly and have the right to hold others that do not conform to the norm accountable, for instance, by imposing fines on them. It is irrelevant for successful coordination and regulation of traffic whether the norm is to drive on the left or on the right side of the road, as long as there is one norm that everyone is aware of and adheres to. In fact, in continental Europe everyone drives on the right side of the road, while in the British Islands everyone drives on the left side of the road. That is, an important feature of norms is that they are context-specific (i.e. driving on the right is correct in France, but not in the United Kingdom; see e.g., Rakoczy and Schmidt 2013, for a review).

Social norms help coordinate behaviour not only in smaller groups such as sports club, groups of friends, families, but also in large ethnic or religious groups or whole nations. Essentially, a group can be any number of people that share a common set of values and/or characteristics and identify themselves with a particular group. Individuals are often members of more than one group (citizens of a nation, members of religious groups, families, sports or work teams, etc.) and these groups might adhere to distinct or even conflicting norms. Sometimes even categorizing people based on arbitrary features such as the colour of their shirt is sufficient to elicit identification with a group and show favouritism towards one's own group (Tajfel et al. 1971).

Group norms may regulate behaviour in different domains and it can often be useful to distinguish between norms that belong in the moral domain and conventional norms (e.g., Turiel 1983). Moreover, conventional norms can often be separated into regulative norms and constitutive norms (Lewis 1969; Searle 1996). We will explain each of these types of norms in the following paragraphs and provide examples to illustrate them.

Moral norms are usually norms that relate to harm and fairness. They may determine, for example, that hitting someone constitutes a harmful action whereas shaking someone's hand is a harmless action or that giving everyone the same share is fair while giving more to the tallest person is unfair. Some cultures or groups may also treat violations of norms pertaining to loyalty such as burning the flag of one's country or norms pertaining to sanctity such as eating certain "impure" foods as harmful and immoral acts (Shweder 1991; Haidt 2012).

In contrast to moral norms, regulative norms coordinate behaviours and usually have the goal of solving a coordination problem (Lewis 1969; Searle 1996). For example, in many places there are norms that regulate traffic to prevent delays and accidents. Traffic lights are one means by which traffic can be coordinated, but giving way to the car that arrives first may achieve this goal just as well. Importantly, regulative norms are context-specific, that is, what may be considered appropriate behaviour in one context may be inappropriate in another. Contexts may be occasions (e.g., it is appropriate to wear a white shirt to a wedding but not to a funeral), relationships (e.g., it is appropriate to greet a friend with a hug but not a business partner) or locations (e.g., it is illegal to smoke in public places such as restaurants, but alright to do so in the privacy of one's home). In contrast, moral norms are less context-specific and often apply more generally. Hitting someone in the face is usually considered a harmful act, irrespective of whether it occurs at a wedding or a funeral, between friends or colleagues, and in public or in private.

A second type of conventional norms is called constitutive norms. These norms are termed "constitutive" because they give rise to other social norms or social institutions (Searle 1996). Constitutive norms make certain rights, duties or obligations possible, that is, without these norms these social entities would not exist. Take the example of money to illustrate what is meant by a constitutive norm: A piece of paper of a certain size and colour counts as a $1 note in trading interactions. Crucially, the piece of paper cannot perform this function by its physical properties alone (e.g. its size, weight or colour), but there needs to be a collective agreement and recognized practice that this piece of paper functions as a "$1 note" (e.g. a store will accept this piece of paper in exchange for goods "worth" $1).

Ownership is another example of a social institution, which gives owners certain rights that determine what they are entitled to do with their property (e.g., use it, sell it, give it away, destroy it, etc.) and regulates what non-owners should or should not do with other's property (e.g. destroy it, taking it without permission, etc.; Honoré 1961; Snare 1972; Kalish and Anderson 2011). Social institutions thus create certain rights, duties, obligation, commitments, titles, and roles that would not exist without these social institutions (e.g., respect for other's property).

In our definition of social norms and institutions, we have repeatedly mentioned that they are mutually agreed on rules, without further elaborating on this particular characteristic. From a psychological perspective, this feature is one of the core elements that sets social norms (and for that matter all types of norms) apart from other types of coordination rules or coordinated behaviour. Humans, unlike any other species on the planet, have a unique ability to create collectively shared norms and agreements and complex social and cultural institutions (Tomasello 2009; Tomasello et al. 2012; Wyman and Rakoczy 2011). These norms and institutions form part of our cultural common ground; that is the way we—as a group—do things and expect other group members to do them.

It has been argued that our ability to create (and adhere to) social norms is grounded in our capacity to engage in shared or "we" intentionality with other members of our species (Gilbert 1992; Searle 1996; Tomasello and Carpenter 2007). Shared or collective intentionality describes the ability to share psychological states with others and, in particular, to share a goal, an action plan to reach this goal, and an understanding of the different roles that are necessary to implement the action plan. For instance, you and I ("we") intend to build a table together. We now have the shared goal to build a table, including a plan of how to procure the materials, how to design it and when and where to meet to complete it (action plan) and a mutual understanding of the different roles needed to build it (e.g. I will be responsible for cutting the wood, you will be responsible for drilling holes, etc.). Importantly, the basic cognitive abilities needed to engage in shared intentionality emerge early in development, already during the second year of life. While children are not yet able to engage in complicated shared goals and activities like building tables (or skyscrapers), they begin to attend to things in the environment jointly with others (joint attention), to engage in cooperative communication (verbal and non-verbal), and to participate in collaborative activities and instructed social learning (see e.g., Tomasello and Carpenter 2007, for a review). These abilities rapidly improve, and by 3 years of age children expect a partner to return to a joint activity, wait for her before continuing an activity, and take on their partner's role when needed, but also acknowledge when they themselves leave a joint task (Gräfenhain et al. 2009, 2013). Furthermore, 3-year-olds will continue to help a partner in a collaborative activity (e.g., to get rewards) even after they have already received their own reward and could easily break off from the activity thus demonstrating their commitment to their partner to complete the joint activity (Hamann et al. 2012).

In summary, social norms are the collectively shared rules of a social group that coordinate and constrain behaviour in context-specific ways. They are thus rules that prescribe how someone ought to behave under certain circumstances, with violations of norms being subject to sanctions and punishment by the group. Next, we will elaborate on when and how young children begin to understand regulative and constitutive social norms (see Tomasello and Vaish 2013, for a review on children's understanding of moral norms).

3 Young Children's Understanding of Social Norms

Children's understanding of social norms can be studied using a range of different methods. Generally speaking, these methods either focus on children's reasoning about norm violations in hypothetical scenarios or they investigate children's reactions to norm violations in practical situations.

Researchers focusing on children's reasoning about norms usually present children with pictures or stories, in which a fictional child violates a norm, and then ask children questions about the protagonist's behaviour (Turiel 1983; Killen and Smetana 2013). These studies have found, for example, that 3- and 4-year-old children reason differently about violations of physical laws (e.g. "Can a little boy lift a heavy sofa?") and social laws (e.g. "Can a little boy wear his shoes in the bath tub?" (Kalish 1998). They have also shown that 3- and 4-year-olds view violations of moral rules (e.g., hitting another child) as more severe than violations of regulative norms (e.g., not sitting in the designated place during story time; Smetana 1981). These studies have in common that they focus exclusively on children's theoretical understanding—or their knowledge—of norms and their violations, but reveal little about children's understanding of the normative force of norms (i.e., that one should do certain things). For the rest of this section, we will thus primarily focus on children's understanding of norms in practice and, in particular, on how young children react when they witness norm violations (Schmidt and Tomasello 2012; Rakoczy and Schmidt 2013). This will help us to identify under which circumstances children first learn about social norms, how they know that something is a norm, how they distinguish between different types of norms and how they themselves create their own norms.

In an early study on children's understanding of social norms, Rakoczy and colleagues first introduced a simple new game to 2- and 3-year-old children (e.g., "This is how we play Daxing!") and then had children observe a hand puppet that played the game in an incorrect way (Rakoczy et al. 2008). Young children protested and criticized the puppet, and 3-year-olds often used language that referred to norms such as "No, one must not do it like that!" When the puppet did not violate any game rules (i.e., she announced that she would simply show the child something), children did not protest. This suggests that young children already understand that people who decide to play a game should adhere to the game's (arbitrary) rules. Young children thus do not just passively follow norms such as game rules. They understand that they might get into trouble if they do not abide to the rules set by adults. Indeed, between around 2 to 3 years of age, children begin to criticize norm violators and to actively enforce norms—even when they themselves are not affected at all by the reprehensible act. Importantly, such active enforcement of norms reveals that children understand that norms determine how one ought to behave and do not just copy an adult's behaviour without understanding the normative nature of this behaviour.

How do young children first learn about social norms? One context in which children may learn about norms is pretend play, in which they pretend that one thing is something else (Walton 1990). For instance, in the banana-phone game children pretend that a banana is a telephone and use it to "call someone", thus assigning a new function (telephone) in a context-specific way to an object. Rakoczy (2008) has investigated 2- and 3-year-old children's understanding of pretence acts: Children watched an adult perform different pretence acts such as pretending that a clothespin was a knife. When a puppet pretended to eat the object, children protested against the puppet's behaviour. However, when the object was declared to be a carrot in the pretend game, children did not protest when the puppet pretended to eat it. Furthermore, 3-year-olds, but not 2-year-olds, also understand that pretended identities can change from one location to another. For example, they understand that a stick may be treated as a toothbrush in one game at one table, but as a carrot in another game at a different table (Wyman et al. 2009). These findings suggest that young children understand that social norms are context-specific and not necessarily valid in all situations, i.e. they understand that an object can have one function in one context but another function in a different context.

Another important fact about social norms, as mentioned above, is that they are group-specific and often only locally recognized. For instance, many people in Western cultures use fork and knife, while people in other cultures may use chopsticks. When do young children understand that such norms are not binding for everyone? Schmidt and colleagues (2012) investigated this question and found that 3-year-olds criticized and protested against moral norm transgressions (a puppet destroyed the experimenter's property) irrespective of whether the norm violator was someone from their own group ("in-group") or someone from a different group or culture ("out-group") (Schmidt et al. 2012). But interestingly, children enforced conventional norms (about simple game rules) only for in-group members, suggesting that they understand that conventional norms are specific to certain groups and hence not binding for members of other groups.

The above-mentioned studies indicate that between 2 and 3 years of age, children understand that social norms are context- and group-specific and thus already begin to grasp some of the essential features of norms. But how do young children identify that a particular action an adult performs is in fact normative (or intended to convey normative information)? Do children need explicit instructions ("Hey, look, now I am teaching you something about how members of this group eat their food.")? Or is it enough for them to observe a member of their group performing a certain act to make inferences about whether this action is a binding social norm (e.g., everyone eats food with chopsticks)? These questions are important since in everyday situations children do not always receive explicit teaching about "how we do things". In order to address this question Schmidt and colleagues assessed whether 3-year-old children understand some simple game actions as binding even though these acts are not explicitly introduced as a norm or a game (i.e., the model did not use any normative language such as "This is the correct way to do it."; Schmidt et al. 2011). Children incidentally watched as an adult confidently performed actions that looked like a game (e.g., using a piece of plastic to push a block across a board until the block falls into a gutter at the end of the board). That is, the model appeared to know how to play the game. Interestingly, children not only imitated the adult's action but later even protested against a puppet who performed a different action with the objects—that is, children inferred that this action must be something everyone should do. Children did not make this inference, however, when the adult demonstrated the action as if she had just invented it spontaneously. Hence it seems that young children are eager to learn norms and do so rapidly, even in the face of sparse evidence. These findings suggest that contrary to a recent theoretical account called "natural pedagogy" (Csibra and Gergely 2009, 2011), it does not seem to be the case that young children mainly use so-called "ostensive cues" (e.g., eye contact, calling the child by her name) to learn that a demonstrated action is normative. Rather, young children seem to pay close attention to the adult demonstrator's intentions and knowledge and the specific context in which acts are presented.

Although children adopt many norms of their social or cultural group, these norms are not always set in stone and may change over time (e.g., smoking used to be allowed in airplanes but is now strictly prohibited). That is, norms can be negotiated, created, and altered. While adults are certainly aware of this and create new norms, it is unclear whether children are already able to create their own norms. The developmental psychologist Jean Piaget analysed children's games of marbles in great detail because he believed that this may be one context in which children actively teach and create their own norms (Piaget 1932). Inspired by this work, Göckeritz and colleagues examined in a recent study whether 5-year-old children would spontaneously create their own norms without any adult guidance (Göckeritz et al. 2014). Groups of three children faced an instrumental task (a marble run) in which they had to coordinate in order to get some reward. Children introduced norms for how to work together successfully and later transmitted these norms to peers who were totally ignorant of the task. They did so using generic normative language (e.g., "One must do it like this!"), suggesting that they understood these norms as binding for others, too.

Besides obligations to do certain things, we also have rights or entitlements to perform certain actions. Any entitlement is closely linked to what others are obliged to do (Rainbolt 2006): When someone is entitled to do something, then others may not just tell the person not to perform the act she is entitled to. In recent work, 3-year-olds' understanding of entitlements was investigated (Schmidt et al. 2013). Children witnessed, as disinterested observers, how an individual forbade another person to play with a toy (and even took it away), even though that person was entitled to play with the toy (because the owner of the toy gave the person permission to use it). Children stood up for the person's right and enforced her entitlement to play with the toy. This suggests that young children have some understanding about what it means to have an entitlement, in particular, in contexts that deal with physical property (We will elaborate on children's understanding of ownership rights and entitlements in more detail in Sect. 4.2).

In summary, the reviewed research suggests that young children are equipped with capacities to rapidly learn the social norms of their culture and to understand the context-relativity and group-specificity of many norms—and this at a very young age. Moreover, young children even enforce norms when others violate them. This reveals something about their motivation to uphold social norms (not just to follow them), perhaps based on identification with their group (Schmidt and Tomasello 2012).

4 Young Children's Understanding of Social Institutions: The Example of Ownership

In the previous section, we have presented evidence that young children come prepared with a general capacity to acquire the norms of their socio-cultural environment. In this section, we will turn our attention to how young children come to understand social institutions, using the example of ownership. Let us begin with a brief definition of ownership and sketch its main characteristics.

Broadly speaking, ownership regulates the control and use of objects. Some philosophers have even claimed that norms of ownership are essential to maintaining peace and harmony by preventing disputes over possessions (Hume

1739/2000). Many scholars have highlighted the relational nature of ownership or as Jeremy Bentham put it (Bentham 1894): "There is no image, no painting, no visible trait, which can express the relation that constitutes property." Importantly, ownership is not just a relation between one person and an object, but is a triadic relation between one person and (at least) another person with respect to objects (Christman 1994; Singer 2010). For instance, it is not sufficient that I claim or know that something is mine; it is also necessary that you recognize my claim and respect it.

Moreover, ownership gives owners a set of rights and duties over their property (Honoré 1961; Snare 1972). Such rights may include the right to exclusively use one's property (e.g., I can use my pencil whenever I like without having to ask anyone for permission), to transfer ownership (I can sell my pencil, gift it to someone etc.), and to exclude others from using it (e.g., to prevent you from using my pencil—unless you explicitly ask me for permission) (Snare 1972). Ownership is thus a social institution that imbues owners with different rights (and duties) that they would not possess otherwise (Kalish and Anderson 2011).

Ownership is not limited to tangible objects such as toys, cars, clothes, land, but may also extend to intangible objects such as ideas. Even though in many Western countries ownership is often understood as private ownership, our definition of ownership applies to other types of ownership such as collective or group ownership, too. But note, that most of the developmental research we discuss in this section focuses on personal or individual ownership.

Ownership is a complex social institution; yet it has been suggested that it is one of the first social institutions that children begin to grasp (Kalish and Anderson 2011). In fact, possession and ownership of objects play an important role early on in life: In Western culture most of young children's conflicts with peers occur over the possession of toys or other objects (Hay and Ross 1982; Shantz 1987; Dunn and Munn 1987; Ross 1996; Hay et al. 2011). In order for young children to develop an understanding of ownership, they need to develop the ability to recognize property relations (e.g. to distinguish their own things from others and to know who owns what) and to acquire the different social norms and rights regulating ownership relations in their socio-cultural group (e.g., the types of property different people are allowed to own, what one is allowed to do with one's property, etc.). We will now look at the development of young children's understanding of ownership, beginning with their ability to relate owners to their possessions and focusing in the main part of this section on their understanding of property rights and norms.

4.1 Identifying and Inferring Ownership

Before 1 year of age, and thus before they are able to speak, infants probably associate persons and objects on a visual basis. For instance, by seeing someone repeatedly with an object they may form expectations about how this person relates to the object in her possession (Blake and Harris 2011). When infants learn to speak during the second year of life, "mine" is often among the first and most frequent words infants utter—at least in Western cultures (Tomasello 1998; Hay 2006). Towards the end of their second year of life, infants are able to identify objects of owners that they are familiar with: for example, when being asked to get their mother's shoes or their own toothbrush they will usually return with the correct object (Fasig 2000; Rodgon and Rashman 1976). By two and a half years of age, children are also able to learn ownership relations between objects and unfamiliar people or people they have never met: for instance, when they are shown a photograph of John and told that a toy belongs to John, they will later fetch or point to the correct object when asked to find John's toy (Blake and Harris 2011; Gelman et al. 2012).

Yet, young children are not always directly told about ownership or know about ownership from repeated experiences with an object (e.g., their own objects or objects belonging to their family members). Often children have very little or only ambiguous information about ownership available to them. For instance, when children see someone playing with a toy, that toy could either belong to the child currently playing with it or to a friend, a sibling, the kindergarten and so forth. Children (and for that matter, adults, too) often have to make an informed guess about who owns an object. Studies with 3- and 4-year-olds (in some cases also 2-year-olds) in North America, the UK, China and Japan have found that children infer that the person who held a toy at the beginning of an interaction (e.g. in a story, cartoon or short video-clip) owns the toy; that is, they will infer ownership based on first possession (Friedman and Neary 2008; Kanngiesser et al. 2015a). From 6 years of age children will also apply this principle to ideas (Shaw et al. 2012). Moreover, young children seem to pay special attention to cues relating to an object's history such as who could have feasibly had an object first or acquired it first (Gelman et al. 2012; Friedman et al. 2013; Nancekivell and Friedman 2014). They also prioritize verbal information (e.g., being told that this is John's car) over visual information (e.g., seeing Peter with a car) (Blake et al. 2012).

Based on the evidence to date, it has been claimed that the first possession principle is one of the earliest (possibly even innate) principles that children use to make inferences about ownership (Friedman 2008; Friedman and Neary 2008). However, in a recent study, 5- to 10-year-old children from a non-industrialized small-scale agricultural group, the Kikuyu (Kenya), watched videotaped interactions of two women playing with an object. Kikuyu children did not apply the first possession principle until 9 to 10 years of age, suggesting that children's socio-cultural environments play an important role in shaping children's use of this principle (Kanngiesser et al. 2015b).

In summary, children as young as 2 years of age already have the ability to relate owners and their property and to make (basic) inferences about who owns what. But does this also mean that young children have an understanding of ownership rights and entitlements? We will turn to this question in the next section.

4.2 Ownership Norms and Rights

Observational studies of ownership conflicts in young Western children have found that parents are often inconsistent in enforcing ownership rights (Ross 1996; Ross et al. 1996, 1990): Parents support the owner of an object equally or even less often than the non-owner. They also frequently stress sharing rather than to support the owner in her right to decide what to do with her object. Since parental interventions influence the outcome of these disputes (e.g., Ross 2013), young children receive conflicting messages about what kind of rights they have over things they own.

Early interview studies seemed to support the idea that an understanding of ownership rights develops late. Hook (1993) asked children between 4 and 15 years of age to judge the badness of a character who does not want to return an object to the first owner after having "stolen", "borrowed", or "found" it or "received it as a gift". While younger children judged all scenarios as equally bad, from 8 years of age children distinguished between stealing and receiving a toy as a gift in their ratings.

However, recent empirical evidence shows that even young children understand something about ownership rights. Rossano and colleagues studied 2- and 3-year-olds' reactions to violations of ownership rights (Rossano et al. 2011). Specifically, they studied if children would intervene if a puppet violated the rights of the child and of a third-party by stealing and throwing away their personal property (e.g. a hat or a scarf). They found that two- and 3-year-olds protested when their own belongings were at stake, while only 3-year-olds sanctioned the puppet for violating the third-party's property rights. Using a similar procedure, a recent study found that 2- and 3-year-old children also protested and made spontaneous reference to ownership for objects that the children had created on the spot (i.e., pictures or play-dough shapes; Kanngiesser and Hood 2014). Young children thus already possess an understanding of ownership rights for their own objects (e.g. intervene when non-owners try to take or throw away their belongings) and generalize these rights to third parties by 3 years of age. This normative understanding of property rights emerges at an age where children begin to develop a general sense of the normative nature of social rules (see Sect. 3).

Young children do not only actively enforce ownership rights, they also apply them when presented with stories about ownership conflicts. For example, a recent study found that from 3 years of age children give priority to owners rather than current users in conflicts about who should get to use an object (Neary and Friedman 2014). In addition, 4- to 8-year-old children believe that borrowers and finders do not acquire the rights to use the property against the wishes of the original owners (Kim and Kalish 2009).

While the previous studies investigated owners' rights, researchers have also studied whether young children understand that ownership rights can be transferred from one person to another. Blake and Harris (2009) presented 2- to 5-year-old children with stories about a child giving away a gift at a birthday party or about a child stealing a toy in the park. From 2 years of age children correctly assumed that stealing does not transfer ownership. In contrast, only 4- to 5-year-olds replied that gift giving transfers ownership to the recipient. Similarly, Kim and Kalish (2009) found that 4-year-olds believed that ownership rights transferred via gift giving; yet, they did not fully understand that ownership rights could be also transferred by selling an object.

Besides these very salient and highly ritualized ways of transferring ownership, Kanngiesser and colleagues investigated in a series of experiments with 3- and 4-year-olds from the UK and from Japan whether they would transfer ownership on the basis that someone had invested labour into creating a new object (Kanngiesser et al. 2010, 2014). British and Japanese children rarely transferred ownership after they (or the experimenter) had only played with the other person's play-dough, that is, they thought that the owner of the materials retained ownership. However, many children transferred ownership to creators that had invested effort into creating something new. Young children thus do not only understand ownership transfers that occur in ritualized ways like gift giving or selling. They also believe that ownership can be transferred after someone has invested labour into creating something new.

Finally, owners do not only have the right to exclude others from using their property or to transfer ownership rights to others, they may also relinquish or give up their ownership rights. Rossano and Tomasello (2014) asked whether children would accept that ownership of an object could actually be given up. 3- and 5-year-old children generally resisted "finders-keepers" claims (i.e., someone claiming ownership of an abandon object) and believed that the original owner retained ownership of an object. However, they could be convinced that someone relinquished ownership of an object when she publicly declared her intention to do so and deposited it in a culturally marked location for this purpose: a trashcan. This is in line with above-mentioned findings that young children uphold ownership of the original owners and resist assigning ownership to finders, unless very explicit communication has occurred.

Taken together, research on young children's understanding of different ownership rights has revealed that young children already grasp some ownership rights and distinguish between ownership transfers that are temporary (e.g., borrowing, playing with some- one's objects) and transfers that are permanent (e.g., gift giving, creating something new). Of course what counts as ownership rights and transfers, who may be entitled to ownership (individuals, groups, etc.), and what entities can and cannot be owned may vary between socio-cultural groups. But as we have argued in the previous section (Sect. 3) children come prepared with the ability to acquire the specific ownership norms (just as all other norms) of their group.

5 Conclusion

We have presented evidence that children from a young age have the capacity to learn, apply and even create their own social norms. The ease with which we navigate our social worlds as adults is thus rooted in our early childhood experiences. As adults we may often be unaware of the norms that shape our own behaviour and influence how we expect others to behave—unless we are confronted with violations of these norms. We usually note when people do not know the rules of how "we" behave. Similarly, young children will already take note and actively correct others if they fail to comply with norms (e.g., play a game the wrong way or take things from other people).

As a species we are predisposed to create normative worlds and socialize children into them. However, children's socialization does not just occur in their family's home. Indeed, it has been found that young children will receive conflicting information about social norms (e.g., parents may tell their child to share and not enforce their child's ownership rights, see Sect. 4.2). As soon as children are exposed to a wider world of other people and particularly to their peers (e.g., when entering kindergarten or preschool), their normative horizon will broaden. Jean Piaget has proposed that interactions with peers are important for developing a fully autonomous understanding of morality and moral behaviour that goes beyond mere obedience to adult authority (Piaget 1932). We suggest that this may apply to most of children's normative understanding and behaviour. In fact, we have presented evidence indicating that young children already create their own norms with peers (see Sect. 3) and that frequent ownership conflicts with siblings and peers may be important for developing a sense of ownership (see Sect. 4.2).

The research reported in this chapter shows that already between 2 and 3 years of age children show an understanding of social norms and ownership rights. This is of particular importance because it suggests that at that young age children are aware (and potentially retain memories) of events that led to violations of their own property rights, of the rights of their family and friends and of the norms that they have learned to adhere to.

To conclude, as every child learns to speak, every child learns the rules of her socio-cultural group. This is not to say that normative behaviour is set in stone and immune to change (in fact, following some norms may turn out to do more damage than good). And certainly as adults there are mechanisms available to us that allow us to attempt to change and challenge the norms of our environment and to set new normative standards for following generations.

Five Questions

1. How do children learn social norms (and which ones) if normative standards (e.g., everyone should wait at a red traffic light) and people's actual behaviour (e.g., people rarely wait at red traffic lights) do not line up?
2. How do children deal with conflicting information about social norms (e.g., Mum says one should wear sandals to school but the head-teacher says it is not allowed)?

3. How easily do young children overwrite social norms they have already learnt and adopt new norms (e.g., the colour of their school uniform has changed and it is no longer correct to wear a red sweater to school)?
4. Why do children sometimes fail to respect others' rights and entitlements (e.g., respect other's ownership rights)?
5. Are there differences across socio-cultural groups in how willing children are to actively sanction violations of social norms (or how they sanction norm violations)?

References

Bentham, J. (1894). *Theory of legislation*. London: Trübner.

Bicchieri, C., & Muldoon, R. (2014). Social norms. In E.N. Zalta (Ed.), *The Stanford Encyclopedia of Philosophy* (Spring 2014 Edition), http://plato.stanford.edu/archives/spr2014/entries/social-norms/.

Blake, P. R., Ganea, P. A., & Harris, P. L. (2012). Possession is not always the law: With age, preschoolers increasingly use verbal information to identify who owns what. *Journal of Experimental Child Psychology, 113*, 259–272.

Blake, P., & Harris, P. (2009). Children's understanding of ownership transfers. *Cognitive Development, 24*(2), 133–145.

Blake, P., & Harris, P. (2011). Early representations of ownership. *New Directions for Child and Adolescent Development, 2011*(132), 39–51.

Christman, J. (1994). *The myth of property: Toward an egalitarian theory of ownership*. New York: Oxford University Press.

Csibra, G., & Gergely, G. (2009). Natural pedagogy. *Trends in Cognitive Sciences, 13*, 148–153.

Csibra, G., & Gergely, G. (2011). Natural pedagogy as evolutionary adaptation. *Philosophical Transactions of the Royal Society B: Biological Sciences, 366*, 1149–1157.

Dunn, J., & Munn, P. (1987). Development of justification in disputes with mother and sibling. *Developmental Psychology, 23*, 791–798.

Fasig, L. G. (2000). Toddlers' understanding of ownership: Implications for self-concept development. *Social Development, 9*, 370–382.

Friedman, O. (2008). First possession: An assumption guiding inferences about who owns what. *Psychonomic Bulletin & Review, 15*, 290–295.

Friedman, O., & Neary, K. R. (2008). Determining who owns what: Do children infer ownership from first possession? *Cognition, 107*, 829–849.

Friedman, O., van de Vondervoort, J. W., Defeyter, M., & Neary, K. R. (2013). First possession, history, and young children's ownership judgments. *Child Development, 84*, 1519–1525.

Gelman, S. A., Manczak, E. M., & Noles, N. S. (2012). The nonobvious basis of ownership: Preschool children trace the history and value of owned objects. *Child Development, 83*, 1732–1747.

Gilbert, M. (1992). *On social facts*. Princeton: Princeton University Press.

Göckeritz, S., Schmidt, M. F. H., & Tomasello, M. (2014). Young children's creation and transmission of social norms. *Cognitive Development, 30*, 81–95.

Gräfenhain, M., Behne, T., Carpenter, M., & Tomasello, M. (2009). Young children's understanding of joint commitments. *Developmental Psychology, 45*, 1430–1443.

Gräfenhain, M., Carpenter, M., & Tomasello, M. (2013). Three-year-olds' understanding of the consequences of joint commitments. *PLoS One, 8*(9), e73039.

Haidt, J. (2012). *The righteous mind: Why good people are divided by politics and religion*. New York: Random House LLC.

Hamann, K., Warneken, F., & Tomasello, M. (2012). Children's developing commitments to joint goals. *Child Development, 83*, 137–145.

Hay, D. F. (2006). Yours and mine: Toddlers' talk about possessions with familiar peers. *British Journal of Developmental Psychology, 24*, 39–52.

Hay, D. F., Hurst, S., Waters, C., & Chadwick, A. (2011). Infants' use of force to defend toys: The origins of instrumental aggression. *Infancy, 16*, 471–489.

Hay, D. F., & Ross, H. S. (1982). The social nature of early conflict. *Child Development, 53*, 105–113.

Honoré, A. M. (1961). Ownership. In *Oxford essays in jurisprudence* (pp. 107–147). Oxford: Clarendon.

Hook, J. (1993). Judgments about the right to property from preschool to adulthood. *Law and Human Behaviour, 17*, 135–146.

Hume, D. (1739/2000). *A treatise of human nature*. Oxford: Oxford University Press.

Kalish, C. (1998). Reasons and causes: Children's understanding of conformity to social rules and physical laws. *Child Development, 69*, 706–720.

Kalish, C., & Anderson, C. (2011). Ownership as a social status. *New Directions for Child and Adolescent Development, 2011*(132), 65–77.

Kanngiesser, P., Gjersoe, N., & Hood, B. M. (2010). The effect of creative labor on property-ownership transfer by preschool children and adults. *Psychological Science, 21*, 1236–1241.

Kanngiesser, P., & Hood, B. M. (2014). Young children's understanding of ownership rights for newly made objects. *Cognitive Development, 29*, 30–40.

Kanngiesser, P., Hood, B. M., & Itakura, S. (2014). The effect of labour on ownership decisions in two cultures: Developmental evidence from Japan and the UK. *British Journal of Developmental Psychology, 32*, 320–329.

Kanngiesser, P., Itakura, S., Zhou, Y., Kanda, T., Ishiguro, H., & Hood, B. (2015a). The role of social eye-gaze in children's and adults' ownership attributions to robotic agents in three cultures. *Interaction Studies, 16*(1), 1–28.

Kanngiesser, P., Rossano, F., & Tomasello, M. (2015b). Late emergence of the first possession ownership heuristic: Evidence from a small-scale culture. *Child Development, 86*, 1282–1289.

Killen, M., & Smetana, J. (2013). *Handbook of moral development* (2nd ed.). New York: Psychology Press.

Kim, S., & Kalish, C. W. (2009). Children's ascription of property rights with changes of ownership. *Cognitive Development, 24*, 322–336.

Lewis, D. (1969). *Convention: A philosophical study*. Cambridge, MA: Harvard University Press.

Nancekivell, S. E., & Friedman, O. (2014). Preschoolers selectively infer history when explaining outcomes: Evidence from explanations of ownership, liking, and use. *Child Development, 85*, 1236–1247.

Neary, K. R., & Friedman, O. (2014). Young children give priority to ownership when judging who should use an object. *Child Development, 85*, 326–337.

Piaget, J. (1932). *The moral development of the child*. London: Kegan Paul.

Rainbolt, G. W. (2006). *The concept of rights*. Dordrecht, The Netherlands: Springer.

Rakoczy, H. (2008). Taking fiction seriously: Young children understand the normative structure of joint pretence games. *Developmental Psychology, 44*, 1195–201.

Rakoczy, H., & Schmidt, M. F. H. (2013). The early ontogeny of social norms. *Child Development Perspectives, 7*, 17–21.

Rakoczy, H., Warneken, F., & Tomasello, M. (2008). The sources of normativity: young children's awareness of the normative structure of games. *Developmental Psychology, 44*, 875–881.

Rodgon, M., & Rashman, S. (1976). Expression of owner-owned relationships among holophrastic 14- to 32-month-old children. *Child Development, 47*, 1219–1222.

Ross, H. (1996). Negotiating principles of entitlement in sibling property disputes. *Developmental Psychology, 32*, 90–101.

Ross, H. S. (2013). Effects of ownership rights on conflicts between toddler peers. *Infancy, 18*, 256–275.

Ross, H., Martin, J., Perlman, M., Smith, M., Blackmore, E., & Hunter, J. (1996). Autonomy and authority in the resolution of sibling disputes. *New Directions for Child and Adolescent Development, 1996*(73), 71–90.
Ross, H., Tesla, C., Kenyon, B., & Lollis, S. (1990). Maternal intervention in toddler peer conflict: The socialization of principles of justice. *Developmental Psychology, 26*, 994–1003.
Rossano, F., Rakoczy, H., & Tomasello, M. (2011). Young children's understanding of violations of property rights. *Cognition, 121*, 219–227.
Rossano, F., & Tomasello, M. (2014). *Preschoolers' understanding of trash and the relinquishing of property*. Manuscript submitted for publication
Schmidt, M. F. H., Rakoczy, H., & Tomasello, M. (2011). Young children attribute normativity to novel actions without pedagogy or normative language. *Developmental Science, 14*, 530–53.
Schmidt, M. F. H., Rakoczy, H., & Tomasello, M. (2012). Young children enforce social norms selectively depending on the violator's group affiliation. *Cognition, 124*, 325–333.
Schmidt, M. F. H., Rakoczy, H., & Tomasello, M. (2013). Young children understand and defend the entitlements of others. *Journal of Experimental Child Psychology, 116*, 930–944.
Schmidt, M. F. H., & Tomasello, M. (2012). Young children enforce social norms. *Current Directions in Psychological Science, 21*, 232–236.
Searle, J. R. (1996). *The construction of social reality*. London: Penguin.
Shantz, C. U. (1987). Conflicts between children. *Child Development, 58*, 283–305.
Shaw, A., Li, V., & Olson, K. R. (2012). Children apply principles of physical ownership to ideas. *Cognitive Science, 36*, 1383–1403.
Shweder, R. A. (1991). *Thinking through cultures: Expeditions in cultural psychology*. Cambridge, MA: Harvard University Press.
Singer, J. W. (2010). *Property law: Rules, policies & practices* (5th ed.). New York: Aspen Publishers.
Smetana, J. G. (1981). Preschool children's conceptions of moral and social rules. *Child Development, 52*, 1333–1336.
Snare, F. (1972). The concept of property. *American Philosophical Quarterly, 9*, 200–206.
Tajfel, H., Billig, M. G., Bundy, R. P., & Flament, C. (1971). Social categorization and intergroup behaviour. *European Journal of Social Psychology, 1*, 149–178.
Tomasello, M. (1998). One child's early talk about possession. *Typological Studies in Language, 36*, 349–373.
Tomasello, M. (2009). *Why we cooperate*. Cambridge, MA: MIT Press.
Tomasello, M., & Carpenter, M. (2007). Shared intentionality. *Developmental Science, 10*, 121–125.
Tomasello, M., Melis, A. P., Tennie, C., Wyman, E., & Herrmann, E. (2012). Two key steps in the evolution of human cooperation. *Current Anthropology, 53*, 673–692.
Tomasello, M., & Vaish, A. (2013). Origins of human cooperation and morality. *Annual Review of Psychology, 64*, 231–255.
Turiel, E. (1983). *The development of social knowledge. Morality and convention*. Cambridge: Cambridge University Press.
Walton, K. L. (1990). *Mimesis as make-believe: On the foundations of the representational arts*. Cambridge, MA: Harvard University Press.
Wyman, E., & Rakoczy, H. (2011). Social conventions, institutions, and human uniqueness: Lessons from children and chimpanzees. In: *Interdisciplinary anthropology* (pp. 131–156). Berlin Heidelberg: Springer.
Wyman, E., Rakoczy, H., & Tomasello, M. (2009). Normativity and context in young children's pretend play. *Cognitive Development, 24*, 146–155.

Family Influences on Offending and Family-Based Intervention

David P. Farrington

Abstract This chapter reviews knowledge about the most important family influences on offending and about the most effective family-based intervention programmes to reduce offending. Prospective longitudinal studies yield the most convincing information about family influences on offending, while randomized experiments yield the most convincing information about the effectiveness of interventions.

A great deal is known about risk factors for offending, but less is known about protective factors. The most important family risk factors include poor child-rearing (poor supervision, harsh or erratic discipline, parental coldness, low parental involvement), teenage parents, child physical abuse or neglect, parental conflict, disrupted families (caused by parental disharmony), criminal parents and large family size.

In risk-focussed prevention, intervention techniques target key risk factors such as poor child-rearing. Home visiting programmes including general parent education, and parent management training that teaches parents child-rearing skills, are both effective in reducing later offending. Named programmes such as The Incredible Years, Triple-P, Functional Family Therapy, Treatment Foster Care and Multi-systemic Therapy, are effective. The financial benefits of these programmes exceed their financial costs. A national prevention agency is needed in all countries to fund and coordinate the delivery of effective prevention programmes.

1 Introduction

This chapter first reviews knowledge obtained in the best research on family influences on offending, and then reviews knowledge obtained in the best research on the effectiveness of family-based interventions.

D.P. Farrington (✉)
Cambridge University, Cambridge, UK
e-mail: dpf1@cam.ac.uk

H. Kury et al. (eds.), *Women and Children as Victims and Offenders: Background, Prevention, Reintegration*, DOI 10.1007/978-3-319-08398-8_8

The best method of establishing that a family factor predicts later offending is to carry out a prospective longitudinal survey, and the emphasis in this chapter is on results obtained in such surveys. The best surveys possess as many as possible of the following features:

(a) a large sample size of at least several hundreds;
(b) repeated personal interviews;
(c) a large number of different types of variables measured from different data sources (which makes it possible to study the effect of one variable independently of others, or interaction effects);
(d) a longitudinal design spanning at least 5 years (which makes it possible to establish causal order, to study the strength of effects at different ages, and to control extraneous variables better by investigating changes within individuals; see Farrington 1988);
(e) a prospectively chosen, community sample (as opposed to retrospective comparisons between prisoners and controls, for example); and
(f) self-reported and official measures of offending (since results replicated with both methods probably provide information about offending rather than about any measurement biases).

I will refer especially to knowledge gained in the Cambridge Study in Delinquent Development, which is a prospective longitudinal survey of over 400 London males from age 8 to age 56 (Farrington et al. 2006, 2009, 2013). Fortunately, results obtained in British longitudinal surveys of delinquency are highly concordant with those obtained in comparable surveys in North America, the Scandinavian countries and New Zealand, and indeed with results obtained in British cross-sectional surveys. For example, a systematic comparison of the Cambridge Study and the Pittsburgh Youth Study showed numerous replicable predictors of offending over time and place, including impulsivity, attention problems, low school attainment, poor parental supervision, parental conflict, an antisocial parent, a young mother, large family size, low family income, and coming from a broken family (Farrington and Loeber 1999).

The best evidence about the effectiveness of family-based intervention programmes has been obtained in randomized experiments, especially those that have included a cost-benefit analysis. A randomized experiment ensures that those who are treated are equivalent before the intervention to those who are not treated, on all possible measured and unmeasured variables. Therefore, it is possible to disentangle the effects of the treatment from pre-existing differences and the influence of all other variables.

2 Family Influences on Offending

Many features of family life predict children's offending. Smith and Stern (1997, pp. 383–384) concluded in their review that:

> We know that children who grow up in homes characterized by lack of warmth and support, whose parents lack behavior management skills, and whose lives are characterized by conflict or maltreatment will more likely be delinquent, whereas a supportive family can protect children even in a very hostile and damaging external environment... Parental monitoring or supervision is the aspect of family management that is most consistently related to delinquency.

In agreement with this, Alan Leschied and his colleagues (2008) found that parental management that was coercive, inconsistent, or lacking in supervision during mid-childhood was a strong predictor of adult criminality, as were parental separation and marital status.

Lipsey and Derzon (1998) reviewed the predictors at age 6–11 of serious or violent offending at age 15–25. The best explanatory predictors (i.e., predictors not measuring some aspect of the child's antisocial behavior) were antisocial parents, male gender, low socio-economic status of the family, and psychological factors (daring, impulsiveness, poor concentration, etc.). Other moderately strong predictors were minority race, poor parent-child relations (poor supervision, discipline, low parental involvement, low parental warmth), other family characteristics (parent stress, family size, parental discord), antisocial peers, low intelligence, and low school achievement. In contrast, abusive parents and broken homes were relatively weak predictors. It is clear that some family factors are at least as important in the prediction of offending as are gender and race.

More recently, Derzon (2009) carried out a meta-analysis of family factors as predictors of criminal and violent behavior (as well as aggressive and problem behavior). The meta-analysis was based on longitudinal studies, but many predictions were over short time periods (less than 4 years in 55 % of cases), many outcome variables were measured at relatively young ages (up to 15 in 40 % of cases), and many studies were relatively small (less than 200 participants in 43 % of cases). The strongest predictors of criminal or violent behavior were parental education ($r = 0.30$ for criminal behavior), parental supervision ($r = 0.29$ for violent behavior), child rearing skills ($r = 0.26$ for criminal behavior), parental discord ($r = 0.26$ for criminal behavior), and family size ($r = 0.24$ for violent behavior). Notably weak predictors were young parents, broken homes, and socio-economic status.

Reviewing these kinds of results reveals the bewildering variety of family constructs that have been studied, and also the variety of methods used to classify them into categories. In this chapter, family factors are grouped into five categories: (a) child-rearing methods (poor supervision, poor discipline, parental coldness and rejection) (b) teenage mothers and child physical abuse or neglect; (c) parental conflict and disrupted families; (d) criminal and antisocial parents and siblings; and (e) large family size. These groupings are somewhat arbitrary and reflect the organization of topics of investigation within the field. For example, harsh discipline is usually studied along with poor supervision but, at the extreme, it could shade into physical abuse. Physical neglect is usually grouped with physical abuse but of course it usually coincides with emotional neglect (cold and rejecting parents). Socio-economic aspects of the family (e.g. family poverty) are not reviewed.

While factors encouraging offending and factors inhibiting offending are both discussed in theories, empirical research overwhelmingly focusses on factors encouraging offending, which are termed "risk factors". Factors that inhibit offending, often termed "protective factors", have rarely been studied, and there is not space to review knowledge about these factors here (see Farrington et al. 2012; Farrington and Ttofi 2011).

2.1 Child-Rearing

Many different types of child-rearing methods predict offending. The most important dimensions of child-rearing are supervision or monitoring of children, discipline or parental reinforcement, warmth or coldness of emotional relationships, and parental involvement with children. Parental supervision refers to the degree of monitoring by parents of the child's activities, and their degree of watchfulness or vigilance. Of all these child-rearing methods, poor parental supervision is usually the strongest and most replicable predictor of offending, as mentioned in the earlier quotation from Smith and Stern (1997).

Many studies show that parents who do not know where their children are when they are out, and parents who let their children roam the streets unsupervised from an early age, tend to have delinquent children. For example, in Joan McCord's (1979) classic Cambridge-Somerville study in Boston, poor parental supervision in childhood was the best predictor of both violent and property crimes up to age 45. In the Cambridge Study, 61 % of boys who were poorly supervised at age 8 were convicted up to age 50, compared with 36 % of the remainder (Farrington et al. 2009).

Parental discipline refers to how parents react to a child's behaviour. It is clear that harsh or punitive discipline (involving physical punishment) predicts offending (Haapasalo and Pokela 1999). In their follow-up study of nearly 700 Nottingham children, Newson and Newson (1989) found that physical punishment at ages 7 and 11 predicted later convictions; 40 % of offenders had been smacked or beaten at age 11, compared with 14 % of non-offenders. Erratic or inconsistent discipline also predicts delinquency. This can involve either erratic discipline by one parent, sometimes turning a blind eye to bad behaviour and sometimes punishing it severely, or inconsistency between two parents, with one parent being tolerant or indulgent and the other being harshly punitive.

Cold, rejecting parents tend to have delinquent children, as Joan McCord (1979) found in the Cambridge-Somerville study. She also concluded that parental warmth could act as a protective factor against the effects of physical punishment (McCord 1997). Whereas 51 % of boys with cold physically punishing mothers were convicted in her study, only 21 % of boys with warm physically punishing mothers were convicted, similar to the 23 % of boys with warm non-punitive mothers who were convicted. The father's warmth was also a protective factor against the father's physical punishment. Childhood neglect predicted self-reported and official offending in the Cambridge Study (Kazemian et al. 2011).

The classic longitudinal study by Lee Robins (1979) in St. Louis shows that poor parental supervision, harsh discipline and a rejecting attitude all predict delinquency. Also, in the Seattle Social Development Project, poor family management (poor supervision, inconsistent rules, and harsh discipline) in adolescence predicted violence in young adulthood (Herrenkohl et al. 2000). Similar results were obtained in the Cambridge Study. Harsh or erratic parental discipline, cruel, passive or neglecting parental attitudes, and poor parental supervision, all measured at age 8, all predicted later juvenile convictions and self-reported delinquency (West and Farrington 1973). Generally, the presence of any of these adverse family background features doubled the risk of a later juvenile conviction.

Laurence Steinberg and his colleagues (1992) distinguished an authoritarian style of parenting (punitively emphasizing obedience) from an authoritative style (granting autonomy with good supervision). In the Cambridge Study (Farrington 1994), having authoritarian parents was the second most important predictor of convictions for violence (after hyperactivity/poor concentration). Interestingly, having authoritarian parents was the most important childhood risk factor that discriminated between violent offenders and frequently convicted non-violent offenders (Farrington 1991).

Most explanations of the link between child-rearing methods and delinquency focus on attachment or social learning theories. Attachment theory was inspired by the work of John Bowlby (1951), and suggests that children who are not emotionally attached to warm, loving and law-abiding parents tend to become offenders. Social learning theories suggest that children's behaviour depends on parental rewards and punishments and on the models of behaviour that parents represent (Patterson 1995). Children will tend to become offenders if parents do not respond consistently and contingently to their antisocial behaviour and if parents themselves behave in an antisocial manner.

2.2 *Teenage Mothers and Child Abuse*

At least in Western industrialized countries, early child-bearing, or teenage pregnancy, predicts many undesirable outcomes for the children, including low school attainment, antisocial school behaviour, substance use and early sexual intercourse. The children of teenage mothers are also more likely to become offenders. For example, Morash and Rucker (1989) analysed results from four surveys in the US and UK (including the Cambridge Study) and found that teenage mothers were associated with low income families, welfare support and absent biological fathers, that they used poor child-rearing methods, and that their children were characterized by low school attainment and delinquency. However, the presence of the biological father mitigated many of these adverse factors and generally seemed to have a protective effect. In the Cambridge Study, teenage mothers who went on to have large numbers of children were especially likely to have convicted children (Nagin et al. 1997). In the Newcastle Thousand-Family study mothers who married as teenagers (a factor strongly related to teenage childbearing) were twice as likely as others to have sons who became offenders by age 32 (Kolvin et al. 1990).

Several researchers have investigated factors that might mediate the link between young mothers and child delinquency. In the Dunedin study in New Zealand, Sara Jaffee and her colleagues (2001) concluded that the link between teenage mothers and violent children was mediated by maternal characteristics (e.g. intelligence, criminality) and family factors (e.g. harsh discipline, family size, disrupted families). In the Rochester Youth Development Study, Greg Pogarsky and his colleagues (2003) found that the most important mediating factor was the number of parental transitions (frequent changes in care-givers). Much research suggests that frequent changes of parent figures predict offending by children (e.g. Krohn et al. 2009; Thornberry et al. 1999).

Children who are physically abused tend to become violent offenders, as Maxfield and Widom (1996) showed in a retrospective study of over 900 abused children in Indianapolis. In the Cambridge-Somerville study in Boston, McCord (1983) found that about half of the abused or neglected boys were convicted for serious crimes, became alcoholics or mentally ill, or died before age 35. Child maltreatment before age 12 was one of the most consistent predictors of violence and serious theft in the Pittsburgh Youth Study (Loeber et al. 2008). In the Rochester Youth Development Study, child maltreatment under age 12 (physical, sexual or emotional abuse or neglect) predicted later self-reported and official offending (Smith and Thornberry 1995). Furthermore, these results held up after controlling for gender, race, socio-economic status and family structure. Also, Margaret Keiley and her colleagues (2001) reported that maltreatment under age 5 was more damaging than maltreatment between ages 6 and 9. The extensive review by Malinosky-Rummell and Hansen (1993) confirms that being physically abused as a child predicts later violent and nonviolent offending.

Possible causal mechanisms linking childhood victimization and adolescent offending have been reviewed by Widom (1994). First, childhood victimization may have immediate but long-lasting consequences (e.g. shaking may cause brain injury). Second, childhood victimization may cause bodily changes (e.g. desensitization to pain) that encourage later aggression. Third, child abuse may lead to impulsive or dissociative coping styles that, in turn, lead to poor problem-solving skills or poor school performance. Fourth, victimization may cause changes in self-esteem or in social information-processing patterns that encourage later aggression. Fifth, child abuse may lead to changed family environments (e.g. being placed in foster care) that have harmful effects. Sixth, juvenile justice practices may label victims, isolate them from prosocial peers, and encourage them to associate with delinquent peers.

2.3 Parental Conflict and Disrupted Families

There is no doubt that parental conflict and interparental violence predict adolescent antisocial behaviour (Buehler et al. 1997; Ireland and Smith 2009). In the Christchurch Study in New Zealand, children who witnessed violence between their parents were more likely to commit both violent and property offences according to their self-reports (Fergusson and Horwood 1998). Witnessing father-initiated violence was still predictive after controlling for other risk factors such as parental criminality, parental substance abuse, parental physical punishment, a young mother and low family income. Parental conflict also predicted delinquency in both the Cambridge and Pittsburgh studies (Farrington and Loeber 1999).

Many studies show that broken homes or disrupted families predict delinquency. In the Newcastle Thousand-Family Study, Israel Kolvin and his colleagues (1988) reported that marital disruption (divorce or separation) in a boy's first 5 years predicted his later convictions up to age 32. Similarly, in the Dunedin study in New Zealand, Bill Henry and his colleagues (1993) found that children who were exposed to parental discord and many changes of the primary caretaker tended to become antisocial and delinquent. In the US National Longitudinal Survey of Adolescent Health, Demuth and Brown (2004) concluded that single-parent families predicted delinquency because of their lower levels of parental supervision, closeness and involvement with children.

The importance of the cause of the broken home was demonstrated by Wadsworth (1979) in the UK National Survey of Health and Development. Boys from homes broken by divorce or separation had an increased likelihood of being convicted or officially cautioned up to age 21, in comparison with those from homes broken by death or from unbroken homes. Homes broken while the boy was under age 5 especially predicted offending, while homes broken while the boy was between ages 11 and 15 were not particularly criminogenic. Remarriage (which happened more often after divorce or separation than after death) was also associated with an increased risk of offending, suggesting a possible negative effect of step-parents. The meta-analysis by Wells and Rankin (1991) also indicates that broken homes are more strongly related to delinquency when they are caused by parental separation or divorce rather than by death.

Most studies of broken homes have focussed on the loss of the father rather than the mother, simply because the loss of a father is much more common. McCord (1982) in Boston carried out an interesting study of the relationship between homes broken by loss of the natural father and later serious offending of the children. She found that the prevalence of offending was high for boys reared in broken homes without affectionate mothers (62 %) and for those reared in united homes characterized by parental conflict (52 %), irrespective of whether they had affectionate mothers. The prevalence of offending was low for those reared in united homes without conflict (26 %) and—importantly—equally low for boys from broken homes with affectionate mothers (22 %). These results suggest that it is not so much the broken home, which is criminogenic as the parental conflict which often causes it, and that a loving mother might in some sense be able to compensate for the loss of a father.

Few longitudinal studies of offending have begun before age 7 or 8. However, in the British Cohort Study of children born in 1970, Joseph Murray and his colleagues (2010) investigated the extent to which very early risk factors (measured up to age 5) predicted self-reported convictions at ages 30 and 34. Murray and his colleagues found that the strongest early predictors were a single mother, a teenage mother, maternal smoking during pregnancy, loss of a biological parent, and family deprivation (low social class, low parental education, poverty, and household overcrowding). The likelihood of a conviction increased with the early risk score, from 17 % to 44 % for boys and from 3 % to 11 % for girls.

In the Cambridge Study, both permanent and temporary separations from a biological parent before age 10 (usually from the father) predicted convictions and self-reported delinquency, providing that they were not caused by death or hospitalization (Farrington 1992b). However, homes broken at an early age (under age 5) were not unusually criminogenic (West and Farrington 1973). Separation before age 10 predicted both juvenile and adult convictions (Farrington 1992a), and it predicted adult convictions independently of other factors such as low family income or poor school attainment; 60 % of boys who had been separated from a parent by their tenth birthday were convicted up to age 50, compared with 36 % of the remainder (Farrington et al. 2009). It seems that broken homes caused hyperactivity, which in turn caused offending (Theobald et al. 2013).

Explanations of the relationship between disrupted families and delinquency fall into three major classes. Trauma theories suggest that the loss of a parent has a damaging effect on a child, most commonly because of the effect on attachment to the parent. Life course theories focus on separation as a sequence of stressful experiences, and on the effects of multiple stressors such as parental conflict, parental loss, reduced economic circumstances, changes in parent figures and poor child-rearing methods. Selection theories argue that disrupted families produce delinquent children because of pre-existing differences from other families in risk factors such as parental conflict, criminal or antisocial parents, low family income or poor child-rearing methods.

Hypotheses derived from the three theories were tested in the Cambridge Study (Juby and Farrington 2001). While boys from broken homes (permanently disrupted families) were more delinquent than boys from intact homes, they were not more delinquent than boys from intact high conflict families. Overall, the most important factor was the post-disruption trajectory. Boys who remained with their mother after the separation had the same delinquency rate as boys from intact low conflict families. Boys who stayed with their father, with relatives or with others (e.g. foster parents) had high delinquency rates. These living arrangements were more unstable, and other research shows that frequent changes of parent figures predict offending. It was concluded that the results favoured life course theories rather than trauma or selection theories.

2.4 Criminal Parents

Lee Robins and her colleagues (1975) showed that criminal, antisocial and alcoholic parents tend to have delinquent sons. Robins followed up over 200 males in St. Louis and found that arrested parents tended to have arrested children, and that the juvenile records of the parents and children had similar rates and types of offences. Joan McCord (1977) also reported that convicted fathers tended to have convicted sons. She found that 29 % of fathers convicted for violence had sons convicted for violence, in comparison with 12 % of other fathers, but this may reflect the general tendency for convicted fathers to have convicted sons rather than any specific tendency for violent fathers to have violent sons.

In the Cambridge Study, the concentration of offending in a small number of families was remarkable (Farrington et al. 1996). Less than 6 % of the families were responsible for half of the criminal convictions of all members (fathers, mothers, sons, and daughters) of all 400 families. Having a convicted mother, father, brother or sister significantly predicted a boy's own convictions. As many as 63 % of boys with a convicted parent were themselves convicted up to age 40. Furthermore, convicted parents and delinquent siblings predicted self-reported as well as official offending (Farrington 1979). Same-sex relationships were stronger than opposite-sex relationships, and older siblings were stronger predictors than younger siblings. Therefore, there is intergenerational continuity in offending.

Similar results were obtained in the Pittsburgh Youth Study. Arrests of fathers, mothers, brothers, sisters, uncles, aunts, grandfathers and grandmothers all predicted the boy's own delinquency (Farrington et al. 2001). The most important relative was the father; arrests of the father predicted the boy's delinquency independently of all other arrested relatives. Only 8 % of families accounted for 43 % of arrested family members. Similarly, in the Dunedin study in New Zealand, the antisocial behaviour of grandparents, parents, and siblings predicted the antisocial behaviour of boys (Odgers et al. 2007). Similar results were obtained in a large-scale criminal record study of all families who had a child born in 2006 in a Dutch city (Junger et al. 2013).

While arrests and convictions of fathers predicted antisocial behaviour of boys, imprisonment of fathers before boys were aged 10 further increased the risk of later antisocial and delinquent outcomes in the Cambridge Study (Murray and Farrington 2005). Interestingly, the effect of parental imprisonment in Sweden (in Project Metropolitan) disappeared after controlling for parental criminality (Murray et al. 2007). This cross-national difference may have been the result of shorter prison sentences in Sweden, more family-friendly prison policies, a welfare-oriented juvenile justice system, an extended social welfare system, or more sympathetic public attitudes towards prisoners (see also Murray et al. 2014).

It is not entirely clear why criminal parents tend to have delinquent children. In the Cambridge Study, there was no evidence that criminal parents directly encouraged their children to commit crimes or taught them criminal techniques. On the contrary, criminal parents were highly critical of their children's offending; for example, 89 % of convicted men at age 32 disagreed with the statement that "I would not mind if my son/daughter committed a criminal offence". Also, it was extremely rare for a parent and a child to be convicted for an offence committed together. The main link in the chain between criminal parents and delinquent sons seemed to be poor parental supervision (West and Farrington 1977). In the Rochester Youth Development Study, Terence Thornberry and his colleagues (2009) concluded that the continuity from parental self-reported offending to child antisocial behaviour was primarily mediated by ineffective parenting and parental stress.

There are several possible explanations (which are not mutually exclusive) for why offending tends to be concentrated in certain families and transmitted from one generation to the next. First, there may be intergenerational continuities in exposure to multiple risk factors. For example, each successive generation may be entrapped in poverty, disrupted families, single and/or teenage parenting, and living in the most deprived neighbourhoods. Second, the effect of a criminal parent on a child's offending may be mediated by environmental mechanisms such as poor parental supervision. Third, this effect may be mediated by genetic mechanisms.

Fourth, criminal parents may tend to have delinquent children because of official (police and court) bias against criminal families, who also tend to be known to official agencies because of other social problems (Besemer et al. 2013). At all levels of self-reported delinquency in the Cambridge Study, boys with convicted fathers were more likely to be convicted themselves than were boys with unconvicted fathers (West and Farrington 1977). However, this was not the only explanation for the link between criminal fathers and delinquent sons, because boys with criminal fathers had higher self-reported delinquency scores and higher teacher and peer ratings of bad behaviour.

2.5 Large Family Size

Large family size (a large number of children in the family) is a relatively strong and highly replicable predictor of offending (Ellis 1988). It was similarly important in the Cambridge and Pittsburgh studies, even though families were on average smaller in Pittsburgh in the 1990s than in London in the 1960s (Farrington and Loeber 1999). In the Cambridge Study, if a boy had four or more siblings by his tenth birthday, this doubled his risk of being convicted as a juvenile, and large family size predicted self-reported offending as well as convictions (Farrington 1992b). It was the most important independent predictor of convictions up to age 32 in a logistic regression analysis (Farrington 1993).

In the National Survey of Health and Development, Wadsworth (1979) found that the percentage of boys who were convicted increased from 9 % for families containing one child to 24 % for families containing four or more children. John Newson and his colleagues (1993), in their Nottingham study, also concluded that large family size was one of the most important predictors of offending. A similar link between large family size and antisocial behaviour was reported by Israel

Kolvin and his colleagues (1990) in their follow-up of Newcastle children from birth to age 33.

There are many possible reasons why a large number of siblings might increase the risk of a child's offending. Generally, as the number of children in a family increases, the amount of parental attention that can be given to each child decreases. Also, as the number of children increases, the household tends to become more overcrowded, possibly leading to increases in frustration, irritation and conflict. In the Cambridge Study, large family size did not predict delinquency for boys living in the least crowded conditions (West and Farrington 1973). This suggests that household overcrowding might be an important intervening factor between large family size and delinquency.

Brownfield and Sorenson (1994) reviewed several possible explanations for the link between large families and delinquency, including those focussing on features of the parents (e.g. criminal parents, teenage parents), those focussing on parenting (e.g. poor supervision, disrupted families) and those focussing on economic deprivation or family stress. Another interesting theory suggested that the key factor was birth order: large families include more later-born children, who tend to be more delinquent. Based on an analysis of self-reported delinquency in a Seattle survey, they concluded that the most plausible intervening causal mechanism was exposure to delinquent siblings. In the Cambridge Study, co-offending by brothers was surprisingly common; about 20 % of boys who had brothers close to them in age were convicted for a crime committed with their brother (Reiss and Farrington 1991).

3 Family-Based Interventions

As mentioned, this chapter aims to summarize briefly some of the most effective programmes for preventing delinquency and antisocial behaviour whose effectiveness has been demonstrated in high quality evaluation research. The focus is especially on programmes evaluated in randomized experiments with reasonably large samples, since the effect of any intervention on delinquency can be demonstrated most convincingly in such experiments (Farrington and Welsh 2005, 2006). I also focus on randomized experiments with long-term follow-ups, which make it possible to determine if effects persist or wear off (Farrington and Welsh 2013), and on evaluations that include a cost-benefit analysis.

The most effective programmes target risk factors for offending. The basic idea of developmental or risk-focussed prevention is very simple: Identify the key risk factors for offending and implement prevention techniques designed to counteract them (Farrington 2000). There is often a related attempt to identify key protective factors against offending and to implement prevention techniques designed to enhance or strengthen them (Catalano et al. 2002). Longitudinal surveys are used to advance knowledge about risk and protective factors, and experimental and quasi-experimental methods are used to evaluate the impact of prevention and intervention programmes.

Risk-focussed prevention was imported into criminology from medicine and public health by pioneers such as Hawkins and Catalano (1992). This approach has been used successfully for many years to tackle illnesses such as cancer and heart disease. For example, the identified risk factors for heart disease include smoking, a fatty diet, and lack of exercise. These can be tackled by encouraging people to stop smoking, to have a more healthy low-fat diet, and to take more exercise.

Risk-focussed prevention links explanation and prevention, links fundamental and applied research, and links scholars, policy makers, and practitioners. The book *Saving Children From a Life of Crime: Early Risk Factors and Effective Interventions* (Farrington and Welsh 2007) contains a detailed exposition of this approach. Importantly, risk-focussed prevention is easy to understand and to communicate, and it is readily accepted by policy makers, practitioners, and the general public. Both risk factors and interventions are based on empirical research rather than on theories. This approach avoids difficult theoretical questions about which risk factors have causal effects.

3.1 Cost-Benefit Analysis

I will describe some of the most important and best-evaluated programmes, with special reference to programmes that have carried out a cost-benefit analysis. The conclusion from the Perry project (discussed later) that, for every $1 spent on the programme, $7 were saved in the long term (Schweinhart et al. 1993) proved particularly convincing to policy makers. The monetary costs of crime are enormous. For example, Brand and Price (2000) estimated that they totalled £60 billion in England and Wales in 1999. There are tangible costs to victims, such as replacing stolen goods and repairing damage, and intangible costs that are harder to quantify, such as pain, suffering and a reduced quality of life. There are costs to the government or taxpayer for police, courts, prisons, crime prevention activities, and so on. There are also costs to offenders—for example, those associated with being in prison or losing a job.

Cohen (1998) estimated that a high-risk youth in the USA cost society about $2 million at 1997 prices. Cohen and Piquero (2009) updated this analysis using new methods, and concluded that the value of saving a 14-year-old high-risk juvenile from a life of crime ranged from $2.6 to $5.3 million at 2007 prices. In the Cambridge Study in Delinquent Development, the total cost of offending by the 400 males from age 10 to age 50 was $50 million at 2010 prices, or £123,000 per male, when self-reported as well as official offending was considered (Raffan Gowar and Farrington 2013).

To the extent that crime prevention programmes are successful in reducing crime, they will have benefits. These benefits can be quantified in monetary terms according to the reduction in the monetary costs of crime. Other benefits may accrue from reducing the costs of associated social problems such as unemployment, divorce, educational failure, drug addiction, welfare dependency, and so on. The fact that offending is part of a larger syndrome of antisocial behaviour (West and Farrington 1977) is good news, because the benefits of a crime prevention programme can be many and varied. The monetary benefits of a programme can be compared with its monetary costs to determine the benefit: cost ratio. Surprisingly few cost-benefit analyses of crime prevention programmes have ever been carried out (Roman et al. 2010; Welsh et al. 2001).

3.2 The Influence of Gerald Patterson

Family programmes are usually targeted on risk factors such as poor parental supervision and inconsistent discipline. The behavioural parent management training developed by Patterson (1982) in Oregon is one of the most influential approaches. His careful observations of parent-child interaction showed that parents of antisocial children were deficient in their methods of child-rearing. These parents failed to tell their children how they were expected to behave, failed to monitor their behaviour to ensure that it was desirable, and failed to enforce rules promptly and unambiguously with appropriate rewards and penalties. The parents of antisocial children used more punishment (such as scolding, shouting or threatening), but failed to use it consistently or make it contingent on the child's behaviour.

Patterson's method involved linking antecedents, behaviours and consequences. He attempted to train parents in effective child rearing methods, namely noticing what a child is doing, monitoring the child's behaviour over long periods, clearly stating house rules, making rewards and punishments consistent and contingent on the child's behaviour, and negotiating disagreements so that conflicts and crises did not escalate.

His treatment was shown to be effective in reducing child stealing and antisocial behaviour over short periods in small-scale studies (Dishion et al. 1992; Patterson et al. 1992). However, the treatment worked best with children aged 3–10 and less well with adolescents. Also, there were problems of achieving cooperation from the families experiencing the worst problems. In particular, single mothers on welfare were experiencing so many different stresses that they found it difficult to use consistent and contingent child-rearing methods. (For a recent review of parent training programmes, see Piquero et al. 2009.)

I will now review the most important types of family-based programmes that have been evaluated. These are home visiting programmes (and especially the work of David Olds), parent training programmes (especially those used by Carolyn Webster-Stratton, Stephen Scott, Frances Gardner and Matthew Sanders), home or community programmes with older children (especially those implemented by James Alexander and Patricia Chamberlain) and Multi-Systemic Therapy or MST (used by Scott Henggeler and Alison Cunningham).

3.3 Home Visiting Programmes

In the most famous intensive home visiting programme, David Olds and his colleagues (1986) in Elmira (New York State) randomly allocated 400 mothers either to receive home visits from nurses during pregnancy, or to receive visits both during pregnancy and during the first 2 years of life, or to a control group who received no visits. Each visit lasted about one and a quarter hours, and the mothers were visited on average every 2 weeks. The home visitors gave advice about prenatal and postnatal care of the child, about infant development, and about the importance of proper nutrition and avoiding smoking and drinking during pregnancy. Hence, this was a general parent education programme.

The results of this experiment showed that the postnatal home visits caused a decrease in recorded child physical abuse and neglect during the first 2 years of life, especially by poor unmarried teenage mothers; 4 % of visited versus 19 % of non-visited mothers of this type were guilty of child abuse or neglect. This last result is important because children who are physically abused or neglected tend to become violent offenders later in life (Widom 1989). In a 15-year follow-up, the main focus was on lower class unmarried mothers. Among these mothers, those who received prenatal and postnatal home visits had fewer arrests than those who received prenatal visits or no visits (Olds et al. 1997). Also, children of these mothers who received prenatal and/or postnatal home visits had less than half as many arrests as children of mothers who received no visits (Olds et al. 1998). Most recently, John Eckenrode and his colleagues (2010) followed up this experiment to age 19, and found that 25 % of the treated children were arrested, compared with 37 % of the controls; the desirable effects were much greater for girls. Steve Aos and his colleagues at the Washington State Institute for Public Policy (WSIPP) calculated that $2.4 are saved for every $1 expended on this programme (Lee et al. 2012). (For reviews of home visiting programmes, see Bilukha et al. 2005; Olds et al. 2007.)

3.4 Parent Management Training

One of the most famous parent training programmes ("The Incredible Years") was developed by Webster-Stratton (1998, 2000) in Seattle. She evaluated its success by randomly allocating 426 children aged 4 (most with single mothers on welfare) either to an experimental group which received parent training or to a control group which did not. The experimental mothers met in groups every week for 8 or 9 weeks, watched videotapes demonstrating parenting skills, and then took part in focussed group discussions. The topics included how to play with your child, helping your child learn, using praise and encouragement to bring out the best in your child, effective setting of limits, handling misbehaviour, how to teach your child to solve problems, and how to give and get support. Observations in the home showed that the experimental children behaved better than the control children.

Webster-Stratton and Hammond (1997) also evaluated the effectiveness of parent training and child skills training with about 100 Seattle children (average age 5) referred to a clinic because of conduct problems. The children and their parents were randomly allocated to receive either (a) parent training, (b) child skills training, (c) both parent and child training, or (d) to a control group. The skills training aimed to foster prosocial behaviour and interpersonal skills using video modelling, while the parent training involved weekly meetings between parents and therapists for 22–24 weeks. Parent reports and home observations showed that children in all three experimental conditions had fewer behaviour problems than control children, in both an immediate and a 1-year follow-up. There was little difference between the three experimental conditions, although the combined parent and child training condition produced the most significant improvements in child behaviour at the 1-year follow-up. It is generally true that combined parent and child interventions are more effective than either one alone.

Stephen Scott and his colleagues (2001) evaluated the Webster-Stratton parent training programme in London and Chichester. About 140 mainly poor, disadvantaged children aged 3–8 who were referred for antisocial behaviour were randomly assigned to receive parent training or to be in a waiting-list control group. The parent training programme, based on videotapes, covered praise and rewards, setting limits, and handling misbehaviour. Follow-up parent interviews and observations showed that the antisocial behaviour of the experimental children decreased significantly compared to that of the controls. Furthermore, after the intervention, experimental parents gave their children more praise to encourage desirable behaviour, and used more effective commands to obtain compliance. This programme was also found to be effective in a later experiment with over 100 children in London (Scott et al. 2010).

Frances Gardner and her colleagues (2006) evaluated the success of the Webster-Stratton programme in Oxfordshire. Over 70 children, aged 2–9, referred for conduct problems, were randomly assigned to receive parent training or to be in a waiting-list control group. Follow-up parent reports and observations again showed that the antisocial behaviour of the experimental children decreased compared with the controls. In a later experiment (Gardner et al. 2010), over 150 problematic children aged 3–5 from disadvantaged neighbourhoods were randomly assigned to receive parent training or to be in a waiting-list control group. The results showed that the treated children improved in parent-rated conduct problems, and that this was mediated by changes in parenting skills.

Matthew Sanders and his colleagues (2000) in Brisbane, Australia, developed the Triple-P Parenting programme. This programme either can be delivered to the whole community in primary prevention using the mass media or can be used in secondary prevention with high-risk or clinic samples. Sanders evaluated the success of Triple-P with over 300 high-risk children aged 3 by randomly allocating them either to receive Triple-P or to be in a control group. The Triple-P programme involves teaching parents 17 child management strategies including talking with children, giving physical affection, praising, giving attention, setting a good example, setting rules, giving clear instructions, and using appropriate penalties for misbehaviour ("time-out", or sending the child to his or her room). The evaluation showed that the Triple-P programme was successful in reducing children's antisocial behaviour. The effectiveness of Triple-P was confirmed in a meta-analysis by Thomas and Zimmer-Gembeck (2007). According to WSIPP (Lee et al. 2012), $6.1 are saved for every $1 expended on Triple-P.

3.5 Other Parenting Interventions

Another parenting intervention, termed Functional Family Therapy, was developed by James Alexander in Utah (Alexander and Parsons 1973). This aimed to modify patterns of family interaction by modelling, prompting and reinforcement, to encourage clear communication between family members of requests and solutions, and to minimize conflict. Essentially, all family members were trained to negotiate effectively, to set clear rules about privileges and responsibilities, and to use techniques of reciprocal reinforcement with each other. The programme was evaluated by randomly allocating 86 delinquents to experimental or control conditions. The results showed that this technique halved the recidivism rate of minor delinquents in comparison with other approaches (client-centred or psychodynamic therapy). Its effectiveness with more serious offenders was confirmed in a replication study using matched groups (Barton et al. 1985; see also Sexton and Alexander 2000). According to WSIPP (Lee et al. 2012), $10.4 are saved for every $1 expended on FFT.

Chamberlain and Reid (1998) in Oregon evaluated treatment foster care (TFC), which was used as an alternative to custody for delinquents. Custodial sentences for delinquents were thought to have undesirable effects especially because of the bad influence of delinquent peers. In treatment foster care, families in the community were recruited and trained to provide a placement for delinquent youths. The TFC youths were closely supervised at home, in the community, and in the school, and their contacts with delinquent peers were minimized. The foster parents provided a structured daily living environment, with clear rules and limits, consistent discipline for rule violations and one-to-one monitoring. The youths were encouraged to develop academic skills and desirable work habits.

In the evaluation, 79 chronic male delinquents were randomly assigned to treatment foster care or to regular group homes where they lived with other delinquents. A 1-year follow-up showed that the TFC boys had fewer criminal referrals and lower self-reported delinquency. Hence, this programme seemed to be an effective treatment for delinquency. Similarly encouraging results were obtained in an evaluation of TFC for delinquent girls (Leve et al. 2005). The effectiveness of TFC has been confirmed in systematic reviews (Hahn et al. 2005; Macdonald and Turner 2007). According to WSIPP (Lee et al. 2012), $4.9 are saved for every $1 expended on TFC.

3.6 Multi-Systemic Therapy

Multi-Systemic Therapy (MST) is an important multiple-component family preservation programme that was developed by Scott Henggeler and his colleagues (1998) in South Carolina. The particular type of treatment is chosen according to the particular needs of the youth. Therefore, the nature of the treatment is different for each person. MST is delivered in the youth's home, school and community settings. The treatment typically includes family intervention to promote the parent's ability to monitor and discipline the adolescent, peer intervention to encourage the choice of prosocial friends, and school intervention to enhance competence and school achievement.

In an evaluation by Scott Henggeler and his colleagues (1993), 84 serious delinquents (with an average age of 15) were randomly assigned either to receive MST or the usual treatment (which mostly involved placing the juvenile outside home). The results showed that the MST group had fewer arrests and fewer self-reported crimes in a 1-year follow-up. In another evaluation in Missouri, Charles Borduin and his colleagues (1995) randomly assigned 176 juvenile offenders (with an average age of 14) either to MST or to individual therapy focussing on personal, family and academic issues. Four years later, only 26 % of the MST offenders had been rearrested, compared with 71 % of the individual therapy group. Later follow-ups to age 29 (Schaeffer and Borduin 2005) and age 37 (Sawyer and Borduin 2011) confirmed the cumulative benefits of MST. Other evaluations by Henggeler and his colleagues (1997, 1999, 2002) have also produced impressive results. According to WSIPP (Lee et al. 2012), $4.4 are saved for every $1 expended on MST.

Unfortunately, disappointing results were obtained in a large-scale independent evaluation of MST in Canada by Leschied and Cunningham (2002). Over 400 youths who were either offenders or at risk of offending were randomly assigned to receive either MST or the usual services (typically probation supervision). Six months after treatment, 28 % of the MST group had been reconvicted, compared with 31 % of the control group, a non-significant difference. Therefore, it is not totally clear how effective MST is when it is implemented independently, although has been successful in Norwegian and Dutch evaluations (Asscher et al. 2013; Ogden and Hagen 2006). Unfortunately, two meta-analyses of the effectiveness of MST reached contradictory conclusions. Nicola Curtis and her colleagues (2004) found that it was effective, but Littell (2005) found that it was not. Nevertheless, MST is a promising intervention technique, and it is being used quite widely in the UK (Jefford and Squire 2004).

3.7 Is Family-Based Intervention Effective?

Evaluations of the effectiveness of family-based intervention programmes have produced both encouraging and discouraging results. In order to assess effectiveness according to a large number of evaluations, Brandon Welsh and I reviewed 40 evaluations of family-based programmes each involving at least 50 persons in experimental and control groups combined (Farrington and Welsh 2003). All of these had outcome measures of delinquency or antisocial child behaviour. Of the 19 studies with outcome measures of delinquency, 10 found significantly beneficial effects of the intervention and 9 found no significant effect. Happily, no study found a significantly harmful effect of family-based treatment.

Over all 19 studies, the average effect size (d, the standardized mean difference) was 0.32. This was significantly greater than zero. When we converted it into the percentage reconvicted, a d value of 0.32 corresponds to a decrease in the percentage reconvicted from 58 % to 42 %. Therefore, we concluded that, taking all 19 studies together, they showed that family-based intervention had substantial desirable effects.

4 Conclusions

A great deal has been learned in the last 40 years, particularly from longitudinal surveys, about risk factors for offending and other types of antisocial behaviour (Farrington and Welsh 2007). Offenders differ significantly from non-offenders in many respects, including impulsiveness, empathy, low intelligence and low school achievement, poor parental supervision, child physical abuse, punitive or erratic parental discipline, cold parental attitude, parental conflict, disrupted families, antisocial parents, large family size, low family income, antisocial peers, high delinquency-rate schools, and high crime neighbourhoods. These differences are present before, during and after criminal careers. While the precise causal chains that link these factors with antisocial behaviour, and the ways in which these factors have independent, interactive or sequential effects, are not well understood, it is clear that individuals at risk can be identified with reasonable accuracy. More longitudinal studies are needed in different countries, with frequent measurement of risk factors and offending.

High quality evaluation research shows that many programmes are effective in reducing delinquency and antisocial behaviour, and that in many cases the financial benefits of these programmes outweigh their financial costs. The best programmes include general parent education, parent management training, pre-school intellectual enrichment programmes, child skills training, teacher training, anti-bullying programmes, mentoring and MST (Farrington and Welsh 2007). Whilst most is known about programmes for boys, there are also effective interventions designed specifically for girls (Hipwell and Loeber 2006). Importantly, early intervention programmes have long-lasting benefits (Dekovic et al. 2011; Farrington and Welsh 2013; Manning et al. 2010).

High quality experimental and quasi-experimental evaluations of the effectiveness of crime reduction programmes are needed in European countries. Most knowledge about the effectiveness of early prevention programmes based on

American research. Ideally, prevention programmes should aim not only to tackle risk factors but also to strengthen protective factors, and both risk and protective factors should be measured and targeted. An important development in recent years has been the increasing use of cost-benefit analysis in evaluating prevention programmes. Cost-benefit analyses of the effectiveness of prevention programmes should be given some priority, and a standard how-to-do-it manual should be developed.

In all countries, there should be an agency whose main mandate is the primary prevention of crime. A national prevention agency could provide technical assistance, skills and knowledge to local agencies in implementing prevention programmes, could provide funding for such programmes, and could ensure continuity, co-ordination and monitoring of local programmes. It could provide training in prevention science for people in local agencies, and could maintain high standards for evaluation research. It could also act as a centre for the discussion of how policy initiatives of different government agencies influence crime and associated social problems. It could set a national and local agenda for research and practice in the prevention of crime, drug and alcohol abuse, mental health problems and associated social problems.

National crime prevention agencies have been established in some countries, such as Sweden (Andersson 2005) and Canada (Sansfaçon and Waller 2001). These agencies have emphasized three main mechanisms: collaboration with other government departments, development of local problem-solving partnerships, and involvement of citizens (Waller and Welsh 1999). These points specify how evidence-based results can be translated into local practice. Each point specifies concrete actions that a national agency can influence at the local level, but programme success ultimately will depend on local persons. A national agency can influence these implementation issues in a number of ways; for example, by developing guidelines on effective practice and making project funding conditional on the use of evidence-based programmes.

A national agency could also maintain a computerized register of evaluation research and, like the UK National Institute of Health and Care Excellence, advise the government about effective and cost-effective crime prevention programmes. Medical advice is often based on systematic reviews of the effectiveness of health care interventions organized by the Cochrane Collaboration and funded by the National Health Service. Systematic reviews of the evaluation literature on the effectiveness of criminological interventions, possibly organized by the Campbell Collaboration (Farrington et al. 2011), should be commissioned and funded by government agencies.

Recently, there have been encouraging developments in the UK. In September 2006, Prime Minister Tony Blair announced an action plan for "social exclusion", which is a general concept including antisocial behaviour, teenage pregnancy, educational failure, and mental health problems (Cabinet Office 2006). This action plan emphasized early intervention, better coordination of agencies, and evidence-based practice (systematically identifying what works and rating evaluations according to methodological quality: see Farrington 2003). It proposed home visiting programmes targeting at-risk children from birth to age 2, implemented by midwives and health visitors, inspired by the work of David Olds (Olds et al. 1998). It proposed that teenage pregnancy "hot spots" would be targeted with enhanced social and relationship education and better access to contraceptives. It proposed multi-agency and family-based approaches to tackle behavioural and mental health problems in childhood, including treatment foster care (Chamberlain and Reid 1998) and multi-systemic therapy (Henggeler et al. 1998). It also proposed interventions for adults with chaotic lives, mental health problems and multiple needs, to try to get more of them into employment. This Action Plan has now been replaced by the Early Intervention Foundation, which was launched by Prime Minister David Cameron in April 2013.

In conclusion, a great deal has been learned about family influences on offending and effective family-based programmes, but mainly from American research. The time is ripe to establish national agencies in all countries that will advance knowledge about family risk factors (from longitudinal studies) and about effective family-based interventions (from randomized experiments and cost-benefit analyses).

Five Questions

1. What are the most important protective factors that predict a low rate of offending among children at risk?
2. What are the most important mediating factors between family influences and offending, and what theories explain these relationships most accurately?
3. What are the most effective family programmes, in reducing offending and in having financial benefits exceeding financial costs?
4. Why do criminal parents tend to have delinquent children, and what are the most effective methods of interrupting this inter-generational continuity?
5. What new longitudinal and experimental studies are needed to advance knowledge about family influences and family interventions?

References

Alexander, J. F., & Parsons, B. V. (1973). Short-term behavioral intervention with delinquent families: Impact on family process and recidivism. *Journal of Abnormal Psychology, 81*, 219–225.

Andersson, J. (2005). The Swedish National Council for Crime Prevention: A short presentation. *Journal of Scandinavian Studies in Criminology and Crime Prevention, 6*, 74–88.

Asscher, J. J., Dekovic, M., Manders, W. A., Van Der Laan, P. H., & Prins, P. J. M. (2013). A randomized controlled trial of the effectiveness of Multisystemic Therapy in the Netherlands: Post-treatment changes and moderator effects. *Journal of Experimental Criminology, 9*, 169–187.

Barton, C., Alexander, J. F., Waldron, H., Turner, C. W., & Warburton, J. (1985). Generalizing treatment effects of functional family therapy: Three replications. *American Journal of Family Therapy, 13*, 16–26.

Besemer, S., Farrington, D. P., & Bijleveld, C. C. J. H. (2013). Official bias in intergenerational transmission of criminal behaviour. *British Journal of Criminology, 53*, 438–455.
Bilukha, O., Hahn, R. A., Crosby, A., Fullilove, M. T., Liberman, A., Moscicki, E., Snyder, S., Tuma, F., Corso, P., Schofield, A., & Briss, P. A. (2005). The effectiveness of early childhood home visitation in preventing violence. *American Journal of Preventive Medicine, 28*(2S1), 11–39.
Borduin, C. M., Mann, B. J., Cone, L. T., Henggeler, S. W., Fucci, B. R., Blaske, D. M., et al. (1995). Multisystemic treatment of serious juvenile offenders: Long-term prevention of criminality and violence. *Journal of Consulting and Clinical Psychology, 63*, 569–587.
Bowlby, J. (1951). *Maternal care and mental health*. Geneva, Switzerland: World Health Organization.
Brand, S., & Price, R. (2000). *The economic and social costs of crime*. London: Home Office (Research Study No. 217).
Brownfield, D., & Sorenson, A. M. (1994). Sibship size and sibling delinquency. *Deviant Behavior, 15*, 45–61.
Buehler, C., Anthony, C., Krishnakumar, A., Stone, G., Gerard, J., & Pemberton, S. (1997). Interparental conflict and youth problem behaviors: A meta-analysis. *Journal of Child and Family Studies, 6*, 233–247.
Cabinet Office. (2006). *Reaching out: An action plan for social exclusion*. London: Author.
Catalano, R. F., Hawkins, J. D., Berglund, L., Pollard, J. A., & Arthur, M. W. (2002). Prevention science and positive youth development: Competitive or cooperative frameworks? *Journal of Adolescent Health, 31*, 230–239.
Chamberlain, P., & Reid, J. B. (1998). Comparison of two community alternatives to incarceration for chronic juvenile offenders. *Journal of Consulting and Clinical Psychology, 66*, 624–633.
Cohen, M. A. (1998). The monetary value of saving a high-risk youth. *Journal of Quantitative Criminology, 14*, 5–33.
Cohen, M. A., & Piquero, A. R. (2009). New evidence on the monetary value of saving a high risk youth. *Journal of Quantitative Criminology, 25*, 25–29.
Curtis, N. M., Ronan, K. R., & Borduin, C. M. (2004). Multisystemic treatment: A meta-analysis of outcome studies. *Journal of Family Psychology, 18*, 411–419.
Dekovic, M., Slagt, M. I., Asscher, J. J., Boendermaker, L., Eichelsteim, V. I., & Prinzie, P. (2011). Effects of early prevention programmes on adult criminal offending: A meta-analysis. *Clinical Psychology Review, 31*, 532–544.
Demuth, S., & Brown, S. L. (2004). Family structure, family processes, and adolescent delinquency: The significance of parental absence versus parental gender. *Journal of Research in Crime and Delinquency, 41*, 58–81.
Derzon, J. H. (2009). The correspondence of family features with problem, aggressive, criminal, and violent behaviour: A meta-analysis. *Journal of Experimental Criminology, 6*, 263–292.
Dishion, T. J., Patterson, G. R., & Kavanagh, K. A. (1992). An experimental test of the coercion model: Linking theory, measurement and intervention. In J. McCord & R. E. Tremblay (Eds.), *Preventing antisocial behavior: Interventions from birth through adolescence* (pp. 253–282). New York: Guilford.
Ellis, L. (1988). The victimful-victimless crime distinction, and seven universal demographic correlates of victimful criminal behaviour. *Personality and Individual Differences, 3*, 525–548.
Farrington, D. P. (1979). Environmental stress, delinquent behavior, and convictions. In I. G. Sarason & C. D. Spielberger (Eds.), *Stress and anxiety*, (vol. 6 pp. 93–107). Washington, DC: Hemisphere.
Farrington, D. P. (1988). Studying changes within individuals: The causes of offending. In M. Rutter (Ed.), *Studies of psychosocial risk: The power of longitudinal data* (pp. 158–183). Cambridge: Cambridge University Press.
Farrington, D. P. (1991). Childhood aggression and adult violence: Early precursors and later life outcomes. In D. J. Pepler & K. H. Rubin (Eds.), *The development and treatment of childhood aggression* (pp. 5–29). Hillsdale, NJ: Lawrence Erlbaum.

Farrington, D. P. (1992a). Explaining the beginning, progress and ending of antisocial behaviour from birth to adulthood. In J. McCord (Ed.), *Facts, frameworks and forecasts: Advances in criminological theory* (Vol. 3, pp. 253–286). New Brunswick, NJ: Transaction.
Farrington, D. P. (1992b). Juvenile delinquency. In J. C. Coleman (Ed.), *The school years* (2nd ed., pp. 123–163). London: Routledge.
Farrington, D. P. (1993). Childhood origins of teenage antisocial behaviour and adult social dysfunction. *Journal of the Royal Society of Medicine, 86*, 13–17.
Farrington, D. P. (1994). Childhood, adolescent and adult features of violent males. In L. R. Huesmann (Ed.), *Aggressive behavior: Current perspectives* (pp. 215–240). New York: Plenum.
Farrington, D. P. (2000). Explaining and preventing crime: The globalization of knowledge – The American Society of Criminology 1999 presidential address. *Criminology, 38*, 1–24.
Farrington, D. P. (2003). Methodological quality standards for evaluation research. *Annals of the American Academy of Political and Social Science, 587*, 49–68.
Farrington, D. P., Barnes, G., & Lambert, S. (1996). The concentration of offending in families. *Legal and Criminological Psychology, 1*, 47–63.
Farrington, D. P., Coid, J. W., Harnett, L., Jolliffe, D., Soteriou, N., Turner, R., & West, D. J. (2006) *Criminal careers up to age 50 and life success up to age 48: New findings from the Cambridge Study in delinquent development.* London: Home Office (Research Study No. 299).
Farrington, D. P., Coid, J. W., & West, D. J. (2009). The development of offending from age 8 to age 50: Recent results from the Cambridge Study in delinquent development. *Monatsschrift fur Kriminologie und Strafrechtsreform (Journal of Criminology and Penal Reform), 92*, 160–173.
Farrington, D. P., Jolliffe, D., Loeber, R., Stouthamer-Loeber, M., & Kalb, L. M. (2001). The concentration of offenders in families, and family criminality in the prediction of boys' delinquency. *Journal of Adolescence, 24*, 579–596.
Farrington, D. P., & Loeber, R. (1999). Transatlantic replicability of risk factors in the development of delinquency. In P. Cohen, C. Slomkowski & L. N. Robins (Eds.), *Historical and geographical influences on psychopathology* (pp. 299–329). Mahwah, NJ: Lawrence Erlbaum.
Farrington, D. P., Loeber, R., & Ttofi, M. M. (2012). Risk and protective factors for offending. In B. C. Welsh & D. P. Farrington (Eds.), *The Oxford handbook of crime prevention* (pp. 46–69). Oxford: Oxford University Press.
Farrington, D. P., Piquero, A. R., & Jennings, W. G. (2013). *Offending from childhood to late middle age: Recent results from the Cambridge Study in delinquent development.* New York: Springer.
Farrington, D. P., & Ttofi, M. M. (2011). Protective and promotive factors in the development of offending. In T. Bliesener, A. Beelman, & M. Stemmler (Eds.), *Antisocial behavior and crime: Contributions of developmental and evaluation research to prevention and intervention* (pp. 71–88). Cambridge, MA: Hogrefe.
Farrington, D. P., Weisburd, D. L., & Gill, C. E. (2011). The campbell collaboration crime and justice group: A decade of progress. In C. J. Smith, S. X. Zhang & R. Barberet (Eds.), *Routledge handbook of international criminology* (pp. 53–63). New York: Routledge.
Farrington, D. P., & Welsh, B. C. (2003). Family-based prevention of offending: A meta-analysis. *Australian and New Zealand Journal of Criminology, 36*, 127–151.
Farrington, D. P., & Welsh, B. C. (2005). Randomized experiments in criminology: What have we learned in the last two decades? *Journal of Experimental Criminology, 1*, 9–38.
Farrington, D. P., & Welsh, B. C. (2006). A half-century of randomized experiments on crime and justice. In M. Tonry (Ed.), *Crime and Justice* (Vol. 34, pp. 55–132). Chicago: University of Chicago Press.
Farrington, D. P., & Welsh, B. C. (2007). *Saving children from a life of crime: Early risk factors and effective interventions.* Oxford: Oxford University Press.
Farrington, D. P., & Welsh, B. C. (2013). Randomized experiments in criminology: What has been learned from long-term follow-ups? In B. C. Welsh, A. A. Braga, & G. J. N. Bruinsma (Eds.),

Experimental criminology: Prospects for advancing science and public policy (pp. 111–140). New York: Cambridge University Press.
Fergusson, D. M., & Horwood, L. J. (1998). Exposure to interparental violence in childhood and psychosocial adjustment in young adulthood. *Child Abuse and Neglect, 22*, 339–357.
Gardner, F., Burton, J., & Klimes, I. (2006). Randomized controlled trial of a parenting intervention in the voluntary sector for reducing child conduct problems: Outcomes and mechanisms of change. *Journal of Child Psychology and Psychiatry, 47*, 1123–1132.
Gardner, F., Hutchings, J., Bywater, T., & Whitaker, C. (2010). Who benefits and how does it work? Moderators and mediators of outcome in an effectiveness trial of a parenting intervention. *Journal of Clinical Child and Adolescent Psychology, 39*, 568–580.
Haapasalo, J., & Pokela, E. (1999). Child-rearing and child abuse antecedents of criminality. *Aggression and Violent Behavior, 1*, 107–127.
Hahn, R. A., Bilukha, O., Lowy, J., Crosby, A., Fullilove, M. T., Liberman, A., Moscicki, E., Synder, S., Tuma, F., Corso, P., & Schofield, A. (2005). The effectiveness of therapeutic foster care for the prevention of violence. *American Journal of Preventive Medicine, 28*(2S1), 72–90.
Hawkins, J. D., & Catalano, R. F. (1992). *Communities that care*. San Francisco: Jossey-Bass.
Henggeler, S. W., Clingempeel, W. G., Brondino, M. J., & Pickrel, S. G. (2002). Four-year follow-up of Multisystemic Therapy with substance-abusing and substance-dependent juvenile offenders. *Journal of the American Academy of Child and Adolescent Psychiatry, 41*, 868–874.
Henggeler, S. W., Melton, G. B., Brondino, M. J., Scherer, D. G., & Hanley, J. H. (1997). Multisystemic Therapy with violent and chronic juvenile offenders and their families: The role of treatment fidelity in successful dissemination. *Journal of Consulting and Clinical Psychology, 65*, 821–833.
Henggeler, S. W., Melton, G. B., Smith, L. A., Schoenwald, S. K., & Hanley, J. H. (1993). Family preservation using multisystematic treatment: Long-term follow-up to a clinical trial with serious juvenile offenders. *Journal of Child and Family Studies, 2*, 283–293.
Henggeler, S. W., Rowland, M. D., Randall, J., Ward, D. M., Pickrel, S. G., Cunningham, P. B., et al. (1999). Home-based Multisystemic Therapy as an alternative to the hospitalization of youths in psychiatric crisis: Clinical outcomes. *Journal of the American Academy of Child and Adolescent Psychiatry, 38*, 1331–1339.
Henggeler, S. W., Schoenwald, S. K., Borduin, C. M., Rowland, M. D., & Cunningham, P. B. (1998). *Multisystemic treatment of antisocial behavior in children and adolescents*. New York: Guilford.
Henry, B., Moffitt, T., Robins, L., Earls, F., & Silva, P. (1993). Early family predictors of child and adolescent antisocial behaviour: Who are the mothers of delinquents? *Criminal Behaviour and Mental Health, 2*, 97–118.
Herrenkohl, T. I., Maguin, E., Hill, K. G., Hawkins, J. D., Abbott, R. D., & Catalano, R. F. (2000). Developmental risk factors for youth violence. *Journal of Adolescent Health, 26*, 176–186.
Hipwell, A. E., & Loeber, R. (2006). Do we know which interventions are effective for disruptive and delinquent girls? *Clinical Child and Family Psychology Review, 9*, 221–255.
Ireland, T. O., & Smith, C. A. (2009). Living in partner-violent families: Developmental links to antisocial behavior and relationship violence. *Journal of Youth and Adolescence, 38*, 323–339.
Jaffee, S., Caspi, A., Moffitt, T. E., Belsky, J., & Silva, P. A. (2001). Why are children born to teen mothers at risk for adverse outcomes in young adulthood? Results from a 20-year longitudinal study. *Development and Psychopathology, 13*, 377–397.
Jefford, T., & Squire, B. (2004). Multi-systemic therapy: Model practice. *Young Minds, 71*, 20–21.
Juby, H., & Farrington, D. P. (2001). Disentangling the link between disrupted families and delinquency. *British Journal of Criminology, 41*, 22–40.
Junger, M., Greene, J., Schipper, R., Hesper, F., & Estourgie, V. (2013). Parental criminality, family violence and intergenerational transmission of crime within a birth cohort. *European Journal on Criminal Policy and Research, 19*, 117–133.

Kazemian, L., Widom, C. S., & Farrignton, D. P. (2011). A prospective examination of the relationship between childhood neglect and juvenile delinquency in the Cambridge Study in delinquent development. *International Journal of Child, Youth and Family Studies, 2*, 65–82.
Keiley, M. K., Howe, T. R., Dodge, K. A., Bates, J. E., & Pettit, G. S. (2001). The timing of child physical maltreatment: A cross-domain growth analysis of impact on adolescent externalizing and internalizing problems. *Development and Psychopathology, 13*, 891–912.
Kolvin, I., Miller, F. J. W., Fleeting, M., & Kolvin, P. A. (1988). Social and parenting factors affecting criminal-offence rates: Findings from the newcastle thousand family study (1947–1980). *British Journal of Psychiatry, 152*, 80–90.
Kolvin, I., Miller, F. J. W., Scott, D. M., Gatzanis, S. R. M., & Fleeting, M. (1990). *Continuities of deprivation? The newcastle 1000 family study*. Aldershot: Avebury.
Krohn, M. D., Hall, G. P., & Lizotte, A. J. (2009). Family transitions and later delinquency and drug use. *Journal of Youth and Adolescence, 38*, 466–480.
Lee, S., Aos, S., Drake, E., Pennucci, A., Miller, U., & Anderson, L. (2012) *Return on investment: Evidence-based options to improve statewide outcomes* (Document no. 12-04-1201). Olympia: Washington State Institute for Public Policy.
Leschied, A., & Cunningham, A. (2002). *Seeking effective interventions for serious young offenders: Interim results of a four-year randomized study of Multisystemic Therapy in Ontario, Canada*. London, Ontario, Canada: London Family Court Clinic.
Leve, L. D., Chamberlain, P., & Reid, J. B. (2005). Intervention outcomes for girls referred from juvenile justice: Effects on delinquency. *Journal of Consulting and Clinical Psychology, 73*, 1181–1185.
Lipsey, M. W., & Derzon, J. H. (1998). Predictors of violent or serious delinquency in adolescence and early adulthood: A synthesis of longitudinal research. In R. Loeber & D. P. Farrington (Eds.), *Serious and violent juvenile offenders: Risk factors and successful interventions* (pp. 86–105). Thousand Oaks, CA: Sage.
Littell, J. H. (2005). Lessons from a systematic review of effects of Multisystemic Therapy. *Children and Youth Services Review, 27*, 445–463.
Loeber, R., Farrington, D. P., Stouthamer-Loeber, M., & White, H. R. (2008). *Violence and serious theft: Development and prediction from childhood to adulthood*. New York: Routledge.
McCord, J. (1977). A comparative study of two generations of native Americans. In R. F. Meier (Ed.), *Theory in criminology* (pp. 83–92). Beverly Hills, CA: Sage.
McCord, J. (1979). Some child-rearing antecedents of criminal behavior in adult men. *Journal of Personality and Social Psychology, 37*, 1477–1486.
McCord, J. (1982). A longitudinal view of the relationship between paternal absence and crime. In J. Gunn & D. P. Farrington (Eds.), *Abnormal offenders, delinquency, and the criminal justice system* (pp. 113–128). Chichester: Wiley.
McCord, J. (1983). A forty year perspective on effects of child abuse and neglect. *Child Abuse and Neglect, 7*, 265–270.
McCord, J. (1997). On discipline. *Psychological Inquiry, 8*, 215–217.
Macdonald, G. M., & Turner, W. (2007). Treatment Foster Care for improving outcomes in children and young people. *Campbell Systematic Reviews, 9*, 2007.
Malinosky-Rummell, R., & Hansen, D. J. (1993). Long-term consequences of childhood physical abuse. *Psychological Bulletin, 114*, 68–79.
Manning, M., Homel, R., & Smith, C. (2010). A meta-analysis of the effects of early developmental prevention programmes in at-risk populations on non-health outcomes in adolescence. *Children and Youth Services Review, 32*, 506–519.
Maxfield, M. G., & Widom, C. S. (1996). The cycle of violence revisited 6 years later. *Archives of Pediatrics and Adolescent Medicine, 150*, 390–395.
Morash, M., & Rucker, L. (1989). An exploratory study of the connection of mother's age at childbearing to her children's delinquency in four data sets. *Crime and Delinquency, 35*, 45–93.

Murray, J., Bijleveld, C. C. J. H., Farrington, D. P., & Loeber, R. (2014). *Effects of parental incarceration on children: Cross-national comparative studies*. Washington, DC: American Psychological Association.

Murray, J., & Farrington, D. P. (2005). Parental imprisonment: Effects on boys' antisocial behaviour and delinquency through the life-course. *Journal of Child Psychology and Psychiatry, 46*, 1269–1278.

Murray, J., Irving, B., Farrington, D. P., Colman, I., & Bloxsom, C. A. J. (2010). Very early predictors of conduct problems and crime: Results from a national cohort study. *Journal of Child Psychology and Psychiatry, 51*, 1198–1207.

Murray, J., Janson, C.-G., & Farrington, D. P. (2007). Crime in adult offspring of prisoners: A cross-national comparison of two longitudinal samples. *Criminal Justice and Behavior, 34*, 133–149.

Nagin, D. S., Pogarsky, G., & Farrington, D. P. (1997). Adolescent mothers and the criminal behavior of their children. *Law and Society Review, 31*, 137–162.

Newson, J., & Newson, E. (1989). *The extent of parental physical punishment in the UK*. London: Approach.

Newson, J., Newson, E., & Adams, M. (1993). The social origins of delinquency. *Criminal Behaviour and Mental Health, 3*, 19–29.

Odgers, C. L., Milne, B. J., Caspi, A., Crump, R., Poulton, R., & Moffitt, T. E. (2007). Predicting prognosis for the conduct-problem boy: Can family history help? *Journal of the American Academy of Child and Adolescent Psychiatry, 46*, 1240–1249.

Ogden, T., & Hagen, K. A. (2006). Multisystemic Treatment of serious behaviour problems in youth: Sustainability of effectiveness two years after intake. *Child and Adolescent Mental Health, 11*, 142–149.

Olds, D. L., Eckenrode, J., Henderson, C. R., Kitzman, H., Powers, J., Cole, R., et al. (1997). Long-term effects of home visitation on maternal life course and child abuse and neglect: Fifteen-year follow-up of a randomized trial. *Journal of the American Medical Association, 278*, 637–643.

Olds, D. L., Henderson, C. R., Chamberlin, R., & Tatelbaum, R. (1986). Preventing child abuse and neglect: A randomized trial of nurse home visitation. *Pediatrics, 78*, 65–78.

Olds, D. L., Henderson, C. R., Cole, R., Eckenrode, J., Kitzman, H., Luckey, D., et al. (1998). Long-term effects of nurse home visitation on children's criminal and antisocial behavior: 15-year follow-up of a randomized controlled trial. *Journal of the American Medical Association, 280*, 1238–1244.

Olds, D. L., Sadler, L., & Kitzman, H. (2007). Programs for parents of infants and toddlers: Recent evidence from randomized trials. *Journal of Child Psychology and Psychiatry, 48*, 355–391.

Patterson, G. R. (1982). *Coercive family process*. Eugene, Oregon: Castalia.

Patterson, G. R. (1995). Coercion as a basis for early age of onset for arrest. In J. McCord (Ed.), *Coercion and punishment in long-term perspectives* (pp. 81–105). Cambridge: Cambridge University Press.

Patterson, G. R., Reid, J. B., & Dishion, T. J. (1992). *Antisocial boys*. Eugene, Oregon: Castalia.

Piquero, A., Farrington, D. P., Welsh, B. C., Tremblay, R. E., & Jennings, W. G. (2009). Effects of early family/parent training programmes on antisocial behaviour and delinquency. *Journal of Experimental Criminology, 5*, 83–120.

Pogarsky, G., Lizotte, A. J., & Thornberry, T. P. (2003). The delinquency of children born to young mothers: Results from the Rochester Youth Development Study. *Criminology, 41*, 1249–1286.

Raffan Gowar, B., & Farrington, D. P. (2013). The monetary cost of criminal careers. In K. Boers, T. Feltes, J. Kinzig, L. W. Sherman, F. Streng, & G. Trueg (Eds.), *Kriminologie, kriminalpolitik, strafrecht (Criminology, crime policy, penal law): Festschrift fur Hans-Jurgen Kerner on the occasion of his 70th birthday* (pp. 441–456). Tubingen, Germany: Mohr Siebeck.

Reiss, A. J., & Farrington, D. P. (1991). Advancing knowledge about co-offending: Results from a prospective longitudinal survey of London males. *Journal of Criminal Law and Criminology, 82*, 360–395.

Robins, L. N. (1979). Sturdy childhood predictors of adult outcomes: Replications from longitudinal studies. In J. E. Barrett, R. M. Rose, & G. L. Klerman (Eds.), *Stress and mental disorder* (pp. 219–235). New York: Raven.

Robins, L. N., West, P. J., & Herjanic, B. L. (1975). Arrests and delinquency in two generations: A study of black urban families and their children. *Journal of Child Psychology and Psychiatry, 16*, 125–140.

Roman, J., Dunworth, T., & Marsh, K. (2010). *Cost-benefit analysis and crime control.* Washington, DC: Urban Institute Press.

Sanders, M. R., Markie-Dadds, C., Tully, L. A., & Bor, W. (2000). The triple P-Positive parenting program: A comparison of enhanced, standard and self-directed behavioral family intervention for parents of children with early onset conduct problems. *Journal of Consulting and Clinical Psychology, 68*, 624–640.

Sansfaçon, D., & Waller, I. (2001). Recent evolution of governmental crime prevention strategies and implications for evaluation and economic analysis. In B. C. Welsh, D. P. Farrington, & L. W. Sherman (Eds.), *Costs and benefits of preventing crime* (pp. 225–247). Boulder, CO: Westview Press.

Sawyer, A. M., & Borduin, C. M. (2011). Effects of multisystemic therapy through midlife: A 21.9-year follow-up to a randomized clinical trial with serious and violent juvenile offenders. *Journal of Consulting and Clinical Psychology, 79*, 643–652.

Schaeffer, C. M., & Borduin, C. M. (2005). Long-term follow-up to a randomized clinical trial of multisystemic therapy with serious and violent juvenile offenders. *Journal of Consulting and Clinical Psychology, 73*, 445–453.

Schweinhart, L. J., Barnes, H. V., & Weikart, D. P. (1993). *Significant benefits: The High/Scope Perry Preschool Study through age 27.* Ypsilanti, MI: High/Scope Press.

Scott, S., Spender, Q., Doolan, M., Jacobs, B., & Aspland, H. (2001). Multicentre controlled trial of parenting groups for child antisocial behaviour in clinical practice. *British Medical Journal, 323*, 194–196.

Scott, S., Sylva, K., Doolan, M., Price, J., Jacobs, B., Crook, C., et al. (2010). Randomised controlled trial of parent groups for child antisocial behaviour targeting multiple risk factors: The SPOKES project. *Journal of Child Psychology and Psychiatry, 51*, 48–57.

Sexton, T. L., & Alexander, J. F. (2000). *Functional family therapy*. Washington, DC: U.S. Office of Juvenile Justice and Delinquency Prevention.

Smith, C. A., & Stern, S. B. (1997). Delinquency and antisocial behavior: A review of family processes and intervention research. *Social Service Review, 71*, 382–420.

Smith, C. A., & Thornberry, T. P. (1995). The relationship between childhood maltreatment and adolescent involvement in delinquency. *Criminology, 33*, 451–481.

Steinberg, L., Lamborn, S. D., Dornbusch, S. M., & Darling, N. (1992). Impact of parenting practices on adolescent achievement: Authoritative parenting, school involvement and encouragement to succeed. *Child Development, 63*, 1266–1281.

Theobald, D., Farrington, D. P., & Piquero, A. R. (2013). Childhood broken homes and adult violence: An analysis of moderators and mediators. *Journal of Criminal Justice, 41*, 44–52.

Thomas, R., & Zimmer-Gembeck, M. J. (2007). Behavioural outcomes of parent-child interaction therapy and Triple-P positive parenting programme: A review and meta-analysis. *Journal of Abnormal Child Psychology, 35*, 475–495.

Thornberry, T. P., Freeman-Gallant, A., & Lovegrove, P. J. (2009). Intergenerational linkages in antisocial behaviour. *Criminal Behaviour and Mental Health, 19*, 80–93.

Thornberry, T. P., Smith, C. A., Rivera, C., Huizinga, D., & Stouthamer-Loeber, M. (1999). *Family disruption and delinquency.* Washington, DC: Office of Juvenile Justice and Delinquency Prevention.

Wadsworth, M. E. J. (1979). *Roots of delinquency: Infancy, adolescence and crime*. London: Martin Robertson.
Waller, I., & Welsh, B. C. (1999). International trends in crime prevention: Cost-effective ways to reduce victimization. In G. Newman (Ed.), *Global report on crime and justice* (pp. 191–220). New York: Oxford University Press.
Webster-Stratton, C. (1998). Preventing conduct problems in Head Start children: Strengthening parenting competencies. *Journal of Consulting and Clinical Psychology, 66*, 715–730.
Webster-Stratton, C. (2000). *The incredible years training series*. Washington, DC: Office of Juvenile Justice and Delinquency Prevention.
Webster-Stratton, C., & Hammond, M. (1997). Treating children with early-onset conduct problems: A comparison of child and parent training interventions. *Journal of Consulting and Clinical Psychology, 65*, 93–109.
Wells, L. E., & Rankin, J. H. (1991). Families and delinquency: A meta-analysis of the impact of broken homes. *Social Problems, 38*, 71–93.
Welsh, B. C., Farrington, D. P., & Sherman, L. W. (Eds.), (2001). *Costs and benefits of preventing crime*. Boulder, CO: Westview Press.
West, D. J., & Farrington, D. P. (1973). *Who becomes delinquent?* London: Heinemann.
West, D. J., & Farrington, D. P. (1977). *The delinquent way of life*. London: Heinemann.
Widom, C. S. (1989). The cycle of violence. *Science, 244*, 160–166.
Widom, C. S. (1994). Childhood victimization and adolescent problem behaviors. In R. D. Ketterlinus & M. E. Lamb (Eds.), *Adolescent problem behaviors* (pp. 127–164). Hillsdale, NJ: Lawrence Erlbaum.

Women's Substance Abuse and Its Impacts on Children's Early Development and Deviant Behaviors

Huan Gao and Jianhong Liu

Abstract According to recent reports from the United Nations, the population of illicit drug users continues to grow globally, particularly in rapidly urbanizing, developing countries. As women's social status increases, so does their involvement in illicit drug use. This article examines from an international perspective the root causes of women's substance abuse, focusing on its socio-legal consequences and impacts on children's early development. Taking a global view, the article outlines what we know about women who become addicted to illicit drugs and explores the role of women's substance abuse in the development of deviant behavior among young children.

1 Introduction

While the United States has a well-documented history of substance abuse research, gender-specific studies did not emerge until the early 1980s after feminist scholarship had advanced our understanding of gender, crime and justice. Prior to the 1980s, studies on women's substance abuse as well as studies on female criminality in general ignored gender as a defining factor. As a result, research on substance abuse focused predominantly on the population of male drug users while women remained virtually invisible to researchers. After several decades a considerable amount of research on women and substance abuse has been published; still, our knowledge about women's substance abuse and its impacts on children's early development and deviant behaviors—especially from an international standpoint—is still limited and falls behind the ever-increasing population of female drug users.

H. Gao
California State University, Stanislaus, CA, USA
e-mail: hgao@csustan.edu

J. Liu (✉)
University of Macau, Taipa, Macau, China
e-mail: jliu@umac.mo

H. Kury et al. (eds.), *Women and Children as Victims and Offenders: Background, Prevention, Reintegration*, DOI 10.1007/978-3-319-08398-8_9

According to the World Drug Report in 2014 (UNODC 2014), between 162 and 324 million people aged 15–64 (3.5–7.0 % of the world's population) abused illicit drugs at least once in 2012. Among them, between 16 million and 39 million people were either regular drug users or had shown drug use disorders or dependence. Cannabis has been identified as the most popular illicit drug based on global, regional, and country-specific reports.[1] Cannabis, the most popular drug among 30 European countries for adults aged 15–64, showed a prevalence rate ranging from 14.2 % (Sweden) to 32.1 % (France) (EMCDDA 2013a). Based on data collected by the Australia Longitudinal Study on Women's Health (N = 9512) in 1996 and 2000, cannabis has become the gateway drug for multiple drug use, with multiple drug use increasing in numbers (Turner et al. 2003).

Concerning the prevalence rate of illicit drug use, it is well-established that a drug of choice is primarily determined by its availability, accessibility and price in a given country. Drug of choice is also related to gender but varies by country[2]: males have been always the dominant drug users across the world regardless of socio-cultural differences and responses of the criminal justice system.[3] However, the gender gap has shrunk in recent years in the misuse of pharmaceuticals. Globally, while only one third of men abused pharmaceutical drugs in 2013, about half of women drug users did, as was revealed in a recent survey (UNODC 2014).[4] Another survey of students aged 15–16 conducted in 2011 among 36 European countries also confirmed this distinctive illicit drug use pattern among women. While boys have continued to show higher percentages of use of all major illicit drugs since data was collected from the first wave in 1995, boys no longer show higher percentages of the non-prescription use of tranquillizers (EMCDDA 2012a). The gender difference in drug use patterns might be relevant to legal sanctions and the public perception. Under such an assumption, women may have tended to use those illicit drugs that carried fewer criminal sanctions and that were found more acceptable by the general public (EMCDDA 2000).

With changes in social contexts and women's increasing roles in society, women's engagement in substance abuse has been rising in recent years; a large increase in female drug use among school-aged students in Europe has been

[1] Cannabis (2.7–4.9 %), amphetamine-type stimulants (2.1 %), opioids (0.7 %) and cocaine (0.45) were the most common illicit drugs abused worldwide.

[2] According to data collected from 22 European Union (EU) member states and Switzerland (where there are 4647 drug treatment centers combined), the gender ratio (male to female) significantly varied among countries (also by drugs): 5.3 (South Europe), 4.3 (East Europe), 3.5 (West Europe), 2.6 (North Europe) (Montanari et al. 2011).

[3] According to a 2013 National Survey on Drug Use and Health (SAMHSA 2014), the primary source of statistical information on substance abuse in the United States, the rate of illicit drug use for persons aged 12 or older was 9.4 % with only a slightly increase (<2 %) as compared to data collected 10 years ago. Men are more likely to use illicit drugs than women across countries; the male to female gender ratio was 11.5 vs. 7.3 %.

[4] This survey included both developed countries and developing countries: Australia, United States of America, Spain, Urban Afghanistan, and Pakistan.

observed since 2005. This increase has been explained as a "cohort effect" among females experiencing gender equality along with increased drug-using opportunities (EMCDDA 2005, p. 17). In particular, increased drug use among women, especially young women, has been witnessed in newly industrialized countries such as China, India, South Africa and Brazil,[5] where society is transforming due to rapid modernization and social change that includes increased drug availability and accessibility, new migrants and employment opportunities for women, more tolerable local culture toward new drugs, and lack of precise legislation to respond to this emerging issue (Gao 2011; Peltzer et al. 2010; UNODC 2002).

For example, a study was conducted in 2010 in a hospital in Brazil based on first-time hospital admissions (N = 761), where the Brazilian public health system offered free treatment programs to patients selected by the government. Crack cocaine-related visits went up quickly for women from 2.8 % to 67.8 %; and new multiple drug use rates also increased during the same time period (Moreira et al. 2010). Besides newly industrialized countries, Moscow, Russia has seen the number of females identified as first time drug users with substance dependence increase tenfold between 1993 and 1999 (EMCDDA 2006). In South Korea, while the rate of alcohol abuse for women has been rising in the past decades, a dramatic age decrease at the onset of drinking was also evident as compared to the older generations in the past 50 years (Kim and Kim 2008).

To improve our understanding of women's substance abuse and to develop evidence based social and criminal justice policies, a growing body of literature has shown a strong demand for more comprehensive data collection with an inclusion of gender-specific variables at the country level and/or at the regional level. Currently, data about women's substance abuse primarily comes from national general population surveys and data collected by researchers/scholars via surveys or in-depth interviews. However, national information systems about substance abuse may not be available in many countries, such as countries in Africa, Asia and South America, where there is an increasing demand for drug treatment and related services.[6,7,8] Even when these treatment modalities were achievable, gender-specific variables were not prioritized by most of these countries, even many European countries.

The objective of this chapter, therefore, is to examine the causes of women's substance abuse from an international perspective, focusing on socio-legal

---

[5] See Internal Monetary Fund 2011 for a full list of newly industrialized countries.

[6] While both sex workers and people who injected drugs were identified as key populations by the World Health Organization (WHO), only 10 % of the people living with HIV were receiving antiretroviral therapy (ART) in Africa, followed by slightly better numbers in Eastern Europe (22 %) and East and Southeast Asia (about 32 %) (WHO 2014).

[7] While the total number of newly infected children with HIV in low-and middle income countries declined by 40 %, one third of pregnant women (about one million) in these countries have not received ART treatment, which was provided to pregnant women infected with HIV (WHO 2014).

[8] Standard antiretroviral therapy (ART) consists of the combination of at least three antiretroviral (ARV) drugs to suppress the HIV virus and stop the progression of HIV disease.

consequences and impacts on children. In particular, the article takes a global view in outlining what we know about women who become addicted to illicit drugs and also explores the role of women's substance abuse in children's early development and how substance abuse contributes to further deviant behaviors among young children. Furthermore, available programs for substance-abusers and their children will be reviewed and the needs of women and their children will be addressed.

2 Social Characteristics of Substance-Abusing Women

While limited information is available on women's substance abuse across the world, still, the scant publications currently available suggest that substance-abusing women share some common characteristics regardless of geographical location and that locality's socioeconomic development. In general, women who experienced drugs occasionally or for recreational purposes show quite different demographics compared to those women who have developed drug disorders or dependence. Women's education, marital history/status, drug-using male partners, and employment status were the most defining characteristics related to women's substance abuse across countries.

In the United States, according to a 2013 survey of adults aged 26 or older, rates of illicit drug dependence were associated with levels of education. College graduates had a lower rate of illicit drug dependence or abuse (0.9 %) than adults with some college education (2.1 %) and adults who did not graduate from high school (2.5 %) (SAMHSA 2014). Based on data collected from the same national survey in 2002 and 2003, a study indicated that over half of women in the U.S. only had a high school degree or equivalent. In that study, risk factors for drug dependence were younger age (between 18 and 25), serious mental illness, imperfect health and undesirable financial situation. In fact, a large percentage of women drug users (20 %) lived below the poverty line with an annual family income less than $20,000 (Simmons et al. 2009). Another study conducted in Australia with 109 women (mostly heroin users) in Canberra and Melbourne found that only 25 % of the women completed year 11 + 12 education and that their employment rate was only 14 % including part-time, full-time and casual jobs, and finally that their household annual income was less than $ 20,000 (Olsen et al. 2014).

For substance-abusing women who live in developing countries, lack of access to formal educational systems is a major obstacle in their lives. For example, in Pakistan, the majority of drug-using women are illiterate, and nearly 66 % of those interviewed never received any formal education.[9] About 60 % of women interviewed were currently married and 50 % lived with their husbands. Low education status greatly limited women's opportunities for seeking jobs beyond

[9] The number was much higher than the illiterate rate for the general population (38 %) (UNODC 2008).

their homes. Women either stayed at home, kept low-paying labor jobs, or engaged in the sex trade (UNODC 2010).[10]

Available studies also illustrate how women's marital history relates to their substance abuse. A study conducted in the Dimapur district of Nagaland, India, indicates that women who had a marriage history were more vulnerable to drug use as compared to single women; married women were more likely to become addicted to drugs under the influence of their drug-using husbands. Surprisingly, it was commonplace that women engaged in the sex trade while staying in a marriage or relationship (Medhi et al. 2012). A study conducted in Liuzhou, China, of female injection drug users (who were also sex workers) found that nearly half of the women were married or cohabited with a partner (Gu et al. 2013). A two-stage cluster survey with 400 female sex workers conducted in Hanoi, Vietnam, also showed similar research findings: one third of participants initiated drug use before engaging in sex work, and many of them had drug-using love mates (Tran et al. 2004).

2.1 Victimization and Women's Road to Substance Abuse

Since gender-specific concerns among drug users were initially addressed in the early 1980s, studies have focused on the root causes of women's substance abuse. A variety of studies has demonstrated that women follow distinct pathways toward substance abuse that are significantly different from men's. Consequently, differing from mainstream research, studies on women's substance abuse have consistently proposed victimization of women as a defining attributor. While large-scale cross-cultural comparison studies on women's substance abuse may not be currently available, individual country-based research has tended to support these findings.

Data collected from 50 drug treatment programs in the United States from 1996 to 2000 showed histories of victimization among participating women: 57.4 % by their parents during childhood and 73.6 % reported abuse by someone other than a parent. Additionally, over half of the women (58.1 %) reported having mental health problems (Conners et al. 2003). Based on a review of studies conducted in Australia and the international literature, Willis and Rushforth (2003) highlighted leading factors in women's substance abuse as the following: parental/familial issues, childhood abuse and neglect, mental illness, lack of social support and association with other drug users. An accumulation of these factors elevates an individual's risk level for using drugs, or sometimes different types of drugs. For example, experiences of sexual or emotional abuse plus pregnancy and depression and living with a drug-using male partner may increase women's risk for being a multiple drug user but not for exclusive cannabis use (Turner et al. 2003).

[10] In the study, women's occupations were limited to the following categories: house wife (36 %), house maid (21 %), sex worker (13 %)

It is well established in the literature that victimization of women during childhood and adulthood in the form of physical, emotional and sexual abuse is more likely to link to illicit drug use. The prevalence rate may vary in different cultural and social settings. For instance, a study conducted in Philippines with urban residents (aged at 35 or over) selected from Quezon City by using systematic sampling suggested that while physical and sexual abuse were not as high as in many other western countries (5.6 % for men vs. 7.5 % for women), nearly half of those respondents reported psychological/emotional abuse (45.7 %) and psychological neglect (87.3 %) (Ramiro et al. 2010).

The immediate consequences of childhood abuse may involve physical or psychological trauma, and long-term effects can interfere with day-to-day functioning. A history of trauma not only impairs women's early development but also extends into women's adulthood, which in turn increases their vulnerability to future domestic violence (Kyzer et al. 2014; Regan et al. 1987). As a result, women may experience multiple forms of abuse in their lives along with mental health issues such as depression and anxiety disorders (Johnson 2004). As a result, illicit drug use by women has been interpreted as women's self-medication—a way of coping with trauma and resisting victimization (Bloom et al. 2003). However, the extent of victimization among women drug users varies with studies, suggesting that women's victimization in childhood and its possible extension to adulthood, only increases women's risk for substance abuse but proceed along differing pathways.

In addition, as revealed in a study of women drug users in India who also worked in the sex trade, participants were mostly from disadvantaged social groups who had been forced to enter the sex trade to satisfy their male partners' or pimps' needs for drugs or money (Kumar and Sharma 2008). This study showed the linkage between women's substance abuse and social inequality in society and how extreme poverty could nullify women's ability to show resistance against their subordinate status in the male-dominant society. In the Northern Province of South Africa, where child sexual abuse prevalence rate was as high as 54.2 %, not only girls (53.2 %) but also boys (56 %) were victims of sexual abuse. Teenagers were easily lured into sexual abuse simply because of small gifts offered by adult males (Madu and Peltzer 2000). In Africa, local beliefs that having sex with young virgin girls may cure sexually transmitted diseases or bring good wealth and fortune have made many young African girls targets of sexual abuse (Lalor 2004; Madu and Peltzer 2000).

On a larger scale, however, is the fact that women's substance abuse and their participation in the sex trade expose them to street violence and further victimization. In a study of female sex workers conducted in Guangxi province, China, about 62 % of women reported partner violence or violence inflicted by their clients (Zhang et al. 2014). Interpersonal violence and substance abuse is highly correlated. Research demonstrates that women who use drugs or drink alcohol are more likely to be battered and injured. In addition, for those substance-abusing women who were older and worked in the sex trade, as shown in a study conducted in Liuzhou

China, inability to make money due to their age has driven many to engage in more risky sexual behaviors by serving more clients with less protection (either with less or no condom use), which exposes the women to a higher risk of contracting HIV (Gu et al. 2013).

Women's pathways to substance abuse are complex, varying with social context, culture and tradition, magnified by a number of mediating and moderating factors (Wiechelt 2008).[11] While one universal model may not be the reality everywhere, it is evident that women's victimization has been one of the most defining factors associated with women's substance abuse across different cultures.

2.2 Social and Legal Consequences of Women's Substance Abuse

Women's substance abuse brings significant social and legal consequences into their lives. Dramatic changes in lifestyle, in particular, bring about frequent contacts with the criminal justice system. While traditionally substance abuse was viewed as a victimless crime, its actual impacts extend far beyond substance-abusing women and their own families to society at large. Regardless of women's criminal history prior to drug initiation, it is generally believed that increasing drug use will be linked to more income-generating illegal activities (Willis and Rushforth 2003).

Connections between women's substance abuse and crimes have been well documented in developed countries. In the United States, among adult parolees or those on supervised release, the prevalence rate for illicit drug or alcohol use was 34.3 % in 2013; for adult probationers, the prevalence rate for illicit drug or alcohol use was 35 % in the same year. Both these numbers were much higher than the general population's rates in the country, as noted previously (SAMHSA 2014). Unfortunately, gender-specific data for the criminal justice population was not available in this report. In Europe, according to data reported by individual EU member states, women comprise between 2 % and 8 % of the prison population, and 9–15 % of them have been convicted of drug offenses. The likelihood that women would be convicted in court varied among countries (EMCDDA 2006).[12]

In terms of substance-abusing women's participation in illegal activities, our knowledge is largely limited by scarce reports from individual countries. While the rates vary with studies, current literature has shown a strong connection with sex work—a main income source for most addicted women. Among European countries, about 60 % of drug-using women have engaged in sex work, but these have

[11] Mediating and moderating factors vary across time, cultures, ethnicities, social roles, class, age, sexual orientation and identity (Wiechelt 2008, p. 974).

[12] Spain, Italy, Austria and Sweden were less likely to convict female offenders, but other countries, such as Germany, Belgium and the United Kingdom were not (EMCDDA 2006).

committed fewer other crimes than men (EMCDDA 2000). A study conducted in two major cities on the Mexico-U.S. border, Tijuana and Ciudad Juarez, suggests that one third of female sex workers have engaged in commercial sex activity since they began injecting drugs (Morris et al. 2012). Among female Russian injection drug users in St. Petersburg, Russia, about one third had a history of sex trading (37 %) (Benotsch et al. 2004). In Pakistan, while female arrestees represented only 4.3 % of total arrestees, most were arrested for drug related offenses[13] (UNODC 2010). A study conducted with female sex workers in Guangxi province, China, indicated that 18.1 % of those participants (N = 1022) reported drug use (Zhang et al. 2014).

Due to increasing concerns about the prevalence of HIV/AIDS, research organized by international organizations has long focused on the connection between commercial sexual activities and injection drug use (IDU). Both female sex workers and people who inject drugs have been identified as key populations (among several others) by the World Health Organization (WHO 2014). In particular, females involved in both injection drug use and sex work not only place themselves in a vulnerable position health-wise but also become the predominant transmitters of HIV to the general population (Medhi et al. 2012; Tran et al. 2004).

Based on observations in India, unprotected sex is a common practice among female sex workers (Kumar and Sharma 2008). In Pakistan 25 % of those interviewed reported selling sex for money, but only 3.7 % of them always used a condom during sexual intercourse (UNODC 2010). An early study conducted in the country also revealed that female sex workers had very minimal knowledge about HIV and its transmission channels—only 22 % of those interviewed knew that HIV could be transmitted by needles/syringes (UNODC 2008). As compared to the non-drug using sex workers, female intravenous drug users (IDU's) tended to be less protected during their commercial sexual activities (11.1 vs. 79.9 %) (Hong et al. 2013). Substance-abusing women also have more sex partners. A study conducted in Sichuan with 1422 sexually active female IDUs reported that 44.3 % of participants had more than one type of sex partner (regular sex partner, non-regular partner, commercial sex partner) (Lau et al. 2011), which resulted in not only increased numbers of HIV infections but also of other infectious diseases[14] (Wang et al. 2011).

---

[13] These crimes included drug use, drug pushing, sex work and other petty crimes (UNODC 2010).

[14] These other diseases include N. Gonorrhea, syphilis, C. trachomatis, and HSV-2 (Wang et al. 2011).

3 Women's Substance Abuse and Children's Early Development

3.1 The Role of Pregnancy for Substance-Abusing Women

Since the normal menstrual cycles of substance-abusing women are interrupted by regular drug use, it is not uncommon that these women ignore the early symptoms of pregnancy (Sawyer et al. 2006; Rosenbaum 1981; Taylor 1993). While pregnancy may become an incentive for some women to quit using drugs, many others may find it difficult to make changes regardless of impending motherhood. However, continuous drug use during pregnancy can be detrimental to a fetus, causing both temporary and permanent consequences. Since the properties of drugs vary, health harms associated with substance abuse during pregnancy vary with substances.

Among many other drugs, it is well-established that alcohol produces almost all of the adverse effects as do illicit drugs (Irner et al. 2014). While cannabis is the most popular illicit drug worldwide, our understanding of its effects on a fetus is still in the developmental stage. A review of the literature suggests that cannabis use may adversely affect neurodevelopment of a fetus, particularly during the critical brain growth phase (Jaques et al. 2014). Cannabis may also contribute to a series of other negative outcomes, such as low birth weight; miscarriage; fetal mortality (EMCDDA 2012b); impaired cognitive functioning, such as eye and hand coordination; and disabilities in hearing, speech and practical reasoning (Irner et al. 2014). The detrimental effects of mothers' substance abuse can be long-lasting, relating to developmental problems at childhood and may include developmental delays, learning disabilities, social disturbances and lifelong health issues (Rohan et al. 2011, p. 159).

Along with premature delivery, low birth weight, and congenital abnormalities, a high rate of neonatal abstinence syndrome was reported for mothers' heroin or methadone abuse in a study conducted in Croatia (Vucinovic et al. 2008).[15] Another study conducted in Denmark exploring long-term developmental effects on children of their mothers' heroin and methadone abuse suggests significant group differences in neonatal abstinence syndrome for both toddlers (34.9 vs. 13 %) and preschoolers (49 vs. 13.5 %) as compared to control groups (Irner et al. 2014). However, an illicit drug itself may not be the only reason for harmful effects on the fetus. Substance-abusing women's poor health care and lack of proper nutrition may also be influential (Burns et al. 2006).

Since taking illicit drugs during pregnancy is generally not tolerated by society at large, collecting information regarding women's illicit drug use from women themselves has proved to be unreliable (Smarsh-Hogan et al. 2006). In many

[15] In this study 71 % of the children showed neonatal abstinence syndrome relating to their mothers' heroin or methadone abuse (Vucinovic et al. 2008).

countries, including developed countries in Europe, identifying substance abuse during pregnancy still remains a challenge (Irner et al. 2014). For example, the study conducted in Spain revealed that while only 1.9 % of mothers admitted using drugs during pregnancy, the results of hair analysis showed overall 16 % positivity for drug abuse during pregnancy (Friguls et al. 2012).[16] However, only a limited number of countries have national databases containing information on pregnant women and their drug-using patterns. Data on the prevalence of drug use among pregnant women are not available for most European countries (EMCDDA 2012b).

In the United States' National Survey on Drug Use and Health in 2013 (SAMHSA 2014), the drug prevalence rate among pregnant women aged 15–44 remained steady (5.4 %) as compared to the result in 2012 (5.0 %) and was much lower than the non-pregnant group (11.4 %). The rate of drug prevalence among pregnant women varied with age: the prevalence rate increased when age decreased.[17] This finding suggests that pregnancy may be an incentive for women to change their drug-using behavior (Taylor 1993). Comparatively, women who were pregnant at younger ages were much more likely to continue their drug use and thereby impose higher risks to their fetuses (SAMHSA 2014). This finding was confirmed by the study conducted in Australia. Besides age, the type of drug abused by pregnant women may also relate to the prevalence rate. Women who abused stimulants had had five or more previous pregnancies than the non-drug group (Burns et al. 2006).

Drug abuse by pregnant women is quite consistent with a country's drug use traditions and culture. For countries like Croatia with a long history of opiate use, research has focused on opiates and their prenatal effects. A study conducted in a Croatian hospital from 1997 to 2007 identified 85 dependence-complicated pregnancies (the prevalence rate was 0.2 %) (Vucinovic et al. 2008). In countries where cannabis has a high prevalence rate, cannabis becomes the drug of choice by pregnant women. Longitudinal research conducted in Australia from 1998 to 2002 that included observations of 416,834 live births suggests that cannabis, opioids and stimulants were the main types of drugs abused by women in that country. The study also found that women may abuse a single drug or multiple drugs at the same time. Comparatively, women who abused stimulants were much more likely to be multiple drug users, and of those who abused multiple drugs, most combined other drugs with cannabis (39 %) or opioids (23 %) (Burns et al. 2006).

Policy and legal frameworks concerning pregnant women across international society see large variations among individual countries: some countries require by law mandatory reporting and/or mandatory treatment while other countries are very lax on their policies regarding pregnant drug users. Among European countries removing children from mothers was not a common practice, suggesting that such a

[16] Drug testing for pregnant women usually incorporates one of these methods: urine toxicology screening, hair testing, or meconium testing.

[17] The prevalence rate was 14.6 % for ages 15–17, 8.6 % ages 18–25, and 3.2 % for ages 26–44 (SAMHSA 2014).

policy was either not in place or seldom was enforced (EMCDDA 2000). One of the biggest concerns is whether strict laws or enforcement of laws may create barriers for women to seek treatment because of fears that they may lose custody of their children. However, in the Netherlands, prenatal supervision orders are issued to mandate that pregnant women enter treatment programs. While issues related to child welfare have been addressed by various European countries, the question of whether the protection should be extended to an unborn child is still largely unsolved (EMCDDA 2012b).

A nationwide survey of directors of substance abuse and child protective services across the United States showed a dramatic change in the mid-1990s. The number of states that defined positive neonatal toxicology as abuse/neglect increased 21 % in 1995; the number of agencies whose definitions conformed to that standard increased by 30 %. Mandatory reporting of positive toxicology in pregnant drug users also increased. Due to the changes in law, criminal prosecution of drug-using women increased from 45 % to 71 % in 1995, but mandatory treatment for pregnant women or women with children saw almost no change (Chavkin et al. 1998).

At the federal level, a clear guideline emerged for early intervention for substance exposed newborns after the Child Abuse Prevention and Treatment Act (CAPTA) (Public Law 93-247) included Keeping Children and Families Safe Act (Public Law 108-36) in 2003 as its component. As a result of this federal action, states have to develop protocols in order to be eligible for receiving federal CAPTA funding. While all 50 states in the United States have in place a mandatory reporting law for child abuse and neglect, only a few states legally define substance exposure in pregnancy as child abuse (Rohan et al. 2011).

Between 1973 and 2005, 413 legal cases of prenatal substance abuse were identified in 44 of the United States, the District of Columbia and federal jurisdictions. Drinking alcohol or using drugs while pregnant were the legal reasons for these arrests (68 % of these cases related to cocaine use). The women arrested were mostly charged with child abuse and neglect (51 %) and drug possession or use (22 %). The women had been reported mostly by health care providers (41 %) and social workers (12 %) (Paltrow and Flavin 2013).

3.2 *Impacts on Children's Early Development*

For substance-abusing women, one of the biggest challenges they have to face in their lives is the prospect of endless abstention or relapse. Even those women who successfully abstain from drug abuse for a relatively long time are never quite sure whether they will accomplish a lifetime of abstinence or whether their current period of abstinence is simply another break in their drug-using careers. Repeated failures of drug abstinence and frequent withdrawal symptoms may worsen women's psychiatric symptoms and further increase their stress levels. While mental health problems can be a risk factor for substance abuse, substance abuse may also trigger further mental problems.

For the above reasons, research has recognized the crucial role of the postnatal environment simply because if potential negative factors are not eliminated, then substance abuse may be elevated because of changes in circumstances (Rohan et al. 2011). Children of substance abusing parents have more adverse life situations as compared to other children. Therefore, they also have a higher likelihood of developing a series of developmental and behavioral problems (Conners et al. 2003). Due to this concern, risk assessment on post-hospital care—right after the women and infants are released from the hospital—becomes crucial. Research suggests that women who score higher risk levels at assessment are much more likely to have their children sent to foster care after they are discharged from the hospital (Irner et al. 2014). The series of risk factors for disruption in primary caregiving among infants of substance abusing mothers were found relevant to the mothers' young age, previous placement of children in foster care, maternal depression, psychosocial characteristics at delivery, and challenging infants due to drug use during pregnancy (Nair et al. 1997, p. 1048).

Even in the United States, which lacks national data about a linkage between substance-abusing mothers and child maltreatment, it is hard to estimate the extent of the problem. The available national report revealed that caregivers' risk factors for maltreating their children varied with geographical location. The risk factor for alcohol ranged from 1.3 % (Ohio) to 47.3 % (South Dakota), and drug abuse ranged from 3.0 % (Arkansas) to 62.6 % (New Mexico).[18] Children of maltreatment not only had a high rate of disability (13.3 %), they also had a high risk of fatal incidents (estimated 1640 children died of these incidents) (Administration for Children and Families 2012).[19] Although both males and females might be potential victims of abuse, a survey conducted in 2005 in three African countries, Zimbabwe, Tanzania and South Africa (N = 11,206), suggested high rates of child sexual abuse among boys (Richter et al. 2014).

Research has shown that parental substance abuse significantly increases the risk of children being abused either physical or sexually. One study used records of newborns at the University of Chicago (Chicago Lying-In Hospital) from 1985 to 1990 and child maltreatment reports from the State Central Registry indicating that 155 out of 513 (30.2 %) children born to substance-abusing mothers were abused or neglected. Among 102 reports relating to neglected and maltreatment (72.6 %), children's natural parents were more likely to be the perpetrators (88.2 %), and

[18] Not all states reported differentiated caregivers' risk factors on alcohol and drug abuse. Therefore, in some states alcohol or drug abuse might have been counted twice.

[19] If a child showed any of the following signs, he or she would be considered as have a disability: intellectual disability, emotional disturbance, visual or hearing impairment, learning disability, physical disability, behavioral problems, or other medical problems (Administration for Children and Families 2010, p. 21).

toddlers were more vulnerable to abuse/neglect as compared to other age groups (Jaudes et al. 1995).[20]

Using data from the United States' National Survey of Child and Adolescent Well-Being (NSCAW), the first study that investigated adolescents involved in the child welfare system (CWS) and their substance abuse, revealed that many of these adolescents were maltreated during their childhood, suffering child neglect (40.7 %), physical abuse (32.1 %) and sexual abuse (14.3 %). The main risk factors associated with caregivers were parental deviant behavior (alcohol and illicit drug abuse), poor mental health issues and arrests, and poor parenting skills (Casanueva et al. 2012). Parental alcohol or drug abuse was one of the biggest concerns because of its relation with mental health, contacts with the criminal justice system and ineffective parenting skills. Social stress associated with substance abuse may be the major risk factor for substance-abusing women to abuse their children (Jaudes et al. 1995). Studies suggest that when both parents are substance abusers, the risk of children being abused will be elevated to a much higher level (Ammerman et al. 1999; Walsh et al. 2003). Unfortunately, substance-abusing women are much more likely to live with alcohol users or drug users and therefore are unable to provide positive influences on their children (EMCDDA 2012b; Kyzer et al. 2014).

Women's substance abuse, together with low income status (even prior to their drug initiation), low education, high unemployment rates, and residential instability renders their already impoverished family finances worse than ever; in particular, their finances become dire when they are incarcerated or participate in long-term residential treatment (Conners et al. 2003). In a study conducted in the United States, the majority of women who entered treatment (85.3 %) were jobless 30 days before they entered treatment; 68.2 % of these women received most of their financial support from others, and many had had their children removed or had given up custody of their children due to a child protection order (35.3 %) (Kyzer et al. 2014). For those substance-abusing women who lived in developing countries with meager social resources, some even took to begging as a main source of income while accompanying their husbands and young children (UNODC 2010).

3.3 Impacts on Children's Substance Abuse

With a growing number of children born to substance-abusing women, how these children are affected by their mothers' substance abuse and whether they will eventually abuse drugs in their lives has become an emerging concern in the literature. While parental substance abuse acts as a strong factor influencing adolescents' drug abuse, researchers also recognize the importance of

---

[20] This finding was confirmed by the recent national report on child maltreatment: Infants aged 2 years old or younger were more vulnerable to abuse and neglect (but not to sexual abuse) (Administration for Children and Families 2012).

environmental factors such as drug availability and peer association (McArdle et al. 2002). Cumulative environmental risk factors at home and in the neighborhood and community are strong predictors for youth substance abuse (Caudill et al. 1994; Kelley 2003). Still, family, as the social institution of children, plays the most important role in children's growth particularly from childhood to early adolescence.

As discussed previously, while mothers' abuse of drugs during pregnancy can be detrimental to children, a maternal history of drug abuse will be more influential and may impose long-term impacts on children's drug use behavior. A study conducted in Washington, DC with crack smokers involved in treatment showed that those who were exposed to maternal substance abuse (during their childhood) rather than parental drug use history showed higher differences as compared to non-history group on both drug use and antisocial behaviors (Caudill et al. 1994). The impacts of mother's substance abuse have proved to have long lasting effects and may extend to children's later lives. Children who witness their mothers getting drunk significantly increase their odds of engaging in risky drinking even while staying at home or alone (Cleveland et al. 2014). Children who witness such incidents may not abuse drugs right away but may have a latent period for drug initiation after they reach transition age (Casanueva et al. 2012).

Given the fact that substance-abusing women are often primary caretakers of children, the question of whether they can develop close bonds with their children is critical. For females, positive relationships with mothers and residing with family show the strongest protection for alcohol use (Cleveland et al. 2014). Another study conducted in five selected European cities suggests that living with both parents and experiencing a positive parent-child relationship significantly reduced levels of drug use in four cities. However, if examining impacts of fathers/mothers on children's drug use behaviors separately, a trustworthy relationship with mother has proved to be a strong protective factor across five sites (McArdle et al. 2002). While having a father or mother with a lifetime history of substance abuse disorder significantly increases the child's risks for substance abuse, parental involvement with the child and quality of communication have been linked with low abuse scale scores for mothers but not fathers (Ammerman et al. 1999).

Long-term devastating substance abuse may create a great deal of trauma in women's lives; for example, they may experience consequent mental health issues, and they are less capable of developing effective parenting skills as compared to non-drug using women. Effective parenting has two dimensions: parental warmth and parental control. Effective interaction and emotional connection, as discussed earlier in this section, together with appropriate control of children's behavior, lead to more effective parenting (Slesnick et al. 2014). However, the prevalence of child neglect by substance abusing parents suggests that effects of parental substance abuse on their children's drug use may be mediated by neglectful parenting (Dunn et al. 2002). In particular, as children grow up, substance-abusing women may have to face more challenges in handling the relationships with older children as compared to younger ones (Slesnick et al. 2014). Related to parental control, current research suggests that youth drug use is strongly linked to parents' disapproval.

Youth are less likely to use drugs if their parents strongly disapprove. For example, youth who perceived strong parental disapproval for trying marijuana showed a much lower percentage of actual drug use than those who did not receive the same response from their parents (4.1 vs. 29.3 %, respectively) (SAMHSA 2014). Besides neglectful parenting, women who abused drugs themselves may not be in the position to raise a strong voice against their children's drug use.

Women's participation in criminal activities often results in frequent contact with the criminal justice system. Either short or long-term incarcerations inevitably impair not only family functioning but also family stability (Conners et al. 2003; Rohan et al. 2011). As a result, children of substance-abusing women are more likely to be placed in foster care. A study conducted in Philadelphia on drug-dependent women indicated that as high as 40 % of those women had had their children placed in foster care (voluntarily or involuntarily). Even in a situation where women could stay with their children, many of them failed to cope with stresses related to parenting (Regan et al. 1987). A study conducted in Sweden also had similar findings: the parents of 37 % of foster children were substance abusers, as compared to only 1 % in the general population. Under Sweden's current policy and practice, children living with substance-abusing parents are seldom removed from their parents unless abuse or neglect is reported (Von Borczyskowski et al. 2013).

In addition, children who grow up in a family with drug and alcohol problems are more likely to develop mental health issues in their critical development stage (Johnson 2004; Ramiro et al. 2010). Frequent incarceration of substance abusing mothers has led to children ending up in foster care or living without biological parents and has not only increased children's risk for drug dependence but often leads to an early onset for drug initiation (Ilomaki et al. 2005). In the Philippines, those who were exposed to adverse childhood experiences saw increased likelihood to use substances and participated in risky sexual behaviors at an early age. Having a family member who abused drugs, suffered from mental illness, or who was incarcerated also increased the children's risk of using drugs or developing their own mental health problems (Ramiro et al. 2010). A study on the relationships between parental substance abuse and adolescents' exposure to violence and mental health issues suggested that parental alcohol use served as a major depressive disorder (MDE), posttraumatic stress disorder (PTSD) and substance abuse/dependence (SA/D); girls had higher likelihood to develop MDE and PTSD while boys were more likely to be related to substance abuse (SA/D) (Hanson et al. 2006).

Consequently, having substance abusing parents not only exposes children to a series of biological and psychological risks at birth, as well as maltreatment during childhood, but also may trigger a series of behavioral problems. Parental substance abuse can be a risk factor for maladjustment among children and adolescents. The research highlighted the intergenerational nature of substance abuse and related problems within substance abuse families. In a longitudinal study conducted in Los Angeles County, California, the United States, researchers found that while substance-abusing mothers' drug problems were significantly associated with developmental and social problems in their children,[21] grandparents' drug use not only predicted mothers' drug problems but also significantly predicted behavior problems of their grandchildren with gender differences (Stein et al. 1993).[22] Importantly, substance abuse and delinquent behavior all shared some common risk factors (Carney et al. 2013), and substance abuse by adolescents is closely associated with other delinquent behaviors, as revealed in the most recent national survey in the United States (SAMHSA 2014).[23]

4 Programs for Substance-Abusing Women and their Children

Since the early 1970s, a small treatment program for substance-abusing women in the U.S. launched by the National Institute on Drug Abuse (NIDA), has increased the number of studies about the nature of women's substance abuse. The distinct character of women's substance abuse, as compared to men's, suggests an urgent need for gender-specific intervention for women (Ashley et al. 2003). While there is increasing demand of addressing women's needs across international society, more information needs to be collected for developing effective gender-specific intervention programs (Wiechelt 2008).

Due to limited social resources, not all countries have equal opportunities to develop intervention programs even for the general drug use population. According to the EMCDDA Statistical bulletin (2013b), the number of clients entering treatment and treatment units by country (N = 30) in 2011 were determined by the treatment capacity of the country. In Europe, countries with extra capacity for receiving clients included Italy, Belgium, Sweden, Turkey, and Germany,[24] while some others, Estonia, Lithuania, Luxembourg, Malta, Norway, and Portugal, had all reached their countries' maximum capacity to receive patients. Unfortunately, these countries did not indicate whether they offered gender-specific programs.

Globally, only one in six drug users has access to or receives drug dependence treatment services each year (UNODC 2014). In the United States, it is estimated that 22.7 million persons aged 12 or older needed treatment for substance

[21] Such problems included fearfulness, hyperactivity, acting out, and psychosomatic complaints.

[22] For boys, impacts were on hyperactivity, acting out, psychosomatic complaints and social problems, and girls only acting out.

[23] Among youths aged 12–17, about 17.0 % of them had gotten into violence and 34.6 % of them had engaged in property crime/petty thefts that were related to substance abuse (SAMHSA 2014).

[24] These countries only partially filled their treatment capacity and had more available facilities or units for new clients: Italy (16.2 %), Belgium (25.9 %), Sweden (42.9 %), Turkey (50 %), and Germany (61.9 %).

dependence in 2013.[25] However, one very small percentage of this population (10.9 %) received treatment at a specialty facility. Among those who were not treated, 4.5 % of them expressed a desire for treatment and made an effort to get into a treatment program (34.8 %). Lack of insurance coverage and the inability to afford treatment themselves (37.3 %) were the most common reasons for not accessing treatment (SAMHSA 2014). These reasons were also the primary conditions that blocked drug users' access to treatment in Australia. Limited opening slots for drug users often meant much longer waiting times (Olsen et al. 2014).

In countries like China, recognized as newly industrialized with a rapidly growing economy, only limited drug-related treatment programs are currently available, not to mention gender-specific programs for women and their children. According to a study conducted in Sichuan Province, China with non-institutionalized female heroin users, there were barely any detoxification treatments available for women in the study. Over half of the study participants were not enrolled in any harm reduction program (Lau et al. 2011). While women heroin users in Kunming, the area with the highest heroin prevalence rate, had access to the government-funded methadone program, there was virtually no other treatment available besides methadone (Gao 2011). In Pakistan, according to the survey, over two-thirds of women drug users desired to receive treatment; however, only 13.2 % of them were treated at least once for drug use. In extreme situations, women drug users used home remedies to temporarily ease withdrawal symptoms during initial abstinence, a method that was also revealed in research conducted in China (Gao 2011; UNODC 2010).

Even when drug treatment is available, programs are more likely available only for people abusing traditional drugs, typically opiate types of drugs, but not for emerging illicit drugs. For example, antenatal and postnatal programs for pregnant opioid users are currently available in some European countries (EMCDDA 2012b). Treatment programs for opiate addiction were well developed in Croatia as compared to other types, such as programs for benzodiazepine (EMCDDA 2000). However, for substances such as amphetamines, replacement therapy was virtually non-existent in most countries (Hjerkinn et al. 2009). Another issue relating to drug treatment programs is the gender ratio among those who enrolled in the given drug treatment programs. While the EU Drugs Action Plan 2009–2012 addressed the issue of gender for substance abuse treatment, general population-based surveys conducted in European countries showed that the male-to-female gender ratio was much higher than that in the drug use population, suggesting that women may have less access to drug treatment as compared to men (Montanari et al. 2011).

As discussed earlier, women drug users are generally the primary caregivers of their children, sometimes the only caregivers in the family. One study revealed that a surprisingly high percentage of children (67.1 %) stayed with mothers who alone

[25] This number was based on criteria specified in the Diagnostic and Statistical Manual of Mental Disorders, 4th edition (DSM-IV) (SAMHSA 2014).

provided legal custody, as compared to fathers who alone provided custody (0.9 %) (Conners et al. 2003). A report from European Union countries suggested that women who enrolled in drug treatment services showed interesting age patterns: most were either under 20 years old or older than 39 years old (EMCDDA 2005), implying that women of child-rearing age might encounter more barriers to participating in drug treatment programs. In Australia, early childhood support in conjunction with drug treatment has proved a successful program strategy (Harvey et al. 2012). Using data collected from 50 drug treatment programs in the United States, one study identified a series of obstacles that women substance users face on their way to recovery, including lack of financial resources and social support, unstable housing, and lack of child care (Kyzer et al. 2014).

While a growing number of intervention programs are being developed, there is an urgent need to establish what is essential for a successful program. A review of more than 30 published works on the effectiveness of substance abuse treatment for women identified six areas of concern: child care, prenatal care, women-only programs, supplemental education sessions, mental health, and comprehensive programming. To be successful, drug treatment programs need to focus on reducing women's barriers to treatment, integrating supplemental programs and improving women's self-esteem and confidence in recovery (Ashley et al. 2003, p. 42).

To gain better knowledge of ongoing substance abuse service programs, researchers in Canada conducted the first national survey with substance abuse service providers for women and their children. The survey gathered 163 responses out of 287 program managers (57 % response rate). The findings indicated that services in Canada were provided in two concentrated areas: Ontario and British Columbia (the most populous provinces). In terms of service types, 53 % of agencies provided services for pregnant women and 46 % for child-related services. Forty-three percent of agencies did not provide on-site services but referred clients to outside providers for pregnancy/parenting and 33 % referred clients to outside providers for child services (Niccols et al. 2010).

When researchers conducted the second national survey with agencies, they focused on the partnerships between different agencies. They found that among a total of 106 agencies, 44 of them had no partnerships at all, and no partnerships were extended to agencies beyond the provincial territory. In Ontario, British Columbia and Alberta, the partnerships between agencies showed 1 or 2 large clusters (large partnership networks), while the rest were scattered with fewer and smaller clusters. Four central agencies in Canada linked others together: addiction treatment, adult mental health, health care and social support agencies. However, in terms of services provided to women and children, very few partnerships were identified for prenatal/postnatal care programs (Sword et al. 2013).

The above discussion suggests that only when substance treatment programs have the potential to address women's needs can they be beneficial and that any narrowly focused program on substance abuse may not make the considerable changes needed for recovery (Ashley et al. 2003). Research suggests that it is a series of cumulative maternal risk factors[26] that predict negative outcomes of women's substance abuse rather than a single factor (Nair et al. 2003). Therefore, research suggested that effective intervention on women's substance abuse should focus on three levels: the individual level (personal coping), family level (parenting styles), and community level (community cohesion and organization) (EMCDDA 2008, p. 13). Due to the complexity of the problem, as illustrated in research conducted in Canada, it is certain that no single agency can perform such a task on its own. A range of multidisciplinary agencies developing long-term interagency partnerships would go a long way toward providing for continuity of care for substance abusing women, their children and families (Harvey et al. 2012).

5 Conclusions

The previous sections briefly discussed women's substance abuse and its impacts on children's development and deviant behaviors, in particular substance abuse, from an international perspective. The paucity of current information regarding women's substance abuse and the extent of the problem presents challenges to the development of evidence-based intervention programs and corresponding social and legal policies across international society. While gender-specific research on women's substance abuse has increased significantly in the past four decades since its emergence, there are still significant gaps in the literature. Currently research and publications in this area of study mainly come from North America, Europe, and Australia. Little is known about women's substance abuse in South America, Africa and Asia, where there is increasing concern about substance abuse issues.

What we have learned from current research is that women's substance abuse has become a global concern and that women's drug use is not only an individual decision but is rooted in social relations and cultural traditions undergoing changing social contexts. For instance, in some Asian countries such as Afghanistan, feeding infants with opiates to placate them is a common practice in the family (UNODC 2009). As reviewed previously, women in developing countries are still in subordinate positions without having gained equal opportunities or even the fundamental right of education, which has resulted in many women drug users who have never received any formal education; thus, the surprisingly high rate of illiteracy. In contrast, research has identified new drug-using trends among women in newly industrialized countries. With rapid modernization and urbanization, women are seeing increased job opportunities along with changing perspectives about drugs and women's gender roles in society while exposing themselves more to the

[26] These risk factors include maternal depression, domestic violence, nondomestic violence, family size, homelessness, incarceration, absence of boyfriend or husband, life events, psychological status, and drug severity. Level of risk was recorded into 4 categories ranging from 2 or less to 5 or more.

emerging drug-using themes (Gao 2011). For the above reasons, conducting further research to understand the nature of women's drug use in its own culture and social context becomes an urgent demand.

Regardless of geographical locations, differences in culture and socio-economic status, women's substance abuse across international society has both distinctive characteristics and similarities. Women's victimization both in childhood and adulthood has been recognized as one of the most prominent risk factors across countries, leading women on the pathway of substance abuse. Many women substance abusers have been victims of child abuse and/or domestic violence; however, their substance abuse in the course of childbearing and childrearing has put their own children in vulnerable positions, either neglected or abused by the women themselves or by other parties. As a consequence, these children have increased risks of abusing drugs or engaging in other deviant behaviors. It is an unfortunate life cycle that transmits intergenerational deviant behaviors from substance-abusing women to their offspring one generation after the next (Dunlap et al. 2002).

For women substance abusers who are also bearers and primary caregivers of children, the impacts of their substance abuse on children's development are found to be prolonged and profound. For this reason, women who engage in substance abuse are barely accepted by society as compared to male substance users. This disparity causes potential barriers for women who would enter treatment programs (Wechsberg et al. 2008; Wiechelt 2008). Recent developments seem to indicate a start in providing the need-based treatment programs not only for women but also for their children. Current research has highlighted the importance of early intervention (during pregnancy in particular) with families and children at high risk and its roles in reducing child abuse of newborns and preventing intergenerational drug abuse and offending (Haabrekke et al. 2014; Hjerkinn et al. 2009).

Evidently, there remains a long way to go in the development of holistic, women-centered intervention programs with continuity of care, including substance abuse treatment, mental health care, prenatal and postnatal care, childcare, social services, psychological counseling etc. In particular, many developing countries with limited social resources, for example, in Africa, Asia and South America, will face huge challenges as compared to developed countries. As advocated by the United Nations, successful programs require whole-government approaches and inter-agency cooperation (UNODC 2010), as demonstrated in the two national surveys of service providers for women substance abusers in Canada. With the continuously growing female substance abuser population globally, the research and discussion in the international arena should focus not only on implementing meaningful gender-specific programs for women, their children and families, but should also be concerned about whether programs successful in other countries fit into their specific cultural needs.

Five Questions

1. What are key components of the most effective programs for sheltering/rehabilitating/serving/? What do these programs do for substance abusing women and children?
2. In order to develop successful programs for women substance users and their children, what kinds of collaborations among agencies need to be established?
3. Due to limited social resources available in many developing countries, what kinds of support from international society should be suggested?
4. To develop evidence-based research on women's substance abuse and its impacts on children's early development, what roles should the individual country's government and criminal justice system play?
5. How can we improve research collaboration at the international level to advance our knowledge of women's substance abuse and its consequences for children?

References

Administration for Children and Families. (2010). Protecting children in families affected by substance abuse disorders. Washington, DC: Children's Bureau, Office on Child Abuse and Neglect.

Administration for Children and Families. (2012). *Child maltreatment 2012*. Washington, DC: U.S. Government Printing Office.

Ammerman, R., Kolko, D., Kirisci, L., Blackson, T., & Dawes, M. (1999). Child abuse potential in parents with history of substance use disorder. *Child Abuse & Neglect, 23*(12), 1225–1238.

Ashley, O., Marsden, M., & Brady, T. (2003). Effectiveness of substance abuse treatment programming for women: A review. *The American Journal of Drug & Alcohol Abuse, 29*(1), 19–53. doi:10.1081/ADA-120018838.

Benotsch, E., Somlai, A., Pinkerton, S., Kelley, J., Ostrovski, D., Gore-Felton, C., et al. (2004). Drug use and sexual risk behaviors among female Russian IDUs who exchange sex for money or drugs. *International Journal of STD & AIDs, 15*, 343–347.

Bloom, B., Owen, B., & Covington, S. (2003). *Gender-responsive strategies: Research, practice and guiding principles for women offenders*. Washington, DC: National Institute of Corrections.

Burns, L., Mattick, R., & Cooke, M. (2006). The use of record linkage to examine illicit drug use in pregnancy. *National Drug and Alcohol Research Centre*. doi:10.1111/j.1360-0443.2006.01444.x.

Carney, T., Myers, B., Louw, J., Lombard, C., & Flisher, A. L. (2013). The relationship between substance use and delinquency among high-school students in Cape Town, South Africa. *Journal of Adolescence, 36*, 447–455. doi:10.1016/j.adolescence.2013.01.004.

Casanueva, C., Stambaugh, L., Urato, M., Fraser, J., & Williams, J. (2012). Illicit drug use from adolescence to young adulthood among child welfare-involved youths. *Journal of Child & Adolescent Substance Abuse, 23*, 29–48. doi:10.1080/1067828X.2012.735514.

Caudill, B., Hoffman, J., Hubbard, R., Flynn, P., & Luckey, J. (1994). Parental history of substance abuse as a risk factor in predicting crack smokers' substance use, illegal activities, and psychiatric status. *The American Journal of Drug and Alcohol Abuse, 20*(3), 341–354.

Chavkin, W., Breitbart, V., Elman, D., & Wise, P. (1998). National survey of the states: policies and practices regarding drug-using pregnant women. *American Journal of Public Health, 88*(1), 117–119.

Cleveland, M., Reavy, R., Mallett, K., Turrisi, R., & White, H. (2014). Moderating effects of positive parenting and maternal alcohol use on emerging adults alcohol use: does living at home matter? *Addictive Behaviors, 39*, 869–878. doi:10.1016/j.addbeh.2014.01.028.

Conners, N., Bradley, R., Mansell, L., Liu, J., Roberts, T., Burgdorf, K., et al. (2003). Children of mothers with serious substance abuse problems: an accumulation of risks. *The American Journal Of Drug And Alcohol Abuse, 29*(4), 743–758. doi:10.1081/ADA-120026258.

Dunlap, E., Golub, A., Johnson, B. C., & Wesley, D. (2002). Intergenerational transmission of conduct norms for drugs, sexual exploration and violation: A case study. *British Journal of Criminology, 42*, 1–20.

Dunn, M., Tarter, R., Mezzich, A., Yanyukov, M., Kirisci, L., & Kirillova, G. (2002). Origins and consequences of child neglect in substance abuse families. *Clinical Psychology Review, 22*, 1063–1090.

European Monitoring Centre for Drugs and Addiction (EMCDDA). (2006). *Annual Report: Selected Issues: A gender perspective on drug use and responding to drug problems*. Libson, Portugal (2), 31–37.

European Monitoring Center for Drugs and Drug Addiction (EMCDDA). (2013a). *(Statistical Bulletin Table GPS-1) General population surveys: Data tables*. http://www.emcdda.europa.edu/stats

European Monitoring Center for Drugs and Drug Addiction (EMCDDA). (2013b). *(Statistical Bulletin Table TDI) Treatment demand: Data tables*. http://www.emcdda.europa.edu/stats13

European Monitoring Center for Drugs and Drug Addiction (EMCDDA). (2012a). *Summary 2011 ESPAD Report: Substance abuse among students in 36 European countries*. Lisbon, Portugal.

European Monitoring Center for Drugs and Drug Addiction (EMCDDA). (2012b). *Pregnancy, childcare and the family: Key issues for Europe's response to drugs*. Lisbon, Portugal.

European Monitoring Center for Drugs and Drug Addiction (EMCDDA). (2008). *Drugs and vulnerable groups of young people*. Lisbon, Portugal.

European Monitoring Center for Drugs and Drug Addiction (EMCDDA). (2005). *Differences in patterns of drug use between women and men*. Lisbon, Portugal.

European Monitoring Center for Drugs and Drug Addiction (EMCDDA). (2000). *Problems facing women drug users and their children* (In EMCDDA 2000 Annual report on the state of the drugs problem in the European Union). Lisbon, Portugal.

Friguls, B., Joya, X., Garcia-Serra, J., Gomez-Culebras, M., Pichini, S., Martinez, S., et al. (2012). Assessment of exposure to drugs of abuse during pregnancy by hair analysis in a Mediterranean island. *Addiction, 107*, 1471–1479. doi:10.1111/j.1360-0443.2012.03828.x.

Gao, H. (2011). *Women and heroin addiction in China's changing society, (Advances in Criminology Book Series)*. New York: Routledge.

Gu, J., Bai, Y., Lau, J., Hao, Y., Cheng, Y., Zhou, R., et al. (2013). Social environmental factors and condom use among female injection drug users who are sex workers in China. *AIDS & Behavior, 18*, S181–S191. doi:10.1007/s10461-013-0434-z.

Haabrekke, K. J., Slimning, K., Walhovd, K. B., Wentzel-Larsen, T., & Moe, V. (2014). The perinatal outcome of children born to women with substance dependence detoxified in residential treatment during pregnancy. *Journal of Addict Disease, 33*(2), 114–23. doi:10.1080/10550887.2014.909698.

Hanson, R., Self-Brown, S., Fricker-Elhai, A., Kilpatrick, D., Saunders, B., & Resnick, H. (2006). Relations among parental substance use, violence exposure and mental health: the national survey of adolescents. *Addictive Behaviors, 31*(11), 1988–2001. doi:10.1016/j.addbeh.2006.01.012.

Harvey, S., Schmied, V., Nicholls, D., & Dahlen, H. (2012). Key components of a service model providing early childhood support for women attending opioid treatment clinics: An Australian state health service review. *Journal of Clinical Nursing, 21*, 2528–2537. doi:10.1111/j.1365-2702.2011.04063.x.

Hjerkinn, B., Rosvold, E. O., & Lindbaek, M. (2009). Neonatal findings among children of substance-abusing women attending a special child welfare clinic in Norway. *Scandinavian Journal of Public health, 37*(7), 751–7. doi:10.1177/1403494809342310.

Hong, H., Xu, G., & Zhang, D. (2013). HIV risk, drug use, and sexual transmission among female sex workers in Ningbo, China. *International Journal of Gynecology and Obstetrics, 121*, 91–95.

Ilomaki, R., Kaartinen, K., Vilo, K., Makikyro, T., Rasanen, P., & Workgroup, S. (2005). Intravenous drug dependence in adolescence. *Journal of Substance Use, 10*(5), 315–326. doi:10.1080/14659890500114334.

Irner, T., Teasdale, T., Nielsen, T., Vedal, S., & Olofsson, M. (2014). Cognitive, emotional and social development in adolescents born to substance using woman. *Scandinavian Journal of Psychology, 55*, 319–325. doi:10.1111/sjop.12134.

Jaques, S. C., Kingsbury, A., Henshcke, P., Chomchai, C., Clew, S., Falconer, J., Abdel-Latif, M. E., et al. (2014). Cannabis, the pregnant women and her child: Weeding out the myths. *Journal of Perinatology, 34*, 417–424. doi:10.1038/jp.2013.180.

Jaudes, P. K., Ekwo, E., Van Voorhis, J. (1995). Association of drug abuse and child abuse. *Child Abuse & Neglect, 19*(9), doi:0145-2134(95)00068-2

Johnson, H. (2004). Key findings from the drug use careers of female offenders study. Trends & Issues in Crime and Criminal Justice. *Australian Institute of Criminology, 289*.

Kim, S., & Kim, W. (2008). Women's alcohol use and alcoholism in Korea. *Substance Use & Misuse, 43*, 1078–1087. doi:10.1080/10826080801914212.

Kelley, S. (2003). Cumulative environmental risk in substance abusing women: early intervention, parenting stress, child abuse potential and child development. *Child Abuse & Neglect, 27*, 993–995. doi:10.1016/S0145-2134(03)00161-3.

Kumar, M. S., & Sharma, M. (2008). Women and substance use in India and Bangladesh. *Substance Use and Misuse, 43*, 1062–1077. doi:101080/10826080801918189

Kyzer, A., Conners-Burrow, N., & McKelvey, L. (2014). Environmental risk factors and custody status in children of substance abusers. *Children and Youth Services, 36*, 150–154. doi:10.1016/j.childyouth.2013.11.020.

Lalor, K. (2004). Child sexual abuse in sub-Saharan Africa: A literature review. *Child Abuse & Neglect, 28*, 439–460. doi:10.1016/j.chiabu.2003.07.005.

Lau, J., Tsui, H., Gu, J., Zhang, J., Zhang, L., Zhang, Y., et al. (2011). Sexual mixing and condom use with different types of sex partners among non-institutionalized sexually active female injecting drug users in Sichuan, China. *AIDS Behaviour, 15*, 86–94. doi:10.1007/s10461-010-9754-4.

Madu, S., & Peltzer, K. (2000). Risk factors and child sexual abuse among secondary school students in the Northern Province (South Africa). *Child Abuse & Neglect, 24*(2), 259–268. doi:10.1016/S0145-2134(99)00128-3.

McArdle, P., Wiegersma, A., Gilvarry, E., Kolte, B., McCarthy, S., Fitzgerald, M., et al. (2002). European adolescent substance use: The roles of family structure, function and gender. *Addiction, 97*, 329–336.

Medhi, G., Mahanta, J., Kermode, M., Paranjape, R., Adhikary, R., Phukan, S., et al. (2012). Factors associated with history of drug use among female sex workers (FSW) in a high HIV prevalence state of India. *BMC Public Health, 12*, 273.

Montanari, L., Serafini, M., Maffli, E., Busch, M., Kontogeorgiou, K., Kuijpers, W., et al. (2011). Gender and regional differences in client characteristics among substance abuse treatment clients in the Europe. *Drugs: Education, Prevention, and Policy, 18*(1), 24–31. doi:10.3109/09687637.2010.504199.

Moreira, M., Barbosa, G., Laranjeira, R., & Mitsuhiro, S. (2010). Alcohol and crack cocaine use in women: A 14 year cross-sectional study. *Journal of Addictive Diseases, 33*, 9–14. doi:10.1080/10550887.2014.882726.

Morris, M., Lemus, H., Wagner, K., Martinez, G., Lozada, R., Gomez, R., et al. (2012). Factors associated with pathways toward concurrent sex work and injection drug use among female sex workers who inject drugs in northern Mexico. *Addiction, 108*, 161–170. doi:10.1111/j.1360-0443.2012.04016.x.

Nair, P., Black, M., Schuler, M., Keane, V., Snow, L., & Rigney, B. (1997). Risk factors for disruption in primary caregiving among infants of substance abusing women. *Child Abuse & Neglect, 21*(11), 1039–051. doi:10.1016/S0145-2134(97)00064-1.

Nair, P., Schuler, M. E., Black, M. M., Kettinger, L., & Harrington, D. (2003). Cumulative environment risk in substance abusing women: Early intervention, parenting stress, child abuse potential and child development. *Child Abuse & Neglect, 27*(9), 997–1017. doi:10.1016/S0145-2134(03)00169-8.

Niccols, A., Dobbins, M., Sword, W., Smith, A., Henderson, J., & Milligan, K. (2010). A national survey of services for women with substance use issues and their children in Canada: Challenges for knowledge translation. *International Journal of Mental Health Addiction, 8*, 310–319. doi:10.1007/s11469-009-9267-4.

Olsen, A., Banwell, C., & Madden, A. (2014). Contraception, punishment and women who use drugs. *BMC Women's Health, 14*(5). doi:10.1186/1472-6874-14-5

Paltrow, L., & Flavin, J. (2013). Arrests of and forced interventions on pregnant women in the United States, 1973–2005: Implications for women's legal status and public health. *Journal of Health Politics, Policy and Law, 38*(2), 299–343. doi:10.1215/03616878-1966324.

Peltzer, K., Ramlagan, S., Johnson, B. D., & Phaswana-Mafuya, N. (2010, November). Illicit drug use and treatment in South Africa: A review. *Substance Use & Misuse, 45*(13), 2221–2243. doi:10.3109/10826084.2010.481594

Ramiro, L., Madrid, B., & Brown, D. (2010). Adverse childhood experiences (ACE and health-risk behaviors among adults in a developing country setting. *Child Abuse & Neglect, 34*, 842–855. doi:10.1016/j.chiabu.2010.02.012.

Regan, D., Ehrlich, S., & Finnegan, L. (1987). Infants of drug addicts: At risk for child abuse, neglect, and placement in foster care. *Neurotoxicology and Teratology, 9*(4), 315–319. doi:10.1016/0892-0362(87)90022-5.

Richter, L., Komarek, A., Desmond, C., Celentano, D., Morin, S., Sweat, M., et al. (2014). Reported physical and sexual abuse in childhood and adult HIV risk behaviour in three African countries: Findings from project accept (HPTN-043). *AIDS Behaviour, 18*, 381–389. doi:10.1007/s10461-013-0439-7.

Rohan, A., Monk, C., Marder, K., & Reame, N. (2011). Prenatal toxicology screening for substance abuse in research: Codes and consequences. *Substance Abuse, 32*(3), 159–164. doi:10.1080/08897077.2011.560526.

Rosenbaum, M. (1981). *Women on heroin*. New Brunswick, NJ: Rutgers University.

Sawyer, K., Wechsberg, W., & Myers, B. (2006). Cultural similarities and differences between a sample of Black/African and colored women in South Africa: Convergence of risk related to substance use, sexual behavior, and violence. *Women and Health, 43*(2), 73–90. doi:10.1300/J013v43n02_05.

Simmons, L., Bada, H., Haven, J., Holz, J., & Whiting, J. (2009). Illicit drug use among women with children in the United States: 2002–2003. *Ann Epidemiol, 19*(3), 187–193. doi:10.1016/j.annedpidem.2008.12.007.

Slesnick, N., Feng, X., Brakenhoff, B., & Brigham, G. (2014). Parenting under the influence: The effects of opioids, alcohol and cocaine on mother-child interaction. *Addictive Behaviors, 39*, 897–900. doi:10.1016/j.addbeh.2014.02.003.

Smarsh-Hogan, T., Myers, B., & Elswick, R., Jr. (2006). Child abuse potential among mothers of substance-exposed infants and toddlers. *Child Abuse & Neglect, 30*, 145–156. doi:10.1016/jchiabu.2005.10.007.

Stein, J., Newcomb, M., & Bentler, P. (1993). Differential effects of parent and grandparent drug use on behavior problems of male and female children. *American Psychological Association, 29*(1), 31–43. doi:0012-1649/93

Substance Abuse and Mental Health Services Administration (SAMHSA). (2014). *Results from the 2013 National Survey on Drug Use and Health: Summary of National Findings*, NSDUH Series H-48, HHS Publication No. (SMA) 14–4863. Rockville, MD: Substance Abuse and Mental Health Services Administration.

Sword, W., Niccols, A., Yousefi-Nooraie, R., Dobbins, M., Lipman, E., & Smith, P. (2013). Partnerships among Canadian agencies serving women with substance abuse issues and their children. *International Journal of Mental Health and Addiction, 11*, 344–357. doi:10.1007/s11469-012-9418-x.

Taylor, A. (1993). *Women drug users: An ethnography of a female injecting community*. Oxford: Clarendon.

Tran, T., Detels, R., Long, H., & Lan, H. (2004). Drug use among female sex workers in Hanoi, Vietnam. *Addiction, 100*, 619–625. doi:10.1111/j.1360-0443.2005.01055.x.

Turner, C., Russell, A., & Brown, W. (2003). Prevalence of illicit drug use in young Australian women, patterns of use and associated risk factors. *Addiction, 98*, 1419–1426.

UNODC. (2014). *World Drug Report 2014*. Vienna: United Nations.

UNODC. (2010). *Female drug use in Pakistan: Mapping estimates, ethnographic results and behavioral assessment*. Pakistan: United Nations.

UNODC. (2009). *Drug use in Afghanistan*. Kabul/Vienna: United Nations.

UNODC. (2008). *Illicit drug trends in Pakistan*. Pakistan: United Nations.

UNODC. (2002). *Women and drug abuse: The problem in India*. Regional Office for South Asia: United Nations.

Von Borczyskowski, A., Vinnerljung, B., & Hjern, A. (2013). Alcohol and drug abuse among young adults who grew up in substitute care: Findings from a Swedish national cohort study. *Children and Youth Services Review, 35*, 1954–1961. doi:10.1016/j.childyouth.2013.09.024.

Vucinovic, M., Damir, R., Vucinovic, Z., Capkun, V., Bucat, M., & Banovic, I. (2008). Maternal and neonatal effects of substance abuse during pregnancy: Our ten year experience. *Yonsei Medical Journal , 49*(5), 705–713. doi:10.3349/ymj.2008.49.5.705.

Walsh, C., MacMillan, H., & Jamieson, E. (2003). The relationship between parental substance abuse and child maltreatment: Finding s from the Ontario health supplement. *Child Abuse & Neglect, 27*, 1409–1425. doi:10.1016/j.chiabu.2003.07.002.

Wang, H., Brown, K., Wang, G., Ding, G., Zang, C., Wang, J., et al. (2011). Knowledge of HIV seropositivity is a predictor for initiation of illicit drug use: Incidence of drug use initiation among female sex workers in a high HIV-prevalence area of China. *Drug and Alcohol Dependence, 117*, 226–232. doi:10.1016/j.drugalcdep/2011.02.006.

Wechsberg, W. M., Luseno, W., & Ellerson, R. M. (2008). Reaching women substance abusers in diverse settings: Stigma and access to treatment 30 years later. *Substance Use & Misuse, 43*, 1277–1279. doi:10.1080/10826080802215171.

Wiechelt, S. (2008). Introduction to the special issue: International perspectives on women's substance use. *Substance Use & Misuse, 43*, 973–977. doi:10.1080/10826080801914188.

Willis, K., & Rushforth, C. (2003). *The female criminal: An overview of women's drug use and offending behaviour*, Trends & issues in crime and Criminal Justice No 264. Canberra: Australian Institute of Criminology.

World Health Organization. (2014). *Global update on the health sector response to HIV*. Geneva, Switzerland: WHO Press.

Zhang, C., Li, X., Chen, Y., Hong, Y., Shan, Q., Liu, W., et al. (2014). Alcohol and other drug use, partner violence, and mental health problems among female sex workers in Southwest China. *Health Care for Women International, 35*(1), 60–73. doi:10.1080/07399332.2012.757317.

Fairness and Trust in Developmental Psychology

Daniel Brugman, Christa Out, and John C. Gibbs

Abstract Fairness or justice is central to moral development. A universal and impartial point of view on fairness has been considered as the final stage of life-span trajectories on moral development. Human rights are viewed as the core of such a fully developed morality. Although the study of fairness implies paying attention to trust, the relationship between fairness and trust has seldom been studied empirically. Fairness and trust are both necessary for and stimulated by cooperation. Fairness depends upon the development of social perspective-taking skills; empathy refers to the affective side of these skills. According to Gibbs' developmental theory of moral motivation, the cognitive judgment of fairness and the affective response of empathy may both become a primary moral motive. Breaches of fairness or empathy can threaten or undermine interpersonal or social trust. In turn, disturbances in the development of trust in early childhood may have long-term negative consequences for the development of social perspective-taking skills and thus affect moral motivation.

1 Introduction

Fairness or justice is central to the development of individual's moral understanding. A universal and impartial point of view on fairness has been considered as the final stage of life-span trajectories on moral development. Human rights are viewed

D. Brugman (✉) • C. Out
Utrecht University, Utrecht, The Netherlands
e-mail: d.brugman@uu.nl; dan.brugman@gmail.com; christavankessel@gmail.com

J.C. Gibbs
Ohio State University, Columbus, OH, USA
e-mail: gibbs.1@osu.edu

H. Kury et al. (eds.), *Women and Children as Victims and Offenders: Background, Prevention, Reintegration*, DOI 10.1007/978-3-319-08398-8_10

as the core of such a fully developed morality.[1] Although the study of fairness implies paying attention to trust, the relationship between fairness and trust has seldom been studied empirically. Fairness and trust are both necessary for and stimulated by cooperation. Fairness depends upon the development of social perspective-taking skills; empathy refers to the affective side of these skills. According to Gibbs' developmental theory of moral motivation, the cognitive judgment of fairness and the affective response of empathy may both become a primary moral motive (i.e. co-primacy). Breaches of fairness or empathy can threaten and undermine interpersonal or social trust. In turn, disturbances in the development of trust in early childhood may have negative long-term consequences for the development of social perspective-taking skills and thus affect moral motivation.

This chapter addresses a number of topics pertinent to fairness and trust. We first pay attention to the definitions of fairness and trust from the perspective of developmental psychology. Next, we summarize Gibbs' theory of the development of moral judgment with a focus on fairness and trust. In studying individual's moral judgment, it becomes clear that breaches of fairness may affect interpersonal trust. Factors affecting the development of moral judgment are introduced, as are concepts that have shown to be of importance in the study of the relationship between moral judgment and behavior. Trust might be of importance for the relationship between moral judgment and behavior because it seems to foster field independence.

Traditionally, developmental psychologists have recognized the development of trust as a milestone in early childhood development and have stressed its consequences for socialization. Currently, Rotenberg and colleagues (see References) have carried out a substantial amount of empirical research on the development of interpersonal trust in childhood and factors affecting this development. Two other

[1] During and after World War II, the intellectual and scientific community stood up to investigate how it could be possible for human beings to show that kind of "inhumanity" to their own mankind. Maslow for example wrote: "it was at that moment that I realized that the rest of my life must be devoted to discovering a psychology for the peace table" (Hoffman 1999, p. 137). After the war the international community vowed never again to allow atrocities like those of World War II happen again. As a result The United Nations was created, which developed The Universal Declaration of Human Rights (United Nations 2014a). The basic ideas are that human rights are rights inherent to all human beings, independent of our nationality, place of residence, sex, national or ethnic origin, color, religion, language, or any other status. All human beings are all equally entitled to our human rights without discrimination. These rights are all interrelated, interdependent and indivisible (United Nations 2014b). In the preamble of The Universal Declaration of Human Rights is stated that the "recognition of the inherent dignity and of the equal and inalienable rights of all members of the human family is the foundation of freedom, justice and peace in the world" (United Nations 2014a). Clearly, equality or fairness appears as a major principle. This is in accordance with for example article 1: "All human beings are born free and equal in dignity and rights" and article 7: "All are equal before the law and are entitled without any discrimination to equal protection of the law". These human rights are central to (inter)national law, and can be viewed as a morality in which the consequences of impartiality and uniformity are fully represented.

types of trust that also have been studied in developmental psychology need to be distinguished: epistemic and moralistic trust.

Although trust has been an important topic of research in developmental psychology, the relationship with fairness has been barely touched upon in research. The development of trusting relationships stimulates cognitive and affective social perspective-taking skills, which affects moral socialization and the development of the understanding of fairness. As a life-span developmental theory, Gibbs' theory of moral judgment development is not particularly sensitive for the study of fairness and trust in early and middle childhood. The moral domain theory is introduced as a plausible alternative. Children distinguish the consequences for interpersonal trust of a transgression in the moral or non-moral domain. Several perspectives on the relationship between fairness and trust are outlined.

2 Fairness, Morality, and Trust: Definitions and Issues

Fairness refers to the ideal of treating people equally or in a way that is right or reasonable (Cambridge dictionary 2014). Scholars have approached fairness from multiple angles. They emphasize that not only the outcome but also the process needs to be examined, because fair outcomes should be the result of fair processes (Holcombe 1983). Procedural fairness might be a necessary precondition to establish trust in the outcome as being fair. In accordance with this view, philosophers also approach fairness as a matter of equity of process. Contributing to judgments concerning fairness are notions of equity, impartiality and uniformity (Rawls 1999; Rescher 2002). Moreover, moral philosophers emphasize the role of moral reasons: "Fairness consists in proportional satisfaction of a certain type of moral reasons" (Broome 1990, p. 91), specifically, moral reasons depending on considerations derived from deserts, agreements, and needs (Hooker 2005). Fairness mostly refers to distributive justice (perceived fairness of an outcome) and procedural justice (making decisions according to fair processes), but also to retributive justice (system of criminal justice based on the punishment of offenders) and restorative or corrective justice (system of criminal justice that focuses on the rehabilitation of offenders).

Beyond the multiple angles on fairness, no consensus currently exists about the meaning of morality (Kagan 2013, pp. 157–160). From a developmental psychology point of view, fairness relates to life-span moral development, especially, the emergence and development of the understanding of morality. Turiel (1983) views morality as "prescriptive judgments of justice, rights, and welfare pertaining to how people ought to relate to each other" (p. 3). Supplementing or competing with this cognitive view on morality, affective and behavioral views can be distinguished, focusing on moral emotions, feelings, and intuitions; and on moral behavior, respectively. One of the major obstacles for agreement, according to Kagan (2013), is that some prefer to apply the word "moral" to those who honor the standards for behavior that a majority in a community regard as the most reasonable response to a given situation, while others insist that the word should apply to those who honor their personally constructed understanding of right and wrong, even if their community disagrees with the agent's judgment. Both notions of morality relate to (neo-) Kohlbergian models of moral judgment development (Colby and Kohlberg 1987; Gibbs 2014; Rest et al. 1999).

Also at issue is the relevance of the intention of the actor. Although some scholars emphasize prosocial behavior per se, others argue that the intention defines whether an action is moral or not. Saving the president's life by stepping accidentally into the trajectory of an assassin's bullet is no moral act, in contrast to our judgment of the same behavior carried out intentionally (cf. Blasi 1999; Nucci 2000). This demonstrates the need for a view on morality that includes some type of cognition.

Trust is the belief that someone is good and honest and will not harm you, or that something is safe and reliable (Cambridge dictionary 2014). As with fairness, trust has been gaining an increasing amount of attention from scholars in various research areas; among those scholars are economists, psychologists and sociologists. Notwithstanding the diverse backgrounds of definers, all definitions contain the components "confident expectations" and "a willingness to be vulnerable" (Rousseau et al. 1998). In their overarching, cross-disciplinary attempt to identify a shared understanding of trust, Rousseau et al. (1998) propose the following definition: "Trust is a psychological state comprising the intention to accept vulnerability based on positive expectations of the intentions or behavior of another" (p. 395).

Different forms of trust can be distinguished: interpersonal trust, which is rooted in early attachment experiences and is expressed as a state (situational determined, i.e., do you trust this person in this situation?); moralistic trust, which also originates in parent-child interactions, but then becomes a moral value like a trait (i.e., do you trust persons in general?); and epistemic trust, which is the cognitive dimension of trust and depends on the social-emotional dimension of trust (i.e., do you trust what this person tells you?). Trust as a state can be distinguished on different social levels: interpersonal trust whereby one person trusts another person, and impersonal trust which describes a person's trust in a system as a whole, e.g., trust in a financial institution.

When the relationship between fairness and trust is discussed, we may ask the question: what type of fairness and what type of trust are involved? In developmental psychology, the focus has mostly been on justice and interpersonal trust as a state.

3 Development of Reasoning Concerning Fairness and Implications for Empathy and Trust

For many years we presented adolescents with moral stories such as the following (Basinger & Gibbs 1987; Boom et al. 2001):

> Bill is a boy of fourteen who would love to camp wild. His father promised him that he was allowed to camp when he himself saved the money. So Bill worked very hard at his part-time job. He spared a hundred dollars that were needed for the camp and even something more. But, just before Bill was going to camp his father changed his mind.
>
> A few friends of Bill's father decided to make a special fishing trip and Bill's father did not have enough money to go with them. He told Bill that he had to give his savings to him. But Bill wanted to camp anyway. He thinks about the possibility not to give the money to his father. Bill has a problem. His father had promised him that he could go to camp when he would earn the money. But Bill can only go to camp if he does not obey his father and does not help him.

This moral story about fairness and trust was presented as Bill's moral dilemma between having his father keep his promise and helping his father. We asked our participants what Bill should do and why, and subsequently classified their judgments into a scoring system of moral development in which a higher stage reflects a more complex weighing of socio-moral perspectives and a deeper understanding of morality (Gibbs et al. 1992; cf. Colby and Kohlberg 1987). According to Gibbs' stage model (Gibbs 2014), moral judgments can be classified into four stages: reasons reflecting only an unilateral or physical perspective (stage 1; e.g., "You should always keep your promise"); reasons reflecting an instrumental exchange (stage 2; e.g., "The parents want the children to keep their promises, so the parents should keep theirs"); reasons reflecting a mutual and pro-social orientation (stage 3; e.g., "When the parents don't keep promises, the children will lose trust and stop believing their parents"), and reasons reflecting standards and institutions (stage 4; e.g., "Society is based on trust, and keeping promises is necessary for the sake of order", or "Honesty is a standard everyone can accept, and you wouldn't want to live in a society where you couldn't trust anyone"). Note that, in this example, trust is viewed by morally mature participants as a state that is threatened or undermined by the father's unfair behavior. Bill depended on his father and intended to accept the consequent vulnerability, because Bill had the positive expectation that his father would allow him to camp if he saved the money by himself. He could not know that his father would break his promise and betray Bill's trust.

According to the developmental model used to analyze Bill's story (Gibbs 2014), then, stage 1 and 2 reasoning constitutes an immature level, preceding a mature level constituted by stages 3 and 4. At the mature level, reference is made to moral values underlying social relationships referring to the physical and psychological integrity of individuals. Also at the mature level, reasons can be distinguished reflecting a standard sequence development entailing some mixture (varying across individuals) of an "embedded" mindset (Type A) and a more "field-independent" and universalized perspective (Type B). For example a statement like "Keeping promises to one's children is very important: a parent needs to

... instill values of ... faithfulness to his or her child" reflects a type A stage 4, while the next statement brings out universalizable ideals (type B) in the parent-child relationship: "It is extremely important to keep promises to children. S/He learns to trust other adults and foster good relationships with children based upon honesty and trust" (Gibbs et al. 1992). The difference between Type A and Type B in Gibbs' model may correspond at least partly to the distinction between standards for behavior of a majority in a community versus personally constructed understanding of right and wrong (cf. Kagan 2013); in this connection, "standards of conscience" is a Type B criterion for classifying moral reasons (Gibbs et al. 1992). Type B moral judgment style might be a prerequisite for moral courage (Gibbs et al. 1992).

Bill's story is constructed in such a way that it minimizes empathy with the father. He is portrayed as a person who uses his parental authority to get what he wants and doesn't seem to care about breaking a promise to his son. However, the story can be easily changed in such a way that we empathize with Bill's father and excuse him for breaking his promise.

> Bill's father had an accident and broke his leg. He needed Bill's money for paying the hospital to heal his broken leg. Bill has a problem. He thinks about the possibility not to give the money to his father. His father had promised him that he could go to camp when he would earn the money. But Bill can only go to camp if he does not help his father to get his broken leg healed.

What would be the right thing to do for Bill in this version of the story? The story is now more morally nuanced. The father still breaks his promise, but has good, "valid" reasons to do so, reasons that Bill may understand and accept. In this case, breaking a promise may not damage trust; indeed, trust may become damaged if Bill would refuse to help his father and still go to camp. Gibbs (2014) presents several examples of morally nuanced or multifaceted situations in which cognition (justice) and affect (empathy) compete for primacy in moral judgment and motivation. In the transition from stage 2 to stage 3 in moral judgment, interpersonal empathy becomes a criterion in moral reasoning development (e.g., Gibbs et al. 1992, p. 71). Affective empathy can be seen as a response that is more appropriate to another's situation than one's own (Hoffman 2000).

Gibbs' four-stage (and existential) model of moral judgment aims to reflect—as did Kohlberg's six-stage model on which it is based (Kohlberg 1984; Lapsley 2006)—the development of moral judgment over the life-span. Following Piaget, developmental theories of moral judgment have tried to describe development toward an impartial and universal moral point of view. For example, in Kohlberg's stage model of moral development, the highest stage (stage 6) is described as follows: "At heart, these are universal principles of justice, of the reciprocity, and equality of the human rights, and of respect for the dignity of human beings as individual persons" (Kohlberg 1971, pp. 164–165). Also at higher levels, trust is considered a basic moral value, because society or human social relationships in general are based on trust (Colby and Kohlberg 1987, p. 21). In Gibbs' model, impartiality, universalizing, and the trust value pertain to the higher (both stage and existential or philosophical) reaches of morality. In stage terms, a breach of fairness means a breach in trust. In stage 3 "moral judgment advances beyond pragmatic thinking to a perspective of mutual trust" (Gibbs et al. 1996, p. 157), and in stage 4 trust and reliability are "necessary for the sake of societal order" (Gibbs 2014, p. 73). Fairness, empathy and trust become intrinsically related in moral judgment during adolescence when the transition takes place from the immature to the mature level.

Fairness, empathy and trust seem to go hand in hand, but that is not necessarily always the case. Tragedies happen. Examples can be found in which judgments of fairness and feelings of empathy are in conflict with each other, and the question arises what will take priority. For example, Korthals (1994) points to the theme of the movie "The Bridge on the River Kwai": Prisoners of war have escaped from the Japanese and return in order to prevent the bridge being built. They have to fire at their former comrades. Should universal justice and the greater good be awarded higher priority than interpersonal empathy? What about the trusting relationships with their former comrades? Many other examples of such tragedies can be found in Vasili Grossman's works: "Do you think it's easy to destroy the lives of children, women, and old men, to feel pity for them in the depths of your soul as you carry out acts of terrible cruelty in the name of the Revolution? . . . believe me . . . there is no truer test of strength or weakness of the soul." (Grossman 2010, pp. 275–276). Bergman's Fanny and Alexander can be seen as an example of parental education in which the strict, cold fairness of the stepfather prevents the development of trusting, empathic family relationships.

Stage models of moral judgment have been applied successfully in many western and non-western countries. Cross-cultural validity for the development of moral judgment has been established up to stage 4 (Gibbs et al. 2007; Snarey 1985). Different kinds of measures are available for different target groups; a measure can be an oral or written interview, a questionnaire, with or without moral dilemmas (Basinger and Gibbs 1987; Brugman et al. 2007; Colby and Kohlberg 1987; Gibbs et al. 1984, 1992; Rest et al. 1999).

Using several moral dilemmas, in which different moral values conflict with each other, different value areas can be probed to tap participants' moral judgment and their notion of fairness. The most widely used measure to assess moral judgment development in adolescents is the Sociomoral Reflection Measure—Short Form (Gibbs et al. 1992), a group-administrable measure without moral dilemmas. All these measures have shown that the development of moral judgment across different values areas (e.g., contract and truth, affiliation, life, property and law, legal justice) is sufficiently reliable to make up one moral judgment score.

Maturity in moral judgment gains as adolescents grow through broader social and educational experience. While positive associations have been found for moral development with (verbal) intelligence, no relationship with gender is found (Walker 2006). A temporary effect has been reported for young adolescents, when girls outperform boys; however, during mid-adolescence this difference disappears (Garmon et al. 1996). In addition, moral judgment is positively related to pro-social behavior, and negatively with antisocial behavior with delinquents scoring lower on moral judgment than non-delinquents (Gibbs et al. 2007; Stams et al. 2006). Delinquents score in particular lower on the value area "property and law" (Brugman and Aleva 2004; Gregg et al. 1994) and sex offenders on the value area "erotic love and sex" (Beerthuizen and Brugman 2012; Van Vugt et al. 2008). The moral judgment level of (juvenile) delinquents typically arrests at the immature level, while normal adolescents grow into the mature level (Gibbs et al. 2007). Individuals with antisocial behavior not only score lower on moral judgment as compared to their peers, but also on empathy (Jolliffe and Farrington 2004, 2007).

The relationship between fairness and trust has seldom been studied empirically. An example to investigate this relationship in adolescents might be Van Ijzendoorn and Zwart-Woudstra's (1995) study on the relationship between attachment representation and moral judgment in college students. These authors hypothesized that adolescents with an autonomous attachment representation (individuals who developed a basis trust in significant others and in their own capacities) would show higher levels of moral judgment, in particular Type B. They found that adolescents with an autonomous attachment representation did not differ in level of moral judgment from adolescents with a dismissing or preoccupied attachment representation. However, adolescents with an autonomous attachment representation showed a higher score on moral Type B reasoning, meaning they had developed a judgment style more independent from conventions and group pressure.

More elaborated conceptual models for moral cognition in relationship with attitude and behavior (both individual and group) have also been proposed (Barriga et al. 2001; Beerthuizen and Brugman 2013; Van der Velden et al. 2010). These models include variables such as cognitive distortions (or moral disengagement, Bandura 2002, i.e. biased processing tendencies, more specifically, inaccurate or rationalizing attitudes, thoughts, or beliefs concerning one's own or other's social behavior), moral identity (a kind of self-regulatory mechanism that motivates moral action), and group moral atmosphere (the norms, values, and meaning systems that regulate informal social relationships in a group and the degree in which these norms and values are shared by the group members). To predict antisocial behavior, self-serving cognitive distortions seem to be of particular importance, while to predict pro-social behavior moral identity plays an important role (Gibbs 2014). These complex models extend beyond the individual level and emphasize also the quality of the moral atmosphere at the group level.

Trust plays also an important role in these constructs, e.g., trustworthiness is viewed as an important moral trait or virtue in adolescent's assessment of moral identity, shared trust as a state is a criterion in group moral atmosphere (Power et al. 1989), and trust as it relates to sharing reciprocally personal information with friends and stimulating cognitive and affective empathy (Rotenberg and Mann 1986). Research found a positive association between moral judgment development and moral identity: higher levels of moral judgment covariate with a stronger sense of moral identity. However, moral identity seems to play a more important role in moral courage than moral judgment (Colby and Damon 1992; Walker and Frimer 2007); as we noted earlier, we need to distinguish in this connection between Moral Type A and Type B (Gibbs et al. 1992). A positive association has also been reported between moral judgment and the importance adolescents attach to moral values (Beerthuizen and Brugman 2013). Negative associations have been reported between moral judgment and self-serving cognitive distortions, which has been shown to be a strong predictor of antisocial behavior in children and adolescents (Barriga et al. 2001; Nas et al. 2008; Ribeaud and Eisner 2010).

Cognitive developmental scholars emphasize that children and adolescents essentially (re)construct their morality from their experiences in social relationships, more fundamentally than their acquisition of moral values from their parents or other educators through transmission by instruction and modeling. Instead of instruction and modeling, social role-taking opportunities are stressed. These opportunities enhance cognitive "decentration" (growing beyond egocentric bias by taking the social perspectives of other individuals and coordinating these different perspectives) (Gibbs et al. 1992). Reflective moral maturity is correlated with gains in cognitive and social perspective taking skills (Walker and Hennig 1997). Besides child-rearing experiences—parents who promote cooperation, engage in moral discussions and encourage prosocial behavior (Pratt et al. 2004)—and peer interactions, close friendships (Schonert-Reichl 1999) promote moral understanding. Peer interactions offer more opportunities for social perspective-taking than adult-child interactions, which will enhance the understanding of fairness and trust. These opportunities also contribute to moral socialization, which has been proposed to play an important role in the development of empathy (Gibbs 2014; Hoffman 2000).

Although there has been a lot of criticism on stage models of moral judgment development (e.g., Lapsley 2006; Nucci 2004), no other empirically based life-span developmental model is available that describes the pathway to mature understanding of fairness as impartial and universal (Colby and Kohlberg 1987; Gibbs 2014; Rest et al. 1999). The criticisms have led to refinements in moral judgment stage models. For example, the concept of stage was replaced by the concept of cognitive schema and consequently, the developmental claims of so-called "hard" stage model were abandoned. One of the problems of the life-span developmental model of moral judgment and the measures based on it is that it pays attention to moral development during childhood only at a global level, although it is acknowledged that experiences in social relationships during childhood may have long term consequences for moral development and socialization. For example, according to Gibbs (2014), a delay in moral judgment development due to poor parental practices (resulting in few social perspective-taking opportunities) may result in antisocial behavior during adolescence. Because trust as an explicit criterion in moral judgment arrives relatively late in individual development, this raises questions about the relationship between fairness and trust in children as they reason at the immature level. Before we tackle that issue, we need to have a closer look at trust.

4 Development of Interpersonal Trust

According to the psychosocial theory of the neo-Freudian Erikson (1963), children gain a sense of trust that the world is good during their first year of life, as they receive warm and responsive care. Bowlby's (1969) ethological theory of attachment strengthens this view. According to Bowlby, the early attachment experiences between a child and his caregiver have profound implications to the child's capacity to form trusting relationships. Attachment is an evolved response to promote survival, which starts with an innate set of behaviors to keep the parent nearby, and ultimately develops into an affectionate bond. This development is supported by emotional and cognitive child characteristics and warm and sensitive parenting. Children develop schemas (internal working models) about the availability of attachment figures, which will serve as a guide for future close relationships (Bretherton and Munholland 1999). When the relationship between parents and children is characterized by consistent, responsive and caring parenting, a secure attachment relationship will develop, whereby children experience an inner sense of safety, security and trust (Bowlby 1973).

Unfortunately, the development of trust is threatened when an insecure (avoidant, resistant or disorganized) attachment style develops. Children with an insecure attachment style are characterized by, respectively, unresponsiveness, clinginess, and confused behavior toward their parent. These behaviors are partially derived from harsh and inconsistent parenting. In particular, parents of disorganized/disoriented children engage in highly maladaptive caregiving (Ainsworth et al. 1978).

Mistrust, instead of trust, for instance, develops when children face maltreatment. Children who were psychologically maltreated during their childhood, are prone to develop maladaptive interpersonal relationships later in life. These relationships are mediated by schemas of mistrust (Crawford and O'Dougherty Wright 2007). For instance, an 8 year old girl who is rejected by her parents, forms schemas about relationships—expectations about how she will be treated based on how she has been treated by her parents. Ultimately, these relationship expectations can become true in her future partner relationships, which are characterized by victimization. This example illustrates that child maltreatment through the development of maladaptive schemas may have serious consequences for future interpersonal relationships. Not only for intimate relationships, but also for peer relationships in general, as physically maltreated children show greater mistrust in peers (Bernath et al. 1993).

Besides the impact of already formed schemas, children will simultaneously form new schemas while interacting with peers, and learn more about the dimensions of trust and the dynamics of cooperation in peer relationships. Reliability is an important basis of trust, because keeping promises adds order to a relationship (Rotenberg 1994). In close friendships, children learn even more of social perspective-taking skills, empathy and compassion than in more superficial peer relationships (Buhrmester and Furman 1986).

In her analysis of the developmental foundations of trust, Flanagan (2003) summarizes that trust is rooted in the sense of security that develops in early nurturing relationships between a child and his parents. Trust is a relational construct and contains the belief that others are fair, with the vulnerability that others might take advantage of us. Children first develop a basic sense of security, which is the origin of a sense of trust in themselves and others. These are the roots of the development of interpersonal (especially, dyadic) patterns of trust (Rotenberg 2010). Interpersonal trust is primarily based on the nature of the specific relationship, is situational determined, and is influenced by immediate social cues and the child's social cognitive development. In the example of Bill and his father, Bill trusted his father because he had the experience that his father will keep to his promise.

According to Rotenberg's view, interpersonal trust is like a state, an ability, which can be acquired. In line with Rousseau et al.'s (1998) definition of trust, Bernath and Feshbach (1995) reviewed the literature on children's interpersonal trust and described a developmental course of trust in friendships. This is combined with recent literature on the consequences to development.

4.1 Early Childhood Development

Using the method of clinical interview, Selman and Selman (1979) found that children in kindergarten and the first grade understand the concept of trust in friendships; they trust their friends indicated by a peer rating (Rotenberg 1984). However, young children's decisions are egocentric and influenced by immediate reward and punishment. They focus primarily on overt, recent, and rewarding peer behavior, while making a decision about trust (Rotenberg 1980). Basically, kindergarten-aged children trust their friends in order to like them and play and share with them.

Low trust and limited friendships will put young children at risk for poor psychosocial functioning (Betts and Rotenberg 2008). In another study, young children with low generalized trust (trust as a state) had fewer friends and—surprisingly—children with high generalized trust experienced more loneliness. Perhaps children with a high generalized trust have higher expectations concerning social relationships, and if these expectations are not met they experience elevated levels of loneliness (Betts et al. 2009), which may suggest that these children cannot adapt their expectations or standards to the relationships they have to deal with.

4.2 Middle Childhood Development

Advanced information processing skills and social perspective taking skills may support the development of a more mature understanding of trust. According to

Selman and Selman's (1979) stage description of friendship and trust conceptions, children from ages 6–12 years, are increasingly concerned with the perspectives of peers and view these perspectives as reciprocal. However, friendships are still guided by self-interests (i.e., "children do what their peers want, and trust that their peers will do the same for them"). Measured with a semi-structured interview using narratives, children in second- and fourth-grade use information about the consistency of their peer's trustworthy behavior. Children also base their trust decision on the likelihood that peers will keep to their promise. Yet, the second-graders are not as accurate as the fourth-graders at the differentiation between their peer's consistent and inconsistent behavior, and they are still somewhat influenced by immediate reward and punishment (Rotenberg and Pilipenko 1983–1984). At the same time, through the ability to perceive and use consistency information, reciprocal cooperation between peers emerges and becomes the basis for mutual trust (Rotenberg and Pilipenko 1983–1984). Rotenberg and Pilipenko argue that mutual trust may be the product of cooperation, because mutual trust is not observed in kindergarten but it is in second-grade.

In middle childhood (9–11 years of age), loneliness is negatively related to trust beliefs. Moreover, when children demonstrate low trusting beliefs and behaviors, an additional risk of loneliness is present. The negative association between loneliness and trust is stronger for girls than for boys (Rotenberg et al. 2004). Interestingly, Rotenberg et al. (2013) found the relationship between trust beliefs and psychosocial functioning not to be linear but curvilinear. Children evidencing high or low (but not moderate) trust beliefs are at risk for psychosocial maladjustment in the form of loneliness, fewer friendships, and more retaliatory aggression.

4.3 Late Childhood Development

Children, ages 9–15 years, become able to view friendship from a third-person perspective (Selman & Selman 1979). At this point, children view friendship as stable, intimate and emotionally supportive. Together with commitment and loyalty, trust forms the basis of this relationship, in which children are able to share intimate feelings and thoughts. Subsequently, intimate sharing will promote friendship and trust. Trust is an important component of friendship because it allows children to handle the vulnerabilities, which occur in intimate friendships. At this age, trust is central to children's friendship expectations, as opposed to secret sharing for second-grade children, assessed using a clinical interview (Furman and Bierman 1984). Due to children's interaction with peers in early and middle childhood, in pre-adolescence trust becomes the "glue" that helps to foster and maintain friendships.

Pre-adolescence development—During pre-adolescence children are able to recognize the importance of trust in friendships (Selman & Selman 1979), and show trust in the form of intimate sharing (Rotenberg 1986). However, intimate sharing is mainly shown in the context of same-sex friends, and continues to expand to opposite-sex friendships. The hypotheses that low trust beliefs promote loneliness from early childhood to adulthood is supported by multiple studies (Rotenberg et al. 2010).

5 Epistemic and Moralistic Trust

A conceptually different aspect of trust, although part of the larger construct, is epistemic trust. Research on the cognitive foundations of trust shows that, as children learn about new objects and situation they cannot always rely on their own judgments, especially when perceptual cues are not present. In such cases, children need to trust others and rely on the testimony of others—epistemic or selective trust (Koenig and Harris 2005). From an early age children show selective trust, while relying on the testimony of others (Harris 2007). Selective trust is the ability to distinguish who should be trusted from who should not, based on their testimony (e.g., Koenig and Harris 2005). Mills' (2013) review on the development of selective trust reveals that 3-year-olds make a more dichotomous selection of who is trustworthy or not. For instance, they do not trust a person who expresses clear uncertainty, but find it more difficult to distinguish a trustworthy person from an untrustworthy person when their testimony is doubtful. Four-year-olds are more selective in their trust in others in the sense that they are more likely to endorse information from a more accurate informant, even when that informant is mostly but not completely accurate. They still tend to struggle when the reasons to doubt are more subtle. It is not until middle childhood that children develop a better sense of how intentions and motivations influence behavior, and understand more complex reasons to doubt, such as persuasion and distortion. Harris (2007) concludes that besides establishing an emotional profile of their caregivers (i.e. emotional reliability in an attachment relationship) due to their emotional dependence, preschoolers also establish a cognitive profile of others, due to their reliance on the testimony of others. Testimony is essential in the process of knowledge acquisition. It is through testimony that children acquire representations of history, science, and religion (Clément et al. 2004).

The social-emotional perspective (interpersonal trust) and the cognitive perspective (epistemic trust) were combined in a study that tested whether infant attachment security influenced the child's trust in the attachment figure as an informant (Corriveau et al. 2009). The results indicated that children prefer information from their mother rather than a stranger, and that the strength of that preference is moderated by their attachment relationship. Avoidant children displayed the least reliance on their mother, secure children displayed a moderate and flexible pattern of reliance, and resistant children displayed the greatest reliance (Corriveau et al. 2009).

Beyond interpersonal and epistemic trust is an internal working model of generalized trust in which individuals think people are basically trustworthy or not, independent of situational factors. Specifically, not every situation gives the opportunity to assess a person's trustworthiness based on experiences with that person or the credibility of that person. For instance, when interacting with a stranger, one must decide whether or not to trust this person, based on the moralistic (generalized) dimension of trust (Flanagan 2003; Uslaner 2002). Uslaner (2001) characterized moralistic trust as a moral value based on a positive view on humanity and beliefs in the goodwill of others. Moralistic trust is treated as a general personality characteristic, and includes the "belief that 'most people' are fair, helpful and trustworthy" (Flanagan 2003, p. 165). Although the foundation of moralistic trust is rooted in a child's early experiences with their parents, moralistic trust is stable over time and is not dependent on daily experiences. Moralistic trust makes it possible to decide to cooperate with someone you do not know. Imagine, for example, that the interaction between Bill and his father was actually the first interaction between Bill and his new stepfather. They do not have a history together, nor could Bill know his stepfather as an untrustworthy person. Thus, interpersonal trust cannot fully explain why Bill would trust his stepfather. A more generalized form of trust (moralistic trust) gives Bill the opportunity to trust his stepfather insofar as Bill trusts other individuals in general, most of the time. Moralistic trust is like a trait or disposition to trust or distrust most people.

To summarize, interpersonal trust arises in attachment, which is an evolved response to promote survival. It starts with an innate set of behaviors to keep the parent nearby, and ultimately develops to an (in)affectionate bond. Children form schemas (expectations about their future relationships) based on their current parent-child relationship. These expectations will be positive or negative depending on whether their parents are trustworthy or not. This does not necessarily mean children are scarred for life during the attachment period, because children form new schemas while interacting with peers and learn more about the dimensions of trust and the dynamics of cooperation in peer relationships. In this way, peer relationships may buffer the effect of maladaptive schemas developed from child maltreatment. However, maltreated children will always have a disadvantage because it is more difficult for them to start trusting peers and subsequently, to form positive schemas. Besides the construction of an emotional profile of others (schemas), children also construct a cognitive profile of others, because they need to rely on the testimony of other to learn about new objects or situations.

Thanks to the development of more complex reasoning skills and cooperation with others, in middle childhood, children are adequately able to rely on the testimony of others, show epistemic trust. Although interpersonal and epistemic trust are part of the same phenomenon, they are two differentiable constructs that interact with each other: the emotional and cognitive state of trust. From these experiences and one's personality characteristics, trust develops into moralistic trust.

6 Factors Affecting the Development of Fairness and Trust

A notion of fairness does not develop in isolation. Its development is affected by other factors important during childhood development, such as cooperation, theory of mind and intentions. Cooperation is necessary for human social functioning, and emerged as an evolutionary benefit. Hamann et al. (2014) identified cooperation as a crucial component for the development of equitable sharing. The results of their study suggested that 3-year-old children tend to share marbles with their partner in a collaborative task (both worked together to receive a reward, one of them received more rewards), and take merit into account (they shared their marbles only when they undeservingly received more). Collaboration is a facilitative context in the development of a notion of fairness, because children in the non-collaborate condition (both worked independently to receive a reward, one of them received more rewards) shared less with their partner, and did not show a sign of merit (they did not share their marbles, when they undeservingly received more).

Both for moral judgments and Theory of Mind (ToM, the understanding that individuals have their own thoughts and wishes) it is necessary to understand intentionality (see Kagan 2013). This explains why many scholars address the interrelatedness between these factors in their research. An example of such a study comes from Killen et al. (2011). Children who did not pass the false belief Theory of Mind task (i.e. failed to understand that their believes or representations about the world may contrast with reality) were more likely to attribute negative intentions to an accidental transgressor (a child accidentally threw away a special cupcake while cleaning the classroom when the cupcake owner was outside) than children who passed the false belief ToM task. Besides, they viewed it as more acceptable to punish the accidental transgressor than did participants who passed the false belief ToM task. The authors give an implication of their results: children who do not have false belief knowledge may be more likely to accuse their friends of wrongdoing unfairly.

Interpersonal trust is established in caring relationships and develops through social relationships with peers. Scholars have also examined factors that enhance the development of epistemic trust. One of these factors is imitation. Through imitation, children develop cognitively, socially and behaviorally (e.g. Bandura 1962) and view themselves as more similar to those they imitate. Over et al. (2013) found that imitation influences social behavior; more specifically, it increases children's trust in the preferences and factual claims of others. A speaker's accuracy also influences a child's willingness to imitate, which subsequently influences social learning (Brooker and Poulin-Dubois 2013). Other factors are benevolence, honesty, and helping behavior.

Children rely on competence and benevolence information when determining whom to trust. More specifically, children aged 3–5 preferred the claims made by a nice person even when that person lacked expertise (Landrum et al. 2013). Besides competence and benevolence, children also consider honesty when they make judgments whether to trust someone or not. Nonetheless, as children develop they give greater weight to information considering the benevolence of a person (good/bad, nice/mean), and they are capable of making differentiated judgments, for instance trusting a lie-teller if this person is helpful (Xu et al. 2014). Young infants show preference to helping behavior (Hamlin et al. 2007). It is this preference which precedes the ability to distinguish between benevolent and malevolent behavior, and ultimately trusting claims made by benevolent persons (Mascaro and Sperber 2009).

There has been a debate on the question whether the development of epistemic or selective trust is related to the development of theory of mind (e.g. false beliefs). Basically, there are two lines of research on the relationship between selective trust and false belief, one that finds a relationship and one that does not. The former line expects that, to judge people's beliefs and intentions in order to decide whom to trust, one should have the notion that other people can have their own distinct beliefs. Researchers along this line cite studies indicating that selective trust and the completion of false belief tasks both show the same age trends starting at age 3 moving to a more differentiated form at age 5 (e.g. Koenig et al. 2004). In line with these ideas, significant positive correlations are found between theory-of-mind performances and scores on the selective trust tasks (DiYanni et al. 2012; Lucas et al. 2013). In contrast, Pasquini et al. (2007) could not demonstrate a relationship between selective trust and the understanding of false belief. It should be noted that Pasquini and colleagues' sample size (41 participants) was much smaller than that of a cross-cultural study conducted by Lucas et al. (2013, 144 participants), who did find a positive association between multiple tasks on selective trust and false belief: children who are faultlessly at false belief are more consistent in trusting an informant. Overall, children's ability to assess false knowledge does seem to facilitate selective trust development. In sum: imitation, helping behavior and social perspective taking leads children to a stance of skeptical trust rather than being naïve theorists.

In sum, development of fairness is affected by cooperation and intentions. Development of trust, on the other hand, is affected by imitation, and helping behavior. Both are influenced by the development of social perspective taking skills (theory of mind).

7 The Relationship Between Fairness and Trust in Children

It can be argued that the causal relationship between fairness and trust is bidirectional. On the one hand, unfair behavior may have consequences for a trusting relationship. As our morally mature research participants judged in the example of Bill, trust as a state between Bill and his father becomes damaged because of the father's unfair behavior. On the other hand, it has been proposed that children with a disorganized or anxious attachment style lack a basic sense of trust which may have consequences for their development of empathy and moral reasoning; children with such an attachment style miss many social perspective-taking opportunities and the sharing of emotions with a sensitive parent (Van Ijzendoorn and Zwart-Woudstra 1995).

The cognitive developmental approach to the study of fairness starts at about 3 years of age, when children can be asked to give a reasoned evaluation of actions (Smetana 1981). At that age, schemas of social expectancies concerning trust have already become established. The domain theory (Smetana et al. 1991; Turiel 1983, 1998, 2006) affords more credit to moral development at a young age (Nucci and Herman 1982; Turiel 1983) than does Piaget's (1932), Kohlberg's (Colby and Kohlberg 1987), or even Gibbs' (2014) theories. Moreover, domain theory proposes a parallel development of several domains of social knowledge beginning in early childhood: the moral, conventional and personal domains. The moral domain concerns rightness, fairness and the welfare of others. The conventional domain concerns rules or behavioral uniformities that is agreed upon in a particular social context and that regulate social interactions within that context. The personal domain refers to acts or decisions that affect the individual, and are personal choices, such as friendships, clothing and leisure activities (Arsenio and Lemerise 2004; Smetana 1989).

The ability to distinguish between domains appears from the way children and adolescents judge hypothetical norm transgressions. An example of a transgression in the moral domain is unfair or threatening behavior (Turiel 1983). Talking in class exemplifies a transgression in the conventional domain. Turiel (1983) designed a set of judgment criteria and justification categories to explore children's judgments. Children consider transgressions in the moral domain to be more serious, less acceptable, more universally wrong, and more independent of authority than transgressions in the conventional and personal domain (Nucci and Nucci 1982; Smetana 1995; Tisak 1995). In the study of Smetana (1981), preschool children indicated that in familiar situations prototypical moral transgression deserved more punishment than prototypical conventional transgressions. As children grow older, the evaluation of moral and conventional transgressions becomes more expansive and refined, no longer restricted to familiar situations, and sensitive to subtle differences between moral and conventional transgressions (Tisak and Turiel 1988). The domain distinction is fully developed at about the age of 9 years.[2]

To examine trust from a domain approach, Kahn and Turiel (1988) studied children's conceptions of trust by examining social expectations in a moral context. The results provided that violations in the moral domain (lying to a friend for personal gain) would diminish intimacy in a friendship, while violations of conventional domain wouldn't. Ultimately, Kahn and Turiel (1988, p. 416) assumed that being let down or being betrayed is necessary to the idea of trust and that the "social conventional expectations lie outside the trust boundary".

[2] For a critique of domain theory, see Gibbs 2010.

Moral evaluations and justifications of moral transgressions have been related in social domain research to antisocial behavior in children and adolescents (Tisak 1995; Tisak et al. 2006). Children displaying antisocial behavior have been found more likely to judge moral transgressions into the direction of conventional (Malti et al. 2009; Nucci and Herman 1982). Astor (1994) found that children with violent behavior show lower moral domain scores than regular children on acts of proactive aggression, but not on acts of reactive aggression. Blair et al. (2001) found that larger deficits in correctly evaluating and justifying moral transgressions were associated with more antisocial behavior in adolescents. Adolescents with higher scores on antisocial behavior are more likely to judge their own moral transgressions as belonging to the non-moral (i.e. conventional or personal) domain, since a non-moral transgression is less threatening to self-esteem (Leenders and Brugman 2005).

Interestingly, psychopathic individuals do not seem to differentiate between moral and conventional transgressions (Blair et al. 1995), while autistic individuals do. This seems to be problematic for the social perspective-taking approach underlying the cognitive approach to moral development, as psychopaths pass the ToM task while autistic people don't. Blair has proposed alternatively to social perspective-taking the violent inhibition mechanism (VIM) in human beings. In normal individuals, the domain distinction would be coupled to VIM, while in psychopaths this process would have been blocked. Nichols (2004) has argued that although autistic people do not pass the elementary ToM task, they do show elementary forms of social perspective-taking, like distinguishing emotional states in another person. This elementary discrimination would be sufficient for the domain distinction (Nichols 2004). Consequently, no alternative explanation for social perspective-taking is needed. According to Cima et al. (2010) psychopaths lack affective empathy and simply "don't care".

We investigated moral evaluation, self-serving cognitive distortions, and antisocial behavior in a group of clinical children (7–12 years old) at a residential treatment institution (Van Boxtel et al. 2013). As expected, the clinical group showed lower levels of moral evaluation, and higher levels of self-serving cognitive distortions and antisocial behavior than the comparison group of normal school children. In addition, cross-sectional relationships were found between moral evaluation, self-serving cognitive distortions, and antisocial behaviour comparable to the relationships found in adolescent samples between moral judgment, self-serving cognitive distortions and antisocial behavior. The question was raised whether in the residential group differences can be found in the strength or the direction of the relationship between moral evaluation, cognitive distortions and antisocial behavior between children that were diagnosed as having reactive attachment disorders (RAD) and children with other types of psychiatric disorders (non-RAD, mostly attention deficit hyperactivity disorder, but also autism, etc.). Children with RAD are viewed as more difficult to treat than children with other types of problems. In a 1-year longitudinal study the direction of the relationships between moral evaluation, self-serving cognitive distortions, and antisocial behavior were investigated. In the RAD group antisocial behavior predicted moral evaluation and cognitive distortions, while the reverse was found in the non-RAD group. Thus, it is important to distinguish between clinical groups when examining the developmental relationship between moral cognitive processes and externalizing problem behavior. For RAD-children, who lack a basic sense of trust, moral-cognitive disorders are an outcome of behavioral problems, while for non-RAD children behavioral disorders are an outcome of interpreting the social environment and their own behavior in a different way. This result seems partly in accordance with the two different directions in the causality of the relationship between trust and fairness.

8 Summary and Policy Implications

Cognitive developmental psychologists study how conceptions of fairness and trust develop over the life-span in many different cultures. They emphasize that children and adolescents essentially (re)construct their conceptions of fairness and trust from their experiences in social relationships. Social perspective-taking opportunities are viewed as permitting a constructive process that is more fundamental than their acquisition of moral values from their parents and other educators through transmission by instruction and modeling. Cooperation fosters cognitive and affective social perspective-taking skills, including the awareness of other individuals having their own desires and views. Reflective moral maturity is correlated with gains in cognitive and social perspective-taking skills. Fairness, empathy and trust become intrinsically related in moral judgment during adolescence. As children mature, and social and educational experiences expand, their moral judgments or concepts of fairness provide an increasingly mature basis for moral values. It is not a surprise that higher levels of moral judgments are positively related to pro-social behaviors, and individuals with antisocial behavior not only score lower on moral judgment as compared to their peers, but also on empathy. Moral judgments extend from an individual level to moral atmosphere at the group and institutional level. At all levels, trust is also viewed as an important moral value.

Actually, the development of trust starts in early childhood. Interpersonal trust (emotional state) arises in attachment. Children develop schemas (expectations about their future relationships) based on the social and affective quality of current parent/educator-child relationships. While interacting with peers, children form new schemas and learn even more about the dimensions of trust and the dynamics of cooperation. Thanks to the development of more complex reasoning skills and cooperation with others, in middle childhood, children are adequately able to rely on the testimony of others, that is, they show epistemic trust (cognitive state). From these experiences and one's personality characteristics, trust develops into moralistic trust. Once these schemas are formed, they establish expectations concerning social relationships. Breaches of these expectancies may damage the social relationships involved.

Besides genetic endowments, the quality of the social interactions between the developing child and the nurturing social environment is critical. Children who lack common social interactions with adults and peers may show disturbances in developing trusting social relationships, deficits in empathic understanding, and a delay in their understanding of fairness. According to cognitive developmentalists, individuals act on their interpretation of events. These interpretations depend on schemas of fairness and trust. Incomplete or poorly developed schemas may have behavioral consequences.

The quality of common social interactions with adults and peers in early childhood foreshadows the close social relationships individuals develop later in life. Understandably, the social and affective quality of early childhood, i.e. sensitive parenting, seems of utmost importance. However, development is never fixed or complete; development remains always possible, even in situations that seem far from ideal. A fully mature moral understanding requires a long process of education and schooling. Future generations will have to find out whether such processes are attainable in countries all over the world.

Five Questions

1. Can you give an example from your own society of the confrontation between a morality based on the behavioral standards of the majority in your society and a morality based on the personal construction of right and wrong as an universal ideal? Argue what needs to have priority in this example and why.
2. Which aspects are distinguished in Gibbs' theory of moral motivation? Give an example in which these aspects interweave and an example in which they conflict with each other.
3. How do you view the developmental order in trust and fairness? Make a distinction between different types of trust.
4. Let's assume that you teach children aged between 5 and 7 years. A pupil approaches you and asks you what to do when s/he is bullied. What advice would you give? Why? Would you advice differ if this student were aged between 11 and 13 years? If so, how?
5. As an educational and developmental psychologist you are asked by a mother about the education of her son. She wants him to become an honest man. What capacities to develop in the child would you stress in your advice to this mother?

References

Ainsworth, M. D. S., Blehar, M., Waters, E., & Wall, S. (1978). *Patterns of attachment*. Hillsdale, NJ: Erlbaum.

Arsenio, W., & Lemerise, E. (2004). Aggression and moral development: Integrating the social information processing and moral domain models. *Child Development, 75*, 987–1002.

Astor, R. A. (1994). Children's moral reasoning about family and peer violence: The role of provocation and retaliation. *Child Development, 65*, 1054–1067.

Bandura, A. (2002). Selective moral disengagement in the exercise of moral agency. *Journal of Moral Education, 31*, 101–119.
Bandura, A. (1962). Social learning through Imitation. In M. R. Jones (Ed.), *Nebraska symposium on motivation*. Lincoln: University of Nebraska Press.
Barriga, A. Q., Morrison, E. M., Liau, A. K., & Gibbs, J. C. (2001). Moral cognition: Explaining the gender difference in antisocial behavior. *Merrill-Palmer Quarterly, 47*, 532–562.
Basinger, K. S., & Gibbs, J. C. (1987). Validation of the sociomoral reflection objective measure-short form. *Psychological Reports, 61*, 139–146.
Beerthuizen, M. G. C. J., & Brugman, D. (2012). Sexually abusive youths' moral reasoning on sex. *Journal of Sexual Aggression, 18*, 125–135.
Beerthuizen, M. G. C. J., & Brugman, D. (2013). Moral value evaluation: A neglected motivational concept in externalizing behaviour research. In K. Heinrichs, F. Oser, & T. Lovat (Eds.), *Handbook of moral motivation: What makes people act morally right?* Rotterdam: Sense Publishers.
Bernath, M. S., & Feshbach, N. D. (1995). Children's trust: Theory, assessment, development, and research directions. *Applied & Preventive Psychology, 4*, 1–19.
Bernath, M. S., Feshbach, N. D., & Gralinski, J. H. (1993). *Physical maltreatment and trust in peers: Feelings, reasons, and behavioral intentions*. Paper presented at the Society for Research in Child Development, March 25–28, 1993.
Betts, L. R., & Rotenberg, K. J. (2008). A social relations analysis of children's trust in their peers across the early years of school. *Social Development, 17*, 1039–1055.
Betts, L. R., Rotenberg, K. J., & Trueman, M. (2009). The early childhood generalized trust belief scale. *Early Childhood Research Quarterly, 24*, 175–185.
Blair, R. J. R., Jones, L., Clark, F., & Smith, M. (1995). Is the psychopath 'morally insane'? *Personality and Individual Differences, 19*, 741–752.
Blair, R. J. R., Monson, J., & Fredrickson, N. (2001). Moral reasoning and conduct problems in children with emotional and behavioral difficulties. *Personality and Individual Differences, 31*, 799–811.
Blasi, A. (1999). Emotions and moral motivation. *Journal for the Theory of Social Behaviour, 29*, 1–19.
Boom, J., Brugman, D., & van der Heijden, P. G. M. (2001). Hierarchical stage structure assessed by sorting moral statements. *Child Development, 72*, 535–548.
Bowlby, J. (1969). *Attachment and Loss, vol. 1: Attachment*. New York: Basic Books.
Bowlby, J. (1973). *Attachment and loss, vol. 2: Separation, anxiety and anger*. New York: Basic Books.
Bretherton, I., & Munholland, K. A. (1999). Internal working models in attachment relationships: a construct revisited. In J. Cassidy & P. R. Shaver (Eds.), *Handbook of attachment* (pp. 89–111). New York: Guilford.
Brugman, D., Basinger, K. S., & Gibbs, J. C. (2007). *Measuring adolescents' moral judgment: an evaluation of the Sociomoral Reflection Measure—Short Form Objective (SRM-SFO)*. Paper presented at the Symposium: Cross-Cultural Research on Moral Reasoning. International Council of Psychologists, San Diego, USA, August 11–14, 2007.
Brugman, D., & Aleva, A. E. (2004). Developmental delay or regression in moral reasoning by juvenile delinquents? *Journal of Moral Education, 33*, 321–338.
Brooker, I., & Poulin-Dubois, D. (2013). Is a Bird an Apple? The effect of speaker labeling accuracy on infants' word learning, imitation, and helping behaviors. *Infancy, 18*, 46–68.
Broome, J. (1990). Fairness. *Proceedings of the Aristotelian Society, 91*, 87–102.
Buhrmester, D., & Furman, W. (1986). The changing functions of friends in childhood: A Neo-Sullivanian perspective. In V. J. Derlega & B. A. Winstead (Eds.), *Friendship and social interaction* (pp. 41–62). New York: Springer.
Cima, M., Tonnaer, F., & Hauser, M. D. (2010). Psychopaths know right from wrong but don't care. *Social Cognitive and Affective Neuroscience, 5*, 59–67.

Clément, F., Koenig, M., & Harris, P. L. (2004). The ontogenesis of trust in testimony. *Mind and Language, 19*, 360–379.

Colby, A., & Damon, W. (1992). *Some do care: Contemporary lives of moral commitment*. New York: Free Press.

Colby, A., & Kohlberg, L. (1987). *The measurement of moral judgment, Vol. 1: Theoretical foundations and research validation*. Cambridge: Cambridge University Press.

Corriveau, K. H., Harris, P. L., Meins, E., Fernyhough, C., Arnott, B., Elliott, L., et al. (2009). Young children's trust in their mother's claims: longitudinal links with attachment security in infancy. *Child Development, 80*, 750–761.

Crawford, E., & O'Dougherty Wright, M. (2007). The impact of childhood psychological maltreatment on interpersonal schemas and subsequent experiences of relationship aggression. *Journal of Emotional Abuse, 7*, 93–116.

DiYanni, C., Nini, D., Rheel, W., & Livelli, A. (2012). "I won't trust you if I think you're trying to deceive me": Relations between selective trust, theory of mind, and imitation in early childhood. *Journal of Cognition and Development, 13*, 354–371.

Erikson, E. H. (1963). *Childhood and society* (2nd ed.). New York: Norton.

Fairness. (2014). *In dictionary.cambridge.org*. Retrieved April 10, 2014, from http://dictionary.cambridge.org/dictionary/british/fairness_1?q=fairness

Flanagan, C. (2003). Trust, identity, and civic hope. *Applied Developmental Science, 7*, 165–171.

Furman, W., & Bierman, K. L. (1984). Children's conceptions of friendship: A multimethod study of developmental changes. *Developmental Psychology, 20*, 925–931.

Garmon, L. C., Basinger, K., Gregg, V. R., & Gibbs, J. C. (1996). Gender differences in stage and expression of moral judgment. *Merrill-Palmer Quarterly, 42*, 418–437.

Gibbs, J. C. (2010). Beyond the conventionally moral [review of nice is not enough]. *Journal of Applied Developmental Psychology, 31*, 106–108.

Gibbs, J. C. (2014). *Moral development and reality: Beyond the theories of Kohlberg, Hoffman, and Haidt*. New York: Oxford University Press.

Gibbs, J. C., Arnold, K. D., Morgan, R. L., Schwartz, E. S., Gavaghan, M. P., & Tappan, M. B. (1984). Construction and validation of a multiple-choice measure of moral reasoning. *Child Development, 55*, 527–536.

Gibbs, J. C., Basinger, K. S., Grimes, R. L., & Snarey, J. R. (2007). Moral judgment development across cultures: Revisiting Kohlberg's universality claims. *Developmental Review, 27*, 443–500.

Gibbs, J. C., Basinger, K. S., & Fuller, D. (1992). *Moral maturity: Measuring the development of sociomoral reasoning*. Hillsdale, NJ: Lawrence Erlbaum.

Gibbs, J. C., Potter, G. B., Goldstein, A. P., & Brentro, L. K. (1996). Equipping youth with mature moral judgment. *Reclaiming Children and Youth, 5*, 156–162.

Gregg, V., Gibbs, J. C., & Basinger, K. S. (1994). Patterns of developmental delay in moral judgment by male and female delinquents. *Merrill-Palmer Quarterly, 40*, 538–553.

Grossman, V. (2010). *The road: Short fiction and articles* (Robert and Elizabeth Chandler, Olga Mukovnikova, Trans.). London: Quercus, Maclehose Press.

Hamann, K., Bender, J., & Tomasello, M. (2014). Meritocratic sharing is based on collaboration in 3-year-olds. *Developmental Psychology, 50*, 121–128.

Hamlin, J. K., Wynn, K., & Bloom, P. (2007). Social evaluation by preverbal infants. *Nature, 450*, 557–559.

Harris, P. L. (2007). Trust. *Developmental Science, 10*, 135–138.

Hoffman, E. (1999). *The right to be human: A biography of Abraham Maslow* (2nd ed.). New York: McGraw-Hill.

Hoffman, M. L. (2000). *Empathy and moral development: Implications for caring and justice*. New York, NY: Cambridge University Press.

Hooker, B. (2005). Fairness. *Ethical Theory and Moral Practice, 8*, 329–352.

Holcombe, R. G. (1983). Applied fairness theory: Comment. *The American Economic Review, 73*, 1153–1156.

Jolliffe, D., & Farrington, D. P. (2004). Empathy and offending: A systematic review and meta-analysis. *Aggression and Violent Behavior, 9*, 441–476.

Jolliffe, D., & Farrington, D. P. (2007). Examining the relationship between low empathy and self-reported offending. *Legal and Criminological Psychology, 12*, 265–286.

Kagan, J. (2013). *The human spark: The science of human development*. New York: Basic Books.

Kahn, P. H., & Turiel, E. (1988). Children's conceptions of trust in the context of social expectations. *Merrill-Palmer Quarterly, 34*, 403–419.

Killen, M., Mulvey, K. L., Richardson, C., Jampol, N., & Woodward, A. (2011). The accidental transgressor: Morally-relevant theory of mind. *Cognition, 119*, 197–215.

Koenig, M. A., & Harris, P. L. (2005). The role of social cognition in early trust. *Trends in Cognitive Sciences, 9*, 457–459.

Koenig, M. A., Clement, F., & Harris, P. L. (2004). Trust in testimony: Children's use of true and false statements. *Psychological Science, 15*, 694–698.

Kohlberg, L. (1971). From is to ought: How to commit the naturalistic fallacy and get away with it in the study of moral development. In T. Mischel (Ed.), *Cognitive development and epistemology*. New York: Academic.

Kohlberg, L. (1984). *Essays on moral development, Vol. 2: The psychology of moral development*. San Francisco: Harper and Row.

Korthals, M. (1994). Over de rol van emoties bij het moreel redeneren. Gibbs' mislukte poging tot integratie van de theorie van Kohlberg met die van Hoffman. [The role of emotions in moral reasoning Gibbs's failed attempt to integrate the theories of Kohlberg and Hoffman]. *Comenius, 14*, 38–49.

Landrum, A. R., Mills, C. M., & Johnston, A. M. (2013). When do children trust the expert? Benevolence information influences children's trust more than expertise. *Developmental Science, 16*, 622–638.

Lapsley, D. K. (2006). Moral stage theory. In M. Killen & J. G. Smetana (Eds.), *Handbook of moral development* (pp. 37–66). Mahwah, NJ: Erlbaum.

Leenders, I., & Brugman, D. (2005). The moral/nonmoral domain shift in relation to delinquent behavior in adolescents. *British Journal of Developmental Psychology, 23*, 65–79.

Lucas, A. J., Lewis, C., Pala, F. C., Wong, K., & Berridge, D. (2013). Social-cognitive processes in preschoolers' selective trust: Three cultures compared. *Developmental Psychology, 49*, 579–590.

Nichols, S. (2004). *Sentimental rules: On the natural foundations of moral judgment*. Oxford: University Press.

Nucci, L. (2000). *The promise and limitations of the moral self construct*. Presidential address delivered at the annual meeting of the Jean Piaget Society, Montreal, Canada

Nucci, L. (2004). Reflections on the moral self construct. In D. K. Lapsley & D. Narvaez (Eds.), *Moral development, self, and identity* (pp. 111–132). Mahwah, NJ: Lawrence Erlbaum.

Nucci, L. P., & Herman, S. (1982). Behavioral disordered children's conceptions of moral, conventional, and personal issues. *Journal of Abnormal Child Psychology, 10*, 411–425.

Nucci, L. P., & Nucci, M. S. (1982). Children's responses to moral and social conventional transgressions in free play settings. *Child Development, 53*, 1337–1342.

Malti, T., Gasser, L., & Buchmann, M. (2009). Emotion attributions and moral reasoning of aggressive and prosocial children. *Aggressive Behavior, 35*, 90–102.

Mascaro, O., & Sperber, D. (2009). The moral, epistemic, and mind reading components of children's vigilance towards deception. *Cognition, 112*, 367–380.

Mills, C. M. (2013). Knowing when to doubt: Developing a critical stance when learning from others. *Developmental Psychology, 49*, 404–418.

Nas, C., Brugman, D., & Koops, W. (2008). Measuring self-serving cognitive distortions with the how i think questionnaire. *European Journal of Psychological Assessment, 24*, 181–189.

Over, H., Carpenter, M., Spears, R., & Gattis, M. (2013). Children selectively trust individuals who have imitated them. *Social Development, 22*, 215–224.

Pasquini, E., Corriveau, K. H., Koenig, M., & Harris, P. L. (2007). Preschoolers monitor the relative accuracy of informants. *Developmental Psychology, 43*, 1216–1226.

Piaget, J. (1932). *The moral judgment of the child.* New York: Free Press.

Power, F. C., Higgins, A., & Kohlberg, L. (1989). *Lawrence Kohlberg's approach to moral education.* New York: Columbia University Press.

Pratt, M. W., Skoe, E. E., & Arnold, M. L. (2004). The development of care reasoning in later adolescence: A longitudinal analysis. *International Journal of Behavioral Development, 28*, 139–147.

Rawls, J. (1999). *A theory of Justice* (Revised ed.). Cambridge: Harvard University Press.

Rescher, N. (2002). *Fairness: Theory and practice of distributive justice.* New Brunswick: Transaction Publishers.

Rest, J. R., Narvaez, D., Thoma, S. J., & Bebeau, M. J. (1999). *Postconventional moral thinking: A Neo-Kohlbergian approach.* Mahwah, NJ: Lawrence Erlbaum.

Ribeaud, D., & Eisner, M. (2010). Are moral disengagement, neutralization techniques, and self-serving cognitive distortions the same? Developing a unified scale of moral neutralization of aggression. *International Journal of Conflict and Violence, 4*, 298–315.

Rotenberg, K. J. (1980). "A promise kept, a promise broken": Developmental bases of trust. *Child Development, 51*, 614–617.

Rotenberg, K. J. (1984). Sex differences in children's trust in peers. *Sex Roles, 12*, 953–957.

Rotenberg, K. J. (1986). Same-sex patterns and sex differences in the trust-value basis of children's friendship. *Sex Roles, 15*, 613–626.

Rotenberg, K. J. (1994). Loneliness and interpersonal trust. *Journal of Social and Clinical Psychology, 13*, 152–173.

Rotenberg, K. J. (2010). The conceptualization of interpersonal trust: A basis, domain, and target framework. In K. J. Rotenberg (Ed.), *Interpersonal trust during childhood and adolescence* (pp. 2–27). New York: Cambridge University Press.

Rotenberg, K. J., Addis, N., Betts, L. R., Corrigan, A., Fox, C., Hobson, Z., et al. (2010). The relation between trust beliefs and loneliness during early childhood, middle childhood, and adulthood. *Personality and Social Psychology Bulletin, 36*, 1086–1100.

Rotenberg, K. J., Betts, L. R., & Moore, J. (2013). The relation between early adolescents' trust beliefs in peers and reactions to peer provocation: Attributions of intention and retaliation. *The Journal of Genetic Psychology: Research and Theory on Human Development, 174*, 450–456.

Rotenberg, K. J., MacDonald, K. J., & King, E. V. (2004). The relationship between loneliness and interpersonal trust during middle childhood. *The Journal of Genetic Psychology, 165*, 233–249.

Rotenberg, K. J., & Mann, L. (1986). The development of the norm of the reciprocity of self-disclosure and its function in children's attraction to peers. *Child Development, 57*, 1349–1357.

Rotenberg, K. J., & Pilipenko, T. A. (1983–1984). Mutuality, temporal consistency, and helpfulness in children's trust in peers. *Social Cognition, 2*, 235–255.

Rousseau, D. M., Sitkin, S. B., Burt, R. S., & Camerer, C. (1998). Not so different after all: A cross discipline view of trust. *Academy of Management Review, 23*, 393–404.

Schonert-Reichl, K. A. (1999). Relations of peer acceptance, friendship, adjustment, and social behavior to moral reasoning during early adolescence. *Journal of Early Adolescence, 19*, 249–279.

Selman, R. L., & Selman, A. E. (1979). Children's ideas about friendship: A new theory. *Psychology Today, 13*, 71–80.

Smetana, J. G. (1981). Preschool children's conceptions of moral and social rules. *Child Development, 52*, 1333–1336.

Smetana, J. G. (1989). Adolescents' and parents' reasoning about actual family conflict. *Child Development, 60*, 105–1067.

Smetana, J. (1995). Parenting styles and conceptions of parental authority during adolescence. *Child Development, 66*, 299–316.

Smetana, J. G., Killen, M., & Turiel, E. (1991). Children's reasoning about interpersonal and moral conflicts. *Child Development, 62*, 629–644.
Snarey, J. (1985). The cross-cultural universality of social-moral development: A critical review of Kohlbergian research. *Psychological Bulletin, 97*, 202–232.
Stams, G. J. M. M., Brugman, D., Dekovic, M., Van Rosmalen, L., van der Laan, P., & Gibbs, J. C. (2006). The moral judgment of juvenile delinquents: A meta-analysis. *Journal of Abnormal Child Psychology, 34*, 697–713.
Tisak, M. S. (1995). Domains of social reasoning and beyond. *Annals of Child Development, 11*, 95–130.
Tisak, M. S., & Turiel, E. (1988). Variation in seriousness of transgressions and children's moral and conventional concepts. *Developmental Psychology, 24*, 352–357.
Tisak, M. S., Tisak, J., & Goldstein, S. E. (2006). Aggression, morality, and delinquency: A social cognitive perspective. In M. Killen & J. Smetana (Eds.), *Handbook of moral development* (pp. 611–632). Mahwah, NJ: Lawrence Erlbaum.
Trust. (2014). *In dictionary.cambridge.org*. Retrieved April 10, 2014, from http://dictionary.cambridge.org/dictionary/british/trust_1?q=trust
Turiel, E. (1998). The development of morality. In W. Damon (Ed.), *Handbook of child psychology* (5th ed.). Vol. 3: N. Eisenberg (Ed.), *Social, emotional, and personality development* (pp. 863–932). New York: Academic Press.
Turiel, E. (2006). Thought, emotions, and social interactional processes in moral development. In M. Killen, & J. G. Smetana (Eds.), *Handbook of moral development* (pp. 7–35). Mahwah, NJ: Erlbaum.
Turiel, E. (1983). *The development of social knowledge: Morality and convention*. Cambridge: Cambridge University Press.
United Nations. (2014a). *Universal declaration of human rights*. Retrieved January 29, 2014, from http://www.un.org/en/documents/udhr/index.shtml
United Nations. (2014b). *The Office of the United Nations High Commissioner for Human Rights (OHCHR)*. Retrieved January 29, 2014, from http://www.ohchr.org/EN/Issues/Pages/WhatareHumanRights.aspx
Uslaner, E. M. (2001, September). Trust as a moral value. Paper presented at the Conference: *Social Capital: Interdisciplinary Perspectives*. University of Exeter, United Kingdom
Uslaner, E. M. (2002). *The moral foundations of trust*. New York: Cambridge University Press.
Van Boxtel, K., Brugman, D., Van de Schoot, R., & Aleva, A. E. (2013). *Moral cognitions and externalizing problem behavior in children: differences between psychiatric disorders*. Poster presented at the 8th International Conference on Child and Adolescent Psychopathology, Roehampton University, London, 15–17 July 2013.
Van der Velden, F., Brugman, D., Boom, J., & Koops, W. (2010). Moral cognitive processes explaining antisocial behavior in young adolescents. *International Journal of Behavioral Development, 34*, 292–301.
Van Ijzendoorn, M., & Zwart-Woudstra, H. A. (1995). Adolescents' attachment representations and moral reasoning. *The Journal of Genetic Psychology, 156*, 359–372.
Van Vugt, E., Stams, G. J., Deković, M., Brugman, D., Rutten, E., & Hendriks, J. (2008). Moral development and solo juvenile sex offenders. *Journal of Sexual Aggression, 14*, 1–11.
Walker, L. J. (2006). Gender and morality. In M. Killen & J. G. Smetana (Eds.), *Handbook of moral development* (pp. 93–115). Mahwah, NJ: Erlbaum.
Walker, L. J., & Frimer, J. A. (2007). Moral personality of brave and caring exemplars. *Journal of Personality and Social Psychology, 93*, 845–860.
Walker, L. J., & Hennig, K. H. (1997). Moral development in the broader context of personality. In S. Hala (Ed.), *The development of social cognition* (pp. 297–327). East Sussex: Psychology Press.
Xu, F., Evans, A. D., Li, C., Li, Q., Heyman, G., & Lee, K. (2014). The role of honesty and benevolence in children's judgments of trustworthiness. *International Journal of Behavioral Development, 37*, 257–265.

Results of the Second Round of the International Self-Report Delinquency (ISRD2) Study: Importance of Education and Social Learning for 12–15 Year Olds

Ineke Haen Marshall

Abstract The first part of this chapter describes the basic structural contours of youth crime and victimization in a comparative perspective; the second part of the chapter focuses on the importance of school, education and social learning. Accordingly, this chapter reports on the results of a large international collaborative study of juvenile delinquency and victimization (International Self Report Delinquency Study—ISRD2) conducted in 30 countries between 2006 and 2008. About 68,000 pupils in grades 7, 8 and 9 (12–15 year old) answered questions about alcohol and drug use, offending, victimization, family, school, friends, neighborhood and attitudes towards violence. Presentation of the results uses six country clusters, based on an expansion of Esping-Andersen's (1990) welfare regimes: Anglo-Saxon countries (liberal model), West-European countries (corporatist model), Scandinavian countries (social democratic model), South European countries (Mediterranean model), Post-socialist countries, and a Latin American group. The overall result is that delinquent behavior and victimization is a rather common, typical experience among most youth. Youth who spend more time with family rather than friends, and youth who like school and perform well are less likely to commit delinquent acts (and be victimized) than their counterparts. This finding is true for all 30 countries in the study.

1 Introduction

This chapter reports on youth crime and victimization in Europe and a handful of non-European countries, using the results from the International Self-Report Delinquency Study (ISRD), a large international collaborative self-report study of delinquency, substance use and victimization. The ISRD project is an ongoing research

I.H. Marshall (✉)
Northeastern University, Boston, MA, USA
e-mail: i.marshall@neu.edu

H. Kury et al. (eds.), *Women and Children as Victims and Offenders: Background, Prevention, Reintegration*, DOI 10.1007/978-3-319-08398-8_11

study of delinquency and victimization among youth, using standardized instruments and data collection procedures. The primary focus has been on Europe, but the ISRD project also includes a number of non-European countries.

2 The International Self-Report Delinquency: Measuring Crime and Victimization in Europe and Beyond

The ISRD project has two primary objectives; (a) Observe and compare differences, similarities, and trends in offending and victimization between countries, (b) Explore and test theoretical issues related to juvenile delinquency and victimization, while maintaining relevance for policy purposes. Data was first collected in 1990–1991 among 13 countries (ISRD1), and in 2005–2008 in 31 countries (ISRD2). The third data collection sweep (ISRD3) is currently on-going, with about 35 partners across the globe (2012–2016). In this chapter, results from the second round of the ISRD (ISRD2) are presented.[1]

A total of 31 countries participated in ISRD2. When analyzing the data for earlier publications, we grouped the ISRD2 countries into six country clusters, using the Esping-Anderson typology elaborated by Saint-Arnaud and Bernard (2003). This clustering appeared to be rather useful, since the country clusters differ significantly with respect to welfare regimes (including youth-related policies), culture, history, and economic prosperity. In this paper, the same country clustering is employed:

- The Anglo-Saxon cluster, including the United States, Canada and Ireland[2];
- The West-European cluster, including Germany, France, Belgium, Netherlands, Austria and Switzerland;
- The Scandinavian cluster, covering all Northern European countries (Finland, Sweden, Norway, Denmark and Iceland);
- The South-European cluster, including Spain, Italy, Portugal, and Cyprus;
- The Post-Socialist countries, comprising the Czech Republic, Poland, Hungary, Estonia, Lithuania, Slovenia, Bosnia, Armenia and Russia;
- A Latin-American cluster, comprising a rather heterogeneous group: Venezuela, Netherlands Antilles, Aruba and Surinam.

Directly comparing survey results from different countries is difficult, since it is always possible that the observed differences are the result from differences in the way the study was conducted (how was the questionnaire administered? How was the sample selected? Were there differences in the wording of the questions, due to

[1] For detailed information on the International Self-Report Delinquency (ISRD) Study, see Junger-Tas et al. (1994, 2003, 2010, 2012), Enzmann et al. (2010), Marshall and Enzmann (2012). Parts of this chapter draw from these published works.

[2] Canada was excluded from some of the analyses because of concerns related to data protection.

translation?). Although the ISRD used a standardized methodology in hopes of minimizing this problem, most of the participating countries had to make some adjustments for their particular situation, resulting in a *contextual standardization*. This means, simply stated, that we need to be cautious when interpreting comparative results. As a general rule, in studies such as the ISRD, we can be pretty confident about findings related to hypothesis-testing of crime theories (since exact comparability between countries is not so important here), but we need to approach strictly descriptive findings (for example, estimates of offending or victimization rates as presented in the next section) with a bit more caution.

The ISRD2 used a mixed sampling strategy, that is, most (21) of the countries drew samples from one or two cities, while nine countries complemented a national sample with an oversampling of one or two cities. For the descriptive analysis presented in the first part of the paper, where the comparability of the samples is important, data from 60 cities are used (n = 40,678) instead of the entire international sample. In the second part of the paper, for theoretical purposes (where the comparability of samples is not crucial), we use the entire sample of 67,883 cases (pupils). Within the selected cities and towns, probability samples of 7th, 8th and 9th grade classrooms were used where the pupils were asked to complete a paper-and-pencil questionnaire within the classroom. Unfortunately, the 30 countries were quite different with regard to cooperation by the schools, the parents, and the pupils, cautioning us once again that direct cross-national comparisons may be misleading. That is, some country samples are more representative of the entire country than others. However, by grouping countries into larger clusters, some of the national idiosyncrasies in sampling cancel each other out to a certain degree. With these cautions in mind, let us now take a look at what those 12–15 year old pupils tell us about their experiences with offending and victimization.

2.1 Delinquency in 60 Cities: Some Expected and Some Unexpected Findings

The young people were asked about 12 behaviors (vandalism, theft, extortion, burglary, bicycle theft, car theft, theft from car, purse snatching, carrying a weapon, group fight, assault, and selling drugs). These behaviors were selected because they make sense in all national contexts and they are considered illegal in all countries involved. For each of these 12 items, they were asked about "ever" (life time prevalence) and "last year" (last year prevalence). Following a tradition in studies of delinquency, we first present a rather general measure of delinquency involvement (overall delinquency); that is, if a pupil answered positive to any of the 12 items listed above, he or she is considered as a delinquent. When looking at the data, we need to keep in mind that this measure covers a broad range of delinquent involvement, ranging from the youth who admits to one act of damaging property (vandalism), to the youth who admits to two assaults, one burglary, and 10 drug deals. Table 1 presents the results

When looking at the lifetime prevalence rates for the individual countries, we see a rather wide range of values, between a low of 22.8 (Cyprus), 25.9 (Portugal) and 27.1 (Venezuela) to a high of 46.3 (Finland), 47.3 (France), 47.4 (Aruba) and 56.2 (Ireland). Thus, Irish youth were twice as likely to report that they "ever" committed some kind of delinquent act as their Venezuelan counterparts. When comparing the averages (for life-time prevalence) for the different country clusters, we see that the Anglo-Saxon cluster, Western European cluster and the Northern European cluster have higher average prevalence rates than the three other groups (Latin America, Mediterranean and Post-Socialist group). A similar pattern is found when looking at "last year" prevalence rates (which overall tend to be lower of

Table 1 Lifetime and "Last Year" delinquency prevalence (%) in 60 cities (n = 43,101) (Adapted from Junger-Tas 2012, Table 3.1, p. 70)

Country/ Cluster	Lifetime prevalence	Last year prevalence	Country/ Cluster	Lifetime prevalence	Last year prevalence
Ireland	56.2	40.1	Czech Republic	39.7	24.5
United States	44.1	28.8	Armenia	29.8	22.0
Canada	36.5	20.1	Estonia	37.5	20.8
Anglo-Saxon	***45.6***	***29.6***	Hungary	45.3	27.0
Germany	47.9	29.0	Lithuania	30.8	19.0
Netherlands	45.8	29.3	Slovenia	28.7	17.2
France	47.3	28.9	Poland	29.4	16.3
Belgium	41.0	25.1	Russia	29.5	17.7
Switzerland	42.9	24.6	Bosnia-Herzeg.	24.5	16.1
Austria	40.6	22.1	***Post-Socialist***	***32.8***	***20.1***
Western Europe	***44.3***	***26.5***	Aruba	47.4	25.5
Denmark	43.0	26.5	Dutch Antilles	40.3	20.1
Finland	46.3	20.7	Surinam	36.0	16.2
Iceland	42.6	20.9	Venezuela	27.1	13.8
Sweden	36.5	19.7	***Latin American***	***37.7***	***18.9***
Norway	33.3	16.6			
Northern Europe	***40.3***	***20.9***			
Italy	39	25.6			
Spain	37.2	21.4			
Cyprus	22.8	15.6			
Portugal	25.9	14.5			
Mediterranean	***31.2***	***19.3***			

course than the "ever" prevalence): Anglo-Saxon and Western European countries on average tend to have the highest levels of self-reported delinquency (29.6 and 26.5 respectively). Another notable observation is the rather *ubiquitous* nature of youth crime: between one-fifth and over half of the youth in the sample admits to ever having done any of the 12 items. Taking into consideration that offending behavior tends to be underreported (because of the so-called social desirability effect), these figures tend to confirm the common observation that engaging in some form of delinquent behavior is a rather common, typical experience among most youth.

Differences between the clusters reflect essentially differences in property crime (higher in Western Europe, Anglo-Saxon countries and Northern Europe), and are much less shaped by differences in violent crime, where there is much more variation between the countries. Typically, policymakers are not so much interested in the many youths who occasionally commit minor property crime; rather they tend to be more concerned about those youth who are involved in *frequent, repeated delinquent behavior*. Our data shows that the large majority of youth who admit to at least one offense have been involved only in relatively minor offenses (such as shoplifting, vandalism, group fights). Only 6 % of the offenders reported exclusively serious offenses (such as burglary, car theft, assault, drug dealing, robbery, theft).[3] Also, most of the offenses are committed infrequently; youths who report committing an offense more than five times during the last year are rare and are mainly found among the non-serious offenders (Junger-Tas 2012, pp. 74–75). Again, it is possible to see a pattern related to country clusters: The Anglo-Saxon, Western and Northern European clusters show that offenders there commit not only more offenses, but they also report a larger *variety* of offenses (i.e. have a higher versatility) than youth in the other clusters.

The ISRD data confirms the observation that males tend to be involved in more frequent and more serious delinquency than females. Also consistent with what we know to be true from many other studies, the gender gap is largest for violent offending, less so for property offending. And, not surprisingly, as in many other studies, shoplifting remains an exception to the gender gap: differences between boys and girls with regard to their involvement in shoplifting are very small. And—last but not least—our data show that most juvenile offending is a group activity (Junger-Tas 2012, p. 85). Even in Latin America, where a relatively larger proportion of offenses are done by solo offenders (compared to the other five clusters), most offenses are done in the company of peers (except purse snatching and assault, where only respectively 37 and 47 % are committed with others) (Junger-Tas 2012, Table 2).

[3] See Junger-Tas (2012) for more details.

Table 2 Last year victimization prevalence rates (in %) by clusters and countries (medium and large cities) (n = 40,000) (Table modified from Gruszczyńska et al. 2012, Table 4.2, p. 98)

	Extortion	Assault	Theft	Bullying	Total criminal victimization
Country clusters					
Ireland	6.3	4.0	19.6	16.2	24.1
United States	5.5	4.7	33.0	20.6	35.5
Anglo-Saxon	***5.9***	***4.3***	***26.4***	***18.4***	***29.9***
Germany	4.8	6.1	29.1	18.5	34.2
Netherlands	4.1	4.9	22.9	14.4	27.3
France	3.4	4.3	15.7	17.7	19.7
Belgium	2.6	2.8	18.6	16.7	21.2
Switzerland	4.0	3.4	27.0	12.4	29.8
Austria	3.3	4.2	25.1	9.7	28.3
Western Europe	***3.7***	***4.3***	***23.2***	***14.9***	***26.8***
Denmark	4.1	3.8	21.2	15.1	24.6
Finland	3.7	2.4	14.9	12.3	18.0
Iceland	1.2	4.1	20.4	9.3	22.5
Sweden	3.1	2.3	25.2	10.0	27.2
Norway	2.7	3.6	23.3	13.4	25.3
Northern Europe	***3.0***	***3.2***	***20.9***	***12.0***	***23.5***
Italy	2.6	3.0	16.8	14.6	19.1
Spain	8.9	1.2	15.9	14.0	22.0
Cyprus	1.7	3.2	14.6	9.8	16.7
Portugal	8.6	1.2	14.2	4.0	18.3
Mediterranean	***5.5***	***2.1***	***15.4***	***10.6***	***19.0***
Czech Republic	3.2	3.3	20.0	10.1	23.5
Armenia	1.1	4.2	9.1	2.4	12.9
Estonia	8.0	6.8	25.0	24.8	31.0
Hungary	12.9	5.9	25.7	17.9	33.2
Lithuania	7.7	2.8	14.4	18.5	20.0
Slovenia	7.2	5.6	34.1	28.0	38.2
Poland	8.2	6.1	19.3	13.9	25.9
Russia	8.8	7.9	13.8	15.7	23.2
Bosnia-Herzeg	10.4	4.7	21.5	6.1	29.0
Post-Socialist	***7.5***	***5.2***	***20.3***	***15.2***	***26.3***
Aruba	5.0	4.7	31.4	19.8	34.6
Dutch Antilles	4.8	7.7	27.5	17.1	32.4
Surinam	6.3	6.2	21.1	9.7	26.3
Venezuela	9.3	4.0	28.6	13.4	33.9
Latin American	***6.3***	***5.7***	***27.2***	***15.1***	***31.8***

2.1.1 Youth as Victims

We know quite a bit about the victimization of adults and older adolescents through the International Crime Victim Survey (Van Dijk et al. 2007), but there is much less information about the victimization of 12–15 year olds, the target group of our study. The ISRD2 survey asked pupils some questions about "some bad things that may have happened to you" in the last 12 months, and then proceeded to ask about having been the victim of extortion or robbery, assault, theft and bullying. Table 2 presents the rates (% of pupils who answered "yes" to questions about particular kinds of victimization) of victimization of the pupils in the 30 countries involved in the study.

The first observation is that being victimized is not an uncommon experience for many youth in our study. Overall, the most likely form of victimization of youth is *theft*: more than 1 in 5 pupils responded that something had been stolen from them the last year. The rates vary between a high of about one-third of kids reported having been the victim of theft [U.S. (33.0 %), Slovenia (34.1 %) and Aruba (31.4 %)] to a low of about one out of every ten kids (Armenia (9.1 %). When comparing cluster averages, Latin America (27.2 %), Anglo-Saxon countries (26.4 %) and the Western European cluster (23.2 %) seem to have the greatest problem with theft. The Mediterranean countries report overall the lowest level of theft victimization (15.4 %), and the Post-Socialist and Northern European countries occupy a middle position (respectively 20.3 and 20.9 %). Here we need to note that (cluster) averages at times only provide part of the picture. Indeed, there appears to be a large degree of variability *within* some of the clusters, in particular in the Post-Socialist cluster (that includes both the lowest—Armenia—and the highest—Slovenia—ranking country).

Bullying also appears to be a fairly common experience among our youth. Interestingly, comparable to the just described theft victimization, both Slovenia (28.0 %) and the US (20.6 %) rank among the top countries. A few countries have a rather low rate of reported bullying [e.g. Armenia (2.4 %), Portugal (4.0 %) and Bosnia-Herzegovina (6.1 %)]. Comparable to what we saw with regard to theft victimization, the Anglo-Saxon country cluster ranks highest (18.4 %), while the Mediterranean cluster ranks lowest (10.6 %).

Extortion/robbery and *assault* are—fortunately—much more infrequent experiences among the surveyed youth. Being threatened and forced to give up some personal property seemed relatively prevalent in a number of the Post-socialist countries [Hungary (12.9 %), Bosnia-Herzegovina (10.4 %), Estonia (8.0 %), Russia (8.8 %) and Poland (8.2 %)], in two Mediterranean countries [Spain (8.9 %) and Portugal (8.6 %)], and in Venezuela (9.3 %). On the other hand, very few youth in Armenia (1.1 %), Iceland (1.2 %) and Cyprus (1.7 %) reported that they had been a victim of robbery. The Post-socialist and Latin American clusters have the highest average prevalence rate (7.5 and 6.3 % respectively), Western and Northern Europe report the lowest average rate (3.7 and 3.0 % respectively), with the Anglo-Saxon and Mediterranean countries occupying a middle position (5.9 and 5.5 % respectively).

The question about assault tries to measure rather serious violent victimization by asking the youngster if—in the last year—"Someone hit you violently or hurt you so much that you had to see a doctor?" A handful of countries report a prevalence rate of more than 5 (out of 100): Russia (7.9 %), Netherland Antilles

(7.7 %), Estonia (6.8 %), Germany (6.1 %), Hungary (5.9 %), Poland (6.1 %), and Surinam (6.2 %). The lowest rates are reported by Spanish and Portuguese adolescents (1.2 %). Comparing averages, we find that Latin American and Post Socialist clusters score highest (5.7 and 5.2 % respectively), Anglo-Saxon and Western European countries are in the middle (4.3 % for both), while Northern Europe and the Mediterranean countries report the lowest average prevalence score (3.2 and 2.1 % respectively).

Focusing on *criminal* victimization only, which excludes bullying, Table 2 shows that the Mediterranean cluster has the lowest *overall* level of criminal victimization (assault, extortion, theft) (19.0 %), whereas Latin America (31.8 %) and the Anglo-Saxon cluster (29.9 %) report the highest averages. When focusing on violent offenses only (assault and extortion/robbery), we find that violent victimization occurs most often in Latin American countries, Post-socialist countries, and Anglo-Saxon countries.

Overlap between Offending and Victimization. We used to think that delinquent youth are separate and distinct from kids who are the victims of violence or property crime. Starting some 20 years ago, criminologists started to re-consider that old assumption, and indeed by now a large body of research has shown that there is considerable overlap between those who offend and those who victimize (see, for example, Schreck et al. 2008). The data from our youth study confirm this conclusion, and we also found a considerable degree of overlap between offending and victimization. That is, kids who report that they are victimized tend to be more likely to report that they commit delinquent acts (see Posick 2013). Unfortunately, our data do not allow us to determine any temporal or causal order, so we cannot conclude that the experience of being a victim *results* in a youngster to be more likely to commit delinquent acts. It is also possible that hanging out with a group of friends in unsupervised settings results in *both* a greater chance of becoming a victim as well as increasing the likelihood of getting into trouble with the law.

2.1.2 A Note of Caution: Correlation is not the Same as Causation

At this point, it is important to stress that in a survey study such as the ISRD, we cannot use the responses to demonstrate cause and effect. Delinquency theories use cause and effect language: poverty causes crime, or lacking self-control causes delinquency. But we have to be cautious in assuming that we can *directly* test these causal links. We ask the students a large number of questions about their family, their experiences in school, their neighborhood, their friends, and their attitudes and beliefs and we also ask detailed questions about offending and victimization. The reason for all these background questions is, of course, to see if any of these are *related* to greater likelihood of delinquency or victimization. For example, many youth surveys have found that youths who have a strong bond with their parents are less likely to be delinquent than their counterparts who do not get along with their parents at all.

Finding such *correlation*, however, does not mean that we then may conclude that low affective attachment to parents *causes* the child to become delinquent. There are many different possible reasons or causes for getting involved in delinquency, and it is very well possible that the parental bond with the child only weakened *after* he or she got involved in delinquency (for a number of other reasons). If we want to draw conclusions about cause and effect, we need to have a study which collects *repeated* data on the child over time (i.e. a longitudinal design such as the Cambridge Study in Delinquent Development). Since the ISRD study collects information about the child only at one point in time, conclusions need to be limited to *correlates* of delinquency and victimization. However, if we find (as we did) that the results of correlational studies such as ours are consistent with those found in studies with a design more suitable for detecting cause-effect, we gain confidence that our conclusions have direct relevance for the testing- and developing of delinquency theories as well as having legitimate policy implications for delinquency prevention.

In earlier publications (Junger-Tas et al. 2010, 2012b), the main findings of our international survey have been presented. For purposes of this chapter, we want to focus primarily on those findings that are related to the role of the school and (social) learning theory (Akers and Jensen 2003).

2.2 *The Role of School and Learning in Delinquency*

There are many different theories which aim to explain why some individuals get involved in delinquency while others don't, or why some teens' delinquent behavior gets worse over time whereas other teens' law-violating behavior remains limited to very minor, sporadic problematic behavior (see, for example, Moffitt 1993). The ISRD project collected information that allows the testing of a number of the most popular theories of youth crime: Social bonding/social control theory (Hirschi 1969; Sampson and Laub 1993), self-control theory (Gottfredson and Hirschi 1990), routine activities/opportunity theory (Cohen and Felson 1979), social disorganization/collective efficacy theory (Bursik and Grasmick 1993; Sampson et al. 1997), general strain theory (Agnew 2005) and social learning theory (Akers 1985). Previous analyses of the ISRD2 data have shown some support for aspects of all of these theories, suggesting that an integration of different theoretical perspectives may be the best way to proceed. Not all theories provide clear policy implications however. In the remainder of this chapter, we want to focus on one of the main life domains of immediate relevance to adolescents: the *school*. Schools are more amenable to policy changes than, for example, the family or the child's personality or aptitudes. The school is the place where formal learning takes place, but it also provides an important context for informal learning (of values and norms, of appropriate and inappropriate behavior).

Formal learning is important, but perhaps even more important are informal learning processes, particularly in the formative adolescent years. Much of the informal learning is shaped by a child's friends and peers who attend the same school.[4] Below we report on what we found out about the relationship between pupils' experiences in school and their level of self-reported delinquency.

2.2.1 School Experiences and Delinquency

The school plays a crucial role in adolescents' lives. It is the place where they spend a large part of their waking hours, where they make and meet friends, where they are exposed to adult role models (teachers) other than their parents, where they learn critical skills needed for functioning in society (reading, writing and mathematics) and where they learn about history, larger society, government, politics, and morality.[5] In many societies, education is also considered a prerequisite for becoming an independent and economically successful adult. Not surprisingly, therefore, there is a large body of scholarship on the link between youngsters' experiences within the school system and problem behavior, such as delinquency and drug use (For example, Cohen 1955; Gottfredson 2001).

Individual School Problems and Delinquency

Anomie or strain theory (Merton 1938, Agnew 2005) hypothesizes that individuals whose path to success is blocked become frustrated and may turn to alternative ways of becoming successful, if not in the eyes of larger society, than at least in the eyes of their peers. And these alternative ways often include delinquency, or other forms of deviant behavior. Over half a century ago, the American criminologist Cohen (1955) wrote in his book *Delinquent Boys* how lower income boys often fail to meet the schools' "middle class measuring rod" of high academic achievement and "proper" social demeanor and clothing. These disadvantaged youngsters then start to form delinquent subcultures with other lower-income boys who experience similar status frustration in the school context. Cohen introduces the notion of *reaction formation* to account for the often negativistic, destructive and malicious character of delinquency. Although Cohen's theory has not gone without challenges, the basic premise of linking problems in school with delinquency and other risky behavior (such as drinking and drug use) has been confirmed time and time again. As we discuss below, ISRD2 data confirm this observation, not just for kids

[4] It goes without saying that the family is the primary and most important socializing influence on a child. That is where most of the informal learning takes place in early childhood. However, in the early teen years, typically, there is a shift of the importance of the family towards friends and peers instead.

[5] In some schools, morality is an explicit part of the curriculum, for example in faith-based schools. Virtually all schools, however, focus on the importance of following rules, and of acceptable and appropriate behavior. Schools have a crucial socializing function, teaching youth the norms and values of society.

in one country, but for the large sample of kids representing 30 countries. But the picture is complicated.

In the ISRD2 questionnaire, a number of questions were related to the student's *performance*: one objective measure (school failure, i.e. repeating a grade) and one subjective measure (self-assessment of achievement, i.e. do the students think they perform better, the same or worse than their classmates?). Students were also asked about their *aspirations* concerning continuing their education after compulsory school. In our sample, repeating classes and below average performance are weakly related to higher levels of delinquency, as are low educational aspirations (Marshall and Marshall 2015), but—as we will discuss shortly—other school-related factors (such as truancy and type of school context) appear to be much more important.

Another important theory in criminology is *social control—or social bonding theory* (Hirschi 1969; Sampson and Laub 1993). In its original form, the theory claims that delinquency is the result of weakened or broken bonds to society (i.e. family, school, peers). The strength of the social bond is measured through four components: *attachment* to significant others (parents, teachers, or friends), *involvement* in conventional activities, *commitment* to conformity, and *beliefs* in the norms of society. The stronger these four social bonds, the lower the likelihood of delinquency. The ISRD asked students whether they *like school* (as a measure of attachment to school). The data show that students who like their school are less likely to get involved in delinquency (Junger-Tas et al. 2012b). The ISRD2 survey also asks about skipping school without a legitimate excuse. And interestingly, we find that *truancy* (skipping school regularly) is a much stronger predictor of delinquency than school performance or liking school (Junger-Tas et al. 2012b, Chapter 12, Lucia et al. 2012).[6] Social bonding theory states that skipping school without an excuse on a regular basis means that the adolescent is not attached to conventional society, that he or she feels there is not much to lose by challenging the conventional norms (i.e. kids are supposed to go to school), and that therefore he or she is free to break the law (Junger-Tas et al. 2012a, p. 332).

The important role of truancy as a risk factor for delinquency is also predicted by *routine activity/opportunity* theory (Cohen and Felson 1979). A major claim of this approach is that everyday life and movements of people are of prime importance in understanding patterns of victimization and crime. In delinquency research, opportunity theory is tested through measuring the availability of opportunities for young people to commit delinquent acts. Truant youth are not under the supervision of responsible adults (parents or teachers), and are likely to hang out in public settings. Hanging out in public places, unsupervised, with large groups of friends has been shown to be a strong set of predictors of delinquency in previous research (Hay and Forrest 2008; Wikstrom et al. 2012). We will come back to this later, but for now it

---

[6] In Lucia and colleagues' (2012) controlled analysis of school-related variables, the strongest contribution in terms of explained variance in versatility of delinquency came from truancy in all 6 country clusters, although the strength of the association varied by cluster (Anglo-Saxon cluster 0.29; West European cluster 0.25, North European cluster 0.28; Southern Europe 0.21; Post-socialist 0.19 and Latin American cluster 0.17) (pp. 215–216).

suffices to note that truant youth probably have a low commitment to following social conventions (low stake in conformity), *and* are without supervision of adults, thereby creating more opportunity for getting into trouble.

Structural School Problems and Delinquency

Doing poorly in school, disliking school, and skipping school are all *individual* characteristics and behaviors of adolescents. Though these individual factors appear to have a link with delinquent behavior,[7] it is important to recognize that schools and their structural characteristics may be more important than the individual features of students (Rutter et al. 1979; Gottfredson 2001 cited in Lucia et al. 2012, p. 234). Schools vary widely in the quality of teachers, strength and rigor of curriculum, physical resources, and composition of student body to mention but a few of the more obvious structural characteristics. These structural characteristics influence undoubtedly the performance, educational aspirations, and amount of truancy of pupils. The ISRD2 questionnaire asked students several questions about their perception of their school functioning and school climate. Based on responses to answers to four questions (there is a lot of stealing in my school; there is a lot of fighting in my school; many things are broken or vandalized in my school; there is a lot of drug use in my school), we created a *school disorganization* scale.[8] Analysis of the international sample shows that school disorganization is a relatively strong correlate of delinquency, that is, youth who attend schools with higher levels of stealing, fighting, vandalism and drug use tend to be more delinquent than kids who go to schools without these problems.[9] Although this is *not* a direct measure of the quality of the school, the teachers, physical structure or curriculum, this measure is an indicator of the amount of disorder that is present in the school context. And this aspect of the *school environment* appears to have a significant influence on individual pupils' delinquent involvement, more so than their performance, repeating classes or educational aspirations. Interesting to mention in this context is that school disorganization also is related to increasing the likelihood of becoming a *victim* of theft or assault (Gruszczyńska et al. 2012, p. 115).

---

[7] These individual-level school factors appear to play a role—albeit small and with some variability—in all six country clusters (Lucia et al. 2012, pp. 215–216).

[8] Mean of the scale is 37.9 (range 1–100); standard deviation = 25.1; Cronbach's alpha = 0.75 which means it is a reliable scale.

[9] Multivariate regression analysis on control variables (age, gender and immigration status) and school variables (repeating classes, educational aspirations, truancy, liking schools, school bonding and school disorganization) with delinquency versatility for the six country clusters shows that the impact of school disorganization was quite comparable in the six country clusters (Anglo-Saxon beta = 0.16; West Europe beta = 0.15; Northern Europe beta = 0.14; Southern Europe beta = 0.12; Post-socialist beta = 0.11; Latin American cluster beta = 0.10; Lucia et al. (2012), pp. 216–217).

Unfortunately, ISRD2 data does *not* include *objective* measures of structural characteristics of schools.[10] In order to get a fuller picture of the role of structural school characteristics, Lucia and colleagues (2012) presented an imaginative analysis of the ISRD2 data by *including country-level educational characteristics*. They made use of an informal survey of the 31 national ISRD2 research partners on educational tracking practices. *Tracking* is the division of students into instructional groups by ability (Lucia et al. 2012, p. 217). In tracked systems, students are placed in different classes within a school, based on their academic abilities. In nine of the ISRD2 countries, a tracking system is used (with 2 or 3 levels), in three countries there is a streaming system (students follow some subject according to their ability in different levels), and in 17 countries there is no differentiation of students according to their abilities (Lucia et al. 2012, pp. 219–220). Tracking systems are most prevalent in Western Europe. From their review of the literature, Lucia and colleagues (2012) conclude that the evidence on the effect of tracking on student achievement and success is mixed. Some researchers argue that it is a more efficient system, shielding lower ability students' self-esteem, whereas others object to the class-bias inherent in this system, and the negative stigma associated with being in a lower track. From the *social learning* perspective, which claims that most delinquent (and other) behavior is learned through interaction with others, tracking implies that a student will be more exposed to peers with comparable abilities, educational aspirations and opportunities.[11]

Lucia and colleagues—in their analysis of ISRD2 data—included as a *second country-level measure* of education, national 2006 PISA scores, produced by a large international study of national differences in educational achievement (reading, mathematics and logical problem-solving). They calculated national PISA means and standard deviations for 21 of the ISRD2 countries for whom this information was available, and used this as a measure of *national educational achievement* (Lucia et al. 2012, p. 221). They also used the amount of variation among pupils at the PISA test as a measure of how well-integrated pupils of various backgrounds are within the school system in a particular country. If there is not a lot of variation in intellectual performance of students in a country, they assumed that social integration of students is higher (Ibidem, pp. 221–222).

Lucia et al. conclude that, with the exception of gender, school-related variables such as school disorganization, the existence of a tracked system and high heterogeneity in intellectual performance among students are the best predictors of serious violent offenses. Countries with high-quality schools (i.e. higher PISA scores) have lower rates of serious violence among their students (228); Egalitarian school system (that is, countries with less variation in intellectual performance by their students) tend to produce less offending than elitist school systems. And,

---

[10] In the third round of ISRD which will be concluded by the end of 2015, for a number of countries we will collect more information on the participating schools so we can conduct more complete analyses than those possible on the ISRD2 data.

[11] See Lucia et al. (2012) for a more in-depth review of relevant research and literature.

finally, countries with a tracked school system have higher rates of serious violence (but not property offenses) as compared to schools without tracking (233). Important to note here is Lucia and colleagues' cautionary statement that "students who are enrolled in the lowest of several tracks... do not commit more often serious violent or property offenses. It is not the individual fate of being in a low track, but *the structural inequality that matters*" (2012, p. 234, emphasis ours). Take away point: Individual-level school factors are less relevant than contextual factors (school structure and climate, or national educational characteristics)

2.2.2 Social Learning and Delinquency

The belief that delinquent behavior should be understood first and foremost as *learned* behavior has been one of the main premises of crime theory since Sutherland (1947) first proposed his Theory of Differential Association many decades ago. Later versions of learning theory have further specified the mechanism and conditions under which such learning takes place (see, for example, Akers 1985). The assumption is that criminal behavior does not differ from other (conforming) behavior in how it is acquired. Akers identifies four key elements that help shape behavior, two of which are especially relevant to the present discussion: (1) *differential association*, the process by which one learns definitions favorable or unfavorable to the law through a process of *social interaction*, and (2) *definitions* which include orientations, rationalizations, definitions of the situation, and other evaluative aspects of right and wrong.[12] With regard to the first element, it has been well-established that adolescents tend to move away from their parents and siblings as the primary sources of interaction and become much more oriented towards peers and friends. Research has shown that *deviance of one's friends* is among the strongest and most consistent predictors of delinquent behavior (Brown et al. 2013, p. 319). The responses of the approximately 67,000 12–16 year old students from 30 countries involved in the ISRD project confirm this observation. They were asked about friends who have committed one or more of five offenses (using drugs, shoplifting, breaking and entering, threats with violence, or beating someone up), and we found that the more delinquent acts committed by friends, the more offenses the juveniles committed themselves. They also tend to commit offenses similar to their friends: if the latter commit shoplifting, they are also more likely to shoplift themselves; this is also the case for burglary and assault (Junger-Tas et al. 2012a, p. 333). And—also consistent with what is found in other studies—the data showed that juvenile delinquency is primarily group behavior (Steketee 2012, p. 254).

We earlier mentioned the importance of school disorganization for delinquency. If we interpret this measure of school disorder as reflecting the amount of deviance committed by peers in school (Junger-Tas et al. 2008), then we can use social

[12] The two other elements are differential reinforcement and imitation (Brown et al. 2013, p. 321).

learning theory as a reasonable theoretical framework. In an (school) environment where delinquency such as drug use, vandalism, fighting and stealing are rather common, one would expect that such behavior soon will be viewed as acceptable and normal.

Social learning theories further assume that *attitudes* are a key component of explaining delinquency, and that these attitudes are transmitted through a process of learning (see previous paragraph). The ISRD2 project included a well-established scale of attitudes towards violence by asking respondents to agree (fully or somewhat) that a bit of violence is part of the fun, one needs to make use of force to be respected, if one is attacked, one will hit back, without violence everything would be much more boring, and it is completely normal that boys want to prove themselves in physical fights with others.[13] We found that pupils with more positive attitudes towards violence tended to have significantly higher levels of involvement in delinquency.

There is More to Learning than Going to School

School is indeed a very important part of adolescents' daily life. The results of the ISRD2 study have shown that performance and achievement in the formal school curriculum are of some relevance to delinquency, but that factors such as disliking school and skipping school regularly are of more importance. We further have discussed how the school context rather than individual achievement, attendance and affective ties with the school impact delinquent behavior (and victimization). Going to a disorderly school increases the chances that a youngster will engage in delinquent behavior him- or herself. The school is not only the setting for formal learning, but also for informal transmission of values, norms and attitudes. Intimately intertwined with the school environment is the impact of friends and peers, who often attend the same school. Friends and peers are primary sources of learning of delinquent values and rationalizations. Our research has clearly shown the important role that delinquent friends play in encouraging delinquent behavior. Youth who spend more time with family rather than friends are less likely to commit delinquent acts (and be victimized) than their counterparts. That may be partly due to closer supervision by parents, but it may also reflect a continuing influence of parental values and beliefs (which are assumed to be more law-abiding).

[13] The responses were transformed to Pomp scores (mean = 33.7, standard deviation = 22.3, Cronbach's alpha = 0.71).

2.3 Conclusions

This chapter reports findings from the Second International Self-Report Delinquency (ISRD2) project, a large international collaborative survey involving almost 68,000 12–15 year old pupils in 30 countries. It is the large size of the sample and the inclusion of 30 some countries that make this study of unprecedented importance. When analyzing the entire combined sample of youth, our findings pretty much align with those of comparable (much smaller) studies in different countries. That is, after analysis of ISRD2 data we find that minor delinquency is a rather common experience for a large proportion of youth; that only a small proportion of youth is involved in high frequency, serious delinquency; that victimization is not an uncommon experience for youth, but only a small proportion of adolescent encounter serious victimization; that there is considerable overlap between offenders and victims; and that much delinquency is group delinquency. We also find that the correlates of delinquency are: being male, having low parental supervision, low attachment to parents, living in a disorganized neighborhood, having a positive attitude towards violence, having a low level of self-control, spending a lot of time with deviant friends hanging out in public places, doing poorly in school, skipping school, disliking school and being registered in a disorganized school.[14] Because we collected comparable data in 30 different countries, we are also able to see if countries differ with respect to which factors are associated with delinquency (and victimization). The comparisons of six country clusters showed some differences in *strength* of associations, but we detected relatively little variation with regard to the *types* of correlates. Considering the wide range of countries involved in the ISRD2 project, this is a very important conclusion concerning the generalizability of commonly used predictors of delinquency.

We cautioned earlier that we should not confuse correlation with causation. That is clearly illustrated by the findings concerning the school-related variables. Here we find that repeating classes goes together with an absence of plans for future education and more truancy. Youths who have future plans are more likely to attend well-organized schools, have a positive bond with schools, and like schools, whereas those who attend disorganized schools do not like school and tend to be truant more often (Junger-Tas et al. 2012a, p. 332). The best school-related predictors of delinquency at the individual level are truancy, attending a disorganized school and not liking school. Furthermore, we also find that the existence of a tracking system, disorganized schools and a high variation in intellectual performance are related to national differences in serious violent offenses. To try to disentangle the micro- and macro-level effects of these different school-related variables remains a daunting task (Lucia et al. 2012).

These theoretical challenges notwithstanding, the insights from IRSD2 do provide some suggestions for policy. After all, following the public health model, we may base sound policy on observed correlates of behavior (even if the theoretical

[14] These correlates vary in significance. See Junger-Tas et al. (2012a, 2012b).

connection is not crystal clear). In earlier work, we have proposed a number of policy implications (Junger-Tas et al. 2012a, pp. 350–353), but here we mention only those related to education. Education is the area which is most amenable to policy intervention, much more so than family, personality, or peers. "If one wishes to prevent delinquency, investing in education should be placed high on the agenda" (Junger-Tas et al. 2012a, p. 351). Here follow, in abbreviated form, the education-related policies proposed in the concluding chapter of *The Many Faces of Youth Crime* (Junger-Tas et al. 2012a, pp. 351–352):

(a) Early education for low income children in order to promote a positive school career;
(b) Development of so-called 'large schools' in deprived neighborhoods. These schools include social services, a longer school day, parent-training programs;
(c) Improve quality of schools, particularly in low income areas by better training and pay for teachers;
(d) In countries with tracking systems, introduce more flexibility allowing students to gradually move to higher tracks.

Policies such as these will not only have an effect on delinquency and crime, but they also will improve the quality of life of future generations by improving opportunities for employment, diminishing inequality and preparing children for their role as global citizens.

Five Questions

1. The International Self Report Delinquency Study (ISRD) uses surveys of 12–15 year old pupils in schools to obtain information about offending and victimization. How does this information differ from that which we have available through official sources, such as police reports? What source provides us with better information: self-reports or official sources?
2. What are the main differences in self-reported offending and victimization between the six country clusters? What are the similarities in offending and victimization across all 30 ISRD countries? Can you think of ways to explain these differences as well as the commonalities among countries?
3. How important is the school when trying to understand and explain juvenile delinquency? In your answer, make reference to the relevant theories as well as the findings of the ISRD2 study.
4. Gender, parental supervision and (deviant behavior of) friends are significantly related to involvement in delinquency in the 30 ISRD2 countries. Explain this, and make use of the theoretical ideas presented in this chapter.
5. Which education-related policy suggestions listed at the end of this chapter do you think are most promising and useful? Based on what you have read in this chapter, can you think of some other policies which could be implemented in order to prevent offending and victimization among youth?

References

Agnew, R. W. (2005). *Why do criminals offend? A general theory on crime and delinquency*. Los Angeles: Roxbury.

Akers, R. L. (1985). *Deviant behavior: A social learning approach* (3rd ed.). Belmont, CA: Wadsworth.

Akers, R. I., & Jensen, G. F. (Eds.). (2003). *Social learning and the explanation of crime*. New Brunswick, NJ: Transaction.

Brown, S. E., Esbensen, F.-A., & Geis, G. (2013). *Criminology. Explaining crime and its context* (8th ed.). New York: Anderson Publishing.

Bursik, R. J., & Grasmick, H. G. (1993). *Neighborhoods and crime: The dimensions of effective community control*. New York: Lexington.

Cohen, A. (1955). *Delinquent boys: The culture of the gang*. Chicago: University of Chicago Press.

Cohen, E., & Felson, M. (1979). Social change and crime rate trends: A routine activity approach. *American Sociological Review, 44*(4), 588–608.

Enzmann, D., Marshall, I. H., Killias, M., Junger-Tas, J., Steketee, M., & Gruszczyńska, B. (2010). Self-reported youth delinquency in Europe and beyond: First results of the Second International Self-Report Delinquency Study in the context of police and victimization data. *European Journal of Criminology, 7*(2), 159–183.

Esping-Andersen, G. (1990). *The three worlds of welfare capitalism*. Princeton, NJ: Princeton University Press.

Gottfredson, D. (2001). *Schools and delinquency*. Cambridge: Cambridge University Press.

Gottfredson, M. R., & Hirschi, T. (1990). *A general theory of crime*. Stanford, CA: Stanford University Press.

Gruszczyńska, B., Lucia, S., & Killias, M. (2012). Juvenile victimization from an international perspective. In J. Junger-Tas, I. H. Marshall, D. Enzmann, M. Killias, M. Steketee, & B. Gruszczynska (Eds.), *The many faces of youth crime: Contrasting theoretical perspectives on juvenile delinquency across countries and cultures* (pp. 95–116). New York: Springer.

Hay, C., & Forrest, W. (2008). Self-control theory and the concept of opportunity: The case for a more systematic union. *Criminology, 46*, 1039–1072.

Hirschi, T. (1969). *Causes of delinquency*. Berkeley, CA: University of California Press.

Junger-Tas, J. (2010). The significance of the International Self-report Delinquency Study (ISRD). *European Journal on Criminal Policy and Research, 16*(2), 71–87.

Junger-Tas, J. (2012). Delinquent behavior in 30 countries. In I. H. Marshall, D. Enzmann, M. Killias, M. Steketee, B. Gruszczyńska, & J. Junger-Tas (Eds.), *The many faces of youth crime: Contrasting theoretical perspectives on juvenile delinquency across countries and cultures* (pp. 69–94). New York: Springer.

Junger-Tas, J., Enzmann, D., Steketee, M., & Marshall, I. H. (2012a). Concluding observations: The big picture. In J. Junger-Tas, I. H. Marshall, D. Enzmann, M. Killias, M. Steketee, & B. Gruszczyńska (Eds.), *The many faces of youth crime: Contrasting theoretical perspectives on juvenile delinquency across countries and cultures* (pp. 329–353). New York: Springer.

Junger-Tas, J., Marshall, I. H., Enzmann, D., Killias, M., Steketee, M., & Gruszczyńska, B. (2012b). *The many faces of youth crime. Contrasting theoretical perspectives on juvenile delinquency across countries and cultures*. New York: Springer.

Junger-Tas, J., Marshall, I. H., Enzmann, D., Killias, M., Steketee, M., & Gruszczyńska, B. (Eds.). (2010). *Juvenile Delinquency in Europe and Beyond. Results of the Second International Self-Report Delinquency Study*. New York: Springer.

Junger-Tas, J., Marshall, I.H., & Ribeaud, D. (2003). Delinquency in an international perspective: The International Self-Reported Delinquency Study (ISRD). The Hague: Kugler Publications.

Junger-Tas, J., Steketee, M., & Moll, M. (2008). *Achtergronden van jeugddelinquentie en middelengebruik*. Utrecht: Verwey-Jonker Instituut.

Junger-Tas, J., Terlouw, G. J., & Klein, M. W. (Eds.). (1994). *Delinquent behavior among young people in the western world: First results of the International Self-Report Delinquency Study*. Amsterdam: WODC–Ministry of Justice, Kugler Publications.

Lucia, S., Killias, M., & Junger-Tas, J. (2012). The school and its impact on delinquency. In J. Junger-Tas, I. H. Marshall, D. Enzmann, M. Killias, M. Steketee, & B. Gruszczyńska (Eds.), *The many faces of youth crime: Contrasting theoretical perspectives on juvenile delinquency across countries and cultures* (pp. 211–236). New York: Springer.

Marshall, I. H., & Enzmann, D. (2012). Methodology and design of the ISRD-2 Study. In J. Junger-Tas, I. H. Marshall, D. Enzmann, M. Killias, M. Steketee, & B. Gruszczyńska (Eds.), *The many faces of youth crime: Contrasting theoretical perspectives on juvenile delinquency across countries and cultures* (pp. 21–68). New York: Springer.

Marshall, C., & Marshall, I. H. (2015). *Jeugdelinquentie in vergelijkend perspectief. Vertellen individuale en nationale analyses hetzelfde verhaal?* Working paper. University of Nebraska-Omaha, School of Criminology and Criminal Justice, Omaha USA.

Merton, R. K. (1938). Social structure and anomie. *American Sociological Review, 3*, 672–682.

Moffitt, T. E. (1993). Adolescence-limited and life-course persistent antisocial behavior: A developmental taxonomy. *Psychological Review, 100*(4), 674–701.

Posick, C. (2013). The overlap between offending and victimization among adolescents: Results from the second International Self-Report Delinquency Study. *Journal of Contemporary Criminal Justice, 29*, 106–124.

Rutter, M., Maughan, B., Mortimore, P., & Ouston, J. (1979). *Fifteen thousand hours: Secondary schools and their effects on children*. London: Open Books.

Saint-Arnaud, S., & Bernard, P. (2003). Convergence or resilience? A hierarchical cluster analysis of the welfare regimes in advanced countries. *Current Sociology, 51*, 499–527.

Sampson, R. J., & Laub, J. H. (1993). *Crime in the making: Pathways and turning points through life*. Cambridge, MA: Harvard University Press.

Sampson, R. J., Raudenbush, S. W., & Earls, F. (1997). Neighborhoods and violent crime: A multi-level study of collective efficacy. *Science, 277*, 918–924.

Schreck, C., Stewart, E., & Osgood, D. (2008). A reappraisal of the overlap of violent offenders and victims. *Criminology, 46*, 871–906.

Steketee, M. (2012). The lifestyles of youth and their peers. In J. Junger-Tas, I. H. Marshall, D. Enzmann, M. Killias, M. Steketee, & B. Gruszczyńska (Eds.), *The many faces of youth crime: Contrasting theoretical perspectives on juvenile delinquency across countries and cultures* (pp. 237–256). New York: Springer.

Sutherland, E. (1947). *Principles of criminology*. Philadelphia, PA: Lippincott.

van Dijk, J. J., van Kesteren, J., & Smit, P. (2007). *Criminal victimization in an international perspective: Key findings from the 2—4-2005 ICVS and EU ICS*. The Hague: Ministry of Justice/WODC.

Wikstrom, P. O., Oberwittler, D., Treiber, K., & Hardie, B. (2012). *Breaking rules: The social and situational dynamics of young people's urban crime*. Oxford: Oxford University Press.

The Role of Justice and Fairness as Global Values: Promoting Public International Law at the (Pre-)University Level

Roger S. Clark

Abstract The United Nations Charter and other international instruments promote justice and international law as cornerstones of peace and security, nationally and internationally. This chapter looks into the avenues and precepts of inculcating an appreciation for international law and international principles (for example those on crime prevention and criminal justice or human rights) through education at the university level and, especially, at the pre-university level. It discusses ways in which relevant learning takes place both in the regular curriculum and in such extra-curricular activities as Model United Nations Conferences, which involve both high school and university students. Various efforts by the United Nations and its Specialized Agencies to stimulate such education are noted, such as "United Nations Academic Impact Initiative". So too is the dearth both of curricular requirements and of teaching materials suitable for teaching the subject at the pre-university level. Note is taken of a handful of excellent teaching aids that *are* available.

1 Introduction

Contributing to an edited work always presents some interesting challenges to the writer. What do the editors really want? I was flattered when the distinguished editors of this large undertaking presented me with the title you are now looking at and asked me to discuss it. My initial reaction, however, was that a chapter on promoting public international law was an awkward fit in a book devoted to the general subject of "Women and Children as Victims and Offenders". A little reflection convinced me that I had made a mistake, for which I have often criticized others, of taking an overly narrow approach to the subject. In particular, I had begun by thinking too much in traditional terms about international law as confined to

The author appreciates the assistance of Marvin Astrada, Daniel Baum, Donald Buckingham, Hays Butler, Valerie Epps, John King Gamble, Libby Giles, Maryella Hannum, Michael Herdman, Ved Nanda, Wes Rist and Tony Smith.

R.S. Clark (✉)
Rutgers University, Camden, NJ, USA
e-mail: rsclark@crab.rutgers.edu

H. Kury et al. (eds.), *Women and Children as Victims and Offenders: Background, Prevention, Reintegration*, DOI 10.1007/978-3-319-08398-8_12

such topics as sources of law (especially treaties and customary law), settlement of disputes between states, the law of the sea (and other issues of resource allocation), the laws of armed conflict (including the abolition of weapons of mass destruction) and the protection of the environment. These are, of course, subjects that might appropriately be addressed in a university or pre-university course on international law—and are. But so also should subjects like human rights (at a broad level of abstraction)[1] or more narrowly children's[2] and women's rights,[3] or the right not to be discriminated against on grounds such as race,[4] gender[5] or disability,[6] to say nothing of peace studies,[7] global citizenship,[8] sustainable development,[9] and—most important in terms of the quinquennial United Nations crime prevention and criminal justice congresses (with the next one in Japan in 2020)—United Nations

[1] Some of the best existing teaching materials are in the area of human rights. See below at notes 70–84.

[2] Notably the Convention on the Rights of the Child (1989), 1577 UNTS 3.

[3] See the Convention on the Elimination of All Forms of Discrimination against Women (1979), 1249 UNTS 13.

[4] See the Convention on the Elimination of All Forms of Racial Discrimination (1965), 660 UNTS 195.

[5] Convention on the Elimination of All Forms of Discrimination against Women, above note.

[6] Convention on the Rights of Persons with Disabilities (2006), 2525 UNTS 3.

[7] See, e.g., on Peace Education in the New Zealand School Curriculum, https://podcasts.otago.ac.nz/nzpeace-ed/peace-education-directory/nz-curriculum/. Departments and programmes with such titles as "Peace and Conflict Studies" and "Global Citizenship" have proliferated in universities world-wide in recent years.

[8] See, e.g., Sobhi Tawil, Education for 'Global Citizenship': A Framework for Discussion, UNESCO Education Research and Foresight Working Papers, No. 7 (August 2013), available at http://www.unesco.org/new/fileadmin/MULTIMEDIA/HQ/ED/pdf/PaperN7EducforGlobalCitizenship.pdf. UNESCO fosters numerous initiatives in schools worldwide through its Associated Schools Project Network (ASPnet), a global network of over 9000 education institutions in 180 countries. See http://www.state.gov/p/io/unesco/c18952.htm. See also Center for International Education and Research (CIER) University of Birmingham, Global Citizenship: The Needs of teachers and Learners, Key Findings, available at http://www.birmingham.ac.uk/Documents/college-social-sciences/education/cier/global-citizenship-report.pdf; Oxfam, Education for Global Citizenship, A Guide for Schools, available at http://www.oxfam.org.uk/~/media/Files/Education/Global%20Citizenship/education_for_global_citizenship_a_guide_for_schools.ashx.

[9] Note UNESCO's work for the United Nations Decade for Education in Sustainable Development (2005–2014), available at http://www.unesco.org/new/en/education/themes/leading-the-international-agenda/education-for-sustainable-development/about-us/.

standards and norms in criminal justice.[10] To revert for a moment to the title of the chapter: women are typically victims in war, but occasionally they are war criminals; child soldiers can be both victims and perpetrators.[11]

So one has to think both about "hard law" (treaties and clear customary law) and about "soft law" (standards that may or may not have found their way into international customary law but which nevertheless have some "weight" when it comes to thinking about law in the present context).[12] Most of the instruments I have just noted can be understood by senior high school students in their original form, although for more junior students it may be necessary to distill their essence.[13]

---

[10] See Compendium of United Nations Standards and Norms in Crime Prevention and Criminal Justice (2006 ed.), available at http://www.unodc.org/unodc/en/justice-and-prison-reform/compendium.html. Looking through the Table of Contents of the Compendium, I noted the following instruments as being particularly relevant in the present context, although there are no doubt others: Standard Minimum Rules for the Treatment of Prisoners, United Nations Standard Minimum Rules for the Administration of Juvenile Justice (the Beijing Rules), United Nations Guidelines for the Prevention of Juvenile Delinquency (the Riyadh Guidelines), United Nations Rules for the Protection of Juveniles Deprived of their Liberty, Guidelines on Action for Children in the Criminal Justice System, Basic Principles on the Use of Restorative Justice Programmes in Criminal Matters, Declaration of Basic Principles of Justice for Victims of Crime and Abuse of Power, Guidelines on Justice in Matters involving Child Victims and Witnesses of Crime, Declaration on the Elimination of Violence against Women, Model Strategies and Practical Measures on the Elimination of Violence against Women in the Field of Crime Prevention and Criminal Justice, and Basic Principles on the Independence of the Judiciary. On the standards and norms in general, see Ram (2012); Redo (2012); Clark (1994). For some excellent teaching material on international criminal justice in general, see Natarajan (2011). For some wider thoughts on international criminal law, see Podgor and Clark (2013).

[11] The Rome Statute of the International Criminal Court has numerous provisions on the protection of victims, especially women and children, and also acknowledges the difficult problem of child soldiers by asserting that the Court has no jurisdiction over any person who was under the age of 18 at the time of the alleged commission of a crime.

[12] My former student, Marvin Astrada, who has had experience teaching in Political Science and International Affairs departments, comments on a draft of this chapter in the present context:

To effectively counter the critique that idealism, which undergirds international law, has little or no effect independent of State power (political realism) on international affairs, it would be wise to inculcate from the inception of pedagogical training ... a comprehensive understanding of the limits as well as the potential for international law to be effective – to maximize its capacity to impact in a meaningful way international affairs.

[13] There have been several efforts to present the Universal Declaration of Human Rights in ways that younger children can appreciate. See e.g., Universal Declaration of Human Rights, Plain Language Version, available at http://www.un.org/cyberschoolbus/humanrights/resources/plain.asp. Amnesty International has produced a creative video using various art forms to explain each article of the Declaration, available at www.youtube.com/watch?v=epVZrYbDVis. Teaching the Universal Declaration is facilitated by its translation into 370 languages; it is the most translated document in the world according to the Guinness Book of Records. See http://www.ohchr.org/EN/UDHR/Pages/SearchByLang.aspx. On disseminating the United Nations crime prevention and criminal justice instruments, especially in universities and specialized training institutes, see Aromaa and Redo (2008).

Then there was the question of "justice and fairness as global values". It also took me a while to realize that that part of the title had probably been stimulated by the remarkable work by Otto Spijkers, *The United Nations, The Evolution of Global Values and International Law*.[14] Dr. Spijkers "characterizes the work of the United Nations as a contribution to a global discussion about the evolution of global values".[15] Typically, the United Nations is "seen as a political organization with various highly ambitious tasks"[16] but Dr. Spijkers posits some useful insights on regarding it from the perspective of its *values*. He quotes the words of Jan Pronk, a Dutch politician and former Special Representative of the United Nations Secretary-General in Sudan:

> The United Nations is also a community of values. Through intensive and continuous international dialogue, a global consensus has been achieved on principles, norms and values. The results are codified in charters, conventions and resolutions. Without all this, the United Nations could never have acted effectively, either in the implementation of programs, or when international intervention is deemed desirable. A history of the United Nations can be written from this perspective: a history about the development of values, in order to better cope, together, with the [global] challenges. The foundation [of such history] is enshrined in the Charter of the United Nations and the Declaration of Human Rights. These texts are about peace, human rights, human dignity, international economic and social cooperation, respect for the principle of equal rights and self-determination of peoples, territorial integrity of all States, and other basic values.[17]

Dr. Spijkers considers how these values are teased out in the Charter and in subsequent actions within the Organization, especially by the General Assembly. While the United Nations standards and norms on crime prevention and criminal justice are not included in the specific examples that he examines, the analysis based on values is highly applicable in this area also.

It is largely values similar to those identified in Dr. Spijkers' work that inform a major initiative launched in 2010 by Secretary-General Ban-Ki-Moon, entitled "United Nations Academic Impact Initiative". This is a global initiative that "aligns institutions of higher learning with the United Nations in supporting ten universally accepted principles in the areas of human rights, literacy, sustainability and conflict resolution."[18] Participating institutions are asked to actively demonstrate support for at least one of those principles each year. The ten principles are:

1. A commitment to the principles inherent in the United Nations Charter as values that education seeks to promote and help fulfil;
2. A commitment to human rights, among them freedom of inquiry, opinion, and speech;

[14] Spijkers (2011).

[15] Id. at p. 4. This is not to deny that there are occasions where the values of major players in the organization are dominant. See Bemis (2000).

[16] Spijkers (2011) p. 4.

[17] Quoted id. pp. 4–5 (interpolation in original).

[18] See the website of the initiative, available at http://academicimpact.org/engpage.php.

3. A commitment to educational opportunity for all people regardless of gender, race, religion or ethnicity;
4. A commitment to the opportunity for every interested individual to acquire the skills and knowledge necessary for the pursuit of higher education;
5. A commitment to building capacity in higher education systems across the world;
6. A commitment to encouraging global citizenship through education;
7. A commitment to advancing peace and conflict resolution through education;
8. A commitment to addressing issues of poverty through education;
9. A commitment to promoting sustainability through education;
10. A commitment to promoting inter-cultural dialogue and understanding, and the "unlearning" of intolerance, through education.

Hundreds of universities worldwide, including my own Rutgers University,[19] are associated with the initiative.

There was a time when International Law was a prominent topic at universities. In my first legal studies at Victoria University in New Zealand in the late 1950s and early 1960s it was a compulsory subject, taught in part by George Barton, a protégé of the great Hersch Lauterpacht, and in part by a then junior scholar, Kenneth Keith, later a member of the International Court of Justice. James Kent's *Commentaries on American Law*, the first great United States legal treatise, based on his lectures at Columbia College beginning in 1794, begins with a Part of nine lectures and 211 pages on The Law of Nations before moving to Part II on the Government and Constitutional Jurisprudence of the United States.[20] In the Preface, Kent has a classic assertion of the value of the subject:

> [T]he knowledge that is intended to be communicated in these volumes is ... of that elementary kind, which is not only essential to every person who pursues the science of law as a practical profession, but is deemed useful and ornamental to those who are to assume places of public trust and to take a share of the business and councils of our country.[21]

I love those words about our subject: "useful and ornamental"! Regrettably, however, the current state of the teaching of international law in universities, and especially in their law schools, is disappointing. It is no longer compulsory at Victoria University, although a large number of students take it. A Report for the

---

[19] Rutgers offers a Summer United Nations Study Program consistent with the Initiative. See https://studyabroad.rutgers.edu/index.cfm?FuseAction=Programs.ViewProgram&Program_ID=10391 on the 2014 offering.

[20] Kent (1858). (First edition published in 1826).

[21] Id. at pp. xi–xii. In modern terms, and no doubt when he was writing, the group to which Kent refers who "assume places of public trust" would include the media. Public commentators about international law on a par with those such as Anthony Lewis or Linda Greenhouse, who have made United States constitutional law accessible to many, are lacking in the international area. The American Society of International Law's *ASIL Insights* series, available at http://www.asil.org/insights/all, is accessible to the educated public.

International Law Association at its Hague Conference in 2010, prepared by the Association's Committee on the Teaching of International Law, summarizes material gleaned from countries worldwide where the Association is represented:

- A clear "outcome" was that despite the best endeavours of all, international law as an undergraduate[22] course remains largely on the periphery of legal studies.
- This was to an extent based on lack of student interest which was, in turn, based, among other things, on a misconception of the relevance of the field for admission to practice (notably in the US system) and its everyday relevance to national law.
- The countries in which international law is a compulsory component of the undergraduate (and practice-oriented) degree represent a clear minority.
- The Committee also noted its surprise at the extent to which EU law competes with international law for space in curricula.[23]

I have taught international law at universities across the globe for five decades (with occasional guest forays into elementary and high schools).[24] Having noted the

[22] The reference to "undergraduate" here may be confusing to some. It is apparently referring to a first degree in law. Note that in the United States and Canada, law is normally a three-year "graduate" degree (culminating in a Juris Doctor degree) in that law students have already completed a 4-year bachelor's degree before coming to law school. In Canada and the United States, study of international law also takes place in "truly undergraduate" programmes in Departments of Political Science or International Relations. Some students in postgraduate law programmes in the US and Canada (Masters in Law and Doctorates in Juridical Science typically) study international law at an advanced level at law schools across the spectrum of prestige. My impression is that it is more common for foreign students than the local ones to take such courses. In most other parts of the world, law is an undergraduate degree in the sense that it is attended by students immediately following secondary school. There are, of course, many graduate programmes in law world-wide that build on what is covered in a first law degree. There are some excellent graduate programmes in what might be described broadly as international relations which have advanced law courses aimed primarily at non-law students. See, for example, the courses offered at the Fletcher School of Law and Diplomacy of Tufts University in Massachusetts.

[23] International Law Association, The Hague Conference (2010), Committee on the Teaching of International Law, available on the internet via Google.

[24] Beginning in the early 1970s, I taught a course on the International Protection of Human Rights and one on the Law of International Organizations (a kind of constitutional and administrative law course on the United Nations and the Specialized Agencies). Later, in the 1980s, I began offering the basic Introduction to International Law course, a course entitled International Criminal Law and Criminal Justice Policy, and one on Foreign Relations and National Security Law. My Law School, which has a broader international curriculum than many American law schools, continues to offer these courses and courses on International Environmental Law, European Law, and Legal Research on International Law. We have occasionally offered one on the Law of the Sea. In the "private" international law area, we have offerings on International Commercial Arbitration, International Business Transactions, International Trade Law and Conflict of Laws. None of the courses in public or private international law are compulsory.

dismal state of university teaching of international law,[25] I decided to make a liberal interpretation of my editors' title and remove in my mind the brackets around "pre" in "(pre-) university" and concentrate for the most part in this chapter on public international law education prior to the university level. I shall, however, indulge myself with occasional references to the university teaching of international law, mostly in footnotes, which I hope will be useful to some readers. The main issues I take up are: can the case be made for teaching some international law before university; is teaching international law pre-university perhaps even a matter of legal obligation and not merely good policy; should international legal issues be introduced at the secondary level, or earlier; what teaching materials are there for a pre-university curriculum; and what educational strategies (classroom exegesis and discussion, extra-curricular competitions, field trips and the like) might be utilized.

2 Making the (Policy) Case for Pre-University Teaching of International Law

The best articulation of the benefits of teaching Public International Law prior to the university level that I have discovered is a 1995 essay by Dr. Donald Buckingham, then a professor at the Law Faculty of the University of Western Ontario in Canada. It appears in the report of the Congress on International Law held at United Nations Headquarters in 1995 in celebration of the fiftieth anniversary of the Organization. His discussion was entitled *"Creating World-Class Citizens: International Law as an Essential Ingredient in Secondary School Education,"*[26] The United Nations

[25] Perhaps this situation in part reflects the difficulties international law has in finding a place in a curriculum which seems increasingly to be swallowed up by "skills" courses. Many teachers/ practitioners in the human rights field have responded with clinical offerings. My colleague, Beth Stephens, for example, has a very popular offering on Human Rights Advocacy and Litigation. In a very thoughtful essay a few years back Professor Gerry Simpson wrote of a "malaise in the teaching of international law resulting from a fear of being confined to the academic peripheries. This fear arises from a sense that international lawyers are deemed not sufficiently like 'real' lawyers by some of our colleagues and not savvy enough about global realities according to some international relations scholars." Simpson (1999) (abstract). As one who has made a living for half a century as an academic, scholar, occasional government legal representative, member of a UN Committee and NGO agitator, I have never felt especially defensive about the "reality" of international law.

[26] Buckingham (1996). The 1995 U.N. Congress was part of the programme of the United Nations Decade of International Law. Authorized by GA/Res/44/23, the Decade had as one of its main purposes, to "encourage the teaching, study, dissemination and wider appreciation of international law." An earlier initiative was the United Nations Programme of Assistance in the Training, Study, Dissemination and Wider Appreciation of International Law, established in 1965 by G. A. Res. 2099 (XX). An important (and continuing) product of that initiative is the United Nations Audiovisual Library of International Law, available at http://legal.un.org/avl/lectureseries.html. The Library contains some presentations that would work at the secondary school level as well as in universities.

Congress had as its rather compelling theme "Towards the Twenty-First Century: International Law as a Language for International Relations." Buckingham's basic argument was that "[p]eace and security, social well-being and economic development, sustainability and distributive justice in the global village all depend on a wide-scale and general acceptance of the language and principles of international law." He noted the paucity (still the case) both of introductory texts on International Law that were suitable for high schools[27] and the absence of professional literature in journals of education, law or international law on teaching international law in secondary schools.[28] His argument proceeded with the exposition of four points: "First, *why* the language of international law is largely learned rather than experienced; second, *who* speaks or could learn to speak the language of international law; third, *what* we, the speakers of the language, must do to teach students the language of international law, particularly in secondary education; and fourth *where* has Canada gone in teaching international law in secondary schools."

As to why the vocabulary has to be "learned" so that "the language of international law must become, like the rule of law is to domestic legal systems, the notion that individuals, institutions and governments of States submit to the law to govern their affairs," Buckingham makes a sophisticated argument based on some of the insights contained in Professor H.L.A. Hart's *The Concept of Law*. Relying on Hart, Buckingham suggests that "law works because the persons that make up the society which the legal system is to serve agree to be bound by it."[29] The internalization of rules in a domestic legal system occurs through direct experience and formal education. Citizens learn about rules by personal encounters with them, what Buckingham calls "experiential osmosis".[30] Moreover, "[f]ormal instruction in the obligations of citizenship is undertaken through State education programmes such as schooling, citizenship training and licensing." This, he suggests, does not work as well at the international level. With international law still to a significant extent a matter of the interactions between independent States, the language is not as internalized as well. Thus it is necessary to rely more on education. I am not entirely convinced that the differences are quite as stark between domestic and international law as Buckingham suggests, but his point about the importance of internalization is certainly true. My own experience in talking to the general public about international law is often the public's surprise that there is such a thing—or that leaders, judges and other public officials take it seriously. Indeed, leaders, judges and other public officials are not always consistent in their attitudes of obedience to international law. Education along the lines of discussing the way in

[27] Sophisticated high school students could no doubt appreciate some readable texts such as Lowe (2007), Bederman (2010); Dixon (2013); Mansell and Openshaw (2013) and Buergenthal and Murphy (2013). Also useful could be contextual readings such as those in Betts (2012).

[28] Buckingham, above at p. 367. One exception he notes was McNemar (1983) (emphasizing importance to creating an informed public of study of international law in colleges and high schools as well as law schools).

[29] Buckingham at p. 359, relying on Hart (1961).

[30] Id.

which States (or at least their officials) internalize international law certainly makes sense.

As to the question who speaks and understands the language of international law, Buckingham draws a distinction between "fluent speakers", "novice speakers", "occasional or tourist-class speakers" and "non-speakers". The first class includes "lawyers in States' foreign services, immigration and trade departments; lawyers in private firms largely involved in international business transactions, or immigration; corporate counsel in legal departments of transnational corporations; lawyers in intergovernmental organizations and non-governmental organizations; and international legal academics."[31] This is an exceedingly small group of society as a whole. Novice speakers, the second group, is a category largely composed of law and political science students. This is a relatively small part of the student body too, at least in North America. Buckingham quotes a 1993 study by Professor Gamble which indicated that only about 45 % of North American students take one or more international law courses during their law school career,[32] and the percentage of those taking it in other departments must be lower. "Occasional or tourist-class speakers", a group of unknown size, is able to "experience" international law "largely though media reports, even if it be second-hand."[33] He suggests that "this group is able to recognize that the language of international law is an important factor in the conduct of international relations. This recognition is a first step to the internalization of international law by a broad group of non-professional speakers."[34] Implicit in his analysis is that this group could become more powerful with exposure to international law in an educational setting. The same must be true, *a fortiori*, of his final group "non-speakers". The challenge is how to get a least a minimal knowledge base to them.

The next challenge Buckingham addresses is how speakers of the language can get more people interested in studying international law at law school. He reports on a small sample of law students (55) at the University of Western Ontario. About 6 % of his sample had previously studied some international law at the secondary school

---

[31] Id. at p. 360.

[32] Id. at p. 361 quoting Gamble (1993) at pp. 122–123. Professor Gamble of Penn State University is Chair of the International Law Association's Interest Group on Teaching and has taught International Law to Political Science students throughout a long career. He reports in an e-mail dated 26 May 2014 observing something of a resurgence in teaching International Law in the United States, including at some "top-notch schools". He attributes some of the neglect in American Political Science departments to the prevalence of empirical teaching and scholarship. The classic study of the teaching of international law is that by Judge Lachs, the late Polish member of the International Court of Justice: Lachs (1982). Devoted in large part to musings about great teacher/practitioners of international law through history, the book contains some interesting material about the state of teaching International Law in universities in Europe and North America (a somewhat disappointing picture it would seem). See especially at pp. 137–150. See also Cheng (1982), which contains useful studies of the teaching on international law in the United Kingdom, France and Austria (and implies that support for such programs in not overwhelming).

[33] Buckingham at p. 362.

[34] Id.

level. "However, 100 % of the students who had previously studied some international law at secondary level also went on to take at least one course during their undergraduate studies (even though their undergraduate majors were as diverse as French, journalism or history) and at least one international law course as part of their legal training."[35] From this, albeit small, sample Buckingham draws a conclusion which has substantial intuitive appeal, namely that "one way to improve the likelihood of students pursuing international legal training in law school is to introduce them to the subject at the secondary school level."[36] Teaching of international law in secondary schools could also have some impact of what Buckingham called "occasional speakers" and "non-speakers". Such education would expand their opportunities to deal with international law messages in the media and to own greater ability to understand current international issues. So, Buckingham sees at least two good reasons for teaching international law in secondary schools:

(a) It will increase the likelihood that students will do further studies in international law;
(b) It will prepare students to identify and understand international legal issues, thereby allowing them to become fully operating members of international society with a respect for international law as the language of international relations.[37]

Finally, Dr. Buckingham addressed the question where his native Canada was going with respect to the teaching of international law in secondary schools.[38] Education is a provincial matter in Canada and at the time only one province, albeit the largest, Ontario, included international law in the secondary curriculum, and

---

[35] Id. at p. 363.

[36] Id.

[37] Id at pp. 363–364. The second argument touches more generally on the necessity to teach international law at all levels of study, including the university level. Marvin Astrada comments:

I would ground the case for international law – as well as orientation for students of international law – in globalization (as historical processes, as a product and producer of norms and values, as an expression of power, as a challenge to State power, as a complex cultural, social, political, economic harbinger of transformation in the modus operandi of international affairs).

See generally Astrada and Martin (2013) pp. 27–33.

[38] I have not been able to find anything systematic about the teaching of international law at high schools throughout the world. Professor Kai Ambos of the University of Gottingen was kind enough to report to me that:

[In Germany] there are no books for the High School, pre-University level. Usually high school students get some basic information about international law from their political science courses and books. Apart from that there is a Federal Agency for Civic Education, the Bundeszentral für politische Bildung, which publishes kind of journals on specific topics, including legal topics (for example recently one on the ICC), see www.bpb.de/die-bpb/138852/the-federal-agency-for-civic-education.

A computer search of United States and other high schools reveals a few random (often private) schools around the globe with international law offerings, but I located nothing systematic at a national, provincial or state level aside from Ontario.

then in the final year.[39] The 1987 version of the Ontario Curriculum, the relevant parts of which were annexed to his article,[40] states in its "description" that "[s]tudents should come to appreciate the scope and limitations of the law as a means of resolving international conflicts and problems." Moreover, "[a]n awareness of the global aspects of law should increase student interest in international legal affairs and enhance their awareness of themselves as 'world citizens'".[41] So far as content was concerned, the Curriculum was divided into "sources and uses of international law", "current concerns of international law" and some "sample teaching and evaluation strategies". Much of the content was similar to the topics that I take up in my survey course for law students, Introduction to International Law, although obviously a secondary school teacher would be able to cover much less ground.

The "sources and uses" were: the United Nations, Charter and Organization; the World Court; international conventions and treaties; territorial disputes, boundaries and international zones; war crimes and crimes against humanity; the problem of international terrorism. "Current concerns" (of which it was suggested teachers should choose at least three topics) were: the use of international boycotts and sanctions; the ownership of world resources; cross-border pollution; citizenship and immigration; terrorism; human rights; the regulations of international trade and investment; diplomatic immunity; extradition; refugees and political asylum. The list is still very relevant a quarter of a century later.

Among the samples of "teaching and evaluation strategies" were these: "Have students investigate and assess the Nuremberg and other post-war tribunals and explore later cases in which the rules developed in these tribunals have or could

[39] Buckingham at pp. 364–367.

[40] Ontario Curriculum (1987), Unit 5. Law and the World Community, reproduced in Buckingham at p. 370. The 2005 version of the Curriculum perhaps emphasizes more the connections between Canadian and International Law. See the general description in Ontario Curriculum, at p. 239, Canadian and International Law:

> This course examines elements of Canadian and international law in social, political, and global contexts. Students will study the historical and philosophical sources of law and the principles and practices of international law and will learn to relate them to issues in Canadian society and the wider world. Students will use critical-thinking and communication skills to analyse legal issues, conduct independent research, and present the results of their inquiries in a variety of ways.

Available at http://www.edu.gov.on.ca/eng/curriculum/secondary/canworld1112curr.pdf. The details, at 244–246, are not all that different from the 1987 version. See also the item "Canada in the World Community", id. at p. 153 discussing Canada's involvement in UN Peacekeeping, the WHO, the Universal Declaration of Human Rights, the Declaration on the Rights of Indigenous Peoples, and the International Campaign to Ban Landmines. Making the domestic law connections strikes a chord with some of my own experience in teaching United States law students. Perhaps my most successful course, Foreign Relations and National Security Law, deals primarily with the inter-relationship between the United States Constitution and International Law. Students quickly appreciate that the Founding Fathers believed in the law of nations (as they called it—see reference to Kent above nn 20–21) and sought to anchor their constitution in its framework. International Law thus has an immediate appeal, even if it is not a subject that is tested directly on the bar examination.

[41] Id. (Ontario Curriculum, 1987).

have been applied"; "Have students analyse the 1982 United Nations Convention on the Law of the Sea for its potential future impact;" and an open-ended one that caught my fancy: "Have students contact an agency such as Amnesty International for materials and information. Using this material as a basis for further research, students then analyse the role, methods and effectiveness of the agency and present findings in the form of a research paper." I like the combination in this last topic of close reading of a text, along with the historical and contemporary research techniques recommended[42] and the various kinds of written and oral outputs that emerge: a debate, an exposition, and evaluation of various modalities of operating. Lots of critical skills are being honed here, over and above the precise content of the exercises.

3 Is Teaching International Law a Matter of Legal Obligation and Not Merely Good Policy?

That introducing international law into the pre-university school curriculum might be a positive international obligation of states was suggested at the turn of the Millenium by Scott Pasternack in the Indiana International and Comparative Law Review.[43] Pasternack coined the word "worldism" for a course that would include "the history, structure and laws of international and regional institutions."[44] In arguing that there is an international obligation to introduce such material into the curriculum, Mr. Pasternack makes a number of arguments which are worth summarizing here.

First,[45] he reminds us of the calls by the General Assembly and ECOSOC to "study the possibility of introducing topics of international law in the curricula of schools at primary and secondary levels."[46] Secondly, he notes the reference in a number of human rights instruments[47] to the purpose of education. A good example is Article 5(1)(a) of the UNESCO Convention Against Discrimination in

[42] Research by students or scholars which involves talking to the people involved and getting the latter's stories, in addition to consulting the printed word (or these days the internet), has always appealed to me as a way to bring a subject to life.

[43] Pasternack (1999–2000).

[44] Id. at pp. 51–52.

[45] Id. at p. 52.

[46] G.A. Res. 45/40 (Annex) (1990) and later resolutions dealing with the United Nations Decade of International Law, discussed above. See also the voluminous other UN and Organization of American States materials discussed by Pasternack at 55–59, including Article 26(2) of the Universal Declaration of Human Rights which proclaims that education "shall promote understanding, tolerance and friendship among all nations, racial or religious groups, and shall further the activities of the United Nations for the maintenance of peace."

[47] The relevant provisions all appear to be derivative from Article 26(2) of the Universal Declaration of Human Rights, above note 46.

Education[48] which insists that "[e]ducation shall be directed to . . . the strengthening of respect for human rights and fundamental freedoms; it shall promote understanding, tolerance and friendship among all nations, racial or religious groups, and shall further the activities of the United Nations for the maintenance of peace." Another (in this case, non-treaty) instrument that Pasternack notes is the 1974 UNESCO Recommendation Concerning Education for International Understanding, Co-operation and Peace and Education Relating to Human Rights and Fundamental Freedoms.[49] In relevant part, that Recommendation reads:

> In order to enable every person to contribute actively to the fulfillment of the aims [set out in the Charter of the United Nations, the Constitution of UNESCO and the Universal Declaration of Human Rights and to] promote international solidarity and co-operation, which are necessary in solving the world problems affecting the individuals' and communities' life and exercise of fundamental rights and freedoms, the following objectives should be regarded as major guiding principles of educational policy

(a) an international dimension and a global perspective in education at all levels and in all its forms;
(b) understanding and respect for all peoples, their cultures, civilizations, values and ways of life, including domestic ethnic cultures and cultures of other nations;
(c) awareness of the increasing global interdependence between peoples and nations;
(d) abilities to communicate with others;
(e) awareness not only of the rights but also of the duties incumbent upon individuals, social groups and nations towards each other;
(f) understanding of the necessity for international solidarity and co-operation;
(g) readiness on the part of the individual to participate in solving the problems of his community, his country and the world at large.[50]

The extent to which statements such as these amount to customary law, binding on members of the international community, is not crucial to the present discussion. It is sufficient to note how strongly they reinforce the value of education in international law, even in the law's soft form.

---

[48] UNESCO Convention against Discrimination in Education (1960), 429 UNTS 93.

[49] Adopted by the General Conference at the eighteenth session of UNESCO, 19 November 1974, available at http://www.unesco.org/education/nfsunesco/pdf/Peace_e.pdf.

[50] Id. operative paragraph 4.

4 Should Teaching of International Law Be Introduced at the Secondary Level, or Earlier?

A reasonable question is whether pre-university study of international law should be confined to the secondary level. Dr. Buckingham thought so:

> Although this view is not universally shared, I think it is unrealistic to expect that the concepts of international law can be introduced any earlier than secondary school. Elementary students do not have the skills or the underlying knowledge base to appreciate international law. It is not until the secondary school years that the political and geographical awareness of students will crystallize sufficiently to look beyond one's borders to the international community.[51]

On the other hand, Jonathan Todres and Sarah Higinbotham, suggest in a very imaginative piece on children's literature, especially on the works of Dr. Seuss,[52] that some such education is already going on, perhaps without being explicitly articulated. A lengthy quote[53] is telling:

> In this emerging field of human rights and literature, and more broadly in the field of law and literature, the relationship between children's literature and children's rights and responsibilities has been overlooked. Yet stories which are often at the center of children's imaginative and creative lives, shape children's understanding, or lack of understanding, of rights. 'Only a tiny minority of the community will ever study law after the ages of around 18 or 19,' writes Ian Ward, 'but the vast majority who encounter a reasonably wide spectrum of children's literature will already have engaged in the jurisprudential debate.'[54]

The authors continue:

> Recently, compelling work on children's literature and law has been done in the areas of legal norms, adoption law, punishment and legal agency, as well as on how children

---

[51] Buckingham (1996) p. 363 n. 14. He added, however, quite fairly:

For a view which implicitly denies this position, see the Centre for Human Rights, *Teaching Human Rights: Practical Activities for Primary and Secondary Schools* (United Nations, New York, 1989).

There was a new edition of this handy 84-page work in 2004. See discussion below at notes 71–81.

[52] Todres and Higinbotham (2013). The authors find some striking connections between Dr Seuss's work and the rights enumerated in the Convention on the Rights of the Child. For my own speculations on the law relating to nuclear weapons and Dr Seuss's *The Butter Battle Book*, see Clark (2013/2014). The latter contribution is part of a major symposium in Volume 58, Number 3 of the Review devoted to the connections between Dr Seuss's work and the law which could be of considerable interest to educators.

[53] Todres and Higinbotham (2013), p. 40.

[54] Id. quoting Ward (1995).

perceive the law through the stories they read. Some of these critical essays have emphasized the formative effect of the imagination in children's understanding of law.[55]

In his "worldism" article,[56] Scott Pasternack, discusses a "still timely" 1976 study on the 1974 UNESCO Recommendation. It was produced for the United States National Commission for UNESCO by Thomas Buergenthal (later a judge on the International Court of Justice) and Judith Torney (a professor of psychology who was one of the drafters on the UNESCO Recommendation).[57] The authors in turn rely on a study from the National Council on Social Studies[58] for these conclusions:

VI. International learning begins early in life.
VII. International learning is cumulative ... what children learn at one age builds upon and is influenced by what they have previously learned.
VIII. The time of middle childhood (grades three through eight) is an important period in international learning.
IX. The beliefs, attitudes, values, and knowledge individuals develop about the world differ—each individual student brings his or her own particular configuration of orientations toward the world.
X. The mass media, especially television and newspapers [and, today, the Internet], play an important role in children's international learning.[59]

Buergenthal and Torney draw some conclusions from this, directed particularly to United States education, but the lesson is far from limited to the United States:

> Positive national identity is established very early and forms part of the child's *perspective* for viewing the activity of other nations and his own, as well as the future of international society. The period before the age of fourteen in especially important because the child's openness to diversity in this period is more likely to foster positive international *attitudes*.

And further:

> The UNESCO Recommendation has given the appropriate breadth of focus ... A new course here or a new extra-curricular project there will not even approximate the degree of understanding of other peoples of the world, their problems and aspirations which will be needed by present-day students to become well-balanced and socially effective adults.[60]

---

[55] Id. with several references to relevant scholarly works. See also their quotation at pp. 44–45 of the work of Howe and Covell:

The evidence shows overwhelmingly that children who learn about and experience their rights are children who demonstrate the fundamentals of good citizenship. They gain knowledge not only of their basic rights but also their corresponding social responsibilities. They develop the attitudes and values that are necessary for the promotion and protection of the rights of others, and they acquire the behavioral skills necessary for effective participation in a democratic society.

Howe and Covell (2007) at p. 7.

[56] Pasternack (1999–2000) at pp. 61–64.

[57] Buergenthal and Torney (1976).

[58] Remy et al. (1975), pp. 39–40.

[59] Id. as quoted in Pasternack at p. 63 (includes Pasternack's interpolated addition of reference to internet).

[60] Buergenthal and Torney at pp. 122–123, quoted in Pasternack at pp. 63–64.

5 Some Curricular Materials for High Schools[61]

Dr. Buckingham, whose very suggestive essay was discussed earlier,[62] was subsequently involved in two book projects that have contributed to the teaching of legal issues in Canadian Schools and which contain discussions of international law: *Learning About Law*[63] and *Understanding the Law*.[64] Another former Canadian law professor, Daniel J. Baum, produced a very widely used volume in 1989, *Thinking About Law*[65] which was revised in 1995[66] and translated into French for use in Quebec and other Canadian provinces with French programmes.[67] In a telephone conversation with me, Mr. Baum stressed the importance in producing such materials (and in teaching them) that the author or teacher not "talk down" to the students and treat them as intelligent human beings.

The best general course for high schools devoted exclusively to general questions of international law that I have located is called Teaching International Law.[68]

[61] At the university level in the United States, most law school courses that I have encountered use one or other of the many collections of cases and materials offered by legal publishers as the primary teaching source. This reflects the pervasive influence of the "case method" in US legal education. Students are often recommended a brief textbook as supplementary reading. Some political science courses use the law school casebooks, with varying degrees of success. One excellent collection, Epps (2013) is aimed at intelligent students without an extensive legal background. My impression is that, in many parts of the world, the main teaching resource is a narrative textbook which is supplemented by a "package" of materials selected by the teacher, rather than materials supplemented by a text.

[62] Above at notes 26–42.

[63] Buckingham et al. (1997).

[64] Dickenson et al. (1996).

[65] Baum (1989).

[66] 1995 edition with Roland Case. Mr. Baum has written widely for high schools and community colleges on a number of law-related topics.

[67] Mr. Baum's most recent work, Baum (2014), while it discusses Canadian domestic law, is a template for addressing complex legal subjects in a manner which is intelligible but not condescending to the target audience. Anyone contemplating strategies to discuss the UN standards and norms on criminal justice with high school students will find Youth and the Law a suggestive model. There are probably lessons to be drawn also from another "domestic law" project, the Marshall-Brennan Constitutional Literacy Project that operates across the United States. Law students, under faculty supervision, teach constitutional law doctrine to high school students, especially in inner cities. See Friedman et al. (2013) (there are several other interesting articles on the topic in the same issue of the Review). See also the work of Street Law, Inc., in which lawyers, law students and teachers work together to teach high school students about law, democracy and human rights, description available at http://www.streetlaw.org/en/home.

[68] Caroline Starbird, Jenny Pettit and Laurel Singleton, Teaching International Law (2004) (part of a series on Concepts in International Relations), available at http://www.worldaffairschallenge.org/wp-content/uploads/2012/01/Teaching-International-Law.pdf. A paperback edition is advertised through a print-on-demand service. An imaginative document that could be useful in high schools, as well as universities and in educating the general public is the American Society of International Law's *International Law: 100 Ways It Shapes Our Lives*, available at http://www.asil.org/education/100-ways.

It was produced at the Center for Teaching International Relations, formerly attached to the International Relations School at the University of Denver.[69] It has various problem-based lessons that raise such issues as the nature of international law, treaties and model laws, public international organizations (mainly on the UN and the WTO), international human rights, international trade law, the role of nongovernmental organizations (NGOs), the law of the sea, labor rights and international environmental law. Some excellent role-playing exercises are included, fostering both litigation and negotiation skills.

A particularly imaginative publication, *ABC: Teaching Human Rights, Practical Activities for Primary and Secondary Schools*,[70] as has been noted,[71] proceeds on the basis that human rights education can and should begin at a very early age. Indeed, the Plan of Action of the United Nations Decade for Human Rights Education, which inspired its publication, suggested the following:

---

[69] The Center is apparently in the process of re-inventing itself as a separate non-for-profit. See http://www.volunteermatch.org/search/org211098.jsp. I suspect that many initiatives such as this ultimately founder on a lack of continuing financial resources.

[70] *ABC* (2004) (revised edition published in 2004 by the Office of the United Nations High Commissioner for Human Rights). The publication was UNHCHR's major contribution to the U.N. Decade for Human Rights Education (1995–2004). The Decade was mandated by G.A. Res. 50/177 of 22 December 1995. In the Plan of Action for the Decade, set out in UN Doc. A/51/506/ Add. 1 of 12 December 1996 at 6, the UNHCHR noted the objective of the Decade thus:

Human rights education under the Decade shall seek both to impart skills and knowledge to learners and to affect positively their attitudes and behaviour, consistent with all other principles set forth in the present Plan of Action and in the international human rights instruments upon which it is based.

The Decade was followed by the World Programme for Human Rights Education, proclaimed by G.A. Res. 59/113 of 10 December 2004. A large number of United Nations programmes and agencies have been cooperating in the World Programme under the aegis of the United Nations Inter Agency Coordinating Committee on Human Rights Education in the School System (UNISACC). The Office of the High Commissioner for Human Rights is the lead agency in this endeavour. See material at http://www.ohchr.org/EN/Issues/Education/Training/WPHRE/FirstPhase/Pages/UNInterAgency.aspx. The Programme has been operating in 5-year phases. The first phase, 2005–2009, focused on human rights education in primary and secondary schools; the current (second) phase, 2010–2014 deals with human rights education for higher education and on human rights training programmes for teachers and educators, civil servants, law enforcement officials and military personnel. As a contribution to the first phase, a consortium led by the Office for Democratic Institutions and Human Rights of the Organization for Security and Co-operation in Europe (OSCE/ODIHR), and including the Council of Europe (CoE), the Office of the United Nations High Commissioner for Human Rights (OHCHR) and the United Nations Educational, Scientific and Cultural Organization (UNESCO) produced a very useful volume, Human Rights Education in the School Systems of Europe, Central Asia and North America: A Compendium of Good Practice (2009). The Foreword to this publication containing 101 examples of good practices describes it as "a resource for practitioners and policymakers as well as a platform for exchange among institutions and individuals." More recently, the OHCHR and UNESCO have produced a document entitled Human Rights Education in Primary and Secondary School Systems: A Self-Assessment Guide for Governments (2012). It has some thoughtful material on practices and on the literature dealing with assessment of the effectiveness of human rights programmes in schools.

[71] Above at n 51.

> Schools, universities, professional and vocational training programmes and institutions should be encouraged and assisted in developing human rights curricula and corresponding teaching and resource materials, with the help of Governments and international donors and programmes for incorporation into formal education at the early childhood, primary, secondary, post-secondary and adult education levels.[72]

Chapter 1 of ABC lays out principal human rights concepts, drawing particular attention to the development of human rights law under the aegis of the United Nations Charter and to the major human rights instruments: the Universal Declaration of Human Rights, the Covenants on Economic, Social and Cultural Rights and on Civil and Political Rights, the International Convention on the Elimination of All Forms of Racial Discrimination, the Convention on the Elimination of All Forms of Discrimination against Women, the Convention against Torture and Other Cruel, Inhuman of Degrading Treatment or Punishment and the Convention on the Rights of the Child. The Children's Convention is of particular significance to pre-university education; the Convention's approach to children's rights emphasizes the inherent dignity of children and insists that "the child should be fully prepared to live an individual life in society, and [be] brought up in the spirit of the ideals proclaimed in the Charter of the United Nations, and in particular in the spirit of peace, dignity, tolerance, freedom, equality and solidarity."[73] This Chapter also contains some pioneering efforts suggesting a step-by-step approach to familiarizing students with human rights concepts at various ages, categories entitled early childhood (ages 3–7), later childhood (ages 8–11), adolescence (ages 12–14) and youth (ages 15–17). There are suggestions about what kinds of concepts, practices, specific human rights problems and which standards and instruments can be introduced at each stage of development. It also makes the important point[74] that opportunities for including human rights themes in the curriculum may vary: "human rights themes may be infused into existing school subjects, such as history, civics, literature, art, geography, languages and scientific subjects, or may have a specific course allocated to them; human rights education may also be pursued through less formal education arenas within and outside schools such as after-school activities, clubs and youth forums."[75] It concludes with some suggestions for

---

[72] Plan of Action, above note 70 at p. 9.

[73] Convention on the Rights of the Child, preambular paragraph 7. Note also UNICEF's Rights Respecting Schools initiative which encourages putting the Convention on the Rights of the Child at the centre of a school's planning, policies, practice and ethos. See http://www.unicef.org.uk/Get-Involved/Your-organisation/Schools/rights-respecting-school-award/. Although the CRC has not been translated into as many languages as the UDHR, UNESCO has it in 58 languages, many of them child-friendly versions. See http://www.unicef.org/magic/briefing/uncorc.html.

[74] *ABC* at p. 18.

[75] In my daughter's high school in New Jersey, a history course on the Holocaust introduced her to some basic notions of human rights and international law. Her teacher was also engaged with the Model United Nations Program, below. No doubt international legal material could be inserted into history courses dealing with the American Civil War (and the Lieber Code on the laws of armed conflict) and on comparable European experience leading to the adoption of the first Geneva Convention in 1864. And see ASIL material below n 83. Slavery and the slave trade is another

pedagogical techniques for human rights education that the authors believe have "proved especially appropriate for human rights education because they encourage critical thinking, both cognitive and affective learning, respect for differences of experience and opinion, and active engagement of all participants in ongoing learning."[76] These are brainstorming, case studies, creative expression (such as drama,[77] graphic arts, song and dance), discussion, field trips/community visits, interviews (of family members, activists or eye-witnesses),[78] research projects, role plays/simulations and visual aids (such as posters, slides, videos and films).

Chapter 2 of ABC is aimed at primary teachers and it fills out some of these general ideas in age-appropriate ways. In particular, it offers suggestions for "nurturing younger children's sense of their own worth and that of others through materials that evoke the human rights principles of human dignity and equality."[79]

Chapter 3 "contains activities for upper primary and secondary school students that are of a more sophisticated nature and deal with current issues."[80]

ABC: Teaching Human Rights is, in short, a very stimulating work[81]

---

obvious area where historical analysis can be combined with some appreciation of the contribution that treaty law (both bilateral and multilateral) made to the abolition of that odious trade. UNESCO has some creative materials on the trade in its Transatlantic Slave Trade project, available at http://www.unesco.org/new/en/education/networks/global-networks/aspnet/flagship-projects/transatlantic-slave-trade/. In respect of "after-school activities", consider for example the presence of Amnesty International or other human rights groups in some high schools. In law schools there is recurrent debate on whether international law should be addressed in bespoke courses or whether it should be "mainstreamed" with modules in other courses. The "best practice" is surely to do both.

[76] *ABC* (2004) at p. 25.

[77] English teachers may find in Shakespeare's Henry V a useful opportunity to introduce students to the law of armed conflict. See Meron (1993).

[78] As an "activist" on such issues as criminal justice, nuclear weapons and the International Criminal Court, I have occasionally been interviewed by local high school students in New Jersey in what seemed each time to be a very creative assignment by an engaged teacher which combines interviewing and writing skills along with substantive learning.

[79] *ABC* (2004) at p. 6.

[80] Id.

[81] As I suggested at the beginning of this chapter, Peace Studies is also an area of the curriculum where issues of international law are inevitably introduced. For a collection of very thought-provoking material aimed at early childhood education and at primary and secondary programmes in the New Zealand School Curriculum, see the website entitled "education4peace" at the University of Otago, a production of the New Zealand National Centre for Peace and Conflict Studies, available at https://podcasts.otago.ac.nz/nzpeace-ed/peace-education-directory/. On the International Baccalaureate and its human rights component, see the chapter in this volume by Elizabeth Stanners, School education and social behavior: teaching aspects of human rights and values. Genocide is another area; the American University, Washington College of Law, has some excellent materials in its Genocide Teaching Project which is aimed at high schools. See http://www.wcl.american.edu/humright/center/rwanda/lesson.cfm.

6 Educational Strategies

Late in 2014, the American Society of International Law (ASIL) posted on its website[82] a set of four curriculum modules designed to support high school teachers seeking to add international law elements to their classrooms.[83] ASIL developed these materials with grant funding support from the Open Society Foundations. These are a free resource on the ASIL website—downloadable and available for anyone to use in any educational setting. Each module is designed to give teachers two 45 min-long classes to be incorporated into topics that are commonly taught in high school history or social studies classes (U.S. Constitution, U.S. Civil War, World War II, and the Civil Rights Movement). Each module provides a variety of teaching topics, links to free, online supporting resources (such as YouTube videos of famous speeches, etc.), and evaluation and classroom exercise materials. Each is also designed to cover some element of how international laws, principles, or standards impacted a particular issue and then look to the present on how those issues are reflected in current national and international settings.[84] These modules are a significant addition to the materials currently available to high school teachers.

Materials such as those just noted are invaluable for an in-class curriculum. Mention should also be made of particularly significant out of class events (or at least partially out of class).[85] A few years ago, I was asked to brief students participating in a high school Model United Nations event. The group was doing a simulation of a meeting of the Third (Social, Humanitarian and Cultural) Committee of the United Nations General Assembly which deals with human rights and social development matters. That part of the programme on which I was asked to

---

[82] www.asil.org/education.

[83] The modules are entitled: The United States Constitution and International Law; The Rules of War: From the Civil War-Era Lieber Code to the Geneva Conventions; The Nuremberg Tribunal: Justice and Accountability; and Lessons Learned: Civil Rights and Human Rights in the United States and the World. The American Bar Association has a program for Civics and Law Academies which can be offered in various formats—in-class or as curricular add-ons. The current materials all address American legal issues, see http://www.americanbar.org/groups/civics/civics_and_law_academy.html, but the format seems to be eminently adaptable to international legal issues.

[84] I am grateful to D. Wes Rist, Director of Education and Research at the ASIL for this information and for a peek at an advanced draft of the materials which are very professionally done.

[85] The following is another example of an extracurricular experience adaptable to international law. The New Zealand Centre for Global Studies (http://nzcgs.org.nz/news-and-events/) hosted a project titled *Global Citizenship in Schools*, involving senior high-school students selected by application. In collaboration with a leading secondary school, Auckland Girls Grammar, the Centre convened a conference in August 2012 (Auckland) and has held seminars on the subject in March 2014 (Waiheke). Report by the students on file with the author. On global citizenship studies, see also references in n 8 above. Libby Giles, the Auckland Girls Grammar teacher directly involved with the Waiheke event, emphasized in an e-mail the need for teacher training to cope with the cross-curricular skills involved in global citizenship education.

speak arose out of the Report of the Commission on Crime Prevention and Criminal Justice on its then most recent meeting. It was clear from the thoughtful questions that followed my talk that the students had entered enthusiastically into the spirit of the event and had done a significant amount of research. Model United Nations events are aimed variously at high school, community college and university students (undergraduate and graduate). Students choose or are assigned particular countries to represent and they then research the position of that country on the relevant issues. The website of the Model UN Headquarters makes the point that "[f]or over 50 years now, teachers and students have benefited from and enjoyed this interactive learning experience. It not only involves young people in the study and discussion of global issues, but also encourages the development of skills useful throughout their lives, such as research, writing, public speaking, problem solving, consensus building, conflict resolution and compromise and cooperation."[86] One exciting exercise in which the groups often engage is the drafting and negotiation of a United Nations Resolution, typically of the General Assembly or the Economic or Social Council, but it is easy enough to set the issues in plenary or committee meetings of Specialized Agencies such as the International Labour Organization or UNESCO. Events can take place within a particular class or school (under the aegis of a class or a Model UN club), but it is common for Conference events to be large and involve numerous schools. There are many opportunities to participate. For example, the National Model United Nations has brought together thousands of students for events in New York, Washington, D.C., Rome and Olomouc in the Czech Republic.[87] In the United States, the United Nations Association[88] and several leading universities[89] have excellent offerings, including events for high school as well as inter-university competition. The Ivy League Model United Nations Conference (ILMUNC) describes itself, with only a little hyperbole, as "the premier Model United Nations for high schools" and attracts students from across the globe. Its January 2015 event took place at the University of Pennsylvania in Philadelphia.[90] A number of groups have produced useful sets of resources for those participating or contemplating participating in the events.[91] My

[86] Model UN, FAQ, available at http://www.un.org/cyberschoolbus/modelun/faq.html.

[87] National Model UN, available at http://www.nmun.org/.

[88] United Nations Association of the United States of America, Model UN: How to Participate, available at http://www.unausa.org/global-classrooms-model-un/how-to-participate.

[89] My own university hosts a well-attended Model United Nations for high schools. See http://modelun.com/rumun/. In addition, the Rutgers University Model UN Travel team reports competing in inter-university competitions in The Hague, Montreal and Puebla, Mexico as well as throughout the United States, available at http://www.ruair.org/model-un-team.html. For an extensive list of high school events, see Bestdelegate, Model United Nations Conference Database, available at http://bestdelegate.com/model-un-conferences-database/.

[90] See Ivy League Model United Nations Conference, available at http://www.ilmunc.com/.

[91] E.g., National Model UN Delegate Preparation Guide (2013), available at http://www.nmun.org/ny_archives/ny13_downloads/Delegate_Prep_Guide2013.pdf. Chen (2009), available at http://www.scribd.com/doc/9717149/Model-United-Nations-Handbook.

international law students who have participated earlier in their academic career in the Model United Nations invariably describe it as a life-enriching experience which was instrumental in encouraging them to proceed with further study and potential employment in the area.

7 Conclusion

Despite some stimulation by exhortations and programmes at the global level, particularly from the United Nations and UNESCO, it can hardly be said that international law is taught widely at either the pre-university or university level across the world. Indeed, as a teacher of international law for half a century, a sad personal reflection upon completing the research for this chapter, is how little the subject is taught even in law schools. All my instincts tell me that the core of teaching in international law should take place in the classroom using interactive materials and informed by the larger context in which international law takes a place. My impression, however, is that currently the best education on the subject that goes on in high schools is through extra-curricular simulations such as Model United Nations events. Nevertheless, I believe that there are significant opportunities to add the study of international law, including information on human rights and social development issues in general and crime prevention and criminal justice issues in particular, in high school curricula. The production of a greater range of suitable teaching materials in many more languages and resources devoted to teacher training in the area should be a matter of high priority.

Five Questions

1. What is the status of international law in the education system in your country? Is it taught in elementary or high schools? If so, is it a stand-alone part of the curriculum, or is it part of other programmes such as civics, social studies or history? At the university level is it compulsory for law students? Is it offered/required in such disciplines as political science or international relations? Should it be much more widely offered/required?
2. Can students be introduced to concepts of international law in elementary school? In high school? If so, what topics are most appropriate?
3. What materials are available for teaching international law in high schools? How is it possible to stimulate the writing and dissemination of such materials? Can governments be persuaded to commission such materials? Should philanthropic organizations put resources into such endeavors?
4. What is the best way to stimulate extra-curricular activities about international law in high schools (e.g., symposia, Model United Nations and other simulations, field trips to the UN or other international organizations)?
5. Are issues of crime prevention and criminal justice (because of their inherent interest) particularly suited to pre-university study? How can such material, which often appears technical and abstract, best be made appealing to younger students?

References

Aromaa, K., & Redo, S. (Eds.). (2008). *For the Rule of Law: criminal justice teaching and training across the world*. Helsinki and Seoul: HEUNI and Korean Institute of Criminal Justice Policy.

Astrada, M., & Martin, F. (2013). *Russia and Latin America: from nation state to society of states*. New York: Palgrave.

Baum, D. J. (1989). *Thinking about Law*. Toronto: IPI Publishing.

Baum, D. J. (2014). *Youth and the Law*. Toronto: Dundurn.

Bederman, D. (2010). *International Law frameworks* (3rd ed.). St. Paul: Foundation.

Bemis, P. (2000). *Calling the shots: how Washington dominates today's UN*. Brooklyn: Olive Branch Press.

Betts, R. (2012). *Conflict after the cold war: arguments on causes of war and peace* (4th ed.). New York: Pearson Longman.

Buckingham, D. (1996). Creating world-class citizens: International law as an essential ingredient in secondary education. In *United Nations, International Law as a language for international relations* 358. The Hague: Kluwer.

Buckingham, D., et al. (1997). *Learning about Law*. Toronto: McGraw-Hill Ryerson. French edition, *Comprendre Le Droit Canadien* (2003). Chenelière McGraw-Hill, Montréal.

Buergenthal, T., & Torney, J. V. (1976). *International human rights and international education*. Washington, DC: Department of State.

Buergenthal, T., & Murphy, S. (2013). *Public International Law in a Nutshell* (5th ed.). St. Paul: West.

Chen, G., (Ed.), (2009). *Model United Nations Handbook*, available at http://www.scribd.com/doc/9717149/Model-United-Nations-Handbook#scribd.

Cheng, B. (Ed.). (1982). *International Law: Teaching and practice*. London: Stevens.

Clark, R. S. (1994). *The United Nations crime prevention and criminal justice program: Formulation of standards and efforts at their implementation*. Philadelphia: University of Pennsylvania Press.

Clark, R. S. (2013). Is *The Butter Battle Book*'s Bitsy Big Boy Boomeroo Banned? What has international law to say about weapons of mass destruction? *New York Law School Law Review, 58*, 655.

Dickenson, D., et al. (1996). *Understanding the Law*. Toronto: McGraw-Hill Ryerson. French language edition Le Droit Candien et International (2004). Chenelière McGraw Hill, Montréal.

Dixon, M. (2013). *Textbook on International Law* (7th ed.). Oxford: OUP.

Epps, V. (2013). *International Law* (5th ed.). Durham, NC: Carolina.

Friedman, J., et al. (2013). Educating young people about law in a disadvantaged city: Rutgers university school of law and the city of Camden, New Jersey. *Denver University Law Review, 90*, 937.

Gamble, J. (1993). *Teaching International Law*. New York: American Society of International Law.

Hart, H. L. A. (1961). *The concept of Law*. Oxford: Clarendon.

Howe, R. B., & Covell, K. (2007). *Empowering children: Children's rights education as a pathway to citizenship*. Toronto: U Toronto Press.

Kent, J. (1858). *Commentaries on American Law* (9th ed.). Boston: Little Brown (1st ed 1826).

Lachs, M. (1982). *The Teacher in International Law (Teachings and Teaching)*. The Hague: Nijhoff.

Lowe, V. (2007). *International Law*. Oxford: Clarendon.

Mansell, W., & Openshaw, K. (2013). *International Law a Critical Introduction*. Oxford and Portland: Hart.

McNemar, D. W. (1983). The task of education: Broadening professional training and public awareness. *Proceedings of the American Society of International Law, 75*, 173.

Meron, T. (1993). *Henry's wars and Shakespeare's Laws: Perspectives on the law of war in the later middle ages*. Oxford: OUP.

Natarajan, M. (2011). *International crime and criminal justice*. Cambridge: CUP.

Organization for Security and Cooperation in Europe et al. (2009). *Human rights education in the school systems of Europe, Central Asia and North America*. Warsaw: OSCE.
Pasternack, S. (1999–2000). The international legal obligation to teach worldism in U.S. classrooms. *Indiana International and Comparative Law Review, 10*, 51.
Podgor, E., & Clark, R. (2013). *Understanding International Criminal Law (3rd ed.)*. New Providence, NJ: LexisNexis.
Ram, C. D. (2012). *Meeting the challenge of crime in the global village: An assessment of the role and future of the United Nations Commission on Crime Prevention and Criminal Justice*. Helsinki: HEUNI.
Redo, S. M. (2012). *Blue criminology: The power of the United Nations to counter crime globally*. Helsinki: HEUNI.
Remy, R., et al. (1975). *International learning and education in a global age*. Silver Spring: National Council for the Social Studies.
Simpson, G. (1999). On the magic mountain: Teaching Public International Law. *EJIL, 10*, 70.
Spijkers, O. (2011). *The United Nations, the evolution of global values and International Law*. Cambridge: Intersentia.
Starbird, C., et al. (2004). *Teaching International Law (on line)*. Denver: Center for Teaching International Relations.
Todres, J., & Higinbotham, S. (2013). A Person's a Person: Children's rights in children's literature. *Columbia Human Rights Review, 45*, 1.
United Nations (2004). *ABC: Teaching human rights, practical activities for primary and secondary schools*. New York and Geneva: United Nations.
United Nations, UNESCO (2012). *Human rights education in primary and secondary schools: A self-assessment guide for governments*. Geneva, Paris, New York: United Nations/UNESCO.
Ward, I. (1995). *Law and literature: Possibilities and perspectives*. Cambridge: CUP.

Legal Education in Transition: Is the *Bologna Process* Responding to Europe's Place in the World?

Emil W. Pływaczewski and Izabela Kraśnicka

Abstract The Bologna Process is a series of ministerial meetings and agreements between European countries, which began in 1999 to ensure the harmonization of the standards and quality of higher education qualifications. Through the Bologna Accords, the process has created the European Higher Education Area. The preoccupation of the Bologna Process with continental Europe has left out from its purview other regions of the world where traditionally European universities have played a leading role.

This article reassesses the Bologna Process against the North American universities' outreach and proposes new avenues for matching it by the European universities.

It will first examine the Bologna Process: its goals, achievements and failures. Special emphasis, as detailed analysis will be put on the mobility component of the Bologna Process—Erasmus program and its potential for the future.

The US system of legal education will be then shortly presented with special emphasis on the clinical legal education as the American method which in regions all over the world promoted not only an effective teaching mechanisms but core, fundamental principles such as rule of law and human rights.

Transatlantic influence of the Bologna Process will also be examined to bring final conclusions for possible international actions in the future. The text is based on data available in 2014.

> The main hope of a nation lies in the proper education of its youth. Desiderius Erasmus (1466–1536)

E.W. Pływaczewski (✉) • I. Kraśnicka
Faculty of Law, University of Bialystok, Białystok, Poland
e-mail: e.plywaczewski@uwb.edu.pl; krasnicka@uwb.edu.pl

H. Kury et al. (eds.), *Women and Children as Victims and Offenders: Background, Prevention, Reintegration*, DOI 10.1007/978-3-319-08398-8_13

1 Introduction

Internationalization of higher education has become a global trend. Initiatives aiming at addressing the modern needs of economy and education have been designed and implemented throughout all regions in the world. International organizations such as the World Trade Organization, the Asia Pacific Economic Cooperation, agencies of the United Nations as well as the regional European institutions (European Union, Council of Europe, Organization for the Economic Cooperation and Development/OECD) have been active not only by gathering data and publishing rankings on the level of education and higher education in particular countries but have also tried to propose some extensive and comprehensive programs of reforms. Those reforms are to help states develop educational programs to establish, improve and facilitate global higher education mobility and quality (Terry 2011, pp. 305–356; Rowland 2013, pp. 123–124).

The European Union (EU) has been especially active in this field. Although education does not fall under the exclusive competences of the Union and Member States are free to decide on their educational systems, the idea of harmonization of some educational standards throughout the EU has been regarded as an element necessary to achieve basic goals of the European integration. Economic benefits of the internal market can be used only if the EU teaches its future professionals how to deal with comparative aspects of instruments and institutions, how to understand and accommodate the cultural, language, social, political and most of all legal differences present in Member States.

It is possible only if students have a chance to freely enjoy the possibility of studying at partner universities in different states provided the programs of foreign exchange will be recognized at their home schools and some common evaluation rules will be established to foster the process. As part of the European internal market freedoms, student mobility is known as the free movement of students (Götzelmann 2010, p. 55). As such it should be accompanied by the quality of education undergoing assurance and possibility of flexible adjustment of teaching methods responding to the needs of the global market.

The 2009 Lisbon reform of the EU has brought some significant changes and clarifications in the complex relation between the Union and its Member States. One of the key issues finally adopted in the text of the main treaties is the list of exclusive powers of the EU along with the list of powers shared between the EU and Member States and the list of powers where the Union's role is limited to a support function.

Education is listed in the Treaty on the Functioning of the EU (TFUE, art. 6), as an area of action where "The Union shall have competence to carry out actions to support, coordinate or supplement the actions of the Member States". As a result Member States may freely shape their educational systems and the Union may only come in as a cooperating partner proposing some ideas or projects but with no power to execute them and force member states to apply them. Harmonization of any educational issues relies therefore on the common acceptance of the twenty-eight EU countries.

Higher education, especially legal education constitutes a very specific, yet crucial platform for possible cooperation and harmonization. Even though Member States of the EU have different legal traditions, combine elements of various legal cultures, and each legal order of each Member State has its own unique specifics, the education of future lawyers seem to have similar elements in most of those systems. In order to practice law it is necessary to obtain an academic degree and further complete some kind of practical training (Lonbay 2011–2012, p. 479).

Through its programs and proposed reforms (see below), the Union has tried to harmonize the higher education systems of the Member States and enable both students and faculty members to enjoy the open borders of the European market as well as to provide ways to extend the reach to non-EU states and regions.

2 The Bologna Process

2.1 Lisbon Origins of the Bologna Process

The Bologna Process originating from the Bologna Declaration of 1999 is commonly associated with the projects, works, efforts and achievements of the EU. It should be therefore clarified that the primary document triggering further actions and laying the foundations for the design and acceptance of the Bologna Declaration was prepared as a result of the joint work of the Council of Europe and the United Nations Educational, Scientific and Cultural Organization's (UNESCO) European program. As such the core ideas of educational freedom, increased students mobility and flexibility of the study periods' recognition have a broader, rather international than European (or strictly EU) background.

The Convention on the Recognition of Qualifications concerning Higher Education in the European Region (Lisbon Convention[1]) was adopted by national representatives meeting in Lisbon on 8–11 April 1997. It has been since then ratified by most European countries, members of the Council of Europe as well as by some non-European states including the United States of America and Australia and the only non-member of the Council of Europe in Europe—Belarus. The Convention had entered into force on February 1, 1999, just a few months before the Bologna Declaration was announced. The aim of the Convention was to oblige its signatories to recognize qualifications obtained while studying at foreign institutions established in other states that had signed the Convention, and to ensure that graduates of secondary education would have access to higher education programs in other signatory states. It laid firm foundations for other European

[1] Convention on the Recognition of Qualifications concerning Higher Education in the European Region Council of Europe Treaty Series No. 165.

projects and still constitutes in fact the only legally binding document within the widely understood Bologna Process, which the EU initiated, more or less successfully implemented in cooperation with its Member States and is continuing it through other initiatives (McKiernan and Birtwistle 2009–2010, p. 516).

The Bologna Process itself engages not only EU Member States but also other European countries—a total of 47 participating states and as such reaches far beyond the EU borders (Kazakhstan as the 47th participating country of the European Higher Education Area was accepted in 2010).

The Bologna Process is closely linked to the Lisbon Strategy operational between 2000 and 2010. As stated in the Report analyzing the Lisbon Strategy, at its beginning in 2000 the EU introduced a very ambitious and challenging goal "to become the most dynamic and competitive knowledge-based economy in the world, capable of sustainable economic growth with more and better jobs and greater social cohesion, and respect for the environment" (The Lisbon Strategy 2000–2010, p. 13). Quality of higher education plays a key role on the road to achieve such goal.

The Bologna Process is comprised of a number of documents, programs, projects, analysis, declarations, frameworks and communications accepted during meetings of the higher education ministers of particular countries as well as through the constant work of national groups preparing those meetings (Terry 2006, pp. 864–865). Problems presented below will be mostly narrowed to issues concerning higher education in the legal studies.

2.2 *High Bologna Hopes for the European Higher Education Area in the Field of Legal Education*

The goal of the Bologna Process, as introduced in the Bologna Declaration of 1999 (Bologna Declaration) was to establish a European Higher Education Area (EHEA). Six objectives leading to this goal include:

1. Adoption of a system of **easily readable and comparable degrees**, also through the implementation of the Diploma Supplement, in order to promote European citizens employability and the international competitiveness of the European higher education system
2. Adoption of a system essentially based on **two main cycles**, undergraduate and graduate
3. Establishment of a **system of credits**—such as in the European Credit Transfer and Accumulation System (ECTS)—as a proper means of promoting the most widespread student mobility
4. Promotion of **mobility** by overcoming obstacles to the effective exercise of free movement
5. Promotion of **European co-operation in quality assurance** with a view to developing comparable criteria and methodologies

6. Promotion of the **necessary European dimensions in higher education**, particularly with regards to curricular development, inter-institutional co-operation, mobility schemes and integrated programs of study, training and research.

The Declaration, it has to be remembered, is not a legally binding document. An ambitious goal and equally ambitious objectives set up by the signatories left their implementation to the decisions made on national levels in every participating state (not only Member States of the EU).

The Declaration however designs more than just general objectives. There are clearly established standards proposed throughout the text. For example objective number 2 cited above is followed by a precise explanation: "Access to the second cycle shall require successful completion of first cycle studies, lasting a minimum of three years. The degree awarded after the first cycle shall also be relevant to the European labor market as an appropriate level of qualification. The second cycle should lead to the master and/or doctorate degree as in many European countries." Such specific terms were used in order to promote common standards in all the participating states. The word "harmonization" however does not appear in the text of the Declaration as it would create too much pressure on the states. After all, education stays within the national powers (Garben 2010, pp. 187–190). The idea is promoted as a voluntary decision made by each country and its higher education community to endorse the principles underlined in the European Higher Education Area. It is not harmonize but to provide tools to connect the national systems of higher education (European University Association).

Each of the objectives presented in the Bologna Declaration responds to the needs of improving legal education, with one exception, crucial to the entire process. Easily readable and comparable degrees are necessary to evaluate the work of law students at different universities given the specifics of teaching methodologies used throughout Europe. The ECTS system (if implemented properly) helps to compare the studying results (both the curriculum itself and the grades obtained by the students) and the workload applied for particular courses. Mobility of students and faculty members is certainly significant an provides opportunity to experience different legal systems, learn about the comparative aspects and obtain a much wider, fuller perspective on the complex dimensions of the European legal systems as well as the unique legal order of the EU. Finally, promotional actions in the fields of European co-operation in quality assurance and necessary European dimensions in higher education serve to assist in the improvement of legal education in changing regional, international and global circumstances. It may and already has had a positive impact on some legal education systems which were considered not good enough for the global market because they were too theoretical and insufficient in terms of teaching necessary skills (Atienza 2011–2012, p. 472).

However the idea of breaking up the study programs into cycles caused various problems and, as a consequence, triggered a series of protests leading to the adoption of different solutions in many European countries. The details of this issue will be presented in the following part of the chapter.

2.3 *Achievements and Disappointments of the Bologna Process*

With all the possible different evaluations of the Bologna Process, one statement seems to be left without much controversy: The Bologna Process has transformed the face of European higher education. This statement opens the first paragraph of the Executive Summary, part of the major Bologna evaluation report: The European Higher Education Area in 2012: Bologna Process Implementation Report. The conclusions of the report contain both—satisfaction and disappointment.

It is undoubtedly a success that 47 countries have on a voluntary basis decided to reform their higher education systems to make studying in Europe open and possible to students from other countries and to improve the quality of education provided. Enrolments in higher education increased between 1999 and 2009, even if the development was not uniform throughout the countries (The European Higher Education Area in 2012, p. 9). This increase however is threatened by present and future significant demographic changes: the European population is ageing. The average percentage of the OECD countries aged over 65 is expected to rise from 14 % in 2005 to 21 % in 2030; at the same time the age group of 18–24 year olds (which constitutes the enrollment group for higher education) will fall on average by 9 % by 2025 (Vincent-Lancrin 2008, pp. 42–43).

Ambitious goals usually require strong financial support. It comes as no surprise that, given the world economic crisis, the European statistics show that there has been an overall decline in higher education expenditure, even if the calculations vary among the countries, and in some states the financial resources dedicated to higher education have grown (The European Higher Education Area in 2012, p. 8 and 23–28).

In all of the 47 Bologna Process countries the system of three cycle studies have been implemented. In 26 countries, as stated in the report, the share of students studying in programs corresponding to the Bologna two-cycle system is 90 % and in 13 other countries 70–89 %, in some countries the legislative procedures are still being adopted (The European Higher Education Area in 2012, pp. 9–10).

There are however areas where education of a uniform 5 to 6 years program is required by national and/or EU law (architects, medical professions, lawyers). In legal education the 2 and 3-year cycles have been implemented only in some countries as the debate continues on what kind of qualifications a lawyer with only a first degree diploma has acquired. The problem received critical reactions from some countries, including a strong response from Germany (Riedel 2005, pp. 59–62). As a result the legal education in Europe varies from country to country. In some states it is offered as a first degree (3-year cycle) program (for example in Malta and Spain), in some it is a uniform masters program, (Czech Republic, Poland), in some, both ways are possible to a obtain law degree (United Kingdom), and some have specific, complex possibilities (France). It makes the exchange programs more complicated as it is difficult to compare the study programs and requirements on different levels of legal education.

The ECTS system has been implemented in most of the countries, and the common rule requires every student in the law program to obtain 60 ECTS credits per academic year. Each course is assigned with a specific number of credits reflecting the workload necessary to complete the course. Students using the mobility programs (such as Erasmus) are usually required to take courses at foreign universities and bring back 30 ECTS credits per semester or 60 ECTS credits per year. It is however very difficult or many times impossible to provide fair evaluation rules for students traveling across Europe. Study programs for regular, national students constitute usually the majority of study programs in the law schools. European students come to British universities to study in English, most European students come to Spain to master Spanish while studying law, and most students go to Germany to practice legal German. They take courses offered in regular study programs for national students. The situation is quite different when, for example, a Polish student chooses a Greek or Danish law school as a destination under the Erasmus program, or a Spanish or British student wishes to come to Poland to study. Those schools usually prepare study programs offered in foreign languages which differ from regular study programs. The number of ECTS credits also changes. For example, a Polish law student who happens to go to the Faculty of Law and Economics of the University of Thessaloniki for a semester or two will be offered a variety of courses taught in English, and each course will be valued at 6 ECTS credits. The same student going to a Danish law school in Copenhagen will be able to take courses offered in English valued at 10 ECTS credits per course. A French-speaking student from any EU state who comes to Paris will be faced with courses offered in French with ECTS assignment between 2.5 and 5 credits per course. In addition similar courses are assigned with a different number of hours and credits (for example the Law of the EU is valued 9 ECTS at the Bialystok Law Faculty in Poland and the same subject is valued 6 ECTS at the Croatian Law School in Rijeka). Navigation through adjustments and possible adaptation of study programs to enable recognition creates a number of challenges for Erasmus coordinators throughout European law schools.

To summarize, four reasons for the reluctance towards the Bologna Process presented by a Austrian law professor seem common and still present for most of the European states and include: 1. The organization of the universities has been subjected to permanent and increasingly radical reforms during the last three decades; 2. Several fundamental changes in the curriculum of the study of law have taken place since the late seventies; 3. there is great uncertainty about the professional perspectives of "bachelors of law"; 4. the number of law students has been continuously declining since 1995 (Posch 2005, p. 208).

3 The Erasmus Program: A Closer Look at the Bologna Mobility Component

3.1 The Erasmus Dimension of the Free Movement of Students in the EU

It is enough to cite one of many famous quotes of Desiderius Erasmus to fully understand why the EU has chosen him as the patron for the exchange program: "The main hope of a nation lies in the proper education of its youth". Erasmus was a very mobile scholar who traveled around Europe studying and teaching at different universities. The EU program under his name (Erasmus also comes as acronym for European Community Action Scheme for the Mobility of University Students) is meant to provide the exact same opportunities to students and scholars of the European higher education institutions.

The program started its operation in 1987 and was originally and with some problems designed by the European Commission to enable mobility of students within the EU. The Commission had to negotiate a compromise with some of the EU member states, which were not necessarily happy to see the funds gathered to establish a new transnational education program as it would be a direct competitor to their own well developed projects offered to students from other countries.

The Erasmus program was incorporated into the Socrates framework education program and existed as the Socrates/Erasmus program between 1999 and 2007 when it was replaced by the Lifelong Learning Program Erasmus (LLP-Erasmus between 2007 and 2014). The newest edition has just come into being as the Erasmus + (Erasmus Plus) program for 2014–2020 and has absorbed all of the past sub-programs and projects such as Erasmus Mundus, Gruntvig, Leonardo da Vinci, Jean Monnet, etc. (Erasmus Guide, p. 10).

The program is designed and supervised by the European Commission, which also plans its budget. The Education, Audiovisual and Culture Executive Agency of the Commission serves as the main executive body for the program. It cooperates and distributes means through a network of national agencies set up in every Member State of the EU.

Each university or other higher education institution wishing to participate in the Erasmus Plus program is obliged to sign and obey the Erasmus Charter for Higher Education (ECHE) confirming that participation in the program is part of its own strategy for modernization and internationalization (Erasmus Charter, p. 1).

The Erasmus program's goals throughout its editions have been extended but the core idea remains to support, improve and facilitate mobility among European and, further, also non-European students and teachers. The European Commission's aim was to make sure that higher education institutions and its members fully benefit from the open borders and freedom to study in different countries—both members of the EU and partner countries.

3.2 *Erasmus Actions in and Outside the EU: Successes and Failures in Numbers*

The Erasmus Program between 1987 and 2014 has experienced both spectacular successes and disappointing failures. It should be underlined that the number of the Member States of the EU within this period has increased from 12 to 28. The statistics and comments presented below will focus on the last edition of the program, namely the LLP-Erasmus program operating between 2007 and 2014 as the most representative one (Romania and Bulgaria joined the EU in 2007 and after only Croatia became a member in 2013). The latest statistics from the European Commission are available for the academic year 2011/2012. This chapter will analyze only the student mobility program, the numbers concerning staff mobility being outside the scope of this presentation.

The goal of the LLP-Erasmus program was to contribute through lifelong learning to the development of the EU as an advanced knowledge society, with sustainable economic development, more and better jobs and greater social cohesion (Preamble to Decision 1720/2006/EC).

Under the LLP-Erasmus, several subprograms were operating among which Erasmus for higher education was the key mobility program for students and faculty staff from the 33 countries benefiting from the program (the list included the 28 Member States of the Union and 5 non-EU countries: Norway, Switzerland, Turkey, Lichtenstein, Iceland).

The success of the LLP-Erasmus Program could be viewed through growing numbers of students using the mobility chances. In 2007/2008 total of 182,697 students travelled to study or train abroad and the number increased in the following years to: 198,523 in 2008/2009, 213,266 in 2009/2010, 231,408 in 2010/2011 and 252,827 in 2011/2012. The last year's record was a 9 % increase. Country statistics show that in the vast majority of Member States the number of Erasmus students have grown in the last years. The average growth in 11 countries reached 8.3 %, some countries (Slovenia, Turkey) went up by 17 %, Denmark by 20 % and Croatia hit the record with 62 %, but it should be noted that Croatia joined the program in 2009/2010. (Erasmus program in 2011–2012: the figures explained, pp. 2–3).

In some countries the number of students using the Erasmus opportunities have grown consistently in the last academic years. A good example is United Kingdom, whose students used to be rather moderately enthusiastic about studying outside their home schools. In 2011/2012 UK students took 13,663 periods of study or work-placement (comparing to 12,833 in 2010/2011 and 11,723 in 2009/2010) the highest number, the British Council notes, since the program was launched in 1987 (British Council Statistics, pp. 1–2). Even if the increase is not very high it is consistent, which brings hope for future growth as well.

From this perspective, LLP-Erasmus may be evaluated as a successful program. The perception changes, however, if we look at the same numbers from a different angle and add some others as well. In 2011/2012 total student population in the 33 participating states was 24 million, which means that only 1 % of all the students used the Erasmus opportunities. This is a very disappointingly low number. There were also some countries where the growth was minimal (e.g. France which achieved 5 % or Bulgaria 1 %) or none (such as Malta, Switzerland). There were some countries which witnessed a decrease in number of outgoing students including Romania—1 % or Cyprus—3 % (Erasmus program in 2011–2012: the figures explained, p. 2).

The European Commission also aimed at some cooperation and mobility programs outside the EU. Two related programs have so far reached outside the EU.

The Tempus program (run between 2000 and 2006 as Tempus III and between 2007 and 2013 as Tempus IV) supported the modernization of higher education in the Partner Countries of Eastern Europe, Central Asia, the Western Balkans and the Mediterranean region, mainly through university cooperation projects. In Tempus IV three main actions were announced for funding: Joint Projects (with relevant themes including curriculum development, enhancing university governance and creating better links between higher education and society at large), Structural Measures (aimed at development and reform of national educational systems in the partner countries to improve, for example, qualification systems, quality assurance, national laws, organization, coordination, accreditation, evaluation and the policy of higher education systems) and Accompanying Measures (comprising dissemination and information activities related to Tempus projects).

The number of applications submitted to the Tempus program witnessed dynamic changes in statistics. For example in the last Tempus IV edition, in the first call a total of 404 applications were submitted from the 27 Members States of the EU, which came into partnerships with institutions from other regions. In 2009 the numbers grew to 457, then dropped to 306 in 2010 to pick up again in 2011 to 423, 530 in 2012 and reach a record of 701 in 2013. The downside however is reflected in the number of accepted projects, for example out of 530, only 108 were approved to be funded including 45 in Eastern Europe, 34 in Southern Mediterranean countries, 24 in the Western Balkans and only 13 in Central Asia. In 2013, out of 701 proposals 171 were approved with a similar geographical diversion (Tempus Statistics). It seems that building extensive partnerships, finding common goals and measures for the projects within EU countries and other regions was difficult and problematic given not only the cultural diversities but also different expectations and project management possibilities.

Another wonderful example in its origins and disappointing in its final outcomes was the Erasmus Mundus program (last edition operating between 2009 and 2013). It aimed at enhancing the quality of European higher education, promoting understanding between peoples as well as contributing to the sustainable development of higher education in third countries whilst avoiding the brain drain and favoring vulnerable groups. It was also to it contribute to the development of human resources and the international cooperation capacity of higher education institutions in Third Countries by increasing the mobility between the EU and these countries. (Preamble to Decision 1298/2008/EC).

Under the Erasmus Mundus program financial support was provided for a total of three Actions in the following subjects: higher education institutions that wished to implement joint programs at postgraduate level (Action 1) or to set up inter-institutional cooperation partnerships between universities from Europe and targeted Third Countries (Action 2). Within those two Actions, individual students, researchers and university staff had the possibility to spend a study/research/teaching period in the context of one of the above-mentioned programs or cooperation partnerships. Finally, any organization active in the field of higher education that wished to develop projects aimed at enhancing the attractiveness, profile, visibility and image of European higher education worldwide was able to apply for grants under Action 3 (European Commission: Erasmus Mundus).

Each call for proposals under Erasmus Mundus indicated the geographical scope of the program. There were several in so-called "slots" or "strands" designed to address different directions. Slots or strands varied through the calls but usually they included a variety of regions: from Balkans, South Africa through Latin America Central, Latin America South, India, Asia East, Asia West, Russia, all countries and republics of former Soviet Union, Israel, ACP states, Arabic states US & Canada, Australia, New Zealand, Japan, The Republic of Korea and other). For each geographical slot or strand a specific number of proposals would be accepted in each call, so the program actually covered the entire globe.

Students from countries all over the world were addresses of these scholarship opportunities. In addition, consortiums of higher education institutions and other subjects were invited to apply for funding for the joint programs and mobility programs (Erasmus Mundus selected projects).

Once again the statistics may seem impressive but they do not fully respond to the needs and abilities of the EU to reach outside its borders in higher education programs and to promote its academic traditions in the world.

According to the European Commission's data the number of students receiving an opportunity to study under the Erasmus Mundus Master Courses grew between 2004 and 2013, however the numbers themselves are not overwhelming. There were 176 countries covered by the program. While in 2004 scholarships were awarded to 140 students, the record in 2013 reached 1966. The total number of scholarships in the analyzed period amounts to 13,957. A breakdown of this number among the countries shows great differences. The highest number of scholarships was granted to students from India (1519), then China (1339), followed with a big gap by 578 in Brazil, 535 in Mexico, 509 in Russia, and 467 in the USA. The numbers decrease further down all the way to 4 in Niger, 2 in Libya, and 1 in Gambia. Lichtenstein, Luxembourg, Suriname have none at all. It should also be noted that number of applicants for each year's edition was much higher, between 20,000 and 35,000 per year (Erasmus Mundus Master Courses).

In Action 2 (and in a sub-program called External Cooperation Window which ran for couple of years) every year only around 20 projects built by the international consortia were selected. In Strand 1 and 2 together all of the world's regions were covered. In 2010 a total of 20 projects were approved for funding, similarly in 2011 a total of 21, in 2012 a total of 16 and finally in 2013, in the last round, a total of 22 projects (Erasmus Mundus selected projects). It should be noted that the minimum requirements for the partnerships composition when applying were not very high—the minimum partnership was to be constituted by five European higher education institutions from at least three EU member states and at least one higher education institution from the third countries. The maximum size of the partnership was however limited to 20 partners (Erasmus Mundus Program Guide, p. 50). A brief analysis of the selected projects confirms that the winning partnerships included between 18 and 20 institutions. In addition, individual calls for proposals within the program gave precise instructions and added requirements of other participating institutions (i.e. NGOs as associated partners), so the total number of participating institutions could reach up to 50. It made the projects very demanding, challenging to manage and supervise, especially that the financial support for the administrative costs provided in the budget was not high (i.e. € 10,000 per year in a 4-year project). There was no possibility of a small or even bilateral cooperation.

Under Action 3 total of 98 projects were implemented including 10 Erasmus Mundus National Structures information projects and 88 projects to promote European Higher Education (Erasmus Mundus selected projects).

Some additional bilateral programs were also implemented between 2007 and 2014. For example the EU-USA Atlantis Program focused on implementing joint or dual transatlantic undergraduate degrees with consortia of higher education and training institutions (The EU-USA Program). It was cancelled in 2011 due to the US Congressional budget reductions (Rowland 2013, pp. 125–126).

3.3 *Erasmus Plus: Hope for the Future?*

Still under the LLP-Erasmus regime, in 2012 at a meeting in Bucharest, higher education Ministers from 47 European countries adopted the Mobility strategy 2020 for the European Higher Education Area (called the Bologna Mobility Strategy) which states that, by 2020, at least 20 % of European higher education graduates should have spent part of their studies abroad (2012 EHEA Mobility Strategy, p. 1). This is a very ambitious goal to achieve given the numbers presented above and the financial crisis still forcing Europeans to cut costs. At the same time investing in higher education, if accompanied by the increase of financial means to support such programs does not have to be argued as a crucial and significant element for the future development of the Union. The numbers have to go up, students have to fully appreciate the "pluses" of the international exchange possibilities, which is possibly why the new mobility program is called Erasmus + (or Erasmus Plus).

As stated on the official website of the European Commission the Erasmus + program aims to boost skills and employability, as well as modernizing Education, Training, and Youth work. The seven year program has a budget of € 14.7 billion constituting a 40 % increase compared to current spending levels of nearly €7 billion (European Commission, Erasmus).

With time, the addressees' geographical scope and goals of the program extended and developed. Presently beneficiaries of the Erasmus + program (for the purpose of this study only elements of the program addressed to higher education will be examined) include:

- students through possibilities of studying at partner universities and possibilities of placements at European institutions,
- academic staff, understood in a large sense (through possibilities of visiting lectures at partner universities as well as short term trainings)
- higher education institutions (through possible transnational partnerships for grant projects on the development of the study programs, curricula, joint degree projects etc.)

Erasmus Plus aims at strong cooperation, not only among the higher education institutions but also emphasizes the need for strong links between the business sector and higher education. It provides for programs to build strategic partnerships and knowledge alliances by inviting business entities to participate in the Erasmus funded projects (Erasmus Plus Opportunities).

Even though the Erasmus Plus program is a program developed by the EU, its geographical scope reaches far beyond the Union's borders, both to the West and to the East. Complete participation in the Erasmus projects (in the frame of so called "program countries") is open to the 28 Member States of the EU as well as to some non-EU countries including: The Former Yugoslav Republic of Macedonia, Iceland, Liechtenstein, Norway, Switzerland and Turkey. In addition, subject to specific criteria or conditions partner countries neighboring the EU may take part is Erasmus projects and those include: Eastern Partnership countries (Armenia, Azerbaijan, Belarus, Georgia, Moldova, Ukraine), Southern Mediterranean countries (Algeria, Egypt, Israel, Jordan, Lebanon, Libya, Morocco, Palestine, Syria, Tunisia, Western Balkans: Albania, Bosnia and Herzegovina, Kosovo, Montenegro, Serbia) as well as the Russian Federation (Erasmus Guide, p. 24).

It should be noted that Switzerland's status is different at the moment. As a result of a popular vote in Swiss cantons in February 2014, the legal basis for the participation of Switzerland in the mobility program has to be negotiated in a separate agreement; until then Switzerland is moved to the category of "partner countries". This change has come as a very surprising and disappointing one for both Swiss students and students from other countries who quite often chose Switzerland and its universities as their exchange destinations: according to UNCESCO, in 2011 there were almost 28,000 EU students studying at Swiss universities in postsecondary programs (Schuetze 2014).

It is worth emphasizing the main features of the Erasmus + Program listed in the Guide. Those include: (1) recognition and validation of skills and qualifications, (2) dissemination and exploitation of project results, (3) open access for educational materials, documents and media produced by Erasmus +, international dimension, multilingualism, equity and inclusion, (4) protection and safety of participants (Erasmus Guide, pp. 11–14). These features are strongly related to the extensive, ambitious objectives of the program set out in the founding Regulation. The

Erasmus + responds to the Europe 2020 strategy for smart, sustainable and inclusive growth which defines the Union's growth strategy for the coming decade to support such growth, setting five ambitious objectives to be reached by 2020, particularly in the field of education, where the aim is to reduce early school-leaving rates to a level below 10 % and to enable at least 40 % of 30–34 year-olds to have completed tertiary or equivalent education.

It also aims to include a strong international dimension, particularly as regards higher education, in order not only to enhance the quality of European higher education in pursuit of the broader ET 2020 objectives and the attractiveness of the Union as a study destination, but also to promote understanding between people and to contribute to the sustainable development of higher education in partner countries, as well as their broader socio-economic development, inter alia by stimulating "brain circulation" through mobility actions with partner-country nationals. (Preamble to Regulation 1288/2013).

With a higher budget, more consolidation within the program and hopefully better awareness of the possibilities to use the funds among higher education institutions of the member states and partner countries, Erasmus Plus might be of crucial importance for outside EU mobility. Since the program has just been implemented, some executive regulations are still to be announced including a draft of the bilateral Erasmus agreement which will be signed between higher education institutions in the EU country and partner institution in the third country. This might bring real benefits of close academic cooperation between institutions, which have already made some efforts of joint projects and programs.

4 Europe 2020 Strategy: Goals for the Present and the Future

The Bologna Process is a dynamic process with new mechanisms and strategies adding to the original ideas.

The Lisbon Strategy period expired in 2010 but already, the EU had prepared and presented another long-term strategy called Strategy Europe 2020, which stand for the EU's 10-year growth and jobs strategy. It was launched in 2010. As stated in the Strategy it is about more than just overcoming the crisis from which European economies are now gradually recovering. It is also about addressing the shortcomings of the growth model and creating the conditions for a smart, sustainable and inclusive growth. Five headline targets have been set for the EU to achieve by the end of 2020. These cover once again, in a very ambitious tone the following: 1. Ensuring 75 % employment of 20 to 64-year-olds, 2. Getting 3 % of the EU's GDP invested into research and development, 3. Limiting greenhouse gas emissions to a certain percentage, 4. Reducing school dropout rates to below 10 %, with at least 40 % of 30 to 34-year-olds completing tertiary education, 5. Ensuring that

20 million fewer people are at risk of poverty or social exclusion (The EU Explained: Europe 2020, p. 3).

Two out of five objectives deal with investment in research and with education, which clearly confirms the role of proper and quality education on all levels in the achievement of the highest possible development of the Union. The Europe 2020 objectives are designed in a challenging tone, with specific numbers to be achieved. It makes the future evaluation of the successes and failures easily ascertainable. It is difficult to calculate the outcomes of the EU actions now in the mid-term of the Strategy period. Hopefully those numbers will also serve as a continued motivation in all the actions undertaken in the future.

The Bologna Process is also examined at the other side of the Atlantic Ocean and commonly viewed as an important development that has dramatically changed legal education in Europe (Terry 2007, p. 252).

5 Legal Education in the United States: Lessons for Europe?

5.1 Legal Education in the US: Main Features

In 2012 President Obama gave a speech to students at the University of Michigan in An Arbor. A quote from this speech may serve to show the American understanding of the firm and stable connection between education (higher education) and economy's success leading to individual success. "Higher education is not a luxury. It's an economic imperative that every family in America should be able to afford. And when I say higher education, I don't just mean 4-year colleges and universities; I also mean our community colleges and providing lifelong learning for workers who may need to retrain for jobs when the economy shifts. All those things cost money, and it's harder and harder to afford." (Remarks by the President on College Affordability 2012).

The total sum of public and private expenditure on education in the United States is one of the highest in the OECD countries. Annual expenditure per student in tertiary education places the US as number 1 among those countries (OECD Country Note 2012, p. 13).

American universities and colleges are among the best schools in all the world reports. Those schools remain the most popular destination for foreign students from other countries (OECD Country Note 2012, p. 11).

Europe has always looked up to its partner on the other side of the Ocean, and the Bologna Process has also been designed in order to become a better-qualified competitor to the United States' higher education system. The differences between the two partners are known and the specifics of the US higher education, especially legal education in its actual form, are worth commenting on.

Studying in the United States is expensive. Studying law in the United States has become incredibly expensive and has led to a serious crisis in the legal education. The best law schools charge high tuition: Harvard's annual tuition reaches 52,000 USD, Columbia University Law School charges 55,000 USD per year and Cornell University Law School 57,000 USD. Adding costs of living, insurance and books, the total cost of a 3-year road to law degree becomes a serious luxury. High tuitions and limited job offers on the legal market have made the situation of future lawyers truly complicated, to the extent that some argue that attending law school is now not a great opportunity but a terrible risk of both economic loss and personal and professional disappointment (Menkel-Meadow 2013, p. 133).

In his recent speech to a crowd of students at the University of Michigan in 2014, the President of the United States said: "Opportunity means guaranteeing every young people access to a world-class education, and that's got to start with pre-K, all the way through higher education. And it means making college more affordable." (Remarks by the President on Minimum Wage). This quote may serve as an indicator of the biggest obstacle for young people to follow their professional dreams.

What does a law student get from the American law school? What is so expensive and what makes studying law financially challenging?

Legal education in the United States is offered on the graduate level. To enter the law school, a candidate must already have a bachelor degree diploma obtained after a 4-year college education. In addition Law School Admission Test (LSAT) results are taken into account in the enrollment procedures along with some other possible requirements such as Grade Point Average note or reference letters.

Education remains a state power in the federal system of the United States. Each state therefore is free to organize its own systems of education including higher education. Despite this freedom, model solutions are adopted throughout the country. There are 200 law schools in the United States accredited by the American Bar Association (ABA). In almost every state only graduates of the ABA-approved law schools are allowed to sit for the bar exam necessary to obtain a license to practice law.

ABA standards require each law school to build a specific curriculum focused on the practical elements of legal education and providing opportunity for lawyering skills training throughout the studies. The basic program lasts for 3 years with a core curriculum offered during the first year followed by a 2-year program individually organized by each student from a number of elective courses offered by the school. No final diploma defense is necessary to obtain the diploma. Upon reception of a required number of credits, students are allowed to graduate with a diploma of doctor of jurisprudence (JD). The JD diploma is a requirement to sit for the bar exam. Positive results of the bar exam allow law graduates to practice in particular state jurisdictions.

There are no apprenticeship or training programs required after the law school, which is a complete turn in history—at the beginning of the existence of the United States, internship in a law firm was the only way to become a lawyer. The origins of an organized legal education are commonly associated with the establishment of the first university school of law, that is Harvard Law School founded in 1817 although legal education at Litchfield Law School had historically marked the beginning of law teaching in the United States in as early as 1775 (McManis 1981, p. 603).

The law school is responsible to teach future professionals not only the theoretical basis of law but also, or even predominantly practical skills such as case analysis, communication with clients, negotiations, legal writing, etc.

As the ABA standards for law school approval state: "an approved law school must provide an opportunity for its students to study in a diverse educational environment, and in order to protect the interests of the public, law students, and the profession, it must provide an educational program that ensures that its graduates:

1. understand their ethical responsibilities as representatives of clients, officers of the courts, and public citizens responsible for the quality and availability of justice;
2. receive basic education through a curriculum that develops:
   (a) understanding of the theory, philosophy, role, and ramifications of the law and its institutions;
   (b) skills of legal analysis, reasoning, and problem solving; oral and written communication; legal research; and other fundamental skills necessary to participate effectively in the legal profession;
   (c) understanding of the basic principles of public and private law; and
3. understand the law as a public profession calling for performance of pro bono legal services". (2013–2014 ABA Standards and Rules of Procedure for Approval of Law Schools, p. ix)

5.2 American Methods Beyond US Borders: A Clinical Case for Social Justice and Women's Rights

The Socratic method and case method are two most popular American teaching techniques used in legal education. The common law system is a natural environment for learning law from judicial decisions. Therefore from the very first class in American law school, students use opinions of the courts (mostly Appellate Courts and the US Supreme Court) to understand the rules of particular laws. The Socratic method has been the one more often criticized, even if from the European point of view, the dialogue between the instructor and students is still a revolution to come in many schools throughout the old continent. Critical thinking skills are valued the most by both law schools graduates and practicing lawyers. Teaching methods necessary to master those skills and make students "think like lawyers" have been dynamically discussed among top law professors and law school authorities for years (Moskovitz 1992, p. 245; Friedland 1996, p. 7; Jennison 2013, p. 8, Patterson 1951–1952, pp. 1 and 17).

One of the revolutionary ideas in legal education, which developed in the United States but has successfully spread to other continents and countries is the clinical legal education which comes down to the simple idea of teaching law by using "real" problems while helping those who cannot afford professional legal advice. Legal clinics are present at every American law school, and taking a clinical course is part of the regular curriculum. In the clinical class students, under the faculty supervision, meet with real clients, members of the local community who come for free of charge legal assistance.

Clinical education responds to the global need of educating students to become sensitive lawyers with an appreciation of the social mission of their profession. In addition it is a method which smoothly develops necessary lawyering skills valued in the American legal profession such as: problem solving, legal analysis and reasoning, legal research, communication, counseling, negotiation. Those skills were indicated as most important in the legal profession in the famous MacCrate Report of 1992 (Pearce 2003, pp. 575–582). It was followed by the Carnegie Report, which concluded that there must be three basic elements to legal education: (1) the learning of legal analysis and analytical thinking; (2) an introduction to practice and practice skills; and (3) the development of a professional identity, also referred to as professionalism or ethics (Jennison 2013, p. 568).

Legal clinics in the US have become fields for the development of the programs specifically oriented towards women's rights issues. At present there are a number of excellently functioning clinics dedicated to solving problems (and teaching students the importance and wide scope of those) relating to family law, domestic violence, child abuse and protection of women's and children's rights. For example The Women and the Law Clinic operating at the American University Washington College of Law often begins representation of clients in child custody and support, domestic violence, and child neglect cases but then expands its services to variety of family law oriented problems (http://www.wcl.american.edu/clinical/women.cfm). The New York University School of Law opened a Reproductive Justice Clinic and Advanced Reproductive Justice Clinic[2] and Georgetown Law decided to go further and reach to other regions of the world where women's rights is almost an unknown concept. The International Women's Human Rights Clinic offers its students opportunity to observe court proceedings and analyze court decisions in Africa. The clinic offers its services through partnerships with local women's rights NGOs in the region.[3]

The clinical teaching method has become popular not only in the United States but worldwide. It became a useful weapon in the fight with deficits in legal education in developing countries which in the 1970s still struggled with a vast number of problems including fundamental issues concerning legal studies such as, for instance, a very academic, theoretical approach to law as a doctrine without any

[2] http://www.law.nyu.edu/academics/clinics/semester/reprojustice).

[3] http://www.law.georgetown.edu/academics/academic-programs/clinical-programs/our-clinics/IWHR/.

links to other fields such as economics or sociology; traditional, only theoretical teaching methods that failed to implement mechanisms to teach legal skills and legal awareness (Legal Education in a Changing World 1975, p. 19).

Taking a particular example, clinical legal education has had a tremendous impact on legal education and social changes throughout apartheid in South Africa. As such it served and still serves as a mechanism not only to assist those in need but also to promote social justice (Maisel 2006, pp. 379–385). South African example is not the only one. Legal clinics have developed successfully also in Latin America and India, mostly in the common law countries.

At the end of the twentieth century, with the wind of political and social change, the clinical method has also come to Europe. Clinical legal education has found a very productive ground especially in Central and Eastern Europe. The case of Poland may serve as a good example. The first legal clinic was established in 1997. Presently every law school in Poland (both public and private) either already has a clinical program or is in the process of implementing one. A great number of students has a chance to "touch" a real legal problem under supervision of an experienced lawyer or faculty member (Krasnicka 2008, pp. 53–54). The Polish experience has been used to promote and develop clinical programs in many other countries, such as the Ukraine, Belarus and many other former Soviet republics. It has also served as a model for China and its legal education. A manual on the basics on clinical education written 10 years ago by the Polish authors has been recently translated into Chinese (The Legal Clinic. The Idea, Organization, Methodology, Peking University Press 2014).

Once the regular clinical programs have been successfully established in this part of Europe, they could possibly serve as fields to the development of more specialized programs such as those addressing women's rights. A thorough, deep study of the legal education in post-socialist countries carried out by an experienced American law professor leaves no doubt that the so called "gender mainstreaming" is far from being fully addressed in Central and Eastern Europe, even in those countries which smoothly went through the transformation and joined the European Union with all its non-discriminatory standards and policies. Legal education is still to adapt its programs to those sensitive and very significant problems (Marcus 2014, pp. 507–568).

Western Europe used to be somehow less enthusiastic about the clinical method for several reasons including the obligatory apprenticeship system existing in most states, the number of enrolment and difficulties in the organization of clinical courses, a better state system of legal assistance for the poor etc. It was also argued that this method is less effective in the civil law traditions (Wilson 2009, pp. 828–839).

The situation has changed even there, because clinical legal education is a perfect tool to fulfill the goals of the Bologna Process, as one of the outcomes of the Bologna Process is to modernize higher education systems in order to provide graduates with competences and skills required for a successful career and active participation in the economy and society (Bücker and Woodruff 2008, p. 614). The Bologna Process, not without problems and challenges to be overcome in a diverse

Europe, brings opportunities to introduce or improve a practical approach to traditional legal education (Hovhannisian 2006, p. 6). Western European Universities slowly open themselves to the idea and, in return, receive the gratitude of students, who are usually very enthusiastic about working on real cases in live client clinics offered by their schools. It goes along with the Recommendation on the Training Outcomes for European Lawyers issued in 2007 by the Council of Bars and Law Societies in Europe (CCBE) where skills similar to those listed in the American MacCrate Report were indicated as necessary for the professional legal services in the EU.

Learning law through clinical programs enables students to become more aware of social problems and needs. Human Rights and the rule of law issues are often strongly emphasized and examples of different attitudes towards access to justice, especially in criminal cases can be observed in a real setting by future lawyers. The rule of law can be advanced through clinical programs, especially in countries struggling with democracy and respect for human rights. Not surprising clinical legal education has become extremely appreciated in China, where law professors started to believe that awareness of the rule of law among representatives of the legal profession plays a major role in the advancement of the principle nation-wide (Milstein 2009, p. 57). New teaching methods gained popularity and with financial support from the United States, a non-profit organization Committee of Chinese Clinical Legal Educators was established attract institutions to become members dedicated to promoting the idea of practical teaching methods. Latest research results show that legal clinics have become a battleground for social change in China (Phen 2005, p. 129).

There have been attempts to promote the rule of law through clinical programs in Iraq, where schools still suffer from the times under a totalitarian regime. Existing law schools continue to use lectures as the main method of education and the struggle to see clinics considered as solutions to social and educational problems is far from over (Hamoudi 2005, pp. 116–118). Other places where clinical legal education has played a significant role in an attempt to promote the rule of law include Jordan (Thomas and Mahasneh 2012) or Palestine where the Human Rights Clinic established in 2006 was the first accredited clinic in the Arab world (Chavkin 2010, p. 14). The latest geographical expansion of clinical legal education is Egypt where the revolutionary transformation finds in the clinical model the role for law school education with special emphasis on social justice (Rosenbaum 2012, p. 43). In all of these projects experienced American law professors, who run clinical programs at their home schools, travel to distant places in the world to train local faculty how to establish, manage and use legal clinic.

The significance of the teaching method which does not only introduce the students to practical lawyering skills, but which also or most of all, ensures their sensitiveness and awareness of the importance of human rights problems, the principle of the rule of law and social justice needs is unquestionable and represents a valuable example of the American "virus" spreading through the world improving legal education and at the same time confirming the leading position of American education in the world.

Naturally, as every method, the clinical model is not free from weaknesses and has been sometimes quite strongly opposed not only by practicing lawyers but also by the American law professors themselves as they realized and pointed to the difficulties in this specific "learning by doing" and "learning by imitating" courses and how actually "critical" clinical instruction can be for the students and how many practical problems concerning ethics in the student-client relation may be created. (Condlin 1983, pp. 325–327; Condlin 1986, pp. 54–55). In addition, the "exotic" method is also, when implemented in its full, complex version, quite expensive (small classes, special training, different workload of instructors, arranged office space within the law school, etc.), which makes it, especially at present, a luxury offer for the law school students.

5.3 The Impact of the Bologna Process on US Higher Education

The worldwide American leadership in research and innovation associated strongly with American prosperity, especially before the financial crisis, constituted one of the fundamental principles of the US educational policy in the world. Announced in 1999 the Bologna Declaration provided for a major reform of European higher education. The reform was and continues to be aimed at strengthening the European position in the educational competition. Not surprisingly, the discussion about the possible influence and threat of the planned European reforms to the leading American position was intense and managed to create initiatives to prepare for what was seen as a "massive European transformation" in higher education (Terry 2007, p. 241).

General issues which not only the United States but also other countries had to deal with after Bologna included adjustments necessary to accept European graduates of the first degree (3-year) programs and also to proceed with recognition based on the ETCS system. Quality assurance and improvement of the study programs throughout Europe certainly influenced the competitiveness in the transatlantic educational relations.

The United States also identified some elements of the Bologna Process that could be adapted into the American system of higher education. In a 2008 report "Learning Accountability from Bologna: A Higher Education Policy Primer", Adelman challenges the assumption that American colleges and universities are "accountable" to those who subsidize them or pay their tuition and fees if they make public their graduation rates, demographic mix, and job placement rates, and throw in a test or two to show that a random sample of their students know how to write or solve a problem. Everybody goes home assured that this is what higher education is about. In his study, Adelman advises American educators to look beyond American borders and points to the Bologna Process as a real development in this direction calling it "the most far-reaching and ambitious reform of higher education ever undertaken" (Adelman 2008, p. 2).

Based on the analysis of the Bologna Process Adelman's report proposes three major reforms to be implemented into the American higher education system: 1. developing detailed and public degree qualification frameworks for state higher education systems and for all institutions in students' major fields, 2. revising the reference points and terms of our credit system; 3. developing a distinctive version of a diploma supplement that summarizes individual student achievement (Adelman 2008, p. 3).

A pilot Tuning USA project initiated by the Lumina Foundation aiming at the harmonization of the curricula may serve as an example of actions undertaken in the United States based on the European experience and is clearly influenced by the Bologna Process. The financial crisis, which hit the United States shortly after such projects were designed, has certainly influenced their speed and extension.

The Bologna reforms have had an impact in other regions of the world as well. Australia initiated a similar process for the Asia-Pacific Region called the Brisbane Process. The Latin American and Caribbean Common Area of Higher Education was initiated by the Inter-American Organization for Higher Education. Some countries in North Africa and the Middle East, although formally not participants of the Bologna reforms, have adopted some of the Bologna principles and mechanisms (Crosier, Parveva 2013, pp. 75–77).

Legal education in the United States is going through the most difficult crisis in its history. The enrollment of students has dropped dramatically, the job market for law graduates is shrinking and the tuition costs have reached levels too high for a majority of Americans, despite the possibility of bank loans. Most expensive programs, including clinical education courses, have to be strongly defended to maintain their position in the curricula (Joy 2012, pp. 311–313). There have been strong, well-argued voices calling for the need to look at American legal education from the economic perspective and to take into account the reality in which there is a "critical disjunction between the number of law schools in the United States, the absolute number of graduates with which they are continuing to 'load' the system, and the competitive conditions of the system represented by the volume of demand for legal services on the part of clients or organizations capable of paying for the provision of those services" (Barnhizer 2010, p. 262). Proposals are made how to react to this emergency. In the on-going debate on the possible actions to stop the crisis are some quite revolutionary ideas such as shortening the legal education program to a 2-year study curriculum completed with a third year of some kind of internship or practical training (Estreicher 2013, p. 606). The concept is not new and has been already positively evaluated by the American Bar Association's Task Force on the Future of Legal Education with the support of the President of the United States himself as a lawyer. On the other hand strong voices of dissent come from various professional groups, including the United States Supreme Court (Scalia 2014, p. 2).

It seems that even if according to American experts, the Bologna Process should act as a "wake-up call" for higher education in the United States (Crosier, Parveva

2013, p. 76), the US legal education has to overcome its own difficulties before it will be ready again to focus on the adjustments to the global market. The national market for lawyers has reached its limits but the number of foreign students increases and saves the finances of American law schools.

The United States retains its position of world leader in research and education. The European efforts to consolidate, harmonize and strengthen higher education systems should be continued to enable the old continent to fight an even transatlantic battle and reach with its academic traditions new regions and markets, thereby opening opportunities for students and faculty.

6 Conclusions

The Bologna Process reforms have brought both reasons for satisfaction and disappointment. One of the biggest disappointments is reflected in the low mobility rates within the EU. The data shows that the majority of the Bologna countries have an incoming and outgoing mobility rate of less than 10 %, with more than half of the countries dropping down to 5 % (The European Higher Education Area in 2012, p. 13), and only symbolic programs allowing for exchanges outside of Europe.

The recently launched Erasmus Plus program should be fully made use of to change the situation. Promoting mobility among students should become a priority of every university administration and faculty policies. The Erasmus Plus bilateral agreements with non-EU countries provide for unique opportunities to develop external relations, not in vast consortia but in smaller, more effective cooperation projects between actual partners.

A lot has been said and written about missed opportunities and failures of Bologna, but there is still room for discussions and common, satisfying conclusions on possible remedies. The European Law Faculties Association could serve as a more vital forum for such discussions and outcomes. Possibly a European system of law school accreditation should be developed, not as a mandatory accreditation but more as a model list of "best practices in legal education" with mechanisms to implement it in interested institutions.

During the ELFA annual meetings, representatives of the American law school associations are present which provides opportunities for some real international ideas. Example of the clinical legal education should be regarded as successful adoption of foreign ideas on national grounds in different legal and academic traditions.

There are model US programs, which Europe could adopt or better develop in its law schools. Clinical legal education promoted globally by the US can bring real benefits and increase the value of European legal education especially though courses teaching students to be aware of problems of access to justice, women's rights and family issues. Skills necessary to face such problems are required and highly valued in every country in today's world. The American-European partnership in promoting these programs and skills in other regions would certainly help to address at least some of the major difficulties.

The time of current negotiations of the Transatlantic Trade and Investment Partnership between the EU and the United States should be used also in terms of rising educational investments.

The old song of increasing the states' expenditure on higher education in research should be still loudly sung throughout Europe. Financial investment in those areas is crucial in the EU-US partnership opportunities as higher education (as commonly agreed) is a key factor in finding a way out of the crisis (Garben 2012, p. 1).

Five Questions

1. How can the EU improve its exchange program policy so that more students use the Erasmus studying abroad possibilities?
2. Is the Bologna Process actually helping the European Union's Member States in the higher education sector through the so far established components?
3. How can EU and USA work on building more powerful transatlantic educational bridge?
4. Is clinical legal education the best method to teach students social justice? Is there any other experience?
5. How can successful programs aiming at women's rights education be transported to the Central and Eastern European universities?

References

Legal Acts

Treaty on the Functioning of the EU, Official Journal of the EU (OJ C 115/47) of 9 May 2008.

The Convention on the Recognition of Qualifications concerning Higher Education in the European Region (Lisbon Convention) http://conventions.coe.int/Treaty/Commun/ChercheSig.asp?NT=165&CM=1&DF=26/01/2010&CL=ENG

Decision No 1720/2006/EC of the European Parliament and of the Council of 15 November 2006 establishing an action programme in the field of lifelong learning.

Decision No 1298/2008/EC of the European Parliament and of the Council of 16 December 2008 establishing the Erasmus Mundus 2009–2013 action programme for the enhancement of quality in higher education and the promotion of intercultural understanding through cooperation with third countries.

Regulation (EU) No 1288/2013 of the European Parliament and of the Council of 11 December 2013 establishing 'Erasmus+': the Union programme for education, training, youth and sport and repealing Decisions No 1719/2006/EC, No 1720/2006/EC and No 1298/2008/EC Text with EEA relevance.

Articles

Atienza, S. (2011–2012). The evolution of legal education in Spain. *Journal of Legal Education, 61*, 468–478.

Barnhizer, D. (2010). Redesigning the American law school. *Michigan State Law Review, 2010*, 249–310.

Bücker, A., & Woodruff, W. A. (2008). The bologna process and German legal education: Developing professional competence through clinical experiences. *German Law Journal, 9*, 575–617.

Chavkin, D. F. (2010). Thinking/practicing clinical legal education from within the Palestinian-Israeli conflict: Lessons from the Al-Quds human rights clinic. *Human Rights Brief, 18*(1), 14–18.

Condlin, R. J. (1983) The moral failure of clinical legal education. In: D. Luban (Ed.), The good lawyer: Lawyers' roles and lawyers' ethics, Rowman & Allenheld, Totowa, N.J (pp. 317–349).

Condlin, R. J. (1986). "Tastes great, less filling": The law school clinic and political critique. *Journal of Legal Education, 35*, 45–78.

Estreicher, S. (2013). The Roosevelt-Cardozo way: The case for bar eligibility after two years of law school. *New York University Journal of Legislation and Public Policy, 15*, 599–617.

Friedland, S. I. (1996). How we teach: A survey of teaching techniques in American law schools. *Seattle University Law Review, 20*, 1–44.

Garben, S. (2010). The Bologna process: From a European law perspective. *European Law Journal, 16*, 186–210.

Garben, S. (2012). *The future of higher education in Europe: The case for a strong base in EU law* (LEQS Paper No 50, pp. 1–44). LEQS, London.

Götzelmann, C. (2010). How free is the free movement of students in the EU? An analysis of third-level cross-border education. *University College Dublin Law Review, 10*, 55–84.

Hamoudi, H. A. (2005). Toward a rule of law society in Iraq: Introducing clinical legal education into Iraqi law schools. *Berkeley Journal of International Law, 23*, 112–136.

Hovhannisian, L. (2006). *Clinical legal education and the bologna process* (PILI Papers No. 2, pp. 3–20). PILI, Budapest - Moscow - New York.

Jennison, B. (2013). Beyond langdell: Innovating in legal education. *Catholic University Law Review, 62*, 643–674.

Joy, P. A. (2012). The costs of clinical legal education. *Boston College Journal of Law & Social Justice, 32*, 309–330.

Krasnicka, I. (2008). Legal education and clinical legal education in Poland. *International Journal of Clinical Legal Education, 13*, 47–55.

Lonbay, J. (2011–2012). The changing regulatory environment affecting the education and training of Europe's lawyers. *Journal of Legal Education, 61*, 479–485.

Maisel, P. (2006). Expanding and sustaining clinical legal education in developing countries: What we can learn from South Africa? *Fordham International Law Journal, 30*, 374–420.

Marcus, I. (2014). The "Woman Question" in post-socialist legal education. *Human Rights Quarterly, 6*, 507–568.

McKiernan, H. H., & Birtwistle, T. (2009–2010). Making the implicit explicit: Demonstrating the value added of higher education by a qualifications framework. *Journal of College and University Law, 36*, 511–564.

McManis, C. R. (1981). The history of first century American legal education: A revisionist perspective. *Washington University Law Quarterly, 59*, 597–659.

Menkel-Meadow, C. (2013). Crisis in legal education or the other things law students should be learning and doing. *McGeorge Law Review, 45*, 133–160.

Milstein, E. (2009). Experimental education and the rule of law: Teaching values through clinical education in China. *Global Business & Development Law Journal, 22*(1), 55–62.

Moskovitz, M. (1992). Beyond the case method: It's time to teach with problems. *Journal of Legal Education, 42*, 241–270.

Patterson, E. W. (1951–1952). The case method in American legal education: Its origins and objectives. *Journal of Legal Education, 4*, 1–32.
Pearce, R. G. (2003). MacCrate's missed opportunity: The MacCrate report's failure to advance professional values symposium. *Pace Law Review, 23*, 575–597.
Phen, P. N. (2005). Clinical legal education in China: In pursuit of a culture of law and a mission of social justice. *Yale Human Rights and Development Journal, 8*(1). Article 3.
Posch, W. (2005). The Austrian view of the Bologna process in legal education. *Slovenian Law Review, 2*, 207–2011.
Riedel, J. (2005). The Bologna process and its relevance for legal education in Germany. *European Journal of Legal Education, 2*, 59–62.
Rosenbaum, S. (2012). The legal clinic is more than a sign on the door: Transforming law school education in revolutionary Egypt. *Berkeley Journal of Middle Eastern & Islamic Law, 5*, 39–71.
Rowland, C. (2013). We can work it out: Putting our best foot forward in international higher education initiatives. *Penn State Journal of Law & International Affairs, 2*, 118–149.
Scalia, A. (2014). *Reflections on the future of the legal academy, 2014 commencement exercises* (pp. 1–8). Williamsburg, VA: William & Mary Law School.
Schuetze, Ch. F. (2014, February 23). Swiss immigration overhaul puts study programs at risk. *New York Times*, http://www.nytimes.com/2014/02/24/world/europe/swiss-immigration-overhaul-puts-study-programs-at-risk.html?_r=0
Terry, L. (2006). Living the Bologna process: Recommendations to the German legal education community from a U.S. perspective. *German Law Journal, 7*, 863–905.
Terry, L. (2007). The Bologna Process and its Implications for U.S. Legal Education. *Journal of Legal Education, 57*, 237–252.
Terry, L. (2011). International initiatives that facilitate global mobility in higher education. *Michigan State International Law, 2011*, 305–356.
Thomas, K. A., & Mahasneh, N. (2012). Learning from the unique and common challenges: Clinical legal education in Jordan. *Berkeley Journal of Middle Eastern and Islamic Law, 5*, 1–38.
Vincent-Lancrin, S. (2008). What is the impact of demography on higher education systems? A forward-looking approach for OECD countries. In: *Higher education to 2030, volume 1: Demography* (pp. 41–103). OECD, Paris.
Wilson, R. J. (2009). Wester Europe: Last hope in the worldwide acceptance of clinical legal education. *German Law Journal, 10*, 823–846.

EU and OECD Documents

Erasmus Guide: Erasmus Plus Programme Guide, Version 3: 09/04/2014. http://ec.europa.eu/programmes/erasmus-plus/documents/erasmus-plus-programme-guide_en.pdf
Erasmus Charter: Erasmus Charter for Higher Education 2014–2020 – Annotated Guidelines, European Commission: http://eacea.ec.europa.eu/funding/2014/documents/annotated_guidelines_en.pdf
European Commission, Erasmus: http://ec.europa.eu/programmes/erasmus-plus/index_en.htm
European Commission: Erasmus Mundus: http://eacea.ec.europa.eu/erasmus_mundus/programme/about_erasmus_mundus_en.php
Erasmus Mundus selected projects: http://eacea.ec.europa.eu/erasmus_mundus/results_compendia/selected_projects_en.php
Erasmus Mundus Master Courses – students selected per year: http://eacea.ec.europa.eu/erasmus_mundus/results_compendia/documents/statistics/cumulative/statistics_by_country_erasmus_mundus_masters_students_selected_each_academic_year,_2004-05_to_2013-14.pdf
Erasmus programme in 2011-2012: the figures explained, European Commission – MEMO 13/647 08/07/2013: http://europa.eu/rapid/press-release_MEMO-13-647_en.htm

Erasmus Plus Opportunities: http://ec.europa.eu/education/opportunities/higher-education/business_en.htm
Tempus Statistics: http://eacea.ec.europa.eu/tempus/results_compendia/statistics_en.php
The EU-USA Programme: http://eacea.ec.europa.eu/bilateral_cooperation/eu_us/index_en.php
The Lisbon Strategy 2000-2010. An analysis and evaluation of the methods used and results achieved, European Parliament 2010: http://www.europarl.europa.eu/document/activities/cont/201107/20110718ATT24270/20110718ATT24270EN.pdf
Bologna Declaration: Joint Declaration of the European Ministers of Education, The Bologna Declaration of 19 June 1999: http://www.ond.vlaanderen.be/hogeronderwijs/bologna/documents/MDC/BOLOGNA_DECLARATION1.pdf
The EU Explained: Europe 2020: Europe's Growth Strategy, Luxembourg 2013: http://ec.europa.eu/europe2020/pdf/europe_2020_explained.pdf
2012 EHEA Mobility Strategy: Mobility strategy for 2020 for the European Higher Education Area (EHEA), EHEA Ministerial Conference, Bucharest, April 26-27, 2012: http://www.ehea.info/Uploads/%281%29/2012%20EHEA%20Mobility%20Strategy.pdf
OECD Country Note, Education at a Glance: OECD Indicators 2012 United States: http://www.oecd.org/unitedstates/CN%20-%20United%20States.pdf

Reports

The European Higher Education Area in 2012: Bologna Process Implementation Report, Brussels 2012: http://epp.eurostat.ec.europa.eu/cache/ITY_OFFPUB/EC-30-12-534/EN/EC-30-12-534-EN.PDF
Legal Education in a Changing World: Report of the Committee on Legal Education in the Developing Countries, International Legal Center, Uppsala 1975.
Adelman, C. (2008). Learning Accountability from Bologna. A Higher Education Policy Primer, Institute for Higher Education Policy Issue Brief, Washington.
Crosies, D., & Parveva, T. (2013). The Bologna Process: Its Impact in Europe and beyond, UNESCO: International Institute for Educational Planning, Paris.

Other Documents

British Council Statistics: Outgoing UK Erasmus Student Mobility by Host Country – 2007–2011: http://www.britishcouncil.org/outgoing_uk_erasmus_student_mobility_by_host_country_-_2007_to_2011.pdf
European University Association: What is the Bologna Process? http://www.eua.be/eua-work-and-policy-area/building-the-european-higher-education-area/bologna-basics.aspx
Remarks by the President on College Affordability, Ann Arbor, Michigan, The White House, Office of the Press Secretary, January 27, 2012: http://www.whitehouse.gov/the-press-office/2012/01/27/remarks-president-college-affordability-ann-arbor-michigan
Remarks by the President on Minimum Wage – Ann Arbor, MI, The White House, Office of the Press Secretary, April 2, 2014: http://www.whitehouse.gov/the-press-office/2014/04/02/remarks-president-minimum-wage-ann-arbor-mi
2013–2014 ABA Standards and Rules of Procedure for Approval of Law Schools, ABA 2013: http://www.americanbar.org/content/dam/aba/publications/misc/legal_education/Standards/2013_2014_final_aba_standards_and_rules_of_procedure_for_approval_of_law_schools_body.authcheckdam.pdf

A Critical Examination of the Contention of the Existence of a Culture Justice Education at the Vienna International School, Austria

Elisabeth Stanners

Abstract What is the foundation for a cultural of justice in a school? Can a curriculum programme alone guarantee that students experience justice and leave school as potential contributors to global justice? Against the background of internationalization and standardization of secondary school education across the world pursued by the United Nations Scientific, Educational and Cultural Organization (OESCD), and academic assessment of the International Baccalaureate (IB) school curricula, this chapter examines the basis for asserting that a culture of justice exists at the Vienna International School (Vienna, Austria). It examines whether the adoption of the three IB curriculum programmes (Diploma Programme, Middle Years Programme and Primary Years Programme) are central to the existence of a culture of justice. It explores research on justice and democracy in education in the context of the Vienna International School and asks which of the characteristics identified as being necessary for justice and democracy to be present exist in the school. The chapter contends that while the curriculum plays a strong part in providing a context in which justice and democracy can be nurtured, this by itself would be insufficient to guarantee the culture of justice that is present in the school and that it is the relationships that exists between all the stakeholders that are key to the existence of a culture of justice at the Vienna International School.

1 Introduction

The Academic Council on the United Nations System convened during the 20-s session of the United Nations Commission on Crime Prevention and Criminal Justice (Vienna, Austria, 2013) an expert panel on "Inculcating Justice in 'Succeeding Generations' by Building a Culture of Lawfulness." This contribution

---

E. Stanners (✉)
Vienna International School, Vienna, Austria
e-mail: estanners@vis.ac.at

H. Kury et al. (eds.), *Women and Children as Victims and Offenders: Background, Prevention, Reintegration*, DOI 10.1007/978-3-319-08398-8_14

is a follow-up to an original invitation extended to the Vienna International School to present an expert practitioner view whether there is a culture of justice in the Vienna International School (VIS). The aim of the chapter is to examine the basis on which this culture of justice may exist and to reference this to research in the field of justice education.

2 Contentions of Education in a Culture of Justice

A recent chapter in The Times (UK) news (Thursday, May 15, 2014, No 71197) was headlined "State Schools don't know right from wrong, says top teacher." He contends: *"State schools are creating amoral children because they spend more time on academic studies than learning right from wrong"*. The contention of the "top teacher" was that schools in which *"extra-curricular activities; learning good values; developing students' characters* [through] *respect for discipline and academic seriousness; sport and culture; citizenship and community; service; environmental awareness; spiritual life and personal responsibility"* [results in] *"young people with emotional intelligence, developed moral understanding and a willingness to make a contribution to society."* This "top teacher" is representing a view that teaching for results [alone] limits the scope of a school to develop the personal characteristics that are of value to society.

As reflected above, there is a popular belief in educational circles that it is a tension to combine an aim of excellent academic success with an education that has as part of its core values a commitment to develop the personal traits of students that will enable them to be resilient in adult life and that prepares them to be contributors to society as a whole. The contention of this chapter is that a commitment to a culture of justice in a school is not at odds with academic excellence but that it goes beyond the curricular frame that a school has chosen to adopt.

3 Explaining the Premises of IB Education

In its Statues, the VIS has chosen to adopt the International Baccalaureate (IB)[1] curriculum programmes: VIS is an "IB World" school, educating students from the age of 3–18 (pre-university) in a continuum of IB programmes. The school's Mission Statement states:

[1] For an explanation of the IB programmes see http://ibo.org/programmes/.

For an academic analysis of international education, including the IB see, for example: http://www.bloomsbury.com/us/international-education-and-schools-9781472510464/.

> Our Mission is to empower all of our students to be successful and responsible in a nurturing and diverse learning community, so that they can achieve their potential in a changing world.
>
> In harmony with the ideals of the IB Learner Profile, and the spirit of the Universal Declaration of human rights, we aim for students to be **inquiring, inspired,** and **involved** lifelong learners.

Ian Hill, a former deputy director-general of the IB has written broadly[2] on the history of the International Baccalaureate. Hill assumes *"that a world class education model is one anchored in a UNESCO description of international education, of which IB programmes are a prominent example in both state and independent schools around the world."* (Hill 2012, p. 356)

The scope of this chapter is not to attempt to match the IB programmes with the UNESCO (1974) recommendation concerning education for international understanding, co-operation and peace and education relating to human rights and fundamental freedom. Instead, it assumes that the IB programmes match the UNESCO (1974) recommendation (see Clark in this handbook) and examines how a culture of justice and lawfulness is built and maintained in an individual school (Vienna International School) in the context of the IB programmes.

4 The Vienna International School, Its Ethos and Cultural Tensions

The Vienna International School is an Association; a not-for-profit entity whose objectives are to provide an education *"for the international community, in particular the needs of the United Nations System and other non-governmental organisations having their seat in Vienna* [as well as] *children of members of the diplomatic community residing in Austria* [as well as] *children of the international business community"* (*Vienna International School Association: Statutes* 2013[3]).

What is not typical of schools globally is the background of the students, given the community that the school serves (the objectives of the Association) and thus the professional profile of the parents. The parents, like the students, spend their days working in a multi-cultural environment focused on work that transcends national and linguistic boundaries. The experience of both students and (the working) parents is similar. Unlike many international schools, there is a relatively stable student population; many students spend a significant proportion of their school lives at VIS.

According to the statutes of the Vienna International School (VIS), *"the VIS Association shall take into account the spirit and principles embodied in the United*

---

[2] For articles critiquing aspects of the IB, its history and programmes, see: https://ibdocs.ibo.org/research/search.php?att=author&term=Hill&type=All.

[3] http://www.vis.ac.at/show_content2.php?s2id=23&language=en.

Nations Charter and the Declaration of Human Rights and the special character of an international education" (Vienna International School Association: Statutes 2013*).*

The school has a capacity of 1400 students and, in present times, operates at full capacity. The school serves "*In particular the needs of the United Nations System and other inter-governmental organisations having their seat in Vienna*" (VIS Statutes, p. 1). The students come from all over the world and truly represent a global cross section: more than 100 different nationalities are represented in the student body. The school is non-selective and educates students across a wide range of academic abilities. The language of instruction is English, but students are admitted, irrespective of their language background.[4] No one language, cultural or religious background is dominant in the student body. While the cross-section of students is culturally and linguistically broad, the educational background of their parents is, in world terms, similar. This factor, together with the chosen careers of the parents in UN and other inter-governmental organisations, are likely to have a significant impact on the possibility of developing a culture of justice in such a student body.

The school has adopted a language policy and practice that promotes the development of bilingualism, recognising the importance of students continuing to develop their mother-tongues (see Cummins 2000). Students of more than 40 different mother tongues receive bilingual diplomas at the completion of school. This commitment goes beyond the belief that bilingualism is limited to a proficiency in language: it reflects a deeply held belief that it is through the development of language that students learn much of their cultural identity.

The school provides a comprehensive extra-curricular programme. Together with service-related activities it results in students being broadly engaged beyond the scope of the academic curriculum. The school is regarded as a second home to many of the students, who are happy to remain there past the end of the normal school day

The Vienna International School has a fully constituted student leadership model that allows students significant democratic rights. Elections for the Student Council and representatives from each class across the Secondary School are held each year. This allows for a process of representation of student views on any topic that they deem needs addressing.

It is important to understand how the adoption of the IB programmes reflects a school's given objectives and impacts its culture. In his chapter "An international model of world class education" (2012), Ian Hill traces the history of the IB from its origins in the International School of Geneva in the 1960s to today when there are four curriculum programmes, spanning from pre-school to pre-university entrance.

[4] This is the case until Grade 10, when students are only admitted if they will have sufficient basis in English to be able to cope with the linguistic demands of the IB Diploma Programme in Grade 11.

Hill (2012) identifies three main reasons for the origin of the International Baccalaureate, which started at the International school of Geneva in 1962:

1. To provide an education which placed emphasis on critical thinking skills;
2. To promote intercultural understanding and provide students with an international perspective;
3. To provide a diploma which would be recognised for access to higher education around the world.

The IBDP (International Baccalaureate Diploma Programme) was the first of three curriculum programmes to be launched by the International Baccalaureate Organisation (IBO). Today there are four programmes: the International Baccalaureate Primary Years Programme (IBPYP); the International Baccalaureate Middle Years Programme (IBMYP); the IBDP; and the International Baccalaureate Careers Certificate (IBCC). These four programmes cover all ages of schooling from the early years to university entrance.

The IB has a mission that encompasses intellectual, social and emotional aims for the development of the whole individual it seeks to educate in its programmes. The International Baccalaureate Mission Statement is:

> [] to develop inquiring, knowledgeable and caring young people who help to create a better and more peaceful world through intercultural understanding and respect. []. These programmes encourage students across the world to become active, compassionate and lifelong learners who understand that other people, with their differences, can also be right. (http://www.ibo.org/mission/)

Of importance to this chapter is the commitment to peace in the world *"through intercultural understanding and respect."* One would assume that it is a given that if such programmes were to be in place in a school, the students would be educated in a culture in which justice were central. However, an examination of the patterns of adoption of the programmes (predominantly the IBDP) globally reveals that this is not necessarily the case as some schools adopt the programme for only a select few. To examine this, it is necessary to consider the requirements of being an IB World School. For this to be the case, a school must fulfil the following (www.ibo.org):

- commitment to the IB philosophy with a focus on international-mindedness;
- a rigorous, comprehensive curriculum encouraging student curiosity and inquiry;
- teachers, leaders, and staff trained in the IB programme and philosophy;
- school leadership and administrative structures that serve its mission and support the IB programme;
- a comprehensive plan for implementation and sustainability of the IB programme.

The character of the students that IB schools educate is not left to any chance: schools have a responsibility to consciously ensure that a student develops a range of characteristics, defined as "The Learner Profile", which, when combined, will ensure "international mindedness": *"IB learners strive to be: inquirers; knowledgeable; thinkers; communicators; principled; open minded; caring; risk-takers; balanced; reflective."* (*http://www.ibo.org/programmes/profile/*)

A significant additional aspect of all programmes that distinguish them from any other curricular programme worldwide is that throughout the programmes students are required to participate in "Action and Service" and that without evidence of this students cannot successfully complete any of the programmes or, significantly, gain the IB Diploma, no matter how well they may do in the assessed aspects of the programme.

In his chapter in the book on the changes needed in international education to address the challenges of the globalised world by George Walker, a former Director General of the IB (Walker 2011), Boyd Roberts (2011) writes: *"It was a brave move, in 1968, to incorporate community service as a mandatory element of the new International Baccalaureate (IB) Diploma Programme (DP)... the IB diploma remains the only academic school-leaving examination qualification with a service requirement."*

Community Service (now termed Service) is a component of "Action" in the IB. The IB says of IB World Schools that they *"value action that encompasses a concern for integrity and honesty as well as a strong sense of fairness that respects the dignity of individuals and groups...Action in IB programmes may involve service learning, advocacy and educating self and others." (IB* 2014)

It is not, therefore, the assessed curriculum alone that ensures that the mission of the IB is fulfilled: the values have to be embedded in all of the elements that make a school: policies; practices; and most importantly validated by the entire school community: teaching staff; administrators; parents and students. The argument of this chapter is that the existence of a culture of justice in a school goes beyond this. In the case of VIS, the choice of adopting an IB programme articulation rests on the premise that these curriculum programmes fit the (already existent) ethos of the school: the school would not and does not recognise its values and ethos as being limited to those of the IB.

The International Baccalaureate Organisation has three regions worldwide: IB Americas (IBA), IB Africa, Europe and the Middle East (IBAEM), and IB Asia Pacific (IBAP). Table 1 shows that, of a total of 4691 schools worldwide offering one of the three IB programmes, just 225 offer all three programmes (4.8 %). VIS is thus in a very small minority of schools worldwide offering a full continuum of IB programmes.

The International Baccalaureate Diploma Programme (IBDP) is now widely valued as an elite education, giving students of high academic ability access to prestigious universities worldwide. As an example, in the US, in addition to the Advanced Placement (AP) programme, the IBDP is used for students who have been identified as being gifted and talented (see, for example, Mayer 2008). Further evidence can be found in Doherty's (2012) study in three Australian schools offering the IB Diploma. The study examines the schools through the lens of 'meritocracy' and confirms the *'consumption of the IB for meritocracy'* and *'for the IBO, it also indicates that the Diploma's reputation in these contexts will work*

Table 1 Schools offering the three IB programmes across the three regions of the International Baccalaureate Organisation worldwide

	IBA	IBAEM	IBAP	Total schools
DP only	*1031*	*601*	*250*	*1882*
MYP & DP	182	44	17	243
MYP only	*443*	*21*	*23*	*487*
PYP & DP	29	41	68	138
PYP & MYP	*63*	*27*	*23*	*113*
PYP, MYP & DP	66	86	73	225
PYP only	*437*	*73*	*149*	*659*
Total schools	2251	893	603	3747
	IBA	IBAEM	IBAP	Total programmes
DP	*1308*	*772*	*408*	*2488*
MYP	754	178	136	1068
PYP	*595*	*227*	*313*	*1135*
Total programmes	2657	1177	857	4691

Source: http://www.ibo.org/facts/schoolstats/progcombination sbyregion

against its wish to increase access and lessen the ongoing critique of elitism' The programme is adopted for these students because of the high level of academic challenge it provides.

In this context, Doherty (2012) refers to Paul Tarc's book 'Global dreams, enduring tensions: International Baccalaureate in a changing world' (2009), which points out possible tensions Three tensions are identified related to citizenship, curriculum and operational goals:

1. The citizenship tension between producing the national and global citizen,
2. The curricular tension between designing an education in itself, and as means to an end, 'enabling access to the next level of education' (p. 24),
3. The operational tension, between the 'global dreams' of the IBO and the more pragmatic goals of local stakeholders, thus 'how IB actually operates in the world' (p. 24).

There therefore appears to exist a tension in the IB context between academic qualification and the mission of the IB. While a school would not be accredited to offer the programme if it were not fulfilling all the requirements set by the IB for World Schools, in cases in which the IBDP is adopted as an option (among others) for students who are academically gifted, does not guarantee that the total ethos of a school will be embedded with the characteristics which would ensure a culture of justice (nor does it mean that one would not exist). The adoption of the IBDP for this purpose does not guarantee any more than the high academic standards that Hill (2012) identifies as one of the original aims of the IBDP. There is evidence to suggest that in these cases the IB only provides a world class education because *"it provides international recognition of an educational process and the measurement of its outcomes expressed in meaningful certification".*

There is a therefore a distinction to be made between the four IB programmes. The IBMYP and IBPYP are different from the IBDP in that they do not provide the elite, international recognition of the IBDP. The tension that now exists is that the certification provided by the IBDP potentially limits the focus on the other values that are so much part of the mission of the IB.

The question then arises as to whether the culture of the school is determined by its curriculum programmes or the curriculum programmes have been chosen because they match the desired mission, philosophy and culture of the school. This is a very cyclic argument, the start of which is difficult to determine. However, the contention of the leaders of the school would be that the curriculum programmes have been chosen because they allow the school to achieve the desired match. This chapter argues that a curriculum programme that includes a commitment to building a more peaceful world (such as the IB programmes) does not necessarily result in schools that have a culture that would inculcate a sense of justice through a "culture of lawfulness" and that the fact that VIS has a culture of lawfulness is not only the result of the curriculum programmes it has chosen to adopt.

Howard Gardner (Gardner 2009) identifies five "kinds of minds" that he believes we should cultivate for the future, two of which are of particular relevance to this chapter: The Respectful Mind and The Ethical Mind. Gardner says that *"the first steps towards a respectful mind begin at home. But for nearly all young people, the atmosphere within the school makes an enormous contribution to the development (or lack of development) of a respectful stance. Education leaders set the tone.* [...] *That is why the ethical tone of a school and a school system is so important. Education in ethics may not begin as early as education for respect, but neither curriculum ever ends."*

Visitors to the VIS often comment on the atmosphere within the school. They use words such as "open, friendly, relaxed" to describe their first impression of the interactions between all those present on the site on a daily basis, particularly the students. It has also been said of students at the VIS that they are too autonomous and exert too many democratic rights. This is a deeply embedded culture in the school and is recognised as having been present from the school's inception. While many aspects of curricula and personnel have changed over time, this has not.

We have little measurable data on which to understand this. One measure is the response to questionnaires that ask students to rate how safe they feel at school. The data points to a school in which students generally feel safe. However, we observe that the relationships between the students and between the adults and students are strong; they are friendly, open and trusting. It is the contention of this chapter that it is this strength of relationship and sense of autonomy that exists in the student body that determines the strong sense of fairness in the school Anecdotally, those who work within the school believe that this comes from the students' experience and understanding of the commitment of the school to ensuring that they are recognised as learners with individual profiles and that they are supported in becoming personally successful with respect to their own abilities and strengths.

Curricula are comprised of three parts: the written curriculum, the taught curriculum and the learned curriculum. A school writes, or adopts, a curriculum (the written curriculum) that more than one teacher may be charged with teaching at any time; the teacher has the autonomy to deliver this curriculum according to his or her own preferred style (the taught curriculum). However, what each individual student learns differs; learning is a structured process that connects itself to past experience, not just in a learning context but also in a social and cultural context.

Gardner and Toope (2011) use the Strengths Based (SB) education definition of Lopez and Louis (2009) *"as a philosophical stance and daily practice that shapes how an individual engages in the teaching and learning process"* and in addition that in SB education there is an emphasis on *"the positive aspects of student effort and achievement, as well as human strengths."* They consider "*A Social Justice perspective on Strengths-based Approaches*", contending that a SB *"engagement involves at least four intersecting sets of educational practices: recognising students-in-context, critically engaging strengths and positivity, nurturing democratic relations, and enacting creative and flexible pedagogies."*

Gardner and Toope (2011) also consider curriculum delivery. A listing of what they discovered from the educators includes: *capitalizing on students' internal and external strengths and using these to create positive learning environments*; using students as *"teachers"*, *"experts"*, *"navigators"* and *"captains" (p. 94)*. Democracy is seen as important, including *"student voice, participation, leadership and self-advocacy"* with the creation of *"non-judgemental, safe and caring learning environments"* and *"active engagement and democratic dialogue"* and "*student involvement in decision-making.*" The power of flexibility and *"a common understanding... that students learn in different ways"* is seen as key, concluding that "*it is educators' on-going ability and flexibility to strive to best serve students in a given situation that is particularly important" (p. 99).*

IB schools, place the learner at the centre.[5] Learner-centred education takes responsibility for designing and presenting the curriculum to students in such a way that each individual student can access it and can be guaranteed to learn from it. Learner-centred education places a responsibility on the school to define the pedagogies that support this type of learning and train teachers accordingly. It places a responsibility on the student to become an autonomous, reflective learner capable of meta-cognitive thinking.

Much research has been done on the practices that lead to improved learning in schools (for example, Hattie 2009). The VIS has considered research and has identified pedagogical and assessment practices for teaching for effective learning, which have been shared with all teachers in written guides.

Weinstock et al. (2009) *"hypothesized that teachers' encouragement of critical thinking in students would predict more autonomous thinking"* p. 139*)*. The

[5] This would contrast with a teacher-centered classroom approach.

research showed that when teachers supported critical and independent thinking in students there was more internalisation of values and more autonomous moral judgement and development.

In its review of teaching and learning practices that support a learning-centred approach, the Vienna International School has recognised constructivism as being central to effective teaching and learning. Learning is constructed: every interaction with new information, through whatever sense or stimulus, builds upon previous experiences to construct each individual's unique way of understanding everything with which they come into contact.

A constructive approach to the learning environment has been shown to relate strongly to democracy and justice education. Ültanir (2012) summarises the work of McNeil 1986; Dewey 1961 and Rovai 2003 on a *"democratic classroom and constructivist learning environment"* (p. 205) with the following definition:

- *Instructional emphasis: Knowledge construction, an environment which supports active and collaborative thinking;*
- *Classroom activities: Learner centred, Socratic, authentic, individual and group work;*
- *Instructor roles: focuses on the student in learning, collaborator, facilitator, encourager, community builder;*
- *Student roles: active, collaborator, constructor of knowledge, self-monitoring.*

The recognition of the importance of building students' strengths is therefore widely developed in the literature. It covers building strengths in the social and emotional domains; in the areas of personal identity (gender, cultural, racial and ethnic); empathy and open-mindedness. Additionally to critical and independent thinking, self-reflection and introspection are important.

"Trust-in-advance" also termed "leap of faith" is identified (in Oser et al. 2008) as a "discourse-oriented concept" which *"manifests a positive view of human nature in fostering positive behaviour and relationships."* An example of this is: *"Teachers who believe and trust in advance that students fundamentally want to participate, to think and to act morally, will treat them in a way that actually helps to advance these attitudes—and the corresponding competencies."* Further, *"there is a positive correlation between social engagement and academic performance (e.g. Seligman 2002 in Oser et al.* 2008*) and that a focus on community can go together with strong academic achievement"* (Bennninga et al. 2006; Oser 2008).

The research literature supports an approach to pedagogy that places the learner at the centre of the model. Learning is thus focused on the student and is flexible, allows students scope to develop an understanding of themselves as learners. Teachers recognise that students learn in different ways and become facilitators who allow students to develop and share their own expertise. There is also a recognition of safe and caring learning environments in which students feel able to develop their own identities and in which achievement is recognised in the positive and a lack of achievement is seen as an obstacle to work collaboratively to overcome.

Olson (2011), looking at fairness in Kohlberg's development theory (Kohlberg 1975), emphasizes the challenges of fairness in a school setting, of the pressure to achieve as an individual. She says that we have an individualistic society which has *"impressed upon us the importance of working alone, independently... Especially as there is an increase pressure in schools to become more competitive (students being evaluated against each other, teachers being evaluated against each other, schools being evaluated against each other)*" (p. 132). She maintains that we must explicitly work toward, and acknowledge, the challenges and benefits of working together, especially with multiple stakeholders in the school.

Oser et al. (2008) ask whether democracy can be learned. They identify *three "forms of the notion of using democracy in education"*. The first is "analytical" and centres on students knowing, for example, how laws come into being. The second is "formal" and involves "competencies and attitudes" in which curriculum is a means for acquiring *"critical thinking, problem-solving, perspective taking, moral reasoning, openness to different points of view and autonomy in thought and action."* (p. 401) The third form is a "Just Community" school-reform approach in which the school becomes the democratic forum and thus the experience is a first-hand one in which the students play a political role in the school life, thus introducing them to "*democracy in a wider society through learning, learning by doing and, most importantly, by convincing students of the importance of democratic action and thus engendering motivation for them to become future active citizens."*

The first two forms above are easily identifiable in the VIS model but the "Just Community", while it is offered to the students through their constitutional rights, is not one of which they take much advantage. As noted above, the school has a fully constituted Student Council with significant rights. It is of importance to this chapter that a comment should be made on how little the students choose to use these rights and to use this forum as a democratically elected body might. Instead, the focus is on social interactions. At the time of writing, the most notable negotiation which had been undertaken was to ensure off-campus privileges were extend to allow Grade 11 students the right to arrive at school for their first class of the day, rather than arrive for registration at the start of the school day.

An answer for this can be found in the work of Biederman and Oser (2006) (in Oser et al. 2008). They *"found that most subjects perceive the given participation opportunities as pseudo-participation*" (p. 408) (the lowest level of participation in their Participation Hierarchy). They found that full participation was not actually something that was desired. Two factors were of importance, one was that with participation came responsibility and this was not something that was sought, and the second was that *"Whatever the level of freedom or autonomy, it is always in the context of adult guidance and collaboration"* (Watson and Brattistich 2006; Oser et al. 2008, p. 408).

Recently a group of teachers at the VIS have been looking at ways to promote the "student voice" in the school. This "voice" is in interesting contrast to the democratic voice of student leadership role and is seen by the students as being something quite separate. These teachers have worked with a group of students who have volunteered to participate. Two particular areas have been identified by the students as in need of addressing: students would like to have more opportunities to give feedback to their teachers and students would like to have more opportunities to recognise and celebrate their cultural heritages.

The research shows that Multicultural Perspectives (MP) are an added consideration. Ponterotto et al. (2008) considers MP in the context of school counselling, in particular strengths-Based School Counselling (SBSC: Galassi and Akos 2007). He argues that, for a strength-based model of counselling to be successful (in the USA), it is necessary that students learn to be able to address the demands of a population that is increasingly culturally diverse. His arguments about the ways in which students need to be prepared can be extended to a consideration as part of the challenge that are implicit in an international school community of students, particularly one such as is found at the VIS. This research extends into the tensions between home and school and argues that for multiculturalism to really to exist in schools, those working with the students need to understand multicultural perspectives. This is an aspect of the work of the VIS (and of international education in general) that needs to be further developed.

Ponterotto et al. (2008) synthesised previous research and identified the strengths most pertinent to living a satisfied life in a culturally diverse environment: *"Among these individual strengths are cultural empathy, open-mindedness, emotional stability, social initiative, flexibility, critical thinking skills, higher states of racial and ethnic identity development, humour, expanded gender role networks, bilingualism, self-reflection and introspection, social activism, and a sense of spirituality or the experiencing of a connectedness among all of life's forces."* (p. 8)

These strengths are ones that are defined in relationships. In a school, they need to be present in numerous relational interactions: student-student; student-teacher; teacher-teacher; teacher-administrator and importantly in the relationship between the school and the home.

The lack of bilingualism in students who have been brought into international education has been a concern. Families have often adapted to their new international context by allowing the development of their children's fluency in English to become the focus. They have undervalued the need to maintain the cultural, heritage language of their families. There are well-researched (Cummins 2000) cognitive benefits of being bilingual (additive bilingualism). However, in terms of developing in students the foundations of a just world, it is also a key element that they should have the understanding of their own culture that is developed through the development of language and a study of the literature that is associated with it. Students who have this grasp of their mother tongue share their sense of their own identity with others. This celebration of identity builds respect for the culture and is a barrier to the development of the prejudices that have led to a lack of justice towards those of other cultures. Bilingualism develops racial, ethnic and cultural identities, which in its turn promotes a sense of respecting and understanding others.

The argument of this chapter does not extend to a consideration of the extent to which the school helps students to address the tensions between the culture and expectations of the school and those of the home. For example, the VIS gives no message of gender difference in any of its approaches or teaching and yet there are girls whose home life reflects a different reality: these students exist in two parallel, conflicting worlds. However there is a basis for believing that these tensions are less pronounced than they might in a national context. The basis for this is the assumption is that the parents are, in the main, working in multicultural contexts, mirroring that of the school, in which there is an international focus and that they therefore have a greater affinity for the experience of their children at school than might otherwise be the case.

The probability of a cultural basis in what is understood of the moral thinking, reasoning and action in which we seek to educate students in international schools would be a factor worthy of further analysis. There are those who would argue that the values of an IB education are very much influenced by the historical influence of Christianity in the development of western cultural understanding. It is not surprising therefore to find research that links the work of Kohlberg and Piaget to that associated with Christian education. Maddix (2011), writing in the Christian Education Journal concludes that *"morality is motivated by doing what is right (justice) and what is good (empathy)."* The cognitive, which is justice, is connected to the affective, which is empathy. He quotes Gibbs (2010) who states that *"the, most plausible position of moral motivation is neither 'affective primacy' (empathy) nor 'cognitive primacy' (justice) but 'co-primacy' (both empathy and justice as primary motives)"* (p. 55).

5 Conclusion

A summary of the research on nurturing democratic relations in schools therefore identifies the need to develop critical thinking skills in students; promoting a sense of personal and cultural identity and ensuring that the following are present: student voice, participation, leadership and self-advocacy; active participation in democratic dialogue; student involvement in decision making, liberty, equity, fairness, respect, human rights and reciprocal duties (see further Clark in this volume). In the context of international education, cultural identity spans the globe and should bring individuals into a democracy that bridges cultural gaps. The limitation on this, as discussed above, may be the notionally pseudo-Christian values on which international education has potentially been based.

This investigation began with the assertion that there is a culture of justice the Vienna International School. The school community, by its very profile, offers the opportunity for an experience of social justice that transcends any of the barriers that are generally present. The choice of the IB curricula programmes for the school has been important in reflecting the value that the school places on international understanding, peace, human rights and fundamental freedom. Additionally, the learner is central to the curriculum programmes, which allow for the adoption of an approach to learning that focuses on the development of the individual and promotes a sense of personal and cultural identity. However, most importantly, there is deeply embedded culture of relationships in the school that supports and nurtures in students the development of a sense of self and personal and group autonomy. It is the contentions of this chapter that the importance of these relationships in creating a culture of justice in a school transcends the other identified factors.

Five Questions

1. To what degree is the voice of those students from non-western traditions compromised by the western values of international schools: do international schools support students to develop an individualised sense of justice with respect to their heritage culture, or do they educate students (only) to understand and work within a western understanding of justice?
2. Can a curriculum programme alone guarantee that students experience justice and leave school as potential contributors to global justice?
3. Is it a tension to combine an aim of excellent academic success with an education that has as part of its core values a commitment to develop the personal traits of students that will enable them to be resilient in adult life and that prepares them to be contributors to society as a whole?
4. Does educational background and chosen career paths in UN and other inter-governmental organisations of the parents of students at the VIS, significantly (positively) impact the possibility of developing a culture of justice in such the student body?
5. To what extent can students be supported to address the tensions between the culture and expectations of the school and those of the home?

References

Cummins, J. (2000). *Language, bilingual children in the crossfire*. Clevedon, UK: Multilingual Matters.

Doherty, C. (2012). Optimising meritocratic advantage with the International Baccalaureate Diploma in Australian Schools. *Critical Studies in Education, 53*(2), 183–196. doi:10.1080/17508487.2012.672329.

Gardner, H. (2009). The five minds for the future. *School Administrator, 66*(2), 16–20.

Gardner, M., & Toope, D. (2011). A social justice perspective on strengths-based approaches: Exploring educators' perspectives and practices. *Canadian Journal of Education, 34*(3), 86–102.

Hattie, J. (2009). *Visible learning: A synthesis of over 800 meta-analyses relating to achievement*. Oxon: Routledge.

Hill, I. (2012). An international model of world-class education: The International Baccalaureate. *Prospects (00331538), 42*(3), 341–359. doi:10.1007/s11125-012-9243-9.

International Baccalaureate. (2014). *MYP: From principles into practice*. Cardiff, Wales: The International Baccalaureate Organisation.

Kohlberg, L. (1975). Just community approach. In *Collected papers from the center for moral education, Chapter 29*, (pp. 1–77). Cambridge, MA.: Harvard Univ., Graduate School of Education.

Mayer, A. P. (2008). Expanding opportunities for high academic achievement: An International Baccalaureate Diploma Program in an Urban High School. *Journal of Advanced Academics, 19* (2), 202–235.

Maddix, M. A. (2011). Unite the pair so long disjoined: Justice and empathy in moral development theory. *Christian Education Journal, 8*(1), 46–63.
Olson, C. (2011). The deep roots of the fairness committee in Kohlberg's moral development theory. *Schools: Studies in Education, 8*(1), 125–135.
Oser, F. K., Althof, W., & Higgins-D'Alessandro, A. (2008). The just community approach to moral education: System change or individual change? *Journal of Moral Education, 37*(3), 395–415. doi:10.1080/03057240802227551.
Ponterotto, J. G., Mendelowitz, D. E., & Collabolletta, E. A. (2008). Promoting multicultural personality development: A strengths-based, positive psychology worldview for schools. *Professional School Counselling, 12*(2), 93–99.
Roberts, B. (2011). Engaging with the community. In G. Walker (Ed.), *The challenging face of international education* (pp. 86–88). Cardiff, Wales: International Baccalaureate Organization.
Ültanir, E. (2012). An epistemological glance at the constructivist approach: constructivist learning in Dewey, Piaget and Montessori. *International Journal of Instruction, 5*(2), 195–21.
Vienna International School Association: Statutes (2013) http://www.vis.ac.at/show_content2.php?s2id=23&language=en
Weinstock, M., Assor, A., & Broide, G. (2009). Schools as promoters of moral judgment: The essential role of teachers' encouragement of critical thinking. *Social Psychology of Education, 12*(1), 137–151. doi:10.1007/s11218-008-9068-9.

Education for Justice: Experiences and Prospects for Further Internationalization

Rosemary Barberet

Abstract This chapter discusses the internationalization of criminal justice education in the United States, highlighting the experiences of John Jay College of Criminal Justice of the City University of New York (USA), a leader in international criminal justice education. Since 2001, it has offered an undergraduate degree in international criminal justice, and since 2010, a Master of Arts in International Crime and Justice. Both programs are unique in the United States and among very few in the world. This chapter discusses the development of the most recent program, the Master of Arts program: its curriculum, faculty, the students it attracts and graduates, and the prospects of these programs for the future. The chapter then moves on to discuss international curricular initiatives in women, crime and criminal justice. It ends with a discussion of why and how nations around the world might encourage similar curricular development, and how the work of intergovernmental organizations such as the United Nations might contribute to such developments as well as benefit from them.

1 Introduction

In the United States and many other parts of the world, the internationalization of higher education is of increasing interest to university administrators, faculty and students. There are few who would deny that the world has become more interconnected and that the speed of communication has greatly increased in recent decades. A high quality university education, therefore, needs to keep pace with these trends, and educate students who are aware of the world outside their national borders, adaptable to change, and possess skills needed in the global marketplace. Criminal justice education, compared to many disciplines, lags behind in its efforts to internationalize, and most higher education curricula in criminal justice offer only elective courses that are international in nature. Despite calls for increased

R. Barberet (✉)
John Jay College of Criminal Justice, New York, NY, USA
e-mail: rbarberet@jjay.cuny.edu

H. Kury et al. (eds.), *Women and Children as Victims and Offenders: Background, Prevention, Reintegration*, DOI 10.1007/978-3-319-08398-8_15

understanding of crime and criminal justice in other countries (comparative criminal justice and criminology), of crimes that cross borders and are thus transnational in nature and of crimes that are offensive to the world order (war crimes, crimes against humanity and human rights violations), most criminal justice and criminology programs throughout the globe are based on research and practice that occur within the confines of the nation-state. This chapter details the internationalization of criminal justice at one institution in the United States, with an eye to examining the particularities of this case study and the lessons it may bring to other systems of higher education around the globe.

2 John Jay College of Criminal Justice

In the United States in the 1950s, many political and civic leaders became increasingly aware of the need for better police officer education. Indeed, police officer education was the main driver for the development of criminal justice education in the United States, and this is not an uncommon driver in other countries of the globe. In the United States, this move to develop police officer education was prompted by the need for the police, as an institution of a democratic society, to improve relationships with the community. In New York City, civic leaders and the New York City Police Department voiced these concerns. In response, in 1954 a Police Science Program was created at the then Baruch School of Business and Public Administration of City College. The program grew and, in 1964, a special committee convened by the Board of Higher Education recommended the establishment of an independent degree granting school of police science. The College of Police Science of The City University of New York (CUNY) was thus established and started admitting students in 1965. Within a year, it became clear that the name assigned to the College did not adequately represent the mission of the college and the college was renamed, in honor of the first Chief Justice of the United States Supreme Court, John Jay (1745–1829) (Markowitz 2008).

Today, John Jay College of Criminal Justice is a large institution offering many different degree programs related to the pursuit of justice, and police officers who study at the college are in the minority. There are 55 certificate, majors, and programs offered, including 26 different undergraduate majors and 13 Master's programs. The most popular majors are criminal justice, forensic psychology, and criminology, and the most popular Master's programs are public administration, criminal justice and forensic psychology. Students now number over 15,000 students (13,000 undergraduate and 2000 graduate students). Annually, the college awards over 3000 degrees, about 500 of which are Master's degrees.

The students at John Jay College of Criminal Justice are 60 % women, 40 % Hispanic, and 25 % African-American. About a quarter are born outside the United States; half speak a language other than English at home. Most are the first in their families to pursue higher education. It is this student profile that contributes to the success of internationalization at John Jay College of Criminal Justice. Ironically, many private colleges in the United States must work hard to attract international students to their relatively homogenous student populations. At John Jay College of Criminal Justice, as at many sister institutions of the City University of New York, low tuition cost (less than $3000 per semester for undergraduate New York resident students) and urban location at one of the country's popular receptor cities for immigrants mean that the "international" students come to the College "naturally." Given that many students were born outside the United States, half are fluent in a language besides English, and most live in very diverse neighborhoods, the push for internationalization is not a "hard sell" on the College campus. It is also the case that many students who have emigrated from other countries have done so due to some kind of injustice—ranging from outright conflict and human rights violations to global economic injustice. Therefore, the quest to study justice-related matters is also, one in fitting with students' backgrounds.

Fulltime faculty at John Jay College of Criminal Justice number 415. They are 46 % women and 29 % minority (defined as Black, American Indian/Alaska Native, Asian or Pacific Islander, or Hispanic). A normal course load at John Jay College of Criminal Justice is 21 credits a year, or seven three-credit courses per year. A three-credit course means 2–3 h of classroom teaching per week.

3 Internationalization of the Curriculum and of Criminal Justice

Higher education institutions in the United States are increasingly internationalizing, yet much of this internationalization is aspirational, more than a reality, on college campuses in the United States. Hudzik (2011) explains the trajectory of internationalization in U.S. higher education, by pointing out the reluctance to internationalize against the background of isolationism in U.S. history and politics. Until the latter half of the twentieth century, "such [international] knowledge was seen neither as a core subject [...] not an important component to creating an educated citizenry or workforce. Such knowledge was nice, a conversation piece, sometimes exotic, but rarely if ever considered broadly necessary" (p. 14). Whereas other regions of the world have been much more attuned to the benefits of internationalism, such as Europe, it is only fairly recently that in the United States, internationalism has come into vogue. A recent report by the Center for Internationalization and Global Engagement of the American Council on Education (ACE) (2012) provides U.S. higher education institutional survey results from 2011 to compare to previous ACE surveys from 2001 and 2006. The results are mixed. Certainly, many more colleges and universities have included internationalization as part of their mission statements and strategic plans, more are assessing how well they internationalize, and more are hiring faculty candidates with international backgrounds or interests. Funding is being devoted to increasing student mobility in study abroad programs, seek partnerships abroad, and recruit international students. Yet much of the curriculum (what are commonly called general education requirements) is not internationalized whereas certain disciplines (majors) may be, and the internationalization that occurs within disciplines is unevenly spread. Foreign language graduation requirements have been steadily declining. Tenure and promotion requirements that reward international activities are rare, in contrast to many other parts of the world that see a scholar's international status as a sign of his or her culminating success.

The internationalization of any discipline in the United States must be understood against this backdrop, but given that criminal justice in any country is a typically sovereign project, the internationalization of studies in criminal justice is a relatively rarity. Again, we are reminded of Hudzik's (2011) comments about internationalization being nice to have but rarely necessary. In the United States, the only certification standards for criminal justice are those of the Academy of Criminal Justice Sciences (www.acjs.org), and these standards are optional (institutions may choose to be certified by the ACJS). These certification standards mention comparative criminal justice as part of the mandated content area of Administration of Justice, for undergraduate and graduate programs in criminal justice. There is no other mention of internationalization requirements, except for that "issues of diversity" must be covered systematically within the criminal justice curriculum, which may be interpreted to encompass some aspects of internationalization. More importantly, because these standards are very focused on what should be taught in a domestic (as opposed to fully internationalized) program of study in criminal justice, neither the undergraduate program in international criminal justice nor the Master of Arts degree program in international crime and justice at John Jay College of Criminal Justice could ever achieve certification from the Academy of Criminal Justice Sciences.

Indeed, the most recent survey on the internationalization of criminal justice (Cordner et al. 2000) is now dated. According to this survey, only about one third of 4-year undergraduate university programs in the United States had an international criminal justice course. The teaching of comparative methodology is also notably absent from criminology curriculum (Barberet 2005). Despite individual faculty member interest and receptivity to international topics, most university students in the United States receive little curricular exposure to international criminal justice topics. Nevertheless, the call to internationalize has been frequent within mainstream criminology (Adler 1996; Bennett 2004; Barberet 2001, 2007; Nelken 2010; Sampson 2013).

4 The Master of Arts Degree Program in International Crime and Justice

The Master of Arts Degree in International Crime and Justice was a logical sequence to the undergraduate major in International Criminal Justice at John Jay College, in existence since 2001, now totaling 523 students and more successful than was ever imagined. Natarajan (in press, 2008, 2002), the program's founding coordinator, has chronicled the development and evolution of this undergraduate degree. The cornerstone of the undergraduate degree in international criminal justice was its encompassing definition of the subject of study, including not just comparative criminal justice and criminology, but the study of transnational crime and violations of international law, and the study of international organizations. Also at its heart was the recognition of the importance of interdisciplinary studies, encompassing traditional criminal justice but also political science, economics, anthropology, sociology, public administration, history, and area studies. The undergraduate degree provides for substantive knowledge, methods, theory and statistics, and a "capstone seminar," a course taken in the student's last year, which synthesizes what has been learned and includes the writing of a senior thesis.

The Master of Arts Degree continued our tradition of international education in criminal justice by opening the possibility of graduate education in this field. It was established with three foundational intentions and goals:

1. To create an interdisciplinary Masters of Arts program that both builds on the content and structure of the undergraduate major in International Criminal Justice and offers advanced knowledge and skills to stimulate critical thinking and research by students;
2. To provide a sophisticated curriculum that enables students to critically discuss current international criminal justice policies and programs, by producing graduates with a truly global outlook, a moral commitment to international justice, and professional competence in the increasingly multicultural workplace;
3. To further establish John Jay College as a center for innovative, interdisciplinary scholarly work in international crime and justice, and to provide an interdisciplinary framework for faculty research collaboration.

These goals were seen to enhance John Jay College's image as a mission-oriented liberal arts college that is dedicated to producing graduates with the needed skills to address the multitude of injustices, social and criminal, in the modern world. The program also contributes to the broader model of criminal justice education by including an international lens through which to analyze both international and domestic criminal justice policies. The program was established with a variety of ultimate exits for students. Students who graduate with a Master of Arts in International Crime and Justice would be competitive as applicants for a variety of doctoral programs, and as job applicants or candidates for promotion in a number of professions (managerial, policy, research). In order to accomplish this, the program is an interdisciplinary one that stresses theory, research methods, and practical applications.

At the time of creation of the Master of Arts Degree Program in International Crime and Justice, there were seven other universities currently offering graduate studies in the area of international criminal justice or criminology: St. Mary's University (Texas, USA), and in the United Kingdom, Nottingham Trent University (LLM), Leeds University, Sheffield University, University of Portsmouth, University of Bangor, and University of Greenwich. These programs had been created in the last 5 years and not all are still in existence today. Over half of these programs are in schools of law (King's College London, Nottingham, Sheffield, Leeds) and the only program in the United States is a specialization of International Relations. Despite the strong move towards internationalization in the field of criminology and criminal justice in the United States, and the interest in the related areas of security studies, including homeland security, there is still only one baccalaureate degree in International Criminal Justice in the United States (John Jay College of Criminal Justice) and no Master's degree. Recently, the University of New Hampshire School of Law has created an International Criminal Law and Justice Online Program.

4.1 Faculty Expertise and Commitment

John Jay College is fortunate to have talented faculty with a strong record of scholarship in international crime and justice, and has made a commitment to increasing the number of faculty with an interest in international criminal justice. Currently there are 23 faculty members specialized in this area, from such disciplines as criminal justice and criminology, sociology, political science, anthropology, and economics. Of these faculty members, six were contracted specifically to teach international criminal justice.[1]

[1] In addition to these faculty, the BA and MA programs have hosted a number of visiting scholars and professors, including Alexis Aronowitz (University of Utrecht, Netherlands), Marcus González Beilfuss (former DG of Migration, Government of Spain), Jamil Dakwar (ACLU, New York), Elisa García España (Universidad de Málaga, Spain), Matti Joutsen (HEUNI, Finland), Her Royal Highness Princess Bajrakitiyabha Mahidol of Thailand, Slawomir Redo (UNODC, Austria), Carolina Villacampa (Universitat de Lleida, Spain). Once a semester, faculty and students gather for a dinner and lecture, which have included such scholars as Anna Alvazzi (Small Arms Survey, Geneva), James Cockayne (UN University, New York) and Andrew Carpenter (UN Police, New York).

4.2 Need for the Program

In the wake of the creation of John Jay College's undergraduate major in International Criminal Justice, New York City became the target of terror. There is no doubt that within the discipline of criminal justice and criminology, students and faculty have developed an increased sensitivity to the problems of global cooperation, peace and security, and most criminal justice practitioners also recognize the need to know more about international issues relating to law, crime and justice. Furthermore, the New York City area is home to millions of recent immigrants, some of who choose to study at the John Jay College of Criminal Justice in order to understand conflict and crime in their nations of origin as well as the United States. Creating a Master of Arts program in International Crime and Justice responded to a real need within the disciplines of criminal justice and criminology to recognize the importance of global affairs in the configuration of crime as well as on the institutions designed to prevent and control it.

As mentioned previously, John Jay College's trademark in internationalizing criminal justice is the fusion of three disciplinary areas: comparative criminology and criminal justice, transnational crime research, and international law and human rights. In recent years, citizens of the world witnessed landmark achievements in the international arena: the creation of the International Criminal Court in 2002 and the entry into force of the United Nations Convention against Transnational Organized Crime in 2003. There are now many more textbooks and monographs on international criminal justice than before, and the success of John Jay College's baccalaureate program in international criminal justice, which has greatly surpassed expectations, was proof that there was a strong student base for advanced studies in this area.

The Master of Arts in International Crime and Justice strengthens the College's commitment to the internationalization of criminal justice education. To date, both Presidents of the College of Criminal Justice have made a strong commitment to the internationalization of the campus. This has been reflected in a number of activities. First, starting in 1992, the College has organized seven international conferences in St. Petersburg, New York City, Dublin, Budapest, Bologna, London, Bucharest, San Juan, Puerto Rico, Marrakech, New York City, and Athens. Second, John Jay College has developed a number of longstanding exchange programs, notably with Bramshill Police Command College in England and with An Garda Siochana in Ireland through the Jerry McCabe Fellowship Program. Besides these programs, John Jay College routinely hosts visiting professors and Fulbright scholars from a variety of countries. John Jay College of Criminal Justice has provided and continues to provide training to the Dominican Republic National Police Force. The College has an articulation agreement with the Center of Security Studies of the Greek Ministry of the Interior, and an exchange with the University of Rome where its staff participated in a joint conference in Rome in 2006 and another in 2008. The College hosts visitors from many police forces and criminal justice agencies from around the world—visits often sponsored by the U.S. Department of State. Finally, three members of the Law and Police Science Department have become members of the Russian Police Training Academy.

Students are further active in a variety of internationally focused extracurricular activities, including the award-winning Model United Nations Team and the International Criminal Justice Club.[2] In 2006 the College's first Director of International Studies and Programs was hired. Since then, the College has embarked on steady offerings of study abroad programs around the globe, created an International Programs Advisory Board and appointed senior administrators to manage international initiatives.

Degree-granting programs must also be responsive to the job market. Dr. Matti Joutsen, a visiting professor at the time of the creation of the Master of Arts Degree Program, identified five distinct job markets for graduates holding a Master of Arts in International Crime and Justice. From the least to the most important, they are: international organizations, NGOs and civil society in general; research and policy; the private sector; private legal practice; and the civil service. I am indebted to Dr. Joutsen for his appraisal, below.

4.2.1 International Organizations, NGOs and Civil Society in General

A number of organizations are directly interested in at least certain aspects of international criminal law: Interpol, the United Nations, Transparency International, and the long list of organizations that have consultative status with ECOSOC and follow the work of the UN criminal justice and crime prevention program. They could appreciate internationally oriented persons who feel comfortable in looking at policy or practice that affects two or more criminal justice systems. However, this job market is weak at present and in the foreseeable future, although these organizations are eager for graduate student interns and would provide placements for students to gain exposure and experience in this area.

---

[2] The Model United Nations team prepares for and participates in the yearly National Model United Nations Conference (NMUN) held in New York City. National Model United Nations Conference (NMUN) is a program sponsored by the National Collegiate Conference Association, a nonprofit organization that advances understanding of the United Nations and contemporary international issues. NMUN New York brings more than 4000 delegates to New York City each spring. Each team represents one country and participates in General Assembly and Security Council deliberations, along with other committees. Delegates deliberate, negotiate, draft and adopt resolutions and reports on a variety of issues on the global agenda. The International Criminal Justice Club (I.C.J.) sponsors a broad range of extracurricular academic and field experiences to International Criminal Justice majors at John Jay College of Criminal Justice.

4.2.2 Research and Policy

International criminal justice is a growing area, and there is every expectation that academic interest in it will grow. John Jay College has the luxury of being one of the first in the field. However, new positions are created slowly, and there is keen competition. Over the next 5 or 10 years, it is doubtful whether more than a handful of universities will be hiring faculty that is specifically interested in international criminal justice. However, with the appropriate balance of interests, a holder of an MA (and, even more, an advanced degree) in international crime and justice could readily compete with generalists.

4.2.3 The Private Sector

A more promising job market can be found in the private sector, where the potential job opportunities would primarily be in (1) major international corporations that find themselves the victims of, or accused of, offences in other countries, and (2) major national corporations that find themselves the victims of transnational offences. An international corporation, if it were a victim of, or accused of, an offence in another country would primarily retain a lawyer in that country. However, one can well imagine that certain types of offences become sufficiently widespread such that a large international corporation would want an expert responsible for developing a company policy for dealing with such cases, and to liaise with the local lawyers to implement the policy. The offence in question could be the traditional offences directed at companies (fraud, shoplifting, embezzlement, corruption) but also the increasingly common transnational organized crime offences (in particular trademark piracy, but also counterfeit pharmaceuticals or unsafe products such as toys). National corporations, in turn, may find themselves the victims of a range of transnational offences, ranging from trademark piracy to fraud to computer crime. Again, the standard practice of national corporations placed in this situation would be to retain a lawyer either in the U.S. or in the country where the offence was alleged to have been committed. But once again, it is possible that national corporations with sufficient prestige or that otherwise are an attractive target for offences may find themselves victimized by offenders from a number of countries, and would therefore want to develop a company policy for such an eventuality. In the near term, this job market is presumably limited. However, it is likely that by the time the MA program is producing its first graduates the leading national and international companies will see the merit in preferring a John Jay MA graduate who specializes in international crime and justice.

4.2.4 Private Legal Practice

While an MA in International Crime and Justice is in no way the equivalent of a law degree, it does provide a greater understanding of how the criminal justice system in other countries works, and what factors are involved in international and transnational cases. Companies, individuals and even governments may find themselves perplexed by international cases, and in need of assistance. Already a quick skim through any copy of the New York Times will show the extent to which cross-border crime or criminal justice issues affects us: fears of unsafe products from China, contested ownership of art or cultural artifacts that have crossed borders, international advance fee fraud, maritime fraud, claims that assets held in New York banks are derived from corruption and should be returned to their country of origin, etc. There are already a large number of law firms that are specifically oriented towards international criminal justice issues. The monetary value at stake even in one individual case of alleged art fraud or alleged maritime fraud can be huge, certainly in the millions of dollars. Such law firms could benefit from the contribution of persons who have become capable of quickly immersing themselves and coming to grips with foreign legal systems, and making the bridge to the U.S. This is already now an appreciable and lucrative job market, one that can only expand.

4.2.5 The Civil Service

The major job market is the civil service—national and local government. On the local (and also state) level, the larger police departments, prosecutor's offices and courts already today have a large number of cases with international connections. Most, of course, can be dealt with by regular staff, who learn through experience how to deal with such complex cases. However, there would seem to be a potential for criminal justice practitioners who already from the outset have the skills to deal with such cases. The bulk of job opportunities, however, can be found in national government. The United States has, for some 40 years, vigorously promoted an active policy of engagement in international criminal justice. According to Andreas and Nadelman (2006), over 2000 U.S. law enforcement personnel were operating abroad by the end of the 1990s. The FBI has over 40 offices abroad, and the INS, the DEA and the State Department's Bureau for International Narcotics and Law Enforcement Matters have all expanded their worldwide reach. On the judicial side, the Department of Justice has had to expand in order to deal with the burgeoning caseload, and the contacts at the Department of State are quick to point out how short-handed they are in persons skilled in treaty negotiation. And when one adds to this equation the imperative needed for competent and effective U.S. personnel to cooperate with their colleagues around the world in anti-terrorism cases, it can be seen that this is clearly a growth area.

Although other countries do not have the same international presence as does the U.S. in criminal justice, also they have had to face the need to recruit capable personnel to deal with international cases. When one further notes that the U.S. will be one of the primary points of contact with the criminal justice systems of other countries, the advantages of learning the ropes of international criminal justice at a U.S.-based academic institution are clear. The job market is thus large and growing, both in the U.S. and in just about every other country in the world. Given the almost complete absence elsewhere of a specialized training in international criminal justice, graduates with an MA in International Crime and Justice would have a clear competitive advantage.

4.3 Students

The program targets four different student markets:

- graduates of our baccalaureate program in international criminal justice;
- graduates of baccalaureate programs in criminal justice and other related disciplines in the social, behavioral and political sciences;
- mid-career professionals working in the area of international criminal justice in the United States:
- criminal justice personnel from other countries and international agencies.

It has been most successful so far in recruiting students from the first three categories. Criminal justice personnel from other countries and international agencies must usually find scholarships to relocate to New York City for the duration of the program, and although several have come from the Turkish and Korean police, they are the minority of students in the program. In general, the students in the program are residents (not necessarily citizens) of the United States. International students are in the minority.

4.4 Admission Requirements

The program seeks individuals who have the background and interest in the field of international crime and justice. Admission to the program is competitive based on the following:

- Eighteen (18) credits of undergraduate level coursework the social, political and behavioral sciences;
- An undergraduate course in statistics;
- An undergraduate economics course;
- GPA of at least 3.0 on a scale of 4.0 (equivalent to an average grade of "B");
- Work experience in international criminal justice;

- Three letters of recommendation;
- Personal interview (where feasible and necessary).

4.4.1 Curricular Design

The MA in International Crime and Justice takes advantage of many existing courses in this area offered by a variety of departments for the existing Master's Degree programs at John Jay College—in particular, those offered for the MA in Criminal Justice and the MA in Public Management. The college has a solid track-record of course offerings that are international in nature, including those leading to a certificate in terrorism studies, and thus the proposed MA in International Criminal Justice builds on existing expertise. It constitutes, nevertheless, a unique new offering at John Jay College of Criminal Justice, emphasizing a global outlook on crime and justice and a solid commitment to the interdisciplinary study of international crime and justice. Core course requirements include a course in international economics, making this program perhaps the only criminal justice master's program in the United States to mandate coursework in this area. This course was incorporated so that students could compete in the job market with others who had studied international relations or international development, as well as to provide students with the tools of economic analysis that would be useful for the study of international monetary institutions, international public management, and crime phenomena such as corruption and the international illicit trafficking of goods and services.

4.4.2 Degree Requirements

The course requirements for the Master of Arts in International Crime and Justice are 36 credits. Students complete the course of study in 2 years fulltime or 4 years part time.

Core Courses *24 credits*

International Crime and Justice Theory (3 Credits)
International Criminology examines the multicultural/cross-cultural nature and etiology of international and transnational crimes including genocide, war crimes, terrorism, money laundering, drug and human trafficking and weapons dealing. The course reviews various perspectives, approaches, and theories of crime and criminality that assist in understanding the development of new forms of crimes worldwide and in developing international crime prevention policies. A critical examination is made of various methodologies in collecting empirical data, and the problems of cross-cultural research will be discussed. The course commences with grounding in theories developed in the cultural context of the United States, and expands to embrace theories from and applying to other regions of the world.

Research Methods in International Crime and Justice (3 Credits)
The purpose of this course is to provide an understanding of the basic use of different methods used to obtaining data in criminology and criminal justice research in comparative, international and global contexts. The focus is equally on thinking statistically and qualitatively. Statistical thinking involves drawing sensible conclusions from various kinds of data by interpreting appropriate statistics. This course covers basic bivariate statistics and some models with multiple independent variables. Qualitative methods focus primarily on participant-observation, on asking questions, on writing field notes, and on the transformation of these primary field data into written ethnographic documents. This is a basic requirement for both doing social science research and for becoming an educated consumer of such research.

Using Computers in Social Research (3 Credits)
This course introduces the use of software programs to search for relationships and patterns in data sets, and to calculate the statistics needed to draw interpretations and conclusions in research reports. It is not international in nature although students are able to work with international datasets of their choosing.

International Economics (3 Credits)
This course is an advanced overview of global development and crime, and international trade and finance, to provide insight into and to critique measures of development. The concepts of international trade and finance are taught by using examples related to transnational crime. The course starts with a review of development, then covers trade including its role in development and then international finance.

Comparative Criminal Justice (3 Credits)
This course uses as a baseline the criminal justice system of the United States, and initial lectures provide an overview of the US system as a basis for comparison. Afterwards, beginning with a contextualization of world cultures, legal families and systems of government, this course studies the commonalities and variations in criminal justice systems around the world, including law enforcement, adjudication and post-sentencing measures. Special attention is paid to the impact of the growth of private security, victim assistance and corruption. Examples are drawn from a variety of political systems.

International Law and the World Order (3 Credits)
The course is an introduction to the study of international law and policy. It addresses the evolution of the international legal process, and explores—through the use of a series of hypothetical and actual problems—the principal challenges to the present world order. In particular, the course analyzes and assesses contending theories on the law/power dichotomy, the origins of international law, the structure of the international legal argument, and evaluates the relevance of the international legal lenses in addressing problems in key issue areas, such as peace and human security, intervention, human rights and humanitarian action, and justice/accountability.

Culture and Identity in a Global Context (3 Credits)
This course examines research on culture, power and identity in international criminal justice. Students are introduced to the concept of culture and how it has been related to contemporary problems and struggles in justice systems between local groups and larger, sometimes global forces. These have included concerns over culturally specific categories of identity such as gender, race, ethnicity, caste, religion, sexuality, or other social and political statuses, such as rights to property, place and behavior. Particular attention is given to the issues emerging from local confrontations with and responses to international criminal justice initiatives around domestic violence, human trafficking, copyright piracy, indigenous rights, governmental corruption, and war crimes. Through an examination of studies from different continents, students learn both the substance of the issues, and the methods, analytical approaches and rhetorical skills of research in the discipline.

Capstone Course in International Crime and Justice (3 Credits)
This course synthesizes the knowledge and perfects the skills gained throughout Masters Coursework and allows students to compare and contrast the multidisciplinary perspectives gained throughout their studies. The course consists of a series of in depth case studies of research, legal cases, or crime events, viewed from various disciplinary perspectives. Currently, program faculty and students are participating on an experimental basis in the U.S. Department of State's Diplomacy Lab project, whereby capstone students complete a semester-long research project of interest to the U.S. Department of State. In the future, capstone seminar projects may be completed for other national or international agencies.

Electives *9–12 credits*

Electives may be selected from the themed lists below or from any of the graduate courses offered at John Jay and CUNY, subject to the approval of the graduate program director.

CRJ 727 Cybercriminology
CRJ 739 Crime Mapping
CRJ 744 Terrorism and Politics
CRJ 747 Terrorism and Apocalyptic Violence
CRJ 759 Comparative Police Administration
CRJ 784 Organized Crime
CRJ 850 Homeland Security and Terrorism
CRJ 796 Homeland Security and International Relations
ICJ/PAD 762 Corruption and the Global Economy
ICJ 801 Crime and Justice in the Balkans
ICJ 802 International Perspectives on Women in Criminal Justice
ICJ 803 The UN Permanent Forum on Indigenous Issues: International Rights and Beyond
ICJ 804 Environmental Crime
ICJ 805 Human Rights and Counterterrorism

ICJ 810 Human Trafficking
PAD 718 International Public Policy and Administration
PAD 746 Comparative Public Administration
PAD 772 International Inspection and Oversight
PSY 705 Psychology of the Victim
PSY 729 Psychology of Terrorism

Students may combine electives in terrorism studies to obtain the Graduate Certificate in Terrorism Studies alongside their Master's Degree. Many of the electives feature the work of the United Nations, such as ICJ802 (International Perspectives on Women in Criminal Justice), ICJ810 (Human Trafficking) and ICJ803 (The UN Permanent Forum on Indigenous Issues), which is offered in the spring semester and includes student observation of the UN Permanent Forum on Indigenous Issues session in New York City).

Students choose one of three tracks to finish their degree. The thesis track allows the student to work one on one with a faculty advisor and produce either a traditional thesis or a publishable journal article. The thesis track is for students who enjoy scholarly research on a particular topic and/or are considering doctoral study. The comprehensive exam is a 5-h, closed book exam on the content of the program's core courses. An optional preparatory course for the exam is offered. The comprehensive examination track is for students who work fulltime and cannot choose other track options. The internship track requires the combination of 280 hours in a placement and completion of an online course taught by program faculty. Placement is undertaken by the college's Center for Career and Professional Development, or can be initiated by the student, subject to the approval of the program director. Students who choose the internship track are frequently seeking the professional experience that such an internship offers. Students obtaining new paid employment in an ICJ-related field at the time of their final track may use their employment as their internship, subject to the approval of the program director.

Students are required to demonstrate foreign language competency in the language of their choice by an oral and written test, which we outsource to LTI, the testing arm of the American Council on the Teaching of Foreign Languages (ACTFL). Credits earned in language study while enrolled in the MA in International Crime and Justice do not count towards degree requirements, and students may prepare for testing however they wish (e.g. college language lab services, course enrollment, private tutoring). Students who have studied in a foreign language through secondary school or beyond may be exempted from testing. To our knowledge, there are very few criminal justice master's programs in the United States with a foreign language proficiency requirement. So far, our students have graduated with proficiency in Arabic, Chinese, Danish, French, German, Hebrew, Hindi, Italian, Japanese, Korean, Lithuanian, Polish, Portuguese, Punjabi, Russian, Spanish, Ukrainian, and Turkish.

4.5 Administration

The program has by-laws, which provide procedures for election of program director for a 3-year term; detail the role and responsibilities of the program director; establish rules for the selection of program faculty; and establish committees for admissions and curricular development. The program avails itself of plentiful library resources, thanks to the years of responding to the demands of the undergraduate major in international criminal justice, and the college's hiring of librarians specialized, or willing to become specialized, in international criminal justice.

4.6 Results and Critical Assessment

Between 50 and 80 students are enrolled at any time in the program, since students can pace themselves with full or part time status. Sixty (60) students have graduated from the Master of Arts Degree Program in International Crime and Justice to date. Virtually all are employed, in such diverse areas as U.S. federal agencies (Homeland Security, Federal Bureau of Investigation), intergovernmental organizations (United Nations), agencies of their national governments of origin (non-United States), and as predicted by Dr. Joutsen, private intelligence firms and the private sector in general (banking, law firms). National enrollments in graduate programs in the United States have decreased over the past several years, yet enrollment in this program has been sustained.

In many ways, the unique story of both the undergraduate and graduate programs in international criminal justice responds to a number of factors that may not be present at other institutions, or may need to be developed. The strong push of our college Presidents to internationalize is corroborated by the findings of the ACE report (2012), which document that throughout the United States, leadership from above is essential in internationalizing the college campus. The presence of a large number of internationally minded students such as at the City University of New York is another factor that guarantees a "natural" student market for these programs. The lure of New York City as a multicultural city and international transport hub, and the presence of United Nations headquarters here to faculty with international interests has helped us hire many faculty members who have substantial experience and interest in internationalization. Finally, the very existence of an entire school of criminal justice (as opposed to just one small program of study) lends itself to diversifying the curricular offerings, with one option being internationalization. Finally, the John Jay "stamp" on international criminal justice—its broadening the subject of study to other disciplines besides criminal justice, and beyond comparative criminal justice to encompass transnational crime and violations of international law, as was initiated in the undergraduate degree offerings—

gives students and faculty a much wider area of teaching and scholarship than that conceptualized at many other U.S. institutions.

Challenges, of course, remain. Graduates employed in the United States sometimes comment that they must argue to their employers the value of what they have studied and how it is relevant to the very local realities of criminal justice work. They are sometimes shocked to see how very insular some U.S. criminal justice agencies can be, in the "real world." Most often, though, they are hired precisely because of their ability to "think outside the box", and for their international experience and foreign language expertise. Faculty, despite embracing innovation, are sometimes frustrated by the lack of textbooks and curricular materials in international criminal justice, although these are increasing, sometimes authored by our own faculty (Andreopoulos et al. 2011; Barberet 2014a; Natarajan 2005, 2011; Smith et al. 2011). More often, faculty are more frustrated by the inability (and impracticality) to span the globe in the same amount of teaching time that other faculty use to cover only one country (i.e. the U.S. criminal justice system). The future will surely hold creative ways to resolve these problems, the development of international criminal justice doctoral study, as well as the expansion of the student market via online learning.

5 International Curricular Initiatives on Women, Crime and Criminal Justice

Part of the course offerings in both the undergraduate and graduate programs in international criminal justice at John Jay College of Criminal Justice include electives on women, crime and justice in international context. These include an undergraduate course called Gender Issues in International Criminal Justice, and a graduate course, titled International Perspectives on Women in Criminal Justice. The development of these initiatives at John Jay College of Criminal Justice is again, unique in criminal justice in the United States and is relevant to the main topic of this volume. Thus, they merit discussion. Again, these topics are not mandated specifically within the certification standards of the Academy of Criminal Justice Sciences, but they are understood to form part of the systematic examination of issues of diversity mandated by these standards. Research and teaching in the area of women and crime in the United States is by no means novel (see Rasche, 2014) but the internationalization of research and teaching on women, crime and justice within criminology is a fairly recent development.

5.1 The Justification for International Curricular Offerings on Women, Crime and Justice

From the 1980s to the present in the Anglo-American world in particular, there has been an explosion of research on women and gender, including research on women and crime. This scholarship tends to feature analyses at the local or national level, and thus coursework in criminal justice also tends to be national in scope (see Luther and Foley, 2011, for a useful syllabus collection focused on women and crime course offerings in the United States). The growth in scholarship on global women's issues (including some research on women and crime) has occurred largely outside the disciplines of criminal justice and criminology, in fields such as international relations, development studies, security studies and public health (See Consortium on Gender, Security and Human Rights for their syllabus collection, reflecting these areas). There has also been substantial development in international policymaking in areas related to women and crime by such organizations as the United Nations and its affiliates, the World Bank (2012) and the World Health Organization, along with others such as the Organisation for Economic Co-operation and Development (OECD). Much of this development has been the result of successful mobilization on the part of the international civil society community that works on women's rights issues, including crime and victimization (United Nations 2005; Kristof and WuDunn 2010). Criminologists are seldom involved in these global debates, and criminal justice students rarely study global issues pertaining to women and crime in criminal justice programs in the United States. Yet it is true that criminology has much to contribute to this scholarship, policy and debates (Rafter and Heidensohn 1995; Gelsthorpe 2002; Pickering and Lambert 2004; Sudbury 2004; Cain and Howe 2008; Renzetti 2013; Barberet 2014b).

The multilateral work of the international community is an important justification for curricular offerings on Women, Crime and Justice. It is important that criminal justice students around the world are aware of relevant international law and the work of international institutions, not just the workings of their own local criminal justice systems. Despite the absence of the United States as a signatory to CEDAW, the Convention on the Elimination of all Forms of Discrimination Against Women, this convention represents the cornerstone of efforts around the globe to work towards gender equality. Specifically related to women, crime and justice, the UN Declaration on the Elimination of Violence Against Women in 1993 represents the first global effort to define violence against women universally. After the 1995 Fourth World Conference on Women in Beijing, the UN General Assembly mandated the UN Commission on the Status of Women to integrate into its program a follow-up process to the conference and to develop its important role in mainstreaming a gender perspective into United Nations activities. Of the critical areas of concern, many of them are relevant to students of criminal justice, and students of Gender Issues in International Criminal Justice routinely attend the NGO parallel events of the annual session of the Commission on the Status of

Women in New York each spring.[3] Indeed, we have reached the twentieth anniversary of the Beijing Conference. The United Nations Security Council resolution 1325 (2000) was a landmark resolution on women, peace, and security. More recently, the United Nations Security Council resolution 1820, paragraph 4 (2008), reaffirmed that sexual violence in armed conflict can be a war crime, a crime against humanity, or genocide. Two additional resolutions, the United Nations Security Council resolution 1888 (2009) and the United Nations Security Council resolution 1889 (2009) strengthen both the United Nations Security Council resolution 1325 and the United Nations Security Council resolution 1820. Recently, the United Nations Security Council resolution 1960 (2010) and the United Nations Security Council resolution 1820 (2013) were approved. This collection of resolutions has been instrumental in linking women to peace and security issues, preventing and demanding accountability for the use of sexual violence in armed conflict, involving women in peacebuilding and recruiting more women peacekeepers and women in criminal justice professions in general. Finally, there are now universal standards for women offenders and prisoners via the UN Rules for the Treatment of Women Prisoners and Non-Custodial Measures for Women Offenders ("The Bangkok Rules"), adopted by the General Assembly in 2010. Gender is considered a cross cutting issue in criminal justice assessment, and UNODC has a special toolkit for this purpose (UNODC 2010). These instruments must all be part of the education of today's young criminologists and form part of the effort to gender mainstream criminal justice education.

5.2 *Curricular Content*

A global examination of women, crime and criminal justice, much like the global examination of criminal justice examined in the first part of this chapter, necessitates a larger field of inquiry and forays into other disciplines. It must cover not only theory and method, but also globalization, development, international law, human rights, and activism. Violence against women should be explored both in peacetime (including son preference, female infanticide, female genital cutting/mutilation,

[3] The persistent and increasing burden of poverty on women; Inequalities and inadequacies in and unequal access to education and training; Inequalities and inadequacies in and unequal access to health care and related services; Violence against women; The effects of armed or other kinds of conflict on women, including those living under foreign occupation ; Inequality in economic structures and policies, in all forms of productive activities and in access to resources; Inequality between men and women in the sharing of power and decision-making at all levels; Insufficient mechanisms at all levels to promote the advancement of women; Lack of respect for and inadequate promotion and protection of the human rights of women; Stereotyping of women and inequality in women's access to and participation in all communication systems, especially in the media; Gender inequalities in the management of natural resources and in the safeguarding of the environment; Persistent discrimination against and violation of the rights of the girl child (Beijing Platform for Action, 1995).

and forced marriage) but also in after armed conflict (including forced conscription, forced pregnancy, ethnic cleansing, sexual torture, sexual slavery, rape in refugee camps, and the involvement of women in peace negotiations and peacebuilding. Sex work, prostitution and trafficking for sexual exploitation in global context require a critical analysis and discussion of the United Nations Convention on Transnational Organized Crime and its protocol to Prevent, Suppress and Punish Trafficking in Persons, especially Women and Children. Women as offenders, prisoners, and criminal justice professionals (including peacekeepers) around the globe also need to be examined, including international norms such as the Bangkok Rules for women offenders and prisoners. Women's other identities based on race, ethnicity, class, and indigenous status are important to cover, as is the importance of featuring issues from the developing and the developed world (Mohanty 2013; Connell 2007). The aforementioned international agreements as well as international institutions charged with engaging or monitoring compliance with these agreements, such as the CEDAW Committee, UN Women, the United Nations Commission on Crime Prevention and Criminal Justice, and the International Criminal Court also demand attention. Both the undergraduate and graduate courses at John Jay College of Criminal Justice cover these topical areas, complementing lectures with documentary films from around the world.

5.3 How Can Countries Encourage the Incorporation of Global Women's Issues in the Criminal Justice Curriculum?

This chapter has argued for the incorporation of international material throughout our curriculum in criminal justice and criminology. By international material, this includes foreign languages, international human rights, the study of transnational crime, and the study of international criminal justice and transitional justice. It also means study abroad, cultural exchanges, and the learning of research methods that can work outside one's native country (Barberet 2004, 2006).

There is a huge need by scholars and policymakers to understand how justice for women is understood and can be delivered in cultural context, in consonance with international norms and research based "best practice". The global criminal justice and international legal response to women's crime and victimization is hugely under researched, particularly newer innovations such as transitional and restorative justice and the work of the International Criminal court. Similarly, there are few evaluations of the effectiveness of gender mainstreaming. There is a demand for monitoring and evaluation of policies and programs in the area of women, crime and justice, both in the developed but particularly in the developing world. Criminological research methods need to be adapted to multicultural, uncertain, transient, and dangerous contexts. There is a strong need to provide research input to international policymakers. The United Nations commissions research reviews, but precious few empirical studies. So much of what we publish in books or journals is not accessible to international policymakers. Encouraging local scholarship is key. Gender machineries such as Ministries for Women (McBride and Mazur 2011) are the natural place for the encouragement of scholarship and teaching on women, crime and criminal justice in global context. Spain, for example, has offered pedagogical grants for years to encourage university professors to mainstream women's issues into their curricular offerings, as well as grants to enable the publishing of scholarly materials on women. Civil society organizations can be encouraged to participate in university activities. National curricula for universities should include women's international issues from the start. Nations must encourage academics to found local associations for criminology, participate in global associations, share syllabi and publish in both local and global outlets.

6 Conclusion

This chapter has covered the development of the international criminal justice undergraduate and graduate curriculum at John Jay College of Criminal Justice in New York City, USA and attempted to elucidate the factors which have led to this rather unique experiment. It is hoped that this short case study will be of use to others considering similar curricular projects, so that in future years, we may be accompanied around the globe by a multitude of varied experiences in the internationalization of criminal justice.

Five Questions

1. What are arguments for internationalizing the criminal justice curriculum?
2. How can an internationalized criminal justice curriculum also respond to domestic interests and priorities?
3. How can countries encourage the development of international criminal justice at institutions of higher education?
4. Why is the study of women within international crime and justice important?
5. What can policymakers learn from academics in these areas, and vice versa?

References

Adler, F. (1996). Our American Society of Criminology, the world, and the state of the art—The American Society of Criminology 1995 presidential address. *Criminology, 34*(1), 1–9.

Andreas, P., & Nadelman, E. (2006). *Policing the globe*. Oxford: Oxford University Press.

Andreopoulos, G., Barberet, R., & Levine, J. (Eds.). (2011). *International criminal justice: Critical perspectives and new challenges*. New York: Springer.

Barberet, R. (2004). Mainstreaming comparative methodology in criminal justice/criminology research methods courses. *International Journal of Comparative Criminology, 4*(1), 112–126.

Barberet, R. (2007). The internationalization of criminology? A content analysis of presentations at American Society of Criminology Conferences. *Journal of Criminal Justice Education, 18* (3), 406–427.
Barberet, R. (2014a). Measuring and researching transnational crime. In P. Reichel & J. S. Albanese (Eds.), *Handbook of transnational crime and justice* (2nd ed.). Thousand Oaks, CA: Sage Publications.
Barberet, R. (2014b). *Women, crime and criminal justice: A global enquiry*. London: Routledge.
Barberet, R. (Guest Ed.). (2005). Thematic issue on criminal justice policy diffusion and Europe. *European Journal on Criminal Policy and Research*, *11*(1).
Barberet, R. (Guest Ed.). (2006). Thematic issue on comparative methods in criminal justice. *Journal of Contemporary Criminal Justice*, *22*(2).
Barberet, R. (2001). Global competence and American criminology—An expatriate's view. *The Criminologist, 1*, 3–5.
Bennett, R. (2004). Comparative criminology and criminal justice research: The state of our knowledge. *Justice Quarterly, 21*(1), 1–21.
Cain, M., & Howe, A. (Eds.). (2008). *Women, crime and social harm*. Oxford and Portland, Oregon: Hart Publishing.
Center for Internationalization and Global Engagement. (2012). *Mapping internationalization on U.S. campuses*. Washington, DC: American Council on Education. http://www.acenet.edu/news-room/Documents/Mapping-Internationalizationon-US-Campuses-2012-full.pdf
Connell, R. W. (2007). *Southern theory: Social science and the global dynamics of knowledge*. Cambridge: Polity.
Consortium on Gender, Security and Human Rights Syllabus Collection. http://genderandsecurity.org/projects-resources/syllabus-collection
Cordner, A., Dammer, H., & Horvath, F. (2000). A national survey of comparative criminal justice courses in universities in the United States. *Journal of Criminal Justice Education, 11*, 211–223.
Gelsthorpe, L. (2002). Feminism and criminology. In M. Maguire, R. Morgan, & R. Reiner (Eds.), *Oxford handbook of criminology* (pp. 112–143). Oxford: Oxford University Press.
Hudzik, J. H. (2011). *Comprehensive internationalization: From concept to action*. Washington, DC: NAFSA. http://www.nafsa.org/uploadedFiles/NAFSA_Home/Resource_Library_Assets/Publications_Library/2011_Comprehen_Internationalization.pdf.
Kristof, N. D., WuDunn, S. (2010). Half the sky: Turning oppression into opportunity for women worldwide. Vintage, New York: Alfred A. Knopf.
Luther, K., Foley, A. (co-chairs) and the Ad hoc Syllabus Collection Committee (Eds.). (2011). Division on women and crime teaching resources: syllabi and assignment collection. Columbus, OH: American Society of Criminology, Division on Women and Crime.
Markowitz, G. E. (2008). *Educating for justice: A history of John Jay college*. New York: John Jay Press.
McBride, D., Mazur, A. (2011). Gender machineries worldwide. Background paper for the World Development Report 2012: Gender equality and development. Washington, DC: World Bank. http://siteresources.worldbank.org/INTWDR2012/Resources/7778105-1299699968583/7786210-1322671773271/McBride-Mazur-Background-Paper-Final.pdf
Mohanty, C. T. (2013). Transnational feminist crossings: On neoliberalism and radical critique. *Signs, 38*(4), 967–991.
Natarajan, M. (2002). International criminal justice education: A note on curricular resource. *Journal of Criminal Justice Education, 13*(2), 479–498.
Natarajan, M. (2008). John Jay's bachelor's degree in international criminal justice. In S. Redo (Ed.), The rule of law: Criminal justice teaching and training across the world. Helsinki, Finland: The European Institute for Crime Prevention and Control.
Natarajan, M. (Ed.). (2005). *Introduction to international criminal justice*. New York: McGraw-Hill Publishing.

Natarajan, M. (Ed.). (2011). *International crime and justice*. New York: Cambridge University Press.
Natarajan, M. (1997). International criminal justice major at John Jay: A success story. In H. Dammer & P. Reichel (Eds.). *Teaching comparative/international criminal justice manual.*
Nelken, D. (2010). *Comparative criminal justice: Making sense of difference*. Thousand Oaks, CA: Sage.
Pickering, S., & Lambert, C. (Eds.). (2004). *Global issues, women, and justice*. Sydney: Sydney Institute of Criminology.
Rafter, N. H., & Heidensohn, F. (Eds.). (1995). *International feminist perspectives in criminology: Engendering a discipline*. Buckingham and Philadelphia: Open University Press.
Rasche, C. E. (2014). The ASC division on women and crime from 30 years out. *Feminist Criminology, 9*(4), 253–269.
Sampson, R. J. (2013). Common concerns, unique cultures? European and American criminology. *ESC Newsletter, 12–13*, 15.
Smith, C. J., Zhang, S. X., & Barberet, R. (Eds.). (2011). *Routledge handbook of criminology: An international perspective*. London: Routledge.
Sudbury, J. (2004). *Global lockdown: Race, gender, and the prison-industrial complex*. London: Routledge.
United Nations. (2005). *Broken bodies, broken dreams: Violence against women exposed.* New York: OCHA/IRIN.
UNODC. (2010). *Gender in the criminal justice system assessment tool*. Vienna: UNODC. http://www.unodc.org/documents/justice-and-prison-reform/crimeprevention/E-book.pdf.
World Bank. (2012). *World development report: Gender equality and development*. Washington, DC: World Bank.

Part III
Children/Juveniles and Women as Victims and Offenders

The Criminal Victimization of Children and Women in International Perspective

Jan Van Dijk

Abstract In this article we will present an overview of the results of the national and international crime victims surveys regarding the distribution of victimization according to age and gender with a focus on violent crime. The results show a consistent inversed relationship between age and criminal victimization by all types of crime. Children are by far the most at risk to be victimized by criminal violence of all age groups. The violence is in large part committed by parents or other caretakers. The relationship between gender and victimization is less straightforward. Men are more exposed to various types of non-sexual violence by strangers, including homicide. Women are more exposed to sexual violence. Exposure to non-sexual violence by intimates is less strongly gendered than sexual violence by intimates according to the results of dedicated surveys on domestic violence among males and females. Cross-national analyses suggest that violence by intimates against females is most prevalent in countries where gender equality is low. However, self-reported victimization rates of violence against women by intimates are also relatively high in countries where gender equality is the highest, such as Scandinavian countries. This paradoxical result seems due to increased sensitivity to acts of less serious violence among female respondents in the latter countries. The various findings concerning the distribution of victimization risks across age and gender are interpreted with lifestyle-exposure theory and feminist perspectives on violence.

1 Introduction

Various theoretical models have been developed to explain how the differential vulnerability of individuals to criminal victimization is determined by their lifestyle or "routine activities" (Hindelang et al. 1978; van Dijk and Steinmetz 1980). In this victimological perspective gender and age are associated with victimization risks

J. Van Dijk (✉)
University of Tilburg, Tilburg, The Netherlands
e-mail: jan.vandijk@uvt.nl

H. Kury et al. (eds.), *Women and Children as Victims and Offenders: Background, Prevention, Reintegration*, DOI 10.1007/978-3-319-08398-8_16

because of structural differences in routine activities of age and gender categories. According to the three factorial risk model designed by van Dijk and Steinmetz (1980) risks are determined by (a) economic or psychological attractiveness of persons as targets of crime; (b) proximity to offenders due to residence or lifestyle; and (c) a lack of social and/or practical protection against crime. To the extent that these three risk factors are related to age and gender, criminal victimization can be expected to be age and gender-related as well.

The link between gender and criminal victimization has been the subject of a specific theoretical perspective. In seminal publications feminist scholars have argued that norms condoning violence against women flourish in male dominated societies (Brownmiller 1975; Dobash and Dobash 1979). In this perspective, women and girls can be expected to be vulnerable for violence by men, especially in countries were gender inequality is most pronounced. In several policy documents of the United Nations violence against women is projected as an expression of gender inequality (United Nations 2006).

An important breakthrough in the gathering of empirical knowledge on criminal victimization is the conduct of large-scale sample surveys on experiences of crime, such as the National Crime Victims Survey of the USA (NCVS), the England and Wales Crime Survey (formerly British Crime Survey) and the Dutch Security Monitor. The considerable sample sizes of these surveys, often consisting of ten thousands of respondents or more, allow for disaggregation of victimization risks for various subsets of the population including gender and age categories. In some countries these disaggregated results of general victimization surveys are supplemented by data from surveys on violence against women (Tjaden and Thoennes 2000), violence between intimates (van Dijk et al. 2010) and on the criminal victimization of children (Finkelhor et al. 2005; Alink et al. 2011; Baier et al. 2006). In addition, results are available of standardized international surveys such the International Crime Victims Surveys (ICVS), the International Violence against Women Survey (IVAWS) and the Violence against Women surveys of the Fundamental Rights Agency of the European Union (FRA 2014).

In this article we will present key results of the national and international surveys just mentioned regarding the distribution of victimization according to age and gender with a special focus on violent crime. We will discuss how these results relate to lifestyle-exposure theory and to the feminist perspective. In the final paragraph we will discuss some policy implications for crime prevention and victim assistance

2 Victimological Risk Analyses: Gender and Age Gaps

Data from general victimization surveys can, as said, shed light on demographic and other social characteristics that may act as risk-enhancing or reducing factors. The oldest and most cited national survey is the National Crime Victims Survey (NCVS) of the USA which has been repeated annually since 1973. In the more

Table 1 Rates of violent victimization by demographic characteristics of victims, 2004, 2012 and 2013, USA National Crime Victims Surveys (NCVS); Bureau of Justice Statistics 2014

	Number of victims[a]			Prevalence rate[b]		
Victim demographic characteristic	2004	2012	2013	2004	2012	2013
Total	3,478,620	3,575,900	3,041,170†	1.4%	1.4%	1.2%†
Sex						
Male	1,925,560	1,917,390	1,567,070†	1.6%	1.5%	1.2%†
Female	1,553,060	1,658,520	1,474,090†	1.3	1.2	1.1†
Race/Hispanic origin						
White[c]	2,474,200	2,186,520	1,860,870†	1.5%	1.3%	1.1%†
Black/African American[c]	475,090	598,100	430,380†	1.7	1.9	1.3†
Hispanici/Latino	373,740	592,230	540,130	1.2	1.5	1.3
American Indian/Alaska Native[c]	34,840	27,980	38,310	3.4	1.9	2.8
Asian/Native Hawaiian/ other Pacific Islander[c]	55,750	105,990	57,300†	0.6	0.8	0.4†
Two or more races[c]	65,010	65,080	114,190†	3.7	2.0	3.6†
Age						
12–17	714,180	617,820	545,370	2.8%	2.5%	2.2%
18–24	800,770	716,360	527,410†	2.8	2.3	1.7†
25–34	624,510	712,600	604,500†	1.6	1.7	1.4†
35–49	885,990	785,440	684,150‡	1.4	1.3	1.1
50–64	393,700	582,760	566,990	0.8	1.0	0.9
65 or older	59,480	160,930	112,760†	0.2	0.4	0.3†
Marital status						
Never married	1,964,120	1,894,560	1,626,980†	2.5%†	2.1%	1.8%†
Married	891,720	966,420	738,410†	0.7	0.8	0.6†
Widowed	45,230	71,370	74,880	0.3	0.5	0.5
Divorced	384,980	465,360	405,420	1.8	1.8	1.6
Separated	180,110	164,500	171,630	3.9	3.3	3.3

Source: Bureau of Justice Statistics, National Crime Victimization Survey, 2004, 2012, and 2013
†Significant change from 2012 to 2013 at the 95 % confidence level
‡Significant change from 2012 to 2013 at the 90 % confidence level
[a]Number of persons age 12 or older who experienced at least one victimization during the year for violent crime
[b]Percentage of persons age 12 or older who experienced at least one victimization during the year for violent crime
[c]Excludes persons of Hispanic or Latino origin

recent, redesigned sweeps the measurement of violence also covers violence by intimates and family members. The most commonly used breakdowns of the NCVS results are those of gender, ethnicity, age and marital status. Table 1 shows results for victimization by violent crime of three sweeps of the survey (2004, 2012 and 2013) (BJS 2014).

The first finding that catches the eye is that in the USA victimization by violence has gone down between 2004 and 2013. The results of breakdowns furthermore

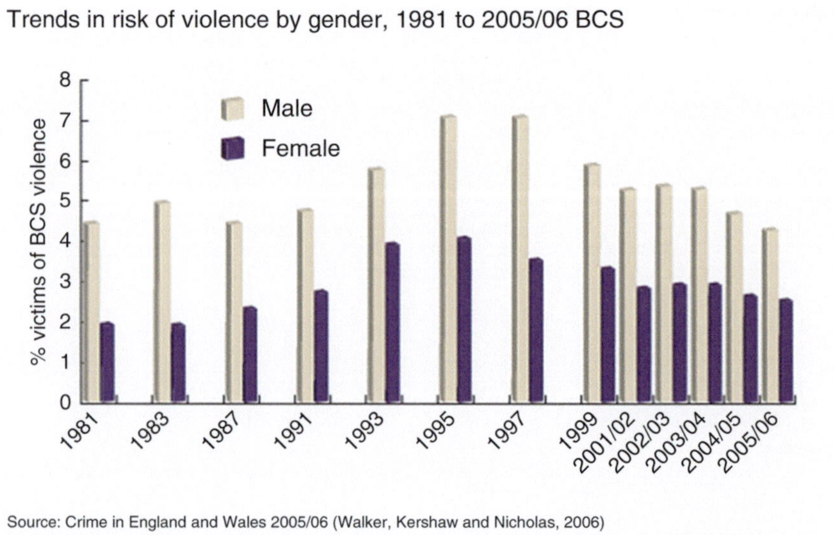

Fig. 1 Trends in risk of violence by gender, 1981 to 2005/2006, British Crime Survey (BCS)

show that men are consistently more at risk to be victimized by violent crime, especially by serious violent crime than women. The picture of the age distribution shows a linear decline with growing age. Children between 12 and 17 years and young adults (18–24) are more at risk than any other age group. Since 2004 the age gap seems to have narrowed somewhat. Ethnicity appears to be systematically related to victimization risks as well. Indian Americans are more at risk across the board and black Americans seem more exposed to serious violence than whites. Marital status seems also relevant with the status of being married acting as protective factor.

We will first revisit the hypothesis of a gender gap in victimization by violent crime found in the USA. This we will do first by looking at the results of several sweeps of one of the largest and oldest European crime survey, the England/ Wales Crime Survey, formerly British Crime Survey. Figure 1 shows results over a period of 25 years (Jansson 2006).

The data from the BCS indicate a curvilinear trend in violent victimization peaking around 1997, just as in the USA. Similar trends have been observed across the Western world (van Dijk et al. 2013). The hypothesis of a gender gap is fully confirmed. The gender gap proves to be even larger than in the USA, with male citizens possessing risks twice as high as those of females. Over the years the gender gap appears to have narrowed somewhat in England/Wales.

The third major national general survey to be consulted on the distribution of victimization across various demographics is the Dutch Security Monitor of the Central Bureau of Statistics (2014) which used a sample of 145.000 respondents of 15 years and older in 2013. Table 2 presents findings concerning the demographics gender, age and ethnicity as well as sexual orientation.

Table 2 Victimization risks of different population groups in The Netherlands; Security Monitor, CBS, The Netherlands

	Violence	Property	All crime
Gender			
Male	2.9	13.5	20.1
Female	1.9	13.9	19.4
Age			
15–24	4.1	19.8	25.9
25–44	3.1	14.8	22.2
45–64	2.0	13.0	19.2
65+	0.9	8.6	12.2
Ethnicity			
Dutch	2.4	13.0	19.0
Other white	2.4	14.2	20.6
Non western	2.7	18.5	24.2
Sexual orientation			
Gay	3.9	19.3	26.7
Lesbian	4.1	18.1	27.1
Bi male	4.6	16.1	22.0
Bi female	2.2	15.1	20.4
Hetero m	3.0	13.4	20.4
Hetero fem	2.0	14.5	20.3

The results regarding the links between age and gender and victimization by violent crime are mostly in line with those from the USA and the UK. Males are more often victimized by violent crime in the Netherlands, as elsewhere, and victimization by violent crime is inversely correlated with age. Risks for property crime are the same for both sexes. Age is inversely related with age for property crime as well.[1] Persons of non-Western origin are more likely to be victimized by any crime.

Uniquely, the latest Dutch national survey allows breakdowns of victimization risks according to sexual orientation. Gays and lesbians are more exposed to both violent and property crimes than heterosexual males and females respectively. An elevated risk also holds for bisexual males but not, or less so, for bisexual females.

So far we have discussed the breakdowns of results from the three largest national surveys on criminal victimization in the world. The International Crime Victims Survey (ICVS), a standardized survey conducted since 1988 six times in altogether over 80 different nations, allows a replication of such risks analyses for a larger selection of nations (van Kesteren et al. 2014). The data from the first three rounds in 1989, 1992 and 1996, covering 54 countries from all world regions, were

[1] In recent versions of many general victimization surveys questions have been added on victimization by internet-based crime. These surveys show that victimization by internet-based crime such as viruses and cyber bullying is most prevalent among the youngest age group (16–24 years) and decreases with age (e.g. Smith et al. 2006).

Table 3 Controlled effects of risk factors (odds ratios) on victimization in 1999; ICVS 2000 (16 Western countries combined)

	Property crime	Contact crime	Sexual crime (women)	Any crime
Age (base = 55+)				
25–54	1.61	1.92	8.05	1.72
16–24	2.04	2.51	15.48	2.31
Gender				
Male	1.02	1.19	n.a.	0.99
Town size (base = <10.000)				
10–100.000	1.33	1.48	1.96	1.39
> 100.000	1.60	1.60	1.51	1.64
Married (base = married)				
Not married	1.18	1.99	2.40	2.29
Going out (base = not often)				
Often	1.22	1.25	1.45	1.23

analyzed using a multivariate analysis to determine how relevant social characteristics influence victimization risks independently of each other (van Dijk 1999b). The results of this multivariate analysis showed that the known risk-enhancing factors age and gender operated in all regions in roughly the same way. Young age was found to be a strong universal risk-enhancing factor. However, the age gap was found to be significantly larger among populations of developed countries than those of developing countries. Victimization by any crime was found not to be gender-related. Other universal risk enhancing factors were found to be high income and an outgoing lifestyle.

Multivariate analyses were made of the controlled risk effects on victimization by different types of crime in the data from 16 Western nations participating in the 2000 ICVS. Included were the demographics age, gender, town size, marital status, and lifestyle (frequency of going out in the evening) (van Kesteren et al. 2000). The results are expressed as odds ratios. An odds ratio is the odds of someone in a certain group (e.g. young age) as being victimized by any crime, divided by the odds of someone in the base group with the lowest risk (55+). In this example the risk of those of young age is 2.31 times higher than of the base group. Results are presented in Table 3.

The results of this multivariate analysis show that being young increases the risk of victimization, especially for contact crimes (threats, assaults and robberies) and sexual crimes (women only). Seniority acts as protective factor against victimization across the board. These results confirm that young people are most at risk. The age factor proves to be the most powerful determinant of victimization risks, independently of other factors. The results concerning gender differentiation are mixed. Risks to be victimized by any crime are roughly equally divided. Risks to be victimized by contact crime (threats, assaults and robberies) are somewhat elevated for men, as also shown by national surveys. The second most important risk factor is the size of one's residence. Inhabitants of large cities are most at risk. An independent risk factor for victimization by contact crime is the status of being single. The frequency of going out at night was found to explain a considerable amount of victimization, especially for sexual crimes. As in the USA, marital status is relevant in the sense that single persons are more at risk. In a subsequent multivariate analysis of data of the ICVS 2005 Van Kesteren included ethnic status. Being a non Western immigrant was found to be an independent risk-enhancing factor across the Western world (van Kesteren 2006).

By and large, the results of multivariate analyses of international victimization data confirm that across the world being young is a major risk factor for victimization by any type of crime and that males run higher risks of victimization by violence. The age gap is also evident in the distribution of homicide. Homicide appears universally to victimize predominantly (young) males. WHO homicide data show the risk for homicide to be the highest for young males (19.4 per 100,000) and young adult males (18.7) (WHO 2002). Risks for females are significantly lower in all age groups (4.5 on average).

In the ICVS, the questions on victimization by sexual incidents (physical harassment, attempted rape or rape) are only put to female respondents.[2] In an analysis of results from all world regions victimization by serious sexual incidents was combined with victimization by non-sexual violence. The use of this comprehensive index of violence reversed the direction of the gender gap: females appeared now to be somewhat more at risk of victimization by violence than males (van Dijk 1999a). In Europe and North America males continue to show higher rates of victimization by violence than females. But in the other regions, the difference goes in the other direction. In Africa, South-Central America and Asia, the percentage of women victimized by any kind of violence is 50 % or more above that of males. In Asia, female victimization by violence is even twice as high as male victimization (van Dijk 1999a). The stereotypical notion that Asian countries are low on violence must be qualified with respect to gender. For Asian women the risks of being violently victimized by either non-sexual or sexual violence are not much lower than for women in Western countries.

3 Dedicated Surveys Among Children

Comprehensive surveys in the tradition of the NCVS apply minimum ages of 12 or 16 years. The ICVS uses samples of 16 years and up. This implies that no data are collected on victimization of young children. In recent years bespoke surveys have been designed to measure various forms of criminal victimization of young chil-

[2] Pilot studies had shown that very few male respondents mention serious incidents of sexual victimization and that the item caused problems for the interviewers in some countries.

dren. In the USA a bespoke survey was conducted among young children between 2 and 17 (Finkelhor et al. 2005). The victimization rates were found to be much higher than those found in the NCVS among young people and adults. The study confirms the pervasive exposure of young people to violence, other crime, maltreatment, and other forms of victimization as a routine part of ordinary childhood in the United States. More than one half of this nationally representative sample had experienced a physical assault in the past year, more than 1 in 4 a property victimization, more than 1 in 8 a form of child maltreatment, 1 in 12 a sexual victimization, and more than 1 in 3 had been a witness to violence or another form of indirect victimization. Only a minority (29 %) had no direct or indirect victimization. Among children victimization risks go up between 2 and 7 and stay more or less at the same level thereafter.

A dedicated survey has been carried out in 2000 in Germany among 11,000 teenagers between 14 and 16 years of age about their experiences with domestic violence. Seven percent of the sample reported to have ever been beaten by parents. Eight percent had seen violence between their parents, usually but not exclusively by their father against their mother (Baier et al. 2006). German children of divorced or separated parents reported on average even higher percentages (30 %). Significantly higher percentages of violence against mothers were reported by children of immigrants, 9 % among Greeks, 32 % among Turks, 25 % among immigrant families from Yugoslavia and 20 % among Russians. The percentages of immigrant families experiencing such violence was higher to the extent that they had resided longer in Germany, suggesting growing tensions between spouses after a longer exposure of women to German norms and values concerning gender equality.

In the Netherlands special victimization surveys have been carried out at the national scale among schoolchildren from 12 to 17 years in 2006 and 2010 (Alink et al. 2011). The questionnaire used was largely based on the internationally tested Parent Child Conflicts Tactics Scale designed by Straus et al. (1998). The report on the 2010 survey among 2000 respondents focuses on acts of physical child abuse by parents, ignoring violence by siblings or peers. The results show that 9 % of Dutch children have experienced physical abuse by parents in the course of last year considered criminal by Dutch official standards (excluding e.g. simple acts of slapping). The percentage of Dutch schoolchildren who felt to have been exposed to parental violence of any kind was twice as high. As in Germany, children of divorced parents were more at risk, as were children of non-Western immigrants. After controlling for education and social-economic status the enhanced risks among children from traditional migrant communities such as Turks and Moroccans disappeared. The enhanced risks among children of new immigrants groups, consisting of asylum seekers, persisted after such controls had been entered.

Although the results from the three countries where such bespoke surveys have been conducted cannot be compared due to differences in focus and measurement tools, the results indicate that young children are significantly more at risk to be victimized by violence than any other age group.[3] In all three nations physical abuse by parents makes up a large part of the victimization by violence of children. These results confirm the general pattern emanating from general surveys that risks to be criminally victimized decrease linearly with age.

4 Bespoke Surveys on Violence by Intimates

In several countries special in depth surveys using very extensive questionnaires with many prompts to assist the respondent in remembering and reporting incidents have been carried out on violence against women, including sexual violence (for an overview see Kangaspunta and Haen Marshall 2012). Such dedicated surveys on violence against women aim to collect information on a wider range of violent acts, specifically also those committed by husbands or other intimate partners. They consequently show higher violent victimization rates among women than the general national victimization surveys or the ICVS (Kangaspunta 2000). Such surveys, once pioneered in Canada, have now been carried out in 70 or more countries across the world.

Globally, on average, an estimated 30 % of women have been victimized by male partner violence at least once in their lifetime (WHO 2002; United Nations 2006). One in ten women has been a victim of intimate partner violence in the course of last year. In a majority of cases women are victimized by both ordinary violence and sexual violence by the same intimate(s).[4]

The violent victimization rates just mentioned go far beyond those found in general surveys and have raised awareness of the pervasiveness of violence against women. It has become clear that general victimization surveys fail to measure the full extent of partner violence. Since the first generation of these bespoke surveys were conducted exclusively among females, the question remains whether partner violence only victimizes women or also men. In the National Violence against Women Survey of the USA from the late 1990 ties male respondents were included. The results show that 1.3 % of surveyed women and 0.9 % of surveyed men reported experiencing such violence in the previous 12 months (Tjaden and Thoennes 2000). In The Netherlands a stand alone survey on sexual or non-sexual violence by intimates was carried out in 2010 among a national sample

[3] In England/Wales a module attached to the national crime survey interviews young children between 10 and 15 years old about crime with a questionnaire that mirrors the one used for adults (Smith et al. 2006). No questions are asked about violence by parents. The experimental results show that 6.9 % of children aged 10–15 had experienced a violent crime in the last 12 months. Boys were around twice as likely as girls to have been victimized (9.5 and 4.1 % respectively). Around 3.1 % of adults had experienced a violent crime in the last year.

[4] Special surveys on sexual attacks in the USA confirm the pervasiveness of sexual violence against women. In the USA nearly 1 in 5 (18.3 %) women and 1 in 71 men (1.4 %) reported experiencing rape at some time in their lives (Black et al. 2011).

Table 4 Incidents of physical and sexual violence in the domestic sphere; results of Dutch violence by intimates survey (van Dijk et al. 2010)

	Males	Females
Hitting with object	7	7
Hitting/biting/stumping	17	17
Threatening with knife	7	6
Wounding with object	2	2
Throwing object	17	18
Destruction property	21	20
Taunting/belittling	18	25
Rape	1	7
Coerced intercourse	3	17
Coerced sexual acts	1	9

of both females and males (van Dijk et al. 2010). The results of the survey can be used to revisit the hypothesis of the gender gap in victimization by partner violence with more comprehensive and detailed data recently collected through a bespoke, gender-neutral survey. Table 4 presents some key results.

The results show that for most types of victimization by non-sexual violence in the domestic sphere there were almost no differences between men and women. Women, however, were five times more likely to have been victimized by sexual violence. Of all forms of violence measured, women made up 60 % of the victims. In the British Crime Survey a self-completion questionnaire module on intimate violence has been added since 2004. Overall, 2.2 % of men and 2.7 % of women in current or former relationships reported experiencing force by partners in the last year (Home Office Bulletin 2008). The finding that partner violence victimizes considerable numbers of males in the USA and that among the Dutch and British populations non-sexual violent victimization by partners is almost as prevalent among males as among females raises doubts about the general applicability of feminist theories on violence against women.[5] Although women are definitely much more exposed to sexual violence than men, victimization by acts of physical violence by partners seems at least in Western countries not to be an unambiguously gendered phenomenon.

5 Cross Country Comparisons of Violence Against Women

A powerful test regarding the feminist hypothesis of a relationship between structural gender inequality and victimization by violence against women is whether such violence is more prevalent among societies where power inequalities between

[5] In Denmark questions on partner violence have been included in the National Health Interview Surveys since 2005. In the 2010 NHIS 1.5 % of women and 0.5 % of men reported having been exposed to physical partner violence in the last year. The Danish findings indicate a decrease of partner violence against women and an increase of partner violence against men in recent years (Helweg-Larsen 2012).

males and females are most pronounced. Cross-national datasets are ideally suited for such analysis. In the United States, Yllö correlated scores on a status of women index with domestic physical violence against women using the nation's various states as unit of analysis (Yllö 1983). The results showed a curvilinear relationship between gender equality and victimization by domestic violence. Victimization rates were, in line with the hypothesis, highest in states where women were the most unequal, as expected. However, more surprisingly, relatively high rates were also found in American states where the status of women was the most equal.

Although the measurement of victimization by violence in the ICVS is limited, this standardised survey allows inter-country comparisons of the levels of victimization of women by both sexual and non-sexual violence at the global level. Analyses of ICVS data on violence, including sexual violence, against women have shown that the level of such violence shows a complex relationship with measures of gender equality. The highest rates of violence against women are found in developing countries where the social position of women is relatively weak. Among developing countries a negative relationship was observed between various measures of gender equality and victimization by sexual violence (Alvazzi del Frate and Patrignani 1995). However, in an analysis of global ICVS data, Kangaspunta (2000) found that in countries which stand at the top end of the gender equality scale, e.g. countries such as the USA, Canada, Finland and New Zealand, women report somewhat *higher* proportions of (relatively minor) sexual incidents than the average (Kangaspunta 2000). This finding suggests that the most "liberated" women are more likely to perceive sexually motivated incidents as criminal behavior than women in nations with greater gender inequality. This result resembles that of Yllö on the curvilinear relationship between gender equality and self-reported domestic violence among American states.

In another secondary analysis of the data of the ICVS 2000, Yodanis (2004) looked at the relationship between measures of gender inequality and victimization by violence and sexual violence separately among 27 Western nations. Her results show a correlation between gender inequality and the prevalence of victimization by sexual violence but no correlation between inequality and prevalence of victimization by non-sexual violence. Taken together, secondary analyses of global ICVS data on violence against women offer qualified support to the feminist hypothesis regarding the epidemiology of such violence. Violence against women of any type is most prevalent in developing nations where gender inequalities are most pronounced. Among developed nations the linkage between gender equality and violence against women is less clearly in evidence. No such relationship was found for non sexual violence and the one for sexual violence seems to be curvilinear rather than linear at the global scale.

Bespoke surveys on violence against women produce more comprehensive data on violence against women than the ICVS. Such surveys have, as mentioned, been carried out in 70 or more nations. Although such surveys yield better data on domestic violence, these data can, for lack of standardization, not be reliably used for comparative purposes. Stand alone victimization surveys on violence against women use divergent definitions of violent behavior against women. Some

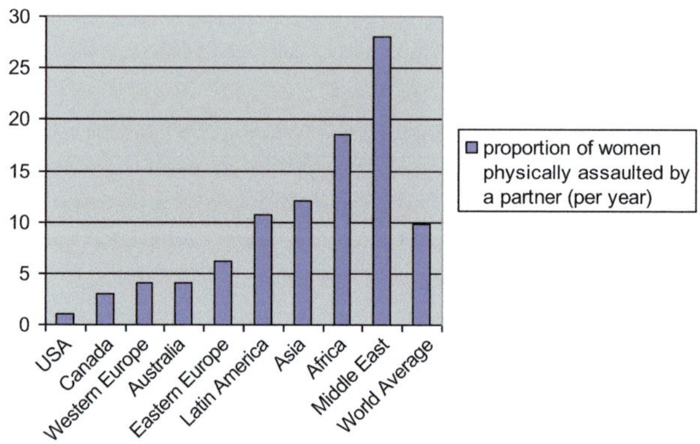

Fig. 2 Percentages of women 15 years and older victimized by violence from intimate partners over the last 12 months of world regions; sources: independently run, dedicated surveys of violence against women in 72 countries (*source*: United Nations 2006; Van Dijk 2008)

questionnaires include non-physical sexual harassment others do not, or to a lesser extent. Since the methodologies used vary within world regions as much as across regions, a comparison of rates of world regions can yet give a tentative insight in the epidemiology of violence against women across the world. Figure 2 presents an overview of regional rates of women victimized by intimate partner violence over the last 12 months according to non-standardized, dedicated VAW surveys.

The regional rates for intimate partner violence show huge variation around a mean of ten. Rates are the lowest in the USA, Canada, Western Europe and Australia (less than 5 % victims). The highest rates are found in Africa (18 %) and in the Middle East (Egypt/Palestina:28 %). Given low overall rates of crime and violence in the Asian region, the medium high rates of intimate partner violence among Asian nations (12 %) is also striking.

In order to develop better comparable information on violence against women, a standardized International Violence Against Women Survey (IVAWS) has been executed in ten mainly developed countries by an international consortium of researchers (Johnson et al. 2008). In 2005 the WHO published results of another standardized international survey on violence against women carried out in ten developing countries, unfortunately using a different questionnaire than the IVAWS (WHO 2005). Lifetime prevalence rates for partner violence in the latter study were 61 % in Peru (province), 49 % in Ethiopia (province), 47 % in Tanzania (province), 43 % in Brazil (province), 42 % in Bangladesh (province), 41 % in Samoa, 34 % in Thailand (province), 31 % in Namibia (city), 23 % in Serbia (city) and 13 % in Japan (city). In most cases women experiencing physical violence had also been sexually abused. Although their results are not strictly comparable, the two standardized surveys on violence against women confirm that male violence against women is more prevalent in developing countries than in developed ones. In all countries were standardized surveys were carried out in both provincial areas and cities, prevalence rates were also found to be higher in provincial areas than in cities. Available evidence from these bespoke surveys, then, suggests that violence against women by partners is more prevalent in less developed countries where women possess lower social status, especially in rural areas of such countries

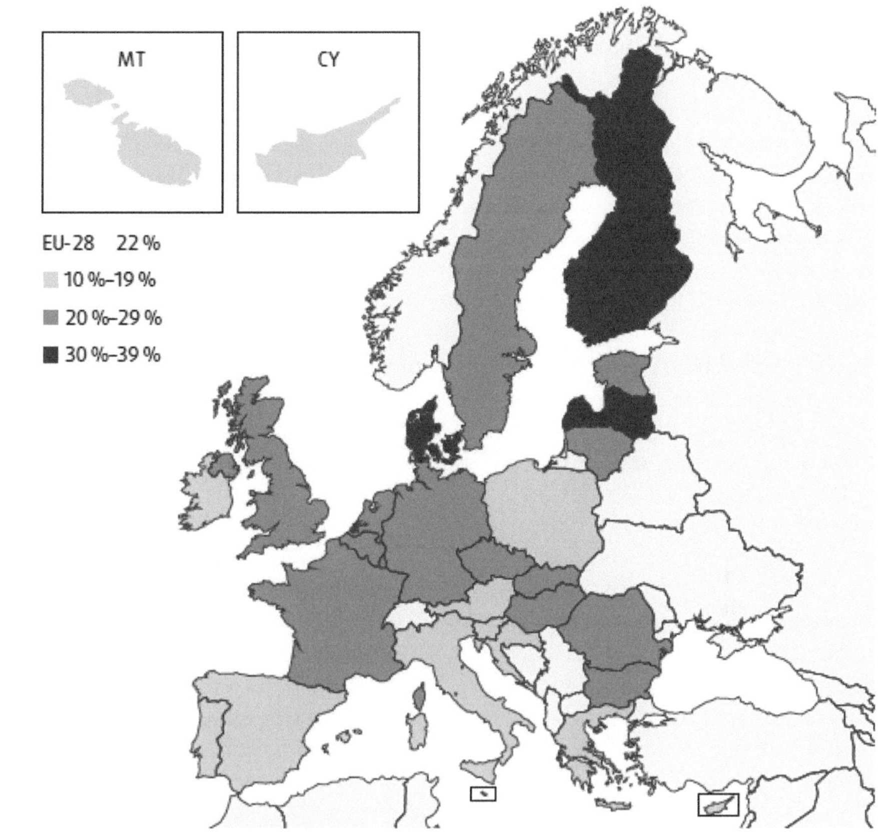

Fig. 3 Physical and/or sexual partner violence since the age of 15, EU-28 (%)

Within the European Union, a fully standardized survey on violence against women was conducted in 2012 among the 28 member states (n = 42.000). Out of all women, who have a (current or previous) partner, 22 % have experienced physical and/or sexual violence by this partner since the age of 15. Figure 3 depicts the distribution of partner violence across the 28 EU-countries.

The mean prevalence rates of the EU are much lower than those found in developing countries in the WHO overview just cited. But, unexpectedly, the results show that within the Union partner violence against women is most prevalent in Denmark (32 %), Finland (30 %) and Latvia (32 %). Nations with the next highest prevalence rates are Sweden (28 %) France (26 %), and the Netherlands (25 %). Since these European countries are consistently rated as those with the highest measures of gender equality, these results fly in the face of the feminist hypothesis. Equally counter-intuitive from a feminist perspective are the relatively low rates of Spain (13 %), Poland (13 %) and Hungary (13 %). The FRA authors themselves caution that inter country difference in victimization, even when measured through a dedicated survey, cannot be taken at face value. Noting the high rates in Nordic countries, they stress that "*gender equality could lead to higher levels of disclosure about violence against women*" (FRA 2014).

Taken together the analyses of the relationship between gender equality and victimization by violence and domestic violence at the macro level show mixed results. From a global perspective the results show an inverse relationship between gender equality and violence against women: violence is most prevalent in countries were the status of women in society is relatively low. This is found in analyses of ICVS data as well as in analyses of data from bespoke surveys on violence against women. However, there are important complications. Among Western nations the linkage with gender equality seems limited to sexual violence as shown by Yodanis (2004). Violence by intimates against women generally tends in the European Union to be higher precisely in nations where the status of women is most equal to that of men. From a global perspective, the cross-sectional relationship between gender equality and violence against women can be graphically described as a long downward slope with a jump at the very end: rates of violence fall considerably with rising equality but the relationship changes direction among the group of countries with the highest values on gender equality. As discussed, an analysis of USA data on gender equality and partner violence against women revealed a similar ski jump-shaped curve.

In line with Kangaspunta (2000) and the researchers of FRA just cited, we interpret the high rates of self-reported victimization by violence in countries such as Finland, Sweden, Denmark and The Netherlands as an artifact of heightened sensitivity to (less serious) acts of sexual or non sexual violence. The paradoxical findings that victimization rates for violence against women show a curvilinear relationship with gender equality should remind us that rates of victim-reported victimization are determined by two independent factors, the acts of violence perpetrated against respondents and the perceptions of these acts by them. With rising gender equality acts of violence against women seem to go down while simultaneously heightening the sensitivity to such acts.

There is some evidence from repeated bespoke surveys in Western nations that over the past 10 years rates of violence against women have stabilized or have even gone down in a selection of Western countries (Kangaspunta and Haen Marshall 2012). Since it seems unlikely that women in these countries have recently become *less* sensitive to violence, the latter result suggest that acts of violence against women have actually dropped. Considering the continued political drive towards more gender equality in these countries, the downward trend of violence against women in Western nations points at a negative relationship between increasing gender equality and violence against women over time. In cross-national comparisons this linkage seems to be somewhat masked by differential sensitivities to violence.

6 Conclusion and Discussion

In this article we have looked at the distribution of victimization risks along the dimensions of age and gender. We will sum up and discuss the findings concerning the age and gender links respectively.

Our findings on age point at a clear and universal inverse relationship between age and criminal victimization for almost all types of crime. According to general victimization surveys risks are universally the highest among the age group of 17–24 years, medium high among adults and the lowest among seniors. Bespoke surveys among young children show that victimization risks reach already relatively high levels at the age of five. The data on high risks of children of victimization by peers and maltreatment by parents are an important supplement to the existing data based on ordinary victimization surveys. They reveal that young children of both genders are more exposed to violent victimization than any other age group. Most tellingly, bespoke surveys among schoolchildren in three Western nations (USA, Germany and the Netherlands) indicate a 1 year prevalence of victimization by parental violence of 10 %. An obvious and pressing research priority for the international crime prevention and criminal justice community would seem the conduct of standardized victimization surveys among school children across the world.

According to the three factorial risk model developed by van Dijk and Steinmetz (1980) victimization risks are, as mentioned, determined by (a) economic or psychological attractiveness as target; (b) proximity to offenders; and (c) a lack of social and/or practical protection against crime. The age-victimization link can to some extent be explained in these terms. First of all, children and adolescents nowadays possess more stealable valuables such as expensive clothes and electronics, than ever before. This explains the new phenomenon of school yard extortion and robbery. More than ever before children and young adults in developed countries have become an attractive target group for acquisitive crime. Secondly, children and young people run high risks because of their proximity to potential offenders. Children are at risk to be victimized in their own homes by dysfunctional parents and siblings. They cannot escape these offenders without running away from home. Older children and young adults are confronted with inescapable offenders in their school environment. Schools are dangerous places for the simple reason that offending universally peaks around the age of 15. The elevated risk of victimization of teenagers mirrors their risks of offending. At a later age, teenagers and students further enhance their proximity to offenders by frequenting the hazardous environment of the night life industry and visiting dubious websites. Thirdly, children and mid adolescents are, in line with the stereotypical images of a victim, physically vulnerable for attacks from older peers and adults. In many cultures violence against children is under certain circumstances still socially condoned as pedagogic tool. Children are expected to undergo such violent punishment passively. Young people also tend to be more risk taking and therefore less inclined to apply preventive measures against criminal victimization. These factors together explain the high exposure of the youngest age groups to criminal victimizations of all sorts.

In our presentation of results of risk analyses we have in passing highlighted some other independent risk factors for criminal victimization besides age, namely ethnicity, marital status (being single), sexual orientation, and lifestyle (extent of leisure time spent outdoors). Ethnicity can act as risk enhancing factor for two reasons. Members of ethnic minority groups tend to live in neighborhoods where more potential offenders reside. They are in addition targeted by offenders with racist motivations. The phenomenon of hate crimes also explains the above average risks of gays and lesbians to be victimized by violent and other types of crime. Finally, the lifestyles of persons in stable families shields them against encounters with strangers. In contrast a non marital status increases proximity to potential offenders, e.g. in the night life industry.

The findings regarding the gender gap in victimization are, as discussed, less straightforward. Risks to be victimised by property crimes are not very different for males and females. Men tend to be more often car owners than women: this explains higher levels of victimization by car-related crimes among men. This is evened out by a somewhat higher exposure of women to theft in public transport. The findings on victimization by violent crime are, as discussed, mixed. According to ordinary victimization surveys young males are significantly more at risk of violence, including lethal violence, by strangers than young females whereas young women are more at risk of sexually motivated attacks. These findings concerning violence in the public domain can also be tentatively explained by our risk model. In a macho culture males are more attractive targets of violent attacks than females to achieve status among peers. Also young males are more likely to spend time in the proximity of potential offenders (other young males). Among young males, victims and offenders show much overlap (Wittebrood and Nieuwbeerta 1999). At the same time, prevailing macho values of chivalry may offer females a measure of protection against attacks by male strangers. On the downside macho values makes young women an attractive target of indecent assaults and other sexual attacks.

Bespoke surveys about violence against women provide more comprehensive and reliable data on violence, especially acts committed by intimate partners. These surveys have revealed extraordinarily high levels of victimization by both sexual and non-sexual violence by intimates among women. Globally, one in three women experience such victimizations during their lifetime and one in ten in the course of last year. Informed by feminist theories, the ubiquity of violence against women has often been portrayed as a manifestation or consequence of gender inequality. The latest versions of these bespoke surveys conducted among samples of both males and females, such as the Dutch and British surveys have complicated the issue. These surveys confirm the gendered nature of sexual violence: females are more at risk than males to be sexually attacked. But these surveys also suggest that physical violence in the domestic sphere victimizes men and women in almost equal measure. Violence between intimates can therefore not be exclusively attributed to gender inequality and/or patriarchal value systems. The understanding of the high prevalence of violence between intimates in countries such as The Netherlands and England and Wales apparently requires other theoretical perspectives besides standard feminist theory.

In order to further explore the links between structural gender inequality and violence at the macro level, we have examined available cross-national datasets. The results of this analysis are ambiguous as discussed. Analyses of the ICVS datasets show that female respondents of developing countries where women possess a relatively low social status, report the highest rates of victimization by violent offences, especially sexual offences. However, the rates of violence against women by intimates are also relatively high in some developed countries where gender equality is more advanced, such as some parts of the USA and several North European countries. In many countries dedicated surveys have been conducted on violence against women, employing specially designed methodologies. To the extent that these surveys are comparable, they confirm that violence against women is most prevalent in developing countries, where gender equality remains comparatively low. Violence against women appears to be more prevalent in rural areas than urban ones. The available evidence from these specialised surveys suggests that violence by intimate partners can indeed be understood as an expression of gender inequality. However, within the European Union the highest rates of victimization by domestic violence are recorded in North European nations where gender equality is comparatively well established. This paradoxical result does not in our view necessarily refute feminist perspectives. It may well be caused by the fact that female respondents in the latter countries hold stricter opinions about what constitutes an act of violence against them than women in less gender equal countries. Increased gender equality, then, seems to have a dual impact on self-reported victimization rates. While gender equality reduces actual violence on the one hand, it increases sensitivity to violent acts on the other. This dual impact should be examined in more detail in future studies on the measurement of victimization by violence against women. Preferably such studies should be carried out with gender neutral samples in order to obtain a more comprehensive insight in the root causes of domestic violence against both genders.

Our overview of research findings on the elevated risks of violent victimization of children and young people underlines the urgent need of more programs of violence prevention. Surveys among children as pioneered by Finkelhor et al. (2005) have revealed staggeringly high prevalences of violent victimization among children. Replications of these surveys in developing nations may reveal even higher prevalences due to traditional modes of parenting. The rampant victimization of children has obvious humanitarian and health implication. It is also a root cause of violence itself. Several studies have found links between direct or indirect childhood experiences with domestic violence and violent offending at later stages in the life cycle (National Crime Prevention 1999; Cicchetti and Valentino 2006). The phenomenon of second generation effects is so common that it has been dubbed the "cycle of violence". The high percentages of teenagers who have experienced domestic violence as a child among second-generation German immigrants deserves mentioning in this respect (Baier et al. 2006). A recent Dutch study showed that 60 % of a representative sample of young males of Moroccan descent had been exposed to domestic violence (Lahla 2013). Problems of violent crime among migrant communities and elsewhere cannot be effectively addressed if no action is taken against widespread practices of child abuse and other forms of domestic violence. Evidence-based approaches of early intervention in at risk families such as Parent-child Interaction Therapy (Thomas and Zimmer-Gembeck 2007; Juffer et al. 2008) should be widely implemented as a form of prevention against violent crime. In this framework suitable arrangements should be created for the provision of non-stigmatizing support for victims of child abuse and for mid-adolescent victims of crime. A qualitative study in Belgium into the criminal victimization of mid-adolescents detected widespread victim blaming by peers and parents and a lack of suitable avenues for support or redress (Vijnckier 2012).

Dedicated surveys on violence against women have raised the awareness of the world community of the seriousness of violent victimization of women by partners. In a report of the World Health Organization on the economic dimensions of interpersonal violence the total costs of intimate partner violence in the USA is estimated at $12.6 billion (WHO 2004). Child abuse is estimated to result in annual costs to the economy of $94 billion or 1 % of the gross domestic product of the USA (WHO 2004). Results on developing countries are scarce but costs of intimate partner violence have been estimated by the WHO to amount to 2 % of the GDP in Chile and 1.6 % in Nicaragua.

The latest versions of these surveys, such as the Dutch survey of 2010, have taught that such violence affects many (young) men as well. This new generation of partner violence victimization surveys will hopefully raise awareness of the pernicious consequences of domestic violence for both genders. Special services for female victims of domestic violence should not be just expanded but also be supplemented by similar services tailored to the needs of male victims.[6]

Five Questions

1. How can it be morally justified that innocent children remain the population group most frequently victimized by serious violent crime ? Why is the promotion of responsible parenting not a priority of crime prevention policies?
2. Isn't it time to address school safety worldwide, e.g. through a Global Programme of the United Nations?
3. Why are standardized international surveys on victimization by common crime, child victimization and partner violence not more widely promoted?
4. Isn't it time to break down taboos on recognizing young men as possible victims of various forms of violence including partner violence and human trafficking?
5. Isn't it time to upgrade the United Nations Declaration of Victims Rights of 1985 into a UN Convention?

[6] In the Netherlands shelter facilities for male victims of domestic violence were provided for the first time in 2008 (Nanhoe 2011). In most other countries such services are still rarely available. The belated provision of services for male victims of crime may well have been the result of a cultural taboo concerning male victimization by intimate partners (Nanhoe 2011).

References

Alink, L., van IJzendoorn, R., Bakermans-Kranenburg, M., Pannebakker, F., Vogels, T., & Euser, S. (2011, August). *De Tweede Nationale Prevalentiestudie Mishandeling van Kinderenen Jeugdigen (NPM-2010)* (Second national prevalence study of abuse of children and adolescents). Leiden: Leiden University.

Alvazzi Del Frate, A., Patrignani, A. (1995). *Women's victimization in developing countries* (Issues & Report, No. 5). Rome: UNICRI Series

Baier, D., Pfeiffer, C., Windzio, M., & Rabold, S. (2006). *Schulerbefragung 2005: Gewalterfahrungen, Schulabsentismus und Medienkonsum von Kindern und Jugendlichen*. Hannover: Kriminologisches Forschungsinstitut Niedersachsen.

Black, M. C., Basile, K. C., Breiding, M. J., Smith, S. G., Walters, M. L., Merrick, M. T., et al. (2011). *The National Intimate Partner and Sexual Violence Survey: 2010 Summary Report*. Atlanta, GA: National Centre for Injury Prevention and Control.

Brownmiller, S. (1975). Against our will, men, women and rape, New York: Bantam Books.

Bureau of Justice Statistics (2014, September 18). *Criminal victimization* (revised). In L. Langton & J. L. Truman (Eds.), Washington, DC: Bureau of Justice Statistics.

Central Bureau of Statistics (2014). Veiligheidsmonitor 2013. Den Haag/Heerlen; Centraal Bureau van de Statistiek (Security Monitor 2013)

Cicchetti, D., & Valentino, K. (2006). An ecological transactional perspective on child maltreatment: Failure of the average expectable environment and its influence upon child development. In D. Cicchetti and D. J. Cohen (Eds.), Developmental psychopathology, risk, disorder, and adaptation (2nd ed., Vol. 3, pp. 129–201). New York: Wiley.

Home Office Bulletin (2008). Crime in England and wales 2006/2007-Supplementary Vol. 2; Chapter 3-Intimate Violence, 31 January 2008.

Dobash, R. E., Dobash, R. (1979). Violence against wives: A case against the patriarchy. London: Open Books.

Finkelhor, D., Ormrod, R., Turner, H., & Hamby, S. L. (2005). The victimization of children and youth: A comprehensive, national survey. *Child Maltreatment, 10*(1), 5–25.

FRA. (2014). *Violence against women: an EU-wide survey; results at a glance*. Vienna: European Union Agency for Fundamental Rights.

Helweg-Larsen, K. (2012, October). Violence in close relationships; the prevalence, nature and development as well as the efforts to combat intimate partner violence among women and men in Denmark. Copenhagen: National Institute of Public Health.

Hindelang, M. J., Garofalo, J., & Godfredson, M. R. (1978). *Victims of personal crime: an empirical foundation for a theory of personal victimization*. Cambridge, MA: Ballinger Publications.

Jansson, K. (2006). *BCS-measuring crime for 25 years*. London: Home Office.

Johnson, H., Ollus, N., & Nevala, S. (2008). *Violence against women; An international perspective*. New York: Springer/HEUNI.

Juffer, F., Bakermans-Kranenburg, M. J., & Van IJzendoorn, M. H. (Eds.). (2008). *Promoting positive parenting: An attachment-based intervention*. Mahwah, NJ: Lawrence Erlbaum.

Kangaspunta, K. (2000). Secondary analysis of integrated sources of data. In A. Del Frate et al. (Eds.), *Surveying crime: A global perspective*. Rome: UNICRI/ISTAT.

Kangaspunta, K., Haen Marshall, I. (2012). Trends in violence against women; some good news and some bad news. In J. Van Dijk, T. Tseloni & G. Farrell (Eds.), *The international crime drop: New directions in research*. Hampshire: Palgrave/MacMillan.

Lahla, E. (2013). *Invisible victims? Ethnic differences in the risk of juvenile violent offending of Dutch and Moroccan-Dutch adolescent boys*. Ph.D. Tilburg University.

Nanhoe, A. C. (2011). *Pionieren in de mannenopvang: Een evaluatie studie na 2½ jaar ervaringmet de opvang en hulpverlening aan mannelijke slachtoffers van (dreiging van) geweld in afhankelijkheidsrelaties in Amsterdam, Rotterdam, Den Haag en Utrecht* (Pioneering in the reception of men: an evaluation study of 2,5 years experience with the reception and support of male victims of violence between intimates in Amsterdam, Rotterdam, The Hague and Utrecht). The Hague: WODC.

National Crime Prevention (1999). *Pathways to prevention, developmental and early intervention approaches to crime in Australia.* (edited by R. Hommel et al.). Canberra: Attorney-General's Department.

Smith P. K., Mahdavi J., Carvalho M., & Tippett N. (2006). *An investigation into cyberbullying, its forms, awareness and impact, and the relationship between age and gender in cyberbullying.* London: Unit for school and family studies, Goldsmiths College, University of London.

Straus, M. A., Hamby, S., Finkelhor, D., Moore, D. W., & Runyan, D. (1998). Identification of child maltreatment with the Parent-child conflict tactics scales: Development and psychometric data for a national sample of American parents. *Child Abuse & Neglect, 22*, 249–270.

Thomas, R., & Zimmer-Gembeck, M. J. (2007). Behavioral outcomes of parent-child interaction therapy and tripl P-positive parenting program: A review and meta-analysis. *Journal of Abnormal Child Psychology, 35*(3), 475–495.

Tjaden, P., & Thoennes, N. (2000, July). *Extent, nature and consequences of intimate partner violence; findings from the national violence against women survey.* Washington, DC: National Institute of Justice.

United Nations (2006). *In-depth study on all forms of violence against women.* Report of the Secretary-General, New York, United Nations (A/61/122/Add.1.).

van Dijk, J. J. M. (1999a). The experience of crime and justice. In G. Newman (Ed.), *Global report on crime and justice. United Nations office for drug control and crime prevention, centre for international crime prevention.* New York: Oxford University Press.

van Dijk, J. J. M. (1999b). Criminal victimization and victim empowerment in an international perspective. In J. J. M. van Dijk, R. G. H. van Kaam, & J. Wemmers (Eds.), *Caring for crime victims.* New York: Criminal Justice Press.

van Dijk, J. J. M. (2008). *The world of crime: Breaking the silence on problems of security, justice and development across the world.* Thousand Oaks: Sage.

van Dijk, J., Tseloni, A., & Farrell, G. (2013), *The international crime drop: New directions in research.* Hampshire: Palgrave/Mac Millan.

van Dijk, J. J. M., & Steinmetz, C. H. D. (1980), The RDC victim surveys 1974–1979, WODC [English translation of report of 1979]. OnderzoekenBeleid/13.

van Dijk, T., Veen, M., & Cox, E. (2010). *Slachtofferschap van huiselijk geweld: aard, omvang, omstandigheden en hulpzoekgedrag.* Hilversum: Intomart (Victimization by domestic violence; nature, prevalence, circumstances and support seeking behavior).

van Kesteren, J. N. (2006). *Hate crime in Europe; Results from the 2005 EU/ICS (ICVS).* Paper presented at the International Symposium of the World Society of Victimology, August 19–26, 2006, Orlando, Florida, USA.

van Kesteren, J., van Dijk, J., & Mayhew, P. (2014). The international crime victims survey: A retrospective. *International Review of Victimology, 20*(1), 49–69.

van Kesteren, J. N., Mayhew, P., & Nieuwbeerta, P. (2000). *Criminal victimisation in seventeen industrialised countries. Key findings from the 2000 International Crime Victims Survey.* The Hague: Onderzoek en Beleid, No. 187. Ministry of Justice, WODC.

Vijnckier, G. (2012). Mid adolescent victims: (Un)willing for help? *International Review of Victimology, 18*, 109–132.

Wittebrood, K., & Nieuwbeerta, P. (1999). Wages of sin? The link between offending, lifestyle and violent victimization. *European Journal on Criminal Policy and Research, 7*, 63–80.

World Health Organization (2002). *World Report on Violence and Health: Summary.* Geneva: World Health Organization

World Health Organization (2004). *The economic dimensions of interpersonal violence.* Geneva: World Health Organization

World Health Organization (2005). *WHO multi-country study on women's health and domestic violence against women*. Geneva: World Health Organization.

Yllö, K. (1983). Sexual equality and violence against women in American states. *Journal of Comparative Family Studies, 14*, 67–86.

Yodanis, C. L. (2004). Gender inequality, violence against women, and fear: A cross-national test of the feminist theory of violence against women. *Journal of Interpersonal Violence, 19*, 655–675.

Global Homicide Mortality Trends by Gender 1950–2010

Tapio Lappi-Seppälä and Martti Lehti

Abstract Most large scale comparative studies on homicide analyses total victimisation rates. Well-known exceptions include historical data-series from Veli Verkko, which showed that the higher the level of violence, the smaller the share of female victims and perpetrators. Consequently also the increases and decreases in lethal violence touch more male victims and perpetrators than female victims and perpetrators. This chapter tests these hypotheses and discusses the current differences in male and female homicide mortality levels with the most extensive available data today. The contribution draws a detailed picture of female and male homicide trends across regions and countries from 1950 to 2010. It furthermore explores the associations between femicide and homicide rates and female-male victimisation ratios and different socio-economic, political and cultural factors.

1 Introduction

Homicides have been a primary target for comparative criminological studies since the beginning of modern criminology with scholars such as Enrico Ferri, Franz von Liszt, Cesare Lombroso, and Veli Verkko in Finland. Historical studies have often treated infanticide as a separate phenomenon, due to its peculiar position as a major social and legal problem in the seventeenth and eighteenth centuries (and even later) and its exceptional long term dynamics (Verkko 1931b, pp. 155–166; Eisner 2008, pp. 293–294). Gender specific differences have received less attention, however, with some notable exceptions.

Veli Verkko's comparative statistical studies on homicide, with the longest existing uninterrupted database of lethal violence starting from 1750, formed a path-breaking foundation for further work in the field (Verkko 1931a, b, 1951). He was also one of the first to attach systematic attention to gender specific differences

T. Lappi-Seppälä (✉) • M. Lehti
Institute of Criminology and Legal Policy, University of Helsinki, Helsinki, Finland
e-mail: tapio.lappi-seppala@helsinki.fi; martti.lehti@helsinki.fi

H. Kury et al. (eds.), *Women and Children as Victims and Offenders: Background, Prevention, Reintegration*, DOI 10.1007/978-3-319-08398-8_17

in homicide victimization. Verkko concluded, on the basis of statistical materials on homicides in Europe, the Americas, East Asia and Oceania between the 1880s and the mid-1920s, that the ratio between male and female victims changed, depending on the overall level of lethal violence. In his comparative studies he reached a conclusion that female homicide mortality is more static than male mortality; and that in countries with low homicide mortality the difference between male and female mortality is smaller than in countries with high homicide mortality.

He summarized his findings in the form of two "laws" (or regularities): (1) First, the higher the level of violence, the smaller the share of female victims and perpetrators (static law). (2) Second, the increases and decreases in lethal violence touch more male victims and perpetrators than female victims and perpetrators (dynamic law). Although these observations may not be universal social laws (as Verkko might have thought), especially the observations concerning the static law were based (by the standards of their time) on fairly reliable and large empirical data. The dynamic law was based mainly on observations on homicide trends in Finland, Sweden and a few European countries during the nineteenth and early twentieth century (Verkko 1951, pp. 53–54), thus, the generalization of those observations to a global regularity is more debatable. One should note that Verkko understood the influence of neonaticide mortality on the mortality levels and gender ratios of low homicide mortality countries and tried to neutralize this influence whenever possible (Verkko 1931b, pp. 155–166). Verkko's own explanation for his observations was "the fact that the woman lives in a somewhat different and more peaceful atmosphere than the man, and that the factors influencing her [life] are not nearly so subject to changes as those affecting a man" (Verkko 1951, p. 54). I.e. he looked for explanations in the different roles of men and women in (Western) society and thought that these role differences protected women from aggravated violence. He did not, however, analyze in detail the structural and context differences between lethal violence against men and women, although his Finnish data would have made possible also this kind of analysis. (His international data did not allow any detailed structural studies.)

Later, similar observations on the more static nature of female homicide mortality have been made by several researchers.[1] Eisner (2008, pp. 307–309) has shown with large western European data that changes in homicide rates between the 1850s and the 2000s were caused mainly by changes in homicide mortality of young men. In his review on long-term homicide trends in Europe, Spierenburg (2012) has come to the conclusion that men have been the dynamic force behind homicide rate variations in Europe since the Middle Ages. In his study on violent crime trends in London, McClintock (1963) linked the differences in the dynamics of male and female homicide mortality to structural differences—the much closer connection of female mortality to intimate partner and domestic violence. Also

[1] See for example (Dunstall 2004; Eisner 2003; Gurr 1981; Gurr 1989; von Hofer 2008; Lindström 2008; Lehti 2001; McClintock 1963; Sharpe 1996; Wikström 1992; Ylikangas 1998; Zahn 1989; Zahn and McCall 1999).

Eisner (2008, p. 308) has found clear differences in the trends of different types of homicide, including a relatively stable long term trend in domestic violence related homicides. In the last few years, the differences in the dynamics of female and male homicide mortality have been discussed, for example, by Marshall and Summers (2012, pp. 60–61) and in the UNODC homicide reports (2011, p. 59; 2013, pp. 48–55). In fact, the context differences and the dominance of intimate partner and domestic violence related crimes in homicides against adult women have received strong global support from structural homicide research (Stöckl et al. 2013; Granath et al. 2011; UNODC 2011, 2013). All these studies show that while lethal violence is dominated by male to male homicides (especially in working age population) and affected by volatile factors (such as socio-political crises and drug-markets), homicides against women are determined by less volatile domestic contexts and experience slower and lesser changes.

The differences between the dynamics of male and female homicide mortality have, however, also been contested. In her study on homicide mortality trends in 18 developed democracies from 1955 to 1980, Gartner (1990) found that during the period both male and female homicide mortality changed usually in the same direction (increased). Also the differences in the mortality levels between the studied countries concerned as a rule both genders in a similar way; female homicide mortality levels were lower than male levels in all the studied countries, but in countries with high base level homicide mortality both male and female mortality levels were higher than corresponding levels in low base level countries. According to Gartner risk factors predicting homicide rates did not vary by gender in her sample of countries. Material deprivation, weak social integration, and exposure to official violence were associated with significantly higher risks of homicide for both genders. For both men and women, the divorce rate was the most important risk factor. Among the demographic indicators, the post-Second World War shift in routine activities away from households appeared to put women at a greater risk of homicide. Chon (2013) came to similar conclusions in his study on female homicide victimization in 124 countries. Unlike Gartner, he did not find any significant correlation between women's homicide mortality risk and educational or social status, but according to him general violent crime predictors related to income equality, gross domestic product and ethnic heterogeneity explained female homicide mortality in the same way as they explained general homicide mortality.

Between the gender specific and the gender insensitive interpretations one can find mediating interpretations. Stamatel (2014) examined female homicide mortality rates in Europe in 1985–2010. In her study covering 33 countries she both described variation patterns in mortality rates between European regions and tested the viability of general homicide predictors, as well as gender-sensitive and context-sensitive explanations as explanations of these variations. According to Stamatel, all three types of explanations contributed toward understanding female homicide mortality rate variations in Europe. Better economic conditions tended to reduce female homicide mortality as well as the collective improvement of the status of women in society; less traditional gender roles on the other hand increased the mortality risk. According to Stamatel also historical legacies and socio-historical contexts contributed significantly to female homicide mortality level differences between countries and regions in Europe.

Basically there exist in modern research, thus, two main approaches concerning homicide mortality of men and women. The first one assumes that lethal violence against men and women is influenced by gender specific factors, and also the explanations are partly or totally different (this can be called as a gender sensitive approach). These differences in the background factors are sometimes stretched even further and it is claimed that homicides against men and women are, in fact, affected by different factors to the extent that we are dealing with two different types of phenomena. Should this be the case, this should have important implications for crime prevention policies: actions that have been targeted against male-victim violence may not be relevant for female-victim violence. The second main approach assumes, on the contrary, that lethal violence against men and women can be explained by the same general predictors (we can call it as a gender insensitive approach). In this case, for example, the crime prevention policies should be effective to reduce lethal violence irrespective of the gender of the victims. The theoretical backgrounds of both approaches are heterogeneous.

This chapter will discuss the current differences in male and female homicide mortality levels as well as changes that have taken place between 1950 and 2010. We do not test the theoretical backgrounds of either of the main approaches but try to describe and compare the changes that have taken place during the last 60 years. However, also a description of trends can be used as a rough test of the approaches. If male and female mortality trends have not correlated or have correlated only weakly with each other in most countries that can be seen as an indicative support for gender sensitive approaches; globally strongly correlating trends would again support gender insensitive approaches.

2 Sources and Method

2.1 Data Sources

We have used as our primary data source the published raw mortality data files of the World Health Organization (WHO) Mortality Database (www.who.int/healthinfo/mortality_data/en/). For Estonia, Latvia, Russia, and Ukraine data prior 1980 have been taken from special sources. The Estonian data are from unpublished cause of death tables kept in the archive of the Estonian Statistical Office (*Eesti Statistikaamet*)—their copies are in the possession of the Institute of Criminology and Legal Policy in Helsinki. The Russian data are from Meslé et al. (1996), the Ukrainian data from Meslé and Vallin (2012). Latvian data have been obtained from Ms Sandra Vitola from the *Latvijas republikas centrālā statistikas pārvalde* (CSB). Post-1970 data for Taiwan are from published cause of death statistics of the Taiwanese Ministry of Health and Welfare (www.mohw.gov.tw). For rate calculations we have used the annual mean population data published by the United Nations Department of Economic and Social Affairs (esa.un.org/unpd/wpp/Excel-Data/population.htm). The time series have been published by the Institute of Criminology and Legal Policy in Helsinki as a part of homicide data collection project).[2]

Our study covers, in principle, all countries where continuous annual data have been available for period from 1950 until 2010. In practice, this means the industrialized countries of Europe, North America, East Asia, and Oceania as well as the larger countries of Latin America. In Africa, only Mauritius has been included, in the rest of Asia (including Middle East), Thailand, Sri Lanka, and Israel. However, in our analyses of today's situation we have included also countries with shorter mortality data time series published either by the WHO or national statistical offices. This data are from the homicide data collection project of the Institute of Criminology and Legal Policy (see, note 2 above).

2.2 Reliability of Data

Cross-national comparative statistical studies on crime are problematic because statistical, legal, criminal policy and substantive factors affect the crime statistics of each country in a different way (Aebi and Linde 2012). Cause-of-death (COD) data are generally superior to criminal justice data as a source for this type of homicide studies; for example, the definition of intentional homicide is based on fairly similar definitions all over the world (Aebi and Linde 2012). However, also COD data have their own problems (Aebi and Linde 2012; Smit et al. 2012; Trent and Pridemore 2012).[3] National studies indicate that there can be substantial differences in the reliability of COD statistics even in Europe (where both COD and criminal justice statics are generally of relatively good quality). For example, structural differences in types of homicide, (related) differences in detection rates as well as forensic medical examination practices affect COD statistics in a similar way as they affect criminal justice statistics (Smit et al. 2012, p. 19).

The problems concern, however, mainly cross-national *crime level* comparisons. *Crime trend* comparisons are more reliable, especially if recording and reporting practices and definitions of crimes in individual countries have not changed substantially during the study period (Aebi and Linde 2012; von Hofer and Lappi-Seppälä 2014). There is no indication of critical changes in the classifications in the COD statistics during the period from the 1950s until 2010 in the studied group of

[2] See www.optula.om.fi/fi/index/julkaisut/verkkokatsauksia-sarja/nrilpcomparativehomicidetimeseriesnrilp-chts.homicidetrendsfrom1950until2012.html. For details, see Lehti 2013.

[3] Information on infant homicides is especially unreliable in both COD and criminal justice statistics (Yarwood 2004; Eisner 2008; Tursz and Cook 2011; Höynck et al. 2012).

countries.[4] In spite of this, operational changes in public health care or criminal justice systems in individual countries may have influenced the comparability of COD data during the period. However, usually this type of changes affect registered male and female mortality in a similar way; because of this we think that such changes (even unknown ones) have not influenced the results significantly.[5]

2.3 The Special Problem of Infanticides

The gravest reliability problems in COD statistics concern the registering of infant homicides, especially neonaticides (victims killed during the first day of their life). It is estimated, that currently even in many European countries (for example, Austria, France, Germany) only 10–20 % of neonaticides are registered in official COD statistics. The registering rate of all infanticides is higher but less than 50 %. On the other hand in some countries, for example, Sweden almost all infanticides are registered. This means that differences in infanticide rates between countries are even in today's Western Europe to a large extent influenced by registering rates only (Ellonen et al. 2014). On the other hand, registered infanticide rates, especially neonaticide rates have decreased sharply in most European countries since the 1950s. There are several factors that have contributed to this drop (which has neither comprised the non-European industrial countries nor the developing countries), one being the medicalization of the birth giving process. Thus, infanticides and especially neonaticides seem to be phenomena that are very distinct from other types of homicidal crime and also phenomena that are covered exceptionally unreliably by official COD statistics. On the other hand, especially in Europe before the 1960s infanticides made up a substantial percentage of (female) homicide deaths—the larger, the longer we go back in time.[6] Because of all this we have used in this study for most of the countries included in the time series analyses data

[4] During the period we examined all the included countries used ICD-classification (International Statistical Classification of Diseases and Related Health Problems, published by the World Health Organization) or its national adaptations in their cause-of-death statistics. The ICD-classification changed three times during the review period: from ICD-7 to ICD-8 in 1968–1970, from ICD-8 to ICD-9 in 1979–1995, and from ICD-9 to ICD-10 in the years following 1994. The changes took place in different years in different countries. Changes in the definition of a death caused by an intentional assault in all four classifications were, however, negligible. Earlier analyses suggest that the first classification change from ICD-7 to ICD-8 influenced infanticide levels but not other child or adult homicide levels in some industrialised countries (Jason et al. 1983). The later classification changes seem not to have had any effect even on infanticide levels (Ellonen et al. 2014).

[5] These kinds of changes when known have been reported in the detailed data source descriptions (see Lehti 2013).

[6] For example, in Norway, infanticides made up in the 1880s 73 %, in the 1950s 7 %, in the 2000s 2 % of female homicide deaths; in Switzerland the figures for the 1950s and 2000s were 28 % and 4 %, in Sweden 10 % and 2 %, and in England and Wales 11 % and 2 %.

that do not include homicide victims less than 1 year of age.[7] This does not mean that we think that violence against infants is less important than violence against older children or adults, but we think that infanticides should be studied as a separate phenomenon because of their distinct characteristics and methodological questions (Ellonen et al. 2014).

2.4 Method and Way of Presentation

The chapter describes the general trend in male and female homicide mortality during a 60 year period in 58 countries. The focus is on the differences and similarities in the trends of both genders. The first part includes a statistical description of the current global male and female homicide mortality levels (Sect. 3) and of the trends in homicide mortality (Sect. 4) and female/male homicide ratio (Sect. 5) between 1950 and 2010 by sub-regions and individual countries. The last section (Sect. 6) explores the possible reasons behind the differences in mortality levels and trends. The factors discussed fall into four main groups. The first group consists of macro-level social and structural indicators discussed usually under strain-disorganization and deprivation theories. The second set consists of state-level political indicators, dealing with political structures and the style and quality of governance. The third group consist of cultural variables, including social values, and attitudes. The fourth group consists of gender specific factors (female adult literacy rate, female economic activity rate, female primary net enrolment rate, gender-related development index, gender empowerment measure and gender equality index). We have calculated bivariate correlates of each factor separately for male and female homicide mortality levels and female/male homicide ratios and looked for possible differences and similarities in their explanative power.

3 Homicide Victims in 2000–2010 by Gender

The section gives an overview of levels of male and female homicide mortality today. First we describe the situation globally, after that follows a more detailed presentation by continents and sub-regions.

[7] If infanticides have been included in the data, a note has been added.

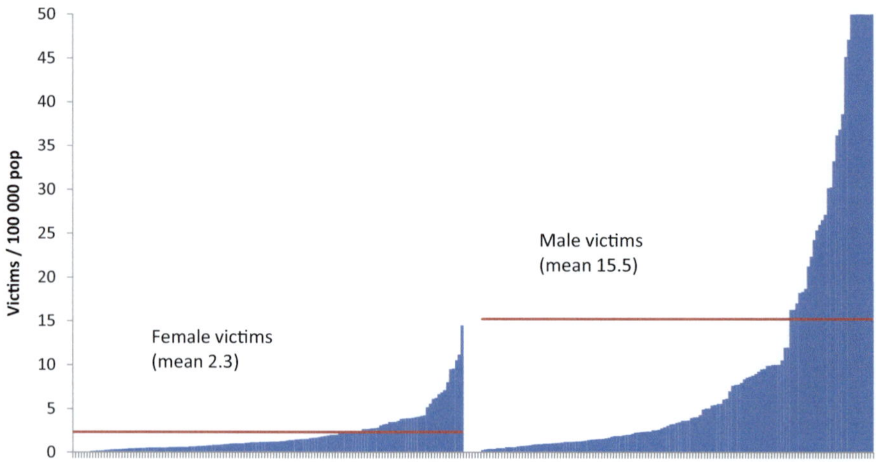

Fig. 1 Female and male homicide mortality rates in 2000–2010 in 134 countries (unweighted global means)

3.1 Global Overview

In 2000–2010, the global mean female homicide mortality rate of 134 countries was 2.3 per 100,000 women annually (when each country was given the same weight in the calculus; the mean rate weighted by populations of the countries for the same period was 2.1). The corresponding male mortality rate was 15.5 per 100,000 men (weighted mean rate 11.9). For every woman killed worldwide there were, thus, approximately five killed men. However, there were huge differences in homicide mortality rates between countries (Fig. 1).

Female homicide mortality varied from close to zero (in some countries with population below 50,000 there were not a single female victim during the whole 10 year period) to little below 15. Male mortality varied from close to zero to 100. For reasons of presentation the scale in Fig. 1 has been cut with a maximum value of 50. The male mortality rate exceeded this in seven countries in the studied group: US Virgin Islands 56, Venezuela 60, Trinidad and Tobago 64, Guatemala 67, Colombia 75, Jamaica 80, and El Salvador 99.

The weighted means adjusting for population size were for both men and women lower, indicating that high homicide rates in numerous small countries lifted the overall global means. Table 1 displays the male and female homicide mortality rates (weighted and unweighted) by continents and sub-regions.[8] Country specific rates are available in Appendix 1.

[8] The rates have been weighted by the mean population of 2010. The unweighted mortality rates show the mean of the national rates of each sub-region, while the weighted rates show the homicide rate of the whole sub-region.

Table 1 Homicide annual mortality rates /100,000 men/women, 2000–2010, by continent and sub-region

Continent	Unweighted		Weighted		Countries
Sub-region	Males	Females	Males	Females	N
Europe	2.9	1.1	5.8	1.9	54
Scandinavia	1.3	0.5	1.4	0.6	5
France/Benelux	1.4	0.8	1.0	0.6	5
German speaking Europe	0.7	0.4	0.6	0.5	4
British Isles	1.2	0.7	1.0	0.4	7
Southwest Eur	1.3	0.5	1.2	0.5	6
Southeast Eur	2.3	0.9	1.3	0.4	11
Baltic	8.5	2.7	8.5	2.8	3
Central-Eastern Europe	1.9	1.0	1.9	0.9	6
Former Soviet Reg (Europe)	8.5	2.8	18.6	5.5	7
Americas	28.4	3.6	29.1	3.3	44
North America	4.3	1.2	8.2	2.2	3
Central America	62.1	6.9	47.4	5.0	7
Sourth America	25.6	2.8	40.7	3.5	12
Caribbean	22.4	3.4	32.0	3.8	22
Asia	5.6	1.3	7.7	1.2	22
West Asia	1.9	0.5	2.6	0.7	4
Southcentral Asia	3.2	0.7	6.0	1.2	2
East Asia	4.5	1.3	1.0	0.6	6
Southeast Asia	8.0	1.1	15.4	1.6	5
Former Soviet Reg (Asia)	8.6	2.2	8.0	2.2	5
Africa	7.5	1.9	17.1	2.5	6
North Africa	5.6	0.3	5.6	0.3	1
East Africa	5.1	2.1	4.1	1.7	4
South Africa	18.7	2.7	18.7	2.7	1
Oceania	3.5	2.3	1.4	0.8	8
Total	11.9	2.1	15.5	2.3	134

Unweighted and weighted means

The lowest mortality rates were in Europe and the highest in the Americas. However, there were substantial differences between sub-regions within each continent. Female homicide mortality was very low in Scandinavia, continental and southwest Europe as well as Western Asia. The highest female homicide mortality rates were to be found in Central America, South America and the Caribbean.

3.2 Europe

We have divided European countries into three main regions (Western, Southern, and Eastern Europe) with further sub-regions based on geographic, historical, linguistic, and cultural traditions. Western Europe has been divided into the Nordic countries (Scandinavia), the British Isles (Ireland, England and Wales and Scotland), German speaking continental Europe, France and the Benelux countries; Southern Europe again into Southwestern and Southeastern Europe. Eastern Europe includes three sub-regions: Central Europe, the Baltic countries, and the former Soviet region (see Appendix 1). On the basis of their history from the late-1940s until the beginning of the 1990s also the Baltic countries belong to the former Soviet region. They also shared largely similar homicide trend profiles with other countries in the group until the mid-1990s, mortality rates exceeding well over all other European regions.

The European annual mean homicide mortality rates in 2000–2010 by gender and country are displayed in Fig. 2.[9] Female rates for Scandinavia and Western Europe ranged from 0.1 in Iceland and 0.3 in Ireland to 1.0 in Finland. The rates in Southern European countries were equally low ranging from 0.2 in Turkey[10] and 0.4 in Italy to 1.8 in Northern Cyprus. In the Central European countries the range was from 0.6 in Poland to 1.5 in Romania. Male homicide mortality followed basically similar profile. However, there were a few significant country level exceptions. Male mortality was exceptionally low (when compared with female mortality) in all three German speaking countries, Slovenia and the Czech Republic. In all these female and male homicide mortality were on almost similar levels.

In the Baltic countries female mortality rates ranged from 2.2 to 3.2; and male rates from 7.6 to 10. Rates in the former Soviet region varied for females from 0.3 in Georgia to 6.9 in Russia; male mortality rates ranged from 1.2 in Georgia to 24.3 in Russia. Compared with Belarus and Ukraine female homicide mortality level was in Russia approximately double and male mortality level more than 2.5 fold higher.

3.3 The Americas and Oceania

The American continent was divided into four sub-regions: North, Central, and South America, and the Caribbean Islands. In North America, Canadian homicide mortality rates were the lowest (0.8 for women and 2.5 for men); in the United States rates were three to fourfold higher (2.5 for women and 8.8 for men). As

[9] Countries with mean annual population below 100,000 in 2000–2010 have been excluded.

[10] According to Turkish police statistics the general homicide rate was 7.8-fold higher than the level shown by published COD statistics in 2003–2010. If we adjust the COD statistics levels accordingly, annual female homicide mortality would have been appr. 1.5 per 100,000 women and male mortality appr. 6.5 per 100,000 men during the period.

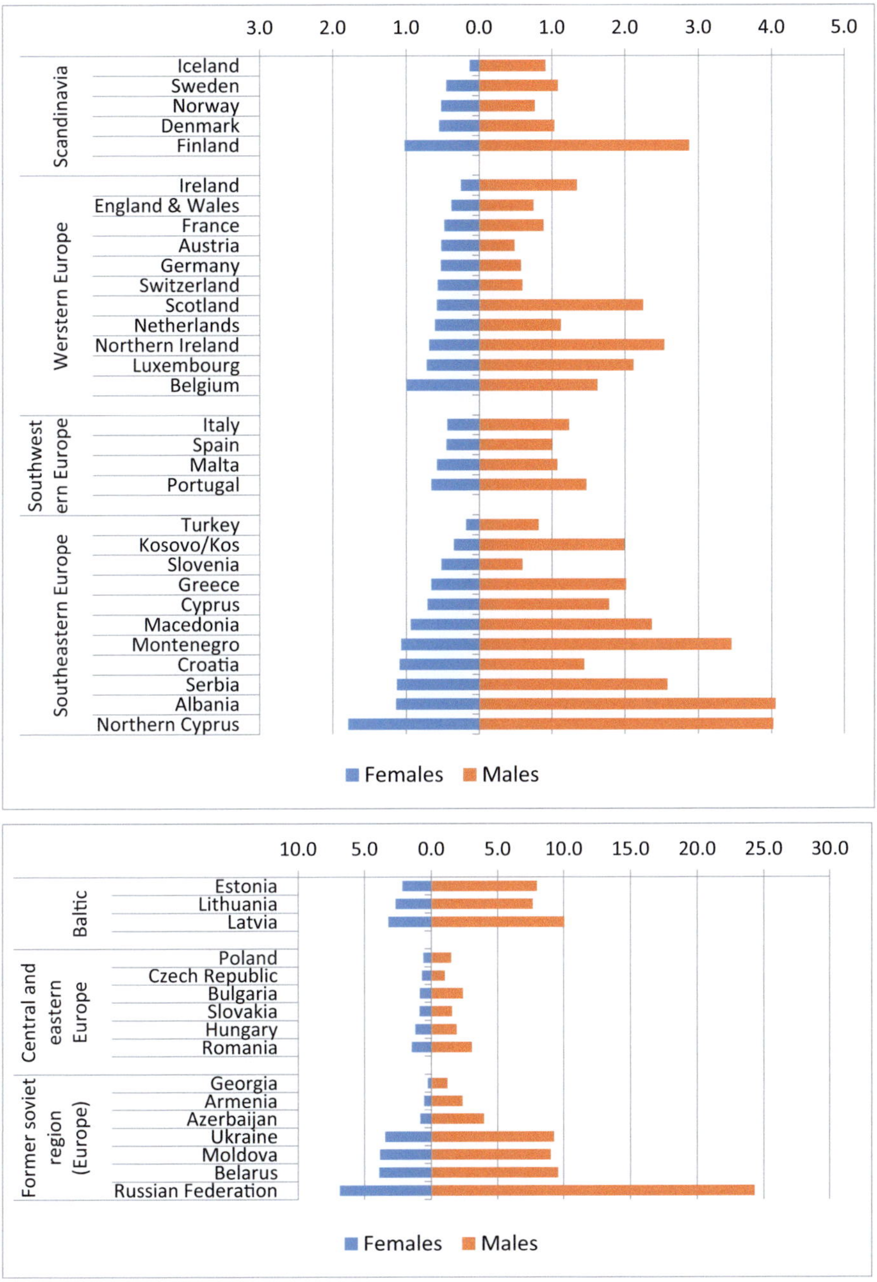

Fig. 2 Mean annual homicide mortality rates by gender, per 100,000 men/women, 2000–2010. Western, Southern and Eastern Europe

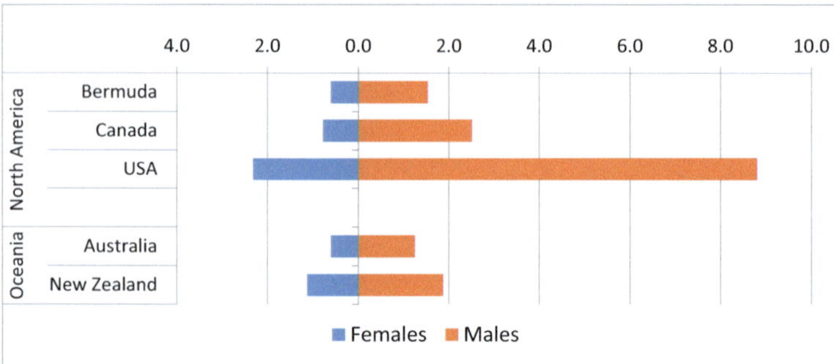

Fig. 3 Mean annual homicide mortality rates by gender, per 100,000 men/women, 2000–2010. North America, Australia, and New Zealand

points of comparison for the United States and Canada we used Australia and New Zealand (because of similar socio-cultural backgrounds). Both scored about the same levels with Canada on female homicide mortality but had clearly lower male mortality levels (Fig. 3).

The base levels of homicide mortality (especially male mortality) were on average much higher in Latin America than in North America or in Australia or New Zealand. Female mortality rates ranged in Central America from 2.5 to over 11, male rates from 16 to 98.5. In the Caribbean, female mortality rates varied from less than 1 to about 9.5, male rates from 5 to 80. In South America, female rates varied between 0.5 and 6.5, male rates between 3 and 75 (Fig. 4).

3.4 Asia and Africa

Homicide mortality rates for both genders were very low in East Asia and the Middle East. In East Asia (Japan, Hong Kong, Macau, South Korea, and Taiwan) female and male mortality were actually more or less on the same level (in Macau and Hong Kong female mortality was even higher than male mortality). East Asian countries resembled in this respect the German speaking Europe; the situation in both regions was similar and exceptional when compared with every other sub-region of the world (Fig. 5). In the Middle East, in spite of low levels, male mortality was clearly higher than female mortality. Female homicide mortality was low by global standards also in Southeast and South Asia, but male mortality was rather high. (We included Central Asia in Europe as part of the former Soviet region.)

Data for African countries were available only for Mauritius, Reunion, Rodrigues, Seychelles, and South Africa. Thus, the data covered mainly the small islands in the Indian Ocean with strong cultural links to South Asia. The only country from continental Africa included in the 2000–2010 analysis was South Africa. Neither the situation in South Africa nor in the islands of Indian Ocean could be regarded as

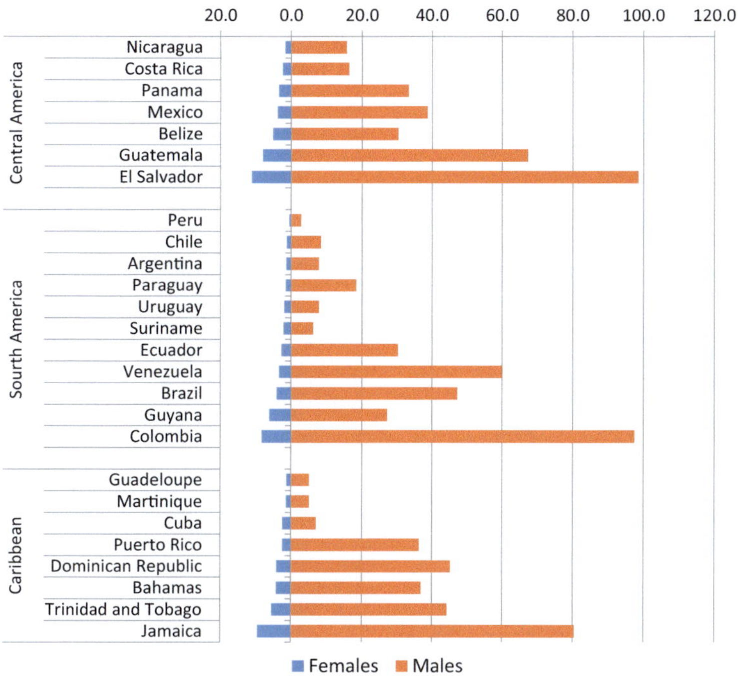

Fig. 4 Mean annual homicide mortality rates by gender, per 100,000 men/women, 2000–2010. Latin America

generalizable for other parts of Africa. The rates in the islands varied between 0.5 and 3 for women; and between 2.5 and 10 for men. The female mortality levels were more or less the same as in the Caribbean islands, but male mortality levels were clearly lower. In South Africa, according to our data based on COD statistics, female homicide mortality was 2.7 and male mortality 18.7 during the period. These rates were probably much too low. According to police statistics, the mean annual general homicide rate was in South Africa in the 2000s 3.6-fold higher than in the COD statistics; if we adjust the COD statistics levels to correspond to those given by the (more reliable) police statistics, female homicide mortality would have been about 10 and male mortality more than 67 per 100,000 men/women a year (Fig. 5).

4 Trends in Homicide Mortality 1950–2010

This section describes the trends in male and female homicide mortality from 1950 until 2010. It gives an overview of mortality rate changes between the 1950s and the 2000s as well as during the last two decades, in the following Sect. 5 we describe

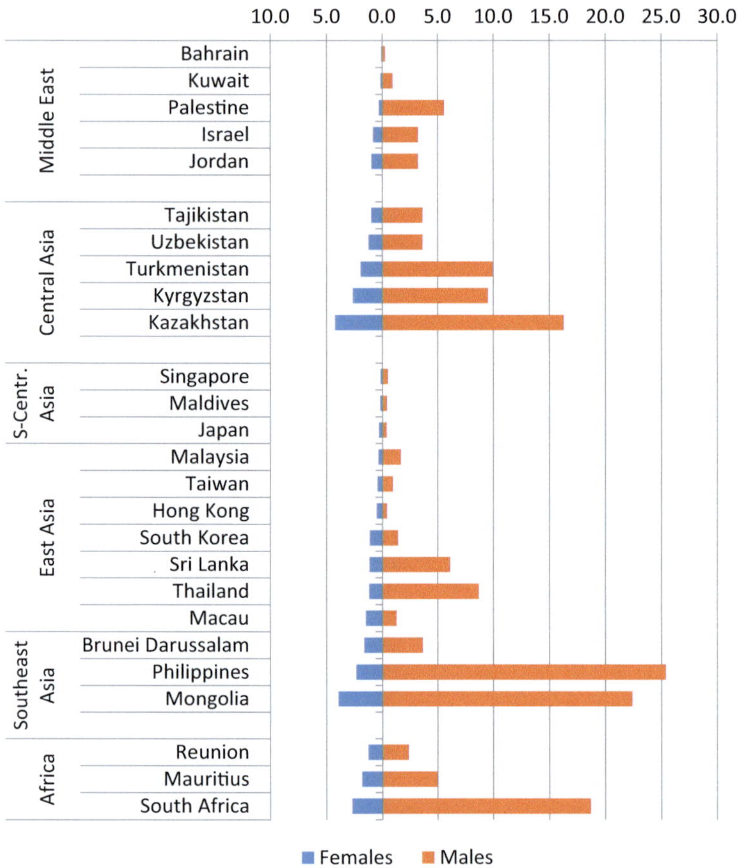

Fig. 5 Mean annual homicide mortality rates by gender, per 100,000 men/women, 2000–2010. Asia and Africa

how these changes have influenced the female/male homicide death ratio, i.e. the relative difference between homicide mortality levels of women and men.

4.1 *General Homicide Mortality Trends*

During the period from 1950 until 2010, homicide mortality was stable neither globally nor in any of the main world regions. Changes occurred, but they were different in different parts of the world.[11]

[11] See for details, Lappi-Seppälä and Lehti (2015). For a longer term analyses in mostly European countries, see Eisner 2008.

The period was characterized in most of Europe and in the non-European English speaking industrialized countries (Australia, Canada, New Zealand, and the United States) by a sharp increase in general homicide mortality beginning in the late 1950s–early 1970s. This increasing trend peaked in the 1990s at the latest, and during the last 10 years homicide rates have been generally declining in the Western world. However, the timings of the beginning of the increasing trend, its peaking, and the start of the decline vary considerably between countries (Lappi-Seppälä and Lehti 2015).

Trends were partly different in Asia. In East Asian countries homicide rates were declining during the whole studied period (or at least during most of it). In Japan, a linear decline started already in the 1950s; in Singapore, Taiwan, and Hong Kong there were more short term variation but a general decrease had begun by the mid-1970s at latest. In Thailand, Sri Lanka, and Israel again, homicide mortality trends were influenced substantially by internal or external conflicts causing sharp peaks in different decades. In Israel and Sri Lanka the mean homicide mortality rate of the 2000s was more or less the same as 50–60 years ago, in Thailand one third lower. In Mauritius, homicide mortality doubled between the 1950s and the 2000s. Also in Latin America, politics and civil unrest seem to have had a strong influence on homicide mortality during the last 60 years. In most Latin American countries homicide rates have been increasing since the 1970s although with substantial short-term variations (Lappi-Seppälä and Lehti 2015).

To sum up, depending on the region the general pattern in homicide mortality trends have differed considerably during the last six decades: roughly we can find at least four different patterns: (1) ∩-curve (Europe, Australia, Canada, New Zealand, the United States), (2) general decline (East Asia), (3) general increase (Latin America), and (4) sharp variations without a general direction (conflict ridden countries in all regions). In the following we look in more detail, whether these patterns have applied in an equal manner to both female and male homicide mortality.

4.2 Europe

4.2.1 Overall View

From the 1950s until the 2000s both male and female homicide mortality increased in all European regions. No clear patterns emerged between genders. In Scandinavia and the British Isles the increase was steepest among men; in all other regions of Europe the situation was the reverse (Fig. 6).

Between the 1990s and the 2000s homicide mortality decreased with one exception (male mortality in the British Isles) in all regions and for both genders. The pattern was also clear: male mortality decreased (although only slightly) more than female mortality. In Europe as a whole, male mortality rates declined between the 1990s and the 2000s 28 % and female rates 22 %. There were, however,

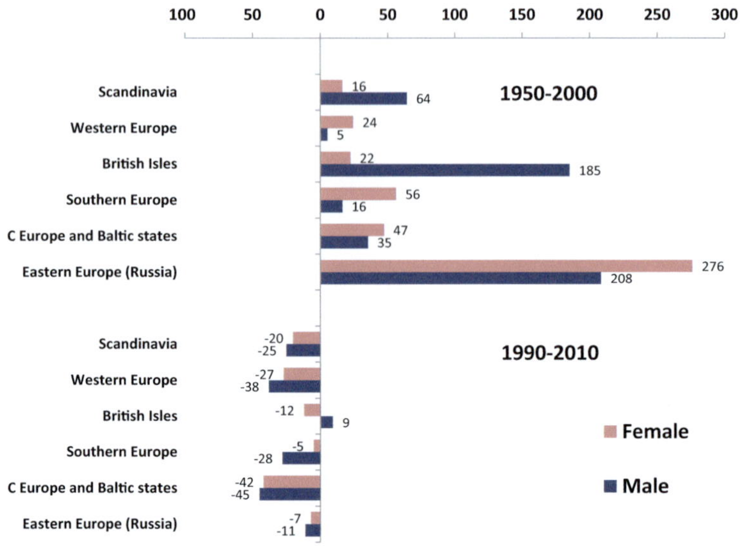

Fig. 6 Percentual change in homicide mortality rates by gender in European regions, 1950–2000 and 1990–2010 (weighted means)

substantial differences between the European regions in the magnitude of the drop (Fig. 6), and these differences became even larger when we looked at the changes in individual countries.

4.2.2 Northern and Western Europe

In Northern and Western Europe (including Scandinavia, the British Isles, France, the Benelux countries, Germany, Austria, and Switzerland) male homicide mortality increased between the 1950s and the 2000s in nine countries and decreased in five (Finland, Germany, Austria, Switzerland, France). Female mortality increased also in nine countries and decreased in four (Finland, Denmark, Germany, Austria). In England and Wales, female mortality levels were the same in the 1950s and the 2000s. Between the 1990s and the 2000s male homicide mortality decreased in all other countries except England and Wales and Ireland; female mortality decreased in every country in the region (Table 2).

Figure 7 displays female and male homicide mortality trends in four western European sub-regions from 1950 to 2010. In order to eliminate short term fluctuations, we have shown the rates as 3-year moving averages.

Perhaps the most striking feature in these diagrams is the general symmetry in mortality trends. Basically female and male homicide mortality evolved during this period in Western and Northern Europe in a similar manner and shared similar trend-changes. The differences were mainly in the details.

Table 2 Change in annual average homicide mortality rates (%) in 1950s/2000s and 1990s/2000s by gender in Europe (regional figures are weighted means[a])

	1950s/2000s		1990s/2000s	
Country/Region	Female	Male	Female	Male
Scandinavia	*+16.7 %*	*+63.8 %*	*−19.8 %*	*−24.7 %*
Denmark	−22.9 %	+58.0 %	−37.3 %	−16.8 %
Finland	−9.7 %	−13.1 %	−23.5 %	−25.7 %
Norway	+116.7 %	+100.0 %	−5.6 %	−32.6 %
Sweden	+6.5 %	+93.8 %	−14.3 %	−24.8 %
Western Europe	*+24.2 % [+25.1 %]*	*+5.0 % [+27.2 %]*	*−26.7 %*	*−37.6 %*
Austria	−3.6 %	−36.6 %	−31.8 %	−46.7 %
Belgium	+69.8 %	+157.1 %	−26.2 %	−25.3 %
France	+13.2 % [+16.2 %]	−42.1 % [+28.1 %][b]	−23.2 %	−27.0 %
Germany	−3.6 %	−36.6 %	−31.6 %	−49.2 %
The Netherlands	+209.5 %	+345.2 %	−9.7 %	−15.9 %
Switzerland	+17.5 %	−12.2 %	−31.5 %	−48.9 %
British Isles	*+21.9 %*	*+185.1 %*	*−11.7 %*	*+8.5 %*
England and Wales	0.0 %	+120.0 %	−11.1 %	+11.4 %
Ireland	+146.2 %	+450.0 %	−11.1 %	+19.2 %
N Ireland[c]	+300.0 %	+708.3 %	−25.9 %	−58.9 %
Scotland	+66.7 %	+477.4 %	−13.6 %	−7.3 %

[a]The regional figures have been weighted by population using the average populations of 1950–2010 (1950s/2000s) and 1990–2010 (1990s/2000s)

[b]The drop in male homicide mortality between the 1950s and the 2000s is caused by Algerian war related homicides both in Algeria (where French inhabitants were French citizens) and metropolitan France. The victims of these killings were mainly men and they caused in 1958–1962 about 3000 extra male homicide deaths while their effect on female homicide mortality were only marginal. If we compare the average rate of the early 1950s (1950–1955, years when homicide rates were not yet influenced by the Algerian war) with that of the 2000s, male mortality increased by 28.1 % and female mortality by 16.2 %

[c]In Northern Ireland both male and female homicide mortality quadrupled in 1970 because of the armed conflict between Catholics and Protestants. Homicide rates have remained high ever since in spite a clear decline in the 2000s

In both Scandinavia and the British Isles, male homicide mortality increased much faster than female mortality from the very low levels of the 1950s until the 1990s (in the British Isles until the 2000s). In Scandinavia, the regional trend was caused by developments in Sweden and Denmark. In Finland, where the base levels in homicide mortality of both genders were in the 1950s substantially higher than in the other three Nordic countries (and still are), homicide mortality of men and women decreased during the studied period, male mortality faster than female. In Norway again, female mortality increased during the six decades faster than male mortality. In the British Isles the trend was a general one comprising all four parts of the islands (Fig. 7).

The regional trend of continental Western Europe concealed two opposite sub-regional trends. In the German speaking countries male homicide mortality

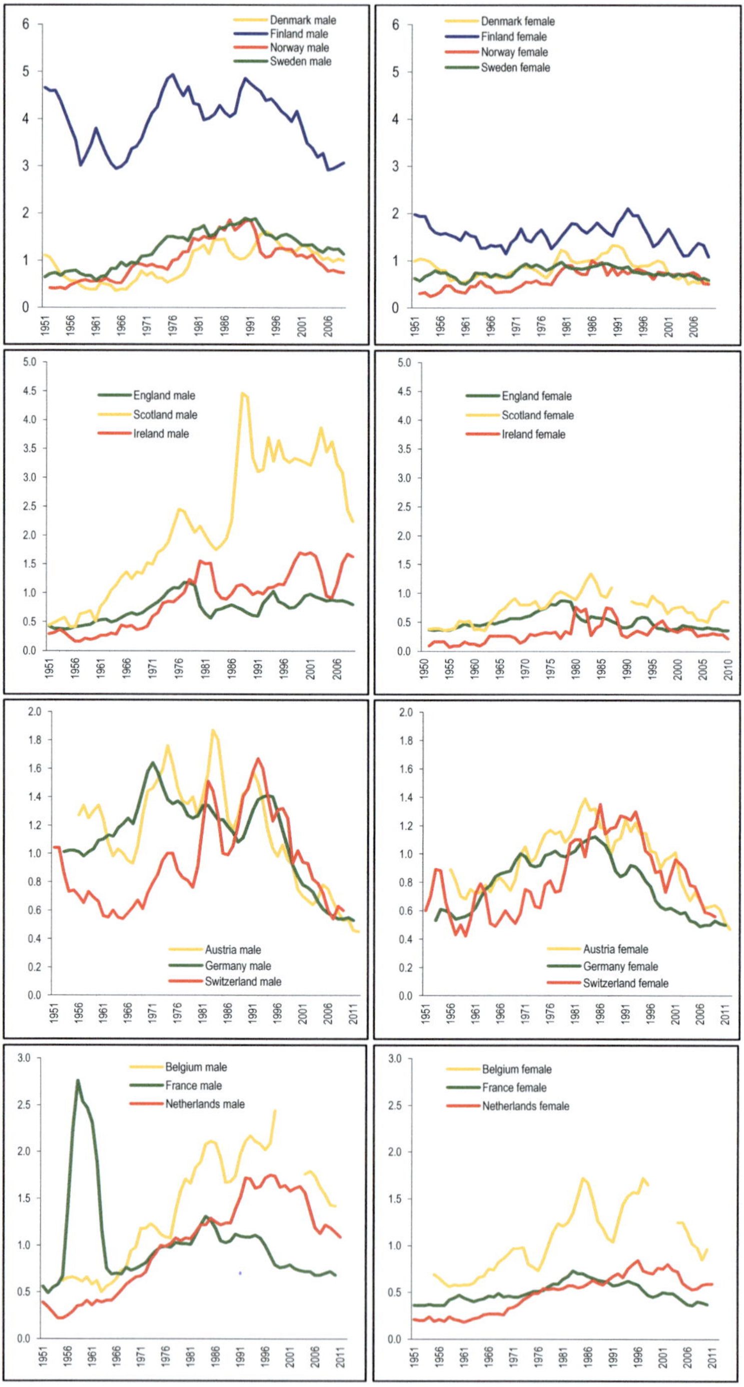

Fig. 7 Male and female homicide mortality trends in Western and Northern Europe in 1951–2010 (victims per 100,000 men/women; 3 year moving averages; *left column* figures show male rates and *right column* figures female rates)

rates decreased radically during the period while female rates stayed stable (Germany, Austria) or increased (Switzerland). In France, Belgium and the Netherlands, male and female homicide mortality rates increased from the 1950s to the 1990s (if we exclude the effect of the Algerian war in France), but this increase was substantially larger in male mortality than in female mortality (Fig. 7).

The most significant deviation from the symmetry of the mortality trends was, however, in the 1950s in France. During the Algerian war in 1957–1962, male homicide mortality was in France almost fivefold higher when compared with the pre-1955 and post-1962 levels, annually this meant 560 extra male homicide victims. The changes in female mortality were more moderate and less clear cut: the average mortality level of 1959–1962 was 28 % higher than the level of 1950–1958 but only 7 % higher than the average level of 1963–1967.

Also during the Troubles in Northern Ireland the increase in male homicide mortality was much sharper than in female mortality. In the 1970s annual average male homicide mortality was in Northern Ireland 29-fold higher than the annual average of 1960–1968; female mortality was "only" fivefold higher. The average level of the period from 1970 to 2000 was in male homicide mortality 20.5-fold and in female mortality 4.4-fold higher than the average of 1960–1968.

4.2.3 Southern and Eastern Europe

In Southern and Eastern Europe male homicide mortality increased between the 1950s[12] and the 2000s in eight countries and decreased in four (Greece, Italy, the Czech Republic, Hungary). Female mortality decreased in Greece and Italy and increased everywhere else. Between the 1990s and the 2000s both male and female homicide mortality decreased in all countries in these regions except in Spain where they increased, but the female mortality only slightly (Table 3).

In these regions, between the 1950s and the 2000s, there was, thus, a general increase in the homicide mortality rates of both genders. This increase was in female mortality substantially faster than in male mortality. In Southern Europe, the regional trend was the result of changes in Spain and Portugal. As mentioned above, in Greece and Italy, both male and female homicide mortality decreased. In Greece, female mortality faster than male mortality, in Italy the decrease was of the same magnitude for both genders (Table 3).

In Central and Eastern Europe the regional trends begin in our study in the 1960s. Neither in Central Europe nor in Eastern Europe was the trend a general one. In Eastern Europe, the weighted regional trend was in practice the Russian trend differing substantially from that in Ukraine. In Central Europe and the Baltic countries, the regional trend corresponded to the developments in Poland, Estonia,

[12] The time series of Bulgaria, Latvia, Poland, Russia, and Ukraine begin in the 1960s. For these countries the comparisons have been made between the mean annual levels of the 1960s and the 2000s.

Table 3 Change in annual average homicide mortality rates (%) in 1950s/2000s and 1990s/2000s by gender in Europe (regional figures are weighted means[a])

	1950s/2000s		1990s/2000s	
Country/Region	Female	Male	Female	Male
Southern Europe	*+56.2 %*	*+15.6 %*	*−4.7 %*	*−27.6 %*
Greece	−43.6 %	−38.1 %	−14.9 %	−14.4 %
Italy	−31.4 %	−31.6 %	−17.2 %	−53.9 %
Portugal	+27.3 %	+2.2 %	−2.8 %	−12.6 %
Spain	+219.4 %	+103.0 %	+14.6 %	+1.5 %
C Europe and Baltic states[b]	*(+46.4 %)*	*(+35.0 %)*	*−42.4 %*	*−45.0 %*
Bulgaria	(+11.1 %)	(+9.3 %)	−35.4 %	−46.3 %
Czech Republic	+19.8 % (+1.5 %)	−8.7 % (+25.3 %)	−30.1 %	−40.9 %
Estonia	+13.4%[c] (+250.6 %)	+44.9 % (+149.7 %)	−46.2 %	−54.4 %
Hungary	+30.4 % (+4.3 %)	−41.2 % (+33.9 %)	−38.0 %	−45.9 %
Latvia (incl. infanticides)	(+122.5 %)	(+94.4 %)	−37.4 %	−40.4 %
Poland	(+67.2 %)	(+35.7 %)	−48.6 %	−45.5 %
Eastern Europe[b]	*(+274.6 %)*	*(+208.4 %)*	*−6.7 %*	*−11.1 %*

[a]The regional figures have been weighted by population using the average populations of 1950–2010 (1950s/2000s) and 1990–2010 (1990s/2000s)
[b]Figures in (brackets) refer to the change between the average levels of the 1960s and the 2000s
[c]In the last years of the Stalin regime, 1950–1954, homicide mortality rates of both men and women were substantially higher than in the second half of the 1950s, some of the killings may still have been related to armed resistance against the Soviet occupation

and Latvia while in Hungary and the Czech Republic male homicide mortality increased faster than female mortality; in Bulgaria the increases were of similar magnitude for both genders (Table 3).

Also in these regions male and female mortality trends were roughly symmetric and shared similar main trend-changes. The clearest deviation from this symmetry was in Hungary and coincided with the 1956 revolution and the years immediately following when male homicide mortality increased by 120 % from the level of 1955 while female mortality increased by less than 30 %; the increase in male mortality lasted also longer than the one in female mortality (Fig. 8).

4.3 Australia, Canada, New Zealand, and the United States

We have treated the English speaking industrial countries in North America and Oceania as a single separate group, partly because of a similar general ∩-curve homicide mortality trend shared with Europe. In all of these countries, both male and female homicide mortality rates have declined during the last 10 years. The average female homicide mortality levels were in the 2000s over 30 % lower than

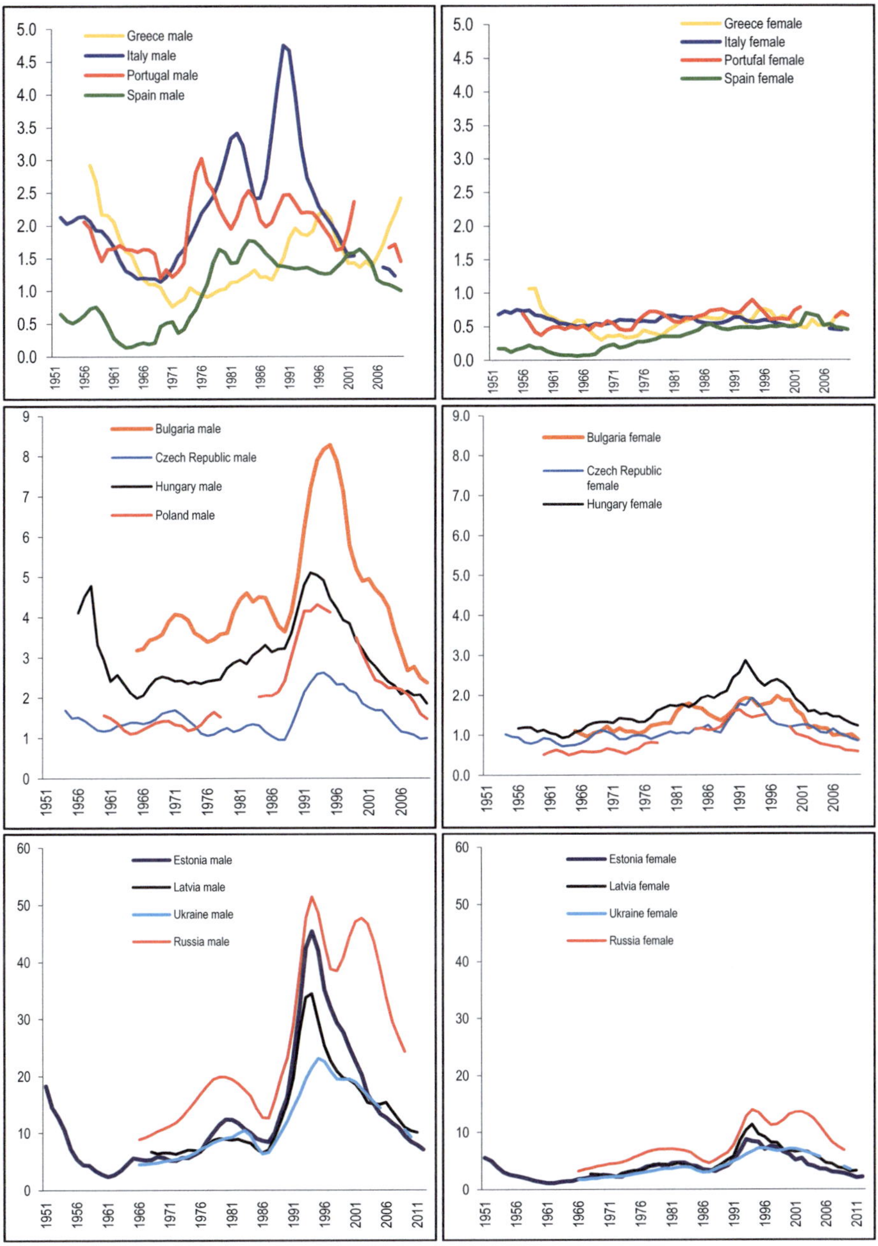

Fig. 8 Male and female homicide mortality trends in Southern, Central, and Eastern Europe in 1951–2010 (victims per 100,000 men/women; 3 year moving averages; *left column* figures show male rates and *right column* figures female rates)

Table 4 Change in annual average homicide mortality rates (%) in 1950s/2000s and 1990s/2000s by gender in North America and Oceania (regional figures are weighted means[a])

	1950s/2000s		1990s/2000s	
Country/Region	Female	Male	Female	Male
North America	*+14.8 %*	*+41.2 %*	*–31.0 %*	*–27.0 %*
Canada	+9.6 %	+90.8 %	–31.0 %	–2.1 %
USA	+15.4 %	+36.0 %	–31.0 %	–29.7 %
Oceania	*–8.3 %*	*+5.2 %*	*–33.3 %*	*–33.3 %*
Australia	–20.0 %	–9.4 %	–38.7 %	–35.3 %
New Zealand	+48.6 %	+75.7 %	–6.1 %	–23.0 %

[a]The regional figures have been weighted by population using the average populations of 1950–2010 (1950s/2000s) and 1990–2010 (1990s/2000s)

the 1990s' levels in North America and Australia, in New Zealand the drop was 6 % (Table 4). In male mortality the decrease rate was 20–30 % in Australia, New Zealand and the United States but only 2 % in Canada.

The longer-term trends differed between Australia and the other three countries. Between the 1950s and the 2000s, male homicide rates increased 35–90 % in the United States, Canada, and New Zealand but dropped 9 % in Australia. Similarly female homicide rates decreased 20 % in Australia but increased 10–50 % in the other three (Fig. 9).

Also in these Western countries male and female mortality trends were roughly symmetric sharing similar main trend-changes during the period. In the long term, however, considering the difference in the relative homicide death risk for men and women, male risk increased in comparison with female risk in all of the countries. In Canada, New Zealand and the United States because of a faster increase in male mortality levels; in Australia, because of a slower drop.

4.4 Asia and Africa

In East Asia, both male and female homicide mortality have declined during the last 10 years. The average female homicide mortality levels were in the 2000s over 30 % lower than in the 1990s in Hong Kong, Singapore, and Taiwan; in Japan the drop was 9 % (Table 5). Male death rates were 20–60 % lower in all of the countries. Also in Sri Lanka and Thailand, male and female homicide mortality have decreased; in Sri Lanka 70–80 %, probably because of a ceasefire in the civil war in 2001–2005.[13] In Thailand, the drop was more moderate. In Israel and Mauritius, male and female homicide mortality increased between the 1990s and

[13] Our data cover the years 2000–2006, data of the last years of the 2000s (when hostilities broke out again) have not yet been published.

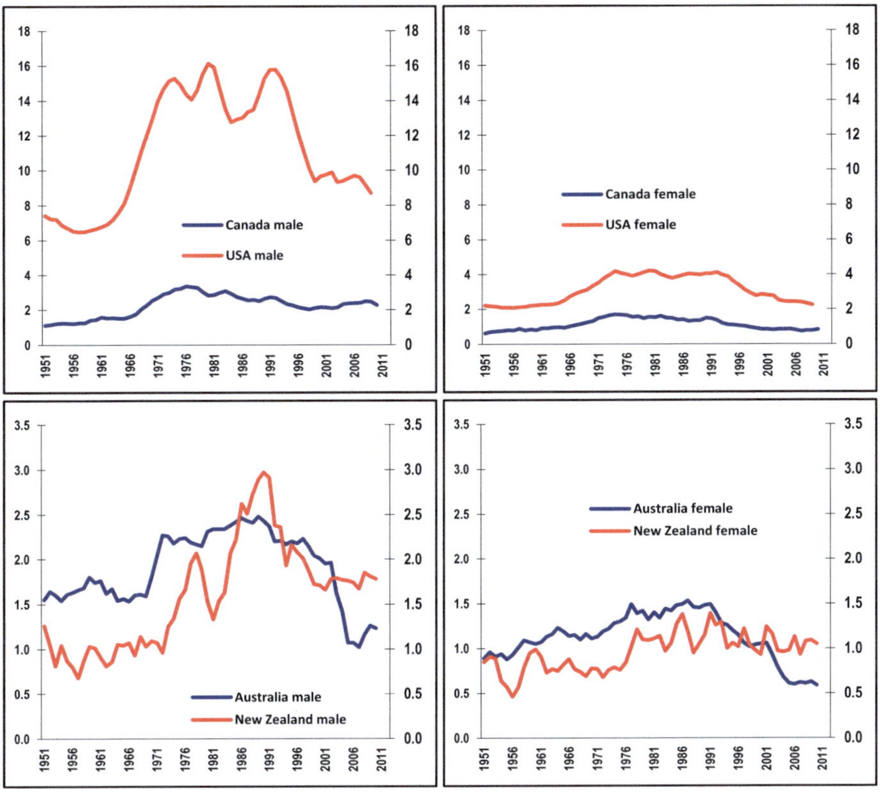

Fig. 9 Male and female homicide mortality trends in Australia, Canada, New Zealand and the United States in 1951–2010 (victims per 100,000 men/women; 3 year moving averages; *left column* figures show male rates and *right column* figures female rates)

the 2000s—in Israel, 130–160 %, probably because of killings related to the second Intifada; in Mauritius, 40–60 % (Table 5).

Between the 1950s and the 2000s, male homicide mortality rates dropped 70–95 % in all East Asian countries. Female mortality rates dropped 65–95 % in Japan, Singapore and Taiwan, but only 10 % in Hong Kong. Also in Thailand, both male and female homicide mortality declined: male mortality by more than 35 % and female mortality by 20 %. In Israel, between the 1960s and the 2000s, male homicide mortality dropped substantially but female mortality increased by 130 %; the drop in male homicide mortality, in spite of the second Intifada, was related to a sharp peak during the War of Attrition between Egypt and Israel in 1969–1970. In 1969, male homicide mortality increased in Israel over 33-fold from the mean level in 1965–1968 while female mortality decreased by one third. The surge in male mortality was short lived, rates returned to pre-surge levels already in 1970. In Sri Lanka, female homicide mortality was 15 % lower in the early 2000s than in the 1950s, while male mortality was 12 % higher. In Mauritius, both male and female

Table 5 Change in annual average homicide mortality rates (%) in 1950s/2000s and 1990s/2000s by gender in Asian countries and Mauritius (regional figures are weighted means[a])

	1950s/2000s		1990s/2000s	
Country/Region	Female	Male	Female	Male
East Asia	*–70.5 %*	*–81.4 %*	*–15.8 %*	*–30.2 %*
Hong Kong	–11.3 %	–73.3 %	–33.7 %	–60.4 %
Japan	–69.4 %	–79.7 %	–8.9 %	–24.3 %
Singapore	–64.7 %	–78.8 %	–38.8 %	–44.9 %
Taiwan (incl. infanticides)	–95.9 %	–95.6 %	–45.7 %	–52.3 %
Other Asia				
Israel	(+126.8 %)	(–26.4 %)	+162.0 %	+130.0 %
Sri Lanka	–15.2 %	+12.4 %	–67.1 %	–79.8 %
Thailand	–20.4 %	–36.0 %	–24.8 %	–19.6 %
Mauritius	+128.0 %	+136.1 %	+58.5 %	+40.7 %

[a]The regional figures have been weighted by population using the average populations of 1950–2010 (1950s/2000s) and 1990–2010 (1990s/2000s)

homicide mortality increased between the 1950s and the 2000s about 130 % (Fig. 10).

Also in the Asian countries studied and in Mauritius male and female homicide mortality trends were mainly symmetric and shared similar trend-changes. The clearest deviation was to be found in Israel and coincided with the 1969 conflict when only male mortality surged while female mortality declined.

4.5 Latin America

In the group of Latin American countries studied, male homicide mortality rates increased by 35 % and female rates by 17 % on average between the 1990s and the 2000s.[14] During the last decade, the general trend in homicide mortality of both genders differed thus radically in Latin America from the one observed in the industrialized countries of Europe, North America, East Asia, and Oceania (Table 6).

There have been, however, substantial differences between countries. Countries where both male and female homicide mortality rates have decreased during the last decade include Mexico, Colombia, Cuba and Puerto Rico; in addition in Paraguay and Barbados female mortality has decreased, while in Uruguay and the Dominican Republic there has been a slight decline in male homicide mortality. Because of the dominant position of Mexico in Central America and Cuba in the Caribbean region, the weighted means for both sub-regions show a moderated decline in homicide mortality of both genders. In South America, during the last decade the weighted

[14] These are unweighted means for the whole group of Latin American countries in Table 3.

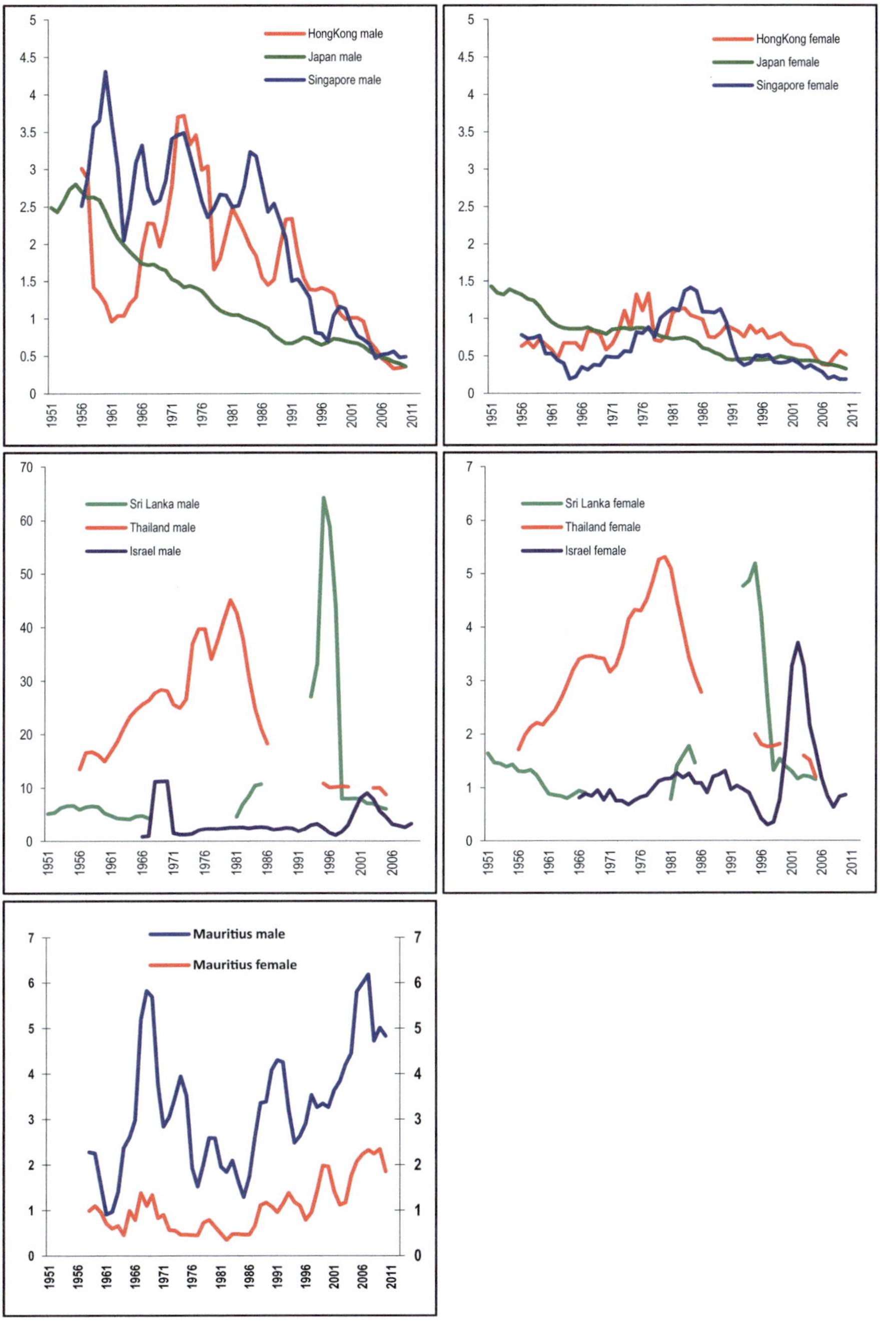

Fig. 10 Male and female homicide mortality trends in Asia and Mauritius in 1950–2010 (victims per 100,000 men/women; 3 year moving averages; *left column* figures show male rates and *right column* figures female rates; the figure for Sri Lanka, Thailand Israel has different scales for men and women)

Table 6 Change in annual average homicide mortality rates (%) 1950s/2000s and 1990s/2000s by gender in Latin America (regional figures are weighted means[a])

	1950s/2000s		1990s/2000s	
Country/Region	Female	Male	Female	Male
Central America	*–6.1 %*	*–17.1 %*	*–4.7 %*	*–12.0 %*
Costa Rica	+31.1 %	+134.1 %	+34.8 %	+46.8 %
El Salvador	+93.6 %	+34.0 %	+48.1 %	+17.9 %
Guatemala	+298.6 %	+270.2 %	+53.9 %	+42.2 %
Mexico	–47.3 %	–62.7 %	–18.7 %	–28.1 %
Nicaragua	–39.4 %	–55.2 %	+14.8 %	+65.0 %
Panama	+42.5 %	+218.7 %	+50.0 %	+50.7 %
South America	*+61.5 %*	*+158.0 %*	*+15.7 %*	*+26.4 %*
Argentina			+10.6 %	+26.8 %
Brazil			+11.0 %	+20.8 %
Chile	+12.6 %	+22.5 %	+68.1 %	+78.2 %
Colombia	+38.3 %	+61.5 %	–20.8 %	–27.0 %
Ecuador	(+81.1 %)	(+122.5 %)	+34.0 %	+27.0 %
Paraguay	(–22.4 %)	(–30.8 %)	–14.0 %	+13.8 %
Uruguay	+23.8 %	–5.7 %	+2.0 %	–1.7 %
Venezuela	+153.7 %	+519.2 %	+82.8 %	+125.6 %
The Caribbean	*+5.4 %*	*+124.0 %*	*–11.9 %*	*–1.2 %*
Bahamas			+21.0 %	+14.7 %
Barbados	+658.5 %	+886.0 %	–18.8 %	+52.1 %
Cuba (incl. infanticides)	(+11.3 %)	(+24.3 %)	–20.5 %	–25.5 %
Dominican Republic	–37.6 %	+65.8 %	+2.3 %	–2.7 %
Puerto Rico	–10.2 %	+365.3 %	–35.4 %	–6.9 %
Trinidad and Tobago	+85.7 %	+441.0 %	+30.0 %	+217.8 %

[a]The regional figures have been weighted by population using the average populations of 1950–2010 (1950s/2000s) and 1990–2010 (1990s/2000s)

mean increase in female mortality has been 16 % and in male mortality 26 % (Table 6).

In the long term, between the 1950s and the 2000s, homicide mortality of both genders decreased in Mexico, Nicaragua and Paraguay. In addition, in two countries (the Dominican Republic, Puerto Rico) female mortality decreased, and in one country (Uruguay) male mortality. In all other countries of the region, during the six-decade period, homicide mortality increased for both genders—male mortality substantially more than female mortality—this in spite the fact that in Latin America men had much higher mortality levels already in the 1950s than women did (Table 6; Fig. 11).

In male mortality, the highest increases between the 1950s and the 2000s were in the Caribbean (Barbados, Puerto Rico, Trinidad and Tobago) and Central America (Costa Rica, Guatemala, Panama). But also Venezuela and Ecuador had increases of over 100 %. In female mortality, the increases were on average substantially

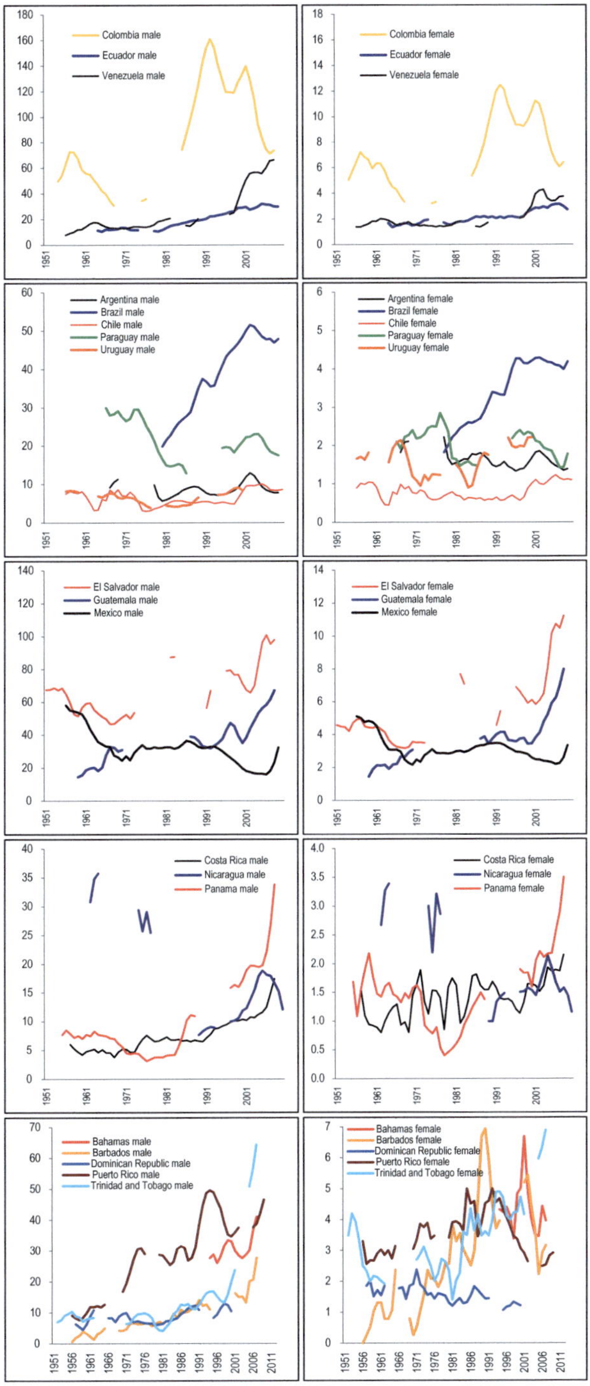

Fig. 11 Male and female homicide mortality trends in Latin America in 1951–2010 (victims per 100,000 men/women; 3 year moving averages; *left column* figures show male rates and *right column* figures female rates; different scales for men and women)

lower. Highest growth percentages could be found in Venezuela, Barbados, Guatemala, and El Salvador (Table 6).

Of the 17 Latin American countries where data from the 1950s onwards were available, in 11 male homicide rates had increased more or decreased less than female rates since the 1950s. The most notable exceptions from this trend were Mexico, El Salvador and Nicaragua (Fig. 11). However, in spite of the differences in sharpness of the changes, the main trend-changes were similar for both male and female homicide mortality also in Latin America during the period.

5 Notes on the Gender Ratio of Homicide Mortality

According to Veli Verkko, the share of female victims should decrease in homicides when the level of lethal violence (dominated by male-to-male homicides) increases and vice versa. In the following we examine briefly these assumptions, both cross-sectionally and over time.

We have calculated a gender ratio of homicide mortality by dividing female mean mortality by male mean mortality in certain time periods. This ratio shows the relative difference between female and male homicide mortality levels. In simple terms, it shows the percentage of female mortality out of male mortality. If the ratio is one or higher, women have higher risk to die as victims of homicide than men; if the ratio is one, men and women have an identical risk; and if the ratio is below one, women have lower homicide victimization risk than men. (For example, a ratio of 0.20 means that there are against every female victim five male victims.)

5.1 *Overview*

There are currently huge differences in the gender ratios of homicide mortality between continents, regions and countries, differences that only roughly follow differences in general homicide mortality rates. In 2000–2010, the global ratio weighted by populations was 0.17. Thus, for every killed adult woman, approximately five adult men were killed worldwide (Table 7).

The lowest ratios are currently found in Latin America and continental Africa, the highest in East Asia and German speaking Europe. In Central and South America, at the moment for every killed woman ten men are killed, in German speaking Europe the corresponding ratio is only 1 to 1.1 and in East Asia 1 to 1.2; i.e., in these two regions, the risk for women to die as victims of homicides is practically the same as for men. They are, however, conspicuous exceptions from a global rule: in all other sub-regions of the world female homicide mortality level is even at its highest only about half of the male mortality level (Fig. 12).

The only countries in the studied group where female homicide mortality was higher in 2000–2010 than male mortality were Austria, Switzerland, and Hong

Table 7 Mean female/male homicide ratios by countries 2000–2012

Region	Country	Female/ Male—ratio	Region	Country	Female/ Male—ratio
Western Europe	Ireland	0.19	North America	USA	0.26
	Scotland	0.26		Canada	0.31
	Northern Ireland	0.27			
	Luxembourg	0.34	Central America	Mexico	0.10
	Finland	0.36		Nicaragua	0.10
	Italy	0.36		Panama	0.10
	Sweden	0.42		El Salvador	0.11
	Portugal	0.45		Guatemala	0.12
	Spain	0.45		Costa Rica	0.15
	England and Wales	0.51			
	Denmark	0.53	South America	Venezuela	0.06
	Netherlands	0.54		Paraguay	0.08
	France	0.55		Brazil	0.09
	Belgium	0.62		Colombia	0.09
	Norway	0.68		Ecuador	0.09
	Germany	0.93		Chile	0.14
	Switzerland	0.97		Argentina	0.18
	Austria	1.08		Peru	0.19
				Guyana	0.23
Eastern Europe	Kosovo/Kos	0.18		Uruguay	0.25
	Azerbaijan	0.21		Suriname	0.35
	Turkey	0.22			
	Armenia	0.23	Caribbean	Puerto Rico	0.07
	Georgia	0.23		Dom. Republic	0.09
	Estonia	0.27		Trinidad and Tobago	0.11
	Albania	0.28		Jamaica	0.12
	Russian Fed.	0.28		Cuba	0.34
	Montenegro	0.31			
	Latvia	0.32	Asia	Philippines	0.09
	Greece	0.33		Thailand	0.14
	Lithuania	0.35		Kuwait	0.16
	Bulgaria	0.37		Mongolia	0.18
	Ukraine	0.37		Sri Lanka	0.19
	Cyprus	0.40		Turkmenistan	0.20
	Macedonia	0.40		Malaysia	0.22
	Poland	0.41		Kazakhstan	0.26

(continued)

Table 7 (continued)

Region	Country	Female/ Male—ratio	Region	Country	Female/ Male—ratio
	Belarus	0.41		Israel	0.26
	Moldova	0.43		Kyrgyzstan	0.28
	Serbia	0.44		Tajikistan	0.28
	Romania	0.49		Jordan	0.31
	Slovakia	0.59		Bahrain	0.32
	Hungary	0.64		Uzbekistan	0.35
	Czech Republic	0.71		Singapore	0.37
	Croatia	0.76		Taiwan	0.46
	Slovenia	0.88		South Korea	0.82
				Japan	0.89
Africa	South Africa	0.15		Macau	1.19
	Mauritius	0.37		Hong Kong	1.36
	Reunion	0.54			
			Oceania	Australia	0.48
				New Zealand	0.60
				Fiji	1.58

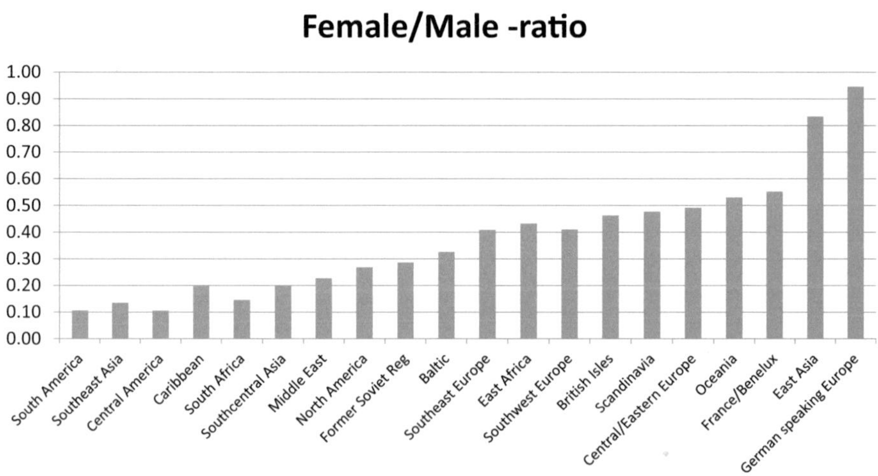

Fig. 12 Mean female/male homicide ratios by sub-regions in 2000–2010

Kong; in addition, more or less even risks for both genders could be found in Germany, Korea, the Czech Republic and Rodrigues. In the other end of the scale were Brazil, Colombia, Puerto Rico, Paraguay, and Venezuela where female

Table 8 Mean female/male homicide ratios and mean general homicide mortality rates by sub-regions in 2004–2012

Sub-region	F/M—ratio	Homicide 2004–2012 (mean)
South America	0.09	21.7
Southeast Asia	0.10	7.6
Central America	0.10	18.6
Caribbean	0.12	17.0
South Africa	0.15	34.3
Southcentral Asia	0.19	3.3
Middle East	0.20	1.9
North America	0.27	5.3
Former Soviet Reg	0.29	9.8
Baltic	0.33	7.1
Southeast Europe	0.39	1.8
East Africa	0.40	15.3
Southwest Europe	0.40	0.9
British Isles	0.41	1.3
Scandinavia	0.43	1.1
Central/Eastern Europe	0.48	1.6
Oceania	0.54	3.6
France/Benelux	0.56	0.8
East Asia	0.61	1.6
German speaking Europe	0.94	0.7

homicide mortality was less than 10 % of male mortality, all were Latin American countries with relatively high homicide levels.

5.2 Comparing Gender Ratios and Homicide Rates Cross-Sectionally

According to Veli Verkko, the gender ratio of homicide mortality should be linearly associated with the general level of lethal violence (Verkko 1951, pp. 50–55). Table 8 displays both gender ratios and overall mean homicide mortality levels by global sub-regions.

When we compare the gender ratios with overall homicide rates, the initial impression is that they are in general correlated; low regional ratios seem to go usually with high homicide rates, and vice versa. To test this association Fig. 13 plots female/male homicide ratios and homicide rates by countries and by regions.

This also indicates that the distribution of victims by gender depends on the overall level of lethal violence. While the global mean female/male homicide ratio is around 0.2, the mean ratio is twice as high in low homicide rate countries, and only about half of that in high homicide rate countries. We have ranked in Fig. 13

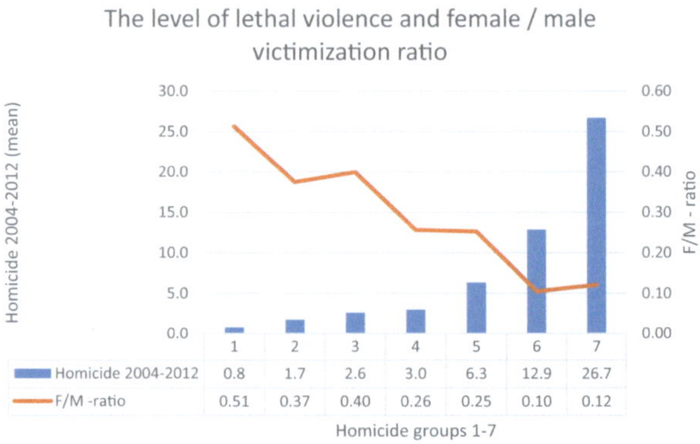

Fig. 13 Mean female/male homicide ratio and overall homicide rate by country groups in 2000–2010

countries (n=134) into seven groups on the basis of overall level of lethal violence, with corresponding data on average homicide levels and female/male homicide ratios. In low homicide level countries with a mean overall homicide rate of 1.4 or less the gender ratio is 0.6 on average. In high homicide rate countries with mean overall homicide rate over 12 the gender ratio is less than 0.15 on average.

Figure 13 suggests a curvilinear association: High homicide rates go with low ratios, but once the level of violence remains low or high enough, this correlation weakens. This can be confirmed with a scatter plot (Fig. 14). The plots in Fig. 14 examine also whether there have been changes in this association over time between the 1950s and the 2000s.

The pattern has remained stable. Female/male homicide ratio seems to be dependent on the overall level of lethal violence: The higher the level, the lower the share of female victims. In other words, Verkko's static law seems to hold, at least this was the case during the six decades from 1950 until 2010.

The global correlation between overall and female homicide rates is currently linear. Should the relative share of female homicides diminish with increasing overall levels, the fir-line should follow a different pattern (skewed upwards). This does not seem to be the case today in a cross sectional setting. This leaves the issue of dynamic laws (changes) open. An initial examination of short term changes, indicate that the connection between the ratio of male and female victims and the changes in homicide levels during the twentieth century has actually more or less followed Verkko's predictions: increase in homicide levels has usually increased the proportion of male victims and vice versa. However, the general proportion of male victims has differed and differs substantially in different cultural-political regions: in Latin America the share of men out of victims has been throughout the twentieth century much higher than in the European cultural area or in East Asia.

There seems also to be clear pattern differences between homicide mortality changes related to internal armed conflicts on one hand and changes related to social crises (or other less dramatic social developments) on the other hand. At least this was the case in the studied group of countries during the post-Second World

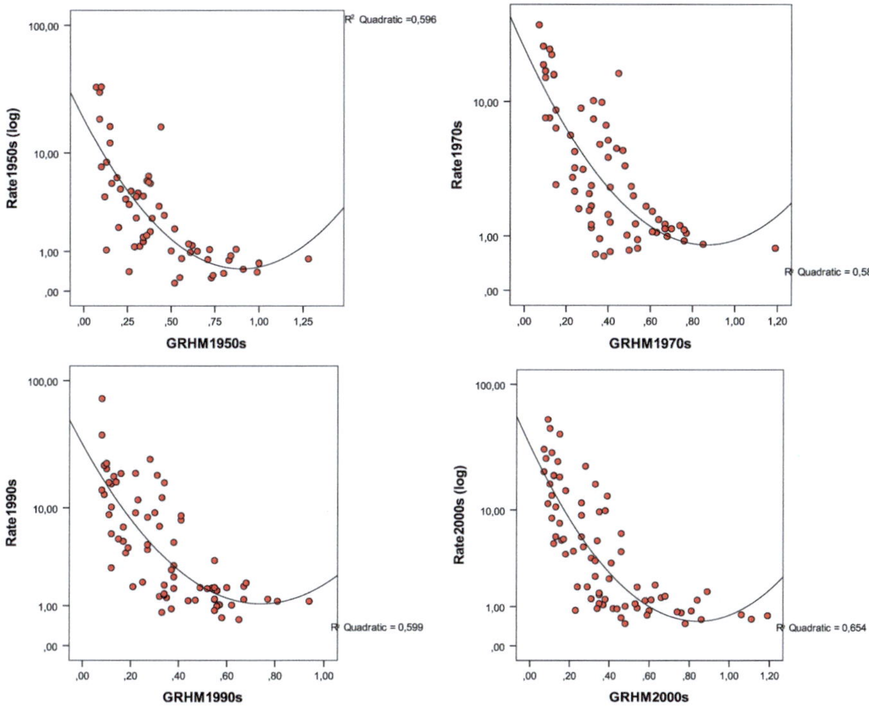

Fig. 14 Female/male homicide ratios and overall homicide levels (logged) from the 1950s to the 2000s globally by countries. (GRHM = Female/male homicide ratio)

War period.[15] Both armed conflicts and social crises usually increased homicide mortality sharply and rapidly, but during armed conflicts these increases were focused on male mortality[16] while during social crises both male and female mortality increased in a more evenly way.

[15] There were several such crises in the studied group, as examples of armed conflicts we used the period of armed resistance in Estonia (1947–1949), the Algerian war in France (1954–1962), the Hungarian revolution (October–November 1956), the conflict in Northern Ireland (1968–1998), the War of Attrition (March, 1969–August, 1970) and second Intifada (2000–2005) in Israel, the first phase of the Sri Lankan civil war (1983–2001), and the Colombian crises of the post-Second World War period. As examples of political crises we used the Stalinist period (1950–1953) in Estonia, and the regime changes in Central Europe, Baltic countries, and Eastern Europe in the late-1980s and during the 1990s.

[16] There were, however, a few exceptions from this rule: the period of armed resistance in Estonia in the 1940s, the period of La Violencia in Colombia from the 1940s until the 1960s, and the second Intifada in Israel in the 2000s increased male and female homicide mortality more or less evenly.

5.3 Summary

In the studied group of 58 countries, between 1950 and 2010, female homicide mortality increased in 37 countries and male mortality in 35 countries; in 31 of them the mortality of both genders increased. This means that in the majority of the countries homicide mortality levels of both men and women are today higher than they were in the 1950s. The trend of the last 20 years has been in the opposite direction: between the 1990s and 2000s, in 41 countries female homicide mortality and in 39 countries male homicide mortality has decreased; in 37 of them the mortality of both genders decreased.

In the majority of the studied countries (30), the female/male homicide ratio changed between the 1950s and the 2000s to the detriment of men, in seven countries the ratio stayed stable. Today relatively more men are killed compared to women than 60 years ago. Between the 1990s and the 2000s also this trend, however, has changed: during the last 20 years, the ratio has increased in 25 countries, decreased in 18 and stayed stable in 15. Globally a general increase in homicide mortality rates of both genders usually decreased the female/male ratio, and a general decrease increased it during the period. However, there were many exceptions from this rule on the country level.

One should also note that in spite of the general increase in the female/male homicide ratio in the studied group during the last two decades, in only a few countries female homicide mortality rates are today higher than male rates. During the whole period with available published homicide mortality data, female homicide mortality rates have continuously been substantially lower than male rates throughout the world. And as the long term trend in the female/male homicide ratio shows, this difference between the genders in the risk to die as victims of homicides has increased during the post-Second World War decades to the detriment of men.

6 Exploring the Correlates

In this section we explore possible explanations for gender related homicide mortality level differences over time and between countries. Most of the analyses are cross-sectional and exploratory; we examine a range of promising explanatory variables rather than test specific criminological hypotheses or theories.

The sample used in the analyses includes the 222 nations from the CHTS dataset that also provide data on imprisonment rates The sample has been divided into three subsamples according to classifications in the 2012 UN Human Development Index (HDI) in order to examine patterns across different level of development (for a similar solution, see Ouimet 2012).

6.1 Previous Research

In our previous work (Lappi-Seppälä and Lehti 2015) we explored explanations for national homicide rate differences over time and between countries. The results showed that societies with high overall homicide levels are characterized by gross income differences, meagre welfare state, high corruption, low social trust, and less effective government. Cross-sectional analyses with a large set of countries and a variety of social, political, and cultural factors provided strong and consistent indications that lethal violence was far more common in countries with large income differences and less well-developed social welfare states than in developed democracies, but also in autocracies (obviously for different reasons). Homicide rates were lower under more effective governments and in less corrupt environments. High-crime societies were characterized by stronger authoritarian and conservative moral views, more collectivist cultures, and lower long term cultural orientations. Demographic considerations—the age-structure and ethnic diversity—played much lesser roles than social-structural, political, and cultural variables. Use of capital punishment, high rates of imprisonment, and extensive use of life sentences were usually associated with high and increasing homicide rates—and not the other way around.

These results were robust across countries of different levels of economic development from all main regions of the world. However, as has been pointed out, homicides against men and women follow different patterns in terms of offense context and victim-offender relations. Female victims are killed to a much larger proportion by their family members or intimate partners and these structural and context differences seem to be global (Stöckl et al. 2013; UNODC 2011 p. 58). This raises the question, whether and to what extent the observations referred above concerning general homicide levels apply to female homicide mortality. To answer this question, we have counted key correlations separately in gender-specific homicide data.

6.2 Comparing Correlates for Homicides Against Men and Women

The explanatory factors that we have investigated here fall into four main groups. The first are macro-level social and structural indicators discussed traditionally in the contexts of strain-disorganization and deprivation theories. The second consists of state-level political indicators, including political structures and the style and quality of governance. The third consists of cultural variables, including social values and attitudes. The fourth includes formal controls and sanctioning practices. The sample used in the following analyses includes the 222 nations from the CHTS dataset that also provide data on imprisonment rates. Also indicators linked more directly with gender-equality have been included. These are female adult literacy rate, female economic activity rate, and female primary net enrolment as % of male

Table 9 Male-victims and female-victims. Bivariate correlations

Correlations (Global sample)	Male victims	Female victims	N (both)
A. Demographics			
Ethnic factionlization (combined linguistic and racial) (Alesina et al. 2002)	0.217*	0.258**	103
Males 15–29 years (%)	0.373**	0.353**	80
Males (%)	−0.067	−0.202	80
B. Development			
Human development index 2005 100-pt scale (UNDP 2007)	−0.427**	−0.489**	97
GDP per capita ppp 2006 (World bank 2007)	−0.298**	−0.366**	104
C. Democracy and Governance			
Effective democracy 2006 (Fuchs and Klingemann)	−0.386**	−0.444**	82
Summary good governance 2006 (Kaufmann et al. 2006)	−0.327**	−0.373**	102
D. Social Policy			
GINI coefficient (UNDP 2004)	0.574**	0.472**	76
Public Social Exp. 2002–2007 % of GDP (IMF)	−0.527**	−0.492**	63
Education (LPI)	0.645**	.602**	71
Health (LPI)	0.566**	.580**	71
E. Trust			
Social	−0.347**	−0.321*	62
Police	−0.305*	−0.400**	60
F. Formal Control			
Prisoners 2010-2013 (mean)	0.192*	0.275**	132
G. Gender Specific Factors			
Female adult literacy rate, 2002 (UNDP 2004)	−0.436**	−0.328**	67
Female economic activity rate (% ages 15 and above) 2002 (UNDP 2004)	−0.085	−0.005	92
Female primary net enrolment, as % of male ratio, 1997	0.117	0.082	71
Gender-related development index (GDI) value 2005 (UNDP 2007)	−0.451**	−0.512**	86
Gender equality index GII (UNDP 2012)	0.549**	0.531**	86

*Significant at the .05 level (2-tailed)
**Significant at the .01 level (2-tailed)

ratio, and more specifically, and the UN gender inequality indexes (GII). The dimensions in GII are reproductive health, empowerment, and labor market participation (Table 9).[17]

[17] The latter was counted for the first time 2010 and it replaces previous GEM and GDI indexes.. Reproductive health covers Maternal Mortality Ratio (MMR) and the adolescent fertility rate (AFR). With a low MMR, it is implied that pregnant women have access to adequate health needs, therefore the MMR is a good measure of women's access to health care. A high AFR, which measures early childbearing, results in health risks for mothers and infants as well as a lack of higher education attainment. The empowerment dimension is measured by the share of national parliamentary seats held by each sex and higher education attainment levels. Access to higher

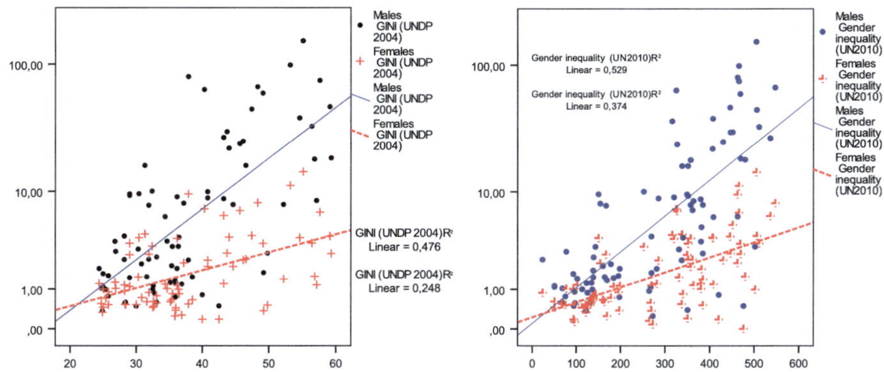

Fig. 15 Correlations between income inequality (*left*) and gender equality (*right*) and homicide by gender

Factors influencing the homicide levels globally seem to be gender-neutral. High male and female homicide mortality rates correlate with the same factors and on an equal manner. No systematic difference can be detected between gender-specific (section G) and general predictors (A–F). The strongest correlations were found between social-policy indicators and gender specific factors. However, the latter correlated in an equal manner with homicide against both genders. The shapes of the correlations are illustrated in scatter-diagrams below (Fig. 15).

6.3 *Explaining Variations in the Female/Male Homicide Ratio*

The same issues may also be approached from the point of view of the female/male homicide ratio and examined whether this ratio correlates in similar manner with the same background factors. The answer to this is affirmative. The female/male homicide ratio is associated with the same factors referred in the previous section and in equal intensity; in fact, the correlations are often even stronger, as the following examples illustrate (Table 10 and Fig. 16):

Social-equality factors and general prosperity indicators hardly serve as factors that can explain the distribution of homicide victims. But these factors do have crucial relevance for the overall level of lethal violence and it seems that in spite of the substantial structural and context differences, these factors are indeed the same and work in a similar way in homicidal crime against both genders.

education expands women's freedom by increasing their ability to question and increases their access to information which expands their public involvement. The labor market dimension is measured by women's participation in the workforce. This dimension accounts for paid work, unpaid work, and actively looking for work.

Table 10 Socio-economic correlates with homicide rates and gender ratios in 2004–2012

	Female-male—ratio	All victims	Male victims	Female victims
HDI 2012 (UNDP)	0.433**	−0.457**	−0.451**	−0.469**
GINI mid 2000s (Lis, WB)	−0.690**	0.584**	0.617**	0.533**
Gender inequality (UN2010)	−0.682**	0.474**	0.569**	0.560**

**Correlation is significant at the 0.01 level (2-tailed)

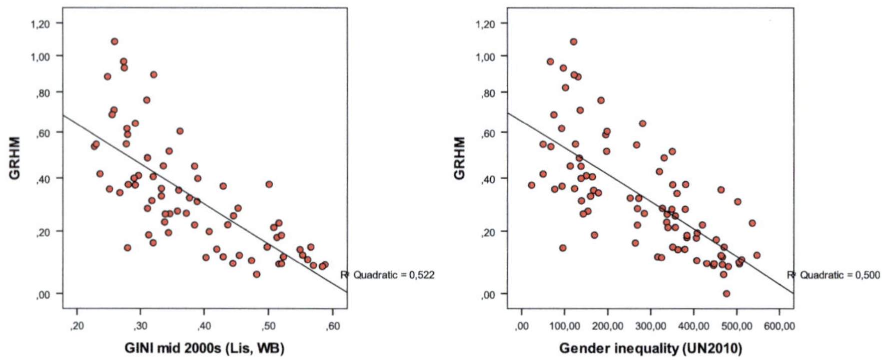

Fig. 16 Correlations between income inequality (*left*) and gender equality (*right*) and female-male homicide ratio

7 Conclusions

In criminological research, there are currently two main approaches concerning lethal violence against men and women. The first one assumes that lethal violence is influenced by gender specific factors and also the explanations are partly or totally different depending on victim's gender (gender sensitive approach). This difference in the background factors is sometimes stretched to such an extent that homicides against men and women are claimed to be two totally different types of phenomena. The second approach assumes that lethal violence against men and women can be explained by the same general predictors (gender insensitive approach). The theoretical backgrounds of both approaches are heterogeneous, and both have found support in earlier studies on gender specific homicide mortality trends. The research topics, country samples, time periods and studied variables have, however, varied in these studies, and the differing results and interpretations can partly be due to these variations. In general (but in varying degrees), the gender sensitive approach has had an important role in historical criminology and feminist criminology while gender insensitive approach has received support among mainstream criminologists.

Irrespective of the differences between theoretical approaches and explanations, there is a general agreement among homicide researchers about significant structural differences between male and female homicide mortality. Research results show that homicides against women follow a different pattern in terms of offense context and victim-offender relations than the crimes against men. Female victims are killed to a much larger proportion by their family members or intimate partners in domestic contexts. These structural differences seem to be global and relatively stable.

In this chapter we have analysed the current male and female homicide mortality levels and mortality trends globally. We have not tested the theoretical backgrounds of either of the main approaches but have described and compared the changes that have taken place during the last 60 years in male and female homicide mortality rates. In addition, regarding these changes, we have explored the explanative power of some key socio-demographic and gender equality related factors using bivariate correlates. On basis of the results we can make conclusions also regarding the general approaches.

Current victimization levels. Today, for every woman killed worldwide there are approximately five killed men. The higher homicide mortality risk of men seems to be a characteristic that is common to the human race irrespective of cultural background, denomination, level of economic development or social system. It also seems to be fairly permanent by nature. There are, however, huge differences in homicide mortality rates of both genders between sub-regions and nations. In 2000–2010, in the studied group of 58 countries the mean annual homicide mortality rate of women varied from zero to 15 victims per 100,000 women; the male rate close to zero to 100 per 100,000 men. The lowest rates for both genders were found in Europe and East Asia; the highest rates in the studied group were in Latin America, however, the group did not include most African and Asian countries. Also the ratio between female and male homicide mortality is not a global constant. The lowest ratios are currently found in Latin America and continental Africa, the highest in East Asia and the German speaking Europe. In Central and South America, for every killed woman ten men are killed, in the German speaking Europe the corresponding ratio is only 1 to 1.1 and in East Asia 1 to 1.2; in these two regions, the risk for women to die as victims of homicides is practically the same as for men (and in a few countries of the regions even higher than for men). They are, however, exceptions from a global rule: in all other sub-regions of the world, female homicide mortality level is even at its highest only about half of the male mortality level. The rate and ratio variations mean that although globally in almost all countries men have a clearly higher risk to be killed than women, the men living in the low homicide rate regions have a much lower homicide mortality risk than the women living in the high homicide mortality regions.

Victimization trends of the last sixty years. Homicide mortality has been stable neither globally nor in any of the main world regions during the post-Second World War period; and depending on region the general pattern in mortality trend has differed considerably. In 1950–2010, there were in the studied group at least four different main patterns: (1) ∩-curve (Europe, Australia, Canada, New Zealand, United States), (2) general decline (East Asia), (3) general increase (Latin America), and (4) sharp variations without a general direction (conflict ridden countries in all regions). When we disaggregated these trends by gender we could see that in all regions the pattern of male and female mortality was usually similar when regarding the main trend changes; this did, however, not mean that male and female trends would have been identical. During the whole 60 year period the female/male homicide ratio changed in a slight majority of the countries to the disadvantage of men. In the last 20 years this trend has been in the opposite direction: between 1990 and 2010 the ratio changed in most of the countries to the disadvantage of women or stayed stable. When we combined the observations on rate changes and those on ratio changes we could see that a general increase in homicide mortality rates had usually decreased the female/male ratio (i.e. male rates had increased more), and a general decrease had increased it (male rates had decreased more). There were, however, many exceptions from this rule on the country level.

Effects of socio-demographic and gender equality factors. We explored explanations for homicide mortality rate, ratio and trend differences between countries and regions by using bivariate correlations of key socio-demographic and gender equality factors on male and female homicide mortality as well as on the female/male homicide mortality ratio. The studied factors that influenced homicide levels globally seemed to be gender-neutral. High male and female homicide mortality rates as well as female/male homicide ratio correlated with same factors and in an almost equal manner. We could also detect no systematic differences between the used gender-specific and general predictors. The strongest correlations we found between social-policy indicators and gender specific factors. However, the latter correlated in an equal manner with homicides against both genders.

Lethal violence against both men and women is more common in countries with large income differences and less well-developed social welfare states. Similarly it is lower against both genders in developed democracies, but also in autocracies (probably for different reasons). Homicide rates are lower under more effective governments and in less corrupt environments. High-homicide-rate societies are characterized by stronger authoritarian and conservative moral views, more collectivist cultures, and lower long term cultural orientations. Demographic considerations—the age-structure and ethnic diversity—play much lesser roles than social-structural, political, and cultural variables. Use of capital punishment, high rates of imprisonment, and extensive use of life sentences are usually associated with high and increasing homicide rates—and not the other way around.

The two approaches. Our results actually seem to confirm some aspect of both the gender sensitive and the gender insensitive approach.

As first shown by Verkko and in more recent times by, for example, Eisner and Spierenburg, male homicide mortality largely determinates the dynamics of general homicide mortality trends—a characteristic that seems to be global and fairly permanent in human societies. The majority of lethal violence is committed (by men) against men but the criminality against men is also much more volatile than homicidal crime (by men) against women. All this is probably related to the structural and context differences between homicides against women and those against men. There may also be links to age dynamics of lethal violence and the age structure differences between perpetrators of crimes against women and crimes against men. Historical studies show that young adult men in their teens and twenties have often been the main force behind trend changes in Western lethal violence; and that the percentage of domestic violence related crimes (and female victims) is usually smaller in their homicides than in the crimes of older men (see, for example, Eisner 2008; Granath et al. 2011; Kivivuori and Lehti 2011).

In spite of these substantial structural and dynamical differences between male and female homicide mortality, it seems, however, that social, control, and economic factors have very similar effects on lethal violence regardless of the gender of victims. Perhaps a little surprisingly, also gender equality related factors seem to influence both male and female homicide mortality in a similar way. Our results do not support the view that homicides against men and women would be two totally different types of phenomena in this respect: what happens in society influences both in a similar way although this influence has usually more radical consequences for male mortality. Nor do our results support the theory that an increase in gender equality and women's participation in public life would increase their risk to die as victims of homicides (as indicated, for example, by Gartner 1990). The increase in female homicide mortality in Western societies during the post-Second World War period seems to have been connected mainly to a general increase in lethal violence, not in women's changed role in society—during the same period male homicide mortality increased even faster. Similarly the decrease in female homicide mortality in Europe and non-European English speaking industrialized countries during the last 20 years has been connected to a general decrease in lethal violence and probably not so much to any gender specific policy actions. However, increasing gender equality seems to increase the *relative* homicide victimization risk for women; this is due to the fact that gender equality seems to go along with general welfare indicators which reduce all types of lethal violence in society, and male victimization decreases then usually even faster than female victimization. Well-governed, legitimate and prosperous democracies are safe—and equal—societies.

Five Questions

1. What are the current victimization rates and how does female- and male victimization differ across regions and countries?
2. How have victimization rates evolved during the last decades in different parts of the world ?
3. Are there differences in femicide and homicide trends?
4. What explains overall differences in lethal violence?
5. What is the role of gender specific factors in explaining female victimization?

Appendix

Table 9 sources

- Males, 15–29 % (2005): UN DESA World Population Database (http://esa.un.org/unpd/wpp/unpp/p2k0data.asp)

- Urban population (% of total WB 2007): The World Bank Database (http://data.worldbank.org/indicator)
- Ethnic fractionalization (Alesina 2002): Alesina et al. (2002).
- GDP per capital PPP 2006 World Bank (2007): The World Bank Database (http://data.worldbank.org/indicator)
- HDI 2012 (UN): UNDP Human Development Reports Database (http://hdr.undp.org/en/data)
- Public Social Exp. 2002–2007, % of GDP (IMF): http://www.ilo.org/dyn/sesame/ifpses.socialdbexp
- GINI Coefficient (UNDP 2004): UNDP Human Development Reports Database (http://hdr.undp.org/en/data)
- Education (LPI): Legatum Institute Prosperity Index (http://www.prosperity.com)
- Health (LPI): Legatum Institute Prosperity Index (http://www.prosperity.com)
- Gender-related development index (GDI) http://hdr.undp.org/en/content/gender-development-index-gdi
- Gender equality index (GII) http://hdr.undp.org/en/content/gender-inequality-index-gii

Total homicide rates and male and female mean homicide mortality rates by continents and regions (victims per 100,000 total population, men and women)

Continent		Homicide			Female/ Male	Years
Sub-region	Country	2004–2012	Males	Females	Ratio	Female/ Male
Europe						
Scandinavia	Denmark	0.8	1.03	0.55	0.53	2009–2011
	Finland	2.1	2.87	1.02	0.36	2009–2011
	Iceland	0.7	0.91	0.13	0.14	2005–2009
	Norway	0.9	0.76	0.52	0.68	2009–2010, 2012
	Sweden	0.9	1.08	0.45	0.42	2010–2012
	All	*1.1*	*1.3*	*0.5*	*0.40*	
France/Benelux	Belgium	1.4	1.62	1.00	0.62	2007–2009
	France	0.7	0.88	0.48	0.55	2007–2009
	Luxembourg	1.3	2.11	0.72	0.34	2007–2011
	Monaco	2.8	1.22	1.22	1.00	2003–2012
	Netherlands	0.9	1.12	0.61	0.54	2010–2012
	All	*1.4*	*1.4*	*0.8*	*0.58*	
German speaking Europe	Austria	0.6	0.48	0.52	1.08	2010–2012
	Germany	0.7	0.57	0.53	0.93	2009–2011
	Liechtenstein	2.8	1.19	0.00	0.00	2004–2012
	Switzerland	0.7	0.59	0.57	0.97	2008–2010
	All	1.2	0.7	0.4	0.57	

(continued)

Continent		Homicide			Female/ Male	Years
Sub-region	Country	2004–2012	Males	Females	Ratio	Female/ Male
British Isles	England and Wales	1.3	0.74	0.38	0.51	2010–2012
	Guernsey (UK)	0.3	0.33	0.32	0.97	2003–2012
	Ireland	0.8	1.34	0.25	0.19	2010–2012
	Isle of Man (UK)	2.1	0.70	1.00	1.43	2003–2012
	Jersey (UK)	3.5	0.69	1.62	2.35	2004–2012
	Northern Ireland	1.6	2.53	0.69	0.27	2009–2011
	Scotland	2.0	2.24	0.58	0.26	2010–2012
	All	1.9	1.2	0.7	0.56	
Southwest Europe	Andorra	1.3	1.87	0.00	0.00	2001–2004
	Gibraltar (UK)	3.5	1.19	1.16	0.97	2007–2012
	Italy	0.9	1.23	0.44	0.36	2008–2010
	Malta	0.9	1.07	0.58	0.54	2007–2011
	Portugal	1.2	1.47	0.66	0.45	2009–2011
	Spain	0.9	1.00	0.45	0.45	2009–2011
	All	1.5	1.3	0.5	0.42	
Southeast Europe	Albania	3.3	4.05	1.14	0.28	2007–2009
	Bosnia and Herzegovina	1.6				
	Croatia	1.5	1.44	1.09	0.76	2009–2011
	Cyprus	1.4	1.78	0.71	0.40	2007–2011
	Greece	1.1	2.01	0.66	0.33	2007–2009
	Kosovo/Kos	1.1	1.99	0.35	0.18	2007–2011
	Macedonia	2.1	2.36	0.94	0.40	2009–2011
	Montenegro	2.0	3.45	1.07	0.31	2005–2009
	Northern Cyprus	2.2	4.02	1.79	0.45	2001–2010
	Serbia	2.2	2.57	1.13	0.44	2009–2011
	Slovenia	0.9	0.59	0.52	0.88	2008–2010
	Turkey	0.5	0.81	0.18	0.22	2006–2008
	All	1.7	2.3	0.9	0.38	
Baltic	Estonia	6.6	7.95	2.16	0.27	2010–2012
	Latvia	8.0	10.03	3.22	0.32	2010–2012
	Lithuania	6.7	7.63	2.68	0.35	2010–2012
	All	2.7	3.5	1.2	0.35	
Central and Eastern Europe	Bulgaria	1.9	2.37	0.88	0.37	2009–2011
	Czech Republic	0.9	0.99	0.70	0.71	2009–2011
	Hungary	1.8	1.87	1.20	0.64	2010–2012
	Poland	1.3	1.48	0.60	0.41	2009–2011
	Romania	2.4	3.03	1.47	0.49	2009–2011
	Slovakia	1.4	1.53	0.90	0.59	2008–2010
	All	1.6	1.9	1.0	0.51	

(continued)

Continent		Homicide			Female/ Male	Years
Sub-region	Country	2004–2012	Males	Females	Ratio	Female/ Male
Eastern Europe (Former Soviet Region)	Armenia	1.6	2.33	0.54	0.23	2009–2011
	Azerbaijan	1.9	3.95	0.84	0.21	2002–2004
	Belarus	7.4	9.54	3.91	0.41	2007–2009
	Georgia	1.2	1.18	0.27	0.23	2007, 2009, 2010
	Moldova	7.0	8.99	3.84	0.43	2009–2011
	Russian Federation	19.2	24.28	6.86	0.28	2008–2010
	Ukraine	7.9	9.24	3.45	0.37	2009–2011
	All	6.6	8.5	2.8	0.33	
Africa						
North Africa	Algeria	8.4				
	Egypt	0.8				
	Libya	2.9				
	Morocco	1.5				
	Sudan	26.4				
	Tunisia	1.4				
	All	6.9				
Central Africa	Angola	27.5				
	Cameroon	17.9				
	Central African Republic	29.2				
	Chad	17.4				
	Congo (Dem Repub of)	24.8				
	Gabon	15.5				
	Sao Tome e Principe	3.7				
	All	19.4				

(continued)

Continent		Homicide			Female/ Male	Years
Sub-region	Country	2004–2012	Males	Females	Ratio	Female/ Male
East Africa	Burundi	28.6				
	Comoros	10.8				
	Djibouti	3.5				
	Eritrea	16.9				
	Ethiopia	22.4				
	Kenya	4.0				
	Madagascar	9.9				
	Malawi	27.0				
	Mauritius	3.7	4.94	1.85	0.37	2009–2011
	Mayotte	1.9				
	Mozambique	14.5				
	Rodriques	4.0	3.35	2.79	0.83	2001–2011
	Reunion	2.0	2.35	1.27	0.54	2001–2009
	Rwanda	21.9				
	Seychelles	6.0	9.91	2.64	0.27	2001–2009
	Tanzania	7.8				
	Uganda	7.3				
	All	11.3	5.1	2.1	0.42	
West Africa	Benin	14.0				
	Burkina Faso	18.1				
	Cape Verde	11.9				
	Cote D'Ivoire	51.3				
	Equatorial Guinea	22.4				
	Gambia	12.2				
	Ghana	13.7				
	Guinea Bissau	18.3				
	Liberia	13.5				
	Mali	13.0				
	Mauritania	15.0				
	Niger	12.0				
	Nigeria	15.0				
	Republic of Guinea	19.9				
	Saint Helene	17.9				
	Senegal	11.5				
	Sierra Leone	24.5				
	Togo	12.3				

(continued)

Continent		Homicide			Female/ Male	Years
Sub-region	Country	2004–2012	Males	Females	Ratio	Female/ Male
South Africa	Botswana	11.7				
	Lesotho	18.1				
	Namibia	20.1				
	South Africa	36.7	18.66	2.72	0.15	2004–2009
	Swaziland	31.1				
	Zambia	30.5				
	Zimbabwe	23.6				
	All	24.5	18.7	2.7	0.15	
Americas						
North America	Bermuda (UK)	2.3	1.52	0.61	0.40	1999–2008
	Canada	1.6	2.51	0.78	0.31	2007–2009
	Greenland	14.7				
	USA	5.7	8.80	2.32	0.26	2008–2010
	All	6.1	4.3	1.2	0.29	
Central America	Belize	16.3	30.26	5.17	0.17	2005–2009
	Costa Rica	8.8	16.27	2.37	0.15	2010–2012
	El Salvador	50.5	98.52	11.17	0.11	2007–2009
	Guatemala	35.4	67.23	8.01	0.12	2007–2009
	Honduras	50.1				
	Mexico	13.6	38.62	3.91	0.10	2009–2011
	Nicaragua	9.1	15.60	1.70	0.10	2008–2010
	Panama	15.0	33.25	3.47	0.10	2007–2009
	All	24.9	42.8	5.1	0.12	
South America	Argentina	5.5	7.75	1.38	0.18	2007–2009
	Bolivia	7.2				
	Brazil	25.2	47.15	4.04	0.09	2007–2009
	Chile	5.1	8.37	1.15	0.14	2007–2009
	Colombia	41.5	97.40	8.30	0.09	2008–2010
	Ecuador	18.8	30.18	2.75	0.09	2008–2010
	French Guyane	9.1	17.00	2.00	0.12	2005–2009
	Guyana	16.5	27.15	6.21	0.23	2006–2008
	Paraguay	11.0	18.30	1.50	0.08	2007–2009
	Peru	1.7	2.75	0.51	0.19	2005–2007
	Suriname	4.3	6.14	2.17	0.35	2000–2009
	Uruguay	4.7	7.74	1.97	0.25	2007–2009
	Venezuela	30.9	60.07	3.44	0.06	2005–2007
	All	14.0	27.5	3.0	0.11	

(continued)

Continent		Homicide			Female/ Male	Years
Sub-region	Country	2004–2012	Males	Females	Ratio	Female/ Male
Caribbean	Anguila	18.6	11.97	1.71	0.14	2000–2009
	Antigua and Barbuda	4.9	5.43	1.48	0.27	2000–2009
	Aruba	5.1	5.57	1.65	0.30	2000–2009
	Bahamas	19.2	36.86	4.18	0.11	2005–2008
	Barbados	12.5	18.19	3.88	0.21	2000–2008
	Cayman	8.0	10.00	3.18	0.32	1999–2009
	Cuba	5.3	6.99	2.37	0.34	2008–2010
	Dominica	6.9	10.00	2.22	0.22	2001–2010
	Dominican Republic	20.7	45.19	4.09	0.09	2009–2011
	Grenada	1.2	0.57	0.75	1.32	2001–2010
	Guadeloupe	3.4	5.04	1.33	0.26	2004–2009
	Haiti	14.5				
	Jamaica	53.5	80.36	9.49	0.12	2010–2012
	Martinique	3.5	5.04	1.38	0.27	2004–2009
	Montserrat	21.1	12.00	0.00	0.00	2001–2010
	Puerto Rico	21.8	36.22	2.40	0.07	2005–2007
	St Lucia	12.5	26.54	9.58	0.36	1998–2008
	St Vincent and the Grenadines	18.4	26.00	6.11	0.24	2001–2010
	St. Kitts and Nevis	16.0	21.25	0.83	0.04	1999–2008
	Trinidad and Tobago	32.6	44.20	5.50	0.11	2006–2008
	Turks and Caicos	9.0	4.29	1.43	0.33	2000–2009
	Virgin Islands (UK)	13.3	5.38	3.08	0.57	1998–2009
	Virgin Islands (USA)	28.5	56.11	5.56	0.10	1998–2007
	All	15.2	21.5	3.3	0.15	
Asia						
Central Asia (Former Soviet Region)	Kazakhstan	12.4	16.26	4.24	0.26	2008–2010
	Kyrgyzstan	6.4	9.50	2.65	0.28	2008–2010
	Tajikistan	2.1	3.62	1.01	0.28	2003–2005
	Turkmenistan	11.8	9.93	1.97	0.20	1996–2098
	Uzbekistan	2.6	3.61	1.25	0.35	2003–2005
		7.1	8.6	2.2	0.26	

(continued)

Continent		Homicide			Female/ Male	Years
Sub-region	Country	2004–2012	Males	Females	Ratio	Female/ Male
Middle East	Bahrain	0.2	0.25	0.08	0.32	2000–2009
	Iran	2.0				
	Iraq	4.4				
	Israel	2.3	3.21	0.84	0.26	2008–2010
	Jordan	7.0	3.22	0.99	0.31	2008–2009
	Kuwait	2.0	0.94	0.15	0.16	2009–2011
	Lebanon	3.1				
	Palestine	3.6	5.56	0.30	0.05	2008–2009
	Qatar	0.7				
	Saudi Arabia	1.1				
	Syria	2.5				
	United Arab Emirates	0.8				
	Yemen	2.3				
	All	2.5	2.6	0.5	0.18	
Southcentral Asia	Afghanistan	3.4				
	Bangladesh	2.7				
	Bhutan	1.4				
	India	2.9				
	Maldives	0.5	0.39	0.20	0.51	2001–2011
	Nepal	3.0				
	Pakistan	6.6				
	Sri Lanka	6.2	6.08	1.18	0.19	2004–2006
	All	3.3	3.2	0.7	0.21	
East Asia	China	1.4				
	Hong Kong	0.5	0.39	0.53	1.36	2009–2011
	Japan	0.4	0.37	0.33	0.89	2009–2011
	Macau	1.6	1.28	1.52	1.19	2003–2008
	Mongolia	11.9	22.37	3.95	0.18	2006–2008
	North Korea	17.1				
	South Korea	1.5	1.41	1.16	0.82	2009–2011
	Taiwan	0.8	0.94	0.43	0.46	2009–2011
	All	35.2	26.8	7.9	0.30	

(continued)

Continent		Homicide			Female/ Male	Years
Sub-region	Country	2004–2012	Males	Females	Ratio	Female/ Male
Southeast Asia	Brunei Darussalam	3.6	3.61	1.66	0.46	2002–2009
	Cambodia	3.7				
	Indonesia	8.5				
	Laos	5.0				
	Malaysia	1.6	1.67	0.37	0.22	2006–2008
	Myanmar	1.6				
	Philippines	17.5	25.35	2.33	0.09	2008
	Singapore	0.4	0.49	0.18	0.37	2009–2011
	Thailand	5.4	8.67	1.20	0.14	2004–2006
	Timor-Leste	9.3				
	Vietnam	2.7				
	All	5.4	8.0	1.1	0.14	
Oceania						
	American Samoa	3.4				
	Australia	0.9	1.24	0.60	0.48	2009–2011
	Cook Islands	5.1				
	Fiji	3.1	2.26	3.58	1.58	2006–2008
	French Polynesia	2.1	0.98	0.49	0.50	1999–2005
	Guam	3.0				
	Kiribati	6.9	1.95	0.00	0.00	1992–2001
	Marshall Islands	1.8				
	Micronesia	0.9				
	Nauru	9.9				
	New Caledonia	2.4	8.53	1.90	0.22	1999–2002
	New Zealand	1.5	1.87	1.13	0.60	2007–2009
	Norfolk Island	55.6	10.53	10.53	1.00	2003–2012
	Palau	0.9				
	Papua New Guinea	14.2				
	Samoa	2.1				
	Solomon Islands	1.3				
	Tonga	1.0	0.49	0.00	0.00	2000–2007
	Tuvalu	9.0				
	Vanuatu	1.0				
	All	6.3	3.5	2.3	0.65	
Total		6.3	10.76	1.97	0.18	

References

Aebi, M. F., & Linde, A. (2012). Crime trends in Western Europe according to official statistics from 1990 to 2007. In J. van Dijk, A. Tseloni, & G. Farrell (Eds.), *The international crime drop: New trends in research* (pp. 37–75). New York: Palgrave Macmillan.

Alesina, A., Devleeschauwer, A., Easterly, W., Kurlat, S., &Wacziarg, R. (2002). *Fractionalization* (NBER Working Paper Series 9411). Cambridge, MA: National Bureau of Economic Research. http://www.nber.org/papers/w9411

Chon, D. S. (2013). A spurious relationship of gender equality with female homicide victimization: A cross-national analysis. *Crime & Delinquency*. First published on 12 July 2013 as doi: 10.1177/0011128713492497.

Dunstall, G. (2004). Frontier and/or cultural fragment? Interpretations of violence in colonial New Zealand. *Social History, 29*(1), 59–83.

Eisner, M. (2003). Long-term historical trend in violent crime. In: *Crime and justice: A review of research* (Vol. 30, pp. 83–142). Chicago: University of Chicago Press.

Eisner, M. (2008). Modernity strikes back? A historical perspective on the latest increase in interpersonal violence (1960–1990*). International Journal of Conflict and Violence., 2*(2), 288–316.

Ellonen, N., Kääriäinen, J., Lehti, M., & Aaltonen, M. (2014). *Trends of infanticides 1960–2009: Comparisons between 28 countries*. Unpublished manuscript, available from the NRILP.

Gartner, R. (1990). The victims of homicide: A temporal and cross-national comparison. *American Sociological Review, 55*, 92–106.

Granath, S., Hagstedt, J., Kivivuori, J., Lehti, M., Ganpat, S., Liem, M., & Nieuwbeerta, P. (2011). *Homicide in Finland, the Netherlands and Sweden. A First Study on the European Homicide Monitor Data*. The Swedish National Council for Crime Prevention Research Report 2011:15. Oikeuspoliittisen tutkimuslaitoksen tutkimuksia 259. Stockholm: Swedish National Council for Crime Prevention.

Gurr, T. R. (1981). *Historical trends in violent crime: A critical review of the evidence* (Crime and Justice Vol. 3). Chicago: The University of Chicago Press.

Gurr, T. R. (1989). *Historical trends in violent crime: Europe and the United States. Violence in America 1: The history of crime*. Newbury Park: Sage.

Höynck, T., Zähringer, U., & Behnsen, M. (2012). *Neonatizid. Expertise im Rahmen des Projekts "Anonyme Geburt und Babyklappen in Deutschland—Fallzahlen, Angebote, Kontexte"*. München: Deutsches Jugendinstitut.

Jason, J., Carpenter, M. M., & Tyler, C. W., Jr. (1983). Underrecording of infant homicide in the United States. *American Journal of Public Health, 73*(2), 195–197.

Kaufmann, D., Kraay, A., & Mastruzzi, M. (2006) *Governance matters V: Aggregate and individual governance indicators for 1996–2005* (World Bank Policy Research Working Paper No. 4012). Washington, DC: World Bank.

Kivivuori, J., & Lehti, M. (2011). Homicide in Finland and Sweden. In M. Tonry, & T. Lappi-Seppälä (Eds.), *Crime and justice in scandinavia* (Crime and Justice Vol. 40). Chicago: University of Chicago Press.

Lappi-Seppälä, T., & Lehti, M. (2015). Cross-comparative perspectives on global homicide trends. In M. Tonry (Ed.), *Why crime rates fall, and why they don't* (Crime and Justice Vol) Chicago: University of Chicago Press.

Lehti, M. (2001). Homicide trends in Finland and Estonia in 1880–1940: Consequences of the demographic, social and political effects of industrialization. *Journal of Scandinavian Studies in Criminology and Crime Prevention, 2/2001*, 50–71.

Lehti, M. (2013). *NRILP comparative homicide time series (NRILP-CHTS)* (National Research Institute of Legal Policy Research Brief 32/2013). Helsinki: National Research Institute of Legal Policy. *http://www.optula.om.fi/1368802881488*

Lindström, D. (2008). Homicide in Scandinavia: Long-term trends and their interpretations. In S. Body-Gendrot, & P. Spierenburg (Eds.), *Violence in Europe: Historical and contemporary perspectives*. New York, NY: Springer.

Marshall, I. H., & Summers, D. L. (2012). Contemporary differences in rates and trends of homicide among European nations. In M. Liem & W. Pridemore (Eds.), *Handbook of European homicide research* (pp. 39–69). New York: Springer.

McClintock, F. H. (1963). *Crimes of violence: An enquiry by the Cambridge institute of criminology into crimes of violence against the person in London* (Cambridge Studies in Criminology XVIII). London: Cambridge University Press.

Meslé, F., Shkolnikov, V. M., Hertrich, V., & Vallin, J. (1996). *Tendances récentes de la mortalité par cause en Russie 1965–1994*. Paris: INED.

Meslé, F., & Vallin, J. (2012). *Mortality and causes of death in 20th century Ukraine*. Paris: INED.

Ouimet, M. (2012). A world of homicides: The effect of economic development, income inequality, and excess infant mortality on the homicide rate for 165 countries in 2010. *Homicide Studies: An Interdisciplinary and International Journal, 16*(3), 238–258.

Sharpe, J. A. (1996). Crime in England: Long-term trends and the problem of modernization. In E. A. Johnson, & E. H. Monkkonen (Eds.), *The civilization of crime: Violence in town and country since the middle ages*. Urbana: University of Illinois Press.

Smit, P. R., de Jong, R. R., & Bijleveld, C. C. J. H. (2012). Homicide data in Europe: Definitions, sources, and statistics. In M. C. A. Liem, & W. A. Pridemore (Eds.), *Handbook of European homicide research: Patterns, explanations, and country studies* (pp. 5–24). New York: Springer.

Spierenburg, P. (2012). Long-term historical trends of homicide in Europe. In M. C. A. Liem, & W. A. Pridemore (Eds.), *Handbook of European homicide research: Patterns, explanations, and country studies* (pp. 25–38). New York: Springer.

Stamatel, J. P. (2014). Explaining variations in female homicide victimization rates across Europe. *European Journal of Criminology, 11*(5), 578–600.

Stöckl, H., Devries, K., Rotstein, A., Abrahams, N., Campbell, J., Watts, C., & Moreno, C. G. (2013). The global prevalence of intimate partner homicide: a systematic review. *Lancet, 382*, 859–865.

Trent C. L. S., & Pridemore, A. (2012). A Review of the cross-national empirical literature on social structure and homicide. In M. C. A. Liem, & W. A. Pridemore (Eds.), *Handbook of European homicide research: Patterns, explanations, and country studies* (pp. 111–136). New York: Springer.

Tursz, A., & Cook, J. M. (2011). A population-based survey of neonaticides using judicial data. *Archives of Disease in Childhood-Fetal and Neonatal Edition, 96*(4), F259–F263.

UNODC. (2011). *Global study on homicide: Trends, contexts, data*. United Nations Office on Drugs and Crime. Vienna: United Nations Office on Drugs and Crime.

UNODC. (2013). *Global study on homicide: Trends, contexts, data*. United Nations Office on Drugs and Crime. Vienna: United Nations Office on Drugs and Crime.

Verkko, V. (1931a). *Henki- ja pahoinpitelyrikollisuuden kehityssuunnan ja tason määräytymisestä I. Tilastollis metodologinen tutkimus*. Helsinki: Valtioneuvoston Kirjapaino.

Verkko, V. (1931b). *Henki- ja pahoinpitelyrikollisuuden kehityssuunnan ja tason määräytymisestä II. Tilastollis metodologinen tutkimus*. Helsinki: Valtioneuvoston Kirjapaino.

Verkko, V. (1951). *Homicides and suicides in Finland and their dependence on national character* (Scandinavian studies in sociology Vol. 3). Köbenhavn: G. E. C. Gads Forlag.

von Hofer, H. (2008). *Brott och Straff i Sverige: Historisk kriminalstatistik 1750–2005: Diagram, tabeller och kommentarer*. Stockholm: Kriminologiska Institutionen Stockholms Universitet.

von Hofer, H., & Lappi-Seppälä, T. (2014). The development of crime in light of finnish and Swedish criminal justice statistics, ca. 1750–2010. *European Journal of Criminology, 11*(2), 169–194.

Wikström, P.-O. (1992). Context-specific trends in criminal homicide in Stockholm 1951–1987. *Studies on Crime & Crime Prevention, 1/1992*, 88–105.

Yarwood, D. J. (2004). *Child homicide: Review of statistics and studies.* Dewar Research. Available at: www.dewar4research.org (retrieved in 31.10.2013).
Ylikangas, H. (1998). *The knife fighters: Violent crime in Southern Ostrobothnia 1790–1825.* (Suomen tiedeakatemian toimituksia, Humaniora 293). Helsinki: Suomen tiedeakatemia.
Zahn, M. A. (1989). Homicide in the twentieth century: Trends, types, and causes. In T. R. Gurr (Ed.), *Violence in America 1: The history of crime* (pp. 216–234). Newbury Park: Sage.
Zahn, M. A., & McCall, P. L. (1999). Homicide in the 20th-century United States: Trends and patterns. In M. D. Smith, & M. A. Zahn (Eds.), *Studying and preventing homicide: Issues and challenges.* Thousand Oaks: Sage.

Women as Victims and Perpetrators of Violence: Empirical Results from National and International Quantitative Violence Research

Monika Schröttle and Kathrin Vogt

Abstract National and international quantitative violence studies show that if women are the victims of physical, sexual and/or psychological violence, it is most often a case of domestic violence by intimate partners—in contrast to men, who are more often victims of violence in public spaces at the hands of persons known or unknown to them, particularly at a younger age, up to around 25–30. Both women and men are primarily victims of violence by male perpetrators. Women comparatively rarely act as perpetrators of severe violence.

The present chapter deals with empirical findings on the extent, causes, backgrounds and consequences of violence against women from national and international empirical research particularly focusing on domestic violence. Furthermore, findings on perpetration of intimate partner violence are critically reflected upon. This includes considerations on the research method and its implications for data interpretation and future research. The chapter shows the value and effectiveness, as well as the limitations, of violence prevalence studies, data collection and data comparison from a methodological and gender-critical perspective.

1 Introduction

National and international quantitative violence studies show that if women are the victims of physical, sexual and/or psychological violence, it is most often a case of domestic violence by intimate partners—in contrast to men, who are more often victims of violence in public spaces at the hands of persons known or unknown to

M. Schröttle (✉) • K. Vogt
Technical University of Dortmund, Dortmund, Germany
e-mail: monika.schroettle@tu-dortmund.de; kathrin.vogt@tu-dortmund.de

H. Kury et al. (eds.), *Women and Children as Victims and Offenders: Background, Prevention, Reintegration*, DOI 10.1007/978-3-319-08398-8_18

them, particularly at a younger age, up to around 25–30. Both women and men are primarily victims of violence by male perpetrators. Women comparatively rarely act as perpetrators of severe violence (see e.g. Black et al. 2011; FRA 2014; WHO 2005; Kapella et al. 2011; Schröttle and Müller 2004; Schröttle 2010; GiG-net 2008).

The present contribution deals with empirical findings on the extent, causes, backgrounds and consequences of violence against women from national and international research particularly focusing on domestic violence. Furthermore, findings on perpetration of intimate partner violence are critically reflected upon in terms of gender comparisons. This includes considerations on the research method and its implications for data interpretation and future research. The findings mainly refer to sociological and criminological violence prevalence research, which, over the past 15 years, has increasingly produced in-depth findings on the victimisation of women (and men) from quantitative data. The authors of the present chapter have been actively involved in quantitative and qualitative research and networking regarding research on violence against women in Europe for many years. They are also involved in coordinating the European Network on Gender and Violence (ENGV, see http://www.engv.org). The present chapter focuses on violence against women and gender-related research on violence as an independent research priority. The issue of violence against children is not dealt with in depth as research on the two issues is subject to different methodological and theoretical requirements. However, at this point it is relevant to underline that violence against women and violence against children within the domestic sphere often overlap or occur together in families affected by violence, and that violence between parents or by the father against the mother always also harms the children present. Therefore, domestic violence against women is always also—either directly or indirectly—a form of violence against the children living in the affected household. Moreover, violence against girls and boys shows a highly relevant gender-specific causal link with later victimisation (and perpetration)—a point that will be addressed again later within the risk factor analysis.

2 The Extent of Violence Against Women: What Do We Know from National and International Studies?

Numerous national and international violence prevalence surveys, carried out in most countries in and beyond Europe, deal with the extent of violence against women.[1] Usually, these surveys are quantitative studies on victimisation through

[1] The number of studies conducted on the prevalence of violence against women has also increased significantly in international terms over the past 10 years. A listing by UN Women shows that by the end of 2012 as many as 99 countries worldwide had conducted research on victimisation of women (cf. UN Women 2013). National and international studies on this issue have also been conducted within European research since 1990 (see e.g. Schröttle and Martinez 2006; EIGE 2012; WHO 2005; FRA 2014).

physical, sexual and/or psychological violence by intimate partners and/or other persons with regard to reported as well as unreported cases. Their methods have been developed further over the past 10 years, particularly within European violence prevalence research, in order to better uncover experiences of sexual and domestic violence, which are often linked to shame (cf. among others Schröttle and Martinez 2006; WHO 2005; FRA 2014). The high prevalence of domestic and sexual violence against women cannot be adequately depicted by crime statistics or general criminological surveys. This is due to the fact that many acts of violence are perpetrated by intimate partners. The affected persons rarely report these cases or see them in the context of crime. Several studies have proven that the level of disclosure of violence against women within police statistics as well as in criminological surveys on various offences is very low—significantly lower than in studies that are specifically designed to uncover sexual violence and domestic violence in partner relationships by using sensitive approaches (cf. Walby and Allen 2004; Wetzels and Pfeiffer 1995; Schröttle and Müller 2004).

Even though methodologically sophisticated studies on unreported cases of violence paint a significantly more realistic picture of the degree to which women are actually affected by violence than criminological and crime statistics-based data, they too will never identify the full extent of the problem as many interviewees will not talk to third persons about these intimate experiences, be it because of shame or because experiences that stressful are often repressed. A current study that was conducted in 28 European states including 42,000 women demonstrated that only about one in seven women who experienced domestic violence reported the most severe violent act to the police. Additionally, only for one case out of three any institutional support (police/court, medical care, counselling/shelters) was involved (cf. FRA 2014: p. 59). The Fig. 1 by Kapella et al. (2011) illustrates the high number of unreported cases of experiences of violence in terms of violence of which institutions are aware and unreported cases uncovered by violence prevalence studies.

Over the past few years, significant international prevalence studies on violence against women have been carried out by the European Union Agency for

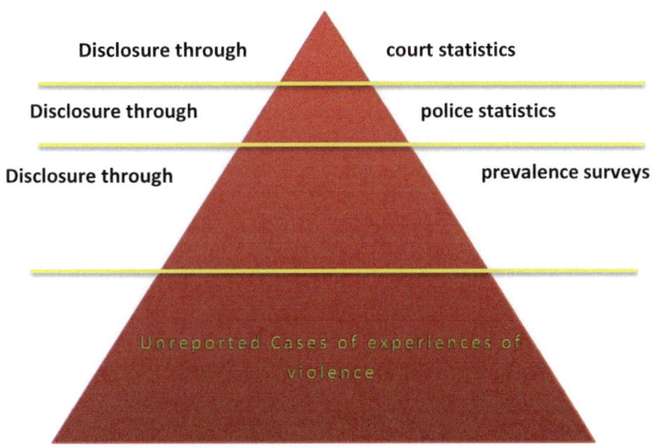

Fig. 1 Unreported cases of experiences of violence (*source*: Kapella et al. 2011: p. 40)

Fundamental Rights (FRA) and the World Health Organization (WHO). The study conducted by FRA is a survey of more than 42,000 women aged 18–74 from 28 EU member states. The WHO study, however, compiles the statements of more than 24,000 women from ten participant countries from all over the world (WHO 2005). Both studies refer to physical, sexual and psychological violence against women at the hands of their partners, as well as other persons known and unknown to them. Trained female interviewers conducted the interviews with the participants face-to-face; they had to be conducted alone, without anyone else present. Within both the European FRA study and the WHO study, the interview was accompanied by an additional written questionnaire for the participants to complete themselves. This questionnaire aimed to allow the women to answer highly sensitive and intimate questions (for example on sexual violence during childhood or on violence committed by their partner) independently, without having to talk about their experiences directly to a third person. Research shows that this and other methods can considerably increase disclosure of violence (Schröttle and Müller 2004; Walby and Allen 2004). In the National Intimate Partner and Sexual Violence Survey in the US, more than 16,000 people (men and women aged over 18) were interviewed over the telephone. Some European researchers doubt that studies conducted over the telephone or in households by postal questionnaires lead to a high level of discovery of unreported cases, as there is always the risk that—especially in control situations that are typical for abusive situations—other people could be present in the household, including the perpetrator of domestic violence (Martinez and Schröttle 2007). This can impede women from speaking about their experiences of violence. For this reason it can be assumed that telephone surveys come along with higher numbers of unreported cases of violence.

The results of the aforementioned studies show that a high number of women are affected by violence, especially by intimate partner violence. Furthermore the levels of identified prevalence differ considerably across the individual countries: within the European FRA study, an average of 33 % of the women interviewed reported having experienced physical and/or sexual violence since turning 15; data between the countries varied between 19 and 52 % (FRA 2014: pp. 28–29). Physical and/or sexual violence at the hands of current and/or former partners experienced an average of 22 % of the women, here data varied between 13 and 32 % (FRA 2014: pp. 28–29) (Fig. 2). The worldwide survey by the WHO cites numbers of intimate partner violence against women between 15 and 71 % (with an average number of 30 %) (WHO 2005: p. 27; WHO executive summary 2005: p. 1). Of the American women, 36 % stated that they had experienced rape, physical violence and/or stalking by an intimate partner (Black et al. 2011: p. 39). Taking mean values, it can be assumed that worldwide at least one in four up to one in three women were affected by physical and/or sexual violence at the hands of their partner and that these rates are significantly higher in some African and South American countries.

Psychological forms of violence committed by current or former partners can include very different acts. They can range from verbal insults and humiliation, to

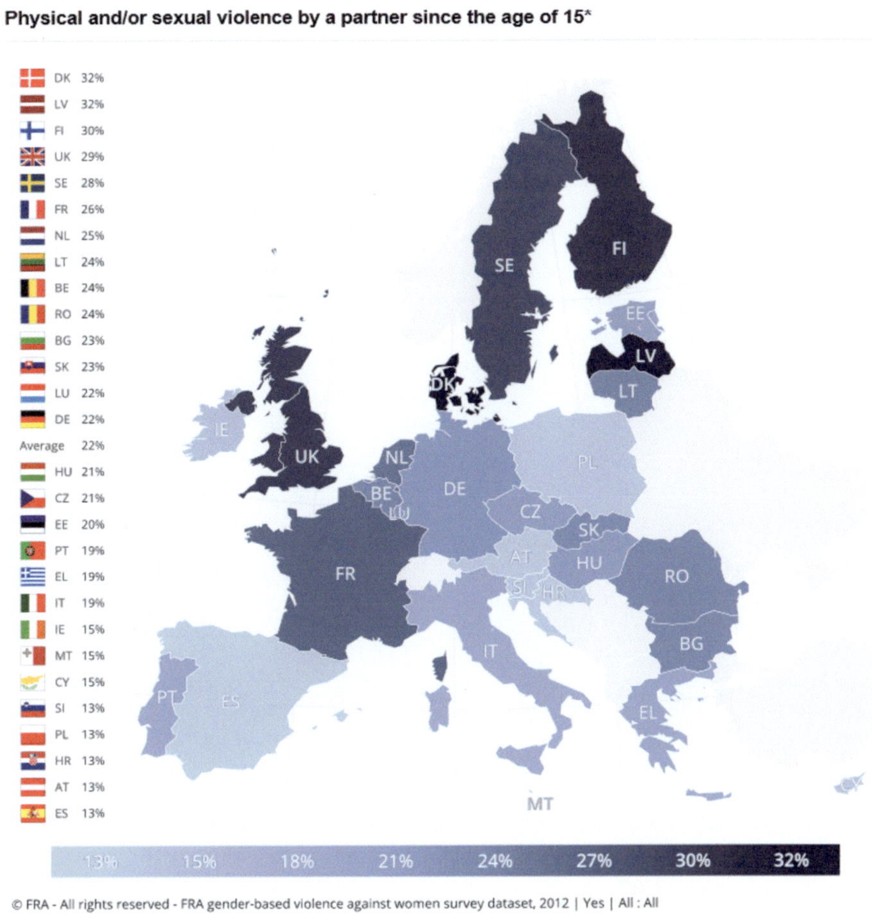

Fig. 2 a–c: Prevalence of violence against women in EU-member-states. *Source*: FRA 2014 (http://fra.europa.eu/DVS/DVT/vaw.php)

threats and to extreme jealousy and control. In the European FRA study, between 31 and 60 % of the women reported having been affected by psychological partner violence (43 % on average) (FRA 2014: pp. 73–74); the WHO identified figures of between 20 and 75 % of women who ever experienced emotionally abusive acts by a former or current partner, depending on the country (WHO 2005: p. 34). Experiences of controlling behaviour by an intimate partner were presented separately in this study. The rate of women reporting these experiences varied from 21 % to almost 90 %, again depending on the country (WHO 2005: p. 36). Finally, 48 % of the American women reported in the US-study having experienced psychological violence at the hands of a partner (Black et al. 2011: p. 45). Based on mean values, worldwide every second to third woman has experienced psychological violence committed by a current and/or former intimate partner.

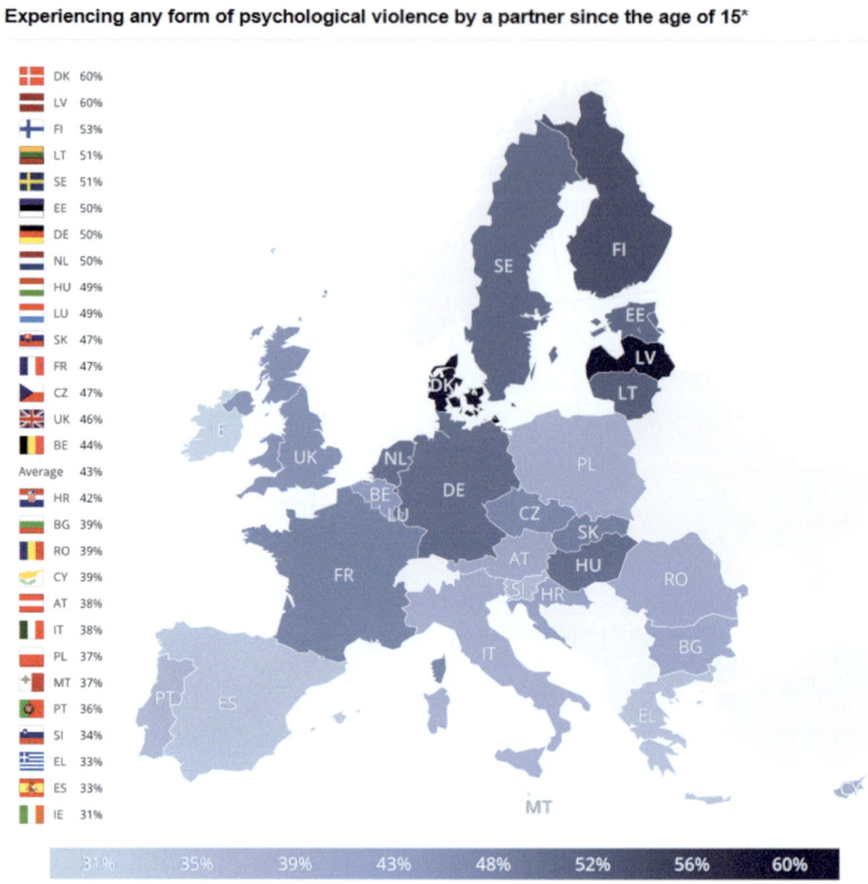

Fig. 2 (continued)

Experiences of sexual violence at the hands of their partner were reported by 6–59 % of the women surveyed in the WHO study (WHO 2005: 27); in the European study, this was reported by 3–11 % of the women (EU average: 7 %) (FRA data explorer 2014). The US study found that 9 % of the interviewed women had been raped by an intimate partner in her lifetime (Black et al. 2011: p. 39).

The number of women who experienced sexual violence by non-partners since the age of 15 varied in the WHO study as well as in the European FRA-study from 1 to 12 % (WHO 2005: p. 44; FRA data explorer 2014; EU average: 6 %). In the US study results for sexual violence are presented in a more differentiated manner. Here 18 % of the women had experienced rape[2] during their lifetime; forms of

[2] Includes completed forced penetration, attempted forced penetration, completed alcohol/drug facilitated penetration.

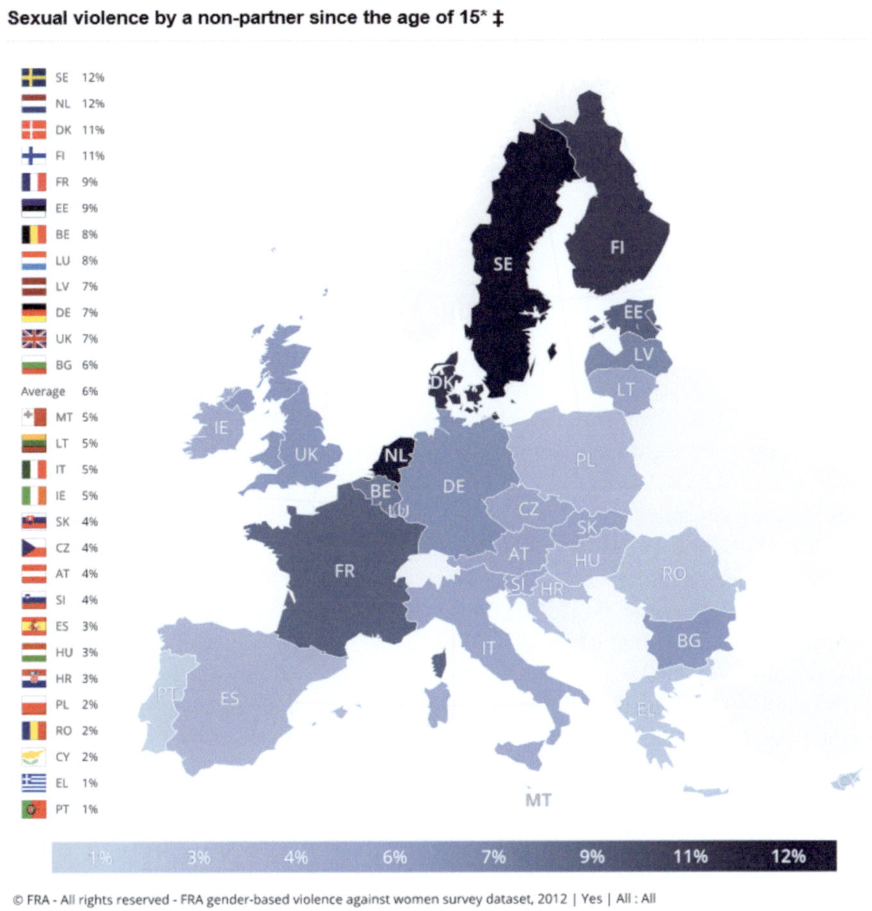

Fig. 2 (continued)

sexual violence other than rape[3] were experienced by 45 % of the women who participated in the interviews (Black et al. 2011: pp. 18–19).

Overall, the results show that high levels of violence against women are present in all countries, including in the Western industrialised nations. Country-specific differences appear to be relevant, but have to be interpreted with care, because both the reporting behaviour of women and the concrete method and conduct of the studies can differ significantly—a fact that can strongly influence the identified levels of prevalence of violence. Due to these facts the data may not necessarily reflect the actual differences of the extent of violence between countries (see for the

[3] Includes made to penetrate, sexual coercion, unwanted sexual contact, non-contact unwanted sexual experiences.

interpretation of prevalence data between countries e.g. Schröttle and Martinez 2006; FRA 2014). Cultural differences between women regarding social, national and ethnical backgrounds can affect the way women talk about their experiences of violence to third persons. Moreover the quality of the training of the interviewers as well as the exclusion of third persons from the interviews can have immense effects on disclosing violence in interviews.

3 Violence Against Women and Health-Related Consequences

Numerous studies from violence and health research show that violence against women may have significant short- and long-term consequences in terms of their health (Arias 2004; Campbell 2002; Campbell et al. 2002; Garcia-Moreno et al. 2005; McCauley et al. 1997; Porcerelli et al. 2003; Roberts et al. 1998; Schröttle and Khelaifat 2008; FRA 2014; WHO 2005; overview on national and international research: Schröttle and Martinez 2006; Schröttle et al. 2008; WHO 2013). According to the World Health Organization (WHO), violence, especially domestic violence, is one of the main health risks for women and children worldwide (Krug et al. 2002).

Research on the health consequences of violence distinguishes between short, medium and long-term health effects. Immediate effects arise from the acute consequences of injuries as well as from psychological and psychosocial problems suffered as a direct result of the violence, for example feeling anxious or threatened, psychological stress, difficulty concentrating, difficulties at work or in studies, increased alcohol or medicine consumption. Moreover, research has described somatic, psychosomatic and psychological impairments as medium and long-term health-related consequences of physical, sexual and psychological violence (on research methods regarding health-related effects within violence prevalence and health research, cf. Martinez and Schröttle 2006, 2007; GiG-net 2008; Schröttle et al. 2008).

According to present surveys, about one half up to two thirds of European women who have experienced violence at the hands of their partner report that this violence resulted in physical injuries (cf. Schröttle and Martinez 2006; FRA 2014). In these surveys, violence against women in intimate partner relationships is linked to physical injuries more often than violence committed by unknown or other persons.

Regarding somatic and psychosomatic complaints resulting from violence against women and children in close relationships, national and international research results point to different aches and pains, gastrointestinal issues, heart and circulatory problems, gynaecological and cerebral problems as well as dermatological issues (cf. among others Brzank et al. 2004; Campbell et al. 2002; Coid et al. 2003; Coker et al. 2000; Felitti 1991; Garcia-Moreno et al. 2005; Golding

1994, 1996; Kimerling and Calhoun 1994; Leserman et al. 1996; McCauley et al. 1995, 1997; Porcerelli et al. 2003; Roberts et al. 1998; Schröttle and Müller 2004; Thompson et al. 2004; Walker et al. 1993). According to a large representative study in the US, the probability of gynaecological problems was considerably higher in the case of abused women than in the control group (McCauley et al. 1995). A secondary data analysis of the representative German study on violence against women (Schröttle and Khelaifat 2008) also documents a highly significant relation between interviewees having experienced violence during their life and their health situation. Women who had been exposed to physical, sexual or psychological violence since the age of 16 evaluated their medical condition more negatively than those who had not been affected. Furthermore, they reported considerably more health complaints such as headache, abdominal pain, stomach and intestinal problems, shaking, nervousness, dizziness, breathing problems and pain in the uterine region. An increased impact on health was discovered when cumulative experiences of violence were reported (for example abuse during childhood and partner violence later on).

According to results of international research, the psychological problems resulting from violence against women are also significant: in particular, participants mentioned depression, stress symptoms, sleep disorders, difficulty concentrating, low self-esteem, anxiety disorders, *posttraumatic stress disorders (PTSD),* eating disorders and suicidal tendencies (cf. among others Bergman and Brismar 1991; Brzank et al. 2004; Campbell et al. 1997, 1995; Campbell 2002; Coid et al. 2003; Danielson et al. 1998; Felitti 1991; Follette et al. 1996; FRA 2014; Gelles and Harrop 1989; Golding 1996; Houskamp and Foy 1991; Kaslow et al. 2002; Krug et al. 2002; McCauley et al. 1995; Porcerelli et al. 2003; Roberts et al. 1998; Schröttle and Müller 2004; WHO 2013).

All results of national and international research indicate significant health-related consequences, and also high costs, caused by the consequences of violence against women and children. These high costs for individuals as well as for society as a whole are especially marked in the case of continued violence, which occurs more often in family and partner relationships.

4 Causes and Risk Factors of Violence Against Women

Unequal gender relationships and discrimination against women are, of course, the central societal background in which violence against women by men takes place. Research also shows that some women are more vulnerable to, or at a higher risk of being victimised than others. There is high interest in research and in practice in identifying risk and protective factors. Several prevalence studies have collected relevant information about this subject, but limited resources have often not permitted multidimensional analyses of factors that are likely to increase or reduce the risk of violence against women and the risk of staying in violent situations or relationships (Schröttle and Martinez 2006: p. 29).

The following factors are predominantly discussed within research:

- Age
- Educational status and socioeconomic resources
- Migration and ethnicity
- Disabilities
- Social isolation
- Alcohol
- Experiences of childhood violence
- Pregnancy
- Divorce and separation
- Power relations between genders.

This chapter can only give a short overview of the most relevant risk factors for violence against women that were found in research.

All studies show that violence during childhood and adolescence dramatically increases the risk of women being victimised during adulthood (ibid.). For example, the German violence prevalence study showed that women who had been victims of parental physical and psychological violence or sexual abuse during childhood and adolescence became victims of intimate partner violence during adulthood twice to four times as often as women who had not been affected by violence during their childhood and adolescence (cf. Schröttle and Müller 2004). The European FRA study (2014) and other European Studies (cf. Schröttle and Martinez 2006) found a strong relationship between experiences of violence during childhood and later life as well. One third of the women who reported physical violence by a current or previous intimate partner also indicated multiple incidents in childhood (FRA 2014: p. 132). In Fig. 3 experiences of physical and/or sexual violence before and since the age of 15 and their correlations are presented.

Early violations of boundaries during childhood and adolescence harm the women's ability to defend themselves against perpetrators as an adult, and/or to distance themselves from violent intimate partners. Perpetrators may specifically pick victims who are or have been impaired in this respect.

Certain living situations or phases in partner relationships also pose an elevated risk of women becoming victims of violence committed by their partner. Examples include starting a family and pregnancy, difficult financial situations, power imbalances in the relationship (and changes to the women's advantage), alcoholism in one or both partner(s), the intention to separate as well as social isolation, which is often also a consequence of violent relationships (Schröttle and Ansorge 2008; Schröttle and Martinez 2006; WHO 2005; FRA 2014: pp. 35 et seqq.). According to national and international violence prevalence studies, women up to their mid-forties—in some studies up to 59 (FRA 2014: p. 35)—are most often affected by intimate partner violence; sexual violence and other forms of violence by non-partners are most often experienced by younger women up to their mid-thirties (ibid.).

In terms of constellations of power in partner relationships, it can be seen that extreme power imbalances to the women's disadvantage, as found in more

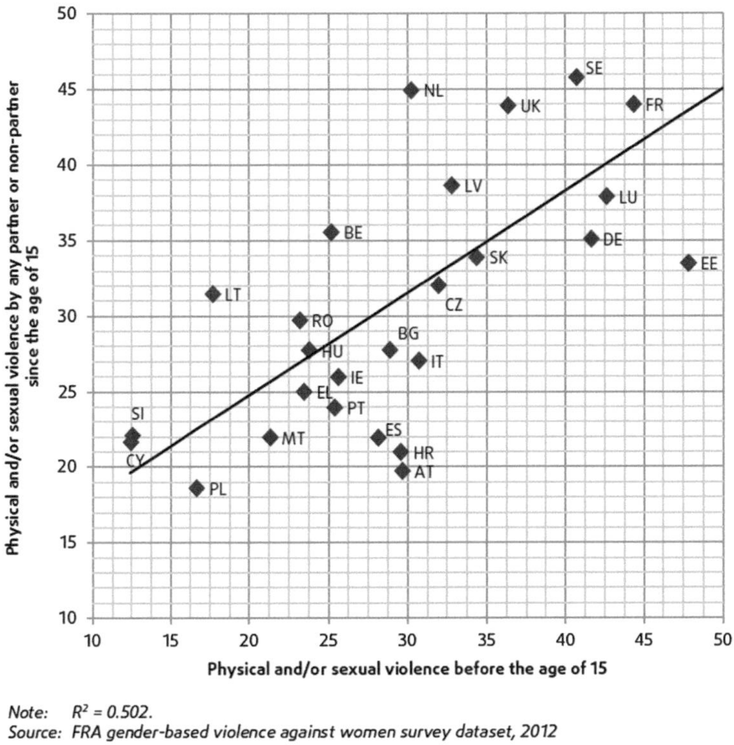

Fig. 3 Physical and/or sexual violence before the age of 15 and since the age of 15 (%). *Source*: FRA gender-based violence against women survey dataset, 2012 (see FRA 2014: p. 133)

traditional and conservative partner relationships, as well as changes and challenges to such power relationships (when the woman gains more independence within the partner relationship due to a high or improving educational, occupational and social status, for instance) can increase the risk of violence being committed by men in partner relationships, or the intensity of violence. The same is true for separation or divorce situations. Women in studies that experienced one or more separations also were exposed to violence in partner relationships considerably more often (ibid.). Thus, a high proportion of the women who had separated themselves from their partner relationships had experienced violence and stalking by partners (ibid.).

As national and international prevalence surveys show in general, the practice of intimate partner violence does not follow a social hierarchy and all social and educational groups can experience violence (Schröttle and Martinez 2006: p. 30). Some studies found that persons that are socially and economically deprived or marginalized are partly at greater risk of not being able to stop or leave violent situations and violent partners, and thus experience higher rates or more intense levels of intimate partner violence. This is partly the case for women from ethnic minority groups, as studies in several countries show (see Thiara et al. 2011) and for women in poor and very traditional societies (see e.g. Panda and Agarwal 2005, Panda et al. 2006, Amaral 2014). Other studies, especially in European countries, found weak or no links between socioeconomic situations, unemployment, alcohol use, low levels of education and intimate partner violence. "The German, Swedish and to some extent also the Finnish study found that the social and cultural spread of violence challenges the notion that the perpetrators predominantly belong to socially disadvantaged or ethnic minority groups. Many well educated, non-alcoholic and employed men exercise intimate partner violence." (Schröttle and Martinez 2006: p. 30). In the German prevalence study higher educated and financially better off women who were older than 45 had reported higher rates of severe violence through current intimate partners than other women (Schröttle and Ansorge 2008).

The European FRA study additionally found gaining more gender equality by means of challenging traditional gender roles by e.g. going out at night to socialise or being in work was found to be a risk factor for intimate partner violence against women as well. Furthermore, employment situations could be risk factors for non-partner violence. Here it was found that the risk to experience sexual harassment was increased for women in higher management positions (cf. FRA 2014: p. 26). The results indicate that violence against women might also function as an instrument to weaken and sanction women who are leaving old, traditional gender roles and relationships.

In some studies the influence of alcohol consumption by perpetrators was confirmed, especially for serious forms of violence, but a high proportion of intimate partner violence was not connected with alcohol abuse on the part of perpetrators (and victims) at all (Schröttle and Martinez 2006; Schröttle and Ansorge 2008). The European FRA survey found high correlations between alcohol consumption by the perpetrator and intimate partner violence (FRA 2014: p. 38).

One of the most vulnerable groups of women with respect to victimisation through violence are disabled women. A current German representative study with 1560 women with disabilities living in households and residential institutions showed that disabled women were affected by violence two to four times more often than women of the average population (see Schröttle et al. 2013; Schröttle and Glammeier 2013). Overall, 25–45 % of women with disabilities (depending on the forms of disability and the current living situation) had experienced intimate partner violence, which is two to five times the rate of the general population. Sexual violence in adult life was reported by 21–43 % of disabled women (depending on the specific group). They were hence affected by sexual violence in adult life roughly two to three times more frequently than the average female population (13 %). Deaf women (43 %) and women with mental disorders (38 %) were worst affected by violence (ibid.).

The study reveals the connection between violence and health impairments/ disabilities in women's lives. Disabled women are not only at a greater risk of being confronted with violence, but also (previous) experiences of violence in the women's lives frequently contribute to health and mental impairments as well as to disabilities later on.[4] A large percentage of the respondents—including those whose disabilities had not occurred until adult life—had already been subjected to a considerable level of violence by parents and other persons during childhood and adolescence. Depending on the investigation group, they were between twice and three times more likely to have been subject to sexual abuse during childhood and adolescence. For many women with disabilities, multiple experiences of violence during childhood that often continue in their adult lives, together with experiences of discrimination in society and specific dependencies, weaken their self-esteem and the ability to set boundaries and defend themselves against violence. Furthermore, they often do not receive shelter and support in and after situations of violence, often because of the lack of accessibility to supporting institutions.[5]

5 Women as Perpetrators and the Theory of Gender Symmetry in Violence Within Partner Relationships

According to present knowledge, women are relatively rarely the perpetrators of severe physical and/or sexual violence, both within and outside of partner relationships. This is shown both by criminological statistics on crimes of violence (with respect to lethal violence) as well as by violence prevalence studies that have asked both women and men about severe violence suffered at the hands of their partner or other perpetrators (GiG-net 2008; Kapella et al. 2011; Watson and Parsons 2005). Where women are found to have committed violence, this is most often in the context of child abuse and child neglect (and of care of elderly family members) (cf. Cicchetti and Carlson 1989; Godenzi 1996; Rabold and Goergen 2013).

The theory of gender symmetry in violence within partner relationships has been periodically cited in populist and anti-feminist discourse since the 1980s. It claims that women and men are victims (and perpetrators) of violence in heterosexual partner relationships in equal measure. Proponents argue that the fact that women and men are equally affected by violence at the hands of their partner had been proven in numerous studies,[6] and that addressing and trying to prevent violence against women and developing corresponding support structures for women affected by violence should therefore be seen as one-sided. The theory of gender symmetry in violence within partner relationships that was discussed relatively objectively in American family violence research in the 1980s, and has since been

[4] This has already been documented by large numbers of national and international studies documenting the connection between health and violence in women's lives. See for an overview: Schröttle et al. (2008).

[5] See also http://women-disabilities-violence.humanrights.at/.

[6] Reference is most commonly made to Archer (2000); for criticism thereof, cf. Gloor and Meier (2003) and Kimmel (2002).

modified by its proponent Murray Strauss, is now periodically referred to in the Anglo-American and European environment whenever new findings from research on high levels of women being affected by violence are presented and/or further socio-political or legal projects in the field of prevention of violence against women are introduced. The gender-symmetry-theory is half true and half false: many empirical studies dealing with conflict behaviours within heterosexual partner relationships show indeed that women and men have experienced and committed physical and/or psychological aggressive behaviours in conflicts within partnerships more or less at the same rate; however, there is a considerable difference between the forms, severity, contexts and consequences of the violence experienced and committed by men and women in partner relationships, meaning that it is necessary to think about different *qualities of violence*. A one-off yell or angry push or a one-off one-sided or reciprocal slap in the face cannot be compared to systematic, chronic and severe violence with the aim of intimidation and control, which women experience considerably more often within partner relationships than men. Both national and international surveys on unreported cases and statistics on deaths point to a considerably higher risk of women experiencing severe, threatening and life-endangering violence in heterosexual relationships worldwide than men (cf. Schröttle 2010; Kapella et al. 2011; Watson and Parsons 2005).

This is also shown in the following graphic from a national study on the prevalence of violence in Ireland (Watson and Parsons 2005), focusing on physical and psychological/emotional violence and the link between different forms of violence in partner relationships. As one of very few gender comparative studies this survey differentiated severe and minor severe abuse in intimate partnerships.

According to the study, women experienced severe forms of physical violence at the hands of their partner twice as often as men (9 % vs. 4 %), and were affected by sexual violence committed by their partner eight times more often than men (8 % vs. 1 %, see Fig. 4). The psychological/emotional violence experienced by women was also more severe than the psychological violence experienced by men (cf. Watson and Parsons 2005). If psychological violence is included in the analysis of physical and sexual violence, then, according to the Irish violence prevalence study, around the same proportions of men and women have experienced some form of physical, sexual or psychological attack by their partner (all forms together, 26 % vs. 29 %). However, at 15 %, the proportion of women affected by forms of severe abuse by their partner was two to three times higher for women than for men (6 %; cf. ibid.). The Austrian prevalence survey found similar results concerning gender differences in levels of violence experienced (cf. Kapella et al. 2011).

In terms of women as perpetrators of violence in partner relationships, previous studies have shown that, in comparisons between the sexes, women more frequently commit reactive violence, and that their acts of violence were often in resistance and reaction to physical and/or sexual violence previously committed by their partner (see next paragraph)—which cannot be sufficiently illustrated in the quantitative data from the family violence studies or other violence prevalence studies.

Michael P. Johnson, an American researcher, distinguishes in his analysis of different surveys about violence in intimate partnerships between different patterns

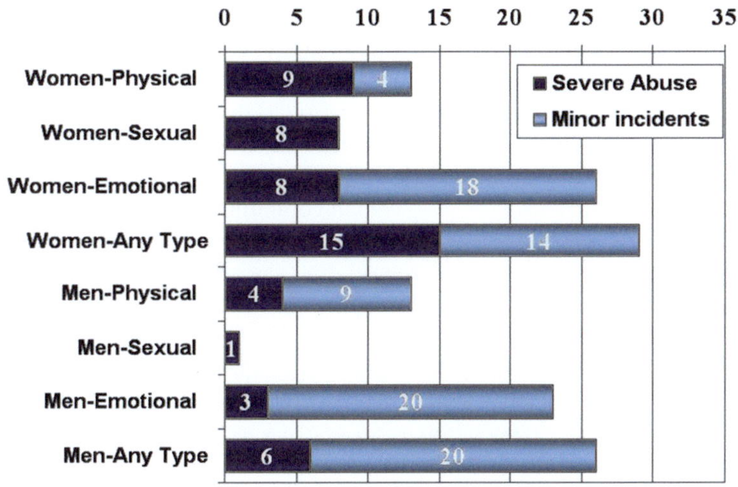

Fig. 4 Lifetime prevalence of severe abuse and minor incidents of different types for women and men (n = 3000). Figure from the presentation "focused approach to domestic violence" by Dorothy Watson; this lecture was held in June 2006 in Valencia, as part of the Crosscutting Workshop of the CAHRV (Coordination Action on Human Rights Violation, cf. www.cahrv.uni-osnabrueck.de) project. Study documentation: Watson and Parsons 2005

of domestic violence, which take into account not only the level of severity of violence, but also the exercise of power and control in partner relationships (cf. Johnson 1995, 2006). According to his analysis, which includes both quantitative data and qualitative studies from the Anglo-American environment, some forms of violence in heterosexual partner relationships are committed reciprocally as a result of concrete confrontations, and generally represent less serious physical attacks; this pattern, which can affect both women and men in equal measure, was described by Johnson—with a somewhat belittling effect in semantic terms—as "common couple violence", and by Gloor and Meier (2003) as a pattern of "violence as spontaneous conflict behaviour". According to Johnson's analysis, other patterns of systematic violence, which cover severe acts of violence and often additional psychological violence and aim to control the partner, were committed less often by women and more often by men.

This includes the pattern of abuse in partner relationships described by Johnson as "intimate partner terrorism" and by Gloor and Meier as "systematic control and violent behaviour". In addition, Johnson described another pattern whereby both partners reciprocally exercise control over the other using violent means, and finally a pattern of "violent resistance", whereby one partner—normally the woman—retaliates after years of abuse by the other partner, sometimes seriously injuring him. Even though they certainly need to be differentiated further in a gender-specific way and for different societies or population groups in empirical research, such patterns of violence in partner relationships are important in order to be able to interpret men's and women's experiences of violence in heterosexual relationships through comparison, and to be able to put them into context.

British violence and gender researcher Marianne Hester investigated cases of one-sided and two-sided partner violence known to the police and found not only that men committed a higher number of violent acts against women and that their acts of violence were more severe, but also that this violence showed stronger patterns of threat and control. Where women committed violence, it was a case of either violence that was not seen as frightening by their partner, or severe violence (including involving weapons), which was often a reaction to previous threats and mistreatment by their partner. In cases of two-sided violence, male partners committed more often and more severe violent acts than their female partners. One-sided severe violence by women against men that was embedded in patterns of fear and control was virtually not found in the study (cf. Hester 2009). Further quantitative studies on victimisation of all genders are required in order to better understand such patterns of one-sided and two-sided violence in heterosexual (as well as homosexual and other) partner relationships in terms of their significance for violence and power structures and for gender relations; furthermore the relevance of other social inequalities in the perpetration and victimisation of violence should be investigated in greater detail.

6 Methodological Requirements for Future Comparable Research on Women (and Men) as Perpetrators and Victims of Violence

The following reflections are primarily based on the authors' research experience from over 15 years of involvement in national and international research into the prevalence of violence, and on extensive methodology discussions within the scope of national and international, and particularly European, research networks on gender-critical violence research (cf. among others the work of the European Coordination Action on Human Rights Violations: www.cahrv.uni-osnabrueck.de, the European Network on Gender and Violence: www.engv.org and the EU Cost-Action on Femicide: www.femicide.net).

The following reflections aim to describe central aspects that need to be taken into account in designing and implementing violence prevalence studies in the field of research on violence against women (and men). On the one hand, they serve to ensure quality and compliance with ethical research requirements, and on the other, they help to avoid classic errors and misinterpretations, which often occur in research in this sensitive topic area.

6.1 *Random Sample Concept and Inclusion of Marginalized Groups*

Particularly in violence prevalence studies, the random sample concepts and methods for finding interviewees that are used must be such to allow to include in the survey target groups that are difficult to reach or difficult to survey. As shown by previous studies, these groups are often highly affected or threatened by violence. These include both persons living in isolation and those in control and dependency situations (for example, within institutions and situations of care, or in situations of extreme domestic violence and control). Furthermore, it is important to include groups of people who are often excluded from population-wide surveys due to a limited ability to communicate in the surveys language, such as ethnic minority groups or those with communicative disabilities, such as the Deaf. If the set-up and method of the study are such that these target groups are not, or are not sufficiently, reached, systematic distortion of the random sample can lead to underestimate the actual extent of violence. Furthermore, the increased rate and level of violence within certain population groups cannot be sufficiently identified. Surveys by post and by telephone, which are often used in criminological studies, also pose a problem in the context of recording domestic violence. It cannot be assumed that victims of extreme domestic violence and control, as well as of violence within institutions, will be able to report their experiences of victimisation truthfully or without fear in surveys by post or telephone as the perpetrator might be present.

Another important aspect of the random sample concept is the fact that a relatively high total number of samples is required in order to be able to present differentiated statements regarding the extent of violence and people affected by violence within different population groups. This is necessary because certain forms of violence only appear in a small percentage of the population (at certain periods). For example, the prevalence of sexual violence against women recorded in studies occupies few percentage points over a 1-year period. This means that if there are not high enough samples the number of cases of affected persons is too low to form a basis for assertions that can be generalised and allow more in-depth (time-, gender-, region-) comparative analyses. In addition, groups of affected persons that are at particular risk (such as persons with a migrant background, persons with disabilities and those living within institutions or on the street) also only represent a small proportion of the total population, and are generally not well represented in representative samples. In this case, it is important to use additional random samples that specifically target these groups with easy-access methods, in order to increase the relevant base of cases (cf. also the implementation in Schröttle and Müller 2004 and Schröttle et al. 2013, as well as the methodological explanations in Thiara et al. 2011).

6.2 Further Development of Recording Tools for Comparative Analyses on Violence

Validated questions and questionnaires on violence and victimisation, and in particular on violence against women, are abundantly available from international, national and regional, as well as institution-related research, and have been used many times in Anglo-American, European and other countries (in the overview of European studies, cf. Martinez and Schröttle 2006; and in the updated overview, cf. EIGE 2013, pp. 9 et seqq.; WAVE 2012). As violence and violence prevalence research constantly developing and learning from previous studies, the recording tools can be used as templates and adapted to suit the relevant aims of the study.

However, there are several methodological requirements and standards that essentially need to be observed and that have proven useful within the scope of prevalence research on violence against women and domestic violence, in order to allow violence to be uncovered and described in a differentiated manner (for methodological discussions and standards, cf. among others Schröttle and Martinez 2006; Martinez and Schröttle 2007). For example, elaborate prevalence studies never explicitly ask whether "violence" has been experienced, as the term "violence" is defined, perceived and mentioned in very different ways by different individuals. In particular, violence in the intimate social environment and close social relationships is often normalised or not classified as violence or an offence, and is not reported to third parties. Therefore, in order to be able to comparatively record and better uncover different forms and dimensions of violence, item lists with concrete, neutrally formulated acts (example: "Were you hit? Kicked? Slapped?" etc.) are normally used.

Research on violence against women (and men) in national violence prevalence studies has thus far used either lists of acts in what are known as "conflict tactic scales" (sometimes in modified form), or independent item lists from violence against women research, for example on violence within intimate partner relationships or sexual violence, or a mixture of the two (Schröttle 2010). The *conflict tactics scales* (CTS) were developed as part of US family violence research in the 1970s, and have since been modified several times (cf. Straus 1990; Straus et al. 1996). Alongside verbal aggression and peaceful models of conflict solution, they cover a wide range of violent physical (and, in later versions, sexual) attacks in partner relationships. The CTS have been widely criticised for focusing, in a gender-neutral way, on violent acts within *couple conflicts*, but insufficiently recording severe systematic abuse, which is often exercised one-sidedly and without previous disputes or conflict situations by men against women (which the researchers that developed the scales subsequently even admit themselves, Straus cited by Godenzi 1996: pp. 164 et seqq.; for criticism on the CTS, cf. Gloor and Meier 2003 and Schröttle 2010). However, the acts contained in the CTS themselves are formulated neutrally, and have been used many times, in a slightly modified form, in violence against women (VAW) surveys as well (for an overview, see: Schröttle and Martinez 2006). Nevertheless, it is important—and herein lies the strength of the VAW surveys—to look into the severity, consequences, contexts and dynamics of violence based on further additional questions. Alongside consequent injuries, this includes recording the threat, frequency and (long-term) psychological and psycho-social consequences of acts of violence, and integrating violence into contexts of control and abuse of power in relationships. Furthermore, it is important to investigate the question of whether one-sided or reciprocal violence was committed, and whether violent attacks occurred at the person's own initiative or as resistance. If this is omitted, then different qualities of violence, dynamics and contextual integration into control and power relationships remain invisible, particularly in the case of gender comparison-based studies and analyses (cf. Schröttle 2010; Gloor and Meier 2003).

Empirical research on sexual violence represents a particular difficulty, on the one hand because it is an extremely sensitive topic that concerns people's private sphere and can be associated with painful, taboo or even traumatic memories, and on the other hand because sexual violence is often not perceived or reported as such, particularly in the case of sexual violence at the hands of an intimate partner or other close person (father, relative). When formulating questions within prevalence studies, it is especially important to strike a balance between questions that cover the acts that were experienced in the most concrete and neutral manner possible and that, at the same time, are sensitive and do not lead the participant to remember situations of sexual violence in too much detail, as there is a risk of retraumatisation. Here, the interviewers must be well trained and explicitly inform the interviewees that they do not have to answer, or can easily skip, certain questions if they so wish.

Another methodologically relevant aspect in the recording of violence within the scope of violence prevalence studies is the recording period. A distinction is generally made between violence during childhood/adolescence and violence during adulthood (from the age of 15, 16 or 18). In most cases, questions are also asked about violence over the last 3 or 5 years and over the last 12 months, in order to differentiate current acts from acts further in the past, and also in order to be able to make age group-specific comparisons in terms of current levels of people affected. However, as the 12-month period frequently used in criminological studies often only reveals low rates of people being affected, and therefore leads to numbers of cases that are too low for meaningful results and comparative analyses, it is advisable to choose larger time frames of 3 or 5 years (possibly as an addition). This also seems logical in light of the fact that for violence within family and partner relationships, as well as for other forms of continued violence within the intimate social environment (bullying, stalking), recording of prolonged violence is highly relevant as regards estimating the severity, quality and consequences of violence.

6.3 Gender Comparison-Based Victimisation Studies

Although worldwide there are several criminological and sociological studies in which men are (also) surveyed on their experiences of victimisation through violence (cf. for example Kapella et al. 2011; Heiskanen and Ruuskanen 2011; Watson and Parsons 2005, to name the more recent studies), well-founded research on violence against men and gender comparison-based violence and victimisation are still in their infancy, particularly because central challenges have still not been solved.

One problem is that reporting on experiences of victimisation can be associated with different taboos and difficulties for men, and this can have an effect on uncovering unreported cases. Males' experiences of being affected as a victim are often normalised and trivialised if they—for example in the context of violence by and between boys—are perceived as a "normal" part of male socialisation, or are dismissed as not worth mentioning (cf. Jungnitz et al. 2007). In addition, there is a tendency to hide and see experiences of being a victim as taboo wherever experiences of powerlessness and sexual violence, for example, are deemed to threaten their masculine identity and cast doubt upon their "manliness" (ibid.), which can be the case with violence in partner relationships and sexual violence.

As long as masculinity is constructed as the opposite of victimisation, weakness and helplessness, many men may find it difficult to report on serious and threatening or very harmful experiences of being a victim in this area. In addition, in the context of violence, boys and men often also have the experience of being a perpetrator, or being both a perpetrator and a victim. Once again, it cannot necessarily be assumed that participants will provide truthful statements that will allow for a realistic estimation of one-sided and reciprocal violence in the context in which it occurred. Socially accepted offences ("tussles between boys or young men") are more likely to be reported than acts from which society is increasingly distancing itself (violence against a relationship partner, rape). There are also indications that women perceive their experiences of being a perpetrator more sensitively, and report them more often, than men, particularly in the case of physical attacks within partner relationships (Kapella et al. 2011; Gig-Net 2008), which can lead to misinterpretations in the gender-based interpretation of results.

A critical investigation of this aspect represents considerable challenges for the research in future studies. The greatest care is therefore required in comparative evaluation and interpretation of male and female experiences of being a victim. Contexts of violence and perpetrator-victim-relationships, forms of violence and different meanings and qualities of violence (levels of severity) should be carefully differentiated and demarcated (also in combination of quantitative and qualitative research), in order to reflect possible differences and similarities in perception and disclosure behaviours. Studies that create superficial comparisons in this respect, or contrast statements on experiences of being a perpetrator and victim without reflection, are highly problematic from a scientific point of view.

6.4 Comparisons in Time, Between Countries and Population Groups

A logical progression from gender comparison-based studies are studies and analyses that go beyond gender-polarising and heteronormative connections and also include experiences of violence by lesbian, gay, transsexual and intersexual persons. In addition, inter-sectional approaches should include different structural categories, such as social/ethnic background, disability, age, education and social status, on an equal level with gender aspects.

The aspects cited in relation to gender comparisons in terms of differences in the perception and disclosure of violence also apply to other comparative evaluations, and should also be systematically taken into account in the interpretation of results. Group-specific differences in people affected by violence as shown in violence prevalence studies must be critically considered and very carefully interpreted, just as differences in the comparison of countries, generations and periods of time.

If, for example, middle-aged and older people report sexual abuse during childhood and adolescence more frequently than younger people (cf. Stadler et al. 2011), this cannot simply be interpreted as a reduction in sexual abuse over a period and generation-based comparison without further investigation. It is known that particularly traumatic experiences of sexual abuse during childhood and adolescence are often repressed and only remembered again later in life (at the age of 35–40 years). This suggests that, in surveys, younger age groups will report sexual abuse less frequently than older age groups. Moreover, country and culture comparisons relating to the extent of violence against women using prevalence data, as well as period-based comparisons, should be investigated very critically (see also FRA 2014; Schröttle and Martinez 2006). It can be assumed that particularly in countries with an active anti-violence policy and PR work on violence against women, taboos will have been broken down and women will both report violence to the police more often and also report violence more often in surveys; this can lead to prevalence studies finding increased levels of violence in these countries, whilst less violence is reported and recorded (in surveys and police statistics) in countries or time periods where higher levels of taboo and rather traditional gender relations are existing. Here there is generally a great risk of misinterpretation of comparative data on the extent of violence (see also FRA 2014). Tools and methods that integrate relevant aspects that influence disclosure behaviours in violence prevalence studies have previously been suggested on individual occasions (cf. Schröttle and Martinez 2006: p. 38)[7] but have not yet been methodologically refined, and are still applied relatively rarely in studies.[8]

[7] Within the CAHRV-research network for comparative studies it was suggested to include "questions about perceptions of violence, about the understanding of questions, and on norms or opinions about disclosing sexual or intimate partner violence." (Martinez and Schröttle 2007).

[8] The authors of the article suggested survey tools that specifically include questions on taboos and hesitation about talking about violence (within the family) for the European surveys (cf. Martinez

7 Summary and Conclusion

The present chapter shows the value and effectiveness, as well as the limitations, of violence prevalence studies—including from a methodological and gender-critical perspective. We tried to show that diverse methodological experiences and findings exist on how corresponding studies should be carried out in a scientifically well-founded manner, but that there is also a need to continually evaluate and further develop these. There are initial approaches to also take into account inter-sectional perspectives in methodological terms and in the evaluation of studies, but there is no systematic and concentrated research and theorisation in this field as yet. There is still a lack of empirically well-founded analyses that focus on the construction and deconstruction of violence, gender, disability, migration and other aspects. What is required to this end is, on the one hand, further theorisation of the entire topic with a clearly stronger empirical reference than before. However, it is also necessary to develop methodological study designs and tools that are suited to gaining further knowledge. This may apply to representative quantitative studies, but is probably best done as a combination of quantitative and qualitative research. In this respect, a targeted expansion of qualitative research, which would also aim at deepening representative quantitative violence prevalence studies, would be a great gain, in order to be able to better profile contexts of occurrence and causality, as well as the significance of violence (in comparative evaluations). This could, and should, be specifically promoted within the framework of existing national and international prevalence surveys and research networks, and be supported by research-supporting bodies.

Five Questions

1. What do we know about the extent and the consequences of violence against women in intimate partner relationships?
2. What are the most relevant risk factors for women to be exposed to violence by intimate partners?
3. Why is the thesis of gender symmetry in intimate partner relationships problematic?
4. What are the most relevant methodological requirements for prevalence research and data comparison with regard to intimate partner violence?
5. What has to be taken into account when data is compared between countries, population groups and in time?

---

and Schröttle 2007: p. 38). However, this suggestion was not pursued within the FRA-survey; thus it cannot be subsequently determined whether the high levels of women affected—for example in the northern European countries as compared with some eastern European states—actually reflect differences in the extent of violence, or merely in disclosure behaviours (cf. FRA 2014).

References

Amaral (2014). Do improved property rights decrease violence against women in India? Job market Paper. (o.O.) http://www.google.co.uk/url?sa=t&rct=j&q=&esrc=s&source=web&cd=3&cad=rja&uact=8&ved=0CC4QFjAC&url=http%3A%2F%2Fwww.birmingham.ac.uk%2FDocuments%2Fcollege-social-sciences%2Fbusiness%2Feconomics%2Fphd-job-market-cvs%2Fsofia-amaral-job-market-paper.pdf&ei=NZSVVLfKCsPmUunngKgL&usg=AFQjCNFfdg6UbiyRpiVek2nnQZa78n98Sw&sig2=sP8uco_PkhWOfnb2APYr9Q&bvm=bv.82001339,d.d24.

Archer, J. (2000). Sex differences in aggression between heterosexual partners. A meta-analytic review. *Psychological Bulletin, 126*(5), 651–680.

Arias, I. (2004). The legacy of child maltreatment: long-term health consequences for women. *Journal of Women's Health, 13*(5), 468–473.

Bergman, B., & Brismar, B. (1991). Suicide attempts by battered wives. *Acta Psychiatrica Scandinavica, 83*(5), 380–384.

Black, M. C., Basile, K. C., Breiding, M. J., Smith, S. G., Walters, M. L., Merrick, M. T., Chen, J., & Stevens, M. R. (2011). The National Intimate Partner and Sexual Violence Survey (NISVS). 2010 Summary Report. National Center for Injury Prevention and Control & Centers for Disease Control and Prevention, Atlanta, GA.

Brzank, P., Hellbernd, H., & Maschewsky-Schneider, U. (2004). Häusliche Gewalt gegen Frauen: Gesundheitsfolgen und Versorgungsbedarf – Ergebnisse einer Befragung von Erste-Hilfe-Patientinnen im Rahmen der S.I.G.N.A.L. – Begleitforschung. *Das Gesundheitswesen, 66*(3), 164–169.

Campbell, J. (2002). Health consequences of intimate partner violence. *Lancet, 359*(9314), 1331–1336.

Campbell, J., Kub, J., Belknap, R. A., & Templin, T. (1997). Predictors of depression in battered women. *Violence Against Women, 3*(3), 271–293.

Campbell, J., Jones, A. S., Dienemann, J., et al. (2002). Intimate partner violence and physical health consequences. *Archives of Internal Medicine, 162*(10), 1157–1163.

Campbell, R., Sullivan, C. M., & Davidson, W. S. (1995). Women who use domestic violence shelters: Changes in depression over time. *Psychology of Women Quarterly, 19*(2), 237–255.

Cicchetti, D., & Carlson, V. (1989). *Child Maltreatment. Theory and research on the causes and consequences of child abuse and neglect*. Cambridge: University Press.

Coid, J., Petruckevitch, A., Chung, W. S., et al. (2003). Abusive experiences and psychiatric morbidity in women primary care attenders. *British Journal of Psychiatry, 183*, 332–339.

Coker, A. L., et al. (2000). Physical health consequences of physical and psychological intimate partner violence. *Archives of Family Medicine, 9*, 451–457.

Danielson, K. K., Moffitt, T. E., Caspi, A., et al. (1998). Comorbidity between abuse of an adult and DSMIII-R mental disorders: Evidence from an epidemiological study. *American Journal of Psychiatry, 155*(1), 131–133.

European Union Agency for Fundamental Rights (FRA) (2014). Violence against women: an EU-wide survey. Main results. http://fra.europa.eu/sites/default/files/fra-2014-vaw-survey-main-resultsapr14_en.pdf. Accessed 28 Nov 2014.

European Union Agency for Fundamental Rights (FRA). Survey data explorer - Violence against women survey. http://fra.europa.eu/DVS/DVT/vaw.php. Accessed 18 Dec 2014.

European Institute for Gender Equality (EIGE) (2012). Women Against Violence in Europe National prevalence surveys. http://eige.europa.eu/literature-and-legislation/women-against-violence-in-europe-national-prevalence-surveys. Accessed 16 Dec 2014.

Felitti, V. J. (1991). Long-term medical consequences of incest, rape, and molestation. *Southern Medical Journal, 84*(3), 328–331.

Follette, V. M., Polusny, M. A., Bechtle, A. E., et al. (1996). Cumulative trauma: The impact of child sexual abuse, adult sexual assault, and spouse abuse. *Journal of Traumatic Stress, 9*(1), 25–35.

Garcia-Moreno, C., Jansen, A. F. M, Ellsberg, M., et al. (2005). WHO Multi-country-study on Women's Health and Domestic Violence against Women. Initial results on prevalence, health outcomes and women's responses. WHO, Geneva.

Gelles, R. J., & Harrop, J. W. (1989). Violence, battering, and psychological distress among women. *Journal of Interpersonal Violence, 4*(4), 400–420.

GIG-net (Forschungsnetz "Gewalt im Geschlechterverhältnis") (2008). Gewalt im Geschlechterverhältnis. Erkenntnisse und Konsequenzen für Politik, Wissenschaft und soziale Praxis. Budrich, Opladen & Farmington Hills.

Gloor, D., Meier, H. (2003). Gewaltbetroffene Männer – wissenschaftliche und gesellschaftlichpolitische Einblicke in eine Debatte. *FamPra.ch, die Praxis des Familienrechts 3*, 526–547

Godenzi, A. (1996). *Gewalt im sozialen Nahraum*. Basel: Helbing & Lichtenhahn.

Golding, J. M. (1994). Sexual assault history and physical health in randomly selected Los Angeles women. *Health Psychology, 13*(2), 130–138.

Golding, J. M. (1996). Sexual assault history and limitations in physical functioning in two general population samples. *Research in Nursing and Health, 19*(1), 33–44.

Heiskanen, M., Ruuskanen, E. (2011). Men's experiences of Violence in Finland 2009. http://www.heuni.fi/material/attachments/heuni/reports/6KGSrDN0Z/HEUNI_report_71_Mens_experiences_of_violence.pdf. Accessed 16 Dec 2014.

Hester, M. (2009). *Who does what to whom? Gender and domestic violence perpetrators*. Bristol: University of Bristol in Association with the Northern Rock Foundation.

Houskamp, B. M., & Foy, D. W. (1991). The assessment of posttraumatic stress disorder in battered women. *Journal of Interpersonal Violence, 6*(3), 367–375.

Johnson, M. P. (1995). Patriarchal terrorism and common couple violence: Two forms of violence against women. *Journal of Marriage and the Family, 57*, 283–294.

Johnson, M. P. (2006). Conflict and control: Gender symmetry and asymmetry in domestic violence. *Violence against Women, 12*, 1003–1018.

Jungnitz, L., Lenz, H. J., Puchert, R., Puhe, H., & Walter, W. (Eds.). (2007). *Gewalt gegen Männer. Personale Gewaltwiderfahrnisse von Männern in Deutschland*. Opladen: Budrich.

Kapella, O. et al. (2011). Gewalt in der Familie und im nahen sozialen Umfeld. Österreichische Prävalenzstudie zur Gewalt an Frauen und Männern. Studie im Auftrag des Bundesministeriums für Wirtschaft, Familie und Jugend. Wien.

Kaslow, N. J., Thompson, M. P., Okun, A., et al. (2002). Risk and protective factors for suicidal behavior in abused African American women. *Journal of Consulting and Clinical Psychology, 70*(2), 311–319.

Kimerling, R., & Calhoun, K. S. (1994). Somatic symptoms, social support, and treatment seeking among sexual assault victims. *Journal of Consulting and Clinical Psychology, 62*(2), 333–340.

Kimmel, M. (2002). Gender symmetry in domestic violence. A substantive and methodological research review. *Violence Against Women, 11*, 1332–1363.

Krug, E., et al. (Eds.). (2002). *World report on violence and health*. Geneva: WHO.

Leserman, J., Drossman, D. A., Li, Z., et al. (1996). Sexual and physical abuse history in gastroenterology practice: How types of abuse impact health status. *Psychosomatic Medicine, 58*(1), 4–15.

Martinez, M., & Schröttle, M. (2006). *State of European research on the prevalence of interpersonal violence and its impact on health and human rights*. Osnabrück: CAHRV. http://www.cahrv.uni-osnabrueck.de/reddot/190.htm. Accessed 18 Dec 2014.

Martinez, M., & Schröttle, M. (2007). *Perspectives and standards for good practice in data collection on interpersonal violence at European level*. Osnabrück: CAHRV. http://www.cahrv.uni-osnabrueck.de/reddot/FINAL_REPORT__29-10-2007_.pdf. Accessed 18 Dec 2014.

McCauley, J., Kern, D. E., Kolodner, K., et al. (1995). The ≫battering syndrome≪: Prevalence and clinical characteristics of domestic violence in primary care Internal Medicine Practices. *Annals of Internal Medicine, 123*(10), 737–746.

McCauley, J., Kern, D. E., Kolodner, K., et al. (1997). Clinical characteristics of women with a history of childhood abuse: Unhealed wounds. *Journal of the American Medical Association, 277*(17), 1362–1368.

Panda, P., Agarwal, B. (2005). Marital violence, human development and womens property status in India. *World Development 33*(5), 823–850, GB. https://www.google.co.uk/url?sa=t&rct=j&q=&esrc=s&source=web&cd=5&ved=0CDwQFjAE&url=https%3A%2F%2Fwww.amherst.edu%2Fmedia%2Fview%2F92357%2Foriginal%2FMarial%252BViolence%25252C%252BHuman%252BDevelopment%252Band%252BWomen%252527s%252BProperty%252BStatus.pdf&ei=NZSVVLfKCsPmUunngKgL&usg=AFQjCNHr2L3S3lA3DlG1csyOMtC_cWKXzg&sig2=5Szi4UQnt7OqP0rVBanjrw&bvm=bv.82001339,d.d24.

Panda, P., Gupta, J., Bulankulame, I., Bathla, N., Chakraborty, S., & Duvvury N. (2006) Property Ownership & Inheritance Rights of Women for Social Protection – The South Asia Experience. Synthesis report of three studies. http://www.google.co.uk/url?sa=t&rct=j&q=&esrc=s&source=web&cd=2&cad=rja&uact=8&ved=0CCkQFjAB&url=http%3A%2F%2Fwww.icrw.org%2Ffiles%2Fpublications%2FProperty-Ownership-and-Inheritance-Rights-of-Women-for-Social-Protection-The-South-Asia-Experience.pdf&ei=NZSVVLfKCsPmUunngKgL&usg=AFQjCNFq1ndYCLtcnnmjpBqgIo-k3RGoKA&sig2=ersGUb5sXSYvy0LxBuxzEg&bvm=bv.82001339,d.d24.

Porcerelli, J. H., Cogan, R., West, P. P., et al. (2003). Violent victimization of women and men: Physical and psychiatric symptoms. *Journal of the American Board of Family Practice, 16*(1), 32–39.

Rabold, S., & Goergen, T. (2013). Abuse and neglect of older care recipients in domestic settings - Results of a survey among nursing staff of home care services in Hanover (Germany). *Journal of Adult Protection, 15*(3), 127–140.

Roberts, G. L., Williams, G. M., Lawrence, J. M., et al. (1998). How does domestic violence affect women's mental health? *Women & Health, 28*(1), 117–129.

Schröttle, M. (2010). Kritische Anmerkungen zur These der Gendersymmetrie bei Gewalt in Paarbeziehungen. *Gender, 1*(2010), 133–151.

Schröttle, M., Ansorge, N. (2008). Gewalt gegen Frauen in Paarbeziehungen – eine sekundäranalytische Auswertung zur Differenzierung von Schweregraden, Mustern, Risikofaktoren und Unterstützung nach erlebter Gewalt. Im Auftrag des Bundesministeriums für Familie, Senioren, Frauen und Jugend. Berlin. https://www.google.de/search?q=schr%C3%B6ttle+ansorge+gewalt&ie=utf-8&oe=utf-8&aq=t&rls=org.mozilla:de:official&client=firefox-a&channel=sb&gfe_rd=cr&ei=IFuUVKGHGIHe8geZx4HABw. Accessed 31 Nov 2014.

Schröttle, M., Hornberg, C., & Bohne, S., et al. (2008). Gesundheitliche Folgen von Gewalt unter besonderer Berücksichtigung von häuslicher Gewalt gegen Frauen. Gesundheitsberichterstattung des Bundes. Heft 42. Robert-Koch-Institut (RKI), Berlin. http://www.rki.de/DE/Content/Gesundheitsmonitoring/Gesundheitsberichterstattung/GBEDownloadsT/gewalt.html;jsessionid=2B3F08D615EA4D274FF9C98F57461C18.2_cid372?nn=2370692. Accessed 4 Nov 2014

Schröttle, M., Müller, U. (2004). Lebenssituation, Sicherheit und Gesundheit von Frauen in Deutschland. Eine repräsentative Untersuchung zur zu Gewalt gegen Frauen in Deutschland. Im Auftrag des Bundesministeriums für Familie, Senioren, Frauen und Jugend. http://www.bmfsfj.de/RedaktionBMFSFJ/Abteilung4/Pdf-Anlagen/langfassung-studie-frauen-teil-eins,property=pdf,bereich=bmfsfj,sprache=de,rwb=true.pdf. Accessed 02 Dec 2014

Schröttle, M., & Martinez, M. (2006). Comparative Reanalysis of Prevalence of Violence against Women and Health Impact Data in Europe – Obstacles and Possible Solutions: Testing a Comparative Approach on Selected Studies. CAHRV, Osnabrück. http://www.cahrv.uni-osnabrueck.de/reddot/D_20_Comparative_reanalysis_of_prevalence_of_violence_pub.pdf. Accessed 01 Dec 2014.

Schröttle, M., Khelaifat, N. (2008). Gesundheit – Gewalt – Migration. Eine vergleichende Sekundäranalyse zur gesundheitlichen und Gewaltsituation von Frauen mit und ohne Migrationshintergrund in Deutschland. Im Auftrag des Bundesministeriums für Familie, Senioren, Frauen und Jugend. Berlin. http://www.bmfsfj.de/RedaktionBMFSFJ/Broschuerenstelle/Pdf-Anlagen/gesundheit-gewalt-migration-langfassung-studie,property=pdf,bereich=bmfsfj,sprache=de,rwb=true.pdf. Accessed 01 Dec 2014.

Schröttle, M., & Hornberg, C., et al. (2013). Lebenssituation und Belastungen von Frauen mit Beeinträchtigungen und Behinderungen in Deutschland. Langfassung. Im Auftrag des Bundesministeriums für Familie, Senioren, Frauen und Jugend. Berlin. http://www.bmfsfj.de/ RedaktionBMFSFJ/Broschuerenstelle/Pdf-Anlagen/Lebenssituation-und-Belastungen-von-Frauen-mit-Behinderungen-Langfassung-Ergebnisse_20der_20quantitativen-Befragung,property=pdf,bereich=bmfsfj,sprache=de,rwb=true.pdf (in German) Accessed 28 Nov 2014 Short version in English: http://www.bmfsfj.de/BMFSFJ/Service/publikationen,did=201652.html?view=renderPrint. Accessed 18 Dec 2014.

Schröttle, M., & Glammeier, S. (2013). Intimate partner violence against disabled women as a part of widespread victimization and discrimination over the lifetime: Evidence from a German representative study. *International Journal of Conflict and Violence, 7*(2), 232–248.

Stadler, L., Bieneck, S., Pfeiffer, C. (2011). Repräsentativbefragung Sexueller Missbrauch 2011. KFN-Forschungsbericht, Nr. 118. Hannover. http://www.kfn.de/versions/kfn/assets/fob118.pdf. Accessed 22 June 2014.

Straus, M. A. (1990). The conflict tactics scale and its critics: An evaluation and new data on validity and reliability. In M. A. Straus & R. J. Gelles (Eds.), *Physical violence in American families: Risk factors and adaptions to violence in 8,145 families* (pp. 49–73). New Brunswick: Transaction Publishing.

Straus, M. A., Hamby, S. L., Boney-McCoy, S., & Sugarman, D. B. (1996). The revised Conflict Tactic Scales (CTS2): Development and preliminary psychometric data. *Journal of Family Issues, 17*, 283–316.

Thiara, R. K., Condon, S., & Schröttle, M. (Eds.). (2011). *Violence against women and ethnicity: Commonalities and differences across Europe*. Leverkusen-Opladen: Budrich.

Thompson, M. P., Kingree, J. B., & Desai, S. (2004). Gender differences in long-term health consequences of physical abuse of children: Data from a nationally representative survey. *American Journal of Public Health, 94*(4), 599–604.

UN Women (2013). Violence against women prevalence data: Surveys by country. http://www.endvawnow.org/uploads/browser/files/vawprevalence_matrix_june2013.pdf. Accessed 01 Dec 2014

Walby, S., & Allen, J. (2004). Domestic Violence, Sexual Assault and Stalking: Findings from the British Crime Survey. Home Office Research Study 276. Home Office, London.

Walker, E. A., Katon, W. J., Roy-Byrne, P. P., et al. (1993). Histories of sexual victimization in patients with irritable bowel syndrome or inflammatory bowel disease. *American Journal of Psychiatry, 150*(10), 1502–1506.

Watson, D., & Parsons, S. (2005). Domestic Abuse of Women and Men in Ireland. Report on the National Study of Domestic Abuse. National Crime Council, Dublin.

WAVE. (2012). Country Report 2012. Reality check on data collection and European services for women and children survivors of violence. A right for protection and support? http://www.wave-network.org/sites/default/files/WAVE%20COUNTRY%20REPORT%202012.pdf. Accessed 16 March 2016.

Wetzels, P., & Pfeiffer, C. (1995). Sexuelle Gewalt gegen Frauen im öffentlichen Raum. Ergebnisse der KFN-Opferbefragung 1992. http://www.kfn.de/versions/kfn/assets/fb37.pdf. Accessed 17 Dec 2014.

World Health Organisation (WHO) (2013). Global and regional estimates of violence against women. Prevalence and health effects of intimate partner violence and non-partner sexual violence. http://www.who.int/reproductivehealth/publications/violence/9789241564625/en/. Accessed 17 Dec 2014.

World Health Organisation (WHO) (2005). Multi-country Study on Women's Health and Domestic Violence against Women. Initial results on prevalence, health outcomes and women's responses. http://www.who.int/gender/violence/who_multicountry_study/en/. Accessed 28 Nov 2014.

Victims but Also Perpetrators: Women's Experiences of Partner Violence

Alexandra Lysova

Abstract Both the United Nations and the World Health Organisation have made serious efforts to address violence against women as a public health and a human rights issue worldwide. Drawing on international scholarship primarily from Western industrialized countries, this chapter critically discusses perspectives on women's experiences of partner violence (PV) as both victims and perpetrators. It emphasizes that partner violence is a dynamic, complex, and multidimensional phenomenon. Researching it needs the examination of its interactional and situational aspects. Integrating attention to the violent dynamics of partner violence with elements of the "violence against women" framework would allow global research to recognize and give voice to women's diverse experiences of partner violence, help reveal its intrinsic, interactional nature, and, as a result, promote a transformational change for crime prevention at the international and domestic level.

1 Introduction

In the last 30 years violence against women as a public health priority and a human rights issue has received substantial attention internationally. Both the United Nations and the World Health Organisation have made serious efforts to examine the prevalence and risk factors of violence against women across different countries, as well as to develop and implement means for its prevention (e.g., Abramsky et al. 2011; Devries et al. 2013; Garcia-Moreno et al. 2006; Jewkes 2002). One of the most common types of violence against women worldwide is domestic or partner violence (PV), which is primarily understood as perpetrated by a male partner (Heise 1998; Krug et al. 2002). There are major negative health consequences of partner violence for women around the world, including injury,

I thank the Trudeau Foundation (Canada) for funding this study and Rosemary Gartner for her comments on the first draft, and her research support for this work.

A. Lysova (✉)
School of Criminology, Simon Fraser University, 8888 University Drive, Burnaby V5A1S6, BC, Canada
e-mail: alysova@sfu.ca

H. Kury et al. (eds.), *Women and Children as Victims and Offenders: Background, Prevention, Reintegration*, DOI 10.1007/978-3-319-08398-8_19

unwanted pregnancy, HIV/AIDS, homicide and suicide (Ellsberg et al. 2008; García-Moreno and Riecher-Rössler 2013).

At the same time, a growing body of interdisciplinary PV studies in industrialized countries, which are in the vanguard of PV research in the world, points to the more interactive and mutually dynamic nature of PV in addition to the prior understanding of PV as a phenomenon with a strict gender dichotomy. For example, studies identify different types of violent relationships (e.g., one-sided violence directed at a woman or a man and mutual violence) (Hamby 2009; Johnson 2008; Olson 2004), distinct psychological types of male and female perpetrators (Babcock et al. 2003; Henning et al. 2006; Holtzworth-Munroe and Meehan 2004; Ross and Babcock 2012; Swan and Snow 2003), and specific characteristics of situations of violence (Collins 2008; Wilkinson and Hamerschlag 2005). Overall, these studies strongly suggest that women's experiences of partner violence are not fully represented by their victimisation at the hands of male partners; women seem more involved in the violent interactions with their intimate partners than it was believed before.

However, studies conducted in industrialised countries may not necessarily be relevant to countries with drastic gender inequality and cultural and religious practices that indirectly or directly mandate violence against women. At the same time, a study that applied the "relationship approach" to violence against women in ten countries in the WHO Multi-country Study on Women's Health and Domestic Violence (e.g., Bangladesh, Brazil, Ethiopia, Namibia, and the United Republic of Tanzania) clearly demonstrated the benefits of examining situational and individual characteristics and experiences of both victims and perpetrators in explaining PV (Abramsky et al. 2011). For example, older age of the women, problematic alcohol use by both partners, men's and women's experiences of non-partner violence prior to their current relationship, and experience of child abuse by both partners increased the risk of violence against women. Moreover, many of the situational and individual risk factors examined in the study affected PV similarly across the ten countries.

A few available multi-national studies[1] that examined PV perpetrated by both males and females imply that research on its dynamic mutual nature should not be restricted to industrialized countries only. One study, which was conducted in 32 countries, including Iran, Tanzania, India, Venezuela, Russia, and South Africa among others, suggested that the most frequent pattern of violence was when both partners were violent, and the next most prevalent pattern was when the *female* partner was the only one to physically attack the male partner (Straus 2008). Despite its limitations (the study drew on a convenience sample of university students most of whom were in dating rather than married or cohabiting relationships, used a cross-sectional design, and did not measure the situational context of violence), this study indicates the relevance of further examination of the

[1] Many multi-national and large national studies still restrict their questions to the victimization of women and do not include questions on perpetration by women.

contextual dynamics of PV from a global perspective.[2] Another multinational study of PV in ten countries in the Americas, i.e., the PAHO[3] Multicentric study, which included questions on physical violence both by a partner and toward a partner by both female and male respondents, found comparable or higher rates of male victimization than female victimization in seven out of ten countries and comparable or higher rates of perpetration reported by female than male respondents in all countries, except in Peru (Ayacucho) (Graham et al. 2008, p. 222). Even though gender differences in reporting violence might perhaps explain some of these findings, this multinational study clearly suggests the need for examining both partners' experiences of violence from a global perspective.

It is also important to recognize that the diverse manifestations of partner violence may necessitate different prevention and treatment strategies. Current policies in many industrialized countries that favour criminal justice responses and have been designed primarily for male perpetrators raise empirical, theoretical, political, and practical concerns (for a review, see Buzawa et al. 2012; Comack and Balffour 2004; Snider 2008). For example, mandatory arrest practices that require police officers to make an arrest in cases of PV appear to restrict victims' ability to control the situation and also dramatically increase the arrest of both parties (dual arrest). Furthermore, court-mandated batterer-intervention programs do not seem to deter most perpetrators, especially those who are chronic and severe batterers (Buzawa et al. 2012). This suggests that more elaborated and diverse approaches that recognize the complex and multifaceted nature of partner violence, including the role of women in the violent interaction, are needed.

Indeed, many scholars and practitioners in industrialized countries now express their support for uniting both men's and women's efforts in reducing PV. Drawing on the empirical scholarship that suggests much more active engagement of women in partner violence as both victims and perpetrators, concerted efforts of male and as well as female partners in preventing PV may prove to be the most effective (for a review, see Hamel and Nicholls 2007; Dutton 2006, 2007; Harris 2006; Stith and McCollum 2011; Stith et al. 2011). It is worth recognizing that WHO has also demonstrated a greater interest in the roles and responsibilities of men and boys in relation to gender equality, which is one of the key protective factors against gender-based violence around the world. For example, the Department of Gender, Women, and Health exhorts on its website that "[w]omen and men need to work

[2] Moreover, some scholars argue for reconsidering the "violence against women" perspective as a framing tool. Without undermining the understanding that women are disproportionally more likely to experience fear and sustain injury as a result of PV than men worldwide, a more gender-neutral frame, such as "gender violence", coupled with continuing efforts to fight inequality based on gender and other marginalized identities, can more accurately capture the experiences of violence, challenge stereotypes, and enhance social policy (Goldscheid 2014).

[3] PAHO stands for the Pan American Health Organization. The survey study was conducted in Argentina, Belize, Brazil, Canada, Costa Rica, Mexico, Nicaragua, Peru, Uruguay, and the United States between 2001 and 2007.

together for greater gender equality and not merely blame each other for the inequalities and inequities…" (WHO 2014).

Drawing on the international scholarship primarily from Western industrialized countries (e.g., the United States, UK, Israel, and Australia) and the results of the author's research in Canada,[4] this chapter critically discusses perspectives on women's experiences of PV as both victims and perpetrators. By treating PV as a dynamic, complex, and multidimensional phenomenon I argue that our understanding of PV will benefit from examining interactional and situational aspects of violent interactions, in addition to larger societal factors. Moreover, the examination of dynamic aspects of violence in global research on PV, along with (not instead of) the "violence against women" framework, would allow us to recognize and give voice to women's diverse experiences of partner violence, help reveal the intrinsic, interactional nature of PV, and, as a result, promote a transformational change at the level of political discourse and social policy.

This chapter first critically reviews the current conceptualizations of PV with respect to female partners as victims and perpetrators of PV. Given its focus on violent dynamics in PV incidents, it also discusses men's experiences of violence as both perpetrators and victims. Then, this chapter introduces interactional and violent event perspectives on PV, and discusses women's part in PV as seen in my study of the incarcerated women's views on the violence dynamics in Ontario, Canada. In conclusion, this chapter discusses the implications of current findings for social policy and future research on PV in a global perspective.

2 Perspectives on Women's Experiences of Partner Violence

Historically, there has been a gradual shift from seeing women as only victims of interpersonal violence to recognition of their more active involvement in PV. This section presents and discusses several major perspectives on female PV perpetration, but is not intended as an exhaustive review of these approaches. First, it briefly discusses the perspective that dominates in PV research and is currently embraced by major international organizations, i.e., the violence against women framework. Then it introduces three perspectives that explain women's involvement in violence, i.e., through their experiences of victimization, as active rational actors, and finally, as a result of women's personality disorders or other psychological malfunction.

[4] Although carried out in Canada, my study has drawn on a group of the most marginalized women in Canadian society, i.e., economically disadvantaged women, many of whom are Aboriginal, serving time in a provincial correctional facility in Ontario, Canada.

2.1 Violence Against Women in the Partner Relationships

Violence against women (VAW),[5] or gender-based violence as it is also commonly known in the PV research literature, has received enormous attention in the international community in the last 20 years. Achievements in our understanding of VAW worldwide have become possible thanks to the efforts of the global organizations, the UN and WHO, which have made VAW a research and policy priority. Although there has been much progress in documenting the magnitude of the problem in many countries (e.g., Devries et al. 2013) and in identifying risk factors for VAW (e.g., Abramsky et al. 2011), some problems are still present. These include a lack of reliable comparative data across countries and underreporting of VAW, especially in developing countries (Palermo et al. 2014). Taking these limitations into consideration, I briefly review recently available data on the estimated prevalence of VAW in the partner relationships globally, main risk factors for, and consequences of violence for women and broader communities.

The most recent comprehensive review of data on PV, based on 141 studies in 81 countries, estimates that in 2010 globally 30 % of women aged 15 and over have experienced physical and/or sexual violence at some point in the intimate relationships (Devries et al. 2013). This study also identified notable regional differences in the prevalence of women's victimization ranging from 16 % in East Asia to 66 % in Central Sub-Saharan Africa. Despite regional variations in the prevalence of VAW, the risk factors appear to be similar across many countries. Specifically, ideologies of male superiority, gender inequality (with the lesser power of women in family and society), along with some situational (e.g., heavy alcohol use by both partners), relationship (e.g., length and type of relationship), and individual (e.g., older age of women and histories of child abuse for both partners) factors, can significantly increase risk of VAW worldwide (Abramsky et al. 2011; Jewkes 2002). VAW in the partner relationships has adverse public health effects on women around the world, including injury, unwanted pregnancy, chronic pain, physical disability, substance abuse, HIV/AIDS, homicide and suicide (Ellsberg et al. 2008). Moreover, negative consequences of violence for women are not always physical and therefore visible; VAW is strongly associated with mental health problems in women, such as posttraumatic stress disorder, depression, suicidal thoughts, substance abuse problems, eating disorders, as well as antenatal and postnatal mental disorders (García-Moreno and Riecher-Rössler 2013). Additionally, there are negative social and economic impacts of VAW on survivors, their families, and the society in general (e.g., Day et al. 2005).

[5] Acknowledging that VAW is a term that collectively refers to various violent acts against women that can be committed by individuals as well as states, this chapter, however, uses this term in relation to the PV.

2.2 Women-Perpetrators as Victims

In the last 40 years in the industrialized countries, views on women's crime and violence have shifted dramatically. After being ignored or denied for some time, women's offending moved into the spotlight after Freda Adler's 1975 book "*Sisters in crime: The rise of the new female criminal*". Despite an ensuing greater readiness to acknowledge female criminality, women's violence was not something that became accepted easily, which arguably contributed to the "male offender/female victim" binary, or what some termed "the myth of the nonaggressive woman" (White and Kowalski 1994) or "the myth of female passivity" (Richardson 2005). Many scholars initially were explicitly discouraged from studying female violence (Holtzworth-Munroe 2005; Straus 1999) but the pendulum has moved and a body of research on female offending began to grow in the 1990s and has continued apace in many industrialized countries.

In the light of the growing data on female criminality, more and more scholars have acknowledged the constraints of the binary "female victim versus male offender" and launched explorations of the issue of female offending. A large group of scholars contextualises female offending in terms of the broader socio-political and economic forces structured around sexual inequality and male oppression, hence, steering towards seeing female victimization as a main explanatory factor of female offending (e.g., Dobash and Dobash 1979; Moe 2004; Chesney-Lind 1989; Chesney-Lind and Pasko 2013; Richie 1996; Stark 2007). In other words, women commit PV (or other crimes and acts of delinquency) because they are physically or sexually victimized in their family of origin and/or in order to cope with the abuse in their intimate relationships.[6]

For instance, studies of delinquent girls uncover the gender-specific socialization patterns in the family, which include physical and sexual abuse of girls, and the further role of the juvenile justice system in the criminalization of girls' survival strategies, which result in female's offending later in life (Chesney-Lind and Pasko 2013; Chesney-Lind 1989). Some other studies document the specific circumstances in which women's survival strategies have been viewed and responded to as lawbreaking behaviour. For example, in their analysis of women who smoke crack and engaged in street-level sex work in New York city, Maher and Curtis (1998) highlighted women's experiences within the context of both male dominated structures and occupational opportunities for women in the informal economy. They suggested that crack cocaine was not a way of liberation for women but rather a coping strategy for women embedded in the context of poverty, violence and disrespect. In the sex-segmented informal economy, women crack smokers often found themselves engaged in street-level prostitution as a means of supporting drug consumption. The "war on drugs" directed against poor minority

[6] This argumentation, however, is rarely applied to male offenders of PV and thus, male engagement in PV continues to be explained by these authors mainly by the motives of control, domination, and oppression of women.

women who used crack cocaine, and changes in the price and nature of sex work, increased women's violent victimisation by male clients, police and neighbourhood youth. Maher and Curtis (1998) suggested that the increased rates of women's participation in "criminal" activities such as robbery and assault more accurately reflects women's continued subjugation and necessitated adaptations to survive rather than "masculinization" of women and a shift away from traditional female roles.

In another study, Richie (1996) develops a gender-entrapment theory that explains the involvement of Black battered women in illegal activities. She argues that these women are not "criminals" but rather "victims of crimes" who were set up or entrapped in their lives by socially constructed conditions, who were deeply misunderstood and betrayed by the loyalty to their families, abused and degraded in intimate relationships and in the end criminalized and stigmatized by the criminal justice system (Richie 1996, p. 5). All these processes taken together comprise what Richie calls "gender entrapment". She argues that Afro-American battered women who were incarcerated for violent, property, drug-related crimes, and prostitution were in fact compelled to commit crimes by their male partners, and also under the pressure of the early childhood experiences, constructed cultural/racial identity, violence in intimate relationships, and negative social factors.

Although many studies in both industrialized and non-industrialized countries indeed support what has come to be known as a victimization-offending hypothesis, this perspective used alone, however, does not seem to represent the complexity of women's violent offending. Specifically, one of the limitations of attributing female offending exclusively to female victimization is that it overlooks or diminishes the weight of the female agency, responsibility, and meaning of their violent behaviour and, on the other hand, tends to essentialize weaknesses and victimhood of women in IPV situations (e.g., Kruttschnitt and Carbone-Lopez 2006; Daly 1998). Indeed, many scholars working in this perspective notably use the passive voice when it comes to illustrating women's lives and their paths to offending, including the titles of their books, e.g., "*Compelled to Crime*". Having said that, this position tends to reject the very human nature of women who occasionally or often feel angry, jealous, envious, strive for control and dominance, have personality disorders, etc. By focusing on the overarching role of a patriarchal context in the victimization of female offenders, this perspective appears to underestimate the potential role of class, race, immigration and other factors that intersect with gender in explaining offending by different women in different contexts.

2.3 Agentic Views on Women's Offending

The scholarship that emerged in several industrialized countries in the late 1990s challenged the myth of a nonaggressive woman (e.g., Baskin and Sommers 1998; Kruttschnitt and Carbone-Lopez 2006) and critiqued the antiagentic representation of women's offending in both the media and the criminal justice system (Allen 1998; Downs 1996; Morrissey 2003). These scholars suggest that female offenders were shown almost invariably as victims rather than as actors in the crimes they committed and that this representation was likely to harm women. Scholars within this perspective argued that by denying the possibility of female agency in violent crimes, the best of intentions actually deny women the full freedom to be human.

Specifically, Allen (1998) documented that the severity of women's violence tends to be moderated (i.e., by referring to the psychological and medical aspects of female crimes), domesticized (by invoking her "feminine" position as a woman, as a mother, and as a wife), and normalised (by considering female crimes as "impersonal misfortunes rather than personal misdeeds", as acts committed "without volition, intention, understanding or consciousness") by psychiatrists and probation officers (Allen 1998, p. 63).

Downs (1996) comes to a similar conclusion about the detrimental effect of the victimisation discourse on female offenders in his book "*More than Victims*" (1996). In it, he discusses the use of the Battered Woman Syndrome (BWS) as a legal defence and shows how the syndrome's logic harms those it is trying to protect. The major flaws of the BWS lie in seeing battered women as lacking the will, responsibility, and mental capacity for handling the situation; its group-based approach to gender justice; its rigidity that can compromise the prospects of defendants who do not fit the stereotypes of the syndrome; and its "excuses" and "justifications" for criminal acts. His study provides a powerful analysis of female victims' role in PV without denying their victimization, minimizing the problem, or exonerating women who killed or injured their male partners. Downs (1996) shows that justice in domestic violence cases can be achieved without sacrificing the presumptions of reason and responsibility. He argues for abandoning BWS in favour of standards of responsibility that provide justice for women (not just those who fit the syndrome) and apply equally to all citizens. In his opinion, the law of self-defence provides a more appropriate framework for treating cases of battered women who resort to lethal force since it addresses their individual situations and does not rely on pseudo-scientific stereotypes of helplessness and lack of will (Downs 1996, p. 223).

Morrissey's (2003) position echoes Downs' (1996) argument in the way that she supports application of the self-defence law rather than any of the syndromes for battered women who kill. In her discussion of battered women who kill, Morrissey (2003) argued that these women need recognition of their accountability for their crimes and acknowledgement of their agency without a concomitant increase in their liability for punishment. These women require a new legal narrative based upon a concept of determined agency whereby battered women might be considered as making a rational choice in killing abusive, life-threatening partners, and at the same time as being coerced into this decision through a lack of societal support and recognition of their situation. Moreover, Morrissey (2003) shows why and how women's violence that cannot be explained in conventional ways (e.g., child abuse or spouse abuse) leads to an essentialist conception of the nexus between sex and gender.

Many other scholars have provided empirical evidence for the diversity of contexts and motives for female violence (Baskin and Sommers 1998; Daly 1998; Gartner and McCarthy 2006; Miller and Mullins 2006). These scholars have challenged antiagentic, passive views on women offenders who were long characterized as inherently evil, sick, or thoroughly affected by early victimization by uncovering a wide range of motives for women's involvement in violent offending. Although some motivations are clearly related to economic and social status, e.g., the desire for money and respect, violence by women is also motivated by gendered considerations, e.g., threats to their status as a good mother or a faithful partner. These studies further espouse the idea of agency and the limited choices these women have.

For instance, a study of 170 women who committed nondomestic violent felony crimes (robbery, assault, and homicide) in New York City (USA), suggested that women were not simply "coerced" or "forced" by male partners and family members into crime but expressed their agency in making personal decisions related to their participation in crime. For example, a common theme in many of the accounts describing assault is that the use of violence was seen by women as a legitimate method to avenge being "dissed" and one of the most effective ways of gaining respect and "saving face" (Baskin and Sommers 1998, pp. 117–118). The study also revealed the importance of other social factors, mainly the neighbourhood environments, in accounting for female violent career patterns.

Female offenders' agency appears to be denied particularly in the cases of infanticide. These women were long seen by criminologists as evil or impotent due to victimhood or madness. Gartner and McCarthy (2006) examined the undetected cases or the "dark figure" of homicides by women hoping that it might provide an alternative explanation for their violent behaviour. Comparing two data sets of homicides in which parents were identified as killers and in which the offender was not identified revealed much more complex characterization of women who killed their children. Some of the women who killed their children but were never identified as such presumably had sufficient resources and a sense of self-preservation to hide their crimes. However, this does not deny that these women might have experienced many other problems, e.g., psychological and structural, that could constrain their choices. At the same time, Gartner and McCarthy (2006) argued that given these constraints women still had agency and ability to make choices in their lives.

A steering committee established by the US Congress to develop a detailed research agenda on violence against women emphasized the importance of further studies on the links between women's PV victimization and offending (Kruttschnitt et al. 2004, p. 87). Based on an extensive review of studies of PV, the authors, however, acknowledged that women's violence against partners could not be completely explained as defensive, i.e., by female victimization only. Thus, a framework that could connect different types of violence in which women play roles of offenders or victims should be considered. In relation to female victimization, the committee found that despite widely held beliefs that the factors behind female victimization differ from those affecting rates of male victimization, risk factors seem to be very similar to those for other kinds of criminal offending and victimization. As a result, the authors called for expansion of both theoretical and empirical models that would provide a better understanding of such female-perpetrated violence, including an examination of individual factors, the environments, and the cultural context of violent women.

Overall, these and other studies reveal the complex aetiology of female offending that extends beyond prior victimisation to many other individual, situational, relationship, and societal factors and reflect the inherent agency of women who commit crime including violent offences. Furthermore, these studies suggest that the myth of the nonaggressive woman can in fact reinforce male power, silence women's voices, impede attempts to solve the problems that lead to female aggression, and deny the acknowledgment that women have power to control others (Langhinrichsen-Rohling 2010; White and Kowalski 1994).

2.4 Psychological Typologies of Women-Offenders

Some scholars, primarily psychologists, have enriched our understanding of female involvement in violence by identifying distinct types of violent women depending on the different context and motivations for the use of violence (Babcock et al. 2003; Henning et al. 2006; Ross and Babcock 2012; Swan and Snow 2003). Similarly to violent men, scholars identify at least two types of women who use violence in the intimate relationship: partner-only (PO) and generally violent (GV) women (Babcock et al. 2003). PO women are those who use violence only in the context of an intimate relationship, often in self-defence, and who have learnt through their adult relationships that violence is an acceptable and effective way to deal with conflict in intimate relationships. Additionally, comparison of perpetrator typologies by gender using a community sample has identified nearly equal rates of men and women who may be classified as partner-only perpetrators (Monson and Langhinrichsen-Rohling 2002). However, the violence of many women in this group was likely a result of poor communication skills in managing interpersonal conflicts whereas men's violence was mainly associated with antisocial characteristics. GV women, on the other hand, are likely to use violence in a variety of situations, including intimate relationships, mostly for the purposes of retribution, gaining compliance or control, and demonstrate many traumatic symptoms (e.g., memory problems, a desire to hurt themselves) (Babcock et al. 2003).

A study of women convicted of PV by Henning et al. (2006) has further demonstrated the heterogeneity of female PV offenders. The authors identified a small group of women (9 %) who were primary aggressors in the relationship, which is close to the proportion of GV women in other classifications. These women used coercive violence and serious aggression with their partners more often than other women; also, they experienced early conduct problems and greater exposure to family violence in childhood than other women convicted of PV. Contrary to researchers' expectations about these women's continuing violence against their male partners, these women were in fact more likely to end as victims in subsequent PV reports than as offenders. One of the explanations is that women's physical aggression may increase the risk for future victimisation. The majority of women who were convicted of PV offenses in the Henning et al. (2006) study, however, were women whom they called victims. Researchers found that in the majority of couples in which women were arrested for PV the male was much more often the primary aggressor than the female, which suggests that women's use of violence in these cases was motivated primarily by self-protection.

Other studies distinguish a type of female offender who engages in coercive control (Robertson and Murachver 2011) and intimate terrorism against their male partners (Hines and Douglas 2010b; Ross and Babcock 2012). Specifically, in a comparative study of men who sought help for PV victimisation and men from the community sample, Hines and Douglas (2010b) found that female partners of the men who sought help were much more likely to hit first during the last physical argument and ever in the relationship than female partners of men from a community sample. Moreover, in comparison with the female partners of men in the community sample, the female partners of men in the help-seeking sample engaged in significantly higher rates and frequency of all types of PV, including controlling behaviors and minor physical aggression. In addition, men in the help-seeking sample were much more likely to sustain injuries resulted from violence by a female partner than men from a community sample did.

Based on these perspectives, it can be concluded that although female offenders have experienced enormous victimisation in their lives (much greater one than women from a community sample), their offending can also be attributed to many other motives, e.g., contextual, individual, and socio-economic. Moreover, many scholars emphasise the decision-making process of offending women in the constraints of the situation. Overall, the studies of female offenders suggest that they are a heterogeneous group who perpetrate crime, including PV, in different contexts and for various reasons. This implies that the explanation of women's engagement in crime and violence may benefit from an integrated approach, i.e., one that combines gender perspectives on the one hand and classical criminological, sociological and psychological theories on the other.

3 Men's Experiences of Partner Violence

Most perpetrators of homicide or nonfatal violence (both within and outside of intimate relationships) who become to be known to the police are men. This fact may explain the predominant research focus of many criminologists and sociologists on men as perpetrators of violence, typically against other men. However, thanks to feminist activists, since the early 1970s the attention of both mainstream and radical criminology was turned to men's violence against women as well. Although men's offending, including homicide, can be accounted for by many factors, i.e., individual (e.g., experience of violence as a child), situational (e.g., alcohol use), structural (e.g., marginal position in society), and cultural (e.g., honour contest), the PV literature in the 1980s and early 1990s has put emphasis on the greater power of men in society and men's needs to control women (e.g., Kurz 1993). However, this one-dimensional and deterministic understanding of men's violence has gradually given way to more complex and elaborated models of men, masculinity, and crime.

One of the approaches to understanding men's violence has focused on viewing gender as a set of practices, and crime as a resource in "doing masculinities". That is, Messerschmidt (1997) examines masculinities (and femininities) as they are reproduced among different races and classes and highlights the process of making of crime based on the analysis of gender, race and class in the making. However, pondering the question why only some men choose to commit crime as a way to accomplish masculinity prompted scholars to seek ways of linking structure and agency in explaining men's violence. Some of these scholars underscore the link between poverty and violence that is mediated through masculine identity. Specifically, "violence against women is thus seen not just as an expression of male powerfulness and dominance over women, but also as being rooted in male vulnerability stemming from social expectations of manhood that are unattainable because of factors such as poverty experienced by men" (Jewkes 2002, p. 1424). In his study of confrontational homicide, Polk (1998) found that extreme violence in defense of honour was quite prevalent among men from the lower social class. In another study, violence against women becomes a norm for Puerto Rican men growing up in New York slums who are pressured by the models of masculinity, on the one hand, but unable to attain them due to unemployment and poverty, on the other (Bourgois 1996).

Within a broader perspective of viewing men as violent offenders, some scholars—predominantly psychologists—identify types of male PV offenders and thus strongly suggest that this is not a homogeneous group (e.g., Dutton 2006; Holtzworth-Munroe and Meehan 2004; Holtzworth-Munroe and Stuart 1994; Johnson 2008). Many scholars agree that there are at least three salient types of male batterers, i.e., generally violent and antisocial batterers (who are likely to engage in moderate to severe levels of marital violence and the highest levels of extrafamilial violence; often demonstrate criminal behaviour, arrests, and substance abuse); dysphoric or borderline batterers (who are likely to engage in moderate to severe levels of marital violence, but not much violence outside of family; often demonstrate emotional lability, intense and unstable interpersonal relationships, jealousy and fear of rejection); and family-only batterers (who engage in the least marital and extramarital violence and whose violence seems to be more situational and related to stress and marital conflict) (Holtzworth-Munroe and Meehan 2004).

However, new scholarship appears to be growing that is intended to hear men's voices about their experiences of violence, including perpetration of and victimization resulted from a female intimate partner's violence. These approaches differ from those described above because they draw on the understanding of men's violence as a complex and multifaceted phenomenon that cannot be attributed to a few factors. Also, men are allowed to describe their perception of the violent incidents without being seen as using the "abuse excuse". For example, the Wood's (2004) study of perspectives on violence against female intimate partners among men who were convicted for PV reveals a rich diversity of men's accounts of their involvement in violence. Although accepting responsibility for violence, all 22 men in her study explained why their actions were "appropriate, reasonable, necessary, within the actor's right and in fact were not that bad as perceived" (Wood 2004, p. 562). Most of the men mentioned being disrespected as men, having the right to control/discipline his woman, and being provoked in the form of verbal aggression and "pushing the button" by their female partners. Most of the men did not see themselves as "real abusers" and regretted that they abused their female partners. Wood (2004) suggests that the heterogeneity of men's accounts of PV may be associated with the conflicting codes of manhood that are present in US society.

Finally, some scholars intend to enrich our understanding of men's experiences of violence by examining men as victims of females' violence in intimate relationships (Hines et al. 2007; Hines and Douglas 2009, 2010a, b; Hines and Malley-Morrison 2001). They find a wide range of PV committed against men by their female partners, including psychological aggression, controlling behaviour, and severe violence in the form of "intimate terrorism". These findings add to the complex picture of men's experiences of PV. Despite these various deliberations concerning male offenders, what still appears to be missing are the considerations that male offenders 'may also be subject to personal frailties, family pressures, and external disadvantages' (Allen 1998, p. 66).

4 Violent Event and Interactional Perspectives on Partner Violence

Despite considerable progress in learning about partner violence in the last 40 years, there are still important gaps. In particular, there is a growing body of research calling for more studies of interactional, situational, and contextual aspects of PV that would incorporate the major theoretical assumptions of leading perspectives on PV and would provide a deeper understanding of the nature and dynamics of violent episodes and the role of both partners in them (e.g., Bell and Naugle 2008; Collins 2008; Heise 1998; Kruttschnitt et al. 2004; Meier et al. 2001; Wilkinson and Hamerschlag 2005; Winstok 2008, 2013). In addition, violent event and interactional perspectives would contribute to a better understanding of the heterogeneity of PV by identifying differences and similarities across various forms and types of PV.

Most PV theory and research tends to conceptualize the main components of PV separately as discrete units of analyses, i.e., perpetrators, victims, and the social situations within which violence takes place. Moreover, the relationships between these discrete components of PV are often formulated as binaries (e.g., victimization versus perpetration, male perpetrators versus female victims). Studies by family violence researchers, criminologists, and recent feminist scholars appear to challenge these simplistic conceptualizations of PV and depict a more complex picture of intimate violence as caused by a wide array of factors at the individual, interpersonal, and societal levels. However, these studies have often failed to conceptualize the factors in ways that emphasize their interrelatedness. Violent event and interactional perspectives provide a useful framework for analysing IPV as a contextualized dynamic process and therefore correct the aforementioned limitations.

4.1 Violent Event and Interaction as a Focus of Analysis

The violent event perspective (VEP) concentrates on the violent *event* rather than certain *actors* and their predispositions, and combines analyses of the perpetrator, the victim, and the context (Meier et al. 2001). In this respect, VEP addresses the specific nature of intimate relationships, in which participants are often active decision makers whose decisions reflect the interaction of motivation and social context and are contingent on the actions of others. A violent event perspective considers violent events as having, first, precursors, i.e., factors that precede and shape the content of events, then transactions, i.e., the interactions involving perpetrators, victims and the immediate environment, and lastly an aftermath, i.e., the consequences of the events for offenders, victims, and the larger community and the reactions of police and criminal justice agencies. To a certain degree, VEP is similar to ecological approaches (e.g., Heise 1998) by identifying different levels of social ecology and the factors that emerge as predictive of violence on each of these levels. On the other hand, VEP focuses on explaining the relationships among these components, which are often seen as separate elements in ecological approaches.

One of the central elements of the violent events framework is an emphasis on the *interaction* between two parties, whose roles of perpetrator and a victim are not fixed and emerge in the process of the violent interaction. The perspective that focuses on interaction and, unlike individual-based approaches, view each partner's behavioural acts and attitudes as embedded in rather than separate from the couple's interaction is interactional perspective.[7] Winstok and his colleagues (e.g., Eisikovits et al. 2002; Winstok 2008, 2013) and some communication researchers (e.g., Gottman and Notarius 2000; Olson 2004; Sabourin 1995) have been among the first to apply an interactional perspective to PV, which they consider to be a result of disrupted interaction. By interaction they generally understand behaviour as comprised of two consecutive acts, e.g., one party's act, such as a slap, leads to the successive act of the other party, such as a punch.

[7] This perspective is not the same as the symbolic interactionist perspective.

Escalation is a focal concept of an interactional approach to PV because it is thought of as an inherent tendency of any conflict, social or interpersonal (Cairns et al. 1994; Eckert and Willems 2003; Winstok 2013). Despite being an essential part of many conflicts, escalation has not been an independent field of basic sociological and criminological research. In the PV context, escalation often represents the process of circular interaction where two parties in an intimate relationship push one another to the intensification of a dispute by adopting changing strategies, taking up new issues and demands, and finally bringing it to the point where physical violence is used. Violent conflict escalation can be viewed as occurring both within and between PV incidents.

4.2 Women's Part in Violent Dynamics in PV Incidents

First and foremost, women are much more likely to perpetrate violence against a male partner in the intimate relationship rather than against a male stranger (Ben-David 1993; Winstok and Straus 2011). From an evolutionary viewpoint, fear is one of the factors that explains this difference. Fear can be seen as an adaptive mechanism, which reduces exposure to physical violence for women. In intimate relationships, women are likely to have reduced fear, which is mediated by the hormone oxytocin (Cross and Campbell 2011). This hormone is required for the establishment of sexual relationships with the partner. On the other hand, oxytocin can also disinhibit aggression toward a partner (Cross and Campbell 2011), which also contributes to the higher propensity of a woman to attack a male intimate partner rather than a male stranger (Winstok and Straus 2011). Other factors that facilitate women's use of violence within intimate relationships (i.e., the private domain) rather than outside (i.e., in the public domain) are the existence of specific psychological instigators to violence at home related to, for example, danger of harming the relationship, behavioural habitual responses to the particular instigators usually learnt at home, and situational aspects suitable for violence often related to an endangered woman's role as wife and mother (Ben-David 1993).

Although not systematically, researchers have examined some important aspects of violent dynamics in partner relationships, i.e., motives for the initial and reactive violence and an overall pattern of involvement in PV, which can be bidirectional (mutual) or one-sided (unilateral). The *initiation of violence* is important to study because partners can attribute their own violence to the allegedly initial violence of the other partner, thus considering their own violence as less serious or as justifiable. Moreover, examination of initial psychological aggression in addition to physical violence may provide a more nuanced picture of the dynamics of PV because psychological aggression can serve as a catalyst or a precipitating factor for physical violence (Infante et al. 1990; Roloff 1996; Stets 1990). Shame theory, for example, argues that traditionally socialized men are particularly vulnerable to humiliation and shame because it exposes their dependency needs, threatens their masculine self-concept, and reveals the limits of their power (Jennings and Murphy

2000). To save face, enraged men, particularly those without good skills to find constructive solutions, may be more likely to react to humiliation with violence against an intimate partner (Retzinger 1991).

Studies suggest that there are gender differences in the prevalence of initiation of psychological aggression and physical violence. For example, women are more likely than men to use mild forms of aggression, including psychological and indirect aggression, as a survival strategy (Bjorkqvist 1994). Indeed, research findings suggest that women report initiation of psychological aggression or physical violence in the majority of PV situations (54 %), followed by partner-initiated aggression or violence (36 %) and mutually initiated aggression or violence in 10 % of the PV incidents (Olson and Lloyd 2005). These findings are in line with other studies showing that women initiate aggression more often than men do (Archer 2000; Straus 1999).

4.2.1 Reaction to Initial Violence

Women's reactions to partners' initial violence can be expressed in two main ways, i.e., de-escalation (no use of violence) and escalation (use of violence). Some manifestations of de-escalation strategies used by women are negotiation and verbal reasoning, complying or agreeing with the accusations, toleration or remaining silent and passive (Dobash and Dobash 1979), and leaving the scene or attempting to withdraw from the situation (Messinger et al. 2011).

Women's use of violence in response to their partners' initial violence has long been associated with self-defence. However, emerging PV studies that impartially investigate the motives for female (and male) violence in response to perceived aggression, provocation, or threat to the relationship suggest that retaliation, punishment, and violent resistance prevail among the explanations for reactive violence committed by either partner,[8] and that self-defence is not consistently a leading motive for female-perpetrated violence (e.g., Gabora et al. 2007; Kruttschnitt and Carbone-Lopez 2006; Straus 2011). Moreover, studies find that accounts of self-defensive aggression even in samples of highly victimized women often are more consistent with retaliation, retribution (Bair-Merritt et al. 2010; Dasgupta 1999; Dobash and Dobash 1984) and what Foshee et al. (2007) identify as the "fed-up" motive and "anger response" and cannot always be clearly distinguished from self-defence (Bair-Merritt et al. 2010; Saunders 1988).

4.2.2 Use of Violence in the PV Incident

A growing body of research suggests that PV can be mutual/unilateral or unidirectional. Mutuality (also known as bidirectional and reciprocal violence) refers to the

[8] For a review, see Flynn and Graham (2010), Caldwell et al. (2009), Miller and Melloy (2006).

perpetration of assault by both partners within the PV incident. It is important to distinguish mutuality from symmetry of PV, which signifies approximately equal rates of perpetration by male and female partners at the population level (Straus 2011). Mutuality appears to be a characteristic of most couples that experience violence (Chiodo et al. 2012; Gabora et al. 2007; Goldenson et al. 2007; Johnson 2008; Kwong et al. 1999; Langhinrichsen-Rohling 2010; Palmetto et al. 2013; Whitaker et al. 2007). Unilateral violence, in turn, can be perpetrated solely by men or by women. Recent studies suggest that the prevalence of PV perpetrated solely by women ranges from 12 % among young women in dating relationships (Palmetto et al. 2013) and in a community sample of violent couples (Ross and Babcock 2012) to 15 % among female perpetrators of PV in federal prison in Canada (Gabora et al. 2007).

Studies suggest that mutual violence may represent a distinct phenomenon compared to a unilateral violent relationship (Caetano et al. 2005). However, there is no consensus in the PV literature on the association of mutuality with the frequency, severity, and rate of injuries to one or both partners. Some studies suggest bidirectional violence is associated with more severe injuries to partners (Caetano et al. 2005; Capaldi et al. 2007; Palmetto et al. 2013; Whitaker et al. 2007), while others find that mutual violence is associated with less severe consequences (Swan and Snow 2003).

4.3 Canadian Study of Women's Roles in the Violent Dynamics

To address the need for more context-inclusive and interaction-based research on violence in intimate relationships, this study draws on violent event and interactional perspectives and has two main objectives. First, it aims to identify the interactional patterns of women's use of violence against their male partners within PV incidents. The second objective is to examine the association between the identified patterns and relevant variables at the individual, relationship, and situational levels. This study relies upon data collected as a part of the Canadian-based *Women's Experiences of Violence: Victimization and Offending in the Context of Women's Lives* study (WEV, hereafter).[9] Women incarcerated in a provincial correctional facility in Ontario, Canada, regardless of their committed offense or history of violence, provided detailed accounts of what happened during PV

[9] The WEV project is a multi-site study of incarcerated women that started with a seed grant from the (U.S.) National Consortium on Violence Research (NCOVR) to Professors Julie Horney, Sally Simpson, Rosemary Gartner, and Candace Kruttschnitt. Professor Rosemary Gartner was subsequently awarded a grant (410-2000-0030) by the Social Sciences and Humanities Research Council of Canada (SSHRC) to collect data in Ontario, Canada. Data were also collected in Baltimore, Maryland (Sally Simpson, PI) and in Minneapolis, Minnesota (Candace Kruttschnitt, PI) using the same study design, instrument, and procedures.

incident(s) that took place during the 3 years prior to their incarceration. Respondents had been imprisoned for a variety of crimes, including property crimes (31 %), violent crimes (24 %), and drug-related crimes (15 %). Three quarters of the respondents were Caucasian, 15 % Aboriginal, and 5 % Afro-Canadians. In general, respondents' socio-economic status was quite low, which is consistent with other research on incarcerated women (Gabora et al. 2007; Richie 1996).

Women were asked to describe incidents of serious violence,[10] which they could remember clearly, and each woman could report up to eight incidents. A total of 135 women reported 295 violent episodes with a partner during the 3 years prior to their incarceration.[11] Neither the sample of women nor the sample of the PV incidents is random or representative of any known population. However, given the focus of my exploratory study on the intra-incident dynamics of PV, this sample is appropriate and allows me to address the research questions. Moreover, self-reported accounts of the respondents' violent interactions rather than directly observed PV incidents provide a valuable account of women's *perceptions* and *understanding* of what has happened to them in the course of these incidents and of the motives for their own actions (Eisikovits and Winstok 2002; Enosh and Buchbinder 2005; Flynn and Graham 2010).

Guided by the violent event perspective described above, the PV incident rather than an individual woman is the unit of analysis in this study. Women provided a narrative account of each incident, describing how the fight began, who did what to whom, who said what to whom, whether weapons were involved, the extent of injury experienced by the combatants, how the confrontation came to an end, and any other details the respondent could remember about the violent altercation. After providing their narrative descriptions, the women were asked a series of structured follow-up questions for each reported incident including questions about the location of the incident, number of bystanders, relationship between opponents, demographic characteristics of the opponent, and use of drugs or alcohol on the part of either opponent, among other details.

Because studies of the interactional dynamics of PV incidents are still in their infancy, I created a coding scheme and applied it to the 295 narratives of IPV incidents. The purpose was to identify whether male and female partners used violence in the entire incident, who initiated physical violence, what the partner's reaction to the initial violence was (i.e., escalation or de-escalation), and whether either partner was injured as a result of the violence. Next, a graduate student ("coder") with training in coding qualitative data and the author separately read and coded ten of the narratives, subsequently assessed for their inter-rater reliability. We then discussed the discrepancies in our coding and reached agreement on the appropriate codes. Next, we independently coded the next ten incidents, which resulted in 95–100 % agreement. After we resolved these discrepancies, the coder

[10] Narratives were not collected about incidents that involved only pushing, shoving, or grabbing where there were no injuries.

[11] All these incidents described violence in heterosexual relationships.

continued coding the rest of the incidents, consulting with the author whenever the coder had questions about a coding decision.

Then, drawing on these observed variables, the Latent Class Analysis (LCA) to identify the classes of PV incidents that represent patterns of violent dynamics was employed. This approach produced a latent unobserved variable with four classes of incidents depending on the types of violent dynamics that characterize them. In almost half of all incidents (Class I), male partners were described as the only one to use violence (49 %). Women in these incidents refrained from any violence, including self-defence, but still sustained injuries in over two thirds of the incidents. In 16 % of the incidents (Class II) women described how they solely perpetrated violence against a male intimate partner. In these incidents, women initiated violence, which was severe in 70 % of the cases (e.g., women described using knife or other sharp weapon, kicked or beat up partners). This can explain injuries to men in over half of these incidents. Two remaining classes of IPV incidents with a nearly similar number of cases in each category, i.e., 19 and 17 %, reflect what may be termed "mutual violence" because both partners appear to be actively engaged in violence in the course of these incidents. The difference between these two classes of the latent variable, however, reflects who initiates violence, men (Class III) or women (Class IV) respectively. Below are reported some of the main findings of the above study, as per its key variables.

4.3.1 Motives for a Violent Incident

This study reveals several salient motives for violence in PV incidents. Some of these motives are gender-specific and some are similar for both male and female partners. The motives that are associated with violence initiated by women are unfair or unjust treatment (e.g., men ignored women's needs and laughed at their concerns), issues about housing (e.g., women became violent if partners tried to evict them from the property), fear of losing custody of their children or that a partner will take or hurt their children. The women's emotions that appeared to prevail in these incidents were anger and fear. For example, a woman reported yelling at a partner who was laughing in response, so that she got very angry and "...just grabbed the knife and tried to stab him in the chest, but he hopped over the couch and I got his foot". It is noteworthy, that this motive often has been associated with homicide perpetrated by men (e.g., Katz 1988). At the same time, this gender-specific motive for women's violence in this study, i.e., perceived disrespect and humiliation from a male partner, has also been documented in other studies of women's violence (e.g., Kruttschnitt and Carbone-Lopez 2006; Miller and White 2003). Incidents in which men initiated violence against a female partner were most often associated with a challenge to their authority, especially if a woman challenged a partner's decision in the presence of his friends. However, in many incidents the motives were similar for both women's and men's initiation of violence, e.g., sexual jealousy, issues about alcohol and drugs, and issues about money.

4.3.2 Consequences of Women's Initiation of Violence

Women admitted initiating physical violence in one third of the incidents, which was severe in 57 % of these cases (e.g., women reported using a knife on a partner, kicking, or beating up a partner). At the same time, this also indicates that in almost half of the initial violent attacks by females their violence was minor (e.g., women most often reported slapping, grabbing, and pushing a male partner). Contrary to the expectations drawn from other research suggesting that male partners are likely to ignore or laugh rather than reciprocate the women's initial, in particular, minor violence (e.g., Miller and White 2003), my study documents that male partners responded violently in over half of these cases (51 %). This violent dynamic resulted in injuries to women in 41 % of the incidents in which women initiated minor violence, and in 32 % of the incidents in which women used severe violence. This finding highlights the potential danger to women of initiating even minor violence toward their partners (Straus 2005). Nevertheless, women's violence, in particular minor or "ordinary" forms, such as slapping or pushing, is often seen as an innocuous way for women to express their anger and frustration and not as an element of violent dynamics that increases their chances of injury and death (Straus 2005).

Two examples below illustrate how minor violence initiated by a woman is associated with men's retaliation.

> We were drinking at home, he had friends of his there, . . . he mentioned something about if he wanted to get laid he was going to pay $20 bucks for the girl outside – I slapped him in the face – he grabbed me around the throat and he said if you ever slap me like that again and I'll kill that – I got the hint – I never touched him again.

The woman who reported this incident went on to explain her behaviour in this way: "I was embarrassed—I had to defend me, I had to defend my reputation in front of his friends—he embarrassed me in front of his friends—I have a habit of striking out at people—it's a problem that has to stop." Another example that demonstrates a similar situation is the following:

> . . .we got in an argument [over the drugs] and I slapped him in the face – he tried to stop me from hitting him – he got so mad and he didn't mean to do it but he already had a knife in his hand – he was cutting up some dope – the back of the knife wacked me in my eye and my eye got all bust open. . .

4.3.3 Diversity of the Motives for Women's Reactive Violence

Women reported reacting with violence in response to men's initial violence in almost a third of the incidents (31 %). In the majority of these incidents (74 %) men's first attack was in the form of severe violence. i.e., women reported that their partners punched them in the head, kicked, pushed them off the stairs resulting in injuries, etc. Until recently, it was commonly believed that most of women's violence against an intimate partner was explained by self-defence. However, reading through the narratives suggests that there are at least four main reasons for women reacting to men's initiation of with violence, i.e., retaliation/anger response (44 %), followed by self-defence (31 %), contestation of power (21 %), and restraining violence (3 %). These findings are consistent with other studies that have identified the diversity of motives for women's use of violence against an intimate partner (e.g., Kruttschnitt and Carbone-Lopez 2006).

Examination of the motives for reactive violence perpetrated by men and women identified salient gender differences. Specifically, men were more likely to use retaliation than women (66 versus 44 %) whereas women were more likely to react violently for self-protection than men (31 and 4 % accordingly). These findings are consistent with the studies that suggest that self-defence is a clearly gendered motive for reactive violence. At the same time, these findings also indicate that self-defence is not necessarily a leading motive for female-perpetrated violence (e.g., Gabora et al. 2007; Kruttschnitt and Carbone-Lopez 2006; Straus 2011). Overall the high percentage of the incidents in which incarcerated women reported reacting violently for the purposes of retaliation or self-protection is in line with a study that found that incarcerated women were less likely to contact the police and more likely to take justice in their own hands (Dugan and Castro 2006).

In my study, *retaliation* was understood as an anger-motivated attempt to hurt the other, to intentionally cause harm to the partner, and to make him feel the pain for instigating violence or offense. Violence motivated by retaliation does not typically have any other instrumental goals but the emotional discharge. Retaliatory violence is rarely associated with fear but rather is spurred by a "tit-for-tat" attitude and anger. In the PV narratives respondents often mentioned such negative emotions as anger, rage, and frustration when they described violence out of retaliation. This excerpt from a narrative describes how the respondent appeared to retaliate in response to her partner's attempt to pick a fight and his violent behaviour.

> ...He said he was cold – I had put the air conditioner on – he got extremely pissed off because I didn't jump up to turn the air conditioner off – I took it that he was trying to pick a fight with me ... he pushed me away, shoved me and I went and I turned around and I smacked him back across the face – his nose was bleeding – he came and fucking threw me and started punching me on the head – this was all over an air conditioner...

Some other studies suggest that it is not always easy to distinguish between two motives for females' and males' PV, i.e., self-defence and retaliation. However, in reading the PV narratives, it became clear that women often indicated that the primary goal of their violence was *self-protection* or "to make him let me go". For example,

> ... I had gone out with the girls and I hadn't come back when I was 'supposed' to. He interpreted that that I was messing around on him... he told me that he was going to teach me a lesson – then he just kind of snapped and started punching me everywhere. I was trying to defend myself – verbally and a little bit physically... I started punching him back but then it turned to me defending myself and trying to block the shots – and then he just kept beating on me and telling me that maybe this would teach me not to mess around...[12]

[12] Because I keep the language used in the narratives intact, the excerpts can contain some mistakes and inappropriate usage of words.

The other common theme regarding motives for reactive violence is what I term a *contestation of power*. This refers to instrumental violence that partners use to get what they want, to insist on their opinion or will, and/or to continue doing something against the other partner's will. For example, several narratives describe situations when partners fight over property and most often female partners strike back in order to stay in the house or apartment:

> . . .Basically he wanted me out [of the house] and I needed some time to secure a place . . . he wanted to throw me out of the house – I stood my ground and said no I'm not leaving – that's when it became really physically violent. . . I was in the bedroom – he grabbed me and sort of physically hit me. . . Prior to getting physically thrown out there was huge verbal abuse – I would dig my heels in and say that I said a right to stay here – when I did dig in my heels it was brutal – biting, hitting, knocked down and dragged out of my house.

Finally, my study identified an additional theme associated with motives for reactive violence, what may be termed the *restraining violence* (or escalation prevention) motive. In the PV narratives, most often male partners attempted to prevent the escalation of female physical fighting by restraining women while they were using violence against them or attempted to harm them with a weapon, or pre-empting an impending violent act against them. The acts that were used by the male partners to prevent escalation of physical fighting were primarily grabbing the respondent's arms and restraining her, shoving her away from him, or pushing her down on the floor and holding her there until she quit trying to hit him or until she calmed down. This motive for typically male reactive violence is identified by Foshee et al. (2007) who created a typology of perpetration events in dating relationships.

The following excerpt from the IPV narratives in my study illustrates this motive:

> It started because I wanted him to buy more dope – I knew he had money - he didn't want to but I pushed and pushed him – It started into a big argument – he wanted to go to bed because it was 2 o'clock in the morning – he said something to me and I got really violent and I pushed him onto the bed – he knows that I get violent so he tried to stop me – he grabbed me, but not in a hurtful way - so I punched him – and then I walked out of the room. . .

4.3.4 Habituation to Violence

One of the salient characteristics of the incidents, described by incarcerated women in my study, is a prevailing sense of normality of violence by women engaged in it. The incident below illustrates it.

> We were just drinking and arguing [I don't remember what the argument was about] and I just threw a beer bottle at his head. I just threw it and it went in the wall – got stuck there in the wall. . .it was just kinda hanging there. We laughed, though. . .that's when we got along

In another incident, a woman describes attacking her partner with a knife and actually cutting his hand in response to her partner's violence. But injuries to a partner and the potential danger to the woman do not seem to restrain the partners from having another beer together.

> I was in the hospital for 2 weeks for psych care – I come home and got my welfare cheque for $490 - we (respondent and partner) bought some beer – we were sitting around drinking – he called me names – fat and ugly – he was drunk and he gets assholish when he's drinking – and he close fist punched me – I got an instant black eye – so I hit him back – and then he just kept it up and I just grabbed the knife and I stabbed him – I'd had enough – that's it that's all – the knife was on the TV – we were outside on the carport – there was an empty TV– there was no guts in it – he saw me coming with the knife and he put his arms up and I stabbed him in the forearm – he called me a fucking bitch and he wrapped his arm up and then he sat back down and had another beer with me...

The sense of normality of violence also emerged from the incidents, in which women after incidents of severe violence would continue relationships with their male partners. The incident below illustrates this situation.

> We were verbally arguing and then I smacked him in the face and then I ran – he got me so I sat down on the couch in the living room – he threw a full bottle of root beer at me – I remember seeing stars so I think it almost knocked me out – I went to the phone and he jumped in the truck and left – I told him never to come back – we stayed broken up for two weeks and then I took him back like a fucking idiot

One of the explanations for the apparent normality of violence in women's intimate relationships stems from the attitudinal differences in relation to violence among people with higher and lower socio-economic status (SES). In other words, adverse social conditions can help form and start social schemes that condone violent-prone attitudes and norms and thus lead to more violence (Markowitz and Felson 1998). Given that women in my study come predominantly from the lower social class, which is reflected in their lower income, fewer years of education, and a lack of legal occupation among others, it is perhaps not surprising that there is greater tolerance of violence among them than among women with higher SES. In addition, due to assortative mating women seem to be likely to date and get into relationships with the men who are similar to them in their attitudes to violence. Hence, risk factors in common to both partners can increase the likelihood of mutual violence in these couples (Palmetto et al. 2013).

4.3.5 Factors Associated with Women's Use of Violence in PV Incidents

To identify associations between various independent variables (i.e. individual, relationship, and situational) and classes of PV incidents, I used the multivariate logistic regression analysis. One of the analyses compares incidents in Class I (i.e., in which men were the only ones to use violence) (Group 1) with incidents in Classes II, III, and IV combined (i.e. in which women used violence against the partner) (Group 2). Incidents in Group 1 were coded "0" and incidents in the Group

2 were coded "1". Among the variables that significantly predicted membership in Group 2 relative to Group 1 are more frequent experiences of child abuse for women (an individual-level variable), shorter relationship length (a relationship–level variable), and unjust behaviour of the partner, women's alcohol use, and women's weapon (situational-level variables). Said differently, women's PV victimisation is associated with women's infrequent experiences of child abuse and staying in longer relationships with their partners. At the situational level, women who become targets of violence are not likely to drink alcohol before the incident or to use a weapon during the incident. Some of these variables have already been found to be associated with women's victimisation and perpetration in other studies (Abramsky et al. 2011; Baskin and Sommers 1998; Babcock et al. 2003; Kruttschnitt et al. 2004; Miller and Mullins 2006; Swan and Snow 2003).

In sum, this study is directed at an under-researched area in the literature on women's experiences of violence in PV incidents, i.e. the sequence of interactions and motivations associated with their use (or non-use) of violence. Although the women in my sample represented a high-risk population and, as research literature suggests, have higher chances than non-criminalized populations to face PV in their lives (Chesney-Lind and Pasko 2013; Gabora et al. 2007; Richie 1996), they reported a great heterogeneity of motives for and patterns of PV including their own use of violence against a male partner. However, it is important to note that because this study refers to heterosexual intimate relationships and is carried out in the Western industrialized country the study's findings cannot be generalized to non-Western countries and to same-sex intimate partner relationships.

5 Conclusion and Implications for Social Policy and Future Research

5.1 Conclusion

This chapter was premised on the idea that it is important to explore both men's and women's contributions to violence in intimate relationships because it is increasingly recognized that to ignore or deny women's capacity for and men's vulnerability to violence limits our understanding of PV and reduces our ability to protect women and men from injury and death at the hands of their intimate partners. Moreover, we cannot longer ignore mounting research in industrialized countries that documents the heterogeneity and diversity of patterns of PV. Many of these studies examined women's explanations for their involvement in violence and found a wide range of motives for their engagement in violent behaviour and thus challenged the overall myth of a nonaggressive woman and antiagentic representation of women's involvement in PV.

The above reported study of PV incidents narrated by incarcerated women in Canada also suggests that women possess much greater agency in perpetrating violence against a male partner than many have argued. In addition, my analysis identified salient patterns of violent dynamics in PV incidents (including incidents in which males and females were dominant perpetrators of violence as well as incidents involving mutual violence), and risk factors at the individual, relationship, and situational levels that are associated with these patterns. For example, women's perpetration of violence was associated with frequent experiences of abuse in childhood, alcohol use, and shorter relationships with their partners. I also found a pronounced prevalence of anger in women's narratives about the situations they perceived as unjust, which appeared to incite their use of initial and reactive violence. Moreover, my findings suggest that women's behaviour in violent situations with their partners is associated with different consequences for women (and men), which opens up opportunities for interventions that help reduce negative consequences of violence.

However, despite women's undoubted involvement in violence as perpetrators, almost half of the incidents in the study described cases of predominantly severe violence perpetrated solely by men against women, cases in which women sustained injures no matter how they attempted to deescalate in response to partners' violence. Moreover, these incidents most often happened when women reported they had challenged their partners' power and authority. This clearly indicates that violence against women by their male partners continues to be a serious problem for women even in the industrialised countries and that the continuing efforts should be made to increase gender equality and fight ideologies supportive of men's superiority.

Given these findings, it may be reasonable to argue that a more nuanced and comprehensive understanding of different dimensions of this phenomenon, ranging from societal and relationship to individual and situational levels, can enhance strategies aimed at preventing and addressing this issue globally. In other words, emphases on different dimensions of this phenomenon should not be seen as excluding each other, but rather as representing different sides of this complex issue, which together can help examine the phenomenon as fully as possible.[13]

5.2 *Implications for Future Research*

The efficiency of the strategies to address partner violence at the individual, relationship, community, and global levels hinges upon our readiness to embrace the conceptualisation of partner violence as a multidimensional and complex

[13] The current scholarship of PV, however, still seems to be torn apart by the heated debates "who is more victim", "who is more violent", and "who deserves more help" (e.g., see issue 16 (4) of the *Aggression and Violent Behaviour* (July, 2011)).

phenomenon by examining different dimensions of this phenomenon. In practical terms, the reported study emphasizes the importance of, for example, collecting information about both women's and men's perceptions and meanings of violence, about perpetration of violent behaviour by both partners, and about the availability of services/sources of help for women as well as for men. Moreover, despite many gender-specific aspects, women's engagement in violence is similar to men's in important respects and hence our understanding of PV may benefit from an integrated approach, i.e., one that combines traditional theories of crime (life-course, situational and personality theories) and violence and gender perspectives (e.g., feminist theories).

At the same time, it is important to be aware of the challenges associated with more agentic views of women's engagement in partner violence for research at the global perspective. First, studies conducted in the industrialised countries may not be necessarily relevant to the non-industrialized or traditional countries with its drastic gender inequality and cultural and religious practices that indirectly or directly mandate violence against women. Hence, further studies are needed. Second, research on this issue especially in traditional societies should abide by principles that put the safety of women first (WHO 2001).

5.3 *Implications for Social Policy*

Prevention and treatment of PV has received considerable attention in the industrialized world as well as globally. Despite this, our knowledge of how to predict and prevent the most dangerous incidents of violence, including lethal cases of PV, is still limited (Kieselbach and Butchart 2012). Moreover, evaluation of nearly universal policies implemented in many industrialized countries in the criminal justice system (e.g., court-mandated treatment programs, mandatory arrest and no-drop prosecution policy) and in treatment (e.g., gender-specific groups for male offenders) provide mixed results (e.g., Babcock et al. 2004; Buzawa et al. 2012). Although relying heavily on criminal justice interventions to limit domestic violence has transformed societal perceptions of PV as a crime and increased the willingness of individuals to accept responsibility for dealing with abuse in their lives, growing evidence suggests that criminal justice interventions alone have limited effects on domestic violence (Buzawa et al. 2012). Instead, the most effective approaches seem to involve cross-agency and cross-community alliances and coordination (e.g., Butchart 2011) and those that rely on scientifically grounded observations about which elements of which interventions are effective for which subgroups (e.g., Miller et al. 2005).

In addition, I argue that a more comprehensive understanding of various patterns of PV not only at the societal or macro-level but also at the micro-level of social ecology, including situational and interactional risk factors and patterns of violent dynamics, can help us develop more nuanced strategies to reduce PV in the industrialized countries as well as globally. The policies to address PV globally can in particular benefit from more context-inclusive and culturally sensitive approaches to PV as some international studies of risk factors for PV (Abramsky et al. 2011) and anthropological studies imply (Merry 2006).

Because a "one size fits all" approach does not seem to work for addressing such a complex and multidimensional phenomenon as PV, carefully tailored interventions for different types of violence and violent types/incidents should be considered. Specifically, unidirectional chronic and severe violence against a partner, whether the perpetrator is a male or female, calls for more offender- and violence-specific types of intervention (i.e., individual treatment programs to address personality disorders and anger issues). In the case of mutual violence in couples, which varies from mild to moderate severity, and where partners have no alcohol abuse or mental health issues that may compromise safety, conjoint couple therapy is seen as most appropriate (Antunes-Alves and Stefano 2013; Trute 1998). Conjoint couple therapy has long been debated in the professional and scientific communities in relation to cases of PV. The major criticism of this approach has been associated with putting victims at greater risk by directing blame at them and in turn reducing or eliminating the legal or moral accountability of perpetrators (Stith and McCollum 2011). At the same time, conjoint therapy appears to address the important issues of the relational dynamics, such as dissatisfaction and distress, and also ineffective interpersonal problem solving skills that other gender-specific interventions such as, for example, batterer intervention programs have overlooked (for review, see Harris 2006).

It is worth mentioning that attention to the situational and international aspects of violent dynamics and relevant policies should be seen as supplementary to rather than competing with continuing efforts to bring greater gender equality and economic stability to societies around the globe. It is also important to emphasise that any violence against another human being is wrong and agentic views on female perpetration of PV that highlight women's agency, rationality and decision-making capability in no way represent the liberation of women or acclaim this kind of resiliency. Research on violence generally concur that violence begets violence and support the idea that any violence, whether against a man, woman or a child, should be stopped.

Five Questions

1. What are the major perspectives on women's experiences of partner violence in addition to a "violence against women" framework?
2. What research tools do we have and use to learn about men's experiences of partner violence worldwide?
3. Can we fully comprehend the nature of partner violence without examining its situational and interactional dimensions?
4. How should research on the woman's use of violence in an intimate relationship be done so as not to imply "blaming the victim" or render her "bad, mad or evil"?
5. How can knowledge about interactional and situational aspects of partner violence, in combination with what is known about societal risk factors, help us improve policies to address partner violence around the globe?

References

Abramsky, T., Watts, C. H., Garcia-Moreno, C., Devries, K., Kiss, L., Ellsberg, M., Jansen, H., & Heise, L. (2011). What factors are associated with recent intimate partner violence? Findings from the WHO multi-country study on women's health and domestic violence. *BMC Public Health, 11*, 109.

Allen, C. (1998). Rendering them harmless: The professional portrayal of women charged with serious violent crimes. In K. Daly & L. Maher (Eds.), *Criminology at the crossroads: Feminist readings in crime and justice* (pp. 54–68). New York: Oxford University Press.

Antunes-Alves, S., & Stefano, J. D. (2013). Intimate partner violence: Making the case for joint couple treatment. *The Family Journal*, published online 21 October 2013 doi: 10.1177/1066480713505056.

Archer, J. (2000). Sex differences in aggression between heterosexual partners: A meta-analytic review. *Psychological Bulletin, 126*, 651–680.

Babcock, J., Green, C. E., & Robie, C. (2004). Does batterers' treatment work? A meta—analytic review of domestic violence treatment outcome research. *Clinical Psychology Review, 23*, 1023–1053.

Babcock, J., Miller, S., & Siard, C. (2003). Toward a typology of abusive women: Differences between partner-only and generally violent women in the use of violence. *Psychology of Women Quarterly, 27*, 151–161.

Bair-Merritt, M. H., Crowne, S. S., Thompson, D. A., Sibinga, E., Trent, M., & Campbell, J. (2010). Why do women use intimate partner violence? A systematic review of women's motivations. *Trauma, Violence, and Abuse, 11*(4), 178–189.

Baskin, D. R., & Sommers, I. B. (1998). *Casualties of community disorder: Women's careers in violent crime*. Boulder, CO: Westview.

Bell, K. M., & Naugle, A. E. (2008). Intimate partner violence theoretical considerations: Moving towards a contextual framework. *Clinical Psychology Review, 28*, 1096–1107.

Ben-David, S. (1993). The two facets of female violence: The public and the domestic domains. *Journal of Family Violence, 8*(2), 345–359.

Bjorkqvist, K. (1994). Sex differences in physical, verbal, and indirect aggression: A review of recent research. *Sex Roles, 30*(3/4), 177–188.

Bourgois, P. (1996). In search of masculinity—violence, respect and sexuality among Puerto Rican crack dealers. *British Journal Criminology, 36*, 412–427.

Butchart, A. (2011). Public health and preventing violence. *BMJ, 342*, d2882. doi:10.1136/bmj.d2882.

Buzawa, E. S., Buzawa, C. G., & Stark, E. (2012). *Responding to domestic violence: The integration of criminal justice and human services* (4th ed.). Thousands Oaks, CA: Sage.

Caetano, R., Ramisetty-Mikler, S., & Field, C. (2005). Unidirectional and bidirectional intimate partner violence among White, Black, and Hispanic couples in the United States. *Violence and Victims, 20*(4), 393–405.

Cairns, R. B., Santoyo, C. V., Holly, K. A. (1994). Aggressive escalation: Toward a developmental analysis. In M Potegan, & J. F. Knutson (Eds.), *The dynamics of aggression: Biological and social processes in dyads and groups* (pp. 225–253). Hillsdale, NJ: Lawrence Erlbaum Associates.

Caldwell, J. E., Swan, S. C., Allen, C. N., Sullivan, T. P., & Snow, D. (2009). Research examining the motivation of women's use of intimate partner violence. Why I hit him: Women's reasons for intimate partner violence. *Journal of Aggression, Maltreatment, and Trauma, 18*, 672–697.

Capaldi, D. M., Kim, H. K., & Shortt, J. W. (2007). Observed initiation and reciprocity of physical aggression in young, at-risk couples. *Journal of Family Violence, 22*, 101–111.

Chesney-Lind, M. (1989). Girls' crime and woman's place: Toward a feminist model of female delinquency. *Crime and Delinquency, 35*(1), 5–29.

Chesney-Lind, M., & Pasko, L. (2013). *The female offender: Girls, women, and crime* (3rd ed.). Thousand Oaks, CA: Sage.

Chiodo, D., Crooks, C. V., Wolfe, D. A., McIssac, C., Hughes, R., & Jaffe, P. G. (2012). Longitudinal prediction and concurrent functioning of adolescent girls demonstrating various profiles of dating violence and victimization. *Prevention Science, 13*, 350–359.

Collins, R. (2008). *Violence: A micro-sociological theory*. Princeton: Princeton University Press.

Comack, E., & Balffour, G. (2004). *The power to criminalize: Violence, inequality and the law*. Winnipeg and Halifax: Fernwood.

Cross, C., & Campbell, A. (2011). Women's aggression. *Aggression and Violent Behaviour, 16*, 390–398.

Daly, K. (1998). Women's pathways to felony court: Feminist theories of lawbreaking and problems of representation. In K Daly, & L. Maher (Eds.), *Criminology at the crossroads* (pp. 135–156). New York: Oxford University Press.

Dasgupta, S. D. (1999). Just like men? A critical view of violence by women. In M. E. Shephard & E. L. Pence (Eds.), *Coordinating community responses to domestic violence* (pp. 195–222). Thousand Oaks, CA: Sage Publications.

Day, T., McKenna, K., & Bowlus, A. (2005). The economic costs of violence against women: An evaluation of the literature. Expert brief complied in preparation for the Secretary-General's in-depth study on all forms of violence against women. http://www.un.org/womenwatch/daw/vaw/expert%20brief%20costs.pdf. Accessed 24 April 2014.

Devries, K. M., Mak, J. Y. T., Garcia-Moreno, C., et al. (2013). The global prevalence of intimate partner violence against women. *Science, 340*(6140), 1527–1528.

Dobash, R. E., & Dobash, R. P. (1979). *Violence against wives: A case against the patriarchy*. New York: Free Press.

Dobash, R. E., & Dobash, R. P. (1984). The nature and antecedents of violent events. *British Journal of Criminology, 24*, 269–287.

Downs, D. A. (1996). *More than victims: Battered women, the syndrome society, and the law*. Chicago: University of Chicago Press.

Dugan, L., & Castro, J. L. (2006). Predictors of violence victimization: National Crime Victimization Survey women and jailed women. In K. Heimer & C. Kruttschnitt (Eds.), *Gender and crime: Patterns of victimization and offending* (pp. 171–194). New York: New York University Press.

Dutton, D. G. (2006). *Rethinking domestic violence*. Vancouver: University of British Columbia press.

Dutton, D. G. (2007). Thinking outside of box: Gender and court-mandated therapy. In J. Hamel, & T. Nicholls (Eds.), *Family interventions in domestic violence: A handbook of gender-inclusive theory and treatment* (pp. 27–59). New York, NY: Springer.

Eckert, R., & Willems, H. (2003). Escalation and de-escalation of social conflicts: The road to violence. In W. Heimeyer & J. Hagan (Eds.), *International handbook of violence research* (pp. 1181–1199). Netherlands: Kluwer Academic.

Eisikovits, Z., & Winstok, Z. (2002). Reconstructing intimate violence: The structure and content of recollections of violent events. *Qualitative Health Research, 12*(5), 685–699.

Eisikovits, Z., Winstok, Z., & Gelles, R. J. (2002). Structure and dynamics of escalation from the victim's perspective. *Families in Society, 83*(2), 142–152.

Ellsberg, M., Jansen, H. A., Heise, L., Watts, C. H., & Garcia-Moreno, C. (2008). Intimate partner violence and women's physical and mental health in the WHO multi-country study on women's health and domestic violence: An observational study. *Lancet, 371*(9619), 1165–1172.

Enosh, G., & Buchbinder, E. (2005). Strategies of distancing from emotional experience: Making memories of domestic violence. *Qualitative Social Work, 4*(1), 9–32.

Flynn, A., & Graham, K. (2010). 'Why did it happen?' A review and conceptual framework for research on perpetrators' and victims' explanations for intimate partner violence. *Aggression and Violent Behaviour, 15*, 239–251.

Foshee, V. A., Bauman, K. E., Linder, F., Rice, J., & Wilcher, R. (2007). Typologies of adolescent dating violence: Identifying typologies of adolescent dating violence perpetration. *Journal of Interpersonal Violence, 22*(5), 498–519.

Gabora, N., Stewart, L., Lilley, K., & Allegri, N. (2007). A profile of female perpetrators of intimate partner violence: Implications for treatment. *Correctional Service Canada, R-175*, 1–10.
Garcia-Moreno, C., Jansen, H. A., Ellsberg, M., Heise, L., & Watts, C. H. (2006). Prevalence of intimate partner violence: Findings from the WHO multi-country study on women's health and domestic violence. *Lancet, 68*(9543), 1260–1269.
García-Moreno, C., & Riecher-Rössler, A. (Eds.), (2013). *Violence against women and mental health: Key issues mental health* (Vol. 178). Basel: Karger.
Gartner, R., & McCarthy, B. (2006). Maternal infanticide and the dark figure of homicide: Beyond the mad, the bad, and the victim. In K. Heimer & C. Kruttschnitt (Eds.), *Gender and crime: Patterns in victimization and offending* (pp. 91–114). New York: New York University Press.
Goldenson, J., Geffner, R., Foster, S., & Clipson, C. (2007). Female domestic violence offenders: Their attachment security, trauma symptoms, and personality organization. *Violence and Victims, 22*(5), 530–543.
Goldscheid, J. (2014). Gender neutrality, the 'Violence Against Women' frame, and transformative reform (August 1, 2013). 84 UMKC L. Rev. Available at SSRN: http://ssrn.com/abstract=2304716 or http://dx.doi.org/10.2139/ssrn.2304716
Gottman, J. M., & Notarius, C. I. (2000). Decade review: Observing marital interaction. *Journal of Marriage and Family, 62*(4), 927–947.
Graham, K., Bernard, S., Munne, M., & Wilsnack, S. (Eds.). (2008). *Unhappy hours: Alcohol and partner aggression in the Americas*. Washington DC: PAHO.
Hamby, S. (2009). The gender debate about intimate partner violence: Solution and dead ends. *Psychological Trauma: Theory, Research, Practice and Policy, 1*(1), 24–34.
Hamel, J., & Nicholls, T. (Eds.). (2007). *Family interventions in domestic violence: A handbook of gender-inclusive theory and treatment*. New York: Springer.
Harris, G. E. (2006). Conjoint therapy and domestic violence: Treating the individuals and the relationship. *Counselling Psychology Quarterly, 19*(4), 373–379.
Heise, L. L. (1998). Violence against women: An integrated, ecological framework. *Violence Against Women, 4*(3), 262–290.
Henning, K., Renauer, B., & Holdford, R. (2006). Victim or offender? Heterogeneity among women arrested for intimate partner violence. *Journal of Family Violence, 21*, 351–368.
Hines, D. A., Brown, J., & Dunning, E. (2007). Characteristics of callers to the domestic abuse helpline for men. *Journal of Family Violence, 22*, 63–72.
Hines, D. A., & Douglas, E. M. (2009). Women's use of intimate partner violence against men: prevalence, implications, and consequences. *Journal of Aggression, Maltreatment & Trauma, 18*(6), 572–586.
Hines, D. A., & Douglas, E. M. (2010a). A closer look at men who sustain intimate terrorism by women. *Partner Abuse, 1*(3), 286–313.
Hines, D. A., & Douglas, E. M. (2010b). Intimate terrorism by women towards men: Does it exist? *Journal of Aggression, Conflict and Peace Research, 2*(3), 36–56.
Hines, D. A., & Malley-Morrison, K. (2001). Psychological effects of partner abuse against men: A neglected research area. *Psychology of Men and Masculinity, 2*, 75–85.
Holtzworth-Munroe, A. (2005). Female perpetration of physical aggression against an intimate partner: A controversial new topic of study. *Violence and Victims, 20*(2), 251–259.
Holtzworth-Munroe, A., & Meehan, J. C. (2004). Typologies of men who are martially violent: Scientific and clinical implications. *Journal of Interpersonal Violence, 19*(12), 1369–1389.
Holtzworth-Munroe, A., & Stuart, G. L. (1994). Typologies of male batterers: Three subtypes and the differences among them. *Psychological Bulletin, 116*(3), 476–497.
Infante, D. A., Sabourin, T. C., Rudd, J. E., & Shannon, E. A. (1990). Verbal aggression in violent and nonviolent marital disputes. *Communication Quarterly, 38*, 361–371.
Jennings, J., & Murphy, C. M. (2000). Male-male dimensions of male-female battering: A new look at domestic violence. *Psychology of Men and Masculinity, 1*(1), 21–29.

Jewkes, R. (2002). Intimate partner violence: Causes and prevention. *Lancet, 359*(9315), 1423–1429.
Johnson, M. P. (2008). *A typology of domestic violence: intimate terrorism, violent resistance, and situational couple violence*. Boston: Northeastern University press.
Katz, J. (1988). *Seduction of crime: Moral and sensual attractions in doing evil*. New York: Basic Books.
Kieselbach, B. S., & Butchart, A. (2012). Strengthening capacity for the prevention of family violence in low-income and middle-income countries. *Injury Prevention, 18*(2), 146.
Krug, E., Dahlberg, L. L., Mercy, J. A., Zwi, A. B., & Lozano, R. (Eds.). (2002). World report on violence and health. WHO. www.who.int/violence_injury_prevention/violence/world_report/en/. Accessed 26 May 2014.
Kruttschnitt, C., & Carbone-Lopez, K. (2006). Moving beyond the stereotypes: Women's subjective accounts of their violent crime. *Criminology, 44*(2), 321–351.
Kruttschnitt, C., McLaughlin, B. L., & Petrie, C. V. (2004). *Advancing the federal research agenda on violence against women/steering committee for the workshop on issues in research on violence against women; Committee on Law and Justice, Division of Behavioural and Social Sciences and Education, National Research Council of the National Academies*. Washington, D.C.: National Academies Press
Kurz, D. (1993). Physical assaults by husbands: A major social problem. In R. J. Gelles & D. R. Loseke (Eds.), *Current controversies on family violence* (1st ed., pp. 88–103). Thousand Oaks, CA: Sage.
Kwong, M. I., Bartholomew, K., & Dutton, A. (1999). Gender differences in patterns of relationship violence in Alberta. *Canadian Journal of Behavioural Science, 31*, 150–160.
Langhinrichsen-Rohling, J. (2010). Controversies involving gender and intimate partner violence in the United States. *Sex Roles, 62*(3–4), 179–193.
Maher, L., & Curtis, R. (1998). Women on the edge of crime: Crack cocaine and the changing context of street-level sex work in New York city. In K. Daly & L. Maher (Eds.), *Criminology at the crossroads: Feminist readings in crime and justice* (pp. 110–134). New York: Oxford University Press.
Markowitz, F., & Felson, R. (1998). Social-demographic attitudes and violence. *Criminology, 36* (1), 117–138.
Meier, R. F., Kennedy, L. W., & Sacco, V. (Eds.). (2001). *The process and structure of crime: Criminal events and crime analysis*. New Brunswick: Transaction Publishers.
Merry, S. E. (2006). *Human rights and gender violence: Translating international law into local justice*. Chicago: University of Chicago Press.
Messerschmidt, J. (1997). *Crime as structured action: Gender, race, class, and crime in the making*. Thousand Oaks, CA: Sage.
Messinger, A. M., Davidson, L., & Rickert, V. I. (2011). IPV among adolescent reproductive health patients: The role of relationship communication. *Journal of Interpersonal Violence, 26* (9), 1851–1867.
Miller, S. L., Gregory, C., & Iovanni, L. (2005). One size fits all? A gender-neutral approach to a gender-specific problem: Contrasting batterer treatment programs for male and female offenders. *Criminal Justice Policy Review, 16*(3), 336–359.
Miller, S. L., & Melloy, M. L. (2006). Women's use of force: Voices of women arrested for domestic violence. *Violence Against Women, 12*(1), 89–115.
Miller, J., & Mullins, C. W. (2006). The status of feminist theories in criminology. In F. T. Cullen, J. Wright, & K. Blevins (Eds.), *Taking stock: The status of criminological theory, advances in criminological theory* (vol. 15). Freda Adler and William Laufer. Piscataway, NJ: Transaction Publishers.
Miller, J., & White, N. (2003). Gender and adolescent relationship violence: A contextual examination. *Criminology, 41*(4), 1207–1248.
Moe, A. (2004). Blurring the Boundaries: Women's criminality in the context of abuse. *Women's Studies Quarterly, 32*(3/4), 116–138.

Monson, C., & Langhinrichsen-Rohling, J. (2002). Sexual and nonsexual dating violence perpetration: Testing an integrated perpetrator typology. *Violence and Victims, 17*(4), 403–428.
Morrissey, B. (2003). *When women kill: Questions of agency and subjectivity*. New York: Routledge.
Olson, L. (2004). Relational control-motivated aggression: A theoretically-based typology of intimate violence. *Journal of Family Communication, 4*, 209–233.
Olson, L. N., & Lloyd, S. A. (2005). 'It depends on what you mean by starting': An exploration of how women define initiation of aggression and their motives for behaving aggressively. *Sex Roles, 53*(7–8), 603–617.
Palermo, T., Beck, J., & Peterman, A. (2014). Tip of the iceberg: Reporting and gender-based violence in developing countries. *American Journal of Epidemiology, 179*(5), 602–612.
Palmetto, N., Davidson, L., Breirbart, V., & Rickert, V. (2013). Predictors of physical intimate partner violence in the lives of young women: Victimization, perpetration, and bidirectional violence. *Violence and Victims, 28*(1), 103–121.
Polk, K. (1998). Masculinity, order, and confrontational homicide. In K. Daly & L. Maher (Eds.), *Criminology at the crossroads: Feminist readings in crime and justice* (pp. 188–208). New York: Oxford University Press.
Retzinger, S. M. (1991). *Violent emotions: Shame and rage in marital quarrels*. Newbury Park, CA: Sage.
Richardson, S. R. (2005). The myth of female passivity: Thirty years of revelations about female aggression. *Psychology of Women Quarterly, 29*, 238–247.
Richie, B. E. (1996). *Compelled to crime: The gender entrapment of battered black women*. New York: Routledge.
Robertson, K., & Murachver, T. (2011). Women and men's use of coercive control in intimate partner violence. *Violence and Victims, 26*(2), 208–217.
Roloff, M. E. (1996). The catalyst hypothesis: Conditions under which coercive communication leads to physical aggression. In D. D Cahn & S. A Lloyd (Eds.), *Family violence from a communication perspective* (pp. 20–37). Thousands Oaks, CA: Sage.
Ross, J. M., & Babcock, J. C. (2012). Gender differences in partner violence in context: Deconstructing Johnson's (2001) control-based typology of violent couples. In L. M. Conradi & R. Geffner (Eds.), *Female offenders of intimate partner violence: Current controversies, research, and treatment approaches* (pp. 58–76). New York: Routledge.
Sabourin, T. C. (1995). The role of negative reciprocity in spouse abuse: A relational control analysis. *Journal of Applied Communication Research, 23*, 271–283.
Saunders, D. G. (1988). Wife abuse, husband abuse, or mutual combat. In K. Yllo & M. Bograd (Eds.), *Feminist perspectives on wife abuse* (pp. 90–113). Newbury Park, CA: Sage.
Snider, L. (2008). Criminalizing violence against women: Solution or dead end? *Criminal Justice Matters, 74*(1), 38–39.
Stark, E. (2007). *Coercive control: The entrapment of women in personal life*. New York: Oxford University Press.
Stets, J. E. (1990). Verbal and physical aggression in marriage. *Journal of Marriage and the Family, 52*, 501–514.
Stith, S. M., & McCollum, E. E. (2011). Conjoint treatment of couples who have experienced intimate partner violence. *Aggression and Violent Behaviour, 16*, 312–318.
Stith, S. M., McCollum, E. E., & Rosen, K. H. (2011). *Couple therapy for domestic violence: Finding safe solutions*. Washington, DC: American Psychological Association.
Straus, M. A. (1999). The controversy over domestic violence by women: A methodological, theoretical and sociology of science analysis. In X. B. Arriaga & S. Oskamp (Eds.), *Violence in intimate relationships* (pp. 17–44). Thousand Oaks, CA: Sage.
Straus, M. A. (2005). Women's violence toward men is a serious social problem. In D. R. Loseke, R. J. Gelles, & M. M. Cavanaugh (Eds.), *Current controversies on family violence* (2nd ed., pp. 55–77). Newbury Park: Sage Publications.

Straus, M. A. (2008). Dominance and symmetry in partner violence by male and female university students in 32 nations. *Children and Youth Services Review, 30*, 252–275.
Straus, M. A. (2011). Gender symmetry and mutuality in perpetration of clinical-level partner violence: Empirical evidence and implications for prevention and treatment. *Aggression and Violent Behaviour, 16*, 279–288.
Swan, S. C., & Snow, D. L. (2003). A typology of women's use of violence in intimate relationships. *Violence Against Women, 8*, 286–319.
Trute, B. (1998). Going beyond gender-specific treatments in wife battering: Pro-feminist couple and family therapy. *Aggression and Violent Behaviour, 3*(1), 1–15.
Whitaker, D. J., Haileyesus, T., Swahn, M., & Saltzman, L. S. (2007). Differences in frequency of violence and reported injury between relationships with reciprocal and nonreciprocal intimate partner violence. *American Journal of Public Health, 97*, 941–947.
White, J. W., & Kowalski, R. M. (1994). Deconstructing the myth of the nonaggressive woman. *Psychology of Women Quarterly, 18*(4), 487–508.
WHO. (2001). *Putting women first: Ethical and safety recommendations for research on domestic violence against women.* Geneva: Author. http://www.who.int/gender/documents/violence/who_fch_gwh_01.1/en/. Accessed 26 May 2014.
WHO. (2014). The role of men in promoting gender equality. http://www.who.int/gender/topics/role_of_men/en/. Accessed 26 May 2014.
Wilkinson, D. L., & Hamerschlag, S. J. (2005). Situational determinants in intimate partner violence. *Aggression and Violence Behaviour, 10*, 333–361.
Winstok, Z. (2008). Conflict escalation to violence and escalation of violent conflicts in intimate relationships. *Children and Youth Service Review, 30*(3), 297–310.
Winstok, Z. (2013). *Partner violence: A new paradigm for understanding conflict escalation.* New York: Springer.
Winstok, Z., & Straus, M. (2011). Gender differences in intended escalatory tendencies among marital partners. *Journal of Interpersonal Violence, 26*(18), 3599–3617.
Wood, J. (2004). Monsters and victims: Male felon's accounts of intimate partner violence. *Journal of Social and Personal Relationships, 21*(5), 555–576.

A Reflection on Women, Girls and Armed Violence

Anna Alvazzi del Frate

Abstract The 20th anniversary of the Beijing Platform for Action is marked by discussion of the post-2015 development framework, prominently featuring achieving gender equality, empowering all women and girls and promoting peaceful and inclusive societies among its goals (Goals 5 and 16 respectively, see UNDESA, Open Working Group Proposal for Sustainable Development Goals. United Nations Sustainable Development Knowledge Platform, 2014). The focus on the Sustainable Development Goals and the recent developments in the policy and research agendas on ending violence against women may represent a unique opportunity for converging efforts towards effective prevention and reduction of many forms of violence impacting on women and girls, in both conflict and non-conflict settings, including firearm violence. This contribution analyzes patterns of female violent deaths and firearm victimization, provides an overview of promising prevention policies and programmes, as well as challenges for monitoring and evaluating progress.

1 Introduction

Gender equality cannot be achieved without addressing all forms of violence against women. The post-2015 development framework places emphasis on this aspect, stressing the link between development, peace and safety/security. The proposed Sustainable Development Goals 5 and 16, respectively aim at achieving gender equality and promoting peaceful and inclusive societies (UNDESA 2014). Progress towards both goals is strictly connected with a drastic reduction—possibly the end—of all forms of violence. Much of the work to meet these goals will depend on practical implementation of a broad set of recommendations that can be seen in recent policy instruments on women, peace and security and firearm control. This unprecedented alignment of agendas may produce effective results in preventing

A. Alvazzi del Frate (✉)
Small Arms Survey, Geneva, Switzerland
e-mail: anna.alvazzi@smallarmssurvey.org

H. Kury et al. (eds.), *Women and Children as Victims and Offenders: Background, Prevention, Reintegration*, DOI 10.1007/978-3-319-08398-8_20

misuse of arms, their illicit trafficking, and advancing towards the elimination of many forms of violence impacting on women and girls, in both conflict and non-conflict settings.

2 Armed Violence, Women and Girls

Violence against women is generally identified with various forms of sexual exploitation and abuse, and relevant information collected on the basis of the experience of survivors. More rarely, studies focus on killings of women. International statistics show that females represent between 16 and 21 % of the total homicide victims (UNODC 2014, p. 13; Geneva Declaration Secretariat 2014b; WHO 2014a, p. 9). The global ratio between female and male victims of homicides translates into an average rate of 2.5 female homicides per 100,000 population, as opposed to 10.8 for males (WHO 2014a, p. 9).

Although there is a correlation between high levels of violence and high numbers of females killed, most of the violent deaths of women and girls occur in settings where there is no declared armed conflict. In 2011, ranking of female homicides were highest in Southern Africa, South America, the Caribbean, and Central America, which also ranked at the top of homicides rates in general (Alvazzi del Frate 2011, p. 119). Nevertheless, numbers of women and girls killed in the most violent contexts, although comparatively higher, only represent a small proportion as opposed to males. In general, the higher the homicide rate in a country, the lower the proportion of women killed. This finding can also be read in the opposite direction, to indicate that the highest proportion of female victims is found in the least violent settings. For example in Europe, where homicide rates are generally low, the proportion of females killed with respect to males is almost twice the global average (31 % as opposed to 16 %, Geneva Declaration Secretariat 2014b).

Analysis of geographical distribution shows further major disparities. For example, in most countries in the Americas, rates of female homicide are much higher than the average, resulting in a regional rate of 4.4 per 100,000 women, almost twice the global rate (Geneva Declaration Secretariat 2014a). The Asia-Pacific region counts only 22 % of the total number of male victims of homicide, but almost double share of female victims, 43 % of the world total (Geneva Declaration Secretariat 2014c).

Violence against women rarely occurs as an isolated incident. It frequently develops in the domestic environment and takes the form of an escalating series of aggressions, which could lead to a fatal outcome. When a woman is killed in these circumstances, there may be further indirect casualties: in many cases the perpetrator commits suicide and/or kills others, including children, witnesses or by passers.

Very frequently, perpetrators of serious violence against women are persons very close to them, especially their current or former partners,[1] as well as other close family members (parents, children, brothers). Violence committed by intimate partners (IPV) represents a risk spread across countries and cultures.

According to a study in the US, the vast majority of women killed had previous experience of domestic violence or stalking (McFarlane et al. 1999), including being physically abused by the same perpetrator, who directed his violence expressly against them (Campbell et al. 2003).

This form of gender-specific lethal violence is frequently called femicide (see Box 1).

Box 1: Defining Femicide

When the victim is a woman, homicide is often redefined as Femicide. According to a definition that dates back to the feminist movement in the 1970s, femicide means the killing of women specifically because of their gender, or "the misogynous killing of women by men" (Radford and Russell 1992). Diana Russell, an architect of the term femicide, indicates that the concept has been in use for centuries. In nineteenth-century Britain, for example, it was used to designate the "killing of a woman" (Russell 2008, p. 3). The feminist movement politicized the use of the word femicide in the 1970s, restricting its meaning to the killing of a woman or a girl based on her sex. With time, this definition has expanded to refer to any killing of a woman. While such an approach dilutes the political connotation of violence against women based on their sex, it facilitates the comparability of cross-national data on lethal violence against women. A number of recent studies and data collection exercises focus on the issue of femicide in a stricter sense. Qualitative studies of the killing of women in Latin America, for example, seek to assess the intent of the perpetrator. Furthermore, some countries in Latin America have implemented specific laws on femicide in recent years, such as Guatemala in 2008, Chile in 2010 and Brazil in 2015. These laws take into consideration the targeting of a woman for misogynous or gender-based reasons and foresee stricter penalties if there is evidence of such circumstances.

Source: updated from Alvazzi del Frate (2011*, p. 116)*

A typology of femicide based on the characteristics of perpetrators could be useful for developing targeted policies to prevent violence. It is generally under-

[1] Many different sources agree. See for example US Bureau of Justice Statistics (http://bjs.ojp.usdoj.gov/content/homicide/intimates.cfm#intgender), WHO et al. (2013) and Stöckl et al. (2013) (it was estimated that as many as 38 % of female homicides globally were committed by male partners while the corresponding figure for men was 6 %).

stood that male perpetrators represent the vast majority and female perpetrators represent a residual portion of all offenders. According to UNODC (2014, p. 13), male perpetrators of intentional homicide represent 95 % globally, but there are regional variations. For example, a mean of 13 % of female offenders was observed in Europe in 2010 (Aebi et al. 2014, p. 80).

Most frequently women know their aggressors, including actual or former intimate partners, friends and acquaintances, as well as known strangers and distant family members. Although statistically less numerous, killings by "unknown perpetrator" describe deaths occurring during armed conflicts, robberies, gang actions, shootings in public places and other unrelated incidents.

2.1 Conflict Settings

Armed conflicts involve a large proportion of civilian casualties, many of them women and girls. Although the majority of casualties are males, the proportion of females killed is increasing. For example, in Syria the percentage of female victims increased from less than 1 % in April 2011 to over 13 % in March 2015 (Humanitarian Tracker 2015).

Female victims in conflict include not only those who lose their lives in indiscriminate bombing or shooting, but also women and girls who are specifically targeted by sexual violence during warfare. Female victimization in conflict settings includes many types of violence, which may be directly or indirectly related to the conflict itself. Any type of hardship and deprivation, including conflict, increases the risk of exploitation of and violence against women. For example, during the 2014 Ebola crisis, cases of domestic and sexual violence dramatically increased in West Africa (IRC 2014).

Women are particularly affected and rarely protected in these situations. Rape is frequently endemic in conflict settings. Perpetrators of violence are civilians, combatants of the opposite or the same faction, as well as peacekeepers. Statistics are scarce, and largely depend on the existence of structures to provide assistance and shelter to victims, which also function as surveillance and reporting mechanisms.

2.2 Firearms and Violence Against Women

Gender-disaggregated statistics which indicate the type of instruments used in violence are scarce at the international level, and available only for a relatively small number of countries. For example, at the time of publication of the Global Burden of Armed Violence 2011, data on firearm killings of women and girls were available for only 24 countries. In this small sample of countries, on average,

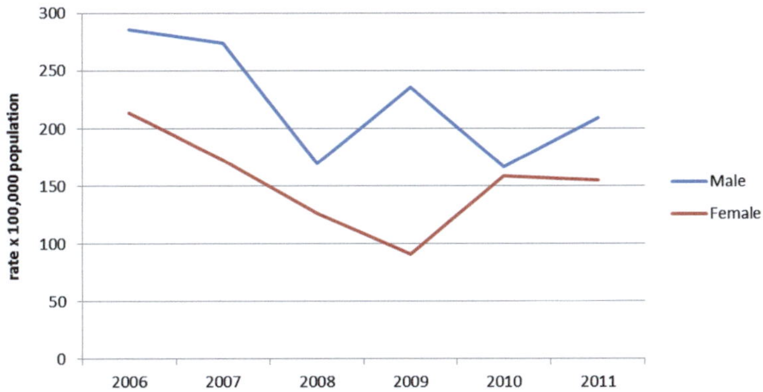

Fig. 1 Non-fatal firearm victimization among male and female respondents aged 12 and older in the United States, 2006–2011 (*Source*: Cohn et al. 2013—elaboration of NCVS data from Appendix 2)

approximately half of the homicides were committed with a firearm in the period 2004–2009, but only one out of three cases with female victims.

Firearm violence often carries high emotional impact on women and girls as witnesses and survivors, irrespective whether firearm incidents occurred in public spaces or domestic contexts. Victimization surveys confirm that crimes against women are less frequently committed with any type of weapon (guns, knives, or anything used as a weapon) than those against men. This is the case, for example, with simple assaults, fights, bullying, pickpocketing, bag snatching and the vast majority of crimes committed against women, children and the elderly, which are generally covered by victimization surveys. Nevertheless, more serious (property) crime committed with firearms tends to involve male and female victims almost equally. For example, analysis of the National Crime Victimization Survey (NCVS) data in the US presented in Fig. 1 (Cohn et al. 2013) reveals that rates for non-fatal firearm victimization among respondents aged 12 and older show similar male/female trends and a relatively small difference between the two. Actually, data indicates that in 2010 the risk was almost equal for male and female respondents.

According to the findings of the International Crime Victim Survey, among the types of incidents covered by the survey, car hijacking was one of the most serious and the one in which firearms were more frequently present, in approximately half of cases, almost equally distributed among male and female victims (ICVS n.d.). Victims described that firearms were mostly used with the purpose to intimidate them and rarely to fire.

Considering that firearms may be used not only to shoot, but also displayed to threaten and intimidate, and that not all bullets kill, their "lethality" is difficult to estimate, especially taking into account gender differences. Available data on the male/female distribution of survivors of non-lethal firearm injuries at the global level suggests that the higher a country's firearm homicide rate, the higher its "case fatality rate". In the 26 countries for which relevant data is available, there is a correlation between the rate of firearm homicides and non-lethal firearm injuries

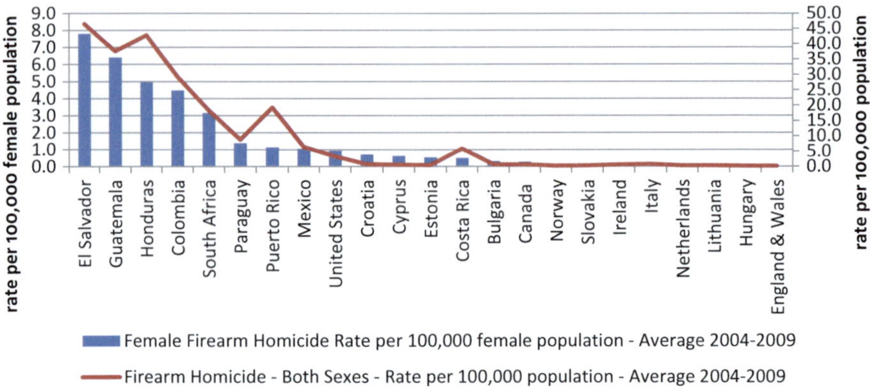

Fig. 2 Rates of firearm homicide (both sexes) and rates of firearm homicide with female victims, various years, various sources (*Source*: Small Arms Survey database)

(0.689, N = 26) (Alvazzi del Frate 2012, p. 92). On average, it has been estimated that for every death as a consequence of gun violence, three victims survive injuries (Alvazzi del Frate 2012). Depending on the context, the type and level of firearm violence, the male/female ratio may vary. For example in Bahawalpur, Pakistan, data from surveillance of firearm injuries resulting from civilian clashes and robbery showed a 5:1 ratio (Niaz and Shujah 2013).

Data shows that women are killed with firearms more frequently in the countries/territories where levels of firearm violence are higher. Where the levels of armed violence are lower, percentages of women and girls killed by firearms are also lower (Fig. 2; Alvazzi del Frate 2012, p. 131).

Figure 2 shows that ranking of countries as regards rate of females killed by firearm and overall levels of homicide by firearm go parallel and see El Salvador, Guatemala, Honduras, Colombia and South Africa at the top. In Honduras and Colombia more than two-thirds of the homicides with a female victim involved the use of firearms.

The availability of firearms in the domestic sphere represents a further factor of risk for women and girls. Van Kesteren (2014) has observed that the availability of firearms has a stronger association with both the killing and suicide of females compared to male victims. Analysis of data on prevalence of firearms and violent deaths from the Global Burden of Armed Violence database confirms such relationship (Shaw 2013, pp. 25–26). The first cross-national study, which concluded that there was a very high correlation between overall prevalence of firearms in a country and the number of female victims of firearm homicide was based on data from 25 high-income countries in 2002 (Hemenway et al. 2002).

Firearms are also associated to cases of homicide-suicide, which most frequently involve the use of guns. A study carried out in South Africa showed that the use of a firearm in femicide increases the probability that the perpetrator commit suicide after the killing (Mathews et al. 2008). Similar findings in Europe indicate that firearms play a predominant role in murder–suicide cases, which are mostly perpetrated by men (Liem and Oberwittler 2012; Shaw 2013, p. 17).

A gender dimension in the use of firearms can also be observed by looking at suicide patterns. At the international level, studies indicate that firearm suicide is more frequent in countries where firearms are more available among civilians, especially in the Americas and also in some European countries (Ajdacic-Gross et al. 2008). Female suicides with firearms are however rare, as women generally chose other mechanisms (notably poisoning by drug overdose, Alvazzi del Frate and Pavesi 2014). The use of guns in committing suicide is more frequent in the Americas than in the rest of the world. On average, in 19 countries in the American continent approximately 22 % of male and 12 % of female suicides were committed with firearms, as opposed to 13 and 2 % respectively in 28 European countries (Ajdacic-Gross et al. 2008).

Figure 3 shows rates of female firearm suicide with respect to 100,000 female population in selected countries for which suicide data is available disaggregated by sex and mechanism. The impact of firearm suicide on female population is highest in the US (a rate of 1.7 women every 100,000 committed suicide with a firearm) and

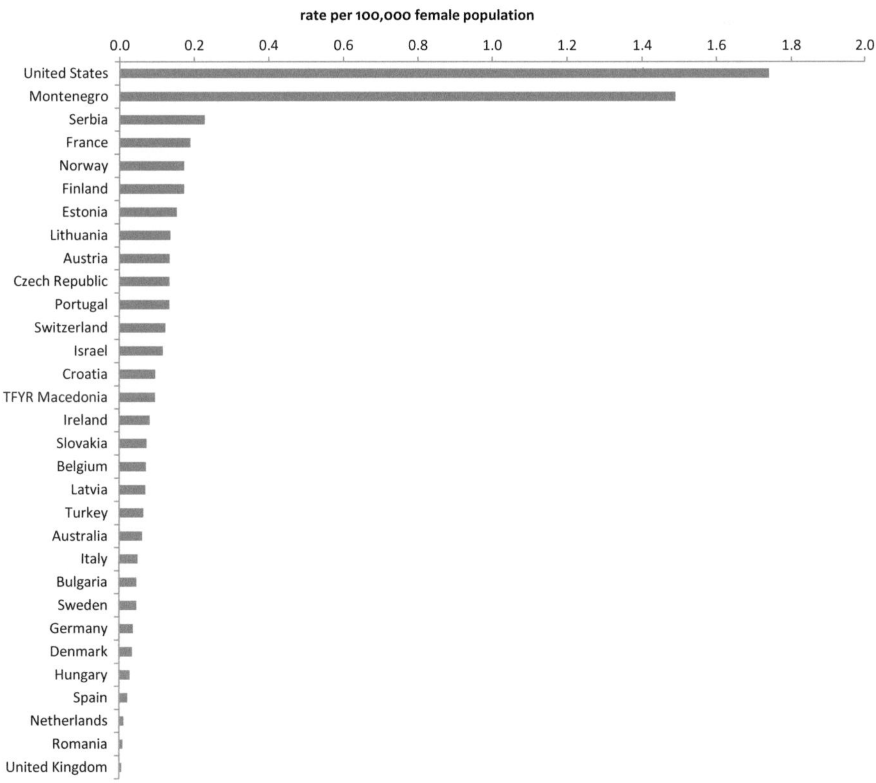

Fig. 3 Female suicides with firearms, by country, 2013 or latest available year (rate per 100,000 female population). *Sources*: WHO (2014b), CDC (2013), OFS (2014), ABS (2014)

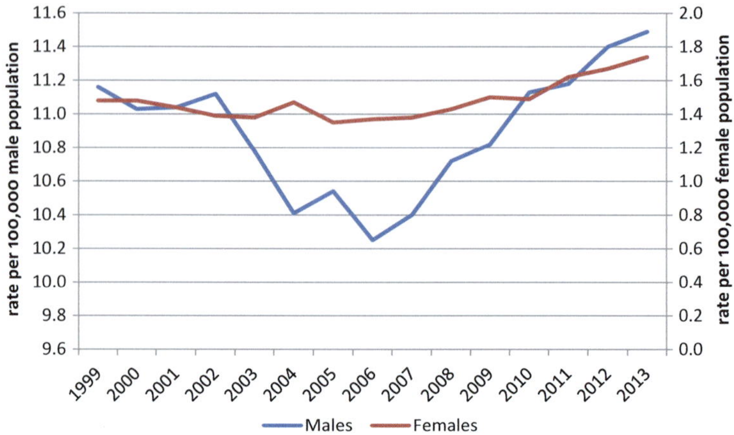

Fig. 4 Suicides with firearms, by sex, United States, 1999–2013 (rate per 100,000 population). *Source of data*: CDC (2013)

Montenegro (1.5), followed at some distance by Serbia (with rates of approximately 0.2 per 100,000).

In the US, more than two-thirds of male suicides and slightly more than one-third of female suicides involve firearms, 57 and 32 % in 2013, a smaller proportion with respect to 1999 (when the percentages were 58 and 36 % respectively, CDC 2013). But due to the overall increase in the number of suicides, especially since 2010 (both female and male firearm suicide increased, by 17 and 3 % respectively, between 2010 and 2013), Figure 4 shows that rates of firearm homicides are much higher than in 1999. Despite a marked difference in rates (male rates are more than 5 times higher than those of females), trends of firearm suicide for males and females in the US show a similar pattern over time.

Comparing Figs. 3 and 4, it can be observed that in the US approximately twice as many women and girls committed suicide with a firearm than those who were killed by using firearms (rates of 1.7 and 0.9 per 100,000 respectively). This proportion applies also to men: suicide has increasingly exceeded homicide since the early '80s as the most common form of fatal firearm violence, until representing 64.0 % of deaths in 2012 (Wintemute 2015).

2.3 Effects of Gun Control Legislation on Firearm Homicide and Suicide

Would stricter access to guns reduce opportunities for suicides? Or would potential suicides look for a substitute method to complete their plan? Research suggests that if a gun is not rapidly available it is unlikely that another method is considered by most persons who intend to commit suicide, at least in the short period (Alvazzi del

Frate and Pavesi 2014). Examples include the period between 1996 and 2002 in Australia, where there was a marked decrease in firearm-related deaths, including homicides, suicides, unintentional shootings, and justifiable homicides following the introduction of stricter private gun ownership legislation (Florquin and Wille 2004, p. 184). A study in Belgium indicates that introduction of legislation restricting civilian possession in 2006 contributed to a substantial decrease in firearm suicides and homicides in the following years (Duquet and Van Alstein 2015). In Canada, a 2010 study of the number of women killed over a six-year period (RCMP 2010) demonstrated that the introduction of a policy limiting the access to firearms in households had reduced the risk of fatal outcomes in case of domestic disputes. Many initiatives aimed at imposing a "cooling off" or "waiting" period for the purchase of firearms intend to prevent impulsive violence, either suicidal or directed towards others. A systematic review of several of such policies carried out in the US, although inconclusive, indicated that a reduction in firearm suicide could be attributable to the introduction of "waiting" periods (Hahn et al. 2003), but did not discuss whether there was any proof that the waiting period served to prevent the suicide with a substitute mechanism.

In South Africa, although statistics on firearm violence have become progressively less available, a 2014 study estimated that the effect of the introduction of the 2000 Firearm Control Act in the country accounted for an estimated 4585 lives saved because of reduced violence across five major cities between 2001 and 2005 (Matzopoulos et al. 2014).

More specifically as regards preventing intimate partner violence (IPV), limiting access to known perpetrators of domestic violence appears as a promising practice. The withdrawal of gun licenses following incidents of intimate partner violence certainly limits the consequences of further violence. Other promising strategies to reduce gun-related IPV include broader awareness campaigns to alert women and girls of the danger of firearms in intimate partner settings, and "cultural" interventions focusing on attitudes to guns and their relation with certain concepts of masculinity (Shaw 2013, p. 18).

Fuller involvement of women in prevention programmes is a good policy per se. For example, women in immediate post-conflict settings are frequently involved in disarmament initiatives. It is important that this involvement results in their full participation and engagement, not only in the specific disarmament initiatives, but also in the longer term peace processes. Many women may have lost either their husband, or brother, or father, and are left with firearms that belonged to them. Some women take an active role in gun collection programs and become active in raising awareness of other women on these issues. In some cases, women turn weapons in on behalf of male family members who would not do that out of fear or distrust in the disarmament process.

The 2014 WHO Global Status Report on Violence Prevention includes a comprehensive overview of measures to regulate access to firearms adopted by nearly all the countries included in the study. These measures include various forms of restriction or limitation of civilian access to firearms, for example "...bans on specified firearms or ammunition, background checks, waiting periods and other licensing requirements, laws to prevent child access, and restrictions for certain settings (for example, school premises, carrying guns in public places, etc.)" (WHO 2014a, p. 35).

3 Women, Peace and Physical Security and Small Arms: Moving on and Measuring Progress

After the UN Convention to eliminate all forms of discrimination against women (CEDAW 1979[2]) and the Inter-American Convention on the Prevention, Punishment and Eradication of Violence Against Women ("Convention Of Belem Do Para" 1994), since the 1995 UN Conference on Women in Beijing, the international community has indicated that the way towards improving the political, economic and social status of women goes through increased respect of women's rights and gender equality. Violence against women is stigmatized throughout the Beijing Declaration and Plan of Action, with reference to both conflict[3] and non-conflict settings.

Despite the awareness of the impact of firearms violence on women and girls, firearms control was not spelled out in international instruments dealing with gender issues. The international community had started equipping itself with instruments aimed at regulating small arms. The Programme of Action to Prevent, Combat and Eradicate the Illicit Trade in Small Arms and Light Weapons in All Its Aspects (2001) made only a short reference to "...the negative impact on women and the elderly" (A/CONF.192/15, para 6). Equally, the UN Protocol Against the Illicit Manufacturing of and Trafficking in Firearms, Their Parts and Components and Ammunition (2001) provides a framework for states to control and regulate licit arms and arms flows, with measures to prevent illicit trafficking and diversion into illegal market, but does not mention any gender-related aspect.

The main agenda on Women, Peace and Security (WPS) is rooted in United Nations Security Council Resolution 1325, which was unanimously adopted in 2000. Building on the Beijing Declaration and Plan of Action, UNSCR 1325 also aims at reducing victimization of women and girls, placing emphasis on the special risk that women face in conflict and immediate post-conflict settings. Resolution 1325 acknowledges the importance of the participation of women and the inclusion of gender perspectives in peace negotiations, humanitarian planning, peacekeeping operations, post-conflict peacebuilding and governance. The resolution seeks, inter

[2] UN Convention on the Elimination of All Forms of Discrimination against Women (CEDAW, 1249 UNTS 13) 1979.

[3] Para 11 of the Beijing Declaration and Platform for Action "Grave violations of the human rights of women occur, particularly in times of armed conflict, and include murder, torture, systematic rape, forced pregnancy and forced abortion, in particular under policies of ethnic cleansing" (Report 1995, chap. I, resolution 1, annex I).

alia, the protection of women and girls from sexual and gender-based violence, including in emergency and humanitarian situations, and the prevention of violence against women through the promotion of women's rights, accountability and law enforcement. Small arms proliferation is an underlying threat to the successful implementation of UNSCR 1325. While the linkages between the proliferation of small arms and poverty, crime, insecurity, and violations of human rights are clear, there is no explicit mention of small arms in UNSCR 1325.

It is only recently that the international community has recognized the need to reconcile the two global agendas on women, peace, and security and small arms, by making cross-references in different UN instruments, which has resulted in mutually reinforcing their mandates (Bastick and Valasek 2014).

3.1 The Small Arms International Agenda Highlighting Women Issues

The outcome documents of the Second Review Conference (2012) and Fifth Biennial Meeting of States (2014)[4] of the UN Programme of Action on Small Arms and Light Weapons highlight both the "victimization", namely the negative impacts of illicit trade in small arms on women, as well as the "empowerment" aspects, underlining the need for increased representation of women in small arms policymaking. The UNSCR 2117 on small arms (2013)[5] also recognizes the impacts of armed violence against women and girls, and stresses the importance to facilitate "women's full and meaningful participation in all policymaking, planning and implementation processes to combat and eradicate the illicit transfer, destabilizing accumulation and misuse of small arms and light weapons in all its aspects" (para 12).

3.1.1 The Arms Trade Treaty

The adoption of the Arms Trade Treaty (ATT) in 2013 and its entry into force on 24 December 2014 represented important steps in promoting shared principles for the regulation of arm trade and control of illicit trafficking. Although the ATT covers all aspects of arms trade, not only small arms, negotiations could not ignore the impact of armed violence and misuse of arms on civilians, particularly women and children. The lively debate during the negotiations about the "gender" aspect resulted in unprecedented language inserted in the text (art. 4(6)(b)), under which states parties will be required to *consider taking feasible measures* to avoid the arms

[4] A/CONF.192/2012/RC/CRP.3/Rev.3 and A/CONF.192/BMS/2014/2 respectively.

[5] S/RES/2117, 26 September 2013.

being used to commit or facilitate gender-based violence or violence against children.

Although the article does not make mandatory either the carrying out of a risk assessment of the likelihood of such violence to occur or denying the transfer in case a perceived risk exists, thus making the provision relatively weak, no other arms control instrument specifically mentions gender-based violence to be considered in the decision-making process. The ATT has therefore advanced in linking the women, peace and security and arms control agendas, despite the strong resistance demonstrated by several states during negotiations.

In the process of facilitating implementation of the ATT, states and regional organizations are focusing on how to become more effective in reducing the risk of weapons being used to commit acts of violence, particularly against women and youth. This will not only result in raising awareness, but also in the identification of good practices in incorporating gender-sensitive approaches in disarmament and arms control programmes, model evaluations and possibly the development of relevant tools to facilitate the inclusion of gender in export assessments covered by the ATT.[6]

3.2 Women and Small Arms: International Commitments

On the women side, the General Recommendation No. 30 of CEDAW on Women in Conflict Prevention, Conflict and Post-Conflict Situations (2013)[7] reinforces the link between control of illicit trade of arms and serious acts of gender based violence, including domestic violence, and recommends that state parties "Address the gendered impact of international transfers of arms, especially small and illicit arms including through the ratification and implementation of the Arms Trade Treaty (2013)" (paragraph 33 (e)).

Another important development was the language used in the "Agreed Conclusions" of the 57th session of the CSW on the Elimination and prevention of all forms of violence against women and girls,[8] which makes specific reference to the concept of femicide (or feminicide), placing emphasis on ensuring accountability and ending impunity for the perpetrators, exploring linkages between serious crime against women and girls and transnational organized crime, strengthening legislation, and in general adopting specific policies to prevent and eradicate violence against women in crime prevention strategies (para 24).

---

[6] See for example the Roundtable organized by UNLIREC on "Incorporating gender and youth approaches when implementing the United Nations Programme of Action on Small Arms (PoA) and the Arms Trade Treaty (ATT)" in November 2014 (http://www.unlirec.org/noticias_det_eng.aspx?id=116)

[7] Committee on the Elimination of Discrimination against Women CEDAW/C/GC/30, 18 October 2013.

[8] http://www.unwomen.org/~/media/headquarters/attachments/sections/csw/57/csw57-agreedconclusions-a4-en.pdf

The General Assembly Resolution on women, disarmament, non-proliferation and arms control[9] was adopted in 2014 and provides a comprehensive framework for action by the international community in the promotion of the role of women (and their empowerment) as "agents for change" in disarmament and arms control (articles 1 and 5), generating knowledge through the collection of disaggregated data on gendered impacts of illicit small arms trafficking (article 4), as well as the development of criteria for national risk assessment about the use of arms to commit gender-based violence or violence against women and girls (article 7, which can be read in synergy with the relevant provisions of the ATT).

4 Measuring Progress, Tracking Results

Measuring violence against women is a challenging task in every context, be that of estimating the extent of the problem (in conflict or non-conflict settings), or within the framework of monitoring trends and measuring change. Well-known methodological challenges exist in counting either *incidence* (i.e., estimating the number of incidents) or *prevalence* (i.e. estimating the number of victims). In many cases, challenges start from definition.

A first definition useful for statistical purposes was included in the 1979 UN CEDAW and referred to gender-based violence (GBV), which was described as follows:

> violence that is directed against a woman because she is a woman, or violence that affects women disproportionately. It includes acts that inflict physical, mental, or sexual harm or suffering, threats of such acts, coercion, and other deprivations of liberty.[10]

The 1993 United Nations Conference on Human Rights provided further specification and defined violence against women as "any act of gender-based violence that results in, or is likely to result in, physical, sexual or psychological harm or suffering to women, including threats of such act, coercion or arbitrary deprivations of liberty, whether occurring in public or private life".[11] The Beijing Platform of Action, adopted in 1995, further elaborated on the need to:

> Promote research, collect data and compile statistics, especially concerning domestic violence relating to the prevalence of different forms of violence against women, and encourage research into the causes, nature, seriousness and consequences of violence against women and the effectiveness of measures implemented to prevent and redress violence against women.[12]

---

[9] A/RES/69/61, 2 December 2014.

[10] Convention on the Elimination of All Forms of Discrimination against Women, Article 1.

[11] A/RES/48/104, Declaration on the Elimination of Violence against Women, Article 1, http://www.un.org/documents/ga/res/48/a48r104.htm (9-12-2010).

[12] Beijing Declaration and Platform for Action, Fourth United Nations World Conference on Women, Beijing 1995, http://www.un.org/womenwatch/daw/beijing/pdf/BDPfA%20E.pdf (9-12-2010), pp. 54–55.

The above definitions contain all the elements necessary to develop a core list of violations for measuring and monitoring violence against women. In this framework, a task force of governmental experts coordinated by the UN Statistical Commission (the "Friends of the Chair"),[13] in 2009 promoted a list of indicators aimed at facilitating the production of statistics on violence against women according to internationally agreed standards. The proposed set of indicators covers the broad areas of physical, sexual and psychological violence as defined by the CEDAW and is a good starting point towards the development of internationally comparable data. The report also indicates the recommendation that one of the indicators deals with lethal violence and is aimed at measuring the "Annual rate of femicides" (para 34). Still, a set of data to allow a fuller understanding of how violence impacts on women and girls should include not only other forms of domestic violence (in addition to IPV), honour killings, and dowry deaths, but also robberies, mass shootings or acts of terrorism, or any other non gender-related act of violence.

Data is still scarce: even considering the most serious forms of violence (killings), gender-disaggregated statistics (actual data collected locally, not estimates) exist only for approximately half of the countries/territories and most frequently do not provide more than top level headers. For example, the level of detail is insufficient to apply a proper classification. Furthermore, some countries may still differentiate some categories of crimes with female victims which may not appear in statistics.

Within the process of establishing the post-2015 framework "data are the lifeblood of decision-making and the raw material for accountability" (IEAG 2014, p. 2). The proposed Sustainable Development Goals (SDGs) 5 and 16 include specific targets to measure progress on reducing violence against women and girls, either as a specific group (target 5.2 on violence against women and girls) or as a result of advancing with the "data revolution" and obtaining more accurate gender-disaggregated data (SDG target 16.1 on reducing all forms of violence and related deaths).

Furthermore, it will be necessary to make efforts to expand the availability of gender-disaggregated data on prevention *programmes* related to violence, especially in low-income countries, for monitoring and evaluating their impacts and results. The Global Burden of Armed Violence has produced a major database, which as of March 2015 includes gender-disaggregated data for 104 countries and data on firearm killings from 175 countries, as well as estimates of the total number of violent deaths for 201 countries and territories (Alvazzi del Frate and De Martino 2015).

[13] The Friends of the Chair group was established by the Statistical Commission at its thirty-ninth session (decision 39/116). It consisted of representatives of Botswana, Bulgaria, Canada, Chile, Ghana, Italy, Mexico (the Chair) and Thailand, as well as several United Nations agencies as observers, with the UN Statistics Division acting as secretariat. The report of the group was presented to the 40th Session of the UN Statistical Commission (E/CN.3/2009/13).

Box 2: Monitoring Implementation of Resolution 1325: Indicators of Women, Peace and Security

Ten years after the adoption of UNSCR 1325 (2000), as the result of the work of a Technical Working Group on Global Indicators, UNSCR 1889 (2009) and the Secretary General's 2010 report to the Security Council on Women and Peace and Security (S/2010/498) established a monitoring system for tracking progress of implementation of UNSCR 1325 based on 26 indicators. As mandated by UNSCR 1889 and as detailed in the Secretary General's 2010 report, two indicators are specifically relevant in linking the gender and physical security agendas. These are indicator 17, which relates directly to the control of small arms, and indicator 14, which aims at monitoring the impact of (armed) violence on women's and girls' physical security. It has been acknowledged that while data is scarce, especially as regards gender-based violence, reliable statistics are necessary to inform humanitarian interventions and for monitoring violence prevention and reduction programmes.

The list proposed by the Secretary-General[14] includes several indicators dealing directly with the measurement of the phenomenon of violence against women and girls, including:

1a Prevalence of sexual violence
1b Patterns of sexual violence in conflict and post-conflict situations
4 Percentage of reported cases of sexual exploitation and abuse allegedly perpetrated by uniformed, civilian peacekeepers and/or humanitarian workers that are acted upon out of the total number of referred cases
14 Index of women's and girls' physical security. Survey-based indicator to measure three dimensions:

- Perceptions of physical security of women and girls (by location, time of day)
- Proxy variables measuring how women's and girls' ability to participate in public life has been affected
- Proxy variables measuring how women's and girls' regular activities have been affected

19 Percentage of referred cases of sexual and gender-based violence against women and girls that are reported, investigated and sentenced

The UN Secretary-General in his report of 2012 on Women, Peace and Security[15] stressed that "The availability and limited control of small arms and light weapons continue to facilitate gender-based crimes, such as rape and other forms of sexual abuse and violence" (UNSC 2012, para. 35). Monitoring progress towards

[14] The indicators are listed on page 15–21 of the Secretary General's Report (S/2010/498).
[15] S/2012/732 of 2 October 2012.

more security for women and girls to be protected from gender-based violence in conflict settings requires effective implementation of UN Security Council resolution 1325 of 2000 (See Box 2).

Finally, General Assembly Resolution 68/191 of 2013 ("Taking action against gender-related killing of women and girls")[16] urges member states to make further efforts to prevent, investigate, prosecute and punish violence against women and girls. In particular, the resolution calls for an end to impunity of those responsible for these serious crimes, aiming at reducing the vulnerability of women and girls which may be the result of ineffective action in this respect. The resolution also invites member States to address the problems of underreporting in the belief that data is crucial to inform the formulation, monitoring and evaluation of relevant laws, policies and programmes (para 7).

5 Conclusions

This chapter has discussed aspects of (lethal) violence against women and girls, with special emphasis on firearm violence. Data shows that violence against women and girls is present across countries and particularly visible in relatively peaceful societies, where women and girls represent a larger portion of the total number of victims. Special attention to firearms and their impacts on women and girls has recently been mandated by the converging agendas of the women, peace and security and small arms. The international community has equipped itself with a range of relevant measures and recommendations aimed at preventing misuse of arms, and their illicit trafficking, including the UN Protocol against the Illicit Manufacturing of and Trafficking in Firearms, Their Parts and Components and Ammunition, Supplementing The United Nations Convention against Transnational Organized Crime, the Programme of Action on Small Arms and Light Weapons, and most recently The Arms Trade Treaty. At the same time, international instruments in the women, peace and security agenda stress the importance of a full involvement of women as prominent actors of change. The chapter has also explored the role of women in this process, including their relation with firearms, not only as victims of crime (stalking, firearm injuries, gender-based killings—femicide) or self-harm (suicide), but also their active involvement in advancing a global agenda to peace and security.

Five Questions

1. The male/female ratio of homicides is skewed in more peaceful countries, showing a higher proportion of female victims. How to go about reducing the lethality of domestic and intimate-partner violence against women and girls?

[16] A/RES/68/191 of 18 December 2013.

2. How to measure whether gun control legislation takes into consideration the impact of firearms on women?
3. What is the role of the crime prevention and criminal justice community in supporting the implementation of the international mandates of the women, peace and security and small arms communities?
4. What kind of domestic frameworks, engaging policy makers, practitioners and civil society, would fully reflect the spirit of the alignment of the women, peace and security and small arms agendas?
5. How to build more capacity for the collection, analysis and dissemination of more data disaggregated by gender, instrument, context and location, with a view to support the prevention and reduction of violence against women and girls?

References

ABS (Australian Bureau of Statistics). (2014). Causes of death. Australia, 2012. http://www.abs.gov.au/AUSSTATS/abs@.nsf/DetailsPage/3303.02012?OpenDocument

Aebi, M., et al. (2014). *European sourcebook of crime and criminal justice statistics 2014* (5th ed.). Helsinki: HEUNI. http://www.heuni.fi/en/index/publications/heunireports/europeansourcebook.html.

Ajdacic-Gross, V., Weiss, M. G., Ring, A., Hepp, U., Bopp, M., Gutzwiller, F., Rössler, W. (2008, September). Methods of suicide: International suicide patterns derived from the WHO mortality database. *Bulletin of the World Health Organization, 86*(9), 726–32. Geneva: World Health Organization. http://www.who.int/bulletin/volumes/86/9/07-043489/en/

Alvazzi del Frate, A., & De Martino, L. (2015). *Every body counts: Measuring violent deaths* (Research Note No. 49). Geneva: Small Arms Survey. http://www.smallarmssurvey.org/about-us/highlights/highlights-2015/highlight-rn49.html

Alvazzi del Frate, A., & Pavesi, I. (2014). *Firearm suicides* (Research Note No. 44). Geneva: Small Arms Survey. http://www.smallarmssurvey.org/about-us/highlights/highlights-2014/rn44-firearm-suicides.html

Alvazzi del Frate, A. (2011) When the victim is a woman. In *Geneva Declaration Secretariat, Global Burden of Armed Violence 2011: Lethal Encounters* (pp. 113–144). Cambridge: Cambridge University Press. http://www.genevadeclaration.org/measurability/global-burden-of-armed-violence/global-burden-of-armed-violence-2011.html

Alvazzi del Frate, A. (2012). A matter of survival. In *Small Arms Survey 2012*. Cambridge: Cambridge University Press. http://www.smallarmssurvey.org/publications/by-type/yearbook/small-arms-survey-2012.html

Bastick, M., & Valasek, K. (2014). Converging agendas: Women, peace, security, and small arms. In *Small Arms Survey 2014: Women and Guns* (pp. 35–63). Cambridge: Cambridge University Press. http://www.smallarmssurvey.org/fileadmin/docs/A-Yearbook/2014/en/Small-Arms-Survey-2014-Chapter-2-EN.pdf

Campbell, J. C., Webster, D., Koziol-McLain, J., et al. (2003). Risk factors for femicide in abusive relationships: Results from a multisite case control study. *American Journal of Public Health, 93*(7), 1089–1097. http://ajph.aphapublications.org/cgi/content/abstract/93/7/1089.

Committee on the Elimination of Discrimination against Women (CEDAW/C/CG/30). (2013, October 18). General recommendation No. 30 on women in conflict prevention, conflict and post-conflict situation.

CDC (Centers for Disease Control). (2013). Fatal injury reports, national and regional, 1999 – 2013. Web-based injury statistics query and reporting system. http://webappa.cdc.gov/sasweb/ncipc/mortrate10_us.html

Cohn, D., Taylor, P., Lopez, M. H., Gallagher, C. A., Parker, K., Maass, K. T. (2013). *Gun homicide rate down 49% since 1993 peak; public unaware*. Washington, DC: Pew Research Center. http://www.pewsocialtrends.org/2013/05/07/appendix-2-additional-tables-on-non-fatal-violent-firearm-crimes/

Convention on the Elimination of All Forms of Discrimination against Women (CEDAW) (1979), A/RES/34/180, http://www.un-documents.net/a34r180.htm

Duquet, N., & Van Alstein, M. (2015, March). *Gun control in Belgium: A review of the effects of the 2006 weapons law*. Brussels: Flemish Peace Institute. http://www.vlaamsvredesinstituut.eu/sites/vlaamsvredesinstituut.eu/files/files/reports/gun_control_in_belgium.pdf

E/CN.3/2009/13. (2008, December 11). Friends of the Chair of the United Nations Statistical Commission on the indicators on violence against women. Note by the Secretary-General.

Florquin, N., & Wille, C. (2004). A common tool: Firearms, violence, and crime. In *Small Arms Survey 2004: Rights at Risk* (pp. 173–211). Oxford: Oxford University Press. http://www.smallarmssurvey.org/fileadmin/docs/A-Yearbook/2004/en/Small-Arms-Survey-2004-Chapter-06a-EN.pdf

Geneva Declaration Secretariat. (2014a, April). Lethal violence in the Americas. Factsheet. Geneva: Geneva Declaration Secretariat. http://www.genevadeclaration.org/publications-resources/gd-publications/lethal-violence-in-the-americas.html

Geneva Declaration Secretariat. (2014b, July). Lethal Violence in Europe, the Caucasus, and Central Europe. Factsheet. Geneva: Geneva Declaration Secretariat. http://www.genevadeclaration.org/publications-resources/gd-publications/info-europe.html

Geneva Declaration Secretariat. (2014c, October). Lethal Violence in the Asia and Pacific Region. Factsheet. Geneva: Geneva Declaration Secretariat. http://www.genevadeclaration.org/publications-resources/gd-publications/lethal-violence-in-asia-and-the-pacific.html

Hahn, R., Bilukha, O. O., Crosby, A., et al. (2003, October). *First reports evaluating the effectiveness of strategies for preventing violence: Firearms laws* (pp. 11–20). Morbidity and Mortality Weekly Report (Centers for Disease Control and Prevention). http://www.cdc.gov/mmwr/preview/mmwrhtml/rr5214a2.htm

Hemenway, D., Shinoda-Tagawa, T., Miller, M. (2002). Firearm availability and female homicide victimization rates among 25 populous high-income countries. *Journal of American Medicine Women's Association, 57*(2), 100–104. http://www.researchgate.net/publication/11379728_Firearm_availability_and_female_homicide_victimization_rates_among_25_populous_highincome_countries/file/d912f5093e30f66993.pdf

Humanitarian Tracker. (2015). Syria Tracker. http://www.humanitariantracker.org/#!syria-tracker/cj00

ICVS (International Crime Victim Survey). (n.d.). Database. http://www3.unil.ch/wpmu/icvs/

IEAG (Independent Expert Advisory Group on a Data Revolution for Sustainable Development). (2014, November). A world that counts: Mobilizing the data revolution for sustainable development. http://www.undatarevolution.org/wp-content/uploads/2014/11/A-World-That-Counts.pdf

IRC (International Rescue Committee). (2014). 9 unexpected consequences of the Ebola crisis on women and girls – and 3 creative solutions. http://www.rescue.org/blog/9-unexpected-consequences-ebola-crisis-women-and-girls

Liem, M., & Oberwittler, D. (2012). Homicide followed by suicide in Europe. In M. Liem & W. A. Pridemore (Eds.), *Handbook of European homicide research: Patterns, explanations and countries studies* (pp. 197–215). New York: Springer.

Mathews, S., Abrahams, N., Jewkes, R., Martin, L. J., Lombard, C., Vetten, L. (2008). Intimate femicide–suicide in South Africa: A cross-sectional study. *Bulletin of the World Health Organization, 86*, 552–558. http://www.who.int/bulletin/volumes/86/7/07-043786.pdf.

Matzopoulos, R., Thompson, M. L., Myers, J. E. (2014, March). Firearm and nonfirearm homicide in 5 South African cities: A retrospective population-based study. *American Journal of Public Health, 104*(3), 455–460. http://ajph.aphapublications.org/doi/pdf/10.2105/AJPH.2013.310650

McFarlane, J., Campbell, J. C., Wilt, S., Sachs, C. J., Ulrich, Y., Xu, X. (1999, November). 'Stalking and Intimate Partner Femicide'. *Homicide Studies, 3*(4), 300–316. http://www.ncvc.org/SRC/AGP.Net/Components/DocumentViewer/Download.aspxnz?DocumentID=39084

Niaz, K., & Shujah, I. A. (2013). Civilian perspective of firearm injuries in Bahawalpur. *Journal of Pakistan Medical Association, 63*(1), 20–4.

OFS (Office fédéral de la statistique, Suisse). (2014). Méthodes de suicide, selon la classe d'âge et le sexe. Neuchâtel: OFS. http://www.bfs.admin.ch/bfs/portal/fr/index/themen/14/02/04/key/01.Document.139169.xls

Radford, J., & Russell, D. (Eds.). (1992). *Femicide: The politics of woman killing*. New York: Twayne Publishers.

RCMP (Royal Canadian Mounted Police). (2010, February). RCMP Canadian firearms program: Program evaluation. Ottawa: RCMP. http://www.rcmp-grc.gc.ca/pubs/fire-feu-eval/eval-eng.pdf

Report of the Fourth World Conference on Women (1995, September 4–15). Beijing. United Nations publication, Sales No. E.96.IV.13.

Russell, D. (2008, May). *Femicide: Politicizing the killing of females*. Paper presented at the Interagency Gender Working Group Meeting on Strengthening Understanding of Femicide, Washington, DC. http://www.igwg.org/Events/femicide.aspx

Shaw, M. (2013). Too close to home: Guns and intimate partner violence. In *Small Arms Survey 2013: Everyday Dangers* (pp. 17–45). Cambridge: Cambridge University Press. http://www.smallarmssurvey.org/publications/by-type/yearbook/small-arms-survey-2013.html

Stöckl, H., Devries, K., Rotstein, A., Abrahams, N., Campbell, J., Watts, C., Moreno, C. G. (2013). The global prevalence of intimate partner homicide: A systematic review. *Lancet, 382*(9895), 859–865.

UNDESA (United Nations Department of Economic and Social Affairs). (2014). Open Working Group Proposal for Sustainable Development Goals. United Nations Sustainable Development Knowledge Platform. https://sustainabledevelopment.un.org/sdgsproposal

UNODC (United Nations Office on Drugs and Crime). (2014). *Global study on homicide 2013*. Vienna: United Nations. http://www.unodc.org/gsh/

UNSC (United Nations Security Council). (2012). *Report of the secretary-general on women, peace and security*. S/2012/732 of 2 October. New York: UN. http://www.un.org/en/ga/search/view_doc.asp?symbol=S/2012/732

Van Kesteren, J. N. (2014). Revisiting the gun ownership and violence link. *British Journal of Criminology, 54*, 53–72. http://bjc.oxfordjournals.org/content/54/1/53.full.pdf

WHO (World Health Organization Department of Reproductive Health and Research), & London School of Hygiene and Tropical Medicine, South African Medical Research Council. (2013). Global and regional estimates of violence against women: prevalence and health effects of intimate partner violence and non-partner sexual violence. Geneva: World Health Organization. http://www.who.int/reproductivehealth/publications/violence/9789241564625/en/

WHO (World Health Organization). (2014a). *Global status report on violence prevention*. Geneva: WHO. http://www.who.int/violence_injury_prevention/violence/status_report/2014/en/

WHO (World Health Organization). (2014b). European Detailed Mortality Database. http://data.euro.who.int/dmdb/. Accessed 18 March 2015.

Wintemute, G. (2015). The epidemiology of firearm violence in the twenty-first century United States. *Annual Review of Public Health, 36*, 5–19. http://www.annualreviews.org/doi/pdf/10.1146/annurev-publhealth-031914-122535.

Women and Children as Victims and Offenders: The Impact of Armed Conflict and Post-Conflict Period Challenges

Vesna Nikolic-Ristanovic and Ljiljana Stevkovic

Abstract The aim of the chapter is to explore the impact of armed conflicts and their consequences on victimization and offending of women and children, and the implications on how a State, international actors and civil society respond. First, the theoretical framework and an overview of available findings about the impact of war on crime is provided, with special emphasis on victimization and offending of women and children. Then, we present a detailed review and analysis of the situation in Serbia during and after armed conflicts on the territory of the former Yugoslavia. In the analysis of the Serbian situation, particular emphasis is put on the long-term impact of war on offending and victimization of women and children through domestic violence and trafficking in persons. In conclusion, the role of the State, civil society and international actors is assessed and recommendations for more timely and appropriate responses are offered.

1 Introduction

Experts who have dealt with war and crime suggest that war, as a phenomenon of social disorganization followed by paralysed or biased formal control, usually creates favourable conditions for an increase of the crime rate, weakens inhibitions, encourages primitive impulses and, in this way, contributes to the temporary transformation of the rate, usual structure, as well as the aetiology and phenomenology of crimes (Gassin 1988, p. 327; Nikolic-Ristanovic 1998a). As emphasised by Bonger, the war drives up almost all factors, which may lead to crime (Bonger, cited in Jamieson 1998).

In line with that, studies which have dealt with the impact of war on crime suggest that war leads to an increase of military related, property and violent crimes, including sexual and domestic violence against women and children, as well as sexual slavery and sex trafficking. War also leads to an increase and changes

V. Nikolic-Ristanovic (✉) • L. Stevkovic
University of Belgrade, Belgrade, Serbia
e-mail: vnikolic@EUnet.rs; stevkoviclj@gmail.com

H. Kury et al. (eds.), *Women and Children as Victims and Offenders: Background, Prevention, Reintegration*, DOI 10.1007/978-3-319-08398-8_21

in the phenomenology of juvenile and female crime. It affects as well the regional dynamics and patterns of crime, and its impact is not restricted only to directly affected territories. There is a spill-over effect that reaches border zones and continues beyond (Reckless 1940, p. 253; Exner quoted in Reckless 1940, p. 253; Kinberg 1960, p. 192; Archer and Gartner quoted in Gassin 1988, p. 327; Gassin 1988, p. 328; Schneider 1987, p. 243; Nikolic-Ristanovic 1998a; Nikolic-Ristanovic 2000a; Nikolic-Ristanovic and Copic 2013; Nikolic-Ristanovic et al. 2014; Rummens and Seat 2003; UNICEF 2009).

The brutalization effect of war on crime lasts longer than the war itself, as the influencing factors on crime continue in the war- and post-war period (Jamieson 1998, 2014; Cockburn 2014). After the war, registered crime rates usually tend to decrease, but crime aetiology and phenomenology as well as the scope of hidden crime continues to reflect complex social, moral and economic consequences of war long after its formal end. The impact of war on family, socialization of youth, as well as on gender and age order, identities and relationships, produces long-term consequences that shape both victimization and offending of women and children.

Bearing all of the above-mentioned in mind, this chapter intends to explore the impact of armed conflicts and their consequences on victimization and offending of women and children, as well as to assess the responses of the state, international actors and civil society toward them. First, we provide the theoretical framework and an overview of available findings about the impact of war on crime, with special emphasis on victimization and offending of women and children in different wars, followed by a detailed review and analysis of the situation in Serbia during and after armed conflicts on the territory of the former Yugoslavia. In the analyses of the Serbian situation the emphasis is put on the long-term impact of war on offending and victimization of women and children through domestic violence and trafficking in persons. In conclusion, we assess the role of the State, civil society and international actors and make recommendations for more timely and appropriate responses.

2 The Impact of War on Crime and Victimization/ Offending of Women and Children

War results in the breakdown of formal and informal control as well as the inability (or at least diminished ability) of groups or individuals in a community or neighbourhood to solve problems collectively. Thus, it is quite understandable that all available theoretical explanations suggest the impact of social disorganisation on crime during the war (Jamieson 1998). More specifically, explanatory models include the impact of war-produced anomie, "temporary reversal" of moral progress, "temporary inversion of prevailing morality", re-traditionalisation of gender roles and intensified expression of a traditional gender order, as well as the economic and social-learning impact of war (Jamieson

1998; Nikolic-Ristanovic 2002, 2011; Jennings and Nikolic-Ristanovic 2013). In addition, we find attempts to explain both "immediate" and "wider origins" (Taylor et al. quoted in Lynch and Groves 1989, p. 56) of crime during the war, starting from a radical perspective, and also using the main assumptions of theories of social disorganization, anomie and social-learning (Nikolic-Ristanovic 1998a).

The breakdown of institutional control in war primarily creates favourable conditions for those who were criminals before the war. Selective and arbitrary arrests affect non-criminals rather than criminals and force people to live in constant fear and legal insecurity since no one knows who should be considered as "a criminal", who are "the police" and who are "the army". Criminals become incorporated into formal control agencies and criminal behaviour is not only unpunished—it is even regarded as desirable as a strategy of inter-ethnic war. Political leaders do not even try to do anything to prevent crimes against civilians, but perceive and pursue the benefits that may arise from these crimes in terms of the terror which serve their aims: ethnic cleansing, demoralization of the enemy and so on. Another use of criminals plays an especially important role at the beginning of the war when law-abiding people still do not feel enough endangered to be ready to go into battle.

As may be expected, criminals are among the first who are ready to use weapons and join the war. The crimes they then commit are welcomed by political leaders as a pretext for a further call to arms, i.e. the creation of a sense of danger to the nation and call for law-abiding people to also join the battle. The lack of any wish to prevent or at least to control the participation of criminals in the war, either as a part of police or paramilitary forces, leads to the assumption that warlords consciously use criminals in order to achieve their aims. This is confirmed by the fact that in the Balkans some criminals went directly from prisons to battle, as well as by the high social positions and important roles in national politics given to some leading criminals involved in the war (Nikolic-Ristanovic 1998a).

While in 'total wars' criminals have usually been involved as combatants because of added demand for all sources of manpower (Cavan 1956, p. 596), civil wars like the one in the former Yugoslavia suggest a different central role. This is not surprising bearing in mind the aforementioned suggestion that it was not so easy for leaders to convince previously law-abiding people, who had been living together for years, to kill each other. To manage this astonishing and terrible mission the leaders had to rely on criminals to materialize both war propaganda and the war itself.[1]

---

[1] How people (men) from former Yugoslavia were reluctant to engage in war is well illustrated by the picture of the average soldier in what was the Yugoslav National Army at the time of the brief war in Slovenia which was the beginning of the disintegration of the former Yugoslavia given by Sherwel: "Most are young conscripts who appear to have little idea what the fighting was about...Many of the captured soldiers are little older than schoolchildren whose paintings still adorn the walls. Several said they had no idea why they were ordered to seize border crossings and many admitted they had given up without firing a shot...The general view among 12 prisoners

However, the social disorganization generated by the war not only encourages criminals to continue with their criminal activity and to be more brutal and greedy. It also promotes criminal activities of those who, before the war, were conformists and law-abiding. As Shoemaker noticed, "the individuals who live in such situations of social disorganization are not necessarily themselves personally disoriented; instead, they are viewed as responding 'naturally' to disorganized environmental conditions" (Shoemaker 1990, pp. 81–2). This is how one can explain the enormous rise of crime in areas both directly and indirectly affected by the war, i.e. the fact that in wartime almost all the people were involved in some kind of criminal activity. In addition, as Jamieson (1998) suggests, reversal of moral progress contributes to crime through the removal of painful restraints on urges for which warfare provides an outlet and expression. The constant death vision and terrifying war consequences on people produce what some authors called "a state of moral vertigo" (Roux, quoted in Jamieson 1998).

According to some authors, women are more prone to moral reversal than men. They explain the increased rate of female violent and economic crime during the war as a consequence of increased shortages of consumer goods and increased family responsibilities of women (Mannheim, quoted by Jamieson 1998) who have to take on also the role of (usually) absent husband or other male family member(s). In addition, the increase of female and juvenile crime may be more pronounced compared to the crime of adult men due to what Archer and Gartner (quoted in Jamieson 1998) call the catharsis model of temporary reversal of moral progress. This means that men are those who primarily have the opportunity to express their violent and otherwise criminal behaviour on warfare, lessening the rate of their violent crime against the civil population (at home). This assumption may be well questioned in the light of the fact that in most contemporary conflicts civilians are the prevailing victims, and bearing as well in mind evidence on the impact of war on gender identities/gender order and male spouse and family violence, which is responsible in great part of war and post-war victimization of women and children.

Learning theories and the theory of anomie may be useful to explain the over-criminalization of society during the war as well. Once violence is made legitimate by war, "people apparently believe that if their leaders can solve problems with violence, it is also a suitable means for them to resort to resolve interpersonal differences" (Archer and Gartner quoted by Conklin 1992, p. 272). This kind of social learning of criminal behaviour during the war is especially characteristic of young people and presents a good framework for the explanation of the rise of violent crimes committed by juveniles (see also Jamieson 1998).

In the process of learning criminal motives the media play an especially important role. Biased information and the presentation of scenes of war violence urge people to go to battle and commit crimes in order to retaliate. Apart from this, the media's idolization of criminals offers a model for the behaviour of a large portion

interviewed was that Yugoslavia's problems have to be resolved without bloodshed" (Sherwell quoted by Korac 1994).

of young people and teaches them that being criminal is far more profitable than conforming.

In addition, people who went to battle and who were not criminals before, learned to become criminal in association with others who were criminals or in response to an excess of attitudes favouring crime (Sutherland 1939, pp. 4–9). Criminal behaviour learned in the war continued to be the way of life for many who came back home (Hentig, quoted in Jamieson 1998). In a war, the prohibition against killing becomes relative which leads to the rationalization of other killings and rendering of human life as worthless (Killias 1991, p. 280). This may, for example, explain the rise of homicides committed by former soldiers in Serbia during the wars in the former Yugoslavia. The other or supplementary explanation, which takes into consideration post-traumatic stress disorder (PTSD) similar to the post -Vietnam syndrome as the individual's reaction to social disorganization, is also applicable. Many of those who were "normal" men before the war and who were manipulated by war propaganda became angry or else had a sense of guilt and were accused of being participants in a politically wrong and "dirty" war. Their potential victims are all those who revive their sense of hopelessness, uselessness and guilt for killings in warfare, especially if they are of the same ethnic origin as the ethnic origin of the offender's wartime enemy. In ethnically mixed families, spouses and/or other members of the family may become their victims as well. It is when soldiers return from war that the wider origins of the crimes they have committed are evident.

Women are especially likely to be victimized when they resist a man's attempts to control them, or otherwise frustrate him in his attempts to assume a position of dominance, i.e. strong and "manly" behaviour (Matsakis 1996, p. 183). Often, man's violence is directed towards children too. Victimization of children may occur alone, or they may be victimized during the violence against their mothers, whether they watch, hear or try to help mother, or suffer direct physical, sexual and/or psychological violence (Nikolic-Ristanovic 2002; Nikolić-Ristanović and Stevković 2010).

Ex-soldiers may be incapable of controlling their rage, or may show extraordinarily intense emotions in normal situations. The study of PTSD among Vietnam veterans showed that there are more problems and more violence in families of Vietnam veterans with PTSD than in families of those without it (Kulka et al. 1990, p. 237). Feeling out of control and emasculated (by his own emotions, which, except for anger, he may view as "feminine"), an ex-soldier may attempt to regain a sense of control and affirm his manhood by battering. And, as Matsakis (1996, p. 183) put it, battering also "helps release the mounting adrenaline caused by his pent-up emotions and inner turmoil". Women's Aid, an Irish NGO from Dublin, reports on the plight of Bosnian women who were made to seek refuge twice—once from the Serbian army who had displaced them from their homes and again from their husbands who used domestic violence as a means of venting their frustration at their own "powerless" situation (McWilliams 1998, p. 128). Male control of women may consist of different forms of violence but may also consists of forcing women into offending, such as committing property crimes, helping the man in killing other people or recruiting other women for sex trafficking (Nikolić-Ristanović 2000b; Nikolic-Ristanovic 2011). Also, in their attempts to defend themselves and their children, women may become offenders by inflicting injuries or killing their abusers.

Another problem that may lead to the abuse of women and children is long-term separation of spouses, which may be the source of conflicts connected to men's frustrations because of difficulties to adapt to a changed division of labour caused by the war. Women's active role and proven ability to undertake both female and male roles in the family may additionally lower a man's already low self-esteem related to his lost role in the family (Andrić-Ružičić 1999, p. 15; Mitić 1997, p. 110; Euler and Welzer-Lang 2000; Moser 2001, p. 47) As pointed out by Connell, violence may result from a man's attempt to re-assert a damaged masculine ego (Connell 1995a, p. 128).

Women and girls are also the majority of victims of sexual violence in war.[2] Rape, sexual slavery and forced prostitution are crimes, which have been committed in all wars, regardless between whom and why they were waged. A woman is raped and/or taken as a sexual slave, i.e. forced into prostitution, in war because she is a woman and because she "belongs" to the man of the enemy side. In addition, in inter-ethnic wars, she is victimized because she belongs to the other (adversary) ethnic group, even when she is married to a man who does not belong to the enemy side (Nikolic-Ristanovic 2000a).

Within the predominantly male character of war, the gap between the man who has power and the woman devoid of power becomes greater than usually. The power of men is increased by weapons, so that an ordinary man becomes unordinary by "entry into the most exclusive male-only club in the world" (Brownmiller 1975, p. 32). On the other hand, women deprived of arms and protection of "their" men, with their class and ethnic belonging, educational and professional status, are exposed to the sexual violence of men.

It is also the rule that rape is committed by the men who belong to the winning side (Brownmiller 1975, p. 47). But since in the war the power relations change very often, rapes by conquerors are replaced by revenge rapes, committed by those who were previously defeated. As a result, there are usually a number of victims on all sides. Nowadays it is obvious that a large number of women are raped in war with extreme cruelty as well as that this is one of frequent ways how men use to confront each other through women's bodies (Nikolic-Ristanovic 2000a). However, in spite of that knowledge as well as in spite of serious and long term consequences for victims, rape in war was and still is "the crime that is by reputation the easiest to charge and the hardest to prove". But, it "has traditionally been the easiest to disprove as well" (Brownmiller 1975, p. 47).

[2] It should not be ignored that, especially in recent civil wars, the number of male victims of sexual violence increased. Men and boys were raped in Bosnia, albeit much less often than women and girls (Gutman 1994; Mazowiecki Report 1993; Bassiouni Report 1994; Helsinki Watch 1993; quoted by Hague 1997, p. 53).

If, in addition to everything mentioned above, we add easy access to weapons during the war as well as the fact that the majority of those who come back from warfare often bring back weapons with them, the rise of violent crimes both during the war and after the war should not be surprising.

War also produces an economic crisis and it, together with anomie, further contributes to the enormous rise of property crimes. War directly and indirectly (as through economic sanctions) affects society's economy and the distribution of work and economic rewards (Shoemaker 1990, p. 98), and encourages the majority of people to turn to various illegal activities. A large number of people who find themselves at a disadvantage by pursuing legitimate economic activities therefore become motivated to engage in illegitimate, delinquent activities. These people are "willing to work or otherwise be productive members of society but, because of the unavailability of employment or an opportunity to develop job skills, they turn to criminality, perhaps out of frustration with their situation or perhaps because of economic necessity" (Shoemaker 1990, p. 98). Thus, the lack of paid jobs and essential goods during the war prompts a large number of people to be involved in traditional property crimes and different illegal activities related to the hidden economy.

The hidden economy offers "temporary alternative employment" and those who take the jobs within it are for the most part honest citizens who were forced into this field as they were unable to find legal jobs. The extent of people's involvement in the illegal activities and the benefit that the state elite derived from this was so big that it was no longer in the interest of the authorities to punish the perpetrators. This led to complete anomie and social disorganisation, and generated a further rise of crime and other forms of deviant social behaviour.

All of the afore mentioned factors enable the development of all types of criminal markets and organised crime which serve as a survival strategy for some and as a method of capital accrual for others. War zones become seedbeds for organised crime related to illegal trade of drugs, fuel, weapons, human organs and human trafficking (Nikolic-Ristanovic 1998a, p. 466).

Related to economic hardships, illegal markets play an important role in the post- war economy as well—despite the re-establishment of the formal economy and the heightened openness of the citizens to the idea of conformity. Once created, criminal organizations only change the field of their illegal activity. Also, people have learnt to earn money through crime so that the system of values has been completely distorted and it is not so easy, especially in the conditions of a destroyed economy, to motivate people to conform again. Both in connection with violent and organised crime such as human and drug trafficking, the war may be seen also as an inversion of prevailing morality (Jamieson 1998), which lasts and produces consequences on crime far beyond the end of armed conflicts.

In close connection to that, the dual trends of a normalisation of large sex industries and regressive changes in gender relations fed into each other, which contributed to the victimisation of women and children through sexual violence, sex trafficking and sexual slavery of large dimensions. In Bosnia-Herzegovina (B-H) and Kosovo, for example, the wartime and post-war periods have seen a gradual evolution in normative heterosexuality, such that both women and men are pushed, or attracted, to take jobs within the sex industry and/or to involve themselves in sex trafficking (Jennings and Nikolic-Ristanovic 2013). Thus, economic incentives and social pressures reinforce each other: both women and men can secure economic survival, as well as social standing by reaffirming their adherence to regressive gender identities (Messerschmidt 1993, p. 122). Sex work can be seen as embodying the types of the dominant, masterful man and the submissive, beautiful and desirable woman. At the same time, economic hardship and the legacy of war (e.g. women-headed households) make it even more difficult for men and women to achieve ideal masculinity and femininity, except through participation in illegal or illicit activities—which, thanks in part to the peacekeeping economy, is more widely available. Consequently, once the sex industry was entrenched by organised crime interests, peacekeepers and local colluders, the foundation was there to continue the business. The cases of Bosnia-Herzegovina and Kosovo demonstrate that peacekeeping economies' impacts are not temporary, but can be lasting, diverse and dispersed (Jennings and Nikolic-Ristanovic 2013).

There are obviously tight interconnections between the economic consequences of war, organised crime, peacekeeping economy and the sex industry, while the explosion of the latter has contributed to regressive changes in gender identities, roles and relations (Jennings and Nikolic-Ristanovic 2013). At the same time, these are the factors that produce the most persistent patterns of both victimisation and offending of women but children as well (Nikolic-Ristanovic 2001).

3 Offending and Victimization of Women and Children in Serbia During the War

The main factors which contributed to the changes in the extent and structure of crimes in Serbia committed during and after the wars in neighbouring countries and on its own territory in the 1990s,[3] include: the closeness of warfare, the fact that a lot of men from Serbia went to battle as well as a severe economic crisis as a consequence of the expenditure of a great part of the state budget on the war to help Serbs in Croatia, Bosnia-Herzegovina and Kosovo, as well as of an enormous influx of refugees and internally displaced people, UN sanctions and NATO airs strikes.[4]

[3] Serbia has borders with Bosnia-Herzegovina and Croatia, i.e. areas which were directly affected by ethnic war, while Kosovo, another directly affected area, was part of its own territory during the armed conflicts in it. Serbia was not directly affected by the wars in Bosnia-Herzegovina and Croatia. The Serbian government never recognized that Serbia was involved in these wars while men from Serbia went into battle and people suffered a lot of its (indirect) consequences. However, Serbia was more directly affected by the ethnic conflicts in Kosovo, as well as by NATO air strikes during the Kosovo conflict.

[4] Social transformation in Serbia was blocked by wars, as well as by the disintegration of the former Yugoslavia, UN sanctions and isolation of the country, which led to the end of communist

Crime in Serbia had its highest level ever in 1992 and 1993, or at the beginning of the war in the former Yugoslavia. This is confirmed by trends both relating to offenders and crime (Nikolic-Ristanovic 1998a; Nikolic-Ristanovic et al. 2014, in print). In 1993, in total 47 % more offenders were reported than in 1990, while the rise of in reported juvenile delinquents was 41 %. In 1994, the number of reported criminal offenders dropped but still remained high in comparison with 1990. The trend in the number of reported offenders in this period was completely different from the trend in the earlier period, 1984–1991, when this number had a stagnating tendency. The crime trend was similar to the trend of reported offenders: the highest level of crime registered by police was in 1992 (1894 per 100,000 population), while in 1993 it started to decrease slightly (183,793 or 1856 per 100,000 population). Statistical data on reported offenders and crime in Serbia for the period 1990–1994 show trends that are very similar to the trends reported for both world wars (Reckless 1940, p. 253; Kinberg 1960, p. 192).

However, in spite of the increase of reported offenders, the number of persons convicted for crimes showed a decreasing tendency. This discrepancy between the number of reported and the number of convicted persons can be explained by the inefficiency of formal control agencies under the influence of the war and the economic crisis. This is further confirmed by the data, which suggest that in 1993 the number of unknown offenders was 75,950, which was almost double the 1990 figure of 39,432.

In terms of crime structure, the rate of property and economic crimes rose significantly. On the other hand, the total number of offenders reported for crimes against life and limb decreased while the number of offenders reported for most serious crimes, such as murders, attempted murders and serious bodily injuries, increased. Generally, the changes in crime structure are most obvious when the most serious crimes are considered. More specifically, illegal possession of weapons, robbery and burglary are among the crimes that reached the highest rate of increase.

Illegal possession of weapons started to be reported during the war, i.e. in 1992 and rose by 346 % during 1994. In comparison with 1990 the number of reported robbery offenses increased by 344 % with far more frequent lethal consequences than previously. Burglaries also showed an enormous increase: the number of persons reported for burglary increased by 115 % (or more than double).

At the beginning of the war, the number of reported assault and battery, robbery and burglary offenders dropped but in the middle period of the war they started to

---

rule no earlier than the year 2000. As a result of ethnic conflicts in neighbouring countries (which were at their peak in 1993), economic sanctions imposed in 1992 and NATO bombing in 1999, Serbia faced a deep economic crisis. In 1993, the country was hit by enormous inflation, which had disastrous effects in terms of both impoverishment of large parts of the population and severe social differentiation, i.e. concentration of assets and power in the hands of the ruling elite and those close to it (G17Plus 2000, pp. 49–50). NATO bombing, with its enormous destruction of plants and infrastructure, also caused large-scale economic damage to the country's already weak economy and returned it to an even more backward state than it was before.

increase rapidly. With some minor oscillations, homicides showed a rising tendency and reached their highest point in 1993 with a 37 % increase in comparison to 1990. The number of reported rape offenders decrease however until 1994 when it started to go up slightly.

The most serious crimes committed by juveniles increased more than adult crimes. The rate of reported juvenile homicides and robberies doubled and burglaries almost tripled in 1994 in comparison with 1990. As with adult rape cases, reported rapes committed by juveniles tended to decrease.

The increase of violent crimes is most striking in big cities such as Belgrade, Serbia's capital. In comparison with 1990, the number of homicides committed in Belgrade in 1995 increased more than three times. Both adult and juvenile homicides were very often committed as a result of conflicts between criminal gangs and, far more than previously, victims were killed by the use of firearms, which were most often in the illegal possession of offenders ("Portret domaćeg ubice", *Vreme*, 1996). Firearms were often brought back from warfare by soldiers or purchased on the black market.[5] There were also refugees among both offenders and victims of violent and property crimes. People of ethnic origin other than Serbian and political opponents were especially vulnerable to becoming victims of homicides and robberies. Although there is no systematic research on crime during the war, available data suggests that those who committed the most serious violent crimes were very often former soldiers. Some of them simply continued to do what they did in warfare but some became violent as the result of posttraumatic stress disorder caused by their war experience. This latter phenomenon began to appear especially after the end of the war (Nikolic-Ristanovic 1998a).

In the absence of research evidence, it is particularly difficult to explain the decrease of reported rapes in Serbia during the war. However, having in mind that rape was widespread in areas directly affected by war as well as the fact that a lot of men from Serbia (many of them with a criminal past) were involved in the war, it may be that this decrease in rape was a temporary consequence of the absence of men who raped during the war. The slight increase in the number of reported rapes during 1994 may confirm this assumption if we bear in mind that at that time soldiers started to return home. In these circumstances their accumulated aggression and war experience made their crimes more brutal and more often led to lethal consequences. According to media coverage, which, with reliable statistics lacking, has become an important source of knowledge about crimes even for academics, it would seem that sexual crimes were more often than previously followed by inhuman cruelty and resulted in the death of the victims, with the offenders remaining unknown to the police even after a series of such cases (Nikolic-Ristanovic 1998a).

A second explanation is that the decrease in reported rapes in Serbia during the war may in fact hide an increase in the number of unreported rape offences, characteristic of the rape in earlier wars as well (Schneider 1987, p. 245). During

---

[5] Every second citizen of Yugoslavia possesses firearms ("Vreme prokriminalne kulture", 1995).

the war, women and men alike had less confidence in the police, who were regarded as more interested in protecting the political regime from its opponents than in resolving crimes. Thus the dark figure of the number of rapes (which was always high) rose significantly during the war, reflecting both general distrust of the police and the particular distrust felt by women who may have been afraid that the police, who were seen to prioritise more "important" duties, would be more sexist and disinterested toward them than ever (Nikolic-Ristanovic 1998a).

Organized crime grew as well because the war created various needs, which could be satisfied by organized crime rather than by legal means. Apart from organized crime connected to the drugs and weapons trade which developed as a direct consequence of the war, UN sanctions imposed on Federal Republic of Yugoslavia—FRY (Serbia and Montenegro) also led to the creation of organizations for the trade of fuel, cigarettes and other scarce goods.

The economic crisis, which had resulted from both the war and UN sanctions led to the criminalization of society on a scale of enormous proportions. Although it was not reported officially, it is well known that during the war, almost every citizen was involved in some kind of illegal activity. Enormous inflation and the impossibility of earning a significant income legally encouraged a large number of people to acquire and use foreign instead of national currency, smuggle and sell deficient goods on the black market or resort to other legally questionable activities in order to survive (Nikolic-Ristanovic 1998a). In such social conditions, when crimes related to the hidden economy became useful and desirable, the state's interest to punish offenders disappeared. This further led to the creation of the status of complete anomie and generated a further rise of crime and other forms of deviant social behaviours (Ćirić 1993, p. 107).

There were indicators that a significant number of young people (about 30 years old but juveniles as well) were involved in organized crime. Older adult criminals hired them since they were cheap: they killed, stole cars, sold or grabbed narcotics for small amounts of money (Radovanović quoted in "Drzavni neprijatelj broj tri", *Vreme,* 1995; for similar information see also Ruggiero and South 1995, pp. 199–200). Some criminals who had left the country and been "successful" elsewhere in their criminal activity before the war, returned to Serbia when the war began, finding more favourable conditions for criminal activities and profit there. Some of these became symbolic carriers of certain messages about national politics and nationalism and as such were idolized in the state media during the war ("Vreme prokriminalne kulture", *Naša borba*, 1995). Many young people found in them their idols and followed their example in engaging in crime. Juvenile and young adults' delinquency was strongly influenced by other adult criminals for whom the conditions created by the war were extremely profitable. The fact that crime is evidently more profitable than law abiding behaviour, i.e. that the nouveau riche are mainly criminals while law abiding people hardly survive, led many young people to see the attractions of crime as a way to gain both social affirmation and profit.[6]

[6] This is vividly shown in famous Serbian movie *Rane* (Wounds) directed by Srdjan Dragojević.

Contrary to the incidence of male crimes, reported female crime showed a decreasing tendency—from 9.5 % of total reported crime in 1990 to 6.4 % in 1994. The number of reported female offenders dropped by 60 % from 1990 to 1994. In time of war women often turn toward the private, domestic sphere, spend a great deal of time taking care of their families' existential needs and are more ready than usual to sacrifice themselves for persons close to them than to respond to violence against them. Thus crimes usually committed by women (thefts, infractions, assaults and batteries and homicides against persons close to them) decreased. However, perhaps predictably, women did begin to commit more crimes connected to their worsened economic position and/or their new position as head of the family (in the absence of male members). It must be acknowledged that these are crimes for which statistics do not provide us with reliable data since they mainly remain unreported. It does seem to be the case that, as in earlier wars (Schneider 1987, p. 244), women became more involved in many illegal acts connected to smuggling and the black market economy, which were generally underreported. Also, in spite of the decrease in the total number of women reported for offences or crimes, the number of women reported for serious property crimes and some violent crimes (not including persons close to them and as a response to an attack) increased. For example, the number of women reported for burglary increased almost four times (224 in 1990 in comparison to 876 in 1994). Also, the number of women reported for robberies (including robberies with lethal consequences) more than doubled (13 in 1990 in comparison to 29 in 1994). However, as for male crimes, the most enormous rise is related to reported crimes of illegal possession of weapons—43 in 1992 in comparison to 234 in 1994 (Nikolic-Ristanovic 1998a).

Findings of an International Crime (Victim) Survey, conducted by the Institute for Criminological and Sociological Research (in cooperation with UNICRI, Italy) in Belgrade during 1996, showed a high victimization rate in the period 1991–1996. As many as 85.4 % of 1094 respondents reported they had been victims of crime during the past five years. But interestingly, the victimization rate was the highest in 1995: 40.9 % of respondents reported being victimized in that year (Nikolic-Ristanovic 1998b). This could be evidence of rising rates of crime triggered by the approaching end of the war in the former Yugoslavia, i.e. by the economic crisis and a status of anomie, which continued to be high some time after the war, even despite the decrease of reported offenders.

During the war, as in times of peace, women were often victims of domestic violence. One of the indicators of the large number of cases of victimization of women within the family during ethnic conflicts was the data on the cases reported to the SOS hotline in Belgrade. The number of women who called the SOS telephone increased from 499 in 1990 to 1377 in 1995 (Nikolic-Ristanovic 1998a).

According to Belgrade SOS hotline statistics, in 12 % of all calls recorded in 1993[7] women reported that molesters were men who were spending some time on

[7] This was the year when the war in Bosnia was culminating, as well as the year when FRY reached the enormous inflation rate and the level of crime reached its highest point.

war territory as soldiers. The analysis of SOS hotline data (Mršević 1999) suggests that molesters are most often (56 %) actual husbands and partners or former husbands and partners (8 %) From the beginning of ethnic wars the number of violent sons has been increasing (from 6.4 % in 1991 to 8.7 % in 1995), reaching its highest point in 1993: 11.4 %. Most often women reported psychological (52.0 %) and physical violence (70.7 %). Women also reported sexual violence (15.5 %) and economic abuse (6 %), and they reported death threats twice more often in 1993 than in the previous years. Also, the use of weapons in domestic violence had been increasing since the beginning of the war. After the beginning of the war some 40 % of women who called the SOS telephone reported that their partners were threatening them by the use of pistols, grenades and similar weapons. According to the Zagreb SOS hot line, a similar situation regarding the impact of war on domestic violence was found in Croatia (Fisher 1994).

Research findings suggest that war-related worsening of spouse and family relationships in Serbia was connected to the disturbance in inter-ethnic relationships, to men's decisions to go to and return from war, to difficulties brought on by forced migration, as well as to feelings of insecurity, powerlessness and existential fears connected to the NATO bombing of Serbia. Research findings suggest that the impact of war is usually combined with the impact of economic difficulties, and that the risk for women to become victims of domestic violence increases with an increase in the presence of both factors in their lives (e.g. often they live in ethnically mixed marriages, are refugees confronted with economic hardships, and their husbands spent some time in war and suffer from post traumatic stress disorder and a crisis of masculinity) (Nikolic-Ristanovic 2002).

At the very beginning of the war in the former Yugoslavia some women reported a so-called "post TV violence syndrome" (Fisher 1994, p. 165). This means that their husbands became very aggressive after watching TV News, Channel 1,[8] since the main war propaganda was affected through this broadcasting. Some men made decisions to go to fight after watching this broadcasting and when women started to speak about their worries and fears for them, their violence broke out. Obviously, men became nervous because they were convinced that they should go and fight but, at the same time, they were faced with a lack of courage to do it. In such cases every reaction of women (wives as well as mothers) might be the source of men's aggression, since it contributed to their frustration related to their difficulty in identifying with widespread cultural images of militarised masculinity. And it is also often connected to their failure to achieve the role of breadwinner.

In addition, the disturbance in inter-ethnic relationships connected to ethnic conflicts in the former Yugoslavia affected the lives of spouses who belonged to different ethnic groups, whether they lived in territories directly or indirectly (such as Serbia) affected by ethnic conflicts. Domestic violence in these cases was usually

[8] Similarly, as pointed out by Kelly, during the Gulf War women told stories of their husbands dressing in army uniforms before beating them, frequently after watching the TV news (Kelly 2000, p.59).

connected to the women belonging to a different ethnic group. The phenomenon of abstract hatred directed against other nationalities was smoothly transformed into a hatred of very close persons such as wives, children, and relatives. In some cases, violence became more drastic because of the wives belonging to a different ethnic group, while in some cases nationalism even provoked violent behaviour from husbands (Nikolic-Ristanovic 2002).

In Serbia, the war affected the creation of an image of tough, dominant and combative masculinity. As Connell (1995, p. 77) pointed out, hegemonic masculinity is strongly connected to the military. Although mythologies of war, past battles and man's role as a soldier have been largely circulating throughout Serbian history (which itself consists of a number of wars), the creation of militaristic masculinity in recent history became especially pronounced at the beginning of the 1990's and as a part of nationalism and war propaganda (Nikolic-Ristanovic 1998a, p. 466). The use of military rituals and the religious consecration of war as inevitable for defending "our brothers" in other parts of the former Yugoslavia, both contributed to the militaristic images of masculinity. It seems that the mechanisms of militarized gender order creation in the former Yugoslavia were quite similar to those found elsewhere (Hatty 2000, p. 128). The deployment of military rituals included use of uniforms, weapons, flags, music—in the media as well as within the broader culture and in everyday life (e.g. in magazines, daily newspapers, on radio and TV, in streets, cafes, restaurants etc.). Cultural models of masculinity which were, as in other wars (Hatty 2000, p. 139), offered during and after the war, included those of the soldier, breadwinner and family man.

On the other side, complementary femininity models included women's sacrifice as mothers and wives (strongly promoted by the Serbian Orthodox Church) as well as women as sexual objects and entertainers of soldier—widely propagated within popular culture. Hence militarised (hegemonic) masculinity and emphasized femininity[9] served as the most powerful cultural models offered to Serbian men and women during most of the 1990's (Nikolic-Ristanovic 2002).

Similar to Vietnam veterans, Serbian men came back home still very dependent on violence. In addition, they felt disappointed in themselves as men as well as deceived and victimized by those in positions of leadership in the military and government. Many of those who were "normal" men before the war and who were manipulated by national politics were later angry or had a sense of guilt and were

[9] Connell's notion of "hegemonic masculinity" and "emphasized femininity" as the culturally idealized forms of gender in a given historical setting. These forms, as further elaborated by James Messerschmidt are "culturally honored, glorified and extolled at the symbolic level in the mass media". "In Western industrialized societies", as stressed by the same author, "hegemonic masculinity is characterized by work in the paid labor market, the subordination of women and girls, heterosexism and the driven and uncontrollable sexuality of men, and underscores practices toward authority, control and aggressiveness". Emphasized femininity is a form that complements hegemonic masculinity and is defined by Connell through compliance with men's desire for titillation and ego stroking and acceptance of marriage and childcare, and on a mass level is "organized around the themes of sexual receptivity in relation to younger women and motherhood in relation to older women" (Connell 1993).

accused of being participants in a politically wrong and "dirty" war (Nikolic-Ristanovic 1998a, p. 476). In addition, they often ended with a lack of self-esteem and marginalised masculinity, since they usually had a problem regaining their earlier status within the family. The lack of stable employment and a strong economic position led them to feel inadequate or betrayed, especially when they were put in a position to be dependent on their partners, as well as when the war led to emancipation and/or empowerment of the partner. Their feeling of powerlessness was especially strong when they were, as Croatian and Kosovo Serbs, put in a situation to surrender and leave their homes as refugees, becoming dependent not only on their wives but on inadequate Serbian state welfare and the mercy of unknown people.

Thus, the men's frustrations were especially emphasized when they were both former soldiers and multiple refugees (e.g. forced to move from one part of Croatia to another and then to Serbia), and when they were dependent on their wives. Also, violent ex-soldiers often had experiences from several wars and this prolonged war experience created both an enormous "dependence on violence" and an enormous feeling of failure and futility as a consequence of unexpected rejection or ignorance by society. As a result, their violent behaviour in the home progressed over time, so that, as one woman told in an interview to the researcher, "from every war they became worse and worse". These findings also agree with findings of research on wife beating in other wars, which show that the coincidence of war-related risks and negative changes in men's social and economic status is especially likely to lead to violence against women (Matsakis 1996, p. 195). The crisis of male identity as a contributing factor to domestic violence connected to war is also connected to a man's feeling of helplessness, i.e. marginalisation as a man, in relation to oppression done by other men who happen to be much more powerful.

Additionally, post-war surroundings sometimes transform women into martyrs: they are expected to suffer the consequences of men's post-war trauma. (Andrić-Ružičić 1999; Corrin 1999, p. 73). As noticed by a Croatian women's organization, "domestic violence, which has always been considered a minor women's problem (if a problem at all), has become a woman's patriotic duty...Their duty is to make the pains of "our soldiers" easier, to be understanding and patient" (Boric and Desnica 1996, pp. 135–6).

As noticed by El-Bushra (2000, p. 80), in the notion of "hegemonic masculinity" "the differences of power and status between men merge with those between men and women, with the result that certain groups of men are allocated characteristics normally associated with women". A similar effect occurred with both soldiers and male civilians during the NATO bombing of Serbia. Research findings (Nikolić-Ristanović and Milivojević 2000, p. 21) show that women mainly reported long-term violence, which either continued with the same intensity or became worse during the bombing. Only occasionally women mentioned that the violence started at that time. Alcohol as a contributing factor to domestic violence increased as well. Women often stated that their husbands' and sons' increased consumption of alcohol was caused by their fear of bombing and "long hours", since they stopped working when the bombing started. Also, some women reported that their mentally ill husbands became more violent because of their worsening health under the stress produced by bombing.

As circumstances which precipitated violence, women often mentioned circumstances directly or indirectly related to bombing. A woman said that she was beaten, since, having in mind intensive bombing in the close neighbourhood and her daughter's fear, she insisted that her husband make the shelter convenient for them. Another woman said that, from the beginning of the bombing her husband became more violent than before since they did not agree in their political assessments of the situation. In addition to beating, several women were expelled from apartments in the middle of the night, when the bombing was the most intense. Men's violence also intensified because of difficulties divorced women faced during the bombing in providing visitation for their children. Sometimes, men also used the bombing as a pretext for not bringing children to see their mother.

As in other wars (Karstedt 1993, p. 145; Moeller 1993, p. 3), in the wars in the former Yugoslavia (both ethnic conflicts and NATO bombing of Serbia), women performed their traditional duties in much more difficult conditions and with more effort than usual (e.g. long periods of time without electricity and water, serious shortages of food and other essential goods, difficult economic conditions and impossibility to use new technology, etc.). But, paradoxically, the re-traditionalisation of the gender division of labour brought by war, i.e. tightening of external patriarchy, also renewed a stronger position of women in the home as a consequence of the fact that the economic crisis made the gender-specific functions of family maintenance especially important (Karstedt 1993, p. 147; Nikolić-Ristanović et al. 1996, p. VII). Another paradox of feminine identity during the war is the fact that many women assume all burdens or a multiple role identity. This is a consequence of the fact that during and after the war, for various reasons, many families function as single parent- or woman-headed households.

However, performing all roles is especially difficult in abnormal war conditions and post-war economic crises. The situation is further aggravated if, at the same time, a woman is living with a man with PTSD, war caused disability and/or with other war related problems, and who is rarely ready to do any domestic work.[10] The situation is especially difficult for refugee women, whether they are in exile alone with children, or together with the husbands who do not have paid jobs and are frustrated as men. In this situation both women and men, but children as well, suffer all the negative consequences of the reverse gender role model of the family (Nikolic-Ristanovic 2002).

Ethnic conflicts in the former Yugoslavia significantly contributed to the vulnerability of women and children to sex trafficking as well. Sexual slavery and sex trafficking were strongly connected to war rapes and forced prostitution. Moreover, methods used for bringing women into rape camps and brothels were extremely

[10] For similar experiences of Vietnam veteran wives see Matsakis (1996), p. 130, and for women in Germany after World War II, Moeller (1993), p. 9.

cruel and humiliating. Although sex trafficking that was closely connected to ethnic conflicts stayed mainly within the borders of war-affected and neighbouring countries, it contributed to the expansion of prostitution and made a good basis for these countries to become attractive destination for trafficking in women from other parts of Eastern Europe. Post-war militarization and the large presence of international organizations further contributed to the growing sex trafficking problem in the Balkans (Picarelli 2002). Together with Bosnia-Herzegovina and Macedonia, Serbia and its then territory, Kosovo, were particularly affected.

In 1999, Human Rights Watch uncovered brothels "filled with women scattered throughout Bosnia", who told Human Rights Watch interviewers that they had been sold from brothel owner to brothel owner, placed in debt bondage, threatened and beaten. One year later, the United Nations report on trafficking in Bosnia confirmed the widespread abuses. The UN identified 260 nightclubs throughout the country, while the estimate given by NGOs is as high as 900, with between 4 and 25 women in each nightclub (Limanowska 2002). The May 2000 HRW Report documented significant local police, international police, and some Stabilization Force (SFOR) complicity in trafficking in women and girls.[11] Also, according to local NGOs, 50 % of clients are internationals, mainly soldiers from SFOR and at least 70 % of all profits from prostitution were estimated to come from internationals, which used to pay different rates and spend more money in bars than local men. A similar situation was found in Kosovo as well, where some higher level police officers were repatriated for suspected involvement in trafficking (Limanowska 2002).

Serbia, owing to its better economic situation at the beginning of the 1990s, was for some time among the main destination countries within Eastern Europe. However, later on, Serbia became mainly a transit country to neighbouring territories, such as Bosnia-Herzegovina and Kosovo where armed forces (including international peace keeping forces) became a large presence, and, through it, to Western Europe. Also, Serbia has been all the time a sending country for trafficked women.

Women's vulnerability to sex trafficking was the result of consequences, which structural changes in post-communist and war-affected countries produced in everyday life and gender identities of both women and men. Thus it is not possible to understand the wave of sex trafficking of women from Eastern and Central Europe without taking into account both macro social and micro (social and individual) risk factors which either predispose or trigger violence against women.

Similarly as shown by the research on new slavery, carried out by the noted British sociologist and antislavery activist Bales (1999), surveys carried out in Serbia and its surroundings showed that slavery flourishes in societies under stress and in extreme poverty. One of the main consequences of social changes brought by war and social transition is the sharpening of social differentiation between a small part of very rich and a large part of poor people, with an almost disappearing middle class. This had important consequences on the creation of different masculinities and femininities as well as on the emergence of different models of family class relations (Hagan 1988).

[11] Human Rights Watch World Report (2001).

On the one side, there was the rise of traditional (hegemonic) masculinity, while, on the other, multiple marginalized masculinities arose as well. Complementary to them is both emphasized and marginalized femininity. In addition, understanding trafficking in women and children is impossible without understanding interconnections between social processes taking place in different parts of the world as well. The example of the Balkans is very telling in that sense, since it shows how women and children are pushed/pulled into trafficking by a combination of war, transition and factors related to globalization. Or, as Picarelli (2002) puts it, this region is an appropriate selection for studying the problem of trafficking, because it serves as a 'microcosm of the trafficking cycle' and provides an insight into the larger transnational nature of trafficking syndicates.

Micro social expressions of macro social factors, such as transition from communism, war and globalization, serve as strong push factors for women's migration, their employment in the sex industry and vulnerability to sex trafficking. The probability to become a victim of trafficking is greater the younger a woman, since young women are more often identified (by themselves and/or by potential recruiters) as sex objects. This is connected with the changes in gender images about sexuality, which are best mirrored in the explosion of beauty/fashion magazines and pornography in Serbia as well as other post communist and war affected societies. (Nikolic-Ristanovic 2002).

Media re-constructed the traditional opposition between men's sexual needs and women as passive sexual objects and men's property, which was further used to justify violence and blame the victim. At the same time, global mass media reinforced this trend through the circulation of stereotyped gender images that are deliberately made attractive for marketing purposes (Connell 2001). In addition, vulnerability to sex trafficking was connected with marginalization and hopelessness related to the difficulty of economic, war-related, family-or similar situation. Both women's desperate state because of their difficult situation and their efforts to find a solution/exit from it contributed to their inaccurate perception of risks, i.e. of a mistaken cost/benefit calculation and the failure to anticipate danger. In the Balkans, foreigners and desperate local women who suffer short and long-term consequences of war are both pushed into sex industry. As stated by Peter Von Behtlemfavy from IOM (International Organisation for Migration), "the number of illegal prostitutes from the Balkans, where close to a decade of war has wiped out many ordinary jobs, has tripled if not quadrupled from 1995 to 2000"(Smith 2000).

In addition, socio-economic changes in everyday lives of both women and men in post-communist countries (e.g. unemployment and/or loss of previous social positions/privileges) played an important role in them becoming involved in prostitution as pimps, and in trafficking as recruiters, traffickers etc., as well. Findings of surveys carried out in Serbia suggest that labour distribution among people involved in trafficking is strongly gendered so that among recruiters (who get the least profit[12]) women participate in equal measure as men, while men dominate in

[12] For example, criminal gangs buy women from recruiters for small amounts of money such as 50–150 $ and resell them for 5000 $ and more.

higher places in the hierarchy. Also, poor and powerless men are usually subordinated to those who lead the "business", i.e. to those having leading roles within the mafia. Thus, the place, which men have within the economic structure usually determines the role they have within the sex industry business as well (e.g. as street pimps, brothel owners, traffickers or clients). Whatever their economic position, and whether women identify themselves as sex objects or are identified as such without their consent, they are always subordinated to men. Therefore, although some men are sometimes subordinated to women as well, both of them are also subordinated to men. Or, to put it otherwise, there are differences between different forms of emphasized femininities (e.g. women involved in trafficking, street prostitutes, call girls, victims of trafficking etc.), and subordinated masculinities, masculinities are always hegemonic in relation to femininities.

As a result of both economic hardships and changes in normative heterosexuality, i.e. gender images about sexuality, both women and men are also pushed/ attracted to take jobs within the sex industry and/or to involve themselves in sex trafficking as offenders within organized crime. Thus, as Messerschmidt (1993) pointed out, both women and men tend to secure economic survival as well as social standing for reaffirming their gender. In addition, children are also pushed to do some simple and low paid jobs such as guiding victims who are passing the border illegally by foot or to stand guard. They are usually subordinated and exploited by higher level criminals, although some time they are forced into committing trafficking by their parents as the part of trafficking as a small scale family business.

During the war, and most often for sometime afterwards, there are several ways in which the push/pull factors for sex trafficking are generated. Unemployment, poverty and lack of prospects in general, resulting from the war, influence both supply and demand for prostitution/trafficking. Desperate women easily became vulnerable to false promises and deception, as well as to different forms of violence. Traffickers exploit the fact that many persons are in vulnerable situations, undocumented and separated from their families. Refugees are especially vulnerable, both while fleeing from war zones and when finding themselves in exile. The most widespread in the region was obviously the trafficking of Kosovo Albanian and Roma refugee women (Bacanovic 2001). Apart from their desperate situation as refugees, they were also vulnerable since once raped (either by Serb forces in the war zone or by traffickers while fleeing it) they knew that their families would never accept them back. Thus, they became involved in sex trafficking much easier than raped women and women from less patriarchal societies did in peacetime (Nurmi 1999). As British feminist researcher Liz Kelly (2000) noticed in Bosnia, one of the most common routes into the sex industry is rape, which makes women "unmarriageable". Armed conflict makes survival of raped women even more precarious. In addition, lack of prospects connected to the war influenced the demand for paid sex by men involved in the army but also by those in the rear.[13]

[13] A good illustration for that is found in the expansion of sex industry in Serbia during NATO bombing 1999.

When a huge international army is also present, as in the case of Bosnia, for example, and newly created demand is not possible to be met by using only local women, trafficking of foreign women from the poorest (post-communist) countries is used for getting additional supply. According to some sources, there is evidence of foreign women working as prostitutes in Bosnia-Herzegovina as early as in 1993.[14]

Lawlessness and corruption, i.e. social disorganization and a state of anomie, had a serious impact on the increase of sex trafficking in Serbia and other war-affected areas as well. The negative impact of war on the functioning of the criminal justice system and the absence of the rule of law in general had obviously an influence on the increase of crime, including especially the increase of violent and organized crime. This further led to the complicity of criminal justice in different forms of the hidden economy and organized crime, with male police officers being either directly involved in trafficking in women or turning a blind eye on it. One important aspect of this latter is also the high level of prejudices among criminal justice officers about victims of sex trafficking, with the consequence that they often treated them as prostitutes or illegal migrants, i.e. criminals, rather than as victims. In Serbia, the international isolation during the regime of former president Milosevic, which meant that ties with Interpol, other international organizations and the police of other countries were severed, was an additional factor which had generated human trafficking.[15]

In sum, as a consequence of many factors, with ethnic intolerance, frustrations of former soldiers and economic hardship being among the main ones, violence against women and children, especially domestic violence, became more serious than earlier. At the same time, cooperation with the police became more difficult because, "given the general surge of violence, they are less inclined than ever to intervene in cases of violence against women" (Fisher 1994, p. 165).

4 Victimization and Offending of Women and Children in Serbia After the War

After 1994, reported crime started to decrease, and although the trends changed directions in different periods, it never again reached the levels of 1993 and 1994. Crime has been predominantly male, with convicted women not exceeding 10 % of all convicted offenders. When compared with other countries of Central and Eastern Europe, Serbia takes a middle position with a reported crime rate of around 1000 per 100,000 population in 2009 (Selih 2012).

---

[14] Jane's Intelligence Weekly, 1 September 2000.

[15] "Montenegro to crack down on human trafficking", *The Associated Press*, December 11, 2000, received through STOP-TRAFFIC @friends-partners.org list on December 11, 2000.

During the 22-year period (1990–2012), the percentage of juvenile offenders of the total registered crime varied between 3 and 8 %, overall about 4 %. The minimum participation of reported juvenile crime was recorded in 2003 (2.5 %), while the highest was recorded in 2000 (6.1 %) and 2010 (7.8 %).

There was a decrease in reported juvenile crime in the post-war years (1994–1999), after which it slightly increased during next two years. Such variable trends of juvenile crime, with alternation of short periods of decline and increase, can also be seen between 2002 and 2012. In addition, since 1998 until the end of the period, fewer juveniles were reported than in 1990, which may indicate a lower tendency of reporting juvenile crime after the 1990s. For example, compared to 1993, when reported juvenile crime was the highest, in 2003 three times less juveniles were reported. Juveniles have been mostly reported for property crimes and crimes against life and body, whereas economic crimes and crimes against freedom and rights of citizen are the least reported juvenile crimes. More concretely, property crimes and economic crimes have decreased during the post-war period, while crimes against peoples' health and crimes against public order and legal traffic have increased (Stevković 2014).

In Serbia older female and male juveniles are more often sanctioned than the younger ones, which is in accordance with the higher proportion of older juveniles of both sexes in juvenile crime. The rate of 14 years-old sentenced females ranged between 17.2 % (2011) and 22 % (2008); that of 15 years-old females was between 26.2 % (2012) and 32.1 % (2008), and females aged 16 had rates between 24.5 % (in 2009) and 34.5 % (in 2011). The lowest rate of 17 years old sentenced females was in 2008 (16.5 %) and the highest in 2012 (26.2 %) (Stevković 2014).

Findings of the third International Self-Reported (Juvenile) Delinquency Study (ISRD3)[16]carried out in 2013 on a sample of elementary and secondary school pupils provide data on life-time victimization and delinquency, as well as data on victimization and delinquency during the last 12 months. When it comes to life-time victimization data, they show that children were mostly victims of domestic violence (55 %), theft (34 %) and bullying (19 %). According to the data on lifetime delinquent behaviour, children mostly reported writings of graffiti (35 %), shoplifting (24 %) and participation in group-fights (13 %). About 11 % of children reported that they had carried a weapon, committed personal theft or been cruel toward animals. The least reported delinquent behaviour is burglary and robbery (about 1 %). These findings show also that 80 % of children used alcohol at least once in their life, while about 20 % at least once tried cannabis.

[16] Serbia participated for the first time in this international survey. Vesna Nikolic-Ristanovic is national coordinator of the survey for Republic of Serbia, while Ljiljana Stevkovic is survey assistant. The data presented in this chapter are preliminary findings of the ISRD3 Serbia.

4.1 Domestic Violence Against and by Women and Children After the War

Available research findings suggest that high levels of domestic violence continue to exist after the war, i.e. that there is a long-term impact of war-related factors on violence against women and children in the family. Among war related factors, the most persistent are: economic deprivation of large proportions, persistent problems in relationships between members of different ethnic groups that live in Serbia, PTSD and other unsolved problems faced by former combatants, long term refugee status of a large number of people and slow resolving of their problems, as well as a large number of weapons that stayed in private possession after the war (Nikolić-Ristanović 2008).

A high level of domestic violence was indicated by data from the first and so far only victimisation survey on domestic violence covering the entire country, carried out by the Victimology Society of Serbia in 2001. These findings reflect the high rate of physical violence in the aftermath of the war and the economic crisis. The survey was carried out on a sample of 700 adult female respondents in seven towns and approximately 40 villages in the Serbian countryside. According to the data obtained, almost every second woman was a victim of psychological abuse (46.1 %), and every third was a victim of physical violence (30.6 %). In 26.3 % of cases women were threatened with physical violence, while sexual abuse was reported in 8.7 % of cases. Most often the perpetrator were men (88.8 % of cases). Spouse abuse was the most prevalent form of domestic violence. In 71.6 % of cases the perpetrator was a husband or a partner, while in other cases perpetrators were fathers, mothers or brothers/sisters (Vidaković 2002, pp. 14 and 15).

More recent surveys suggest slightly higher level of domestic violence in the northern parts and slightly lower level of domestic violence in the central parts of Serbia (Petrović 2010; Babović et al. 2010) compared to findings from the 2001 survey (Vidaković 2002). For example, the 2009 domestic violence survey, carried out in the province Vojvodina on a representative sample of 516 adult women, found that 33.9 % of them suffered from physical violence, 49.8 % suffered from psychological violence, while 27.3 % of women said that they experienced threats of physical violence. 8.3 % of women were exposed to a threat by weapon, while in 6.2 % of cases, the abuser actually used a weapon during the violent act. 18.6 % of women said that they were victimised by stalking and 9.1 % through sexual violence. Violence occurred more than 10 times in 42.3 % of cases. Husbands or ex-husbands/partners were dominant among the abusers (79.0 %). 24.9 % of the abusers had war experience (as volunteers or regular soldiers) and 22.2 % of them used a weapon during the last violent act. 53.6 % of abusers were violent under the influence of alcohol (Petrović 2010).

The impact of war is evident from the findings about the share of war participants among abusers, as well as from the findings that suggest a connection between war participation and the use of weapons in domestic violence incidents. Findings from the 2010 survey show that domestic violence committed by former soldiers is particularly dangerous and that it is more widespread compared to 2001. This may suggest that society needs to tackle this problem more seriously than it did it before. Violence against women was often accompanied by direct and indirect victimisation of children. 49.7 % of children were present during the last act of sexual and/or physical violence against their mother. Children were also directly victimized, mostly through physical violence, during the last act of violence against the mother—35.6 %. Violence against children resulted in physical injuries in 50 % of the cases of directly victimised children. In 17.7 % of cases violence was not an isolated episode: the abuser ordinarily abuses children. The percentage of injured children reported in the 2009 survey was higher compared to 2001, while the percentage of directly victimised children was a bit smaller. Findings of the 2001 and 2009 surveys showed a significant influence of both direct childhood victimization of girls on their exposure to violence in adulthood and of boys' direct exposure to violence in the family of origin on their violent behaviour in adulthood (Nikolić-Ristanović and Stevković 2010). The same significant influence of direct and indirect childhood victimization of boys on their violent behaviour in adulthood is confirmed in Stevkovic's survey carried out on a sample of 252 male and female inmates in a maximum security prison for men and only prison for women in Serbia (Stevković 2013).

An epidemiological survey on child abuse and neglect carried out during 2011 and 2012 on a sample of 4027 pupils aged 11, 13 and 16 showed that nearly 70 % of children experienced psychological or physical violence at least once during their life. 8 % of children had experienced sexual violence, while 5 % of them had suffered contact sexual abuse. More than a third of the children were indirectly victimized at least once during their life. This survey showed that girls are more exposed to psychological violence, while boys are more vulnerable to sexual and physical violence (Ispanovic-Radojkovic et al. 2012). Data of registered cases of violence against children, obtained from centres for social work, showed that, on average, two out of 1000 children are victims of some form of violence or neglect. In accordance with data from the epidemiological survey, the most prevalent is psychological abuse, while the least prevalent is sexual abuse (Stevkovic et al. 2013). Findings of the International self-reported study on juvenile delinquency (ISRD3 Serbia)[17] carried out in 2013 on a sample of elementary and secondary school pupils showed that almost 55 % of children were directly victimized by their parents at least once in their life, while almost 30 % had had that experience during the last 12 months of their life. In accordance with findings of the above mentioned surveys, the most prevalent form of violence is psychological, while the least prevalent are severe forms of physical violence. Sexual victimization was not the subject of this survey. Fathers were dominant among the abusers.

[17] Serbia for the first time participated in this international survey. Vesna Nikolic-Ristanovic is national coordinator of the survey for Republic of Serbia, while Ljiljana Stevkovic is survey assistant. The data presented in this chapter are preliminary findings of the ISRD3 Serbia.

On the other hand, children are also violent towards their parents and other members of family. The survey that Stevkovic carried out for the purposes of her PhD dissertation[18] on a sample of 1344 pupils aged 12–19 show that almost 30 % of children use psychological violence against their mother and/or father. 14 % of children had hit their mother and/or father at least once, while 4 % used more severe forms of physical violence. 20 % of children used psychological violence against their siblings, slightly more against brothers than against sisters. Almost the same percentage of children reported that they had hit their brother (19.6 %) or sister (19.3 %) at least once in their life. 9.5 % of children reported more severe forms of physical violence used against a brother, and 8 % against a sister. Data from this survey show that juveniles are also violent towards their grandparents. 18 % of them reported being psychologically violent against their grandmother and 4 % against their grandfather. 8 % of children reported less severe forms of physical violence against their grandmother and 3 % of children against their grandfather Less than 1 % of children reported more severe forms of violence against their grandmother and/or grandfather.

All available survey findings suggest that economic deprivation negatively affected family relationships and that economic marginalisation of men was a significant predictor of their violent behaviour. In that regard two risky patterns of gender roles were identified: 1. The man or another family member is the breadwinner rand the woman is economically dependent on him; 2. The man is economically dependent on his female partner (reversal of traditional male–female gender roles) or on another family member (Nikolic-Ristanovic 2002). Another significant predictor of domestic violence identified by surveys concerns ethnically mixed families, which is in obvious connection with interethnic relationships disturbances caused by ethnic conflicts (Nikolić-Ristanović and Petrović 2010).

In the absence of prompt state response and assistance, and without adequate legal protection for victims, domestic violence often has tragic results. Victims of domestic violence are sometimes killed by their abusers, and there have been cases when women have taken justice into their own hands, assaulting or killing their abusers. A woman may attempt or even succeed in committing suicide, sometimes killing her children at the same time. For example, one woman in Serbia jumped from a bridge into a river together with her two children. She and one of her children survived, while the other child died, and she was imprisoned for murdering her child (Nikolić-Ristanović 2000b). Unfortunately, as recent research findings show, the answer of the criminal justice system is more prompt and efficient in punishing the victim who responded to the abuse then to protect her as a primary victim (Nikolić-Ristanović 2013).

Domestic violence victimization survey findings suggest that, in spite of the introduction of good legislation, victims are often dissatisfied with the work of the police. Only 23.2 % of victims of domestic violence in the 2009 Vojvodina victimization survey reported the crime to the police, However, this is more than the percentage shown in the findings from the 2001 domestic violence victimization

[18] Ljiljana Stevkovic carried out her PhD quantitative survey as a part of ISRD3 Serbia survey.

survey for the entire Serbia, which was 16.8 %. Most of those who reported domestic violence were not satisfied with the reaction and/or attitudes of the police.

Since in 2001 there were no laws in Serbia that would explicitly forbid domestic violence, it is interesting to compare these findings with the findings from the 2009 Vojvodina survey. These findings suggest that a lot of old problems with police attitudes toward victims of domestic violence still existed. Most of the victims (56.8 %) still were not satisfied with the work of the police. As the reason for their dissatisfaction they most often mentioned that the police did not do anything, or did not do enough to help and protect them. Besides, one of the reasons for dissatisfaction is also seen in the discourteous attitude of police officers towards female respondents, which includes yelling, persiflage and blaming. Findings of another domestic violence survey carried out in Central Serbia in 2010 confirmed the above-mentioned findings: 46 % of domestic violence victims said that they were not at all satisfied with police reaction, 32 % said that the police helped them but not enough, while only 22 % stated that the police had helped them very much (Babović et al. 2010).

Research on the practice of prosecutors and courts in domestic violence cases showed that after receiving a crime report prosecutors usually do not talk with victims at all and, thus, miss the opportunity to provide them with important information (Konstantinović-Vilić and Petrušić 2007). In those cases where prosecutors received the report directly from the victim, it has been noticed that they tended to ask the victim to think again whether she really wanted prosecution. Prosecutors usually ask the victim whether she is in favour of prosecution, although there is no legal base to ask that question. If the victim, mostly because of fear from the abuser's retaliation, does not give her approval to prosecute, the prosecutors often decide not to prosecute on the ground of insufficient evidence, although other evidence was available (Konstantinović-Vilić and Petrušić 2004, 2007).

4.2 *Trafficking in Persons Against and by Women and Children After the War*

As already stressed, during the war people learned to earn money through crime so that the system of values has been completely disturbed and it is not so easy, especially in the conditions of a destroyed economy, to motivate people to conform again. This produced long-term consequences and still has a significant impact on organized crime given the large illegal labour market in Serbia, particularly for migrant smuggling, and human and drug trafficking (Nikolic-Ristanovic 2004, 2009, and 2012).

In the post-war period, demand for sex work is further increasing with the arrival of peacekeeping troops, private military companies that accompany them[19] and a

[19] Private military companies provide an assortment of services to the armed forces and the US government as well as to foreign governments and international organizations, and it is a rapidly

large number of various international organizations. In addition, in international protectorates such as Bosnia-Herzegovina and the UN administered territory of Kosovo, where the government and law enforcement have been under complete control of the international community, large international police forces and an army of administrative workers are present as well. As examples of the Philippines, Okinawa and Thailand (Euler and Welzer-Lang 2000) show, there is the danger that the war and/or post-war increase in prostitution will be transformed into a peace-time institutionalization of the sex industry as well. Also, it is well known that the sex industry develops and the vulnerability of women to sex trafficking increases with the building of military bases. Thus, although otherwise an international presence may be temporary in the region, prostitution and related trafficking in women may become a long-term problem in the Balkans solely in connection to the emergence of new military bases.

Findings of the survey carried out by the Victimology Society of Serbia shortly after the final end of wars on the territory of the former Yugoslavia, identified 960 female and 94 child victims of trafficking (Nikolic-Ristanovic et al. 2004). Female victims were mostly trafficked for sexual exploitation, domestic work and marriage, while male victims were trafficked primarily for labour exploitation, including begging and delinquency (Ćopić 2009). Both male and female children were trafficked for begging, but also for sexual and labour exploitation, marriages, delinquency, etc.

After the war Serbia increasingly became a country of origin as well, with women and children from Serbia being trafficked to other parts of the former Yugoslavia, which were directly affected by war, such as Bosnia, Croatia and Kosovo, but also to Macedonia and Montenegro. Over time, trafficking in children and men compounded the existing trafficking of women. Also, trafficking for sexual exploitation became less visible then before and tended to be disguised behind legal activities. Recently there has been an increase in the number of identified victims of trafficking in people (especially of men) with legal documents and, as in other Balkan countries, of an internal and regional trafficking in women and children[20] (Ćopić 2009). Women and children who are citizens of Serbia nowadays make the majority of identified victims of trafficking.[21]

growing business. In just ten years, the private military industry has grown from a handful of companies to hundreds, with its income rising from millions of dollars a year to an estimated $100 billion a year (source: http:/salon.com/news/featiue/2002/06/26/bosnia.print.html). As stated in the report from the Turin 2002 Conference on Trafficking, Slavery and Peacekeeping, private contractors supplementing or overseeing the staffing requirements for the peacekeeping operation on behalf of some Member States or providing them with services, equipment and/or supplies, are found to be directly involved in trafficking of women from Eastern Europe (Picarelli 2002).

[20] The trends are based on the data about identified victims, whose number changed over time, but stayed all the time very low.

[21] http://www.mup.gov.rs/cms_lat/sadrzaj.nsf/zrtve-i-zastita-zrtava.h, retrieved on 18 August 2014

One recent analysis (Nikolic-Ristanovic 2012) suggests that between 2004 and 2009 the overall number of persons reported for trafficking in Serbia was 367, out of which 364 were adults and 3 were minors. However, the number of accused and convicted persons is much lower. 96 persons were accused (95 adults and one minor), while 84 were convicted (83 adults and one minor). Most of the persons reported, prosecuted and convicted are male adults, although females and minors also figure in the statistics.

The number of reported, prosecuted and convicted minors in this period was very small. One minor was reported in 2007 for trafficking children for adoption, and two in 2009 for human trafficking. Only one of those minors was prosecuted and convicted, the one indicted for trafficking in children for adoption. However, the number of reported, prosecuted and convicted women is quite significant. For example, women made up 16 out of 71 persons reported in 2007, and 12 out of 39 in 2008. This means that women comprised between one third and one quarter of those reported for trafficking. A similar gender ratio exists when those prosecuted and convicted for human trafficking are considered. Namely, women made up 4 out of 16 persons prosecuted and 3 out of 14 persons convicted for trafficking in 2007. In 2008 women made up 6 out of 23 persons prosecuted and 4 out of 18 persons convicted for human trafficking. In general, convicted traffickers in Serbia have mostly low educational level and are unemployed, with their occupations reflecting their education (Nikolic-Ristanovic 2011). Traffickers seem to be mostly persons without a previous criminal record, suggesting the attractiveness of "organised crime" as a labour market for people who struggle to find legal jobs (Nikolic-Ristanovic 2011).

After the war, some of the criminals who were connected to the ruling elite used privatisation to legalize their activities and used the profit made for investments in legal jobs and privatised enterprises. The other part continued with their criminal economic activities or moved on to other activities that were more profitable and carried less risk, such as trafficking in humans. They continued to get rich in the sphere of the illegal economy and they began to take on the role of the "employer" within it: arrangers/investors and managers. But, the lowest level are marginalised, war-stricken individuals and those with the lowest socio-economic status who are forced, in order to cope with economic difficulties and problems related to migration, to continue to look to the informal markets for cheap commodities and documents that they could not get legally. Research conducted in the majority of the post war societies point to the particular vulnerability of the war participants regarding the aforementioned (Nitzschke 2003, p. 1). Under such conditions, these people were put in a situation, where it was tempting to ask for or accept a job in the sphere of trafficking in people. Closely related to this category of traffickers, the available data on trafficking in humans as a form of organised crime in Serbia and in other countries alike points to the existence of a relationship between structural victimisation caused by war, the development of the informal economy and the risk of criminalisation of formerly law abiding citizens who have since then turned to illegal activities (Studdard 2004).

The Serbian survey findings also suggest that those who were low-level traffickers during the war advanced and acquired managerial or higher positions. As a result, they themselves were able to recruit young people, especially drivers, who found themselves to be in an unfortunate economic situation. However, this applies primarily to male traffickers. With the women on the low level the war did not play a significant role in upward mobility but instead gender marginalisation, partner violence and transition played a significant role. Women began working in the illegal economy under the coercion of their partners, but in some cases their first encounter with the informal economy was related to the transition and opening of the borders of Eastern Europe (i.e. smuggling of commodities). The partners who got them into human trafficking had either the same or a higher position than they had (they were usually recruiters or coordinators of the recruiters' network).

But, rarely, women also had higher positions in the trafficking business, especially as managers ("madams") or brothel and night-bar owners. In this case, the war could also have an impact on women shifting their economic position to earn money in this way. One such woman, convicted for trafficking women for sexual exploitation in her night bar/brothel in Serbia, explained in the interview for the research carried out by the Victimology Society of Serbia that she started to smuggle alcohol during the war in Croatia, and opened a night bar in Kosovo immediately after the arrival of the KFOR (Nikolic-Ristanovic 2011).

People continued to look for jobs in the informal and criminal economy in the post conflict period as well. This could be explained by the lack of distinction between licit and illicit behaviour and the associated habits they formed to look for jobs informally. Also, the wider social and economic context in Serbia also furthered this tendency because of the insufficient availability of legal jobs and income. This was compounded by both the slow recovery of ruined institutions and the lack of citizens' trust in those institutions. Moreover, the economic situation in Serbia is still extremely difficult since the negative consequences of transition have been added to the serious consequences of war affecting the living standard and overall everyday life of people (Nikolić-Ristanović 2008), as well as the corruption of the ruling elite.

A Survey on sex trafficking victims in Serbia carried out by the Victimology Society of Serbia—VDS, Fafo AIS and Sør-Trøndelag University College (Norway) in 2004/5, i.e. in the after-war period and immediately after the introduction of the criminal offense of trafficking in persons, also provides examples of both good and bad practices in police attitude toward victims. Bad practices include either direct involvement of the police in trafficking or their inappropriate, i.e. stereotypical, humiliating and stigmatizing questioning and otherwise bad treatment of victims. Good practices, on the other hand, include establishing a friendly relationship, being supportive and giving the victim time to relax, asking questions in an appropriate way and at the appropriate place, female police officer interviewing the victim, providing information and offering assistance, etc. The survey on victims of sex trafficking in women came across a case from the Special Court trial, where both the presiding judge and the prosecutor intervened at every single attempt of defence lawyers to discredit or insult the victim (Nikolic-Ristanovic 2005).

Findings of a more recent VDS survey on male victims of trafficking in Serbia (Nikolic-Ristanovic 2009) suggest that the activity of the police related to the victims of trafficking in human beings is mostly limited to referral and urgent accommodation of victims. The Survey also showed that the police themselves do not offer the victims, or, potential victims (for example, victims of smuggling in human beings, or street children), any other form of direct assistance (for example, providing of information, or distribution of information leaflets on the rights and possible forms of assistance); nor do they refer the victims to a broader range of institutions and services which could be of assistance in case they should need it—like general services for victims of crime, Roma organizations, or services intended for handicapped persons or persons with special needs. It is obvious that the limitations of such a practice have especially negative consequences on the support and assistance provided to male child victims of internal trafficking, as for them the cooperation of the police and the centres for welfare services and the broader circle of NGOs is of great importance. Finally, experiences of victim support services in Serbia also suggest a high level of dissatisfaction of victims with the police (Brankovic 2009; Nikolić-Ristanović et al. 2006; Kovacevic 2007; Kovačević-Lepojević and Radaković 2008).

5 Concluding Observations and Recommendations

Available findings suggest that the war produces a long-term impact on crime, which is particularly emphasised when victimisation and offending of women and children is in question. Although some time after the war registered crime usually starts to decrease, hidden forms such as domestic violence, sexual violence, juvenile delinquency as well as organised crime, in particular trafficking in persons, continue to be serious social problem. They reflect lasting changes of the socioeconomic structure and overall context of post-war society, which is overburdened with economic problems and other consequences of the war on the everyday life of people. In post communist countries, such as Serbia, the transition to capitalism has serious additional impact as well. In particular is difficult position of the refugees and ex-combatants, who for a long time stay on the margins of society, both in terms of their socio-economic status and the inappropriate treatment by the state. In the aftermath of ethnic conflicts there is also a low level of tolerance toward ethnic and other social and cultural differences, which shape various criminal behaviours, including victimisation/offending of women and children. All that usually occurs in the framework of very weak institutions and in the absence or bad functioning of the rule of law.

However, social responses to victimisation of women and children are usually initiated already during the war by feminist and victim activists—often by those local supported by international ones. In Serbia, similarly as in many other war-affected countries, women's groups and feminist researchers contributed toward greater visibility of the problems of domestic violence victims, as well as those of victims of sexual violence and sex trafficking. During the 1990s, Serbian women's groups' activists established SOS hotlines, shelters and counselling services for women and children. The development of these victim services was particularly intensified after the social changes in 2000. Thus, the first victim services in Serbia were specialised services for women and child victims of violence. Women's groups put the issue of violence against women on the public agenda, emphasising that domestic violence was not a private matter but a social problem, which requires serious discussion and solutions. Children's groups also advocated for the rights of children and juvenile offenders. However, in spite of strong advocacy campaigns, and humanitarian and counselling/support activism, because of their anti-war and anti-Milosevic position during the 1990s, their activities were not acknowledged and supported by the state until 2000. This contributed to the low number of war- and crime-affected people they were able to help during the war and the low efficiency of their actions. In addition, the support of the international community was rather late and insufficient.

Since the end of war and the political changes in 2000, many positive results have been achieved for women and children, as well as for other crime victims (see more in: Lindgren and Nikolic-Ristanovic 2011). The most important development was related to legal changes that accepted most of the international standards, but there were also some efforts toward education of professionals, inter-sector cooperation and some practical improvements as well. New laws have been passed, including the Law on Juvenile Offenders and the Protection of Child Victim, and existing laws have been re-examined and modified. In addition, various policy documents, such as strategies, national action plans and protocols have been adopted. Programs for abusive men have been created. But with a few exceptions of non-governmental activities not much has been done in practical terms to help juvenile- and women offenders to reintegrate into society.

The most important legal and policy changes were initiated and advocated by Serbian non-governmental organisations, which now got a larger support of international organisations and donors. Since 2000, and in particular following Serbia's progress in the EU accession process, international support started to be oriented toward institutional reforms, encouraging partnership between NGOs and the state. Apart from its obvious positive impact, this also had as an unwanted side effect the disappearing of funding for NGOs since international funding wasn't replaced by the sustainable state funding. As a consequence many NGOs that developed high expertise in supporting women and children had to cease their activities, while the state institutions still do not have the capacity to offer timely and quality service to the large number of women and children that need it.

In sum, in spite of many important changes in post war period, in Serbia as well as in other war affected countries, women and children are not treated properly either as victims or as offenders. The lack of timely and adequate protection and support of victims during the war has continued afterwards as well. There is an obvious lack of dealing with victimisation and offending of women and children as a part of overall post-war social context, i.e. as a social rather then as a legal problem. However, unlike in some other countries that were more directly affected by war such as Croatia and Bosnia, war rape is hardly mentioned in any post-war discussion and advocacy campaign in Serbia.

As we hope to have been able to show in this chapter, both victimisation and offending of women and children, in particular by domestic violence and sex trafficking, are largely connected to structural and identity changes produced by war. Thus, we assume that factors that cause a deep and long lasting state of anomie, social disorganisation as well as moral and identity crises need to be dealt as early as possible, in a holistic way and by all actors, on a national and international level. The suggested holistic and complex way of dealing with crime in war affected societies requires also more critical assessment of the role played by both local and international actors, during as well as after the war. However, that is the way in which war affected societies are hardly dealt in any part of the world so far. Bearing that in mind, we hope that this chapter may help shifting the attention of experts and policy makers more seriously in that direction.

Five Questions

1. What should be done and by whom to reduce victimization of women and children during wartime?
2. Which are the measures that may be successful in reducing offending risks of women and children during the war?
3. How should the society deal with the long-term impact of war on victimisation and offending of women?
4. What should be done after the war to reduce the likelihood of victimisation and offending of children?
5. What should be done on a national and international level to improve capacities for the elimination of the negative influence of war-related factors on victimization and delinquent behaviour of women and children?

References

Andrić-Ružičić, D. (Ed.) (1999). Ne/ziveti sa nasiljem (Not/Living with Violence). *Drugi pogled* (Vol. 2). Zenica: Medica Zenica.

Babović, M., Ginić, K., & Vuković, O. (2010). *Mapiranje porodičnog nasilja prema ženama u Centralnoj Srbiji (Mapping of domestic violence against women in Central Serbia)*. Beograd: Uprava za rodnu ravnopravnost.

Bacanovic, O. (2001). Zeni zrtvo na trgovija so luge (Women victims of traffic in people). *Annual Journal of the School of Security - Skopje*,104–116.

Bales, K. (1999). *Disposable people*. Berkley, Los Angeles, London: University of California Press.

Boric, R., & Desnica, M. (1996). Croatia: Three years after. In C. Corrin (Ed.), *Women in a violent world, feminist analyses and resistance across Europe* (pp. 133–150). Edinburgh: Edinburgh University Press.

Branković, B. (2009). *Odgovor na neme krike – Mapiranje usluga koje pružaju nevladine organizacije u Srbiji u oblasti rodno zasnovanog nasilja* (The answer to the silent screams - Mapping services provided by non-governmental organizations in Serbia in the field of gender-based violence). Beograd: UNDP.

Brownmiller, S. (1975). *Against our will: Men, women and rape*. New York: Fawcett Columbine.

Cavan, R. S. (1956). *Criminology*. New York: Thomas Y. Crowel Company.

Ćirić, J. (1993). Hiper-inflacija - kriminološki i krivičnopravni problemi (Hyper-inflation - criminological and criminal law problems). *Zbornik Instituta za kriminološka i sociološka istraživanja, 22*(1), 104–117.

Cockburn, S. (2014). A continuum of violence: Gender, war and peace. In R. Jamieson (Ed.), *The criminology of war* (pp. 357–377). Surrey: Ashgate.

Conklin, J. (1992). *Criminology*. New York: Macmillan Publishing Company.

Connell, R. W. (1993). *Gender and power – Society, the person and sexual politics*. Cambridge: Polity.

Connell, R. (1995). Masculinity, violence and war. In M. Kimmer & M. Messner (Eds.), *Men's lives* (pp. 125–131). Meedham Heights: Allyn and Bacon.

Connell, R. (2001). Masculinities and globalization. In M. S. Kimmel & M. A. Messner (Eds.), *Men's lives* (pp. 56–71). Needham Heights: Allyn and Bacon.

Ćopić, S. (2009). Karakteristike trgovine muškarcima u Srbiji (Characteristics of male trafficking in Serbia). In V. Nikolić-Ristanović (Ed.), *Trgovina muškarcima u Srbiji (Male trafficking in Serbia)* (pp. 77–124). Beograd: Viktimološko društvo Srbije i Prometej.

Corrin, C. (1999). Rethinking citizenship: Analyses and activism in Central and Eastern Europe. *The Journal of Communist Studies and Transition Politics, 1*, 64–82. "Državni neprijatelj broj tri", *Vreme,* 1995

El-Bushra, J. (2000). Transforming conflict: Some thoughts on a gendered understanding of conflict processes. In S. Jacobs, R. Jacobson, & J. Marchbank (Eds.), *States of conflict* (pp. 66–86). London-New York: Zed Books.

Euler, C., & Welzer-Lang, D. *Developing best professional practice for reducing sexual abuse, domestic violence and trafficking in militarised areas of peacetime Europe*. (2000). Project No. 98/043/WC Report. Leeds: Leeds Metropolitan University.

Fisher, E. (1994). War, women and democracy. In *Test the west: Gender democracy and violence* (pp. 163–177). Vienna: Austrian Federal Ministry of Women's Affairs.

G17Plus. (2000). *Bela kniga Miloseviceve vladavine* (White Book of Milosevic's Regime). Belgrade: B92.

Gassin, R. (1988). *Criminologie*. Paris: Dalloz.

Gutman, R. (1994). *Svedok genocida (Witness of genocide)*. Zagreb: Durieux.

Hagan, J. (1988). *Structural criminology*. New Brunowich, New Jersey: Rutgers University Press.

Hague, E. (1997). Rape, power and masculinity: The construction of gender and national identities in the war in Bosnia-Herzegovina. In R. Lentin (Ed.), *Gender and catastrophe* (pp. 50–64). London and New York: Zed Books.

Hatty, S. (2000). *Masculinities, violence and culture*. London: Sage.

Human Rights Watch World Report. (2001). http://www.hrw.org/legacy/wr2k1/. Accessed 2002 June

Ispanovic-Radojkovic, V., Hanak, N., Vlajkovic, A., & Tenjovic, L. (2012). BECAN *Epidemiological survey on child abuse and neglect in the Republic of Serbia, research report*. Belgrade: Faculty for Special Education and Rehabilitation (unpublished). http://www.becan.eu. Accessed 15 June 2014.

Jamieson, R. (1998). Towards a criminology of war in Europe. In V. Ruggiero, N. South, & I. Taylor (Eds.), *New European criminology* (pp. 480–506). London: Routledge.

Jamieson, R. (2014). Introduction. In R. Jamieson (Ed.), *The criminology of war* (pp. XIII–XXXV). Surrey: Ashgate.

Jennings, K., & Nikolić-Ristanović, V. (2013). Political economies of peacekeeping, local gender relations and sex trafficking victimisation: Peacekeepers as patrons? *International Perspectives in Victimology, 7*(2), 36–45.

Karstedt, S. (1993). The impact of social crises on dissocial and problem behavior of women: Effects on sex differences across the life course. *Soziale Probleme, 4*, 139–166.

Kelly, L. (2000). Wars against women: Sexual violence, sexual politics and the militarised state. In S. Jacobs, R. Jacobson, & J. Marchbank (Eds.), *States of conflict* (pp. 45–65). London-New York: Zed Books.

Killias, M. (1991). *Precis de criminologie*. Bern: Editions Staempfli & Cie SA.

Kinberg, O. (1960). *Les problems fondamentaux de la criminologie*. Paris: Editions Cujas.

Konstantinović-Vilić, S., & Petrušić, N. (2004). *Krivično delo nasilja u porodici: pravna praksa u Republici Srbiji (Criminal offense domestic violence: legal practice in Republic of Serbia)*. Niš: Ženski istraživački centar za edukaciju i komunikaciju.

Konstantinović-Vilić, S., & Petrušić, N. (2007). *Krivično delo nasilja u porodici - aktuelna pravosudna praksa u Beogradu i Nišu (Criminal offence of domestic violence – actual legal practice in Belgrade and Nis)*. Belgrade: Autonomni ženski centar and Ženski istraživački centar za edukaciju i komunikaciju Niš.

Korac, M. (1994). Representation of mass rape in ethnic-conflicts in what was Yugoslavia. *Sociologija, 36*(4), 496–512.

Kovačević, M. (2007). Služba VDS info i podrška žrtvama - analiza rada Službe u 2006. godini (VDS info and victim support - the analysis of the work of VDS info and victim support in 2006). *Temida, 9*(2), 41–49.

Kovačević-Lepojević, M., & Radaković, D. (2008). Služba VDS info i podrška žrtvama: analiza rada u 2007. godini (VDS info and victim support - the analysis of the work of VDS info and victim support in 2007). *Temida, 10*(3), 78–96.

Kulka, R., Schlenger, W., Farrbank, J., Hough, R., Jordan, B. K., Marmer, C., et al. (1990). *Trauma and the Vietnam war generation*. New York: Brunner/Mazel Publishers.

Limanowska, B. (2002). *Trafficking in human beings in South-eastern Europe*. Belgrade: UNICEF.

Lindgren, M., & Nikolic-Ristanovic, V. (2011). *Crime victims: international and Serbian perspective*. Belgrade: OSCE.

Lynch, M. J., & Groves, W. B. (1989). *A primer in radical criminology*. Albany: Harrow and Heston Publishers.

Matsakis, A. (1996). *Vietnam wives*. Lutherville: The Sidran press.

McWilliams, M. (1998). Violence against women in societies under stress. In R. E. Dobash & R. P. Dobash (Eds.), *Rethinking violence against women* (pp. 111–140). Thousand Oaks: Sage.

Messerschmidt, J. (1993). *Masculinities and crime*. Lanham: Rowman and Littlefield Publishers.

Mitić, M. (1997). *Porodica i stres – izmedju poraza i nade (Family and stress – between defeat and hope)*. Beograd: Institut za psihologiju.

Moeller, R. (1993). *Protecting motherhood: Women and the family in the politics of post-war West Germany*. Berkley and Los Angeles: University of California Press.

Moser, A. (2001). The gendered continuum of violence and conflict: An operational framework. In C. Moser & F. Clark (Eds.), *Victims, perpetrators or actors?* (pp. 30–51). London and New York: Zed Books.

Mršević, Z. (1999). Mesto i uloga domaćeg nasilja u kriznim periodima (The place and the role of domestic violence in the periods of crises). In M. Djilas, S. Nedović, & A. Jovanović (Eds.), *Ostvarivanje ekonomskih i socijalnih prava* (pp. 426–445). Beogradski centar za ljudska prava: Beograd.

Nikolic-Ristanovic, V. (1998a). War and crime in the former Yugoslavia. In V. Ruggiero, N. South, & I. Taylor (Eds.), *The New European criminology* (pp. 462–480). London: Routledge.

Nikolic-Ristanovic, V. (1998b). The international crime victim survey in Belgrade (FRY). In *The international crime victim survey in Countries in transition - national reports* (pp. 547–565). Rome: UNICRI.

Nikolic-Ristanovic, V. (Ed.) (2000a). *Women, violence and war*. Budapest: CEU Press.

Nikolić-Ristanović, V. (2000b). *Od žrtve do zatvorenice: nasilje u porodici i kriminalitet žena* (From victim to prisoner: domestic violence and women's crime). Beograd: Viktimološko društvo Srbije, Institut za kriminološka i sociološka istraživanja and Prometej.

Nikolic-Ristanovic, V. (2001). Children as multiple victims of war. *Peace Review, 13*(4), 577–582.

Nikolić-Ristanovic, V. (2002). *Social change, gender and violence: Post-communist and war-affected societies*. Dordrecht, Boston, London: Kluwer Academic Publishers.

Nikolic-Ristanovic, V. (2004). Illegal markets, human trade and transnational organised crime. In P. Van Duyne, M. Jager, K. von Lampe, & J. Newell (Eds.), *Threats and phantoms of organised crime, corruption and terrorism* (pp. 117–139). Nijmegen: Wolf Legal Publishers.

Nikolic-Ristanovic, V. (2005). What victims went through and how they survived? In L. Bjerkan (Ed.), *The life on one's own: the rehabilitation of victims of trafficking for sexual exploitation* (pp. 71–118). Oslo: Fafo.

Nikolić-Ristanović, V. (2008). *Preživeti tranziciju: svakodnevni život i nasilje nad ženama u postkomunističkom i posleratnom društvu (Surviving transition: everyday life and violence against women in postcommunist and postconflict society)*. Beograd: Službeni glasnik.

Nikolic-Ristanovic, V. (2009). Victimogenic and criminogenic factors of male trafficking in Serbia. In V. Nikolić-Ristanović (Ed.), *Male trafficking in Serbia* (pp. 219–243). Belgrade: Viktimološko društvo Srbije and Prometej.

Nikolic-Ristanovic, V. (2011). Trafficking in humans and illegal economy in war and post-war society. In P. Van Duyne & J. Spencer (Eds.), *Flesh and money: Trafficking in human beings* (pp. 181–202). Nijmegen: Wolf Legal Publishers.

Nikolic-Ristanovic, V. (2012). Human trafficking between profit and survival. In A. Selih & A. Zavrsnik (Eds.), *Crime and transition in Central and Eastern Europe* (pp. 205–227). New York, Heidelberg, Dordrecht, London: Springer.

Nikolić-Ristanović, V. (2013). *Praćenje primene zakonskih rešenja o nasilju u porodici u Srbiji: nalazi pilot istrazivanja (Monitoring the application of domestic violence legislation in Serbia: pilot survey findings)*. Belgrade: UNWOMEN. Available at: http://www.vds.org.rs/ElektronskePublikacijeEng.htm.

Nikolic-Ristanovic, V., & Copic, S. (2013). *Dealing with interethnic conflicts in Serbia and the place of restorative justice and victims (Deliverable 6.1. of FP7 project ALTERNATIVE - Developing Alternative Understanings of Security and Justice through Restorative Justice Approaches in Intercultural Setting within Democratic Societies)*. Leuven: KU Leuven Institute of Crimnology. Available at: http://www.vds.org.rs/File/Deliverable_6_1_Research_report_on_dealing_with_conflicts_by_NGOs_and_the_state.pdf.

Nikolić-Ristanović, V., & Milivojević, S. (2000). Viktimizacija žena nasiljem u porodici: uticaj socijalnih faktora vezanih za društvene promene i životnu dob (Victimization of women by domestic violence: the impact of social factors connected to social change and age). *Temida, 1* (3), 20–28.

Nikolić-Ristanović, V., & Petrović, N. (2010). Faktori koji utiču na izloženost žena nasilju u porodici (Factors affecting the exposure of women to domestic violence). In V. Nikolić-Ristanović (Ed.), *Nasilje u porodici u Vojvodini (Domestic violence in Vojvodina)* (pp. 55–77). Novi Sad: Pokrajinski sekretarijat za rad, zapošljavanje i ravnopravnost polova.

Nikolić-Ristanović, V., & Stevković, Lj. (2010). Karakteristike fizičkog i seksualnog nasilja u porodici-analiza poslednjeg slučaja nasilja (Characteristics of physical and sexual domestic violence-analysis of the last case of violence). In V. Nikolić-Ristanović (Ed.), *Nasilje u porodici u Vojvodini (Domestic violence in Vojvodina)* (pp. 79–91). Novi Sad: Pokrajinski sekretarijat za rad, zapošljavanje i ravnopravnost polova.

Nikolić-Ristanović, V., Mrvić-Petrović, N., Konstantinović-Vilić, S., Knežić, B., & Stevanović, I. (1996). *Žene Krajine: Rat, egzodus i izbeglištvo (Women of Krajina: War, Exodus and Exile)*. Beograd: Institut za kriminološka i sociološka istraživanja.

Nikolic-Ristanovic, V., Copic, S., Simeunovic-Patic, B., Milivojevic, S., & Mihic, B. (2004). *Trafficking in people in Serbia*. Belgrade: OSCE.

Nikolić-Ristanović, V., Kovačević, M., & Ćopić, S. (2006). Viktimizacija i iskustva žrtava kriminaliteta sa državnim institucijama – analiza podataka Službe VDS info i podrška žrtvama (Victimisation and experiences of victims of crime with state institutions – the analysis of VDS info and victim support data). *Temida, 9*(2), 11–19.

Nikolic-Ristanovic, V., Copic, S., Petrovic, N., & Saciri, B. (2014). *Conflicts, security and justice in intercultural context of Serbia* (Deliverable 6.2. Research report on interethnic conflicts and citizens' perception of security). Belgrade: Victimology Society of Serbia. Available at http://www.vds.org.rs/File/Deliverable_6.2_Research_report_on_interethnic_conflicts_and_citizens_security_p.pdf. And http://www.alternativeproject.eu/assets/upload/Deliverable_6.2_Research_report_on_interethnic_conflicts_and_citizens_security_perceptions_.pdf

Nikolic-Ristanovic, V., Koturovic, D., & Papamalis, F. (2014, in print). Criminology, crime and criminal justice in Serbia. *European Journal of Criminology*.

Nitzschke, H. (2003). *Transforming war economies: Challenges for peacemaking and peace building*. New York: International Peace Academy. http://www.ipacademy.org. Accessed 25 October 2008.

Nurmi, R. (1999, December 2–4). *Mobile Russian Prostitution in Finland. Chapter presented at the 32nd Triennial Conference of the International Abolitionist Federation. Breakdown of Borders*. Denmark: Copenhagen.

Petrović, N. (2010). Rasprostranjenost nasilja u porodici u Vojvodini (The scope of domestic violence in Vojvodina). In V. Nikolic-Ristanovic (Ed.), *Nasilje u porodici u Vojvodini (Domestic violence in Vojvodina)* (pp. 25–53). Novi Sad: Pokrajinski sekretarijat za rad, zapošljavanje i ravnopravnost polova.

Picarelli, J. (2002). *Trafficking, slavery and peacekeeping (A conference report)*. Turin: UNICRI.

Reckless, W. (1940). *Criminal behaviour*. New York and London: McGraw-Hill Book Company.

Ruggiero, V., & South, N. (1995). *Eurodrags: Drug use, markets and trafficking in Europe*. London: UCL Press.

Rummens, J. A., & Seat, R. (2003). *Assessing the impact of the Kosovo conflict on the mental health and well-being of newcomer Serbian children and youth in the greater Toronto area*. Toronto: Joint Centre of Excellence Research on Immigration and Settlement.

Schneider, H. J. (1987). *Kriminologie*. Berlin: Walter de Gruyter.

Selih, A. (2012). Crime and crime control in transition countries. In A. Selih & A. Zavrsnik (Eds.), *Crime and transition in Central and Eastern Europe* (pp. 3–36). New York: Springer.

Shoemaker, D. (1990). *Theories of delinquency*. New York-Oxford: Oxford University Press.

Smith, J. (2000, July 25). Sex trade enslaves East Europeans migrant women brutalized in Burgeoning Business. *The Washington Post*. http://www.highbeam.com/doc/1P2-542571.html. Accessed 10 October 2014.

Stevković, Lj. (2013). Uticaj rane nasilne vikctimizacije na nasilni kriminalitet odraslih (*Influence of early violent victimization on violent criminal behaviour in adulthood*). Master thesis (unpublished). Beograd: Fakultet za specijalnu edukaciju i rehabilitaciju.

Stevković, Lj. (2014). Obim, struktura i dinamika maloletničkog kriminaliteta u svetu i u Srbiji (Scope, structure and dynamics of juvenile crime in the world and in Serbia). In V. Nikolić-Ristanović & Lj. Stevković (Eds.), *Maloletnička delinkvencija u svetu i Srbiji: trendovi i društveni odgovori* (Juvenile delinquency in the world and in Serbia: trends and social responses) (pp. 23–38). Beograd: Prometej i Fakultet za specijalnu edukaciju i rehabilitaciju.

Stevkovic, Lj., Petkovic. N., Tenjovic, L., & Ispanovic-Radojkovic, V. (2013). *Case-base surveillance study: Serbia report* (unpublished). Belgrade: Faculty for Special Education and Rehabilitation. http://www.becau.eu. Accessed 25 March 2013.

Studdard, K. (2004). *War economies in a regional context: Overcoming the challenges of transformation*. New York: International Peace Academy. http://www.ipacademy.org. Accessed 25 October 2008.

Sutherland, E. (1939). *Principles of criminology*. Philadelphia: Lippincott.

UNICEF. (2009). *Machel Study 10-year strategic review: Children and conflicts in changing world*. http://www.unicef.org/publications/files/Machel_Study_10_Year_Strategic_Review_EN_030909.pdf. Accessed 19 June 2014.

Vidaković, I. (2002). Rasprostranjenost nasilja u porodici (Prevalence of domestic violence). In V. Nikolic-Ristanovic (Ed.), *Porodično nasilje u Srbiji (Domestic violence in Serbia)* (pp. 13–72). Beograd: Viktimološko društvo Srbije and Prometej.

A Biopsychosocial Model of Female Criminality: Implications for Assessment and Evidence-Based Treatment Approaches

Martin Peper, Sandy Krammer, and Dorothee Klecha

Abstract Female delinquency is a complex phenomenon that calls for a transdisciplinary, biopsychosocial model of explanation. In this chapter, we organize the phenomena associated with female criminality in the context of a tentative multilevel meta-model. Offending behavior is explained as a result of critical developmental patterns of interaction and information processing that emerge between multiple layers of biopsychosocial structure. Important etiological factors, risk characteristics and treatment goals that are specific for women are summarized. Findings of the cognitive, affective and social neurosciences as well as of behavioral and neurobiological genetics are interleaved with this model to expand the traditional criminological scope. Neuropsychological constructs help to bridge the gap between biological and psychosocial theories and contribute to a better understanding of critical intrapersonal and social processes.

1 Introduction

Comparatively little research has dealt with offending behavior in women (Lewis 2006). As all delinquent behaviors, it is a highly complex phenomenon that has been investigated from different theoretical perspectives. A comprehensive model covering the full range of social, psychological and biological phenomena has previously been considered useful for both medicine in general (Engel 1977) and for criminology in particular (Jeffery 1977, 1990). To provide a transdisciplinary basis for research, assessment and treatment, several biopsychosocial integration models have been recommended for the forensic sciences (e.g. Agnew 2014; Fishbein 2003; Robinson and Beaver 2008; Ross and Hilborn 2008).

M. Peper (✉)
University of Marburg, Marburg, Germany
e-mail: peper@uni-marburg.de

S. Krammer • D. Klecha
University of Bern, Bern, Switzerland
e-mail: sandy.krammer@fpd.unibe.ch; dorothee.klecha@fpd.unibe.ch

H. Kury et al. (eds.), *Women and Children as Victims and Offenders: Background, Prevention, Reintegration*, DOI 10.1007/978-3-319-08398-8_22

Despite these attempts, a broad causal theory of criminal behavior that also accounts for gender differences is not yet in sight. With respect to methods and concepts, current criminological and forensic research traditions remain extremely heterogeneous (see e.g. Heidt and Wheeldon 2014 for review). These domains typically refer to different but interacting levels of structure to explain delinquent behavior. Here, we present a tentative multilevel meta-model to organize and explicate the phenomena associated with female criminal behavior. Hopefully, this contributes to improving the basis for integrated research, assessment and treatment approaches.

In this model, a ***first level*** of explanation refers to culture, society and its institutions that generate superordinate factors such as gender-based concepts influencing individual action. Gender roles, stereotypes and beliefs represent socially constructed categories that are believed to maintain a system, in which women typically have disproportionate lower social and political power as compared to men. At the level of social systems, social hierarchy and inequality could be associated with group-based oppression against women, lack of power, reduced individual opportunities for action, and, at worst, delinquent action. In general, the definition of delinquency and current legal policy such as "war on drugs" in the US (Bloom et al. 2004) may have an effect on delinquent behavior.

There is a multitude of psychological and psychiatric findings on personality related determinants that constitute a ***second level*** of explanation. Thus, forensic research and its applied fields of work have focused on personal criminogenic factors such as antisocial personality traits, antisocial attitudes and social incompetence, impaired emotion regulation and impulsiveness (e.g. Dittmann and Ermer 2002).

A ***third level*** of explanation refers to personal relationships that provide a context for the development of delinquent behavior. It is well known that female delinquent behavior occurs more often in close social relationships. For example, the offense could be associated with partnership conflicts and women may even support and participate in offenses of their male partners. Problematic relationships may promote the social construction of attitudes that enhance the likelihood of criminal behavior.

Cognitive and affective information processing and its neuropsychological underpinnings represent a ***fourth level***. This provides a basis for all higher-level intrapersonal processes and refers to different domains of neurocognitive function including cognition, emotion and the control of action in situational contexts.

Moreover, a large body of recent research has investigated the biological and neurophysiological phenomena associated with delinquent behavior. The early literature on gender differences already explored biologically motivated factors such as lower physical power, instability, impulsivity, substance dependence, or factors associated with reproductive and hormonal functioning that have been attributed a role in delinquent behavior (e.g. Fishbein 1992; Walsh 2002). In contrast, recent research has increasingly elaborated on the neurobiological mechanisms that provide the underpinnings of gender differences in healthy subjects and persons with mental disorders (e.g. Frey and Dias 2014; Haimov-Kochman and Berger 2014). We will discuss below that this neurobiological evidence represents a category of its own, which provides new ideas but also causes some problems if it is to become integrated into a transdisciplinary biopsychosocial model (see Sect. 4.3).

There is no doubt that, in both genders, the conditional network of social, personal and situational factors of criminal acts is multifactorial (e.g. Dittmann and Ermer 2002; Nedopil 2007). Nevertheless, a comprehensive structural model would be helpful to equally account for social, psychological as well as biological influences. How is information transmitted and transformed across the different levels? How can gender-specific factors be accounted for?

Although these issues are unlikely to be answered in a short chapter, we provide some clues as to how the complex factors underlying female criminal behavior could be integrated. For this purpose, we adopt a multidisciplinary metatheoretical framework and review selected evidence from the literature on female criminal behavior placing special emphasis on recent neurobiological findings. We employ a generalization of the Coordinated Management of Meaning theory (e.g. Pearce and Cronen 1980; Pearce 2007; Pearce and Pearce 2000) to categorize the various phenomena (see Sect. 3). Originally, this metatheory comes from interpretive social science, and, corresponding to the tradition of symbolic interactionism, it assumes that multiple social contexts are constituted through communication and, conversely, influence communication and meaning during social interaction. As a theory of practice, it explains how a disadvantageous flow of information between these levels or layers of social structure produces unfavourable repetitive interactional patterns or loops.

In reviewing the personal and social factors of female delinquency, we interlink clinical and criminological information with recent results from the cognitive, social and affective neurosciences. The necessity of introducing neuroscience findings into the present criminological context is justified by the fact that the way how a person interprets episodes, relationships, self and others is mediated by multilevel memory representations. A theory of delinquent action must account for the fact that the above levels of information are all represented and integrated within the offender's neurocognitive system. However, these representations of meaning systems are subject to permanent plasticity and modulation depending on basic biological predispositions and vulnerabilities that also need to be considered. Given the prominent "gender gap" in deviant behavior, it is particularly important to inspect pertinent contributions from the life sciences.

The necessity of integrating biopsychosocial models has previously been recognized in the context of the transdisciplinary model for medicine (Engel 1977) and, more specifically, in the criminological domain (e.g. Jeffery 1977; Ross and Hilborn 2008). Although all of these models suggest syntheses of behavioral, cognitive, social and biological approaches, they appear to have bypassed criminology. Even though the affective and social cognitive neurosciences claimed to have made considerable progress, pertinent findings have not been taken into account in an appropriate manner by the criminological sciences (Ross and Hilborn 2008).

The reluctance to take note of biological explanations might be comprehensible for historical or ideological reasons. However, it is much more important to consider metatheoretical aspects associated with basic categorical differences referring to social, psychological and biological sciences. Therefore, we discuss in Sect. 4 that, for several reasons, a comprehensive biopsychosocial model of female criminality appears to be a long way off. Although a tentative meta-model is suggested, we believe that fundamental problems remain that need to be addressed by future research focusing on specific subunits of the model.

In Sect. 5, we inspect potential consequences for the applied forensic field such as pretrial and risk assessment as well as treatment. With reference to the latter, forensic programs intend to modify the factors that are central in the conditional network of criminal acts (Dittmann and Ermer 2002). In particular, forensic psychotherapy attempts to transform meaning systems such as attitudes and life scripts through communication. For this purpose, convincing multidisciplinary models of female delinquency are needed, which explain how the transformation of meaning occurs and how the symbolic-interactive and the systemic-biological categories can be integrated so that more representative, evidence-based assessment and treatment approaches can be created.

2 Offending Behavior in Women

Obviously, women's role in crime is not limited to the passive victim's role but includes actively committed crimes as well. However, relative to male criminal behavior, female delinquency is less salient ("gender gap"): women show a lower number of criminal records with less than about one quarter of total crimes (Hollin and Palmer 2006), they tend to be older at first imprisonment, imprisoned less frequently, and detained for shorter periods of time over the lifespan (e.g. Messina et al. 2003).

Whereas male offenders typically show a broad range of all types of offenses, a generally lower number of violent crime and sexual offenses is observed in females. Serious female crimes are commonly related to close social relationships with the spouse or children as victims (e.g. Rossegger et al. 2009; Trube-Becker 1974). Female crimes typically entail traffic offenses or property delinquency that corresponds to the higher proportion of female clients with a greater opportunity of shoplifting of consumer goods. Due to vocational reasons, women are less likely to commit serious economic crimes. Nevertheless, current statistics do not represent the dark figures of female crimes that might include a broader range of offenses such as false statements and alibis or complicity.

As a consequence, women are also underrepresented in treatment programs for offenders with mental disorders; however, there is a trend of a growing number of women participating in rehabilitation programs (e.g. Moloney et al. 2009). Thus, institutions should account for gender differences in their programs by inspecting the particular needs and treatment requirements (e.g. Covington 2008). Although gender specific risk factors have been largely ignored previously, the recent approaches are more aware of this issue and take into account gender specific risk factors of relapse and related treatment requirements.

A meta-analysis in both female and male adolescents showed that antisocial behavior, attitudes, personality traits and antisocial peers predicted delinquency

(Jones Hubbard and Pratt 2002). In both genders, criminal history, unemployment and substance abuse play a central role (McIvor 2007). Significant risk factors such as financial burdens, poor education, social problems, previous trauma, as well as mental and physical disorders have been identified (e.g. Blanchette 2002; Hartwell 2001; Hollin and Palmer 2006; Jones Hubbard and Pratt 2002), though it remains unclear whether these factors are actually gender-specific or whether gender-neutral factors have the same effects in both genders. The most salient gender related factors are summarized below.

2.1 Biological Determinants

Sociological and feminist theories have typically viewed delinquent behavior as a product of acquired gender roles directing women towards greater conformity and social adaptation (Walsh 2002). The differential socialization hypothesis of males and females ("blank slate") implicates that, under similar environmental conditions, men and women would show similar crime rates. Nevertheless, males have a greater propensity to show a multitude of problem behaviors and personality traits that are associated with delinquency (e.g. Walsh 2002). This "gender gap" pertaining to crime types and rates cannot be explained exclusively by cultural and socialization differences (Fishbein 1992).

When sex hormone levels (testosterone, sex hormone binding globulin) are introduced into models to predict adolescents' problem behavior, an absorption of age-related variance has been observed suggesting that hormonal effects have a considerable power to explain a broad range of behaviors such as the excessive search for experiences and feelings ("sensation seeking"; Udry 1995; Walsh 2002). There is little doubt that the facilitating effects of hormones are particularly problematic when occurring in adolescents with poor reasoning, planning and emotion regulation abilities due to immature prefrontal cortex (PFC) functioning.

Pre- and postnatal exposure to sex hormones has been identified as the main cause of differential brain development and subsequent behavioral and cognitive gender differences (e.g. Collaer and Hines 1995). It is a well-accepted finding that early exposure to sex hormones leads to permanent behavioral change (Morris et al. 2004). Women typically show greater levels or numbers of sex hormone (estrogen, progesterone) receptors within the serotonin, dopamine and γ-aminobutyric acid systems; sex hormones influence emotion regulation and cognitive functioning as they modulate neurotransmission and stimulate plasticity in a number of brain regions such as the prefrontal cortex, hippocampus, amygdala, and hypothalamus (see Lokuge et al. 2010; Haimov-Kochman and Berger 2014, for reviews).

Within-subject changes of hormone levels may also influence behavior. Hormonal fluctuations that occur during the menstrual cycle as well as long-term hormonal changes associated with menarche, menopause or pregnancy have also been attributed a role in specific intraindividual behavioral changes (e.g. Haimov-

Kochman and Berger 2014). Sacher et al. (2013) reviewed nine studies that investigated the effects of sex hormone variation during the menstrual cycle suggesting that the functions of a wide range of cerebral regions and related emotional functions as well as cognitive regulation of emotion appears to be influenced by subtle fluctuations of hormone levels.

Some of the dysexecutive problems (i.e. impairment of central control functions such as working memory, planning, reasoning, flexibility, control and supervision of behavior, inhibition of emotional and motivational impulses) observed in women with Attention Deficit Hyperactivity Disorder (ADHD) could be related to fluctuations of sex hormones levels (Frey and Dias 2014; Haimov-Kochman and Berger 2014). Although effects of sex hormones on problem behaviors generally appear to be stronger in males than in females, there is evidence that neuropsychological dysfunction due to hormonal influences is also present in female offenders and related to aggressive behaviors (Daoust et al. 2006; Rocha et al. 2014). Nevertheless, it has been suggested that females appear to show a lower susceptibility to such hormonal effects and it may require a greater impact of adverse environmental conditions to stimulate problem behaviors and delinquency in females (Walsh 2002).

2.2 *Mental Health*

Female offenders are affected by mental disorders to a greater extent than men (Hollin and Palmer 2006; Messina et al. 2003). About 80 % of imprisoned women meet the criteria of a mental disorder, most commonly depression, personality disorders, addictive disorders and Post-traumatic Stress Disorder (PTSD; Butler and Allnutt 2003; Teplin et al. 1996; Zlotnick 1999). A greater number of mental health problems were also observed in female adolescent perpetrators as compared with corresponding boys (McCabe et al. 2002). The prevalence rates for Antisocial Personality Disorder (APD) and Borderline Personality Disorder (BPD) were typically increased as compared to the general population (Jordan et al. 1996). However, the predictive power of psychopathic personality traits in a forensic context appears to be lower in women (Eisenbarth 2014).

Trauma exposure and related disorders play a central role in the history of female offenses (Moloney et al. 2009; Krammer et al. 2015). Male and female adolescent perpetrators showed significant differences to the disadvantage of girls with respect to different types of childhood trauma (McCabe et al. 2002). In a meta-analysis, physical and sexual abuse experiences were predictive of delinquency in girls (Jones Hubbard and Pratt 2002). Indeed, an increased lifetime risk in late adolescence for sexual abuse and assault committed by adults and peers (self-report) was found in 26.6 % of 17-year-old females, whereas lifetime experience was only 5.1 % in boys (Finkelhor et al. 2014).

2.3 *Addictive Disorders*

Substance abuse is a typical problem behavior in adolescents and frequently co-occurs with conduct disorder (Vermeiren 2003). Offenses are often related to substance abuse, the latter being closely related to trauma exposure (Covington 1998). The prevalence rate of substance abuse as assessed by diagnostic interview in female adolescent delinquents may range up to 87 % (Myers et al. 1990). Imprisoned women often show serious substance abuse as well as a pattern of use that is different from males (Messina et al. 2003): whereas hedonistic aspects appear to prevail in men, women may show a pattern of "self-medication" to treat physical or mental pain (Hollin and Palmer 2006).

Taken together, there is some overlap with respect to criminogenic risk factors in men and women, but several gender-specific factors can also be identified. However, this overlap does not mean that these factors are etiologically equivalent in men and women (cf. Hollin and Palmer 2006). Rather, it seems likely that different conditions, constellations and contexts may lead into a final common pathway of criminal development. Moreover, these factors can be conceived of as multilevel phenomena with mutual interdependencies, reciprocal relationships and different degrees of aggregation. These dependencies have not been sufficiently reflected with respect to their potential etiological implications or statistical effects on risk modelling.

3 Biopsychosocial Explanations of Female Delinquency

Typically, biopsychosocial explanations refer to constructs that are located in different structural levels or layers of a nomological network, that is, to a hierarchical system providing evidence for the validity of these constructs. There is no doubt that information processing at the bottom layers of individual action feeds forward to higher layers of social organization such as relationships and life scripts, which in turn feed back to influence lower layers. A family of models that accounts for potential recursive transformation processes between layers has been stimulated by the assumptions of symbolic interactionism.

Here, we adopt a generalized version of the Coordinated Management of Meaning theory to reconstruct delinquent development in women (Pearce 2007). This is motivated by the fact that this theory has provided interesting contributions to the metatheoretical understanding of multilevel phenomena in applied fields of work such as clinical psychology and communication theory as well as criminology (e.g. Sundarajan and Spano 2004). Figure 1 illustrates this multilevel model, which provides the framework for the subsequent review of etiological factors of female delinquency and crime.

In the following sections, we adopt a person-centered view starting at the personality layer moving way down in the hierarchy to basic mental dysfunctions.

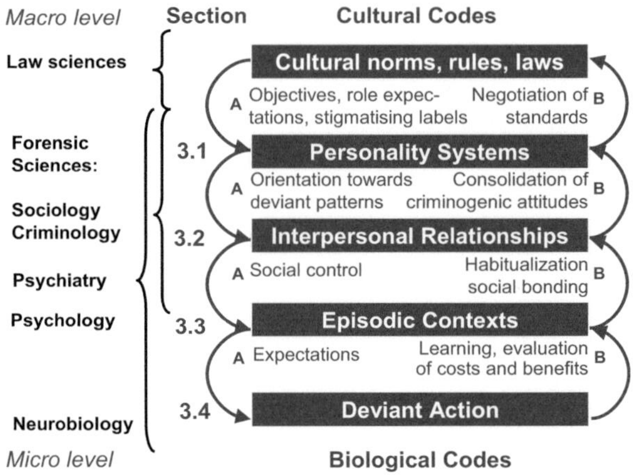

Fig. 1 Hierarchical biopsychosocial meta-model of coordinated processes as conceptualized by different domains of criminological research (*left*). *Arrows* specify (A) *top-down* regulative rules that determine how lower layer processes have to be adapted according to the pertinent higher order context; (B) *bottom-up* constitutive rules explain how meaning at a lower layer determines meaning at the higher order context (see text for explanation)

At the level of *personality*, we summarize criminogenic personality factors that include disorders, cognitive plans, attitudes, life styles and scripts. At the level of *interpersonal relationships,* problematic interaction processes and chronic social stress due to partnership crises are considered. At the level of *situational and episodic contexts*, acute stress (e.g. mental overload, physical disease or personal blows of fate) is relevant; in particular, we discuss the effects of traumatic stress and physical harm including abusive experiences and its chronic effects and their biological concomitants. Finally, we explain *neuropsychological functions* that may facilitate or inhibit delinquent behavior in women. Specific biological predispositions and vulnerabilities will also be considered at each level. Note that genetic influences and gene-environment interactions will be discussed separately (Sect. 4.4).

3.1 Personality

Female prisoners exhibit a wide range of correlated personality traits and comorbid disorders: Antisocial Personality Disorder (APD), Borderline Personality Disorder (BPD) and trauma related disorders as well as depression and anxiety are common (e.g. Mulder et al. 1994; Rogstad and Rogers 2008; Warren and South 2006). These disorders are briefly reviewed and neurobiological correlates are highlighted. In particular, we focus on structural findings pertaining to the volume of grey and white matter of the brain or of neural pathways (cf. structural magnetic resonance imaging, MRI) and on functional alterations that can be assessed by means of functional magnetic imaging (fMRI; e.g. task-related increases of blood oxygenation indicating neural activation) or positron emission tomography (PET; an imaging technique that assesses blood flow or metabolism in the brain to identify hypoactivity such as reduced glucose metabolism or hyperactivity such as elevated metabolism).

3.1.1 Antisocial Personality Disorder

The diagnosis of APD is highly controversial due to comorbidities and heterogeneity of the construct (see Glenn et al. 2013 for a review). A base rate of APD was found to be 21 % in imprisoned women (Fazel and Danesh 2002) with one third also showing symptoms of psychopathy (Warren and South 2006). A prevalence of 18 % of self-reported symptoms of APD was found in a sample of female inmates, which was significantly lower than in males (24 %; Coolidge et al. 2011). Although most women do not meet the diagnostic criteria or exceed critical thresholds, they are likely to show various conduct problems. Psychopathy in women was associated with higher rates of imprisonment due to violent and non-violent crimes (Louth et al. 1998).

On the behavioral level, female offenders with APD are likely to show impulsive behaviors, aggressiveness and emotional dysregulation (e.g. Veit et al. 2002). In general, APD is characterized by hypoemotionality, little anticipation of negative consequences and fear conditioning as well as poor emotional empathy. Male patients with APD may show impaired emotion regulation and inappropriate social behavior since rules are disregarded and action is insufficiently adapted to the situational context, with no or only little anticipation of negative consequences. Reduced regulation and inhibition of aggressive behavior has been associated with decreased prefrontal functioning.

Neurobiological correlates of APD. Most insights into psychobiological and neurobiological correlates of APD and psychopathy have been gained in male offenders. These results show that different subtypes of APD with and without psychopathy are associated with specific neurobiological alterations (see Glenn et al. 2013, van Honk and Schutter 2006 for reviews). Male patients with APD showed a significant reduction in prefrontal gray matter (Raine et al. 2000; Yang et al. 2005). In particular, a recent study reported that offenders with APD and psychopathy showed bilateral reductions of grey matter volumes in the anterior rostral prefrontal cortex (Brodmann area 10) and temporal poles (areas 20 and 38) as compared with offenders without psychopathy and controls (Gregory et al. 2012). In violent perpetrators, a decreased cerebral perfusion was found in frontal brain areas (e.g. Soderstrom et al. 2002). However, it remains unclear to what extent these findings may be extrapolated to women.

Projections of the prefrontal serotonin (5-hydroxytryptamin, 5-HT) system have been attributed a major role in the inhibition of impulsive-aggressive behaviors, hostility and delinquency as well as suicidal behavior (e.g. Seo et al. 2008). Decreased serotonin metabolites have been associated with self-injurious behavior.

The serotonin system has also been associated with the suppression of impulsive and aggressive behaviors (e.g. Gunter et al. 2010; Iofrida et al. 2014). A high density of serotonin receptors was found in the PFC connecting the amygdala with subcortical areas. Aggressive tendencies, behavioral problems and emotional dysregulation were correlated with modulations in serotonin metabolism (Davidson et al. 2000; Seo et al. 2008). In particular, impulsive behavior and aggressiveness have been associated with genetic serotonin polymorphisms and a dysregulation of the serotonergic network in APD (e.g. Aluja et al. 2009). Serotonergic dysregulation appears to be associated with a reduced absolute number of 5-HT receptors, abnormal receptors and serotonin metabolite levels.

In the amygdala, which is a medial-temporal lobe structure providing automatic emotional activation and conditioning functions, no volumetric changes were found (in contrast to patients with BPD). Subjects with APD showed an increase in amygdala activity when being confronted with threatening stimuli or during the acquisition phase of a conditioning experiment (Schneider et al. 2000; Veit et al. 2002). Kiehl and colleagues (2001) found a poor activation of the amygdala when the subjects were confronted with emotional words. In a conditioning paradigm, the antisocial group showed increased activity of the amygdala and dorsolateral prefrontal cortex during the acquisition of conditioned associations as compared to healthy subjects (Schneider et al. 2000). Antisocial subjects with psychopathy showed an increased activity during acquisition but poor anticipatory fear and associated amygdala and orbitofrontal cortex (OFC) reactions in the extinction phase suggesting that these subjects were emotionally less responsive to conditioned stimuli, so that negative consequences predicted by conditioned cues were not anticipated (Veit et al. 2002).

The hippocampus is a medial-temporal lobe structure serving as a recorder of autobiographic episodes and declarative facts. It has been reported that the volume of the bilateral dorsal hippocampi was significantly correlated with psychopathy scores (as assessed with the Psychopathy Checklist-Revised, PCL-R; Hare 2003) in alcohol-abusing violent perpetrators (Laakso et al. 2001). Raine and colleagues (2004) found an asymmetry in the anterior hippocampus in imprisoned psychopaths as compared to non-criminal "psychopaths" and healthy individuals. The deficient fear conditioning and affect regulation in psychopaths could also be attributed to this reduction of hippocampus volume. In sum, however, most of the above findings have been obtained in male inmates and further research is needed to explore whether this can be extrapolated to female offenders.

3.1.2 Borderline Personality Disorder (BPD)

The group of patients with BPD typically includes a larger proportion of women (80 %; Paris 2004). Since criminal acts are socially sanctioned by law enforcement and the opportunity of expansive behavior is limited by gender roles, women tend to show self-injurious behavior to achieve a short-term reduction of excessive emotional activation that has potentially been fueled by prior long-term social conflict.

Self-reports of symptoms of BPD were twice as likely in female inmates than in males; psychotic and depersonalization symptoms were also exceeding the number of male reports (Coolidge et al. 2011). Typical behavioral symptoms include impulsive behaviors, verbal and nonverbal aggression, emotional instability and poor affect regulation as well as antisocial behavior and poor action monitoring. The neural correlates of some of these symptoms have also been explored by structural and functional brain imaging work as summarized below.

Neurobiological correlates of BPD. Brain imaging findings suggest that patient groups with BPD and APD show overlapping structural, functional and behavioral abnormalities. Important neuroanatomical correlates of these disorders were alterations in the prefrontal cortex, amygdala, hippocampus and the serotoninergic system. Structural brain imaging studies of the predominantly female BPD group showed smaller volumes of several brain regions than controls. For instance, the right-hemispheric gray matter in the orbitofrontal and anterior cingulate cortex (e.g. Lyoo et al. 1998; Ruesch et al. 2003) and the connections between the left and right anterior cingulate cortices (Ruesch et al. 2010) were reduced.

Moreover, a volume reduction from 8 to 24 % was found in the amygdala of BPD patients as compared with healthy controls (e.g. van Elst et al. 2003; Whittle et al. 2009). Some studies reported a gray matter reduction in the left amygdala without further volume or density differences in gray or white matter (e.g. Ruesch et al. 2003). A trend towards a reduced amygdala volume was observed in BPD patients with a history of sexual or physical abuse (Driessen et al. 2000). A significant amygdala reduction of 21 % was found in BPD patients with a history of sexual abuse (Schmahl et al. 2003a). However, a larger amygdala volume was found in a BPD group with an additional diagnosis of depression than in patients without this diagnosis (Zetzsche et al. 2006). The reduced amygdala volume was associated with dysregulated and exaggerated emotional reactions and emotional instability, for example, when viewing emotional pictures (Herpertz et al. 2001) or faces (Donegan et al. 2013).

A reduction of hippocampal volume was found both in BPD and APD patients with psychopathy: Driessen and colleagues (2000) reported a trend of a reduced hippocampal volume of 16 % in BPD patients with a history of sexual or physical abuse compared with healthy individuals. Schmahl and colleagues (2003a) found a significant volume rseduction in the hippocampus of 13 % in BPD patients with a history of sexual abuse. Van Elst and colleagues (2003) observed a significant volume reduction in 20 % of BPD patients as well as a reduction in the left orbitofrontal cortex, the right anterior cingulate and amygdala.

Functional brain imaging studies showed altered activation patterns in BPD suggesting OFC dysfunction (Driessen et al. 2004) and metabolic changes in the prefrontal and cingulate cortex (Schmahl et al. 2004), frontal hypermetabolism in an anxious BPD subgroup (Juengling et al. 2003), and frontal hypometabolism in an impulsive-aggressive subtype (Soloff et al. 2003). Changes in serotoninergic neurotransmission in BPD have also been investigated by Positron Emission Tomography (PET): a pharmacological stimulation of serotonin release showed a reduction in the serotoninergic activity in the OFC, cingulum, dorsolateral PFC and temporal lobe (Soloff et al. 2003, 2000).

The prefrontal alterations in BPD have been associated with reduced inhibitory functioning (Kunert et al. 2002). Differential activations of the OFC and ACC could be associated with processes of implicit or explicit affect regulation (e.g. Minzenberg et al. 2007). The different activation patterns in fearful versus impulsive-aggressive subgroups suggest different types of interactions between the frontal monitoring system and limbic brain systems as a result of different emotion regulation strategies.

As previous traumatic experiences prevail in many patients with BPD, functional imaging studies have also focused on emotional memory processes. In patients with BPD and PTSD, not only reduced volumes of the amygdala and hippocampus but also deficient memory functioning were found (Irle et al. 2009; Vermetten et al. 2006). While memories of abuse experiences were stimulated, a hyperperfusion is typically observed in orbitofrontal and dorsolateral prefrontal areas as well as the anterior cingulated cortex (ACC); however, this was absent in women with BPD (Schmahl et al. 2004). Moreover, memories of situations of abandonment also resulted in a reduced blood flow in the medial prefrontal cortex and ACC (Schmahl et al. 2003b).

3.1.3 Posttraumatic Stress Disorder (PTSD)

Posttraumatic stress disorder (PTSD) is, in addition to depression and substance abuse, more prevalent in incarcerated women than in corresponding samples from the general population (e.g. Hollin and Palmer 2006; Teplin et al. 1996). A systematic literature review indicated that the prevalence of PTSD is considerably increased in offenders (Goff et al. 2007). Concerning potentially traumatic events (PTE) and subsequent PTSD, there is a gender-bias to the disadvantage of incarcerated women. Evidence indicates that this might be associated with a higher risk of future criminal behavior. As PTSD is associated with individual coping strategies after PTE, this issue is further discussed in Sect. 3.3.

Taken together, patients with BPD typically show an increased emotional reactivity due to impaired emotion regulation. Reductions of prefrontal and orbitofrontal activation by emotional stimuli have been observed. As the OFC and ACC play important roles in inhibiting ascending aggressive impulses and in motivational, emotional and social behaviors, the presence of corresponding disorders in BPD comes as no surprise. A reduced amygdala and hippocampus volume has been associated with emotional instability, impulsivity and poor memory functioning in these patients. It is likely that these findings can be extrapolated to female inmates with BPD. Female prisoners are also highly exposed to several other mental health constraints, the majority of which being related to traumatization and its sequelae (aftereffects) such as PTSD.

3.2 Social Relationships

Criminal behavior in women is often accompanied by precarious social situations (e.g. homelessness, unemployment of parents, poverty) or difficult family relationships (e.g. family conflicts, "broken family", poor parental care, tense family relationships, alcohol abuse of the spouse, etc.). While male conflict resolution is typically characterized by delinquent and expansive behaviors, women tend to respond to social conflict with passive, internalizing, or autoaggressive reactions such as depression, addictive and self-injurious behaviors. Violent crimes committed by women are often the result of long-term social conflict and a history of abusive relationships.

Compared with homicides committed by males, female homicides more often occur within close social and family relationships, as many victims are family members (e.g. own child or partner). The motivation for killing a partner/spouse often appears to stem from a history of social instabilities (e.g. previous provocations, jealousy due to extramarital relations of the partner, failure of marriage or relationship, fear of being abandoned, termination of an abusive relationship). In this sense, the criminal act appears to be an inappropriate problem-solving strategy in response to the underlying psychological, social, and financial conflicts. The role of women in less serious crimes appears to be limited to providing supportive services (e.g. drug courier services, lures, false alibis), that is, a participation in the criminal subculture of males. Thus, women participate in the crimes of their male partners rather than executing these crimes themselves. Accordingly, female involvement in these crimes also occurs on the grounds of unfavorable relationships.

Taken together, precarious interpersonal relationships are well known environmental risk factors of female delinquency. In problematic relationships, criminogenic tendencies of the partners may have a mutually reinforcing effect so that learned attitudes and behaviors consolidate and are incorporated into the personality system. Moreover, a long-term history of social conflict and abusive events may lead to unstable relationships. These in turn give rise to inappropriate problem-solving strategies including aggressive acts against self and others. Thus, relationships are shaped by adverse events and experiences and, conversely, provide a context for delinquent attitudes and behaviors to develop.

3.3 Episodic Life Events

A multitude of episodic life events or changes in momentary social contexts such as divorce or job loss may significantly affect the individual. However, exceptional events not always have a harmful intensity and should not be confused with potentially traumatic events (PTE) as defined by ICD-10. PTE can lead to long-term consequences, potentially resulting in stress dependent disorders such as

Posttraumatic Stress Disorder (PTSD). Generally, incarcerated women show a greater rate of traumatization than male inmates or women in the general community. For example, Messina and colleagues (2003) compared female and male inmates with a focus on childhood and adulthood traumatization: 25 % of the female and 14 % of the male group were found to have experienced PTE during childhood, while 25 and 3 %, respectively, experienced PTE during adulthood.

Even greater prevalence rates for PTE among incarcerated women were reported by other studies (e.g. 87 %, Zlotnick 1997; 98 %, Green et al. 2005). With reference to the type of trauma, 70 % of a sample of incarcerated women experienced physical abuse by a parental caregiver during childhood, and 59 % experienced any form of sexual abuse (Browne et al. 1999). 81 % had experienced sexual abuse at any time during their life (Singer et al. 1995). This gender-based disadvantage is also evident in adolescent delinquents, with girls more often reporting PTE than boys (McCabe et al. 2002), in particular, sexual abuse (Baglivio et al. 2014).

Corresponding to this gender bias to the disadvantage of women with reference to PTE, the same bias is observed pertaining to posttraumatic sequelae. According to Zlotnick (1997), the prevalence of PTSD diagnosis in a sample of incarcerated women was 48 % with a lifetime prevalence of 20 %. A German study showed slightly greater lifetime rates among incarcerated women (30 %). Greater rates of PTSD were found in adolescent, delinquent girls as compared to non-delinquent girls and to delinquent boys (Cauffman et al. 1998); in contrast, incarcerated males showed lower rates (e.g. a 1-month prevalence rate of 4 %).

Trauma and PTSD may affect other aspects of health: incarcerated women with a lifetime or current PTSD typically show a high comorbidity rate of major depression, substance abuse, and borderline personality disorder (Zlotnick 1997). The intensity of experienced trauma appears to be associated with both mental disorders (axis I) and personality disorders (axis II) (Driessen et al. 2006). Incarcerated women with both childhood traumatization and addictive disorders show, among other disorders, elevated suicide risk, eating disorders, alcoholism, sexual diseases and hepatitis (Messina and Grella 2006).

Although traumatization is seen as a potential pathway to crime (Salisbury and van Voorhis 2009), only little information is available on traumatic experiences and the mechanisms that elicit, maintain and reset deviant developments. However, when trauma is interpreted as a potential precursor of a delinquent development, it is useful to consider how such an event is processed. Though PTE is a necessary precondition that produces symptoms and instigates a type of maladjustment, which, in turn, may lead to criminal development, it is not sufficient. There are further factors that influence this relationship. The multifactor PTSD model of Maercker (2009) suggests that prior traumatization, (younger or older) age, (low) education, certain personality traits, and (female) gender can be considered as pre-traumatic risk factors.

Furthermore, peri-traumatic factors may be relevant: The severity of a PTE is associated with trauma sequelae, and there is an "overall additive effect of the contribution of cumulative trauma to symptom complexity" (Cloitre et al. 2009, p. 405). According to this, the relation between PTE in adulthood and PTSD symptom complexity depends, up to a certain extent, on the presence of PTE during childhood, that is, on pre-traumatic factors. Thus, prior traumatization can be considered a risk factor for further traumatization and subsequent PTSD. Moreover, social-interpersonal factors influence the relation between PTE and corresponding stress symptoms: Dysfunctional disclosure refers to an inability to express PTE through feelings and emotional responding (Müller and Maercker 2006). Social acceptance is also an important aspect as positive reactions and the acknowledgment of the individual's status as a trauma victim or survivor may have alleviating effects on PTSD (Maercker 2009). It has been suggested that PTSD symptomatology is elicited by a social-interpersonal cascade (Maercker et al. 2009).

Another hypothesis suggested that the loss of resources provokes further losses and the acquisition of resources becomes increasingly difficult (Hobfoll 1989). Thus, persons who have low resources or lost resources have an increased probability to lose further resources as well as facing difficulties keeping their remaining social resources and developing new ones. As a result of traumatization, the persons concerned might become increasingly "antisocial" and, due to the progressive loss of resources, they are being drawn into a "social loss spiral" (Krammer et al. 2013). The social deficits may increase to such a degree that this development finally results in antisocial behavior and delinquency.

Another hypothesis refers to the "cycle of violence" suggesting that victims or survivors of victimization will consequently tend to victimize others (Widom 1989). For example, 80 % of those incarcerated women, who reported PTE in childhood, also reported PTE in adulthood (Browne et al. 1999). PTE during childhood was correlated with an increased amount of years in prison during adulthood (Kopp et al. 2009), and the number of PTE during childhood was associated with the lifetime number of arrests (Messina and Grella 2006).

Taken together, the development of maladaptive processes and delinquent behaviors subsequent to PTE does not solely depend on the occurrence of traumatic life events. According to the multifactorial PTSD model, further factors before, during and after PTE contribute to maladaptive processes (e.g. Maercker 2009). However, trauma does not affect criminal behavior directly or exclusively. Rather, maladjustment such as PTSD is mediated by several factors or processes, among them: (a) social-interpersonal factors affecting traumatization (and possibly vice versa); (b) further mental disorders that augment a delinquent development; (c) a vicious circle of violence.

3.3.1 Neurobiological Correlates of PTSD

The consequences of trauma and PTSD on the structural and functional integrity of the brain have also been investigated for many years (see Irle et al. 2013; O'Doherty et al. 2015 for reviews). Exposure to long-term stress associated with elevated cortisol levels is believed to give rise to hippocampal alterations (glucocorticoid hypothesis; e.g. Sapolsky et al. 1986). A recent meta-analysis of brain volumes has confirmed significant reductions (medium effect sizes) of hippocampal, amygdala and ACC volumes in PTSD groups as compared with healthy controls (O'Doherty et al. 2015).

Reduced hippocampal volumes have not only been observed in male patients with PTSD, for example, due to war incidents (e.g. Bremner et al. 1995), but also in women exposed to childhood sexual trauma (Bremner et al. 1997; for a review see Karl et al. 2006) with structural alterations being associated with the duration and intensity of PTSD (e.g. Bremner et al. 1997, 1995; Gilbertson et al. 2002; Irle et al. 2005). Prolonged stress may affect the inhibitory functions of the hippocampus and thus facilitate subsequent stress responses and corticoid levels. The extent of hippocampal volume loss in patients with PTSD has also been found to be associated with functional changes such as memory deficits (Irle et al. 2005; Weniger et al. 2008).

However, non-traumatized twins of war veterans also showed smaller hippocampal volumes without having been exposed to trauma previously (Gilbertson et al. 2002). Since the hippocampal volume shows some heritability, this may be considered a pre-traumatic factor, which may in turn influence other pre- as well as peritrauma factors such as those described in the preceding section (e.g. Maercker 2009). Early in the course of development, prenatal glucocorticoid exposure due to high maternal cortisol might contribute to the transgenerational transmission of PTSD risk (Yehuda and Biere 2007) and potential alterations of hippocampal structure. In adults, elevated glucocorticoid levels (and related structural effects) could be associated with the antecedent emotion regulation abilities rather than with the consequences of the trauma. By contributing to effective emotion regulation, the hippocampus may have an effect on resilience to adverse environmental events.

Other brain regions involved in emotion regulation such as the cingulate gyrus have also been found to be reduced in patients with PTSD (Rauch et al. 2003; Schmahl et al. 2003a; Weniger et al. 2008, 2009). Volume reductions of the cingulate may also negatively affect emotion regulation as poor cingular and prefrontal mechanisms may disinhibit amygdala activity (e.g. Rauch et al. 2006). However, it remains unclear whether PTSD is associated with a reduced amygdala volume or whether this only applies to patients with BPD (Schmahl and Bremner 2006).

Dissociative phenomena as well as reduced pain sensitivity observed in patients with PTSD and BPD could be functionally important as this averts sensory overload in stress situations. Dissociation was also correlated with brain activity in superior parietal regions and a reduction of activity in the temporal lobe in these patients (e. g, Ludäscher et al. 2010; Kraus et al. 2009). Patients with dissociative disorders are thus prone to show a style of continued downregulated or hypomodulated limbic activity that might not only result in changes of functional connectivity, but also in a decrease of tissue volume (Irle et al. 2013).

3.4 *Control of Action and Behavior*

Neurocognitive problems are not uncommon in prison populations and a high prevalence of cognitive impairment can be expected independent of gender. For instance, Coolidge and coworkers (2011) reported evidence that neuropsychological dysfunction, as assessed by self-report questionnaire, was more frequently reported by adult male prisoners than by males that were not incarcerated. The complaints included perceived memory problems, attention and hyperactivity problems, feelings of easily getting lost, changes in taste and smell, as well as a number of unspecific symptoms such as problems with balance, headaches, physical problems, and dizzy spells. Cognitive and emotional impairment has also been recorded in inmates with APD and psychopathy (Blair 2003; Glenn and Yang 2012; Patrick 2007). However, changes of neurocognitive functioning are still poorly investigated in women (Anton et al. 2012). In the following sections, we summarize selected evidence for the domains of cognitive and emotional functioning.

3.4.1 Cognitive Functioning and ADHD

Moffitt (1993) suggested that neuropsychological impairment represents an important class of vulnerability factors, specifically in adolescents showing life-course persistent antisocial behavior. Distinct patterns of neurocognitive functioning were found in antisocial and psychopathic subgroups (Anton et al. 2012). However, individuals with little or medium antisocial risk do not necessarily show prominent symptoms of executive dysfunction: early neuropsychological work employing standardized tests to assess cognitive deficits and intelligence only found weak to moderate effect sizes in antisocial offenders with some consistent findings referring to problems in verbal and executive functioning (see Henry and Moffitt 1997).

A model of male psychopathy suggested that a failure to attend to additional, peripheral information while adapting behavior may cause a neglect of threatening consequences so that the behavior cannot be changed in the presence of distress cues (Patterson and Newman 1993). In women with APD, attentional and executive problems were found as indicated by deficits to process conflicting contextual information (Vitale et al. 2007) or to reallocate attention during goal-directed behavior (MacCoon et al. 2004).

A significant comorbidity of Conduct Disorder und ADHD with its two dimensions of inattention and hyperactivity-impulsivity has been observed in adolescents. In particular, the prevalence of ADHD appears to be higher in delinquent adolescents than in the normal population (Vermeiren 2003). In boys with previous conduct disorder and ADHD, APD and ADHD are also more likely to co-occur in later adulthood (e.g. Mannuzza et al. 1998). Nevertheless, conduct disorder und ADHD remain relatively independent categories (cf. Vermeiren 2003).

Because externalizing behaviors are more salient in adolescent males and internalizing disorders and anxiety occur more frequently in females, boys are more likely to be referred to ADHD assessment (Rucklidge and Tannock 2001). As a consequence, ADHD might be underdiagnosed in females, although similarities with respect to dysexecutive symptoms exist (Skogli et al. 2013). Thus, it appears to be inappropriate to apply the male-based ADHD literature to female groups (Haimov-Kochman and Berger 2014).

Prevalence rates for ADHD in juveniles in correctional settings in the US and Canada appear to range from 20 to 30 % (Odgers et al. 2005). Little is known about the prevalence of ADHD in female offenders. Rösler and coworkers (2009) found a lifetime prevalence of ADHD of 24.5 % in a German sample of adult female offenders, which showed an age-dependent decline. Six-month prevalence rate was 21 % for females juveniles incarcerated in the US (Teplin et al. 2002). Ulzen and Hamilton (1998) found ADHD in 18 % of their incarcerated adolescent females. In another group of female juveniles, the prevalence of ADHD as determined by diagnostic interview was 20 % (Myers et al. 1990). Since adult patients, who suffered a trauma with severe physical injuries, also exhibited an increased ADHD prevalence (Kaya et al. 2008), it is likely that this can be extrapolated to adult female offenders, who experienced trauma as outlined above.

3.4.2 Emotion Regulation

Self-reports of anxiety, depression and PTSD suggested that emotional problems occur more often in female inmates than in males (Coolidge et al. 2011). Investigations of emotional behavior indicated that women with APD show increased emotion facilitation (Lorenz and Newman 2002), emotional hyperarousal to affective information associated with poor emotion regulation (e.g. Sargeant et al. 2011), as well as disinhibited reactions to emotionally significant cues (e.g. Sylvers et al. 2010).

However, subjects with APD and psychopathy may also show autonomous hyporeactivity with a decrease of autonomic responding in anticipation of aversive stimuli. For example, some female offenders with psychopathy showed less startle potentiation than controls while viewing unpleasant pictures, indicating a blunted emotional response (Sutton et al. 2002). However, reliable information on the specific emotion-processing deficit in female offenders is still missing (Anton et al. 2012).

In contrast to APD, women with BPD showed affective instability including elevated reactivity of mood and feelings of emptiness. Psychophysiological findings in BPD indicated affective hyperarousal to emotional stimuli (e.g. Ebner et al. 2007) or more frequent and prolonged states of aversive internal tension (e.g. Stiglmayr et al. 2001). Women with BPD, who repeatedly committed self-injurious acts, also showed analgesia and reduced pain perception (Schmahl et al. 2006). These findings are likely to be generalizable to forensic populations with BPD.

Deficient responding to emotional distress cues also affects empathetic emotions. Although many antisocial offenders possess the potential to infer mental states in others (thoughts, feelings, beliefs, knowledge, and intentions), they might not be able to empathize (Blair et al. 2005). Empathy is a multi-component function involving perspective taking, imagination, empathic concern and personal distress (e.g. Davis 1983). In contrast, developing a "theory of mind" of another person is a cognitive function, as it is not necessary to become emotionally involved (Singer and Lamm 2009): it serves to predict and explain the behavior of others.

The ability to anticipate and experience how another person feels, what it feels like for another person to experience a certain emotion has been increasingly investigated in recent years. However, gender differences in offenders are not yet well understood. It could be hypothesized that male offenders with psychopathic traits may show fundamental problems in emotional empathy, whereas female offenders with traumatic experiences predominantly have intact empathetic functions but fail to focus attention to distress cues (see also Sect. 3.1).

The presence of previous traumatic experiences has been used to distinguish a secondary from a primary subtype of psychopathy in male offenders (Porter 1996). Although secondary psychopaths show the same antisocial behaviors as the primary subgroup, this behavior results from traumatic experiences (Blackburn et al. 2008). Secondary psychopathy may thus show a high level of anxiety and stress susceptibility (e.g. Fowles and Dindo 2006). Taken together, it can be hypothesized that female offenders are more likely to entail a larger proportion of the secondary subtype showing a greater level of impulsivity, as well as states of strong activation or dissociation during aversive events.

3.4.3 Neurobiological Correlates

The mechanisms underlying gender-specific neurocognitive differences in delinquent samples are poorly understood. Thus, we draw upon the general literature to discuss some of the neural underpinnings of action and behavior control. General factors that favor antisocial behavior have been mentioned above (see Fishbein 2003 for a review): alterations of cognitive executive functioning such as poor behavioral inhibition, dysfunctional decision making and goal-oriented behavior, poor social behavior adaptation, and reduced sensitivity to behavioral consequences.

Neuroscience research has focused on the processing of reward, punishment and other types of adaptively relevant processes that rest upon elementary component functions such as the registration and monitoring of aversive and appetitive stimulus qualities, maintenance of motivationally relevant information, shifting of contingencies, and inhibition or reversal of inappropriate responses (e.g. Blair 2001, 2004). These basic "executive emotions" appear to be implemented as specific hardwired mechanisms of the ventral and medial prefrontal cortex interacting with limbic brain structures (Blair 2001; Peper 2009).

The associated mechanisms have been conceptualized by comprehensive neuropsychological models, the most elaborated being the Reinforcement Sensitivity Theory framework (RST; e.g. Gray and McNaughton 2000; Wallace and Newman

2008). The constructs suggested by RST have been used to explain antisocial and psychopathic behavior for several decades (e.g. Newman et al. 2005). According to the RST model, the type and degree of antisocial disorders are reflected by reactions of the subjects to punishment, reward, and conflict (see Peper and Chavanon 2011 for a review).

RST explains these personality traits in terms of differential sensitivities within three behavioral systems that are associated with reward processing (*Behavioral Approach System,* BAS), punishment or conflict processing (*Behavioral Inhibition System,* BIS), and fight, flight, or freezing reactions (*Fight Flight Freezing System*, FFFS). Typically, offenders maximize the amount of obtained reward (i.e. BAS hyperactivity) regardless of negative or conflictual signals (i.e. BIS hyporesponding). As the BAS responds to all appetitive stimuli and generates positive emotions (cf. McNaughton and Corr 2008), it is also likely to control behavior in female offenders stimulating a high degree of reward-orientation, impulsiveness, as well as addictive and high-risk behaviors.

A poor BIS could be responsible for a reduced detection and resolution of conflicts between concurrent goals; this is also associated with low anxiety and poor inhibition of ongoing behaviors. Poor processing resources to resolve motivational conflicts and to evaluate risks and errors may result in fearlessness and hazardous life styles that are also predictive of delinquency (see Eisenbarth et al. 2012).

Reduced pain perception in BPD was found to be associated with a reduced activity in the anterior ACC and amygdala and an increased activity in the dorsolateral PFC as compared to controls (Schmahl et al. 2006). If this applies to female offenders with BPD, the BIS and FFFS activity would be lower in this subgroup, that is, punishing interventions are less likely to modify behavior due to the poor sensitivity of these systems (Peper and Chavanon 2011).

Moreover, as summarized above, executive and cognitive functioning including the control of emotions are modulated by hormonal influences. Hormones not only have permanent structural effects on the developing nervous system but also modulate the substrates of the above systems such as the prefrontal cortex, hippocampus, amygdala, and hypothalamus. Dysexecutive problems in women with ADHD have been attributed to fluctuations of sex hormone levels (Frey and Dias 2014). Moreover, the cognitive control of emotion is modulated depending on between- and within-subject variations of hormone levels in women (e.g. Haimov-Kochman and Berger 2014; Sacher et al. 2013). Although this is still poorly understood, it is likely that these findings also apply to female prison populations.

4 A Biopsychosocial Model of Female Delinquency

Criminological research has been working since decades on the problem of how multifactor models of criminality can be designed in order to integrate biological, psychological, social, and situational/environmental explanations (see Glueck and Glueck 1950; Jeffery 1977, 1990; McCord and McCord 1959; Ross and Hilborn 2008). Although comprehensive models, which offer a more representative perspective on criminal phenomena, are desirable, these attempts have remained incomplete and inconsistent (Agnew 2014; Robinson and Beaver 2008). Possible reasons for this lack of integration may be found in the extremely heterogeneous and partially incompatible nature of methods and constructs that are characteristic for the different domains (Fahrenberg 2013). This issue cannot be resolved here; however, an attempt is made to reconstruct female delinquency in the context of a general multilevel framework.

Divergent anthropological convictions, constructs, and methodologies of current criminological sub-disciplines are not readily reconciled. A core problem is that the criminological and (neuro-) biological concepts that have been summarized herein come from different categories and are defined in the networks of partially incompatible scientific traditions. The unreflected association of incompatible perspectives may even give rise to category errors (Fahrenberg 2013). For example, contemporary forensic MRI research appears to show a propensity for reductionist interpretations and related category errors. The latter refers to the fact that physiological data does not permit us, in principle, to decode the *content* of mental activity as this requires *additional introspective and contextual information.* Although a wealth of structural and functional neurophysiological data is now available—the rules of how these physiological patterns can be allocated to complex mental phenomena and meaning systems remain largely unknown.

In our tentative biopsychosocial model of female delinquency, we first discuss the qualitative aspects that are related to the interpretation of contextual information and the transformation of meaning across hierarchical levels. In a second step, we outline the organismic and more automatic processes that have been conceptualized by neurobiological and genetic research.

4.1 *Multilevel Model*

Above, we have explained delinquent behavior as an emergent phenomenon of information processing in a multi-layer structure of social reality. A meta-model of different, interacting system levels has previously been conceptualized in the CMM framework (e.g. Cronen et al. 1982; Pearce 2007; cf. Sect. 3) and attempts have been made to apply this model to the criminological domain (see Sundarajan and Spano 2004). We have argued above that this extended hierarchical model could be adopted to interpret criminogenic phenomena such as criminogenic beliefs, attitudes, and related behaviors. Here, criminal action is seen as a final product of recurring reflexive processes. It is based on the assumption that the execution of specific acts consolidates higher-level contexts, and, in turn, the same contexts determine lower level processes.

Thus, this interactionist framework suggests that layers of meaning are recursively connected, that is, they are circular and reflexive (Pearce 2007). Moreover, criminal acts are conceived of as determined not only by one specific social context but also by a multiplicity of superordinate contexts (cf. arrows A at the left hand side of Fig. 1). Conversely, individual criminal behaviors may influence these contexts, giving rise to changed relationships with peers or family and, at worst, consolidate as criminogenic attitudes and personality systems (cf. arrows B at right hand side of Fig. 1).

Delinquent action is thus interpreted as an emergent property of meaning systems that are co-constructed by social interaction in the context of relationships and individual life scripts. This multilevel framework is coordinated on the basis of two types of rules that connect and constitute the layers: (a) regulative rules that determine how action has to be adapted so that it is situationally appropriate (arrows A), and, (b) constitutive rules that explain how meaning at one level determines meaning at another level (arrows B) (cf. Cronen et al. 1982).

More specifically, *regulative rules* determine how individuals should act or respond in specific contexts. These context-dependent rules guide present and future action drawing upon memories and expectations of previous events. Obviously, the ability to regulate behavior according to insights into the situational inappropriateness or violation of explicit rules and laws is reduced in many offenders. *Constitutive rules* describe how social information is extracted from events and integrated so that this can be used to interpret future events or social situations. In forensic populations, this type of learning could be deficient or dysfunctional as subjects with social deficits may fail to attribute a different meaning to a given situation (for example, other than hostile) and to adapt their behavior accordingly.

In forensic psychiatry, the biopsychosocial model has traditionally been described as a hierarchically structured multi-dimensional concept of mental disease (Nedopil 2007). Subjective experience and behavioral phenomena that emerge within specific social contexts are interpreted here as an extension and integration of biomedical concepts. Cross-sectional research approaches typically employ heterogeneous and multidisciplinary factors to predict delinquency in terms of a linear combination of relevant parameters. From a developmental perspective, typical trajectories or longitudinal patterns that lead into crime ("pathways to crime") have been studied (see Brennan et al. 2012; Daly 1994).

In contrast, the generalized symbolic interactionist meta-model posits a hierarchy of social contexts with mutually coordinating layers. Here, delinquency is seen as a developmental pattern of (social) interaction that is established through reciprocal processes of communication or, more generally, adverse patterns of information exchange between layers. How can the phenomena of female delinquency be reconstructed in this model?

4.1.1 Diminution of Social Power and Marginalization

The affiliation to social structures and their associated benefits such as higher education or a favorable vocational environment have been described in terms of "social assets" of the individual (Salisbury and Van Voorhis, 2009). Young perpetrators appear to believe that their behavior increases these "assets" by creating a more powerful status or identity (Barry 2006). In female offenders, a reduction of social power is typically associated with delinquent behavior. In particular, a disadvantageous educational or professional situation was directly associated with imprisonment (Salisbury and van Voorhis 2009). In their typology of delinquent developments in women, Brennan and colleagues (2012) described a "socialized subcultural pathway with less victimization and few mental health problems" (p. 1496) differentiating younger, single women and stressed mothers on one hand and older isolated women on the other, all suffering from serious social exclusion.

From an interactionist perspective, social power could be conceived of as a socially constructed category at the level of the pertinent subculture. An interaction hypothesis would suggest that marginalized women suffering from low social power would select deviant behaviors as a means to define their power and consolidate their affiliation at the subculture level. Conversely, their "status" within the subculture would create regulative rules, which determine that certain types of deviant action could be considered appropriate within the specific subcultural context.

4.1.2 Development of Aggressive and Antisocial Life Scripts and Personality Traits

Brennan and coworker (2012) described a cluster of "aggressive antisocial women", who are characterized by an extreme risk of further offenses. This group, which contained about one tenth of their sample of female offenders, showed lifelong sexual and physical abuse, mental health problems and further deficits. Two patterns of interactions appear to be etiologically important: a first involves higher order social contexts as the offender is gradually marginalized and excluded from social networks of society. A second mechanism suggests that a lower layer of social relationships such as an antisocial family situation promotes a development of hostile and antisocial attitudes and scripts at the personality level.

The results of a qualitative case analysis suggested a coordination of the layer of personal scripts and the layer of social relationships (DeHart 2008): A dysfunctional relationship with significant others may foster the transition to delinquency by undermining personal self-esteem: "Their family and social networks often tended more toward perpetration or collusion than positive support. Their role models were often corrupt, and living contexts permeated with poverty, addiction, and violence"(DeHart 2008, p. 23). Thus, in interactionist terms, a negative self-concept may gradually increase the probability of antisocial behaviors, which, in turn, influences the quality of social relationships.

4.1.3 Dysfunctional Interpersonal Relationships

Various situational determinants and social environmental factors have been described that predict female delinquency. A model of Salisbury and Van Voorhis (2009) focused on interpersonal relationships and their influence on victimization and deficits in women. Dysfunctional relationships fostered victimization experiences in adulthood and negatively influenced aspects of the self and of mental health. This corresponds to findings of Daly (1992) indicating that a dysfunctional relationship with violent attacks ("battered women") was associated with delinquent acts. About one quarter of the sample of Brennan and coworkers (2012) contained "battered women", most of whom experienced physical and sexual abuse in conflicted relationships as well as substance abuse. A second subtype included slightly older and childless women with unsafe housing.

These typological findings may be supplemented with qualitative considerations implicated by the interactionist model. For example, the hierarchical model has been applied to augment interpretations of how events of family violence emerge and are re-created through communication at different levels of social systems (Sundarajan and Spano 2004). Domestic violence is seen here as an emergent property constructed through communication resulting in an abusive relationship; continued patterns of adverse interaction might finally lead to delinquent action.

This account suggests that violence could be established in relationships when one of the partners places his or her *personality or self* as the dominant context, whereas the other views the *relationship* as the dominant context. In a gradual process, the partner, who is interested in maintaining the relationship, gives up her or his autonomy to the benefit of the partner, who is interested in maintaining a self-concept of an "important" or "powerful" person. When such episodes become a habit, a pattern of power differences is established that might finally culminate in an abusive relationship and violent acts. As a stable abusive relationship develops, the forces of the adverse pattern begin to supersede all other factors that normally influence the control of action (Sundarajan and Spano 2004).

As summarized above, abusive relationships or similar long-term conflicts are often a context of violent crimes committed by women. A typical aim of the criminal behavior of women is to resolve specific social conflicts of personal needs or expectations in the context of a precarious social relationship. The criminal act or different types of internalizing or auto-aggressive reactions including addictive and self-injurious behaviors can be interpreted as inappropriate strategies of regulation by either ending the problematic relationship or by decreasing its adverse consequences. Thus, elements from the hierarchy of meaning appear to gain the power to overrule other influences that usually control action. Conversely, involvement in conventional relationships and attachment to meaningful persons such as a caregiver or spouse may have resilient effects (cf. Hirschi 1969).

4.1.4 Dysfunctional Regulation Following Traumatic Events

The effects of early experiences of abuse on female delinquency should not be underestimated (Salisbury and van Voorhis 2009). It has been shown that sexual abuse predicts early delinquency (Simpson et al. 2008). A narrative approach of DeHart (2008) showed an association between victimization during childhood and later life and the onset of delinquent activities. Childhood trauma has an indirect effect on delinquency in later life; among the mediating factors there are disorders such as PTSD, depression, anxiety as well as substance abuse. The latter has been interpreted as an attempt of self-medication to downregulate stress symptoms (e.g. Covington 1998; Daly 1992; Hollin and Palmer 2006).

From an interactionist view, trauma is not a sufficient reason for PTSD and delinquency to develop. A traumatic event is an episodic experience that triggers emotional responses as well as reflexive processes and interpretations that make the meanings of that event. Corresponding to the social constructionist idea, the traumatized person uses habitual rules for the interpretation of the event. In the same way as social resources help to cope with the adverse event, however, deficient interpersonal relationships to significant others may contribute to maladaptive processes.

A first interaction hypothesis would suggest that victimized persons tend to victimize others, that is, once multiple events have established an abusive type of relationship, these rules tend to govern future action ("cycle of violence"). A second hypothesis suggests that, as a result of traumatization, persons with low social resources develop antisocial attitudes and scripts, which, in turn, makes a further loss of resources more likely. This process may be seen as a "social loss spiral" that finally leads into delinquency. However, the nature of the reciprocal relation of traumatic events and problematic social-interpersonal developments ("social-interpersonal cascade") is still poorly investigated in delinquent women.

4.1.5 Chronic Substance Abuse

Two offender clusters of Brennan and coworkers (2012) included about one third of their sample and contained primarily drug-offending women of different age groups, who were or were not parenting. Substance use was not comorbid with prior trauma experience. Despite a high social and economic functioning and job readiness, these groups contained a high percentage of single or unmarried women. There is empirical evidence that delinquency associated with drug abuse has a chronic course (Shechory et al. 2011). These "drug-connected women" (Daly 1992) only show low dependency but pursue their delinquency within the context of the family or personal relationships. The nature of these relationships needs to be inspected to evaluate the importance for the maintenance of drug consumption and vice versa.

4.2 Neuropsychological Dysfunction

The coordination of information processing between higher system layers as described above rests upon an intact encoding, consolidation, and maintenance of social information within declarative and episodic memory systems. However, this assumption is not warranted as the functional integrity of neurocognitive and -affective systems that run these processes cannot be assumed in many offender subgroups (see Blair 2001; Peper and Chavanon 2011 for reviews). Indeed, alterations of cognitive executive functions, behavioral inhibition, dysfunctional decision-making and goal-oriented behavior, poor social behavior adaptation and reduced sensitivity to behavioral consequences are relevant factors that promote antisocial behavior (Fishbein 2003).

As summarized above, previous abuse experiences and situations of abandonment may negatively influence emotional memory processes in many female offenders. Furthermore, emotion regulation capacities may be affected, in particular, in subjects with BPD. The RST-framework provides a useful perspective for conceptualizing basic neuropsychological processes in offenders (e.g. Wallace and Newman 2008). RST suggests that it is highly probable that female offenders with a history of trauma experiences have frequent and strong emotional FFFS activations. New situations are likely to be interpreted as a proximal threat and the augmented FFFS thus triggers fight-responses (verbal and nonverbal aggression), and negatively reinforced impulsive behaviors.

The processes involved may also be conceptualized in a model of recursively connected levels of information processing: firstly, a traumatized person implements a pattern of extreme emotional downregulation to cope with previous abuse or adverse experiences (high BIS); secondly, this is used to manage threatening consequences, conflicts or distress cues. However, this also implies a low sensitivity to punishment cues giving rise to reduced inhibitory functioning and impulsive behaviors (see Peper and Chavanon 2011).

Thus, when pursuing a goal, these difficulties to attend to information that indicates, whether response execution was adequate or not, may facilitate inappropriate behaviors. The BIS typically initiates the allocation of attention towards novel or incompatible information that emerges outside the focus of attention. However, if information is not attended (such as cues signaling changes in reinforcement), it cannot be used to adapt or regulate behavior during choice processes or deter from antisocial behavior (cf. Wallace and Newman 2008). Because many offenders do not show deterrence by punishment or appropriate conflict processing, the assumption that this group would be able to make rational decisions in the face of punishment is basically at fault.

Similar as in male offenders, it seems likely that subgroups may show different profiles of behavioral and cognitive alterations associated with unfavorable BIS functioning: some may have a poor attentional capacity, whereas others show low working memory and cognitive control (e.g. Patterson and Newman 1993; Sadeh and Verona 2008). The observations on ADHD and poor executive functioning in females as reported above may also be relevant in this context. Finally, for women with chronic addictive disorders without additional problems (Brennan et al. 2012), the RST predicts a high BAS activity.

4.3 *Neurobiological Individuality*

Recent neurobiological research has added new data sources and explanatory models to the field of female offenders. Individual differences in antisocial behaviors are explained here in terms of variations of brain structure and function (see e.g. Peper 2009; Peper and Chavanon 2011 for reviews). The prefrontal regions, the ACC and related brain regions show structural and functional alterations in many male offenders, which are also likely to occur in female groups. Different types of interactions between the frontal monitoring system and limbic areas have been described depending on personality traits and emotion regulation strategies. This information has been used to define offender subgroups (e.g. Glenn et al. 2013).

A comprehensive neurobiological model in women would have to cover the whole range of genetic, functional, structural and endocrinological findings. However, such a model is currently not in sight. A model of Fishbein (2003) identifies environmental, genetic and prenatal risk factors, which influence the development of neuroanatomical substrates including the prefrontal cortex, limbic structures, connections between PFC and limbic structures, the autonomic nervous system and the endocrine system (HPA axis).

However, neurobiological concepts do not constitute another bottom layer of the current hierarchical model. It represents a parallel and fundamentally different domain of variables indicative of biological individuality. The neurobiological underpinnings that implement intra-individual information processing represents a category of its own and the rules of how this relates to the levels of meaning still remain obscure.

The brain is the organ that produces meaning by providing the mechanisms of perception and action and permits us to construct a meaningful reality from otherwise incoherent situational stimuli. Nevertheless, brain activity does not help us to understand the meaning of individual criminal actions as this requires introspective and contextual information as argued above. The analysis of the coordination and transformation of meaning as described by the current interactionist model requires explicit, that is, introspectively accessible and communicable information.

Beyond levels of meaning, however, the activity of "speechless" brain regions that control emotional and motivational functioning and modulate system states are not or only poorly accessible through introspection. Neurobiological approaches thus provide additional information to better understand the implicit mechanisms that control emotion, motivation and that resolve conflicts between internal needs, expectations and contextual factors. However, it is beyond the scope of this chapter to provide a comprehensive review of all relevant contributions (see Walsh 2002, Walsh and Ellis 2003 for reviews).

4.4 Behavioral and Neurobiological Genetics

A pertinent problem of biopsychosocial criminology is what is "innate" and what is "instilled", that is, how do genetic and environmental influences contribute to variations in antisocial behavior. If personality, social relationships, parenting, and life events are finally accompanied by detectable changes in brain structure and function—what remains "biologically innate"? Is offending behavior ultimately produced by genetic or by environmental factors?

Social science research has focused on the question of how a problematic socialization and antisocial development are influenced by contextual factors such as relationships, parenting, role models and instruction. Our hierarchical model has suggested that multiple environmental contexts give rise to recursive processes and mutual interdependencies of levels during development. However, personality is also a product of multi-genetic influences; research in behavioral genetics has shown that various environmental *and* genetic influences may shape personality phenotypes.

Because a biopsychosocial model cannot ignore the effects of genetic influences and gene-environment interactions (Walsh 2002), we briefly review significant contributions of behavioral and neurobiological genetics below. Since we cannot provide a full account of all assumptions and findings of this field here (see Dick 2011; Plomin et al. 2008 for introductions), we focus on selected results from quantitative and molecular behavioral genetics. An attempt is made to discuss the relevance of this research in the context of female delinquency and to reflect potential implications for the present model.

An extensive behavioral genetics literature investigated the relative contributions of environment and genome to explain the variation of phenotypes defined on the grounds of personality traits, psychopathology, or specific problem behaviors. The multiple data sources of behavioral genetics are highly complex. Figure 2 provides a rough outline of these multilevel data structures and their relationship to the current biopsychosocial model.

Research in behavioral genetics has consistently demonstrated that personality traits are associated with genetic variation (e.g. Goddard et al. 2009; Plomin et al. 2008). Moreover, there is no doubt that the assumption, a single gene would explain variations of a complex behavior, trait or psychopathology, is an oversimplification. It has since been widely accepted that multiple genes interact with environmental influences to produce behavioral tendencies or traits rather than a specific behavioral outcome.

To be effective, the transcription process of specific genes or groups of genes must possess the capability to be selectively activated or deactivated in response to specific environmental signals or physiological challenges. Regulatory regions of

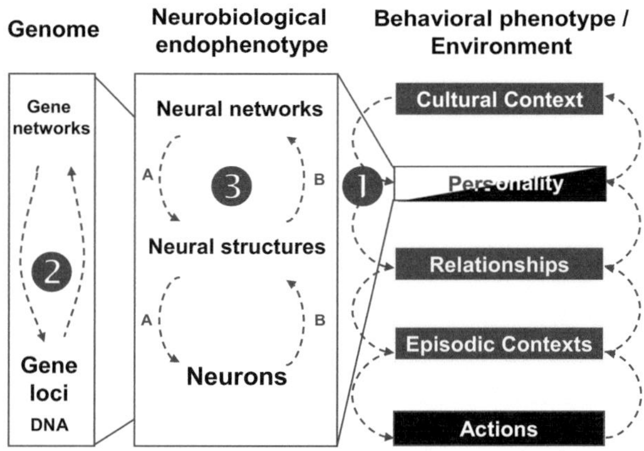

Fig. 2 Overview of data sources of behavioral and neurobiological genetics. *Left column*: genetic data (e.g. gene coding for the serotonin receptor). *Middle column*: neurobiological endophenotypes (e.g. variations of structural and functional connectivity of the prefrontal or anterior cingulate cortex) are constituted by epigenetic rules (A: higher level network activity wires lower level structures in response to environmental input), and genetic rules (B: gene expression at the cellular level gives rise to neurobiological endophenotypes). *Right column*: the personality phenotype is differentiated with respect to a temperament component (e.g. extraversion or impulsiveness) and a life script or personal construct component, which is more influenced by environmental factors. Note that the behavioral phenotype is embedded in multiple environmental contexts (*black boxes*, see Fig. 1). Most relevant research approaches include the following: (1) quantitative behavioral genetics model the variance of personality traits and psychopathology in the context of shared and non-shared environments; (2) molecular genetics estimate the association of individual polymorphisms and behavioral variability; (3) neurobiological and imaging genomics assess associations between selected candidate genes and structural or functional neuro-endophenotypes

the DNA act as activators or repressors of genes and thus change the amount of expressed genes or the temporal-spatial expression pattern. Thus, a first answer to the nature-nurture problem in criminology relates to the fundamental insight that exclusive explanations on the grounds of the genome or the environment are basically at fault; rather, regulation and interaction processes are at the focus: which genes are expressed or activated in which group and under which circumstances?

4.4.1 Quantitative Behavioral Genetics

Quantitative behavioral genetics has traditionally used twin, adoption, and family study approaches to estimate the relative proportion of variance that can be attributed to genetic or environmental sources (e.g. Kim 2009). It is a well-known finding that the heritability coefficient h^2 (which is a comprehensive estimate of additive genetic influences) of criminality measures ranges between 0.30 and 0.40 (Lykken 1995). In contrast, personality traits associated with criminality such as fearlessness, aggressiveness, sensation seeking, or impulsiveness show greater heritabilities (e.g. Plomin et al. 2008; Walsh 2002). For example, the twin method showed mean estimated heritabilities for the five major factors of personality (i.e. openness, conscientiousness, extraversion, agreeableness, and neuroticism) of 0.55, with greater estimates for the two temperament factors of extraversion (0.64) and neuroticism/emotional instability (0.70). Since the adoption method yields lower genetic variance estimates, the coefficient is typically lower for the mean total score (0.30), as well as for extraversion (0.46) and neuroticism (0.14).

Lykken attributed the lower heritability of criminality and greater genetic estimates for extraversion and emotionality instability to the fact that parents may have greater control over behavior than over personality traits. This may be specifically true for females as the behavior of girls is typically much more subject to social control, including a lower number of expansive behaviors than males even though trait levels are similar (see Sect. 3.4). As adolescent males are more likely to become involved with criminal justice authorities, this may increase concordance rates between male twin pairs and reduce h^2 (Walsh 2002). Conversely, however, it may be hypothesized that the lower base rates yield greater additive genetic effects in females. However, multivariate modeling of female and male twin data did not corroborate substantial gender differences of shared environmental and additive genetic influences on externalizing disorders (e.g. Kendler et al. 2003).

Nevertheless, previous research has underlined the importance of gene-environment interactions ($G \times E$) or gene-environment correlations (rGE) as well as of potential gender-specific differences of these interactions. It is a well-known fact that genetic and environmental differences may be correlated as certain genomes occur more frequently or infrequently in certain environments. For instance, a girl might actively select a peer group showing fearless and reckless behaviors as this corresponds to her need for stimulation and sensation seeking (active rGE). The physical education teacher may recognize the robust temperament of the child and place her in a martial arts group (reactive rGE). The girl might grow up with relatives genetically showing a similar temperament, who create a corresponding family environment and parenting style thus adversely affecting the quality of family relationships (passive rGE). Another type of $G \times E$ environment interaction might involve genetic changes due to drug or medication use or lifestyle factors.

Because twin studies possess less power to explain shared environmental influences (Burt 2009), this variance component might have been underestimated. Burt (2009) suggested that the shared environmental mechanisms that contribute to problematic behaviors possess a hierarchical structure. Depending on the level, environmental influences may have different effects on psychopathology: for instance, the subcultural level (e.g. poverty, disadvantageous neighborhood) may have a more general effect on offending behavior, whereas the relationship level (e.g. couple relationship, parent–child relationship etc.) may have more specific effects. We agree with Burt (2009), who suggested to analyze subsets of the hierarchy (e.g. family-level variables) using statistical multilevel modeling. The current biopsychosocial model confirms the usefulness of multilevel models and provides some ideas pertaining to the reciprocal association of environmental contexts (i.e. corresponding to an environment-environment interaction component not yet considered in a quantitative behavioral genetics model of criminality).

4.4.2 Molecular Genetics

Molecular genetics aim at estimating the influence of individual DNA polymorphisms (i.e. interindividual variations of adenine and guanine, cytosine, and thymine in the DNA called Single Nucleotide Polymorphisms, SNPs) on interindividual variability in susceptibility to or protection against a variety of disorders (e.g. Goddard et al. 2009). Thus, molecular genetic prediction studies test for associations between thousands of polymorphisms and a selected number of personality traits. The genetic basis of temperament traits appears to be related to sets of genes, which include at least 10–20 different genes (e.g. Reif and Lesch 2003), some of which will be briefly summarized in the following sections.

We have described personality above as the product of social construction processes shaping cognitive attitudes, plans and life scripts, which are embedded in recursive processes at different contextual levels. In contrast to these facets of personality, which are the product of social construction processes, the level of basic temperament traits is more likely to be influenced by genetic effects. In particular, neurobehavioral indicators of tempertament traits may be candidates for genome-wide association studies rather than the multifaceted, heterogeneous and environment-dependent facets of personality or related disorders (e.g. Reif and Lesch 2003).

An integrated regulation of basic personality and temperament functions requires a fine-grained interaction of neurotransmitter and hormone systems (Montag and Reuter 2014). At the level of the brain, these different but interacting neurotransmitter systems have been seen as the endophenotypic, biological counterpart of personality. An increasing number of studies demonstrated significant associations between the individual neurochemical architecture and interactions of gene polymorphisms. The following examples clarify that aggressive, impulsive and antisocial tendencies can be associated with genetic variation (e.g. Noblett and Coccaro 2005).

The propensity for impulsive and aggressive behaviors has been linked to hypofunction of the serotonergic system (see Seo et al. 2008 for a review). Serotonergic dysfunction, specifically low levels of the serotonin genotype 5-HT2A, was found in offenders (Berggard et al. 2003), and the 5-HT1B receptor has been linked to antisocial behavior and APD (Huang et al. 1999; Lappalainen et al. 1998). Subjects with the short-form allele of the 5-HT transporter gene (5-HTTLPR) polymorphism showed more pronounced anxiety levels (Jacob et al. 2004). The 5-HAT transporter gene was also associated with increased amygdala activation (Caspi et al. 2003; Hariri et al. 2002) and inversely related with a life history measure of aggression (Coccaro et al. 1996).

The serotonin system has inhibitory effects on the dopamine system thus linking impulsivity to dopamine disinhibition, which, in turn, is likely to be associated with increased reward sensitivity (Seo et al. 2008). The findings concerning the polymorphisms of the dopaminergic system show some association with antisocial behavior (e.g. Grigorenko et al. 2010; Guo et al. 2007). The long allele of the dopamine D4 receptor gene D4DR appeared to be positively associated with extraversion and novelty seeking and negatively associated with conscientiousness (Benjamin et al. 1996; Noblett and Coccaro 2005).

In male subjects, the phenotype of impulsive-aggressive behavior tendencies and mental retardation was also associated with a mutation in the monoaminergic neurotransmission (MAO-A) gene (C936T) that has been linked to dysfunctional MAO-A activity (this deficiency leads to increased brain concentrations of NA, 5HT and dopamine; e.g. Brunner et al. 1993). Similarly, the catechol-O-methyltransferase (COMT), which is also involved in the degradation of catecholamines, has been linked to aggression, in particular in patients with schizophrenia (Noblett and Coccaro 2005).

As the quality of interpersonal relations, especially those experienced during childhood, is an important source of (shared) environmental variance, gene x environment interactions are increasingly being explored at the relationship level. For example, an important study of Caspi et al. (2002) showed that maltreatment during childhood interacted with a polymorphism in the promoter region of the MAO-A gene suggesting that previously maltreated (male) subjects with greater MAO-A expression were less likely to develop antisocial problems in adulthood. Thus, the genotype may have moderated the children's sensitivity to adverse social relationships during childhood. Moreover, a significant gene-environment gender effect has been shown for the above 5-HT transporter gene polymorphism, indicating an increased risk of neglect in affected females and an increased risk of abusing marijuana in neglected females (Vaske et al. 2012).

It may also be hypothesized that subjects who show a specific polymorphism of the dopaminergic DRD2 gene might be less likely to profit from socially stimulating environments. This is because subjects with this polymorphism are more likely to show schizoid traits, that is, social detachment with a lack of interest in social relationships and a tendency towards a solitary lifestyle (Noblett and Coccaro 2005).

The level of episodic life events provides a non-shared environmental variance in the first place. However, rare traumatic events may be experienced differently depending on genetic influences. For example, dysfunctional stress regulation under unique adverse conditions in some persons but not in others has been attributed to a differential reactivity of the hypothalamic-pituitary-adrenal (HPA) axis. Several polymorphisms have been associated with HPA axis responsiveness, but those of two corticosteroid receptors (high-affinity mineralocorticoid receptor; lower-affinity glucocorticoid receptor) appear to have a particularly negative effect, as they are associated with suboptimal cortisol secretion after psychological stress involving a subsequently increased vulnerability of the organism (Derijk 2009).

These examples illustrate the complexities of behavioral genetic effects associated with gene-gene interactions such as those controlling serotonergic and dopaminergic neurotransmission, as well as gene-environment interactions. This suggests that predictions at the level of temperament traits could be improved by taking greater account of gene-environment interactions (e.g. Benjamin et al. 2000). Inconsistencies across studies could in part be due to poor modeling of these interaction patterns. Moreover, due to the underrepresentation of female subjects in the investigated samples, some of these genetic findings must be considered difficult in terms of generalizability (e.g. Noblett and Coccaro 2005).

These genome-wide association studies or studies that are restricted to a small number of candidate genes have been subject to further methodological criticism (see Powell and Zietsch 2011). The validity of conclusions is restricted by problems such as inadequate validation procedures or lack of correction for multiple testing. Although previous twin studies have shown a certain genetic basis of personality traits, associations of polymorphisms and personality traits could be more prominent and reliable. Individual polymorphisms showed relatively small effects to be of statistical significance with the available sample sizes (Verweij et al. 2010). Since prediction and genomic profiling studies suffer from low effect sizes, a larger number of polymorphisms with small individual variances would have to be aggregated to detect combined effects.

In addition to traditional behavioral genetics that clarified the various G x E influences on behavior, personality or psychopathology, a growing body of research in the field of neurobiological and neuroimaging genomics has begun to assess associations between candidate genes and structural or functional neuro-endophenotypes (e.g. Hariri et al. 2002; Sweitzer et al. 2012). Given the difficulties to detect truly significant associations between polymorphisms and personality traits, researchers have turned to the identification of associations between genome and structural and functional variables of neural networks (cf. "imaging genetics"; e.g. Sweitzer et al. 2012).

The neural architecture of the brain is based on a common pool of genes that has evolved during phylogeny. For example, social neuroscience has demonstrated that there are innate and hard-wired neurobiological mechanisms for socio-emotional information processing. Interactions with the environment induce adaptive changes of structural and functional connectivity of brain regions during ontogeny. Thus, the degree to which neurocognitive systems are functional at a certain time of life depends on previous gene-environment interactions during development. In other words, neuroplasticity induced by G x E interactions may alter the microstructure, regional brain volume and allocated functional space.

Thus, neurobiological variation cannot be readily attributed to either environmental or genetic influences but needs to be decomposed into a genetic and an environmental component, the latter being stimulated by shared environments (cultural, family context etc.) as well as by non-shared contexts (individual life events, trauma etc.). As neuroimaging data and neurophysiological measures co-vary with behavioral function, successful brain imaging genomics rest upon similar assumptions concerning the reliability and validity of the selected neural measures.

5 Implications for Assessment, Treatment and Prevention

Gender inequalities in offenders and potential implications for forensic assessment and treatment procedures have been internationally recognized (e.g. United Nations Office on Drugs and Crime 2009). Information on gender-specific risk- and need structures and, in particular, reliable information pertaining to the etiology of female delinquency is required to design new assessment, treatment and prevention strategies. In the following, we discuss problems and potential implications for assessment, treatment and prevention and consider some ideas arising from the suggested model.

5.1 Assessment

The assessment of women-specific criminogenic risks and needs and the classification of female offenders according to their risk and need pattern is a central challenge in the context of intervention programs or personalized treatment approaches (e.g. Blanchette 2002). In addition to gender-neutral risk factors, a significant number of factors specific for women have been summarized above, such as social exclusion, poor education, social-interpersonal problems, previous traumatization, as well as specific mental and physical disorders (e.g. Brennan et al. 2012; Hartwell 2001; Hollin and Palmer 2006; Jones Hubbard and Pratt 2002).

Although there is some variation across studies, a common observation is that prevalence rates of psychiatric diagnoses and comorbid substance use disorder are greater in female offenders. Discrepant findings may be due to different degrees of professional training using pertinent diagnostic assessments, to the adequacy of the selected diagnostic instrument as well as to the time point, at which the assessment is performed (Easton et al. 2008). However, these factors do not explain away the different rates of psychiatric and substance disorders between male and female offenders suggesting that an appropriate treatment specific to women is warranted (e.g. Easton et al. 2008).

In a large sample of offenders, Van der Knaap and colleagues (2012) showed that while most risk-assessment procedures for men are also applicable in women, some risk factors had a differential impact: in women, emotional problems were more strongly associated with general recidivism and violent relapse, whereas home and work environment, education and relationships with friends were more salient in men.

However, the detection of risk factors or offender prototypes is not always convincing. If cross-sectional or longitudinal patterns are detected, cross-validation procedures and replications with different offender samples from different institutional contexts and cultural backgrounds are indispensable to confirm the findings. Cluster solutions or prediction models defined on the basis of longitudinal or historical data must be replicated within independent samples. Etiological interpretations of developmental trajectories in women would require different approaches such as quasi-experimental single case designs that take into account personal contextual factors. Because many findings appear to be population- or culture dependent, the generalization of the observed predictions, patterns or pathways remains questionable.

The suggested multilevel biopsychosocial model that includes different layers with variable degrees of data aggregation clarifies some inherent problems that complicate risk assessment and prediction: Firstly, most criminological research focuses on linear predictor-criterion relationships. In contrast, we suggested above that delinquent action is embedded in a system with a "reentrant architecture", in which recursive processes coordinate actions and higher level constructs.

This interactionist framework also has methodological implications. In addition to global risk factors, it emphasizes the role of interaction processes to explain deviant developments. It suggests a multimodal assessment of quantitative *and* qualitative information at different system levels. Subjective representations of pertinent levels or contexts could be analyzed by performing narrative analyses *and* by assessing quantitative data from behavior observation, ratings or interaction analyses etc. The selected variables could be stratified and aggregated according to the suggested hierarchical structure. Moreover, the multiple layers of contextual information and corresponding patterns of situational factors or rules that are perceived in certain institutional settings or contexts could be considered in greater detail.

Secondly, the success of a prediction depends on the symmetry of the predictor relative to the selected outcome variable. Thus, a variable derived from a lower level of the hierarchy is often less reliable and thus less likely to successfully predict a higher-level criterion. Finally, different construct levels of the hierarchy may give rise to different types of category errors, that is, construct systems are partially incompatible or asymmetric with respect to their level of generality. Due to the poor methodological and conceptual compatibility, only subunits of the system are likely to be studied successfully.

The recent attempts to assess (neuro-) biological and/or genetic data that are associated with criminological data ultimately aim at improving clinical risk assessment. However, this remains an intricate endeavor as category errors may occur. The rules of how patterns of brain activity might be used to predict the criminogenic intentions or attitudes of (female) offenders will, in principle, not be decrypted as this requires additional introspective data and higher level contextual information. Many previous brain imaging studies, including those that explored the consequences of trauma, suffer from poor qualitative and quantitative description of the traumatic processes, and social moderator variables making it difficult to disentangle the relationship between the relevant antecedents, concomitants and consequences of these events.

Moreover, the progressive assessment of genomic data has fostered the hope that clinical risk analyses in the public health sector could be improved (Belsky et al. 2013). At present, however, it is uncertain whether this potential improvement in risk assessment would influence medical decision-making in a way to improve treatment outcome. In the forensic setting, many genetic and environmental factors contribute to delinquent behaviors as described above. Associations of genomic data and temperament traits, psychopathology and criminal behavior are highly complex. Even when all the genetic factors would be known, it is unlikely that "diagnosis by genetic testing"would be seriously considered in clinical practice (Belsky et al. 2013).

Genetic influences are obscured by gene-environment interactions and it is unclear whether these interactions occur in a gender-specific manner. Because there is little pertinent research on female offenders, the exact nature and extent of gender-specific genetic effects remain unclear. Given that twin studies yielded relatively small gender differences of additive genetic effects, it seems reasonable to assess the influences of gender-specific contexts to a greater extent.

The assessment of the situational specificity of offending behaviors is associated with methodological problems. For instance, when a problem behavior occurs in one context but not in another, this also depends on the number of informants, that is, whether the disorder or offense has been sufficiently validated (Burt 2009). The specific pattern of prevailing genetic or environmental influences depends on the degree of aggregation across situational contexts; higher estimates of genetic influence are achieved when information is obtained from multiple informants (Burt 2009). Thus, because female offenses occur less frequently and in fewer contexts with fewer informants available, a lower proportion of genetic influences would be expected in women.

Taken together, offending behavior in women is not produced by either environmental or by genetic factors, but the behavioral and neurobiological endophenotypes are a product of lifetime gene-environment interactions. Because the brain wires lower level structures in response to environmental input according to epigenetic rules and, at the same time, cellular mechanisms of gene expression give rise to neuro-endophenotypes, both sources of variation need to be accounted for to disentangle the factors that shape the neurobiological and psychosocial individuality. Thus, in addition to the specific environmental influences that are effective in women, a multimodal assessment of candidate genes, structural or functional neuro-endophenotypes, neuropsychological functioning as well as personality factors would be helpful to capture gender-specific developments.

5.2 *Treatment*

Etiological assumptions concerning delinquent development in women have a direct relevance for the design of appropriate treatment strategies (e.g. Brennan et al. 2012). The necessity to implement gender-sensitive interventions within correctional institutions that focus on the specific needs of women during or after the time of imprisonment has been recognized for several years. Several cognitive-behavioral and multifocal programs have been developed (see Van Voorhis 2012): the "Female Offender Treatment and Employment Programme" (California Department of Corrections and Rehabilitations, see www.cdcr.ca.gov), the "Moving On" program (Van Dieten and MacKenna 2001), the "Forever Free" program (e.g. Prendergast et al. 2002), "Helping Woman to Recover and Beyond Trauma" (Covington 2003; 2008), as well as the "Reasoning and Rehabilitation for Girls and Young Women 2" program (Ross et al. 2008).

These programs have been developed in the English-speaking world to better prepare female offenders for a life in freedom (Van Voorhis 2012). Such programs typically convey knowledge pertaining to coping skills, interpersonal and parenting skills, health competence as well as skills related to lifestyle, household and professional matters. As empirical evidence is still scarce, further research is needed to gradually improve and adapt these programs (e.g. Krammer et al. 2014). In the context of these program developments, the current interactionist model might provide some assistance.

As summarized above, female offenders are more likely than male offenders to suffer from mental disorders, which are often the result of domestic violence and sexual abuse. As antisocial attitudes and life scripts are conceived of as constructed through communication acts that occur in the context of adverse social relationships, it is important to design the rehabilitation program in a way that further adverse communication is avoided. The development of a positive self-concept may help decrease the probability of antisocial behaviors. For example, strengthening resources (e.g. through increasing self-confidence, and improving healthy relationship patterns) are important issues of trauma therapy in offenders (Covington 2000).

Moreover, features of the therapeutic context are specifically important to ensure the success of treatment and to avoid dysfunctional methods of emotion regulation associated with previous trauma (Pepi 1998). Social-interpersonal factors are, for example, highly relevant to women with PTSD (Brewin et al. 2000). The program "Seeking Safety" (Najavits 2002) suggests environmental elements signaling safety (e.g. protection from sexual assault and substance use) to foster a mutual, understanding relationship between the participant and the therapist. Similarly, many programs train their staff to recognize vulnerable women, to support them and to report pertinent problems to the health service. Relationship-based individual therapy and milieu therapy are modalities that also focus on the social relationship level.

The majority of women in prison are mothers (Hollin and Palmer 2006). The separation from their children causes a breakdown of family relationships and is associated with feelings of guilt, shame, frustration and depression. The absence of mothers also interferes with the already unstable family situation (Sheehan et al. 2007). The social space after release from prison is particularly important as the mothers return to an unchanged family situation (Chesney-Lind 2004). If re-integration turns out to be difficult, family life remains impaired imposing a continuing source of emotional stress on children and their mothers. Since this appears to contribute to mental disorders and intramural problems as well as postmural probation failure, the intervention also needs to focus on the social relationships at home. Thus, prior to release from prison, preparations must be made to ensure a continuation of health care and support.

Given the high prevalence of chronic substance abuse, forensic programs must also treat the addictive disorder. Women often use drugs to cope with emotional states (Pepi 1998). Due to the common occurrence of substance abuse and delinquency, it has been suggested that the crime rate can be reduced by treating these comorbidities (Covington 2000). In an extension of the "Helping Women to Recover" program (Covington 2000), trauma therapy is applied along with the treatment of the addictive disorder. Treatment for substance abuse should also be tailored to the needs of women (Langan and Pelissier 2001; World Health Organization 2007). The effectiveness of this treatment, however, should be re-examined using objective indicators of substance use to rule out continued use or symptoms associated with withdrawal (e.g. Easton et al. 2008). Because substance abuse appears to be a coping strategy in the face of traumatic experiences and is a frequent comorbidity of PTSD (Najavits et al. 1997), the trauma itself needs to be addressed as well (Lüdecke et al. 2010). The success of a gender-specific intervention has been demonstrated in women with sexual and physical abuse reducing substance use and depression scores (Saxena et al. 2014).

Finally, at the level of neuropsychological functioning, a multitude of intervention and rehabilitation procedures is available to professionally treat the dysexecutive syndrome as well as learning and memory disorders etc. (e.g. Wilson et al. 2003). Given that many neuropsychological problems can be found in inmate populations (e.g. Coolidge et al. 2011), an objective assessment and neuropsychological treatment of these deficits can be recommended to optimize rehabilitation (Peper and Chavanon 2011).

5.3 Prevention

Primary prevention is aimed at risk groups such as marginalized women with low social power, in particular, single mothers or isolated women suffering from serious social exclusion. Addiction prevention, stress management and all kinds of programs directed at improving interpersonal, parenting, household and professional skills are likely to prevent the occurrence of risk factors (e.g. Van Voorhis 2012). *Secondary* prevention programs might be directed at certain groups of PTSD patients or patients with APD/BPD, who were previously legally inconspicuous or children and adolescents, who have a conduct disorder and have contact with drugs to prevent substance abuse. *Tertiary* prevention would aim at vulnerable women at risk following imprisonment and forensic rehabilitation. As many women are detained only for short periods, the continuation of treatment must be organized on time.

The identification of women at risk is complicated by the fact, however, that gender specific criminogenic risk factors are still poorly investigated in women. It has been critically discussed whether procedures for risk identification are gender neutral. A prospective study of gender differences investigated the predictive validity of various risk instruments (Coid et al. 2009). The predictive validity of these instruments showed some gender differences: the PCL-R (Hare 2003) and HCR-20 (*Historical Clinical Risk Management-20*, see Douglas et al. 2013) subscale were associated with new violent offenses in women. However, no predictive power of the HCR-20 was found in a different sample of 80 female offenders (Eisenbarth et al. 2012). Whereas the VRAG predicted violent crimes in women, the PCL-R score and antisocial lifestyle score were predictive of general recidivism. The Level of Service/Case Management Inventory (LSI/CMI), which measures risk and need factors in adolescent and adult offenders also showed a high predictive validity for criminal recidivism both in women and men (Andrews et al. 2012). This may be attributed to the predictive power of the substance abuse factor in women.

A first women-specific instrument is the "Women's Risk/Needs Assessment" (WRNA; Van Voorhis et al. 2008), which comprises both traditional gender neutral as well as women-specific risk factors. The WRNA probation trailer, which was developed to be used in combination with the LSI-R, suggests the following women-specific areas of interest: employment and financial situation, housing safety, anger/hostility, current symptoms of depression, abuse as child or adult, parental stress. In addition to the trailer, there also exists a WRNA stand-alone instrument that includes both gender-neutral as well as women-specific items. Although risk and need instruments help to locate the major risk factors, the mechanisms of how a dysfunctional relationship, for example, is constituted by communicative acts (e.g. Sundarajan and Spano 2004), is not unraveled; this requires additional and more specific analyses.

6 Conclusions

In recent years, the forensic sciences as well as rehabilitation institutions have increasingly focused on gender-specific characteristics of offender populations. International research has highlighted the women-specific features pertaining to etiology, risk characteristics and treatment goals. These findings are not only relevant for designing individual treatment programs, but also for customizing general conditions of detention in women's prisons. The literature on female offenders has provided important insights into individual offenses, disorders, diagnoses, problems as well as (neuro-) biological and genetic correlates that have improved our understanding of risks and needs when planning women-specific treatments.

Female offending behavior has been described as the final pathway of diverse developmental patterns. Some of these have been explained by poor social power and marginalization in society. Others focus on the level of antisocial life scripts and aggressive personality traits. Dysfunctional interpersonal relationships, which are the result of adverse social interaction processes, play an important role in many cases of criminal development. Traumatic events may be followed by dysfunctional regulation processes at several system levels, constituting thus another important pathway into crime. Finally, substance abuse and neuropsychological dysfunction are more closely related to basic information processing deficits associated with the neurobiological and genetic individuality of the offender.

Gender differences in offenders need to be further investigated and this information should be mapped onto a comprehensive etiological model to better justify decisions in the context of risk assessment and treatment planning. A more representative model of female delinquency is necessarily a multidisciplinary model. Although a unitary biopsychosocial model still appears out of criminological reach, the hierarchical model suggested above may at least clarify some basic issues such as layers of organization, reciprocal processes and mutual interdependencies of levels. According to this, a diversity of environmental mechanisms contribute to problematic behaviors: depending on the hierarchical level, environmental influences may be more general (e.g. subculture, poverty) or more specific (e.g. couple or parent–child relationships).

Forensic psychotherapy typically aims at transforming meaning systems of offenders. The presented model reaffirms the fact that there are multiple contexts that need to be scrutinized with the aim of improving interaction and communication. The model also suggests that the symbolic-interactive transformations of meaning within and between contexts of (sub-) culture, relationships and personal life scripts could finally be reconciled with research on the more "speechless" and automatic processes that control action and behavior at the level of neurobiological functioning.

However, the suggested hierarchical meta-model also identifies a series of problems concerning the multidisciplinary science of criminology. The above considerations clarify that the layers are associated with different scientific stances characterized by divergent anthropological views and methodological traditions. A specific problem is associated with overly simplistic reductionisms, that is, explanations that explicate "molar" phenomena with reference to "molecular" phenomena. These reductionisms run the risk of committing serious category errors. Statistical issues associated with data aggregation and reliability in a hierarchical multilevel model have important implications not discussed in detail here. Thus, a biopsychosocial model implies several unsolved conceptual and methodological incompatibilities of the forensic sciences.

Hopefully, the hierarchical meta-model may help to clarify some of the problems associated with female delinquency and to stimulate new solutions in the fields of criminological research, forensic assessment as well as rehabilitation programs. Although it still remains uncertain as to how concepts from different criminological disciplines translate to one another, some integration attempts appear to be successful. An example at the micro-level is the reinforcement sensitivity theory as this associates neurobiological and neuropsychological constructs with specific personality traits and functions that have a predictive value in the criminological domain.

Five Questions

1. To explain female offending behavior, multiple system levels and contexts must be considered. As criminology refers to subsets of these phenomena, how can research results pertaining to (neuro-) biological and genetic individuality be integrated in such a way that a more comprehensive and gender-sensitive etiological model of offending behavior in women can be established? How would new research approaches have to be designed to define and assess critical patterns of transformations of information within and between the levels or contexts of (sub-) culture, relationships, personal life scripts, and neuropsychological functioning?
2. What are the options for forensic treatment programs if a greater focus is to be placed on systemic interaction and communication processes? What types of diagnostic and intervention methods are useful to influence critical interaction patterns and to modify the meaning system of offenders?
3. If neuroscience and behavioral genetics provide additional information, how may this improve our understanding of the intrapersonal mechanisms that control criminal action? In particular, it might be of interest how learning, emotion, motivation and conflict resolution improve as a function of gene-environment interaction. How may neuroscience findings affect the design of new treatment programs?
4. The identification of women at risk is important for preventive and rehabilitation purposes. As criminogenic risk factors are still poorly investigated in women, new risk and need instruments have been introduced. What is their additional value and how will these instruments have to be adapted for use in different countries?
5. Taking into account the critical patterns of episodes, interactions and relationships, what are potential implications for the general conditions of detention of women to avoid further trauma and to support rehabilitation?

Acknowledgements This chapter was written while the first author was supported by the Forensic Psychiatry Service, University of Bern, Switzerland. I thank the editors for helpful suggestions as well as K. Lenz, who supported the final language editing.

References

Agnew, R. (2014). *Toward an unified criminology: Integrating assumptions about crime, people, and society*. New York, NY: New York University Press.

Aluja, A., Garcia, L. F., Blanch, A., De Lorenzo, D., & Fibla, J. (2009). Impulsive-disinhibited personality and serotonin transporter gene polymorphisms:association study in an inmate's sample. *Journal of Psychiatric Research, 43*, 906–914.

Andrews, D. A., Guzzo, L., Raynor, P., Rowe, R. C., Rettinger, L. J., & Brews, A. (2012). Are the major risk/needs factors predictive of both female and male reoffending? A test with the eight domains of the level of service/case management inventory. *International Journal of Offender Therapy and Comparative Criminology, 56*, 113–133.

Anton, M. E., Baskin-Sommers, A. R., Vitale, J. E., Curtin, J. J., & Newman, J. P. (2012). Differential effects of psychopathy and antisocial personality disorder symptoms on cognitive and fear processing in female offenders. *Cognitive, Affective, & Behavioral Neuroscience, 12*, 761–776.

Baglivio, M. T., Jackowski, K., Greenwald, M. A., & Howell, J. C. (2014). Serious, violent, and chronic juvenile offenders. *Criminology & Public Policy, 13*, 83–116.

Barry, M. (2006). *Youth offending in transition: The search for social recognition*. Abingdon: Routledge.

Belsky, D. W., Moffitt, T. E., & Caspi, A. (2013). Genetics in population health science: Strategies and opportunities. *American Journal of Public Health, 103*, S73–S83.

Benjamin, J., Li, L., Patterson, C., Greenberg, B. D., Murphy, D. L., & Hamer, D. H. (1996). Population and familial association between the D4 dopamine receptor gene and measures of Novelty Seeking. *Nature Genetics, 12*, 81–84.

Benjamin, J., Osher, Y., Kotler, M., Gritsenko, I., Nemanov, L., Belmaker, R. H., et al. (2000). Association between tridimensional personality questionnaire (TPQ) traits and three functional polymorphisms: Dopamine receptor D4 (DRD4), serotonin transporter promoter region (5-HTTLPR) and catechol O-methyltransferase (COMT). *Molecular Psychiatry, 5*, 96–100.

Berggard, C., Damberg, M., Longato-Stadler, E., Hallman, J., Oreland, L., & Garpenstrand, H. (2003). The serotonin 2A–1438 G/A receptor polymorphism in a group of Swedish male criminals. *Neuroscience Letters, 347*, 196–198.

Blackburn, R., Logan, C., Donnelly, J., & Renwick, S. J. D. (2008). Identifying psychopathic subtypes: Combining an empirical personality classification of offenders with the Psychopathy Checklist-Revised. *Journal of Personality Disorders, 22*, 604–622.

Blair, R. J., Mitchell, D. G., & Blair, K. (2005). *The psychopath: Emotion and the brain*. Oxford, England: Blackwell Publishing.

Blair, R. J. (2001). Neurocognitive models of aggression, the antisocial personality disorders, and psychopathy. *Journal of Neurology, Neurosurgery, and Psychiatry, 71*, 727–731.

Blair, R. J. (2003). Neurobiological basis of psychopathy. *The British Journal of Psychiatry, 182*, 5–7.

Blair, R. J. (2004). The roles of orbital frontal cortex in the modulation of antisocial behavior. *Brain and Cognition, 55*, 198–208.

Blanchette, K. (2002). Classifying female offenders for effective intervention: Application of the case-based principles of risk and needs. *Forum on Correctional Research, 14*, 31–35.

Bloom, B., Owen, B., & Covington, S. (2004). Women offenders and the gendered effects of public policy. *Review of Policy Research, 21*, 31–48.

Bremner, J. D., RandalI, P. R., Vermetten, E., Staib, L., Bronen, R. A., Mazure, C., et al. (1997). Magnetic resonance imaging-based measurement of hippocampal volume in posttraumatic stress disorder related to childhood physical and sexual abuse -a preliminary repalt. *Biological Psychiatry, 41*, 23–32.

Bremner, J. D., Randall, P. R., Scott, T. M., Bronen, R. A., Seibyl, J. P., Southwick, S. M., et al. (1995). MRI-based measurement of hippocampal volume in patients with combat-related posttraumatic stress disorder. *The American Journal of Psychiatry, 152*, 973–981.

Brennan, T., Breitenbach, M., Dietrich, W., Salisbury, E. J., & van Voorhis, P. (2012). Women's pathway to serious and habitual crime. *Criminal Justice and Behaviour, 39*, 1481–1508.

Brewin, C. R., Andrews, B., & Valentine, J. D. (2000). Meta-analysis of risk factors of posttraumatic stress disorder in trauma-exposed adults. *Journal of Consulting and Clinical Psychology, 68*, 748–766.

Browne, A., Miller, B., & Maguin, E. (1999). Prevalence and severity of lifetime physical and sexual victimization among incarcerated women. *International Journal of Law and Psychiatry, 22*, 301–322.

Brunner, H. G., Nelen, M., Breakefield, X. O., Ropers, H. H., & van Oost, B. A. (1993). Abnormal behavior associated with a point mutation in the structural gene for monoamine oxidase A. *Science, 262*, 578–580.

Burt, S. A. (2009). Rethinking environmental contributions to child and adolescent psychopathology: A meta-analysis of shared environmental influences. *Psychological Bulletin, 135*, 608–637.

Butler, T., & Allnutt, S. (2003). *Mental illness among New South Wales' prisoners*. Matraville, New South Wales: NSW Corrections Health Service.

Caspi, A., McClay, J., Moffitt, T. E., Mill, J., Martin, J., Craig, I. W., et al. (2002). Role of genotype in the cycle of violence in maltreated children. *Science, 297*, 851–854.

Caspi, A., Sugden, K., Moffitt, T. E., Taylor, A., Craig, I. W., Harrington, H., et al. (2003). Influence of life stress on depression: Moderation by a polymorphism in the 5-HTT gene. *Science, 5631*, 386–389.

Cauffman, E., Feldman, S., & Watherman, J. (1998). Posttraumatic stress disorder among female juvenile offenders. *Journal of the American Academy of Child and Adolescent Psychiatry, 37*, 1209–1216.

Chesney-Lind, M. (2004). *The female offender: Girls, women and crime (2nd ed)*. Thousand Oaks, CA: Sage Publications.

Cloitre, M., Stolbach, B. C., Herman, J. L., Kolk, B. V. D., Pynoos, R., Wang, J., et al. (2009). A developmental approach to complex PTSD: Childhood and adult cumulative trauma as predictors of symptom complexity. *Journal of Traumatic Stress, 22*, 399–408.

Coccaro, E. F., Kavoussi, R. J., & Sheline, Y. I. (1996). Impulsive aggression in personality disorder correlates with tritiated paroxetine binding in the platelet. *Archives of General Psychiatry, 53*, 531–536.

Coid, J., Yang, M., Ullrich, S., Zhang, T., Sizmur, S., & Roberts, C. (2009). Gender differences in structured risk assessment: Comparing the accuracy of five instruments. *Journal of Consulting and Clinical Psychology, 77*, 337–348.

Collaer, M. L., & Hines, M. (1995). Human behavioral sex differences: A role for gonadal hormones during early development? *Psychological Bulletin, 118*, 55–107.

Coolidge, F. L., Marle, P. D., Van Horn, S. A., & Segal, D. L. (2011). Clinical syndromes, personality disorders, and neurocognitive differences in male and female inmates. *Behavioral Sciences & the Law, 29*, 741–751.

Covington, S. (1998). Women in prison: Approaches in the treatment of our most invisible population. *Women and Therapy Journal, 21*, 141–155.

Covington, S. (2000). Creating gender-specific treatment for substance-abusing women and girls in community correctional settings. In M. McMahon (Ed.), *Assessment to assistance: Programs for women in community corrections* (pp. 171–233). Latham, MD: American Correctional Association.

Covington, S. (2003). *Beyond trauma: A healing journey for women*. Center City, MN: Change Companies.

Covington, S. (2008). *Helping woman to recover: A program for treating substance abuse. Facilitator's guide, revised edition for use in the criminal justice system*. San Francisco, CA: Jossey-Bass.

Cronen, V., Johnson, K., & Lannaman, J. (1982). Paradoxes, double binds and reflexive loops: An alternative theoretical perspective. *Family Process, 21*, 91–112.

Daly, K. (1992). Women's pathways to felony court: Feminist theories of lawbreaking and problems of representation. *Review of Law and Women's Studies, 11*, 10–52.

Daly, K. (1994). *Gender, crime, and punishment*. New Haven, CT: Yale University Press.

Daoust, S., Loper, A., Magaletta, P., & Diamond, P. (2006). Neuropsychological dysfunction and aggression among female federal inmates. *Psychological Services, 3*, 88–96.

Davidson, R. J., Putnam, K. M., & Larson, C. L. (2000). Dysfunction in the neural circuitry of emotional regulation: A possible prelude to violence. *Science, 289*, 591–594.

Davis, M. H. (1983). Measuring individual differences in empathy: Evidence for a multidimensional approach. *Journal of Personality and Social Psychology, 44*, 113–126.
DeHart, D. D. (2008). Pathways to prison: Impact of victimization in the lives of incarcerated women. *Violence Against Women, 14*, 1362–1381.
Derijk, R. H. (2009). Single nucleotide polymorphisms related to HPA axis reactivity. *Neuroimmunomodulation, 16*, 340–352.
Dick, D. M. (2011). An interdisciplinary approach to studying gene-environment interactions: From twin studies to gene identification and back. *Research in Human Development, 8*, 211–226.
Dittmann, V., & Ermer, A. (2002). *Multifaktorielle Bedingungen delinquenten Verhaltens. Diagnostik und Therapie psychischer Störungen* (pp. 1047–1077). Stuttgart: Kohlhammer.
Donegan, N. H., Sanislow, C. A., Blumberg, H. P., Fulbright, R. K., Lacadie, C., Skudlarski, P., et al. (2013). Amygdala hyperreactivity in borderline personality disorder: Implications for emotional dysregulation. *Biological Psychiatry, 54*, 1284–1293.
Douglas, K. S., Hart, S. D., Webster, C. D., & Belfrage, H. (2013). *HCR-20V3: Assessing risk of violence, user guide*. Burnaby, Canada: Mental Health, Law, and Policy Institute, Simon Fraser University.
Driessen, M., Beblo, T., Martens, M., Piefke, M., Rullkoetter, N., Silva-Saavedra, A., et al. (2004). Posttraumatic stress disorder and fMRI activation patterns of traumatic memory in patients with borderline personality disorder. *Biological Psychiatry, 55*, 603–611.
Driessen, M., Herrmann, J., Stahl, K., Zwaan, M., Meier, S., Hill, A., et al. (2000). Magnetic resonance imaging volumes of the hippocampus and the amygdala in women with borderline personality disorder and early traumatization. *Archives of General Psychiatry, 57*, 1115–1122.
Driessen, M., Schroeder, T., Widmann, B., von Schonfeld, C., & Schneider, F. (2006). Childhood trauma, psychiatric disorders, and criminal behavior in prisoners in Germany: A comparative study in incarcerated women and men. *Journal of Clinical Psychiatry, 67*, 1486–1492.
Easton, C. J., Devine, S., Scott, M., & Wupperman, P. (2008). Commentary: Implications for assessment and treatment of addictive and mentally disordered offenders entering prisons. *The Journal of the American Academy of Psychiatry and the Law, 36*, 35–37.
Ebner-Priemer, U. W., Welch, S. S., Grossman, P., Reisch, T., Linehan, M. M., & Bohus, M. (2007). Psychophysiological ambulatory assessment of affective dysregulation in borderline personality disorder. *Psychiatry Research, 150*, 265–275.
Eisenbarth, H. (2014). Psychopathische Persönlichkeit bei Frauen. Diagnostik und experimentelle Befunde im forensischen Setting und in der Arbeitswelt. *Nervenarzt, 85*, 290–297.
Eisenbarth, H., Osterheider, M., Nedopil, N., & Stadtland, C. (2012). Recidivism in female offenders: PCL-R life-style factor and VRAG show predictive validity in a German sample. *Behavioral Sciences and the Law, 30*, 575–584.
Engel, G. L. (1977). The need for a new medical model: A challenge for biomedicine. *Science, 196*, 129–136.
Fahrenberg, J. (2013). Zur Kategorienlehre der Psychologie: Komplementaritätsprinzip, Perspektiven und Perspektiven-Wechsel, ebook psydoksulbuni-saarlandde/volltexte/2013/4723/pdf/Zur_Kategorienlehre_der_Psychologiepdf.
Fazel, S., & Danesh, J. (2002). Serious mental disorder in 23,000 prisoners: A systematic review of 62 surveys. *Lancet, 16*, 545–550.
Finkelhor, D., Shattuck, A., Turner, H. A., & Hamby, S. L. (2014). The lifetime prevalence of child sexual abuse and sexual assault assessed in late adolescence. *Journal of Adolescent Health, 55*, 329–333.
Fishbein, D. (1992). The psychobiology of female aggression. *Criminal Justice and Behaviour, 19*, 99–126.
Fishbein, D. (2003). Neuropsychological and emotional regulatory processes in antisocial behaviour. In A. Walsh & L. Ellis (Eds.), *Biosocial criminology: Challenging environmentalism's supremacy* (pp. 185–208). New York, NY: Nova.

Fowles, D. C., & Dindo, L. (2006). A dual-deficit model of psychopathy. In C. J. Patrick (Ed.), *Handbook of psychopathy* (pp. 14–34). New York: Guilford.

Frey, B. N., & Dias, R. S. (2014). Sex hormones and biomarkers of neuroprotection and neurodegeneration: Implications for female reproductive events in bipolar disorder. *Bipolar Disorders, 16*, 48–57.

Gilbertson, M. W., Shenlon, M. E., Ciszewski, A., Kasai, K., Lasko, N. B., Orr, S. P., et al. (2002). Smaller hippocampal volume predicts pathologic vulnerability to psychological trauma. *Nature Neuroscience, 5*, 1242–1247.

Glenn, A. L., Johnson, A. K., & Raine, A. (2013). Antisocial personality disorder: A current review. *Current Psychiatry Reports, 15*, 427.

Glenn, A. L., & Yang, Y. (2012). The potential role of the striatum in antisocial behavior and psychopathy. *Biological Psychiatry, 72*, 817–822.

Glueck, S., & Glueck, E. T. (1950). *Unraveling juvenile delinquency*. New York, NY: Harvard University Press.

Goddard, M. E., Wray, N. R., Verbyla, K., & Visscher, P. M. (2009). Estimating effects and making predictions from genome-wide marker data. *Statistical Science, 24*, 517–529.

Goff, A., Rose, E., & Rose, S. (2007). Does PTSD occur in sentenced prison populations? A systematic review. *Criminal Behaviour and Mental Health, 17*, 152–162.

Gray, J. A., & McNaughton, N. (2000). *The neuropsychology of anxiety* (2nd ed.). Oxford: New York, NY.

Green, B. L., Miranda, J., & Daroowalla, A. (2005). Trauma exposure, mental health functioning, and program needs of women in jail. *Criminology and Penology, 51*, 133–151.

Gregory, S., Ffytche, D., Simmons, A., Kumari, V., Howard, M., Hodgins, S., et al. (2012). The antisocial brain: Psychopathy matters. *Archives of General Psychiatry, 69*, 962–972.

Grigorenko, E. L., DeYoung, C. G., Eastman, M., Getchell, M., Haeffel, G. J., & Klinteberg, B. A. (2010). Aggressive behavior, related conduct problems, and variation in genes affecting dopamine turnover. *Aggressive Behaviour, 36*, 158–176.

Gunter, T. D., Vaughn, M. G., & Philibert, R. A. (2010). Behavioral genetics in antisocial spectrum disorders and psychopathy: A review of the recent literature. *Behavioral Sciences & the Law, 28*, 148–173.

Guo, G., Roettger, M. E., & Shih, J. C. (2007). Contributions of the DAT1 and DRD2 genes to serious and violent delinquency among adolescents and young adults. *Human Genetics, 121*, 125–136.

Haimov-Kochman, R., & Berger, I. (2014). Cognitive functions of regularly cycling women may differ throughout the month, depending on sex hormone status; a possible explanation to conflicting results of studies of ADHD in females. *Frontiers in Human Neuroscience, 8*, 191. doi:10.103389/fnhum201400191.

Hare, R. D. (2003). *Manual for the revised psychopathy checklist* (2nd ed.). Toronto, ON, Canada: Multi-Health Systems.

Hariri, A. R., Mattay, V. S., Tessitore, A., Kolachana, B., Fera, F., Goldman, D., et al. (2002). Serotonin transporter genetic variation and the response of the human amygdala. *Science, 297*, 400–403.

Hartwell, S. (2001). Female mentally ill offenders and their community reintegration needs: An initial examination. *International Journal of Law and Psychiatry, 24*, 1–11.

Heidt, J., & Wheeldon, J. P. (2014). *Introducing criminological thinking: Maps, theories, and understanding*. Thousand Oaks: Sage.

Henry, B., & Moffitt, T. E. (1997). Neuropsychological and neuroimaging studies of juvenile delinquency and adult criminal behavior. In D. M. Stoff, J. Breiling, & J. D. Maser (Eds.), *Handbook of antisocial behavior* (pp. 280–288). New York, NY: Wiley.

Herpertz, S. C., Dietrich, T. M., Wenning, B., Krings, T., Erberich, S. G., Willmes, K., et al. (2001). Evidence of abnormal amygdala functioning in borderline personality disorder: A functional MRI study. *Biological Psychiatry, 50*, 292–298.

Hirschi, T. (1969). *The causes of delinquency*. Berkley, CA: University of California Press.

Hobfoll, S. E. (1989). Conservation of resources: A new attempt at conceptualizing stress. *American Psychologist, 44*, 513–524.
Hollin, C. R., & Palmer, E. J. (2006). Criminogenic needs and women offenders: A critique of the literature. *Legal and Criminological Psychology, 11*, 179–195.
Huang, Y. Y., Grailhe, R., & Arango, V. (1999). Relationship of psychopathology to the human serotonin 1B genotype and receptor binding kinetics in postmortem brain tissue. *Neuropsychopharmacology, 21*, 238–246.
Iofrida, C., Palumbo, S., & Pellegrini, S. (2014). Molecular genetics and antisocial behavior: Where do we stand? *Experimental Biology and Medicine, 239*, 1514–1523.
Irle, E., Lange, C., & Sachsse, U. (2005). Reduced size and abnormal asymmetry of parietal cortex in women with borderline personality disorder. *Biological Psychiatry, 57*, 173–182.
Irle, E., Lange, C., Sachsse, U., & Weniger, G. (2009). Further evidence that post-traumatic stress disorder but not dissociative disorders are related to amygdala and hippocampal size reduction in trauma-exposed individuals. *Acta Psychiatrica Scandinavica, 119*, 330–331.
Irle, E., Lange, C., Sachsse, U., & Weniger, G. (2013). Neurobiologie komplexer Traumafolgestörungen. In M. Sack, U. Sachsse, & J. Schellong (Eds.), *Komplexe Traumafolgestörungen: Diagnostik und Behandlung von Folgen schwerer Gewalt und Vernachlässigung* (pp. 8–32). Stuttgart: Schattauer.
Jacob, C. P., Strobel, A., & Hohenberger, K. (2004). Association between allelic variation of serotonin transporter function and neuroticism in anxious cluster C personality disorders. *The American Journal of Psychiatry, 161*, 569–572.
Jeffery, C. R. (1977). Criminology: Whither or whither? *Criminology, 15*, 283–286.
Jeffery, C. R. (1990). *Criminology: An interdisciplinary approach*. Englewood Cliffs, NJ: Prentice-Hall.
Jones Hubbard, D., & Pratt, T. C. (2002). A meta-analysis of predictors of delinquency among girls. *Journal of Offender Rehabilitation, 34*, 1–13.
Jordan, B. K., Schlenger, W. E., Fairbank, J. A., & Caddell, J. M. (1996). Prevalence of psychiatric disorders among incarcerated women: II. Convicted felons entering prison. *Archives of General Psychiatry, 53*, 513–519.
Juengling, F. D., Schmahl, C., Hesslinger, B., Ebert, D., Bremner, J. D., Gostomzyk, J., et al. (2003). Positron emission tomography in female patients with borderline personality disorder. *Journal of Psychiatric Research, 37*, 109–115.
Karl, A., Schaefer, M., Malta, L. S., Dörfel, D., Rohleder, N., & Werner, A. (2006). A meta-analysis of structural brain abnormalities in PTSD. *Neuroscience and Biobehavioral Reviews, 30*, 1004–1031.
Kaya, A., Taner, Y., Guclu, B., Taner, E., Kaya, Y., Bahcivan, H. G., et al. (2008). Trauma and adult attention deficit hyperactivity disorder. *Journal of International Medical Research, 36*, 9–16.
Kendler, K. S., Prescott, C. A., Myers, J., & Neale, M. C. (2003). The structure of genetic and environmental risk factors for common psychiatric and substance use disorders in men and women. *Archives of General Psychiatry, 60*, 929–937.
Kiehl, K. A., Smith, A. M., Hare, R. D., Mendrek, A., Forster, B. B., Brink, J., et al. (2001). Limbic abnormalities in affective processing by criminal psychopaths as revealed by functional magnetic resonance imaging. *Biological Psychiatry, 50*, 677–684.
Kim, Y. K. (2009). *Handbook of behavior genetics*. New York: Springer.
Kopp, D., Spitzer, C., Kuwert, P., Barnow, S., Orlob, S., Lüth, H., et al. (2009). Psychische Störungen und Kindheitstraumata bei Strafgefangenen mit antisozialer Persönlichkeitsstörung. *Fortschritte der Neurologie Psychiatrie, 77*, 152–159.
Krammer, S., Simmen-Janevska, K., & Maercker, A. (2013). In Richtung "Komplexe PTBS": Die deutsche Version des Trauma Symptom Inventory (TSI) zur Erfassung komplexer Traumafolgen. *Psychotherapie, Psychosomatik, Medizinische Psychologie, 63*, 318–326.

Krammer, S., Linder, Y., Peper, M., Covington, S., & Klecha, D. (2015). Traumatisierung und psychische Gesundheit bei inhaftierten Frauen in der Schweiz. *Schweizerische Zeitschrift für Kriminologie, 2*, 27–40.

Krammer, S., Peper, M., & Klecha, D. (2014). Wirksamkeit des Programms "Reasoning and Rehabilitation" Revised für inhaftierte Frauen in der Schweiz. *Forensische Psychiatrie, Psychologie, Kriminologie, 9*, 29–37. doi:10.1007/s11757-014-0287-y.

Kraus, A., Esposito, F., Seifritz, E., Di Salle, F., Ruf, M., Valerius, G., et al. (2009). Amygdala deactivation as a neural correlate of pain processing in patients with borderline personality disorder and co-occurrent posttraumatic stress disorder. *Biological Psychiatry, 65*, 819–822.

Kunert, H. J., Herpertz, S., & Saß, H. (2002). Frontale Dysfunktionen als ätiologische Faktoren bei der Borderline-und Antisozialen Persönlichkeitsstörung? In H. Förstl (Ed.), *Frontalhirn: Funktionen und Erkrankungen* (pp. 291–313). Berlin: Springer.

Laakso, M. P., Vaurio, O., Koivisto, E., Savolainen, L., Eronen, M., Aronen, H. J., et al. (2001). Psychopathy and the posterior hippocampus. *Behavioural Brain Research, 118*, 187–193.

Langan, N. P., & Pelissier, B. (2001). Gender differences among prisoners in drug treatment. *Journal of Substance Abuse, 13*, 291–301.

Lappalainen, J., Long, J. C., & Eggert, M. (1998). Linkage of antisocial alcoholism to the serotonin 5-HT1B receptor gene in 2 populations. *Archives of General Psychiatry, 55*, 989–994.

Lewis, C. (2006). Treating incarcerated women: Gender matters. *The Psychiatric Clinics of North America, 29*, 773–789.

Lokuge, S., Frey, B. N., Foster, J. A., Soares, C. N., & Steiner, M. (2010). The rapid effects of estrogen: A mini-review. *Behavioural Pharmacology, 21*, 465–472.

Lorenz, A. R., & Newman, J. P. (2002). Deficient response modulation and emotion processing in low-anxious Caucasian psychopathic offenders: Results from a lexical decision task. *Emotion, 2*, 91–104.

Louth, S. M., Hare, R. D., & Linden, W. (1998). Psychopathy and alexithymia in female offenders. *Canadian Journal of Behavioural Science, 30*, 91–98.

Ludäscher, P., Valerius, G., Stiglmayr, C., Mauchnik, J., Lanius, R. A., Bohus, M., et al. (2010). Pain sensitivity and neural processing during dissociative states in patients with borderline personality disorder with and without comorbid posttraumatic stress disorder: A pilot study. *Journal of Psychiatry & Neuroscience, 35*, 177–184.

Lüdecke, C., Sachsse, U., & Faure, H. (2010). *Sucht -Bindung -Trauma: Psychotherapie von Sucht und Traumafolgen im neurobiologischen Kontext*. Stuttgart: Schattauer.

Lykken, D. (1995). *The antisocial personalities*. Hillsdale, NJ: Lawrence Erlbaum.

Lyoo, I. K., Han, M. H., & Cho, D. Y. (1998). A brain MRI study in subjects with borderline personality disorder. *Journal of Affective Disorders, 50*, 235–243.

MacCoon, D. G., Wallace, J. F., & Newman, J. P. (2004). Self-regulation: Context-appropriate balanced attention. In R. F. Baumeister & K. D. Vohs (Eds.), *Handbook of self-regulation: Research, theory, and applications* (pp. 422–444). New York: Guilford Press.

Maercker, A. (2009). *Posttraumatische Belastungsstörungen* (3rd ed.). Heidelberg: Springer.

Maercker, A., Mohiyeddini, C., Müller, M., Xie, W., Yang, Z. H., & Wang, J. (2009). Traditional versus modern values, self-perceived interpersonal factors, and posttraumatic stress in Chinese and German crime victims. *Psychology and Psychotherapy: Theory, Research and Practice, 82*, 219–232.

Mannuzza, S., Klein, R. G., Bessler, A., Malloy, P., & Lapadula, M. (1998). Adult psychiatric status of hyperactive boys grown up. *The American Journal of Psychiatry, 155*, 493–498.

McCabe, K. M., Lansing, A., Garland, A., & Hough, R. (2002). Gender differences in psychopathology, functional impairment, and familial risk factors among adjudicated delinquents. *Journal of the American Academy of Child and Adolescent Psychiatry, 41*, 860–867.

McCord, W., & McCord, J. (1959). *Origins of crime*. New York, NY: Columbia University Press.

McIvor, G. (2007). The nature of female offending. In R. Sheehan, G. McIvor, & C. Trotter (Eds.), *What works with women offenders* (pp. 1–22). Devon: Willan Publishing.

McNaughton, N., & Corr, P. (2008). Central theories of motivation and emotion. In G. G. Berntson & J. T. Cacioppo (Eds.), *Handbook of neuroscience for the behavioral sciences*. Hoboken, NJ: John Wiley and Sons.
Messina, N. P., Burdon, W. M., & Prendergast, M. L. (2003). Assessing the needs of women in institutional therapeutic communities. *Journal of Offender Rehabilitation, 37*, 89–106.
Messina, N., & Grella, C. (2006). Childhood trauma and women's health outcomes in a California prison population. *American Journal of Public Health, 96*, 1842–1846.
Minzenberg, M. J., Fan, J., New, A. S., Tang, C. Y., & Siever, L. J. (2007). Fronto-limbic dysfunction in response to facial emotion in borderline personality disorder: An event-related fMRI study. *Psychiatry Research, 155*, 231–243.
Moffitt, T. E. (1993). Adolescence-limited and life-course-persistent antisocial behavior: A developmental taxonomy. *Psychology Review, 100*, 674–701.
Moloney, K. P., van den Bergh, B. J., & Moller, L. F. (2009). Women in prison: The central issues of gender characteristics and trauma history. *Public Health, 123*, 426–430.
Montag, C., & Reuter, M. (2014). Disentangling the molecular genetic basis of personality: From monoamines to neuropeptides. *Neuroscience and Biobehavioral Reviews, 43*, 228–239.
Morris, J. A., Jordan, C. L., & Breedlove, S. M. (2004). Sexual differentiation of the vertebrate nervous system. *Nature Neuroscience, 7*, 1034–1039.
Mulder, R. T., Wells, J. E., & Bushnell, J. A. (1994). Antisocial women. *Journal of Personality Disorders, 8*, 279–287.
Müller, J., & Maercker, A. (2006). Disclosure und wahrgenommene gesellschaftliche Wertschätzung als Opfer als Prädiktoren von PTB bei Kriminalitätsopfern. *Zeitschrift für Klinische Psychologie und Psychotherapie, 35*, 49–58.
Myers, W. C., Burket, R. C., Lyles, B., Stone, L., & Kemph, J. P. (1990). DSM-III diagnoses and offenses in committed female juvenile delinquents. *Bulletin of the American Academy of Psychiatry and the Law, 18*, 47–54.
Najavits, L. M. (2002). *Seeking safety: A treatment manual for PSTD and substance abuse*. New York, NY: Guilford Press.
Najavits, L. M., Weiss, R. D., & Shaw, S. R. (1997). The link between substance abuse and posttraumatic stress disorder in women. *American Journal On Addictions, 6*, 273–283.
Nedopil, N. (2007). *Forensische Psychiatrie: Klinik, Begutachtung und Behandlung zwischen Psychiatrie und Recht*. Stuttgart: Thieme.
Newman, J. P., MacCoon, D. G., Vaughn, L. J., & Sadeh, N. (2005). Validating a distinction between primary and secondary psychopathy with measures of Gray's BIS and BAS constructs. *Journal of Abnormal Psychology, 114*, 319–323.
Noblett, K. L., & Coccaro, E. E. (2005). Molecular genetics of personality. *Current Psychiatry Reports, 7*, 73–80.
Odgers, C. L., Burnette, M. L., Chauhan, P., Moretti, M. M., & Dickon Reppucci, N. (2005). Misdiagnosing the problem: Mental health profiles of incarcerated juveniles. *The Canadian Child and Adolescent Psychiatry Review, 14*, 26–29.
O'Doherty, D. C., Chitty, K. M., Saddiqui, S., Bennett, M. R., & Lagopoulos, J. (2015). A systematic review and meta-analysis of magnetic resonance imaging measurement of structural volumes in posttraumatic stress disorder. *Psychiatry Research, 232*, 1–33. doi:10.1016/j.pscychresns.2015.01.002.
Paris, J. (2004). Gender differences in personality traits and disorders. *Current Psychiatry Reports, 6*, 71–74.
Patrick, C. J. (2007). Getting to the heart of psychopathy. In H. Herve & J. C. Yuille (Eds.), *The psychopath: Theory, research, and social implications* (pp. 207–252). Mahwah, NJ: Erlbaum.
Patterson, C. M., & Newman, J. P. (1993). Reflectivity and learning from aversive events: Toward a psychological mechanism for the syndromes of disinhibition. *Psychological Review, 100*, 716–736.
Pearce, W. B. (2007). *Making social worlds: A communication perspective*. Oxford: Blackwell.

Pearce, W. B., & Cronen, V. (1980). *Communication, action, and meaning: The creation of social realities*. New York, NY: Praeger.
Pearce, W. B., & Pearce, K. A. (2000). Extending the theory of coordinated management of meaning (CMM) through a community dialogue process. *Communication Theory, 10*, 405–423.
Peper, M. (2009). Neurobiologische Emotionsmodelle. In G. Stemmler (Ed.), *Enzyklopädie der Psychologie: Themenbereich C Theorie und Forschung, Serie 4, Band 3: Psychologie der Emotion* (pp. 21–79). Göttingen: Hogrefe.
Peper, M., & Chavanon, M. L. (2011). The neuropsychology of punishment. In H. Kury & E. Shea (Eds.), *Punitiveness: International developments* (Vol. 3, pp. 231–290). Bochum: Brockmeyer.
Pepi, C. (1998). Children without childhood: A feminist intervention strategy utilizing systems theory and restorative justice in treating female adolescent offenders. In J. Harden & M. Hill (Eds.), *Breaking the rules: Women in prison and feminist therapy* (pp. 141–145). New York, NY: Haworth.
Plomin, R., McClearn, G. E., DeFries, J. C., & McGuffin, P. (2008). *Behavioral genetics* (5th ed.). New York, NY: Worth Publishers.
Porter, S. (1996). Without conscience or without active conscience? The etiology of psychopathy revisited. *Aggression and Violent Behavior, 1*, 179–189.
Powell, J. E., & Zietsch, B. P. (2011). Predicting sensation seeking from dopamine genes: Use and misuse of genetic prediction. *Psychological Science, 22*, 413–415.
Prendergast, M. L., Hall, E. A., & Wellisch, J. (2002). *Outcome evaluation of the forever free substance abuse treatment program: One year post-release outcomes, NCJ 199685*. Washington, DC: National Institute of Justice, US Department of Justice.
Raine, A., Ishikawa, S. S., Arce, E., Lencz, T., Knuth, K. H., Bihrle, S., et al. (2004). Hippocampal structural asymmetry in unsuccessful psychopaths. *Biological Psychiatry, 55*, 185–191.
Raine, A., Lencz, T., Buhrle, L., LaCasse, L., & Colletti, P. (2000). Reduced prefrontal grey matter volume and reduced autonomic activity in antisocial personality disorder. *Archives of General Psychatry, 57*, 119–127.
Rauch, S. L., Shin, L. M., & Phelps, E. A. (2006). Neurocircuitry models of posttraumatic stress disorder and extinction: Human neuroimaging research - past, present, and future. *Biological Psychiatry, 60*, 376–382.
Rauch, S. L., Shin, L. M., Segal, E., Pitman, R. K., Carson, M. A., McIlilullin, K., et al. (2003). Selectively reduced regional cortical volumes in post-traumatic stress disorder. *Neuroreport, 14*, 913–916.
Reif, A., & Lesch, K. P. (2003). Toward a molecular architecture of personality. *Behavioural Brain Research, 139*, 1–20.
Robinson, M. B., & Beaver, K. M. (2008). *Why crime? An interdisciplinary approach to explaining criminal behavior*. Durham, NC: Carolina Academic Press.
Rocha, N. B., Fonseca, D. A., Marques, A. B., Rocha, S. A., & Hoaken, P. N. (2014). Cognitive function is associated with prison behaviour among women in prison but not with subjective perception of adjustment to prison. *Crime Behaviour Mental Health, 25*, 389–402. doi:10.101002/cbm1937.
Rogstad, J. E., & Rogers, R. (2008). Gender differences in the contributions of emotion to psychopathy and antisocial personality disorder. *Clinical Psychology Review, 28*, 1472–1484.
Rösler, M., Retz, W., Yaqoobi, K., Burg, E., & Retz-Junginger, P. (2009). Attention deficit/hyperactivity disorder in female offenders: Prevalence, psychiatric comorbidity and psychosocial implications. *European Archives of Psychiatry and Clinical Neuroscience, 259*, 98–105.
Ross, R. R., Gailey, Y., Cooper, W., & Hilborn, J. (2008). *Reasoning and rehabilitation 2 for girls and young women: A prosocial competence training program*. Ottawa: Cognitive Centre of Canada.
Ross, R. R., & Hilborn, J. (2008). *Rehabilitating rehabilitation: Neurocriminology for treatment of antisocial behaviour*. Cognitive Centre of Canada: University of Ottawa, Ottawa.

Rossegger, A., Wetli, N., Urbaniok, F., Elbert, T., Cortoni, F., & Endrass, J. (2009). Women convicted for violent offenses: Adverse childhood experiences, low level of education and poor mental health. *BMC Psychiatry, 9*, 1–7.

Rucklidge, J. J., & Tannock, R. (2001). Psychiatric, psychosocial, and cognitive functioning of female adolescents with ADHD. *Journal of the American Academy of Child and Adolescent Psychiatry, 40*, 530–540.

Ruesch, N., Bracht, T., Kreher, B. W., Schnell, S., Glauche, V., Il'yasov, K. A., et al. (2010). Reduced interhemispheric structural connectivity between anterior cingulate cortices in borderline personality disorder. *Psychiatry Research, 181*, 151–154.

Ruesch, N., van Elst, L. T., Ludaescher, P., Wilke, M., Huppertz, H. J., Thiel, T., et al. (2003). A voxel-based morphometric MRI study in female patients with borderline personality disorder. *NeuroImage, 20*, 385–392.

Sacher, J., Okon-Singer, H., & Villringer, A. (2013). Evidence from neuroimaging for the role of the menstrual cycle in the interplay of emotion and cognition. *Frontiers in Human Neuroscience, 7*, 374.

Sadeh, N., & Verona, E. (2008). Psychopathic personality traits associated with abnormal selective attention and impaired cognitive control. *Neuropsychology, 22*, 669–680.

Salisbury, E. J., & van Voorhis, P. (2009). Gendered pathways: A quantitative investigation of women probationers' paths to incarceration. *Criminal Justice and Behavior, 36*, 541–566.

Sapolsky, R. M., Krey, L. C., & McEwen, B. S. (1986). The neuroendocrinology of stress and aging: The glucocorticoid cascade hypothesis. *Endocrinol Reviews, 7*, 284–301.

Sargeant, M. N., Daughters, S. B., Curtin, J. J., Schuster, R., & Lejuez, C. W. (2011). Unique roles of antisocial personality disorder and psychopathic traits in distress tolerance. *Journal of Abnormal Psychology, 120*, 987–992.

Saxena, P., Messina, N. P., & Grella, C. E. (2014). Who benefits from gender-responsive treatment? Accounting for abuse history on longitudinal outcomes for women in prison. *Criminal Justice and Behavior, 41*, 417–432.

Schmahl, C., Bohus, M., Esposito, F., Treede, R. D., Di Salle, F., Greffrath, W., et al. (2006). Neural correlates of antinociception in borderline personality disorder. *Archives of General Psychiatry, 63*, 659–667.

Schmahl, C., & Bremner, J. D. (2006). Neuroimaging in borderline personality disorder. *Journal of Psychiatric Research, 40*, 419–427.

Schmahl, C., Verrnetten, E., Elzinga, B. M., & Bremner, J. D. (2003). Magnetic resonance imaging of hippocampal and amygdala volume in women with childhood abuse and borderline personality disorder. *Psychiatry Research, 122*, 193–198.

Schmahl, C. G., Elzinga, B. M., Vermetten, E., Sanislow, C., McGlashan, T. H., & Bremner, J. D. (2003). Neural correlates of memories of abandonment in women with and without borderline personality disorder. *Biological Psychiatry, 54*, 142–151.

Schmahl, C. G., Vermetten, E., Elzinga, B. M., & Bremner, J. D. (2004). A positron emission tomography study of memories of childhood abuse in borderline personality disorder. *Biological Psychiatry, 55*, 759–765.

Schneider, F., Habel, U., Kessler, C., Posse, S., Grodd, W., & Müller-Gärtner, H. W. (2000). Functional imaging of conditioned aversive emotional responses in antisocial personality disorder. *Neuropsychobiology, 42*, 192–201.

Seo, D., Patrick, C. J., & Kennealy, P. J. (2008). Role of serotonin and dopamine system interactions in the neurobiology of impulsive aggression and its comorbidity with other clinical disorders. *Aggression and Violent Behavior, 13*, 383–395.

Shechory, M., Perry, G., & Addad, M. (2011). Pathways to women's crime: Differences among women convicted of drug, violence and fraud offenses. *Journal of Social Psychology, 151*, 399–416.

Sheehan, R., McIvor, G., & Trotter, C. (2007). *What works with woman offenders*. Devon: Willan Publishing.

Simpson, S. S., Yahner, J. L., & Dugan, L. (2008). Understanding women's pathways to jail: Analysing the lives of incarcerated women. *The Australian and New Zealand Journal of Criminology, 42*, 84–108.

Singer, M. I., Bussey, J., Song, L. Y., & Lunghofer, L. (1995). The psychological issues of women serving time in jail. *Social Work, 40*, 103–113.

Singer, T., & Lamm, C. (2009). The social neuroscience of empathy. *Annals of the New York Academy of Sciences, 1156*, 81–96.

Skogli, E. W., Teicher, M. H., Andersen, P. N., Hovik, K. T., & Oie, M. (2013). ADHD in girls and boys-gender differences in co-existing symptoms and executive function measures. *BMC Psychiatry, 13*, 298.

Soderstrom, H., Hultin, L., Tullberg, M., Wikkelso, C., Ekholm, S., & Forsman, A. (2002). Reduced frontotemporal perfusion in psychopathic personality. *Psychiatry Research, 114*, 81–94.

Soloff, P. H., Meltzer, C. C., Becker, C., Greer, P. J., Kelly, T. M., & Constantine, D. (2003). Impulsivity and prefrontal hypometabolism in borderline personality disorder. *Psychiatry Research, 123*, 153–163.

Soloff, P. H., Meltzer, C. C., Greer, P. J., Constantine, D., & Kelly, T. M. (2000). A fenfluramine-activated FDG-PET study of borderline personality disorder. *Biological Psychiatry, 47*, 540–547.

Stiglmayr, C. E., Shapiro, D. A., Stieglitz, R. D., Limberger, M. F., & Bohus, M. (2001). Experience of aversive tension and dissociation in female patients with borderline personality disorder - a controlled study. *Journal of Psychiatric Research, 35*, 111–118.

Sundarajan, N., & Spano, S. (2004). CMM and the co-construction of domestic violence. *Human Systems, 15*, 45–58.

Sutton, S. K., Vitale, J. E., & Newman, J. P. (2002). Emotion among females with psychopathy during picture perception. *Journal of Abnormal Psychology, 111*, 610–619.

Sweitzer, M. M., Donny, E. C., & Hariri, A. R. (2012). Imaging genetics and the neurobiological basis of individual differences in vulnerability to addiction. *Drug and Alcohol Dependence, 123*(Suppl 1), 59–71.

Sylvers, P., Brennan, P. A., Lilienfeld, S. O., & Alden, S. A. (2010). Gender differences in autonomic indicators of antisocial personality disorder features. *Personality Disorders: Theory, Research and Treatment, 1*, 87–96.

Teplin, L. A., Abram, K. M., & McClelland, G. M. (1996). Prevalence of psychiatric disorders among incarcerated women. *Archives of General Psychiatry, 53*, 505–512.

Teplin, L. A., Abram, K. M., McClelland, G. M., Dulcan, M. K., & Mericle, A. A. (2002). Psychiatric disorders in youth in juvenile detention. *Archives of General Psychiatry, 59*, 1133–1143.

Trube-Becker, E. (1974). *Frauen als Mörder*. München: Goldmann.

Udry, J. R. (1995). Sociology and biology: What biology do sociologists need to know? *Social Forces, 73*, 1276–1278.

Ulzen, T., & Hamilton, H. (1998). The nature and characteristics of psychiatric comorbidity in incarcerated adolescents. *Canadian Journal of Psychiatry, 43*, 57–63.

United Nations Office on Drugs and Crime (UNODC). (2009). *Gesundheit von Frauen im Strafvollzug: Beseitigung von Ungleichheiten zwischen den Geschlechtern im Strafvollzug*. Kopenhagen: WHO.

Van der Knaap, L. M., Alberda, D. L., Oosterveld, P., & Born, M. P. (2012). The predictive validity of criminogenic needs for male and female offenders: Comparing the relative impact of needs in predicting recidivism. *Law and Human Behavior, 36*, 413–422.

Van Dieten, M., & MacKenna, P. (2001). *Moving on facilitator's guide*. Toronto: Orbis Partners.

Van Elst, L. T., Hesslinger, B., Thiel, T., Geiger, E., Haegele, K., Lemieux, L., et al. (2003). Frontolimbic brain abnormalities in patients with borderline personality disorder: A volumetric magnetic resonance imaging study. *Biological Psychiatry, 54*, 163–171.

Van Honk, J., & Schutter, D. J. (2006). Unmasking feigned sanity: A neurobiological model of emotion processing in primary psychopathy. *Cognitive Neuropsychiatry, 11*, 285–306.

Van Voorhis, P. (2012). On behalf of women offenders: Women's place in the science of evidence-based practice. *Criminology and Public Policy, 11*, 111–145.

Van Voorhis, P., Salisbury, E., Wright, E., & Bauman, A. (2008). *Achieving accurate pictures of risk and identifying gender responsive needs: Two new assessments for women offenders*. Cincinnati, OH: University of Cincinnati Center for Criminal Justice Research.

Vaske, J., Newsome, J., & Wright, J. P. (2012). Interaction of serotonin transporter linked polymorphic region and childhood neglect on criminal behavior and substance use for males and females. *Development and Psychopathology, 24*, 181–193.

Veit, R., Flor, H., Erb, M., Hermann, C., Lotze, M., Grodd, W., et al. (2002). Brain circuits involved in emotional learning in antisocial behavior and social phobia in humans. *Neuroscience Letters, 328*, 233–236.

Vermeiren, R. (2003). Psychopathology and delinquency in adolescents: A descriptive and developmental perspective. *Clinical Psychology Review, 23*, 277–318.

Vermetten, E., Schmahl, C., Lindner, S., Loewenstein, R. J., & Bremner, J. D. (2006). Hippocampal and amygdalar volumes in dissociative identity disorder. *The American Journal of Psychiatry, 163*, 630–636.

Verweij, K. J. H., Zietsch, B. P., Medland, S. E., Gordon, S. D., Benyamin, B., & Nyholt, D. R. (2010). A genome-wide association study of Cloninger's temperament scales: Implications for the evolutionary genetics of personality. *Biological Psychology, 85*, 306–317.

Vitale, J. E., Brinkley, C. A., Hiatt, K. D., & Newman, J. P. (2007). Abnormal selective attention in psychopathic female offenders. *Neuropsychology, 21*, 301–312.

Wallace, J. F., & Newman, J. P. (2008). Reinforcement sensitivity theory and psychopathy: Associations between psychopathy and the behavioral activation and inhibition systems. In P. J. Corr (Ed.), *Reinforcement sensitivity theory of personality* (pp. 398–414). Cambridge: Cambridge University Press.

Walsh, A. (2002). *Biosocial criminology: Introduction and integration*. Cincinnati, OH: Anderson Publishing.

Walsh, A., & Ellis, L. (2003). *Biosocial criminology: Challenging environmentalism's supremacy*. New York, NY: Nova.

Warren, J. I., & South, S. C. (2006). Comparing the constructs of antisocial personality disorder and psychopathy in a sample of incarcerated women. *Behavioral Sciences and the Law, 24*, 1–20.

Weniger, G., Lange, C., Sachsse, U., & Irle, E. (2008). Amygdala and hippocampal volumes and cognition in adult survivors of childhood abuse with dissociative disorders. *Acta Psychiatrica Scandinavica, 118*, 281–290.

Weniger, G., Lange, C., Sachsse, U., & Irle, E. (2009). Reduced amygdala and hippocampal size in trauma-exposed women with borderline personality disorder and without posttraumatic stress disorder. *Journal of Psychiatry & Neuroscience, 34*, 383–388.

Whittle, S., Chanen, A. M., Fornito, A., McGorry, P. D., Pantelis, C., & Yücel, M. (2009). Anterior cingulate volume in adolescents with first-presentation borderline personality disorder. *Psychiatry Research, 172*, 155–160.

Widom, C. (1989). Child abuse, neglect and violent criminal behaviour. *Criminology, 27*, 251–271.

Wilson, B., Herbert, C. M., & Shiel, A. (2003). *Behavioural approaches to neuropsychological rehabilitation: Optimising rehabilitation procedures*. New York, NY: Psychology Press.

World Health Organization (2007). Health in prison: A WHO guide to essentials in prison health. WHO Regional Office for Europe. Retrieved from: www.eurowhoint/__data/assets/pdf_file/0009/99018/E90174pdf.

Yang, Y., Raine, A., Lencz, T., Bihrle, S., LaCasse, L., & Colletti, P. (2005). Volume reduction in prefrontal gray matter in unsuccessful criminal psychopaths. *Biological Psychiatry, 57*, 1103–1108.

Yehuda, R., & Biere, L. M. (2007). Transgenerational transmission of cortisol and PTSD risk. *Progress in Brain Research, 167*, 121–135.

Zetzsche, T., Frodl, T., Preuss, U. W., Schmitt, G., Seifert, D., Leinsinger, G., et al. (2006). Amygdala volume and depressive symptoms in patients with borderline personality disorder. *Biological Psychiatry, 60*, 302–310.

Zlotnick, C. (1997). Posttraumatic stress disorder (PTSD), PTSD comorbidity, and childhood abuse among incarcerated women. *Journal of Nervous and Mental Disease, 185*, 761–763.

Zlotnick, C. (1999). Antisocial personality disorder, affect dysregulation and childhood abuse among incarcerated women. *Journal of Personality Disorders, 13*, 90–95.

Criminalizing Women: Global Strategies for Denying Female Victimization

Meda Chesney-Lind and Syeda Tonima Hadi

Abstract Global statistics show that nearly a third of the world's girls and women will be the victims of violence. Women who are victimized have long known that they live in communities that blame them for their injuries due to patriarchal values. Global trends suggest that increasingly this victim blaming is being formally incorporated into law. This chapter explores the women's criminalization of women's victimizations in four areas: the merging of religion and law to criminalize female sexuality and sexual expression; the demonization and sexualization of "enemy" women as a justification for mass rape in wartime; the criminalization of reproductive rights; and the use of courts to punish victims of sexual abuse who run away from their abusers. Through this discussion, the authors suggest that the pattern of criminalizing women and girls' victimization requires both research to document and action to challenge the "legal" abuse of women and enforcement of patriarchal privilege.

1 Introduction

Global statistics on victimization show that nearly a third of the world's girls and women will be the victims of violence against them, often from intimates (World Health Organization [WHO] 2013). Regional estimates show prevalence rates of intimate partner violence and non-partner sexual violence combined ranging from 27.2 to 45.6 %. (Africa 45.6 %, Americas 36.1 %, Eastern Mediterranean 36.4 %, Europe 27.2 %, South-East Asia 40.2 %, Western Pacific 27.9 %) (WHO 2013). WHO pointed out that the variation in the prevalence of violence seen within and between communities, countries and regions, highlights the fact that violence against girls and women is not inevitable, and that it can be prevented. The United Nations General Assembly "Updated Model Strategies and Practical Measures on the Elimination of Violence against Women in the Field of Crime Prevention and Criminal Justice" (UN doc. A/RES/65/228, annex) inscribe in this prevention objective.

M. Chesney-Lind (✉) • S.T. Hadi
University of Hawaii at Manoa, Honolulu, HI, USA
e-mail: meda@hawaii.edu; syedahadi@gmail.com

H. Kury et al. (eds.), *Women and Children as Victims and Offenders: Background, Prevention, Reintegration*, DOI 10.1007/978-3-319-08398-8_23

For this reason, it is vital to explore sources of the global variations in gendered violence. Specifically, there is a need to address the economic and sociocultural factors that foster a culture of violence against women. This also includes the importance of challenging social norms that support male authority and control over women and sanction or condone violence against women; reducing levels of childhood exposures to violence; reforming discriminatory family laws; strengthening women's economic and legal rights; and eliminating gender inequalities in access to formal wage employment and secondary education. (WHO 2013)

Despite mounting evidence of the high prevalence of violence against women, many cultures worldwide tend to blame girls and women for their victimizations (often saying they brought it on themselves):

> In the case of non-partner sexual violence, women are blamed for deviating from accepted social roles, for being in the wrong place, or for wearing the wrong clothes. In the case of partner violence, women are blamed for talking to another man, refusing sexual intercourse, not asking permission from their partner (e.g., for going out, visiting their family), or for not conforming to their role as wives/partners in some other way. (WHO 2013: p. 31)

The centrality of victim blaming is more or less understood in the area of violence against women. What is perhaps less clear is that this victim blaming can be formalized through laws that not only blame but also punish women either for their victimization or fore seeking to escape victimization and their abusers. The mechanisms for criminalizing and punishing women vary across the globe.

Since violence against girls and women is such a vast problem, and the site of such violence is frequently the home, one wonders whether classic theorizing about delinquency and crime applies at all to girls' and women's victimization let alone girls' and women's offending. Recall that much of classic theory and research in criminology was really built upon notions of urban youth subculture, the slum, and the streets—so the field saw its role as basically predicting and explaining public male crime and mostly male victimization (Chesney-Lind 2014).

Since the abuse of such a vast number of girls and women persists, one has to ask hard questions not only of crime researchers but also the system that promises justice and the prevention of victimization—the police, the courts, and the prisons. Certainly, if the goal of criminal justice systems worldwide is safety and the prevention of criminal victimization, it has failed girls and women spectacularly. While there are some encouraging signs globally (Hadi and Chesney-Lind 2014), there is mounting evidence that girls and women cannot count on the criminal justice system to provide them with protection from male violence let alone stay out of the endorsement of male privilege in patriarchy.

Instead, there is evidence globally that many girls and women who start off as victims are often punished as criminals, particularly when they are victimized within the family. In Afghanistan, for example, approximately 600 women and girls are imprisoned for "moral crimes", according to a report by the Human Rights Watch (2012); this represents a 50 % increase in the last year and a half. The report indicated that almost all the girls in juvenile detention and about half of the women in Afghan prisons had been arrested for "moral crimes". These "crimes" usually involved flight from unlawful forced marriage, domestic violence, or alleged relationship outside of marriage where in reality the women had been raped or forced into prostitution.

The Human Rights Watch study (2013) reported that when girls and women went to the police in need of immediate help or protection, they were instead often arrested. Running away from a forced marriage (often to much older men), abusive relationship, physical violence, rape, or forced prostitution should clearly not be criminal acts, but the report documents that police often arrest the women based on complaints filed by their husbands or relatives. Prosecutors routinely ignore evidence that support the women's accounts of their situations and the logic behind their running away or fleeing abuse. Finally, judges often convict solely on the basis of "confessions" given by the women in the absence of their lawyers and "signed" without having been read to the women who cannot read or write. After conviction, women routinely face long prison sentences, in some cases more than 10 years (Human Rights Watch 2013).

One might assume that such blatant judicial involvement in the enforcement of male privilege and female subjugation can only be found in extremely conservative and religious societies like those mentioned above, but that would be incorrect. As noted earlier, the earliest history of the juvenile justice system in the United States clearly shows that this "justice" system was heavily involved in punishing girls for parental defiance and sexual expression. Nor is this a pattern that is clearly relegated to the past. Currently, in the U.S., arrests of girls account for over nearly a third of all arrests of young people (Federal Bureau of Investigation 2012), and many of these girls are being held for a wide range of behaviors that violate parental authority: "running away from home"; being "a person in need of supervision", "a minor in need of supervision", "incorrigible", "beyond control", "truant"; or in need of "care and protection". Although not technically crimes, these offenses can result in a youth's arrest and involvement in the criminal justice system. In 2009 (the last year for which we have complete data on runaway arrests) status offenses account for 15 % of arrests for girls—with the offense of runaway alone accounted for 10 % of girls' offenses. Comparatively, status offenses account for only 9 % of boys' arrest and runway only for 3 % of boy's arrests.

In the chapter, we will explore the practice of criminalizing girls and women for violating or challenging systems of patriarchal control. We will explore four particular examples of this phenomenon:

(a) the blurring of religion and law to criminalize female sexuality;
(b) the demonization and sexualization of "enemy" women as a justification for mass rape in wartime;
(c) the criminalization of reproductive rights;
(d) the use of courts to punish victims of sexual abuse;

We are using these issue areas to try to establish that there is a direct interface between. women's victimizations globally and systems that both punish the victim and avoid punishing the assailants. We also want to sketch out the ways that the criminal justice system is either implicated, circumvented or even complicit in the enforcement of systems of patriarchal privilege.

2 Blurring Religion and Law: A Danger for Girls and Women

Sharia Law gained its prominence in the second half of the twentieth century with the emergence of the question of Palestine, and the rise of Islamist movements, which sought a merging of religion and politics (Hosseini 2010). *Fiqh*[1]-based penal laws were revived in codified form in Libya in 1972, in Pakistan with the enforcement of Hudud Ordinances in 1979, in Iran (1979), Sudan (Penal Code 1983 and Criminal Act 1991), and Yemen (Penal Code 1994). The same has occurred at a provincial level in Kalantan state in Malaysia (Syariah Criminal Code Act 1993), several states in Nigeria (1999–2000), and Aceh Territory in Indonesia (2009). In other cases, such as Afghanistan under the Taliban (mid-1990s to 2001), in Algeria since the rise of the Islamic Salvation Front, and in Somalia for many years, there are reports of the arbitrary application of Islamic penal laws. Hosseini (2010), in his analysis of these trends noted their significance for women:

> They presented the "Islamisation" of law and society as the first step to bring about their vision of a moral and just society, as a remedy for the problems of rising criminality, corruption and 'immorality' that they understood be the consequence of the mixing of sexes. This spoke to the masses, and played on the popular belief among Muslims that Islam is the essence of justice, thus no law that is 'Islamic' could be unjust… Tapping into popular demands for social justice, the Islamist rallying cry of "return to Shari'a" led to regressive gender policies, with devastating consequences for women: compulsory dress codes, gender segregation, and the revival of out-dated patriarchal and tribal models of social relations…the Islamists criminalised – and thus politicised – areas of sexual and moral behaviour that previously had not been the concern of the state, and thus facilitated the enforcement of their authoritarian and patriarchal interpretations of the law. (Hosseini 2010, p. 9)

In Sharia law, there are specific provisions for punishment for crimes such as unlawful sexual intercourse (sex outside of marriage and adultery), wine drinking (sometimes extended to include all alcohol drinking), theft, and highway robbery. The punishment is known as Hadd, which includes: flogging, stoning, amputation, exile, or execution. (Johnson and Vriens 2013). In Iran, for example, sex before marriage is punishable by 100 lashes, but married offenders are sentenced to death by stoning (BBC News Middle East 2010). In May 2006, a criminal court in East Azerbaijan province (Iran) found a 43 year old mother of two, Sakineh Mohammadi Ashtiani, guilty of having had an "illicit relationship" with two men following the

[1] *Fiqh* jurisprudence, literally means "understanding", and denotes the process of human endeavor to discern and extract legal rulings from the sacred texts of Islam, that is, the Qur'an and the Sunna (the Prophet's practice, as related in the hadith, or traditions). (Hosseini 2010).

death of her husband. Despite her denial of the accusation, she was given 99 lashes after being charged and has been in prison since 2006. She was later sentenced to death by stoning. Amidst an international outcry, Ms. Ashtiani's sentence of stoning to death was not carried out by the Iranian Government. However, as of the 2012 report by Amnesty International, Ms. Ashtiani remains imprisoned in north-west Iran apparently still facing a stoning sentence (Amnesty International 2012).[2]

In Pakistan, rape is dealt with the Hudud Ordinances (Plett 2006). These criminalize all sex outside marriage, known as Zina. (Plett 2006; Amnesty International in Asia and Pacific n.d.) However, the Ordinance excludes marital rape from the definition of that offence. The Hudud law puts all the burden of proof on the rape victims, the women who report that they have been raped. The rape survivors are asked to provide proof, which involves producing four male witnesses of the rape. The inability of the survivor to produce four male witnesses will result in the presumption of them committing Zina while the rapists go free. In these cases, women and people of other faiths than Islam cannot be called as witnesses. According to The Human Rights Commission of Pakistan, every two hours woman is raped in Pakistan and every eight hours woman is subjected to gang rape (Amnesty International in Asia and Pacific n.d.; Plett 2006). In such circumstances, a combination of social taboos, discriminatory laws such the Hudud, and victimization at the hands of the police are key reasons in Pakistan that many rapes remain unreported (Amnesty International in Asia and Pacific n.d.).

Although actual instances of stoning, flogging, amputation, or exile as a result of judicial sentences remain rare (or are rarely reported), wherever classical penal laws have been revived, and in whatever form, nearly all those sentenced under Zina laws have been women (Hosseini 2010). In many instances, women have been brought to court on the basis of false accusations by family members or neighbors, or have been punished by non-state actors and communities (Hosseini 2010; Hadi and Chesney-Lind 2014).

While precise statistics are scarce, the UN estimates thousands of women are killed annually in the name of family honor. Reports submitted to the United Nations Commission on Human Rights show that honor killings have occurred in Bangladesh, Great Britain, Brazil, Ecuador, Egypt, India, Israel, Italy, Jordan, Pakistan, Morocco, Sweden, Turkey, and Uganda (Mayell 2002). In countries not submitting reports to the UN, the practice was condoned under the rule of the

[2] In 2010, Ms. Ashtiani appeared in front of a camera for Press TV confessing and recounting how she murdered her husband. Her 22-year-old son played the part of her husband in the broadcast (The Guardian 2011). Human rights campaigners described it as a forced confession, distracting world attention from Iran's legal position against international human rights (The Guardian 2011). Press TV is Iran's English-language state television station and has its main overseas office in London, where many of its programmes are made. People in Iran do not have access to the channel. Opponents of the Iranian regime believe the channel is used for propaganda purposes (The Guardian 2011).

fundamentalist Taliban government in Afghanistan, and has been reported in Iraq and Iran (Mayell 2002).

In Bangladesh, despite the banning of Fatwa, a form of religious sanction issued by informal village councils to resolve local disputes, local authorities can still insist that women be publicly beaten when accused of adultery or having a child out of wedlock (BBC News South Asia 2011). Recent incidents include the public lashing of a 14 year old girl and a 40 year-old woman, both accused of adultery in two different villages of Bangladesh. Both victims died after as a result of the severe injuries caused by their beatings (BBC News South Asia 2011).

In north-eastern Afghanistan a woman was strangled and killed by her mother-in-law for the "crime" of giving birth to a third daughter (Sarwary 2012). The birth of a boy is usually a cause for celebration in Afghanistan, but not so with girl babies, since girls are generally seen as a burden. Sadly, it is not uncommon for women in Afghanistan to be abused if they fail to give birth to boys. Another high profile media story of Aisha in Afghanistan revealed that her nose and ears were cut off—with the approval of a Taliban commander—by her abusive husband as punishment for running away (BBC News South Asia 2010). The 18-year-old was reportedly given away by her family in childhood and was subsequently married to a Taliban fighter. His family abused her, and she ran away but was recaptured and mutilated by her husband (BBC News South Asia 2010).

The events of stoning, flogging, and amputation are penalties prescribed oftentimes to control women's sexuality. However, women are restricted and penalized in many ways for seeking even basic human rights, particularly freedom of movement and access to education. Education is critical in providing a path to a successful and productive future. Yet, under strict Islamic laws, women's movements are restricted in such a way that the right to education is difficult to achieve. In Saudi Arabia, for example, girls' access to education is controlled by making men their guardians and thus giving them the power to say whether or not girls will have access to education (Equality Now 2011). Moreover the Saudi official policy on girls' education reflect extreme gender stereotypes: "The purpose of educating a girl is to bring her up in a proper Islamic way so as to perform her duty in life, be an ideal and successful housewife and a good mother, ready to do things which suit her nature such as teaching, nursing and medical treatment" (Equality Now 2011). Male guardians have the authority to prevent girls from continuing their studies at all levels, including graduate and postgraduate studies. In addition, permission is needed from a male guardian in choosing a field of study. The male guardianship system also imposes restrictions on women who are in educational institutions, as they are often not allowed to leave the premises even in case of illness without a male guardian. In fact, Saudi women report that in many educational institutions female teachers and students are locked in during teaching hours and students are not allowed to leave the premises unless a male guardian or designated driver comes to collect them (Equality Now 2011).

We also have witnessed even more extreme attempts of groups in various parts of the world seeking to prevent girls from being educated. Take the now well-known case of Malala Yousafzai, a 16 year old activist advocating female education in Pakistan, who was shot in her head and nearly killed by the Taliban while on a school bus (BBC 2013). A more recent tactic employed by Pakistani Taliban to stop girls and women from seeking education have been acid attacks. The Taliban throw acid in the girls' faces to scar them for life in hopes this will deter other girls from seeking an education (Khan 2012).[3] There are other extremist Islamic groups, not just the Taliban, one most recently emerging is the Boko Haram in Nigeria. The group caught global attention by their recent abduction of some 200 school girls (BBC News Africa 2014). The term Boko Haram means "Western education is sinful". This group of militants has been engaged in a violent campaign against the Nigerian Government since 2009 and preaches against girls' education. In justifying their recent abduction of the school girls, Boko Haram stated, "the girls should not have been at school and should get married instead" (BBC News Africa 2014).

3 Demonizing Women's Images to Justify Brutal Violence

Whether charged for having an "illegitimate" relationship outside marriage, defying roles assigned to women and girls by societal norms, or denying male guardianship, women have been victimized, criminalized, and hence re-victimized both legally (e.g., with the implementation of "Sharia") as well as through informal community rulings. Often, the means of criminalizing them has been to label them as "bad" (often in reference to their sexuality or assumed sexual behavior) and then institute the punishment. Indeed, once a woman has been labeled as "bad" or "out of control", men do not even need to go through the legal route to punish them. This can often be exemplified in the state of conflict or war.

Throughout the 1994 Rwandan genocide, widespread sexual violence, directed predominantly against Tutsi women, occurred in every prefecture (Nowrojee 2005). Every part of the Rwandan environment was a location for rape, often multiple gang-rapes (Nowrojee 2005). Between 100,000 and 250,000 women were raped during the 3 months of genocide (United Nations 2014). Such a massive number of rape incidents were fueled by a deliberate political effort that justified rape by "demonizing" Tutsi women's images. A Women's Media Center report (2012) stated that the largely Hutu-controlled print media and radio broadcasts helped stir up hatred against Tutsi women, often through the use of cartoons that portrayed women as sex objects (The Women's Media Center 2012). Tutsi women were alleged to be "sexual weapons" that would be used by the Tutsi to weaken and ultimately destroy the Hutu men (The Women's Media Center 2012). Ultimately, the overtly partisan media generated propaganda that fueled sexualized violence in Rwanda perhaps more than in any other conflict.

[3] 'Acid throwing is frequently used as a weapon in Pakistan to punish women for acts that allegedly bring dishonor to the family, or just to enact revenge' (Khan 2012).

In an examination of international justice from the perspective of rape survivors from the Rwandan genocide, United Nation's Research Institute for Social Development (UNRISD) elaborated:

> Women were held individually and in groups as sexual slaves for the purposes of rape. Women were not just raped behind closed doors, they were raped on the streets, at checkpoints, in cultivated plots, in or near government offices, hospitals, churches and other public buildings. They were raped to death using sharp sticks or other objects. Their dead bodies were often left naked and spread-eagled, with nearby pools of blood and semen, in public view. The hate propaganda before and during the genocide fuelled the sexual violence by demonizing Tutsi women's sexuality. . .Sexually subjugating and mutilating Tutsi women was a way to attack the ethnic group and to punish the women. The sexual violence directed at the women during the Rwandan genocide was part of the attack against the Tutsi, which is why the ICTR in its first judgment (Akayesu) ruled that rape was an act of genocide. . .Political, administrative and military leaders at the national and local levels as well as heads of militia directed, encouraged or permitted the killings and sexual violence to further their political goals: the destruction of the Tutsi as a group (Nowrojee 2005, p. 2).

The mass rape of women in Rwanda also had a range of negative health implications for those who survived. Many became HIV positives since men with HIV purposefully raped and infected women; husbands abandoned wives who had been raped; women suffered forced pregnancies and induced abortions on themselves; gonorrhea and syphilis were just a couple of the STDs women suffered as a result of rape (Women's Media Center 2012). The actual incidence of rape was only the beginning of a lifelong punishment for victims. Often the survivors of the mass rape even regretted being alive. Here are the comments of a survivor, who was gang-raped and later witnessed the killing of family members, 10 years after her assault:

> I regret that I didn't die that day. Those men and women who died are now at peace whereas I am still here to suffer even more. I'm handicapped in the true sense of the word. I don't know how to explain it. I regret that I'm alive because I've lost my lust for life. We survivors are broken-hearted. We live in a situation which overwhelms us. Our wounds become deeper every day. We are constantly in mourning (Women's Media Center 2012: 27).

This scenario of demonizing women and punishing them, often with unimaginable brutality, is not unique to the case of Rwandan genocide. Many times warring parties find girls and women easy targets for torture and murder, activities often encouraged and permitted by their political, administrative, and military leaders (though clearly war crimes).

Such trends are evident globally from UN agencies estimates (2014): more than 60,000 women were raped during the civil war in Sierra Leone (1991–2002), more than 40,000 in Liberia (1989–2003), up to 60,000 in the former Yugoslavia (1992–1995), and at least 200,000 in the Democratic Republic of the Congo since 1998 (UN 2014). A more recent/ongoing crisis is the case of Sudan. In March 2003, after decades of tension, fighting erupted in Sudan's western Darfur region between Sudanese government forces and rebel groups such as the Sudanese Liberation Army and the Justice and Equality Movement (Women's Media Center 2014). Over the next few months, tens of thousands of Darfuris fled. Government troops and allied militia forces, called the Janjaweed, attacked villages and internally displaced persons camps, systematically raped women, and murdered whole communities. These patterns of rapes and gang rapes have continued in the later years and have spilled over into neighboring eastern Chad (Stop Rape Now 2009). It has been reported that sexual violence has increased alarmingly during the past 5 years, with repeated cross-border incursions of Janjaweed militias from Sudan, the presence of Chadian rebel groups occasionally clashing with Government forces, and inter-communal fighting of local militias (Stop Rape Now 2009).

For the survivors of gang rape in Sudan, the physical pain is only the beginning of suffering. Often times, rather than killing the women after raping them, many of the rapists purposely keep women alive, marking them with wounds, as a cruel gesture to continue punishing and stigmatizing them as victims of sexual assault. Marking the women ensures that they will not be accepted by their families or considered good enough to marry (Women's Media Center 2014). And horribly, this tactic succeeds since rape survivors are many times rejected by families and community. Some relatives even threaten to kill survivors. A commonly held belief in Sudan that causes further pain to women who had been raped is that unwanted sex cannot make a woman pregnant. So if she becomes pregnant, it was not through rape. In addition, pregnancy outside of marriage is illegal in Darfur, leading to the arrest of women who become pregnant through rape. A report by The Guardian (2014) features the case of a teenager who was raped by seven men in Sudan, now faces possible sentence of death by stoning charged with adultery. The 18-year-old Ethiopian, who is 9 months pregnant, is being held in a police cell and until recently was sleeping on a bare concrete floor without a mattress or suitable food or clothing (The Guardian 2014).

One of the chief problems with gendered violence in wartime is that when there are efforts to address the harms visited upon people, it is the victimization of males rather than females that receives attention. This pattern was clearly seen in the South African situation where the Truth and Reconciliation Commissions tended not to hear from or include much discussion of the victimization of women, particularly the sexual assaults of women. The authors who reviewed the files said that this pattern is explained by a number of factors, including the women's own reticence to discuss their victimizations, the way that the commission itself defined human rights violations, and finally the fact that there remains a culture of violence against women in post-apartheid South Africa (Borer 2013).

In times of conflict, then, rape is a weapon of warring parties. It is a means of punishing the enemy using civilian women's bodies. Ironically, though, existing and tenacious patriarchal values mean that women thus victimized are somehow blamed for their own rapes and further ostracized. In some cultures, this even results in formal, legal criminalization as was seen in Sudan.

4 Criminalizing Women's Right to Reproductive Health

Efforts to criminalize [or re-criminalize] family planning and abortion places the criminal justice system firmly in the center of patriarchal controls on girls and women's behavior, particularly since women's sexual and reproductive health is a matter of grave concern worldwide. The World Health Organization estimates that 19 million unsafe abortions take place every year (Ahman and Shah 2002). Despite the adverse impact on women's health, roughly one-third of the world's women live in countries with strict abortion legislation that do not allow women to opt for abortion under any circumstances or only in extreme cases of rape, incest, or where the woman's health is in serious danger (Mishra 2001). Moreover, whether legal or illegal, induced abortion is usually stigmatized and frequently opposed by political and/or religious groups (Grimes et al. 2006). Today, despite all sorts of medical advances, women worldwide still do not have the power to make their own sexual and reproductive choices without government interference.

Women's right to control their sexuality and reproduction has become an international struggle, with strong opposition emerging from organized religious groups like the Catholic Church and other sexually conservative religions. Maguire (2003) analyzing the case of contraception and abortion in the international arena stated:

> What is not notoriously difficult to say is that religions seriously affect national and international policy on contraception and abortion. The Vatican from its unduly privileged perch in the United Nations along with the 'Catholic' nations, newly allied with conservative Muslim nations, blocked reference to contraception and family planning at the United Nations conference in Rio de Janeiro in 1992. This alliance also disrupted proceedings at the 1994 UN conference in Cairo and impeded any reasonable discussion of abortion. As the then Prime Minister Brundtland of Norway said of the Rio conference: 'States that do not have any population problem — in one particular case, even no births at all [the Vatican]—are doing their best, their utmost, to prevent the world from making sensible decisions regarding family planning' (p. 13).

Maguire (2003) argued, most of the world's religions originated at a time when the global population was 50–450 million people in comparison to 6 billion at the beginning of the second millennium and thus the laws and edicts articulated at that time to guide (control) human behavior is not applicable now.

The control over women's choices on reproductive health is evident globally. In Nepal women are criminalized for attempting abortion, even when their pregnancies are the result of rape or incest. In 1997 a nationwide prison study conducted by CREHPA, an NGO in Nepal, revealed that approximately 20 % of women prisoners were in custody on charges of abortion (Mishra 2001). Moreover, the existing law in Nepal does not draw a clear distinction between abortion and infanticide. Thus, while abortion has a maximum punishment of one and a half years, infanticide can expose a woman to punishment for murder, which includes life imprisonment and confiscation of all her property (Mishra 2001). Often times this gap in law is misused by neighbors and/or family members having designs over the women's property, or those seeking revenge.

In Indonesia Amnesty International's research has highlighted a number of legal provisions, including in the Criminal Code, which restrict access to sexual and reproductive rights or have a chilling effect on the provision of sexual and reproductive health information and services (Schlitt 2011). Specifically, there are concerns that new Pornography Law (No. 44/2008) could be interpreted in a way that would criminalize sex education. One activist told Amnesty International: "If people feel uncomfortable and think I am promoting sex, this can be a problem... it always depends on community leaders... if they are very fundamentalist then there is a high chance [we will be arrested]" (Schlitt 2011).

In 2008, draconian legal provisions came into force in Nicaragua, which criminalizes abortion in all circumstances (Schlitt 2011). The situation is so desperate that the Inter-American Commission on Human Rights had to demand of the Nicaraguan Government to provide medical treatment for a young woman suffering from cancer. She was denied the treatment she needed because the 2008 law criminalizes even unintentional harm to the fetus, a risk that her treatment for cancer entailed (Schlitt 2011).

In India, The Medical Termination of Pregnancy Act (MTP Act) of 1972 allows women access to abortion in a few limited circumstances, but does not see abortion as a right (Mishra 2001). The MTP Act permits termination of pregnancy on the grounds that the continuance of pregnancy involves risk to the life of the woman or of grave injury to her physical and mental health and where substantial risk exists of the child being born with serious physical or mental abnormality. The Act restricts abortions to be only performed at government hospitals and only by their registered medical practitioner. While providing women with the legal option for abortion, the MTP Act grants the decision making power to the government medical personnel, not the women. In Bangladesh, although population control is a major national objective, abortion is still illegal except when the pregnancy results from rape or threatens the life of the mother (Islam 1982). In such cases, the decision to terminate the pregnancy must be made by three licensed medical practitioners, yet again taking away all decision making power from the women.

While restrictive abortion laws or laws criminalizing abortion, poor maternal and reproductive health services, and, social, cultural and religious obstacles appear to be the factors keeping women from taking control over their own bodies, especially in the developing world, one might expect that the situation is better in the developed world where abortion and contraception use has been legalized for decades with decent health care services available. For example, abortion has been legal since 1973 in the U.S. with between 1.2 and 1.4 million abortions taking place annually (Fried 2000). There are virtually no mortality or health complications from abortion. However, Fried (2000) stated, "Activists worldwide have learned that the legalization of abortion is necessary but not sufficient to insure the availability of safe abortion to all women who seek it" (p. 177). Women in prison, young women, women who have been raped, "undocumented" women, and women with few economic resources are often denied abortion services. Federal funding does not cover abortions, except in extreme circumstances like rape, incest, or if the woman's life is in danger (and not every state complies with such exceptions).

Because of constant efforts of anti-choice groups, abortion providers are marginalized within the medical profession, often threatened and physically attacked, and women who have abortions are stigmatized, stereotyped as selfish, or portrayed as hapless victims incapable of making their own decisions (Fried 2000).

Finally, over the past decade, it has gotten much more difficult for women in the United States to access safe and legal abortion services, according to a new study by the Guttmacher Institute (Nash et al. 2014). Much of this is a product of various states enacting abortion restrictions, some so severe that they essentially render abortion unavailable. In 2013, 22 states enacted 70 abortion restrictions. As a result of these sorts of changes the Guttmacher Institute concluded that the proportion of women living in restrictive states went from 31 to 56 %, while the proportion living in supportive states fell from 40 to 31 % over the same period (Nash et al. 2014).

Lastly, the Supreme Court of the United States issued a decision on June 30, 2014 regarding women's access to both contraception and abortion that privileged the religious belief's of the owners of a private, for profit corporation over the ability of their employees to gain access to a range of contraceptive services. In a 5-to-4 vote, they held that the contraceptive mandate in the recently passed Affordable Care Act—which requires employers to provide health insurance coverage for contraception—could not be applied to closely held for-profit corporations with religious objections to some forms of contraception. This means these employers can refuse to pay for contraceptive services for their employees (regardless of their faiths or medical situations) (Horowitz 2014). On the heels of that decision, the court also extended this religious "protection" to a small religious college raising fears that employees in these sorts of institutions could also be denied coverage for contraception. Significantly, all three women justices issued an opinion against this decision (New York Times 2014).

The struggle to establish women's rights to control their sexuality and reproduction, in both the developing and developed world, is far from over. The efforts of anti-choice religious and political groups hinder decades of feminist advocates' efforts to prevent the re-criminalization of contraception and abortion. Despite the statistics revealing thousands of women dying worldwide from abortion complications because safe and legal services were not available to them, national policies, laws, and conservative social and community groups still do not permit women to make healthy life choices. Women's power over their own bodies, in short, is under attack worldwide.

5 Criminalizing Girls' Survival: Girls Pathways to Arrest

For many years, statistics showing large numbers of girls arrested for status offenses were taken to be representative of the different types of male and female delinquency in the United States (and elsewhere in the global north). However, self-report studies of male and female delinquency (which ask school-age youth if they have committed delinquent acts) do not reflect the dramatic differences in misbehavior found in official statistics. Specifically, it appears that girls charged with these noncriminal status offenses have been, and continue to be, significantly overrepresented in court populations (Chesney-Lind and Pasko 2013).

It has long been known that a major reason for the presence of many girls in the juvenile justice system was because their parents insisted on their arrest. After all, who else would report a youth as having "run away" from home? In the early years of the juvenile justice system, parents were the most significant referral source; in Honolulu, for example, nearly half (44 %) of the girls who appeared in court in the 20s and 30s were referred by parents (Chesney-Lind 1971).

The fact that parents are often committed to two standards of adolescent behavior is one explanation for these disparities—one that should not be discounted as a major source of tension even in modern families. Despite expectations to the contrary, gender-specific socialization patterns have not changed very much, and this is especially true for parents' relationships with their daughters (Ianni 1989; Kamler 1999; Katz 1979; Orenstein 2000; Thorne 1993). Even parents who oppose sexism in general feel "uncomfortable tampering with existing traditions" and "do not want to risk their children becoming misfits" (Katz 1979, p. 24). Girls can also clash with their parents around issues of gender identity in families committed to hetero-normative sexuality, a concern that is surfacing in recent research on girls on the streets in the juvenile justice system (Irvine 2010; Schaffner 2006).

Whatever the reason, parental attempts to adhere to and enforce the sexual double standard will continue to be a source of conflict between them and their daughters. Another important explanation for girls' problems with their parents that has received attention only in more recent years is that of physical and sexual abuse. Looking specifically at the problem of childhood sexual abuse, it is increasingly clear that this form of abuse is a particular problem for girls.

Reviewing the limited research on girls' pathways into official delinquency suggests that a focus on life experiences, particularly childhood ones, plays a unique role in girls' risk of offending. Focusing mostly on female offending, the "pathways" research indicates that childhood trauma is a defining feature in the lives of many female offenders, and it is often related to one's likelihood of committing crimes (to name a few: Belknap and Holsinger 2006; Bloom et al. 2002; Gaarder and Belknap 2002; Schaffner 2006; Zahn 2009). Girl offenders are more likely than their male counterparts to come from troubled families and negative peer groups, to have chemically dependent and/or criminally involved parents, and to suffer from sexual, emotional and physical abuse in their homes (Acoca 1998; Giordano 2010; Leve and Chamberlain 2004; Piquero et al. 2005; Riehman et al. 2003). Not surprising then, these volatile relationships and abusive experiences precipitate running away (their escape strategy) and increase exposure to criminal opportunities and further victimization on the streets (Acoca 1998; Brannigan and Brunschot 1997; Chen et al. 2004; Flowers 2001). They also underscore female juvenile offenders' high rates of co-existing mental health and substance abuse disorders (Abram et al. 2008; Bailey and McCloskey 2005; Bloom et al. 2002; Fishbein et al. 2009; Liu 2004; Schaffner 2006).

Indeed, the pathways literature shows a strong connection between sexual abuse and girls' delinquency. Girls are three times more likely than boys to be the victims of child sexual abuse (Sedlak and Broadhurst 1996); such abuse tends to be intra-familial and their sexual victimization tends to last longer and have more serious consequences than stranger abuse (Bergen et al. 2004; Finkelhor 1994; Jacobs 1993). The imposition of adult sexuality on children disrupts their psychosexual development, and among its effects are promiscuity, rebellion, feelings of shame and guilt, and a loss of self-esteem. Once girls reach puberty, they often come to the realization that their experiences are different from those of their peers and begin to withdraw. Many "hold a distorted image of their own bodies", which may "lead them to expect that their worth will only be acknowledged when they permit sexual access" (Boyer and James 1982). Further, the girls may learn "that the most effective way to communicate with adults is through sex" (Campagna and Poffenberger 1988) and view themselves as commodities. Boyer, in her research on female prostitution in Seattle, found a direct relationship between sexual abuse of girls and their subsequent involvement in prostitution (Boyer 2008). Widom also found that victims of child sexual abuse are 27.7 times more likely to be arrested for prostitution as adults than are non-victims (Widom 1995).

6 Some Rescue: The FBI's Dubious War on Street Girls[4]

One new risk that runaway girls must contend with is being "rescued" by police and other law enforcement agencies as "victims" of sex traffick. While sexual exploitation of girls is a serious problem globally, some of the ways these issues are politically and legally framed are extremely problematic (Berman 2003). This is particularly acute when it comes to the issue of juvenile runaways and the survival sex that often accompanies girls' lives on the streets. For example, the FBI recently announced with great fanfare that it had "rescued" 105 youth and arrested 150 "pimps" for prostitution in 76 cities, including Boston, Denver, and San Francisco. The three-day raid, dubbed "Operation Cross Country", was the largest in a decade-long FBI initiative aimed at what they called the persistent threat of child prostitution (Yost 2013). But if you look closely, the FBI's rescues look less like real heroism, and more like a photo op.

First of all, the people rescued weren't small children. They were almost teens, girls and young women, 13–17 years old. According to the FBI's lead investigator, virtually all "come from runaway or group homes, and they feel like this [prostitution] is the only way for them to survive on the street".

[4] This section of the chaper is adapted from an op ed that first appeared on the blog *Feministing* on August 26, 2013. The co-author on the op ed is Lisa Pasko. http://feministing.com/2013/08/26/some-rescue-the-fbis-dubious-war-on-street-girls/.

Second, the girls would almost certainly not characterize what was happening as a "rescue". Images on the video accompanying the FBI's press release showed girls in handcuffs. As noted earlier, for centuries, law enforcement and other elements of the juvenile justice system have sought to eliminate prostitution, often incarcerating young women for long terms for "sexual immorality" or "for their own protection". Now, they are being "rescued" and offered services of dubious quality that typically involve social stigma and detention.

In fact, many of these girls have already experienced the woefully inadequate services available to runaway youth. Girls who are on the streets usually have suffered sexual and other violent abuses in their homes and in alternative settings like foster home. The journal Child Maltreatment reports there are some 100,000 substantiated cases a year. Sexual abuse of girls occurs at earlier ages and for longer periods than boys' abuse, and girls' abusers are more likely to be family members. It is no surprise that some run away from home.

Once girls run away, as noted earlier, they sometimes turn to teen prostitution in order to survive. The social context that produces teen prostitution and survival sex is a sad mix of broken and dysfunctional families, abused and traumatized youth, defunded social services, adults willing to exploit desperate youth, and privileged older, wealthier men who have absorbed the cultural idea that they should buy sex. It's worth noting that while the FBI proudly reported on rounding up over 100 women, and 100 "pimps"—often men of color—they made no similar mention of any broad effort to arrest the thousands of clients, or "johns" who make the whole system function financially.

Government leaders and police often fail to acknowledge their own complicity in further stigmatizing girls engaged in survival sex. The FBI's multi-city raid involved officers enforcing standard laws related to prostitution or solicitation, meaning that many of these so-called "rescues" involved little more than "rounding up the usual suspects".

Periodic law enforcement raids change none of these realities. Nor do they change the fact that crucial local, state, and federal dollars that used to fund services for girls on the run from abusive families have been devastated by draconian budget cuts. Federal sequestration alone is predicted to bring a 56 % cumulative reduction in juvenile justice funds that once provided states with vital, community-based services for troubled families and alternative care.

"They (girls) usually get into this because they are running away from something else," Oakland, California, police Lt. Kevin Wiley declared. "It goes way beyond law enforcement to solve this epidemic" (Yost 2013). The Trafficking Victims Protection Act of 2000 and its re-authorizations define commercially-sold girls as victims (Department Of State. The Office of Website Management 2006), but most state laws allow for girls under 18 to be charged as prostitutes. Advocacy groups have tried to pass Safe Harbor laws, which mandate that any girl under 18 who has been sexually exploited be treated as a victim, not a criminal, and placed in safe treatment facilities that provide medical and mental health services. Only 25 % of states have passed such legislation. Even then, "victims" in these states often find their "rescue" home is a shelter or detention facility. With no system for helping teens put their lives on track, putting handcuffed girls in patrol cars is far from a rescue. It's more like a round trip ticket to a visit with a broken detention system, followed by a return to the street.

7 Conclusions

Criminology, as a field, has long focused on crime and justice issues of the global north (particularly the United States). Even when moving internationally, the field has largely developed along the lines first identified by the earliest criminologists, focusing on urban problems, problems of youth, (particularly male youth) and issues of poverty and subculture. If it interfaced with the criminal justice system, it did so "administratively" using data drawn from that system somewhat uncritically (Lee and Laidler 2013). As a result, it failed to critically analyze the role of the criminal justice system in perpetuating class, race and gender privilege. For this reason, we argue that the field is particularly ill equipped to deal with the global scourge of violence against women.

This chapter has showcased several instances where the criminal justice system is either explicitly or implicitly being deployed to deny women's victimization, even going so far as to criminalize it. First, we explored the risks that girls and women face when religious systems and values are co-mingled with those of the state and those values become codified into law. Quickly, rather dramatic constraints on women's liberty and sexuality are imposed, often in the name of religious piety and even national pride. Many examples of this can be found in countries affected by Sharia law, but those are not the only societies that afford examples of this problem.

Demonization of women's sexuality, particularly in the time of warfare, is yet another example of the way that violence against women is normalized by political and legal mechanisms. In this case, in particular, the role of media is showcased, since the media (particularly corporate media) are major vehicles for the transmission of partisan and misogynistic messages to those engaged in warfare against the other group. Systematic violence against women, particularly rape (and even murder) in wartime is thus justified by showcasing the dangerous sexuality of the women of the other group. Even more shocking is the fact that the victims of such violence and degradation are themselves blamed by their own groups as culpable. Here, we see the peculiar and horrific way that patriarchal norms trump even the strongest bonds within groups who have been engaged in conflict. When men are victimized and tortured, for example, the victims of wartime injury and suffering are attended to while celebrating their fortitude and sacrifice. Yet, when women are the victims, and they are harmed, they are blamed for their victimization and shunned.

The worldwide denial of girls and women's access to reproductive rights is another clear example of the complicity of patriarchal attitudes about female sexuality and the legal and criminal system. Globally, women are at increasing risk when they seek to terminate pregnancies that are unwanted or even dangerous too them, and this pattern again, is seen in both the global north and south. The fact that the United Nations has recently considered the explicit denial of abortion services, even in the face of imminent physical harm to the girl or women, as torture, is ample evidence that this often religiously motivated restriction exposes the ways that formal laws enforce male privilege and put girls and women at risk.

Finally, there is the issue of prostitution and/or trafficking. Here we have argued that much of the hysteria about this problem in the global north comes at the expense of young girls who are on the run from abusive families. While the problem of selling young girls in marginalized countries into early marriage or even prostitution is no doubt a problem, the spread of the "trafficking" rhetoric into the first world, and the ways in which that new frame are being codified into federal law (and federal law enforcement) is clearly problematic and, in the US case, an extension of centuries of interest in policing the sexuality of girls, often in the name of "protecting" them.

Criminologists, particularly feminist criminologists interested in the study of patriarchy need to focus on global data on the response to violence against women. These data increasingly suggest that, contrary to notions that the law exists outside of cultural and religious norms and mores, this is not the case. Instead, many complementary and troubling arrangements can be found as we have highlighted in this contribution. This also explains how the criminal justice system was able, for so long, to trivialize and ignore girl's and women's horrific victimizations. Instead, it might be fruitful to explore the ways in which the system ostensibly set up to protect members of society from harm actually criminalizes girls and women's victimizations and their survival strategies.

Five Questions

1. What are the dimensions of the problem of violence against women globally? If these figures are correct, what is the significance of these data for the criminal justice system?
2. Given the spread of *Sharia* law globally, what is the significance of this spread? Are there any situations in the global north that show this same confluence between religious beliefs and legal policies? If so, what are these?
3. Wartime has long been accompanied by the rape of the "enemy's" women. What is the social and political meaning of this phenomenon, and what can be done to challenges these practices?
4. Discuss the significance of global efforts to criminalize and re-criminalize abortion on the status of women globally. What is the meaning of this trend?
5. The juvenile justice system has long policed girls' sexuality. How did the system do this historically, and how is it doing this today (in the case of the federal initiative on victims of trafficking)? Is this good news for girls or not?

References

Abram, K. M., Choe, J. Y., Washburn, J. J., Teplin, L. A., King, D. C., & Dulcan, M. K. (2008). Suicidal ideation and behaviors among youths in juvenile detention. *Journal of the American Academy of Child & Adolescent Psychiatry, 47*(3), 291–300. doi:10.1097/CHI.0b013e318160b3ce.

Acoca, L. (1998). Outside/Inside: The violation of American girls at home, on the streets, and in the juvenile justice system. *Crime & Delinquency, 44*(4), 561–589. doi:10.1177/0011128798044004006.

Ahman, E., & Shah, I. (2002). Unsafe abortion: Worldwide estimates for 2000. *Reproductive Health Matters, 10*, 13–17.

Amnesty International (2012). Iran: Sakineh Mohammadi Ashtiani's fate unclear while lawyer languishes in jail. http://www.amnesty.org.au/news/comments/29297/. Accessed May 23 2014.

Amnesty International in Asia and Pacific (n.d.). Hudood Ordinances: The Crime and Punishment for Zina. http://asiapacific.amnesty.org/apro/aproweb.nsf/pages/svaw_hudoo. Accessed 5 July 2012.

Bailey, J. A., & McCloskey, L. A. (2005). Pathways to adolescent substance use among sexually abused girls. *Journal of Abnormal Child Psychology, 33*(1), 39–53. doi:10.1007/s10802-005-0933-0.

BBC News Africa (2014). Nigeria kidnapped girls'shown in Boko Haram video. http://www.bbc.com/news/world-africa-27373287. Accessed 514 May 2014.

BBC News Middle East (2010). Halt stoning of Iran 'adulterer' - Human Rights Watch. http://www.bbc.co.uk/news/10545062. Accessed May 23 2014.

BBC News Asia (2013). Shot Pakistan schoolgirl Malala Yousafzai addresses UN. http://www.bbc.co.uk/news/world-asia-23282662. Accessed 3 September 2013.

BBC News South Asia (2011). Bangladesh Lifts Fatwa Ban but Forbids Enforcement. http://www.bbc.co.uk/news/world-south-asia-13379016. Accessed 5 July 2012.

BBC News South Asia (2010). Mutilated Afghan Girl Aisha Gets New Nose. http://www.bbc.co.uk/news/world-south-asia-11530849. Accessed 5 July 2012.

Belknap, J., & Holsinger, K. (2006). The gendered nature of risk factors for delinquency. *Feminist Criminology, 1*(1), 48–71. doi:10.1177/1557085105282897.

Bergen, H. A., Martin, G., Richardson, A. S., Allison, S., & Roeger, L. (2004). Sexual abuse, antisocial behaviour and substance use: Gender differences in young community adolescents. *Australian and New Zealand Journal of Psychiatry, 38*(1–2), 34–41.

Berman, J. (2003). Popular strangers and crises (Un)bounded: Discourses of sex-trafficking, the European political community and the panicked state of the modern state. *European Journal of International Relations, 9*(1), 37–86. doi:10.1177/1354066103009001157.

Bloom, B., Owen, B., Deschenes, E. P., & Rosenbaum, J. (2002). Improving juvenile justice for females: A statewide assessment in California. *Crime & Delinquency, 48*(4), 526–552. doi:10.1177/001112802237128.

Borer, T. A. (2013). Gender war gendered peace. In: M. Chesney-Lind, & M. Morash (Eds.), 2011. *Feminist Theories of crime. Volume in Theoretical criminology series* (pp. 523–547). Surrey, UK: Ashgate Publishing Limited

Boyer, D. (2008). *Who pays the price? An assessment of youth involvement in prostitution in Seattle*. Seattle: Human Services Department.

Boyer, D., & James, J. (1982). Easy money: Adolescent Involvement in prostitution. In S. Davidson (Ed.), *Justice for young women*. Seattle: New Directions for Young Women.

Brannigan, A., & Van Brunschot, E. G. (1997). Youthful prostitution and child sexual trauma. *International Journal of Law and Psychiatry, 20*, 337–354.

Campagna, D. S., & Poffenberger, D. L. (1988). *The sexual trafficking in children: An investigation of the child sex trade*. Co: Auburn House Pub.

Chen, X., Tyler, K., Whitbeck, L., & Hoyt, D. (2004). Early sexual abuse, street adversity, and drug use among female homeless and runaway adolescents in the Midwest. *Journal of Drug Issues, 34*, 1–22.
Chesney-Lind, M. (1971). *Female Juvenile Delinquency in Hawaii*. University of Hawai'i at Manoa, Honolulu, HI. Master's Thesis.
Chesney-LInd, M., & Pasko, L. (2013). *The female offender: Girls, women, and crime*. Thousand Oaks: SAGE.
Chesney-Lind, M. (2014). Gendered pathways into delinquency. In F. Cullen, P. Wilcox, J. Lux, & C. Jonson (Eds.), *Sisters in crime revisited: Bringing gender into criminology*. London: Oxford University Press.
Department Of State (2006). U.S. Laws on Trafficking in Persons. http://www.state.gov/j/tip/laws/ . Accessed January 8 2014.
Equality Now (2011). Saudi Arabia: Give women equal opportunities to education & end male guardianship over women. http://www.equalitynow.org/node/785. Accessed August 20 2013.
Federal Bureau of Investigation (2012). Crime in the U.S. 2011. http://www.fbi.gov/about-us/cjis/ucr/crime-in-the-u.s/2011/crime-in-the-u.s.-2011. Accessed January 7 2014.
Finkelhor, D. (1994). The international epidemiology of child sexual abuse. *Child Abuse & Neglect, 18*(5), 409–417. doi:10.1016/0145-2134(94)90026-4.
Fishbein, D., Miller, S., Winn, D. M., Dakof, G., Zahn, M. A. (2009). Biopsychological factors, gender, and delinquency. http://www.rti.org/publications/abstract.cfm?pubid=13583. Accessed May 23 2014.
Flowers, R. B. (2001). *Runaway kids and teenage prostitution: America's lost, abandoned, and sexually exploited children*. Westport, CT: Greenwood Press.
Fried, M. G. (2000). Abortion in the United States: Barriers to access. *Health and Human Rights, 4*, 174–194.
Gaarder, E., & Belknap, J. (2002). Tenuous borders: Girls transferred to adult court. *Criminology, 40*(3), 481–517. doi:10.1111/j.1745-9125.2002.tb00964.x.
Giordano, P. C. (2010). *Legacies of crime: A follow-up of the children of highly delinquent girls and boys*. New York: Cambridge University Press.
Grimes, D. A., Benson, J., Singh, S., Romero, M., Ganatra, B., Okonofua, F., et al. (2006). Unsafe abortion: The preventable pandemic. *The Lancet Sexual and Reproductive Health Series, 368*, 1908–1917.
Hadi, S. T., Chesney-Lind, M. (2014). Silence and the criminalization of victimization: On the need for an international feminist criminology. In: H. Bershot, & Arrigo (Eds.), *Forthcoming: Routledge Handbook on International Crime and Justice Studies*. London: Routledge.
Hosseini. Z. M. (2010). Criminalizing sexuality: Zina laws as violence against women in Muslim contexts. http://lastradainternational.org/lsidocs/islamic.pdf. Accessed January 7 2014.
Horowitz, P. (2014). Hobby Lobby is Only the Beginning. New York Times. http://www.nytimes.com/2014/07/02/opinion/for-the-supreme-court-hobby-lobby-is-only-the-beginning.html?_r=0. Accessed July 10, 2014.
Human Rights Watch (2012). Afghanistan: Hundreds of Women, Girls Jailed for 'Moral Crimes'. http://www.hrw.org/news/2012/03/28/afghanistan-hundreds-women-girls-jailed-moral-crimes. Accessed 5 July 2012.
Ianni, F. A. J. (1989). *The search for structure: A report on American youth today*. New York: Free Press.
Irvine, A. (2010). We've had three of them: Addressing the invisibility of lesbian, gay, bisexual, and gender nonconforming youths in the juvenile justice system. *Columbia Journal of Gender and Law, 19*, 675.
Islam, S. (1982). Case studies of indigenous abortion practitioners in rural Bangladesh. *Studies in Family Planning, 13*, 86–93.
Jacobs, J. L. (1993). Victimized daughters: Sexual violence and the empathic female self. *Signs, 19* (1), 126–145.

Johnson, T., Vriens, L. (2013). Islam: Governing Under Sharia - Council on Foreign Relations. http://www.cfr.org/religion/islam-governing-under-sharia/p8034. Accessed August 23 2013.
Kamler, B. (1999). *Constructing gender and difference: critical research perspectives on early childhood*. Cresskill, N.J.: Hampton Press.
Katz, P. A. (1979). The development of female identity. *Sex Roles, 5*(2), 155–178.
Khan, S. (2012). Pakistani Taliban target female students with acid attack. http://edition.cnn.com/2012/11/03/world/asia/pakistan-acid-attack. Accessed September 3 2013.
Lee, M., & Laidler, K. J. (2013). Doing criminology from the periphery: Crime and punishment in Asia. *Theoretical Criminology, 17*, 141–157.
Leve, L., & Chamberlain, P. (2004). Female juvenile offenders: Defining an early-onset pathway for delinquency. *Journal of Child and Family Studies, 13*, 439–452.
Liu, R. X. (2004). The conditional effects of gender and delinquency on the relationship between emotional distress and suicidal ideation or attempt among youth. *Journal of Adolescent Research, 19*(6), 698–715. doi:10.1177/0743558403260020.
Mayell, H. (2002). Thousands of Women Killed for Family 'Honor'. http://news.nationalgeographic.com/news/2002/02/0212_020212_honorkilling.html. Accessed August 23 2013.
Maguire, D. C. (Ed.). (2003). *Sacred rights: The case for contraception and abortion in world religions*. Cary, NC: Oxford University Press.
Mishra, Y. (2001). Unsafe abortions and women's health. *Economic and Political Weekly, 36*, 3814–3817.
Nash, E., Gold, R. B., Rowan, R., Rathbun, G., & Vierboom, Y. (2014) Laws Affecting Reproductive Health and Rights: 2013 State Policy Review. http://www.guttmacher.org/statecenter/updates/2013/statetrends42013.html. Accessed May 14.
New York Times (2014). Editorial: Hobby Lobby's Disturbing Sequel. http://www.nytimes.com/2014/07/09/opinion/hobby-lobbys-disturbing-sequel.html. Accessed 20 July 2014.
Nowrojee, B. (2005). *'Your justice is too slow': Will the ICTR fail Rwanda's rape victims?* Geneva: UNRISD.
Orenstein, P. (2000). *Schoolgirls: Young women, self-esteem, and the confidence gap*. New York: Anchor Books.
Piquero, N. L., Gover, A. R., MacDonald, J. M., & Piquero, A. R. (2005). The influence of delinquent peers on delinquency does gender matter? *Youth & Society, 36*(3), 251–275. doi:10.1177/0044118X04265652.
Plett, B. (2006). How Pakistan's Rape Reform Ran Aground. http://news.bbc.co.uk/2/hi/south_asia/5346968.stm. Accessed 5 July 2012.
Riehman, K., Blutenthal, R., Juvonen, J., & Morral, A. (2003). Adolescent social relationships and the treatment process: Findings from quantitative and qualitative analyses. *Journal of Drug Issues, 33*, 865–896.
Sarwary, B. (2012), Afghan Woman Is Killed 'For Giving Birth to a Girl'. http://www.bbc.co.uk/news/world-asia-16787534. Accessed 5 July 2012.
Schaffner, L. (2006). *Girls in trouble with the law*. New Brunswick, N.J.: Rutgers University Press.
Schlitt, S. (2011). Rights – not criminalization – for girls and women, says UN health expert | Amnesty's global human rights blog. http://livewire.amnesty.org/2011/10/24/rights-not-criminalization-for-girls-and-women-says-un-health-expert/ Accessed August 20 2013.
Sedlak, A., & Broadhurst, D. (1996). *National study of the incidence of child abuse and neglect*. Rockville, MD: Wetstat.
Stop Rape Now (2009), Update from the field: Darfur. http://stoprapenow.org/uploads/features/pdfDarfur_UN_ACTION_Update_Sept_25.pdf. Accessed May 10 2014.
The Guardian (2014), Pregnant teenager alleging gang-rape charged with adultery in Sudan. http://www.theguardian.com/world/2014/feb/18/sudan-pregnant-alleged-rape-victim-charged-adultery. Accessed 10 May 2014.

The Guardian (2011). Ofcom clears Iranian TV station over woman's murder reconstruction: State-run Press TV showed Sakineh Mohammadi Ashtiani describing her alleged role in her husband's death. http://www.theguardian.com/media/2011/mar/23/ofcom-iranian-tv-murder-reconstruction. Accessed 10 May 2014.
Thorne, B. (1993). *Gender play: Girls and boys in school*. New Brunswick, N.J.: Rutgers.
United Nations (2014). Background Information on Sexual Violence used as a Tool of War. http://www.un.org/en/preventgenocide/rwanda/about/bgsexualviolence.shtml. Accessed May 23 2014.
Widom, C. (1995). *Victims of childhood sexual abuse — later criminal consequences*. Washington, DC: Office of Juvenile Justice and Delinquency Prevention.
The Women's Media Center (2014). Country Profile: Darfur Sudan. http://www.womenundersiegeproject.org/conflicts/profile/darfur-sudan. Accessed May 23 2014.
The Women's Media Center (2012). Rwanda. http://www.womenundersiegeproject.org/conflicts/profile/rwanda. Accessed May 10 2014.
World Health Organization (2013). Global and regional estimates of violence against women: Prevalence and health effects of intimate partner violence and non-partner sexual violence. http://www.who.int/reproductivehealth/publications/violence/9789241564625/en/index.html. Accessed 1 July 2013.
Yost, P. (2013). Child prostitution: Raids rescue 105 young people. http://bigstory.ap.org/article/fbi-raids-rescue-105-kids-forced-prostitution. Accessed January 7 2014.
Zahn, M. A. (2009). *The delinquent girl*. Philadelphia: Temple University Press.

Societal Responses to Sexual Violence Against Women: Rape Myths and the "Real Rape" Stereotype

Barbara Krahé

Abstract Sexual violence is an omnipresent threat to women's sexual well-being, physical and mental health all over the world. In addition to the impact of the victimization experience itself, many survivors are faced with negative social reactions when they disclose it to third parties, which amount to a form of secondary victimization and differ from reactions toward victims of other forms of violent crime. Negative reactions and stereotypic judgments about victims of sexual violence can also be found to operate in the legal handling of sexual violence allegations, playing a part in the widely observed "justice gap" for victims of sexual assault. This chapter examines the role of stereotypes and myths about rape in understanding societal responses to survivors of sexual violence. After presenting prevalence rates of sexual assault worldwide, the process of attrition is examined, from the occurrence of a sexual assault to the potential conviction of a perpetrator in a court trial. A large body of international research shows that attrition may be linked to the influence of extra-legal factors, particularly the tendency to blame the victim and exonerate the perpetrator, which reflect socially shared myths and stereotypes about rape. Evidence will be presented showing the impact of rape myths and stereotypes on the handling of rape complaints by members of the criminal justice system and by the general public. The chapter concludes with a review of potential strategies for challenging rape myths and stereotypes and reducing their influence in the criminal justice system.

B. Krahé (✉)
University of Potsdam, Potsdam, Germany
e-mail: krahe@uni-potsdam.de

H. Kury et al. (eds.), *Women and Children as Victims and Offenders: Background, Prevention, Reintegration*, DOI 10.1007/978-3-319-08398-8_24

1 Introduction: The Social Construction of Sexual Violence Against Women

Sexual violence is a serious and omnipresent threat to the sexual well-being, physical and mental health of women across the world. It is not confined to assaults by strangers but permeates women's personal sphere, including the relationships with their intimate partners. A recent comprehensive review of the international knowledge base revealed that, worldwide, 7.2 % of women from the age of 15 reported the experience of sexual violence from a non-partner during their lifetime (Abrahams et al. 2014). This overall rate disguises a wide variability between regions, with the highest rate found for sub-Saharan Africa (21 %) and the lowest rate found for the region of southern Asia (3.3 %). In a parallel review of violent victimization by an intimate partner that included data from 81 countries, it was established that 30 % of women reported having experienced sexual and/or physical violence from an intimate partner (Devries et al. 2013). Again, the prevalence rates varied widely between countries. In combination, the two reviews suggest that the threat of sexual victimization by strangers, acquaintances, and intimate partners is a reality for every woman, but that women in some parts of the world are more vulnerable than in others.

A large body of research has documented the severe consequences of sexual victimization on women's mental and physical health that places a heavy burden on the individual victim but also on societies as a whole (Martin et al. 2011). At the same time, societal responses to victims of sexual violence have been fraught with problems. Many survivors experience negative reactions from their social environment that feel to them like a "second assault" (Williams and Holmes 1981). These negative responses lead to a silencing of victims and a general silence about the reality of sexual violence (Ullman 2010), which means that the large majority of sexual assault cases remain unnoticed and unsanctioned. The silencing process is also reflected in the criminal justice handling of sexual assault and the fact that only a small proportion of reported sexual assaults result in the conviction of the perpetrator.

This chapter examines how public attitudes and stereotypic beliefs affect the way sexual assault cases are handled by society, including the criminal justice system. It will be argued that misconceptions about rape and stereotypes about the character and behavior of "genuine" victims play a role in the reluctance of survivors to come forward and the low conviction rates of cases that are reported. They contribute to the secondary victimization of affected women, resulting in a "justice gap" for survivors of sexual assault (Temkin and Krahé 2008). Following a brief review of the evidence on the scale of attrition in sexual assault cases, we will examine the widely shared stereotype of the "real rape" and the extent to which it infiltrates judgments about victims and perpetrators, not just by members of the public but also by actors in the criminal justice system, such as police officers and judges. It will be argued that the reliance on stereotypic beliefs and the resulting tendency to blame the victim undermines the normative requirement of a data-driven assessment of "the facts and the evidence" and that this problem affects judgments about sexual violence to a disproportionate degree compared to other types of violent crime (Bieneck and Krahé 2011). This calls for potential strategies for reducing the impact of schematic processing in judging sexual assault cases, which will be discussed in the final part of the chapter.

2 The Problem of Attrition

For the present purposes, attrition may be broadly defined as the difference between the number of sexual assaults that take place and the number of assaults for which a perpetrator is convicted. In a more specific sense, attrition denotes to the process by which cases are dropped from the criminal justice system once they have been reported to the police (Jehle 2012). Attrition is a phenomenon that is generally characteristic of criminal offences, but there is evidence to suggest that it is particularly high in the domain of sexual assault. Attrition may be traced to various stages of the criminal justice handling, from reporting an assault via police investigation to prosecution and, finally, the trial verdict. At each of these stages, rape myths and stereotypes have been shown to play a role in affecting the decision to drop or pursue the case.

By far the largest dropout of cases happens very early on in the process, namely at the reporting stage. It is well-documented from victimization surveys that only a small percentage of sexual assault survivors report their experience to the police. In the United States, an analysis of unreported crime for the period of 2006–2010 estimated that about 211,200 rapes and sexual assaults went unreported to police in each of these years and that the percentage of unreported cases was higher for rape or sexual assault (65 %) than for robbery (41 %) or aggravated assault (44 %) over the 5-year period (Langton et al. 2012). Data from three waves of the Crime Survey in England and Wales from 2007 to 2011 revealed that only 15 % of women who identified themselves as the victim of a serious sexual offense indicated that they had reported the incident to the police (Ministry of Justice, Home Office and the Office for National Statistics 2013). This figure is highly similar to a recent representative survey in Germany in which only 15.5 % of women who experienced a sexual assault reported it to the police (Hellmann 2014). A review of evidence from victimization surveys in Australia, Canada, England and Wales, New Zealand, and the United States established a mean reporting rate of 14 % (Daly and Bouhours 2010).

Once a sexual assault is reported to the police, attrition continues in several steps within the criminal justice system (Lonsway and Archambault 2012). A comparative analysis of attrition rates in 22 European countries revealed that the percentage of reported cases that ended in a conviction varied widely (Lovett and Kelly 2009). For the year 2006, the rates were highest in Luxembourg with 85 % of all reported cases ending in a conviction, and they were lowest in Scotland, where only 3 % of reported cases led to a conviction. The figures for all 22 countries in descending order of conviction rates are presented in Table 1.

Table 1 Convictions as proportions of reported cases in select European countries for the year 2006 (Lovett and Kelley 2009, p. 21)

Country	Conviction rate	Country	Conviction rate
Luxembourg	85 %	Austria	17 %
Hungary	80 %	Cyprus	16 %
Lithuania	44 %	Finland	15 %
Slovenia	42 %	Greece	14 %
Latvia	42 %	Belgium	13 %
Slovakia	28 %	Germany	13 %
Italy	27 %	Portugal	12 %
Czech Republic	26 %	Sweden	10 %
France	25 %	Ireland	7 %
Denmark	22 %	England and Wales	6 %
Switzerland	18 %	Scotland	3 %

Evidence of high attrition from the reporting to the conviction stage also comes from non-Western jurisdictions. For example, a case-tracking analysis from South Africa conducted in 2003 found that only 4.1 % of rape reports made to the police by women over the age of 18 resulted in a conviction (Vetten et al. 2008, p. 53).

Explaining the variations between countries is difficult because many factors, including differences in the legal definitions of rape, the fundamental principles of legal systems, and recording practices may affect attrition rates (see Jehle 2012, for a review). However, Lovett and Kelly (2009) identified a general pattern of "classic attrition" whereby increases in reporting rates are accompanied by decreases in conviction rates. This pattern is illustrated very clearly in the figures presented for Germany in Table 2, which shows that from 2000 to 2007 the rate of reported rape per 100,000 women increased by 11.5 %, whereas the rate of conviction decreased by 48.1 % during the same period.

Table 2 further reveals that the divergence of reporting and conviction rates over time is not found for other forms of violent crime. For assault, the increase in reports is roughly matched by the increase in convictions, for robbery, reports remained at a stable rate with a small decline in convictions (Aebi et al. 2006, 2010). These figures suggest that the loss of cases from reporting to conviction is greater for sexual assault than for other violent offences. Although comparisons with other crimes are fraught with methodological problems, this evidence suggests that attrition rates in sexual assault cases are higher than for other offences of violence against the person (Temkin and Krahé 2008, Chap. 1).

Comparing the number of reported rapes against the number of cases ending in a conviction sheds light on the overall scale of the attrition process. A closer look at different stages of the prosecution process yields more specific information as to when cases are weeded out of the system. It reveals that many cases are dropped at the police investigation stage. Many of the cases in which a suspect is identified are not forwarded to the prosecution. Again, there is evidence that attrition is higher at

Table 2 Convictions as a proportion of reported cases of rape, assault, and robbery in Germany (Source: European Sourcebook of Crime and Criminal Justice Statistics. 3rd edition, 2006, and 4th edition, 2010; Aebi et al. 2006, 2010)

	Rate per 100.000 women	2000	2001	2003	2007	% Change 2000–2007
Rape	Incidence	7.2	7.7	8.8	8	+11.1
	Convictions	2.7	1.5	1.6	1.4	−48.1
Assault	Incidence	448	464	519	593	+32.3
	Convictions	71	73	82	102	+43.6
Robbery	Incidence	47	46	47	44	−6.8
	Convictions	13	13	13	13	0

this stage for sexual assault than for other violent crimes. For example, in England and Wales, the rate at which the police "no-crimes" a report (i.e., decides that in fact no crime took place) has been found to be higher for sexual assault than for other forms of violent crime. In 2010/11, almost 12 % of rapes that were initially recorded by the police were later "no-crimed", which compares to a rate of 3 % for grievous bodily harm with intent. The two offences are similar in their annual prevalence rates and in terms of the sentence they carry, and the higher no-criming rate for rape is qualified as "a considerable problem" (Her Majesty's Inspectorate of Constabulary [HMIC] and Her Majesty's Inspectorate for the Crown Prosecution Service [HMCPSI] 2012, p. 20). These "no-crimed" cases are then removed from the official crime statistics. The comprehensive five-country review by Daly and Bouhours (2010) mentioned earlier found that across countries 65 % of reported cases were dropped at the police stage. The number of cases is further reduced in the subsequent stages of the criminal justice proceedings (see Spohn and Tellis 2012, for a review), and attrition appears to remain disproportionately high for sexual assault compared to other offences. Taking the example of Germany, Jehle (2012) found that the conviction ratio (i.e., the percentage of convicted persons relative to suspects) was 17 % for rape, 24 % for homicide, and 29 % for robbery. For the UK, a report by the Crown Prosecution Service (CPS) showed that in 2010/11 a suspect was charged in no more than 40 % of rape cases referred to the CPS, but it is worth noting that the figure increased to 62 % in 2013/14. Of these, about 60 % ended in a conviction of the defendant (Crown Prosecution Service 2014).

In combination, these examples from victimization surveys and official crime statistics show that only a small number of rapes end in court and, ultimately, in the conviction of the perpetrator. They also show that the rate of attrition appears to be higher than for other violent crimes. To explain why sexual assaults are particularly likely to go unreported or, if reported, to be dropped from the criminal justice system, the following sections will discuss the role of stereotypic beliefs and myths that influence perceptions and evaluations of sexual assault cases.

3 Stereotypes and Myths About Rape

The "real rape" stereotype holds that alleged sexual assaults have to meet a number of features in order to qualify as a genuine report of sexual victimization (Temkin and Krahé 2008). These include a perpetrator who is a stranger to the victim, an assault that happens out of the blue in a remote outdoor location, and a victim who puts up active resistance to fight off the assailant (Anderson 2007). It is blatantly clear from a variety of sources that the "real rape" stereotype is a misconception. Victimization surveys as well as police records have shown that in the majority of sexual assaults the victims know their attackers, that they often do not suffer physical injuries and succumb to the threat of violence without physical resistance. For example, in the representative survey by Hellmann (2014), three quarters of women who reported a sexual assault were assaulted by a former or current partner, and only 7.1 % of the assaults were committed by a stranger. The finding that the majority of sexual assaults are committed by someone who is known to the victim, often in the victim's own home, is confirmed by studies from other countries (e.g., Kilpatrick et al. 2007, for the USA; Smith et al. 2011, for England and Wales).

The "real rape" stereotype is not only *descriptive*, specifying the characteristics of a typical rape, it is also *prescriptive* in that it lays down the criteria a case must meet in order to be judged to qualify as rape. It is this prescriptive aspect which is particularly problematic because cases that fail to meet one or more of the defining features specified by the stereotype are less likely to be accepted as genuine rapes (McKimmie et al. 2014). Experiences of sexual assault that do not match the circumstances laid out in the "real rape" stereotype are often met with disbelief and suspicion.

In fact, even victims themselves may find it difficult to identify their experience as a sexual assault if it does not match the real rape stereotype. In this line of research, women are presented with behavioral descriptions of rape (forced sexual intercourse where the assailant used or threatened to use physical force or the victim was too incapacitated to resist) and are also asked, in a separate question, whether they have ever been raped. Women who answer "yes" to the behavioral item but "no" to the question of whether they have ever been raped are considered "unacknowledged rape victims", because they do not see themselves as victims despite reporting experiences that meet the defining features of rape. According to a review by Littleton, Rhatigan, and Axom (2007), studies have revealed rates of unacknowledged victims in college student samples between 40 and 70 %. Unacknowledged rapes differ systematically from acknowledged rapes in terms of characteristics linked to the "real rape" stereotype: they are more likely to be perpetrated by a partner with whom the victim had previous sexual contact, less likely to be physically violent and involve active victim resistance, and more likely to happen to women who were intoxicated at the time of the assault (Littleton et al. 2007).

These features are at odds with the characteristics defining the "real rape" and suggest that women who were sexually assaulted in circumstances not matching the stereotype are less likely to report because they fail to identify their experience as a sexual assault. This conclusion is further supported by a study by Kahn et al. (1994), who showed that victims of acquaintance rape were less likely to acknowledge their experience as rape if their script of the *typical* rape situation was that of the stranger rape scenario. These findings show that the narrow prescriptive definition of the "real rape", which excludes a large proportion of assaults experienced by women, plays a key role in the first stage of the attrition process, namely the self-identification as a victim of sexual violence.

The "real rape" stereotype not only affects victims' evaluation of their experience, it also affects their decision to report. Victims who were assaulted in circumstances close to the "real rape" stereotype are more likely to report to the police than victims assaulted in circumstances not covered by the stereotype, such as in their own or the perpetrator's home or by someone they know (e.g., Felson and Paré 2005; Kelly et al. 2007; Starzynski et al. 2005). Studies analyzing why women decide against reporting rape to the police found that many victims expect members of the police and the judiciary to hold negative attitudes about rape victims and are likely to treat women with suspicion when they claim to have been raped (e.g., Cohn et al. 2013; Hellmann 2014; see also Sect. 4 below).

Beyond women's self-identification as victims, there is evidence that the "real rape" stereotype has a systematic impact on attrition rates in that cases that do not meet the standard set by the stereotype are more likely to be removed from the system. Several studies have shown that cases involving a non-stranger assault are less likely to proceed through the criminal justice system (see Alderden and Ullman 2012a, for a review). For example, an analysis of 465 cases reported to the police in the United States found that a suspect was more likely to be arrested when the victim showed active resistance and that a decision to press felony charges was less likely when the alleged perpetrator was an acquaintance, relative or intimate partner (Alderden and Ullman 2012a; see also Tasca et al. 2013). Jordan (2004) analyzed 164 alleged rapes in police files from New Zealand, looking for features that characterized cases which the police categorized as "possibly true/false" or "false". Compared to cases considered as genuine, cases in these two categories more frequently involved a victim who was drunk or under the influence of drugs, who delayed reporting, who had previous consensual contact with the accused, who had reported rape before, was intellectually impaired, and who was perceived as "immoral".

In a study analyzing police files in England, only 18 % of the 105 cases examined eventually came to trial or resulted in a caution of the offender (Brown et al. 2007). By far the highest loss (74 % of all cases dropped) occurred at the police investigation stage. Cases that were referred by the police for prosecution were more likely to involve the use of violence, presence of injuries, and immediate reporting. Similar findings came out of a comprehensive analysis of attrition rates in the European Union that drew on prosecution statistics, file tracking analyses, and expert interviews (Lovett and Kelly 2009). The authors of the report concluded that "the closer assaults were to the stereotypes of rape and rapists the more likely they were to result in a conviction", leading them to ask for a revision of legal responses to sexual assault that acknowledges the reality of women's sexual victimization as a form of gender-based violence (Lovett and Kelly 2009, p. 112).

Thus, there is substantial empirical evidence from different countries and different legal systems that sexual assault cases are less likely to be acknowledged, reported and to proceed through the criminal justice system if they fail to meet the defining criteria of the "real rape" stereotype, reflecting the impact of extra-legal factors on the handling of sexual assault cases. As documented conclusively by victimization surveys and case file analyses, this narrowly defined scenario is at odds with the reality of sexual assaults on women, and its pervasive influence results in impunity for a large proportion of sexual aggressors. One underlying mechanism is a shift of the blame for sexual assault from the perpetrator to the victim, even among victims themselves (Perilloux et al. 2014). Another is the undermining of victim credibility that amounts to the stigmatization and secondary victimization of women who disclose a sexual assault experience that is at odds with the notion of a "real rape". Moreover, the fact that the cases that do proceed through the criminal justice system tend to be the ones that are closest to the stereotype creates a self-perpetuating cycle by suggesting that "genuine" rape charges (i.e. those that result in the prosecution and conviction of a perpetrator), are characterized by the features laid down in the "real rape" stereotype (Brown and Horvath 2009).

The "real rape" stereotype is closely linked to a wider network of beliefs about sexual violence that is captured in the concept of *rape myth acceptance*. Rape myths represent "descriptive or prescriptive beliefs about sexual aggression (i.e., about its scope, causes, context, and consequences) that serve to deny, downplay or justify sexually aggressive behavior that men commit against women" (Gerger et al. 2007, p. 425). Rape myth acceptance is part of a cluster of negative attitudes and behavior toward women, such as sexism and sexual aggression, and there is evidence to suggest that men endorse rape myths to a greater extent than do women (Suarez and Gadalla 2010). Findings from a range of studies show that individuals accepting rape myths or holding traditional gender role beliefs tend to assign less blame to the perpetrator and more blame to the victim of a sexual assault (see Edwards et al. 2011; Temkin and Krahé 2008, for reviews). Furthermore, it has been found that individuals accepting rape myths are more susceptible to contextual information, such as victim-perpetrator relationship, when rating victim and perpetrator blame. Therefore, rape myth acceptance is a key construct in seeking to explain individual differences in perceptions and judgments about sexual assault.

4 Myths and Stereotypes in Criminal Justice Responses to Rape

The police are the first port of call for victims who decide to report a sexual assault and thus serve as the gatekeepers to the criminal justice system. Police officers have considerable discretion in assessing sexual assault charges and in deciding about the course of action that follows from a report. Therefore, it is critical to examine the potential influence of rape stereotypes on police decision-making. Moreover, research has shown that the degree of empathy that police officers show toward victims in the initial interview predicts victims' decision to take their case to court (Maddox et al. 2011).

As noted above, victims frequently cite fear of being treated badly by police, lawyers, or other parties in the justice system as a reason for not reporting a sexual assault (Cohn et al. 2013; Fisher et al. 2003). Empirical research exploring responses to rape victims by members of the police lend some support to victims' concerns. Although not all studies substantiate the expectation that police responses to rape victims are often unsympathetic (e.g., Frazier and Haney 1996; LeDoux and Hazelwood 1985), there is considerable evidence demonstrating police officers' understanding of rape is influenced by the "real rape" stereotype and their acceptance of rape myths (LaFree 1981; O'Keefe et al. 2009; Rose and Randall 1982).

In a study with police officers in Germany, participants were asked to identify the prototypical features that characterized different rape categories, such as a typical rape, a dubious rape, or a false complaint (Krahé 1991a). When describing a "typical" rape, they selected features such as a young victim, attacked outside by a stranger who was psychologically disturbed, with severe psychological consequences. The typical features assigned to a "dubious" and a "false" rape complaint were very different. In this category, the complainant was assumed to be an older woman (above the age of 40), who was heavily drunk at the time of the alleged assault, claiming to have been assaulted by a friend or acquaintance in his or her own home, and made no attempt to resist. Police officers' prototypes of rape were highly similar to those identified in a student sample (Krahé 1991b), supporting other evidence that police officers' beliefs about rape are largely in line with the views held by the general public.

In a study with police officers in England, Maddox et al. (2012) conducted interviews with experienced police officers on how their evaluations of rape complainants as reliable or unreliable were influenced by psychological symptoms displayed by the victim, followed up by a survey of a larger sample of officers about their perceptions of women who make a sexual assault complaint. From the interview data, the authors extracted three distinct victim prototypes: (a) the "real" victim, who is intelligent, well dressed, upset, vulnerable, and wants to go to court, (b) the "mad" victim, who has mental health issues and comes across as vague and irrational, and (c) the "bad" victim that is perceived as overtly sexual, cold, and unemotional.

The authors point out that many of the characteristics that police officers named as indicating "mad" or "bad" victims could be linked to the symptomatology of post-traumatic stress disorder (PTSD; Krippner et al. 2012; Martin et al. 2011). In the subsequent quantitative survey, police officers rated a set of characteristics listed by the interviewees of the first study as informing the categorization of a victim into one of the three categories. The clustering of characteristics largely replicated the three categories identified before. For example, in line with the "good victim" prototype, 40 % of respondents believed that immediate reporting by a victim indicates reliability (compared to 55 % who thought early reporting was not diagnostic of reliability), whereas in line with the "bad victim" stereotype 15 % thought alcohol or drug use by the victim indicated unreliability. Just under 50 % of respondents believed in a "gut feeling something is not right" as an indicator of complainant reliability, which raises the possibility that gut feelings may be influenced by stereotypic notions about rape victim behavior.

In a Swedish study, police officers estimated the rate of false complaints to be significantly higher for rape than for other violent crime, such as domestic assault, nondomestic battery, and mugging (Ask 2010). The study also found that three-quarters of the police officers surveyed considered the statement that a victim's emotional expression is an indicator of veracity to be partly, rather, or totally true (Ask 2010). These results confirm earlier findings from a Dutch study with police officers conducting interviews with rape victims. Officers who saw a simulated statement in which the victim's self-presentation came across as numbed rated her as significantly less credible than those who had seen an emotional self-presentation (Winkel and Koppelaar 1992). Reading signs of reliability and truthfulness from the victim's behavior and emotional expression is misguided because, as noted by Maddox et al. (2012), many of these signs are attributable to the traumatizing effect of the sexual assault.

Studies measuring rape myth acceptance in police samples indicate that stereotypic and victim-blaming beliefs are prevalent to a significant extent in this group. In a study with police officers in Singapore, 51 % of participants endorsed the statement "Many women claim rape if they have consented to sexual relations but changed their minds afterwards", and 57 % agreed with the statement "Accusations of rape by bar girls, dance hostesses, and prostitutes should be viewed with suspicion" (Ward 1995). No more than 57 % correctly identified the statement as false that "most alleged rapes involve extensive physical injury". In a study with male police officers from South Korea, Lee et al. (2012) found a mean score of rape myth acceptance of 2.58 on a scale ranging from 1 to 5, indicating substantial support for victim-blaming beliefs.

Studies from the United States suggest similar conclusions. On the basis of interviews with police and district attorneys, Stewart et al. (1996) reported a widespread assumption that genuine rape victims would report to the police immediately. Page (2007) found that 45 % of police officers indicated that they would be unlikely or very unlikely to believe a woman who claims to have been raped if she was a prostitute, and almost 20 % said they would be unlikely or very unlikely to believe her if the man she was accusing was her husband (see also Page 2010).

There is evidence to show that police officers' beliefs about rape also affect their professional behavior. A study by Rich and Seffrin (2012) found a significant negative association between the acceptance of rape myths and victim interviewing skills. In addition, acceptance of rape myths was negatively linked to the willingness to cooperate with rape victim advocates (Rich and Seffrin 2013).

Little research has been conducted into individual differences within the group of police officers in their responses to sexual assault victims. Some studies have shown that the endorsement of rape myths and stereotypic view about rape complainants is lower among police officers who received some form of special training in handling rape complaints (Ask 2010). In the study by Rich and Seffrin (2013), the link between rape myth acceptance and victim interviewing skills was no longer significant when professional characteristics, such as sexual assault education and knowledge of victim interview techniques, were included in the analysis, and Page (2007) found significantly less endorsement of rape myths the more experienced officers were in conducting rape investigations. However, Sleath and Bull (2012) did not find any effects of years of professional experience or specialized training on the tendency to blame the victim in a sexual assault scenario. Based on these findings, it is yet unclear to what extent professional experience or the promotion of specialized skills in dealing with rape complaints may suppress the impact of rape myth acceptance on responding to victims or on the willingness to cooperate with advocates acting on the victim's behalf.

With regard to officer gender, some studies found evidence that female officers tend to hold more positive attitudes toward victims than do male officers (Brown and King 1998; Schuller and Stewart 2000; Page 2007), but others did not find a significant difference (Sleath and Bull 2012; Wentz and Archbold 2012). Even if female police officers were less accepting of rape myths, this does not necessarily indicate that they are more victim-oriented in their decision making. Alderden and Ullman (2012b) found in their analysis of more than 300 rape files that female officers were less likely to arrest a suspect than their male colleagues, controlling for a number of case-related characteristics, such as victim resistance, use of weapons, and victim-perpetrator relationship. These data are inconsistent with the notion that female officers may be more sympathetic to victims of sexual assault.

Beyond file analyses and surveys with police officers, interviews and surveys with women who reported a sexual assault about their experience with the police provides information about the extent to which rape myths and stereotypes affect the interactions between the police and rape complainants. These sources indicate that many victims perceive the police as unsympathetic and treating them with suspicion. An interview study with rape survivors in Britain concluded that "the legal system and society continue to revictimize victims of rape through mythology and faulty perceptions that surround rape" (Wheatcroft et al. 2009, p. 265). Of the victims surveyed by Campbell et al. (2001), 52 % described the way they were treated by the police and the criminal justice system as unhelpful and having aggravated their problems. Only 35 % found the treatment they received supportive. Treatment by medical professionals did not fare much better: Fewer than half of respondents (47 %) had perceived it as supportive. In contrast, rape crisis centers were regarded as helpful by 75 % of victims who turned to them for support. Analyzing police files of 440 rape reports, Anders and Christopher (2011) found that the closer a rape case was to the "real rape" stereotype and the closer the victim came to being a "real victim" (e.g., by *not* engaging in risky behavior, *not* drinking, *not* having had sex with the alleged assailant on a previous occasion), the higher the perceived police support, which in turn predicted the likelihood that victims decided to aid the police in the prosecution of their assailants. Support from social service providers was also perceived as higher the more stereotypic the case.

In-depth interviews with rape victims who had reported to the police revealed both negative and positive experiences of police treatment (Frazier and Haney 1996; Temkin 1999). Critically, a substantial proportion of victims stated they would decide against reporting if they were victimized again. The experience of secondary victimization in the course of rape reporting can aggravate problems in coping with the assault. Perceived secondary victimization by members of the criminal justice system was associated with a significantly higher incidence of post-traumatic stress disorder symptoms (Campbell et al. 1999). The two forms of secondary victimization that were regarded as most damaging by victims were doubts about their credibility and the assessment of their complaint as not sufficiently serious to warrant further investigation.

Overall, the findings reviewed in this section demonstrate that police officers share the misconceptions about rape that are prevalent in society at large. The findings concerning police officers' belief in rape myths and their reliance on the "real rape" stereotype in assessing the credibility of rape complaints highlight the role of extra-legal factors in accounting for attrition rates at the police investigation stage (Lea et al. 2003). It is also clear from the evidence reviewed in this section that police officers tend to draw on their personal beliefs about rape, including the vague notion of their "gut feelings", in their professional interactions with rape complainants. This infiltration of professional decision making by personally held beliefs is unsurprising: Social psychological research has long demonstrated that stereotypic thinking, which occurs largely automatic and facilitates fast information processing on the basis of heuristic judgments, cannot be simply "switched off" (e.g. Kunda 1999).

5 Rape Myths and Victim Blaming in Society at Large

There is large-scale evidence to show that rape myths are prevalent across the world (e.g., Nayak et al. 2003; Ward 1995), with the bulk of the evidence coming from Western societies. For example, a representative survey conducted in London in 2010 revealed that 18 % of participants agreed with the statement "Most claims of rape are probably not true", and 28 % thought that a rape victim should take some responsibility if she dressed "provocatively" (The Havens 2010). In a survey commissioned by Rape Crisis Scotland in 2007, only 28 % of respondents "agreed a lot" with the statement that women are never to blame for being raped. An

American study by Basile (2002) found that 31 % of men and 19 % of women denied that a husband having sex without his wife's consent constitutes rape, and Kahlor and Morrison (2007) found that college students estimated that 19 % of rapes were false reports. A study with college students in Pakistan found that 40 % of men and 26 % of women disagreed with the statement "There can be rape in marital relationship". In the same study, 32 % of men and 20 % of women agreed with the statement that "a woman who is raped is not worthy of being another man's wife" (Kamal et al. 2010). In a survey of medical students in India, 63 % of male and 68 % of female participants agreed with the claim that "most charges of rape are unfounded", and 46 % of men and 35 % of women disagreed with the statement that "a woman can be raped against her will" (Chudasama et al. 2013).

In addition to creating a general climate of distrust and negative evaluation of rape victims, such beliefs may have an immediate impact on legal decision-making in countries that rely on juries of lay members of the community, such as in the Anglo-American world. In their "story model" of jury decision-making, Pennington and Hastie (1992) propose that juries reach a verdict by comparing the different "stories" that evolve in the course of a trial and adopting what they believe to be the "best" story. In identifying the best story, they are guided not only by the trial evidence, but also by their world knowledge and pre-conceived notions of what makes a convincing story. In line with this model, stereotypic beliefs about rape can be seen as part of jurors' world knowledge and schematic expectations, both of which influence their evaluation of a case and may contribute to the rate of attrition in the final stage of the process from trial to conviction.

Findings from a study by Finch and Munro (2005) on juror reasoning in rape cases involving intoxicants are consistent with the *Story Model*. Using focus groups and a simulated jury trial, they found a strong tendency to blame the victim and deny that non-consensual intercourse amounted to rape, even in cases where the defendant had interfered with the woman's drink to make her intoxicated. Participants in this study constructed a story that held the woman responsible for her own safety and stressed her ability to give or withhold consent even under the influence of strong doses of intoxicants. In a subsequent study using the same methodology, participants drawn from the general public were unwilling to find a defendant guilty if the victim had not fought back because she was in a frozen state or if she did not display visible signs of emotion during the trial despite clear evidence that force was used by the defendant (Ellison and Munro 2009a). The authors concluded that their findings falsify "any suggestion that jurors in rape cases can be entrusted to leave their personal prejudices and stereotypical preconceptions behind them when they enter the courtroom" (Ellison and Munro 2009a, p. 13).

To examine the influence of rape myths and stereotypes on judgments of victim blame, a large body of evidence has used the methodology of the "mock jury paradigm". In this paradigm, participants are asked to adopt the role of jurors when judging rape cases presented in the form of short descriptions or "vignettes" (Bieneck 2009). Unlike the realistic trial simulation and group deliberation used by Munro and colleagues, the majority of studies conducted within the mock jury paradigm obtains judgments from individual participants. In the vignettes, the case information of interest, such as victim resistance or relationship to the perpetrator, may be systematically varied, whereas other information can be held constant, facilitating conclusions about the causal impact of different pieces of information on judgments of victim blame. Research studying predictors of victim blame in rape cases has focused on three main groups of variables: (1) perceiver variables, (2) victim variables, and (3) variables related to the situational context of the assault.

5.1 Attributes of the Perceiver

Many studies have looked at characteristics of the persons who make the judgment about a rape scenario. The most widely studied variable in this category is gender, with a large body of evidence showing that men are more inclined to blame the victim than women are (e.g., Earnshaw et al. 2011; see Pollard 1992, for a review of earlier studies). It is clear from a number of studies that the gender difference is due, at least in part, to a difference between men and women in their acceptance of rape myths. Past research has shown that rape myths are more widely accepted among men than among women (see the comprehensive review by Suarez and Gadalla 2010, and the meta-analysis by Anderson et al. 1997).

Several studies have provided data on a direct link between rape myth acceptance and attributions of blame to the victim when making judgments about specific cases (e.g., Krahé et al. 2007; Romero-Sánchez et al. 2012). In a British study with more than 2000 members of the public, more blame was attributed to the victim and less blame to the perpetrator in a rape scenario the more participants subscribed to rape myths (Temkin and Krahé 2008, Study 3). The findings match those of earlier studies with undergraduate law students in Britain and graduate law students in Germany (Krahé et al. 2008; Temkin and Krahé 2008, Study 2). Other research has shown that the more individuals endorse rape myths, the less likely they are to regard a sexual assault vignette as rape and to think that they would convict the assailant (McKimmie et al. 2014). Although men endorse rape myths to a greater extent, the link between rape myth acceptance and victim blame also holds for women (Basow and Minieri, 2011). Studies that considered both rape myth acceptance and perceiver gender showed that gender differences in the extent to which perceivers blame victims and perpetrators may be attributed to men's and women's differential subscription to rape myths (Temkin and Krahé 2008).

Few studies have looked at attitudes associated with increased sympathy for a victim of rape and decreased attributions of blame. The concept of "rape empathy" was introduced to describe differences in the extent to which perceivers understand the traumatic nature of a rape experience and feel sorry for the victim (Deitz et al. 1982). High-empathy observers were found to attribute more blame to the rapist, less blame to the victim and were more likely to find the defendant guilty than observers low on rape empathy (Weir and Wrightsman 1990). Miller et al. (2011) showed that perceivers with a history of sexual victimization expressed greater empathy with the victim of a rape scenario and attributed less blame to her than perceivers who had no experience of sexual victimization.

5.2 Victim Characteristics and Behavior

Research in this category has addressed the impact of information about the victim on attributions of blame. The first studies on victim blame in rape cases concentrated on victim respectability as a critical variable, operationalized by marital or occupational status. The evidence points overwhelmingly toward a negative relationship between respectability and victim blame: The more respectable the victim appears to be, the less she is blamed. Victim blame in a violent stranger rape scenario was higher when the victim was described as a shop assistant than when she was described as a schoolteacher (Krahé 1985). Other studies, using more extreme manipulations of respectability and social status, for example, presenting the victim either as a prostitute or a catholic nun, found the same effect (Luginbuhl and Mullin 1981).

Information about the complainant's past sexual behavior also critically affects attributions of blame. MacCrae and Shepard (1989) showed that observers who thought the victim was a virgin considered the assault to be more serious, assigned more blame to the perpetrator and less blame to the victim, and recommended a harsher sentence for the perpetrator than observers who were told the victim was promiscuous. Other studies found that the complainant was seen as less credible and more to blame when they heard she had engaged in consensual sexual activity with the defendant during a prior intimate relationship (Schuller and Hastings 2002).

In an experimental simulation conducted by Winkel and Koppelaar (1991) in The Netherlands, an alleged rape victim reported the assault either in a very emotional or in a calm and composed way. Participants who saw the emotional victim regarded her as more credible, less responsible for the attack, and more cautious in her behavior prior to the assault than did participants who saw the calm and composed victim, despite the fact that the events both victims reported were exactly the same. In a Norwegian study, a rape victim who showed an incongruent emotional expression (e.g., smiled) when recounting her rape experience was considered by participants to be less credible, and they were less inclined to return a guilty verdict in her case as compared with the case of a rape victim who showed a neutral or congruent (distressed) emotional expression (Kaufmann et al. 2003). Similarly, a Canadian study by Klippenstine and Schuller (2012) found that men were more certain that a victim's account qualified as rape when her emotional expression matched their expectation of a typical rape victim.

5.3 *Contextual Variables*

Attributions of blame are also affected by information about the background against which a sexual assault takes place. The two most widely studied variables are the victim's behavior in the assault situation and information about a prior relationship between victim and perpetrator. Attributions of blame were shown to be influenced by information about the victim's behavior in and around the assault situation. Victims who engaged in behaviors incompatible with female gender role expectations were more likely to be blamed than role-conforming victims. If the victim was portrayed as having been drunk, she was perceived as less credible and the perpetrator was seen as less likely to be culpable compared to a sober victim (Schuller and Wall 1998). A Spanish study showed that the victim was blamed more when she had accepted an alcoholic drink from the man who then assaulted her than when she had accepted a coke (Romero-Sánchez et al. 2012).

Furthermore, observers referred to information about whether or not a victim showed active resistance in their assessment of victim blame. Studies have shown that participants attributed more blame to the victim if she had not fought back, especially when assaulted by a non-stranger (McKimmie et al. 2014), and perpetrators were judged more leniently when the woman showed only verbal but no physical resistance (Hannon et al. 1995). On the other hand, Branscombe and Weir (1992) found that participants attributed less blame to the perpetrator and recommended a more lenient sentence if the victim had actively fought back than if the victim had not shown physical resistance. They argued that physical resistance against a male attacker represents role-discrepant behavior for women and may reduce sympathy with the victim. In combination, these findings suggest that victims are faced with a no-win situation when it comes to the issue of physical resistance as an indicator of their credibility.

As far as information about a prior relationship between victim and perpetrator is concerned, the "real rape" stereotype posits that "genuine" rapes happen between strangers. Therefore, victims who claim they were raped by an acquaintance or a current or former partner are up against the stereotype. This is reflected in a reduced certainty that a rape has occurred, reduced perpetrator blame, and increased victim blame in acquaintance rapes as compared to stranger rapes, which was found in a large number of studies (e.g. Viki et al. 2004). Findings by Krahé et al. (2007) showed that victim blame increased the closer the relationship with the perpetrator. It was lowest in the stranger rape, followed by the rape by an acquaintance, and highest in the cases where the perpetrator was a former sexual partner. Ratings of perpetrator blame showed a parallel pattern, with blame ratings in the acquaintance and ex-partner rape scenarios being significantly lower than in the stranger rape.

Furthermore, even if perceivers are prepared to accept that an assault by an acquaintance or an ex-partner is rape, they see it as less serious and less harmful for the victim than an assault by a stranger (Ben-David and Schneider 2005). In research by Krahé et al. (2008, Study 2), graduate law students in Germany were presented with rape scenarios that varied with respect to victim-perpetrator relationship (stranger, acquaintance, or ex-partner) and coercive strategy (whether the perpetrator used physical force or exploited the victim's incapacitation due to alcohol) and completed a measure of rape myth acceptance. In addition, half of the participants were provided with the legal definition of rape prior to reading the case scenarios, the other half received no such information. For each case scenario, participants were asked to make attributions of victim and perpetrator blame and to recommend a sentence in case the perpetrator was found guilty.

Victim blame increased and perpetrator blame decreased the closer the prior relationship between victim and perpetrator, and the more participants endorsed rape myths. Using force against a stranger was seen as deserving a longer sentence than using force against an acquaintance, which in turn was seen as deserving a longer sentence than the rape of an ex-partner. Whether or not participants were provided with the legal definition of rape prior to reading the scenarios had no effect on their attributions of victim and perpetrator blame or on their sentencing recommendations. Thus, there is no support in these data for the assumption that reliance on schematic conceptions about rape is due to a lack of relevant knowledge about the law that might impede a proper data-based assessment and interpretation of the evidence.

As shown by Bieneck and Krahé (2011), the effects of information about a prior relationship between victim and perpetrator on attributions of blame to the victim and the perpetrator is specific to rape. Participants were presented with a series of vignettes describing either a rape or a robbery in which the perpetrator was a stranger, an acquaintance, or a former partner and either used physical force or exploited the victim's incapacitated state due to alcohol. Attributions of blame to the victim were generally higher in the rape cases than in the robbery cases. In addition, victims of rape were blamed more if the perpetrator was an acquaintance or a former partner than if he was a stranger. By contrast, ratings of victim blame in robbery cases were unaffected by information about a prior relationship between victim and perpetrator. The top half of Fig. 1 shows the findings. Attributions of blame to the perpetrator mirrored these findings. The perpetrator in the rape scenarios was blamed less the closer the relationship to the victim, while ratings of perpetrator blame in the robbery cases were not affected by information about the relationship between victim and perpetrator.

Moreover, if the victim of the rape scenario was portrayed as having been unable to resist the assailant because she was incapacitated by alcohol, the victim was blamed more than if the perpetrator used physical force, as shown in the bottom half of Fig. 1. The perpetrator was blamed less in the alcohol-related rapes than in the force-related rapes. In the robbery scenarios, whether the perpetrator used force or exploited the fact that the victim was incapacitated had no effect on perceptions of victim or perpetrator blame.

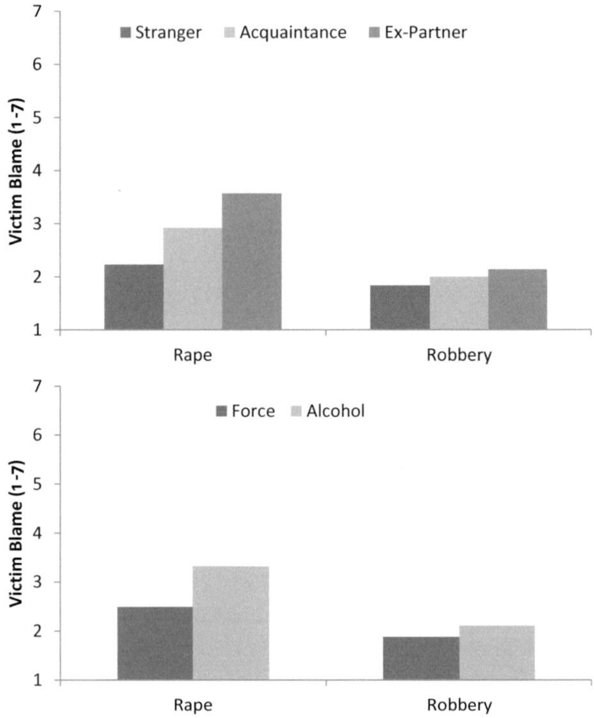

Figure 1 Ratings of victim blame for rape and robbery as a function of victim-perpetrator relationship (*top panel*) and coercive strategy used by the perpetrator (*bottom panel*) (based on Bieneck and Krahé, 2011)

5.4 Interaction of Perceiver, Victim, and Contextual Variables

The findings reported so far showed the individual effects of perceiver, victim, and context variables. In addition, several studies have provided evidence that these influences work in combination, as statistically evidenced in interaction effects. For instance, while women and men did not differ in their perceptions of victim and defendant credibility in a stranger rape scenario, men rated the victim as less credible and the defendant as more credible than did women in an acquaintance rape scenario (McKimmie et al. 2014). The more perceivers accepted rape myths and stereotypes, the more susceptible they were found to be to information potentially suggesting victim blame. Information about victim dress (short vs. long skirt) had a stronger effect on attributions of victim blame in observers scoring high as compared to low on rape myth acceptance (Workman and Orr 1996). Similarly, only observers high on rape myth acceptance assigned more responsibility to the victim who had shown role-discrepant behavior (drank on her own in a pub) than to the victim whose behavior was compatible with female gender role prescriptions (worked late in the office; Krahé 1988).

Taken together, the research reviewed in this section highlights the influence of a variety of factors extraneous to the case at hand or outside the legal definition of rape on judgments about victims and perpetrators. Findings based on responses from student samples are corroborated by studies with participants drawn from the general population and with samples from members of the police and prospective lawyers. They show that rape cases are assessed against the background of widely shared, normative perceptions of role-conforming behavior for women that restrict the range of what is considered a "genuine" rape and provide a basis for assigning responsibility to victims of rape. The more perceivers blame the victim, the less sympathy they have for the victim and the less likely they are to consider a defendant guilty (Sperry and Siegel 2013).

On a methodological note, most of the findings are based on hypothetical cases, and authors are aware that conclusions about their implications for legal decision-making in the real world must necessarily be tentative. However, this methodological approach enables researchers to study the impact of information about victim and perpetrator on observers' judgments, holding other aspects of the case constant, which would not be possible with real-life cases.

6 How to Dispel Rape Myths and Reduce Their Impact on Legal Decision-Making?

The previous sections have shown that misconceptions and stereotypic thinking about rape are widespread in society at large and are also influential in criminal justice responses to sexual assault, which is seen as contributing to the high rate of attrition in rape cases. Recent years have seen a growing awareness of this problem and a consensus that these myths and stereotypes need to be challenged and replaced by a more realistic understanding of the characteristics, circumstances, and consequences of sexual assault. Two main approaches may be distinguished to achieve this goal. The first is to educate the public and the actors in the criminal justice system about the reality of rape. The second is to introduce measures that are designed to reduce the impact of rape myths and stereotypes in the criminal justice system. Both approaches will be discussed briefly in this section (see Krahé and Temkin 2009; Temkin and Krahé 2008, for more detailed reviews).

Efforts at dispelling rape myths in the general public typically take the form of rape awareness campaigns. A number of such campaigns have been launched, such as the "This is not an invitation to rape me" originally started in the United States or the "We believe you" campaign in the United Kingdom.[1] Their purpose is to educate the public about what constitutes rape and provide factual information that contradicts prevailing rape myths.

However, few of these strategies have been subjected to a systematic evaluation of their effectiveness, and for those measures that have been evaluated, success

[1] http://www.thisisnotaninvitationtorapeme.co.uk/; http://www.mumsnet.com/campaigns/we-believe-you-campaign-rape-myths-busted.

appears to be limited and short-lived in its effect (see Temkin and Krahé 2008, Chap. 10, for an overview). An experimental evaluation of a rape awareness poster campaign launched by the British Home Office established that the posters had no effect on reducing participants' tendency to blame the victim in a rape scenario and one poster even lead to an increase of victim blame attributions (Temkin and Krahé 2008; Study 3). To be effective, campaigns need to be based on established theories of attitude change and persuasion, otherwise they may produce counterproductive results. For example, a common approach in campaigns challenging rape myths is to first mention a myth and then confront it by a statement of the facts or the truth. This approach of emphasizing myths has been shown to be counterproductive in research on social information processing because recipients later tend to falsely remember the myths as facts (a phenomenon called the "truth bias"; Skurnik et al. 2005). This is true especially when the myths are consistent with the person's pre-existing attitudes and beliefs (Lewandowsky et al. 2012). Therefore, effective communications challenging rape myths should emphasize the facts, not the myths (Gemberling and Cramer 2014), and they should offer a plausible alternative narrative that perceivers can draw on to make sense of a rape allegation (Lewandowsky et al. 2012).

At the trial stage, a potential strategy for dispelling rape myths could be the introduction of *expert testimony*. In the common law world, expert testimony is designed to inform jurors about matters relevant to the case that are outside their experience and knowledge. Given the prevalence of misconceptions about rape, it is easy to build a case for claiming that essential facts about rape are outside the average juror's experience and knowledge and that there is a need for expert testimony to be introduced in rape trials. Its purpose is to educate jurors about common reactions to rape by providing general information about typical victim behavior, not to relate this information to the case at hand or offer a statement about the credibility of the respective account (Lonsway 2005).

The critical question about this form of expert testimony is whether it is effective in reducing the impact of rape stereotypes on the evaluation of rape charges. As argued above, rape stereotypes are particularly influential in cases that deviate from the notion of the "real rape", such as rape by a dating partner or rape involving alcohol. Ellison and Munro (2009b) compared three expert testimony conditions in simulated rape trials in which the cases contained certain rape myth features (delayed reporting, calm demeanor, lack of resistance, absence of injuries). In the first condition, a psychological expert read out evidence at the beginning of the trial that these features are common in rape cases and do not indicate a lack of credibility of the victim's account. In the second condition, the information that disconfirmed rape myths was included in the judge's guidance to the jury at the end of the trial. In the third condition no expert testimony was provided at all. Juries' deliberations in each condition were coded and analyzed to examine the effectiveness of the expert testimony. The results showed a mixed picture: Whereas juries in the two conditions that received expert testimony were less likely to consider delayed reporting and calm demeanor as information undermining the credibility of the victim's account, no such effect was found for lack of resistance, which reduced jurors' perceptions of credibility in all three conditions. Whether the myth-dispelling information was delivered by the expert early in the trial or presented by the judge toward the end did not make a difference in effectiveness. However, whether similar effects would be obtained in real trials is an open question. For example, the absence of an effect of the timing of the expert evidence may be due to the short duration of the 75-minute trial simulation compared to the length of an actual rape trial (see also Temkin 2010). Looking at the role of the judge's instructions to the jury, Gray (2006) found that mock jurors in a date rape cases who were told by the judge that false accusations are rare thought it more likely that the alleged defendant was guilty than those who were told that false accusations are sometimes made, attesting to the impact of information delivered by the judge.

However, in adversarial justice systems expert witnesses called in by the prosecution may be challenged in cross-examination or contradicted by an expert called by the defense, and since the two parties have conflicting interests, they are likely to deliver divergent messages. Spanos et al. (1991–1992) found that although expert testimony dispelling rape myths made jurors more likely to disbelieve the defendant's claim that sexual intercourse with the complainant was consensual and increased the frequency of guilty verdicts, this effect was reversed when the expert was cross-examined by the defense. To deal with this problem, Gemberling and Cramer (2014) recommend that when rape myths are raised in the course of the trial, experts should address the myths but accompany them with a clear warning about the inaccuracy of these statements.

In addition to challenging the content of rape myths and their relevance for making case-based judgments, an important task is to promote the quality of jurors' decision-making. Reliance on myths and stereotypes reflects a heuristic mode of information processing, which is a swift and superficial way of processing guided by rules of thumb and mental shortcuts (Fiske and Neuberg 1990) and prevents jurors from engaging in the thorough evaluation of "the facts and the evidence" demanded in a trial. Social cognition research has suggested a variety of strategies for promoting data-driven, careful information processing and reducing the reliance on preconceived schematic ideas. One such strategy is to hold people accountable for the judgments and decisions they make by asking them to justify them afterwards. Krahé et al. (2007, Study 2) applied this strategy to the processing of information about sexual assault. One group of participants was told prior to reading a number of rape scenarios that a group of 12 mock jurors would be randomly selected from their midst at the end of the study to justify their judgments of victim blame and perpetrator liability in response to one of the scenarios (accountability group). The other half rated the cases without expecting to have to justify their judgments afterwards, representing the control condition. Among participants scoring high on rape myth acceptance, those in the accountability group attributed more blame to the victim of an ex-partner rape than did those in the control condition. Although the accountability manipulation failed to have a general effect in terms of suppressing reliance on rape schemata, it was successful in the most problematic case, i.e. the combination of a non-stereotypic ex-partner case judged by participants who strongly believed in rape myths. This finding suggests a two-pronged approach for tackling the impact of rape myths, namely challenging the content and relevance of rape myth in judging rape cases and improving the quality of the decision-making process by promoting more thorough and data-driven evaluations of the evidence.

Beyond the potential strategies for dispelling rape myths and reducing their impact on the legal processing of rape complaint discussed in this section, a wide range of legal measures have been discussed and/or implemented to improve the handling of rape complaints. A review of these measures is beyond the scope of the present chapter (see, for example, Horvath et al. 2011; Temkin 2010; Temkin and Krahé 2008). One measure that directly reflects the awareness of the detrimental role of victim stereotypes is the introduction of "rape shield laws" which are designed to keep questions about the victim's sexual history out of rape trials (see Temkin and Krahé 2008, for a review). However, trial observations, interviews with judges, and a number of exceptions to the inadmissibility of sexual history evidence raise questions about the extent to which these restrictions work in practice (e.g., Kelly et al. 2006; Schuller and Klippenstine 2004).

Disillusionment about the ability of the criminal justice system to serve justice in rape cases has led some researchers to explore alternatives to the criminal trial and make suggestions for radical changes of the way in which sexual assault charges are dealt with. Aiming to give greater weight to the needs of survivors, the concept of "restorative justice" has been introduced into the debate on rape reform, and first concepts for its implementation have been developed (Koss 2006; Koss et al. 2004; see also Wemmer and Cyr in this volume). It is based on a philosophy that emphasizes empowerment for rape survivors, acceptance of responsibility by offenders, repairing harm, and strengthening social support (Koss 2006). Proponents of a restorative justice approach regard it as an alternative for dealing with selected sexual offences, particularly first-time offences involving a prior relationship between the parties, nonpenetrative sexual acts, and the use of minimal force (Koss et al. 2004).

7 Summary and Conclusion

This chapter has examined societal beliefs about rape and their impact on the way society responds to victims of sexual violence. Although a systematic international data base is still lacking, the chapter has brought together studies from a range of different countries that all converge on a common conclusion: There is a widely shared stereotype of the "real rape" that is squarely at odds with the reality of the sexual victimization of women, yet serves to inform the social perception of victims and their credibility. The "real rape" stereotype is embedded in a wider network of attitudes and beliefs about the appropriate conduct of women, the circumstances under which a rape can or cannot occur, and the extent to which victims are to blame for being sexually assaulted.

These misconceptions were shown to undermine the sanctioning of sexual violence against women at every step of the way, from the occurrence of a sexual assault to the verdict in the court trial. The research reviewed in this chapter shows that victims whose assault experience does not conform to the "real rape" stereotype are less likely to identify themselves as victims and to report their experience to the police. Police handling of rape cases was shown to be affected by the same stereotypical notions, as reflected in a greater likelihood of non-stereotypical cases to be dropped. Decision-making about rape cases studied in the mock jury paradigm has reflected adherence to schematic information processing on the basis of rape myths and stereotypes about the characteristics of "genuine" complaints. The more cases deviate from the "real rape" stereotype and the more perceivers believe in rape myths, the greater the tendency to blame the victim and exonerate the perpetrator. This was found to be true in experimental studies not only for student samples or members of the general public but also for prospective lawyers, even when they were reminded of the legal definition of rape immediately prior to assessing the case material. It was also shown that the reliance on extra-legal information resulting in a shift of the blame from the perpetrator to the victim is specific to sexual assault and does not occur in judgments about other violent crimes.

In combination, this extensive body of evidence has shown that stereotypical thinking and decision-making about rape is deep-seated and hard to eradicate. Legal scholars, policy makers, and victim support agencies have therefore been seeking to develop effective measures for dispelling rape myths and stopping them from infiltrating legal decision-making through a range of different approaches. Rape awareness campaigns and the introduction of expert testimony are examples discussed in the present chapter. Unfortunately, systematic evaluations of these efforts are rare, and success is not easy to measure. However, there is a growing recognition of the need for change, not least reflected in expert analyses, such as the Stern review (Home Office 2010).

It has become clear in the course of this chapter that the vast majority of studies addressing the role of rape myths and stereotypes on social responses to victims of rape have been conducted in the Anglo-American research literature, with a smaller body of research from other Western countries but virtually no evidence from the non-Western world. At the same time, it is clear that different cultural constructions of sexuality, gender relations, and the right to sexual self-determination are critically important in shaping societal responses to women's experiences of non-consensual sex. Building up a cross-cultural approach to the social context and construction of sexual violence is a key task for future research.

Five Questions

1. How do the figures for attrition in sexual assault cases compare to other forms of violent crime and is there a justice "gap" that is specific to sexual assault?
2. How can the influence of the "real rape" stereotype on legal decision-making about rape be empirically assessed?

3. What are rape myths and what role do they play in the secondary victimization of sexual assault survivors?
4. What evidence is there to demonstrate that decision-making about sexual assault cases at different stages of the criminal justice system is influenced by rape myths and stereotypes?
5. What strategies could be used to challenge rape myths and reduce the influence of rape stereotypes on societal responses to sexual assault?

References

Abrahams, N., Devries, K., Watts, C., Pallitto, C., Petzold, M., Shamu, S., et al. (2014). Worldwide prevalence of non-partner sexual violence: A systematic review. *The Lancet, 383*(9929), 1648–1654.

Aebi, M. F., Aromaa, K., Aubusson de Cavarlay, B., Barclay, G.,Gruszczyñska, B., von Hofer, H., et al. (2006). *European sourcebook of crime and criminal justice statistics* (3rd ed.). Retrieved February 22, 2016, from: http://wp.unil.ch/europeansourcebook/printed-editions-2/third-edition.

Aebi, M. F., Aubusson de Cavarlay, B., Barclay G., Gruszczyńska, B., Harrendorf, S., Heiskanen, M., et al. (2010). *European sourcebook of crime and criminal justice statistics* (4th ed.). Retrieved February 22, 2016, from: http://wp.unil.ch/europeansourcebook/printed-editions-2/printed-editions.

Alderden, M. A., & Ullman, S. E. (2012a). Creating a more complete and current picture: Examining police and prosecutor decision-making when processing sexual assault cases. *Violence against Women, 18*, 525–551.

Alderden, M. A., & Ullman, S. E. (2012b). Gender difference or indifference? Detective decision making in sexual assault cases. *Journal of Interpersonal Violence, 27*, 3–22.

Anders, M. C., & Christopher, F. S. (2011). A socioecological model of rape survivors' decisions to aid in case prosecution. *Psychology of Women Quarterly, 35*, 92–106.

Anderson, I. (2007). What is a typical rape? Effects of victim and participant gender in female and male rape perception. *British Journal of Social Psychology, 46*, 225–245.

Anderson, K. B., Cooper, H., & Okamura, L. (1997). Individual differences and attitudes toward rape: A meta-analytic review. *Personality and Social Psychology Bulletin, 23*, 295–315.

Ask, K. (2010). A survey of police officers' and prosecutors' beliefs about crime victim behaviors. *Journal of Interpersonal Violence, 25*, 1132–1149.

Basile, K. C. (2002). Attitudes toward wife rape: Effects of social background and victim status. *Violence and Victims, 17*, 341–354.

Basow, S. A., & Minieri, A. (2011). "You owe me": Effects of date cost, who pays, participant gender, and rape myth beliefs on perceptions of rape. *Journal of Interpersonal Violence, 26*, 479–497.

Ben-David, S., & Schneider, O. (2005). Rape perceptions, gender role attitudes, and victim-perpetrator acquaintance. *Sex Roles, 53*, 385–399.

Bieneck, S. (2009). How adequate is the vignette technique as a research tool in psycho-legal research? In M. E. Oswald, S. Bieneck, & J. Hupfeld-Heinemann (Eds.), *The social psychology of punishment of crime* (pp. 277–271). Chichester: Wiley.

Bieneck, S., & Krahé, B. (2011). Blaming the victim and exonerating the perpetrator in cases of rape and robbery: Is there a double standard? *Journal of Interpersonal Violence, 26*, 1785–1797.

Branscombe, N. R., & Weir, J. A. (1992). Resistance as stereotype inconsistency: Consequences for judgments of rape victims. *Journal of Social and Clinical Psychology, 11*, 80–102.

Brown, J. M., Hamilton, C., & O'Neill, D. (2007). Characteristics associated with rape attrition and the role played by scepticism or legal rationality by investigators and prosecutors. *Psychology, Crime & Law, 13*, 355–370.

Brown, J., & Horvath, M. (2009). Do you believe her and is it really rape? In M. Horvath & J. Brown (Eds.), *Rape - Challenging contemporary thinking* (pp. 325–342). Cullompton: Willan Publishing.

Brown, J. M., & King, J. (1998). Gender differences in police officers' attitudes towards rape: Results of an exploratory study. *Psychology, Crime and Law, 4*, 265–279.

Campbell, R., Sefl, T., Barnes, H. E., Ahrens, C. E., Wasco, S. M., & Zaragoza-Diesfeld, Y. (1999). Community services for rape survivors: Enhancing psychological well-being or increasing trauma? *Journal of Consulting and Clinical Psychology, 67*, 847–858.

Campbell, R., Wasco, S. M., Ahrens, C. E., Sefl, T., & Barnes, H. E. (2001). Preventing the "second rape": Rape survivors experiences with community service providers. *Journal of Interpersonal Violence, 16*, 1239–1259.

Chudasama, R. K., Kadri, A, M,, Zalavadiya, D., Joshi, N., Bhola, C., & Verma, M. (2013). Attitude and myths towards rape among medical students in Rajkot, India. *Online Journal of Health and Allied Sciences, 12*, 16. Retrieved February 22, 2016, from: http://www.ojhas.org/issue47/2013-3-4.html.

Cohn, A. M., Zinzow, H. M., Resnick, H. S., & Kilpatrick, D. G. (2013). Correlates of reasons for not reporting rape to police: Results from a national telephone household probability sample of women with forcible or drug-or-alcohol facilitated/incapacitated rape. *Journal of Interpersonal Violence, 28*, 455–473.

Crown Prosecution Service (2014). *Violence against women and girls. Crime report 2013-2014.* Retrieved August 15, 2014, from: http://www.cps.gov.uk/data/violence_against_women/vawg_2013_14_report.html.

Daly, K., & Bouhours, B. (2010). Rape and attrition in the legal process: A comparative analysis of five countries. *Crime and Justice: A Review of Research, 39*, 565.650.

Deitz, S. R., Blackwell, K. T., Daley, P. C., & Bentley, B. J. (1982). Measurement of empathy toward rape victims and rapists. *Journal of Personality and Social Psychology, 43*, 372–384.

Devries, K. M., Mak, J. Y. T., García-Moreno, C., Petzold, M., Child, J. C., Falder, G., et al. (2013). The global prevalence of intimate partner violence against women. *Science, 340*(6140), 1527–1528.

Earnshaw, V. A., Pitpitan, E. V., & Chaudoir, S. R. (2011). Intended responses to rape as functions of attitudes, attributions of fault, and emotions. *Sex Roles, 64*, 382–393.

Edwards, K. M., Turchik, J. A., Dardis, C. M., Reynolds, N., & Gidycz, C. A. (2011). Rape myths: History, individual and institutional-level presence, and implications for change. *Sex Roles, 65*, 761–773.

Ellison, L., & Munro, V. E. (2009a). Turning mirrors into windows? Assessing the impact of (mock) juror education in rape trials. *British Journal of Criminology, 49*, 363–383.

Ellison, L., & Munro, V. E. (2009b). Reacting to rape: Exploring mock jurors' assessments of complainant credibility. *British Journal of Criminology, 49*, 202–219.

Felson, R. B., & Paré, P. P. (2005). The reporting of domestic violence and sexual assault by nonstrangers to the police. *Journal of Marriage and Family, 67*, 597–610.

Finch, E., & Munro, V. E. (2005). Juror stereotypes and blame attribution in rape cases involving intoxicants. *British Journal of Criminology, 45*, 25–38.

Fisher, B. S., Daigle, L. E., Cullen, F. T., & Turner, M. G. (2003). Reporting sexual victimization to the police and others: Results from a national-level study of college women. *Criminal Justice and Behavior, 30*, 6–38.

Fiske, S. T., & Neuberg, S. L. (1990). A continuum of impression formation, from category-based to individuating processes: Influences of information and motivation on attention and interpretation. *Advances in Experimental Social Psychology, 23*, 1–74.

Frazier, P. A., & Haney, B. (1996). Sexual assault cases in the legal system: Police, prosecutor, and victim perspectives. *Law and Human Behavior, 20*, 607–628.

Gemberling, T. M., & Cramer, R. J. (2014). Expert testimony on sensitive myth-ridden topics: Ethics and recommendations for psychological professionals. *Professional Psychology: Research and Practice, 45*, 120–127.
Gerger, H., Kley, H., Bohner, G., & Siebler, F. (2007). The Acceptance of Modern Myths About Sexual Aggression (AMMSA) Scale: Development and validation in German and English. *Aggressive Behavior, 33*, 422–440.
Gray, J. M. (2006). Rape myth beliefs and prejudiced instructions; Effects on decisions of guilt in a case of date rape. *Legal and Criminological Psychology, 11*, 75–80.
Hannon, R., Hall, D. S., Kuntz, T., Van Laar, S., & Williams, J. (1995). Dating characteristics leading to unwanted vs. wanted sexual behavior. *Sex Roles, 33*, 767–783.
Hellmann, D. (2014). *Repräsentativbefragung zu Viktimisierungserfahrungen in Deutschland.* Hannover: Kriminologisches Forschungsinstitut Niedersachen. Retrieved September 1, 2014, from: www.kfn.de/versions/kfn/assets/fob122.pdf.
Her Majesty's Inspectorate of Constabulary (HMIC) and Her Majesty's Inspectorate for the Crown Prosecution Service (HMCPSI) (2012). *Forging the links: Rape investigation and prosecution.* Retrieved August 14, 2014, http://www.hmic.gov.uk/publication/forging-the-links-rape-investigation-and-prosecution/.
Home Office (2010). The Stern Review. A report by Baroness Vivien Stern CBE of an independent review into how rape complaints are handled by public authorities in England and Wales. Retrieved February 22, 2016, from: http://www.equalities.gov.uk/pdf/Stern_Review_of_Rape_Reporting_1FINAL.pdf.
Horvath, M. A. H., Tong, S., & Williams, E. (2011). Critical issues in rape investigation: An overview of reform in England and Wales. *The Journal of Criminal Justice Research, 1*(2), 1–18. Retrieved February 22,2016, from: http://eprints.mdx.ac.uk/6983/4/Horvath%252C%2520Tong%2520%2526%2520Williams%2520%25282011%2529.pdf.
Jehle, J. M. (2012). Attrition and conviction rates of sexual offences in Europe: Definitions and criminal justice responses. *European Journal of Criminal Policy and Research, 18*, 145–161.
Jordan, J. (2004). Beyond belief? Police, rape, and women's credibility. *Criminal Justice, 4*, 29–59.
Kahlor, L., & Morrison, D. (2007). Television viewing and rape myth acceptance among college women. *Sex Roles, 56*, 729–739.
Kahn, A. S., Mathie, V. A., & Torgler, C. (1994). Rape scripts and rape acknowledgement. *Psychology of Women Quarterly, 18*, 53–66.
Kamal, A., Shaikh, A. I., & Shaikh, M. A. (2010). Comparative analysis of attitudes and perceptions about rape among male and female university students. *Journal of Ayub Medical College Abbottabad, 22*, 108–110. Retrieved October 10, 2014, from ayubmed.edu.pk/JAMC/PAST/22-2/Anila.pdf.
Kaufmann, G., Drevland, G. C. B., Wessel, E., Overskeid, G., & Magnussen, S. (2003). The importance of being earnest: Displayed emotions and witness credibility. *Applied Cognitive Psychology, 17*, 21–34.
Kelly, L., Temkin, J. and Griffiths, S. (2006). Section 41: *An evaluation of new legislation limiting sexual history evidence in rape trials.* London: Home Office Online Report 20/06. Retrieved September 20, 2014, from: http://webarchive.nationalarchives.gov.uk/20130128103514/http://www.homeoffice.gov.uk/rds/pdfs06/rdsolr2006.pdf.
Kelly, L., Horvarth, M., Uzelac, G, Lovett, J. (2007). *Rape in the 21st century: Old behaviours, new contexts and emerging patterns.* Full Research Report ESRC End of Award Report, RES-000-22-1679. Swindon: ESRC. Retrieved August 15, 2014, from: http://www.esds.ac.uk/doc/5827%5Cmrdoc%5Cpdf%5C5827userguide.pdf.
Kilpatrick, D. G., Resnick, H. S., Ruggiero, K. J., Conoscenti, L. M., & McCauley, J. (2007). *Drug-facilitated, incapacitated, and forcible rape: A national study.* Washington, DC: U.S. Department of Justice. Retrieved September 1, 2014, from: https://www.ncjrs.gov/pdffiles1/nij/grants/219181.pdf.

Klippenstine, M. A., & Schuller, R. (2012). Perceptions of sexual assault: Expectancies regarding the emotional response of a rape victim over time. *Psychology, Crime & Law, 18*, 79–94.

Koss, M. P. (2006). Restoring rape survivors. Justice, advocacy, and a call for action. *Annals of the New York Academy of Sciences, 1087*, 206–234.

Koss, M. P., Bachar, K. J., Hopkins, C. Q., & Carlson, C. (2004). Expanding a community's justice response to sex crimes through advocacy, prosecutorial, and public health collaboration: Introducing the RESTORE program. *Journal of Interpersonal Violence, 19*, 1435–1463.

Krahé, B. (1985). Verantwortungszuschreibungen in der sozialen Eindrucksbildung über Vergewaltigungsopfer und -täter. *Gruppendynamik, 16*, 169–178.

Krahé, B. (1988). Victim and observer characteristics as determinants of responsibility attributions to victims of rape. *Journal of Applied Social Psychology, 18*, 50–58.

Krahé, B. (1991a). Police officers' definitions of rape: A prototype study. *Journal of Community and Applied Social Psychology, 1*, 223–244.

Krahé, B. (1991b). Social psychological issues in the study of rape. In W. Stroebe & M. Hewstone (Eds.), *European review of social psychology* (Vol. 2, pp. 279–309). Chichester: Wiley.

Krahé, B., & Temkin, J. (2009). Addressing the attitude problem in rape trials: Some proposals and methodological considerations. In M. Horvath & J. Brown (Eds.), *Rape: Challenging contemporary thinking* (pp. 301–321). Cullompton, UK: Willan.

Krahé, B., Temkin, J., & Bieneck, S. (2007). Schema-driven information processing in judgments about rape. *Applied Cognitive Psychology, 21*, 601–619.

Krahé, B., Temkin, J., Bieneck, S., & Berger, A. (2008). Prospective lawyers' rape stereotypes and schematic decision-making about rape cases. *Psychology, Crime & Law, 14*, 461–479.

Krippner, S., Pitchford, D. B., & Davies, J. (2012). *Post-traumatic stress disorder*. Santa Barbara, CA: Greenwood Press.

Kunda, Z. (1999). *Social cognition*. Cambridge, MA: MIT Press.

LaFree, G. D. (1981). Official reactions to social problems: Police decisions in sexual assault cases. *Social Problems, 28*, 581–594.

Langton, L., Berzofsky, M., Krebs, C., & Smiley-McDonald, H. (2012). Victimizations not reported to the police, 2006-2010. *National Crime Victimization Survey, Special Report*, ncj 238536. Retrieved August 11, 2014, from: http://www.bjs.gov/content/pub/ascii/vnrp0610.txt.

Lea, S. J., Lanvers, U., & Shaw, S. (2003). Attrition in rape cases: Developing a profile and identifying relevant factors. *British Journal of Criminology, 43*, 583–599.

LeDoux, J. C., & Hazelwood, R. R. (1985). Police attitudes and beliefs toward rape. *Journal of Police Science and Administration, 13*, 211–220.

Lee, J., Lee, C., & Lee, W. (2012). Attitudes toward women, rape myths, and rape perceptions among male police officers in South Korea. *Psychology of Women Quarterly, 36*, 365–376.

Lewandowsky, S., Ecker, U. K. H., Seifert, C. M., Schwarz, N., & Cook, J. (2012). Misinformation and its correction: Continued influence and successful debiasing. *Psychological Science in the Public Interest, 13*, 106–131.

Littleton, H., Rhatigan, D. L., & Axom, D. (2007). Unacknowledged rape: How much do we know about the hidden rape victim? *Journal of Aggression, Maltreatment and Trauma, 14*, 57–74.

Lonsway, K. A. (2005). *The use of expert witnesses in cases involving sexual assault*. Violence against Women Online Resources. Retrieved October 12, 2007, from: http://www.mincava.umn.edu/documents/commissioned/svandexpertwitnesses/svandexpertwitnesses.pdf.

Lonsway, K. A., & Archambault, J. (2012). The "Justice Gap" for sexual assault cases: Future directions for research and reform. *Violence Against Women, 18*, 145–168.

Lovett, J., & Kelly, L. (2009). *Different systems – similar outcomes? Tracking attrition in reported rape cases across Europe*. Retrieved August 12, 2014, from: http://www.cwasu.org/publication_display.asp?pageid=PAPERS&type=1&pagekey=44&year=2009.

Luginbuhl, J., & Mullin, C. (1981). Rape and responsibility: How and how much is the victim blamed? *Sex Roles, 7*, 547–559.

MacCrae, C. N., & Shepard, J. W. (1989). Sex differences in the perception of rape victims. *Journal of Interpersonal Violence, 4*, 278–288.

Maddox, L., Lee, D., & Barker, C. (2011). Police empathy and victim PTSD as potential factors in rape case attrition. *Journal of Police and Criminal Psychology, 26*, 112–117.

Maddox, L., Lee, D., & Barker, C. (2012). The impact of psychological consequences of rape on rape case attrition: The police perspective. *Journal of Police and Criminal Psychology, 27*, 33–44.

Martin, S. L., Macy, R. J., & Young, S. K. (2011). Health and economic consequences of sexual violence. In: J. W. White, M. P. Koss, A. E. Kazdin (Eds.), *Violence against women and children* (Vol. 1: Mapping the terrain, pp. 173–195). Washington, DC: American Psychological Association.

McKimmie, B. M., Masser, B. M., & Bongiorno, R. (2014). What counts as rape? The effect of offense prototypes, victim stereotypes, and participant gender on how the complainant and defendant are perceived. *Journal of Interpersonal Violence, 29*, 2273–2303.

Miller, A. K., Amacker, A. M., & King, A. R. (2011). Sexual victimization history and perceived similarity to a sexual assault victim: A path model of perceiver variables predicting victim culpability attributions. *Sex Roles, 64*, 372–381.

Ministry of Justice, Home Office and the Office for National Statistics (2013). *An overview of sexual offending in England and Wales: Statistics bulletin.* Retrieved August 11, 2014, https://www.gov.uk/government/uploads/system/uploads/attachment_data/file/214970/sexual-offending-overview-jan-2013.pdf.

Nayak, M. B., Byrne, C. A., Martin, M. K., & Abraham, A. G. (2003). Attitudes toward violence against women: A cross-nation study. *Sex Roles, 49*, 333–342.

O'Keefe, S., Brown, J. M., & Lyons, E. (2009). Seeking proof or truth? Naturalistic decision-making by police officers when considering rape allegations. In M. Horvath & J. Brown (Eds.), *Rape: Challenging contemporary thinking* (pp. 229–254). Cullompton, UK: Willan.

Page, A. D. (2007). Behind the blue line: Investigating police officers' attitudes toward rape. *Journal of Police and Criminal Psychology, 22*, 22–32.

Page, A. D. (2010). True colors: Police officers and rape myth acceptance. *Feminist Criminology, 5*, 315–334.

Pennington, N., & Hastie, R. (1992). Explaining the evidence: Tests of the story model for juror decision making. *Journal of Personality and Social Psychology, 62*, 189–206.

Perilloux, C., Duntley, J. D., & Buss, D. M. (2014). Blame attribution in sexual victimization. *Personality and Individual Differences, 63*, 81–86.

Pollard, P. (1992). Judgements about victims and attackers in depicted rapes: A review. *British Journal of Social Psychology, 31*, 307–326.

Rich, K., & Seffrin, P. (2012). Police interviews of sexual assault reports: Do attitudes matter? *Violence and Victims, 27*, 263–279.

Rich, K., & Seffrin, P. (2013). Police officers' collaboration with rape victim advocates: Barriers and facilitators. *Violence and Victims, 28*, 681–696.

Romero-Sánchez, M., Megiás, J. L., & Krahé, B. (2012). The role of alcohol and victim sexual interest in Spanish students' perceptions of sexual assault. *Journal of Interpersonal Violence, 27*, 2230–2258.

Rose, V. M., & Randall, S. C. (1982). The impact of investigator perceptions of victim legitimacy on the processing of rape/sexual assault cases. *Symbolic Interaction, 5*, 23–36.

Schuller, R. A., & Hastings, P. A. (2002). Complainant sexual history evidence: Its impact on mock jurors' decisions. *Psychology of Women Quarterly, 26*, 252–261.

Schuller, R., & Klippenstine, M. A. (2004). The impact of complainant sexual history evidence on jurors' decisions: Considerations from a psychological perspective. *Psychology, Public Policy, and Law, 10*, 321–342.

Schuller, R. A., & Stewart, A. (2000). Police responses to sexual assault complaints: The role of perpetrator/complainant intoxication. *Law and Human Behavior, 24*, 535–551.

Schuller, R. A., & Wall, A. M. (1998). The effects of defendant and complainant intoxication on mock jurors' judgments of sexual assault. *Psychology of Women Quarterly, 22*, 555–573.

Skurnik, I., Yoon, C., Park, D. C., & Schwarz, N. (2005). How warnings about false claims become recommendations. *Journal of Consumer Research, 31*, 713–724.

Sleath, E., & Bull, R. (2012). Comparing rape victim and perpetrator blaming in a police officer sample. Differences between police officers with and without special training. *Criminal Justice and Behavior, 39*, 646–665.

Smith, K., Coleman, K., Eder, S., & Hall, P. (Eds.) (2011). *Homicides, firearm offences and intimate violence 2009/10. Supplementary Volume 2 to Crime in England and Wales 2009/10.* London: Home Office Statistical Bulletin HOS 01/11. Retrieved August 3, 2014, from: http://www.homeoffice.gov.uk/publications/science-research-statistics/research-statistics/crime-research/hosb0111/hosb0111?view=Binary.

Spanos, N. P., Dubreuil, S. C., & Gwynn, M. I. (1991–92). The effects of expert testimony concerning rape on the verdicts and beliefs of mock jurors. *Imagination, Cognition and Personality, 11*, 37-51.

Sperry, K., & Siegel, J. T. (2013). Victim responsibility, credibility, and verdict in a simulated rape case: Application of Weiner's attribution model. *Legal and Criminological Psychology, 18*, 16–29.

Spohn, C., & Tellis, K. (2012). The criminal justice system's response to sexual violence. *Violence against Women, 18*, 169–192.

Starzynski, L. L., Ullman, S. E., Filipas, H. H., & Townsend, S. M. (2005). Correlates of women's sexual assault disclosure to informal and formal support sources. *Violence and Victims, 20*, 417–432.

Stewart, M. W., Dobbin, S. A., & Gatowski, S. I. (1996). "Real rapes" and "real victims": The shared reliance on common cultural definitions of rape. *Feminist Legal Studies, 4*, 159–177.

Suarez, E., & Gadalla, T. M. (2010). Stop blaming the victim: A meta-analysis on rape myths. *Journal of Interpersonal Violence, 25*, 2010–2035.

Tasca, M., Rodriguez, N., Spohn, C., & Koss, M. P. (2013). Police decision making in sexual assault cases: Predictors of suspect identification and arrest. *Journal of Interpersonal Violence, 28*, 1157–1177.

Temkin, J. (1999). Reporting rape in London: A qualitative study. *The Howard Journal, 38*, 17–41.

Temkin, J. (2010). "And always keep a-hold of nurse for fear of finding something worse": Challenging rape myths in the court room. *New Criminal Law Review, 13*, 710–734.

Temkin, J., & Krahé, B. (2008). *Sexual assault and the justice gap: A question of attitude*. Oxford: Hart Publishing.

The Havens (2010). *Wake Up To Rape Research Summary Report*. Retrieved February 22, 2016, from: http://www.zerotolerance.org.uk/vaw/resources?page=1&type=28&subject=30.

Ullman, S. E. (2010). *Talking about sexual assault: Society's response to survivors*. Washington, DC: American Psychological Association.

Vetten, L., Jewkes, R, Sigsworth, R., Christofides, N., Loots, L., & Dunseith, O. (2008). *Tracking Justice: The attrition of rape cases through the Criminal Justice System in Gauteng*. Johannesburg: Tshwaranang Legal Advocacy Centre, the South African Medical Research Council and the Centre for the Study of Violence and Reconciliation. Retrieved October 10, 2014, from www.csvr.org.za/docs/tracking_justice.pdf.

Viki, G. T., Abrams, D., & Masser, B. (2004). Evaluating stranger and acquaintance rape: The role of benevolent sexism in perpetrator blame and recommended sentence length. *Law and Human Behavior, 28*, 295–303.

Ward, C. (1995). *Attitudes toward rape*. London: Sage.

Weir, J. E., & Wrightsman, L. S. (1990). The determinants of mock jurors' verdicts in a rape case. *Journal of Applied Social Psychology, 20*, 901–919.

Wentz, E., & Archbold, C. A. (2012). Police perceptions of sexual assault victims: Exploring the intra-female gender hostility thesis. *Police Quarterly, 15*, 25–44.

Wheatcroft, J. M., Wagstaff, G. F., & Moran, A. (2009). Revictimizing the victim? How rape victims experience the UK legal system. *Victims and Offenders, 4*, 265–284.

Williams, J. E., & Holmes, K. A. (1981). *The second assault: Rape and public attitudes*. Westport, CT: Greenwood Press.

Winkel, F. W., & Koppelaar, L. (1991). Rape victims' style of self-presentation and secondary victimization by the environment. *Journal of Interpersonal Violence, 6*, 29–40.

Winkel, F. W., & Koppelaar, L. (1992). Perceived credibility of the communicator: Studies of perceptual bias in police officers conducting rape interviews. In F. Lösel (Ed.), *Psychology and law: International perspectives* (pp. 219–232). Berlin: DeGruyter.

Workman, J. E., & Orr, R. L. (1996). Clothing, sex of subject, and rape myth acceptance as factors affecting attributions about an incident of acquaintance rape. *Clothing and Textiles Research Journal, 14*, 276–284.

Justice and Family Issues in Shia: Dealing with Domestic Violence

Batoul Pakzad and Hassan Alipour

Abstract The fact that domestic violence against children or women exists in Shia communities across the Muslim World cannot be denied, however the causes of such violence are not different from other communities. In fact, personal, geographical, cultural and economic issues are considered to be as effective elements in domestic violence as in other parts of the globe and, like there, this violence sometimes is justified through the misinterpretation of the contexts of religious sources. Religion should be studied in its entirety together with all its rulings and conditions, however in justifying violence and promoting acts of force based on religion, the emphasis is only on those interpretable subjects that indeed have selective and personal aspects. Family issues in the Shia tradition depend on a dynamic jurisprudence. Hence, some jurisprudents have attempted to interpret religious laws in a correct and up-to-date manner and expressed some new thoughts about women, such as equalizing the amount of blood money between men and women, preferring women over men as caretakers of children, or disapproving of ill-treatment of women by men. These new approaches have been reflected in the laws of Iran as the most populated Shia State. The method of the current research is an analytical method based on Islamic sources combined with a statistical approach. The current research focuses on the basis of justice in Shia families and the causes of domestic violence. The findings of this research show that the justice in Shia families is based on the balance of rights instead of equity.

B. Pakzad (✉)
Islamic Azad University, North Tehran Branch, Tehran, Iran
e-mail: b_pakzad@iau-tnb.ac.ir

H. Alipour
Shahrekord University, Shahrekord, Iran
e-mail: hassan.alipour@gmail.com

H. Kury et al. (eds.), *Women and Children as Victims and Offenders: Background, Prevention, Reintegration*, DOI 10.1007/978-3-319-08398-8_25

1 Introduction

Family status and the position of the woman in the Islamic societies have been shaped within the context of a cultural, religious and geographical framework. Cultural, geographical and religious conditions of the Islamic communities around the globe are not uniform; hence understanding family status and domestic violence just through a religious approach is not feasible. Establishing an irrefrangible relationship between them and the religious primary rules is impossible because of differentiations on geographical and cultural grounds. Accordingly, it is a false assumption about assessing the deficiencies and defects in the family, especially domestic violence in the Islamic societies, based on religious orders. Nevertheless, one cannot ignore the dominant role of religion in shaping a Muslim family, as the religion affected by geographical and cultural factors has a great impact on them as well. Therefore, to understand the issues of family and domestic violence, we should consider three components: religion, geography and culture.

The Islamic religion as the most powerful factor in forming a Muslim family has influenced the family in two ways: a model-oriented way and a competitive one. The model-oriented way is influenced by the verses of the Holy Qur'an and the Last Prophet's behavior regarding family relationships. Here, the effective role of religion is unique and common for all Muslims. The numerous references to women throughout a long and profound Sura (chapter) of the Holy Qur'an, and the Prophet's respectful behavior towards women, that was emphasized by God within the Qu'ran, all are well-founded and practical models for a cohesive family with fairly equal rights. The competitive impact has its origin in sectarianism. After the Prophet's death, the dispute over his succession led to the formation of Islamic sects, each of them having its own jurisprudential system. The more important Muslim sects are Imamites (the Twelvers), Shafi'ite, Hanbalite, Hanafite and Malikite, which are also classified into two major groups as Sunnite and Shia. Shia is the second-largest denomination of Islam, comprising 25 % of the total Muslim population in the world. From the Sunnite sects, the Shafi'ite school is somehow near to the Shia and the Imamites school, and with the exception of some matters, there is an approximate consensus between the jurisprudents of the Shia and the Shafi'ite. The formation of the Islamic jurisprudence and the inference of Islamic primary sources by great Islamic sects caused them to compete in the acquisition of religious knowledge, so that in the different branches of jurisprudence a number of disputes occurred in connection with jurisprudential issues, which were effective in regulating family relations. This competitive impact has itself originated from the geographic environment plus the character traits of the legal experts and the racial, political and social attitudes, so that the opinions of followers about the family and women have varied from sect to sect.

The geographic situation of Islam is the second effective factor that has affected not only the family, but also the religion itself. The world of Islam has covered all kinds of climates as well as inhabitable places. From the westernmost point of Africa, in the desert, to the easternmost point of Asia, covered by rain forest, the people and countries that follow Islam are different. The Islamic Laws, the further they are from the center of legislation, i.e. Arabian countries, are accompanied by alterations. In this context, referring to different attitudes of Muslim communities towards the veil is useful. As a result, it is absolutely impossible to perceive family relations in the world of Islam only by a pattern of one or more Muslim countries. Indeed, the geographic conditions have weakened the Islamic principles or changed some features of them.

Culture, as another important factor, plays a considerable role in family relationships and domestic violence. The emergence of Islam has not just eradicated the domestic cultures, but has cautiously encountered the prevailing cultures regulating the relations between man and woman. The major part of family culture, which has been shaped through many years and belongs to certain regions, is under the influence of more powerful cultures. However, it seems that Islam is the creator of it and/or has accepted it, while the culture in contrast with the religion has different effects without any obligation or duty imposed, and powerfully affects the nations. The age of obligation or imposed duty begins only with puberty, when a person starts carrying out the religious rules and commands, whereas culture is from birth imposed on human beings, and it is obvious that sometimes a Muslim's native culture is prevalent over his or her religion. From this perspective, studying family issues and domestic violence against women in Shia communities, and comparing it with the Sunnite communities, must be accomplished through considering geographical and cultural conditions along with religion.

This chapter only deals with the status of women in Shia communities, and merely involves females, both children and adults, as about male children, except in certain cases, there is no considerable discussion in the Islamic law. In addition, some related issues in Sunni communities are discussed as well.

2 Family Status in the Shia Tradition

The shaping of a Shia family is influenced by religious (holy), personal and regional patterns. Some jurisprudential comments by Imamites apparently seem to indicate that the opinions of this Islamic sect about women in comparison with other sects are more severe or limited; for example, Imamites believe that if a mother stole a piece of property from her child and the proper requirements were given, the amputation of the mother's hand would be feasible. Shafi'ites, Hanbalites, Hanafites, and Malikites on the other hand agree that there should be no such punishment of the mother as amputation (Mousavi Bojnourdi 2003, p. 205). In addition, Imamites believe in temporary marriage, while other Sunnite sects do not.

2.1 The Role of the Holy Patterns in Shaping the Family Status

The holy patterns are God's inspirations and ordinances about regulating the family relationship. There are many impressive and important women in the Qur'an including Bilqis the Queen of Sheba, Sareh, the wife of Prophet Abraham, Asiya, the wife of Pharaon and the mothers of the Prophet Moses and Jesus (Satari 1996, p. 39). God in the first verse of Surat An-Nisa implicitly emphasizes the equality of man and woman, when He says: "Who created you from one soul and created from it its mate and dispersed from both of them many men and women (male and female)." This sage preface of a surah regarding women, named An-Nisa (women), expresses the equality of man and woman in the Creator's sight. In addition, here God guides the Muslims to be mindful of their relatives and family members, including males and females. Therefore, the Qur'an, at the time of its revelation to the Prophet, has paid more attention to the woman, although one may say that, concerning the equality of man and woman, there was no need to have a special surah in the name of women, and all surahs should have been revealed to address males and females. Yet other surahs have also considered women, including An-Nur (Light) that refers to some rules regarding women, just to show that the Qur'an has not addressed women only in An-Nisa. As emphasized by Javadi Amoli, one of the Shia intellectuals, the primary addressing of the Qur'an is not based on gender. With a view to the content, the Qur'an reveals that the perfections of humans can be found in the originology, eschatology, revelation and propheciology; that is, the perfection depends on having a Divine world-view; i.e. the world has an Origin named Allah and His most beautiful attributes, and an end named the Return, which includes resurrection, hell, and paradise. And between this beginning and end is the straight path, in which there is revelation and prophecy. Because in the context of the universe, there is nothing more than the Origin and the Return, and the relationship between the Origin and the Return (the Beginning and the End); therefore, there are three principles of religion: originology, eschatology, and propheciology. This is expressed by the saying of Ali ibn-Abi-Talib (The first holy Imam in Shia) "God gives his blessing to someone who knows from where he came, where he is and where he shall go," and is a comment on the three principles of religion.

Comprehending these three principles is not linked to being a man or a woman, meaning that neither being a man is a condition, nor being a woman is a hindrance. The prophets of Allah who invited people to these three principles did not send out specific invitations for men, nor did they deprive women from being invited. When the Holy Qur'an by the blessed Prophet says: "My way, and that of my followers, is to call you to God with full perception", this invitation includes all human beings. But in An-Nisa and other surahs, women are not equal with men. In addition, a phrase like "Women are like fields for you" is a comment on women's subordination. Yet, Dr. Morteza Motahari, the author of "Rights of Women in Islam" (2003, p. 2) in the preface of his book said: "The Qur'an sees woman as she is in nature. Hence, there is an entire harmony between the Qur'an's decrees and the laws of nature. Woman in the Qur'an is the same woman in nature." From this perspective, the personality traits of women explain the inequalities between men and women, so there is no likelihood of criticizing it at the time of the revelation of the Qur'an.

Besides the generalized status of women and the family in the Qur'an, the female characters mentioned in the Qur'an imply that women behave as men on the basis of human nature. Often, some women like Moses's mother, Asiya (Pharaoh' wife), Jesus's mother, and the Prophet's wife were charged with preparing the ground for the advent of a messenger of God. Occasionally, there are complaints about some women who were conspirators such as Abu Lahab's (the prophet's uncle's) wife. However, the positive traits of women in the Holy Qur'an are more remarkable. The Qur'anic great women had particularly important roles in fostering great men, and without their maternal and pure personalities no messenger would have appeared from their womb. In this way, holy patterns gave a positive and sophisticated image of the status of women, and could be used for regulating family relations and their interaction.

2.2 The Role of Personality Patterns in Family Interaction

Personality patterns in religions are the most important behavioral sources for their followers. The followers of any religion attempt to adjust their behavior to their religious leaders' behavior. In the Shia sect more influential female personalities are found than in other religions. Characterizations of successful women who showed great love for their families like Fatima (the Prophet's daughter and Imam Ali's wife), and Zaynab, the daughter of Ali ibn-Abi-Talib, were not irrelevant to Shia political conditions. During history, the Shias were strictly under the control of the Umayyad and Abbasid Caliphates, so that the Shia men had no opportunity for political power.

These conditions created a relatively equal status of men and women among the Imamites to consolidate the followers of this religion against the threats of governments. Additionally, the personality of Fatima as mother of two Imams (Hasan and Hossein, the first and second Shia's Imams), and mediated mother of ten other Imams of the Imamites had a great impact on the family relationships of the Shias. The innocence of these Imams and the lack of permission to portray them because of their holiness, focused, more than anything else, on the personality of Fatima. Therefore, consecration permeated into jurisprudential principles.

In addition, anywhere that there is an utterance by Imams in the orders and acts of worships, the addressing of Fatima is a necessary part. Gradually, the family relationships between Fatima and Ali ibn-Abi-Talib became a prominent model for the Shia followers, and in general led to a proper position of women in the Shia family. Even a majority of Shia men in honor to Fatima have ignored their rights of polygamy and tried to reconstruct the life of Ali and Fatima. However, the pattern of Ali and Fatima is fragile for a Shia family. These two characters lived together when they were young; and Fatima died when she was still very young. Hence, the pattern of their lives for a Shia family (husband and wife) usually ends at their youth, and other components are highlighted. With other sects, personality patterns have historical effects, and the memories of past lives will not be typically renewed as Shias in today's living.

2.3 The Role of Regional Traditions in Family Behavior

The environment has a remarkable role in the Shia and Sunnite families. The appearance of Islam in the dry region of Arabia has modified the regional traditions regarding woman and the family, but it has never removed all their rules. The warm and desert environment of many Islamic countries in the Middle East provides some concrete and tangible realities for a Muslim family. In fact, these realities are sometimes more effective than the formal and metaphysical realities of religion. There is a huge gap between theory and historical truth. In other words there is a big space between thought and practice. However, in practice women despite of some respect are often despised and restricted (Bousquet 1975, p. 37). The study of religious history shows that every religion depends on the rules established under the shadow of the regional and cultural traditions. The scattering of Islamic sects in different geographical regions has changed the attitudes towards woman and family. In a desert environment, the presence of woman in society is invisible and the conditions are very male-oriented. In a mountainous environment, the presence of woman alongside the man is more visible; and in a rainy environment, a woman appears like a man in society. While in all these three environment Islamic principles are relatively unified, the variety of family attitudes on the basis of regional changes is well visible throughout the south, center and north of the Islamic Republic of Iran.

Regional traditions have affected the approach to the implementation of Islamic laws, so that it differs from country to country, and in a country, from place to place, and for this aspect, there is no difference between religious sects. In a Sunni family near the border of Iran and Pakistan, the desert environment affects the presence of women in the society and her validity in the family. On the other hand, Kurdish and Sunni populations near the border of Iran and Iraq represent good conditions for women and relatively modern family relations. The effect of regional traditions is automatic and compulsory and does not signify the predominance of one sect or the families of a region over other sects or other families in different regions. Thus, this difference shows the effects of various causes besides religion in a Muslim family.

In the highlands, the relationships in a Shia family depend on the regional traditions. Regarding family relationships, a Shia family may not be able to implement Islamic rules exactly. The presence of the Shias, in typical mountainous areas sometimes with a suitable climate and the influence of cultural traditions imposed so many years ago in regions like Iran and Iraq, has caused the men and women to behave in ways that are not exactly the same as prescribed in Islamic sources.

3 An Analysis of Women's Problems in the Family

The movement of advocating women's rights is quite justly insisting on this point that a major part of women's problems and the inequality of their rights compared to men is hidden in a traditional attitude towards women. The major part of traditional attitudes towards women emanates from religious rules. As mentioned, however, traditional attitudes towards women are not regulated only by religion, and separating other contributing factors from religious approaches is not always easy. Women's problems with the religious approach in the family are as follows:

3.1 Participation in Home, Community Control

Some Islamic laws support the claim that a Muslim woman must stay at home instead of contributing to society through her work because of protecting the dignity and gravity of her family. A woman has a primary role at home, whereas socially her position is secondary. In the personality patterns of Shias, there are women like Fatima and Khadija (the Prophet's wife), who had primary roles at home but socially were under the supervision of their husbands. In a Muslim family, the husband is the head of the family and the one who makes decisions about housing the family members. Without the permission of her husband, a wife is not allowed to go out of the house. From this point of view, a wife is more profitable for her family, especially for her husband, than for society. Yet in such a context, she is free to shoulder some important responsibilities such as judgment, congregational prayer leadership (imamat) and being an Islamic governor. In less important tasks, it is her husband who can prevent his wife from being in society.

However, religious approaches to restrict the women are not the same. About women working outside the home, the Hanafieh said, "A woman, who works and does not stay at home, if her husband wants her to stay at home, and she does not accept, will be deprived of alimony payment." Furthermore, other religions altogether say, "She is not permitted to leave the house." Shafi'ites and Hanbalites believed that if she goes out by herself, even with her husband's permission, her alimony fails (Mughniyah 1987, p. 348). In addition, an adult daughter is dependent for marriage on the authority of her father. But in regional traditions, generally the authority of the father is extended to other rights of an adult girl. In the view of Hanaifieh, an adult female, either virgin or widow, can decide herself on her marriage and nobody can have authority over her. Shafi'ites, Hanbalites and Malikites believed that the decision about the marriage of a virgin and/or widow must be made by her and her guardian (Mughniyah 1987, p. 286). With the Imamites, it is generally agreed that the marriage of a virgin girl is subject to the permission of her father.

Of course, in all Islamic sects women are not completely restricted to their home. Women can make a contrary provision before their marriage; alternatively, they can content their husband with relinquishing his headship as the marriage condition. Furthermore, in other Islamic social laws sometimes there are some exponents for the independent presence of women. For example, the Shia, Shafi'ites and Malikites believe that for undertaking Hajj, there is no provision for the presence of the husband or an intimate. If a woman can support herself, hajj is essential for her. Hanbalites and Hanaifieh have said that the presence of her husband or an intimate is a provision for her hajj (Mughniyah 1987, p. 176).

3.2 Unreal Equality: Real Inequality

In Islam, women are respected inside the home, but outwardly, they are not equal with men. In the Shia approach, with regard to personality patterns, typically there is a difference between motherhood and womanhood. A mother enjoys great esteem, and as the Prophet said to his daughter Fatimah, "Heaven is under the feet of mothers," and in a dominant approach "God accepts mothers' prayers." This mother-oriented approach finds meaning only when she stays at home with her children; otherwise, in the case of being outside the home and away from her children or in the absence of a child, she is a woman, and a woman without the attribute of motherhood does not enjoy equal respect. Hence, the formal equality persuades women to be married very soon; but accessing this formal equality is simultaneous with losing the position of equality in the social environment.

It can be said that formal equality is a mental image that a man has about a woman, but real equality is a mental image that a woman has for her own self-respect. Therefore, the mentality of men, although it is respectful towards women, does not necessarily mean that women consider it as equality. In the fourth verse of An-Nisa, a man with financial means and observance of justice can be simultaneously married to two, three, and ultimately four women, which is not created by Islam, but merely permitted (Tabatabai 1976, p. 130). Therefore, seemingly polygamy in the Qur'an is contingent on two conditions: a tangible condition, which is the financial support, and a moral condition, which is the observance of justice. These two conditions beside the legislative philosophy of this verse, i.e., selecting a mate from unaccompanied and unprotected women, give very limited permission to men to be polygamous. However, this, in the mind of a woman, can be only a negative phenomenon and, accordingly, the formal equality in enjoying financial support as well as justice will ultimately be considered as an inequality. This condition for polygamy is not identical in all jurisprudential approaches; and the unequal status of a woman is not necessarily always upheld in favor of the man. For example for Hanbalites, if a husband makes a conditional contract with his wife not to get married to another woman, this condition and the contract will be valid (Mughniyah 1987, p. 268). Nowadays this method is mentioned under the terms and conditions of a marriage contract. In fact, a woman at the time of marriage stipulates a condition with the man that in the case of being married again to another woman she would have the right of getting a divorce. Yet, for Hanbalites, Shafi'ites, Malikites and Imamites this condition is null and the contract is null.

Polygamy among Islamic sects, however, must comply with the terms of marriage. First, polygamy should be in the framework of a permanent marriage. Also, Hanifes, Hanbalites and Shafi'ites agree on the equality of men and women from the aspects of Islam concerning freedom, career and descent. But, Imamites and Malikites believe that the equality of men and women is only based on religious criteria (Mughniyah 1987, p. 290). The Imamites, unlike other Islamic sects, do not believe in the absolute permanence of marriage, but that besides four permanent wives a man can have temporary marriages. Temporary marriage can be considered as inequality for a permanent wife and as equality for a temporary wife. Hence, the temporary marriage for Imamites is included amongst the Islamic rules, but it is not often applied and depends to other conditions.

In marriage, the voluntary acceptance of the woman is a condition. She can decide to accept or reject a marriage offer. The age of marriage is the same as the age of puberty. All Islamic sects have prescribed age and physical criteria for being an adult. For Imamites the age of puberty, specifically in imitation of personality patterns like the marriage of Ali and Fatima, for a girl is full 9 lunar years (entering into 10 lunar years), and for a boy it is full 15 lunar years (entering into 16 lunar years). These ages are the beginning points of the rights and duties of females and males respectively. Although Imamites claim that a preterm puberty for girls justifies their premature presence in society and beside the adults, they challenge at the same time some obligations such as criminal responsibility. The Shia among Islamic sects has the lowest age of criminal responsibility for girls. In the Shia jurisprudence, a girl by reaching 9 lunar years is known as criminally liable and any criminal acts she commits are punishable. The Islamic Penal Code of 2013 (1392) about offenses related to discretionary correction ignores that point of view and determines the age of criminal liability as reaching 16 lunar years.

The age of puberty in other Islamic sects is higher. For Hanbalites and Shafi'ites the puberty age of both boys and girls is 15. The Malikites consider it to be 17 for boys and girls. And for the Hanifeh the ages of puberty for boys and girls are 18 and 17, respectively. The low marriage age in some Islamic sects often caused girls at a young age or without any knowledge of family pressure to be married, which is not directly related to Islam.

Regarding other family issues, a certain inequality of man and woman can be seen, such as the alimony of a man to a woman. The Muslims have reached a consensus on this matter that the marriage is a cause for relation and alimony obligations and commanded by God.

For the Imamites, Hanbalites and Hanaifieh alimony will not fail if the wife becomes sick. But, for the Malikites it would fail, if the sickness of the wife were very acute (Mughniyah 1987, p. 340). The jurisprudents have limited the alimony to nutrition, clothing and housing, and are not against the medical treatment of a wife, and even some of them have said explicitly that it is part of alimony and the obligation of the husband. In the opinion of the Hanaifieh, providing fruits and medical treatment is not the obligation of a husband when there is a dispute between spouses. The book of Javaher Emameh states that the wife has no right to request medicine and the fees of bloodletting and bathing except in cold weather. Seyed Abulhasam Esfahani stated in his book (Vasileh): "if a wife has a usual sickness and needs medical treatment, the husband is obliged to pay related costs. But if a wife's disease is rare and incurable and the treatment of her is costly, it is not part of alimony and the husband in not obliged to pay for it." (Mughniyah 1987, p. 346).

In the view of the Imamites, in the case of madness of the wife, the husband cannot dissolve the marriage, but he can ask for a divorce. For some Islamic sects, the insanity of a wife can be associated with the dissolution of the marriage by her husband. It has even been said that in the case of a wife's insanity prior to any sexual relationship with the husband, no dowry is paid to the wife (Mughniyah 1987, p. 395).

3.3 Two Different Aspects of the Issue of Domestic Violence

The third problem of women in the family is the issue of violence. Some fields of domestic violence are rooted in religion and regulations, however some are related to traditions that are about to change: for instance that the blood-money (financial worth of the life in Islam) of women is only half of that of men, or that fathers are not punished for committing a crime against their daughters. Both may lead to the promotion of violence against women. A woman for killing a man should pay half of the blood money to the man. However, the majority of public jurisprudents believe that a male murderer, contrary to a female murdered, will be punished without paying the half-blood-money by the avenger of blood, except the Hanbalites who agreed with the Imamites (Mousavi Bojnourdi 2006, p. 133). In the Penal Code of 2013 (1392), the Iranian Community goes in the direction of not exactly implementing all the rules of Shia jurisprudence. In this new law, if a woman or her relatives, in some cases, are not able to pay blood money for the punishment of a criminal man, the government may help with the payment. In addition, in the new law, with the government paying half of a woman's blood money, the amount of blood money of men and women has become equal. Also, the punishment of stoning women by putting them in a hole to make their condition worse has been forgotten to a large extent. The anti-violence measures taken to protect women in the Islamic community are thus comparable with other communities. The anti-violence campaign should, however, be accompanied by the knowledge of cultural, regional and religious factors. Yet, the advocates of women's rights in Islamic societies have taken an imitative approach copied from the West.

Without paying attention to the fact that religion is not the only and real cause of inequality, they try to justify it from the viewpoint of religion, while the reality is different. Looking at the various approaches of Islamic sects makes it clear that religion is not inflexible in front of social changes, place and time requirements, or regional and cultural components. The anti-violence campaign against punishment by the advocates of women's rights leads to an oppositional situation in religion and society, on one hand, and in patriarchal traditions, on the other hand, which has no benefit except that the status of women in an Islamic community becomes worse.

Another aspect of increasing violence against women is their attitude to use violence themselves. In the Islamic societies, beside the advocates of excessive anti-violence, there are women who consider the use of violence as their right and justify such a situation in the light of religion and regional cultures. They assume that a weak person being under the protection of a strong person is in an unequal position. A woman for attaining the protection of her man sometimes should assist in applying violence through a play of manhood authority.

The sense of violence acceptance, specifically in Muslim societies, leads to a fragile situation, which is even worse for divorced women in such a way that society's culture and pressure imply that violence at home is better than violence in society. A husband may commit acts of violence at home, and of course, this violence is justifiable and gives meaning to a religious and native life. However, violence against a woman who is divorced may be done by anybody in society. Thus, in the occurrence of society violence it is better for a woman to be under the shadow of domestic violence. Given the hurt resulting from a position of women opposing retributive violence in the relationship between man and woman, on the one hand, and the toleration of active violence by women on the other hand, it may be concluded that a major part of family problems in Muslim society does not relate to religion, although religion has the ability to be its justifier. Indeed, the main cause of women's problems in the Muslim communities is a very deep gap between women who are anti-violence and women who are violence-oriented and consider it as womanly.

4 The Role of Shiism in the Field Of Domestic Violence

Although there are no official statistics regarding domestic violence in Shia societies, the records provided by a number of organizations indicate that there is a high rate of violence against women. According to the Iran National Security Yearbook 2013–2014, p. 134: "in 2013, Violence against women occupied the third place among antisocial behaviors; following Addiction and Child abuse." There was a higher rate of violence in poorer provinces than in other provinces. There was an 88 % rate of violence among "Kurdish" families. In 2014, 41 % of the women referred to the health centers were the victims of domestic violence. In addition, 66 % of Iranian women become victims of domestic violence (Iran's National Security Yearbook 2014–2015, p. 135).

The role played by religion in the increase of domestic violence in the country which houses the largest Shia population in the world, Iran, is not obvious. On one hand, the increase of violence in large cities or central provinces is only loosely related to religion, as people in large cities usually do not firmly practice religious teachings; and the majority of people in border provinces, such as the Kurdish ones, are Sunnite. On the other hand, the increase of violence in poorer provinces is most probably a sign of the role religion plays in domestic violence. Therefore, two different approaches may be chosen while observing the role of Shiism in domestic violence.

4.1 An Approach Linked to the Lack of the Role of Religion in Domestic Violence

The practical rules in Shiism are rooted in the Qur'an and Hadith [the teachings of Prophet Mohammad and the 12 Imams]. The Qur'an and Qur'anic texts mostly hold men and women as equals and introduce no situation in regard to which systematic and permanent acts of domestic harshness or violence are permitted. The Qur'an attempts to depict men and women as equals. This equality, of course, is in their creation and origin. According to verse Al-A'raf, line 189: "It is He Who has created you from a single person (Adam), and (then) He has created from him his wife [Hawwa (Eve)], in order that he might enjoy the pleasure of living with her." And according to Al-Bagara, line 187: "They are Libas [i.e. body cover, or screen, or Sakan, i.e. you enjoy the pleasure of living with her; man and wife fit, protect, cover, etc. one another as clothes fit bodies] for you and you are the same for them".

The fact that men and women are of the very same origin is a solid proof that in the eyes of the All-Creator men are in no way superior which would permit them to resort to domination and violence towards women. According to verse Ar-Rum, line 21: "And among His Signs is this, that He created for you wives from among yourselves, that you may find repose in them, and He has put between you affection and mercy. Verily, in that are indeed signs for a people who reflect." The Qur'an attempts to equalize men and women in their social relationships and communications as well. According to At-Taubah, line 71: "The believers, men and women, are Auliya' (helpers, supporters, friends, protectors) of one another, they enjoin (on the people) Al-Ma'ruf (i.e. Islamic Monotheism and all that Islam orders one to do), and forbid (people) from Al-Munkar (i.e. polytheism and disbelief of all kinds, and all that Islam has forbidden); they perform As-Salat (Iqamat-as-Salat) and give the Zakat, and obey Allah and His Messenger. Allah will have His Mercy on them." And in a number of occasions, the Qur'an speaks to men and women together and in perfect equality: verse Al-Ahzab, line 35: "Verily, the Muslims (those who submit to Allah in Islam) men and women, the believers, men and women, (who believe in Islamic Monotheism), the men and the women who are obedient (to Allah), the men and women who are truthful (in their speech and deeds), the men and the women who are patient (in performing all the duties which Allah has ordered and in abstaining from all that Allah has forbidden), the men and the women who are humble (before their Lord Allah), the men and the women who give Sadaqat (i.e. Zakat, and alms, etc.), the men and the women who observe Saum (fast) (the obligatory fasting during the month of Ramadan, and the optional Nawafil fasting), the men and the women who guard their chastity (from illegal sexual acts) and the men and the women who remember Allah much with their hearts and tongues (while sitting, standing, lying, etc. for more than 300 times extra over the remembrance of Allah during the five compulsory congregational prayers) or praying extra additional Nawafil (prayers of night in the last part of night, etc.) Allah has prepared for them forgiveness and a great reward (i.e. Paradise)." In the Islamic instructions, all forms of violence towards innocent humans are forbidden and there is great emphasis on the observance of social relations, as the blessed Prophet says: "Nobody does violence, unless he/she has gone to hell."

The above-mentioned texts from the Qur'an, along with many Shia traditions which describe how the Prophet and Imams treated women, as well as the qualities of character introduced in Shiism, prove that domestic harshness in the Islamic societies cannot be explained by, or attached to religion; on the contrary, a husband cannot inflict punishment on his wife, in other words, with a view to administering the punishment, a woman does not differ from others (See: Mousavi Bojnourdi 2006, pp. 55–64) - see also: Women and Penal Law: Collection of articles, the results of working group efforts, and the documents from the First International Conference on Women's Rights and Penal Law in the Past, Present and Future, 2004; under supervision of Dr. Mehra, N. Salsabil Publication. (2005). Punishing a woman is contingent upon proving her guilt in front of a judge, and administrating it is reliant upon the judge's decision.

4.2 An Approach Linked to the Excessive Role of Religion in Family Violence

According to another approach, in Shia and also in other Islamic societies, religion plays the dominant role in domestic violence. One subject that matters a great deal in Islamic societies concerns family rules and traditions and the social attitudes towards women, no matter how profoundly the fundamental and civil laws emphasize the equality of women's position with that of men. As a matter of fact, when it comes to an official and fundamental standpoint regarding the law in Islamic countries, two different approaches can be distinguished. The first approach is based upon the legal execution of "Sharia" laws. In countries such as Saudi Arabia and Iran the application of Sharia laws is prioritized over the application of parliament laws. In Iran, "law" is mostly based upon Sharia regulations and teachings. The other approach is based on prioritizing sanctioned laws over Sharia laws. In countries such as Turkey and Malaysia, the family [matrimonial] relationships are actually based on laws, which are not bound to the Islamic Sharia. In spite of all this, domestic violence takes place in the confinement of walls, which are made of religious and cultural traditions; traditions so strong and ingrained that no sanctioned law established and no human rights conviction accepted by Islamic countries may penetrate through. Therefore we may conclude in most Islamic societies, Shia ones included, that the application of the Sharia is more easily accepted than the application of sanctioned laws.

The approach, which believes religion to be the main source of [domestic] violence in Shia societies, introduces quite a few indications and symptoms, the four most prominent ones being the following:

First, *the Sharia permission, which enables husbands to punish their wives*: Based on a number of theories extracted from the wording of line 34 of verse An-Nisa', husbands are permitted to punish their wives according to the pattern and conditions mentioned in this line. The line reads: "Men are the protectors and maintainers of women, because Allah has made one of them to excel over the other, and because they spend (to support them) from their means. Therefore the righteous women are devoutly obedient (to Allah and to their husbands), and guard in the husband's absence what Allah orders them to guard (e.g. their chastity, their husband's property, etc.). As to those women on whose part you see ill-conduct, admonish them (first), (next), refuse to share their beds, (and last) beat them (lightly, if it is useful), but if they return to obedience, seek not against them means (of annoyance). Surely, Allah is Ever Most High, Most Great." The contents of this line are generally based upon the concept of "enjoining [on the people] Al-Ma'ruf (i.e. Islamic Monotheism and all that Islam orders one to do), and interdicting [acting] against Al-Munkar (i.e. polytheism and disbelief of all kinds, and all that Islam has forbidden)"; and explains the hierarchical order according to which a man may deal with his wife. In spite of this fact, the phrase "striking the wife" mentioned as the final stage of this encounter may be a permission to commit physical violence against women. In the view of some jurisprudents, a husband can administer a variety of punishments on his wife. According to this opinion, in all wrongdoings of his wife a husband is both a judge and an executer.

Second, *the permission of men's headship over women*: This section of the above-mentioned line (An-Nisa', 34), which reads: "Men are the protectors and maintainers of women, because Allah has made one of them to excel over the other", has been reflected upon in narratives and proverbs, and eventually in the civil laws of Islamic countries as well. According to article 1105 of the civil Code of Iran (1928), the headship in the married couples' relationships belongs to the husbands. Although a one-person-head often leads to status and cohesion in the family, it may also be accompanied by violence. Since the security policies which are established in business relationships between the superintendents and the underlings do not exist in a family, it is naturally very possible for the chairman's actions to tend towards harshness, violence and [physical] punishment to oblige the subordinates [in this case, wife and children] to act upon his bidding.

Third, *the inequality of the value of life of women compared to that of men*: Although there is no reference in the Qur'an to the value of life of women, according to both Sunnite and Shiá narratives the compensation to be made should a woman be slain is established to be half the amount of the compensation should the slain be a man. According to these regulations, should any damage be inflicted upon any man or woman, and should this damage amount up to one third the value of wergild for a man's life (which is to be the equivalent value of 33 camels out of 100 camels), the appointed compensation is to be equal, whether the victim be male or female. But if the damage inflicted upon a woman amounts to any value higher than one third of the wergild, the compensation is to be reduced to half of that same value for a man. The new Penal Code ruled, however, that the government should pay the other half of the blood money.

It should be pointed out that, should the conditions of punishment not be met, the man or men who have inflicted physical injuries upon a woman or women, shall endure, under any circumstances, a punishment of judiciary discretion in the form of imprisonment [punishments of judiciary discretion are not defined or determined by Qur'an or Hadith, but by the verdict of a Judge].

Fourth, *"Sexual Violence" remains undefined in family [matrimonial] relationships in Islamic societies*: In Shia and Sunnite religious jurisprudence, the concept of sexual violation of a woman is only applicable when the man or men involved are other than the woman's husband. If the husband attempts to have sexual intercourse with his wife without her consent, according to the concept of sexual violation, he has not committed any misdemeanor. However, should any physical injury be inflicted upon the woman, or should the sexual intercourse be forced upon her during the menstrual period, the husband will be sentenced to guarantee the execution of compensation or atonement. Likewise, should a woman fall victim to sexual violence from her husband, she is permitted to demand a divorce and is given the right to divorce, due to the rules which regard "distress and constriction".

In such cases, the act committed is not defined as sexual violation, for the act of adultery [the closest concept to sexual violation in Islam] cannot be committed by a husband towards his wife. This concept, therefore, is prone to pave the way for sexual harshness to be committed by the husbands towards their wives.

4.3 An Approach to the Role of Religion, Besides Other Factors, in Family Violence

The third approach views the role of religion in domestic harshness in a temperate and moderate light. The truth is that from a religious point of view, the right of husbands to commit acts of harshness and/or violence towards women is not fundamentally established; and in spite of a number of exegeses based on the outward appearance of lines of the Qur'an and also a number of narratives in this regard, harshness towards women cannot be justified only by means of religion (see: Khomeini et al. 1986, p. 305 and Tabatabai et al. 1996). In other words, there exists a difference between the cause of harshness and the justification of harshness. The cause of harshness can be found in the factors, which directly result in the harshness directed at women. When studying the causes of violence in Shia countries, Iran in particular, it can be inferred that religion is not the main factor in begetting violence. Rarely has a man been seen who has committed harshness or violence towards a woman or women solely on the grounds of enforcing and/or executing Sharia commandments.

Islam introduces the fundamental elements in forming a family on the basis of affection and kindness. In reality, domestic harshness in Shia societies resembles the harshness in all other societies of the world. A research performed in Tehran

(Ahmadi et al. (2008), pp. 70–73) separated the factors, which caused domestic harshness or violence into four categories which are:

1. Cultural and social factors such as unawareness and cultural weaknesses in the community, character traits such as distrust, fury and hot temper, drug and alcohol abuse, and male chauvinism on the men's side, avarice and ostentatious manners on the women's part, and poor communicational skills and the inability to resolve disputes through dialogue or to jointly settle the problems, lack of adherence to religious practices, and/or wrong deductions and incorrect interpretations of Sharia laws.
2. Economic factors such as: financial instability, poverty and unemployment, low income and poor state of family welfare, financial dependence of wives on their husbands, class difference between the husband's and wife's families; and the conflict between women's right to ownership and financial independence with the men's lawful position as head of the family.
3. Legal and statuary factors such as: incorrect inferences from Sharia laws, inadequacy of laws and lack of legal, social and governmental protection and support for women.
4. Medical factors such as: genetic diseases and disorders, psychological problems, drug abuse, infertility of one party, lack of cultural and intellectual capacity to seek aid from psychotherapists and psychologists.

The known environmental, cultural and economic factors such as addiction, discrepancies in social status, poverty, etc., are the main causes of harshness and violence. In addition, a number of wrong religious beliefs and incorrect Sharia interpretations play a substantial part in justifying domestic harshness. A Muslim man may justify his harsh manners with the fact that the Sharia has not permitted the wife to take a separate residence, or even leave the house, without the consent of her husband.

The truth is that religion, along with other factors, is used to justify the acts of harshness committed in Islamic societies; and the main reason for such justification is that people who commit acts of violence have a poor perception of the generality of Sharia commandments and misinterpret them, and they unintentionally or knowingly take advantage of the fact that their victims lack proper perception as well. Nowadays, most of the Muslim life styles are affected by media. Then Advertising media in the modern world are often focused on external conduct and do not take into account the whole of Islamic commandments. Through such advertisements usually only the instances, which have been stated around 14 centuries ago, and have little affinity with today's society, are endorsed. And most importantly, these advertisements and external studies have not been able to, or have not wanted to, distinguish between two essential facts. The two facts are: religion is not the cause of domestic harshness, only the justification of it in a number of cases. And even this justification is due to the perpetrators [and/or the victims] poor insight into Islamic fundamentals and Sharia.

Another important fact to be taken into consideration is that a number of Sharia laws, which regard family matters are not firmly enforced in Shia societies, due to the necessities of daily life. And regarding such matters, the ones who have to apply the Sharia law [the clergy, the mullahs] do not consistently attempt to enforce the respective rules and teachings upon the community. As an example, the legal age of marriage in Iran is 13 years of age for girls and 15 years of age for boys. In 2013, however, the average age of marriage has been 22.1 years of age for girls and 27.4 years of age for boys. Another example is that according to Islamic Sharia, wives are obliged to practice obedience to their husbands; and one of the conditions of obedience is to reside in the residence determined by their husbands, and that wives do not possess the right to leave the residence except with the consent of their husbands. Despite the existence of this rule, should a woman refuse to practice obedience, and/or be disobedient to her husband, no executive guarantee may be practiced upon her above termination of her alimony [in Islamic term: it is a determined amount of money which the husband is obliged to pay his wife on a regular basis throughout the whole marriage, and which the wife is permitted to spend and use to satisfy her personal needs and desires]. Moreover, women are not obliged to reside in their husbands' residence, and/or to practice obedience towards their husbands against their [women's] will. This fact proves that in Shia communities, in matrimonial relationships in particular, people's will and taste, and the present social and cultural conditions, play a much more effective role compared to the role played by religious attitudes.

5 The Capabilities of Shia Guidance to Counter Domestic Violence

Shi'ism, in comparison with other Islamic sects, is more introverted. In the Shia approach, words such as Innocence, Waiting, and Human Soul are the axis around which ethical, historical, and even behavioral discourses take form. The evidences mentioned below bring to life the position of women in Shia attitudes. The believe that Fatima as the wife of Imam Ali and mother of other Imams was a holy person and that one of the next generation's sons who has temporarily disappeared until the time when he will come back to save the lives from sin, positively impacts on the situation of women from the Shia's perspective. Chastity is valued immeasurably among women, who look up to Fatima [Prophet Muhammad's daughter and Imam Ali's wife], who is known to be innocent and incarnate without sin, and they are waiting for a person who is said to restore the lost rights of Shia Muslims, and who is begotten by Fatima. And most important of all is the emphasis placed upon "human soul and spirit", in regard to which there is no distinction between women and men. In truth, "The divine school supposes the soul to be the whole truth of a human being although the body is necessary and essential as well. Islam says: Disclosure [of divine words] is bestowed [upon the Prophet] with the purpose of teaching and education, of refining oneself and illuminating humans. At this point equality or distinction of man and woman is subtractive of the designated issue, not of the designated predicate. It means the pivot of teaching and education is human life and life is neither male nor female; and in origin no man or woman exists." (Javadi Amuli 1999, p. 21).

This inwardly and spiritual approach of the Shia faith has in fact been influential in family [matrimonial] relationships and permits us to speak of the actual capabilities of the Shia approach to deal with domestic violence. These capabilities can be divided into three sections.

5.1 The Hierarchical Capabilities in the Family

The rights and duties of men and women in the family have been applied in such a way that proves that Islam has placed no heavier responsibilities upon any of the two parties, in order to prevent harming one or the other. Taking into consideration the generally weaker bodily capabilities of women compared to that of men, which is an undeniable natural truth, has resulted, however, in women's rights to be viewed through the same perspective. Rights such as alimony and dowry [in Islam both are to be paid to women] in marriage support the wife financially, and at the same time may be abused by husbands to enforce harshness. Moreover, the right of headship in the family is bestowed upon the husband.

The fact that women are denied social rights such as witnessing in court or to take part in primal Jihad [wars that ensure safety and spreading of Islam] do not necessarily mean inequality of women in Sharia attitudes. These differences in [attitudes towards] men and women do not prove men's superiority in society, but explain his greater responsibilities. Despite all this, the question here is whether there exists in Islamic society equality and assimilation between men's and women's rights, or a balance? The Shia viewpoint does not accept equality and assimilation between men's and women's rights in all aspects; this is due to gender differences and also differences in ability between men and women. This viewpoint, however, believes a balance should be established between men's and women's rights. Therefore, any right that a man may possess is matched by a proportionate and adequate right for the woman. The challenge that appears at this point is that equality and assimilation of rights can be observed but how can it be proved that there exists in Shia societies a balance between the rights of men and women? And how is it to be measured?

The balance between men's and women's rights is subordinate to three viewpoints: social, sanctioned by law, and intellectual. Socially, Muslim societies face a challenge where the equality of rights for men and women are concerned. This challenge has originally and generally emerged from movements formed in western countries. Muslim societies have not yet begun to really feel the necessity of equal rights for men and women. And from a subjective perspective, a balance of rights seems to be more generally accepted than an equality of rights. Through observing the sanctioned laws as well, a balance between the rights and duties of men and women is more generally accepted. To give an example, even if the wergild for a [slain] woman is half the wergild for a man, or the fact that the punishment for adultery is more severe for women, in apostasy the women's punishment is less severe; and in rebelling against the [religious] governor, women, unlike men, are not subjected to a "Baaghi" verdict [Baaghi is referred to a person who fights or conspires against the Imam]. And should the penalty be in the form of whiplash, women are in a better position, since their bodies are covered [in Islam, the law that dictates that a woman's body be covered in public overrides the form of any punishment]. This balance of sanctioned laws is in many cases able to provide women with better conditions. From an intellectual perspective as well, the accepted viewpoint in Shia societies is that the duties and hardships men endure are much greater than those women endure. Despite this truth, Shia societies are influenced by women's claim to rights. In fact, women claim rights more than they claim duties; and duties are still placed upon the shoulders of men. Such an attitude has had the result that the approach seeking balance works better in favor of women than the approach seeking equality and assimilation of rights. In recent years the women's protests led to reduce the unequal distance between men's and women's rights. In addition the women's movements led to the legal obligation of governments to pay the other half of the blood money and also to some other limitations for men's second marriages.

5.2 *Women's Society as Protective Factors from Domestic Violence*

Women's duties in family and society may be prone to criticism if the aim is equal rights for women; if however the principal aim is security and the fight against violence, the potential of the Sharia is considerable. Criminological observations indicate that many precautionary measures conflict with personal freedom and rights. Islam recognizes domestic and social violence towards women as an important topic; therefore the Sharia attempts to prevent violence against women by means of establishing a number of precautionary measures. Against domestic violence [committed by husbands] exposing their bodies, and against social violence concealing their bodies are the most significant precautionary measures and duties proposed to women.

Cooperation of wife and husband and their mutual obedience towards each other's legal desires eliminate the causes of domestic violence. As can be read in line 71 of verse Al-Taubah, the relationship between men and women is based upon gentleness, not stipulations. This line reads: "The believers, men and women, are Auliya' (helpers, supporters, friends, protectors) of one another, they enjoin (on the people) Al-Ma'ruf (i.e. Islamic Monotheism and all that Islam orders one to do), and forbid (people) from Al-Munkar (i.e. polytheism and disbelief of all kinds, and all that Islam has forbidden)". The family stipulations exist not to enforce discrimination, but to enforce an administrative guarantee to protect the gentleness [which shall exist] between husband and wife against deviation.

Women's covering in public is a very potent implement against social violence as well. Although the Hijab (it covers the woman's body except the face and hands) brings a number of limitations, its influential role cannot be ignored. It is due to this fact that even today the Faghih [the religious scholars and jurists in Islam] still stress the wearing of the Hijab, although they are aware of the modern world. These questions have been presented to a number of Shia faghih: "Is the Hijab indispensable according to religious rules? What is the verdict on people who neglect it?" The answers the faghih have proposed are homogeneous and at the same time flexible:

Ayatollah Khamenei: The principle of Hijab is indispensable according to religious rules, a number of branches concerning it, however, may not be essential. Inattentiveness towards and failure to comply with the principle of Hijab is a sin.

Ayatollah Tabrizi: The principle of Hijab for women is indispensable according to religion and the verdict against those who are inattentive towards it is the same verdict as being inattentive of other religious obligations.

His Excellency Ayatollah Safi: the principle of execution of Hijab is in fact one of the obligations of religion and should a Muslim woman renounce it, she shall be a heretic. But being only inattentive towards it, while not renouncing it, it shall only be recognized as debauchery.

His Excellency Ayatollah Sistani: The principle of Hijab is indispensable for Sharia [Shia way of life] and is mentioned in the Qur'an. But those who are inattentive to it are not necessarily renouncing the Prophet; but neglecting Hijab is a sin.

His Excellency Ayatollah Makarem-E-Shirazi: Yes, Hijab is a principle of religion. [However,] Should a person renounce it and should they not know it is a principle, it will not result in their apostasy.

His Excellency Ayatollah Bahjat: Inattentiveness to Hijab is a sin and wearing the Hijab is obligatory (according to the website listed at the sources).

Wearing the Hijab and social limitations women are obliged to practice are due to Sharia attitudes towards women's weaknesses. The Prophetic Hadith [A proverb articulated by Prophet Muhammad], which announces: "[the whole of a] Woman is allegedly genitalia" indicates that women are indeed weak [and vulnerable] and protecting them is mandatory. Therefore, most of the limitations that have been established for women in Islamic societies can be justified not by the women's gender but by their being [physically] weak compared to men.

5.3 The Flexibility of Family Rules and Regulations to Suit Contemporary Requirements

Attempts to bring topics of jurisprudence and the dynamism of Sharia knowledge up to date are two of the main traits of Shia jurisprudence. Such qualities in Shia attitudes have helped develop the position of women over time and to constantly improve their situation compared to the past. Adjusting juridical sentences with the requirements of time and place is accepted by both early and contemporary faghih [religious scholars and jurists].

Of the early faghih, Shamsuddin Mohammad Amuli known as the "First Martyr" (who is one of the most outstanding Shia faghih), believed that the sentences are allowed to go through changes and evolutions with the ebb and flow of times and traditions. "[Fluctuations] such as expenses over women and family; for such matters tend to follow temporal traditions of their time and also the fate of variations and revenue" (Mirshamsi 2001, p. 164). Another faghih, All-knowing Helli, also believes and states that the "sentences in Islamic Sharia relate to interests; and interests change by changes in time, [and] differentiate by differentiations in obligations. Therefore, a specific verdict or rule may benefit a people at a specific time, but be considered vice and prohibited for another people at another time." Even a long time ago, when women's rights and freedom were not considered, Shia faghih were known to have shown greater openness in regard to women's issues. For instance, the "Second Martyr", a faghih of the Imamiyeh sect, attempted in the book "Masalek Al-Afham" to clarify the meaning of line 34 of An-Nisa' verse and stated: "is a husband permitted to personally attempt to correct [by punishment] his wife in regard to matrimonial matters and/or matters which are not related to rights of sexual desire? Or should he relegate this deed to the governor? There exist two statements regarding this issue. The more reliable statement declares the husband is to be considered alien towards all the wife's affairs except those related to rights of enjoyment and residence; even if the wife's deeds disturb the husband's affairs in life or damage his possessions and/or income" (Ibid). Such a viewpoint expressed six centuries ago has profoundly impeded the husband's right to punish the wife. This is the opinion of Shaykh Tusi and Judge Ibn Barraj. In the Tafsir Al-Kabir, which is one of the best-known tafsirs (commentaries) in the Shafi'ite sect, regarding this verse, Al-Shafi'I said, "Although beating is permitted, but abandoning it is better." Or, in al-Tafsir Tabari, Muhammad ibn Jarir al-Tabari said, "Regarding the spouses' quarrel, it has been expressed that the beating is contingent upon the disobedience" (Abdul Hamid Ahmad Abu-Soleima 2001, p. 74)[1] (See also: Al-Talebi 2005, pp. 65–75: The author is a Sunni religious scholar who believed that based on historical and sociological conditions, women

[1] See also: Al-Talebi (2005), pp. 65–75: The author is a Sunni religious scholar who believed that based on historical and sociological conditions, women beating was permitted, but now by disappearing of such conditions it should be absolutely prohibited.

beating was permitted, but now by disappearing of such conditions it should be absolutely prohibited).

Line 18 of verse Az-Zukhruf is one of the Qur'an's lines commonly cited when attempting to declare women unable to hold social positions, judgeship included. The line reads: "(Do they then like for Allah) a creature who is brought up in adornments (wearing silk and gold ornaments), and in dispute cannot make herself clear?" A more profound understanding can, however, be observed through lines 16–19:

16. "Or has He taken daughters out of what He has created, and He has selected for you sons?" 17. "And if one of them is informed of the news of (the birth of) that which he set forth as a parable to the Most Beneficent (Allah) (i.e. of a girl), his face becomes dark, gloomy, and he is filled with grief!" 18. "(Do they then like for Allah) a creature who is brought up in adornments (wearing silk and gold ornaments), and in dispute cannot make herself clear?" 19. "And they make the angels who themselves are slaves to the Most Beneficent (Allah) females. Did they witness their creation? Their evidence will be recorded, and they will be questioned."

A number of Sunnite and Shia exegetes such as Tabari, Beyzaavi and Tabresi declare the phrase "a creature who is brought up in adornments" refers to "women". Other exegetes such as Seyuti and Tabresi himself, in another exegesis, interpret the line's intent to be "idols"; for idols are unable to dispute (Alavi 2006, p. 166). This exegesis is more suited because of the historic truth that idols were commonly depicted as female and were dressed in adornments. The early faghih are also known to have interpreted line 18 of verse Az-Zukhruf in a broadminded way, declaring from an Islamic perspective that women may not be labeled unable to make themselves clear.

Revision of traditional standpoints towards women can be frequently observed by the contemporary Shia faghih. According to Abolghasem Gorji, a contemporary Iranian jurisprudence researcher and jurist, husbands possess no right to strike disobedient wives; for to strike is a form of punishment, and punishment is beyond common people and belongs to the duty of the government. Just as the execution of other limitations and Ta'zir [punishments applied to the offenses for which no punishment is specified in the Qur'an (sanctioned punishments)], takes place following the proof of offence, according to the verdict determined by a judge, so should such a case be relegated to the court of law (Mirshamsi 2001, p. 165).

Ayatollah Sane'i is a contemporary faghih who has brought numerous positive changes to jurisprudential rulings dealing with women. He has forcefully declared his argument based on the climate and geographical differences between Iran and Saudi Arabia and the Hadith reasons, regarding the concept of girls reaching puberty at the age of 13 [many Islamic laws regarding daily prayers, religious duties, and matrimony are firmly attached to this concept]. He believes as well: "Each and every Mujtahed [Islamic priest], who is qualified is nominated to perform advocacy; and among people, the eligibility of execution [of a sentence] regarding the public interest—where Islam offers no specific sentence—may only be approved by the people and a majority of votes. Legitimacy is reached by their unanimity or majority of votes and/or consent." According to his viewpoint:

"Masculinity brings no superiority to this matter and even the Sharia does not single out the superior [when a sentence is involved] and any person qualified to perform advocacy, may announce such sentences eligible to execution (specially in matters regarding women and family rights)." This is due to the fact that the conditions, which permit a person to become a judge could be applied for women as well, therefore these conditions possess universality and inclusion [they are applicable to women as well]. In regard to equality of compensation, Ayatollah Sane'i declares: "The Qur'an lines declare 'human life' as honorable. Therefore the family of the slain is enabled to take vengeance upon the slayer, without being obliged to pay [the slayer's family] any expense as the difference in wergild".

In regard to the concepts applying to women following their matrimony, the new regulations introduced by Ayatollah Sane'i are particularly noteworthy. Such as: "In cases where the wife is the sole heir, in addition to receiving her lawful share [1/4th of the inheritance], what remains of the husband's wealth should advisably be passed unto the wife as well. This approach is more compatible with justice and closer to discretion."[2] Another example is: "A divorce base on the aversion of living with the partner is mandatory for husbands, which means, should the wife absolutely loath her matrimonial life and return the dowry to the husband, or reimburse him with some wealth, and request a divorce, the husband is bound to divorce the wife. And should he refuse to obey, the court owns jurisdiction is above the husband's intent, and is able to declare the wife divorced." In the case of a mother's rights to be guardian, this faghih has proved, on the basis of the general information from the Qur'an and tradition, that mothers possess the right to custody, and that the mothers' right is superior to that of forefathers. He explains: "What has been reputed in regard to the right to custody belonging specifically and firmly to the father's forefather is debatable and unable to be the foundation upon which a jurisprudential verdict should be made".

The line "Men are the protectors and maintainers of women, because Allah has made one of them to excel over the other, and because they spend (to support them) from their means" [line 34, verse An-Nisa'], is explained by Ayatollah Khamene'i, Iran's contemporary Supreme Leader, as follows: "It means that the husband is charged with caring for the household. The husband should work. The family's sustenance is his responsibility. All the wealth the wife possesses is hers [only] but the family's sustenance is not her responsibility. We do not declare the women obliged to obey the men in all and every aspects, no. Such a declaration exists neither in Islam nor in Shariah [Shia Sharia]. The line 'Men are the protectors and maintainers of women' does not mean that the wife is bound to obey her husband in all affairs" (Khamenei.ir).

In this very regard, most contemporary faghih and exegetes disprove of the dominance and superiority of men over women. According to a number of contemporary exegetes of the Qur'an, husbands are charged with social affairs,

[2] In traditional approaches, when the husband passes away, and the wife is the only heir, she would receive only one fourth of her husband's wealth, and the rest would belong to the Islamic governor.

financial decisions, attempting and striving to earn an income, supplying the requirements of the household and family management; and since husbands are charged with earning an income, superintending the household [family members] is their responsibility as well. But the husband is not allowed to expect any privilege due to this superintendence! No. This is an executive task and a duty, and this line should be considered as defining duty, not granting a privilege (Makarem-E-Shirazi, Tafsir E Nemune [Exegesis Exemplar], Book 3, Javadi Amoli, p. 365).

According to Ayatollah Boejnuerdi, a Shia Faghih, no man is allowed to be married to two women simultaneously. The [concept and rules of] polygamy are meant for the caretakers of orphans. In fact [wherever and whenever] the Qur'an approves polygamy, prior are mentioned the orphans and derelict women. This line [such lines] was meant to apply particularly in times of war during which derelict women and their children faced financial, economical, etc., hardships. Therefore approval of polygamy is neither due to men's vigor nor due to women as the weaker sex, but to rectify problems. A number of contemporary Shia faghih view polygamy as excluded in the Shia tradition (http://moosavibojnourdi.blogfa.com).

6 Conclusions

The Shias among the Muslim communities believe in the Imamat of Ali ibn-Abi-Talib in succession to the Prophet. Although the Shia itself is classified into a number of sects, the majority of Shias believe in the continuation of the Imamat from Ali ibn-Abi-Talib to the Hidden Imam, who is now alive. Shia means follower, here the intention is to imitate the speech and the behavior of the 12 Imams, and because of that these followers are called Imamites.

In comparison with other Islamic sects, the Shia sect has two significant features. Firstly, the Shia refuses to follow arbitrary rules as well as participate in jihad (struggle) and violent acts, except by the permission of the Infallible Imam. As the Shias do not have access to the Infallible Imam, they do not have the permission to perform divine judgments arbitrarily and to commit acts of violence against anybody. Hence, violent actions against women or preventing them from education or forcing them into a compulsory marriage have no place in Shia. The Shia groups according to the Sharia regulations do not have the permission to act in this way. Indeed, in contrast with Sunni there is no force for Jihad to promote the Islam in Shia, therefore there is no violence against other Muslims and non-Muslim. It could be concluded that the use of any violence against women is highly prohibited in Shia as well.

Secondly, the Shia jurisprudence is being adapted to changes in place and times. Although the resources of jurisprudence of the Shia in comparison with the Sunnite are more limited, its judgments are more applicable to today's needs, because of its adherence to the Infallible Imam's representatives, who are the contemporary jurisprudents. The dynamics of Shia jurisprudence regarding women, particularly after the Islamic Revolution of Iran in 1979 (1357), has affected the rules and regulations.

Three decades of experience after the revolution showed that the Shia has a flexible approach to family relations and women's issues. In addition, after the revolution, more changes have been in relation to women. These lawful changes prove that a religion with legislative and political power, in comparison with a religion without such power, is in accord with the time and place requirements. Studying all legal developments shows a harmony between jurisprudential regulations and daily issues, the most significant of which can be summarized as follows:

In the laws after the revolution, a husband has never been permitted to punish his wife. Although the traditional interpretation of sura 34 of An-Nisa is about the punishment of women, none of the laws of Islamic countries refer to the husband's right to punish his wife, and if it still occurs, it is due to social conditions and traditions. For instance, in Afghanistan, the reason for the ban on women leaving home without a male has been explained by the presence of foreign forces or domestic terrorists, something that has threatened the safety of women and has become a rooted tradition in the social culture. Also, in the Islamic rules, compulsory marriages are in no way considered lawful. A daughter has a right to choose her future husband freely.

Particularly, in the Imamite sect as well as in general jurisprudence, the marriage contract is made through the offer and its acceptance; and the intention and consent are the elements of authenticity of this contract, like of other contracts. In the case of compulsion, the marriage contract will be invalid and null; and if there is reluctance, the validity can only be achieved through the consent of the woman. In this regard, it should be noted that in Islamic societies, especially in the Shia jurisprudence, female genital mutilation practiced in some countries is not lawful and has no juridical base; it is only considered as a tradition.

Furthermore, in some Acts of the Penal Code some steps have been taken in favor of the equality of lives of men and women. According to Article 550 of the new Islamic Penal Code of Iran, the atonement for a woman homicide is half of the atonement for a man. Paying half of a man's blood money for a woman is only a Sharia rule, otherwise, according to the law the blood money of a woman must be paid the same as for a man. In this regard, the first step was taken in 2008 (1387), when the legal excuse of paying full blood money of a man to a woman was in accord with the adaptive acceptance of insurance funds. As stated by this law, the insurer is bound to compensate the damages imposed on losers up to the insurance policy liabilities, without considering the gender and religion. The additional amount of money determined by the court shall be considered as accident insurance. In the provision of Article 551 of the Islamic Penal Code, it is assumed that in all crimes in which the victim is not a man, an amount equal to the balance of blood money, up to a man's blood money, should be paid by the physical damage fund.

The priority of a woman's life and health over her fetus has been recognized, regardless of the equality of the lives of women and men. Thirty years ago, in the Shia community of Iran, a mother was not allowed to have an abortion, even if the existence of the fetus presented a risk for the mother, and if she aborted, she was faced with punishment. Now the jurisprudents have accepted that a remedial abortion involves no civil and criminal penalties for the mother, and even if a mother gets an abortion, she shall not incur a punishment and a discretionary penalty and only must pay its blood money. Indeed, the legal and jurisprudential developments in recent years have granted an opportunity to women for getting an abortion during the early months.

In the new Islamic Penal Code, the application of fixed penalties has been very limited, and women under the age of 19 have been exempted from prison as well as from physical punishment; instead they are kept in a correction and rehabilitation center. Besides, in a juridical sentence, if the judge realizes that a female under the age of 19 lacks sufficient wisdom and understanding, or even if he has only doubts about it, there will be no physical punishment and/or prison for the female under 19. Since 2013 (1392), non-governmental organizations advocating feminism can file an action on behalf of the offended woman, albeit the offender was her husband, and follow it through till the final stages. In kindergartens and schools, anyone associated with young boys and girls is obliged to report physical and sexual violence as well as early marriages to the legal authorities.

Regarding the family, the woman's status has been improved constantly. In the case of the separation of a wife from her husband, the right of taking care of children, until they reach the age of seven, is given to women and in this regard men have no right. Even after 7 years of age, if a mother can prove that taking care of her child or children is beyond the competence of the father, the court can give the right of care to the mother. The right of heritage has also been increased for women, and they inherit from the whole property of decedent. A wife, if she does not receive her alimony, can refuse to live with her husband and allegedly does not need to obey him. Even in the case of her absence from the family, there has been no anticipation of enforcing a law in this regard. The above-mentioned legislative changes are only part of updating the Shia jurisprudence. With the role of the Guardian Council in approving the current laws, one should not assume that these changes have occurred without the input of jurisprudence; on the contrary, all legislative changes are primarily studied by jurisprudents, and only after their approval will it be approved as legislation. For instance, one of the provisions of the Shia jurisprudence has been the ages of marriage for girls and boys, respectively 9 and 15, which according to some traditions had been sanctified as the marriage ages of Ali (A) and Fatima (A). However, some recent jurisprudents concerning the age requirements have stated that the marriage age for girls is 13. This jurisprudential approach has been formalized in the law, and now in the Islamic Republic of Iran, no girl can be married before 13.

Furthermore, some specific legislation for the protection of women and children and against domestic violence has been adopted in a number of Muslim countries, such as Malaysia,[3] Arabia and Lebanon.

[3] Since 1994, Malaysia has determined to make some laws for protecting women and children being victimized by domestic violence. It must be also noted that these specific laws must be

The aforementioned discussions presented in this chapter suggest the absence of merely jurisprudential and Sharia grounds for violence against women, and the presence of Islamic laws, particularly in the Shia jurisprudence, for eradicating violence against women in the Islamic countries. The enactment of laws to combat violence against women in the Islamic countries confirms this allegation: in Malaysia, the Domestic Violence Act was approved already in 1994, in Afghanistan, The Law on Elimination of Violence against Women in Afghanistan, issue, 2009, and in Lebanon, The Law on the Protection of Women from Domestic Violence 2010 and in Pakistan The Anti-domestic Violence Act 2013.

Five Questions

1. What are the elements of family status and the position of women in Shiite Islam?
2. Is there possibly a connection between domestic violence in Shiite societies and the four sources of this religion's rules, i.e., Koran, Hadith [the teachings of Prophet Mohammad and the 12 Imams] Wisdom and Consensus?
3. What is the religious background of domestic violence in Shiite communities?
4. In Shiism, how can we distinguish between resorting to violence and justifying it?
5. To what extent have Shiite rules concerning the family, particularly with regard to the approach taken by contemporary jurisprudents and new legislations, provided justice between the rights of men and women and gained on international standards?

References

Abu-Soleima, A. H. A. (2001). Hit the woman a way to resolve marital disputes. *Islamic Knowledge*, *24*, U.S.A.

Ahmadi, B., Shams, M., Shariat, M. Ebrahimpour, A., Pourreza, A., Mahmoodi, M., & Younesian, M. (2008). The viewpoints of women and men in tehran and experts on domestic violence against women in Iran. *The Journal of Health University and the Institute of Health Research*, *2*, 67–81. Tehran, Iran.

Al-Talebi, M. (2005). Women punishment by beating: historical approach from the An-Nisa Verse 34 and 35 Qur'an. Translate to Farsi: Mehdi Mehrizi, Baztab Andisheh, 64.

Bousquet, G. H. (1975). l'Etique sexulle de l'Islam, Nouvelle edition, Parise, France.

Javadi Amuli, A. (1999). *Women in the mirror of glory and beauty*. Osra Publication, Tehran, Iran.

Mirshamsi, F. (2001). The principles of women' rights and obligations in marriage from viewpoint of Imamites Jurisprudence. Islamiyeh Publication, Tehran, Iran.

Motahari, M. (2003). *The women's rights in Islam*. Sadra Publication, Tehran, Iran.

Mousavi Bojnourdi (2003), Interview, http://www.mashreghnews.ir/fa/news/302665

---

interpreted and followed in accordance with the context of criminal law. The Anti-Domestic-Violence Law, was enacted in 1994, and since its enactment came into force. Certainly, Malaysia laws on regulating domestic violence may not go against the fundamentals of Islam. As said, Malaysia is a country with a maximum population of Muslims and is sensitive to the protection of the Islamic principles.

Mousavi Bojnourdi, M. (2006). Violence against women from the religion perspective, *Baztab Andisheh, 64*. Tehran, Iran.
Mousavi Khoee, S.A., Mabani Takalomeh Al-mekhaj, Najaf Publication, Matbaeh Al-adaab, Baghdad, Iraq.
Mughniyah, M. J. (1987). *Comparative jurisprudence of the five religious schools* (K. Pourjavadi, Trans.). The Islamic Foundation Publication, Qume, Iran.
Satari, J. (1996). *Woman's personality in the Iranian culture* (2nd ed.). Markaz Publication, Tehran, Iran.
Tabatabai, M. H. (1976). *Sprituality of Shiism*. Qum, Iran.
Tabatabai, M. H. (1996). *Tafsir Al-Mizan*. Qum, Iran: The Islamic Publication Office.
The Anti-domestic Violence Act in Pakistan, 2013.
The civil law code of Iran, 1928.
The Domestic Violence Act in Malaysia, 1994.
The Islamic Penal Code of Iran, 2013.
The Law on Elimination of Violence against Women in Afghanistan, issue (989), 2009 Ministry of Justice, Islamic Republic of Afghanistan.
The Law on the Protection of Women from Domestic Violence in Lebanon, 2010
Women and Penal Law: Collection of articles, the results of working group efforts, and the documents from the First International Conference on Women's Rights and Penal Law in the Past, Present and Future, 2004; under supervision of Dr. Mehra, N. Salsabil Publication. (2005).
http://www.khamenei.ir
http://www.makarem.ir
http://www.saanie.com
http://www.sistani.org
http://www.vahid-khorasani.ir/intro_flash.html

Forced Marriage in Islamic Countries: The Role of Violence in Family Relationships

Mehrdad Rayejian Asli and Mojgan Amrollahi Byouki

Abstract Forced marriage deprives men and women of their fundamental rights. It is a form of marriage that is not based on freedom and full consent of one or both parties concerned but on physical or emotional pressure. It can bring about devastating consequences for both partners and therefore has been proscribed by international instruments as well as domestic legislations in most countries including Islamic ones. Physical forms of violent victimization such as assault, burning, or in extreme cases, murder, and emotional forms like insult and verbal abuse are among the harmful consequences of forced marriage. Improper social norms, distorted religious beliefs, and social and cultural problems have fuelled the expansion of forced marriage in Islamic countries. Unfortunately, the phenomenon continues despite the recent efforts made by governments and human rights supporters within these countries. To eradicate forced marriage, Islamic countries must follow the Islamic religious ordinances prohibiting this kind of marriage, fulfill their international obligations in terms of proper legislations for proscribing forced marriage, (consult professionals and experts of Islamic jurisprudence), and use the mass media and all public and private resources to raise public awareness about its harmful effects.

1 Introduction

Forced marriage and its concomitant violent victimization, have been a persisting issue in most societies—regardless of their religious, cultural, economic, social, and ideological differences—and can be thought of as a global problem which goes beyond a particular history or culture. In forced marriage, one or both partners are

M.R. Asli
Tarbiat-Modares University, Tehran, Iran
e-mail: rayejianasli@modares.ac.ir

M.A. Byouki (✉)
University of Freiburg, Freiburg im Breisgau, Germany
e-mail: mojgan_amrolahi@yahoo.com

H. Kury et al. (eds.), *Women and Children as Victims and Offenders: Background, Prevention, Reintegration*, DOI 10.1007/978-3-319-08398-8_26

forced to marry, without their own consent, by parents, relatives, or sometimes even by the norms or the culture that governs their society, with all the harmful consequences such a marriage may entail.

The focus of the present chapter is on the prevalence of forced marriage and its consequences in Islamic countries.[1] In fact, what has occurred in these countries is influenced by their culture, habits, customs, traditions, and some social, political and economic settings rather than by Islamic ordinances.[2] Arguably, there are at least as many interpretation of Islam as the number of Islamic countries, which draw on their traditions, beliefs, as well as their cultural and historical background to explain what is intended by Islamic rules.[3]

In addition to inequalities rooted in class differences and social structures, the Muslim community is facing a number of inconsistencies that stem from the multiple political and cultural systems, ethnical-racial identities, underdevelopment, and historical background.[4] Therefore, when it comes to "forced marriage and its associated violence in the Islamic World", the first question to have in mind is which country we are speaking of. Which Islamic country has its legislation based on the explicit Islamic ordinances and traditions of the Prophet Muhammad? Is it Afghanistan or Iraq, or may be Iran, Pakistan, Malaysia, Turkey, or Bangladesh?[5] Which of these countries base their policies on *Sharia* (Islamic ordinances or jurisprudence)?

When looking at forced marriage and the violence resulting from it that largely targets women in Islamic countries, it becomes clear that discrimination and violence against women are not prescribed by Islam; rather it is the socio-cultural contexts of Islamic communities that justifies, or even gives legitimacy to inequality, oppression, discrimination and violence against women, including as a result of forced marriage.

---

[1] The Islamic World consists of Muslim countries or non-Islamic ones with a considerable Muslim population. An Islamic country, according to the Organization of the Islamic Conference, is a country where Muslims represent the majority of the population.

[2] Zibakalam (2000), p. 33.

[3] Molaverdi (2005), p. 17.

[4] Shahida, F. (2011). Women Culture and Identity in the Muslim Community, Hamshahri Newspaper (cited in R.I.S.S).

[5] A statistical study in Bangladesh confirmed that men in this country regard assaulting their wives as a naturally acceptable practice. According to a study by the Iranian Students' News Agency (ISNA), despite the relative progresses made over the last decades in terms of the role and position of women in Bangladesh society, most men in this country still believe that abusing their wives is not a disapproved practice. The study also showed that 89 % of Bangladeshi men in rural areas think that they can corporally punish their wives to correct their behaviors. Furthermore, 83 % of men living in urban areas hold the same belief. Moreover, 93 % of men in urban areas and 98 % of men in rural areas of Bangladesh believe that a true man must be a violent man and that women must tolerate these difficulties to keep their families from breaking down (www.alef.ir, code news 219 17).

In this chapter, we describe forced marriage and its consequences in Islamic countries, and give some suggestions how to prevent and to eliminate violent victimization arising from forced marriage within these jurisdictions.

2 An Overview of Definition of Family and General Principles of Marriage in Islam

The family is the oldest social community, essentially formed through marriage. It is a natural group that has been in place since the beginning of human life. In other words, family is the core of social life. It protects the spouses and the children born in wedlock and provides an environment, which maintains national and ethical traditions and promotes emotional growth. A family formed based on free will not only promote cooperation and solidarity but also give protection to its members and social health and wellbeing. Arguably, the family is an entity that determines the level of human social life. Members of a family hear, see, and institutionalize particular values, norms, and rights, including human rights. The international human rights system has taken this into consideration and defined the protection of marriage and the family as a high priority. A number of declarations and recommendations have been made on this topic and much research has gone into it. Each is emphasizing a particular issue, such as forced marriage and its undesirable consequences.[6,7] States are required to provide a number of measures to protect women from forced marriage by creating a consensus and by raising public awareness about the devastating outcomes of this form of marriage.

Family, in its limited sense, is a social entity formed through marriage and completed by childbearing. (An alternative definition describes family as an entity consisting of a number of members living together based on common goals and interests.[8]) Islam defines family as a group consisting of members with civil, legal, and spiritual characters and is formed by a legitimate marriage in which a man and a woman are pronounced husband and wife and bound by new rights and obligations.

In Islam, marriage is based on a contract, in which one party, usually the man, proposes (offer) and the other party, normally the woman, accepts the proposal (acceptance). The contract will be valid only if made by the two parties or their

[6] Research Department, Iranian Islamic Human Rights Commission (2009), p.169.

[7] From a criminological perspective, women are particularly victimized by men as a result of sexual assaults and other abuses often discussed as "violence against women". These criminal behaviors are typically studied as domestic violence, particularly spousal abuse in the literature of criminology and victimology. Rayejian Asli (2013), p. 84. In Iran, for example, despite some protections provided for in criminal laws, the research shows that certain kinds of women victimization including spousal abuse or femicide have become widespread especially during last decade. Rayejian Asli (2006), p. 191.

[8] Family in Islam, http://www.tebyan.net/newindex.aspx?pid=21643

representative in the presence of two just witnesses. In Sunni Islam,[9] only permanent marriage is allowed, while Shiite (or Shi'a) Muslims (*Imamia*)[10] permit both permanent and temporary marriage (mut'ah or *sigha*).[11] In Islamic jurisprudence (fiqh), which is the basis of civil and criminal law in Islamic countries, the consent and free will of both parties are the essence of a marriage contract, the absent of which will render the contract null and void. Therefore, the cases in which a boy or a girl is forced by his/her parents to marry are regarded as oppressive practices and cardinal sins by Islam and may not construe a true marriage unless the parties later give their consent to such a marriage.[12] There are some hadiths[13] (Sunnah or tradition) recommending consultations with the elders of the family for marriage. However, the final decision should be made by the parties involved in the marriage.

> The Qur'an is internally consistent because it is a divine revelation. The Qur'an repeatedly describes the relationship between husband and wife as one of tranquility, affection, and mercy. Further, it enjoins husbands to live with their wives in kindness or leave them amicably.[14]

---

[9] "All the Muslims agree that Allah is One, Muhammad (S) is His last Prophet, the Qur'an is His last Book for mankind, and that one day Allah will resurrect all human beings, and they will be questioned about their beliefs and actions. There are, however, disagreements between the two schools in the following two areas:

1. The Caliphate (successorship/leadership) which the Shi'a believes that it is the right of the Imams of Ahlul-Bayt/Ahlul-Bait (the immediate family of Muhammad which is also called the Householders).
2. The Islamic ordinances when there is no clear Quranic statement, nor is there a Hadith (Tradition) upon which Muslim schools have agreed.

The second issue is rooted in the first one. The Shi'a bound themselves to refer to Ahlul-Bayt for deriving the Sunnah of Muhammad (S). They do this in conformity with the order of the Prophet reported in the authentic Sunni and Shi'i collections of traditions beside what the Qur'an attests to their perfect purity." http://www.al-islam.org/shiite-encyclopedia-ahlul-bayt-dilp-team/major-difference-between-shia-and-sunni.

[10] The *Shi'a* or Shiite branch (also called *Imamiah)* follows the 12 infallible *(Ma'soom)* leaders *(Imams)* from the Household of the Holy Prophet (the Householders or *Ahlul-Bayt)*. This branch of Islam originated in the life of the Holy Prophet under the flag of *Imam Ali* (the son in law of the Prophet), who officially became the fourth Caliph (*Khalifa)* after the departure of the Holy Prophet. The second branch, the *Sunni* school of Islam, came into existence during the second century of the *Hijrah,* i.e., the immigration of the Prophet Mohammad and His companions from Mecca to Medina, in 622 A.D. There are four different *Sunni* schools: the *Hanafi,* founded by Abu-Hanifah (696–767 A.D.); the *Maliki,* founded by Malik IbnAnas (715–795 A.D.); the *Shafe'i,* founded by Al-Shafei'i (767–820 A.D.); and the *Hanbali,* founded by Ahmad IbnHanbal (780–885 A.D.). Because *Shi'a* ordinances have had the greatest influence on Iranian law, the discussion of Islamic law in this article will reflect the *Shi'a* school of law rather than the *Sunni* schools of law, which may present different rulings or understandings respectively (see my comment on p. 9). Ebrahimi (2005), p. 460.

[11] Van Oerven Johaness (2010), p. 255.

[12] Rahmani (2005), p. 50.

[13] Sayings of the Holy Prophet.

[14] Al Hibri (2003), p. 204.

A valid marriage bond, according to Islam, is a marriage based on Islamic ordinances. Otherwise, the children born to such parents will be regarded as illegitimate and may not enjoy the rights of legitimate children.

A Muslim man can marry a non-Muslim woman while a Muslim woman may not marry a non-Muslim man. The reason is the following: a Muslim man who marries a non-Muslim woman will face no restriction on practicing Islamic ordinances and may also encourage his wife to practice Islam, while a Muslim woman who marries a non-Muslim man will have difficulties in practicing Islam and fulfilling her Islamic obligations.[15] This is because according to Islam a woman who receives alimony from her husband must obey his commands otherwise she will be considered a disobedient.

In a valid marriage bond, based upon the Islamic ordinances, a dowry is determined. A dowry is an amount of money or property granted by the husband to the wife as a social guarantee, which helps the wife maintain her financial independence in the case of divorce or death of the husband.[16] In addition, according to norms and traditions prevailing in many Islamic countries, the girl's family, or in some cases the boy's family will be required to provide a bridal dowry (furniture, kitchen utensil, appliances, *etc.*) to begin a decent married life. These customs create difficulties for families that cannot afford such gifts, and poorer families consequently give their consent for a marriage of their daughters with usually older men who offer to provide the bridal dowry. But also the bridegroom is sometimes requested by the woman's family to give extravagant amounts of money or gold coins and this leads men to marry girls who do not ask for such hardly affordable gifts. The girls in this form of marriage do not feel being equal with their husbands in terms of social position, and this can give rise to extreme disagreements resulting in domestic violence or other forms of victimization.

This domestic violence or victimization continues through a vicious cycle since the woman may not apply for divorce, and even if she is entitled to do so under national legislations, it may be too difficult to prove the violence or victimization she has suffered. According to Islam, a man can usually apply for divorce without proof of misconduct. In other words, a man is not required to provide a reason for divorce while a woman, in order to obtain divorce approval from the court, must provide evidence showing that she has been abused or victimized by her husband since it is generally believed that men are more reasonable and realistic in making decisions than women, who often decide based on their emotions.[17] The factors discussed above increase physical and emotional domestic violence in Islamic countries in an unbridled fashion.

---

[15] Van Oerven Johaness (2010), pp. 156–157.

[16] Ibid.

[17] Ibid.

3 A Historical Review of Forced Marriage in Islam

Forced marriage, whether in the pre-Islamic or post-Islamic era, has existed under different names and for a variety of reasons. In the early Islamic period, the major victims of this practice were women for their relatively lower social position. At the dawn of Islam, ignorant Arabs used to bury their daughters alive,[18] showing thus that women had no value compared to men.

Before Islam, fathers were allowed to decide on the marriage of their daughters who had no right to object to this decision. In some cases, two men were allowed to exchange their daughters as each other's wives. In pre-Islam Arabia, there were two forms of marriage other than the regular form. In the first form, a man was forced to "lend" his wife to another man and to keep away from her. In the second type of marriage, a group of less than ten men married one woman and the child born to this marriage belonged to only one of these men. It shows that the ancient Arab community objectified women and regarded them as objects enslaved through marriage.[19]

Islam banned these forms of marriage.[20] Islam explicitly provided for equal human dignity for women and men who, according to Islamic rules, are created from the same essence. In the traditions of the Holy Prophet (Muhammad) and religious leaders, great efforts have been made to make inhuman practices against women obsolete.[21] Islam gave women, as free and independent beings, the right to choose their husbands,[22] which is clearly an important right promoting the survival and significance of the family within society.

For this purpose, reference can be made to the concrete way Muhammad dealt with the marriage of his daughter, Fatima. When Alī-ibn-Abī-Tālib proposed to Fatima, Muhammad let his daughter decide.[23] According to religious and historical evidence, the Holy Prophet let his daughter decide on these proposals without himself being involved in accepting or rejecting them. Finally, Fatima picked Ali as her husband completely on her own will.[24] The Holy Prophet actually wanted to teach the ethnicity-and-tribe-oriented Arabs that their daughters have the right to choose and that this decision should not necessarily be based on the consent of the father, since the daughter has to live with her husband for the rest of her life. Therefore, the father may not be allowed to force his daughter to marry someone he

[18] As a form of criminal victimization, infanticide is an old phenomenon, which is prevalent in various forms within human societies, including in pre-Islamic era. For further study, see: Rayejian Asli and Azizi (2013).

[19] Khamenei (1992), p. 24.

[20] Ibid, p. 88.

[21] Universal Rights of Women and Children, p. 1.

[22] Khamenei (1992), op. cit, p. 87.

[23] Babazadeh (1989), p. 36.

[24] http://www.islamicinsights.com/religion/clergy-corner/the-marriage-of-imam-ali-and-lady-fatima.html.

regards suitable or to forbid her from marrying someone he regards as unsuitable. Giving a girl the right to choose her husband, especially at a time when fathers had the final say on any issue in families, was a completely unprecedented practice.[25] The practice supports the idea that girls should be allowed, and not forced, to decide on their own future.

4 Different Types of Forced Marriage in Islamic Countries

Depending on the norms and traditions governing Islamic countries, forced marriage may exist in different forms.

4.1 Compensation Marriage

The practice of forced marriage for ending feuds has been prevalent in some Islamic countries. When a member of a girl's family murders a person, the elders gather to resolve the dispute by forcing the girl to marry a member of the victim's family. The girl often leads a slave-like life in her new family and in most cases experiences criminal victimization in the form of violence and abuse. The major problem in this area is the lack of the rule of law and lack of intervention by judicial entities of the Islamic countries to prevent such forced marriages. (Compensation is an unfair tradition, which deprives a woman of all her basic rights, sending her to a new home as a slave.[26])

4.2 Exchange Marriage

Exchange marriage is another form of forced marriage in Islamic countries. It is often the result of a lack of financial means, which may lead two families to exchange their daughters to reduce marriage expenses since no bridal dowry will be required in an exchange marriage. However, it is quite likely that one of the daughters in an exchange marriage is not willing to marry, and even if this is not the case, one daughter may face difficulties in her married life because of problems including domestic violence occurring in the other family. It often leads to unwanted problems including denial of substantial rights or experiencing victimizations in various forms from assault to abuse.[27]

---

[25] Ibid.

[26] For more information see, Bernabeo (2011).

[27] Ibid.

4.3 Forced Marriage of Children

Although marriage is an essential right in the human society, it entails a series of conditions including mutual consent, reaching the given minimum age for marriage, and formal registration of the marriage. Failure to observe these conditions will constitute a breach of the right to marriage. Forced marriage of children, also called "early marriage", leads to such problems as runaway children, mental disorders, suicide, high mortality rates among mothers and babies, and the denial of the right to education which, particularly in the long term, adversely influence social, economic, and political rights of women. In other words, early marriage is often accompanied by the denial of rights of the child, including the rights to enjoyment, education, living with parents, *etc*. and seriously hampers the actualization of inherent potentials of children.[28] This is confirmed by a report of UNICEF, showing that girls forced to marry at early ages will not experience complete physical and psychological growth.

The common view in Islamic countries holds that girls should marry as soon as they reach puberty in order to prevent pre-marriage sexual relationships, yet girls and boys are given limited opportunity to choose their age of marriage and their partner since Islam imposes restrictions on pre-marriage relationships prohibiting boys and girls from meeting each other beyond the ordinances of *Sharia*, giving thus young people few opportunities to get to know each other beyond the legal norms and rules of Islam. In this way, an acceptable marriage remains the one based on familial relationships and the consent of the father.

It should be noted that most Islamic countries require virgin girls to obtain their father's consent prior to marriage. A marriage bond made without consent given by the father—or patrilineal grandfather or guardian in cases where the father has died—will be considered null and void.[29] If the father or the guardian unreasonably withholds his consent, the girl may refer her case to the court to obtain a permit if the relevant conditions have been met.

However, there are disagreements in this regard between the old and new Islamic jurisprudence. A number of Muslim scholars argue that guardians must have the right to give or withhold consent for two reasons: virginity and minority. According to their argument, even the girls who have reached puberty must be protected by their guardians.[30] Therefore, girls may not marry in the absence of such consent,

---

[28] Research Department, Iranian Islamic Human Rights Commission (2009), p. 72.

[29] Countries like Iran, Afghanistan, Jordan, Syria, Iraq, Lebanon, Yemen, Indonesia, Philippines, Malaysia, Pakistan, Sri Lanka, Nigeria, Algeria, Tunisia, Morocco, and Senegal require consent of the guardian. In cases where the consent is unreasonably withheld, the court may issue a marriage permit by considering relevant conditions.

[30] In the Islamic Republic of Iran, girls are required to obtain the consent of their father or patrilineal father for marriage. Article 1043 of Civil Code provides that "a virgin girl, even one who has reached puberty, must obtain the consent of her father or patrilineal father for marriage, and in cases where this consent is unreasonably withheld, the girl may refer the case to a court, along with complete information about the man she intends to marry, conditions of marriage, and

and some scholars even believe that the father or patrilineal grandfather may force his daughter or granddaughter to marry, but they recommend to obtain the girl's consent in such cases.[31] It shows that a number of scholars in the past believed that girls could not decide on their own marriage. Some current scholars take a more lenient approach by indicating that the father or the grandfather shall not be entitled to the guardianship over an adult virgin girl who may independently decide on her own marriage.[32]

As an acceptable practice in law, an adult person is no longer covered by guardianship and can decide for his or her own good. (In such case, thus, there is no need for guardianship, regardless of gender.) Therefore, girls are not required to obtain consent from fathers or patrilineal grandfathers since requirement for obtaining such consent will constitute a forced marriage.

It should be noted that in most Islamic countries the minimum age of marriage for both genders is 18. However, even in countries where this minimum age has been set, parents or legal guardians may ask a court to issue a permit for early marriage and the court may issue such a permit by reviewing the relevant conditions. As seen later, in some countries parents may force a 10- to 13-year-old girl to marry under special conditions upon a court approval. Such cases of early marriage are obviously in conflict with the rights recognized by international standards, particularly those contained in the Convention on the Rights of the Child (CRC), which defines a child as a person below the age of 18 regardless of their gender (Article 1). Despite the fact that Islamic states may join the CRC and require that their domestic legislations be amended accordingly, many of these countries have in effect neutralized the provisions of the CRC by including a proviso[33] which states that they will be enforceable only if they are consistent with the ordinances of Islam (*sharia*). This results in a denial of substantial rights of the child, like the right to free will and making decision on getting married after physical and intellectual maturity, which is the age of 18 based on a general agreement by all member states.

---

dowry, to obtain a permit from the court (currently the Family Court) and register the marriage." (amended according to the IRR Civil Code 1991).

[31] Tusi, AbiJafar Muhammad, Al-Khalaf, vol. 4, p. 255.

[32] Al-Feiz Al-Kashani, Mohammad Hossein, Mafatih Al-Sharaya, Majma Al-Zakhayer Al-Islamia (1971), Vol. 2, 1401AH, p. 265. This is a volume of a series of Fiqi (Islamic) books entitled "Al-Sharaya" from the cited Arabian authors.

[33] A number of Islamic states have incorporated vague and ambiguous provisos into the CRC. These include, but are not limited to: Afghanistan, Iran, Saudi Arabia, and Qatar. For example, Iran has included a proviso that states that those provisions of the CRC, which are inconsistent with the domestic legislations and Islamic ordinances will not be enforceable. Although not apparently illegal, such provisos are in conflict with the CRC provisions on the age of minority, discrimination against children, and blood money *(diyah)* for girls and boys. Upon signing the CRC, Afghanistan issued an interpretation document, which states "the Government of the Republic of Afghanistan hereby declares that it preserves certain provisos for all provisions of the CRC which are not consistent with *Shari'a* or enforceable domestic legislations."

Given the importance of this issue, we review the minimum age of marriage in a number of Islamic countries in different regions of the world including the Middle East, Southeastern Asia, South Asia, and a number of African countries.

4.3.1 Iran

According to the Iranian Civil Code (ICC), girls can marry when they reach the age of 13 while the age of marriage for boys is 15.[34] However, a father, upon his own discretion and approval of court, may force his underage son (under 15) or daughter (under 13) to marry without the requirement of obtaining his/her consent, and if he or she, after reaching the age of majority, claims that the marriage has not been in his/her best interests, they may get a divorce. However, the adverse social and emotional impacts of such a divorce on the interests of children are obvious. By criticizing the low age of marriage in Iran and the fact that girls may be forced to marry upon a court's approval when they are under 13, it should, however, be pointed out that such an approval will completely depend on the judge's decision since a judge at a court in Tehran may reject such an application while judges in courts of small towns may grant approval due to traditions and norms governing these communities. The claim can be supported by official statistics provided by Statistical Centre of Iran:

Official statistics released by the Islamic Republic between 2006 and 2011 involving girls below 10 year of age, 10–14 and 15–19 in a number of provinces in Iran indicate a staggering increase of 6448 marriages for the three age groups. The Statistical Centre of Iran reports that the number of girls forced to marry is higher than that of boys: 24,506 girls under 14 compared to 5519 boys between 10 and 14 years old. According to the national census of 2006, the number of married children between 10 and 18 years old was 848,000. The Journal of Sociology of Iran also reported an increasing number of early marriages in the 2000s. The report describes such married girl as "child mothers".[35] Within the period 2006–2011, the ratio of marriages involving girls compared to those among adults grew by 45 %. Statistics indicate the number of girls under the age of 15 who were registered to marry increased from 33,383 in 2006 to 39,831 in 2011. This indicates a 40 % increase in the percentage of girl children below the age of 15 who were forced to marry. Such an increase is even more significant given the fact that the population in the same age range decreased by 394,302. From a different angle, on average 177 typical primary and secondary girl schools are shut down because their student bodies are forced to marry and perform domestic and sexual duties expected of these children as married women. Statistics released in 2012 indicated

[34] Article 1041, ICC states that "Marriage of girls before the age of 13 and of boys before the age of 15 (solar years) will be subject to the guardian's consent and observance of conditions upon court discretion."

[35] Sharq Newspaper (2012), p. 19.

that close to ten million Iranian children over the age of six were illiterate. Furthermore, the mortality rate for married girls below the age of 15 is five times higher than those over the age of 20 due to childbirth complications. Furthermore, experts warn of a surge in mental illness, suicides, teenage runaways and girls turning to sex work. According to recent data released by Iran's Association of Children's Rights, 449 girls were married in 2009 before reaching the age of 10 and as many as 716 girls were married under the age of 10 in 2010, a 59 % increase in one year.[36,37]

4.3.2 Syria

The minimum age for marriage is 18 for boys and 17 for girls. However, there are measures to provide for marriage of girls and boys at the age of 13 upon the consent of the father or patrilineal grandfather, proper physical conditions, and court approval. In cases where the court decides that the age of betrothed parties is not suitable, the judge may withhold the permit for marriage.

Each party requires the consent of his/her guardian, even if they are legally considered major. Marriage must be registered and an application must be submitted to the judge.[38]

4.3.3 Iraq

The minimum age of marriage for both genders is 18. A marriage permit may be obtained from the judiciary for persons under the age of 15 if the person is qualified in terms of physical conditions and guardian's consent (which should not be unreasonably withheld). No other relative or third party may prevent the marriage of a qualified person.[39]

4.3.4 Kuwait

No minimum age has been set for marriage, and puberty and psychological health will suffice. However, marriage might not be registered for boys under 17 and girls under 15. If one party is younger than this age at the time of laying claim, or the claim is not supported by a well-established marriage deed, the claim will be

[36] http://www.ohchr.org/Documents/Issues/Women/WRGS/ForcedMarriage/NGO/JusticeFor Iran.pdf. p. 2.

[37] The General Manager of the Registry of Hormozgan reports registration of five early marriages in which the wives are children under 10 (Sharq Newspaper; op. cit. p. 19).

[38] Damdari (2010), p. 99.

[39] Ibid. p. 186.

subject to "freedom of choice" but the girl or the boy may not make the contract without the consent of the guardian.[40]

4.3.5 Indonesia

The minimum age of marriage for men and women has been set 19 and 16, respectively. Early marriage however may be allowed upon parental consent and court discretion. The marriage bond will be valid only if the parties give their consent, unless otherwise specified by the religious rules governing couple relationships.[41]

According to UNICEF, "in the years 2000 to 2009, 22 percent of women 20 to 24 years old were married or in union before they were 18."[42]

4.3.6 Philippines

The minimum age of marriage is 15 for boys and the age of sexual puberty for girls (girls are assumed to reach puberty at the age of 15). The court of *sharia* may, upon the request by the guardian, issue a permit for marriage of a girl who is between 12 and 15, provided that she has reached puberty.

The marriage of minors is called betrothal and may be terminated by either party within four years after reaching the age of puberty, provided that the marriage bond was not based on free will and neither the father nor the patrilineal grandfather had been involved as guardian. Illegal enforcement of a marriage bond may result in imprisonment and/or a fine. A valid marriage bond requires free will of the parties involved as well as the presence and consent of the guardians.[43]

4.3.7 Jordan

The minimum age of marriage is 16 for men and 16 for women. Underage marriage is criminalized and penal sanctions are provided for such a marriage. Underage marriage will be in no way considered legal if (1) the wife has become pregnant and delivered the baby before an application for annulment has been submitted or (2) either party had just reached the minimum age of marriage by the time the marriage bond has been made. In cases where a marriage bond is made between a woman younger than 18 years of age and a man 20 or more years older than she, the

---

[40] Ibid. pp. 155, 156.

[41] Ibid. p. 186.

[42] Country Report on Human Rights Practices for 2012: Indonesia. http://www.refworld.org/docid/517e6e27f.html

[43] Ibid., pp. 208, 209.

judge will have to verify whether the wife has consented to the marriage and whether this has been in her best interest.[44]

4.3.8 Algeria

The minimum age for marriage is 21 for men and 18 for women. This provision however is flexible and may change upon necessity, interests, or court discretion. Marriage imposed by the guardian—whether the father or someone else—is strictly prohibited since it may force a woman to marry a man against her own will. The Family Law of the country defines the making of the marriage bond as a responsibility of the guardian, whether the father or a relative. But the guardian may not prevent his daughter from marrying a man if it is in her best interest. However, the father may object to the marriage of his virgin daughter provided that this is in his daughter's interests. A judge may issue a permit for marriage if the father unreasonably withholds his consent.[45]

4.3.9 Morocco

The minimum age of marriage is respectively 18 and 15 for men and women. However, there is room for judicial discretion in case of "fear of immorality" for men under the age of 18. Marriage under the age of majority requires the father's consent and if the father refuses to give consent, the parties may bring the case before a court. The father's right to force a marriage under special condition has been invalidated by amendments made in 1993. A fatherless girl or a girl who has chosen a guardian on her own free will may apply for entering a marriage bond.[46]

5 The Consequences of Forced Marriages in Islamic Countries

As noted earlier, choosing someone to marry may be the most important decision made by anyone in his or her life and plays a significant role in their common future.

Religious teachings, human rights instruments, and domestic legislations of many Islamic countries call therefore for freedom of choice as a substantial right of any person while rejecting any form of forced marriage. At the national level, most Islamic countries define thus a correct and valid marriage bond as a marriage based on mutual consent.[47]

[44] Ibid, p. 66.

[45] Ibid, p. 301.

[46] Ibid, p. 186.

[47] Civil Code of Afghanistan, 1976, Art. 497.

Forced marriage brings about many adverse effects and years of suffering for couples. There are alarming statistics in Iran about women and girls who commit suicide or run away from home. Girls now run away from their homes as early as they reach 14, compared to a previously reported age of 16. Yet worse, the figure grows by 15–20 % annually.[48] Studies have revealed that in 12.5 % of cases unsuccessful marriages are among the major causes for running away from home.[49]

Suicide is another devastating consequence of forced marriage. Although scholars believe that suicide in itself is not considered a major issue in Iran as the statistics indicate that suicide figures in Iran are at a much lower level compared to other countries, particularly western countries, the rate of suicide in Iran compared to previous years has increased.[50]

A closer look at the available suicide statistics over the past few years shows a marked increase in some provinces, in particular in poorer provinces, placing Iran third among Islamic countries and only topped by Sudan and Tunisia.[51]

Since Islam highly disapproves of suicide, many families attempt to hide cases of suicide within the families and refuse to admit its existence. Further efforts are required to do away with the taboo of suicide in order to facilitate proper identification and prevention of this detrimental phenomenon.[52]

Self-immolation has become a prevalent form of suicide, particularly in the disadvantaged provinces. It is the most painful type of suicide often regarded as a call for help. A study conducted in Lorestan[53] demonstrated that 85 % of self-immolators commit suicide to escape from the unbearable pain caused by domestic espousal disputes, unsuccessful marriages with considerable age disparity, matrimonial violence and assault, and pressure from prevalent views held by the common people.[54]

To summarize, despite the legal prohibitions and religious bans on forced marriage and its painful consequences, marriage based on free will and mutual willingness remains a rare practice in some Islamic countries that have retained particular tribal traditions and social norms. In many cases, the potential spouses cannot even meet each other before marriage and are led to a forced marriage arranged by others. Some may later become satisfied with their lives, but many remain dissatisfied and had initially been unaware of its consequences.[55]

Although forced marriage has been prohibited by Islamic ordinances and domestic legislations of most countries, it is still on the rise because of improper law

---

[48] http://www.daneshju.ir/forum/sitemap/t-89187.html

[49] http://www.daneshju.ir/forum/sitemap/t-89187.html

[50] http://golshn12.blogfa.com/post/3471

[51] Ibid.

[52] http://www.salamatnews.com/news/103198

[53] A province in western Iran with a high rate of unemployment, poverty, and domestic violence.

[54] Ibid.

[55] Rahmani, S. A., A Guide to Family Law in Afghanistan, p. 57.

enforcement and the presence of incorrect beliefs and traditions in a number of countries including the one discussed below.

5.1 United Arab Emirates

The early marriage of girls is a common practice in the UAE, particularly in its rural areas, and the fact that priority is given to cousins[56] and relatives indicates characteristics of a tribal system.[57]

In making a decision for the marriage of a girl, the first person to decide is her father, followed by her brothers. Although recently some families ask for the opinion of the girl, this is only a formality. It should be noted however that educated girls in the UAE have found the courage and the power to play a key role in choosing their future husbands.[58]

The average divorce rate in the UAE for people under the age of 40 is 69 %, since these people often get married when they are younger than 15, which is not a suitable age for marriage. In fact, this indicates the incorrectness of some beliefs and practices in the UAE and reveals that early marriage does not prevent deviant behavior and is not in the best interest of females in the long run.[59]

Forced marriage in the UAE is a major cause of victimization and violence against women, particularly domestic violence and abuse by husbands. Although the government has taken a number of measures to prevent such violence and punish violators, social pressure and unacceptable traditions are among the major obstacles preventing women from presenting their cases. The problem, however, cannot be overlooked, and abused women should be protected by law and entitled to litigation through access to justice.

5.2 Afghanistan

Current legislations on marriage and family life in Afghanistan are unclear and in conflict with the constitution and international standards. The Civil Code of Afghanistan contains provisions on marriage, annulment, and protection of families, but there is no enforcement guarantee and no sanctions. For example, Article 66 of the Civil Code states that "marriage as a bond referring to explicit acceptance of an immediate and continuous relationship can be made in a single session." Or Article 70 stipulates that "a boy will be qualified for marriage at the age of 18 and a

[56] Many Muslims believe that a marriage between cousins is a heavenly bond blessed by God.

[57] Report by the IRR Embassy in Doha (1997), p. 1.

[58] Ibid.

[59] Molaverdi (2005), p. 50.

girl must reach the age of 16 in order to be qualified for marriage." However, most girls are forced to underage marriage during their childhood.

As mentioned before, there are no sanctions to guarantee the enforcement of the law, and most cases of marriage in Afghanistan lack mutual consent, particularly the consent of girls. Relevant conditions on age and legal provisions on marriage are not properly observed, and women in this country are clearly experiencing gender-based discrimination.[60]

5.3 Iran

Iran, like many other Islamic countries, is facing the adverse effects of forced marriages, which often target women as their victims.[61] Research has shown that emotional violence constitutes a remarkable portion of violence against women in forced marriages. Some believe that this type of violence is more common than physical violence. Spousal neglect, as the most common type of emotional abuse, affects 63.1 % of women, followed by contempt and degradation (37.5 %), insults and offensive words by husbands (30 %), financial deprivation and refusal to pay alimony (18.8 %), mistrust and suspicion (17.5 %), withholding permission for leaving the house (15.6 %), refusal to have sex (19 %), forbidding work and employment (11.3 %), and eviction (6.9 %).[62] Most cases of violence remain undiscovered, and almost all cases presented are dismissed before reaching a court.

Admittedly, there are no actual statistics on domestic violence caused by forced marriage in Iran. A review of relevant cases reveals many incidents of repeated offenses. In 55 % of the cases, petitioners reported previous incidents of assault, and the absence of explicit reports on such incidents in other cases does not mean that women file a lawsuit at the first instance of violence by their husbands. Studies show that many women tolerate violence, refraining from bringing a legal action for a wide range of reason such as shame, fear of losing face, fear of poverty, rejection by families, threats to their lives and that of their children, problems in legal proceeding, and believing that the law favors men.[63]

---

[60] Forsythe (2009).

[61] "Khoon-bass" (Cease-blood) as a prevalent traditional custom in the south-west and south of Iran is linked to forced marriage. According to the custom, when a murder occurs in a tribe or ethnic group, members of the tribe or group seek to end the conflict through reconciliation instead of resorting to blood disputes, and "Khoon-bass" is a peaceful resolution upon which a girl of the murderer family or group, often without her consent, marries a man of the murder victim's family. In recent years, there have been some debates about a national register of "Khoon-bass" as a cultural heritage (Sharq Newspaper, No. 1629, 2012, p. 19). Research shows that marriage followed by "Khoon-bass" may lead to some forms of criminal victimization including honor killing, which will be discussed later. (Bakhtiarnejad 2009, p. 24).

[62] Entekhab Newspaper (2003a).

[63] Entekhab Newspaper (2003b).

5.4 Indonesia

Despite the prohibition of forced marriage by the legislations, Indonesia is experiencing a wide range of problems in this area, particularly in rural communities. Although evidence on violence against women after a forced marriage is missing, the government has admitted unprecedented increase in this type of violence.[64]

Cultural norms regard couple problems as private issues, and thus incidents of domestic violence against women are rarely reported. The police can charge husbands for assault, but the prevalent social practices make them reluctant to do so.[65]

5.5 Pakistan

Forced marriage is widely practiced in Pakistan. Violence against women as a result of forced marriage can be observed in different forms throughout the country. Women live under unacceptable conditions with no protection from men's violence. Although the Pakistani Constitution prohibits the assaulting of wives by their husbands and gives women the right to freely choose or get divorced from their partners, norms and some ordinances of *Shari'a* which state women are owned by men supersede the law.[66]

In addition, another form of victimization of Pakistani females is selling them in forced marriage. Parents sell their young girls for marriage or prostitution to recover from poverty and lack of financial and political support. Unfortunately, lack of the government's commitment to resolve problems caused by forced marriage is a major obstacle in promoting decent conditions of life for women in this country.[67]

There is no safety net for women who run away from their violent traumatic married lives. No social security, welfare services or association have been devised for these women. There is a shelter known as a detention house for this purpose in each city, and courts send girls and women to these houses for rehabilitation. The shelters in fact serve as a home for women, who have been rejected by their families and abused by anti-social groups.

Almost one-third of residents of these houses are women escaping from unbearable marriages, rejected by their families, or seeking divorce. Half of them are girls running away from their home since their fathers would not allow them to marry the

---

[64] Molaverdi (2005), op. cit., p. 161.

[65] Country Report on Human Rights Practices: Indonesia cited in: April 2013.

[66] Shareef Malik (2013).

[67] Rights and Protection Provided to Trafficked Women and Children, Trafficking of Women and Children in Pakistan, 1996, p. 37.

person they love or would force them into an arranged marriage. These girls are rejected by society and their only hope is to marry poor, but good men who cannot find a wife elsewhere.[68]

5.6 *Kuwait*

Violence against women as a result of forced marriage is a pressing issue in Kuwait. According to local experts, domestic abuse occurs in about 15 % of marriages.[69] The police and courts generally attempt to informally resolve domestic disputes and may require the abusing spouse to sign a statement confirming that the abusive behavior will be discontinued. The police refer serious cases to the Department of Psychiatry. Courts have convicted many husbands of abusive behavior toward their wives.

In Kuwait, there are still traditions stating that domestic affairs including domestic violence should not be made public, and such traditions have led to refraining from filing lawsuits against abusive husbands, inadequate law enforcement and informal dispute resolution.[70]

6 Honor Killing Caused by Forced Marriage in Islamic Countries

Domestic violence caused by forced marriage, which often victimizes vulnerable women is a global issue rooted in culture, lifestyle, and gender inequality. Honor killing is an extreme form of violent victimization relatively common in Islamic countries. Females forced into marriage later feel they cannot continue living under these conditions and end up outside their houses seeking ways to make up for their emotional and sexual frustrations or looking for an ideal man who can give them an experience of a life based on mutual love. Yet, having an affair with another man is strictly prohibited by Islam as a cardinal sin. The prevalent norms and traditions in Islamic countries strongly disapprove of such a behavior, and in most families there is no room for forgiving a married woman for having an extramarital affair, and the adulterous woman may even end up being murdered. Sometimes, Islamic countries

---

[68] Ibid.

[69] Country Report on Human Rights Practices: Kuwait, cited in: April 2011, http://www.refworld.org/docid/4da56db4af.html

[70] Molaverdi (2005), op. cit. p. 62.

permit honor killing through formal legislation[71] and in some cases through informal mechanism under the pressure of outdated beliefs and customs.

Girls and young women are the victims of such disastrous practices usually perpetrated by fathers, brothers, uncles, or cousins to save the face of a family, tribe, or clan. Upon the discovery of the murder, the perpetrator is not prosecuted as there is no private complaint.[72]

As noted earlier, honor killings usually occur in Islamic countries, including Jordan, Pakistan, Iraq, and some provinces of Iran,[73] where having an extramarital affair is regarded as an unforgivable sin. For instance, a report by Iranian Police in 2010 indicated that 15 women in Ahwaz[74] have been victimized in honor killings, amounting to 24.5 % of all murders in this city. The number has decreased compared to the statistics for 2006 (35 %) in Ahwaz. According to the District Attorney of Ahwaz, some customs and traditions, "like arranged cousin marriages are the cause of honor killings which occur when a person marries someone other than his or her cousin."[75] Jordan is another case with a high rate of honor killings. According to official statistics provided by the Jordanian government, between 1994 and 2005, 25–30 women have lost their lives annually as a result of honor killings, which constitute around 13 % of all family murders in this country. Annual reports by UNICEF show that on average 23 women and girls fall victim to honor killing in Jordan annually.[76]

A related issue in Islamic countries is that men of families and tribes try to assert their "manhood". When an incident occurs targeting the honor of a family, all members of the family and tribe wait to see how the man of the targeted family will respond. What distinguishes honor killings from other types of murder however is the preplanning and premeditated nature of this type of murder by asking the members of the family, particularly the mother, for their consent. Honor killings

---

[71] For example, Article 630 of the Islamic Penal Code of Iran states that "a man who catches his wife fornicating with another man, knowing that his wife has given consent to adultery, may kill both of them on site and may kill the fornicating man if the wife has not given consent to adultery. The same applies to assault and battery." Or according to Articles 340 and 98 of the General Penal Code of Jordan, "a man who kills or injures his fornicating wife and/or her accomplice will be exempt from any form of punishment." In addition, Article 548 of the Syrian Penal Code provides that "a man may not be punished for killing his wife, daughter, or sister and the fornicating man if he sees them during fornication."

[72] The Islamic penal system provides for a right of relatives of the murdered person known as "right to *qisas*" which is compared to talion, in Latin lex talionis, which was developed in early Babylonian law and is present in both biblical and early Roman law. It says that criminals should receive as punishment precisely those injuries and damages they had inflicted upon their victims. *Qisas* or talion law is also known as the "eye-for-an-eye" principle. *Encyclopedia Britannica*, Keshavarz and Naseri Moghaddam (2010).

[73] Cases of honor killing are often reported in southern or western provinces.

[74] Capital city of Khuzestan, an Iranian province.

[75] http://www.fa.wikipedia.org/wiki

[76] Women and the Other Side of the Coin: a Review of Global Life Conditions for Women, Section III, Human Rights Watch (2014), p. 3.

are not reported to judicial authorities or in some cases reported as suicide, self-immolation, electrocution, a fall, or that the person is missing. These norms are passed down from one generation to the next as a cultural heritage giving social acceptance to collective ardor. In some Islamic societies, despite the historical changes and explicit legislations concerning individual freedoms and legal punishment, such laws are often disregarded by tribal and family vigilantes.

To prevent honor killings, authorities must, among other things, admit the fact that honor killing is an instance of violence that is wholly in conflict with Islam's principles and ordinances, particularly human dignity, and that legislations must be amended to provide more severe and certain punishments for honor killers, including fathers, brothers, and husbands. Nationally and internationally recognized principles, as the principle of respecting human life and the principle of legality in criminal law must be incorporated into public education. Changes in customs and traditions rooted in certain regions should be facilitated by raising awareness and promoting cultural acceptance for criminalizing insults and offensive and coercive behaviors. Measures should be taken to teach people that refraining from honor killing does not harm the honor of a person, or his family or clan to such an extent that he is forced to commit such a crime. This could be done by making use of mass media, schools, and education. Experts, religious scholars, and influential figures should be united in the battle to eliminate such unacceptable practices.

7 Prohibition of Forced Marriage in International Law and Challenges in Implementing International Norms within Islamic Jurisdictions

Laws and regulations concerning families, like other provisions of international law, are the result of international processes, which are often different from domestic legislative processes in terms of their particular complexities and subtleties. Many actors, including states, governmental and non-governmental organizations, the media, public opinions, and a variety of temporal and spatial conditions, are involved in the process of adopting an instrument in the international arena.

Substantial rights and protections for women, including equality of spouses in forming the family, prohibition of forced marriage, and the elimination of unacceptable norms and traditions concerning marriage, can be clearly extracted from the provisions of international rules and instruments.

Article 16 of the Universal Declaration of Human Rights, Article 23 of the International Covenant on Civil and Political Rights, Article 16 of the Convention on Elimination of Discrimination against Women, Article 10 of the International Covenant on Economic, Social, and Cultural Rights, and many other international instruments call for mutual consent and emphasize it as a basic element in marriage. For example, Article 23 of the International Covenant on Civil and Political Rights states that:

(1) The family is the natural and fundamental group unit of society ...
(3) No marriage shall be entered into without the free and full consent of the intending spouses...

As noted before, the most important right in family settings is the equal rights of men and women to marry and have a family based on their own will, free of pressure by family and society. According to international human rights law, establishing this right requires (1) removal from marriage any form of limitation related to ethnicity, race, nationality, language, religion, *etc.* and (2) free will to decide on marriage upon mutual consent, free of any obstacle that violates the right to free choice in marriage and forming a new family; existing obstacles must be eliminated. In short:

- The right to marriage must be recognized for men and women upon reaching the age of marriage[77];
- The right to marriage should be exercised with no restriction in terms of race, nationality, religion, *etc.*[78];
- Marriage bonds should be made based on free and complete mutual consent[79];
- Women and men should be given equal rights to marriage and protected against early or forced marriage[80];
- A minimum age for marriage should be set, particularly for girls,[81] since the underage cannot decide and consent based on free will; and
- The requirement for obtaining the permission of a girl's guardian should be eliminated and girls should be allowed to marry men from other religions.[82]

International obligations, by their legal nature, have different effects on domestic laws and practices of Islamic countries. These must be required to revise and, if necessary, amend or eliminate regulations, procedures, guidelines, and norms that violate these obligations and to provide necessary measures to meet their commitments in terms of legal, judicial, and executive requirements, otherwise they will be held responsible for breaching their international obligations and will face the pressure from public opinions for the neglect or the denial of human rights. In concrete terms, Islamic countries must effectively devise and implement international norms concerning different human rights, particularly rights of women, to protect them from forced marriage and its harmful consequences. They also should domestically develop practical Islamic models as a positive contribution to a global

[77] Article 23(2), the Covenant on Civil and Political Rights.

[78] Article 16(1), the Universal Declaration of Human Rights; Article 16(1-b), Convention on Elimination of Discrimination against Women, 1249 UNTS 13.

[79] Article 23(2), the Covenant on Civil and Political Rights and Statement 16 of the Committee of Economic, Social, and Cultural Rights.

[80] Article 16(1), Section A, Convention on Elimination of Discrimination against Women, 1249 UNTS 13.

[81] Joseph et al. (2005), p. 610.

[82] Ibid, pp. 610–611.

process. The main concern of Islam is perfection and protection of human dignity regardless of race, ethnicity, and tribal association. Any form of violence, especially violence against women and children, has been prohibited by the holy book of Muslims (*Qur'an*). Religious scholars and jurists, thus, have to explain many of these Islamic principles and ordinances, which in numerous cases are in line with international standards and promote basic human rights to freedom of choice. This will make it possible to freely choose a life partner and prevent the negative effects of practices that are no longer acceptable.

In short, the family is facing basic challenges both at the international and national levels in Islamic countries, and proper understanding of these challenges based on knowledge and legal principles is an urgent necessity to prevent irreversible harms for girls and women today and for next generations.

8 Conclusion

A major challenge faced by women, particularly in Islamic countries, is a wide range of victimization and violence caused by a variety of reasons including forced marriage.

Despite many efforts made by Islamic countries to prohibit forced marriage with its often devastating consequences—including amendments to constitutions and civil codes, raising the minimum age of marriage, creating special centers for processing women's complaints and punishing violators—these efforts have had limited success. The reasons are manifold: lack of proper judicial organizations, poor enforcement of laws, and also historical causes of female victimization in traditional cultures and societies.

A major problem in Islamic countries is the denial of the right to marriage based on mutual consent despite it being provided for by domestic legislations as well as international instruments. Forced marriage remains a common practice in Islamic countries where most couples still enter into traditional marriage arranged by their parents, and both parties, particularly girls, have a limited role in choosing their spouse. Compensation marriages or exchange marriages are other types of forced marriage prevailing in some Islamic countries. Women in these countries have to tolerate violence and victimization by their husbands and their relatives. These women either have to endure these conditions for the rest of their lives or try to escape, even by putting an end to their miserable lives. Some run away from home only to find themselves being captured or abused by those who want to take advantage of them or by drug- and prostitution gangs.

Although domestic legislations of most Islamic countries or international standards adopted by these countries emphasize the protection of the family, complying with the provisions on mutual consent and minimum age of marriage, and despite the measures taken by most countries to raise the minimum age, there are numerous instances of underage marriage. Unfortunately, inadequate law enforcement and administration of justice have resulted in violating the rights of women to freely choose their husbands. Because of a lack of judicial offices to register marriages, many regions, particularly in remote and rural areas, do not require such registration although this is necessary for legalizing the marriage and to ensure the enjoyment of legal rights by both parties. Many women are therefore not entitled to the rights arising from marriage because they cannot register their marriage. In the case of a forced marriage, they will also have to put up with different forms of violence and victimization, including physical, sexual, and emotional violence. Since observance of norms and traditions are more prominent in Islamic countries, many instances of victimization, particularly domestic violence, are regarded as private issues and husbands can continue their abuses without any fear of being prosecuted and/or punished. Women have no possibility to escape from these forms of violence since in many of these countries police and judicial authorities ignore their cases despite the presence of legislations concerning the protection of women and the prohibition of forced marriage.

Women have difficulties accessing the courts to denounce their husbands because they worry about losing their honor or they are afraid of being returned to their homes, suffering even worse victimization or being forced into prostitution or an adulterous relationship, only to be arrest by the police and convicted by the courts, despite their being the victims, not the offenders. In other words, women not only see their rights denied by their own families and society, but also receive no proper protection from the judicial authorities and the justice system.

The following recommendations and proposals could pave the way for greatly reducing the different forms of victimization of women presented in this chapter:

1. Criminal and civil legislations should be revised or amended to establish the prohibition of early and forced marriage;
2. In particular, forced marriage should be criminalized and those involved in this practice, the groom, witnesses, and those officiating at the wedding as well as family member should be punished by appropriate criminal sanctions. Also, domestic legislations should be revised to criminalize and severely punish offenders of honor killings;
3. The adverse impacts of forced marriage should be included in school- and university textbooks;
4. Proper measures should be developed to identify the root causes of forced marriage and appropriate legislations should be passed considering particularly the facts and realities in Islamic countries;
5. Institutions and protective mechanisms should be established to guarantee the enforcement of relevant laws and the administration of justice;
6. Unacceptable anti-women beliefs in social cultures and norms of urban and rural areas should be eliminated by seeking help from influential local and religious figures;
7. The judicial system including the courts should be strengthened to facilitate access to justice for women;
8. Police officers should be trained in identifying and investigating cases of forced marriage and referring the cases for prosecution;

9. Governments should develop measures and mechanisms to protect women or girls escaping from forced or early marriage through governmental and non-governmental organizations and to help their acquittal from false charges like running away from home;
10. Non-governmental organizations (NGOs) and civil activists should contribute to raising public awareness about the negative consequences of forced marriages, particularly among men, by seeking help from religious leaders;
11. A comparative study on forced marriage between Islamic Rules (Shari'a) and international instruments

Five Questions

1. What are the different forms of forced marriage covered by International Instruments compared to Shari'a?
2. Have Islamic Rules (Shari'a) provided women with effective protection against forced marriage?
3. Could Islamic Rules (Shari'a) be successful to cover all kinds of forced marriage?
4. Is there any significant progress about forced marriage in Shari'a compare to the non-Islamic countries?
5. What can the Islamic Countries do to eliminate forced marriage?

References

Al Hibri, A. Y. (2003). An Islamic perspective on domestic violence. *Fordham International Law Journal*, *27*, Article 8.

Al-Kashani, A.-F., Mohsen, M., Al-Sharaya, M., Al- Zakhayer Al Islamia, M. (1971). Iranian National Library, Vol. 2, p. 104. Tehran, Iran (AH).

Babazadeh, A. A. (1989). *Marriage and human rights* (Vol. 5, 1st ed.). Iran: Badr Publishing, Al-Habi Al-Ameli, Z., Al-Howza Al- Ruza Al-Bahia fi Sharh Al-Lama Al-Dameshqia, Maktaba Ayatollah Al-Marashi Al- Najafi.

Bakhtiarnejad, P. (2009). Fajeeye Khamush: ghatlhaye namusi [The silence trajedi, Honor killing]. Unpublished study

Bernabeo, P. (Ed.) (2011). *Modern Muslim societies*. Library of Congress Cataloging in Publication Data. Singapore: Marshall Cavendish.

Convention on Elimination of Discrimination against Women. (1981). 1249 UNTS 13 (entered into force 3 September 1981).

Country Report on Human Rights Practices for 2012: Indonesia. http://www.refworld.org/docid/517e6e27f.html

Country Report on Human Rights Practices: Kuwait, cited in: April 2011. http://www.refworld.org/docid/4da56db4af.htm

Damdari, S. M. (2010). *Islamic family law: A critical appraisal of 38 countries*. Iran: University of Qom.

Ebrahimi, S. N. (2005). Child custody, (Hizanat) under Iranian law: An analytical discussion. *Family Law Quarterly*, *39*(2), 459–479.

Encyclopedia Britannica, at: www.britannica.com/topic/581485/contributors; Keshavarz, A., Naseri Moghaddam, H. (2010). A Contemplation on Denial of the Right to Qisas for Couples.

Entekhab Newspaper. (2003a) November 29, 2003.

Entekhab Newspaper. (2003b) October 21, 2003.
Forsythe, D. P. (Ed.) (2009). *Encyclopedia of human rights* (p. 6). New York: Oxford University Press.
Human Rights Watch. (2014). Women and the other side of coin. A Review of Global Life Condition for Women. http://www.hrw.org/.../human-rights-watch-submission...
Joseph, S., Jenny, S., & Melissa, C. (2005). *The international covenant on civil and political rights*. Oxford: Oxford University Press.
Khamenei, S. M. (1992). *Rights of women: A comparison of human and civil rights of women in Islam and the universal declaration of human rights*. Tehran, Iran: Tak Publishing.
Molaverdi, S. (2005). *Eliminating violence against women in Islamic countries*. Tehran: Hoghoghdan Publishing.
Rahmani, S. A. (2005). Thinking the Foundations of Renovating Afghanistan, Kabul, Women Rights Protection Committee.
Rayejian Asli, M. (2006). Iranian criminal justice system in light of international standards relating to victims. *European Journal of Crime, Criminal Law and Criminal Justice*, *14*(2), 185–207.
Rayejian Asli, M. (2013). Introducing a general theory on victimology in criminal sciences. *The International Journal of Humanities of the Islamic Republic of Iran (Scientific Research Quarterly)*, *20*(3), Tarbait-Modares University, Tehran, Iran.
Rayejian Asli, M., & Azizi, M. (2013). A comparative study on infanticide in the light of a criminological-legal approach. *Comparative Law Researches (Scientific Research Quarterly)*, *18*(3), (Tom 81), Autom, Faculty of Humanities, Tarbiat-Modares University, Tehran, Iran.
Report by the IRR Embassy in Doha (1997).
Rights and Protection Provided to Trafficked Women and Children, Trafficking of Women and Children in Pakistan. (1996).
Research Department, Iranian Islamic Human Rights Commission. (2009). Latest Events on the Rights of Women and Children.
Shahida, F. (2011). Women culture and identity in the Muslim community. Hamshahri Newspaper (cited in R.I.S.S).
Shareef Malik, S. (2013). Pakistan. Federal Secretary. Ministry of Human Rights Government of Pakistan. During the 57th Session of the United Nations Commission on the Status of Women (CSW), Pakistan Permanent Mission to the United Nations, New York.
Sharq Newspaper. (2012). Consistency of Child Marriage in Iran: Five Early Marriages under 10 Registered in the South of Iran, No. 1425
Sharq Newspaper. (2012). National Register of "Khoon-bass" is not justifiable, No. 1629.
Tusi, AbiJafar Muhammad, Al-Khalaf, Vol. 4.
Van Oerven Johaness, A. (2010). *Human rights or religious rules? Empirical research in religion and human rights*. Library of Congress Cataloging in Publishing Data, Brill Publishing, Netherlands.
Zibakalam, S. (2000). Islam, west, women, and reforms. *Farzaneh Quarterly*, *3*(10), 73.

Women and Children as Victims and Offenders: The Case of De-Notified Tribes in India

Milind Bokil and Vijay Raghavan

Abstract De-Notified and Nomadic Tribes, which were called "criminal tribes" during the colonial rule, are one of the most subjugated sections in modern India. The colonial administration enacted the Criminal Tribes Act (CTA) in 1871 based on the notion of hereditary criminal class in contemporary Europe, incorrect understanding of the Indian caste system and the social causes of criminality in India, and in a bid to establish law and order in the subcontinent. The CTA, which mostly targeted the nomadic, wandering and peripatetic communities, not only violated the basic dignity of human life but also criminalized millions of individuals. In independent India, the CTA was repealed but later replaced by the Habitual Offenders Act, which retained many of the provisions of the CTA, and led to the continued labeling and criminalization of the DNTs. This process further led to the marginalization and social exclusion of the DNTs, and their ending up becoming de-citizenized. Women and children had to bear the brunt of the criminalization process, in terms of institutional and structural violence—poor access to food security, education, healthcare, social protection and justice delivery. As DNTs were criminalized through the creation of a colonial discourse, their reintegration needs to be informed by an alternate body of liberating knowledge from sociology and criminology. The chapter argues that the vicious circle forcing the DNTs to remain in the criminal nexus can be broken through concerted efforts by the State, community associations of DNTs, civil society and DNT individuals. Specific suggestions informed by criminological theory can bring about a desired change for integrating the succeeding generations and establish a just, egalitarian and violence-free society.

M. Bokil (✉)
Pune, India
e-mail: msbokil@gmail.com

V. Raghavan
Tata Institute of Social Sciences, Mumbai, India
e-mail: vijay.r@tiss.edu

H. Kury et al. (eds.), *Women and Children as Victims and Offenders: Background, Prevention, Reintegration*, DOI 10.1007/978-3-319-08398-8_27

1 Introduction and Background

Prior to becoming independent in 1947, India was under British colonial rule for about a hundred and fifty years. A number of legislations were passed by the colonial administration during this period for consolidating the control over this vast land mass. One of the most notorious legislations among them has been the Criminal Tribes Act of 1871 (CTA). The Act was passed as it was felt expedient to provide for the registration, surveillance and control of certain tribal communities termed as "criminal by birth". The basic operational modality was that if the local government had reason to believe that any tribe, gang or class of persons was addicted to the systematic commission of non-bailable offences, then it could report the case to the Governor General of India and request the latter's permission to declare such tribe, gang or class to be a criminal tribe.

British control over India happened gradually since the arrival of the East India Company (EIC) at the beginning of seventeenth century. The company subjugated the local rulers one by one and annexed their provinces to its dominion. The Company's rule ended after the Indian Rebellion[1] in 1857. Following the Government of India Act of 1858 the British Crown took control and India became a colony of the British Empire. The process of enactment of various laws and legislations had begun during the Company's rule but it was after the 1857 rebellion that they were systematized, with the legislative and juridical framework followed in Britain being applied to India.

In the initial years of consolidation, that is, in the first half of the nineteenth century, the British administration was confronted with two kinds of law and order situations. The first was the resistance from and uprising of various tribal communities living in the hilly and forest areas. After the defeat of the Maratha Empire in 1818, there was no major political power opposing the British rule and the hundreds of small and big princely states had accepted British dominion. The ruling classes and the social elites accepted British supremacy and began to learn English to take benefit of the jobs and employments offered by the colonial rulers. However, tribal societies like Bhils, Santhals, Mundas, Hos, Garos and Nagas living in the interior, core zones of the country did not succumb to British rule. They continued to wage war from their respective bastions till they were finally subjugated in the mid-nineteenth century. Apart from these large tribal societies, there were also a number of smaller and scattered tribal communities which did not accept British rule and continued their resistance through various ways. The rebellion of 1857 was led by the rulers of the princely states but it was backed by a number of tribal

[1] The Indian rebellion, which is also known as the "Sepoy Mutiny" against the East India Company (EIC), was a result of a combination of years of misrule by the EIC and precipitating social, political, economic and religious factors. For a more detailed understanding, read Heather Streets (2001), retrieved from http://www.sdstate.edu/projectsouthasia/Resources/upload/The-Rebellion-of-1857-Streets.pdf.

communities. The British administration had therefore formed an official perception of these tribes as "savage", "predatory", "violent" and "uncivilized".

The second aspect of the law and order situation was posed by bandits, dacoits, thieves and other unruly elements. After the defeat of the resisting forces in 1857 and after the dismantling of the armies of the previous rulers, a considerable number of individuals had taken to crime and were roaming the countryside. They particularly targeted the travellers and traders. Among them, a secret brotherhood of murderers and plunderers came into existence, popularly known as "thugs". The thugs did not just loot the people but also mercilessly strangled them to death. A great deal of fear and chaos about them prevailed in the countryside, especially in the north, north-western and central parts. A special Thugee and Dacoity Department was therefore established to combat this menace (Devy 2000). The Thugee phenomenon not only prompted the British administration to take stringent measures against these gangs but also to think about the nature of crime and criminality among Indian society. As noted by scholars, in the colonial administrative discourse, group criminality in Indian society was seen as emanating from the structure of the Indian society, especially its divisions into castes and tribes (Kumar 2004).

Scholars (Radhakrishna 2001; D'Souza 2001; Bokil 2002a) have identified a number of reasons why the British introduced the CTA. The emergent discourse on this issue makes a case that these communities came into conflict with the colonial rulers on a number of counts. Many of these communities were forest dwelling or forest-dependent communities who lived by hunting, taming of wild animals to be used in battles by local rulers (for example, the Bhartiya-Iranis were known for trading in horses, the Chapparbands supposedly prepared make-shift camps and temporary platforms atop trees for the kings to hunt in forests and during battles),[2] or to be used for entertainment purposes (for example the snake charmers, the Makadwalas who tamed monkeys, or Vaghwale-Shahswho tamed the Indian sloth bears to perform various acrobatics and "human" gestures), grazing of cattle on forest land, and preparing medicinal herbs from plants found in the forests. With the British staking claim on these virgin forests for commercial use and making sleepers from forest wood to lay railway tracks across the country so as to serve their economic and political interests, these tribal groups came in their way; some of them resisting the taking over of the forests and even waging intermittent battles with them. Due to their cultural and occupational past as hunters and warriors, they could not be easily defeated.

The second aspect was the phenomenon of nomadic tribes in India. India was known as a land of villages (or village republics) organized around settled

---

[2] The other narrative about Chapparbands is that they used to make coins during the reign of the princely states prior to British occupation. After the coming of the EIC and the gradual annexation of princely states, the Chapparbands lost their occupation, with the replacement of local coins by the new currency which was introduced throughout colonial India. The Chapparbands "rebelled" against colonial rule by making fake coins, being experts in making coins, to earn their livelihood and hurt the British economy.

agriculture and a sophisticated system of division of labour (also known as caste system). The Indian village society, evolved since the chalcolithic times (Bronze Age), had developed a complex system of patron-client relationships, called as *jajmani* system. Under this system, various artisan castes (like blacksmiths, cobblers, carpenters, barbers, potters, tailors and others) provided their services to the peasants and were paid in kind. The patron-client relationships were hereditary and ran over generations. The villages acquired so-called "self-sufficiency" mainly due to these patron-client relationships. Though these artisans satisfied the village needs, a number of nomadic and peripatetic communities also frequented the villages, who sold a variety of goods (salt, bamboo and cane baskets, ropes, stone-implements, needles, knives, swords, woolen blankets, herbal medicines, beads, trinkets, perfumes, and so on) and extended various services (for example, stone dressing, thatching, smithy, and animal husbandry).

The nomadic groups also consisted of religious minstrels, bards, astrologers and entertainers like acrobats, snake-charmers, bull-deckers, dancers, singers, storytellers, jugglers and so on. Besides, a number of pastoral nomads also visited the countryside with their flocks of sheep, goat, cows, horses and camels. They grazed their animals in the fields and benefitted the farmers with manure, quality breeds and products like wool, hide and meat (Bokil 2002b).

It has been estimated by anthropologists that nomadic groups in India existed about two thousand years ago (Misra and Misra 1982, p. 6). Indian village society was incomplete without the nomads. The significance and utility of nomads was very well understood and their travel routes and relationships were respected. The colonial administrators however did not grasp the significance of the nomads nor did they appreciate the nomadic way of life. Scholars have pointed out that the nomads' lack of property and supposed lack of due regard for others' property was seen to be a threat to the established order and a number of prejudices (including the European prejudices against the Gypsies/Roma) operated against them (Radhakrishna 2001, pp. 9–12). From the law and order perspective, the problem was that owing to their nomadic way of life, it was difficult for the colonizers to pin them down or torment them—they did not own agricultural land and therefore crops, so the land and agricultural revenue laws could not be used to bring them to book, or lived in *pucca* houses which could be damaged; in addition, they could not be easily traced to wage "face to face" battles.

As part of the administrative consolidation process, British rulers also started collecting ethnographic information about Indian communities. British officers were encouraged to document information about local castes and tribes, and their understanding served as a basis while enacting the legislations. However, barring some exceptions, these studies were not carried out by trained social scientists. Although the officers worked meticulously, most often their understanding was distorted as the reality was too complex to perceive. Gradually, over a period of time, detailed accounts about the "immoral" lifestyles, "illegal" occupations, and "loose" social mores and cultural practices of many such communities were constructed by British officers who served in the district administration, police and forest departments, paving the way for a "body of knowledge" which legitimized the "criminal tendencies" of these communities. For example, Lieutenant General George MacMunn, a British Army officer, in his book *The underworld of India*, wrote, "*[T]hey are absolutely the scum, the flotsam and jetsam of Indian life, of no more regard than the beasts of the field.*" T. V. Stephens, a British official of the time, while introducing the CTA bill, said, "*. . . people from time immemorial have been pursuing the caste system defined job-positions: weaving, carpentry and such were hereditary jobs. So there must have been hereditary criminals also who pursued their forefathers' profession*" (D'Souza 1999, p. 3576). The Inspector General of Bombay Presidency, Mr. M. Kennedy, wrote a volume titled "Criminal Classes of the Bombay Presidency."

While these accounts did document the lives and cultures of the communities in astounding detail and remain treasure houses of great anthropological value, they also stand out in terms of the implicit bias and prejudice with which the peoples and their lives were documented, and the complete lack of understanding of embedded local cultures, which were reflected in these accounts. In hindsight, they emerge as systematic attempts to malign the communities as backward, retrograde and immoral. These documents laid the foundation for the introduction of the CTA.

The other rationale for the introduction of the CTA, as pointed out by scholars, is the deliberate or otherwise supplanting of the caste system logic to make a case that if these communities were engaged in criminal occupations, it was logical to assume that in a caste-ridden society, these occupations too were transferred from one generation to another. It was therefore safe to conclude that these criminal occupations were hereditary in nature, just as a male child born into the Brahmin community would have to take to reading the scriptures or performing religious ceremonies, or a male child born into the cobbler community would be forced to take to the same occupation. The twin pillars of this discourse—that there were communities who were traditionally into criminal occupations and that this was carried on along caste lines—created a watertight argument to enact the CTA. With time, more and more communities were included in the CTA; the defining process became more and more loose and arbitrary, it became a tool in the hands of the rulers to fetter communities proving to be a nuisance or creating disturbance in the modernizing project of India.

The CTA was thus an important landmark not just in the social history of India but also in Indian criminology because it coined the term "criminal tribes" for the first time. In conclusion, researchers have summarized the factors contributing to the formation of the CTA as (1) the notion of "hereditary criminal class" in contemporary Europe, (2) the understanding of tribes committing various types of crime in India as belonging to a definable caste of hereditary criminals within the Hindu social system, (3) the understanding that crime was a profession passed on from one generation to another, (4) the pressure on colonial administration to identify precise social causes for criminality in India, and (5) the belief that with social policies and programs the criminal tribes could be weaned away from their traditional occupations (Radhakrishna 2001, pp. 2–8).It has been pointed out that British administration drew deliberate parallels between the thugs and the criminal tribes and made a case for the institution of the CTA (Nigam 1990).

Initially, the CTA was applicable only to the north-west provinces and a north-central region of Oudh. An amendment was carried out in 1897, which allowed the words "tribe", "gang" and "class" to include any portion or members of a tribe, gang or class. Another amendment introduced a provision for establishing and maintaining reformatory settlements for children (persons between the age of four and eighteen). In the initial years of the passing of the 1871 Act, the usual method was to put into prison the members who were apprehended. However, it was realized that this affected their families adversely as women and children were subjected to great financial and emotional stress. It was also noticed that the released prisoners were worse off than before. By that time, agencies such as the Salvation Army had begun experimenting to re-socialize, reform and settle these essentially nomadic and itinerant communities and released prisoners. From these experiments, the idea of settlements was born. In 1908, the Criminal Tribes Settlement Act was passed which allowed the provincial governments to plan the settlements (Simhadri 1991, p. 25; Tolen 1991).

In 1911, the CTA was revised to cover all of India. The Act was made more comprehensive and it clearly specified the provisions for the notification and registration of members of criminal tribes, restrictions on their movements, the provisions for settlements and schools, rules for meeting the objects of the Act and the penalties and procedures associated with it (Simhadri 1991, pp. 119–161). Following this Act, the local governments in different parts of the country altogether notified more than a hundred and fifty communities.

The CTA has been justifiably condemned as one of the most oppressive legislations. It not only violated the basic dignity of human life but also stigmatized thousands of people as criminals. The most damaging fact was that it essentially targeted the nomadic, wandering or peripatetic communities. Scholars have pointed out that "(A) historical explanation of the phenomenon of the Criminal Tribes Act thus lies not only in the generalized fact of a number of communities losing their livelihood, and beginning to be considered criminal, but equally in the social prejudices of persons in authority towards them" (Radhakrishna 2001, p. 36). Although the legislation was aimed at reforming the criminal tendencies and facilitating the resettlement of nomadic communities, in actual practice it became a draconian legislation in the hands of police administration. Another characteristic feature was that after 1911, the task of managing the settlements throughout the country was entrusted to the "Salvation Army", a religious organization identified with imperial aims and projects of England. The reform measures included employing the inmates of the settlements in agriculture or private industries. The aim was not just to rid the society of the pestilential and predatory activities of a criminal section but also to integrate the "rising" generation into the mainstream of society as law-abiding citizens either as peasants or wageworkers in private enterprises (Radhakrishna 2001, p. 17).

This orientation and the latter measures aiming at resettlement of the criminal tribes connect us with the issue at hand, that is, making suggestions for the succeeding generations to be reintegrated into the society. After India became Independent in 1947, the CTA was repealed in 1952 but was later replaced by the

Habitual Offenders Act (HOA), which was purportedly passed to deal with habitual offenders, but retained many of the provisions of the CTA. As the CTA was repealed, the barbed wire settlements were removed and the notified criminal communities were declared as “de-notified”. Hence the term De-notified and Nomadic Tribes (DNTs).

Following the welfare orientation of the democratic State, a number of social development programs were also started for the benefit of the DNTs. The Indian Constitution (adopted in 1950) had two schedules annexed: the Schedule of Castes, which included the previously untouchable castes (SCs), and the Schedule of Tribes, which included the tribal communities (STs) living in forests and mountains. The communities listed in the Schedules were guaranteed Constitutional protection and positive discriminatory action on the part of the State. A number of welfare and development programs were also proposed for them. As the Schedules of Castes and Tribes were prepared state wise, some of the DNTs were varyingly grouped into the SCs and STs. However, many of them were left out of the Schedules. Those who were left out were later included into what is called as “Other Backward Classes” (OBCs). Though at present the DNTs are grouped into one of the three categories, considerable anomalies exist in their enumeration and classification which create serious impediments in getting justice and facilitating development. For example, the Banjaras are included in the ST in Rajasthan, as SC in Karnataka but in states like Maharashtra they are grouped into a separate state-level category of DNTs. The “Phase-Pardhis” are included in the STs in Maharashtra but their counterparts, the Haran Shikaris or Gaon-Pardhis are categorised under the DNTs. Similarly, the Kaikadis in the Vidarbha region of Maharashtra are grouped under the SCs but those from the rest of the state are under the DNTs. The same Kaikadis are categorized as STs in Andhra Pradesh (Bokil 2002a). Such anomalies are plentiful and at times result into conflicts for aspiring the Scheduled statuses (Singh 2008).

The Habitual Offenders Act, 1952 is concerned with individuals and not with communities but in actual practice the police administration, inheriting the colonial mindset and operational manuals, has continued to harass and oppress the communities as before. The United Nations’ Committee on Elimination of Racial Discrimination in its 2007 report has noted with concern that the so-called de-notified and nomadic tribes, which were listed for their alleged “criminal tendencies” under the former Criminal Tribes Act (1871), continue to be stigmatized under the Habitual Offenders Act (1952) (art. 2 (1) (c)) and recommended that India should repeal the HOA and effectively rehabilitate the DNTs concerned.[3] The National Human Rights Commission of India has also recommended the repeal of the HOA (Devy 2006, p. 34).

The Indian media is routinely galore with the stories of police and social brutalities on these communities. The DNTs were traditionally stigmatized as

[3] UN CERD (2007). http://daccessddsny.un.org/doc/UNDOC/GEN/G07/442/00/PDF/G0744200.pdf/OpenElement.

thieves, pickpockets, robbers, dacoits, bandits, distillers, boot-legers, beggars, parasites and amoral people. They were socially ridiculed, ostracized, humiliated, exploited and at times feared. This situation has not changed significantly for communities like Pardhis, Kanjar-Bhats, Sansis, Chharas, Nats, Banjaras, Takaris, Wagharis, Sikligars and for many others. The welfare and developmental measures have also not been very efficacious in changing their livelihood conditions and ushering in a process of development. Secondly, there is no active agency to address human rights violations. The changes that have occurred in some communities are mainly due to their own internal initiatives and dedicated efforts by some social workers. A National Commission on Nomadic Tribes, Semi-Nomadic Tribes and De-Notified Tribes was appointed in 2003 to look into their conditions and make appropriate recommendations. The Commission submitted its report in 2008, but it has neither been made public nor acted upon by the Government of India. As of date, the DNTs remain a fragmented, differentiated and social excluded set of underprivileged communities.

2 The Criminalisation of DNTs: Emerging Issues

The CTA identified more than 150 communities all over the country. As mentioned earlier, the powers for notifying and registering the communities were vested with each local government, which notified these communities for the whole province or part thereof (districts). For the want of space, it would not be practical to give a countrywide list of ex-criminal tribes. As an illustration, the list of tribes notified in Bombay Presidency (which covered the present state of Gujarat, Western Maharashtra and parts of North Karnataka) is provided in Table 1.

Although the list mentioned above pertains to the then Bombay Presidency, the situation is representative of the whole country. This is because the Presidency lay at the confluence of northern and southern India and was inhabited by communities coming from both the directions. The communities like Bhil, Tadvi, Kathodi and Koli were native hill tribes whereas those of Mang, Berad and Ramoshi were part of the village society in southern Maharashtra and north Karnataka. Waghari, Dharala, Baori were part of the Gujarat rural society. Minas were the hill tribes of Aravalis in Rajasthan. The Banjaras and Rajput Bhamptas also originated from Rajasthan. Bhar and Pasi came from the northern states of Punjab and Uttar Pradesh whereas Waddar, Mang-Garudi, Kaikadi and Katbu originated on the Deccan plateau. Pardhi and Sansi (Kanjar-Bhat, Chhara or Bhantu) roamed all over western India. The point to be noted here is that only a couple of communities like Bhar, Pasi and Bhamptas were solely involved in the so-called criminal occupations. Their numbers were small. Futgudi was more of a group of persons committing crimes in Bombay Presidency. The rest had traditional occupations of their own and operated within the livelihood niches carved out historically.

In traditional Indian society, only the term "Bhampta" (meaning cheat) signified a hereditary criminal identity. Although members committing these so called

Table 1 Criminal tribes in Bombay Presidency[a]

S. No.	Name of the tribe	Traditional occupation
1	Bauriah also called Dehliwal, Malpura, Kairwada or Kerara and Badak	Cheating, thieving
2	Berad also called Bedar, Talwar, Naik-Makkalu or Walmiks	Village servants as guards and night-watchmen; agriculture and agricultural labor
3	Bhampta (Rajput) also called as Pardeshi-Bhampta or any other appellations	Spice-trading, pick-pocketing and pilfering
4	Bhampta (Takari) also called Ghantichor, Uchalla, Kall-Wadru, Tudug-Wadru, Girni-Wadru, Wadari, Kamati, Pathrut, Bestars or Dongs, Dasaru or other appellations	Stone dressing and stone-work but also known as bundle thieves, lifters and pocket cutters
5	Bhar	Burglary and dacoity
6	Bhil	Hill farming, agricultural and forest labor
7	Chapparband	Thatching of huts, making coins
8	Dharala	Agriculture
9	Futgudi	Burglary
10	Kaikadi also called Korcha, Korwa, Pamlor, Telagu-Dhangar or Javeri or other appellation	Basket-weaving, broom-making, entertaining, snake-charming, animal husbandry.
11	Kammi	Iron work
12	Katbu	Fishing and tattooing
13	Kathodi or Katkari	Makers of Catechu, fishing, hunting and gathering, sale of minor forest produce
14	Koli	Hill-farming, agricultural labor, sale of minor forest produce.
15	Lamani also called Lambada	Trading of grains, salt and other merchandises; transporters and army-contractors
16	Mang	Rope making, field-labor, village service
17	Mang-Garudi	Snake-charming, buffalo-shaving and trading
18	Marwar-Baori also called Gujarat-Baori, Marwar-Waghari, Salat-Waghari or Baghari	Coining, begging and wandering.
19	Mina	Hunting, gathering, hill-farming.
20	Oudhia	Begging, wandering
21	Pardhi also called Phase-Pardhi, Raj-Pardhi, Waghari-Pardhi, Takari or Takankar, Haran-Shikari, Advichinchar or Chigri-Betgar, Nirshikari or Phasechari or other appellation	Hunting, gathering, makers of grinding-stones (Takari)
22	Pasi	Burglary and dacoity
23	Ramoshi	Village servants as guards and night watchmen, agriculture

(continued)

Table 1 (continued)

S. No.	Name of the tribe	Traditional occupation
24	Sansia also called Beria, Gujarat-Bhat, Kanjar, Nat, Chhara or Gujarati-Kolhatis	Hunting, gathering, distilling, animal herding, agriculture, trading
25	Tadvi	Hill farming, hunting, gathering
26	Vanjari also called Banjari, Rajput or Charan-Vanjari	Trading in grains, salt and other merchandises, animal husbandry
27	Waddar also called Bhandi-Waddar, Ghanti-Waddar, Mann or Mati-Waddar, Kall-Waddar or Wadari	Stone dressing, stone work, earth work, building and construction
28	Waghari	Hunting, gathering, wandering, begging

[a]The list of tribes is as per the Munshi Committee Report (1937)

crimes were penalized by the village society, no other community was ever identified as hereditary criminals. The crime committed by these communities was usually petty thefts of agricultural produce and household things. This was by and large tolerated by the peasant society. Only some of the members of the ex-criminal tribes were involved in major crimes like robbery and dacoity. They usually did not commit murder. The thugs who became notorious for heinous crimes were actually a sect assembled from lone, cast-away individuals. It was not a caste in the Indian parlance. Traditional Indian society's disposition towards these sections was different than the colonial rulers.

When this situation is studied from a criminological perspective, a number of issues come to the fore.

(a) The main concern today is that some of the members of the DNTs are still involved into serious and petty crimes. These acts not only force them into a vicious circle of "crime commission-punishment-recidivism-retribution" but also invite the wrath of the polity and society. Such acts instigate the police to (1) target entire communities and (2) harass innocents, especially women and children. The offences committed by these individuals are often non-bailable and include theft, robbery, dacoity and housebreaking. These offences are sometimes accompanied by violence resulting in serious injury or even death of the victims. When such incidents occur, they receive wide publicity in the local and regional media and lead to a great deal of public outcry. Police respond to this pressure through a fire-fighting mode and arrest those individuals that have a history of crime. Very often, when the accused are unknown, they raid the habitats of the ex-criminal tribes and arrest their members upon mere suspicion. When male members are not found, they coerce women and children to disclose the names and whereabouts. It has been a historical practice on the part of police to take family members as hostages. Custodial harassment of the accused and their family members has been a routine phenomenon. Cases of custodial deaths are frequently reported in local and regional media (Ramakrishnan 2013).

(b) Apart from suffering police repression, women and children have to bear the brunt of this situation in a number of ways. The absence of earning male members forces the women to search for livelihoods and take care of the households. In the present case, this means resorting to manual wage-labor, which is difficult to obtain, especially in the rural areas where they get easily identified as DNTs and are socially stigmatized. They also find it difficult to access State sponsored employment guarantee schemes, due to the same reason. In urban areas they are ridiculed because of their distinctive clothing, lifestyle and behavior. If wage-labor is not available, then the family resorts to begging. Hundreds of instances of DNT families resorting to begging in big cities or railway platforms are noted. However, in most of the states begging is an offence, as a vestige of the colonial mindset of criminalizing the urban "unruly" poor (Chambliss 1960; Tarique and Raghavan 2011). In order to fight the criminal cases lodged against the men in court, the female heads of the households have to assemble a considerable amount of financial resources. Due to poor access to free legal aid by the State (Dhanuka 2013), arranging for competent advocates at the bail and trial stages comes at a heavy cost and becomes extremely difficult for a poor, wage-earning, often illiterate or semi-literate person. The money cannot be gathered through wage-labor or begging and the woman has to either take a loan at usurious rates of interest or may have to resort to prostitution or crime. Thus they turn from victims to offenders and are further plunged into the vicious circle.

(c) Children of arrested DNTs are most vulnerable because the family support in most cases is weak. A study by Prayas (2002) on children of women prisoners in two cities in India highlights the situation of children left outside while the mothers are in prison. The study shows that children may suffer neglect and deprivation, drop out from schools, lack access to nutritional meals or even miss meals, be forced out of their houses by relatives or caretakers, be unable to buy medicines or go to a doctor during illness, face trauma and stress due to imprisonment of the parent, have to take on adult roles to take care of younger siblings, and run away from home unable to take the stress. Activists working with DNT groups reveal that children of arrested or imprisoned DNTs suffer many of these problems, apart from the additional social stigma of being the child of a DNT.

(d) Another factor forcing the DNTs to continue with crime is the nexus formed between police, offenders and traders. It has been historically documented that the local landlords, moneylenders, goldsmiths, village officials and police were party to the crimes committed by the DNT members. Many of the crimes were committed at the behest of local landlords. The moneylenders and local officials like *patils*/*deshmukhs*[4] were the custodians of the loot. Gold and silver could not be brought into currency without the active involvement of

---

[4] Patel or Patil was the lowermost police functionary in the village whereas Deshmukhs were traditional revenue collectors.

goldsmiths. The police not only sought bribes but at times also helped the criminals. The police also needed the services from the DNT members either as informers or alibis. These relationships spanning over time, formed a complex nexus from which the community members could not escape. In the present times these nexuses still exist, which prevent the DNTs from getting out of the vicious circle.

(e) A major impediment in releasing the DNTs from the bondage of crime are the various procedures followed by the police for maintaining so-called law and order. Among other things, it includes a "police diary" (different from "police station diary").[5] It has been observed that at present the police compel the members of DNT to carry this on their person and bring it to the police station for verification at regular intervals. This has been the legacy of the articles 3, 10 and 12 of the CTA (1911), wherein the members were registered with the local authorities and had to present themselves at the appointed time for a roll call. They had to also give account of their movements. A certificate to this effect was issued by the lowermost, village level police representative (for example, the *police patil* in the state of Maharashtra). The latter practice continues till today in many villages. The police are also found to exhibit a "history sheet" of criminals at the police station, which very often lists the names of the DNTs. False documents are routinely created to implicate the members. These practices happen because the HOA is still in force and the mentality of the police has not changed; in their perspective DNTs are still seen as born criminals.

(f) The present system of justice in India is not just slow but also very expensive. Cases linger in lower courts for months increasing the trauma of the prisoners under trial. Although there exist many landmark judgments and judicial orders by the Supreme Court of India and numerous High Courts regarding the prevention of ill-treatment and torture of prisoners under trial, their right to medical examination and legal support, release on bail or Personal Recognizance Bond, and to speedy trial and disposal of cases, these orders are not implemented at the ground level due to a plethora of reasons (Madhurima 2010; Murali 2006; Dholakia 2000). The District Legal Services Authorities are mandated to provide free legal aid to prisoners under trial but they seldom function effectively. It has been observed by the apex court in its judgment of February 15, 1983 that "Legal assistance to a poor or indigent accused, arrested and put in jeopardy of his life or personal liberty, is a Constitutional imperative mandated not only by Article 39A but also by Articles 14 and 21 of the Constitution."[6] State Legal Services Authorities have been constituted in

[5] A police diary is a small notebook that the police may ask a suspect to maintain which records his/her attendance in the local police station, as and when called to the police station. A Station House Diary is a basic legal document maintained in every police station which records all official actions taken by the police, including registration of complaints, arrest and detention of suspects, help provided to citizens in distress, actions taken to maintain law and order, etc.

[6] Sheela Barse versus State of Maharashtra on February 1983, cited at 1983 AIR 378, 1983 SCR (2) 337. (http://indiankanoon.org/doc/174498/).

all the states but they are unable to provide free and competent legal services to indigent prisoners, due to structural and implementation bottlenecks (Raman and Ventakraman 2006; Mathivanan n.d.; Ivaturi 2013). It has been observed by lawyer-activists working for the DNTs that if the accused received prompt legal aid, then many of the false and fictitious cases filed against them could be immediately disposed of.

3 Looking at DNTs Through a Criminological Lens: From Functionalism to Postmodernism

The preceding sections trace the history and journey of the social construction of the DNTs into a criminal category and how this process impacted them at the social, psychological, economic and political levels. From being proud and self-reliant communities with distinct cultures and occupations, which performed specific socio-economic functions in village society and the polity in pre-colonial times, they were reduced to being treated as unruly populations who needed to be disciplined in the Foucauldian sense (Baxstrom 2000) and re-socialized, so that they could join the productive labor force of an industrial, modernizing economy, which British rule brought with it.

It is in this context that we need to understand the so-called criminal behavior of DNTs along the criminological continuum. An attempt is being made in this section to locate DNTs within some of the major criminological theories that have emerged over time.

3.1 Functionalism

The *functionalist* perspective, which emerged in the nineteenth century and has continued through the twenty-first century, was built on a positivist approach. Durkheim (1938) viewed crime as a "normal" phenomenon; it serves a purpose that is necessary in society i.e. to prepare for changes that are necessary in future. It is indicative of the need for reform in society (Moyer 2001, p. 56). Merton (1968) later developed Durkheim's concept of *anomie* as a condition, which occurs when there is a mismatch between the *culturally prescribed goals* and *institutionally available means* in a given society. Once anomie occurs, individuals experience strain and adapt differently. Crime according to him is one of the *modes of adaptation*, when the *institutional means* are not available to an individual to achieve the *culturally accepted goals* of society, and is a result of a society in disequilibrium (Moyer 2001, pp. 61–62).

From this functionalist perspective, the DNTs were viewed by the colonial powers as a threat to their rule and in establishing law and order in British India, owing to their nomadic lifestyle and their rather unconventional occupations, like hunting and fighting wars. This also involved the using and manufacturing weapons. For example, the Sikh-Sikligars were engaged in the making of swords and sharpening knifes, or the Phase-Pardhis were experts in catching birds by the use of a noose rope, and this skill was used by some of them in committing thefts. Many of these communities earned a living by entertaining the public like the Dombaris¸ who performed acrobatics on the rope, the Nats and the Kolhatis, who were into singing and dancing, the Sapelas, Saperas or Saapwales, who were snake-charmers, and the Bazigars and Sansis who were experts in jugglery and acrobatics, the latter also known to be cattle traders and warriors (Maharaja Ranjit Singh, a warrior king from Punjab, who ruled from late eighteenth to early nineteenth century, was supposed to be a Sansi (Singh 1965). These communities and their occupations were similar to the Victorian imagery of the Gypsies who the British identified as being vagabonds, tramps and criminals, and hence matched their idea of an unruly and uncontrollable population. The CTA was used to criminalize these communities, to keep them under check, forcibly reform and "settle" them, and thus maintain order in British India (Economic and Political Weekly 2007; 2008).

3.2 *The Chicago School*

The *Chicago* School sociologists examined crime at the macro level through *ecological* studies that dominated the early part of the twentieth century, and at the micro level through case studies of suicides and delinquent gangs and life histories of delinquent youth and of professional or habitual offenders. Conwell and Sutherland (1956) now famous *differential association theory* propounded that crime was a learnt behavior through the process of socialization in groups. According to him, a person's tendency to conform or deviate depends on the relative frequency of association with others who encourage conventional behavior or norm violation. The learning includes *techniques* of crime commission as well as the *drives, motives, rationalizations* and *attitudes*. Delinquency occurs when there is an excess of definitions favorable to law violation over definitions unfavorable to law violation (Carrabine et al. 2004, p. 56).

Simhadri (1991) used this approach to analyze the DNTs and is perhaps the only one to look at them through a criminological lens. In his seminal work, he traced the history of some of these communities and explained their criminal behavior by using the differential association theory. He contested the "born criminal" theory popularized by the British and claimed that the DNTs took to criminal behavior owing to a range of socio-economic factors, such as their economic backwardness, lack of education and loss of traditional livelihoods. By applying Sutherland's theory, he tried to prove that the DNTs learnt criminal occupations from one generation to another through early childhood socialization and peer group association, against the backdrop of lack of educational and alternative livelihood opportunities for the community.

Simhadri's study was based on secondary sources that he could lay his hands on. Most of these sources consisted of existing accounts on DNTs, many of them by British officers, who were prejudiced against these communities, for reasons highlighted earlier. He arrived at his findings and conclusion based on the analysis of this secondary data. Given the fact that he did not collect empirical or primary data, it stands to question whether these findings can be taken at face value, especially given the biased nature of the knowledge available about the DNTs. Simhadri's study is very important from the point of view that it contributed to a paradigm shift in understanding the criminal behavior of DNTs—from a Lombrosian to a sociological perspective. It is an important study also from the point of view of an attempt to explain the criminal behavior among members from these communities, due to reasons such as loss of traditional livelihoods and the inability to find alternative livelihoods resulting from the processes associated with the application of the CTA.

However, the study falls short in terms of its unquestioning approach towards the truth and validity of the secondary sources which formed the basis of its conceptual journey. While it may be true that some members of the DNT communities may have adopted a criminal lifestyle at some point in time, to assume that all members of these communities uniformly took to crime needs to be interrogated with greater academic rigor, especially in the light of recent studies and writings about them. It is our contention therefore, that Simhadri's study, while making an important contribution towards furthering the boundaries of existing knowledge about criminality among the DNTs, indirectly resulted in reinforcing the idea that criminality was an unquestioned reality and a facet of the lives of these communities.

Sub-culture theories explaining gang formations among adolescent youth were made popular by Cohen (1955). Later, Cloward and Ohlin (1960) attempted to integrate Merton's anomie theory and Sutherland's differential association theory to explain the evolution of delinquent sub-cultures. According to them, the culturally accepted goal of achievement of economic success is internalized by most individuals in society, but the opportunities available to achieve this goal differ across neighborhoods. This gave rise to specific subcultures depending on the opportunities available in specific neighborhoods. The primary among them in this context were *criminal*, *conflict/violent* and *retreatist/drug* sub-cultures (Carrabine et al. 2004, p. 60).

It is tempting to apply the sub-culture theories to explain criminal behavior among youth from the DNTs. However, we would like to add the same caveat here as has been highlighted in our analysis of Simhadri's work. For example, an unpublished study on the socio-economic situation of minorities within DNTs by TANDA[7] has thrown some light on gang formations within Sikh-Sikligars,

[7] Towards Advocacy, Networking and Developmental Action (TANDA), a Field Action Project of Centre for Criminology and Justice, Tata Institute of Social Sciences, Mumbai is working with

especially during the nineteen eighties and nineties, and on criminal network formation within Bhartiya-Iranis at the present time. While it is possible to understand criminal gang formations among some DNT youth through the sub-cultural lens, there is no attempt being made to extend this proposition to DNT youth in general, most of whom are part of the informal labour market in rural and urban areas, as highlighted in a study conducted by Agrawal and Sinha (2012) about the Pardhi community, which is much maligned as a community engaged in criminal activities.

3.3 Control Theories

The cornerstone of the control theories is the assumption that self-control serves as a restraint from criminal actions, and this self-control derives from a positive self-concept. The self-concept in turn, develops as a result of interactions with parents and family members, and later with teachers and peers. They also emphasize *free will* and define criminal behavior as a result of rational choice. Yet at the same time, they see behavior as imposed. The question they are primarily concerned with is 'why doesn't everyone commit crimes?' rather than 'why do people commit crimes?' (Moyer 2001, pp. 131–139).

Hirschi (1969) proposed the *"social attachments or bonds"* theory whereby he linked offending behavior to the level of commitment and attachment to, and belief in society. According to this theory, delinquency occurs when an individual's attachment or bond to society gets weakened or broken. He further proposed that a person's bond to mainstream society is based on four elements—*attachment, commitment, involvement* and *belief*. When belief in the values of society is present in conjunction with involvement, commitment and attachment, deviancy is rare (pp. 27–30).

If one looks at the situation of DNTs as has been highlighted in earlier sections, it is easily possible, given the treatment meted out to them due to the application of the CTA and later the HOA (post-independence) indiscriminately against them, that these communities would have little attachment, commitment, involvement and belief in society. This also explains the resistance offered by many of the DNT communities to civil society intervention, as has been the experience of social activists and NGOs working with them. This is especially true of those communities against whom the police routinely takes legal action, merely based on the suspicion that they may be involved in criminal activities, for example the Pardhis, the Sikh-

Nomadic and De-notified Communities (NT-DNTs). TANDA works towards "creating self-reliant NT-DNTs and ensuring the realisation of their constitutional and entitlement rights, as citizens of India". TANDA strongly believes that NT-DNTs should organise themselves to advocate for their rights and dignity. The project aims to play the role of a change agent through generating knowledge, capacity building and networking with different stakeholders on relevant issues towards policy advocacy.

Sikligars,[8] and the Bhartiya-Iranis. It should come as no surprise if under these circumstances, some members of these communities took to crime, as they may have had little stake in society and incentive to abide by the social norms and values.

3.4 Interactionist School

The formal origin of the Interactionist School in criminology or labeling theories can be traced to Frank Tannenbaum (1938). According to him, most criminals come from the same social backgrounds and possess the same characteristics as common citizens. What distinguishes them is their coming into contact with the criminal justice system. The offender label stamped on the criminal leads to a change in his identity, from a citizen to a criminal. The individual becomes a deviant through a *tagging* process following his or her involvement in an "innocent misadjustment" that has been dramatized by society. Due to this labeling, he/she becomes the very thing that society finds repugnant. The person becomes a criminal by *dramatization of evil* through a tagging and labeling process (Moyer 2001, pp. 164–5).

Lemert (1951) attempted to develop a systematic, comprehensive theory of deviance and audience reaction processes. He came up with the path-breaking concepts of *primary* and *secondary* deviance. Norm violations that invite little reaction from society and have little effect on a person's self-concept can be termed as primary deviance. But the labeling of the same act by society and criminal justice agencies as deviant or criminal behaviour leads to secondary deviance, by which an individual engages in repeated norm violation and begins to take on a deviant identity (Orcutt 1983, p. 227).

Becker's *Outsiders* (1963) is perhaps the most comprehensive treatment of the problems of audience reactions and secondary deviance. Becker was very critical of traditional sociology that viewed deviance as a conceptual category that resulted from a consensus in society as to what was functional for the group as a whole. Such actions only helped in labeling individuals as "outsiders". Becker suggested that creation of rules and their enforcement is not necessarily a universally agreed-on phenomenon; "instead, they are the object of conflict and disagreement, part of the political process of society" (Becker 1963, p. 18).

For Kitsuse (1962), deviance is the interactional process through which audiences define and react to others as deviant. They *interpret* behavior as deviant, *define* persons who so behave as a certain kind of deviant and then proceed to *treat* them in ways considered appropriate by them. They assign deviant meanings to

[8] The Sikligars are variously worded as Sikalgars, Siklagars, Shikalgars, etc. in various texts and government documents. We have used the word as spelt by Sher Singh 'Sher' (1966), who has written an authoritative account about the Sikh-Sikligars titled *The Sikligars of Punjab: A Gypsy Tribe*, New Delhi: Manoharilal Munshiram Publishers Pvt. Ltd.

behavior through a complex, subjective process that draws upon indirect evidence, such as rumors, as well as direct observations of how people act in situational settings. They then subjectively define the actor into a deviant category; and engage in "retrospective interpretation" of the actor's past behavior as evidence that he or she has always been a deviant (Orcutt 1983, p. 233).

Goffman was another Symbolic Interactionist who influenced the growth of criminology in the sixties and seventies. In his second major work, *Stigma* (1963), Goffman defined stigma as attributes that are deeply discrediting' to an individual; he distinguishes three types: *abominations of the body* (physical deformities), *blemishes of individual character* (societal labeling through records of unemployment, imprisonment, mental illness, homosexuality, etc. and as being weak-willed, treacherous, dishonest, etc.) and *tribal stigma* of race, nation and religion (contamination of all members of the particular family through lineages). Through a process of interaction between the individual and the social audience, a person is first *stigmatized* and then becomes what the stigma implies. Once the stigma is acquired, it is very difficult to overcome it (Moyer 2001, pp. 180–1).

The Interactionist School developed the premise that crime was socially constructed, and suggested that criminal justice policy may have unanticipated negative consequences on individuals and communities. The labeling theories, the concept of audience reaction and the impact of social stigma apply very well to understand the criminalization process of the DNTs in colonial and post-independence India. They were first systematically labeled as criminal tribes through a process of tagging and dramatization of evil, on the basis of the detailed accounts about each of the communities, whereby a body of knowledge was created highlighting their immoral and criminal behavior. The labeling process was helped along by the spread of tales and rumors highlighting their criminal behavior by the dominant classes which constituted the social audience.

This resulted in the DNTs being socially stigmatized and then socially excluded from the mainstream. They were trapped in a vicious cycle of: being labeled as criminal tribes through the CTA—criminal action by the police—social stigmatization—exclusion from social life and discrimination—ghettoization—loss of traditional livelihoods due to processes of modernization and industrialization—exclusion from the market and the new economy due to lack of relevant education and skills—lack of alternative livelihoods—forced into wage labor and loss of cultural (pride) identity—some members' entry into crime—arrest and criminal action by police—generalization about the community as a whole as a criminal tribe—repeated and indiscriminate criminal action against community members—forced into debt to deal with legal consequences of arrest and imprisonment—deeper entrenchment into crime to pay off debts—further reinforcement as a criminal community by police and society. For example, the TANDA study referred to earlier shows that while some members of the Bhartiya-Iranis (earlier engaged in selling horses) and Sikh-Sikligars (making weapons for kings) have taken to crime due to the loss of traditional livelihoods, majority of the Bharatiya-Iranis are engaged in running small shops, and the Sikh-Sikligars are into making and selling iron-made utensils and doing carpentry work. The data clearly shows that most members from these communities have not taken to crime as an occupation. Yet, they are treated as criminals by the police and society. Respondents of the study revealed to the TANDA research team that they get randomly "picked up" by the police whenever a crime occurs near their area and neighboring communities view them with suspicion. The areas inhabited these communities are known as "bad and unsafe neighborhoods" and this contributes to the labeling of their youths and prevents them from getting jobs.

3.5 Conflict Theories and the Radical School

The seventies and the eighties were largely dominated by *Conflict* theories, a school of thought, which was a logical extension of theories that emerged from the Interactionist School. They focused on the economic and political nature of crime and traced crime to the ills of the capitalistic society. According to the radicalists, any discussion on crime includes concepts such as imperialism, racism, sexism and other forms of exploitation. They re-conceptualize crime as a violation of human rights (Bohm 1982, pp. 567–71).

One of the most important works in *radical* criminology was Quinney's (1970) *The Social Reality of Crime*. According to Quinney, criminal behavior is *formulated* and *applied* by powerful interests against those with whom these interest groups are in conflict with. The powerful interests intervene at all stages in which criminal definitions are created and applied. The *social reality of crime* is constructed by the ruling class, which benefits them through the legal system they create. Crime control is, in reality, class control (Moyer 2001, pp. 208–10).

Quinney's theory fits well to interpret the process of criminalization of DNTs over time, as explained in the earlier sections. A body of knowledge was created leading to a "discourse" on DNTs and their criminal behavior in the Foucouldian sense. It is interesting to note that many of these communities had offered stiff resistance to the occupation of land and forests by the British as such occupation came in direct conflict with the livelihoods and lifestyle of the DNTs. Their nomadic lifestyle was seen as an irritant to the establishment of orderly rule in British India. Whether the introduction and application of the CTA was an outcome of a cultural clash or a deliberate strategy to demoralize and sedentarize the DNTs is open to debate and further investigation (beyond the scope of this chapter). However, it did lead to cementing the criminal identity of the DNTs and in the creation of a social reality of crime, which may have had little to do factual reality.

Another important work in this tradition is Reiman's (1979) *The Rich Get Richer and the Poor Get Prison*. Throughout his writings, he emphasized that the ideology of the criminal justice system places emphasis on the individual and the poor to divert attention away from the evils of the social order. Reiman (1979) highlighted that the poor get arrested out of proportion to their numbers for the crimes the poor generally commit such as burglary, robbery, assault, etc. When it comes to crimes that the poor do not have an opportunity to commit such as financial frauds, environmental crimes, serious tax evasion, etc., the State and the criminal justice system takes a comparatively benign view (Carrabine et al. 2004, p. 77).

Viewed from Reiman's point of view, one can see that the poor, especially those coming from marginalized sections, are disproportionately represented in arrest and prison statistics in India. The Scheduled Castes (SCs), the Scheduled Tribes (STs), the Other Backward Classes (OBCs) and Muslims are over-represented in prisons across the country (Raghavan and Nair 2013). The percentage of DNTs is not separately mentioned in these statistics, and they are subsumed under the category of SCs, STs and OBCs.[9] But most social activists working with DNTs will testify that they get arrested routinely on mere suspicion based on their social identity, rather than on the basis of facts and evidence. Once arrested, they find it difficult to get bail due to lack of competent legal aid. If and when they do get bail, they are not able to find suitable sureties to get released. It is a proven fact the world over that the chances of conviction increase substantially if an accused remains in custody, especially if he/she does not have access to a legal aid. This may be particularly true of DNTs languishing in prison, since efforts by the family to ensure acquittal may get weakened due to poverty, lack of legal awareness and social support, and acceptance of the tag of criminality on them. Once convicted, the road to multiple convictions is a foregone conclusion, owing to the bias against them. Soon, they acquire the tag of being a "history-sheeter" or a habitual criminal leading to further legal actions such as application of the HOA or preventive detention laws.

3.6 Critical Criminology

A key work in this continuing left history of conflict theories is Taylor, Walton and Young's (1973) *The New Criminology*. They argued that existing crime theories had ignored the wider and structural issues in explaining crime and the material conflicts at the root of the criminal process. They further claimed that earlier theories were deterministic in their assumptions and gave little role to the creative human actor willing to commit crimes and had inadequate epistemologies. They even criticized the radical theories as nothing more than a "form of moral gesture". A new position began to appear from their work, which was based on the "materiality" of crime. *Left realists,* on the other hand, tried to combine the concerns of traditional criminologists with the concerns raised by Marxist and Neo-Marxist

[9] The DNTs are not enumerated as a distinct category in the Census and other official statistics. They are subsumed either under the SCs, or the STs, or the OBCs in different states, based on various criteria identified by different state governments for enumeration purposes. The politics of this enumeration process is based on contesting claims by different communities about their level of socio-economic backwardness and the clout they enjoy in the polity of the state. The fact that DNTs do not exist as a separate category except in one or two states (for example in Maharashtra), is evidence of their inability to stake claim in the political and democratization processes, and their continued subjugated status.

School. This analysis highlights *the square of crime*—the State, society, the offender and the victim, and that the causes of crime lie in the structural inequalities. Crime is produced by *relative deprivation*—a perceived disadvantage arising from a specific comparison—and *marginalization*—where people living on the edge of society and outside of the mainstream with little stake in society overall (Carrabine et al. 2004, p. 79).

Structural inequalities have led to the systematic marginalization of the DNTs in India. From communities who played a useful and sometimes critical role in the economy and polity in pre-colonial times, the DNTs were gradually reduced to losing their cultural and social identity, traditional occupation, and pride and self-respect, through structural factors. The onset of British rule brought with it, far-reaching changes in the mode and relations of production—from an agrarian and feudal economy to an industrializing and capitalistic society. These changes created a demand for people with new skills and formal (English) education. In this process, large sections lost their traditional occupations over time, especially those who served the non-agricultural needs of the village economy, for example artisans and craftsmen. These were replaced by goods produced through mass-production. Communities possessing a range of specialized skills were gradually made redundant. For example, the traditional healer was replaced by the modern doctor and the hospital; the entertainer was replaced by cinema and other modern means of entertainment, the trader who brought goods to the village on the back of the horse or the donkey was replaced by the railway network which now transported goods in bulk, the artisan who made the grain grinder from stone was replaced by the mechanized grain grinder, and so on. Some DNTs who lost their traditional livelihood included pastoralists and hunter-gatherer nomads (shepherds and small game hunters like the Dhangars, Kuruba and Pardhis), providers of community services (blacksmiths like the Ghisadi, stone dressers like the Vadars, transporters and salt traders like the Banjaras, roof-thatchers like the Chapparbands) and entertainers (acrobats and jugglers like the Dombaris and Nats, and snake charmers like the Madaris) (Economic and Political Weekly 2008).

Many of these occupations belonged to the DNTs. Due to their nomadic lifestyle, the DNTs were unable to take to formal education and gradually got left behind in the race for acquisition of new and marketable skills. The application of the CTA and the later HOA, crippled their road to progress, broke their morale and dented their self-respect, into becoming self-defeating and rebellious communities. The State did not make any concerted efforts to create conditions that would help in their reintegration, for example policy initiatives to provide access to land and housing rights, improve access to education and healthcare, prevent illegal arrests, promote their arts and crafts, and arrange for their re-training and re-skilling to match market needs. These barriers have ensured that the situation of DNTs has more or less remained the same in the postcolonial period.

3.7 Postmodernism

Young's (1999) *Exclusive Society* explores three types of divisions in society: economic—where people get excluded from the labor market, social—where sections get excluded from civil society, and the expansion of the criminal justice system—which excludes more and more people from their daily lives. From the 1960s, society is changing from one whose accent was on assimilation and incorporation to one that separates and excludes (p. 7). Pluralism, large-scale immigration of people and glimpses of other societies makes everyone a potential deviant. In this scenario, "crime becomes a defining feature of modern societies". *Postmodernists* emphasize that there is no one story of crime to be told. It seems according to them that the time for "grand truths" is over. There is a turn towards local cultures and multiplicity of stories.

A postmodern understanding of DNTs would therefore mean understanding the situation of each of the DNT communities in their specific cultural and local contexts. It may be misleading to put all DNT populations under one umbrella and develop a theoretical formulation based on this homogenized understanding. The time has come to carry out micro studies of each DNT group in their rural and urban contexts. For example, Agrawal and Sinha's (2012) study of the Pardhi community in Mumbai city shows that most of them live on the margins of society, lack citizenship documents, housing and basic amenities and are engaged as honest wage laborers. Such studies, especially using the constructivist (instead of a positivist) approach, can change the discourse around DNTs in the long run, and the historical injustice done to them (categorizing them as criminal tribes) can be reversed. The reports and documents produced by local civil society organizations working with DNT groups can be analyzed to understand their situation, which can be further enriched through interviews with local activists working in those areas. The politics behind the process of criminalizing the DNTs need to be recognized, and a new "bottom-up" body of knowledge needs to be created, which recognizes the violation of human rights of the DNTs and leads to a process of conscientization among them.

3.8 Risk Society

Another emerging theme in understanding crime is the concept of *risk society*—that we live in a society today, which has risks attached to almost every activity we are involved in. New technology has brought along with it new dangers to people's lives and to the planet itself. For Beck (1992), this risk society has replaced the *class society* of the industrial era. According to Giddens (1999), this leads to a *calculative attitude* in individuals and institutions to deal with issues of risk, trust and security in these troubling times. Risk exists on a global scale and yet is also personalized as it is linked to people's subjective concerns about their identity. In such a scenario, the focus is no more on justice and equality but on *managing risks* and *developing security systems* to counter the risks. This thinking has had an impact on criminology too. Garland (1996) says that the "culture of high crime societies" has led to the development of two contradictory criminologies—*criminology of the self* and *criminology of the other*. The former views the offender as a rational consumer of a society where crime is a normal, common aspect of modern life. The latter sees crime as behavior of the *alien other* and represents criminals as dangerous members of distinct racial or social groups, bearing little resemblance to *us* (Carrabine et al. pp. 103–7).

The creation of the risk society is an outcome of a sense of alienation among individuals from each other, arising out of high levels of individuation of aspirations across society. The aspirational society has also led to a dangerous process of "othering", which then helps in blaming the ills of society on particular individuals and social groups. The image of the dangerous criminal, devoid of human feelings and engaging in brutal acts of violence and cunning is an emergent theme in this othering process. This process allows the State and civil society to dilute or reverse basic human rights of these individuals, which civilizations have fought hard to attain, as non-negotiables for all individuals in society. Gradually, this may lead to the creation of a hard State with harsh laws and the undermining of the human rights *regime*. In such an environment, it becomes difficult to espouse the cause of marginalized groups being processed by the criminal justice system.

One can see this process being played out in the last decade or so in India. The media spotlight on terror attacks and rising instances of brutal violence against women and children has spurred an active civil society response in recent years and has pushed crime and criminal justice response into the public domain, forcing political parties and the establishment to take a hard view on the same. It has become increasingly difficult to highlight issues such as overreach by the police, custodial violence, prison conditions, and a reasoned dialogue to strike at the root of the reasons for increasing violence in society. In such an environment, changing the dominant discourse on marginalized groups like the DNTs is an uphill task.

3.9 Summing Up

As is evident from the above discussion, a vast range of theoretical perspectives based on varied ontological and epistemological paradigms can be applied to explain criminality, alleged or otherwise, among the DNTs. The literature on theory suggests that the world of crime is too complex to be captured by monolithic explanations. It would be appropriate therefore to carefully select those which seem to apply more to the criminal behaviour being studied through this chapter i.e. involvement of DNTs in crime.

In the opinion of the authors, the interactionist perspective, specifically the labelling, the radical, the critical and the postmodern theories can be best applied to understand DNTs through the criminological lens. It is our attempt in this section to make a claim that DNTs were criminalised through the creation of a discourse, which was then legitimized by legal definitions with the introduction of the CTA, and subsequently the HOA in the post-independent India. This process led to the marginalisation and social exclusion of the DNTs, and their ending up becoming de-citizenised. The impact of this process fell on their women and children, who had to bear the brunt of the criminalisation process, in terms of access to food security, education, and healthcare. The story of the criminalisation of the DNTs is a classic example of victimisation of marginal groups by the State and society. The ghettoization of these communities accompanying the criminalisation process has ensured that the winds of social change in terms of empowerment of women and advancement of child rights, has largely not touched these communities. External oppression and exploitation has allowed the tightening of traditional leadership and patriarchal social control within the communities. While there has been a marked improvement in the status of women and children through the women's and the child rights movements in the larger society, women and children from the DNT communities continue to live under oppression and seclusion.

4 Suggesting a Roadmap for Reintegration of Women and Children

Though the criminal tribes were subjected to an inhuman legislation, the need for their integration into the rest of the society was acknowledged right from the beginning. In the initial years this consisted of the ideas of reformation and resettlement. Article 17 of the CTA 1871 stated that "The local government may, with the sanction of the Governor General in Council, place any tribe, gang or class which has been declared to be criminal, or any part thereof, to a reformatory settlement." The amendment carried to CTA in 1897 further elaborated these provisions:

> 17A. (1) The Local Government may establish and maintain reformatory settlements for children and may separate and remove from their parents and place in such a reformatory settlement the children of the registered members of any tribe, gang or class which has been declared to be criminal
>
> (2) For every reformatory settlement for children established under sub-section (1) a Superintendent shall be appointed by the Local Government.
>
> (3) The Superintendent of a reformatory settlement of children shall be deemed to be the guardian, within the meaning of Act No. XIX of 1850 (*concerning the binding of apprentices*), of every child detained in such settlement; and such Superintendent may make in this behalf, apprentice such child under the provisions of the aforesaid Act.
>
> Explanation: The term 'children' in this section includes all persons under the age of eighteen and above the age of four years (Simhadri 1991, pp. 124 and 130).

The idea of reformatory settlements was further expanded to establishing industrial and agricultural settlements in the revised CTA of 1911. The latter CTA also introduced the idea of industrial, agricultural or reformatory schools for children.

However, these were meant to be reformatory schools under the Reformatory Schools Act of 1897 and it was believed that children admitted into such schools would be understood as youthful offenders within the meaning of that Act. The Reformatory Schools Act was meant to reform and rehabilitate delinquent and "uncontrollable" children, a category coined under the definition of child in children's acts framed by various states in the early part of twentieth century under British rule. The introduction of the children's act in India provided for the care, protection and rehabilitation of neglected children as well as truant or delinquent children through institutional means, under the *parens-patriae* philosophy of the State. In contrast, pre-colonial India traditionally viewed children as the responsibility of the family and the community, with a rather tolerant and non-institutional approach towards them. The institutional approach of the children's acts was in sharp contrast to the community-based approach, and created a new category of social problem where none existed earlier. The underlying aim of the institutional and settlement approach towards deviant and so-called deviant populations was to convert them into productive and industrious labor for the new economic order created by the British rule.

After 1911, a number of settlements were established in different parts of the country. The settlements were industrial, agricultural or reformatory. In Bombay presidency, one reformatory settlement, thirteen industrial settlements and two agricultural settlements were established. From the very start of the criminal tribe settlements it was believed that it was desirable to utilize the agencies of private societies and in particular missionary societies in the management of settlements. In the Bombay province various missionary establishments were entrusted with this responsibility whereas in South- and North-India this was handed over to the Salvation Army. Later on, non-missionary indigenous organizations were also involved. Some of the settlements and free colonies were directly managed by the government (Munshi 1939, pp. 52–69). Although the settlements were considered to be a positive attempt towards integration, in actual practice they were not designed with altruistic purposes in mind. As pointed out by Radhakrishna, this was an attempt to forcefully transform the itinerant communities into industrial wage-workers, and in this process the social and cultural resources gathered over generations were wiped out with the violence of change that each of these stages implied (Radhakrishna 2001, p. 21).The Criminal Tribe Act Inquiry Committee, appointed under the chairmanship of K. M. Munshi in 1939, opined that the main objective of the Criminal Tribes Act was to safeguard the rights of society against anti-social influence and its secondary aim was the reformation of the criminal tribes—a reformation, which, in its early stages, had to be carried out against the will of its members (Munshi 1939, p. 26).

Activists from the DNTs have strongly condemned the barbed wire settlements as exploitative and inhuman because they were nothing but open jails. The restrictions imposed on the interns were extremely rigid and although educational and vocational opportunities were provided by the settlement administration, the branding as 'criminals' was further reinforced. A detailed study of the application of the CTA to the tribes of the Bawarias, the Sanorias, the Aherias and Harburahs of the

Punjab provinces between 1871 and 1895 has concluded that resettlement of the criminal tribes was envisaged as an apprenticeship not in successful agriculture but in the virtues of moral livelihood itself (Nigam 1990, p. 286). A number of autobiographies of the settlement inmates in the regional languages have further corroborated this. The settlements were finally removed by a symbolic gesture of cutting the barbed wire at the hands of the first Prime Minister of India, Pandit Jawaharlal Nehru in 1952. The settlements, therefore, cannot be considered as an ideal approach to reintegration.

After Independence and after the repeal of the CTA, further attempts towards welfare and development of the ex-criminal tribes were made by individual state governments. As mentioned earlier the Constitutional Schedules (SCs and STs) provided some protection to the included communities but in the absence of due awareness, this has not been effectively utilized. The nomadic and ex-criminal tribes not included in the Schedules have been totally deprived of these benefits.

By 1960, linguistic reorganization of the country was completed, and the responsibility of looking after the welfare and development of the DNTs was entrusted to the respective state governments. The plight of the DNTs, however, did not receive due attention until in the late eighties when a series of autobiographies of writers and activists from the communities (along the lines of *dalit* literature) were published. These autobiographies and the resurgence of activism after 1977 brought out the historical injustice meted out to these communities. A number of action groups and activists in different parts of the country, both from DNTs and middle-classes, started championing the cause of the DNTs. The state agencies undertook welfare and development schemes and opened up hostels and residential schools. However, these were undertaken more from the standpoint of 'social welfare' than that of reintegration. They have therefore provided limited results, and the socio-economic condition of the DNTs have not improved significantly. As mentioned earlier, the Ministry of Social Justice and Empowerment (Government of India) constituted a National Commission for De-Notified Nomadic and Semi-Nomadic Tribes (NCDNT) which submitted its report in 2008. The Commission has comprehensively looked into the matter and has made more than seventy recommendations to change the plight of the DNTs. The National Advisory Council of the Government of India constituted a Working Group on DNTs in 2012 which has also made a number of useful recommendations.[10] However, all of these have been at the level of recommendations, and concrete policy and program changes have not been effected.

It has been mentioned earlier that almost all the DNTs had some kind of traditional occupations. These occupations have not remained constant as they have been affected by a number of social, economic and ecological factors (Bokil 2002b).The DNTs have been making appropriate changes in their occupations and are resorting to various livelihood options on their own. They have been striving

[10] http://zeenews.india.com/news/nation/nac-recommends-inter-ministerial-task-force-for-dnts_771094.html.

silently and perseveringly to change their situation. Traditionally, nomadic communities have been settling down and are adopting various strategies to respond to the changing markets. Some of the successful examples have been documented by scholars (Salzman 1988). A number of community based organizations have emerged among them which have tried to change the situation from within. The communities which were enlightened by the larger, social transformative movement in the country have made due changes in their ways of life and have also tried to spread the message to other communities. Some communities have moved to urban areas and have tried to uplift their status through education and acquisition of newer skills. Many individuals from the communities have also shown excellence in the chosen fields and have become exemplary role-models for the rest.

Despite these efforts, the need for genuine and permanent integration of these communities has been felt stronger than ever before. Atrocities against the ex-criminal communities have not decreased and social prejudices have not significantly changed. Very often, the DNTs are subjected to mob-violence under the garb of vigilante justice, and the victims of violence are turned into culprits (Radhakrishna 2008). Despite repeated efforts, the police administration has not shown due sensitivity and the crime-nexus has not been broken. Further, the State and society have not paid attention to the special needs of women and children, who are mostly victims as belonging to the supposed offender-families.

Against this background, our basic argument for facilitating reintegration, particularly of women and children, is that the vicious circle forcing the DNTs to remain in the criminal nexus needs to be broken. Borrowing from the Left Realist criminological concept of the *square of crime*,[11] we visualize four principal agencies for reintegration:

1. State (legislature, executive and judiciary),
2. Community Associations of the DNTs,
3. Civil Society (NGOs and activist groups working with DNTs),
4. DNT Individuals.

The square is schematically presented as below followed by a discussion about the role of each peg of the square

[11] The left realists tried to combine the concerns of traditional criminologists with the concerns raised by Marxist and Neo-Marxist School, by viewing *inner city crime* as a growing and serious problem. This analysis highlights *the square of crime*—the State, society, the offender and the victim. All four factors need to be looked at for all types of crime (Carrabine et al. 2004, p. 79).

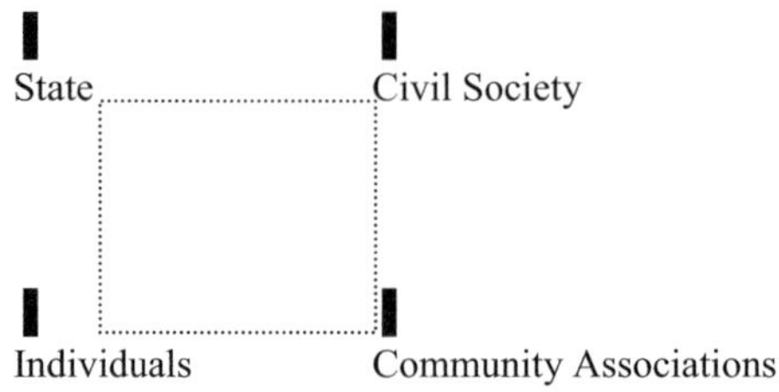

(1) The State began the process with the repeal of the CTA but did a great disservice by enacting the HOA later. Therefore, as first step, the HOA needs to be repealed. Legend has it that the detailed accounts about the occupations, cultural practices, lifestyle, habitat and *modus operandi* of DNTs continues to be taught at police training schools and academies, in order for the police to identify the communities wherever they are posted for effective crime prevention and detection. This retrograde and anti-Constitutional practice needs to be forthwith stopped. All arrested persons, especially those from the DNT communities, should be provided with competent and free legal aid by the State, as per its Constitutional obligation. The State should implement a scheme whereby families of arrested DNTs are given financial assistance for their subsistence and to ensure that their children do not drop out of education. Special provisions should be made under the Right to Education (RTE) Act to ensure the education of DNT children, especially girl children. Similar provisions need to be made to ensure access to healthcare of DNT women and children.

(2) Civil society has to make concerted efforts towards empowering DNT women and ensure the protection of the rights of DNT children. This could be done through the formation of self-help groups, which could become a medium of financial inclusion of these groups as well as a forum to create awareness about their legal rights and government schemes for the poor and the marginalized sections. Awareness will also have to be created among the larger society about the historical injustice done to DNTs through creation of a new discourse about them, which is in consonance with the principles of an equitable and rights-based society.

(3) Community associations of the DNTs can be viewed as victim-rights groups—those fighting for their basic human rights against a discriminatory social order. They would need to spread awareness within the DNTs to restore their self-pride, their arts and crafts, their music, dance and culture, and change their social identity from the existing "criminal" to an image of "self-reliant" and proud communities in search of alternate livelihoods. They need to rewrite their history and rediscover their cultural past, with the help of academics and activist organizations. They also need to develop legal competences to fight against the atrocities committed by the police and society against them. At present, virtually every community has formed its own association and has also federated the local units. However, they need to have proper orientation to make their work effective.

(4) The individuals from DNTs, the last peg of the square, too have a role to play in changing the discourse. At a time when rational choice theories are an important element in current debates in criminology, we need to acknowledge the role that individual will or choice plays in life-changing, decision-making processes. The question asked by control theorists of "why do only some people commit crimes" continues to defy clear answers. Rational choice theorists point to individual will or choice, while critical criminologists tend to downplay this question and focus on larger and structural factors that lead to crime. At the end of the day, the individual element refuses to go away whenever we discuss human action, and in this case, crime. We would therefore like to locate this factor in our discussion, both in terms of entry into and exit from crime. As Henry Thomas Buckle had once said, "society prepares the crime; the criminal commits it".[12]

The specific roles that each agency is expected to play are summarized in Table 2.

The table brings out the fact that although certain functions are being carried out by each of these agencies, additional roles are warranted, particularly from the point of view of integrating women and children and for ensuring justice and development for succeeding generations. Specific suggestions to this effect are presented below.

Table 2 Agencies of reintegration

No.	Agency	Present role and function	Additional roles required
1	State	Social welfare and ad-hoc development measures from time to time	Protection of human rights, sensitization of police and development administration, meticulous implementation of the Right to Education Act
2	Community associations	Community mobilization, acting as pressure groups	Social reform, grievance redress, legal support, internal conscientisation, political enfranchisement.
3	Civil society organizations	Community development programs, income and employment generation activities, legal aid, etc.	Policy-advocacy, networking, alliance building and support DNT associations.
4	Individuals	Victims, strugglers	Empowered and active agents of change

[12] http://web.inter.nl.net/hcc/rekius/buckle.htm.

5 Recommendations

Sr. No.	Recommendation	Rationale
State		
1	Repeal the Habitual Offenders Act, 1952.	The HOA is an extension of the CTA. Repealing this legislation will prevent the tagging and labeling and subsequent criminalization of DNTs.
2	Introduce a special legislation to prevent the atrocities against the DNTs along the lines of the Scheduled Castes and Scheduled Tribes (Prevention of Atrocities) Act. 1989, or include DNTs in the existing legislation.	This will act as a structural deterrent to commit atrocities against the DNTs and make the institutional means available to the DNT communities to counter the hegemony of the dominant social groups in society and bring about a change in the audience reaction.
3	Establish a National Commission and state level DNT Commissions along the lines of the SC/ST Commissions to hear the cases of atrocities against the DNTs and redress the grievances.	
4	Activate the District Legal Services Authorities and ensure that accused persons from the DNTs receive free and competent legal aid.	This will ensure access to justice to DNTs falsely accused of commission of criminal offences and help break the social reality of crime.
5	Set up an impartial grievance redressal mechanism at the district and state level to monitor and take action against errant police officials, in terms of discrimination or illegal action against members of the DNT communities.[13]	This will act as a structural deterrent against police atrocities against the DNTs and break the square of crime.
6	(a) Effectively implement the Right to Education Act to ensure that every child from the DNTs receive free and quality education either through inclusion in local schools or by setting up boarding schools at district level, along the lines of the Navodaya Vidyalayas[14] set up by the government to provide quality education to talented children from tribal areas. (b) Provide scholarships to DNT students from secondary school to post-graduation and doctoral levels, along the lines of such scholarships given to SC/ST students.	Ensuring access to education will have a transformational effect on self-image, social identity and livelihood opportunities of the DNTs and may also lead to social reform within the communities, especially with regard to the status of women and children. This will also break the vicious circle of differential association, if any, and foster a knowledge society.

(continued)

[13] The Supreme Court has passed an order to all states and Union Territories to implement the recommendations of the National Police Commission, which has recommended the setting up of such bodies, among its many far-reaching recommendations. For more details, see http://www.humanrightsinitiative.org/index.php?option=com_content&id=199%3Asupreme-court-directives-on-police-reform&Itemid=98.

[14] www.navodaya.nic.in/.

7	Provide homestead plots to DNT families (with joint titles to husband and wife) at village and taluka places and include DNT families in all government-sponsored mass housing schemes for the poor and socially marginalized populations in urban areas.	This is a basic step towards social inclusion as DNT communities, which have been able to settle down (of their own volition), have been gradually able to find their rightful place as citizens and end their relative deprivation and marginalization.
8	Provide necessary identity documents like ration cards, caste certificates, domicile certificates, voter identity cards, etc. to all the DNTs through a time-bound and camp approach[15] program.	This will increase the self-esteem of DNTs and make them proud and honorable citizens and stakeholders in society.
Community associations		
1	Mobilize and conscientize members to adopt a 'zero tolerance' approach towards crime.	This is to help break the vicious circle of crime, and encourage members to participate in the rule of law society.
2	Initiate a social reform movement from within to eliminate gender- and community-based violence and eradicate blind faith and superstitions.	This will facilitate attachment and commitment to society and increase belief and involvement in wider society.
3	Take steps towards raising awareness on human rights and empowering the communities, through organizing awareness camps, in collaboration with the district legal services authorities and human rights organizations.	This will enable the DNTs to recognize and fight the human rights violations committed against them by the State and society and change the discourse around the DNTs.
4	Adopt the 'watch dog' role towards police actions and social welfare agencies.	To fight bias and prejudice in State agencies against the DNTs and facilitate inclusion in social protection measures provided by the State.
5	Institute local support structures for women and children in distress and facilitate legal support to DNT members.	This will help in providing first-line victim-support services to affected women and children, and link them with long-term services, if required.
6	Reduce the importance of traditional caste councils (*jat-panchayats*) and institute participatory, gender egalitarian and secular arbitration mechanisms.	This will have a transforming effect on the social relations within the community and reduce norm violation and anomic conditions.
Civil society organizations		
1	Undertake research and policy advocacy on behalf of and with DNTs and bring about desirable policy and program changes.	This will facilitate factual knowledge and break the social reality of crime.
2	Provide legal and motivational support to community associations of DNTs.	This will lead to empowerment of DNTs and link them with larger processes of social change.

(continued)

[15] Under this approach, the district collector or other competent authority, along with officials from all concerned departments organizes a camp for DNTs, whereby documents are issued to individuals based on oral depositions by the community members, rather than the typical approach of issuing citizenship documents on the basis of the applicant providing certain 'eligibility' documents/certificates.

3	Demonstrate efficient and effective models of livelihood generation and reintegration of DNTs, with special focus on women and children.	To accelerate labor market inclusion
4	Raise voice against police atrocities and social brutalities and file public interest litigations as and when required.	To prevent the violation of human rights.
5	Organize vocational and skill development programs for the women and children from the DNTs and facilitate their interface with the market economy.	This will help in the economic reintegration of DNTs within market society and help improve their overall socio-economic situation.
6	Facilitate organization of DNT women into self-help groups or similar collective structures and initiate a process of socio-economic and political empowerment.	This is to help combat gender-based violence and crime within DNTs and promote equity and social justice.
7	Establish schools and hostels for children of DNTs.	This will help prevent primary and secondary deviance and facilitate social inclusion.
DNT individuals		
1	Make a rational choice of desistance from involvement in criminal activities.	This will reinforce self-control based on free will and lead to a realization that involvement in crime is a zero-sum game.
2	Make efforts to foster feelings of fraternity and sorority within the community.	This will reduce the sense of alienation and help rebuild their social identity.
3	Engage with community associations and civil society organizations.	To reduce relative deprivation and marginalization to facilitate reintegration.
4	Take responsibility for children's education and well-being.	To increase the human social capital and integrate the succeeding generations with the broader society.
5	Take responsibility to create gender-sensitive and violence-free family and community structures.	

6 Conclusion

The DNTs are one of the most deprived and marginalized sections in India today. They have been the victims of colonial and historical wrongs, social stigmatization, governmental apathy and inadequate internal awakening. The previous generations have suffered considerable injustice and have borne the brunt of social exclusion. Women and children have been the worst victims. The time has come that these historical injustices are redressed and the discourse is changed towards the reintegration of the present and succeeding generations. So far, the plight of DNTs has been sociologically understood but it has not been sufficiently analyzed through a criminological lens. However, criminological insights and methodologies can not only contribute to a more refined understanding of the issue but also provide practical ways for amelioration of the situation. Policy makers and development practitioners need to take note of the criminological findings. This is a classic instance where the so called offenders are actually the victims of structural violence. Social inclusion of the DNTs and their reintegration, therefore, becomes not just the aspiration or need of the victims but also the obligation of the State and responsibility of society. It can come about by changing the discourse around the DNTs through the united efforts of all concerned: the State, civil society, communities and the victims; and through a comprehensive and practical set of policy and program measures. This is essential not just to reduce crime but to also build a society free of injustice, violence and discrimination.

(The authors gratefully acknowledge the financial support provided by Terre des homes, Germany, South Asia Coordination Office, Pune, for the preparation of this paper. Assistance and cooperation by Nirman, Pune; TANDA, Mumbai and various other DNT organizations is also thankfully acknowledged. The usual disclaimers apply)

Five Questions

1. Who are the De-Notified and Nomadic Tribes (DNTs) of India? Trace the processes and highlight the reasons which led to the criminalization of the DNTs by the passing of the Criminal Tribes Act in the colonial era and later the Habitual Offenders' Act in the post-independence period.
2. What has been the impact of the criminalization process of the DNTs on their social, economic and political life, especially with regard to their women and children?
3. Draw a co-relation between the situation of DNTs with some of the criminological theories. Discuss any theory/ies, which you think best relates to their situation, with examples or illustrations.
4. Highlights the steps that need to be taken at various levels to ameliorate the situation of the DNTs and lead to their reintegration, especially their women and children.
5. The criminalization of the DNTs by the colonial administration was an attempt by the British to subjugate and sedentarise essentially itinerant communities with a proud past and culture, by changing the discourse around them. It is therefore necessary that any attempt to reclaim their space in the social mainstream must be preceded or accompanied by changing this discourse. Discuss, in the light of efforts made by the State, civil society and the DNT communities in post-independence India towards the social reintegration of the DNTs.

References

Agrawal, P., & Sinha, M. (2012). *A report on the status of Pardhis in Mumbai city*. Mumbai: TISS.

Baxstrom, R. (2000). Governmentality, bio-power and the emergence of the Malayan-Tamil subjects on the plantations of colonial Malaya. *Crossroads: An Interdisciplinary Journal of Southeast Asian Studies, 14*(2), 49–78. Stable URL: http://www.jstor.org/stable/40860736

Beck, U. (1992). *Risk society: Towards a new modernity*. London: Sage.

Becker, H. S. (1963). *Outsiders: Studies in the sociology of deviance*. New York: The Free Press.
Bohm, R. M. (1982). Radical criminology: An explication. *Criminology, 19*, 565–589. doi:10.1111/j.1745-9125.1982.tb00439.x.
Bokil, M. (2002a, January 12). Denotified and nomadic tribes: A perspective. *Economic and Political Weekly, 37*(2), 148–154.
Bokil, M. (2002b, January). Facing exclusion: The nomadic communities in Western India. *Indian Journal of Social Work, 63*(1), 33–45.
Carrabine, E., Iganski, P., Lee, M., Plummer, K., & South, N. (2004). *Criminology: A sociological introduction*. London and New York: Routledge.
Chambliss, W. J. (1960). A Sociological analysis of the law of vagrancy. *SocialProblems, 12*, 67–77. Stable URL: http://www.jstor.org/stable/798699
Cloward, R. A., & Ohlin, L. E. (1960). *Delinquency and opportunity: A theory of delinquent gangs*. New York: Free Press.
Cohen, A. K. (1955). *Delinquent boys: The culture of the gang*. Glencoe, IL: Free Press.
Conwell, C., & Sutherland, E. H. (1956). *The professional thief: By a professional thief*. Chicago: University of Chicago Press.
D'Souza, D. (1999, December 18). De-notified tribes: Still 'criminal'? *Economic and Political Weekly, 34*(51), 3576–3578.
D'Souza, D. (2001). *Branded by law: Looking at India's denotified tribes*. New Delhi: Penguin Books.
Devy, G. (2000). For a nomad called thief. *India International Centre Quarterly, 27*(2), 55–57, MARGINALISED (SUMMER 2000). Retrieved from http://kalidas-shinde.blogspot.in/2012/12/journal-on-nomadic-tribes-india.html
Devy, G. (2006). *A nomad called thief: Reflections on Adivasi silence*. Hyderabad: Orient Longman Pvt. Ltd.
Dhanuka, M. (2013). The great divide: Theory and practice of criminal defence laws in India. *Criminal Justice Matters, 92*(1), 22–23. doi:10.1080/09627251.2013.805370.
Dholakia, H. C. (2000). Legal aid for under trial prisoners. *Kashmir University Law Review, 7*, 27–37.
Durkheim, E. (1938). The rules of sociological method. New York: The Free Press. Retrieved from http://comparsociology.com/wp-content/uploads/2013/02/Emile-Durkheim-Rules-of-Sociological-Method-1982.pdf.
Economic and Political Weekly. (2007, October 6). Denotified and nomadic tribes - A nowhere existence. *Economic and Political Weekly, 42*(40), 4020.
Economic and Political Weekly. (2008, October 4). Branded for life. *Economic and Political Weekly, 43*(40), 6–7.
Garland, D. (1996). The limits of the sovereign state. *The British Journal of Criminology, 36*(4), 445–471.
Giddens, A. (1999). Risk and responsibility. *Modern Law Review, 62*(1), 1–10.
Goffman, E. (1963). *Stigma: Notes on the identity of spoiled identity*. Englewood Cliffs, NJ: Prentice Hall.
Heather Streets. (2001). Retrieved from http://www.sdstate.edu/projectsouthasia/Resources/upload/The-Rebellion-of-1857-Streets.pdf
Hirschi, T. (1969). *Causes of delinquency*. California: University of California Press.
Ivaturi, R. S. (2013). *Evaluation of legal aid and legal literacy - tools of social justice*. Ph.D. Thesis, Tirupati: Sri Padmavathi Women's University. Retrieved from http://shodhganga.inflibnet.ac.in/handle/10603/7785
Kitsuse, J. I. (1962). Societal reaction to deviance: Problems of theory and method. *Social Problems, 9*, 247–256.
Kumar, M. (2004, March 6). Relationship of caste and crime in colonial India: A discourse analysis. *Economic and Political Weekly, 39*(10), 1078–1087.

Lemert, E. M. (1951). *Social pathology: A systematic approach to the theory of sociopathic behaviour*. New York: McGraw-Hill.
Madhurima. (2010, March). Undertrial prisoners and the criminal justice system. *Supreme Court Cases, 2*, 25–31. Retrieved from http://www.humanrightsinitiative.org/new/2010/undertrial_prisoners_&_criminal_justice_system.pdf
Mathivanan, T. (n.d.). Legal aid: Issues, challenges and solutions – an empirical study. Retrieved from http://www.hcmadras.tn.nic.in/legalaid-issues.pdf
Merton, R. K. (1968). *Social theory and social structure*. New York: Free Press.
Misra, P. K., & Misra, R. (1982). Nomadism in the land of Tamils between 1 A.D and 600 A.D. In P. K. Misra & K. C. Malhotra (Eds.), *Nomads in India*. Calcutta: Anthropological Survey of India.
Moyer, I. (2001). *Criminological theories: Traditional and non-traditional voices and themes*. London: Sage Publications.
Munshi, K. M. (1939). *Report of the criminal tribes enquiry committee*. Bombay: Government of Bombay.
Murali, K. (2006, September 16–22). Institutional apathy towards undertrial prisoners. *Economic and Political Weekly, 41*(37), 3936–3938.
Nigam, S. (1990). Disciplining and policing the "criminal by birth", part 2: The development of a disciplinary system, 1871–1900. *The Indian Economic and Social History Review, 27*(3), 257–287.
Orcutt, J. D. (1983). *Analyzing deviance*. Homewood III: Dorsey Press.
Prayas. (2002). *Forced separation: Children of imprisoned mothers*. Mumbai: Tata Institute of Social Sciences.
Quinney, R. (1970). *The social reality of crime*. Boston, MA: Little, Brown.
Radhakrishna, M. (2001). *Dishonoured by history: Criminal tribes and British colonial policy*. Hyderabad: Orient Longman.
Radhakrishna, M. (2008, January 12). Crime of vigilante justice. *Economic and Political Weekly, 43*(2), 16–18.
Raghavan, V., & Nair, R. (2013). Over-representation of Muslims: The prisons of Maharashtra. *Economic and Political Weekly, 48*(11), 12–17.
Ramakrishnan, N. (2013). *In custody: Law, impunity and prisoner abuse in South Asia*. New Delhi and Colombo: Sage Publications India Pvt. Ltd. and South Asians for Human Rights (SAHR).
Raman, R., & Ventakraman, N. (2006, June 7–9). *Grafting faith: Legal aid services in India*. Paper presented at the Third International Conference on Therapeutic Jurisprudence, Perth, Western Australia. Retrieved from http://www.aija.org.au/TherapJurisp06/Papers/RamanNisha.pdf
Reiman, J. (1979). *The rich get richer and the poor get prison*. New York: Willey.
Salzman, P. C. (1988). From nomads to dairymen: Two cases from Gujarat. *Economic and Political Weekly, 23*(31), 1582–1586.
Simhadri, Y. C. (1991). *Denotified tribes: Asociological analysis*. New Delhi: Classical Publishing Company.
Singh, B. P. (2008). Ex-criminal tribes of Punjab. *Economic and Political Weekly, 43*(51), 58–66.
Singh, 'Sher', S. (1966). *The Sikligars of Punjab: A gypsy tribe*. New Delhi: Manoharilal Munshiram Publishers Pvt. Ltd.
Singh, "Sher", S. (1965). *The Sansis of Punjab: A gypsy and denotified tribe of Rajput origin*. New Delhi: Munshiram Manoharilal Publishers Pvt. Ltd.
Tannenbaum, F. (1938). *Crime and the community*. Boston: Ginn and Co.
Tarique, M., & Raghavan, V. (2011, October 3). India's war on its poor. *50.50 inclusive democracy*. Retrieved from http://www.opendemocracy.net/5050/mohammed-tarique-vijay-raghavan/indias-war-on-its-poor
Taylor, I., Walton, P., & Young, J. (1973). *The new criminology: For a social theory of deviance*. London/New York: Routledge, Taylor and Francis Group.

Tolen, R. J. (1991, February). Colonising and transforming the criminal tribesmen: The salvation army in British India. *The American Ethnologist, 18*(1), 106–125. Stable URL: http://www.jstor.org/stable/645567
UN CERD. (2007). Report. http://daccessddsny.un.org/doc/UNDOC/GEN/G07/442/00/PDF/G0744200.pdf/OpenElement
Young, J. (1999). *The exclusive society*. London: Sage Publications.

Victimisation and Delinquency of Minors in Central-European Countries

Witold Klaus, Irena Rzeplińska, and Dagmara Woźniakowska-Fajst

Abstract Hungary, Poland and the Czech Republic are three former post-socialist countries that have a great deal in common, both from a historical and a socio-economic perspective, despite their considerable differences. There are also many similarities in how crime and criminality have changed in these countries over the past 30 years. For all their many shared attributes, however, there are visible differences in the criminality and victimisation of their youth. The Czech Republic seems to have the fewest juvenile issues, while Hungary has the highest level of crime in the region. Hungary, Poland and the Czech Republic also differ in their juvenile justice systems and the ideology underpinning their response to juvenile offences.

1 Introduction

Many international studies on criminality tie all the post-communist countries together. The assumption underlying this expedient is that they are similar enough to be grouped together and then compared with other countries that have been similarly grouped (e.g. Junger-Tas et al. 2012). This expedient is sometimes necessary when comparing a lot of diverse countries (Elder 1976). It should be remembered, however, that countries grouped this way can often differ from each other considerably. This is certainly the case with the "post-socialist" countries. This group normally comprises Central Europe (The Czech Republic, Poland, Slovakia, Hungary, and often Bulgaria and Romania), the Balkans (Albania and

W. Klaus (✉) • I. Rzeplińska
Department of Criminology, Institute of Legal Studies, Polish Academy of Sciences, Nowy Swiat 72, Warsaw 00-330, Poland
e-mail: witold.klaus@gmail.com; irenkarzeplinska@wp.pl

D. Woźniakowska-Fajst
Institute of Legal Studies Polish Academy of Sciences and Warsaw University, Warsaw, Poland
e-mail: daga.wozniakowska@gmail.com

H. Kury et al. (eds.), *Women and Children as Victims and Offenders: Background, Prevention, Reintegration*, DOI 10.1007/978-3-319-08398-8_28

the former Yugoslavia), the Baltic States (Estonia, Lithuania and Latvia), and Russia and the former republics of the United Soviet Socialist Republics (USSR), including Armenia, Georgia, Moldova, Ukraine, etc. There are enormous historical and socio-economic differences between these countries and regions. The only thing that binds them is that they were under communist regimes for a time. These regimes, however, also differed significantly from one another. At the very least, we might mention their different levels of openness to the outside world, which exhibited enormous differences (e.g. between the former Yugoslavia and the USSR), the varying degrees of control and oppression in Central Europe (e.g. in Poland and Czechoslovakia as opposed to Romania), and the different roads these countries traversed after the fall of communism—the countries that have joined the EU, the Balkan countries with their subsequent wars, and the former republics of the USSR (excluding the Baltic States). This group can therefore be said to have more differences than similarities at present.

2 Changes in Crime in Central Europe Over the Years

The countries of Central Europe (The Czech Republic, Poland and Hungary) have a great deal in common when viewed against this background.[1] This is the case from both a historical (the rebuilding of statehood during the two world wars, and the manner in which the communist regime was installed, the way it functioned, and attempts to overthrow it through strikes and insurgency) and a socio-economic (being an EU member state for 10 years) perspective. These countries also happen to have a great deal in common when it comes to changes in criminality over the last 30 years, viz. a sharp increase in criminality in the wake of the collapse of the communist system, followed by a systematic drop, which is observable in the Czech Republic and Hungary from 1995 and which began in Poland 10 years later. This trend varies considerably from that of e.g. the countries of the former Yugoslavia (Šelih 2012, pp. 17–20).

This discrete and inordinately high (on average twice as much in the first year and even four times as much over 10 years) increase in crime immediately following the constitutional and political transformations of the 1990s, while typical of Central Europe, is not found elsewhere (Válková 1995; Rozum et al. 2006; Kossowska et al. 2012; Kerezsi 2014). This raises the question of what might have caused this phenomenon. Eisner's modernisation theory can be invoked here (Eisner 1995, p. 19). This holds that economic modernisation, which inevitably introduces social changes, brings about an increase in crime by its very nature. The

[1] No reference is made to Slovakia in this analysis, as there is insufficient data on crime in that country. By that is meant not just "dry" statistical data but also analyses conducted by Slovakian criminologists that would enable such data to be interpreted. Slovakia has not participated in any international comparative criminological, victimisation (ICVS) or self-report studies.

increase in crime in this part of Europe is obviously due to a variety of factors, including an increase in material goods to steal (through an increase in opportunities for theft) and a subsequent increase in consumerist attitudes (i.e. increased motivation) accompanied by progressive social stratification as a result of some people becoming rapidly enriched and others becoming just as rapidly impoverished.[2] There has been more social mobility (both within each country and as a result of being able to travel abroad), the police have changed the way they record crimes (so as to better reflect the actual crime rate), and rapid and revolutionary legal changes have opened up many more opportunities for abuse and led to respect for the law among the public being steadily eroded in a part of Europe (especially Poland) where it has never been particularly high (see Šelih 2012, pp. 25–28; Kossowska 2015).[3] Increasing anomie was also a significant factor. This was caused by a weakening of social institutions and the deficiency of those public institutions responsible for social integration (Enzmann and Podana 2010, p. 202). Some authors consider anomie to be the result of the social changes brought about by the transition from a communist to a capitalist system (Válková 1995, pp. 46–47), but as Kossowska (2014) observes, this cannot fully account for this change. Kossowska points out that the decadent period of socialism, viz. the 1980s, was one of profound and worsening social disorganisation. This accompanied the progressive erosion of the state and the grip of the communist authorities. The results could be observed in full during the first few years after the change (Poland was examined but similar things probably occurred in other countries in the region). Eisner believes that social change brought about by modernisation and the increasing similarity of countries being transformed into countries with similar socio-economic systems should result in the composition and intensity of crime in those countries becoming increasingly similar as well (Eisner 1995, p. 19). It can now generally be said that Central European societies are becoming more similar to Western countries in terms of the composition of crime and its changing trends. However, this does not necessarily mean a similar intensity (although its sudden growth from the 1990s can be considered the beginning of the trend towards a flattening out of these levels), as Central European countries still generally have lower crime levels than Western European countries despite this growth (Smit et al. 2012; Gruszczyńska and Heiskanen 2012). This trend has long been apparent, particularly when it comes to reported crimes, which reflect official statistics. This

[2] In the Czech Republic, for example, property crimes can definitely be said to dominate the recorded crime figures, accounting for 70.8 % of all criminal acts in 2003 (Rozum et al. 2006, p. 50). In Hungary, property crimes accounted for 78.4 % in 1996 and 62 % in 2005 (Kerezsi and Lévay 2008, p. 247). A similar fall in the percentage of property crimes can be observed in Poland—from 75.6 % in 1989 to 65.1 % in 2001 (Kirwil 2004, p. 51; Krajewski 2004, p. 386).

[3] During the socialist period, not only were official statistics falsified to meet the demands of the communist authorities, but a significant proportion of crimes were not even reported due to a strong aversion to the police ("citizens' militia" at the time) on the part of the citizenry (Kossowska 2015). While it is difficult to estimate the scale of this phenomenon, ICVS studies from 1991 show that barely one in three crimes were reported in Poland at the time (Van Dijk et al. 2007b, p. 110).

can be explained by the low crime reporting rates and the deficient statistical systems in this part of Europe (Gruszczynska and Gruszczynski 2005, p. 345).[4]

A completely different picture emerges when the victimisation data from the ICVS (International Crime Victims Surveys) are examined.[5] Poland had long been one of those European countries where the threat of victimisation was greatest and has only been in the middle of the range for the past few years (the threat of being robbed is particularly high in Poland). Hungary, on the other hand, currently has one of the lowest victimisation indexes among the countries surveyed (although it has a noticeably high threat of burglary). Both countries also have a high incidence of corruption (Van Dijk et al. 2007a, b).[6] Studies on the capitals of all three countries conducted in 2000 reveal that Prague had the greatest number of criminal occurrences, followed by Budapest and then Warsaw. Prague was found to be one of the most dangerous capital cities in Europe. The crime rate in Warsaw was average. Burglary and car theft were common in Prague (and in Budapest) (Alvazzi del Frate and Van Kesteren 2004).

It is also worth noting that 'when observing crime trends, one may sometimes have the impression that crime in Central and Eastern Europe occurs with a delayed effect (compared with Western Europe). In some countries and for some types of crime, the trends in Central and Eastern Europe are similar to those in Western Europe. The dynamics of assaults in Czech Republic, Hungary and Poland are similar to those observed in Western Europe. The same holds true for the dynamics of robbery and theft' (Gruszczynska 2004, p. 134). This means that the trend of falling crime, noticeable worldwide, can currently be observed in Central Europe as well (Gruszczyńska and Heiskanen 2012).[7] There have been many attempts to explain this phenomenon, although the main—albeit not overly optimistic—conclusion drawn from the studies conducted so far is that 'when levels of crime surpass certain levels, they start to fall for endogenous reasons, irrespective of the economy (or government policies).' (Van Dijk et al. 2012, p. 311). The escalation of crime has also resulted in an increasing fear of it in society. Fear of becoming a victim of crime was one of the main social anxieties expressed in surveys in the early 1990s. This fear assumed irrational dimensions due to exaggerated media

---

[4] Research generally shows a low level of reporting crime and confidence in the police as a means of controlling crime in Central and Eastern Europe (Van Dijk 2010, pp. 641–643). Confidence, however, has been growing markedly over the past 25 years and has recently been around the middle of the range among the countries surveyed (Van Dijk et al. 2007b, pp. 110–116). Significant differences in the reporting of specific types of crime are also apparent (assaults are the most seldom reported) as are differences between countries—Poland had the lowest level in the region (even lower than the Baltic States) (Gruszczynska 2004, pp. 125–126).

[5] Unfortunately, Poland is the only country in the region that has participated in the ICVS regularly since 1991. Hungary only joined in 2003/2004, while the Czech Republic only took part in 2000 and even then only Prague was involved.

[6] Corruption in Europe only occurs more frequently in Bulgaria (twice as often as in Central Europe and four times more frequently than the average for the countries surveyed), than in Poland and Hungary.

[7] This trend does not apply to assault and rape, although the latter only applies to Western Europe and not the EU member states that joined the Union after 2004.

reporting.[8] The media frequently and eagerly began writing about crime as soon as censorship was abolished. The most serious and cruel incidents were shown, and this sent a clear message that crime was everywhere and anyone could fall victim to it. The conviction that crime was rampant and that juveniles were largely responsible for it became widespread.[9] They were supposedly starting out on the road to crime at an increasingly younger age, and according to the media picture and public perception, their acts were increasingly brutal (Krajewski 1996; Rozum et al. 2006, p. 50; Kossowska et al. 2012). On the basis of these fears, some politicians made fighting crime part of their political programmes, sustaining the fear of crime (which was actually falling) in society in order to derive political capital and win elections. This resulted in increasingly punitive legislation and a harsher penal policy. This policy was liberalised in line with human rights thinking in Central Europe in the 1990s, but revisited in the twenty-first century, where a gradual tightening of penal policy can be observed. The best example of this is the increase in the number of regulations tightening criminal liability and the consequent increase in the number of people imprisoned (Lévay 2012; Klaus et al. 2011; Kossowska et al. 2008).

3 Juveniles in the Justice Systems of Selected Countries in the Region

Each of the three countries in the region has framed its administration of justice for juvenile offenders independently. Each national legislature has set a different minimum age at which a juvenile is liable to be penalised for an offence, formulated different purposes for responding to juvenile offenders and provided different kinds of sanctions applicable to them. The differences begin right at the stage of setting the minimum age at which a juvenile is liable to be penalised for an offence—13 in Poland, 14 in Hungary and 15 in the Czech Republic.[10] The age limit for criminal

[8] In 2000, 57 % of the residents of Prague, 53 % of Warsaw and 52 % of Budapest did not feel safe going out after dark. This was average for Central and Eastern Europe (51 %) but more than twice as high as Western societies (24 %) (Alvazzi del Frate and Van Kesteren 2004, pp. 19–20).

[9] This is because of the prevailing conviction that crime is popular in the media when children are involved, i.e. when a child is either a perpetrator or a victim. Jewkes (2010) discusses this trend in the position the media has adopted towards children and teenagers. This is associated with the ambivalent relationship that a large part of society has with young people. She demonstrates that some of the anxiety about and fear of youth is the result of teenagers engaging in different types of behaviour and adopting different cultural patterns than their parents and grandparents did when they were children. And as children are the future of the nation, any deviant behaviour on their part is viewed through the prism of the moral decline of society. "For the media, then, deviant youth is used as a shorthand ascription for a range of gloomy and fatalistic predictions about spiralling levels of crime and amoral behaviour in society at large." (Jewkes 2010, p. 58).

[10] Younger juveniles are liable for "depravity". The Family Court therefore responds to behaviour that is unlawful or inappropriate for their age by applying educational measures (Klaus 2009, pp. 100–108).

liability likewise varies—17 in Poland (despite contravening the UN Convention on the Rights of the Child) and 18 in Hungary and the Czech Republic. These differences can only be explained by each country having developed its own traditions (Wójcik et al. 2008, pp. 188, 201).

It is worth emphasising that although education is the purpose of responding to juvenile offenders in every system analysed in this text, this purpose is worded differently in the legislation of each country. It is a basic principle of dealing with juveniles in Hungary. The purpose of sanctions targeted at juveniles in the Czech Republic is to prevent them from committing offences and engaging in depraved behaviour in the future and to integrate them into society. The application of educational measures is associated with offering them assistance (Wójcik et al. 2008, pp. 236–237, 201–202). The good of the child is the guiding principle in juvenile proceedings in Poland. The proceedings in juvenile cases are not adversarial and the purpose of the measures applied to juvenile offenders is to educate them and help them cope with the situations in which they find themselves (Bojarski et al. 2014, pp. 50–63).

The Polish, Czech and Hungarian systems similarly differ in their implications for juvenile offenders. Juveniles in Poland are mostly subjected to educational measures, e.g. being issued reprimands, being obliged to engage in or refrain from certain conduct, and above all, to repair or compensate any injury or damage caused, being subjected to appropriate supervision on the part of their parents or guardians, being placed on probation, and being sent to juvenile reform school. In exceptional cases, the court can also resort to correctional measures, such a placing the juvenile in a juvenile detention centre (Woźniakowska-Fajst 2010, pp. 325 et seq.). Similar sanctions are applied in Hungary and the Czech Republic. Czech courts can apply educational and protective sanctions, non-custodial sanctions as an alternative to incarceration (with or without probation), and mediation between the juvenile offender and the injured party. The Hungarian Criminal Code provides for informal intervention (postponement of the indictment, mediation) and special sanctions for juveniles, viz. reform school, probation and supervision by a probation officer, community service (only applicable if at least 16 when the sentence is imposed) and fines (ordered when the offender has his or her own income or assets). Both legislatures also cater for the option of incarcerating juveniles, although this has to be of shorter duration than would be the case for adults, e.g. the term cannot exceed 5 years in Hungary (Wójcik et al. 2008, pp. 202–203; Válková and Hulmáková 2010, pp. 253–255; Váradi-Csema 2010, pp. 681–685).

All three systems provide for juveniles to be vested with adult criminal liability in exceptional circumstances and retain the option of ordering a penalty, albeit less than the maximum, in addition to a custodial sentence. The Polish Criminal Code (Art. 10 § 2) provides that a juvenile aged 15 and above who commits an especially grave offence (homicide, grievous bodily harm, violent rape, robbery, etc.) can be held accountable as an adult, provided that this is warranted by the circumstances of the case and the stage of development, attributes and personal circumstances of the offender. The decision to refer a case to the Criminal Court is made by a Family Court judge (who can hear the case alone as part of the Court's jurisdiction).

Fig. 1 The number of juvenile offenders convicted by the Criminal Court pursuant to Art. 10 § 2 of the Criminal Code and the most serious crimes they committed in Poland in 2004–2013

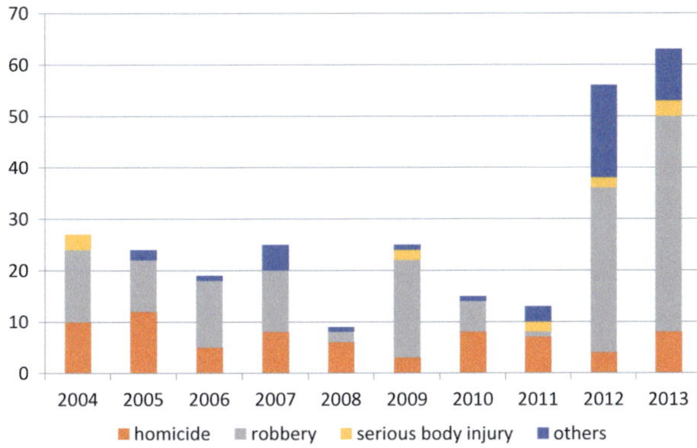

Source: Polish Ministry of Justice

Any penalty ordered by the Court in such a case, however, cannot exceed two thirds of the maximum statutory penalty for the offence in question and the Court can additionally order a commutation in exceptional circumstances. As illustrated in Fig. 1, experience shows that Polish Family Court judges seldom transfer juvenile cases to the Criminal Court (Rzeplińska 2007). The Criminal Court decided fewer than 30 cases annually until 2011. Figure 1 shows that the number of cases heard by the Criminal Court increased in 2012–2013. While the percentage increase is striking, this means still only a few dozen cases per annum. Examining the makeup of the penalties imposed, however, reveals that the most serious, i.e. imprisonment of more than 8 years, are only ordered in a handful of cases every year. A little over half the sentences in the last 2 years shown were suspended, while 23 % (2012) and 33 % (2013) were non-custodial. The Criminal Court does not appear to be imposing particularly severe sentences on juveniles, despite the Family Court recently transferring more cases to it.

Czech Statute No. 218/2003 deems juvenile offenders criminally liable to the extent that their intellectual (having the capacity to control their actions) and moral (understanding the social danger of the deeds they have committed) development warrant it. Any custodial sentence imposed on a juvenile must be lighter than the same sentence imposed on an adult in similar circumstances, and a wide range of rehabilitative and educational measures are to be applied while it is being served. These measures should continue even after the juvenile has completed his or her term of incarceration (Wójcik et al. 2008; Válková and Hulmáková 2010, pp. 253–255). Hungarian criminal law provides for juvenile criminal responsibility between the ages of 14 and 18. Juveniles are liable to the same penalties as adults, albeit with certain restrictions. A custodial sentence cannot exceed 5 years, or 10 or 15 years for very grave crimes (Váradi-Csema 2010, pp. 683–684).

Poland, Hungary and the Czech Republic all have courts that specialise in hearing juvenile offence cases and can therefore be designated “juvenile courts”. Entrusting the courts with juvenile offences is in accord with the UN Convention on the Rights of the Child (adopted by the UN General Assembly 20 November 1989).

Art. 40 Para. 2 Pt. (iii) of the Convention states that any child suspected of or charged with infringing the criminal law should be guaranteed of having his or her case heard according to law by an independent judicial body without delay. The Convention further grants any juvenile suspected of, charged with, or found guilty of infringing the criminal law the following rights:

- to be presumed innocent;
- to be informed promptly and directly of the charges against him or her, and, if appropriate, through his or her parents or legal guardians, and to have legal or other appropriate assistance in the preparation and presentation of his or her defense;
- to have the matter determined without delay by a competent, independent and impartial authority or judicial body in a fair hearing according to law, in the presence of legal or other appropriate assistance and, unless it is considered not to be in the best interest of the child, in particular, taking into account his or her age or situation, his or her parents or legal guardians;
- not to be compelled to give testimony or to confess guilt;
- If considered to have infringed the penal law, to have this decision and any measures imposed in consequence thereof reviewed by a higher competent, independent and impartial authority or judicial body according to law.

These procedural guarantees set out in the Convention and implemented for juvenile offenders in domestic justice systems ensure that juvenile offenders are granted the right to a fair trial in criminal proceedings. Central Eastern European countries have implemented these rules in their legal systems. The following UN resolutions also play an important role in shaping the administration of juvenile justice and executing penalties, including incarceration, which is applicable in exceptional cases: the UN Standard Minimum Rules for the Administration of Juvenile Justice (UN General Assembly Resolution No. 40/33 adopted 29 November 1985); UN Guidelines for the Prevention of Juvenile Delinquency (UN General Assembly Resolution No. 45/112 adopted 14 December 1990); and the UN Rules for the Protection of Juveniles Deprived of their Liberty (UN General Assembly Resolution No. 45/113 adopted 14 December 1990). These resolutions all carry special moral and political weight and countries generally try to incorporate their provisions into their legal systems. These UN resolutions were taken into consideration when drafting the current versions of the provisions regulating the Polish, Czech and Hungarian juvenile justice systems. The fall of communism and the introduction of democratic government led all three countries to join the Council of Europe and to ratify the European Convention for the Protection of Human Rights and Fundamental Freedoms in the early 1990s. This was pivotal in getting them to amend their criminal procedural systems for juvenile offenders so as to comply with the requirements of the right to a fair trial and to respect the principle of the good of the child.

Thomas Hammarberg, Council of Europe Commissioner for Human Rights in 2006–2012, said "In juvenile justice there should be no retribution. The intention is to establish responsibility and, at the same time, to promote re-integration."[11] In Hammarberg's view, there are two parallel tendencies in administering justice to juvenile offenders in Europe. The first is to lower the age of juvenile criminal liability and to apply isolation (incarceration and special penalties for juveniles that consist in isolating them) to an increasingly greater number of children at an increasingly younger age for committing an increasingly greater number of types of crime. This is what happened in Poland, where the age of juvenile criminal liability for the most serious offences was lowered from 16 to 15 when the new Criminal Code came into effect in 1997. The second tendency, which retains the spirit of the UN Convention of the Rights of the Child, is to avoid criminalising juveniles in favour of imposing a variety of non-custodial, social, educational and protective measures as an alternative to incarceration. Both tendencies can be observed in the Polish, Czech and Hungarian systems described here, i.e. on the one hand they all recognise and apply mediation (albeit on different scales and with a lot of difficulties, e.g. in Poland), while on the other, there are tendencies towards subjecting juvenile offenders to harsh and isolating treatment, and rationalising this on the grounds of the growing number of very brutal crimes committed by juveniles. Criminological studies, however, show that brutal and serious juvenile crime has always been marginal. It cannot be denied that juveniles should be held liable for their actions, but what they need more than anything is assistance, support and education, and not just a penal, retributive response.

4 Juvenile Crime in the Czech Republic, Poland and Hungary

Juvenile crime generally follows the overall crime trends described above, although these three countries can be said to have even more similarities in this respect. The official reported crime statistics show that the number of crimes committed by juveniles in every country in the region generally increased until the mid-1990s and then began to fall. This trend is clearly evident in the Czech Republic (Válková and Hulmáková 2010), Hungary (Váradi-Csema 2010) and Poland (Fig. 2).[12] Huge

[11] Presentation "The human rights dimension of juvenile justice" at the Conference of Prosecutors General of Europe, Moscow 5–6 July 2006, retrieved from: https://wcd.coe.int/ViewDoc.jsp?id=1017235 [access: 30 June 2014].

[12] It is worth noting that, according to official data in Poland, the number of juveniles committing offences has been systematically falling for years, although the number of juvenile crimes has been increasing. These data seem to lend themselves to two explanations. On the one hand, the labelling theory is applicable, as is the increasing preference, noticeable in Poland, to respond formally to juvenile offences, i.e. by reporting them to the police instead of having them resolved between parents or at school. On the other hand, this may have to do with the increasing stratification of society. This will result in a reduction in the overall number of children and youth committing offences while at the same time making children from more socially excluded backgrounds feel increasingly demoralised and commit more offences as a result.

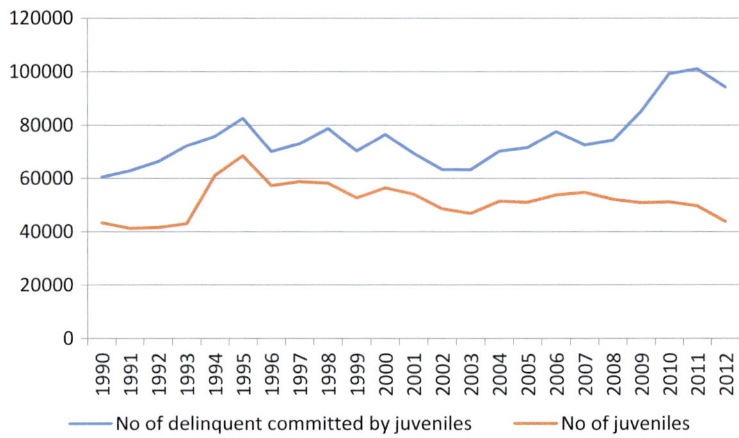

Source: Polish Police Headquarters

Fig. 2 The number of juvenile offenders and offences they committed in Poland in 1990–2012

similarities between Budapest, Kraków and Prague become apparent when their 1990s crime rates per 100,000 population are compared, especially when juxtaposed with the figures for Hamburg, which was surveyed concurrently (Neubacher et al. 1999, pp. 540–544).

The similarities are significantly greater, however, when juvenile crime in Central Europe is considered. It is difficult to determine which country is being described when reading the descriptions of this criminality, as the trends and conclusions frequently apply to every country in the region. Juveniles most often commit crimes against property. As a rule, this is extraordinarily typical of the criminality of this group of offenders. The public, however, are most afraid of violent crimes, especially robberies. The statistical data show that incidents of this type comprise a significant portion of juvenile crime, as well as an overall increase in violent crimes committed by juveniles (cf. Fig. 3). At the same time, studies show that "an analysis of the crime of robbery confirms that many such crimes which formally meet all the criteria of robbery do so chiefly because the offender (...) used violence (or more often threat of violence) for personal gain because it seemed at the time the best way to achieve the objective of the attack. Robbery thus often arises as excess in the context of the clients' property offences." (Večerka 2005, p. 127, similarly Klaus 2009, pp. 157–168). Therefore, while these acts bear weighty names, they are most often not overly brutal.

Central European studies on juvenile offenders reveal many similar characteristics in their profiles.[13] They typically come from lower class, and often broken, families. They are often denied the opportunity to be properly socialised, as their

[13] These studies were mostly based on official materials, i.e. data from court records and the records of public custodial and rehabilitative institutions.

Fig. 3 Police statistics on the changes in selected types of crimes committed by juveniles in Poland in 1990–2012

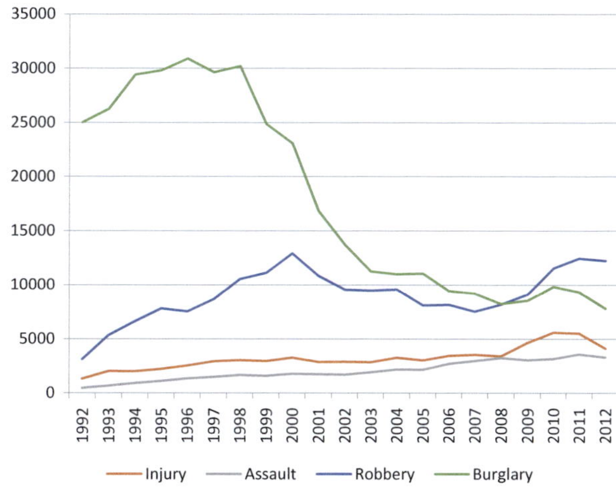

Source: Polish Police Headquarters

families are poorly educated and have a poor attitude to work. Such families do not encourage their children to develop properly, as they do not see the need or do know how to go about it. Many juveniles also experience problems in school from early childhood. They often play truant, repeat classes and start committing petty crimes at a young age.[14] They sometimes commit these offences out of boredom or a desire to do something exciting. Alcohol often drives them to engage in risky behaviour (Váradi-Csema 2010, p. 678; Večerka 2009, p. 124; Večerka 2005, pp. 126–128; Klaus 2009; Woźniakowska-Fajst 2010). Various youth surveys conducted around the world show that young people have very similar ways of spending their free time. These results are independent of the country in which the survey was conducted. "Adolescents (...) spent their time in remarkably similar ways; most of their time was spent in solitary activities, followed by peer, family, and community/sports activities. Also, some interesting differences were found by sex. Consistent with previous work, males spent a smaller proportion of their time in the family context than females, while females spent less time in community/sports activities. (...) Spending time in the family context seemed to buffer adolescents from norm-violating behaviors, while spending time with peers in unstructured and largely unsupervised activities was most predictive of deviant behaviors." (Vazsonyi et al. 2002, pp. 415, 418).

The official statistics presented above, however, should come with a caveat. While statistics have been able to show an increase in juvenile crime—both in total and per 100,000 population (particularly concerning violent crime, cf. Stańdo-Kawecka 2010, pp. 999–1001)—in recent years, this growth is not only not evident in self-report studies, but the very opposite can be observed, viz. a distinct decrease

[14] Criminological studies demonstrate that committing larceny at a young age is a valid indicator of criminality in later life (Batawia et al. 1965; Żabczyńska 1983, pp. 127–131).

in the number of offences committed by juveniles (Enzmann and Podana 2010, pp. 202–203).[15] What the statistics reveal and how they should be interpreted needs to be borne in mind: 'neither as a true representation nor as a distorted reflection of the activities of a criminal justice system. Instead, these statistics should be seen as reflecting specific processing procedures and methods of crime control' (Neubacher et al. 1999, p. 554).

As the statistical data do not give a clear picture of crime, the results of the self-report studies conducted in Central Europe are worth presenting. Such studies were conducted in 12 European countries, including Poland (in Warsaw), in 1993.[16] Warsaw comes across as relatively safe vis-à-vis other countries and is ranked in the middle in terms of the frequency of offences committed by juveniles. The most common offences (committed by half the respondents) were thefts and burglaries. A significant proportion of young people had also participated in fighting (26 % of boys and 11 % of girls). The data on robberies were interesting. These were committed by only 2 of 701 respondents (Kossowska et al. 1995). This contradicts the information presented above about the statistically significant growth in juvenile robberies in Poland at the time. The next Polish studies, conducted using a nationwide sample in 2000, revealed few changes in the picture of juvenile crime in Poland. Theft is still the most common type of offence (as many as 42 % of the young people surveyed had taken money from their parents without their knowledge and one in three had stolen from shops), taking part in fights was on a similar level (one in four of those surveyed admitted to this). As many as one third had beaten someone else during the past year, although this seldom resulted in serious injuries. There was, however, a significant decrease in the number of burglaries—from 20 % in 1993 to 6 % in 2000 (Kossowska 2007, pp. 451–454).

The next survey was conducted in the capitals of six new EU member states, including Warsaw and Prague, in 2006–2007.[17] It is worth emphasising that this survey shows that, as with the statistical data described above, these two countries have convergent patterns of criminality, despite the differences that are sometimes apparent between them. Prague had the greatest frequency of juvenile offences of all the countries surveyed (45 %). The figure for Warsaw was 35 %. Prague youth were at the forefront for such crimes as violent offences (fighting, carrying weapons, vandalism, etc.) and shoplifting. A similar pattern of criminality is noticeable when it comes to gender. On average, one in two boys and one in four girls had committed offences (i.e. offences where there is no clear differentiation between the sexes, e.g. shoplifting, and using and selling illicit drugs). On the other

[15] Self-Reported Delinquency studies conducted in 1998–2001 and International Self-Reported Delinquency (ISDR) studies conducted in 2006.

[16] England and Wales, Belgium, Finland, Greece, Spain, the Netherlands, Northern Ireland, Germany, Poland, Portugal, Switzerland and Italy are the countries that took part. Although each country used the same survey form, the sample was selected differently. This makes it difficult to compare the results. The surveys were nationwide in some countries but restricted to certain cities in others (Kossowska et al. 1995, p. 99).

[17] The Czech Republic, Cyprus, Estonia, Lithuania, Poland and Slovenia.

hand, the two cities varied in their level of youth alcohol consumption, which was rather high in Prague (85 %) and relatively low in Warsaw (71 %). Prague youth began consuming alcohol at a younger age—32 % of 13-year-olds drank beer and 21 % drank vodka. The respective figures for Warsaw were 19 % and 8 %. The trends in Poland and the Czech Republic are likewise identical when the two countries, and not just their capitals, are examined. Shoplifting was the offence most frequently committed by young people, followed by group fighting, carrying weapons and destroying property. Significant differences were apparent in the intensity of the first two of these offences—they were considerably more common in the Czech Republic than in Poland (Steketee et al. 2008; Steketee and Gruszczyńska 2010). Fundamental differences between the two countries were also apparent in the attitude of young people living in the capital to school. This institution was assessed considerably more critically in Warsaw, where one in three declared that they did not like their school (as compared with one in four in Prague). This attitude translated into a higher level of truancy (27 % of teenagers in Warsaw compared with 8 % in Prague) and offences being committed more frequently on school grounds—theft (49 % vs. 36 %) and fighting (54 % vs. 37 %). Only destruction of school property was at the same level in both capitals (Steketee et al. 2008, p. 127).

Hungarian youth were surveyed at the end of the 1990s and in 2011. The first survey showed that Hungarian youth exhibited less deviant behaviour than those in the other countries (Vazsonyi et al. 2002).[18] This is probably due to Hungarian people being brought up in more traditional families and spending much more time together with their families than their peers in other countries. The most recent survey (Görgen et al. 2013; Albert and Tóth 2013) shows that the most common deviant behaviour exhibited by Hungarian youth is carrying items that can be used in a fight (almost one in four boys) and fighting (20 % of boys and 12 % of girls).[19] Crimes against property, too, are all too common. Youth alcohol consumption is also a serious problem. As many as 40 % of junior school pupils admitted to drinking at least once during the past year and 37 % of the teenagers surveyed had been drunk several times during the past month (this is a significantly higher average than the 24 % recorded in the other countries surveyed).

The 2006 International Self-Report Delinquency Study (ISRD2) made it possible to compare all three countries. This showed that Hungary had the highest percentage of juveniles committing offences, and Poland the lowest (cf. Fig. 4). Hungary also recorded one of the highest juvenile crime rates of all the 31 countries studied.[20] Taking the study as a whole, 37.9 % of young people on average claimed to have committed at least one offence during their lives (similar to the Czech

[18] This was simultaneously conducted in Denmark, the USA and Switzerland.

[19] This was also conducted in Belgium, Spain, Germany, Portugal and Slovenia.

[20] The highest crime rates were recorded in Ireland, Germany, France, Finland and Aruba, with the Netherlands, Denmark and Iceland not far behind. The juvenile crime rates of the remaining countries never exceeded 40 %.

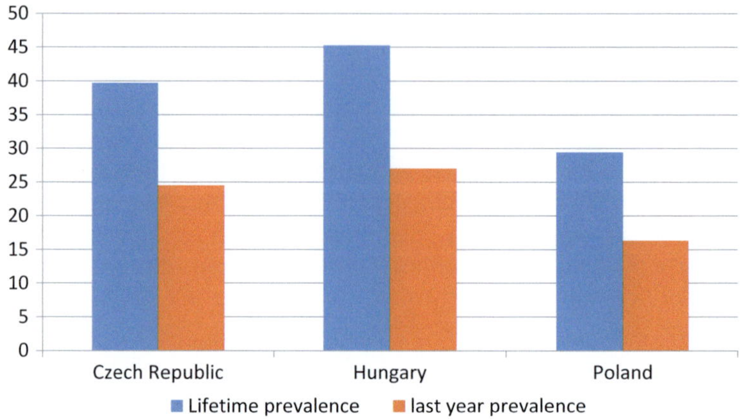

Source: Junger-Tas et al. 2012, p.70

Fig. 4 Juvenile crime in the Czech Republic, Hungary and Poland as per the International Self-Report Study of Delinquency (ISRD2)

Republic) and 22.1 % during the previous year. The Czech Republic, Hungary and Poland vary in terms of the gravity of the offences committed by young people. The overwhelming majority of offences everywhere were obviously relatively minor, e.g. shoplifting, vandalism, group fights, carrying weapons (knives) and hacking. Of those who had committed an offence in the year prior to the study, however, 24 % of the Polish respondents had committed an offence deemed serious.[21] This compares with 18 % of Hungarians and 16 % of Czechs. When particular types of crimes committed in the year prior to the study are compared, property crimes in large and medium cities were most frequent in the Czech Republic. This country was the regional leader (along with Slovenia) when it came to minor offences of this type (approx. 7.5 %). When it came to major offences of this type, however, it was Poland that appeared most frequently, although the differences between countries were not all that great and this type of crime was not all that common, fluctuating between 1 % and 2 % of the survey population. The order for minor violent crimes committed in the year prior to the study follows the general trend and the incidence fluctuates around 19 % in Hungary and 11 % in Poland. Serious crimes are at a similar level of around 2–3 % in each of the countries surveyed (Junger-Tas et al. 2012, pp. 69–74).

Unfortunately, the ISRD2 seldom compares individual countries with each other or cites detailed data in this area. Rather, it focuses on comparing groups of countries. Estonia, Lithuania, Slovenia, Bosnia and Herzegovina, Russia, Armenia, and the three countries mentioned above were included in one group of post-socialist countries. This comprised the largest group in the study in terms of the

[21] The following are acknowledged as such: theft, burglary, theft of bike/motorcycle, auto theft, theft from a motor vehicle, robbery, assault, dealing in drugs.

number of countries. It should be noted that there are significant differences between the individual countries in this group (this is a recurring regularity for each group of countries). Central and Eastern European countries can be described as relatively safe in terms of the threat of juvenile crime when compared with the others. The greatest threat was noted in English-speaking countries[22] and in Western Europe.[23] Central and Eastern Europe, on the other hand, had the lowest percentage of young people committing offences (Junger-Tas et al. 2012, pp. 69–75). This trend is noticeable in each of the countries mentioned in the survey from the early 1990s.[24]

There are still two issues worth noting in a comparative context. The first is the link between crime and gender. As mentioned, people in Central European societies are convinced that crime among girls is on the increase. While it can be said, taking Poland as a case in point, that the overall role of women and girls in crime, especially aggressive crime, has been statistically increasing, this growth still appears insufficient to warrant social anxiety (cf. Habzda-Siwek and Grzyb 2013). The ISRD2 study shows that when all the participating countries were compared, Central and Eastern Europe had the largest gender gap and the least girls committing offences, especially the most serious ones. This may be because a great deal of control is exercised over girls in this region. Girls here spend relatively a lot of time with their families and small circles of friends (up to three people) (Junger-Tas et al. 2012, pp. 80, 198–200).

Typically for this region, young people have very little attachment to school—half the teenagers here do not like their school. A fifth of those surveyed noticed some disruption in their place of learning in the form of illegal behaviour on the school grounds (fights, thefts, vandalism and illegal drugs). This was lower than the figure for English-speaking and Western countries (37.2 % and 28.6 % respectively) but still high enough (Junger-Tas et al. 2012, pp. 223–225). At the same time, the study shows the enormous impact of school and the prevailing atmosphere there on the behaviour of young people: "pupils in disorganized schools are about 3 times more likely to commit serious violent offenses compared to those attending schools without such characteristics" (Junger-Tas et al. 2012, pp. 227–228). On the other hand, a series of organisational factors in the educational system that prevent criminal behaviour can be observed in Central and Eastern Europe, e.g. schools are egalitarian and pupils are not divided into better and weaker categories during the early years of their education (i.e. there is a one track system).[25] Separating pupils and grouping together those who have low social capital, and who are often

[22] As represented by Ireland, the USA and Canada.

[23] The Netherlands, Germany, France, Belgium, Switzerland and Austria.

[24] Unfortunately, there is no way to compare the changes in individual counties and regions over a period of years. This is because of changes in how the questions have been formulated and the countries grouped in particular studies.

[25] Although an increasing trend to segregate pupils at the high school level can be observed in Poland in recent years (cf. Klaus 2015).

"problem" pupils as well, gives them no way of learning other models of behaviour, and strengthens their own negative attitudes, as they only have each other for company and have no friends from other socio-cultural backgrounds. A correlation between good school results and a low level of serious crime has also been observed (Junger-Tas et al. 2012, pp. 232–234). The PISA (Programme for International Student Assessment) results show that Central and Eastern Europe performs reasonably well in this area and continues to achieve better results from one study to the next.

5 Victimisation of Minors

Child and youth crime victims is an emotionally charged issue practically everywhere. It crops up in media discussions and political speeches. Public broadcasts are more newsworthy whenever children are involved (Jewkes 2010, p. 57). Some categories of wrong inflicted on minors stand out by dint of their scale and/or the gravity of the conduct of the perpetrator(s). Of all the crimes that do harm to minors, violent crimes (especially violence in the home and at school) and sexual crimes are definitely the ones that require the most effective reaction possible from the state, as well as an awareness on the part of the citizenry and the courage to respond. Procedural guarantees for minors harmed by crime are another serious problem, especially in the context of having to implement Directive 2012/29/EU of the European Parliament and of the Council establishing minimum standards on the rights, support and protection of victims of crime.

It is widely known in victimology that it is young people who most often fall victim to crime. How young? Data from different countries show that it is most often people aged 16–24 (cf. Home Office 2006). Are these data completely reliable? Not necessarily. Children are excluded from most national and international victimisation surveys. The UN handbook on designing these kinds of surveys states that the 'target population in victimization surveys is usually defined by age or gender' (UN 2010, p. 25). By way of example, it mentions that the accepted age of respondents is 14 in Italy, 16 in England and Wales and 18 in some other countries. People under the ages of 18 and 16 are, however, included in direct victimisation surveys (both national and international), although as they are conducted separately from adult surveys, they are also analysed separately and not compared with them. A commonly accepted methodology is to combine victimisation and self-report surveys in a single questionnaire and to address questions on victimisation and crime to the same respondents. This is simpler from both an organisational and a substantive standpoint, as delinquency and victimisation are correlated. Young offenders are more frequently vulnerable to being victimised than children who do not commit crimes, as they are more likely to come from disadvantaged social backgrounds (Junger-Tas et al. 2012, p. 95).

It is difficult to compare data on violence towards children in Central Europe. To get some idea of the scale of the problem, the Hungarian Ombudsman stated that there are about 6000 child victims of violent crime every year in Hungary, a country

Table 1 Sentences handed down by Polish courts in 2013

Type of crime	No. of underage victims
Homicide	34
Causing grievous bodily harm	24
Causing non-grievous bodily harm	220
Affray and battery	212
Punishable threat	373
Stalking	54
Rape	202
Sexual intercourse with a minor under 15 years	659
Abuse of a family member	3885
Child support evasion	12,075
Theft	228
Burglary	169
Robbery	357

Source: Polish Ministry of Justice

of 8 million (Hungarian Ombudsman 2012). Minors accounted for 53 % (911 people) of victims in domestic violence cases in the Czech Republic (which has a population of more than 10 million) in 2009. Almost 86,800 cases of domestic violence, in which 22 % (19,250 people) of the victims were children, were reported to the police in Poland (more than 38 million people) in 2013.[26] Polish courts also impose around 4000 sentences for domestic violence offences in which children are victims every year. Table 1 shows the number of final judgements in criminal cases in which the victims were minors in 2013.

The International Self-Report Delinquency Study 2 (ISRD-2), conducted in 2005–2007, shows that the victimisation of children aged 12–15 in Poland, Hungary and the Czech Republic is not at this level. These surveys show that, among the "post socialist countries" (Estonia, Lithuania, Poland, the Czech Republic, Hungary, Russia, Armenia, and Bosnia and Herzegovina), Hungary reported the most harm (33.2 % of respondents) from crimes such as robbery, assault, theft and bullying, while Armenia reported the least (12.9 %). The results for "post-socialist countries" do not diverge significantly from other groups. Latin American countries had the highest overall victimization rate (31.8 %, mostly consisting of assault and theft) and Mediterranean Europe the lowest (19 %). Northern Europe (23.5 %) and Western Europe (26.8 %) had the same level of victimisation as the post-socialist countries, although Polish and Hungarian children declared decidedly more harm from robbery and assault than children in these two regions (Junger-Tas et al. 2012, p. 98).

From the data in Table 2, it can be seen that the level of victimisation of Polish teenagers was closest to the mean for the group. All categories of victimisation were

[26] Data from Polish Police Headquarters http://statystyka.policja.pl/st/wybrane-statystyki/przemoc-w-rodzinie/50863,Przemoc-w-rodzinie.html accessed June 2013.

Table 2 ISRD-2 prevalence rates (%) by country

	Robbery	Assault	Theft	Bullying	Total criminal victimization
Post-socialist countries combined	7.5	5.2	20.3	15.2	26.3
Poland	8.2	6.1	19.3	13.9	25.9
Czech Republic	3.2	3.3	20.0	10.1	23.5
Hungary	12.9	5.9	25.7	17.9	33.2

Source: Junger-Tas et al. (2012), p. 98

below (sometimes significantly below) average in the Czech Republic, whereas Hungary had a level of victimisation that was very high, and as already mentioned, the highest in the group. These figures are extremely difficult to interpret. The ICVS shows that Hungary had one of the lowest victimisation rates in the surveyed countries during roughly the same period. The highest level of victimisation of minors in Hungary in the ISRD-2 correlates to the highest level of juvenile crime in the surveyed countries. The situation, however, appears to be different in Poland and the Czech Republic. While Polish children declared the lowest participation in deviant behaviour, the level of victimisation was average. Czech children committed more offences than their Polish counterparts but declared a slightly lower level of victimisation. One possible explanation for this is that a greater proportion of the offences committed by Polish children harm physical persons (e.g. assault and robbery). This is evident from both police statistics and the ISRD-2 surveys (Enzmann et al. 2010, pp. 172–173).

So far as specific crimes are concerned, one of the most serious experiences of victimisation is being robbed. Boys are generally more at risk than girls. The ISRD-2 surveys indicate that the risk of being robbed is three times greater for boys on average. The differences between girls and boys are even greater in Central Europe. Polish and Czech boys were robbery victims 4 times more often than girls, while Hungarian boys were robbery victims 7 times more often. These results are obviously influenced by cultural factors (Junger-Tas et al. 2012, p. 99). It is interesting to note, however, that boys were only robbed twice as often as girls according to surveys conducted in Kraków, Poland, in 1999 (Krajewski 2001, p. 154). Regardless of sex, the likelihood of being robbed increases with age, although Czech studies have produced the surprising result that this risk actually decreases with age in that country (Junger-Tas et al. 2012, p. 101). As for victimisation in the capitals of the surveyed countries, nearly twice the difference in the risk of being robbed was observed in Warsaw (7.7 %) and Prague (4 %) (Steketee et al. 2008, p. 110).

Bullying is becoming an ever more frequent experience of school life, although whether this is entirely due to increasing occurrences or whether there is also greater sensitivity and more formal responses to violence between pupils is not known. Any assessment of the scale of bullying obviously depends on the survey methodology. The ISRD-2 indicates that bullying victimisation remains pretty much average in Poland, that the level of harassment in the Czech Republic is fairly low (compared with Scandinavian countries, where benchmark programs to prevent violence in schools have been conducted for years) but that Hungary has one of the highest levels of all the countries that took part in the survey. At the same time, Wendy Craig surveys from the same period indicate that the Czech Republic has a noticeably low level of bullying (which would concur with the ISRD-2 surveys) (Craig et al. 2009), but so does Hungary (PREVNet 2009). The Czechs, who performed well in the two studies, were concerned about the brutalisation of school life and announced that 20 % of pupils experienced bullying in 2000 (Ginter 2000). Polish surveys from 2011 show that verbal abuse (insult, ridicule, humiliation, etc.) is the most common form of violence in school and that almost two thirds of pupils fall victim to it. One in three respondents had experienced wilful physical violence in the form of being pushed or beaten and 7 % had encountered serious physical violence (i.e. using dangerous weapons and resulting in bodily injury). Relational violence (exclusion from the group, manipulation, slander, etc.) affected 41 % of Polish pupils (Komendant-Brodowska et al. 2011, pp. 3–4). Polish studies indicate that 9 % of children can be considered victims of bullying. Bullying is an experience that more often affects boys than girls. Girls more frequently fell victim to bullying in Hungary (8.7 % compared with 5.7 % of boys), although boys more frequently perpetrated this form of violence (Buda and Szirmai 2010, p. 8). One boy in ten and one girl in fifteen was a victim of torment in Poland (Komendant-Brodowska et al. 2011, p. 9).

Violence and abuse towards children has only been perceived as a social problem in Central Europe since the early 1990s. During the communist period, domestic violence was a private matter and institutional violence (perpetrated in schools, orphanages, juvenile detention centres, etc.) was not spoken of at all. The Committee for the Protection of Children's Rights, a social organisation constituted to combat various forms of harm to children, only came into existence in Poland in 1981. Along with democracy and capitalism, however, the fall of the communist regime ushered in greater sensitivity to violence in the home and violence inflicted on children. NGOs concerned with children's rights sprang up in every Central European country and every government in the region initiated and supported campaigns of various sorts aimed at informing the public as to what violence towards children was and inculcating a sense of responsibility, especially in adults, for reporting any suspicions of violence towards children. These activities are ongoing in Poland, Hungary and the Czech Republic, as there remains a great deal to be done. These campaigns have highlighted a variety of problems associated with a higher level of sensitivity to violence and new forms of it over the years (Poremska 2008). A campaign to draw attention to the issue of psychological violence towards children was launched in Poland in 2013. Increasing attention is also being paid to cyberbullying.

Protecting children from sexual predation is an important child care objective in Central Europe, as it is everywhere else. Cohabiting with a person under the age of 15 years is punishable in Poland and the Czech Republic—even with the consent of the minor and even on his/her initiative. In Hungary, the minimum age for consensual sex is 14. Offenders are severely punished in the case of victims under 12 years (HRR: Hungary 2011).

The high dark figure for sexual violence makes it difficult to gauge the extent of this type of crime. Accepted research methods and the definition of sexual violence also have an influence on the extent of crime uncovered (Sajkowska 2002, pp. 1–2). To quote from a Czech report: 'according to an ongoing 15-year study conducted by sexologists at the medical school of Charles University in Prague, 10 percent of children in the country have experienced sexual abuse; 7 percent were sexually abused at least once, while 3 percent experienced such abuse repeatedly' (HRR: Czech 2011). Polish police register approx. 2000 reports concerning cases of sexual exploitation of people under the age of 15 annually, of which some 700 result in convictions.[27]

Another problem with protecting children from sexual predation is the exploitation of minors in the pornographic industry. Every country in Central Europe has signed the Convention on Cybercrime and penalises the production, distribution and possession of pornographic materials involving minors.[28] Poland only made the possession of child pornography punishable in 2005, although work on tightening criminal liability and introducing EU regulations to protect children from crimes of a sexual nature was in progress at the time of writing (2014). These new measures are intended to more effectively and efficiently combat the producers and consumers of child pornography as well as those who profit from child prostitution. This is why the amendments impose penalties for recording, storing and possessing pornography involving children under the age of 18. Possessing pornography involving children under the age of 15 (with no intention of trafficking) had previously been penalised. The amendments simply raised the age limit.[29] In the Czech Republic, by contrast, possessing child pornography was penalised in an atmosphere of scandal. Austrian police had broken up an online child pornography ring in early 2007. A lot of people were arrested for possessing pornographic images of children, including 60 from the Czech Republic, where downloading and possessing such images were not criminalised at the time. Amendments had been made to the Czech Criminal Code but these had been rejected by the Senate, i.e. the Upper House of Parliament. The Act was only passed after a second vote in the autumn of 2007 (Konviser 2007).

Possessing materials utilising graphically produced images (drawings, computer graphics, etc.) of a minor is likewise penalised in Poland. It is prohibited to produce, record, procure, store and/or possess pornographic materials involving a minor of 18 years of age or under with an intent to distribute them and to distribute or publicly present pornographic materials involving a minor. There are few

[27] Data from Police Headquarters: http://statystyka.policja.pl/st/kodeks-karny/przestepstwa-przeciwko-6/63501,Seksualne-wykorzystanie-maloletniego-art-200.html and the Ministry of Justice in the possession of the authors.

[28] Poland is the only Central European country that has not ratified the Convention.

[29] Parliamentary Paper No. 2016.

convictions for this type of crime, e.g. there are 20–30 convictions for presenting pornographic materials to people under the age of 15 annually. There were 18 convictions for using minors to produce pornographic materials in 2012, but only 5 in 2013. Moreover, only a few people are convicted for recording pornographic images of children under the age of 15 every year.[30]

Given their shared histories and similar geographical location (neighbouring more powerful countries), sexual tourism has become a common problem for Poland, Hungary and the Czech Republic. While there are many definitions of sex tourism, they are all essentially grounded in men and women travelling from economically advanced to poorly developed countries with a view to purchasing sexual services from the local men, women and children. This conduct may have several causes. The most common is being able to engage in behaviour that is prohibited in the tourists' home countries (e.g. homosexual or child sex), but there is the additional possibility of enjoying sexual services in anonymity and at prices below those in their own countries (Borzyszkowski 2011). While sex tourism is most often associated with countries such as Thailand, Cuba and the Dominican Republic, it is definitely a problem in Central Europe. It has been observed that once countries such as Thailand and the Philippines tightened their criminal policy towards paedophiles in the mid-1990s, child prostitution businesses started relocating to Central and Eastern Europe, especially Poland, Estonia, Russia and Hungary (Campbell and Connolly 1997). It was not just the opening of the borders in this part of Europe that drew paedophiles, but also the degree of police corruption, as this made it easy to carry on illegal activities. Little has changed in 20 years.

British police claim that sexual tourism is more and more frequently occurring in the USA and a range of European countries with similar social, economic and cultural conditions (CEOP 2013). Movement between Germany, Austria and the Scandinavian countries, and Poland, Hungary and the Czech Republic, has been renewed since the borders between Eastern and Western Europe came down in 1990. Europeans from behind the 'Iron Curtain' travelled to the West as tourists, businesspeople and hired workers, but also as perpetrators and victims of crime. In the early 1990s, it became popular for minors to make short (only a few hours) excursions from Poland to Germany and then return by train after quickly stealing from supermarkets there (Kurzępa 2010, p. 99).

Juvenile prostitution is another way to obtain money by exploiting the proximity with the affluent West. This is effectively sex tourism in reverse: children prostituting themselves go to richer countries in search of clients. Boys and girls both engage in this conduct, although their clients are almost exclusively men (Kurzępa 2010). One of the reasons that young people embarked on prostitution excursions in the early 1990s was the enormous wealth gap between Western and Central Europe. A girl was paid around 4 EUR for providing a sexual service in Budapest in the mid-1990s. The connection between the sexual exploitation of children (for pornography as well as prostitution) and rampant poverty was also noted at the time.

[30] Data from the Ministry of Justice in the possession of the authors.

This greatly affected socially excluded (i.e. the poorest and least educated) Roma families (Szabo 1996). The situation on the Czech-German border at the turn of the twenty-first century was dire. A 2003 UNICEF report stated that 'A key reason for the increasing demand is that larger numbers of sex tourists specifically request children.' (Staff 2004). Sexual services were even provided by children as young as six. They would stand at service stations, bus stops and in supermarkets and accost potential clients from Germany. The youngest children were procured by their mothers (Siegel and Senna 2007, p. 48).

It is difficult to assess the scale of sexual exploitation of children in Central Europe. Gabriela Kühn (2014, p. 12), citing the report 'End Child Prostitution Child Pornography & Trafficking of Children for Sexual Purposes (ECPAT)', says that approximately 20,000 German tourists sexually exploit children and 4–5000 Swedes seek contacts with minors on sexual tourism trips. How many of them make their way to Central Europe is not known.

The previously mentioned huge economic differences between regions that were a major cause of child prostitution as recently as 10 years ago, still prevail. The income differentials across particular countries are not as glaring as they were, but many Central European children still suffer from poverty. Surveys conducted by the Nobody's Children Foundation in Poland show that the commercial sexual exploitation of children remains a very real problem. For the Polish (as opposed to Ukrainian) children surveyed, the main motivation for turning to prostitution was no longer excruciating poverty or dire material circumstances, but a desire for material gain and acquiring new gadgets (Włodarczyk and Hamela 2011, p. 14).

So how do Central European countries go about tackling the issue of child prostitution and sex tourism? The first method is to improve the legislative framework. Hungary, Poland and the Czech Republic are required to adopt *Directive 2011/92/EU on combating the sexual abuse and sexual exploitation of children and child pornography* and *Directive 2011/36/EU on preventing and combating trafficking in human beings and protecting its victims* as part of their domestic legislation as EU member states. Hungary introduced a new criminal code in 2013. With regards to prostitution, the novelty of the New Criminal Code is a new provision that specifically prohibits child prostitution. Penalties apply to any person who aspires to gain financial benefits from the prostitution of another person under the age of eighteen, any person who provides compensation for the sexual services of another person under the age of eighteen, any person who supports himself wholly or in part from the earnings of a person engaging in prostitution under the age of eighteen, and any person who maintains or operates a brothel, or provides financial means for the operation of a brothel where a person under the age of eighteen engages in prostitution (section 203 of Hungarian Criminal Code).

It is illegal to facilitate or derive a benefit from the prostitution of another person under Czech law. Until 2010, the age of the victim was considered an aggravating circumstance: when the victim was between 15 and 18 years of age, penalties ranged from 2 to 8 years' imprisonment and from 5 to 12 years' in cases when the victim was under 15 (ECPAT 2006). This construction was abandoned in the new criminal code that came into effect in 2010. The new procuring provision, which concerns deriving a benefit from the prostitution of another person, does not apply to people under the age of 18, who are protected by the more stringent provisions on trafficking in human beings.[31] Czech police investigate dozens of cases of commercial sexual exploitation of children every year (46 in 2010 and 96 in 2012). (HRR: Czech 2011, HRR: Czech 2013).

"Child prostitution" is not defined in Polish law. A minor is not criminally liable for providing sexual services for financial gain in Poland, although the fact that the minor is prostituting him or herself is evidence of moral depravity. A minor can appear in the Family Court, which may apply educational measures. As mentioned above, sexual contact with a person under the age of 15 is prohibited in Poland. Inducing a minor to engage in commercial sexual acts is punishable in the case of the minor being 15 or over but under 18. There is, however, a legal loophole in Poland that needs to be closed, viz. benefitting from the services of a minor prostituting him or herself is only punishable when the client initiates the contact. The client is not liable to any penalty when the child initiates the contact (Kühn 2014, p. 21). The Polish criminal code also penalises the obtaining of any financial gain from a third person practising prostitution, facilitating prostitution or inducing others to practise it with a view to obtaining financial gain, and coercing others into prostitution by means of violence, threats or deception or by exploiting a dependent relationship or any critical situation in which the victim finds him or herself. The police confirm dozens of such cases every year (generally around 30, although there were a record 63 in 2002 compared with only 17 in 2013).[32] It is interesting to note that the ratio of the number of confirmed cases and the number of cases decided by the courts where the victims were minors is not constant. The number of juvenile crime victims coerced into prostitution changes dramatically from year to year. Not a single sentence in a case where the victim was a minor was handed down in 2013 (see Table 3).

Sixteen European countries are involved in the "Don't Look Away" campaign in order to more effectively prevent the commercial sexual exploitation of children, especially in sex tourism. These countries have set up Internet platforms that contain educational materials and which enable disturbing situations to be reported. This new tool is intended to mobilise society into no longer remaining indifferent to suspicious contacts between adults and children. People who frequently travel or work in the tourist industry can be particularly helpful here. Poland and the Czech Republic, but unfortunately not Hungary, are involved in the campaign.

[31] E-note website, European NGOs Observatory on Trafficking, Exploitation and Slavery, http://www.e-notes-observatory.org/legislation/czech-republic/ (downloaded June 2014).

[32] Police Headquarters statistics: http://statystyka.policja.pl/st/kodeks-karny/przestepstwa-przeciwko-6/63504,Zmuszanie-do-prostytucji-art-203.html, downloaded June 2013.

Table 3 Coercion to prostitution: the number of cases confirmed by the police and decided by the courts where the victims were minors

	2003	2004	2005	2006	2007	2008	2009	2010	2011	2012	2013
Number of cases confirmed by the police	47	46	35	42	55	35	33	28	19	26	17
Number of cases decided by the courts where the victims were minors	No data	23	5	1	24	5	26	4	11	1	0

Source: Polish Ministry of Justice

6 Children's Rights in Criminal Trials

Directive 2012/29/EU establishing minimum standards on the rights, support and protection of victims of crime is of major importance to all EU countries. This naturally includes Poland, Hungary and the Czech Republic. The main point to note for the purposes of this chapter is that the Directive contains detailed regulations on protecting children. Framework Decision 2001/220, which the Directive supersedes, did not even mention children as being special participants in criminal trials. Article 1 of the Directive, which sets out its objectives, emphasises that 'Member States shall ensure that in the application of this Directive, where the victim is a child, the child's best interests shall be a primary consideration and shall be assessed on an individual basis. A child-sensitive approach, taking due account of the child's age, maturity, views, needs and concerns, shall prevail. The child and the holder of parental responsibility or other legal representative, if any, shall be informed of any measures or rights specifically focused on the child' (Paragraph 2). The Directive further notes that children are to be afforded special protection from secondary victimization and retaliation (Art. 22).

The Directive makes another major change by defining 'child' more broadly than does the Convention on the Rights of the Child. The Convention states that a child is any person under the age of 18 but adds 'unless under the law applicable to the child, majority is attained earlier' (Art. 1). A child within the meaning of the Directive is any person under the age of 18. This is a significant change for every Central European country as they all have legislation that provides for people under the age of 18 entering into marital relationships and thereby attaining their majority. Boys and girls can enter into marital relationships once they have turned 16 in the Czech Republic (Boele-Woelki et al. 2005, p. 56). In Hungary, people over the age of 16 are additionally required to show a strong reason and the guardianship authority has to approve it in advance in the presence of their parents.[33] Only the

[33] See more at: accessed: June 2014.

bride can be a child in Poland and she has to be at least 16. Such a marriage requires the consent of the courts. Consideration is to be given as to whether there are pressing reasons and the family is well established (Art. 10 Family and Guardianship Code). Also important, although they are only a non-binding recommendation, are the *Guidelines of the Committee of Ministers of the Council of Europe on child-friendly justice* published by the Council of Europe in 2010.

Both Art. 24 of the Directive and the Guidelines of the Council of Europe place special emphasis on examining children by implementing special measures especially for them. The examination of children during preliminary proceedings should be audiovisually recorded and then used as evidence in subsequent judicial proceedings in order to prevent the trauma of having to repeatedly recount painful memories. In the Czech Republic "the ministries of interior and justice implemented use of special interviewing rooms for child victims and witnesses. A child victim is not required to give additional testimony in any future court proceedings when specially trained police follow the special interview requirements (including the presence of psychologists and, in some cases, judges and defence attorneys)" (HRR: Czech 2011).

The educational components of the specifics of working with children are included in the professional training of the Hungarian police force. Comprehensive training, however, is not provided in this area. The investigative authorities do what they can to ensure that children are only interviewed once, and in cases where interviewing the child would occasion additional harm, they can request that the prosecutor order that the child be heard by the investigative judge. Up until 2014, the police had to ensure that each county had at least one room that could be used to conduct a congenial interview. This is clearly not overly ambitious. The Hungarian Ombudsman believes that too few interview rooms could contribute to additional harm to the child by prolonging the proceedings in cases where the only available interview room is a long way from the residence of the child. Those working in the justice system are already overburdened with work without the additional burden of having to travel to other towns and cities to interview children (Hungarian Ombudsman 2012, p. 30).

Poland has more than 300 places where children can be interviewed in conditions congenial to them. While this "congeniality" varies in degree, more than 70 of these places have a certificate from the Ministry of Justice and the Nobody's Children Foundation that not only vouches for their safety (e.g. any interview of a child is guaranteed to be conducted solely by a judge with the assistance of a psychologist and in a place where the accused is not admitted) but also shows that children can rest assured of a sense of intimacy through the use of pastel colour schemes and the provision of toys.[34] At the same time, certified places have to have audio-visual equipment available so as to meet the requirements of the justice system. Since the beginning of 2014, every interview of a child victim has had to

[34] Other people, e.g. the prosecutor and the lawyer of the accused, can be present in another room while the interview is being held.

be held in a room adapted for this purpose in order to comply with the material provisions.[35] The Polish provisions guarantee child victims of crime adequate protection in addition to access to rooms in which they can be interviewed in appropriate conditions. For example, in cases of violent crimes, unlawful threats, crimes against freedom and liberty, crimes against sexual freedom and morality, and crimes against the family and custody, child victims under the age of 15 at the time of being interviewed are only interviewed as witnesses if their testimony is deemed to have a significant bearing on the case. On principle, children aged 15 and under are only interviewed once, unless material circumstances come to light. This can also apply to older minors, although there is a concern that interviewing them in normal conditions can negatively affect their psychological health. It is mandatory to register an interview of a child and only a reproduction of the picture and sound of the interview can be played back at the court hearing. A psychologist must be present at the interview.

Central Europe is no trailblazer when it comes to protecting the rights of child crime victims. This part of Europe still takes a fairly patronising and paternalistic approach to children. On the other hand, however, Poland, Hungary and the Czech Republic have been continually striving for higher standards of caring for children and protecting their rights at every stage of criminal trials in the 25 years or more that have elapsed since these countries set out on the set to democracy and during their 10 years as EU members.

Five Questions

1. What impact on the severity and type of crime had a history of Czech Republic, Hungary and Poland as post-communist countries? What distinguish them from other countries, both Western and Eastern Europe, and is this diversity still present today?
2. What measures should be applied to minors—educational or criminal? Which ones are more effective in preventing recidivism?
3. What are the similarities and differences between the countries of Central Europe in the field of juvenile delinquency? How can you explain them?
4. What, in your opinion, could be done to prevent sexual tourism in Central Europe?
5. What are the similarities and differences in policy of Central European countries towards victimization of minors?

[35] Art. 185a, 185b and 185d of the revised Criminal Procedure Code. These provisions came into effect at the beginning of 2014.

References

Albert, F., & Tóth, O. (2013). Gloomy future ahead? – Results of the YouPrev project in Hungary. In T. Görgen, B. Kraus, A. Taefi, M. J. Bernuz Beneitez, J. Christiaens, G. Meško, H. Perista, & O. Tóth (Eds.), *Youth deviance and youth violence* (pp. 61–84). Münster.

Alvazzi del Frate, A., & Van Kesteren, J. (2004). *Criminal victimisation in Urban Europe: Key findings of the 2000 International Crime Victim Surveys, United Nations Office on Drugs and Crime*. Retrieved from: http://www3.unil.ch/wpmu/icvs/files/2012/11/CriminalVictimisationUrbanEurope.pdf [2 June 2014].

Batawia, S., Kołakowska, H., Strzembosz, A., & Szelhaus, S. (1965). Wyniki badań dalszych losów nieletnich i młodocianych recydywistów (katamnezy w 443 przypadkach) [The subsequent fate of minor and juvenile recidivists: a follow-up study of 443 cases]. *Państwo i Prawo, 4*, 556–574.

Boele-Woelki, K., Braat, B., & Curry-Sumner, I. (Eds.). (2005). *European family law in action. Volume III. Parental responsibilities*. Hart Publishing.

Bojarski, T., Kruk, E., & Skretowicz, E. (2014). *Ustawa o postępowaniu w sprawach nieletnich. Komentarz* [Act on Proceedings Involving Minors: Commentary]. Warsaw: LexisNexis.

Borzyszkowski, J. (2011). Problem zdefiniowania i klasyfikacji seksturystyki. *Turystyka kulturowa* [The Problem of Defining and Classifying Sex Tourism: Cultural Tourism], *1*, 19–31.

Buda, M., & Szirmai, E. (2010). School bullying in the primary school. Report of a research in Hajdú-Bihar County (Hungary). *Journal of Social Research & Policy, 1*, 49–68.

Campbell, D., & Connolly, K. (1997). *Inside story: Europe's sex supermarket money buys a lot in Eastern Europe, including children willing to sell their bodies for a pair of trainers*. The Guardian London (UK), 17 December 1997.

CEOP. (2013). *Threat assessment of child sexual exploitation and abuse*. Child Exploitation and Online Protection Centre. Retrieved from: www.ceop.police.uk/Documents/ceopdocs/CEOP_TACSEA2013_240613%20FINAL.pdf [accessed June 2014].

Craig, W., Harel-Fisch, Y., Fogel-Grinvald, H., Dostaler, S., Hetland, J., Simons-Morton, B., et al. (2009). A cross-national profile of bullying and victimization among adolescents in 40 countries. *International Journal of Public Health, 54*, 216–224.

ECPAT. (2006). *Report on the status of action against commercial sexual exploitation of children*. Czech Republic. Retrieved from: http://www.ecpat.net/sites/default/files/Global_Monitoring_Report-CZECH_REPUBLIC.pdf [June 2014].

Eisner, M. (1995). *The effects of economic structures and phases of development on crime*. In Crime and Economy. Reports Presented to the 11th Criminological Colloquium (1994), Strasbourg, pp. 13–52.

Elder, J. W. (1976). Comparative cross-national methodology. *Annual Review of Sociology, 2*, 209–230.

Enzmann, D., Marshall, I. H., Killias, M., Junger-Tas, J., Steketee, M., & Gruszczynska, B. (2010). Selfreported youth delinquency in Europe and beyond: First results of the Second International Self-Report Delinquency Study in the context of police and victimization data. *European Journal of Criminology, 7*(2), 159–183.

Enzmann, D., & Podana, Z. (2010). Official crime statistics and survey data: Comparing trends of youth violence between 2000 and 2006 in cities of the Czech Republic, Germany, Poland, Russia, and Slovenia. *European Journal on Criminal Policy and Research, 16*, 191–205.

Ginter, J. (2000). *The School Sadists: The horror of Bullying in Czech schools*. Pravo 27 May.

Görgen, T., Evenepoel, A., Kraus, B., & Taefi, A. (2013). Prevention of juvenile crime and deviance: Adolescents' and experts' views in an international perspective. *Varstvoslovje: Journal of Criminal Justice & Security, 4*, 531–550.

Gruszczynska, B. (2004). Crime in Central and Eastern European countries in the enlarged Europe. *European Journal on Criminal Policy and Research, 10*, 123–136.

Gruszczynska, B., & Gruszczynski, M. (2005). Crime in enlarged Europe: Comparison of crime rates and victimization risks. *Transition Studies Review, 12*(2), 337–345.
Gruszczyńska, B., & Heiskanen, M. (2012). Trends in police-recorded offences. *European Journal on Criminal Policy and Research, 18*, 83–102.
Habzda-Siwek, E., & Grzyb, M. (2013). Płeć a przestępczość. O problemie dysproporcji płci wśród sprawców przestępstw z użyciem przemocy [Crime and gender: The gender ratio of violent offenders]. *Archiwum Kryminologii, 35*, 95–136.
Home Office. (2006). *Crime in England and Wales 2006/2007*.
HRR: Czech. (2011). *2011 Human Right Report: Czech Republic*. Retrieved from: http://www.state.gov/j/drl/rls/hrrpt/2011/eur/186344.htm [June 2014].
HRR: Czech. (2013). *2013 Human Right Report: Czech Republic*. Retrieved from: http://www.state.gov/j/drl/rls/hrrpt/humanrightsreport/index.htm#wrapper [June 2014].
HRR: Hungary. (2011). *2011 Human Right Report: Hungary*. Retrieved from: http://www.state.gov/j/drl/rls/hrrpt/2011/eur/186359.htm [June 2014].
Hungarian Ombudsman. (2012). *Child-friendly justice. From the Ombudsman's Perspective*. Retrieved from: http://www.ajbh.hu/documents/14315/131278/Child-friendly+justice+from+the+Hungarian+Ombudsman's+perspective/53bc5136-3d2a-40d2-b576-2ea6a5b2f979;jsessionid=7B4B101C32C12C5E1F0B846344B3C7FD?version=1.0 [June 2014].
Jewkes, Y. (2010). *Media and crime*. Sage.
Junger-Tas, J., Marshall, I. H., Enzmann, D., Kilias, M., Steketee, B., Gruszczynska, B., et al. (2012). *The many faces of youth crime. Contrasting theoretical perspectives on juvenile delinquency across countries and cultures*. Springer.
Kerezsi, K. (2014). Challenges of criminality in Hungary: Anything new under the sun? *Proceedings of Criminology, 73*, 13–29.
Kerezsi, K., & Lévay, M. (2008). Criminology, crime and criminal justice in Hungary. *European Journal of Criminology, 5*(2), 239–260.
Kirwil, L. (2004). Changes in the structure of crime during the transition period in Poland. *International Journal of Sociology, 34*(3), 48–82.
Klaus, W. (2009). *Dziecko przed sądem. Wymiar sprawiedliwości wobec przestępczości młodszych nieletnich* [Children before the courts: The justice system and young juveniles]. Warsaw.
Klaus, W. (2015). Preventing criminality – The social policy of preventing social exclusion. In K. Buczkowski, B. Czarnecka-Dzialuk, W. Klaus, A. Kossowska, I. Rzeplińska, P. Wiktorska, D. Woźniakowska-Fajst, & D. Wójcik, *Criminality and criminal justice in contemporary Poland: Sociopolitical perspectives*. Ashgate.
Klaus, W., Rzeplińska, I., & Woźniakowska-Fajst, D. (2011). Punitivity in Polish law, public opinion, and penal policy. In H. Kury & E. Shea (Eds.), *Insecurity and punitiveness* (pp. 245–268). Bochum.
Komendant-Brodowska, A., Giza-Poleszczuk, A., & Baczko-Dombi, A. (2011). *Przemoc w szkole. Raport z badań "Szkoła bez przemocy"* [Violence in school: A "School Without Violence" report]. Retrieved from: http://www.scdn.pl/images/stories/RAPORTY2011/24.pdf [June 2014].
Konviser, B. (2007). *Czech Bill On Child Porn Faces Resistance*. Washington Post 3 September 2007.
Kossowska, A. (2007). Obraz przestępczości współczesnej młodzieży [The criminality of contemporary youth]. In K. Krajewski (Ed.), *Nauki penalne wobec problemów współczesnej przestępczości [Penal studies on the problems of contemporary crime]* (pp. 447–456). Kraków: Wolters Kluwer.
Kossowska, A. (2015). Social change and criminality – Mutual relationships, determinants and implications. In K. Buczkowski, B. Czarnecka-Dzialuk, W. Klaus, A. Kossowska, I. Rzeplińska, P. Wiktorska, D. Woźniakowska-Fajst, & D. Wójcik, *Criminality and criminal justice in contemporary Poland: Sociopolitical perspectives*. Ashgate.

Kossowska, A., Buczkowski, K., Klaus, W., Rzeplińska, I., & Woźniakowska-Fajst, D. (2012). The role of politicians and the media in society's perception of crime. In A. Šelih & A. Završnik (Eds.), *Crime and transition in Central and Eastern Europe* (pp. 37–63). Springer.
Kossowska, A., Krawczyk, J., & Rzeplińska, I. (1995). Zachowania dewiacyjne młodzieży w Warszawie w 1993 r. (Self-report study) [The deviant behaviour of Warsaw youth in 1993 (Self-report study)]. *Archiwum Kryminologii, 21*, 81–103.
Kossowska, A., Rzeplińska, I., Woźniakowska, D., & Klaus, W. (2008). Criminal policy based on fear of crime (Case of Poland). In H. Kury (Ed.), *Fear of crime – Punitivity, new developments in theory and research* (pp. 371–391). Bochum: Universitätsverlag Brockmeyer.
Krajewski, K. (1996). Fear of crime and criminal law reform in post-communist societies. In: B. Szamota-Saeki & D. Wójcik (Eds.), *Impact of political, economic and social change on crime and its image in society* (pp. 147–155). Warsaw.
Krajewski, K. (2001). Przemoc w doświadczeniach życiowych młodzieży. In A. Gaberle (Ed.), *Przestępczość i zachowania dewiacyjne dzieci i młodzieży w Krakowie* [Crime and deviant behaviour in Kraków children and youth] (pp. 111–194). Zakamycze.
Krajewski, K. (2004). Crime and criminal justice in Poland. *European Journal of Criminology, 1*(3), 377–407.
Kühn, G. (2014). Komercyjne wykorzystywanie seksualne dzieci w kontekście podróży i turystyki [Commercial sexual exploitation of children in travel and tourism]. *Dziecko Krzywdzone 13*(1), 11–32.
Kurzępa, J. (2010). *Młodzież pogranicza – "świnki", czyli o prostytucji nieletnich* [Borderland youth – On teenage prostitution]. Impuls.
Lévay, M. (2012). Penal policy, crime and political change. In A. Šelih & A. Završnik (Eds.), *Crime and transition in Central and Eastern Europe* (pp. 117–153). Springer.
Neubacher, F., Walter, M., Válková, H., & Krajewski, K. (1999). Juvenile delinquency in Central European cities: A comparison of registration and processing structures in the 1990s. *European Journal on Criminal Policy and Research, 7*, 533–558.
Poremska, M. (2008). Child pornography on the Internet in Central Europe. *Masaryk University Journal of Law and Technology, 1*, 105–117.
PREVNet. (2009). *Bullying: Cross-cultural consistency*. Retrieved from: http://www.prevnet.ca/sites/prevnet.ca/files/fact-sheet/PREVNet-SAMHSA-Fachsheet-Bullying-Cross-Cultural-Consistencies.pdf [June 2014].
Rozum, J., Kotulan, P., & Tomasek, J. (2006). Robberies in Prague. *European Journal on Criminal Policy and Research, 12*, 49–60.
Rzeplińska, I. (2007). Nieletni skazani w warunkach art. 10 § 2 k.k. [Juveniles Convicted Pursuant to Art. 10 § 2 of the Criminal Code]. In K. Krajewski (Ed.), *Nauki penalne wobec problemów współczesnej przestępczości* [Penal studies and the problems of contemporary offences] (pp. 507–518). Kraków.
Sajkowska, M. (2002). Wykorzystywanie seksualne dzieci. Ustalenia terminologiczne, skala zjawiska, oblicza problemu społecznego [Sexual exploitation of children: The terminological determinations, scale and face of a social issue]. *Dziecko Krzywdzone, 1*, 5–28.
Šelih, A. (2012). Crime and crime control in transition countries. In A. Šelih & A. Završnik (Eds.), *Crime and transition in Central and Eastern Europe* (pp. 3–34). Springer.
Siegel, L., & Senna, J. (2007). *Introduction to criminal justice*. Thompson Wandsworth.
Smit, P., Van Eijk, A., & Decae, R. (2012). Trends in the reaction on crime in criminal justice systems in Europe in 1990–2007: A comparison of four European regions. *European Journal on Criminal Policy and Research, 18*, 55–82.
Staff, P. F. (2004). *Europe Tackles Pedophilia Cases; Belgium's Long-Awaited Trial of Dutroux is just One Example of a Larger Pedophilia Problem, from Portugal to the Czech Republic*. The Christian Science Monitor 9 March 2004.
Stańdo-Kawecka, B. (2010). Poland. In F. Dünkel, J. Grzywa, P. Horsfield, & I. Pruin (Eds.), *Juvenile justice systems in Europe: Current situation and reform developments* (pp. 991–1026). Forum Verlag Godesberg.

Steketee, M., & Gruszczyńska, B. (2010). Juvenile delinquency in six new EU member states. *European Journal on Criminal Policy and Research, 16*, 111–125.

Steketee, M., Moll, M., Kapardis, A., Buriánek, J., Dekleva, B., Gruszczyńska, B., et al. (Eds.). (2008). *Juvenile delinquency in six new EU member states: Crime, risky behavior and victimization in the capital cities of Cyprus, Czech Republic, Estonia, Lithuania, Poland and Slovenia*. Verwey-Jonker Instituut.

Szabo, C. (1996). *Child prostitution growing in region: Sex tourism is fueling trend, police say*. Budapest Sun 5 September 1996.

UN. (2010). *Manual on victimization surveys*. Geneva.

Válková, H., & Hulmáková, J. (2010). Czech Republic. In F. Dünkel, J. Grzywa, P. Horsfield, & I. Pruin (Eds.), *Juvenile justice systems in Europe: Current situation and reform developments* (pp. 253–304). Forum Verlag Godesberg.

Válková, J. (1995). The impact of socio-economic changes on crime in the Czech Republic. In B. Szamota-Saeki & D. Wójcik (Eds.), *Impact of political, economic and social change on crime and its image in society* (pp. 45–59). Warsaw.

Van Dijk, J. (2010). The international crime victims survey. In M. Herzog-Evans (Ed.), *Transnational criminology manual* (Vol. 2, pp. 631–650). Nijmegen: Wolf Legal Publishers.

Van Dijk, J., Manchin, R., Van Kesteren, J., & Hideg, G. (2007a). *The burden of crime in the EU, a comparative analysis of the European Survey of Crime and Safety (2005 EU ICS)*. Brussels, Gallup Europe.

Van Dijk, J., Tseloni, A., & Farell, G. (2012). Conclusions – Understanding international crime trends: A summing up. In J. Van Dijk, A. Tseloni, & G. Farrell (Eds.), *The international crime drop: New directions in research* (pp. 300–320). Palgrave Macmillan.

Van Dijk, J., Van Kesteren, J., & Smit, P. (2007b). *Criminal victimisation in international perspective: Key findings from the 2004–2005 ICVS and EU ICS*. WODC.

Váradi-Csema, E. (2010). Hungary. In F. Dünkel, J. Grzywa, P. Horsfield, & I. Pruin (Eds.), *Juvenile justice systems in Europe: Current situation and reform developments* (pp. 671–720). Forum Verlag Godesberg.

Vazsonyi, A. T., Pickering, L. E., Belliston, L. M., Hessing, D., & Junger, M. (2002). Routine activities and deviant behaviors: American, Dutch, Hungarian, and Swiss Youth. *Journal of Quantitative Criminology, 18*(4), 397–422.

Večerka, K. (2005). Juvenile offenders at the turn of the millennium. In Z. Karabec & M. Scheinost (Eds.), *Selected results of research activities of ICSP in the years 2002–2004* (pp. 121–129). Prague: Institute of Criminology and Social Prevention. Retrieved from: http://www.ok.cz/iksp/docs/316.pdf [2 June 2014].

Večerka, K. (2009). Youth in a criminological perspective. In M. Scheinost (Ed.), *Selected results of research activities of ICSP in the years 2002–2004* (pp. 116–125). Prague: Institute of Criminology and Social Prevention. Retrieved from: http://www.ok.cz/iksp/docs/359.pdf [2 June 2014].

Włodarczyk, J., & Hamela, M. (2011). *Komercyjne wykorzystywanie seksualne dzieci i młodzieży. Postawy wobec problemu* [Commercial sexual exploitation of children and young people: Attitudes to the problem]. Warsaw. Retrieved from: http://fdn.pl/badania-postaw [June 2014].

Wójcik, D., Buczkowski, K., Czabański, J., & Jankowski, M. (2008). Wymiar sprawiedliwości wobec nieletnich w wybranych krajach [Justice for juveniles in selected countries]. *Prawo w działaniu, 3*, 187–240.

Woźniakowska-Fajst. (2010). *Nieletnie. Niebezpieczne, niegrzeczne, niegroźne?* [Underage, dangerous, naughty and harmless?]. Warsaw.

Żabczyńska, E. (1983). *Przestępczość dzieci. Etiologia i rozwój* [Child criminality: Aetiology and development]. Warsaw.

Sexual Abuse of Children in Comparative and International Perspective

Rossella Selmini

Abstract Child sexual abuse (CSA) is a chronic problem that can occur in any family or any country. National governments, international organizations, and non-governmental organizations have given it increasingly high priority in recent decades. Scholars also have given CSA increased attention though more at clinical case-study than at policy levels. Some basic epidemiological conclusions can be drawn. Girls are at considerably greater CSA risk than boys, but in some places boys also experience high levels of victimization. Perpetrators are much more likely to be male than female, and family members or acquaintances than strangers. Victimization is not only by adults but also by young people. Cross-national knowledge is underdeveloped. Comparative studies are rare, partly because they are expensive and complicated to organize but also because of fundamental differences in legal and research definitions of the behaviours studied. Only a few countries have successfully established long-term surveys and data series that provide a solid empirical basis for describing CSA and changes in its nature, prevalence, and incidence. The US data provide a firm basis for concluding that the incidence of CSA in that country has dropped substantially since the early 1990s in parallel with drops in rates of violence generally and sex crimes specifically. The CSA research mission is to build the tools and infrastructure to learn what is happening today, and has happened over time, cross-nationally and in all individual countries, in order to develop better policies at the national and international level.

1 Introduction

Sexual assaults against children and young people became in recent decades a major governmental concern throughout the world, the European Union, international organizations (especially the United Nations) and the non-governmental organizations (NGOs). Many hundreds of campaigns and preventive programmes

---

R. Selmini (✉)
University of Minnesota, Minneapolis, MN, USA
e-mail: rselmini@umn.edu

H. Kury et al. (eds.), *Women and Children as Victims and Offenders: Background, Prevention, Reintegration*, DOI 10.1007/978-3-319-08398-8_29

have been launched in the last 30 years to reduce sexual violence against children—in its different forms—and to improve children's well-being. Violence against women and against children are now definitively global issues, and their conceptualization as human rights issues helped raise public, media, and institutional attention and concern for the wellbeing of succeeding generation. Sexual violence against women and children is increasingly understood to be an intolerable behaviour in more and more contexts and it has been criminalized by many countries around the world (Frank et al. 2009).

Despite widespread public concern and a remarkable number of studies and reports on the subject, scientific knowledge on rape of young people and children sexual abuse generally remains limited at national and international levels. Cross-national studies are impaired by a paucity of reliable data, as a result of differing legal and cultural definitions of the phenomena. Like many other forms of violence that relate to domestic settings[1] and to behaviours that are not easy to talk about—many abusive sexual incidents are never reported to the criminal justice and welfare systems. Crimes against dependent people, such as children and the elderly, are more affected than many other crimes by the problem of the dark number. The true number of incidents is unknown and unknowable, partly because victims are insufficiently autonomous to disclose their victimizations to official institutions and agencies.

In this article I explore several issues related to rape and sexual abuse of children, starting with an attempt to define the kinds of behaviours that should be considered to be child sexual abuse (CSA). I then discuss the characteristics of the data available for a better understanding of the problem and major methodological issues that bedevil efforts to understand and document it nationally and internationally. Some national cases, concerning which research on sexual violence against children is more advanced, are examined, as is the relevant research literature, in order to summarize knowledge about the problem and the most important risk factors. I then focus on knowledge concerning CSA trends and the recent sharp declines in the United States. The latter has important scientific and political implications. Some suggestions for improvement of future research conclude the article.

2 Definitions of Child Sexual Abuse

Child sexual abuse is one sub-category in the broader category of child maltreatment and abuse. A broad definition encompasses many criminal behaviours. Definitions of CSA vary from very general to very detailed, and from narrower to broader. A short and general definition that focuses on the intentionality of the

[1] Rape and sexual abuse occur in diverse settings and not only in the family. However, in many countries the majority of cases of child sexual abuse is perpetrated in the family.

perpetrator and on the age of the victim is offered, for instance, by Bolen and Gergely (2014, p. 59): "the wilful violation of an underage child." According to the World Health Organization (WHO), sexual abuse can be defined as "the involvement of a child in sexual activity that he or she does not fully comprehend, is unable to give informed consent or for which the child is not developmentally prepared, or else that violates the laws or social taboos of society" (quoted in Williams and Weeks 2014, p. 15). This definition is much more detailed, the element of "age" is translated in practical examples, and it takes into account that behaviours may have different social and cultural meanings.

Many years ago, Finkelhor defined child sexual abuse as "sexual contact with a child that occurs as result of force or in a relationship where it is exploitative because of an age difference or caretaking responsibility" (Finkelhor 1991, p. 79). This definition remains timely, and like the WHO definition captures different aspects of the phenomenon.

One of these aspects, and a critical one, is age. The age at which a child is able to give consent differs from country to country and is defined by national legislations. This age is usually 18, but in many countries it is earlier, at 16 or 14, or even 12. This aspect of CSA is strongly related to different legal traditions and cultural practices and it becomes critical to keep in mind when we need to compare CSA across countries.[2] Age is also important because different forms of CSA occur more frequently at different stages in childhood.

The category of CSA includes a wide range of different behaviours, not all of which in many places are legally defined as crimes. Though almost all forms of CSA are serious and have serious consequences, the most brutal behaviour included in CSA is rape, which implies sexual contacts with penetration (vaginal, oral, or anal). Differently from adults, for whom issues of consent and of threats or use of force are pertinent legally and practically, for children, in all countries' criminal laws, any unlawful sexual intercourse or intrusion is rape.

Other forms of CSA—also defined as sexual molestation—are sexual activities with a child with physical contact (kissing, touching outside the clothing). In a broader concept, sexual activities without contact (verbal sexual molestation, indecent exposure, etc.) are considered abusive. In short, CSA—in many legal, scientific, and common sense definitions—usually includes rape, other sexual activities with physical contact, and sexual activities without contact and without consent.

Another important aspect of CSA is the perpetrator's characteristics. Sexual activity, in Finkelhor's definition, includes forced rape, but also any other forms of sexual contacts between a child and an adult or a peer. In the United States, when this definition was offered, there was at the time a tendency to restrict the definition of sexual abuse by limiting the categories of perpetrators (only adults against children, for instance, or only caretakers but not strangers). Over the years, this

[2] Even in the same country, as in the United States, there are legal differences across states about ages of victims.

narrower approach to sexual abuse disappeared and there is now in the United States general agreement that the CSA category should not be limited by characteristics of perpetrators. Therefore, sexual abuse can be perpetrated by peers or adults; by parents, relatives, friends, or strangers; by caregivers, or by other people who do not have any responsibility for the children. Rape may be committed by unknown perpetrators or by parents, step-parents, friends, relative, or acquaintances. Rapes or unwanted sexual contacts or molestations may also be committed by teachers or members of staffs of residential facilities and detention centres, and in settings different from home, including schools, religious institutions, and shelters.

That peers or other young people can perpetrate CSA is a relatively new and important acknowledgment in studies in this field. It helped change ideas about CSA as an activity perpetrated only or almost exclusively by adult perpetrators in positions of authority.

It should be clear by this point that the conceptualization of CSA is undergoing a process of enlargement that includes above all the characteristics of perpetrators and the kinds of behaviours at issue. From theoretical, empirical, and practical points of view, this is one of the most important recent developments in efforts to understand, document, and prevent this form of child abuse.[3] Over the years, understanding of the problem of sexual violence has changed remarkably, moving from prototypical cases of a family member sexually assaulting a child in an intimate setting or assault by an unknown molester in the neighbourhood to broader formulations that include peer relationships and more organized and less intimate contexts, where children's right are violated in different ways and where children are subjected to intolerable forms of violence.

3 Changing Contexts and Forms of CSA

Social change and global social problems affect CSA as they do many other criminal or violent behaviours. Global processes, such as national and international migrations, wars, religious conflicts, conflicts between traditional practices and new values of human rights, and the enormous changes that new technology has brought into interpersonal relationships, are affecting CSA. These broader processes necessitate a new conceptualization of CSA that reconsiders both the contexts in which CSA occurs and the kind of behaviours it should incorporate in our time.

In the following pages I consider the *contexts* in which CSA occurs and then examine some new—or relatively new—*forms* of CSA related to the processes that

[3] It is worth noting that the broadening process has also occurred for several decades in relation to the concept of child maltreatment in general, with the inclusion of new behaviours that are now considered (and increasingly criminalized) as child abuse, such as neglect, emotional abuse, and exposing children to other forms of family violence.

I just described. Forms and contexts of CSA are strongly interconnected and sometimes some of these new behaviours overlap. For instance, commercial sexual exploitation of children can occur in the family, on the Internet, or in the context of migrant trafficking. Child pornography can be considered as a separate form of CSA, but there is little doubt that most of its occurrence is related to commercial sexual exploitation of children. Categorization and conceptualization of CSA is an increasingly challenging task, especially if the complexities that are emerging have to be considered on a global scale.

3.1 CSA in the Family

According to a United Nations report on violence against children, CSA—like overall child abuse –can be analysed according to the different main contexts in which it occurs: the family, the educational system, other institutions like care and detention centres, the workplace, and the community (Pinheiro 2006).

The family is the context in which sexual violence against children was first investigated and at which, above all in the past, the interventions of government and agencies were mostly addressed. This context remains the most important for understanding CSA, although, as already mentioned, other places where children spend their lives—or their time, as in the case of the Internet—are becoming increasingly relevant. CSA in the family is characterized by the domestic setting and by known perpetrators (parents, step-parents, relatives, fiends) and it affects more girls than boys. Risk for this form of CSA increases with gender (girls) and age (older children). The concept of "family" for CSA is a broad one and mostly identifies a domestic setting, with perpetrators that include also relatives and friends.

Globalization and the reconceptualization of CSA in terms of human rights have broadened the concept of sexual abuse in the family to embrace practices that are common in some countries but that are now usually considered a violation of human rights and have been condemned and stigmatized by many governments, international agencies, NGOs, and advocacy groups. These include forced early marriages and genital mutilations.

Child marriages are forms of CSA because they facilitate sexual contact of an adult with a child and can therefore be seen as a form of "persuasion, inducement, enticement, or coercion of a child to engage in sexually explicit conduct" (Williams and Weeks 2014, p. 17). In this case, sexual abuse of children may overlap with commercial sexual exploitation, because sometime forced sex with family members and early marriages are the outcome of contractual agreements between families in which children are treated as commodities.

A 2014 UNICEF report estimates that 700 million women now alive were married when they were younger than 18, and about 250 million when they were younger than 15. Early marriages are a critical issue in some specific areas of the world, including South Asia and sub-Saharan Africa, where are located the

10 countries with the highest rates of early marriage in the world. Early marriages are disproportionately higher for young girls (who are often married to much older adults) than for boys, though even males in many countries are married while still children in family-arranged marriages. Poor girls of rural areas are most at risk of early marriage (UNICEF 2014).

Genital mutilations are also widely considered a form of CSA which affect young girls in some areas of the world.[4] In 29 countries, almost all concentrated in Central and Eastern Africa, 125 million of women living today are estimated to have been mutilated (UNICEF 2013). The real figure is still unknown. Research in this field has improved a great deal in recent years and we know much more than formerly about this practice that is at the same time a form of gender violence and a form of child abuse.[5]

3.2 CSA in Institutions and in the Community

Reports of the United Nations and of the World Health Organization also direct public attention toward sexual violence in educational settings. This seems to be a serious problem above all in schools in Africa, Central America, and some areas of Asia (Pinheiro 2006). In Africa the problem of violence in school is reported by many different sources and seems to be widespread and especially dangerous in relation to diffusion of HIV, extreme brutality, and societal blaming and stigmatisation of victims (Pinheiro 2006). Little systematic information is available on sexual violence against children in religious school or boards, although recent press news that raise the issue have generated widespread concern and debate among the public.

One more context where children and adolescents may be victims of rape and forced sexual activity are diverse institutions and residential care facilities for abandoned children, children in detention centres, and children in prison in countries were criminal institutionalization of young people is permitted. In these contexts, children can suffer from violence by other young or older inmates and by institutional personnel. The phenomenon is largely undocumented and unmeasured, since these institutions, much more than schools or similar settings,

---

[4] Although studies and reports available on this problem focus only on female genital mutilations, there is an increasing and very controversial debate about other practices that are seen by some as forms of genital mutilation for boys, including male circumcision (Williams and Weeks 2014, p. 16).

[5] Pinheiro (2006) estimates that 100–140 million girls have been subjected to a form of genital mutilation in the world. UNICEF (2013) reports many detailed findings and rates, above all for African countries, such as Egypt, Sudan, and Somalia, where the highest percentages of women have been mutilated (respectively 91 %, 88 %, and 99 %). Many communities from these countries continue with this practice after migration to Europe or North America. Figures on this transplanted tradition are largely unknown.

are unregulated and difficult for external authorities to monitor. Victims have no contacts with the outside world that allow them to disclose their experiences.[6]

Finally, children and adolescents suffer sexual violence and rape in the world outside, or, as a UN report by Pinheiro (2006) defines it, in "the community." This context includes cases of rape and sexual violence by strangers, dating violence, and other sexual abuse by peers. All these forms of violence are more common for young adolescents then for children. Dating violence, which includes rape and sexual abuse, occurs in the context of dating or courting relationships and involves adolescents between 12 and 18, though some studies also take into consideration older teens and young adults. There is increasing concern about sexual violence among adolescents especially in industrialized countries where contacts between boys and girls are not forbidden by cultural or religious traditions (Pinheiro 2006). Data on this phenomenon are available only for some few areas, above all North America and to a lesser extent Europe. This form of sexual abuse is at the border between child and gender abuse.

In less industrialized countries, and especially in Asia and South America, but also in some Eastern European countries, sexual abuse of children in the community is mostly related to violence by strangers and particularly affects more vulnerable groups, such as young girls and boys living in the streets. These children are also more at risk of commercial sexual exploitation and being trafficked for sexual purposes. Knowledge of CSA in the community is scant, and no systematic data are available or gathered (Pinheiro 2006).

3.3 CSA in New and Old Forms

The concept of CSA is becoming increasingly broader. In recent times sexual abuse of children has taken different forms, and new ways to exploit children have been discovered. Better knowledge of what occurs in a wide range of countries, as a by-product of globalization processes and a product of persistent campaigns by international agencies, has led to greater knowledge of practices and behaviours that, according to prevailing sensibilities, are considered CSA. Examples include the above-mentioned cases of child marriages and genital mutilations. Some transnational phenomena, like increased migration and related forms of transnational crime, have increased the risk for some groups of children involved in national and international migration processes. Finally, new technologies offer new opportunities and new modalities for CSA throughout the world. Commercial sexual exploitation of children, pornography, and child prostitution are new or greatly expanded forms of CSA that are characterized by their occurrence more often in the world

[6] There are in the world an estimated 8 million young people in institutional care (Pinheiro 2006). Although it is impossible to estimate the cases of sexual violence, it is reasonable to assume that rape and sexual abuse affect a remarkable number of children in this situation.

outside the family or in the world of the Internet.[7] "New" is not entirely correct, because, sexual exploitation of children, child pornography and child prostitution are not "new" phenomena: what is different from the past is that there are new modalities for involving children in these crimes and that we know much more about their worldwide diffusion. I first examine CSA on the Internet, because it is in this context that many of these forms of CSA can occur.

3.3.1 CSA Online

Online sexual abuse is a broad category that includes many different behaviours and that often overlaps with—or is conducive to—other forms of CSA. Children and teen agers are increasingly involved in sexual violence online. Its character has changed radically in the past decade (Richardson 2011). The traditional images of a child's picture stolen for the market of pornography or of sexual offenders who try to contact children through the web no longer capture the multifaceted varieties of sexual violence against children online. The different harms that can affect children when using new technologies have been recently conceptualized in three different forms: online harm from content (when children are passively exposed to pornographic materials); online harm from contact, which occurs when the child is targeted as a participant by an adult or another child in activities that represent forms of sexual abuse; and harm as a result of online conduct, as when the child undertakes risky behaviours creating or uploading images or pornographic materials, or when the child actively contacts people online (Livingstone and Haddon 2009; UNICEF 2011).

The Internet enables easier and faster distribution of materials and communications within paedophile communities (Kloess et al. 2014). It also makes kids more independent and able actively to be involved in risky behaviours. Traditional risky behaviours are now paralleled by new behaviours in which the roles of victims and perpetrators are blurred. Online sexual violence, thus, now refers to a wide range of behaviours that include sexting (the sharing of sexualized images or text through mobile phones or similar devices), usually because of peer pressure or for financial gain, grooming, and bullying, all potentially conducive to sexual exploitation and prostitution (Richardson 2011, p. 289; Mitchell et al. 2007). It has been said that in the artificial and virtual world of Internet, "Sexual violence can be seen as a spiral rather than as a spectrum of different types of isolated acts" (Richardson 2011, p. 290).

A UNICEF (2011) report observes that risks increase not only when children use the Internet at home without supervision, but also in countries where it is not commonly available at home, especially in poor families. Children use Internet

[7] Yet, the boundaries between home and family contexts and extra domestic settings are often unclear, as in cases of child pornography committed by parents or relatives or through the Internet and social networks.

cafes, where the possibility of a real, physical contact with a potential perpetrator is higher. Smartphones also increase the risk of children's involvement in sexual abuse because of larger autonomy in use of cell phones compared with computers (UNICEF 2011). Yet, the risk is higher in Europe and North America, the contexts where we can also find some empirical analysis of this—relatively—new phenomenon.

A survey of risks European teenagers are exposed to online shows that 50 % are potentially at risk of grooming and dangerous contacts because of disclosure of private information, of seeing pornography (40 %), of seeing violent or hateful content (33 %), of being bullied, harassed, or stalked (17–20 %), of receiving unwanted sexual comments (10 %), and (the most dangerous) of meeting an online contact offline (8 %) (Richardson 2011).

In the US, an emerging body of literature and research is addressing new challenges that characterize sexual abuse. A Youth Internet Safety Survey was launched by the Crime against Children Research Centre (CCRC) in 1999–2000, repeated in 2005, and again in 2010. The CCRC survey tracks the number and characteristics of threats against young people that can occur when using new technologies. Examples include unwanted sexual solicitations, aggressive solicitation, distressing sexual solicitations, cyber-bullying, unwanted exposure to sexual materials, and sexting. The most recent report on trends shows that some of these behaviours have decreased since 1999 (including unwanted sexual solicitations and distressing sexual solicitations) and others including sexting are stable or increasing (Mitchell et al. 2014).

A recent report on Europe shows that, despite concerns about online sexual abuse, its risk is much less relevant than for other forms of CSA, and that online risks are real, but less important than risks at home, in school, and in the community (Livingstone and Smith 2014).[8]

The following forms of CSA are connected to online abuse. The Internet increased remarkably the opportunities for perpetration of these criminal behaviours.

3.3.2 Commercial Sexual Exploitation

Definitions of commercial sexual exploitation of children (CSEC) may be narrower or broader. One broader and clear definition is offered by Mitchell and Jones (2013, p. 1): "sexual exploitation of a child that occurs at least in part for the financial or economic gain of a particular party." The economic gain may also be non-monetary (e.g. food, protection).

[8] A comment on this report by Finkelhor (2014, p. 655) raises interesting issues—from scientific and policy perspective—on the "alarmist narrative" that surrounds online CSA and urges a more critical and scientific approach.

Here is a more detailed definition: "Such exploitation is the sexual abuse by an adult or by a peer of a person under the age of 18, and remuneration in cash or in kind to the child or to a third person or persons. The child is treated as a sexual object and as a commercial object. The child may be used for prostitution or for the making of pornography. The commercial sexual exploitation of children constitutes a form of coercion and violence against children, and amounts to forced labour and a contemporary form of slavery" (O Briain 2006, p. 7).

Under this "umbrella" are crimes like the production and sale of child pornography, juvenile prostitution, and the trafficking of children for sexual purposes. Mitchell and Jones (2013, p. 2) remind us that, looking internationally, we can find other forms of commercial sexual exploitation of children These include the mail-order bride-trade, early forced marriages, and young people working in sex clubs.

There is not much information on these phenomena. The National Online Victimization Study conducted in the United States by the CCRC found that many offenders know their victims (39 %), and 23 % were family members, while only 17 % were met online. The rest were pimps. These forms of abuse nonetheless can be related to organized crime, or to the Internet.[9] Victims of these crimes are often troubled kids, with a story of irregular conduct, running away from home, or dropping out of school frequently. Compared with victims of non-commercial sexual exploitation, these young people and children may suffer additional violence, like being assaulted, being compelled to participate in child pornography, or being given drugs and alcohol (Mitchell and Jones 2013).

Behaviours usually included in commercial sexual exploitation of children are juvenile prostitution, child pornography, and trafficking of young people for sexual purposes. Juvenile prostitution—not necessarily related to use of the Internet—encompasses a variety of situations, all characterized by exchanges of money or other goods and sex (Mitchell and Jones 2013). Knowledge about organized, pimp-led networks of prostitution is low. Individual juvenile prostitution is better investigated through self-report studies or use of other quantitative surveys. Prostitution of children and adolescents can be transnational, as in the case of sex tourism (Berardi 2011). Trafficking in child pornography may be organized by individuals acting alone or as part of organized networks that involve many. Systematic knowledge of this phenomenon is low and most cases are only discovered through police investigations.

Trafficking of children for sexual purposes has for many years received attention from international agencies and national governments, alongside with the general problem of trafficking. Many actions have been taken to fight against this crime at

[9] A detailed in-depth study of sexual exploitation of children online (both commercial and not) describes behaviours, patterns, and stages of this form of CSA (Kloess et al. 2014).

international and national levels.[10] Once again, however, it is remarkably difficult to find reliable and detailed information on this form of sexual exploitation of children.[11] Often it is the result or even the origin of a trafficking operation (O Briain 2006, p. 7). In 2012 there were estimated to be 35 million migrant children in the world (UNICEF, quoted by McLeigh 2013, p. 1062). Sexual exploitation is a serious risk above all for children of minorities and children who are undocumented. Sexual exploitation can be the primary purposes of trafficking, or trafficking for other purposes can end up, especially for girls, in sexual exploitation (Dottridge 2008, p. 15).

More reliable estimates of human trafficking have been available since the beginning of 2000. However, usually these statistics do not distinguish among the different purposes of trafficking (and therefore information on sexual purposes is missing) or there are no data on the ages of trafficked persons. Many countries carry on national studies but use different definitions, and thus make comparison across countries impossible. We know that trafficking of children is an important national and global issue. However we do not know whether it is increasing or decreasing, and we know very little about the characteristic of victims, perpetrators, and events despite efforts by many researchers and organizations to find relevant information.[12] There is general agreement that trafficking is especially a problem for children in some countries and regions, for children living in the street or from poor backgrounds, and for children of ethnic minorities. Trafficking in children generally, and for sexual purposes in particular, are mostly problems for the most vulnerable children in the most underdeveloped areas of the world, and in areas in which there are racial, ethnic, or other violent conflicts and wars.

4 Doing Research on CSA

The main problem in understanding rape and sexual abuse of children internationally is related to the limited availability and questionable reliability of sources of information. These problems concerning children are worse than for rape and

[10] See the *Optional Protocol to the UN Convention on the Rights of the Child on the sale of children, child prostitution, and child pornography* and the *UN Protocol to Prevent, Suppress, and Punish Trafficking in Persons, Especially Women and Children* (the "*UN Trafficking Protocol*", also known as the "*Palermo Protocol*"), supplementing the UN *Convention against Transnational Organized Crime*. After 2000, when these UN documents were issued, many states reformed their legislation to meet the standards required by the UN documents. At the European level, the Council of Europe Convention on Action against Trafficking in Human Beings, adopted in 2005, warrants mention.

[11] According to O'Connell Davidson (2013, p. 1073) the number of trafficked children is impossible to measure and we need to be extremely cautious about accepting estimates and figures commonly offered.

[12] See for instance the attempt to offer more detailed information on the characteristics of victims, perpetrators, and trafficking schemes in O Briain (2006).

sexual abuse of adults, because the dark number is presumably much higher and the variety of legal definitions in different countries is larger than for other crimes.

Rape and sexual abuse against adults are among the most underreported crimes. However, the same crimes committed against children are probably much more underreported. For children, disclosure of abusive sexual experiences with a known—and even more with an unknown—person, is much harder than for adults. Reporting is hard for adult victims of sexual violence because they are ashamed, fearful, worried about not being believed, or fearful of retaliation, or they do not trust the police. Many of these motivations are also present for child victims, but the most important reason why sexual violence against children is largely unknown to official institutions is because of the age of the victims. That affects both their capacity to look for protection from an official agency and their emotional vulnerability.

Many countries have developed strategies to encourage victims to report sexual crimes: in the case of children, these strategies are more complicated and are usually based on reinforcing the likelihood that reliable third parties will report. The establishment of a network of reliable third parties (usually family doctors, pediatricians, social welfare agents, teachers, and similar professional) proved to be very successful in unveiling cases of sexual abuse and in offering additional information on the subject (Brosig and Kalichman 1992; Kalichman 1999).

The global CSA literature is enormous, yet the national and international knowledge is still very limited. Comparison across countries is a complex task because of the lack of standardized, common protocols and guidelines for the gathering of data on CSA. Official statistics—sexual abuses and rapes reported to the police—are extremely limited because of underreporting and, at the international level, by differences in legal definitions and statistical recording procedures.

Epidemiological studies, though very important for better understanding, are in most cases based on different concepts and methodologies and are not comparable across time or space. Many studies are based on the prevalence of child sexual abuse, that is, on the fraction of population that experienced sexual abuse during childhood. Other studies are based on the incidence, that is, on cases of child abuse in a specific period—usually the year before the investigation. Still other studies are based on small, one-time clinical samples. Some are based on public health approaches. Some deal with CSA in the general context of child maltreatment (this is typically what happens in national studies based on welfare agency data) or in the context of violence in the family.[13]

Synthesizing this huge range of empirical studies is not easy. There are four main sources of data on CSA: data from official crime statistics (rarely used because of the problem of dark number); data from welfare, educational, or public health systems; data from victimization or similar, or youth-dedicated surveys; and, for comparison purposes, meta-analyses of empirical research at a cross-national

[13] For an in-depth analysis of methodological challenges in research on child abuse in general, see Fallon et al. (2010).

level. Some studies—mostly qualitative—with offenders, parents, and professionals may enrich understanding, but they are useless for comparison purposes.

1. Data from the welfare system. These data are gathered by professionals (and sometimes non-professionals) and communicated to a welfare or public health agency. This source of information, though less limited than police data systems that do not capture a substantial fraction of CSA cases, are limited nonetheless. A large but unknown percentage of cases are also not reported to the welfare system. These data are available in detailed and over time only in a few countries (the United States, Canada, England and Wales, Australia) and they are not usually focused on CSA but on overall child maltreatment.
2. Data from the criminal justice system. In all countries, these data suffer many limitations concerning rape and sexual abuse of children. The dark number is presumably very high: if we consider that only 10–20 % of adult rape is reported to the police in western countries (Selmini and McElrath 2014), we can reasonably hypothesize that the percentage of unreported cases for children and young people is much higher. In a remarkable number of countries there are no police recorded data that distinguish between ages of victims.[14] Differences in legal definitions of criminalized behaviours and used in statistical procedures fundamentally limit comparative use of police data.
3. Victimization surveys and similar self-report studies. Diverse types of surveys investigate child CSA, many of them retrospectively. This means that the survey is addressed to adults concerning CSA. Limitations are evident (e.g., forgetting, confabulation, other memory problems, out-of-date information, etc.). Though there is general agreement for ethical reasons and because of the sensitivity of the subject that targeted surveys of young children are impossible, some studies have been based on interviews with adolescents or young adults about (recent) past experiences of CSA. This approach offers more reliable data than do adult self-reports. Comparison of findings from these surveys across countries is often impossible because of different methodological choices, different sampling methods, different sample sizes, and different questions used.
4. Meta-analyses based on in-depth review of surveys in different countries aim to estimate reliable figures of both incidence and prevalence rates of CSA. They are extremely useful for comparative purposes, though they suffer from limitations that derive from the sources of information available in each country.

CSA is also investigated by means of small-scale clinical studies, small local surveys, and other types of qualitative or quantitative research, including studies on perpetrators, usually incarcerated offenders.[15] These studies are mostly useful to investigate why people commit sexual violence against children, or for

[14] This was true in the United States in the past (Finkelhor 1991, p. 82) and remains true in other countries.

[15] Finkelhor observes that offenders incarcerated for sexual violence against children are an unrepresentative fraction of all sexual offenders: those who are recidivists, who have prior criminal records, who could not afford an effective defence, and whose victims were not family members (Finkelhor 1991, p. 82).

identification of risk factors. In most cases findings are not generalizable, though, of course, they contribute in different ways to improved understanding.

5 What Do We Know?

Despite the limitations and the methodological challenges just mentioned, our knowledge of CSA has improved remarkably in recent years at national and international levels. Here I discuss some of the most important findings from a variety of sources of information, first cross-nationally and then with a focus on selected areas and countries where more reliable data are available.

5.1 *What Do We Know Internationally?*

Many organizations and institutions are gathering data and information on CSA. These include the UN, UNICEF, the WHO, and the Council of Europe. They and many individual academics around the world have produced a remarkable amount of data.

The United Nations commissioned an in-depth study of child abuse across countries in 2006 (Pinheiro 2006). The report constitutes a fundamental source of information on the main characteristics of CSA and is based on a review of the existing literature. It estimates that 150 million girls and 73 million boys under 18 years had experienced a rape or other form of unwanted sexual abuse. At least 7 % of females (ranging up to 36 %) and 3 % of males (ranging up to 29 %) reported sexual victimisation during childhood. Between 14 and 56 % of the girl were abused by relatives or step-parents (up to 25 % of sexual abuse of boys).

An international survey by WHO (2005), dedicated to violence against women, retrospectively investigated experiences of sexual violence in childhood. A section of a standardized population-based household survey was dedicated to CSA before the age of 15.[16] Findings show that experiences of CSA before age 15 ranged from 1 to 21 % and that the majority of perpetrators were family members, relatives, or acquaintances. Many studies have shown that percentages of family members as perpetrators vary across countries, but it is always the largest category.[17]

---

[16] Twenty-four thousand women were interviewed in ten countries (Bangladesh, Brazil, Ethiopia, Japan, Namibia, Peru, Samoa, the former Serbia and Montenegro, Thailand, and Tanzania) on experiences of sexual violence (unwanted sexual contact and rape) before age 15.

[17] Other international surveys have been conducted by international agencies, including the International Society for the Prevention of Child Abuse and Neglect (ISPCAN), which launched the World Perspective on Child Abuse. The findings are not available on line but only in secondary literature. Main findings however, show that countries differ greatly in their capacity to offer reliable information (Williams and Weeks 2014, p. 24). The authors mention the Child Abuse

Table 1 Estimates of prevalence of CSA (total, contact, and penetrative)

Types of CSA	Female	Male
Total CSA	19.1 % (16.3–22.2)	7.0 % (5.0–9.7)
Contact CSA	21.2 % (17.8–25.0)	10.7 % (6.6–16.8)
Penetrative CSA	15.1 % (19.9–17.7)	6.9 % (5.0–9.5)

Sources: Data adapted from Ji et al. (2013, Table 3, p. 619) and based on Stoltenborgh et al. (2011, Table 2, p. 85)

More detailed information on the cross national prevalence of CSA are offered by meta- analysis studies, whose overall findings seem to demonstrate that, despite the local peculiarities, sexual abuse of children is an international phenomenon that displays some similar patterns across the world (Pereda et al. 2009).

A recent study reviewed empirical studies in 28 countries from 5 continents in the period 1998–2008 (Pereda et al. 2009). It compared its results with an earlier analysis by Finkelhor (1994) and it showed that outside the United States, the subject remained nearly unexplored. It reported that the highest prevalence rate was in Africa and the lowest in Europe and that overall global prevalence rates were 19.7 % for girls and 7.9 % for boys.

A similar, more recent, and more comprehensive review, using meta-analytical models, surveyed the prevalence of child sexual abuse in 217 publications from around the world between 1980 and 2008 (Stoltenborgh et al. 2011). About 10 million people were involved in these studies. The global prevalence of CSA was estimated to be 11.8 %, with a significant gender gap: girls reported 18 % prevalence compared with 7.6 % for boys (Stoltenborgh et al. 2011, p. 89). These findings are very close to those of Pereda and colleagues. Once again, male perpetrators were the majority.

Table 1 summarizes the main findings of meta-analyses on the prevalence of CSA for boys and girls, distinguishing between contact and penetrative CSA (Stoltenborgh et al. 2011).

The validity of comparison of prevalence rates across countries and continents is highly contested generally and above all for behaviours, like intimate partner violence and child abuse, that are deeply affected by cultural attitudes and gender dynamics. The studies just mentioned found slightly different prevalence across the world, with the study by Stoltenborgh et al. (2011) showing very low rates of child sexual abuse not only in Europe but also in Asian regions.[18] The highest prevalence rates were found in Latin America (22 %), even though in these countries, as the researchers point out, popular culture does not encourage disclosure of sexual

Retrospective Screening Tools, developed in 2004, as a very promising means to measure CSA on a global scale, because the survey questions take into consideration local cultural peculiarities in definition of the behaviours, in order to maximize the standardization and comparability of results. For more details, see Williams and Weeks (2014, p. 27).

[18] An issue that will be investigated by Ji et al. (2013) and that I investigate below concerning China.

violence experiences, individualism is a less important value than elsewhere, and family ties and traditions are strong (Frìas and Erviti 2014).

The fundamental question is the explanation for the finding: Are different prevalence rates related to different attitude towards reporting or do they capture a real difference in the occurrence of child sexual abuse (Stoltenborgh et al. 2011, p. 89)? Some researchers argue that in some contexts child sexual abuse is widespread, as in Africa where prevalence rates as high as 64 % have been found (Meinck et al 2014). The hypotheses offered to explain the higher prevalence rates are higher risks of sexual violence because of isolation of families and children, traditional gender roles giving men authority over girls and children, and the fear of HIV that leads to the search for younger partner, etc. (Mbgaya 2010). This does not consider that victims in African countries are probably less ready to disclose their experiences to surveyors than are people in less traditional societies. Unfortunately, all these hypothesis are just speculations and any of these conclusions is tentative.

Many studies on CSA do not take official statistics into account because they represent only a small fraction of sexual abuses and rapes of children. These studies can be useful at national levels, especially when law enforcement data are detailed and complete (Snyder 2000), but there is strong reluctance among researchers to use data from official statistics for international comparisons. Even so, these data can make understanding of the phenomenon more complete. A short examination of what is available at the international level can improve the discussion on the quality of data on CSA. The only longitudinal international source of information on levels of sexual violence against children is the database created by the United Nations Office on Drugs and Crime.[19] A broad category that includes statutory rape, child pornography offences, procuring a child for prostitution, and other offences related to sexual exploitation of children was created in order to gather information from many different countries. Data are available from 2003 to 2012 for 98 countries across the world.

Data are collected by means of a survey that is completed by national governments (often by different institutional agencies). It is plausible to suppose that data are not gathered in all countries with the same accuracy or strictly following the definitions set out in the survey. UNODC, however, provides some information on countries that do not meet the standard definitions, and it is therefore possible to single out subjects on which we can assume that definitions are very similar. When the definitions are acceptable, there remains an important difference among countries about ages of the children: in most cases the age of consent is 18 years, but a variety of different ages are used in different countries.

[19] The database, defined as the 'United Nations Surveys on Crime Tremds and the Operations of the Criminal Justice Systems (CTS)', is available on-line at: www.unodc.org/en/data-and-analysis/glotip.html.

Table 2 Increase, stability and decrease of CSA, selected countries, reported offences, 2003–2012

Increasing	Stable	Declining
Kenya, Costa Rica, Colombia, El Salvador, Bolivia, Chile, The Russian Federation, Armenia, Finland, Lithuania, Hungary, Moldova, Serbia, Sweden, New Zealand, England and Wales	France, The Philippines, Trinidad and Tobago, Egypt, Norway, France, Italy, Portugal, Greece, Slovakia	Japan, Austria, Bulgaria, The Czech Republic, Belgium, Latvia, Ukraine, Croatia, Germany, The Netherlands

Source: UNODC. Selection of countries with available data for at least 8 years with no breaks

One more problem in these data are breaks in time series: only a few countries provided data for the all the 10 years considered.[20] For a majority of countries it is impossible to analyse the data longitudinally. In several cases, moreover, there are huge variations between years that do not seem easy to explain, even though the database contains information on changes in law and changes in recording systems for some countries.

We have also to consider differences in counting rules. A well-known problem affects analyses of crime data cross-nationally, which is relevant above all for offences such as pornography and sexual exploitation of children. Some countries base their counting rules not on the single offence but on the number of offenders (Aebi 2008). That in CSA cases could be significant, for instance in cases where many people are involved in the organization of sexual exploitation or distribution of pornography.

For all these reasons, the available cross-national data from official statistics provide no credible basis for real understanding of this phenomenon, although they may possibly be useful for understanding trends across time in CSA reporting. Data from countries where there are no or only few breaks in the UNODC data series paint the picture shown in Table 2.

These informations can be used to complement other studies on crime trends and when analysing official reactions to CSA. Though limited, they may provide a small piece of information that could be useful to reconstruct the whole picture of CSA.

5.2 *What Do We Know Nationally*

5.2.1 In the United States

Information available in the United States on child abuse in general and on rape and sexual abuse of children are detailed, rich, and relatively reliable. Many sources of

[20] These countries are: Chile, Japan, The Philippines, The Czech Republic, Hungary, Finland, Latvia, Lithuania, Norway, England & Wales, Croatia, Portugal, Slovenia, Serbia, Belgium, France, and Germany.

information offer clear pictures of behaviours, of features of victims and perpetrators, of risk factors and of the historical trends.

A federal law, The Child Abuse Prevention and Treatment Act (CAPTA), (42 U.S.C. § 5101), as amended by the CAPTA Reauthorization Act of 2010, established a general, standard definition of child abuse, which includes sexual abuse, and represents the minimum standards American states must meet. Child abuse and neglect are defined as "*Any recent act or failure to act on the part of a parent or caretaker which results in death, serious physical or emotional harm, sexual abuse or exploitation; or an act or failure to act, which presents an imminent risk of serious harm.*"

The definition refers to the four major types of maltreatment of children: phsysical abuse, psychological and emotional abuse, neglect and sexual abuse.[21]

All 50 states, the District of Columbia, and the U.S. Territories have their own laws on child maltreatment that satisfy the federal standard. They also have reporting laws that mandate that designated professionals and institutions report suspected child abuse and neglect to the federal Child Protective Services Agency.[22]

In 1988, CAPTA established a federally sponsored system for the collection of data across the country; this is the National Child Abuse and Neglect Data System (NCANDS). Data are submitted annually by all states. Child Protective Services maintain the CANDAS data base after screening all reports. There are 23 years of longitudinal data available in the United States from 1990 to 2012. In this data system, CSA is defined as follows: "A type of maltreatment that refers to the involvement of the child in sexual activity to provide sexual gratification or financial benefit to the perpetrator, including contacts for sexual purposes, molestation, statutory rape, prostitution, pornography, exposure, incest, or other sexually exploitative activities" (US Department of Health and Human Services 2013).

The latest NCANDAS report on child maltreatment indicated 63,527 substantiated or indicated cases of CSA in 2010 (US Department of Health and Human Service 2013).[23] This represents 9.2 % of all reported abuse of children in the US, a percentage that has been stable during the last 5 years. Though there is general agreement that this system captures only a small fraction of all sexual abuses, NCANDAS offer much information on risk factors for victims and perpetrators and on treatment of child abuse.

As Table 3 shows, sexual abuse is the least common form of child abuse in the US, as it is in other countries where similar analyses have been made.

---

[21] Research in the US and elsewhere shows that these types of maltreatment often occur together.

[22] Professionals who must report child abuse include teachers, police officers, lawyers, and social services staff. CPS also receives reports from non-professionals (friends, neighbours, relatives) and from "other sources." The largest numbers of reports are from police, education, and social services personnel.

[23] In substantiated cases, abuse definitely occurred. In indicated cases there is only a strong suspicion (Bolen and Gergely 2014, p. 61).

Table 3 Selected maltreatment types of victims by age, 2012, United States

Number						Percent				
Age	Medical neglect	Neglect	Physical abuse	Psychological maltreatment	**Sexual abuse**	Medical neglect	Neglect	Physical abuse	Psychological maltreatment	**Sexual abuse**
<1–2	5212	157,713	30,689	12,371	**1660**	33.2	29.7	24.6	21.4	**2.6**
3–5	2456	111,770	21,327	11,518	**8802**	15.6	21.0	17.1	19.9	**14.0**
6–8	2157	88,314	20,883	10,331	**10,827**	13.7	16.6	16.8	17.8	**17.2**
9–11	1925	68,383	17,619	9280	**11,600**	12.3	12.9	14.1	16.0	**18.4**
12–14	2097	58,491	18,308	8229	**16,560**	13.4	11.0	14.7	14.2	**26.3**
15–17	1806	44,800	14,887	5936	**13,133**	11.5	8.4	12.0	10.3	**20.9**
Unborn, unknown, and 18–21	52	1770	831	215	**354**	0.3	0.3	0.7	0.4	**0.6**
Total	15,705	531,241	124,544	57,880	62,936					
Percent						100.0	100.0	100.0	100.0	100.0

Source: US Department of Health and Human Services (2013, p. 21)

A second data system, the National Incidence Study, based on cases selected by the welfare system, has been conducted 4 times (once each decade starting in 1974[24]). It estimates the number of incidents of child abuse and neglect in the country each year, using reports from professionals described as "sentinels."[25] The study includes both incidents reported to the authorities and incidents that are not reported but were observed by the sentinels. The study also gathers demographic details about victims and their families and has proved useful in identifying risk and protective factors for child abuse. The NIS applies two definitional standards in parallel: the Harm Standard and the Endangerment Standard. The Harm Standard is a relatively narrow and objective child abuse standard: it "requires that an act or omission result in demonstrable harm in order to be classified as abuse or neglect" (Sedlak et al. 2010, p. 2). The Endangerment Standard is broader, more "subjective." It includes all children who meet the Harm Standard plus others who have not been harmed but who are believed to be at risk. The fourth NIS identified 135,000 cases of CSA, a rate of 1.8 per 1000 children (it was 3.2 per 1000 in 1993).

The most important limitations of these national surveys are that they do not capture CSA in the community (Bolen and Gergely 2014, p. 61) and, for CSA, are not crime-specific. Yet, their importance for monitoring child abuse and improving policies and programmes is evident. Other national surveys level, such as the National Crime Victimizations Survey, do not interview people younger than 12 and do not cover CSA. Only the National Violence Against Women Survey, a one-time dedicated survey that retrospectively asked about CSA experiences of girls has done that.

Attempts to design more tailored surveys have been made by the Crime Against Children Research Centre, where the National Survey of Children Exposure to Violence was designed (Finkelhor et al. 2009a). Adolescents and children were interviewed in 2008 about several forms of sexual victimization from birth to age 17. These were sexual contact or fondling by a known or an unknown adult or by another child or teen, attempted or completed intercourse, exposure or "flashing," sexual harassment, and consensual sexual conduct. A prevalence rate of about 10 % was found for sexual contact, non-contact incidents, and sexual harassment (with a much higher percentage for the age group 14–17, 28 %, and for girls). The incidence rate was 6 % for both children and adolescents (Finkelhor et al. 2009a).

---

[24] NIS 4 took place in 2005–2006.

[25] A "sentinel" is a professional who had contact with children and families in "police and sheriffs' departments, public schools, day care centers, hospitals, voluntary social service agencies, mental health agencies, the county juvenile probation and public health departments, public housing, and shelters for runaway and homeless youth and for victims of domestic violence" (Sedlak et al. 2010, p. 2).

Table 4 Forms of sexual abuse by level of substantiation, Canada, 2008

Primary category of maltreatment[a]	Number of investigations	Rate per 1000 children	Percent
Physical abuse	17,212	2.86	20 %
Sexual abuse	**2607**	**0.43**	**3 %**
Neglect	28,939	4.81	34 %
Emotional maltreatment	7423	1.23	9 %
Exposure to intimate partner violence	29,259	4.86	34 %
Total substantiated investigations	85,440	14.19	100 %

Source: Canadian Incidence Study of Reported Child Abuse and Neglect—2008, p. 31
[a]Primary is the form that best describes the investigated maltreatment. Sexual abuse was rarely found in combination with other forms of abuse

5.2.2 In Canada

Data available in Canada are from crimes reported to the police. Additional data are available from the welfare system, with a national sample investigation similar to the NIS study in the United States. Combined, these two sources provide a good picture of CSA in Canada.

The Canadian Incidence Study of Reported Child Abuse and Neglect-2008 (CIS-2008) is the third nation-wide examination of the incidence of reported child maltreatment and the characteristics of children and families investigated by child welfare authorities (Lefebvre et al. 2012; Afifi 2011). In the latest survey, sexual abuse represented the least common form of child maltreatment: 3 % of all child abuse, with an incidence rate of 0.43 per 1000 (Public Health Agency of Canada 2010). See Table 4.

Canadian official statistics on CSA are more detailed and accurate than in most countries. They offer a remarkable amount of information, despite inevitable underreporting.[26] According to the Canadian legal definition of sexual violence, there are three different levels: Sexual assault level 1 (sexual assaults with a weapon or causing bodily harm), level two (aggravated sexual assaults) and "other sexual crimes."[27] In 2011, there were 9597 incidents of police-reported sexual assault of any level against a child or youth, for a rate of 140 per 100,000 (Brennan 2012; Canadian Centre for Justice Statistics 2011). In the same year, 3822 "other sexual offences" were reported to the police for a rate of 11 per 100,000, which represents a 3 % increase compared with 2009. This is one of the few violent crimes that is increasing in Canada, and data from 2012 show it to be continuing (Perrault 2013). The increase was related to sexual touching and luring a child via a computer,

[26] Unreported crime nationally has been estimated in 2009 at 88 % (Canadian Centre for Justice Statistics 2011).

[27] "Other sexual crimes" include offences that primarily address incidents of sexual abuse directed at children such as sexual interference, sexual exploitation, invitation to sexual touching, luring a child via computer and incest (Canadian Centre for Justice Statistics 2011, p. 20).

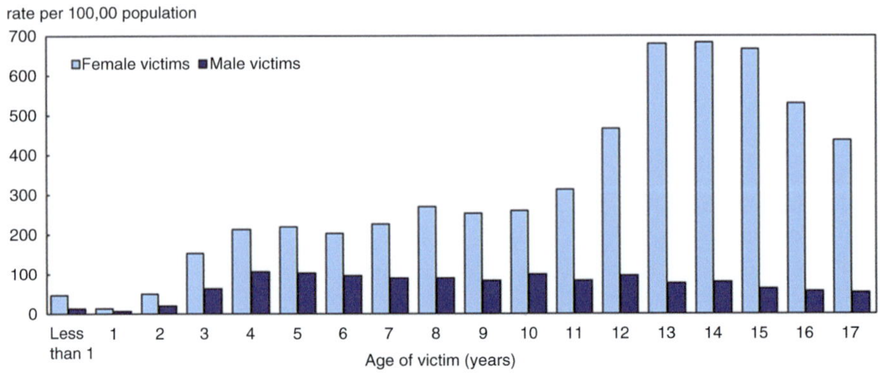

Fig. 1 Male and female victims of sexual assaults (all types), rates per 100,000 population, by age, Canada. Source: Canadian Centre for Justice Statistics, Incident-based Uniform Crime Reporting Survey, 2011

whereas other behaviours in the category were stable. Sexual violence of levels 1, 2, and 3 has been stable since 2003. Child pornography increased 40 % in official statistics in 2011 compared with 2010, as a result of a campaign targeting this behaviour (Brennan 2012).

Data from Canada reinforce our knowledge and confirm many of the most commonly observed patterns of violence against children in industrialized countries. The majority of offenders was known to the victims (89 %), with family members as perpetrators in 35 % of cases. Victims of assaults by family members are usually younger than other victims (below 11 years). The majority of victims are girls, and the gender gap increases as girls get older. Sexual assaults against girls increase at age 12, peak at 15, and then start to decline. Sexual victimization of boys remains stable (Canadian Centre for Justice Statistics 2011). See Fig. 1.

5.2.3 In Central and South America

Despite increasing attention from the public and state institutions towards violence against women and children, and the enactment of many new laws, child abuse and CSA are understudied in many Central and South American countries. There are no cross-national studies for this region and no information is publicly available from national surveys or police data. Most of the literature on CSA consists of small clinical studies or legal analyses with sparse or no empirical data. Some few studies available confirm this lack of research which is attributes to a number of different factors (Knaul and Ramirez 2005; Frìas and Erviti 2014).[28]

[28] Though referring only to Mexico, this summary of conditions that make problems more acute is probably valid for some other countries in Central and South America: the rooted Catholic traditions, for instance, tend to stigmatize sex-related issues; more traditional family models impede individual autonomy, keeping sex issues, including violence, among things people do not talk about (Frìas and Erviti 2014, p. 776).

According to international reports, CSA is a particularly acute problem in Central and South America because of a concentration of social, cultural, and economic conditions—where gender inequality is a relevant issue (Knaul and Ramirez 2005)—that affect children's well-being in general and their exposure to violence in particular. Conditions of life of young people and children in urban deprived areas, poverty, unemployment, and the absence of social support and protection create a context in which violence is widespread, tolerated, and pervasive.

The concept of "violence in chain" elaborated by Auyero and Burbano de Lara (2012) in an ethnographic study of violence in a particular neighbourhood in metropolitan Buenos Aires captures in a few words the conditions of young people and children that are characterized by daily experiences of many forms of violence in the street, at school, and by the police. CSA is but one part of a larger set of problems facing young people.

Only a few studies shed light empirically on the incidence and prevalence of sexual abuse, often in the context of a broader analysis of gender violence, for single countries and for adolescents. For instance, Frìas and Erviti (2014), using data from a Mexican representative national survey of students attending public schools,[29] developed a detailed analysis of risk factors for forced sexual intercourse and unwanted sexual contacts without penetration. Of students in the sample, 6.7 % reported that they had been victims of one of these experiences (forced sexual intercourse was less common, 1.7 %). Sexual abuse from partners or friends was the most common experience, followed by sexual abuse in the family. As in findings of many similar studies, unknown perpetrators were uncommon. As the "violence in chain" concept suggests, victims of sexual abuse are part of a vulnerable group that experiences other forms of violence or witnesses different forms of family and community violence (Frìas and Erviti 2014, p. 784).

One more study, mostly based on data from WHO (2005) and small-scale national studies, reports that the prevalence of sexual violence against children (only girls) before 15 years is as high as 20 % in Lima and 18 % in Peru. From these and similar data for other countries of the area, the authors draw the conclusion that, despite the lack of rigorous prevalence estimates, sexual violence (in general, including CSA) is an issue of major concern for the LAC region (Contreras et al. 2010).

5.2.4 In China

Some international reviews of studies on the prevalence of CSA show that some Asian countries have lower rates than countries on other continents: 11.3 % for female (compared to a cross-national rate of 18 %) and 4.1 % for boys, compared to

[29] The "National Survey on Exclusion, Intolerance, and Violence in Public Institutions of High School Level Education" was carried out in 2007 with interviews of 16,700 adolescents.

an international rate of 7.6 (Pereda et al. 2009; Stoltenborgh et al. 2011). This finding has been tentatively explained with arguments based on methodological problems in Chinese studies and in relation to historical sociological, religious, and cultural tradition of that society (Stoltenborgh et al 2011; Ji et al. 2013).

A recent meta-analysis of studies on CSA in China (including many studies in the original language, usually not considered in international reviews), based on data collected in 27 general population surveys involving a total of 75,409 participants, sought to shed light on CSA in the most populous Asian country (Ji et al. 2013). The authors' starting point was the large difference in prevalence rates found by studies in China, ranging from 2 to 35 %. This sophisticated review, which encompasses contact, penetrative, and non-contact sexual abuse of children, found an estimated prevalence of 15.3 % for total sexual abuse for females (1 % for penetrative sexual abuse and 9.5 % for contact CSA). For boys, the estimated prevalence rate was 13.8 % (total sexual abuse), 8.0 % for contact sexual abuse, and 0.9 for penetrative (Ji et al. 2013). These figures are closer to those of other areas in the world.

Their conclusions confirm the findings of previous studies concerning the prevalence rate of CSA for girls, that in China is remarkably lower than in other countries (above all penetrative CSA, 1 % compared to the international prevalence rate of 15.1 %.). Concerning boys, this study found a higher prevalence rate (13.8 %) than the international one (7 %) and a much lower rate of penetrative abuse (0.9 % compared to 6.9 % at the international level). This finding, according to the authors, is explained by various factors including the broad questions used in some Chinese studies and coded as non-contacts (Ji et al. 2013, p. 619).

5.2.5 In Europe[30]

Research and scientific work on sexual abuse against children are rare in Europe. They mostly relate to psychological and health issues linked to the experience of violence, or to legal analyses in defining sexual abuse and in differentiating rape against children from rape against adults. Empirical research on the phenomenon is underdeveloped and comparison across Europe is made almost impossible by national differences in legal definitions and counting rules.

More information, however, has been made available by the *European Sourcebook of Crime and Criminal Justice* (ESCCJ), a project addressed at producing

[30] I have not mentioned overall Asia, Australia and New Zealand, and Africa. Except for Australia and New Zealand, information and research on CSA in these places is very fragmented and very few data are available—as was the case for Central and South America. For Australia, a systematic gathering of data from the child welfare system is underway, with an annual study of incidence and prevalence, similar to the US NIS and the Canadian CIS. According to this study, CSA constituted 14 % of all child abuse, with a remarkable difference between jurisdictions (Australian Institute of Family Studies 2013; Bolen and Gergely 2014, p. 63). Some information on CSA in Africa is available in Pinheiro (2006) and Meinck et al. (2014).

European statistics on crime for all countries after efforts at standardization of definitions in order to make the data more reliable and comparable.[31] The ESCCJ reports police data on "sexual abuse of minors" for the period 2003–2007., The standardized definition includes "sexual intercourse, or any other form of physical sexual contact, with a person below the age of consent" (Aebi et al. 2010, p. 358). Where possible, the category includes all sexual intercourse or any other form of sexual contact committed without violence, attempts, and acts committed by adults or people under the age of consent. Verbal and non-physical molestation, child pornography, and acts considered to be rape are not included.[32]

The ESCCJ data do not allow comparisons across countries, because of differences in legal definitions. They offer however a broad picture of police reported sexual abuse (some forms, at least) against children in a number of European countries and they may be helpful in understanding trends in reporting of CSA. However, the time series is too short (2003–2007) for any attempt to understand changes in police-reported CSA.

Recently, the European Union published the first European victimization survey on violence against women (FRA – European Union for Fundamentals Right 2014). The study includes a section on experiences of sexual violence (different forms, including sexual forced intercourse) in the childhood and it represents the first general European picture on the prevalence of this crime in the European context, with interviews to 42,000 women in 28 countries. The study uses a retrospective approach—women interviewed are asked about their experience of sexual violence before the age of 15—and suffers therefore of some methodological limitations. However, it offers a broad and very informative picture on our issue. The more relevant findings of this recent study are that 12 % of women (21 million of women) experienced some forms of sexual abuse during their childhood, with the highest rates in countries like France, The Netherlands and the United Kingdom (20 %) and the lowest (less than 4 %) in Bulgaria, The Czech Republic, Poland, Romania and Portugal. One more interesting finding of this study is the lower percentage of family member perpetrators compared to other studies across the world, with unknown people representing the 51 % of all perpetrators. 97 % of perpetrators were men, confirming the "gendered" nature of sexual abuse against children (FRA – European Union for Fundamental Rights 2014, pp. 125–128).

More data on the incidence and prevalence of child sexual abuse in Europe can be found in national studies and in meta-analyses. A recent review of empirical

[31] The ESCCJ is sponsored by the European Council and several European governments. It was started in 1993. Four editions have been published, covering the period from 1990 to 2007 and many European countries. The fifth edition will be available in 2014 and it will cover the years from 2007 to 2012, thus allowing analyses of trends. The 2010 report discusses the project's methods and processes (Aebi et al. 2010). For detailed discussions of the challenges faced in compiling the ESCCJ, see Aebi et al. (2010) and Harrendorf (2012).

[32] Acts considered rape were included only for a few countries: Latvia, Poland, Slovakia, Switzerland (only police data) and Turkey (only conviction data). In all other countries rape of children was included in the general category of rape.

research in Europe by Lalor and McElvaney (2011) offers additional information. The picture is, however, very fragmented, and comparisons of prevalence rates must be taken with caution, since these studies are based on different methodologies, have different aims, and focus on different forms of child sexual abuse and different contexts (family, school, residential facilities, etc.).

Concerning the prevalence of sexual violence against children, the authors mention several studies that offer a broad picture of some European countries in cross-national perspective. Among these studies, one on Austria, Belgium, Denmark, Finland, France, Germany, The Netherlands, Sweden, Spain, Switzerland, Spain and United Kingdom, warrants mention. In these 11 countries, prevalence rates ranged from 6 to 36 % for girls and from 1 to 15 % for boys (Lalor and McElvaney 2011, p. 23).

Other studies investigate the phenomenon at regional levels, as, for example, the Baltic Sea Regional Study on Adolescent Sexuality and the Balkan Epidemiological Study on Child Abuse and Neglect. The Baltic Sea Regional Study investigated three forms of CSA (indecent exposure, indecent touch and sexual intercourse), interviewing 20,000 people around age 18. For all five countries included (Estonia, Lithuania, Norway, Poland, Sweden), the lifetime rate of indecent exposure was 14.2 % for boys and 21.9 for girls. Rates of indecent touching were 16.7 % for boys and 37.0 % for girls. Findings on sexual intercourse show a difference from the majority of research findings in the rest of the world, with a slightly higher rate for boys (11.9 %) than for girls (10 %), due to the much higher male rates in Poland and Lithuania (Lalor and McElvaney 2011, pp. 26–27).[33]

The Balkan study[34] (BECAN) is a European funded FP7 Project. It involves an epidemiological study of child abuse and neglect in the general population for 11-to-16 year old children who were attending or had dropped out of school. The same survey[35] was carried out in all the countries over 3 years, with results made available in 2013. This is the largest survey ever conducted on this subject and at the European level, with 55,729 students involved. It represents an interesting model for improvement and further development of sub-regional studies in the field.

Both prevalence and incidence rates were estimated. The main findings showed that sexual intercourse and sexual unwanted contacts were less frequent than other

[33] For additional details, see Mossige et al 2007.

[34] The participating countries were: Albania, Bosnia and Herzegovina, Bulgaria, Croatia, the Former Yugoslavian Republic of Macedonia, Greece, Romania, Serbia, and Turkey. Information is available online at http://www.becan.ue.

[35] Items explored: (1) Did someone make you upset by speaking to you in a sexual way or writing sexual things about you? (2) Did someone make you watch a sex video or look at sexual pictures in a magazine or computer when you did not want to? (3) Did someone make you look at their private parts or wanted to look at yours? (4) Did someone touch your private parts in a sexual way, or make you touch theirs? (5) Did someone make a sex video or take photographs of you alone, or with other people, doing sexual things? (6) Did someone try to have sex with you when you did not want to?

forms of CSA with rates that ranged from 6.7 % for sexual violence in the former Yugoslav Republic of Macedonia to 20 % in Greece. Contact violence at least once in lifetime ranged from 3.0 % in Serbia to 10 % in Greece. Data on the gender of victims are incomplete in some national reports and the majority of sexual and contacts violence were experienced in the family or involved known perpetrators.

Lalor and McElvaney (2011, p. 27) describe another European cross-national study in 2006 that included Belgium, England (UK), France, Germany, Ireland, Italy, The Netherlands, and Spain. The overall sample was much more limited (2356 cases) than in the regional surveys. Data are from child protection services and not from self-report surveys. Sexual contact with penetration accounted for 6 % of all CSA, with remarkable differences among countries (very low rates in Ireland, Spain, and Italy, and a very high rate, 28 %, in Belgium). Sexual contacts represented 24 % of all cases, with a huge difference between Belgium (53 %) and Ireland (2 %). Overall non-sexual contact was lower than other forms of CSA. Findings show variations across countries that are not easy to explain and that may result from methodological problems relating to the sources of information and limited sample size.

Despite a fragmentation of initiatives and problems in making comparisons, in many European contexts research on CSA is improving, with many efforts to find more comparable tools for investigation.[36] At the national level, data and information are fragmented. I discuss England and Wales, a European country for which information is available in English.[37]

5.2.6 In England and Wales (UK)

In England and Wales (UK), research on CSA is well developed and information is detailed, regularly updated, and available in historical series from different sources. Data from child welfare agencies based on incidents reported to professionals show that CSA represented 9 % of all abuses in 2009—a rate similar to that found in the United States by NCANDAS. Incidence rates were 0.2 per 1000 girls and 0.1 per 1000 boys (Bolen and Gergely 2014, p. 63).

A targeted victimization survey, the Survey of Child Safety and Victimization, was carried out in England and Wales (UK) in 2009.[38] It investigated all forms of

[36] An example is a project for designing a common survey on CSA in five Nordic countries (Helweg-Larsen 2009). This interesting report also includes an overview of existing empirical research on CSA in the Nordic countries.

[37] The Netherlands is another European country which has reliable information on CSA. It replicated the US NIS survey in 2005. CSA was the lowest of all forms of child abuse and even lower than in the US (4 % of all maltreatment). For in-depth information, see Euser et al. (2010).

[38] See Radford et al. (2010). A similar survey was carried on in 1998–1999. However, only some of the questions remained unchanged in the second study 10 years later and it is impossible to compare the results concerning children under age 18. In the 2009 survey, interviews were conducted through a CASI system with: 2160 parents or guardians of children under 11 years of age; 2275 young people between ages 11 and 17; and 1761 young adults (18–24).

child maltreatment at home, in schools, and in the community, including sexual abuse by contact, as part of the broader category "severe maltreatment."[39] Sexual abuse by contact represented 0.5 of all maltreatment of children younger than 11. Sexual abuse was 4.8 % of all forms of violence for children between 11 and 17 years. This survey confirms many of the findings from other surveys in other countries: the majority of perpetrators are male (adults or young people) known to the victims, though parents and guardians were responsible for only 1.7 % of violent acts. The large majority of victims were girls and a large amount of perpetrators (65.9 %) were other children or people younger than 18 (Radford et al. 2010). One more finding, that seems to be a common pattern, is that sexual abuse is but one of several forms of maltreatment children experienced. This has been defined as polyvictimization (Finkelhor et al. 2009b).

Other data on rape and sexual abuse of children are available from police statistics. A recent report of the UK government that combines findings from victimization surveys[40] and police statistics found that there were 13,610 sexual offences in 2013–2014 involving children under the age of 13 (National Office of Statistics 2014). This is the highest number since 2003 and represents an increase of 26 % compared to the previous year. The increase was higher for rape and sexual assaults against boys (+35 %) than for girls (+21 %). Other "sexual activity involving children" increased by 33 %. The increase in reporting is attributed to governmental efforts to encourage notification of CSA and to recently adopted programs to improve police capacity to respond to CSA victims as a consequence of notorious cases of lethal violence against children that attracted media and public attention (National Office of Statistics 2014).

6 The Main Risk Factors

Finding common patterns concerning risk factor in the literature on CSA is not an easy task. However, despite differences in methodology, in sources of information, and in cultural, social, and economic difference across countries and continents, some common findings from the studies reported here may be identified.

First, CSA is much more a problem for girls than for boys. Gender is the most important and common risk factor internationally for rape and other forms of sexual abuse.

[39] The following behaviours are included in this category: physical sexual contact, assault by penetration (rape or oral sex) and non—penetrative acts (masturbation, kissing, touching outside the clothing). Non contact sexual abuse also was investigated, though very few data on this behaviour are available.

[40] For several years the Crime Survey for England and Wales (long known as the British Crime Survey) has included a module dedicated to violence against children from 10 to 15. There are no questions about sexual abuse.

Second, age is also important, with the group aged between 11 and 17 being most at risk but, unlike for gender, there are remarkable variations across countries and even in the same country.

Third, perpetrators are in most case known persons, though there are huge variations according to the type of CSA and the sources of information. Welfare agency reports show higher involvement by parent and stepparent perpetrators compared with studies drawing on other sources, which show higher rates of friends, relatives, and acquaintances. In the majority of studies that we have examined, however, unknown perpetrators are a small fraction of overall perpetrators. Studies of older children and teenagers, such as the BECAN study in Europe, shed light on different kinds of perpetrator risk factors. In these age groups, violence by other adolescents is significant compared to family and other known perpetrators. This finding makes an important change in prevailing conceptions of CSA that has relevant scientific and policy implications.

Other risk factors have been found in many studies, however they cannot be generalized as the gender and age findings can be. Often they relate to specific contexts, countries, or areas (Bolen and Gergely 2014, p. 68). Race/ethnicity,[41] the family size, family conflicts, single parenthood, absent mothers, alcohol and substance abuse, psychological problems, and developmental delays have often been shown to be correlates of CSA, but only in some contexts.

Other risk factors are even more specific, for example, HIV in CSA abuse in Africa (Pinheiro 2006). The fear of HIV led adults to have sex with younger people who were assumed to be healthier than older people. HIV, however, is also a consequence of CSA.

Social and cultural patterns of conduct and the dynamic of gender roles in particular societies represent important risk factors for some forms of CSA. So, on a macro-level, do globalization, migration, and urbanization (Pinheiro 2006).

CSA remains an understudied problem. Even so, we can draw lessons from research around the world to improve our knowledge of these forms of criminal behaviour and to implement more effective policies.

7 Is Child Sexual Abuse Declining?

Scientific debate on the possibility that rates of violence are declining generally have become widespread in recent years, starting from the observation of declines in all types of different forms of violent crime in the United States (Tonry 2014).

[41] In the US, only NIS- 4 found that black girls and boys were more often sexually abused than white and other ethnic group girls, a finding attributed to technical changes in statistical procedure (Sedlak et al. 2010, p. 9). NIS–4 also found that children not enrolled in school were more at risk of CSA.

Violence against children in the United States, including sexual abuse, shows a similar decline. It is unclear whether this is a global trend.

The issue was first addressed in 2006 by Finkelhor and Jones, who noticed that early in the 1990s, after 15 years of increase, the incidence of sexual abuse appeared to decline, alongside other forms of violent juvenile victimization. Other indicators of social maladjustment of children and teenagers (like running away, teen suicide, and teen pregnancy) also were decreasing in the same period (Finkelhor and Jones 2006, p. 689). In the 2006 analysis, both intra-familial and extra-familial sexual abuse were declining. More recent data show that sexual abuse by strangers was mostly stable and declined only slightly in 2004 (Chaffin and Jones 2011).

The general decline continued in the United States after 2006. Recent data show a 61 % decline between 1990 and 2009 in sexual abuse incidents involving children younger than 18 reported by NCANDAS (Chaffin and Jones 2011). The decline is clear and evident also in other sources of information, including police data (Finkelhor et al. 2014). The National Incident Study show a comparable decline (−47 %) in the period 1993–2005 (Sedlak et al. 2010, p. 7). The National Crime Victimization Survey (NCVS) for the same period shows a 52 % decline in juvenile sexual victimization (for teenagers 12–17 years old), with the decline occurring for known pepetrators, whereas unknowm rates of offenders are stable (Chaffin and Jones 2011).

The multiplicity of consistent findings from diverse data sources has led some scholars to conclude that a true decline in sexual abuse cases occurred in the second part of the 1990s and is continuing. Rates of physical abuse also are declining. The only stable or rising form of child maltreatment is neglect.

For the United States, the decline in child sexual abuse has been analysed in the context of general downward trends of various forms of physical violence, including rape and sexual offences against adults. Some factors that are invoked as hypotheses to explain the general drop in violent crime may also relate to the decline in sexual abuse of children. Other causes may be more crime-specific. Finkelhor and Jones (2006), for instance, speculate that incarceration may have played a role in the decrease of sexual abuse, considering the tripling of sex offenders incarcerated between 1986 and 1997, although this explanation does not work for other type of crime. Demographic changes—above all the reduction in unwanted children and the increase in later marriages—may also have played a role. So may the economic prosperity that characterized the US during the 1990s.[42] Other crime-specific factors mentioned by scholars are the diffusion of preventive programs and improvements in psychopharmacological treatment of offenders and potential offenders (Chaffin and Jones 2011; Finkelhor and Jones 2006).

For sexual offences and rape of adult women there is also a clear decline shown by both American police and victimization survey data. Situations in other

[42] The decline, however, continued even during the period of economic recession after 2007. This suggests that cultural and other changes are more relevant in explaining changing attitudes towards sexual violence.

countries are not so clear-cut because of paucities of reliable data and long sequences of victimization surveys. Reported rape seem to be increasing in many European countries, with a few victimizations surveys showing stability (Sweden and UK) (Selmini and McElrath 2014). There are some signs—though the data must be considered with caution—that violence in the family against women is also decreasing (Kangaspunta and Marshall 2012).

The implications of these changes for adults are important for the understanding of patterns of sexual violence against children, even though the two phenomena are different. For instance, if the declines that have occurred in the United States can be shown to have occurred in many other countries, we could hypothesize that violence generally, including gender violence and violence against children, is becoming less frequent. Important and widespread cultural changes in the tolerance of violence may be occurring in our societies, at least in the western world.

The American data that I briefly summarized cannot be confirmed for other countries from data for most other parts of the world, because most countries lack comparative longitudinal quantitative data. In Canada, data from The Canadian Incidence Study of Reported Child Abuse and Neglect (CIS) suggest a decline in the number of substantiated CSA child welfare cases across the country (though information on sexual abuse in particular is not available). However, methodological problems in comparisons of data from different waves of the CIS make it impossible to draw confident conclusions about trends in violence against children (Public Health Agency of Canada 2010). Moreover, other source do not confirm this decline and researchers have concluded that Canada is probably not following the same pattern as the United States (Collin-Vezina et al. 2010). For Europe, we have no clear indication on this issue, although the recent study published by FRA (2014, p. 125) shows that younger women report less experiences of sexual abuse in the childhood than older women, thus suggesting that an overall decline of this crime is occurring in Europe as well.

Despite the fact that a sharp decline in CSA is for now clearly observable only in the United States, understanding this decline is also for Western countries and worldwide extremely important both for scientific and policy reasons.

8 New Directions for Research

Almost all reports and studies on sexual abuse of children begin and end with complaints about difficulties in understanding this phenomenon and about the scarcity and unreliability of data. This survey once again demonstrates how important it is to improve data collection methods and the quality of data if CSA issues are to be understood nationally or internationally.

The most accessible data are from the criminal justice system. In some countries in the industrialized world, good-quality police data—although seriously limited by the dark number problem—can offer some important information on events, victims, and perpetrators. In many countries, this detailed information is not reliably available. These problems are important in Europe and on other continents. Police data systems are often inconsistent and unsystematic. Lack of standardization fundamentally impedes cross-national comparisons.

Concerning adults, victimization surveys provide an important source of additional information that not only can overcome the problem of the dark number, but also offer detailed knowledge of victims' experiences. For children, however, this methodology is not easily applicable and we need therefore to develop better tools in order to study their victimization. Self-report surveys, for instance, could target samples of young adolescents who can be interviewed on their past—and therefore more recent than for adults—experience of sexual violence. Some recent surveys of this kind, which I discussed above, can provide models for use elsewhere with adjustments relating to local peculiarities.

Concerning welfare system data, only some countries can rely upon this source of information. At the European level, for instance, efforts should be made to improve the quality of the different national systems and to strengthen capacities for cross national comparisons.

A better understanding of CSA would improve and enrich the ways it is addressed. Evaluation studies of prevention programs, for example, are largely non-existent but are transparently important to efforts to understand what is, and is not, working to reduce CSA.

I see five main priorities for research that can improve understanding of CSA and the effectiveness of policy responses:

1. Standardization of legal definitions, official data systems, and survey research instruments to facilitate comparisons;
2. Further development of longitudinal studies;
3. Greater inter-disciplinarity in order to combine data and experience from the welfare, criminal justice, and public health systems;
4. Greater attention to the needs of areas of the world where research is seriously underdeveloped and under-funded;
5. Greater focus on evaluation of the effects of policy initiatives.

National governments, international agencies, and NGOs around the world are making huge efforts to improve understanding and handling of CSA. This article has shown that despite the problems discussed and the limitations of existing studies, our knowledge is constantly improving. We need to keep moving forward.

Five Questions

1. Which are the main methodological challenges in doing research on child sexual abuse?
2. How do globalization and social change affect child sexual abuse?
3. Which kind of studies are more promising for a better understanding of child sexual abuse?
4. Which arguments have been used to explain the decline of child sexual abuse in the US and how much is the decline generalizable to other countries?
5. How would you define child sexual abuse: as a psychopathological problem, as a gender violence problem, as a crime, as a human right issue. . .?

References

Aebi, M. F. (2008). Measuring the influence of statistical counting rules on cross-national differences in recorded crime. In: K. Aromaa & M. Heiskanen (Eds.), *Crime and criminal justice systems in Europe and North America 1995–2004* (pp. 200–218). Helsinki: European Institute for Crime Prevention and Control, affiliated with the United Nations.

Aebi, M. F., et al. (Eds.). (2010). *European sourcebook of crime and criminal justice statistics–2010* (4th ed.). The Hague: Boom Juridische uitgevers.

Afifi, T. O. (2011). Child maltreatment in Canada: An understudied public health problem. *Canadian Journal of Public Health, 102*(6), 459–461.

Australian Institute of Family Studies. (2013). Child protection in Australia 2011–2012. www.aifs.gov.au/cfca/index/php

Auyero, J., & Burbano de Lara, A. (2012). In harm's way at the urban margin. *Ethnography, 13*(4), 531–557.

Berardi, G. (2011). Engaging the travel and tourism sector in protecting children from sexual exploitation. In: Council of Europe, *Protecting children from sexual violence. A comprehensive approach* (pp. 303–312). Strasbourg: Council of Europe.

Bolen, R. M., & Gergely, K. (2014). Child sexual abuse. In J. R. Conte (Ed.), *Child abuse and neglect worldwide* (Vol. 1, pp. 59–94). Santa Barbara: Praeger.

Brennan, S. (2012). *Police reported crime statistics in Canada 2011*. Ottawa, ON: Statistics Canada.

Brosig, C. L., & Kalichman, S. C. (1992). Clinicians' reporting of suspected child abuse: A review of the empirical literature. *Clinical Pyschology Review, 12*, 155–168.

Canadian Centre for Justice Statistics. (2011). Family violence in Canada: A statistical profile. Ottawa, ON: Statistics Canada. www.statcan.gv.ca.

Chaffin, M., & Jones, L. (2011, January14). Declining rates of child sexual abuse and what this really means. *NCAC Webinar*, National Children's Advocay Center.

Collin-Vezina, D., et al. (2010). Is child abuse declining in Canada? An analysis of child welfare data. *Child Abuse & Neglect, 34*, 807–812.

Contreras, J. M., et al. (2010). Sexual violence in Latin America and the Caribbean: a desk review. Pretoria: Sexual Violence Research Initiative.

Dottridge, M. (2008). *Child trafficking for sexual purposes*. ECPAT International report.

Euser, E., et al. (2010). Prevalence of child maltreatment in the Netherlands. *Child Maltreatment, 15*, 5–17.

Fallon, B., et al. (2010). Methodological challenges in measuring child maltreatment. *Child Abuse & Neglect, 34*, 70–79.

Finkelhor, D. (1991). Child sexual abuse. In M. Rosenberg & M. A. Fenley (Eds.), *Violence in America: A public health approach* (pp. 79–94). New York: Oxford University Press.

Finkelhor, D. (1994). The international epidemiology of child sexual abuse. *Child Abuse&Neglect, 18*, 409–417.

Finkelhor, D. (2014). Commentary: Cause for alarm? Youth and internet risk research. A commentary on Livingstone and Smith (2014). *Journal of Child Psyhcology and Psychiatry, 55*, 655–668.

Finkelhor, D., & Jones, L. (2006). Why have child maltreament and child victimization declined? *Journal of Social Issues, 62*, 685–716.

Finkelhor, D., et al. (2009a, October). *Children exposure to violence: A comprehensive national survey*. Juvenile Justice Bulletin. US Department of Justice.

Finkelhor, D., et al. (2009b). Pathways to poly-victimization. *Child Maltreatment, 14*, 316–329.

Finkelhor, D., et al. (2014). Trends in children's exposure to violence, 2003 to 2011. *JAMA Pediatrics*. doi:10.1001/jamapediatrics.2013.5296

FRA (European Union for Fundamental Rights). (2014). *Violence against women: An EU-wide survey. Main results*. Luxenbourg: Publication Office of the European Union.

Frank, D. J., et al. (2009). The global dimensions of rape-law reform: A cross-national study of policy outcomes. *American Sociological Review, 74*, 272–290.
Frìas, M. S., & Erviti, J. (2014). Gendered experience of sexual abuse of teen agers and children in Mexico. *Child Abuse & Neglect, 38*, 776–787.
Harrendorf, S. (2012). Offence definitions in the European sourcebook of crime and criminal justice statistics and their influence on data quality and comparability. *European Journal of Criminal Policy and Research, 18*, 23–53.
Helweg-Larsen, K. (2009). *Framework for Nordic youth surveys on child sexual abuse and exposure to violence outside and in the family. TemaNord 2009:540*. Copenaghen: Nordic Council of Ministers.
Ji, K., et al. (2013). Child abuse in China: a meta-analysis of 27 studies. *Child Abuse & Neglect, 37*, 613–622.
Kalichman, S. C. (1999). *Mandated reporting of suspected child abuse: Ethics, law, and policy* (2nd sub edition). Washington, DC: American Psychological Association.
Kangaspunta, K., & Marshall, I. H. (2012). Trends in violence against women: Some good news and some bad news. In J. van Dijk et al. (Eds.), *The international crime drop. New directions in research* (pp. 103–133). Basingstoke: Palgrave Macmillan.
Kloess, J. A., et al. (2014). Online child sexual exploitation: Prevalence, process and offenders characteristics. *Trauma, Violence & Abuse, 15*, 126–139.
Knaul, F., Ramirez, M. A. (2005). *Family violence and child abuse in Latin America and the Carribbean. The cases of Columbia and Mexico*. Technical paper series, Unpublished research report, Inter-American Development Bank, Sustainable Development Department, Washington, DC
Lalor, K., & McElvaney, R. (2011). Overview of the nature and extent of child sexual abuse in Europe. In: Council of Europe, *Protecting children from sexual violence. A comprehensive approach* (pp. 13–43). Strasbourg: Council of Europe.
Lefebvre, R., et al. (2012). *Sexual abuse investigations by level of substantiation in Canada in 2008*. Toronto, ON: Canadian Child Welfare Research Portal.
Livingstone, S., Haddon, L. (2009). *EU kids online*. Final report. LSE, London. EC Safer Internet Plus Programme Deliverable DS6.5.
Livingstone, S., & Smith, P. K. (2014). Annual research review: Harms experienced by children user of online and mobile technologies: The nature, prevalence and management of sexual and aggressive risks in the digital era. *Journal of Child Psychology and Psychiatry, 55*, 635–654.
Mbgaya, C. V. (2010). *Child maltreatment in Kenia, Zambia and the Netherlands. A cross cultural comparison of prevalence, psychopathological sequelae, and mediation by PTSS*. Leiden: Drukkerij Mostert.
McLeigh, J. D. (2013). Protecting children in the context of international migration. *Child Abuse & Neglect, 37*, 1056–1068.
Meinck, F., et al. (2014). Risk and protective factors for physical and sexual abuse of children and adolescents in Africa. A review and implications for practice. *Trauma, Violence & Abuse, 15*, 1–27.
Mitchell, K., & Jones, L. (2013, November). Internet facilitated commercial sexual exploitation of children. Crime against Children Research Centre.
Mitchell, K., et al. (2007). Online requests for social pictures from youth: Risk factors and incidents characteristics. *Journal of Adolescent Health, 41*, 197–203.
Mitchell, K., et al. (2014, February). *Trends in unwanted online experiences and sextings*. Final report. Crime against Children Research Centre paper
Mossige, S., et al. (Eds.). (2007). *The Baltic Sea regional study on adolescents' sexuality*. NOVA report 18/07. Norwegian Social Research, Oslo, Norway.
National Office of Statistics. (2014). *Crime in England and Wales, year ending March 2014*. Statistical Bulletin. https://www.ons.gov.uk
O Briain, M. (Ed.). (2006). *Combating the trafficking of children for sexual purposes. Questions and answers*. ECPAT Netherlands report. Available on-line http://www.humantrafficking.org.

O'Connell Davidson, J. (2013). Telling stories: Child migration and child trafficking. Stories of trafficking obscure the realities for migrant children. *Child Abuse & Neglect, 37*, 1069–1079.
Pereda, N., et al. (2009). The international epidemiology of child sexual abuse: A continuation of Finkhelor (1994). *Child Abuse & Neglect, 33*, 331–342.
Perrault, S. (2013). *Police reported crime statistics in Canada 2012*. Ottawa, ON: Statistics Canada.
Pinheiro, S. P. (2006). *World report on volence against children*. Geneva: United Nations.
Public Health Agency of Canada. (2010). *The Canadian incidence study of reported child abuse and neglect- 2008: Major findings*. Ottawa ON. http://www.phac-aspc.gc.ca/cm-vee/csca-ecve/2008/cis-eci-01-eng.php.
Radford, L., et al. (2010). *Child abuse and neglect in the UK today*. National Society for the Prevention of Cruelty to Children. Report available online www.nspcc.org.uk.
Richardson, J. (2011). Awarness raising to combat online sexual violence. In: Council of Europe, *Protecting children from sexual violence. A comprehensive approach* (pp. 289–299). Strasbourg: Council of Europe.
Sedlak, A. J., et al. (2010). *Fourth national incidence study of child abuse and neglect (NIS–4): Report to congress, executive summary*. Department of Health and Human Services, Administration for Children and Families, Washington, DC.
Selmini, R., & McElrath, S. (2014). Violent female victimization trends across Europe, Canada and the US. In M. Tonry (Ed.), *Why crime rates all and why they don't. Crime and justice: a review of research* (Vol. 43). Chicago: University of Chicago Press.
Snyder, H. N. (2000). Sexual assaults of young children as reported to law enforcement: victims, incident and offender characteristics. Statistical report, US Bureau of Justice.
Stoltenborgh, M., et al. (2011). A global perspective on child sexual abuse: Meta-analysis of prevalence around the world. *Child Maltreatment, 16*, 79–101.
Tonry, M. (2014). Why crime rates are falling throughout the Western world. In M. Tonry (Ed.), *Why crime rates all and why they don't. Crime and justice: a review of research* (Vol. 43). Chicago: University of Chicago Press.
UNICEF. (2011). *Child safety online: Global challenges and strategies*. Florence: Unicef.
UNICEF. (2013). *Female genital mutilation/cutting: A statistical overview and exploration of the dynamics of change*. New York: Unicef.
UNICEF. (2014). *Ending child marriages. Progress and prospects*. New York: Unicef.
US Department of Health & Human Services. Administration for Children and Families, Administration on Children, Youth and Families, Children's Bureau. (2013). *Child maltreatment 2012*. http://www.ac.nes.gov/programs/cb/research-data-technology/statistics-research/child-maltreatment.
WHO. (2005). *Multi-country study on women's health and domestic violence against women*. Geneve: WHO.
Williams, L. M., & Weeks, E. G. (2014). Defining and measuring child maltreatment. In J. R. Conte (Ed.), *Child abuse and neglet worldwide* (Vol. 1, pp. 9–35). Santa Barbara: Praeger.

Trafficking in Persons: The Involvement of Women and Children

Kristiina Kangaspunta, Fabrizio Sarrica, and Raggie Johansen

Abstract The crime of trafficking in persons involves women disproportionately, both as victims and as offenders. Women comprise a majority of the detected victims of this crime, and women are also prosecuted and convicted of trafficking in persons in a far larger proportion than for nearly any other crime. Children are frequently detected as victims. Drawing on findings from the United Nations Office on Drugs and Crime *Global Report on Trafficking in Persons 2012*, this chapter examines some of the patterns of trafficking in persons as detected and reported by countries worldwide. It examines some of the reasons why women and children are particularly vulnerable to this crime, and looks at offending patterns and forms of exploitation from the global and regional perspectives.

1 Introduction

While many cases of trafficking in persons start as attempts to improve the conditions of life, sometimes circumstances transform those attempts into incidences of exploitation and abuse. Inequalities and societal values help create vulnerabilities that make potential victims of trafficking in persons easy targets for criminals intent on profiting from those individuals' hopes of a better life. Recruiting and exploiting a vulnerable person is relatively easy and often carries a low risk of detection.

The chapter is based on the findings presented in the Global Report on Trafficking in Persons 2012, published by the United Nations Office on Drugs and Crime (UNODC) and it presents the results of the analyses of data collected from the Member States covering the period 2007–2010. The results are presented keeping in mind the limitations of the official statistics, so the chapter is not aiming at presenting the prevalence of trafficking persons but focuses on the patterns and flows of detected human trafficking cases.

K. Kangaspunta (✉) • R. Johansen
Global Report on Trafficking in Persons Unit, UNODC, Vienna, Austria
e-mail: kangaspunta@unodc.org; raggie@gmail.com

F. Sarrica
United Nations Office on Drugs and Crime UNODC, Vienna, Austria
e-mail: fabrizio.sarrica@unodc.org

H. Kury et al. (eds.), *Women and Children as Victims and Offenders: Background, Prevention, Reintegration*, DOI 10.1007/978-3-319-08398-8_30

Women and children are often among the most vulnerable persons to become trafficking victims. In many societies, women are less empowered than men. This is true in terms of gender inequality in access to education and work opportunities and access to a fair and timely justice system, as well as attainment of human and social rights (UN Women 2011). At the same time—and perhaps more significantly in terms of risk of becoming a victim of traffickers—this is also true in terms of physical strength, which makes females more vulnerable than males to exploitation through use of force or threats.

Children, both boys and girls, are clearly more vulnerable than adults, as they are neither mature enough nor legally empowered to make their own life decisions. They are dependent on guardians who may not always have their best interest at heart. Children, as a result of their lack of experience, are also prone to trusting others easily, which can be used by criminals to exploit them.

2 Victims

There is a common perception that women and children are more vulnerable than adult men to becoming victims of trafficking in persons. This perception is reflected in the full name of the Protocol to Prevent, Suppress and Punish Trafficking in Persons, Especially Women and Children (United Nations 2000) which singles out the trafficking of women and children as issues of particular concern.

A UNODC study on the patterns and flows of trafficking in persons collected profiles of some 43,000 victims officially detected by national authorities worldwide between 2007 and 2010 or more recently. The analysis of the data confirms the need for special attention to these two categories of victims. Women and children are the two most frequently reported groups of trafficked persons.

2.1 Women as Trafficking Victims

The majority of the above victims were women who were 18 years of age or older. Women comprise the bulk of victims detected globally. This suggests that being a woman in many parts of the world entails those vulnerabilities that may lead to victimization through trafficking in persons. An analysis of the data for 2009 confirms the age/gender patterns recorded during the whole reporting period as presented in Fig. 1.

Taking into account the number of trafficking victims detected in 2009 who were girls under the age of 18, the total proportion of female victims was 76 % of all victims. In particular, in 2009 the share of detected victims who were female was also about three quarters of all victims. However, the share of female victims is slightly lower in 2006 (UNODC/UN.GIFT 2009a, b) than in 2009 (Fig. 2).

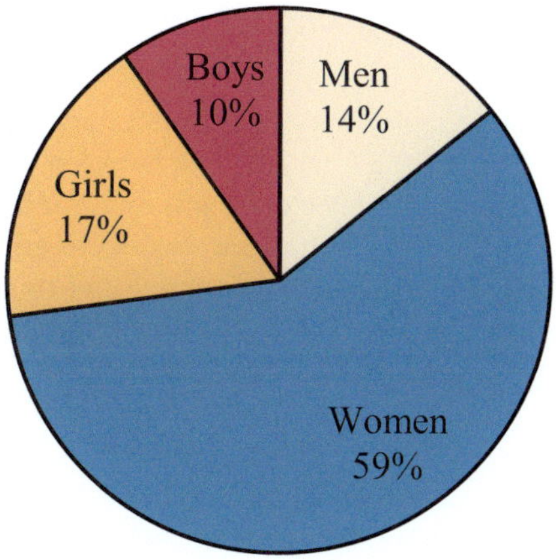

Fig. 1 Gender and age profile of victims detected globally, 2009

Fig. 2 Share of female victims detected globally, by age, 2006 and 2009

The share of women and girls among detected victims over the past few years has been decreasing somewhat. In particular, in recent years there has been an evident reduction of the share of detected adult women, which has been partially offset by an increased share of girls among the detected victims of trafficking.

Nonetheless, trafficking in persons remains a crime with a strong gender connotation. Adult women represent the bulk of female victims. Trafficking of girls accounts for about 15–20 % of the total number of victims detected between 2007 and 2010 (or more recently), representing the second largest category of detected trafficking victims globally and this share has been increasing in recent years. This increase should be seen in the light of the overall increasing share of children among trafficked victims detected recently.

2.2 Children as Trafficking Victims

The share of detected child victims under 18 years of age among those whose age profile was known accounted for a total of 27 % between 2007 and 2010. Among these, girls were more frequently detected than boys. On average, of every three trafficked children detected by the authorities, two were girls and one was a boy. Between 2007 and 2010, the share of boys among the total number of detected victims was in the range of 8–10 %, while girls accounted for about 15–20 %. This reinforces this crime's characteristics with respect to gender and emphasizes the circumstances creating vulnerabilities that push females to become victims of trafficking in persons.

When comparing the proportion of child trafficking detected between 2007 and 2010 (about 27 %) to the proportion recorded between 2003 and 2006 (around 20 %), a general increase of detected child trafficking at the global level can be discerned. This finding is further corroborated by the fact that more than 20 countries recorded a clear increase in the proportion of child trafficking detected in the period 2007–2010 compared with the period 2003–2006. In recent years, the increase has been greater for girls: in 2003, 11 %; in 2006, 13 % and in 2009, 17 % of detected victims were girls (Fig. 3).

The scale of child trafficking varies greatly between regions, subregions and countries. During the period 2007–2010, children accounted for about 16 % of the trafficking victims detected in Europe and Central Asia. North and South America recorded a proportion of child victims at some 27 %, which is in line with the global average. South Asia, East Asia and the Pacific recorded a proportion higher than the global average: about 40 % of all victims detected between 2007 and 2010 were children. In Africa and the Middle East, children comprised a large majority of the victims reported (Fig. 4).

European countries have a comparatively greater capacity to detect and report on trafficking in persons, whereas African countries have a lesser capacity. As a result, global statistics tend to reflect European patterns disproportionately compared with patterns in Africa. Trafficking in persons in Africa is characterized by a high proportion of child victims. Conversely, countries in Europe record a limited share of child victims.

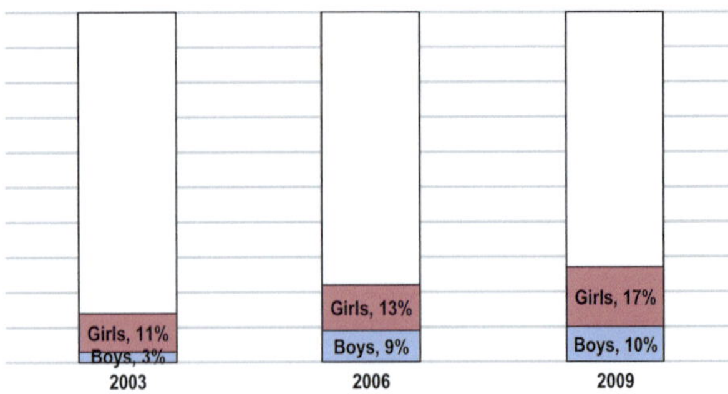

Fig. 3 Share of child victims detected globally, by gender, 2003, 2006 and 2009

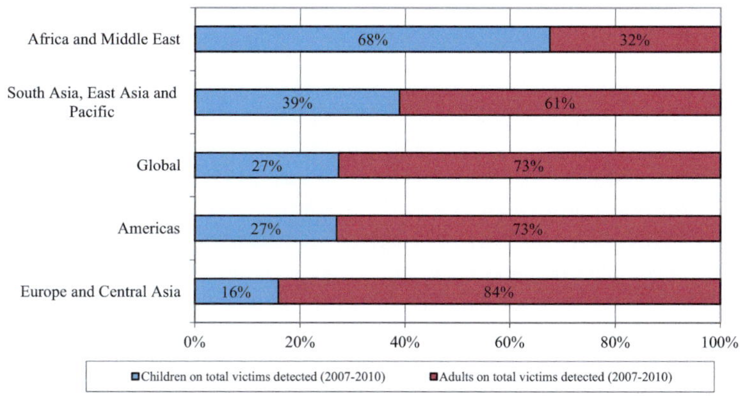

Fig. 4 Share of child victims detected, by region, 2007–2010

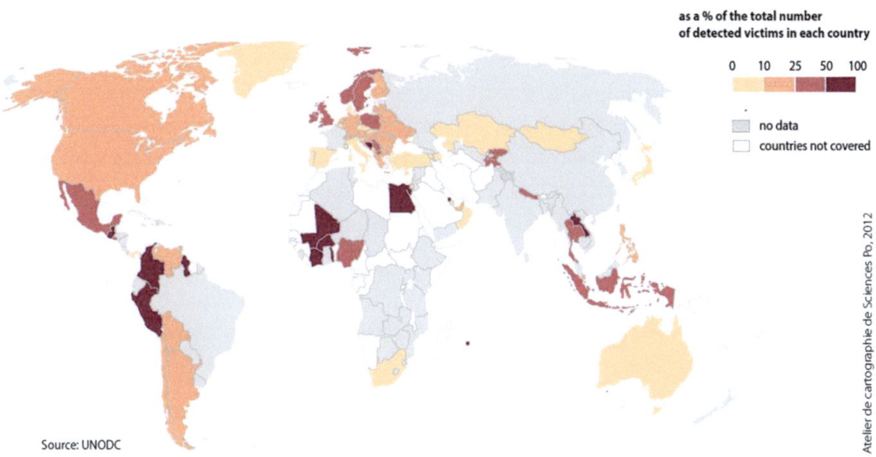

Fig. 5 Share of children among the total number of victims detected, by country, 2007–2010

The aggregated values tend to obscure important differences at the local level. Child trafficking appears to be less frequent than adult trafficking when values are compared at the global level. However, when the regional- and country-level data are considered, it is clear that during the reporting period, in many countries, children were more frequently detected as trafficking victims than were adults.

Figure 5 shows that children were more frequently detected as victims of trafficking in persons on the African continent, in the Andean countries, in South-East Asia and in the Western Balkans.

The share of men among the total victims detected globally is not insignificant. Between 2007 and 2010, men represent about 15 % of the victims over the reporting period. Similar percentages were recorded during the 2003–2006 period, which indicates that the global share of men detected remained relatively constant during the whole decade.

It should be emphasized that official statistics stemming from law enforcement reporting may not always be representative of the human trafficking situation in each country. Enforcement efforts may emphasize certain manifestations of the crime, which could lead to over- or underrepresentation of some types of trafficking. From the currently available data, a limited number of adult men were identified as victims of trafficking in persons; particularly in sub-Saharan Africa and in East Asia. This is likely to be more due to the limited detection capacity in these regions rather than a contained severity of this form of trafficking. More efforts are needed to enhance knowledge and awareness about the trafficking of men.

3 Exploitation

Trafficking in persons happens mostly because of money as some human beings exploit others in order to gain profits. The traffickers leverage their power versus the victims to force them to carry out certain tasks in conditions the victims would not accept if they were free to decide. Exploitation may take many forms. The Trafficking in Persons Protocol lists a number of purposes that the trafficking may have which can be grouped in three categories:

(a) Exploiting the prostitution of others or other forms of sexual exploitation;
(b) Forced labour or services, slavery or practices similar to slavery, servitude;
(c) Removal of organs.

The majority of the detected trafficking victims were sexually exploited between 2007 and 2010. In 2010, about 58 % of the victims detected were trafficked for sexual exploitation (Fig. 6). One victim in three was trafficked for forced labour, slavery or servitude whereas about 0.2 % of the victims detected were trafficked for the removal of organs. A relatively large share (6.4 %) of the victims detected in 2010 were trafficked for purposes not specifically mentioned in the Trafficking in

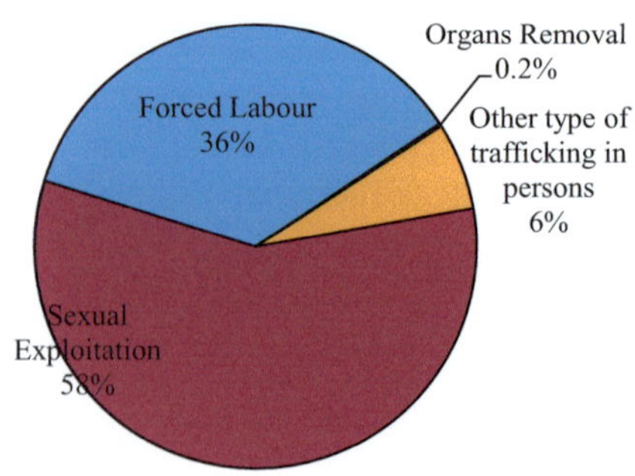

Fig. 6 Distribution of victims detected globally, by form of exploitation, 2010

Persons Protocol, including begging, forced marriages, illegal adoption, participating in armed combat and committing crime (usually petty/street crime).

When the national figures are aggregated into a global total, the picture that emerges shows that trafficking in persons for sexual exploitation is more frequently detected than trafficking for forced labour globally. This result may not be fully representative of the global situation with regard to detected victims, however, as countries in Europe and the Americas detect more victims than the other regions which means that exploitation patterns that are prominent there may affect the global total disproportionately. As a consequence, the share of trafficking for forced labour reported here (36 %) is likely to still be an underestimation compared to trafficking for sexual exploitation.

Furthermore, the lower detection rate of trafficking in persons for forced labour compared to sexual exploitation is probably due to the generally lower visibility of this form of trafficking, as well as historical limitations and/or partial nature of the legislation in many countries that only considered trafficking for sexual exploitation until very recently. This also has an impact on the gender of the detected victims: women and girls are often victims of sexual exploitation as well as other forms of trafficking such as forced labour. On the other hand, men are seldom victims of sexual exploitation, which is the most commonly detected form of trafficking. As official records may not capture those victims who are exploited in forms of trafficking other than sexual exploitation, trafficking in men may be even more hidden than trafficking in women.

The detection rate of trafficking for forced labour is increasing, however. The share of detected victims who were trafficked for forced labour was about 18 % in the year 2006. This share appears to have doubled in the last few years, to 36 % of the total number of victims detected in 2010 (Fig. 7).

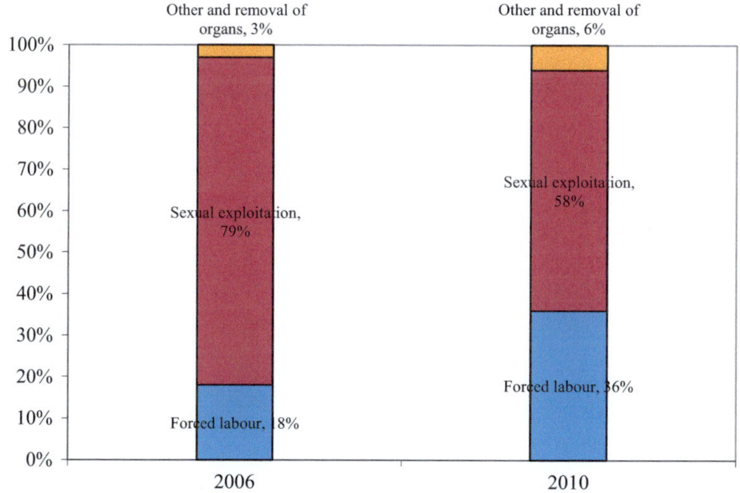

Fig. 7 Victims detected globally whose exploitation was known, by form of exploitation, 2006 and 2010

The share of victims trafficked for purposes other than forced labour and sexual exploitation doubled between 2006 and 2010, albeit from a very low level. Within the "other" category, child begging is the form most frequently reported, accounting for about 1.5 cent of the total number of victims detected between 2007 and 2010. During this period, trafficking for begging was detected and reported in 19 countries around the world. Cases of trafficking for the purpose of illegal adoption have been detected in 15 countries. About 0.6 % of the total number of victims were trafficked for mixed sexual and labour exploitation. Trafficking in children for use as combatants appears to be concentrated in a limited number of countries. Cases of trafficking for forced marriages, for the production of pornographic material and for the use of body parts for rituals have also been reported in a number of countries.

4 Women as Traffickers

While most of the known victims of trafficking in persons are women and children, the vast majority of the detected offenders are adult males. The exact proportions of male involvement vary between countries and regions, however. Based on information provided by 51 countries regarding the gender of people prosecuted for trafficking in persons, as well as data from 56 countries regarding the gender of those convicted between 2007 and 2010, males comprise some two thirds of those involved in the trafficking process. There is no significant gender profile distinction between those prosecuted and convicted (Fig. 8).

In comparison, data collected through the United Nations Survey of Crime Trends and Operations of Criminal Justice Systems (UNODC 2014) on convictions for all crimes in 66 countries during the 2006–2009 period show that most countries indicate a female offending rate below 15 %. The average share is some 12 %, with only a few countries reporting shares above 20 %.

Although a clear majority of those receiving a criminal justice response for trafficking in persons are men, trafficking in persons is a crime with a relatively

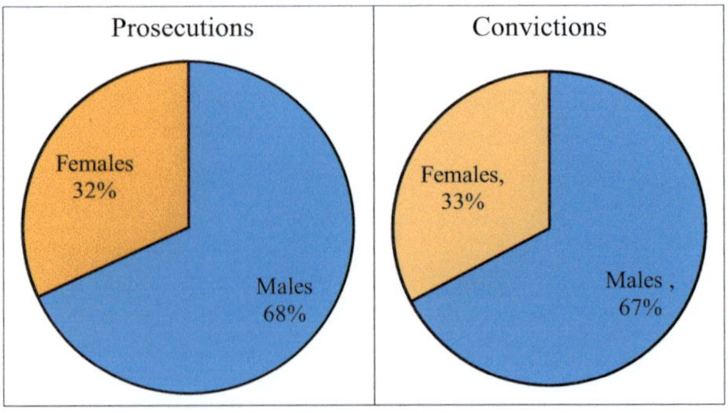

Fig. 8 Persons prosecuted and convicted, by gender, global average, 2007–2010

high rate of female involvement. In fact, the relative prominence of female offending rates related to trafficking in persons is a clear exception within the criminological taxonomy. Few other crimes record this level of female participation.

This result deserves closer attention, beyond the representation of what emerges from criminal justice statistics. It is not necessarily surprising that a crime with such a strong gender connotation in terms of victims (75–80 % are females) reflects this in terms of the profile of the offenders. As a matter of fact, the data show that there may be a link between the profile of the victims and that of the offenders. In particular, there is a positive correlation between the share of underage females detected as victims and the share of women convicted for trafficking in persons (Fig. 9).[1] The countries that detect a relatively high percentage of girl victims also see women found guilty of trafficking more frequently, and conversely, in countries where women are less frequently convicted, there are fewer girls among the victims. This suggests that women traffickers are relatively likely to participate in forms of trafficking related to the exploitation of girls, in relation to whom adult women could have more power to leverage than men.

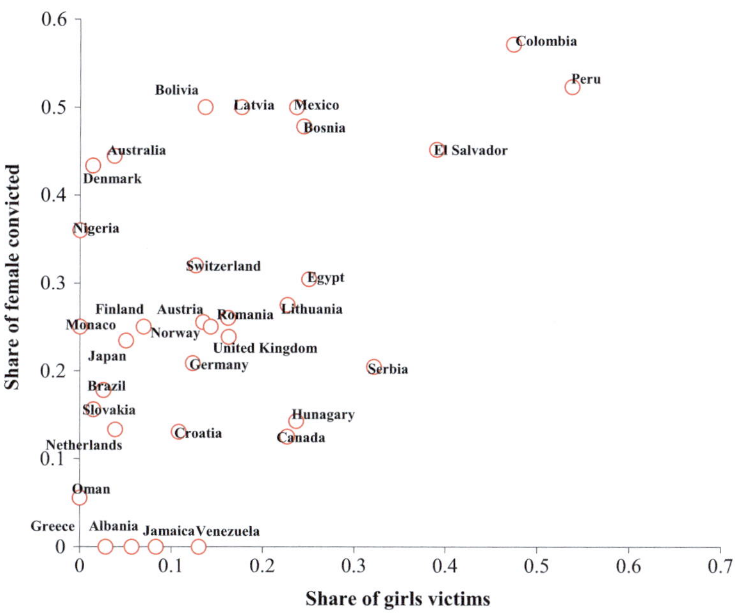

Fig. 9 Correlation between share of girls detected as victims and the share of women convicted for trafficking in persons during the period 2007–2010

[1] A parametric correlation conducted on the percentage of the underage females on the total victims and the percentage of women convicted on total persons convicted gives a Pearsons' coefficient of +508; Sig: 0,003. The correlation was conducted among the variables provided by the 33 countries that provided data on both variables.

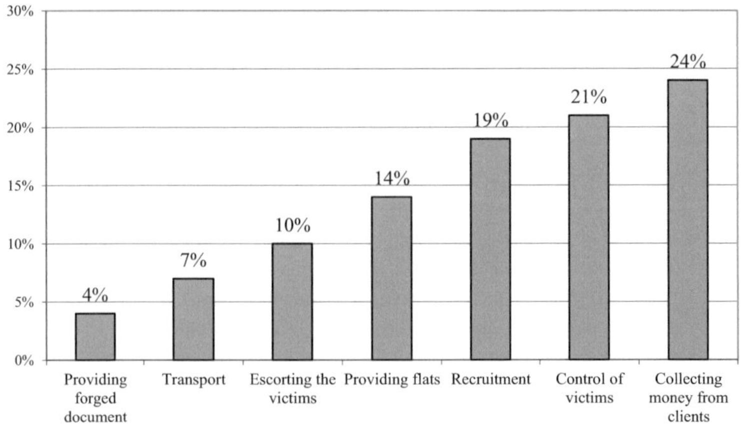

Fig. 10 Activities where women were engaged in the trafficking process in Italy; share of the total number of females convicted between 1996 and 2003

This quantitative result provides support to the hypothesis that female offending is particularly connected to sexual exploitation, which has been noted in a number of qualitative studies. Some of these indicated the emergence of women as traffickers in the late 1990s (See Ciconte 2005 and Surtees 2008), and more recently in 2008. Figure 10 represents the results of a study conducted on Eastern European trafficking networks operating in Italy in the late 1990s, which showed that women were becoming more numerous among those convicted of trafficking in persons.

What is the nature of female involvement in trafficking in persons for sexual exploitation, and what role do these women play? As reported in the chart, and in other qualitative studies (IOM 2001, Denisova 2004; UNICRI 2005; UNODC 2007 and Surtees 2008), in the networks involved in sexual exploitation women are normally used for activities such as guarding the victims where the exploitation takes place, whether it is the street or a brothel, or to receive cash from the clients. These networks also widely use women as recruiters of victims as they may be more easily trusted by other females, who are more vulnerable to this type of trafficking.

This suggests that women traffickers are often placed in low-ranking segments of the trafficking networks to carry out duties that are more exposed to the risk of being caught and prosecuted than men traffickers. As a consequence, a large share of women traffickers may also reflect the higher likelihood of this group to be identified compared to male traffickers, as well as a possible investigative and prosecutorial focus on low-level perpetrators in some countries (OSCE 2010, pp. 56–58).

Some womenmay have been trafficked themselves and have managed to "work their way up" to manage other victims (Siegel and de Blank 2010). The passage from the role of the victim to the role of the exploiter has been documented in the case, for instance, of Nigerian trafficking groups exploiting girls and women from Nigeria (Carling 2006; Carchedi and Orfano 2007 and UNICRI 2004). However, it must be kept in mind that the victims who become members of the criminal group exploiting other victims usually stay at the bottom levels of the traffickers'

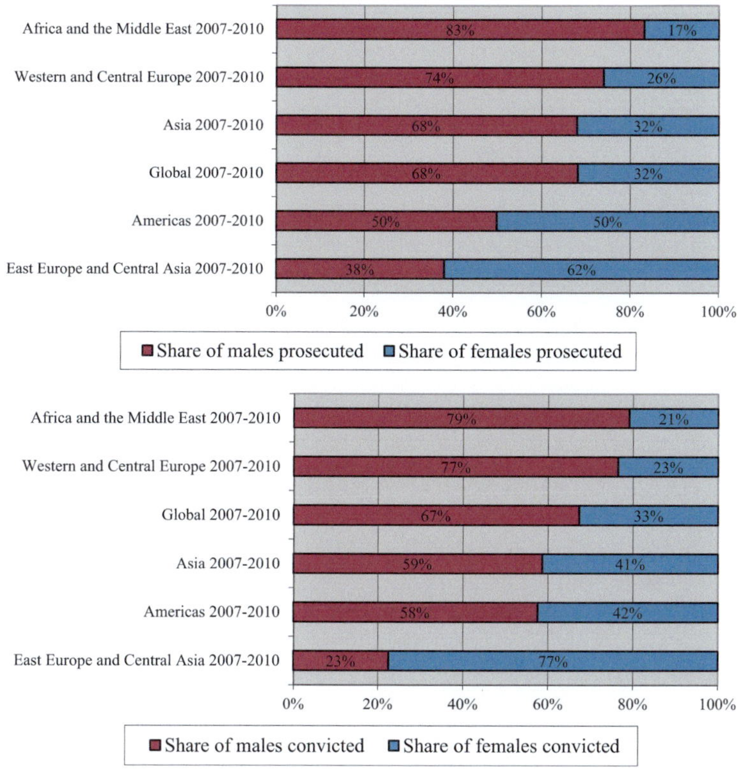

Fig. 11 Share of persons prosecuted and convicted of trafficking in persons, by gender; regional averages, 2007–2010

hierarchy. These women may have another member of the same group still exploiting them. Some countries do not report any differences concerning the gender profile of human traffickers compared to other crimes. Moreover, qualitative studies have indicated that some trafficking networks have historically been male-driven, as in the case of Albanian trafficking groups (Ciconte 2005).

While women traffickers are more likely to be involved in the trafficking of girls for sexual exploitation, their prominence, as well as their roles in the trade, may change according to a combination of factors. The role of the country in the trafficking flow, for example, may make female involvement more or less likely. More sociological aspects, such as the broader roles of women in society, are also influential. The wide regional differences found in prosecutions and convictions reflect these considerations.

Trafficking in Eastern Europe and Central Asia, for example, is strongly gender characterized, with a share of women among those prosecuted and convicted around and above 60 % between 2007 and 2010. In other parts of the world, female offending rates are much lower, for example in Western and Central Europe and in Africa and the Middle East (Fig. 11).

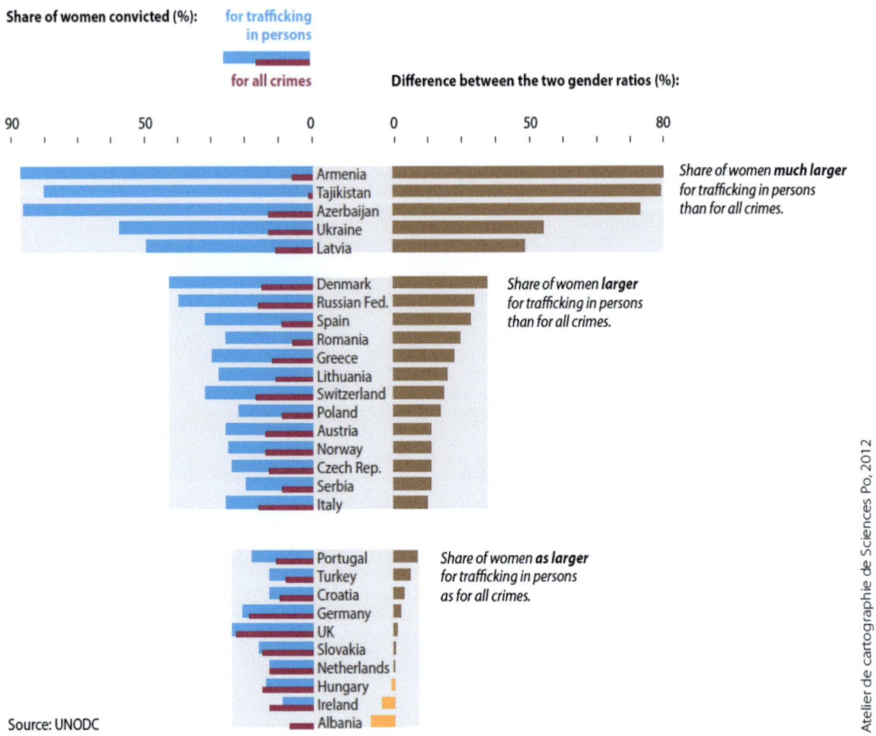

Fig. 12 Share of women convicted of trafficking (2007–2010) and of all crimes (2006–2009)—selected countries in Europe and Central Asia

Countries in Eastern Europe and Central Asia report very high rates of female participation in trafficking in persons-related crimes, above 50 %, with peaks above 70 % in the south Caucasus (Fig. 12). This high rate is constant for the period from 2006 to 2010 (UNODC/UN.GIFT 2009a, b, 47 and UNODC 2012, pp. 54–55). Most victims in the region are women trafficked for sexual exploitation, which is the form of trafficking in which female traffickers are particularly involved. However, the high rate of female involvement cannot be explained by the profile of the victims alone. A law enforcement focus largely limited to lower-ranking segments of the trafficking network—where women are more likely to be found—could be another explanatory factor, though additional research would be needed to explain why.

5 Responses

Faced with recurring challenges, Member States decided to ensure that the next steps in the fight against trafficking in persons were taken without denying the positive impact of the Trafficking in Persons Protocol. In 2010, just a few months short of the tenth anniversary of the adoption of the Protocol, Member States renewed their commitment to the fight against trafficking in persons when the General Assembly adopted the *United Nations Global Plan of Action to Combat Trafficking in Persons* (A/RES/64/293) (2010).

The Global Plan of Action requests that Member States and the international community take action against trafficking in persons in the following areas of prevention and protection:

Prevention of Trafficking in Persons

- Address factors that make people vulnerable:
  - Poverty
  - Unemployment
  - Inequality
  - Humanitarian emergencies (armed conflicts, natural disasters)
  - Sexual violence
  - Gender discrimination
  - Social exclusion
  - Marginalisation
  - Culture of tolerance against violence against women, youth and children
- Address all forms of trafficking in persons.
- Include trafficking in persons in the United Nations work on:
  - Economic and social development
  - Human rights
  - Rule of law
  - Good governance
  - Education and natural disaster
  - Post-conflict reconstruction
- Implement comprehensive policies and action in line with policies on:
  - Migration
  - Education
  - Employment
  - Gender equality

(continued)

- Empowerment of women
- Crime prevention

- Conduct research and share best practices.
- Develop process for the identification of victims and reinforce the provision of identity documents.
- Promote awareness raising to discourage the demand and promote human rights education.
- Focus on demand and trafficking for labour exploitation, and educate consumers on goods and services produced as a result of trafficking in persons.
- Strengthen the capacity of law enforcement, immigration, education, social welfare, labour and other relevant officials to prevent trafficking in persons, in cooperation with civil society.

Protection of and Assistance to Victims of Trafficking in Persons

- Promote and protect the rights of victims, reintegrate them into the community and treat them as victims of crime making sure that they are not penalized for having been trafficked.
- Review and strengthen services and referral mechanisms.
- Strengthen the capacity of those likely to encounter victims: law enforcement personnel; border control officers; labour inspectors; consular or embassy officials; judges and prosecutors; peacekeepers and other relevant sectors including civil society.
- Protect the privacy and identity of victims and ensure their safety as well the safety of their family members.
- Provide assistance and services for the physical, psychological and social recovery and rehabilitation of trafficked persons including special services such as access to prevention, treatment, care and support services for HIV and AIDS and other blood-borne and communicable diseases.
- Consider adopting measures to permit victims to remain in destination countries.
- Ensure a safe and preferably voluntary return of victims to their origin country.
- Adopt labour laws which provide legal rights and protections for workers that would limit their risk of being trafficked.
- Provide appropriate assistance and protection in the best interest of the child tochild victims.
- Establish the United Nations Voluntary Trust Fund for Victims of Trafficking in Persons, Especially Women and Children.
- Adopt measures for compensation.
- Acknowledge the important role of civil society organizations.

(continued)

- Ensure victims' access to justice.
- Provide victims with a reflection period.

The Global Plan of Action requests that Member States and the international community take action against trafficking in persons in the following areas of prosecution and partnerships:

Prosecution of Crimes of Trafficking in Persons

- Criminalize and prosecute all forms of trafficking in persons including attempting, participating and directing other persons to commit an offence as well as organized criminal groups' involvement in trafficking in persons.
- Ensure the liability of all categories of perpetrators of trafficking in persons, including the liability of legal persons and entities.
- Enhance investigation and prosecution and ensure proportionate penalties: use systematically freezing and confiscation of assets .
- Make use of the available technical assistance.
- Investigate, prosecute and punish corrupt public officials who engage in trafficking in persons and promote a zero-tolerance policy against corruption.
- Strengthen cooperation among countries to address crimes that can be linekd to trafficking in persons such as money-laundering, corruption, smuggling of migrants and all forms of organized crime.
- Exchange information among relevant authorities.

Strengthening of Partnerships Against Trafficking in Persons

- Enhance cooperation among UN bodies and other international organizations particularly in relation to capacity building, support the Inter-Agency Coordination Group against
- Trafficking in Persons and encourage UN bodies and other international organizations to assist Member States and improve the coherence and efficiency of delivery.
- Encourage cooperation, share of best practices and mutual legal assistance at the national, bilateral, regional and international levels.
- Promote cooperation among different stakeholders such as authorities, civil society, private sector, media, workers' and employers' organizations, law enforcement agencies.
- Requests UNODC to collect information and report biannually on patterns and flows of trafficking in persons.

6 Conclusion

The majority of detected trafficking cases are of sexual exploitation even though the share of forced labour cases is increasing. Since sexual exploitation often victimizes women it is not a surprise that women and girls form the majority of those victims that are known to the authorities. The share of women has somewhat declined during the last years. At the same time, the share of detected girl victims has increased which could indicate that the traffickers are turning to the exploitation of younger victims. This phenomenon is, however, restricted to girl victims since the share of both adult men and boys as trafficking victims has increased during the recent years. It should also be noted that female offenders are particularly involved in trafficking in girls.

There is a significant regional variation in terms of the share of child victims. The largest share can be found in Africa and the Middle East, which may have been affected by the current legislation on trafficking in persons in the region. Several African countries criminalize only child trafficking or they have changed their legislation just recently to cover also other forms of trafficking in persons. This may result in an overrepresentation of child victims in official records. However, when considering countries with long-standing and comprehensive legislation on trafficking in persons, the share of detected child trafficking in this region is still larger than the global average.

While the majority of the offenders are men, the share of female offenders is exceptionally high for human trafficking crimes. Also in this case there is considerable regional diversity. In East Europe and Central Asia, the majority of offenders are women. For example, some of the countries of the former Soviet Union have a much larger share of women convicted of human trafficking than of other crimes.

Five Questions

1. What are the factors that make women vulnerable to trafficking in persons?
2. What are the factors that make children vulnerable to trafficking in persons?
3. How could trafficking in women and children be prevented?
4. What can the number of those victims identified by the authorities tell about the trafficking situation in a country? What does it not tell?
5. Why women are more involved in human trafficking than in other crimes as offenders?

References

A/RES/64/293, United Nations Global Plan of Action to Combat Trafficking in Person, 30 July 2010.

Carchedi, F., & Orfano, I. (2007). *La tratta di persone in Italia, La tratta di persone in Italia. Evoluzione del fenomenoedambiti di sfruttamento*. Franco Angeli: Milano.

Carling, J. (2006). Migration, Human Smuggling and Trafficking from Nigeria to Europe, IOM. Available at: http://publications.iom.int/bookstore/free/MRS23.pdf.

Ciconte, E. (2005). The trafficking flows and routes of Eastern Europe. WEST Project ref. N. 2A071. WEST, Bologna.
Denisova, T. (2004). Trafficking in Women and Children for Purposes of Sexual Exploitation. Zaporizhie State University. Available at: http://www.childtrafficking.com/Docs/denisova__no_date___traffic.pdf.
IOM. (2001). *Deceived migrants from Tajikistan: A study of trafficking in women and children*. Dushanbe: International Organization for Migration.
OSCE (2010).Analyzing the Business Model of Trafficking in Human Beings to Better Prevent the Crime. Available at: http://www.osce.org/cthb/69028?download=true.
Siegel, D., & de Blank, S. (2010). Women who traffic women: The role of women in human trafficking networks. *Dutch Cases, Global Crime, 11*(4), 436–447.
Surtees, R. (2008). Traffickers and trafficking in southern and eastern Europe. *European Journal of Criminology, 5*(1), 39–68.
UN Women (2011) Progress of the World's Women 2011–2012: in Pursuit of Justice, New York. Available at: http://progress.unwomen.org/pdfs/EN-Report-Progress.pdf.
UNICRI (2005). Trafficking in Women from Romania into Germany: Comprehensive Report. Available at: http://www.childtrafficking.com/Docs/tra_romania_germany_0607.pdf.
UNICRI (2004) Trafficking of Nigerian Girls to Italy, Turin.
United Nations (2000). Protocol to Prevent, Suppress and Punish Trafficking in Persons, Especially Women and Children, Supplementing the United Nations Convention against Transnational Organized Crime., 2337 UNTS 319.Available at: http://www.unodc.org/unodc/en/treaties/CTOC/index.html#Fulltext.
United Nations Global Plan of Action to Combat Trafficking in Person (2010). General Assembly resolution 64/293 (A/RES/64/293) 12 August 2010.
UNODC (2007). An Assessment of Referral Practices to Assist and Protect the Rights of Trafficked Persons in Moldova.Available at: http://www.unodc.org/documents/human-trafficking/Moldova_Assmt_May07.pdf.
UNODC/UN.GIFT (2009a). Global Report on Trafficking in Person. Available at: http://www.unodc.org/unodc/en/human-trafficking/glotip.html.
UNODC (2012). Global Report on Trafficking in Persons 2012. Available at: www.unodc.org/glotip.html.
UNODC (2014). United Nations Survey of Crime Trends and Operations of Criminal Justice Systems. Available at: http://www.unodc.org/unodc/en/data-and-analysis/United-Nations-Surveys-on-Crime-Trends-and-the-Operations-of-Criminal-Justice-Systems.html.
UNODC/UN.GIFT (2009b). Global Report on Trafficking in Persons. Available at: http://www.unodc.org/unodc/en/data-and-analysis/glotip.html.

Exploring Hidden Spaces: Sexual Abuse of Girl Children in India

Swati Shirwadkar

Abstract The present research review explores different aspects of sexual abuse of girls, focusing largely on an Indian context. In spite of progress and new opportunities of education, social and structural divides, traditional cultural practices and gender inequality are some factors that make particularly girl children vulnerable and an easy victim for sexual abuse. The measures taken by the state to control this danger as well as their limitations to address the issue are discussed in the context of the changing social situation in India to bring out multiple aspects that underlie the sexual abuse of children. These complex factors suggest the need of a stronger effort to improve education and awareness with integrated efforts to control the threat.

1 Introduction

Victimization of the vulnerable and exploitation of the defenceless has existed throughout human history. Young ones, though valued by their societies, are sometimes subjected to different forms of victimization and abuse even by their own family, normally considered as the safest place for them to be. In such cases the caregivers themselves exploit the dependents. Child abuse and victimization is present in all societies but the way it is seen, understood and dealt with may differ from society to society, depending largely on the social and cultural framework. With the onset of globalization and related processes, several forces are unleashed which may not necessarily create better opportunities for all but in fact may have created new patterns with deterritoralization of victimization and child abuse. Not only are the earlier geo-political boundaries now more or less blurred, but the cultural and social boundaries of class, ethnicity, culture and religion become flexible to act in favour of the exploitation and abuse with the emerging new global market, changing social dynamics and a potential backlash from these factors. The

S. Shirwadkar (✉)
University of Pune, Pune, India
e-mail: swati@unipune.ac.in

H. Kury et al. (eds.), *Women and Children as Victims and Offenders: Background, Prevention, Reintegration*, DOI 10.1007/978-3-319-08398-8_31

problems that were plaguing the societies, especially for those members who remain on the margins, still persist in spite of the new changes. Many developing countries are presently undergoing a transition that has created new opportunities, such as individual freedom and easy access to technology but also new forms of exploitation, abuse and victimization, with emerging inequalities, new aspirations and sharper social and structural divides while the earlier safety networks continue to diminish.

Against this background this chapter, through a comprehensive research review, explores different aspects of child victimization and abuse, particularly of girl children, focusing largely on an Indian context. The cultural context of the issue will help in understanding as well as in addressing the problem. The measures taken by the state to control this danger as well as their limitations to address the issue will also be discussed in the context of the social situation in India, and the research review will bring out the multiple layers that underpin the sexual abuse of children. It will explore the dynamics of social forces that propagate domination and exploitation and contribute to victimize children into sexual abuse, while at the same time looking at the larger picture.

Since child sexual victimization and abuse exists in all societies, scholars have debated the reasons and factors that result in abusive situations. However, as Finkelhor points out, theories about child sexual victimization must be viewed against the true backdrop, i.e. a vast ignorance of the forces governing the development and expression of sexual behaviour in general. Indeed, as argued by him, the fact that many child victims fail to report their experiences to anyone, including their parents, is powerful evidence that the experience is surrounded by conflict (Finkelhor 2005). The WHO includes all forms of physical and emotional ill-treatment, sexual abuse, neglect, and exploitation that results in actual or potential harm to the child's health, development or dignity (World Health Organization 2010). Researchers have brought out some basic components that are included in the US definition of child abuse and neglect from 1978. The definition includes extra-familial as well as intra-familial abuse, and sexual experience includes both physical and non-physical contact, as well as the factor of authority and power of the abuser and the age of consent. In the context of sexual relations, incest is usually defined as illegal (Barnett et al. 2005). Similarly, researchers include in sexual behaviour acts such as fondling of the body, penetration of the child's body by non-sexual objects or by the offender's sexual organ and also non-contact behaviour, such as voyeurism or pornography (Gelles and Conte 1990). The terms sexual abuse, sexual assault or child victimization may vary in legal interpretations in different countries. For example, in India, it is only after the amendment of the rape law in 2013 that the definition is broadly worded to include offences that were not included earlier and hence was limited in legal interpretation.[1]

[1] After the Delhi gang rape case in December 2012, the rape law was amended in 2013. The definition is now broadly worded with acts like penis penetration or any object or any part of body to any extent, into the vagina, mouth, urethra or anus of another person or making another person

Though the danger of child sexual abuse in its different forms exist in Indian society, talking about it becomes very difficult given the social context. Hence collecting data on the topic remains a challenge. Recently a study on child abuse was conducted which included child sexual abuse in India. For this study, The Ministry of Women and Child Development of the Government of India adopted the WHO definition of child sexual abuse for its study. It includes "inappropriate sexual behaviour with a child, fondling a child's genitals, making a child fondle an adult's genitals, sexual assault (intercourse, incest, rape and sodomy), exhibitionism and pornography" and that these acts are "committed by a person responsible for the care of a child or related to the child (for example a baby-sitter, parent, neighbour, relative, extended family member, peer, older child, friend, stranger or a day-care provider)" (Ministry of Women and Child Welfare 2007, p. 4).

The major findings of the study brought out that 53.22 % of children reported having faced one or more forms of sexual abuse, and among them 52.94 % were boys and 47.06 % were girls. This shows that the common perception in India that it is the girl who has to be protected (due to the importance of chastity) is wrong, even a male child needs protection. However, one has to also keep in mind that reporting an abuse may be difficult and shameful for a girl in an Indian setting. Among the respondents, 21.90 % children reported facing severe forms of sexual abuse, 50.76 % other forms of sexual abuse, and 5.69 % were sexually assaulted.[2] Half of the abusers (50 %) were persons known to the child and in a position of trust and responsibility.

The report also brings out that most children did not report the matter to anyone, only 3 % of children or their families told the police about it (Ministry of Women and Child Development 2007). Voluntary organizations have also produced some statistics regarding child sexual abuse. A study by a voluntary organization surveyed 2211 school children, from different backgrounds (Save the Children and Tulir 2006). Out of a total of 2211 child participants, 939 boys and girls reported sexual abuse, of which 39 % were females. The definition used in the study includes any behaviour by an older or more powerful person, ranging from exhibitionism, making the child touch the offender's private parts or touching the child's private parts, or making the child watch pornography or having oral, vaginal, anal sexual intercourse.

The study concedes that the stigma associated with "loss of virginity" and the general silence on the subject, especially for girls, may have led to underreporting. It has to be noted that there is a lack of availability of systematically collected

do so, apply of mouth or touching private parts now constitutes the offence of 'sexual assault'. For more information, see: http://en.wikipedia.org/wiki/Criminal_Law_(Amendment)_Act,_2013#Changes_in_law.

[2] Child sexual abuse was prosecuted under the following sections of Indian Penal Code: I.P.C. (1860) 375—Rape, I.P.C. (1860) 354—Outraging the modesty of a woman, I.P.C. (1860) 377—Unnatural offences. There were many limitations and loopholes for these. After the Protection of Children from Sexual Offences Act (POCSO) of 2012, a variety of offences are recognized as punishable. For more information, see: http://wcd.nic.in/childact/childprotection31072012.pdf.

official statistics over the years, and that the Protection of Children Against Sexual Offences Bill, 2011 regarding child sexual abuse was passed by Parliament only recently and entered into force on May 22, 2012. Overall, there is some increase in crimes against women in India, as per the National Crime Records Bureau of India. The data is not desegregated by age, but shows that crimes against women reported under the Indian Penal Code (IPC) and Special and Local Laws (SLL) during the year 2011 has increased by 7.1 % over the year 2010 and by 23.4 % over the year 2007. This demands attention to the issue of crimes against women in general and the issue of sexual abuse of girls in particular.

2 Different Perspectives in the Field of Study

Earlier the understanding of the issue was mostly moralistic or medical. Sexual abusers were seen as psychopathic, moral degenerates. But researchers have shown that only a small proportion of offenders fall into this category (Cohen and Boucher 1972). There are theories about victims as well, such as the sexually acting-out child, actively encouraging the adult, or the sexually defenceless child who has a passive outlook. Theories about the family context look at social isolation that may cause incest or role confusion, such as a father treating a daughter as a wife. The fear of abandonment is also an element that helps to explain why a sexual relation of incest is tolerated (Finkelhor 2005; Wiehe 1998).

One of the most believed and common perception and explanation of abuse is that alcohol and drug addiction are the reason. There is a substantial association between alcohol use and child abuse but research points out that they are associated factors and not the cause (Gelles 1993). As far as the abuses within the family are concerned, it is the nature of family that makes it difficult to pin down the reasons for violence within the family. Gelles and Straus identified unique characteristics of the family as a social group that contribute to making the family a violence-prone institution, such as structural arrangements and cultural acceptance of physical violence in most societies or conflicts in relationships due to intimacy. But in a later article, Straus and Hotaling pointed out the irony that these same characteristics and mode of organization of family relationships based on love also make it a supportive and intimate environment (Gelles and Straus 1979; Straus and Hotaling 1980). With the success of the women's movement, feminist theory became a major theoretical model in explaining family violence in asserting the role of gender and power as key elements of domestic violence (Yllo 1993). However, the South Asian women's movement has expressed its dissatisfaction with the mainstream feminist movement which tends to focus on only one dimension of women's lives—the violent relationship (Alexander and Mohanty 1997; Bhattacharjee 1997). In a South Asian context, the specific socio-cultural context and multiple layers of domination also need to be considered (Shirwadkar 2004) while addressing the issue of child sexual abuse.

Social changes that took place during the twentieth century contributed to the success of the child saving movement (Finkelhor 1996). Specialized professionals such as legal advocates, nurses, school teachers and counsellors started taking an interest in saving the children; another reason was the empowerment of women due to which they could advocate for children (as quoted in Barnett et al. 2005).

2.1 Background and Historical Context

A glimpse into the history of societies may reveal that child abuse existed in most societies even though the arrival of a child is usually celebrated. However, if the problem exists and persists, the pattern of retaliation shows that most societies try to hide the issue if the abuse takes place within the family, which is usually considered as a private space outsiders or the state should not encroach on. Awareness about abuse that takes place within the family and of the rights of children is comparatively recent. Child sexual abuses existed in many societies, sometimes having a societal acceptance. However, to understand and interpret the meaning of such relations also depends on the context of the present society; hence the way cultural meanings of past social practices are seen today may be different.

Studies on sexuality show that Greek and Roman societies considered women and children as having subordinate status, and power was reflected in the satisfaction of sexual pleasures of males in particular (Mottier 2008). There is no clear evidence if practices such as male adults fondling boys were condemned (Barnett et al. 2005). Most societies controlled sexual interactions through incest taboos, customs and practices, and particularly female sexuality in the period of socialization.[3] Though family and the larger kin group remained the major controlling factor, it was also supported and controlled by the community, neighbourhood and sometimes even by the peer group through the language of sexual abuse (Weeks 2010). Some myths and beliefs contribute to child sexual abuse which existed not only earlier but even today. For example, folk beliefs circulated in nineteenth century Europe that intercourse with a child virgin could cure venereal diseases (Mottier 2008), and the same seems to be still prevalent in South Asian countries.

Totally unfounded myths such as that raping a child can cure HIV/AIDS intensify the problem (Das and Li 2010). It also has to be noted that in the past and even in the present it is the vulnerable and helpless who become the victim of pervert pleasures. Macho pleasures from sexually abusing and torturing very young girls slowly came out into the open in the post-war period when the public sphere

[3] The term "socialization" has usually been applied to the developmental process by which neonates come to be recognized as competent members of society. However, increasingly, the process is understood as how people internalize the values, attitudes and norms of the culture or the society throughout the life-course.

started making its impact. Mottier documents how the media brought out the hidden horrors of sexual rackets that used to indulge in violence by upper class British "gentlemen", who revelled in sexual torture of young girls. Thanks to their reporting, the age of consent was subsequently pushed in the U.K. from 13 to 16 because of the public debate on the issue (Mottier 2008).

2.2 The South Asian Context and India

The understanding of the "family" and the larger kin group may differ from society to society. While the common understanding of family in the developed Western world may largely be a nuclear one, the perception in the developing societies may include several other members who are related. In Asian and, particularly, South Asian developing societies, the joint family and the larger kin group influence the socialization that ingrain the traditional roles of children within the largely patriarchal family structure. There were some common factors such as age hierarchy within the matriarchal families as well. Ideas and practices related to respect, honour, and shame were always strong and remain so to a large extent even today. There were cases from some countries governed by *Shari'a* law where women were punished for being raped, in spite of a global outcry. Many Asian societies are governed by patriarchal norms and the subordination of women. If sexual assault or rape takes place, the victim is stigmatized for life and sometimes excluded by society. Challenging male authority and prerogatives by any indirect means such as going out in public or having a school education could also be seen as a challenge to the existing structure that underscores patriarchal norms that govern not only the private space of the family but also the public space such as gainful employment or work.

However, one should also take note of cultural specificities in different regions that add several overlapping layers to the situation (Shirwadkar 1998). Some theoretical perspectives look at families in western developed societies as masculinity oriented (Brown et al. 2013). This is particularly the point of view of gender analysts (Jasinski 2001). Studies on criminal exploitation of children point out the commodification of women, male authority within the family and power and control of the male within the family (Ndolo 2010; Azonhoume 2010; Mtimkulu 2010). In the context of developing societies, particularly of South Asian societies such as India, people are generally seen as located within the multiple social relations that intersect class, caste and gender, apart from various nuances of social and cultural specificities of regions and communities and the colonial context. Micro studies have brought out the regional variations in cultural practices but have also highlighted the variations in structure and institutions across the nation (Karve 1965; Madan 1975; Srinivas 1976). In many regions, the importance of a patriarchal joint family, age-status, hierarchy and the role structure not only emphasize the submissive behaviour of females but also demand prescribed role behaviour (Dube 2001; Shirwadkar 1998). It is argued that practices like dowry that become a continuous source of extraction from the girl's maternal family (Deolalikar and Rao 1998; Jejeebhoy 1998) have a colonial context; the practice of "*Streedhan*" (woman's possession) degenerated into a practice of extracting dowry in an exploitative way and resulting in pauperization and strengthening of the male hegemony (Talwar-Oldenberg 2002). Emphasis on the marital status puts pressure not only on the girls but also on their maternal family to "marry them off" at the right time rather than wasting money on the "*paraya dhan*" (someone else's property) for her education.

In the Indian context, the identity of a female child is influenced by several complex and dynamic factors (Shirwadkar 2009). It is influenced through primordial loyalties such as religion, caste, language and history, combined with cultural beliefs and practices that now intersect and take new forms with the onslaught of Bollywood culture and satellite TV (Chananna 1996; Dern'e 1999; Kishwar 1999; Segal 1999). The notion of value of having a male child as a successor makes a girl child not desirable. Resource distribution is not just on the basis of gender but it is also intersected by the ideas of entitlements that are tied with the role set of different communities. Access to education, health and nutrition may not reach a girl child equally due to the existing ideology of a particular community (Dube 2001).

All these factors make the situation of female children precarious, resulting in a skewed sex ratio due to the preference for sons in some regions (Mulay 2009). States in the northern part of India, such as Punjab, Haryana and Delhi, having a better per capita income, show a more skewed sex ratio, and studies have noted the misuse of sex determination tests in these states. However, micro studies point out nuances, such as having one daughter may not be a crisis situation but having a second one may be perceived as such (Patel 2010).

It is not just the economic prosperity that is centrally important to many people. There are other competing and compelling beliefs and traditions which intersect and limit the envisioned idea of human development. Though a daughter also has her importance in rituals, practices and, recently, even in education and other achievements, society makes her aware of her short stay in the natal family.

3 Child Marriage

The problem of child marriage exists in many societies, from Malawi in Africa to a diverse country like India, even though India is now seen as an emerging economy. Girls were married at a fairly advanced age in the *Vedic* period (ca. 1750–500 BCE), as indicated by the evidence from scriptures. However, around 200 AD the age of marriage was lowered and early marriages increased in medieval times (Altekar 1959). The already vulnerable position of a girl child becomes more difficult due to the high value given to family cohesiveness and status in the society if abuse occurs. This is particularly true for sexual abuse because heterosexual sex, for females, is generally perceived as permissible but legitimized only in a marital context (Jejeebhoy 2000). Hence there is also a stigma for women and girls who have any form of physical sexual contact with men. Though there is some change in metro cities, in most places and communities the situation remains the same. On the one hand there is ignorance about sexual relations and the dangers for the adolescent girls and, on the other hand, there are new risks due to changing social spaces with the fast paced process of globalization. The norm of seclusion of girls from puberty onwards does not give the girls a chance for much exposure to the outside world. Studies on the profile of the young adolescents in India show that in many regions, without education, skills and employment opportunities, girls are caught in a web of ignorance, poor reproductive health, early marriage and lifelong dependency (Ramasubban and Jejeebhoy 2000). Though homosexuality does exist in the society, it too has a stigma. However, men could be excused by the community in case of violation of the taboos but the female is always blamed.

While male sexual activity outside marriage is condoned (seen as an activity that is usually done because he is a "real" man or *Mard*, who is bound to do it and hence it should be accepted), adolescent girls face severe restrictions, stigma, violence, exploitation and lack of informed choices (Abraham 2003; Bott and Jejeebhoy 2003; Jejeebhoy 2000; Jejeebhoy et al. 2004). Obviously the burden of stigma and exploitation is inversely borne by females.

This becomes a major factor in small societies mainly responsible for the early marriages of girls. It is a known fact that there are restrictions on public participation of a girl child, her space and time being restricted through metaphors, proverbs and the actual controlling of movement by her family, brother or kin group. For example, a proverb in the Oriya language equates a daughter with "*ghee*" (melted butter): both are valuable but both begin to stink if not disposed of in time (Dube 2001). Thus it becomes important to control and protect her till she gets married. It is pointed out that expectations regarding marriage remain traditional among both adolescent boys and girls but a double standard is reflected in gender relations and expectations (Jejeebhoy 2000). With such constraints and the high value placed on female chastity, early marriage continues to be the norm in many parts of India, especially in rural areas. The Child Marriage Act 1929 and the subsequent Amendment Act 1978 prevents that children get married at too early an age, putting the marriage age for girls at 18 years and for boys at 21 years. The Act is applicable to all communities in India. However, child marriage is also dealt with through various personal laws and local community practices.

Though the legal age for marriage is 18 years for females and 21 for males, women are usually "married off" early to avoid any unwanted consequences. In many cases, the age of the girl is not disclosed to avoid legal problems. Though adolescent and child marriages are now declining, there are regional variations in the age of marriage and this affects the access to better life chances such as education. Parts of northern states in India still suffer from a "gender gap". A study on child abuse by the government concedes that there is a decline in the female/male ratio (or number of girls for every thousand boys), with a maximum in the 0–6 years age bracket with 927 females per 1000 males (Government of India 2007). Biologically, female mortality in the first year of life (beyond the first month) should be lower than male mortality. In India as a whole the child mortality rate for girls is higher than boys; the number of deaths of girls age 1–4 years per 1000 children reaching age 1 year, is 61 % higher than for boys. However, it drops sharply with better economic status and education (Kishor and Gupta 2009; Shekher and Hatti 2010). This brings out that poorer households tend to neglect the girl child. There are several overlapping reasons for this, such as neglect of the girl child due to poverty, preference of a son, blind beliefs, and high maternal mortality (Government of India 2007). The discrimination against girls may be reflected in various ways such as neglect in medical attention except in serious conditions, hard work in the household (usually fetching water from the river or wells is work done by women), bad nutrition and food intake due to poverty, combined with preference given to sons for the limited resources (Padmanabha 2010). Other studies observe that the preference for sons, particularly among the peasant communities, increasing rates of dowry, and cultural factors that emphasise patriarchy are some reasons for the discrimination against girls (Shekher et al. 2010). These factors are also responsible for early marriages and the missed opportunities of education for girls. The retention rate of children in school at the primary level of education is 71.01 % and girls' enrolment in school at primary level is 47.79 % (Government of India 2007). The report also points out that not only the available resources for children's welfare are low but even the utilization of the resources is not effectively done to achieve the outcomes.

It is a well known fact that in many rural hinterlands the allocated amount from the government budget never reaches or is not efficiently utilized, apart from the leakages and siphoning of funds due to frauds. This contributes to the already vulnerable position of the girls who want to avail themselves of an education. As the age level increases, there are more girl dropouts; this is especially related to the age of puberty (Dube 2001; Chanana 1990). Sexuality of girls becomes important as it is women who are responsible for maintaining the family honour (*Izzat*) and the boundary maintenance of caste groups (Dube 2001). In South Asian countries like India, Bangladesh or Pakistan, the concept of honour is very much related to structural factors such as maintaining the power of patriarchy, caste or religion and community. It makes the family and the girls live in fear of social and community pressure, of gossip and at times even of becoming a social outcaste (Kishwar 1999). Though there is some tolerance for inter-caste marriages or even "live-in" relationship in recent years, it is limited mostly to metropolitan areas or the educated higher class or higher middle class. Even today sometimes there are cases of "honour killings" of girls having sexual relations or marrying outside the caste group. The *Khap Panchayat* (community court of the *Khap* community in North India) openly challenged the legal provisions and protections for such cases. The analysis of some autobiographies and literature from the Marathwada region and former (before the re-organization of states) Hyderabad State under Nizam rule shows that earlier, if a woman was violated, there was no option for her but to commit suicide (Shirwadkar 1998; Pagdi 1969). The situation has slowly changed after the independence of India in 1947, and today one sees more reporting of sexual assaults or sexual abuse of girl children in the media that used to remain unreported earlier. The brutal and inhuman Delhi rape and torture case drew international media attention, and many cases of rapes, including gang rapes are being reported which, till recently, used to remain hidden. The incident also created a lot of awareness by the public outrage it caused, protests against the state for failing to protect women and the debate sparked by the incident.

Though there is an overall decline in the practice of child marriage, the tendency towards marrying off girls at an early age still persists to control their sexuality and fertility. Stigma and boundaries of sexuality as well as the importance of chastity of women puts pressure on the girl and the family to be not only vigilant but also silent if any untoward incidence occurs. This is seen more in lower middle classes or in urban fringes and in rural areas where families do not have any options to avoid public suspicions and observation. They also need to depend on the kin- and neighbourhood support network. The social pressures and justifications adversely affect the life chances of a girl child. She is denied access to education, better reproductive health and may have to undergo forced sexual relations at an early age. These pressures also deny the girl child the right to non-discrimination on the basis of age and gender (Sagade 2009).

3.1 Early Marriage, Forced Sex and Missed Opportunities

In many countries across the globe, the age of marriage particularly for girls was a matter to be decided by either social practices or the males. With the importance of debates in the public sphere, there was awareness about the implications of forced sex for young girls.

Against the backdrop of the debates that followed after the "Phulmani case" (of the child wife who was 11 years old and died due to forceful intercourse by her 35 year old husband in 1889), and the subsequent bills passed by the colonial regime after the public debate on the age of marriage and the age of consent in 1891, India and the Indian legal system have gone a long way to bring about changes within the society and in legal provisions to protect women in such cases. Recently the Law Commission of India, in its report of 2008, has recommended that the age of marriage should be equal for both boys and girls at 18 years (Law Commission of India 2008). This is to equalize the legal provisions to give freedom of choice to the young (with a recommendation that the age of sexual consent should be 16) and also to curb misuse. Though legal amendments have been made, the implementation of the law is still challenging as it is difficult and slow to bring about changes in society.

Studies have shown that there are regional as well as rural–urban variations in the age of marriage (Ramasubban and Jejeebhoy 2000). Within the marital framework, having sexual intercourse becomes a prerogative of the husband and refusal to comply may invite domestic violence. Adolescents, especially the younger girls are not fully aware of the resulting health problems and may prefer to keep quiet about them. A study reports that in the age group of married women of 15–19 years, one out of every four had abnormal vaginal discharge, 16 % reported experiencing painful intercourse, and 4 % reported bleeding after intercourse. There is a lack of clinical reporting in such cases (Kulkarni 2003). The same study also notes that nearly one out of every three female adolescents was illiterate.

A review of qualitative studies that present excerpts from studies from different parts of India indicates that early sexual experience of a newly married adolescent woman is traumatic and painful ranging from violence to submission to sex due to fear of abuse (Santhya and Jejeebhoy 2010). Since marriage provides the legitimate framework as well as entitlement of the husband for sexual intercourse, adolescent girls cannot say anything about the relationship that is usually not talked about openly, especially in the marital house. Early (mostly arranged) marriage leaves the girl at the mercy of the husband's family for the continuation of her education or for better health facilities and so on, which are rarely taken care of by the husband's family.

National family health survey data for Maharashtra state show that the gender disparity is quite evident in the school-age population in the state, with 75 % of girls age 6–17 years attending school, compared to 81 % of boys in the same age group. The gender disparity in school education increases with age, particularly in rural settings. In the age group of 11–14 years, 84 % of boys and 75 % of girls attend school but in the age group of 15–17 years, only 32 % of girls are attending school, according to the recent National Family Health Survey of India (IIPS and Macro International 2008). Though there is a decline in the trend of marriage below the age of 18 years, it is still slow. A recent UNICEF report points out that there are more child marriages in rural areas than in urban areas: 52.5 % in rural and 28.2 % in urban areas got married before 18 years of age. The report also notes that there is a higher incidence of domestic violence, particularly sexual violence for young brides (UNICEF 2012).

3.2 *Forced Sex*

In spite of the high value placed on marital relationship, adolescent girls from rural and urban areas are enticed into pre-marital sexual activity, often being lured with love and promise of marriage. Whereas girls expect romantic attachment, for boys the aim is more of a sexual conquest, sometimes entrapment into coercive sex bordering on rape (Ramasubban and Jejeebhoy 2000). Different perceptions of sexual relationships and subsequent entrapment of girls are reported, such as going from "brother–sister" relationship (to make intimate friendship look like a legitimate one) or "asking for friendship" to finally using a girl as a "time-pass" (Abraham 2002) and forcing the girl into sexual relations to prove her commitment. Girls who leave the family due to reasons such as family fights, job search, or visiting relatives are often lured and victimized into forced sex or sexual assault. A study by an NGO in Delhi brings out how girls are coerced into such a relationship. Some studies have reported risky sexual behaviour among different sections of the young population (Jejeebhoy et al. 2004; Abraham 2003; Sodhi and Varma 2003) wherein the girl obviously suffers. Jejeebhoy points out the National AIDS Control Organization, Government of India (NACO) data as well as data collected from different states that report on casual sexual experience, bringing risks and violence in the sexual activity for the girls (Jejeebhoy et al. 2004).

Another study conducted in an urban area reports that in the majority (82 %) of cases, the perpetrators of abuse were people close to the child or adolescent, who enjoyed a position of power, trust and respect in the household, such as uncles, cousins, and a small percentage of even fathers and brothers or some distant relatives. In some other cases, the abusers were neighbours, family friends or even trusted domestic help. Interestingly, the study also brings out that the abuse occurred more often in cases of victims from the nuclear type of family background than from the joint or the extended type; also that the families, though appearing normal, were characterized by strained relationships between parents, domestic violence and neglect (Gupta and Ailawadi 2010). It has to be remembered that in an Indian setting there is a common practice of frequently visiting relatives, staying at each other's houses or entrusting the children to friends and neighbours, colleagues or other informal networks, where such abuse is likely to take place. Close kinship relation patterns can act as an informal control over abuse; however, the same may also act as a trap. The study reported multiple consequences for the abused victims, including psychological, emotional and sexual health hazards in later life (Gupta and Ailawadi 2010, p. 180). Another study by a voluntary organization brings out that out of the total of abusers who had sexual intercourse with children, 41 % were friends and family acquaintances such as friends, family friends, teachers, neighbours or domestic help; and 28 % were abused by members of the extended family such as uncles, aunts or cousins (Save the Children and Tulir 2006).

3.3 Families, Cultural Practices and Structural Constraints

Families from some communities are not aware that they contribute to the abuse and exploitation of girls because of constraints of class, caste or due to cultural practices. Since communities in developing countries face problems of livelihood due to poverty, some cultural practices are found useful by them for the livelihood of the family. In case of some developing countries like India, the colonial background has also contributed to the pauperization of some communities or in establishing new practices such as prostitution for the (British) army. The colonial political economy displaced many communities from their livelihood by introducing new legal and economic structures, and also by criminalizing some communities.

As an effect, women from some "criminalized" communities turned to prostitution and forced their daughters into it. It became a practice in some tribes from the northern part of India, to send their daughters into prostitution. While largely economic reasons have pushed some communities like Bedia, Kanjar, Kolta,

Sansi, Jahat, Banchra into the practice of sending girls for prostitution, cultural practices such as *Devdasi* or *Jogin* has also encouraged families to send their daughters into prostitution. Efforts of government and non-government organizations have to some extent created greater awareness about the harm of the traditional practice of "*Devdasi*" but it still persists in some regions of the Southern part of India, particularly Karnataka and parts of Maharashtra State from the South West. It has now become a platform for entering into prostitution rackets in bigger cities.

The *Devdasi* tradition started in old times for serving the God. Singing and dancing in the temple to praise God was an earlier tradition, and classical Indian dance tradition flourished with that practice. Traditionally, girls from the upper castes or even elites used to serve God in the temple. As an impact of the colonial regime, the patrons of the temple and the economic stability of temples diminished. Over many years the practice faded and other castes, especially the lower castes, adopted this tradition. *Devdasi*, *Jogin*, and *Murali* are names for women who were connected to the temple service or supposed to be involved in dancing in the temple or for festivals such as *Jatras* and *Utsavs* (village fares and celebrations) that were connected to religion.[4]

Over the years the tradition that started out as serving the God slid into serving men, who visited the temple or were potential patrons, and eventually the practice turned into village prostitution. Hence the art of singing and dancing too began having a stigma attached to it, as women's public space became more restricted and women connected to these arts were associated with *Ganika* or courtesans.

The *Devdasi* tradition is, however, multifaceted and it is difficult to find exact evidence of the nature of the practice and the women involved (Ortmann 2013). Usually the girl was "given away" for the "temple service" even before puberty because she was pure at that time. Later, after puberty, she was married to the God.

In the course of time, the practice deteriorated from temple service to village prostitution. Though the exact time of decline is not known, it is believed that it happened after the Muslim invasions and later in colonial times (Ortmann 2013). Later, due to this association, women, who entered into the profession of entertainment such as dance and drama, were invariably related to prostitution and were stigmatized. Poverty and other reasons combined with social stigma pushed lower caste women into this practice. States such as Karnataka, Andhra Pradesh and Goa

[4] A *Devdasi* (Sanskrit: *Dev* is God or *Devi* is Goddess; *Dasi* is a female who serves the God) is a girl dedicated to worship and service of a deity or a temple for the rest of her life. *Murali* is the name for a female child (*Waghya* for a male child) who is given away for service of the Deity, *Khandoba*. There is a traditional practice of giving away the first child for the service of God, in the Jejuri area of Maharashtra State, India. The practices of *Devdasi, Murali, Jogin* are similar and prevalent in some parts of south and western India. In Karnataka state, the Goddess *Yellamma* is worshipped by *Devdasis*.

passed Acts to prevent the *Devdasi* practice and prostitution. Combined efforts of activists and legal provisions have curbed the practice to some extent.[5]

3.4 Child Trafficking, Prostitution and Expanding Flesh Trade

Trafficking of children linked to prostitution is the fastest growing trade the world over and particularly so in developing countries. Currently the USA has downgraded the ranking of Thailand and Malaysia for failure to meet minimum standards for the elimination of human trafficking including sex trade (U.S. Department of State 2014). Globalization and increasing consumerism have exacerbated the other related factors such as poverty, illiteracy, backwardness and ignorance resulting in the sale or luring of children into the trade. Increasingly the age level of prostitutes is going down with the growing demand for child trafficking from particular areas.

Migrants, even occasional travellers, especially women and children from Burma or Laos, who come to visit relatives in Thailand, are watched by gangs at bus and railway stations. They are snatched and drugged to send them for trafficking. A study on young prostitutes shows how the steadily growing market of flesh trade has suffered setbacks due to the growing menace of HIV infection and hence the rising demand for younger girls. The gangs in sex trade systematically cultivate the rural areas for drawing adolescent girls into the trade, who then land up at the lowest end of the market. The author points out the cultural factors complicated by a growing economy (Bales 2002). Some Asian cultures emphasize offering gifts and serving as much as possible to guests, friends or kin group members. Field studies have shown that this is manifested in some societies such as in Thailand or India by men having drinking outings combined with visits to brothels—even as an entertainment for friends (Bales 2002; Pelto 2000). Such practices are instrumental in legitimizing prostitution.

It is also noted that increasingly younger girls are in demand for prostitution (Singh and Singh 2012, p. 15). For example, an 11–12 years old girl gets a higher price in the Thai sex market (Bales 2002). Human Rights Watch records that the average age of girls trafficked from Nepal to India dropped from 14–16 in the 1980s to 10–14 years in 1994 (Human Rights Watch 1995). The wrong ideas and myths such as that sex with a virgin can cure venereal diseases and that it is also "safe", has fuelled an increasing trend of procuring younger girls for trafficking. Young

[5] Karnataka, Andhra Pradesh, Goa, Maharashtra are adjoining states, from the south and south-west of India, having the practice of "Devdasi" or similar practice by different names. Overlapping factors such as poverty, illiteracy and strong blind beliefs use to promote the practice, but there is an element of pride also since there is a belief of relating to God. Hence state and the activists had to intervene to stop such practices with legal bans and creating awareness, resulting in the decline of the practice.

adolescents are usually ignorant, not aware of sex education and without any experience, and thus become an easy prey for traffickers. Studies show the mapping of trafficking of adolescent girls from Nepal, Bangladesh and the North-East regions of India. They are lured into the trade in the Indian metropolitan cities, the Middle East and Pakistan (Choudhary and Das 2012). There are particular routes such as from 24 Parganas—a district in the state of Bengal—girls are trafficked to metropolitan cities like Kolkatta, Mumbai and Delhi; from Bangladesh to Delhi, Mumbai, Kolkatta; from Hyderabad to Dubai, Karachi or Mumbai (Bhartiya et al. 2012).

Delhi is a major destination state for trafficking of children from almost all the states of the country as well as from Bangladesh and Nepal. The supply states from the North-East are Assam, Nagaland and Sikkim; and West Bengal, Jharkhand, Orissa and parts of Bihar from the eastern states (Matiyani and Chattoraj 2010).

Looking at the factors responsible for the trafficking of children, particularly of girls, we find several. Moreover, the interplay between different factors in the context of globalization has created new challenges. The vulnerability of some children increases due to poverty, ignorance, lack of a social network, social capital, gender and discrimination, apart from other factors. The invasion of satellite TV and other new technologies and fast changes in life style have created new aspirations of quick money and a better life that pushes adolescent girls into the trap of traffickers. There are several cases where girls from rural areas are lured by the promise of "better jobs" that will make them and their family better off by working in a big city, only to ultimately land up in brothels in red light areas. Sometimes the girls are sold off by their parents due to sheer poverty but at times also for satisfying the greed and vices of parents. There are instances reported in the media of daughters being sold for a pittance, such as an alcoholic father selling his daughter to buy a bottle of liquor. While in the state of Maharashtra, which is one of the developed states, the reported crime rate of "buying/selling minor girls for prostitution" is 33.33 % of total cases, the registered crime rate of selling girls for prostitution in West Bengal is much higher at 69 % (National Crime Records Bureau 2013).

The recorded crime is usually lower than the actual rate. Migrant children are particularly vulnerable all over the world. Within India, girls from North-Eastern states migrate to cities like Delhi or Mumbai for work. Their parents are in remote hilly rural areas where easy access of communication is not possible. Adolescent girls, who work as trusted domestic help, soon get enchanted by the city life and romantic affairs which lure them to bars and massage parlours that finally launch them into prostitution. The case of Pinky (name changed) in an ongoing field study conducted by the author (unpublished) documented how one adolescent girl from a remote North-Eastern area left a secure, caring family for her "boyfriend", whom her parents also did not know. Her family was promised good money by her boyfriend and she just left for a better paying job of "parlour", the dangers of which her parents were hardly aware of. In a few other recently registered cases with the Pune police it was found that a majority of the rescued girls from brothels had come from Bangladesh because of a promise of work with good pay. That in the state of West Bengal reported crime of "procuring of minor girls" is as high as

39.7 %, followed by Bihar with 15.8 %, and in the North East state, Assam with 10.5 % compared to the southern states of Karnataka (5.56 %) or Maharashtra (3.83 %) is not a surprise. There is a steady increase in this crime from 2009 to 2013. Reported incidents of human trafficking recorded an increase of 10.9 % in 2013 compared to 2012 (National Crime Records Bureau 2013). A number of overlapping reasons may be responsible for minors, especially girls, to get trapped into an abusive situation and further exploitation. Poverty, porous borders and the lure of a luxurious life style sends the young girls from Bangladesh via West Bengal to accept controversial work as "bar girls". Children who do not have a good family life run away and fall prey to the trap of traffickers or land themselves into an abusive situation.

Illiteracy and low education may also drive them towards earning easy money through prostitution. In metro cities such as Delhi, where jobs for street children or poor migrants are not easy to find, girls become an easy prey for pimps. The same is true for minors doing odd jobs in small scale industries or parlours, who sometimes get sexually abused and then shift to prostitution for easy money (Matiyani and Chattoraj 2010). The government data on the crime of selling minor girls for prostitution in West Bengal may be related not only to poverty but also to a past history of feudalism in rural areas. The area is also troubled by a constant problem of large numbers of illegal migrants from Bangladesh. Another state, Maharashtra, which is industrially developed, has a metropolitan city like Mumbai that attracts migrants from different areas, the most vulnerable among them for sexual abuse being children.

The growth of a consumerist culture has promoted and lured very young girls into the sex industry that traps them into easy money and a flashy life style. Police and the media report that there is an increase in the number of school- and college girls in cities, who are lured into the business of "call girls". A sharp increase in the number of people visiting brothels at the time of festivals has been reported in the media. Globalization and new technology have worsened the problem. Police reports show that young adolescent girls, who are brought in for prostitution, are given hormonal injections to enhance their figures. Once the girls are coerced into the profession, they get accustomed to it. News of girls running away from the rescue homes, back to their profession are often reported in newspapers. Sometimes there are reports in the national newspapers and channels about rescue operations, where the trapped girls refuse to go with the police. Many times rescue models do not address structural barriers thus providing unsatisfactory solutions (Magar 2012). Evidently they cannot go back to the villages not just because of the stigma but also because the city life offers them money. Poor conditions of rescue homes and lack of trained personnel are some reasons for the rescued victims to run away and return to prostitution (U.S. Department of State 2014).

Increased per capita expenditure leaves the poor searching for higher income alternatives, human trafficking and prostitution being one of the easier solutions (Reddy 2012). A global monitoring report by an international organization to "end child prostitution, pornography and trafficking for sexual purposes" brings out the high incidence of re-trafficking of rescued children in India (ECPAT 2006). Sex trafficking is prohibited under the Immoral Traffic Prevention Act, but there are reported incidents of inaction by law enforcement agencies and lack of political will to combat trafficking and protect the victims (U.S. Department of State 2014), The corruption in police force and political functionaries and officials hamper the efforts to curb the practice.

3.5 Globalization, New Technologies and Sexual Abuse of Girls

With globalization and the unleashing of the forces of the media as well as easier access to the cyber world, the market together with a changing culture is providing various challenges, also in developed countries. In the U.S., child pornography is punished with 15–30 years imprisonment yet the menace still exists. Cell phone sex talk has gone beyond control in the U.S. and in Japan, and world wide it has become a multi-billion dollar business (Ebbe 2010).

With such huge profits, it is not surprising that the most vulnerable, the children, become an easy prey for traffickers and abusers even in developing countries, where it may be easier to set the traps for children. With fast-paced but lop sided changes in developing countries, new challenges arise. Indeed, in the present social context in India issues related to sexuality and abuse of children and adolescents have become more crucial. A deeper understanding of the problem not only reveals its multi-faceted nature but also brings out complexities that are enmeshed in the structural aspect and the ongoing forces of change in the society. In this context, it becomes necessary to understand the issue by locating it in the present socio-cultural context. The forces of globalization have brought the hidden issues related to sexuality out of the dark cupboards that were not to be discussed openly before. The age of sexual maturity has dropped, especially in the developed countries (Mottier 2008) and similarly in the affluent urban upper classes of developing countries.

The new generation kids are engulfed by the images beamed out by the market world. Consumerist attitudes have given rise to the use of hi-tech tools without much conscience concerning the use of it. Adolescents and youth are bombarded with sleazy ads and images through TV, the cyber world, life-style magazines and "page three" material and hence are in a tricky situation. Increasing consumerism has created a craze for clothes that expose more skin. In the increasing importance of body show, India is not left far behind. Advancement and modernity (which is generally understood by the common public as being westernized) have not provided people with a discursive understanding of sexuality, or understanding obtained through rational analysis. Youth is caught between a value system that is undergoing change and uncontrolled access to technical gimmicks. Several cases of misuse of technology were reported in the media. Cases such as sexual exploitation of adolescent girls by powerful people in Jammu and in Kerala, the Pune case of using a web-cam to watch the young girls while changing, the Delhi case circulating sex clips of a school girl to the whole class and friends, several sms scandals later, and sex rackets from Dhule and Ahmednagar to exploit young girls are just a few examples, followed by several similar reports later on. In recent years there is a clear increase in technology-related sex crimes (Shirwadkar and Asha 2005). Cyber pornography related to girl children is still a big business worldwide.

With the spread of education and the advancement of technology there is also more socio-economic mobility. In the past decade, the absolute number of illiterates has also gone down. There is an avalanche of global media and a market that has reached the rural areas in some way or another. Though there is a lack of basic infrastructure to satisfy the basic needs of the rural poor, consumer goods are fast catching up in rural areas. Recent reports in the media showed that the combination of poverty with increased aspirations due to a visible consumer market has the unwelcome consequence that tribal girls in remote areas are sexually exploited by urban contractors. In the tribal belt of Western Maharashtra there were several cases of adolescent girls being sexually exploited. A field study carried out by the author revealed that several tribal girls within the Raigad district were sexually exploited and made pregnant by *Thekedars* (contractors) who lured them not only with money but with cheap things such as hairpins, cheap bangles, necklaces and so on (Shirwadkar, Construction of safe motherhood 2013, unpublished). The poverty ridden adolescent girls get attracted to these small trinkets due to promotion of consumerism even in rural areas. The contractors now also come from outside the state due to increasing "development" projects and business and have no interest in them apart from exploitation and profit. One has to understand the context of tribal practices in this case. Unlike for other "caste" villagers, for tribes, sex before marriage is not a taboo and there is an understanding of taking responsibility in case the girl becomes pregnant. Sex is not seen necessarily in a marital framework. However, this is limited to the couples within the tribal community. Usually, the urban contractors exploit the girls and then leave them suffering after a while. This situation was also brought up officially by the minister of tribal welfare, and subsequently the state government announced to look into the matter. The outcome or the steps taken are not known. To curb such exploitations, there has to be a strong political will combined with efforts to create awareness among poor people. The increased visibility and aspirations for consumer goods promoted through media networks in the rural area and the resulting impact of the same in an era of globalization evidently has a darker side.

Recent reports in the media show that the attitude and behaviour towards sexuality show a significant change in the sexual behaviour of young people. Several new problems related to sexual abuse and violence arise due to the changes. Different forms, including extreme forms of violence, are now seen, such as attacks on girls by the "spurned" lovers. Even though a girl may be totally unaware of someone falling in "love" with her, she may be attacked with acid or burnt because of a possessive machismo attitude. In such cases it is not only a violation of dignity and safety but also a denial of her right to life. In most cases where victims survive, they end up giving up their education or employment because of their disfigurement, apart from several other factors. Bangladesh and India has witnessed several such cases. Activists and non-government organizations are trying to document these issues and promote debates on such cases. Recently the Supreme Court, while expressing displeasure over the lack of seriousness of the government regarding the menace, has ordered the government to limit over-the-counter acid sales and to make it mandatory to give reasons as well as provide identification while purchasing it.[6] The Law Commission of India submitted its report to the Indian government in 2009 and proposed to include acid attacks as specific offences in the Indian Penal Code and to make a law for the compensation of victims of the crime—this in response to petitions filed by activists. After the horrific gang rape and murder case in Delhi, public wrath pressurized the government to amend the Indian Penal Code; after a parliamentary debate, causing bodily harm by throwing or administering acid (or even attempting to) was included as an offence.

Unmarried adolescent girls become an easy prey for sexual harassment especially in the rural hinterlands in some states of India and also in Bangladesh, because of which families think it is wiser to withdraw the girls from school. A study based on self-reported data on sexual harassment in rural Bangladesh revealed that 35 % of girls experienced sexual harassment, 34 % girls experienced unwanted sexual attentions, and 14 % sexual intimidations. Also, higher education of girls heightened the risk of being sexually harassed (Alam et al. 2010). A study of a slum in Delhi shows that one of the main reasons parents take girls out of school is the rampant sexual harassment in and on the way to school. The study says that about 7 % of girls reported that they discontinued their studies for fear of sexual harassment and about 40 % of girls mentioned that, though it was not cited as the main reason, they were scared of going alone to the school (Chug 2011).

3.6 *Sex Tourism*

With the world becoming closer and more connected, there is a fast growth in the tourism industry. Unfortunately, the dark side of this is the growth of sex tourism. There are some "favoured" destinations in the world that are known for it. For example, after the economic boom in the eighties, the tourism industry in Thailand thrived and also sex tourism (with suggestive advertisements such as "smooth as silk"). Even during World War II, countries like Malay and Burma were hot destinations for prostitution. Girl children from Laos and Burma are still hunted and trapped into sex tourism.

Even rising unemployment may force the young to drop out of education to enter into the unorganized sector, in which sex tourism is a lucrative market. In India, Goa is a "destination" for sex tourism especially for paedophiles, who have been using young girls and boys also for pornography for a long time. When the reports of the case of Freddy Peats, who was of European origin, hit the media headlines and the issue of sex tourism in Goa attracted national attention, it was a rude

[6] For details, please see: http://nlrd.org/resources-womens-rights/acid-attacks/acid-attacks-latest-judgements-of-supreme-courthigh-courts/supreme-court-order-on-acid-attacks.

awakening to the existence of child sex tourism that was just the tip of the iceberg. He was convicted and his conviction was upheld by the High court. Peats was operating an international network of paedophiles in Goa by luring many homeless young children in his shelter home (Sen 2010) where more than two thousand photographs of nude boys and girls, some engaged in sex, were recovered. The case also revealed how children were being used by paedophiles from European countries. NGOs have pointed out that places that have good beaches seem to be an attraction for sex tourists of various types.

Tourist spots such as Puri or Kovalum have proven to be danger zones even for very young children, from 8 years onwards, who are lured into the business. Children from fishing communities, beach boys and others are lured with easy money by a range of tourists (Singh and Singh 2012).

3.7 Sexual Abuse in Private Space

Unfortunately, rape, molestation and sexual assault of children neither have any age limit nor is there a limitation of who could be a perpetrator. There are cases where even babies and toddlers are sexually abused or raped. Shockingly, sexual abuse or assault may even take place within the private space of the family. In a developing country like India, where the family remains an important institution, it becomes difficult to collect data on issues that are usually not publicly discussed. In most cases, only extreme forms of abuse come out in the open. Though it is known that a significant number of girls and boys are abused within the family, the issue remains poorly documented (Gupta and Ailawadi 2010). There is a tendency to deny it if anything goes wrong within the family. According to a government survey of 12,447 children in the age group of 5–18 years old, conducted by the Ministry of Women and Child Development in 2007, 53.22 % of children in the 5–12 year groups faced one or more forms of sexual abuse. The number is large, and it is shocking to see that 50 % of abusers are known to the child or in a position of trust and responsibility.

Usually child sexual abuse occurs as contact or interaction between a child and an older or more knowledgeable child or adult. It may be perpetrated by a stranger, or a sibling, or even a parent or a relative. It has to be understood that there is an absolute, asymmetrical power relation between the victimized child and the perpetrator as the child is dependent on the adult when the child is being used as an object of gratification for the older child's or adult's sexual needs. These contacts or interactions are carried out against the child, using force, trickery, bribes, threats, or pressure as pointed out by many scholars and international organizations. Power relations between children and adults are usually built on trust between them, especially among family members or the family circle. It is this trust that makes child sexual abuse invisible. This is also why many cases of child sexual abuse take place within the family, where members are fully trusted. Hence it is pointed out by many scholars and organizations that child sexual abuse is often caused by people who are well known to the child, whom the child places his or her great trust in, such as fathers, uncles, brothers and cousins. They are usually male members of the family. In the South Asian context, distant family relations, also neighbours and even co-workers are people who are trusted to look after the child. Social practices such as leaving a child to stay with relatives help a parent in absence of social security but may in some cases also have a contrary effect. Often unsuspecting mothers entrust a child to a relative or neighbour.

Sometimes due to other occupations, the child is left alone when relatives will take the opportunity to misbehave or assault the child. In an incident, a girl complained that her brother raped her when she was an adolescent and the family pressured her to keep quiet (Gupta and Ailawadi 2010). The same study found that perpetrators of sexual abuse were mainly male family members (36 %), predominantly uncles and cousins, although 4 % of victims reported a father or brother as the perpetrator and 3 % reported abuse by distant family members, including a brother-in-law, a sister's prospective father-in-law, stepfather and stepbrother. Trusted persons such as neighbours, family friends or domestic help were abusers in 46 % of cases (Gupta and Ailawadi 2010, pp. 172–173). While a family is a place in which children usually grow up safely, it is also a place that can create a great deal of factors to cause child abuse. Social and cultural practices may protect the child at times but they may create situations in which the victim is forced into silence.

Due to the concept of family honour, stigma and patriarchal structure, women often hesitate to complain about child abuse within the family, and family honour is an issue for the larger community as well. The belief of the community in patriarchal norms and ideas of status can be so strong that it may be carried even to a new place and a new country. In a qualitative study of Indian immigrants in Canada it was found that a particular religious community from the Northern part of India advised a mother to go back home (India) when she complained about the sexual abuse of her daughter by her husband. This was also because the abuser was a prominent political community leader. There was strong community pressure on the mother not to speak out because the community's reputation might suffer a setback (Shirwadkar 2004).

In spite of strong normative sanctions for women, sexual exploitation of minors continues to exists. Studies also provide evidence for the abuse of boys. Adolescent boys are enticed into sexual relationships and used for sexual gratification. There are some studies that report the initiation into sexual activity even of adolescent boys by a relative or a *bhabhi* (brother's wife) or an "auntie" who is an older woman (Pelto 1999; Abraham 2002). Though it is difficult to have reliable data collected by government agencies on this theme, cases reported in the media bring out some shocking violation of incest taboos, human rights and dignity. Qualitative and micro studies show that the problem reported must be only the tip of the iceberg.

3.8 *Child Rape, Victims and Offenders in the Light of Media Reports*

Many cases come up where children are raped by known persons, strangers or even the police, while in custody. The legal amendment to the rape law in India was made because of persistent efforts by the women's movement and the media in the aftermath of a rape case, where a minor tribal girl, Mathura, was raped in police custody and the perpetrators were acquitted. Even with legal amendments, the situation still needs to be improved. In a report recently published by the government, the top five states with the highest proportion of registered rape cases as a percentage of the total crime records of India are as follows: Madhya Pradesh: 19.11 %, Uttar Pradesh: 12.18 %, Maharashtra: 10.74 %, Andhra Pradesh: 7.18 %, and Chhattisgarh; 6.08 % (National Crime Records Bureau 2012, p. 17). The higher number of cases are in the Northern part of India where ideas about the subordination of women are stronger. Recently a prominent political leader and former chief minister of a large state in the Northern part of India created an uproar by commenting about rape cases that "boys will be boys" so they may make mistakes, whereas it is the girl who should be blamed for going out with a boy.

The recent brutal and horrifying case of the rape of a young woman in Delhi has brought out other related issues that are now debated in the media and parliament, such as the age of a "juvenile" (Deccan Chronicle, 2 December, 2013). One of the accused, the youngest and the most brutal of the lot, was legally a minor. After this case, there were several reports in the media about cases of minors raping minors, also in gangs. Media reports claimed that the number of rapes committed by juveniles had more than doubled from 485 in 2002 to 1149 in 2011, and the recent statistics of the National Crimes Records Bureau indicates that 1175 cases of rape by juveniles were registered. This has prompted the Ministry of Women and Child Welfare to take note of the issue. Another case happened in Mumbai, which got a lot of attention because the victim was a journalist and in that case too, one of the perpetrator was a minor (The Hindu, 15 July, 2014). After the Delhi gang rape case, there was a debate about raising the age of juveniles in India and whether raising the age due to the international pressure was a wise decision to take. When it became known after the Delhi case verdict that the most brutal juvenile offender was to be sent to a special juvenile home with a minimum tariff, the parents of the girl were shattered and felt cheated, saying that it was a crime to be born as a girl (Bhatt 6 September 2013; Kannampilly 31 August 2013).

4 Efforts to Control Child Sexual Abuse

With rising awareness of the problem, consistent efforts of activists and NGOs as well as legal measures taken, the reporting of child sexual abuse has been increasing. It became clear that the legal provisions to protect children had loopholes. Child sexual abuse was prosecuted under the same sections of the Indian Penal Code (IPC from 1860) as offences against adults. For instance, art. 375: rape (which did not protect male victims), art. 354: outrage against the modesty of woman, and art. 377: unnatural offences, were not defined in a way to include the protection of girls and also of male children.

Several activists and NGOs that were working on the issues related to family violence, particularly violence against women, noted the shortcomings and existing problems. Sakshi, an NGO that worked on the issue and acted as a pressure group by spearheading the efforts to curb child sexual abuse, filed a petition in the Supreme Court of India to declare that "rape" under the Indian Penal Code (Art. 375) should include all forms of forcible penetration. Sakshi claimed that the current interpretation of the law, limiting rape to forcible penile/vaginal penetration only, violated the provisions of the Indian Constitution and was not consistent with India's international commitments such as to the U.N. Convention on the Elimination of all Forms of Discrimination Against Women (CEDAW, 1249 UNTS 13). The Court upheld the existing definition of rape as forcible penile/vaginal penetration thus refusing to include other forms of penetration within the ambit of rape as defined under IPC, art. 375. However, the court also ordered the Indian law commission to examine the issues raised by Sakshi. The report of the commission suggested that the offence of rape should be gender neutral and it should include a range of sexual offences and not just penile penetration of the vagina.

Against this background, it was a great achievement that the new POCSO Act of 2012 (Protection of Children from Sexual Offences Act) was passed in Parliament and came into force on 14 November 2012. The model guidelines of the POCSO Act for the use of professionals and experts hail the Act as a comprehensive law to provide for the protection of children from sexual assault, sexual harassment and pornography. It also considers the existing problems that a child may be facing while undergoing judicial procedures and assures child friendly mechanisms at all stages of carrying out the process of justice (Ministry of Women and Child Development, Government of India 2013).

The Act defines as child a person of less than 18 years of age, regardless of gender. It is gender neutral and does recognize all penetrative or non-penetrative assaults as sexual abuse. It includes also sexual harassment and pornography. As qualified perpetrators it lists not only the family, police, teachers, doctors and several other people having power over the child but also the people who traffic children for sexual purposes, and it prescribes stringent punishment. It also compels the public to report if they have any knowledge of a case of child sexual abuse. It takes also care of secondary victimization of the child, which adds to the trauma of the victim, for example, if the handling of child victims is done by unspecialized personnel of the police or the justice delivery system, or if the child is subjected to repeated questioning and is made to relive the traumatic experience again. The media, too, have a responsibility not to disclose the identity of the victim.

Having a sound legal provision, however, does not mean that the situation will improve immediately. Many times, the politicians forget their responsibility and disclose the name of victims while making their statements.

There are some cases such as that of an adolescent sport star driven to suicide because of sexual abuse by a high-ranking police officer.[7] The case hit the headlines but could not really give justice to the victim (Singh 2010). The officer used his political influence in the case. The girl was expelled from the school, her brother was arrested and tortured under a false case, further, people were sent to stigmatize her family. With unbearable pressures and harassment of the family, the 14-year-old girl committed suicide. The case filed against the perpetrator was dragged out by influential officers who had the support of political leaders. Finally after many years of a prolonged fight by the family and activists, he was convicted but immediately released on bail. Such cases not only bring out the severe limitations of a law that remains on paper, but also the misuse of political power of the state.

The new Act makes provisions for a special court to conduct in camera proceedings for a speedy trial. Procedural delays by courts have been a problem before the Act was implemented. There have been many cases that took several years before they came up for their first hearing. By the time of the first hearing, children would no longer be minors. A study by Virani (2000) cites a few examples, such as the case of a girl who was repeatedly abused by her brother in 1985, but her case came only up for hearing on 14 February 2000. She told the court after 15 years that she had not made any statement to the police and that the content of the first information report was not true. In another example, a complaint that a girl had been raped by her stepfather was filed in 1986, but the case came only up in court in March 2000. By that time the victim was an adult woman, married with two children. She reversed her statement in court.

There are also many instances of abused children having to make frequent court appearances usually due to delaying tactics of the perpetrator. For instance, in December 2009 a 14-year-old girl was admitted to a hospital with many bruises and cuts on her body. She appeared in court 18 times, and she thinks it is not over yet. She is now a young teenager and cannot bear it any longer, especially as many people keep on asking her about what happened. She does not want to relive her past, wants to be left alone and cannot bear the peer pressure (Human Rights Watch 2013).

To address the issue, the Act advises a systematic "multi-sectoral" approach to enhance the recovery of the child and reduce the risk of health problems and trauma. It acknowledges that a coordinated response from police, courts, psychologists, counselors and social service providers is needed. Given today's situation it seems there is a long way to go. The national media often report sexual abuse of

[7] For details, see: http://en.wikipedia.org/wiki/Ruchika_Girhotra_Case.

minors by school bus drivers, but in many instances the school boards try to silence the case and to shirk their responsibility, they even refuse to admit the child in the school.[8] This shows the need to change the attitude of different agents who should be involved in the protection of children.

5 Conclusion

Child sexual abuse exists in all societies but the understanding and measures to control it differ due to the variations in structural, social and cultural factors along with the forces and pace of change. Since these many different factors complicate the existence, extent and measures to control the problem, the effort of providing at least basic security to a child becomes a challenge, particularly in developing countries. To understand the issue in the social and cultural context of a particular society may help in addressing the issue and to identify measures.

Legal measures are no doubt important not only to curb the menace but also to boost the morale of the victims so that they can come out and speak up. However, if the other sectors of society are not in tune with the legal measures, the latter remain on paper. State-run programs may not be a good answer as well. For example, juvenile shelter homes exist for victimized children but the way they are organized and run have invited a lot of criticism and negative reporting. A judge of the Indian Supreme Court criticized the facilities for "being run like brothels" (Sakal Daily 23 February, 2001). There were reports about sexual abuse, homosexuality and a free flow of liquor and *bidis* (cheap country made cigarettes without filters), and also of violent clashes as a usual practice (Mukundan 2010; My Name is Today 2004). For welfare provisions, there has to be a strong political and administrative will. In the absence of it, the programs not only fail but may become another trap of exploitation.

Child sexual abuse needs to be looked at in the social context, and the complexities of power and domination within the given framework have to be unraveled. Addressing the issue and efforts to protect the children will be successful only if efforts on different levels are consistent. Since the government programs of developing countries have several limitations and the NGO efforts are not enough to reach all, community resources also need to be tapped. Due to the awareness and debates in the media, there seems to be increased reporting of incidents. This needs to be translated into a channelized force to create more awareness and to build up

[8] To give an example: an 11-year-old school girl was raped by the school bus driver and attendant. When her parents complained to the school, the school authorities took a long time to act on it and finally asked the parents to withdraw their daughter from the school to protect the driver! Moreover, when the parents went to enrol their daughter in another school, they were denied admission as the other school thought it would get negative publicity (The Indian Express 26 April, 2014).

community pressure on the perpetrators. Simultaneously, the political and administrative will also has to be strong to make it a success.

Five Questions

1. Is the issue of sexual abuse of girl children in South Asian societies different from that in developed countries?
2. Would getting rid of some traditional cultural practices give better access to life chances to minors in developing countries like India?
3. Should the developing countries accept the international standards to make amendments in their legal provisions?
4. What could be the measures to control the sexual abuse of minors by minors?
5. Are legal measures helpful to control the menace of child sexual abuse?

References

Abraham, L. (2002). Bhai-bahen, true love, time-pass: Friendships and sexual partnerships among youth in an Indian metropolis. *Culture, Health and Sexuality, 4*(3), 337–353.

Abraham, L. (2003). Risk behaviour and misperceptions among low-income college students of Mumbai. In S. Bott, S. Jejeebhoy, I. Shah, & C. Puri (Eds.), *Towards adulthood: Exploring the sexual and reproductive health of adolescents in South Asia* (pp. 73–77). Department of Reproductive Health and Research, WHO.

Alam, N., Roy, S., & Ahmed, T. (2010). Sexually harassing behaviour against adolescent girls in rural Bangladesh. Implications for achieving millennium development goals. *Journal of Interpersonal Violence, 25*(3), 443–456.

Alexander, M. J., & Mohanty, C. T. (1997). Introduction: Genealogies, legacies, movements. In M. J. Alexander & C. T. Mohanty (Eds.), *Feminist genealogies, colonial legacies, democratic futures* (pp. xii–xiii). New York: Routledge.

Altekar, A. (1959). *The position of women in Hindu civilization. From prehistoric times to the present day* (2nd ed., pp. 34–105). Delhi: Motilal Banarasidass.

Azonhoume, A. (2010). Criminal abuse of women and children in Benin. In O. N. Ebbe & D. K. Das (Eds.), *Criminal abuse of women and children* (pp. 137–147). Boca Raton: CRC Press, Taylor and Francis Group.

Bales, K. (2002). Because she looks like a child. In B. Ehrenreich & A. R. Hochschild (Eds.), *Global woman-nannies, maids and sex workers in the new economy* (pp. 207–229). New York: Holt Paperbacks.

Barnett, O., Miller-Perrin, C. L., & Perrin, R. D. (2005). *Family violence across the lifespan: An introduction* (pp. 8–9, 89–90). Thousand Oaks: Sage publications.

Bhartiya, A., Verma, A., & Dwivedi, G. (2012). Child trafficking in India. In A. K. Singh, A. P. Singh, & P. A. Khan (Eds.), *Trafficking in women and children in India. Emerging perspectives, issues and strategies* (pp. 404–425). New Delhi: Serials Publications.

Bhatt, M. (2013). *Heinous crimes by minors on the rise, shows NCRB data*. New Delhi Tele Vision, http://www.ndtv.com/article/india/heinous-crimes-by-minors-on-the-rise-shows-ncrb-data-415367. Accessed 31 July 2014.

Bhattacharjee, A. (1997). The public/private mirage: Undomesticating violence work in the South Asian immigrant community. In J. Alexander & C. T. Mohanty (Eds.), *Feminist genealogies, colonial legacies, democratic futures* (pp. 308–329). New York: Routledge.

Bott, S., & Jejeebhoy, S. (2003). Adolescent sexual and reproductive health in South Asia: An overview of findings from the 2000 Mumbai conference. In S. Bott, et al. (Eds.), *Towards adulthood. Exploring the sexual and reproductive health of adolescents in South Asia* (pp. 3–28). Department of Reproductive Health and Research, WHO.

Brown, M. L., Chesney-Lind, M., & Stein, N. (2013). Patriarchy matters: Toward a gendered theory of teen violence and victimization. Girls, women and crime. In M. Chesney-Lind & L. Pasko (Eds.), *Girls, women, and crime* (2nd ed., pp. 21–38). L.A.: Sage Publication.

Chanana, K. (1990). The dialectics of tradition and modernity and women's education in India. *Sociological Bulletin, 39*(1&2), 75–91.

Chananna, K. (1996). Introduction. In A. M. Shah, B. S. Baviskar, & E. A. Ramaswamy (Eds.), *Social structure and change, Vol. 2: Women in Indian society* (pp. 13–32). New Delhi: Sage.

Choudhary, J., & Das, M. (2012). Combating human trafficking with NGOs in North-East states: Some suggestive roles. In A. K. Singh, A. P. Singh, & P. A. Khan (Eds.), *Trafficking in women and children in India. Emerging perspectives, issues and strategies* (pp. 490–508). New Delhi: Serials Publications.

Chug, S. (2011). *Dropout in secondary education. A study of children living in slums of Delhi.* Occasional Papers, National University of Educational Planning and Administration, New Delhi, pp. 22–25.

Cohen, M. L., & Boucher, R. (1972). *Misunderstandings about sex criminals: Sexual behaviour* (pp. 57–62).

Convention on the Elimination of All Forms of Discrimination against Women, 1249 UNTS 13.

Das, K., & Li, J. (2010). Introduction. In: Ebbe & Das (Eds.), *Criminal abuse of women and children: An international perspective* (p. xix). Boca Raton: Taylor and Francis.

Deccan Chronicle. (2013). *Delhi gang rape case: SC seeks centre's reply on laws on juvenility*, http://www.deccanchronicle.com/131202/news-current-affairs/article/delhi-gang-rape-case-sc-notice-centre-plea-victims-father. Accessed 09 August 2014.

Deolalikar, A., & Rao, V. (1998). The demand for dowry and bride characteristics in marriage: Empirical estimates from rural south-central India. In M. Krishnaraj, R. Sudarshan, & A. Shariff (Eds.), *Gender, population and development* (pp. 122–140). New Delhi: Oxford University Press.

Dern'e, S. (1999). Making sex violent: Love as a force in recent Hindi films. *Violence Against Women, 5*, 548–575.

Dube, L. (2001). *Anthropological explorations in gender: Intersecting fields* (pp. 87–117). New Delhi: Sage.

Ebbe, O. (2010). The scope and causes of criminal abuse of children. In O. Ebbe & D. Das (Eds.), *Criminal abuse of women and children: an international perspective* (pp. 47–71).

ECPAT. (2006). *Global monitoring report on the status of action against commercial sexual exploitation of children, India* (p. 12). ECPAT International.

Finkelhor, D. (1996). Introduction. In J. Briere, et al. (Eds.), *The SPCA handbook on child maltreatment* (pp. ix–xiii). Thousand Oaks: Sage, as quoted in Barnett O, Millern-Perrin C, Perrin R (eds.) 2005, Family violence across the lifespan, an introduction. Sage: Thousand Oaks, p. 8.

Finkelhor, D. (2005). Sexually victimized children. In R. Bergen, J. L. Edleson, & C. M. Renzetti (Eds.), *Violence against women. Classic papers* (pp. 42–55). Boston: Pearson Education Inc.

Gelles, J., & Conte, R. J. (1990). Domestic abuse and sexual abuse of children: A review of research in the eighties. *Journal of Marriage and Family, 52*, 1045–1058.

Gelles, R. J. (1993). Alcohol and other drugs are associated with violence-they are not its cause. In R. J. Gelles & D. R. Loseke (Eds.), *Current controversies on family violence* (pp. 182–196). Newbury Park: Sage Publication.

Gelles, R., & Straus, M. (1979). Determinants of violence in family: Toward a theoretical integration. In W. Burn, R. Hill, F. Nye, & I. Reiss (Eds.), *Contemporary theories about the family* (pp. 549–581). New York: Free Press.

Government of India. (2007). *Study on child abuse: India 2007* (pp. 5–6). Ministry of Women and Child Development, Government of India.

Gupta, A., & Ailawadi, A. (2010). Childhood and adolescent sexual abuse and incest: Experiences of women survivors in India. In S. Jejeebhoy, I. Shah, & S. Thapa (Eds.), *Sex without consent: Young people in developing countries* (pp. 171–185). Jaipur: Rawat Publications.

Human Rights Watch. (1995). *Rape for profit. Trafficking of Nepali girls and women to India's brothels*. 12,5(A), http://www.hrw.org/reports/1995/India.htm. Accessed on 29 September 2014.

Human Rights Watch. (2013). *Breaking the silence. Child sexual abuse in India* (pp. 45, 46). U.S. A.: Human Rights Watch.

IIPS and Macro International. (2008). *Maharashtra. National Family Health Survey (NFHS-3) India 2005-06* (pp. 3–4). Mumbai: IIPS.

Jasinski, J. L. (2001). Theoretical explanations for violence against women. In C. M. Renzetti, J. L. Edleson, & R. K. Bergen (Eds.), *Sourcebook on violence against women* (pp. 15–16). Thousand Oaks: Sage Publications.

Jejeebhoy, S. (1998). Wife beating in rural India: A husband's right? Evidence from survey. *Economic and Political Weekly, 33*, 855–862.

Jejeebhoy, S. (2000). Adolescent sexual and reproductive behaviour: A review of the evidence from India. In R. Ramasubban & S. Jejeebhoy (Eds.), *Women's reproductive health in India* (pp. 40–101). Jaipur: Rawat Publications.

Jejeebhoy, S., Sathya, K. G., Verma, R. K., Caleb, L. V., Mahendra, V. S., Widge, A., et al. (2004). Setting the stage. In S. Jejeebhoy (Ed.), *Looking back and looking forward* (pp. 3–22). New Delhi: Population Council, Rawat Publications.

Kannampilly, A. (2013). *Teenager sentenced to three years in Delhi gang-rape case*, Yahoo News, https://uk.news.yahoo.com/india-court-scheduled-first-verdict-gang-rape-case-004706609.html#lICLX8n. Accessed on 31 July 2014.

Karve, I. (1965). *Kinship organization in India*. Bombay: Asia Publishing House.

Kishor, S., & Gupta, K. (2009). *Gender equality and women's empowerment in India* (pp. 7–17). National Family Health Survey (NFHS-3) India 2005-06. Mumbai: Indian Institute of Population Sciences.

Kishwar, M. (1999). *Off the beaten track: Rethinking gender justice for Indian women* (pp. 151–160). New Delhi: Oxford University Press.

Kulkarni, S. (2003). The reproductive health status of married adolescents as assessed by NFHS-2, India. In S. Bott, S. Jejeebhoy, I. Shah, & C. Puri (Eds.), *Towards adulthood. Exploring the sexual and reproductive health of adolescents in South Asia* (pp. 55–58). WHO.

Law Commission of India. (2008). *Proposal to amend the prohibition of child marriage act, 2006 and other allied laws* (Report no. 205, pp. 6–7). Government of India.

Madan, T. N. (1975). Structural implications of marriages in North India. *Contributions to Indian Sociology, 9*(2), 1–81.

Magar, V. (2012). Rescue and rehabilitation: A critical analysis of sex workers' anti-trafficking response in India. *Signs, 37*(3), 619–644.

Matiyani, H., & Chattoraj, B. N. (2010). Prostitution and trafficking for the purpose of commercial sexual exploitation in Delhi. *The Indian Journal of Criminology and Criminalistics, xxxi*(2), 29–50.

Mottier, V. (2008). *Sexuality: A very short introduction* (pp. 4–51, 105). Oxford: Oxford University Press.

Mtimkulu, L. (2010). Criminal exploitation of women and children: A South African perspective. In O. N. Ebbe & D. K. Das (Eds.), *Criminal abuse of women and children* (pp. 161–184). Boca Raton: CRC Press Taylor and Francis Group.

Mukundan, A. (2010). *Study of welfare module in the government run children's residential institutions in the state of Maharashtra*. Ph.D. thesis (unpublished), University of Mumbai, Mumbai.

Mulay, S. (2009). Declining sex ratios in Maharashtra: Gift of technological advance. In S. Shirwadkar (Ed.), *Family violence in India: Human rights, issues, actions and international comparisons* (pp. 189–209). Jaipur: Rawat Publications.
My Name is Today. (2004). Sex abuse stink from juvenile home. *Hindustan Times, XII*(2&3), 67.
National Crime Records Bureau. (2012). *Crime in India 2012. Statistics* (p. 405). NCRB, Ministry of Home Affairs, Government of India.
National Crimes Records Bureau. (2013) *Crime in India* (pp. 79–81, 98–100). Ministry of Home Affairs, chapters, 5 & 6-A.
Ndolo, G. (2010). Criminal exploitation of women and children: The Kenyan experience. In O. N. Ebbe & D. K. Das (Eds.), *Criminal abuse of women and children* (pp. 125–136). Boca Raton: CRC Press Taylor and Francis Group.
Ortmann, B. (2013). The use of religious resources in interreligious development cooperation: The case of oppressive body constructions among Devdasi and Dalit children. In M. Tamcke & J. Gladson (Eds.), *Body, emotion and mind* (pp. 1–26). Zurich: Lit Verlag.
Padmanabha, P. (2010). Foreword. In T. V. Sekhar & N. Hatti (Eds.), *Unwanted daughters. Gender discrimination in modern India* (pp. IX–XV). Jaipur: Rawat Publications.
Pagdi, S. M. (1969). *Jeevan Setu*. Pune: Continental Prakashan.
Patel, T. (2010). Risky lives: Indian caught between individual rationality and public good. In T. V. Sekhar & N. Hatti (Eds.), *Unwanted daughters. Gender discrimination in modern India* (pp. 16–37). Jaipur: Rawat Publications.
Pelto, P. (1999). Sexuality and sexual behaviour: The current discourse. In S. Pachauri & S. Subramanian (Eds.), *Implementing a reproductive health agenda in India: The beginning* (pp. 539–585). New Delhi: The Population Council.
Pelto, P. (2000). Research on sexuality and sexual behaviour in India: The 1990s. In R. Ramasubban & S. Jejeebhoy (Eds.), *Women's reproductive health in India* (pp. 40–133). Jaipur: Rawat Publications.
Ramasubban, R., & Jejeebhoy, S. (2000). Introduction. In R. Ramasubban & S. Jejeebhoy (Eds.), *Women's reproductive health in India* (pp. 13–39). Jaipur: Rawat Publications.
Reddy, V. R. (2012). A comparative analysis of various factors influencing human trafficking in India. In A. K. Singh, A. P. Singh, & P. A. Khan (Eds.), *Trafficking in women and children in India. Emerging perspectives, issues and strategies* (pp. 216–232). New Delhi: Serial Publications.
Sagade, J. (2009). Age of marriage and debate of human rights. In S. Shirwadkar (Ed.), *Family violence in India: Human rights, issues, actions and international comparisons* (pp. 82–113). Jaipur: Rawat Publishers.
Sakal Daily. (2001). *Government shelters are like brothels: Justice Usha Mehra's comments*, February 23, Pune, p. 3.
Santhya, K., & Jejeebhoy, S. (2010). Young women's experiences of forced sex within marriage: Evidence from India. In S. Jejeebhoy, I. Shah, & S. Thapa (Eds.), *Sex without consent. Young people in developing countries* (pp. 59–73). Jaipur: Rawat Publications.
Save the Children and Tulir. (2006). *Doesn't every child count?* (pp. 15–16). Sweden: Save the Children.
Segal, U. (1999). Family violence: A focus on India. In *Aggression and violent behavior* (Vol. IV, pp. 213–231).
Sen, S. (2010). *Human rights and inhuman wrongs* (p. 22). New Delhi: Gyan Publishing House.
Shekher, T., & Hatti, N. (2010). Introduction – Unwanted daughters: Gender discrimination in modern India. In T. Shekher & N. Hatti (Eds.), *Unwanted daughters. Gender discrimination in Modern India* (pp. 75–103). Jaipur: Rawat Publishers.
Shekher, T., Hatti, N., & Bhat, P. (2010). From "fertility control" to "gender control"?: Evidences of daughter discrimination in rural south India. In T. Shekher & N. Hatti (Eds.), *Unwanted daughters. Gender discrimination in Modern India* (pp. 75–103). Jaipur: Rawat Publishers.
Shirwadkar, S. (1998). *Women and socio-cultural changes* (pp. 39–56, 192). New Delhi: Gyan Publishing House.

Shirwadkar, S. (2004). Canadian domestic violence policy and Indian immigrant women. *Violence Against Women, Sage Publication, 10*(8), 860–879.

Shirwadkar, S. (2009). Desh-Pardesh: Indian immigrants and Canadian domestic violence policies. In S. Shirwadkar (Ed.), *Family violence in India: Human rights, issues, actions and international comparisons* (pp. 82–113). Jaipur: Rawat Publishers.

Shirwadkar, S., & Asha, K. (2005). *Sexuality and reproductive health of youth: Socio-legal and health dimensions* (pp. 34–52). Occasional Paper, Department of Sociology, University of Pune.

Singh, K. (2010). *The Rathore case highlights how the law views sexual assault as a trivial crime* (pp. 16–29). Frontline, 27, 02, http://www.frontline.in/static/html/fl2702/stories/20100129270201600.htm. Accessed on 31 July 2014.

Singh, A. K., & Singh, A. P. (2012). Trafficking women and children: An overview. In A. K. Singh, A. P. Singh, & P. A. Khan (Eds.), *Trafficking in women and children in India. Emerging perspectives, issues and strategies* (pp. 1–91). New Delhi: Serials Publications.

Sodhi, G., & Varma, M. (2003). Sexual coercion among unmarried adolescents of an urban slum in India. In S. Bott, S. Jejeebhoy, I. Shah, & S. Puri (Eds.), *Towards adulthood. Exploring the sexual and reproductive health of adolescents in South Asia* (pp. 91–94). Department of Reproductive Health and Research, WHO.

Srinivas, M. N. (1976). *The changing position of Indian women*. Delhi: Oxford University Press.

Straus, M., & Hotaling, G. (1980). Culture, social organization and irony in the study of family violence. In G. Hotaling & M. Straus (Eds.), *The social causes of husband-wife violence* (pp. 10–11). Minneapolis: University of Minnesota.

Talwar Oldenberg, V. (2002). *Dowry murder: The imperial origins of a cultural crime* (pp. 1–30). Oxford: Oxford University Press.

The Hindu. (2014). *Shakti mills rapes: Two juveniles convicted, sent to reform school, 15 July 2014.* http://www.thehindu.com/news/cities/mumbai/shakti-mills-rapes-two-juveniles-convicted-sent-to-reform-school/article6213615.ece.

UNICEF. (2012). *Child marriage in India. An analysis of available data (2012)* (pp. 6–25). New Delhi: United Nations Children's Fund.

US Department of State. (2014). *Trafficking in persons report*. US Department of State, Diplomacy in action, 205, pp. 372–376, http://www.state.gov/j/tip/rls/tiprpt/2014/?utm_source=NEW+RESOURCE%3A+Trafficking+in+Persons+Report+2014&utm_campaign=2014.07.16+NEW+RESOURCE%3A+Trafficking+in+Persons+Report+2014.

Virani, P. (2000). *Bitter chocolate: Child sexual abuse in India* (pp. 151–152). India: Penguin.

Weeks, J. (2010). *Sexuality* (3rd ed., p. 28). London: Routledge.

Wiehe, V. (1998). *Understanding family violence. Treating and preventing partner, child, sibling and elder abuse* (pp. 23–27). Thousand Oaks: Sage Publications.

World Health Organization. (2010). *Child maltreatment* (Fact sheet no. 150). Geneva, Switzerland: WHO.

Yllo, K. (1993). Through a feminist lens: Gender, power and violence. In R. J. Gelles & D. R. Loseke (Eds.), *In current controversies in family violence* (pp. 47–62). Nubury Park: Sage Publication.

Sexual Abuse Within the Family: The Intergenerational Transmission of Victimhood and Offending

Catrien Bijleveld, Jessica Hill, and Jan Hendriks

Abstract This chapter provides an overview of research carried out on 185 juvenile male sex offenders who received treatment in a residential center. We examined their and their parents' history of sexual abuse. Specifically we tested hypotheses relating to the mechanisms linking offender and victim status in cases of sexual abuse within families, i.e. intra-familial abuse. Our findings offer most support for a social learning theory of sexual abuse. Juvenile sex offenders either from families where intra-familial abuse has occurred or who have a father with a history of sexual abuse against children occurring during their childhood have an increased risk of themselves abusing children, rather than peers. Juvenile sex offenders who themselves have been the victim of intra-familial abuse, or who have a sibling that has suffered intra-familial abuse, have an increased risk of committing intra-familial sexual abuse.

1 Introduction

Parental delinquent behavior is an important explanatory factor in the delinquent behavior of their children (Besemer and Farrington 2012; Farrington 2002) and having delinquent family members consistently predicts an individual's delinquency (Thornberry 2009). Research has found that having a delinquent father

---

This chapter is an updated version of Bijleveld, C.C.J.H. and Hendriks, J. (2007). Gezin en seksueel misbruik. *Tijdschrift voor Criminologie, 49*, pp. 123–136.

C. Bijleveld (✉)
Vrije Universiteit Amsterdam, Amsterdam, The Netherlands

NSCR Institute for the Study of Crime and Law Enforcement, Amsterdam, The Netherlands
e-mail: cbijleveld@nscr.nl

J. Hill
NSCR Institute for the Study of Crime and Law Enforcement, Amsterdam, The Netherlands
e-mail: j.hill@nscr.nl

J. Hendriks
Vrije Universiteit Amsterdam, Amsterdam, The Netherlands
e-mail: j.hendriks@vu.nl

H. Kury et al. (eds.), *Women and Children as Victims and Offenders: Background, Prevention, Reintegration*, DOI 10.1007/978-3-319-08398-8_32

roughly doubles the conviction risk for a male child (Bijleveld and Wijkman 2009; Farrington 1995). Moreover many studies have found that having a parent who has been convicted of a crime is related to self-reported delinquency, antisocial behavior in late adolescence and adulthood, as well as serious high frequency or violent delinquency (e.g., Bijleveld and Wijkman 2009; Farrington et al. 2001; van de Weijer et al. 2014). This continuity in offending from one generation to the next, i.e. when the same behavior is observed in parent and child, is also referred to as intergenerational transmission (Besemer 2012; Liefbroer 2005).

As yet the mechanisms behind this phenomenon are unclear. One possibility is parenting style. There are indications that inconsistent discipline and authoritarian parenting are associated with antisocial behavior in childhood. Similarly, poor supervision and permissiveness have also been linked to antisocial behavior (Derzon 2010; Hoeve et al. 2011; Leschied et al. 2008). Another explanation commonly put forward, which draws on social learning theory (Akers 1985; Bandura 1971), is that children model their (antisocial) behavior on that of their parents. Notably, research which supports this mechanism found that the sons of violent offenders only themselves become violent offenders if their fathers remain married to their mothers, i.e. if the sons were more likely to witness and 'learn' their father's behavior (van de Weijer et al. 2015). Alternatively, intergenerational transmission could be the result of children and parents sharing the same criminogenic environment. A further explanation is that traits associated with antisocial behavior are hereditary (Beaver 2013; Niv et al. 2013). Much research on intergenerational transmission has focused either on aggressive behavior (e.g., Besemer 2012), violent offending (e.g., van de Weijer et al. 2014), or on conviction data (Farrington 2011). More recently this phenomenon has been examined for other types of criminal behavior, such as intimate partner violence (Franklin and Kercher 2012), sexual abuse victimization (Testa et al. 2011), and child abuse (although see review by Thornberry et al. 2012). However, to date little research has focused specifically on the intergenerational transmission of sex offending (for an exception see Van de Weijer et al. 2015). In the literature on sex offending a range of explanations for the etiology of this crime are put forward. One such explanation is intra-familial sexual abuse victimization, hence the relevance of investigating their co-occurrence within families.

In this chapter we examine the possible link between sex offender and victim statuses of parents and children. We first outline the extent to which our sample of juvenile sex offenders comes from families where sexual abuse has occurred. Next we examine whether the type and method of sexual abuse that these juvenile offenders commit is related to that of their parents and/or their own victim experiences. Lastly we investigate whether and in what way having a parent who is a victim of sexual abuse is a risk factor for the child becoming a victim of sexual abuse.

2 Literature Review

2.1 *Sexual Victimization of Sex Offenders*

Many studies have found that a relatively high percentage of sex offenders, particularly abusers of children, report being the victim of sexual abuse during childhood. In a systematic review of the literature Seto and Lalumière (2010) found that across studies on average 46 % of adolescent sex offenders reported having experienced sexual abuse. This prevalence rate is considerably higher than that found in the general population. For example, in results of a meta-analysis examining self-reported childhood sexual abuse across the world the rate of male victimization was estimated to be around 8 % (Stoltenborgh et al. 2011), compared to 18 % for females.

Male victims of child sexual abuse are at risk of a variety of different problems (Easton 2012). Early research into male victims of child sexual abuse found that negative outcomes of abuse were reported by 15 to 39 % of victims (Holmes and Slap 1998). Sexual abuse suffered by males that involves force, penetration and/or physical injury has been specifically linked to an increase in problems experienced in later life (Easton 2012). Consequences of child sexual abuse for males range from having an increased risk of a multitude of psychiatric disorders (Chen et al. 2010) and psychopathic symptoms (Maniglio 2009) to an increased likelihood of displaying risky sexual behavior (Homma et al. 2012). Male victims of sexual abuse have also been found to have an increased risk of suicide (Maniglio 2011) and drug and alcohol use (Enoch 2011). Moreover, whilst percentages remain small, male victims of child sexual abuse have a higher risk of becoming a sex offender than non-victims (Ogloff et al. 2012).

Research has found that sex offenders who target children are more likely to have been the victims of sexual abuse than non-offenders (Jespersen et al. 2009; Whitaker et al. 2008) and that juvenile sex offenders are more likely to have family members who had suffered child sexual abuse (Ryan et al. 2011). Trickett et al. (2011) in a longitudinal mixed retrospective and prospective study found that both physical and sexual abuse were transmitted across generations and that mothers of sexually abused daughters had experienced unstable and harsh childhoods. Tomison (1996) reported that in cases of "incest families" both parents had grown up in chaotic, dysfunctional families, with issues surrounding conflict, divorce, alcohol abuse, and sexual abuse. Previous research has also found that the chance of sexual abuse in the second generation is higher when sexual abuse in the previous generation was of a serious nature (Zuravin et al. 1996). These findings indicate therefore that sex offending and sexual abuse victimization may be transmitted from one generation to the next. However, in drawing this conclusion caution is required, as many of the studies carried out on intergenerational transmission of abuse lack the necessary methodological means to unequivocally state this (Thornberry et al. 2012).

2.2 *Intergenerational Transmission of Sexual Offending*

In the introduction we referred to mechanisms whereby the risk of delinquent behavior is transferred from one generation to the next. Whilst many of the mechanisms discussed in the literature equally apply to sex offending, mechanisms exclusive to sex offending also occur. We will now outline four mechanisms by which sexual abuse can lead to the victim turning offender from one generation to the next, and so perpetuating the cycle of abuse.

Van Beek and Mulder (2002) report that when children are within the family and at a young age exposed to pornography, violence, or sexual abuse of themselves or others, this can lead to cognitive reasoning, such as 'controlling sexual urges is impossible' or 'the victim does not experience pain or injury'. This type of cognitive reasoning allows the child to cope with the situation. However, it can lead to the rationalization and normalization of the event, known as "cognitive distortions". Cognitive distortions have long been used to describe child abusers' thinking (e.g., Abel et al. 1984). Ward's implicit theory (Ward and Siegert 2002), and the extension of this incorporating extended mind theory (Ward and Casey 2010), argue that these cognitive distortions are the result of schemas relating to beliefs about victims. These schemas help or give abusers the ability to act out on these beliefs. Sexual abuse can thus act as a "guide" to consequent atypical sexual behavior when no disciplinary feedback from the environment is given (Seto and Lalumière 2010). As a result paraphilic disorders may develop.[1] The chance of these cognitive distortions and paraphilic disorders occurring may arguably be greater when the abuse takes place within the closed setting of the family from which the child is unable to "escape". According to this reasoning we would therefore expect increased paraphilic disorders amongst children abused within the family.

Another possible mechanism is social learning. Children learn certain behavior patterns from their parents, so that if the parent abuses the child, or one of their siblings, the child is likely to pick up and model this behavior. Estes and Tidwell (2002) found that boys who had been victims of intra-familial sexual abuse were more likely to display challenging sexual behavior than those who had been abused outside of the family. According to this mechanism we would therefore expect children who have been abused within the family, or who have witnessed another child within the family being abused by a parent or stepparent, to copy this behavior. They are also more likely to victimize their siblings than other children.

The third mechanism focuses not on the transmission of sex offending per se but on the risk of sex offending. In this theory, based on psychoanalysis, the mother plays a crucial role. The suggestion is that sexually abused women choose partners who resemble their fathers. However, this partner is likely to turn their attention to the children rather than their partner, particularly in situations when the relationship

[1] Paraphilic disorders are described in the DSM-5, as atypical sexual interests where persons either feel distress about their interest, have a sexual desire or behavior which causes harm, distress or injury to others, or a desire for sexual behaviors against unwilling persons or persons unable to give consent.

is in trouble or when the mother is unable due to psychological or medical reasons to sexually gratify her partner (Lev-Wiesel 2006). Several studies have demonstrated the intergenerational transfer of risk from mother to daughter, whereby sexually abused mothers are more likely to have daughters who are sexually abused (Faller 1989; McCloskey 2013; Trickett et al. 2011). A further less direct way in which a mother can contribute to the abuse of her children is if she allows her children to stay with or be looked after by the father who abused her. DiLillo and Damashek (2003) found that children who had contact with their mother's abuser were more likely to be sexually abused by this same offender. Whilst mothers can of course abuse their child(ren) themselves (see Wijkman et al. 2011), facilitating their abuse by a partner or grandparent indirectly transmits risk of sexual abuse from one generation to the next. According to this mechanism we would expect children of sexually abused mothers to have a higher likelihood of being sexually abused by their father, stepfather, or grandfather.

Finally it is also possible that sexual delinquency is partly hereditary (Moffitt et al. 2011; Raine 2013). Research which has examined this hereditary element has often however lacked an explanation as to how exactly the transfer from one generation to the next takes place. In order to address this issue research such as twin studies is required (see for an example of a twin study on aggression Niv et al. 2013). Nevertheless, genetic transfer of risk is a relevant mechanism for the intergenerational transmission of sexual abuse, by which we would expect children to commit the same kind of sexual abuse as their biological parents.

2.3 Methodological Issues Concerning Research on Sexual Victimization and Abuse

Salter and colleagues (2003) find that the risk of sexual offending by child abuse victims is, in absolute numbers, not considerable. From a group of 224 male victims of abuse 19 victims turned offender over a period of 7–19 years. In nearly all these cases their victim was a child. However, one of the problems of studies examining the relationship between prevalence of sexual victimization and offending is that the prevalence varies according to the severity of the abuse. For example, "child sexual abuse" can range from hands-on abuse, such as rape and sexual assault, with or without penetration, to hands-off abuse, such as exhibitionism, exposure to pornography, etc. (Young et al. 2011). Another significant problem is that sexual offenders may attempt to rationalize their abusive behavior as being caused by their own sexual victimization (Barbaree and Langton 2006). Besides these problems concerning definition and rationalization, two further issues regarding research on the effects of victimization of sexual abuse on offending arise. Firstly, the majority of studies are retrospective. In retrospective studies whilst outcomes of abuse can be examined, the risk of transmission cannot be determined. We cannot know how many parents have *not* transmitted a certain characteristic or behavior onto their children. The strength of studies such as that from Trickett, Putnam and colleagues (2011), Salter and colleagues (2003), and Price and colleagues (2002) is that in using a (semi) prospective set-up they are in a better position to examine the issue of intergenerational transmission.

A further problem with many studies on sexual abuse is that different kinds of sexual abuse are not recognized. Abuse by a schoolteacher, where the home could be a place of refuge, and abuse by a parent, where the home is the source of the abuse, is often not differentiated. Intra-familial abuse has been shown to be more damaging than extra-familial abuse (Magalhães et al. 2009). Rasmussen and colleagues (1992) found that the relationship between juvenile and offender is of great importance in how the abuse is dealt with and processed. Glasser and colleagues (1994) showed that the risk of offending in cases of intra-familial sexual abuse was double that of extra-familial abuse. Rayment-McHugh (2003) reported that the risk of sexual re-offending is higher amongst victims of sexual abuse by a family member. However, these findings are not universal; other studies have found little differences between intra vs. extra familial abuse victims (see Hébert et al. 2006; McClure et al. 2008). Nevertheless, in order to determine whether the risk of negative outcomes is greater for victims of sexual abuse within the family, distinguishing between these different types of sexual abuse is vital.

Studies which find only a small risk of sex offending amongst abused males, have generally examined males abused by non-family member(s) (Salter et al. 2003; Price et al. 2002). In cases such as these the likelihood of the crime being reported is much higher and the child and their family are more likely to receive victim support. As a consequence of this, abuse by a non-family member has a higher chance of being included in prospective studies. In contrast, abuse which takes place within the family, especially if it represents an ongoing cycle of dysfunction and violations of sexual norms, is much more likely to remain hidden, only coming to light in extreme cases. Consequently the extent of the damage done to the victims in these cases is likely to be higher, whilst the chance of these cases coming to the attention of the authorities is lower. This results in their underrepresentation in prospective studies.

Whilst in the current study we are not able to address all of these methodological issues we nonetheless shed further light on risk factors relating to juvenile sex offenders, specifically the role of sexual abuse within the family. We explore the explanatory power of each of the four mechanisms discussed relating to how sexual abuse victimization can lead to sex offending. We specifically distinguish between sexual abuse within the family and abuse by non-family members, i.e. intra-familial vs. extra-familial abuse.

3 Hypotheses

According to the first mechanism described above children abused within the family have a higher risk of distorted cognitive reasoning and consequently paraphilic disorders, than children abused by non-family members. This leads to the following hypothesis:

1. Paraphilic disorders will be more common among victims of intra-familial sexual abuse than victims of extra-familial sexual abuse.

According to the second mechanism described above, social learning theory states that children model their behavior on that of parents and other family members. We would expect therefore that children from families where abuse between members takes place would display an increased risk of copying this behavior, i.e. abusing their siblings. This leads to the following hypothesis:

2a. Victims of intra-familial abuse and children from families where there has been at least one intra-familial abuse victim are more likely to victimize a brother or sister than victims of extra-familial sexual abuse or non-victims.

This hypothesis can be extended. If we consider that children copy behavior in general we would expect children with a parent or stepparent who abused (a) child (ren) to have an increased risk of also committing such sexual abuse. The following hypothesis therefore does not refer specifically to abuse of family members but to abuse of children in general.

2b. Children with a parent or stepparent who has committed sexual offenses against children will be more likely to commit such offenses themselves.

For social learning to take place the child has to have "witnessed" the behavior it models. We therefore place children whose parents committed the sexual abuse before the child was five in the reference group, so that only parental behavior that the child can have observed and remembered is included.

Next we test two hypotheses related to the third mechanism discussed above, that the intergenerational transmission of sex offending is indirectly passed through the mother.

3a. Mothers who are the victim of sexual abuse are more likely to have a child that is the victim of sexual abuse.

Specifically:

3b. Mothers who are victims of sexual abuse are more likely to choose a partner who abuses their child than mothers who are not victims of sexual abuse.

According to the fourth mechanism, that sex offending has a hereditary element, we hypothesize the following:

4. Children of parents who have at any point in their lives committed a sexual offense against (a) child(ren) are more likely to commit such an offense themselves.

In this case, in contrast with hypothesis 2b, only offenses committed by biological parents and also offenses committed prior to the birth of the child are included. In this case stepparents are included in the reference group.

4 Method

4.1 Sample

Our starting sample was composed of 185 juvenile male sex offenders. In the Netherlands, the country where the study took place, persons aged 12–17 years are considered a juvenile; criminal behaviors by juveniles constitute crimes. All juveniles had either committed and confessed to, or had been convicted of at least one hands-on sexual offense (some offenders were screened under civil law and/or under the age of 12). All have received treatment for the sex offense at an institution specialized in treatment of juvenile sex offenders. The treatment for sex offenders at this facility typically lasted 2 years. Thus, the sample comprises young males who have committed serious sex offences and who nearly always had severe personality and/or family problems as well.

The sample of 185 males includes almost the entire cohort of sex offenders treated at the institution between 1988 and 2004 (a very small number of offenders had missing or empty records and thus could not be included). Part of this sample has previously been reported upon by Hendriks (2006). Our study adds information on the biological, step, foster, and adoptive parents of these boys. Of the 185 boys in the sample 387 parents were traced: 153 fathers, 174 mothers, 19 step fathers, 5 step mothers, 1 foster father, 1 foster mother, 3 adoptive fathers, and 3 adoptive mothers.

4.2 Treatment Records

The scoring tool for sex offenders used previously by Hendriks and Bijleveld (2005), including information on personality, family characteristics, self-reported and official delinquency data, formed the basis of analysis of the treatment records. The scoring tool was augmented for this study with questions concerning the presence of an intra-familial sex offender within the family, whether other family members had been victims of intra-familial sexual abuse, whether the mother had been the victim of sexual abuse, as well as other information concerning sexual behavior within the family. Short qualitative descriptions of the family situations were also included.

In cases where the offenders themselves had been the victim of sexual abuse this was recorded as "certain" if the offenders or their parents/carers had confirmed it to be so. In cases where the therapist strongly suspected victimization to have occurred, or when the offender indicated that this had occurred, but the parent (s) did not confirm this, "indication" or "suspected" was recorded. In classifying sexual abuse as intra-familial we refer to the definition of incest according to Kouratovsky (2004): all sexual contact between family members where there is no question of mutual consent, where it occurs against the will of the child, or when this contact, due to emotional pressure, dominance or coercion by the offender, cannot be refused. A family member refers to all those included in the immediate family unit, thus step- and foster parents, partners of parents, and any adults or children co-habiting with the family.

The treatment records and details of the parents and carers of the juvenile offenders were blind coded. First the family information was coded. Following this information concerning criminal records of the parents was collected. A second independent coder checked a sample of 10 % of the treatment records. Inter-coder reliability was either sufficient or high.

4.3 Criminal Records

Of the 387 traced parents the criminal records for 6.5 % of them could not be checked due to incomplete personal details. Offenses for which the parent was found not guilty, or for which there was doubt as to their guilt (e.g., a technical dismissal that occurs mostly when the prosecutor believes the case will end in acquittal), were not included in the analysis (see Hendriks and Bijleveld 2005). For convictions lacking an offense date, this was estimated to be 1 year prior to the dismissal date or the date the case was combined with another case against the same defendant. For uncompleted cases a missing offense date was estimated to be on 1 January of the year in which the offense came to light. The vast majority of criminal record information was obtained by the reference date 1 April 2005.

4.4 Study Design and Analysis

This study is partly retrospective, partly prospective. As we start with a sample of juvenile offenders, rather than a sample of sexually offending parents, we cannot draw any conclusions as to the risk of intergenerational transmission of sex offending from parent to child. In this respect we cannot determine the extent to which a history of sexual abuse and a sexually deviant family environment leads to juvenile sex offending.

However, we are able to prospectively examine whether a sexual abuse history increases the risk of certain types of sex offending. We can determine whether fathers who have abused children in turn have children who also abuse children. We are also able to determine whether, for this particular sample, sexually abused mothers are more likely to choose an abusing partner than those who have not been the victim of sexual abuse. We test all our hypotheses using odds ratios (OR).

5 Results

5.1 Juvenile Sex Offenders

All boys had committed at least one hands-on sex offense. Seventy-five percent of the sample was of Dutch descent. Average age at time of the offense was 14 years and 4 months. The juvenile offenders were variably described in their treatment records as highly neurotic, impulsive, having below average intelligence, and vulnerable to stress, with low moral development and low to very low self-esteem. Behavioral disorders were commonly diagnosed (38 %), as well as ADHD (10 %), with pervasive developmental disorder (from the autistic spectrum) diagnosed in 6 % of cases. For 22 % of the offenders this was not their first conviction for a sexual offense. Paraphilic disorders were confirmed in 17 % of cases, and for a further 17 % these were suspected.

Nearly 45 % of the juvenile sex offenders had been sexually abused. Of these boys we can be sure that 25 (14 %) had been the victim of intra-familial abuse, and there were indications that a further 10 boys (6 %) had also been victims of intra-familial abuse. From a further 15 % (27 boys) there were strong indications that they had been sexually abused.

Concerning the sex offenses for which the boys had been convicted, almost half did not involve any physical violence, and slightly over half did not involve any verbal violence. The age of their victims ranged from 1 to 77 years, and of these 62 % were female, 16 % male, and nearly 20 % had abused males and females. Slightly more than 42 % had abused one victim, 20 % two victims, 10 % three victims, and 4 % had abused more than 10 victims. Nearly 37 % had abused at least one victim from within their immediate family. If all relatives are included this rate increases to nearly 42 %. The offenders had abused either exclusively children, or exclusively peers or adults.

5.2 *Families*

Information could not be found on three of the offenders' families. One in three offenders came from a two-parent family. For 27 of the juvenile offenders either one or both of their parents had died, and in four of these cases the mother had committed suicide. In 49 of the families alcohol abuse was present and in ten families drug use was an issue. One in seven families had experienced unemployment. Domestic violence was reported for one in four of the families. Psychopathy was recorded as a problem for parents in one in six of the families. Of all the parents more than 60 % suffered from learning difficulties and/or emotional disorders, and a third had themselves been emotionally and/or physically abused.

In 17 families (9 %) children had been regularly exposed to either pornography or sex between parents from a young age. For six of the offenders there had been regular sexual contact between cousins, nieces, and nephews. Five of the parents worked in prostitution or in the escort business. In contrast, in 11 cases there was no discussion or education within the family concerning sex, and these families were extremely tight knit and insular. In a further 19 families (10 %) there was "irregular" sexual behavior within the family that could not be categorized, e.g. parents sexually abused animals or parents encouraged their children to play sex games. In total 59 of the 182 families (32 %) were scored as having risk factors relating to sexual behavior.

Nearly 47 % of the 359 parents for whom criminal records could be traced had been registered for prosecution for a crime. One in four of the fathers and one in 16 of the mothers had been convicted of a violent crime. Nearly 10 % of the fathers and 3.5 % of the mothers had been registered for a sex offense. It is difficult to compare these figures to that of the general population due to a lack of information on the prevalence of sex offending in the Netherlands. Nevertheless, it seems likely that the prevalence is higher. In total amongst all parents 33 had been convicted of a sex offense. These included 10 cases of non-penetrative non-coercive abuse of a minor, in five of these multiple times, seven cases of intercourse with a child under 12 years, in all of these multiple times, and seven cases of intercourse with a child under 16 years. Three of the fathers had committed a sex offense prior to the birth of the juvenile sex offender.

In addition to the parental criminal records, the offenders' treatment files also provided information on self-reported parental sex offending. There were some discrepancies between the criminal records and treatment files, with some cases whereby the parent was recorded as a sex offender in the criminal record but not in the treatment file or vice versa. We used a combination of both self-report and official records to indicate offender status, in all cases indicating whether there was certainty or just suspicion that the parent had offended. From this information we can say that nearly one in six fathers had committed a sex offense, increasing to nearly one in five when cases of suspected offending are included. For mothers this is respectively 3 and 4 %. In cases where the mothers sexually abused their children, nearly all the fathers also abused these children (6 of the 7 cases). In cases where the father sexually abused their children one in four mothers also abused them. Stepmothers, foster parents and adoptive parents did not, as far as we know, commit any sexual abuse. Four of the fathers had themselves been victims of sexual abuse, and two of these had abused children. Nineteen of the mothers had been victims of sexual abuse and one of these had abused children. For stepfathers there was very little information concerning their victim status.

5.3 *Hypothesis Testing*

In order to test our first hypothesis we compare victims of intra-familial sexual abuse with victims of extra-familial sexual abuse. Whilst 16 of the 22 victims of intra-familial sexual abuse, certain and suspected, were diagnosed with paraphilic disorders, 30 of the 59 victims of extra-familial sexual abuse were also diagnosed with paraphilic disorders. The odds ratio was not significant (OR = 2.58, CI (95 %) 0.89-7.52, N = 81). This hypothesis is therefore rejected. It appears that victimization of intra-familial sexual abuse does not lead to an increased risk of paraphilic disorders.

In order to test hypothesis 2a we examined whether children who had been abused themselves or who had a sibling who was the victim of intra-familial sexual abuse were more likely than the other juvenile sex offenders to have abused a brother or sister. Our results confirm this hypothesis. In cases where we could be sure that intra-familial sexual abuse had occurred offenders were more likely to have abused a brother or sister (OR = 3.025, CI (95 %) 1.287-7.114, N = 185). Furthermore when sexual abuse occurred amongst any relatives, i.e. not only within the immediate family, the chance of the offender abusing a child was also higher in all cases (OR = 2.672, CI (95 %) 1.034-6.903, N = 182), as well as in cases where we could be certain sexual abuse had occurred (OR = 3.094, CI (95 %) 1.207-7.929, N = 182).

In order to test hypothesis 2b we examine whether sexual offenses against a child by a father or stepfather increased the risk of such sexual offenses, either intra- or extra-familial, by his child. The results confirmed this to be true for fathers. Children of fathers who had committed a sexual offense against a child were more likely to have abused their sibling(s), i.e. a child (OR = 3.754, CI (95 %) 1.434-9.83, N = 185). However, neither sexual offenses against children by step-fathers (OR = 1.075, CI (95 %) 0.272-3.948, N = 185) nor by mothers (OR = 4.242, CI (95 %) 0.8-22.487, N = 185) increased the risk for such sexual offenses in their children.

In testing both these hypotheses, cases where sexual offending against children by the parents occurred before the child was 5 years old, and therefore was not likely to have witnessed the offending, were included in the reference group. On the whole given our results we conclude that when sexual offending behavior occurs within the family we see similar sexual offending behavior in the child.

Neither of the hypotheses (3a and 3b) concerning risk related to victimization of the mother were confirmed in our analyses. We did not find that the risk of being a victim of intra-familial sexual abuse was higher for children of mothers who themselves had been victim of intra-familial sexual abuse (OR = 0.77), CI (95 %) 0.166-3.564, N = 185). Similarly, mothers who had been the victim of intra-familial sexual abuse were not more likely to choose a partner who abused their children than mothers with no history of intra-familial sexual abuse (OR = 1.25, CI (95 %) 0.43-3.63, N = 185).

In order to test whether the data support a hereditary explanation for intergenerational transmission of sex offending we examined all sexual offenses against children carried out at any time by biological parents. Offenses by step-parents were included in the reference group. Our results do not support this hypothesis for fathers: OR = 2.027, CI (95 %) 0.77-5.338, N = 182, or for mothers: OR = 3.459, CI (95 %) 0.407-29.384, N = 182.

6 Discussion

The present study examined a group of juvenile sex offenders in order to determine the extent to which a history of sexual abuse affects later sex offending behavior. Specifically we tested whether the four mechanisms, which explain the intergenerational transmission of sex offending and victimization in the literature, were supported. Our research made use of a rich and detailed, valid and reliable dataset comprised of official conviction data, as well as data from a treatment center for juvenile sex offenders.

We found that a large number of the juvenile sex offenders had a history of sexual abuse. We know that nearly half of all offenders had definitely suffered sexual abuse, with this number increasing to 60 % if we include all those for whom there was a strong suspicion that abuse had occurred. Prevalence of sexual abuse amongst this group is therefore far higher than found in the general male population. Of our sample who had suffered abuse nearly one in five was likely the victim of intra-familial sexual abuse.

We found a strong relationship between coming from a family where incestuous behavior occurred and the juvenile sex offenders victimizing their siblings. It appears that it is not always necessary to be the victim of intra-familial sexual abuse, rather simply growing up in a family where sexual abuse occurs also increases the risk of later intra-familial sex offending. In these situations the father appears to be the "role model". We found that sexual offending against children by the father significantly increased the risk of similar sexual offending by the son. These findings, which confirm hypothesis 2a and 2b, support the social learning theory of intergenerational transmission of sex offending. Taken together with the findings of van de Weijer and colleagues (2015), there is an increasing body of evidence that social learning is an important mechanism in the intergenerational transfer of crime.

We did not find that the victims of intra-familial sexual abuse had a higher prevalence rate of paraphilic disorders. We also did not find support for the link between incestuous victimization of the mother and increased risk of victimization of the child. Neither was there support for the hypothesis that mothers who had been victims of intra-familial sexual abuse were more likely to have a partner who abused their children. Lastly our results did not indicate that sexual offending is hereditary.

However, in interpreting our results it is important to bear in mind that our sample was composed of a group of serious sex offenders presenting a myriad of problems, for whom residential treatment was deemed necessary. Furthermore, it is likely that offenders in our sample have committed more sexual offenses than the one for which they are officially registered. Nevertheless, this does not diminish the importance or validity of our findings, given that our conclusions are based on a comparative analysis between groups within this sample, e.g., between victims of intra- and extra-familial abuse.

A further limitation of our study is that we are unable to draw conclusions concerning the sexual offending behavior of all victims of intra- or extra-familial sexual abuse. Prospective, longitudinal studies collecting data from two or more generations over an extended period of time are the only means by which to draw these conclusions. It is vital that such studies include victims of intra-familial sexual abuse, given that our results indicate that these victims are at greater risk than those who suffer sexual abuse by non-family members. Another limitation of our study is that by using an all-male sample we can only draw conclusions concerning male victims and offenders of sexual abuse. As we know that many more females than males are victims of intra- and extra-familial sexual abuse, this provides a further motive for future longitudinal and prospective research in this area.

In conclusion our findings indicate that being the victim of intra-familial sexual abuse increases the risk of victims who become offenders to commit these same kinds of sex offenses, i.e. against children and siblings. Specifically we found this to be the case for families where sexual abuse had occurred, in which the abuse is in some way seen as "normal", and where the father is the abuser. This research therefore strongly indicates that in the treatment of sex offenders it is imperative that the family situation and history is considered. This need is further illustrated by the fact that in this sample following the incarceration of their children for a sex offense certain parents (two fathers and one mother) continued on to commit further sexual offenses against children. It is therefore of great importance that not only the juvenile offender, but also their family is involved in the treatment process.

Five Questions

1. How do you explain why growing up in a family where incestuous behavior occurred increases the risk of becoming an intra-familial offender?
2. What is the most serious methodological shortcoming in this study?
3. Is it possible to reconcile the findings of this study (that support the social learning theory of intergeneration transmission of sex offending) with a theory that supports a genetic explanation for sex offending behavior?
4. If money, time and access to sample populations were no objective, what features would a research study for determining the mechanisms behind the intergenerational transfer of sex offending include?
5. What implications do the findings have for intervention and treatment of juvenile sex offenders?

References

Abel, G. G., Becker, J. V., & Cunningham-Rathner, J. (1984). Complications, consent, and cognitions in sex between children and adults. *International Journal of Law and Psychiatry, 7*, 89–103. doi:10.1016/0160-2527(84)90008-6.

Akers, R. L. (1985). Social learning theory and adolescent cigarette smoking. *Social Problems, 32*, 455–473.

Bandura, A. (1971). *Social learning theory*. New York: General Learning Press.

Barbaree, H. E., & Langton, C. M. (2006). The effects of child sexual abuse and the family environment. In H. E. Barbaree & W. L. Marshall (Eds.), *The juvenile sex offender* (pp. 58–78). New York: Guildford Press.

Beaver, K. M. (2013). The familial concentration and transmission of crime. *Criminal Justice and Behavior, 40*(2), 139–155. doi:10.1177/0093854812449405.

van Beek, D., & Mulder, J. (2002). De rol van cognitieve vervormingen in het plegen van pedoseksuele delicten en hun plaats in de behandeling. *Tijdschrift Voor Seksuologie, 26*, 79–86.

Besemer, S. (2012). Specialized versus versatile intergenerational transmission of violence: a new approach to studying intergenerational transmission from violent versus non-violent fathers: Latent class analysis. *Journal of Quantative Criminology, 28*, 245–263. doi:10.1007/s10940-011-9141-y.

Besemer, S., & Farrington, D. P. (2012). Intergenerational transmission of criminal behaviour: Conviction trajectories of fathers and their children. *European Journal of Criminology2, 9*(2), 120–141. doi:10.1177/1477370811422801.

Bijleveld, C. C., & Wijkman, M. (2009). Intergenerational continuity in convictions: A five-generation study. *Criminal Behavior and Mental Health, 19*(2), 142–155.

Chen, L. P., Murad, M. H., Paras, M. L., Colbenson, K. M., Sattler, A. L., Goranson, E. N., et al. (2010). Sexual abuse and lifetime diagnosis of psychiatric disorders: Systematic review and meta-analysis. *Mayo Clinic Proceedings, 85*, 618–629. doi:10.4065/mcp.2009.0583.

Derzon, J. H. (2010). The correspondence of family features with problem, aggressive, criminal, and violent behavior: A meta-analysis. *Journal of Experimental Criminology, 6*(3), 263–292. doi:10.1007/s11292-010-9098-0.

Dilillo, D., & Damashek, A. (2003). Parenting characteristics of women reporting a history of childhood sexual abuse parenting characteristics of women reporting a history of childhood sexual abuse. *Child Maltreatment, 84*, 319–333.

Easton, S. D. (2012). Understanding adverse childhood experiences (ACE) and their relationship to adult stress among male survivors of childhood sexual abuse. *Journal of Prevention & Intervention in the Community, 40*(4), 291–303. doi:10.1080/10852352.2012.707446.

Enoch, M.-A. (2011). The role of early life stress as a predictor for alcohol and drug dependence. *Psychopharmachology, 214*(1), 17–31. doi:10.1007/s00213-010-1916-6.

Estes, L. S., & Tidwell, R. (2002). Sexually abused children's behaviours: Impact of gender and mother's experience of intra- and extra-familial sexual abuse. *Family Practice, 19*(1), 10–12.

Faller, K. C. (1989). Why sexual abuse? An exploration of the intergenerational hypothesis. *Child Abuse and Neglect, 13*, 543–548.

Farrington, D. P. (1995). The development of offending and antisocial behaviour from childhood: Key findings from the Cambridge study in delinquent development. *Journal of Child Psychology and Psychiatry, 36*, 47–63.

Farrington, D. P. (2002). Key results from the first forty years of the Cambridge study in delinquent development. In T. P. Thornberry & M. D. Krohn (Eds.), *Taking stock of delinquency: an overview of findings from contemporary longitudinal studies* (pp. 137–183). New York: Academic/PlenumPublishers.

Farrington, D. P. (2011). Families and crime. In J. Q. Wilson & J. Petersilia (Eds.), *Crime and public policy* (pp. 130–157). New York: Oxford University Press.

Farrington, D. P., Jolliffe, D., Loeber, R., Stouthamer-Loeber, M., & Kalb, L. M. (2001). The concentration of offenders in families, and family criminality in the prediction of boys' delinquency. *Journal of Adolescence, 24*, 579–596. doi:10.1006/jado.2001.0424.

Franklin, C. A., & Kercher, G. A. (2012). The intergenerational transmission of intimate partner violence: Differentiating correlates in a random community sample. *Journal of Family Violence, 27*(3), 187–199. doi:10.1007/s10896-012-9419-3.

Glasser, M., Campbell, D., Glasser, A., Leitch, I., & Farrelly, S. (1994). Cycle of child sexual abuse: Links between being a victim and becoming a perpetrator. *British Journal of Psychiatry, 179*, 482–494.

Hébert, M., Parent, N., Daignault, I. V., & Tourigny, M. (2006). A typological analysis of behavioral profiles of sexually abused children. *Child Maltreatment, 11*(3), 203–216. doi:10.1177/1077559506287866.

Hendriks, J. (2006). Jeugdige zedendelinquenten: subtypen en recidive. PhD thesis, Vrije Universiteit Amsterdam.

Hendriks, J., & Bijleveld, C. C. (2005). Recidive van jeugdige zedendelinquenten na residentiële behandeling. *Tijdschrift Voor Seksuologie, 29*, 150–160.

Hoeve, M., Semon, J., Gerris, J. R. M., Van Der Laan, P. H., & Smeenk, W. (2011). Maternal and paternal parenting styles : Unique and combined links to adolescent and early adult delinquency. *Journal of Adolescence, 34*(5), 813–827. doi:10.1016/j.adolescence.2011.02.004.

Holmes, W. C., & Slap, G. B. (1998). Sexual abuse of boys. *JAMA, 280*(21), 1855–1862.

Homma, Y., Wang, N., Saewyc, E., & Kishor, N. (2012). The relationship between sexual abuse and risky sexual behavior among adolescent boys: A meta-analysis. *Journal Fo Adolescent Health, 51*(1), 18–24. doi:10.1016/j.jadohealth.2011.12.032.

Jespersen, A. F., Lalumière, M. L., & Seto, M. C. (2009). Sexual abuse history among adult sex offenders and non-sex offenders: A meta-analysis. *Child Abuse and Neglect, 33*, 179–192. doi:10.1016/j.chiabu.2008.07.004.

Kouratovsky, V. G. (2004). *Voorwaardelijk behandeld. Evaluatie van het project incestdaderbehandeling*. Rotterdam: WLP.

Leschied, A., Chiodo, D., Nowicki, E., & Rodger, S. (2008). Childhood predictors of adult criminality: A meta-analysis drawn from the prospective longitudinal literature. *Canadian Journal of Criminology and Criminal Justice, 50*(4), 435–467.

Lev-Wiesel, R. (2006). The process of coping with domestic violence in adult survivors of childhood sexual abuse. *Journal of Child Sexual Abuse, 15*(2), 23–42. doi:10.1300/J070v15n02.

Liefbroer, A. C. (2005). Valt de appel nog steeds niet ver van de boom?

Magalhães, T., Taveira, F., Jardim, P., Santos, L., Matos, E., & Santos, A. (2009). Sexual abuse of children. A comparative study of intra and extra-familial cases. *Journal of Forensic and Legal Medicine, 16*(8), 455–459. doi:10.1016/j.jflm.2009.05.007.

Maniglio, R. (2009). The impact of child sexual abuse on health : A systematic review of reviews. *Clinical Psychology Review, 29*(7), 647–657. doi:10.1016/j.cpr.2009.08.003.

Maniglio, R. (2011). The role of child sexual abuse in the etiology of suicide and non-suicidal self-injury. *Acta Psychiatrica Scandinavica, 124*(1), 30–41. doi:10.1111/j.1600-0447.2010.01612.x.

McCloskey, L. A. (2013). The intergenerational transfer of mother-daughter risk for gender-based abuse. *Psychodynamic Psychiatry, 41*(2), 303–328.

McClure, F. H., Chavez, D. V., Agars, M. D., Peacock, M. J., & Matosian, A. (2008). Resilience in sexually abused women: Risk and protective factors. *Journal of Family Violence, 23*, 81–88. doi:10.1007/s10896-007-9129-4.

Moffitt, T. E., Ross, S., & Raine, A. (2011). Crime and biology. In J. Q. Wilson & J. Petersilia (Eds.), *Crime and public policy* (pp. 53–87). New York: Oxford University Press.

Niv, S., Tuvblad, C., Raine, A., & Baker, L. A. (2013). Aggression and rule-breaking: Heritability and stability of antisocial behavior problems in childhood and adolescence. *Journal of Criminal Justice, 41*(5), 285–291. doi:10.1016/j.jcrimjus.2013.06.014.

Ogloff, J. R., Cutajar, M. C., Mann, E., Mullen, P., Wei, F. T. Y., Hassan, H. A. B., et al. (2012). Child sexual abuse and subsequent offending and victimisation: A 45 year follow-up study. *Trends and Issues in Crime and Criminal Justice, 440*, 1–6.

Price, L., Maddocks, A., Davies, S., & Griffiths, L. (2002). Somatic and psychological problems in a cohort of sexually abused boys: A six year follow up case-control study. *Archives of Disease in Childhood, 86*, 164–168.

Raine, A. (2013). *The anatomy of violence: The biological roots of crime*. New York: Random House.

Rasmussen, L. A., Burton, J. E., & Christopherson, B. J. (1992). Precursors to offending and the trauma outcome process in sexually reactive children. *Journal of Child Sexual Abuse, 1*(1), 33–48. doi:10.1300/J070v01n01.

Rayment-McHugh, S. (2003). Sibling incest offenders as a subset of adolescent sexual offenders. *Justice Response of Alternative Resolution Conference in Adelaide*. Australian Institute of Criminology.

Ryan, G., Leversee, T. F., & Lane, S. (Eds.). (2011). *Juvenile sex offending: Causes, consequences, and correction*. Hoboken, NJ: Wiley & Sons.

Salter, D., Mcmillan, D., Richards, M., Talbot, T., Hodges, J., Bentovim, A., et al. (2003). Development of sexually abusive behaviour in sexually victimised males #: A longitudinal study. *The Lancet, 361*, 471–476.

Seto, M. C., & Lalumière, M. L. (2010). What is so special about male adolescent sexual offending? A review and test of explanations through meta-analysis. *Psychological Bulletin, 136*(4), 526–575. doi:10.1037/a0019700.

Stoltenborgh, M., van Ijzendoorn, M. H., Euser, E. M., & Bakermans-Kranenburg, M. J. (2011). A global perspective on child sexual abuse: Meta-analysis of prevalence around the world. *Child Maltreatment, 16*, 79–101. doi:10.1177/1077559511403920.

Testa, M., Hoffman, J. H., & Livingston, J. A. (2011). Intergenerational transmission of sexual victimization vulnerability as mediated via parenting. *Child Abuse & Neglect, 35*(5), 363–371. doi:10.1016/j.chiabu.2011.01.010.

Thornberry, T. P. (2009). The apple doesn't fall far from the tree (or does it?): Intergenerational patterns of antisocial behavior—the American Society of Sriminology 2008 Sutherland address. *Criminology, 47*(2), 297–325.

Thornberry, T. P., Knight, K. E., & Lovegrove, P. J. (2012). Does maltreatment beget maltreatment? A systematic review of the intergenerational literature. *Trauma, Violence, & Abuse, 13*, 135–152. doi:10.1177/1524838012447697.

Tomison, A. M. (1996). Intergenerational transmission of maltreatment. *Issues in Child Abuse, 6*. Retrieved from http://www.aifs.gov.au/nch/issues6.html.

Trickett, P. K., Noll, J. G., & Putnam, F. W. (2011). The impact of sexual abuse on female development: Lessons from a multigenerational, longitudinal research study. *Development and Psychopathology, 23*, 453–476. doi:10.1017/S0954579411000174

Van de Weijer, S.G., Thornberry, T.P., Bijleveld, C.C.J.H., & Blokland, A.A.J. (2015). Parental divorce and the intergenerational transmission of crime. In A.A.J. Blokland & P. Lussier (Eds.), *Sex offenders. A criminal career approach.*Chichester. UK: John Wiley & Sons, Ltd.

Van de Weijer, S. G., Bijleveld, C. C., & Blokland, A. A. J. (2014). The intergenerational transmission of violent offending. *Journal of Family Violence, 29*(2), 109–188.

Ward, T., & Casey, A. (2010). Extending the mind into the world: A new theory of cognitive distortions in sex offenders. *Aggression & Violent Behavior, 15*(1), 49–58.

Ward, T., & Siegert, R. J. (2002). Toward a comprehensive theory of child sexual abuse: A theory knitting perspective. *Psychology, Crime & Law, 8*(4), 37–41. doi:10.1080/10683160208401823.

Whitaker, D. J., Le, B., Karl Hanson, R., Baker, C. K., McMahon, P. M., Ryan, G., et al. (2008). Risk factors for the perpetration of child sexual abuse: A review and meta-analysis. *Child Abuse & Neglect, 32*, 529–548. doi:10.1016/j.chiabu.2007.08.005.

Wijkman, M., Bijleveld, C. C., & Hendriks, J. (2011). Female sex offenders: Specialists, generalists and once-only offenders. *Journal of Sexual Aggression, 17*(1), 34–45.

Young, T. L., Riggs, M., & Robinson, J. L. (2011). Childhood sexual abuse severity reconsidered: A factor structure of CSA characteristics. *Journal of Child Sexual Abuse, 20*(4), 373–395. doi:10.1080/10538712.2011.590124.

Zuravin, S., McMillen, C., DePanfilis, D., & Risley-Curtiss, C. (1996). The intergenerational cycle of child maltreatment: Continuity versus discontinuity. *Journal of Interpersonal Violence, 11*, 315–334.

"Violence Against Children Sells Very Well". Reporting Crime in the Media and Attitudes to Punishment

Thomas Hestermann

Abstract All over the world, the media paint a different picture of crime and violence than police statistics do. The media do not report on crimes, which occur especially often but on those which cause a great stir. The more drastic a crime, the more closely associated it is with sexual violence, the greater the chance of its being presented in detail. In order to reach a wide audience, the media stir up emotions, especially sympathy with the victim and fear of violence. At the center of such reports stands the victim of the crime—but it is an idealized victim, who is preferably young and female.

Against the background drawn from the international mass media panorama, the results of the research at the Macromedia University in Hamburg and Berlin (Germany) confirm the above with regard to Germany. This type of reporting has consequences that are similar, irrespective of the country. It is above all television, which shows the world as a frightening and dangerous place. This increases the call for tough sentencing. As a result, politicians come under pressure to introduce stiffer penalties—not as a reaction to real developments in criminality but as a reaction to assumptions about criminality.

1 Introduction

The media are a key to understanding the world. We use them to learn about events and developments which are of relevance to our lives but which lie beyond our immediate sphere of perception. However, the media hardly show the normal and generally known but present the surprising and the new. It is thus inappropriate to expect the media to show the world as it is in its entirety, quite apart from the fact that every picture of the world arises in the eye of the beholder and there is no *one* general understanding of reality.

When motorists, for example, listen to the traffic news to find out quickly about conditions on the roads, they want a quick report on accidents, traffic jams and cars going the wrong way on the freeways so that they can change their route if

T. Hestermann (✉)
Macromedia University of Applied Sciences, Hamburg/Berlin, Germany
e-mail: hestermann@medienbuero.net

H. Kury et al. (eds.), *Women and Children as Victims and Offenders: Background, Prevention, Reintegration*, DOI 10.1007/978-3-319-08398-8_33

necessary. They expect a selection of these incidents based on clear rules. No one wants to listen to traffic news, which lists all the roads on which the traffic is flowing normally, only to mention the comparatively rare disturbances in passing. Such a report would be a more representative picture of the reality on the roads but would be completely dysfunctional. In journalism, the same basic principle applies as for the analyzing and controlling of group processes according to the concept of theme-centered interaction: disturbances take precedence (Cohn 1975).

2 Current State of Research

It can thus be expected of reports on criminality that they pay more attention to an especially serious offense than to a slight breach of the rules. The situation, however, becomes complicated when media do not just magnify the important and the interesting like a magnifying glass, but distort and coarsen, when they show one thing and cut out another. Then they lead to misperceptions, which can prove fatal for a society.

2.1 The Inflation of Death on Television: Some Insights from the International Panorama

A comparison of various crimes of violence shows that the media are most interested in those which end fatally. On an international scale, analyses of US journalism, for example, reveal that drastic violence, in particular murder and manslaughter, are reported on disproportionally often (Chermak 1995; Gruenewald et al. 2009; Buckler and Travis 2005). Studies show unanimously that about every second victim of crime on whom German television reports has died (Grimm et al. 2005, p. 120; Krüger 2008, p. 70; Winterhoff-Spurk 1994, p. 57; Groebel and Gleich 1993, p. 102). Groebel and Gleich conclude from this: “The killing of people has become in part a normal program element” (Groebel and Gleich 1993, p. 73). This emphasis on especially serious offenses is frequently criticized. Bourdieu speaks of sensation as a selection criterion (Bourdieu 1998, p. 25).

More recent studies also take a look at the increased significance of sexual violence for journalistic selection processes. According to Baurmann, the perception of sexual violence in partnerships and of sexual abuse of children in particular were freed of taboos in the 1970s and 1980s, first in the USA and then in Europe (Baurmann 2004, p. 436). Since then, more and more findings have revealed a particularly intensive focus on sexual violence (Schulenburg 2007, p. 1; Reuband 2007; Proctor et al. 2002, p. 357). It is therefore not astonishing that reporting on both sexual and fatal violence is increasing in intensity. In fact, a sharp increase in the number of reports on sexually motivated murders of children has been observed in Germany since the 1990s (Schneider et al. 2005). According to Albrecht, it is precisely sexually motivated murders of children which provide all the features "which are required for scandalizing and for corresponding media presentation" (Albrecht 2004, p. 506).

A paradigm shift can also be seen in India, albeit very much later. Currently only every hundredth case of sexual violence in India is reported to the police. However, especially dramatic cases of sexual violence such as the group rape of a student in Delhi in December 2012 and the group rape of a young woman on the orders of village elders in West Bengal in 2014 have been the subject of many media reports in India and worldwide (Raj and McDougal 2014).

The readiness to report crimes is increasing parallel to a growing public awareness in India. Shakuntala sees the rape in Delhi, which provoked outrage all over the world, as a turning point which is bringing sexual violence against women and criminality as a whole increasingly into focus in India: "No doubt this case of rape has created a critical space for the discourse of social justice in the media and has forever changed the way Indian journalists cover crime, policing and corruption" (Shakuntala 2013).

The media have played a key role in making perpetrators fear legal consequences on more than one occasion—for example, after the death of a young actress in Delhi in 1999. The perpetrator, the son of an influential politician, was first acquitted due to hesitant police investigations and the fact that several witnesses had been bribed. Following journalistic research, the culprit was finally sentenced after all. "The press ended up being more productive than the judicial system in bringing out the truth behind rumors of bribery", writes Alvarez (2011).

Fishman (1980) proves how little media trends can be explained with official statistics. He analyzes the sharp rise in the reporting on criminality against old people in the fall of 1976 in New York City, while at the same time the number of offenses reported to the police dropped. Fishman speaks of a "crime wave" which is in essence a wave of *reported* crime (Fishman 1980, p. 5; cf. Cavender and Fishman 1998, pp. 3–15; Fishman 1978, pp. 531–543; Vasterman 2005). Such a wave had already been known about 50 years before—the reporter Lincoln Steffens describes how he himself triggered off a wave of reports on break-ins also in New York City: "I enjoy crime waves. I made one once" (Steffens 1931, p. 285).

How little reporting follows statistical data is also proven by a recent experiment held in the Columbian capital of Bogotá. While some regions of Latin America show the highest homicide rates in the world, the homicide rate in Columbia more than halved between 2001 and 2011. However, this positive development does not play a role either in the media or in public perception. A research team tested the effect of objective information by giving test persons statistical data on the development of criminality. It was seen that such data considerably increased the feeling of safety and trust in the police and that these feeling were still noticeable 3 weeks after the initial survey. The effect is smaller if test persons consume a considerable amount of reporting on criminality (Ardanaz et al. 2013). The stereotypes of violent criminals prove to be strong, as Pereira et al. prove in experiments with test persons from Spain and Brazil (Pereira et al. 2013).

Reporting on crime is a centuries-old tradition. Early examples of criminal reporting include the German "Erweiterte Unholdenzeitung", an illustrated pamphlet on crime and its punishment from the year 1590 (Höbermann 1989, p. 13). According to reports from the seventeenth century, newspapers of that time picked up on incidents such as child murder, theft and adultery (Stieler 1969, p. 61). From 1792 to 1795, the writer and poet Friedrich Schiller wrote reports on extraordinary legal cases and was convinced: "In the whole history of mankind, no chapter is more informative for the heart and mind than the annals of his aberrations" (Tekolf 2005, p. 7).

Systematic examinations of criminal reporting have been known since the end of the nineteenth century. Speed sees in New York newspapers a noticeable tendency towards the terrible: accordingly, newspapers do not report on the really important events but on the sensations and catastrophes (Speed 1893, p. 710, as per Schulz 1989, p. 135; cf. Garofalo 1981, p. 321; Fenton 1910; Swanson 1955, pp. 416 f.).

The theory is often raised that reporting on violence is a crowd-puller and that program planners therefore often include it in their programs. Muckenhaupt sees in "Cassandrian" headlines simply a form of news marketing (Muckenhaupt 1998, p. 123). Kerbel, US television journalist and lecturer, supports the theory "if it bleeds, it leads" in a book of the same name (Kerbel 2000; cf. Gross 2006, 4; Karl 2006, p. 66; McManus 1994). This is assumed to a particularly great extent for sexual crimes (Friedrichsen 2004, p. 199; cf. Friedrichsen 2002; Roithmeier 1994, p. 100). The German public radio station DeutschlandRadio announces: "Red light and blue light are always a safe bet" is rule of thumb in editorial departments—of private and public television channels alike (Mayr 2006).

There are, however, doubts in German television journalism that violence attracts a large audience per se and on a permanent basis. Dieter Lesche, former director of the German private television channel RTL, considers the experiment of winning over a mass audience with mainly violent items of news to have failed (Lesche 2001, p. 46; cf. Patterson 2000; Ludwig and Pruys 1998, pp. 586 f.). Doubts regarding the permanently high attractiveness of violence are reinforced by Ruhrmann and Göbbel who had journalists assess different news factors in an online survey. Of the 22 given features of reporting, the news factor referred to as "Violence/Aggression", which was defined by the threat and use of violence, reached position 13 only (Ruhrmann and Göbbel 2007, pp. 40–42). As far as journalism is concerned, the subject of criminality is thus only the key to a high level of audience attention if it emotionalizes in a special way.

2.2 *The Ideal Victim: Childlike and Female*

While earlier reports often revolved around the motives of the perpetrator, since the 1980s there has been an increasing focus on the victim of the crime. Mass media experts speak of the victim as the central symbolic figure (Katz 1987, p. 52; cf. Garland 2002, p. 11; Friedrichsen 2004, p. 201), whereby it is not the victim in general who is of interest but a picture of an ideal victim, the "worthy victim"(Gruenewald et al. 2009). The preferred victim is innocent and helpless. As a result of this stereotyping, journalists are particularly interested in women and children as victims.

Still at the end of the 1970s, Zenz observes that violence towards children is taboo in Germany. Up to that time, no case of child abuse, however cruel or even fatal, had ever generated attention for more than a day (Zenz 1978, pp. 21–23).

Derwein (1995, p. 137) analyzes the reporting of four German newspapers in 1988. In so doing, he lists the ages of the victims of killings (murder and manslaughter) and compares them with police criminal statistics. As Derwein does not specify his sources further, his data were newly calculated on the basis of the police statistics of the year 1988 (Bundeskriminalamt 1989, p. 97). The results of this calculation show that attention is now focused on the child victim: based on criminal statistics, victims under 14 are now reported on 2.8 times more often than their age group appears in the statistics, people of 60 years and older are reported on only half as often as they appear in the same.

This trend has clearly grown and can be observed on an international scale. Proctor et al. (2002) compile demographics of reported criminality and see a clear tendency to report increasingly on violence against children (cf. Chermak 1995; Peelo et al. 2004). Friedrichsen describes the social cohesion resulting from the collective empathy which, according to her, is triggered off especially by the reporting on crimes against children. However greatly a society is divided into other smaller worlds, however little unity there is on social standards—on this point there is overwhelming unanimity. "The need for this feeling of belonging is satisfied in the 'uprising of the decent' and other similar mood-setting formulas" (Friedrichsen 2004, p. 199; cf. Paoli 2004, p. 304). According to Cohen, violence against children, and above all sexual violence, leads to a real panicky sense of vulnerability (Cohen 2003, p. xvi).

A similar tendency can be observed as regards the increase in attention paid to the female victim, however with various findings. At the end of the 1970s, an analysis of the content of the Chicago Tribune gives a value of 37.3 % for female victims of violence and thus an under-average representation of the same (Graber 1980, p. 56). An analysis of German daily newspapers gives a similar value: in reports on murder and manslaughter in the year 1988, victims were female in 34.2 % of all cases—a figure which is lower than the 52.8 % recorded in police criminal statistics (Derwein 1995, p. 130; Bundeskriminalamt 1989, p. 97).

According to an analysis of German television news programs at the beginning of the 1990s, victims of violence are mainly or exclusively female in only 1.9 % of reports, in 72.4 % they are mainly or exclusively male (Groebel and Gleich 1993, p. 104). In an analysis of television violence in the broadest sense, which was carried out 11 years later, the share of female victims is clearly higher at 27.5 % (Grimm et al. 2005, p. 198).

Proctor et al. (2002, p. 360) show an increase in reporting on violence against female victims. Reijnders (2005) considers the young, female victim to be a stereotype which modern television formats use in the same way as the ballads of the 19th century. Sexual violence against women increasingly became a subject for television in the 1990s (Custers and van den Bulck 2012, p. 2).

A series of studies is devoted to the question whether foreign suspects are particularly stigmatized. Answers to this question differ. Bohn et al. criticize German local reporting which nearly only features Sinti and Romany people when they are under suspicion of having committed a crime (Bohn et al. 1995, pp. 166–183; cf. Jäger et al. 1998). Dixon and Linz find a distorted representation of minorities. According to them, Afro-Americans and Latinos appear in US television news programs mainly as suspects, more rarely as victims (Dixon and Linz 2000, pp. 547–573; cf. Oliver 1994). Welch sees clearly tendentious reporting at the expense of dark-skinned Americans: "In American society, a prevalent representation of crime is that it is overwhelmingly committed by young black men" (Welch 2007, p. 276).

Some studies come to opposite findings. In an experimental study, Carter finds that students writing a report about a violent break-in are less likely to presume that a suspect is guilty if they consider him to be dark-skinned than if they consider him to be white (Carter 1959). According to Derwein, foreign suspects are more likely to be under-represented in reports in German daily papers as compared with police statistics (Derwein 1995, p. 112). In her examination of the local reporting of a South German newspaper, the "Schwäbische Tagblatt", between 1975 and 2000, Saleth comes to the following conclusion: "A clearly negatively colored representation of foreign suspects could not be confirmed" (Saleth 2004, p. 145). Coleman (2011) finds that students of journalism make no distinction in their reporting when the same case studies are presented with individuals of different skin color.

2.3 *The Significance of Emotions: Fear and Sympathy*

Hoffmann borrows from the poetics of Aristotle the idea that "like classical tragedy", reporting on criminality arouses "fear and sympathy, it deals with the failure of human existence, the archaic nature of physical violence, the suffering of the victim, the irruption of the irrational into everyday rationality" (Hoffmann 1992, p. 58). Even if fear in particular is regarded as a consequence of media violence, empathy is as well a frequent emotional echo (Früh 2001, pp. 145–147). According to Voß (2002), the feeling of threat arising from extremely shocking violent incidents is closely linked with feelings such as grief and sympathy.

Media psychology studies describe empathy as a pre-condition for fear but also as a consequence in its own right. Zillmann presumes that representations of danger and suffering trigger off both fear for oneself and empathy with others (Zillmann 2004, p. 119).

Fear in particular is described as an emotional effect of reporting on violent criminality (Cantor 2003, 213). Cavender and Bond-Maupin (1993, 307) consider criminality to be the ideal subject with which to express the fear of city life and the feeling of danger associated with it. Ruhrmann and others generally classify crime subjects as "subjects of fear" (Ruhrmann 2005; Maier et al. 2006, p. 26; Ruhrmann and Göbbel 2007, p. 65; cf. Früh 2001, p. 142 f.; Smaus 1978, p. 193). Altheide considers it to be an essential function of the media to mass-produce fear (Altheide 2002, p. 23; cf. Altheide et al. 2001; Hestermann 2010, 2014).

An analysis of the content of printed texts and television programs showed that in reports of the Los Angeles Times and in the main news programs of the US channel ABC, the word "fear" was used most often in the context of crime (Altheide 2002, p. 70). Kerbel reports on debates in US news journalism, according to which above all professionals in local television news programs consider it a good idea to report on violent criminality so as to create fear and thus guarantee audience figures. Fear is a primary human reaction which in extreme cases rivets the viewer to such an extent that he is no longer able to change channels (Kerbel 2000, p. 106).

2.4 How the Media Increase the Call for Tough Sentences

The sustained fire from the media has consequences. An emotionalizing report on criminality, which shows an especially terrible crime and an especially pitiful victim sparks off reactions. The correlation between media consumption and the call for stiffer sentences has been a subject of research both nationally and internationally. The latter phenomenon, i.e. the urging for vengeance through severe sentences instead of reconciliation and re-socialization, is referred to as punitivity.

Morris (1997) proves the influence of media reporting with a clear example: while police statistics recorded a drop in violent criminality between 1991 and 1995, the main news programs of the three US-wide television channels ABC, CBS and NBC quadrupled the number of their reports on such crimes. In Gallup polls, the number of people who considered violence and criminality to be the most urgent social problem then rose from 9 to 49 % (Morris 1997, p. 108). Similarly in Germany, there is an ongoing discussion on the effects of violence reporting on a more severe crime policy (Walter 1994, 1999; Windzio et al. 2007, pp. 7–8; Pfeiffer et al. 2004; Rückert 2003; Leutheusser-Schnarrenberger 2000, 2012; Hestermann 2003, 2011, 2012, 2014).

The influence of television in particular and of the various program formats has been examined in the past. Formats proving to have a particularly great influence are tabloid-style TV shows (Reuband 2010) or TV news programs (Chiricos et al. 1997, cf. Eschholz et al. 2003). In accordance with previous studies, Sotirovic (2003) confirms the strong influence of television on punitive attitudes such as support for the death penalty.

The following correlations can be shown concretely: in the study of Roberts and Indermaur (2007), which refers to Australia, the viewers in the survey who use commercial TV channels as their main source of news show more punitive attitudes. This finding was confirmed in a further Australian study (Spiranovic et al. 2012). A longitudinal study from Germany also proves that watching news programs on private TV channels significantly increases punitive attitudes, whereas reading quality newspapers leads to a lower level of punitivity (Windzio et al. 2007). This result was found to be true for all levels of education. The same finding was confirmed in a cross-sectional survey in which news consumption on the Internet was considered (Baier et al. 2011).

Krause shows with an experimentally supported survey in Guatemala that the consumption of crime news particularly in tabloid media increases distrust in government and hence the support for authoritarian crime control. "The two measures of distrust in government—distrust in criminal justice institutions and blaming the government for a rise in crime—are the only attitudes significantly affected by exposure to crime news." (Krause 2014).

With reference to the correlation between media consumption and crime-related variables, the degree to which a program format takes on a tabloid character is of decisive importance. People who use news programs on private TV channels or read tabloid newspapers overestimate the development of criminality more; the use of quality media goes along with a lower overestimation (Pfeiffer et al. 2004, 2005; Windzio and Kleimann 2006; Windzio et al. 2007).

Windzio and Kleimann (2006) examine the correlation between media use, perception of criminality and penal attitudes in a structural equation model; their analyses are, however, based only on a cross-section and not on a longitudinal study. The result is an indirect effect of the use of private TV news programs on punitivity via the perception of criminality as well as a direct effect. A differentiated look at the patterns of media usage (Windzio et al. 2007)—also by means of a structural equation model—shows that the consumption of quality media works in the opposite direction: it reduces punitive attitudes both directly and indirectly via a lower overestimation of the development of criminality.

There are currently hardly any content analyses on the differences, which may exist between various online media. This is all the more surprising as a very large number of people now get their information online. Studies presume that online media consumption also has an influence on punitivity. To what extent formats differ systematically with regard to their reporting has hardly been researched. Salter (2013) confirms a growing influence of the social media on the severity of sentences.

Rosenberger and Callanan (2011) predict that the growing linking of television with online forums will favor shocking descriptions of crime, which may in turn affect punitivity. Xie and Newhagen (2012) come to the conclusion that mobile information on criminal cases has clearly higher effects on the fear of criminality in both the short and long term (and therefore possibly on punitivity, too) than stationary media use.

Content analyses combined with audience research provide answers on how the consumption of quality media compared to tabloid media affects the attitudes to punishment of the viewers or readers. The findings thereof suggest on the one hand that quantitative discrepancies arise due to the fact that tabloid media report on criminality more frequently and more conspicuously. All the more relevant are initial findings, which show that attention should be paid to the content of reporting. The way in which victim and perpetrator are presented or whether tougher sentences are demanded seems to vary from media to media. Studies devoted to the question of content are, however, very rare.

2.5 *Is the Audience an Object of Media Influences or a Subject in the Selection of Media Contents?*

Gerbner and Gross (1976) first presumed that there were one-sided causal correlations, according to which people who watch television for more than 5 h a day consider the world to be especially threatening. In later essays, the research group led by Gerbner comes to the conclusion that there is interaction between audience and media producers: "Television neither simply 'creates' or 'reflects' images, opinions, and beliefs. Rather, it is an integral aspect of a dynamic process" (Gerbner et al. 1994, p. 23; cf. Burkart 2004, p. 332; Baumann 1995, p. 35).

This model has become largely accepted in recent media research. For example, Chiricos et al. (2000, 757) describe TV viewers to be influenceable and independent to the same degree: "Consumers of TV programs are subjects as much as objects." This supposition follows the dynamic-transactional approach developed by Früh and Schönbach (1982) as a model for the choices made in journalism, in particular for those made by the audience (Früh and Schönbach 1982, 2005; Schönbach and Früh 1984). They refer to interaction between media and audience as inter-transaction.

"In the process of mass communication, communicator and recipient thus set conditions on the one hand and are confronted with the conditions of the other party on the other; both are therefore passive and active at once" (Früh and Schönbach 1982, 79). The dynamic-transactional approach takes up lines of research which are directed at the effects of the media and thus the question what the media do with people. And it includes research on audience decisions in media behavior, which looks into what people do with the media (Früh and Schönbach 2005, p. 13; Burkart 2004, pp. 239–248; Bonfadelli 2004, pp. 184–187; Maletzke 1998, p. 69f).

Früh and Schönbach emphasize that they are interested in looking at both the audience and media producers. They see their model as neither communicator-oriented, such as the effect approach, nor recipient-oriented as the user approach but as *process-oriented* (Früh and Schönbach 1982, p. 85). According to their model, the increased audience orientation in journalism does not in any way mean that journalistic behavior can now be explained mechanically with the needs of the viewers and that the once criticized self-reference of the media has now turned completely into a reference to the audience. Journalistic behavior is not just the result of the will of the audience. "Cause and effect, dependent and independent variables are woven together very closely in an oscillatory interaction" (Früh and Schönbach 1982, p. 77; cf. Schulz 1997, p. 45 f.; Weischenberg and Scholl 1998, p. 121).

2.6 The Death of an 11-Year Old Girl and the Socialization of Fear and Anger

When 11-year old Lena was found murdered in a parking garage in the small North German town of Emden on one of the first days of spring in 2012, the news of the violent crime spread across the country within a few hours. Radio and television stations reported the incident and the Internet played a central role: sparked off by media reports, a wide front of hate against the still unknown perpetrator quickly arose from debates in the social networks. Feeling that the crime stood for the failure of the state, some people spread archaic fantasies of punishment—using their full names.

A close link between television and the Internet was seen the next day when Emden police held a press conference, which was broadcasted and live-streamed by several TV stations. A large number of *Facebook* users showed little interest in details connected with solving the crime but demanded draconian measures instead—the hanging of the perpetrator immediately on his arrest, for example.

Mass media contributed toward the socialization of fear and anger. In many TV reports, it could be seen how the camera zoomed in on a pool of blood at the scene of the crime. The news program *RTL Aktuell* described Emden as the "town in mourning". Nearly all German news programs showed the arrest of a 17 year-old suspect, in handcuffs and before the eyes of the neighbors. He was remanded in custody. In contrast to the abstract presumption of innocence, it was the impact of the pictures spread by the media, which led countless people to believe that the murderer had now been found—and that at the same time the danger from sexual offenders was growing.

"The media play an important role as intermediaries between the virtual spheres of television and the Internet, for example, but also between the abysses of violent criminality and the everyday life of the normal citizen" writes Gisela Friedrichsen (2012, p. 45), reporter on court cases for the German news magazine *Der Spiegel*. In her view, picture-supported information has a very special dynamic. "The bare facts often come across as dry and boring in print, a text can sometimes be hard to understand and long-winded. Words can be contradicted, pictures cannot."

After pictures of the arrest of the suspect in Emden had circulated, an 18 year-old *Facebook* user called for people to storm the police station and lynch the suspect. Dozens of people actually gathered in front of the Emden police station and stayed there late into the night. There was, however, no violence. A short time later, it was found that the suspect was innocent. The real murderer was arrested soon afterwards.

3 Empirical Findings

Over and above this reported individual case, the question thus presents itself—according to what patterns do media makers report on violent criminality? Do these patterns differ from channel to channel and program to program? Reporting on violent criminality was long considered the domain of TV channels, which have to exist on the market as commercial enterprises. The public TV stations, which are mainly financed by television and radio license fees and hardly by advertising, seemed to have a completely different understanding of journalistic quality.

What is correct here is that news programs on German private channels report on violent criminality in Germany about four times as much as their public competitors. However, a completely different picture emerges if one considers the popular tabloid television magazines—during the period of the survey, no other format is seen to contain as many reports on violence as the public television programs *Brisant* (ARD) and *hallo deutschland* (ZDF) (Fig. 1). This is one of the results of an interdisciplinary research project led by the author in the Criminological Research Institute of Lower Saxony, accomplished with new data on television reports in 2012, which were collected at the Macromedia University in Hamburg and Berlin.

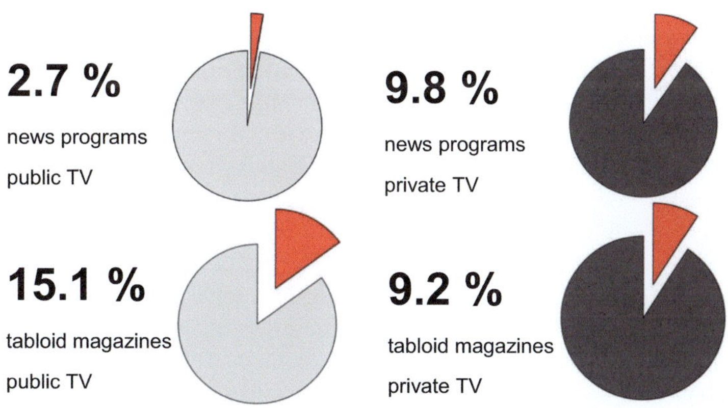

Fig. 1 Percentage of violent reporting as per channels and formats. N = 249 broadcasts of main evening news programs (without weather) and 79 broadcasts of tabloid magazines of the eight most watched German TV channels from three calendar weeks in March, April, and May 2012, in the case of the "Tagesschau" over complete months. The proportionate length of reports on violent criminality in Germany is shown. *Source*: own research at Macromedia University, Germany

What do television producers hope to achieve by reporting on violence? According to which criteria do they select crimes and people? Do sex and crime guarantee high viewing figures? In order to explain journalistic mechanisms in television reporting on violent criminality, 33 program planners were interviewed. With their anonymity ensured, these men and women of all ages, from reporter to editor-in-chief, from public and private television, gave insight into their patterns of interpretation and action. What they said in qualitative research interviews was compared with the results of a standardized analysis of 249 broadcasts of news and 79 broadcasts of tabloid magazines from three program weeks in 2012 which contained 257 reports on violent criminality in Germany.

The linking of these two methods shows astonishing results—astonishing in the sense that media studies are skeptical about comments made by journalists and presume instead that media producers act on instinct and hardly understand their own behavior. And even if they did just once, that they would refuse to give their insights (Kepplinger 2004, p. 90). In fact, journalists do act according to certain conventions but are often not aware of these conventions. For this reason, journalistic patterns of action can only be investigated to a certain extent in standardized interviews. However, if media planners are able to open up and express themselves in their own language in qualitative interviews, they reveal patterns which reflect their actions very precisely and which can be proven with the help of standardized contents analyses.

3.1 In Focus: Murder, Manslaughter and Sexual Violence

Following the theory of newsworthiness, it can be filtered out from the comments of the TV professionals that a number of news factors are important in the reporting of violence—the severity of an act of violence, for example. Media producers closely link the interest which they assume the audience to have in violent criminality with drastic forms of violence, especially with the breaking of the taboo of killing. The editor of a public TV news program is convinced "Murder is simply a subject for everyone", and even more so when it is committed for reprehensible motives such as sexual lust.

In fact, 65 % of all violent crimes reported on during the period surveyed are killings. Compared with police case numbers, sexual murders are reported on 74 times more often than other fatal violence. This leads to a dramatic distortion of reality. In reporting on violence, sexual murders make for a share, which is 27,600 times higher than that found in police statistics (Fig. 2).

It is above all perceived criminality as opposed to actual criminality, which determines the content of reporting. What is important are the viewing figures and not the statistics of the police and criminologists. The explosion in the number of reports on child sexual murders (Schneider et al. 2005) can thus be explained by the high degree of involvement on the part of the audience, while the number of these extremely rare offenses has fallen further in a long-term comparison. "I only serve a

Fig. 2 Figures showing the degree to which television distorts the representation of violence. PCS n = 836,754 cases of violence in the year 2012 recorded in police criminal statistics (police crime statistics of Germany, as per Bundeskriminalamt 2013, pp. 20, 130, 287–309). TV n = 246 television reports which refer to individual crimes of violence in Germany during the period of the study (three program weeks in the year 2012). *Source*: own research at Macromedia University, Germany

Offense	PCS n	PCS %	TV n	TV %	Factor
Sexual murders	11	0.001	68	27.6	**27,600**
Killings without sexual murders	605	0.1	92	37.4	**374**
Attempted killings	1,588	0.2	17	6.9	**34.5**
Sexual offenses	45,823	5.5	19	7.7	**1.4**
Bodily harm without robbery	546,495	65.3	27	11.0	**0.2**
Robbery and other violent offenses	242,232	29.0	23	9.3	**0.3**
Total	836,754	100.0	246	100.0	

market" explains a reporter and adds that anyone who refuses the "stirring-up machinery" of the media because he or she does not wish to arouse groundless fears is laughed at in editorial departments.

Serious crimes generate a lot of attention while everyday violence, which is wide-ranging and therefore a real experience and risk for many people, hardly appears in the media. What initially seems to contradict this is that journalists in an on-line survey named the factor reach to be the most important criterion of their news selection process (Ruhrmann and Göbbel 2007, pp. 41–43). However, it would seem that reach is important in the sense of *perceived* threat. The extent of (assumed) fear on the part of the audience dictates journalistic selection and thematizing strategies.

"A story is relevant and its telling justified if it *could* take place in your home or mine", says a magazine editor from private television. According to the interviewees, perceived reach increases if the horror takes place within the realm of the familiar, as a reporter from public television reveals: "Family dramas are interesting because one thinks that could possibly happen in my family, possibly to my neighbors around the corner."

The consequence of this is not only to show certain offenses more frequently but also to emphasize the everyday character of the scenery—a strategy with which the boundaries of the awful are removed. The scene of the crime thus becomes a normal home in which terrible things happen nonetheless. The similarity of external conditions nurtures the fear that the boundaries between the safe zone in front of the television and the dangerous place that is shown on television will become blurred. This combination of the familiar and the frightening, of consonance and surprise, is described by the interviewees as the "spooky factor".

Finally, the tension has to be released when the culprit is driven out of the dark and is arrested. An important element is that police and justice are seen as having power over illegal violence. In this case, the journalistic interest in a happy ending is combined with the urge of the police force to promote a positive image of itself. "This is a very hypocritical system", criticizes a magazine editor, when the police deliberately present the journalists with an arrested suspect "to shoot him down" because they, the police, want to show that their search for the culprit has been successful (Hestermann 2010).

3.2 "German Perpetrator, German Victim, is Best"

Those interviewed emphasize that statistics are hardly a measure of journalistic selection. Even those who work in the editorial departments of public television channels see themselves under pressure to feature statistically irrelevant subjects if they think these will move a large audience. For, from a journalistic point of view, subjective reach is important in order to involve and bind the audience. Subjective reach is increased when the focus of interest is on people whose circumstances correspond with the target group. It is therefore assumed that the latter will not be very interested in reports on people from other cultures. An editor of one of the tabloid magazines on public television sums it up as follows: "German perpetrator, German victim, is best." A disproportionally low percentage of explicitly foreign victims in the TV reports examined, namely 3.2 %, corresponds with this assumption. Since the characteristics of suspects have less influence on the selection process, their share, namely 8.5 %, is not as disproportionally low when compared with police statistics.

With the exclusion of foreigners particularly as victims of violence, a discriminating effect arises: in news reports, non-Germans appear almost four times as often as suspects than as victims of violence. Police statistics on the other hand show—in as far as they are comparable—more or less equal percentages.

A further news factor, which is of central importance in the reporting on violence is the polarity between the victim of the crime and the culprit (who may occasionally also be a woman). Since the middle of the 1980s, victims of crime have moved to the center of media interest—a trend, which was observed in the USA before it came apparent in Germany (Baurmann 2004; Hestermann 1997). Victims are seen as the key figures of frightening reports on violence, as symbols of the challenge of collective identity (Katz 1987, p. 52; Garland 2002, p. 11).

This tendency can be clearly proven in modern television journalism. The victim is at the center of the report on violence—in as far as he or she fulfills certain expectations. From a journalistic point of view, the ideal victim is childlike, female and indigenous, and of course innocent. Television producers presume that the fate of such a victim will move the audience and consider it to be very important to arouse emotions in the viewers, primarily sympathy with the idealized victim and fear for oneself and one's loved ones.

3.3 *Child Violence as an Article for Sale*

"If one sees the subject of child violence as an article for sale, it sells very well because it always supplies a certain topic of conversation, an emotional topic and simply drama", says an editor. A recording of numerous socio-demographic features of the people shown on television reveals an idealizing of the victim. Taking the same number of violent crimes registered with the police, children younger than 14 years of age are reported on 21 times more often than victims of crime who are 60 and older (Fig. 3).

In police statistics, the share of children under 14 who are victims of the reported crimes equals 9.5 %, while in TV reports it equals 57.6 %. The share of victims of violence 60 and older amounts to 13.8 % in police statistics and only 4.0 % on television. Source: own research at Macromedia University, Germany.

In as far as they speak generally about victims, the interviewees talk without exception of females as the leading figures of reporting. "It's bad if the victim doesn't look nice", says one reporter, "if someone kills his wife, and she looks like a dragon." Or the sad eyes of a maltreated girl are described as a central motif—in any case it is girls and women who are commented upon. Indeed, content analysis confirms that this pattern is relevant for journalistic decisions. Crime reports on television focus on offences with mostly female victims.

While police statistics show that the victims of reported violent crimes are mostly male (59.9 %), less than every third victim of violence shown on television is a man (30.6 %) (Bundeskriminalamt 2013, pp. 41 and 130).

The idealized victim is innocent of the crime—this is assumed per se in the case of children. On the other hand, cases which are not clear-cut are avoided. Crimes of violence in red-light districts, for example, are hardly mentioned as it is presumed that the attitude of the audience towards such victims of crime will be at best ambivalent and that empathy is out of the question, as a journalist from a private television channel explains: "What is then often said is, who will sympathize with someone who sleeps with twenty men a day." (Hestermann 2009).

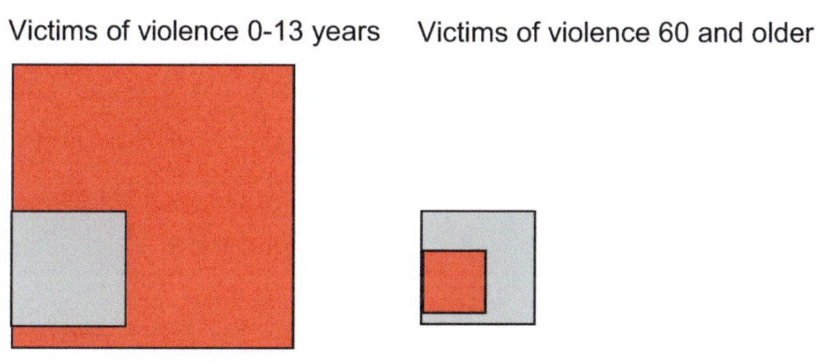

Fig. 3 Children generate a lot of attention as victims of violence, older people are ignored. Number of victims known to the police: *grey*, share of appearances in television reports on violence: *red*. n = 224 victims of violence from 246 television reports which refer to individual crimes of violence and include information about the age of the victims during the period examined (three program weeks in 2012)

The victim of crime should appear as a figure of light in the media in the opinion of an editor of a magazine on private television. “We need a main protagonist, we need a supporting actor: we need a hero, we need a villain.” This explains why journalistic interest, particularly in tabloid journalism, is directed at getting victims of crime—or other people who speak for them—in front of the camera.

3.4 No Sympathy with the Perpetrator

Program producers focus primarily on the victims and those close to them and aim to personalize their suffering and their overcoming of the same, because the journalists interviewed are convinced that seeing someone who reveals his or her feelings brings him or her closer to the audience. What is desirable for victims of crime, however, also proves effective if the figure of the suspect is allowed to take shape. Identification with the culprit is not envisaged though. The culprits remain shadowy, demons in the sense of the word—and thus confirm the thesis of the demonizing of evil (Pfeiffer 2004).

Reports which aim at empathy for a suspect who, for example, was himself once a victim of violence might confuse the audience. One television editor said that he would never write that a defendant had himself been abused by his parents. “Never ever! That doesn’t pull anymore. We would then entertain sympathy for the culprit.” According to the interviewees, ambivalences lessen the effect of a report and are avoided in favor of a personalizing of the side of the victim. Those interviewed express the fear that they might reduce the guilt of the perpetrator if they examine his motives and past life: explanations are equated with excuses. The fact that explanations are not given is not because they are not available but because journalists do not even look for them.

At the same time, those surveyed clearly reject expressions which pass judgment and which are sometimes used in tabloid newspapers and by journalists themselves when speaking about defendants. “Television is currently trying very hard to be grown up, private television, as well. And there are efforts to achieve a high level of political correctness”, says a TV producer from a private channel. “We report, but we don’t say ‘the beast’, ‘the sex beast’, ‘the monster’, or ‘the scumbag’.”

3.5 Child Abusers in the Stocks

Many journalists do not distinguish sensitively between suspects and those condemned. They often reach verdicts of guilt long before the courts and also when suspects deny the accusations made against them. People who are suspected of sexually abusing children are seen as a “swine” or “real scum”. “People who do such things shall never feel safe”, said a reporter who lured suspected pedophiles in front of the camera with a teenager as a decoy. In such cases, some of the journalists interviewed think it is a good idea to pillory in the literal sense of the word—that is, to punish suspects by uncovering them and exposing them to attacks from the public. Fantasies go as far as causing suspects to commit suicide.

These fantasies are, however, rarely realized. Senior television staff consider it unacceptable for such desires for punishment to be fulfilled. Open attacks and visible exposure are taboo. If the desire for punishment becomes visible, interviewees in senior positions claim to remove this from broadcast material. "We take that all out", says a magazine editor, "because we then suddenly find ourselves in the role of the executioner—and we don't want to be that." And an editor of a public television news program adds that a personal preference or an antipathy is a reason not to show a report in the first place.

The television professionals interviewed revealed that when they report on criminal violence, the audience's fear of crime is of central importance to them. However, they do not want to distress their audience. The fear has to be dissipated so it does not become a lasting burden for their viewers and allow for openness for new emotions to be created. And the television audience's sympathy with suffering people is seen as finite. "We have to reconcile the viewer", is said in one of the research interviews, "so that he doesn't lose his lust for life. He has to switch on again tomorrow."

Does violence guarantee high viewing figures as is sometimes assumed? Only to a certain extent say television producers—only when it is good for emotionalizing. Journalists from private television are of the opinion that violence has to be "measured out in homeopathic doses like chili". In the editorial departments of public television, the predominant opinion is that their audiences expect a reserved style of reporting. For this reason, the percentage of reports on violence is especially low.

It is only in the tabloid magazines on public television that violence is measured out in high doses. For the audiences of these shows, who are on average in their mid-sixties, seem to have a greater tendency to be afraid of criminality and to appreciate the numerous reports on the cruel world out there. People who are frightened of something, says a magazine editor from public television, "naturally let themselves be inspired by such reports".

4 Conclusion

The reporter on court cases for the German news magazine *Der Spiegel,* Gisela Friedrichsen (2012), criticizes an increasing emotionalizing in the presentation of crime, which revolves mainly around the victims. As she sees it, they are marketed by so-called victim lawyers and misused as icons of injury in order to stir up the mood against the defendant. According to Friedrichsen, the battle for public opinion and the published opinion already begins before the court case and she warns that the media should not succumb to the temptation to act as a pillory.

Ulrich Meyer, a television reporter of many years' standing, nuances this question differently: "For us today polarizing means: people to whom life has done violence want to see themselves on television as victims, or at least as affected and want to see: who is responsible? Who is the bastard behind all this, who is the culprit? If a television report of this kind is to work for viewers, we need someone who is responsible, a culprit." (Meyer 2012, p. 62).

For the former German Minister of Justice Sabine Leutheusser-Schnarrenberger (2012, p. 8), the functionalizing of the media as a pillory is incompatible with the structure of public discourse. According to her, the power of the media, which feeds off the freedom of the press, is not an end in itself. "The way in which journalists report crimes determines the form of the reality represented. The media have a responsibility." But how do the media fulfill this responsibility? And, in view of the growing power of the audience, which expresses itself increasingly via digital channels, the question should be raised: how does the audience do fulfill its responsibility?

Violent criminality is constructed on television according to rules, which can be explained by the interpretations and actions of media producers and in particular by their assumptions about their audiences. The finding of the research group led by Gerbner that the world of television is created with the aim to win over the public is thus confirmed (Gerbner et al. 1980, p. 707). What is surprising is that this theory, which refers to the fictional representation of violence on television, is also valid for reporting. Reports on criminality are obviously produced according to similar patterns as crime dramas.

Should reporting on criminality show the symptomatic and as it were illustrate the temperature curve of a society? Does it want to keep on reproducing the—assumed—clichés of the audience, even if these take on a life of their own? The real creative achievement of journalism lies in the conveying of that which in the eyes of the journalist concerns people, even it does not interest them from the start. It is a question of making the important interesting, as the former president of CNN International Networks, Chris Cramer, demands (Scheithauer 2001).

Journalism compiles contents, which should find their audience. Television programs which disregard the needs of the viewer in an attempt to set high standards cannot unfold their potential. Nonetheless, it should be asked what the information provided by television is worth if reporting relies on strong emotions and, by idealizing the victim, constructs an unambiguity which is out of touch with life. Violent criminality cannot be explained without recognizing the ambivalences of human relationships. It cannot be represented without nuances, cannot be explained without contradictions. Therefore a new debate on professional responsibility and quality in journalism is needed—also and all the more so with a view to the audience.

At the same time, television producers have a personal responsibility towards the people with whom they come into contact. For the victims of violence, crimes are real in their pain and their loss. As objects of media processing, victims become a part of a play. It is cynical when journalists speak of violence towards children as an article for sale. Media producers should not lose sight of the fact that they are reporting on people and that they must prevent those who are suffering from becoming traumatized a second time.

Moreover, journalists must realize that they change a society if they stir up fears without thinking. Fear is not a good adviser—neither in our daily lives nor in political reality. A society, which is governed by fears instead of rationality tends to greater strictness and tougher sentencing but does not become safer for it.

Journalistic responsibility also extends to those who fall under suspicion, possibly wrongly so. Some of those interviewed speak angrily of suspects as being detestable. They base their judgments on the moment instead of on lengthy court cases. As understandable as their anger occasionally may be, they need to reflect upon their emotions if they are to act responsibly. Finally, in everyday journalism, court-proof evidence is hardly mentioned, only suspicions—which can also prove to be wrong.

In daily journalism, there is hardly room for feelings and stress. Unlike in the police force, supervision is unheard of in many editorial departments. It is therefore hardly possible to reflect upon the emotions of the moment or even upon professional cynicism. Media studies have also hardly concentrated on violence with a view to those who encounter it and process it for the media. Research in this area could make its contribution not only to a founded discussion on quality and responsibility, but also to bring a greater awareness that the afore mentioned dynamic process of “creating” or “reflecting” images, opinions, and beliefs, especially when it unwarrantedly stirs the fear of violence, may throw off the balance of criminal and penal policy of any country, even of one which most profoundly pursues the precepts of sustainable, that is well balanced, socio-economic development.

For the present study, journalists from across Germany’s television landscape have provided insights into the media ghost train and have shown themselves to be most willing to talk about their patterns of decision and action—and as open to a self-critical examination of these patterns. Their openness and curiosity give rise to hope for a fruitful discussion—and for more journalistic responsibility in Germany, if not also elsewhere.

Five Questions

1. What are the motives of journalists when they report on crime?
2. Why are media images so different from the picture that is drawn by statistical data?
3. What do the victims have in common who are reported on most often?
4. How does journalism influence society and specifically crime politics?
5. Is the audience an object of media influences or a subject in the selection of media contents?

References

Albrecht, H.-J. (2004). Öffentliche Meinung, Kriminalpolitik und Kriminaljustiz. In M. Walter, H. Kania, & H.-J. Albrecht (Eds.), *Alltagsvorstellungen von Kriminalität – Individuelle und gesellschaftliche Bedeutung von Kriminalitätsbildern für die Lebensgestaltung* (pp. 491–520). Münster: LIT.

Altheide, D. L., Gray, B., Janisch, R., et al. (2001). News constructions of fear and victim: An exploration through triangulated qualitative document analysis. *Qualitative Inquiry, 7*(3), 304–321.

Altheide, D. L. (2002). *Creating fear: News and the construction of crisis*. New York: Walter de Gruyter.

Alvarez, L. (2011). Justice for Jessica: A Human Rights Case Study on Media Influence, Rule of Law, and Civic Action in India. Honors Theses, Paper 49. Online: http://diginole.lib.fsu.edu/uhm/49.

Ardanaz, A., Corbacho, A., & Ruiz-Vega, M. (2013). Mind the Gap: Bridging Perception and Reality with Crime Information. Inter-American Development Bank. Online: http://www.inesad.edu.bo/bcde2013/papers/BCDE2013-28.pdf.

Baier, D., Kemme, S., Hanslmaier, M., Doering, B., Rehbein, F., & Pfeiffer, C. (2011). Kriminalitätsfurcht, Strafbedürfnisse und wahrgenommene Kriminalitätsentwicklung. Ergebnisse von bevölkerungsrepräsentativen Befragungen aus den Jahren 2004, 2006 und 2010 KFN-Forschungsbericht 117). Hannover: Kriminologisches Forschungsinstitut Niedersachsen.

Baumann, U. (1995). Das Bild des Opfers in der Kriminalitätsdarstellung der Medien. Ergebnisse einer Untersuchung. Mainzer Schriften zur Situation von Kriminalitätsopfern, Band 13. Mainz: Weißer Ring.

Baurmann, M. C. (2004). Monster und Supermänner? Mythen und Realitäten über Tatverdächtige, Straftäter und die polizeiliche Ermittlungsarbeit. In: Walter, M., Kania, H. and Albrecht, H.-J. (Ed.): Alltagsvorstellungen von Kriminalität. Individuelle und gesellschaftliche Bedeutung von Kriminalitätsbildern für die Lebensgestaltung (Kölner Schriften zur Kriminologie und Kriminalpolitik, Band 5) (pp. 435–455). Münster: Lit.

Bohn, I., Hamburger, F., & Rock, K. (1995). Polizei und Presse. Eine Untersuchung zum "staatlich genährten" Rassismus am Beispiel der Berichterstattung über Sinti und Roma, Jahrbuch für Antisemitismusforschung (4), 166–183.

Bonfadelli, H. (2004). *Medienwirkungsforschung I. Grundlagen und theoretische Perspektiven. 3 überarbeitete*. Konstanz: UVK.

Bourdieu, P. (1998). *Über das Fernsehen*. Frankfurt am Main: Suhrkamp.

Buckler, K., & Travis, T. (2005). Assessing the newsworthiness of homicide events: An analysis of coverage in the Houston Chronicle. *Journal of Criminal Justice and Popular Culture, 12*(1), 1–25.

Bundeskriminalamt (1989). Polizeiliche Kriminalstatistik (PKS) 1988. Wiesbaden: Bundeskriminalamt.

Bundeskriminalamt (2013). Polizeiliche Kriminalstatistik (PKS) 2012. Wiesbaden: Bundeskriminalamt.

Burkart, R. (2004). Kommunikationswissenschaft. Grundlagen und Problemfelder. Umrisse einer interdisziplinären Sozialwissenschaft (4., überarb. u. akt. Aufl.). Wien, Köln und Weimar: Böhlau.

Cantor, J. (2003). Media violence and interventions: The roles of communication and emotion. In B. Jennings, D. Roskos-Ewoldsen, & J. Cantor (Eds.), *Communication and emotion. Essays in honor of Dolf Zillmann* (pp. 287–306). Mahwah, NJ: Erlbaum.

Carter, R. E. (1959). Racial identification effects upon the news story writer. *Journalism Quarterly, 36*(3), 284–290.

Cavender, G., & Bond-Maupin, L. (1993). Fear and loathing on reality television. An analysis of "America's most wanted" and "unsolved mysteries". *Sociological Inquiry, 63*(3), 305–317.

Cavender, G., & Fishman, M. (Eds.). (1998). *Entertaining crime. Television reality programs.* New York: Aldine du Gruyter.

Chermak, S. (1995). *Victims in the news: Crime and the American news media.* Boulder, CO: Westview Press.

Chiricos, T., Eschholz, S., & Gertz, M. (1997). Crime, news and fear of crime: Toward an identification of audience effects. *Social Problems, 44*(3), 342–357.

Chiricos, T., Padgett, K., & Gertz, M. (2000). Fear, TV news, and the reality of crime. *Criminology, 38*(3), 755–785.

Cohen, S. (2003). *Folk devils and moral panics* (3rd ed.). London: Taylor and Francis.

Cohn, R. (1975). *Von der Psychoanalyse zur Themenzentrierten Interaktion.* Stuttgart: Klett-Cotta.

Coleman, R. (2011). Color blind: race and the ethical reasoning of Blacks on journalism dilemmas. *Journalism and Mass Communication Quarterly, 2*(88), 337–351.

Custers, K., Van den Bulck, J. (2012). The cultivation of fear of sexual violence in women Processes and moderators of the relationship between television and fear. *Communication Research, XX*(X), 1–29.

Derwein, C. (1995). *Wie wird Kriminalität in der Presse dargestellt, ist die Darstellung wirklichkeitsfremd und gibt es Entsprechungen im Vorstellungsbild der Bevölkerung? Dissertation an der Universität Frankfurt am Main.* Frankfurt a. Main: Selbstverlag.

Dixon, T. L., & Linz, D. (2000). Race and the misrepresentation of victimization on local television. *Communication Research, 27*(5), 547–573.

Eschholz, S., Chiricos, T., & Gertz, M. (2003). Television and fear of crime: Program types, audience traits, and the mediating effect of perceived neighborhood racial composition. *Social Problems, 50*(3), 395–415.

Fenton, F. (1910). The influence of newspaper presentations upon the growth of crime and other anti-social activity. *The American Journal of Sociology, 16*(3), 342–371.

Fishman, M. (1978). Crime waves as ideology. *Social Problems, 25*(5), 531–543.

Fishman, M. (1980). *Manufacturing the news.* Austin, USA: University of Texas Press.

Friedrichsen, G. (2002). Mord und Medien. In: Egg, R. (Ed.): Tötungsdelikte - mediale Wahrnehmung, kriminologische Erkenntnisse, juristische Aufarbeitung. Kriminologie und Praxis, Schriftenreihe der Kriminologischen Zentralstelle (36). Wiesbaden: Kriminologische Zentralstelle, 21-30.

Friedrichsen, G. (2004). "Unheilige Allianzen" und die Macht der Bilder: Einige Bemerkungen zur zunehmenden Emotionalisierung der Kriminalberichterstattung. In M. Walter, M., Kania, H. and H.-J. Albrecht (Ed.), Alltagsvorstellungen von Kriminalität. Individuelle und gesellschaftliche Bedeutung von Kriminalitätsbildern für die Lebensgestaltung. Kölner Schriften zur Kriminologie und Kriminalpolitik (5), 199-207. Münster: Lit.

Friedrichsen, G. (2012). Wie die Medien Emotionen schüren: Kriminalität als Nervenkitzel, in: Hestermann, T. (Ed.): Von Lichtgestalten und Dunkelmännern. Wie die Medien über Gewalt berichten (pp.43–57). Wiesbaden: Springer VS.

Früh, W. (2001). *Gewaltpotentiale des Fernsehangebots. Programmangebot und zielgruppenspezifische Interpretation.* Wiesbaden: Westdeutscher Verlag.

Früh, W., & Schönbach, K. (1982). Der dynamisch-transaktionale Ansatz. Ein neues Paradigma der Medienwirkungen. *Publizistik, 27*(1), 74–88.

Früh, W., & Schönbach, K. (2005). Der dynamisch-transaktionale Ansatz III: Eine Zwischenbilanz. *Publizistik, 50*(1), 4–20.

Garland, D. (2002). *The culture of control: Crime and social order in contemporary society.* Oxford: Oxford University Press.

Garofalo, J. (1981). Crime and the Mass media: A selective review of research. *Journal of Research in Crime and Delinquency, 18*(2), 319–348.

Gerbner, G., & Gross, L. (1976). Living with television. The violence profile. *Journal of Communication, 26*(2), 173–199.

Gerbner, G., Gross, L., Signorielli, N., & Morgan, M. (1980). Television violence, victimization, and power. *American Behavioral Scientist, 23*(5), 705–716.

Gerbner, G., Gross, L., Morgan, M., & Signorielli, N. (1994). Growing up with television: The cultivation perspective. In: J. Bryant, & D. Zillmann (Ed.), *Media effects. Advances in theory and research (S.)* (pp. 17–41). Hillsdale, NJ/Hove, UK: Lawrence Erlbaum Associates, Publishers.

Graber, D. A. (1980). *Crime news and the public*. New York: Praeger.

Grimm, P., Kirste, K., & Weiß, J. (2005). Gewalt zwischen Fakten und Fiktionen. Eine Untersuchung von Gewaltdarstellungen im Fernsehen unter besonderer Berücksichtigung ihres Realitäts- bzw. Fiktionalitätsgrades. Berlin: Vistas.

Groebel, J., & Gleich, U. (1993). *Gewaltprofil des deutschen Fernsehprogramms: eine Analyse des Angebots privater und öffentlich-rechtlicher Sender*. Opladen: Leske und Budrich.

Gross, K. (2006). Covering Crime in Washington, D.C.: Examining the Nature of Local Television News Coverage of Crime and its Effect on Emotional Response, Forschungspapier R-28. Cambridge, USA: Joan Shorenstein Center, John. F. Kennedy School of Government, Harvard University.

Gruenewald, J., Pizarro, J., & Chermak, S. (2009). Race, gender, and the newsworthiness of homicide incidents. *Journal of Criminal Justice, 37*, 262–272.

Hestermann, T. (1997). *Verbrechensopfer – Leben nach der Tat*. Reinbek: Rowohlt.

Hestermann, T. (2003). *Raub, Gewalt und Nervenkitzel. Jugendgewalt und Jugendkriminalität: Ursachen und Auswege* (10th ed.). Hilden: Deutsche Polizeiliteratur.

Hestermann, T. (2009). Das ideale Opfer: jung, weiblich, deutsch. Wie das Fernsehen Gewaltkriminalität darstellt und warum es kaum über Menschenhandel berichtet. *Politische Studien, 60* (427), 47–53.

Hestermann, T. (2010). *Fernsehgewalt und die Einschaltquote. Welches Publikumsbild Fernsehschaffende leitet, wenn sie über Gewaltkriminalität berichten*. Baden-Baden: Nomos.

Hestermann, T. (2011). "Gewalt an Kindern verkauft sich sehr gut": Fernsehberichterstattung über Gewalt. tv diskurs, *15*(1), 44–49.

Hestermann, T. (2012) (Ed.). Von Lichtgestalten und Dunkelmännern. Wie die Medien über Gewalt berichten. Wiesbaden: Springer VS.

Hestermann, T. (2014). Die Gespenster sind unter uns. Dämonisierung in der Berichterstattung über Gewaltverbrechen. In: D. Baier, & T. Mößle (Ed.), *Kriminologie ist Gesellschaftswissenschaft. Festschrift für Christian Pfeiffer zum 70. Geburtstag*. Baden-Baden: Nomos, 261-277.

Höbermann, F. (1989). *Der Gerichtsbericht in der Lokalzeitung: Theorie und Praxis*. Baden-Baden: Nomos.

Hoffmann, A. v. (1992). Attraktion ohne Recherche. Die Kriminalität als Stoff der Medien. *Medium, 22*(2), 58–61.

Jäger, S., Ruth, I., Jäger, M., & Cleve, G. (1998). Von deutschen Einzeltätern und ausländischen Banden: eine Diskursanalyse. *Jungle World, 2*(46).

Karl, C. (2006). Kriminalitätsberichterstattung im Fernsehen: Eine vergleichende empirische Untersuchung zu den Entscheidungsprozessen und zur Vorgehensweise von Journalisten bei der Kriminalitätsberichterstattung anhand zweier ausgewählter TV-Regionalmagazine in den USA und in Deutschland. Magdeburg: Hochschule Magdeburg-Stendal (FH).

Katz, J. (1987). What makes crime news? *Media Culture and Society, 9*(1), 47–75.

Kepplinger, H. M. (2004). Problemdimensionen des Journalismus. Wechselwirkung von Theorie und Empirie. In: Martin Löffelholz (Hrsg.): Theorien des Journalismus: Ein diskursives Handbuch. (2 Ed, pp. 87–106). Wiesbaden: VS.

Kerbel, M. R. (2000). *If it bleeds, it leads. An anatomy of television news*. Boulder, Colorado, USA: Westview Press.

Krause, K. (2014). Supporting the iron fist: Crime news, public opinion, and authoritarian crime control in Guatemala. *Latin American Politics and Society, 56*(1), 98–119.

Krüger, U. M. (2008). InfoMonitor 2007: Unterschiedliche Nachrichtenkonzepte bei ARD, ZDF, RTL und SAT.1. *media perspektiven, 53*(2), 58–83.

Lesche, D. (2001). Fröhlicher Kannibalismus TV-News in der Krise? *message, 3*(2), 43–47.

Leutheusser-Schnarrenberger, S. (2000). Medien als Kriminalpolitiker? In: Bundesministerium der Justiz (Ed.), Kriminalität in den Medien (pp. 182–188.). Godesberg: Forum-Verlag.

Leutheusser-Schnarrenberger, S. (2012). Die Macht der Medien ist kein Selbstzweck. In T. Hestermann (Ed.), *Von Lichtgestalten und Dunkelmännern: wie die Medien über Gewalt berichten* (pp. 7–10). Springer VS: Wiesbaden.

Ludwig, H.-W., & Pruys, G. M. (1998). Gewaltdarstellungen im Fernsehen. Die öffentliche Debatte und die Produktion. In W. Klingler (Ed.), *Fernsehforschung in Deutschland: Themen – Akteure – Methoden (Südwestfunk Schriftenreihe 1, Teilband 2)* (pp. 579–596). Nomos: Baden-Baden.

Maier, M., Ruhrmann, G., & Klietsch, K. (2006). *Der Wert von Nachrichten im deutschen Fernsehen: Ergebnisse einer Inhaltsanalyse 1992–2004*. Düsseldorf: Landesanstalt für Medien Nordrhein-Westfalen.

Maletzke, G. (1998). *Kommunikationswissenschaft im Überblick. Grundlagen, Probleme, Perspektiven*. Opladen: Westdeutscher Verlag.

Mayr, G. (2006). Zwischen Emotionen und Rationalität. Im Strafrecht will die Große Koalition lediglich ergänzen und nachbessern. Hintergrund Politik. [Radio] Deutschlandradio Kultur-Sendung, 14. November 2006. Sendemanuskript. Berlin: Deutschlandradio Kultur.

McManus, J. H. (1994). *Market-driven journalism: Let the citizen beware?* Thousand Oaks, CA: Sage.

Meyer, U. (2012). Das Privatfernsehen als Opfer-TV, in: Hestermann, T. (Ed.): *Von Lichtgestalten und Dunkelmännern. Wie die Medien über Gewalt berichten* (pp. 50–64). Wiesbaden: Springer VS.

Morris, N. (1997). Crime, the media and our public discourse. In J. Q. Wilson, et al. (Hrsg.), *Perspectives on Crime and Justice. 1996-1997 Lecture Series* (99–121). Washington: National Institute of Justice.

Muckenhaupt, M. (1998). Boulevardisierung in der TV-Nachrichtenberichterstattung. In Holly, W. & B. U. Biere (Ed.): Medien im Wandel (pp. 113–134). Opladen: Westdeutscher Verlag.

Oliver, M. B. (1994). Portrayals of crime, race, and aggression in "reality-based" police shows: A content analysis. *Journal of Broadcasting & Electronic Media, 37*(2), 179–192.

Paoli, L. (2004). Verbrechensfurcht und organisierte Kriminalität: "Die Russen-Mafia". In: M. Walter, H. Kania, & H.-J. Albrecht (Ed.), *Alltagsvorstellungen von Kriminalität – Individuelle und gesellschaftliche Bedeutung von Kriminalitätsbildern für die Lebensgestaltung* (287–310). Münster: Lit.

Patterson, T. E. (2000). Doing well and doing good. How Soft News and Critical Journalism Are Shrinking the News Audience and Weakening Democracy – And What News Outlets Can Do About It. Joan Cambridge, Massachusetts: Shorenstein Center on the Press, Politics and Public Policy, John F. Kennedy School of Government, Harvard University.

Peelo, M., Francis, B., Soothill, K., Pearson, J., & Ackerly, E. (2004). Newspaper reporting and the public construction of homicide. *British Journal of Criminology, 44*, 256–275.

Pereira, M. E., Álvaro, J. L., Garrido, A., Machado, D., Dantas, G., Modesto, J. G. N., et al. (2013). The expression of stereotypes of criminals and human rights defenders: A comparative study. *anales de psicología, 29*(2), 565–572.

Pfeiffer, C. (2004). Dämonisierung des Bösen. Frankfurter Allgemeine Zeitung, *56*(55), 9.

Pfeiffer, C., Windzio, M., & Kleimann, M. (2004). Die Medien, das Böse und wir. Zu den Auswirkungen der Mediennutzung auf Kriminalitätswahrnehmung, Strafbedürfnisse und Kriminalpolitik. *Monatsschrift für Kriminologie und Strafrechtsreform, 6*, 415–435.

Pfeiffer, C., Windzio, M., & Kleimann, M. (2005). Media use and its impacts on crime perception, sentencing attitudes and crime policy. *European Journal of Criminology, 2*(3), 259–285.

Proctor, J. L., Badzinski, D. M., & Johnson, M. (2002). The impact of media on knowledge and perceptions of megan's law. *Criminal Justice Policy Review, 13*(4), 356–379.

Raj, A., & McDougal, L. (2014). Sexual violence and rape in India. *The Lancet*, *383*(9920), 865, Elsevier. Online: http://bibliobase.sermais.pt:8008/BiblioNET/Upload/PDF6/004076.pdf.

Reijnders, S. (2005). The people's detective: True crime in Dutch Folklore and popular television. *Media, Culture and Society, 27*(5), 635–651.

Reuband, K.-H. (2007). Steigende Kriminalitätsbedrohung, Medienberichterstattung und Kriminalitätsfurcht der Bürger. In H. Hess, L. Ostermeier, & Paul, B. (Ed.), Kontrollkulturen. Texte zur Kriminalpolitik im Anschluss an David Garland (pp. 71–86). Weinheim: Juventa.

Reuband, K.-H. (2010). Subjektives Kriminalitätserleben im Kontext gesellschaftlicher Transformation. Kriminalitätsfurcht der Ostdeutschen im kollektiven Verlauf und individueller Erinnerung. In A. Groenemeyer (Ed.), Wege der Sicherheitsgesellschaft. gesellschaftliche Transformationen der Konstruktion und Regulierung innerer Unsicherheiten (S.) (pp. 112–162). Wiesbaden: VS.

Roberts, L. D., & Indermaur, D. (2007). Predicting punitive attitudes in Australia. *Psychiatry, Psychology and Law, 14*(1), 56–65.

Roithmeier, K. (1994). *Der Polizeireporter. Ein Leitfaden für die journalistische Ausbildung.* Konstanz: UVK.

Rosenberger, J. S., & Callanan, V. J. (2011). The Influence of media on penal attitudes. *Criminal Justice Review, 36*(4), 435–455.

Rückert, S. (2003). Kriminalität, Medien und Kriminalpolitik. In: E. Minthe (Ed.), Neues in der Kriminalpolitik. Kriminologie und Praxis, Schriftenreihe der Kriminologischen Zentralstelle (42) (pp. 39–47). Wiesbaden: Kriminologische Zentralstelle.

Ruhrmann, G. (2005). Nachrichten zum Fürchten. *Message, 7*(1), 94–96.

Ruhrmann, G., & Göbbel, R. (2007). Veränderung der Nachrichtenfaktoren und Auswirkungen auf die journalistische Praxis in Deutschland. Online: www.netzwerkrecherche.de/docs/ruhrmann-goebbel-veraenderung-der-nachrichtenfaktoren.pdf.

Saleth, S. (2004). Jugendkriminalität im Spiegel der Lokalpresse: Eine Gegenüberstellung der Berichterstattung des Schwäbischen Tagblatts und der Statistik der Jugendgerichtshilfe Tübingen im Zeitraum 1975-2000. Tübingen: Eberhard Karls-Universität Tübingen.

Salter, M. (2013). Justice and revenge in online counter-publics: Emerging responses to sexual violence in the age of social media. *Crime, Media, Culture, 9*(3), 225–242.

Scheithauer, I. (2001). "Wir sind weder Bote noch Botschafter": CNN-International-Chef Chris Cramer über das Selbstverständnis des weltweiten Nachrichtensenders. Frankfurter Rundschau, September 20th.

Schneider, B., Arnold, A.-K., & Greve, W. (2005). Exponentieller Anstieg. Neue Studie zur Berichterstattung über Sexualmorde an Kindern: mehr Beiträge, weniger Emotionen. *Message 7*(1), 97.

Schönbach, K., & Früh, W. (1984). Der dynamisch-transaktionale Ansatz II: Konsequenzen. *Rundfunk und Fernsehen, 32*(3), 314–329.

Schulenburg, C. (2007). Dying to Entertain. Violence on Prime Time Broadcast TV: 1998 to 2006. Los Angeles, CA: Parents Television Council.

Schulz, W. (1989). Massenmedien und Realität. Die "ptolemäische" und die "kopernikanische" Auffassung. In: M. Kaase, & W. Schulz (Ed.), Massenkommunikation. Theorien, Methoden, Befunde. Sonderheft der Kölner Zeitschrift für Soziologie und Sozialpsychologie, 135-149.

Schulz, W. (1997). *Politische Kommunikation. Theoretische Ansätze und Ergebnisse empirischer Forschung zur Rolle der Massenmedien in der Politik.* Opladen: Westdeutscher Verlag.

Shakuntala, R. (2013). Covering rape: The changing nature of society and Indian journalism. University of Wisconsin, Center of Journalism Ethics. Online: http://ethics.journalism.wisc.edu/2013/03/19/covering-rape-the-changing-nature-of-society-and-indian-journalism/.

Smaus, G. (1978). Funktion der Berichterstattung über Kriminalität in den Massenmedien. *Kriminologisches Journal, 10*(3), 187–201.

Sotirovic, M. (2003). How individuals explain social problems: The influences of media use. *Journal of Communication, 53*, 122–137.

Spiranovic, C. A., Roberts, L. D., & Indermaur, D. (2012). What predicts punitiveness? An examination of predictors of punitive attitudes towards offenders in Australia. *Psychiatry, Psychology and Law, 19*(2), 249–261.

Steffens, L. (1931). *The autobiography of Lincoln Steffens*. New York: Harcourt, Brace.
Stieler, K. (1969). Zeitungs Lust und Nutz. Vollständiger Neudruck der Originalausgabe von 1695, hrsg. von Gert Hagelweide. Bremen: Schünemann.
Swanson, C. E. (1955). What they read in 130 daily newspapers. *Journalism Quarterly, 32*(4), 411–421.
Tekolf, O. (2005). Schillers Pitaval. Merkwürdige Rechtsfälle als ein Beitrag zur Geschichte der Menschheit, verfasst, bearbeitet und herausgegeben von Friedrich von Schiller 1792, kommentiert von Oliver Tekolf. Frankfurt am Main: Eichborn.
Vasterman, P. (2005). Media-hype: Self-reinforcing news waves, journalistic standards and the construction of social problems. *European Journal of Communication, 20*(4), 508–530.
Voß, P. (Ed.). (2002). *Wem gehört der Rundfunk? Medien und Politik in Zeiten der Globalisierung*. SWR Schriftenreihe – Medienpolitik (Vol. 2). Baden-Baden: Nomos.
Walter, M. (1994): Gedanken zur Bedeutung von Kriminalität in den Medien. In P.-A. Albrecht (Hrsg.), Festschrift für Horst Schüler-Springorum zum 65. Geburtstag (pp. 123–136). Köln, Berlin, Bonn, München: Heymann.
Walter, M. (1999). Von der Kriminalität in den Medien zu einer bedrohlichen Medienkriminalität und Medienkriminologie? *DVJJ-Journal, 10*(4), 348–354.
Weischenberg, S., & Scholl, A. (1998). *Journalismus in der Gesellschaft: Theorie, Methodologie und Empirie*. Opladen: Westdeutscher Verlag.
Welch, K. (2007). Black criminal stereotypes and racial profiling. *Journal of Contemporary Criminal Justice, 23*(3), 276–288.
Windzio, M., & Kleimann, M. (2006). Die kriminelle Gesellschaft als mediale Konstruktion? Mediennutzung, Kriminalitätswahrnehmung und Einstellung zum Strafen. *Soziale Welt, 57*(2), 193–215.
Windzio, M., Simonson, J., Pfeiffer, C., & Kleimann, M. (2007). Kriminalitätswahrnehmung und Punitivität in der Bevölkerung - Welche Rolle spielen die Massenmedien? Ergebnisse der Befragungen zu Kriminalitätswahrnehmung und Strafeinstellungen 2004 und 2006.KFN-Forschungsbericht Nr. 103. Hannover: Kriminologisches Forschungsinstitut Niedersachsen.
Winterhoff-Spurk, P. (1994). Gewalt in Fernsehnachrichten. In M. Jäckel & P. Winterhoff-Spurk (Eds.), Politik und Medien. Analysen zur Entwicklung der politischen Kommunikation (pp. 55–70). Berlin: Vistas.
Xie, W., & Newhagen, J. E. (2012). The effects of communication interface proximity on user anxiety for crime alerts received on desktop, laptop, and hand-held devices. *Communication Research, XX*(X), 1–29.
Zenz, G. (1978). Einleitung zur deutschen Ausgabe. In: R. E. Helfer, & C. H. Kempe (Eds.) *Das geschlagene Kind* (pp. 17–34). Frankfurt am Main: Suhrkamp Taschenbuch.
Zillmann, D. (2004). Emotionspsychologische Grundlagen. In R. Mangold, P. Vorderer, & G. Bente (Eds.), *Lehrbuch der Medienpsychologie* (pp. 101–128). Göttingen u.a.: Hogrefe Verlag für Psychologie.

Epilogue

I have recently attended the United Nations Congress on Crime Prevention and Criminal Justice in Doha, Qatar, where Member States adopted the "Doha Declaration on integrating crime prevention and criminal justice into the wider United Nations agenda to address social and economic challenges and to promote the rule of law at the national and international levels, and public participation".

This wider United Nations agenda involves the United Nations sustainable development goals for the period 2016–2030.

My own international law education and one and a half year involvement as the President of the Economic and Social Council, the United Nations' principal organ for coordination and policy guidance with regard to its development agenda, prompts me to contribute a few reflections on the meaning of justice which is necessary to end poverty and fight inequalities, promote safe and peaceful societies and strong institutions.

This book addresses the impact of socio-economic inequality in countering crime and victimization of women and children. Building a safe and peaceful future for women and children—the "succeeding generations"—is the leitmotif of all its contributors.

This very focused call in the name of justice to end absolute poverty—the root cause of crime—should be an invitation for all the United Nations entities to "deliver as one" in achieving the agreed goals of sustainable development. Partnerships of all kinds will become ever more important involving government agencies, the private sector, civil society, academia, philanthropic foundations and faith-based organizations. This collaboration will prove critical for the implementation of the new development agenda.

The Thirteenth UN Congress on Crime Prevention and Criminal Justice stressed the need to integrate crime prevention, criminal justice and other rule-of-law aspects into the domestic educational systems. It called for awareness-raising programmes that convey key values based on the rule of law, to be accompanied by economic and social policies promoting equality, solidarity and justice, and

H. Kury et al. (eds.), *Women and Children as Victims and Offenders: Background, Prevention, Reintegration*, DOI 10.1007/978-3-319-08398-8

reaching out to young people, as agents of positive change. The Congress emphasized that education for all young people, including the eradication of illiteracy, is fundamental for the prevention of crime and corruption. Equally, the promotion of a culture of lawfulness that supports the rule of law and human rights while respecting cultural identities is important. In this regard, the Congress also pointed at the fundamental role of youth participation in crime prevention efforts. The Congress emphasized the need to create a safe, positive and secure learning environment in schools, as well as protecting children from all forms of violence, harassment, bullying, sexual abuse and drug abuse. Educators and practitioners from many countries contributed to this book with different perspectives, hopefully broadening our understanding of conditions around the world.

I hope that the book's gender and age-specific research will contribute to policy recommendations regarding women and youth to be more fully inscribed into the wider post-2015 United Nations development agenda.

Finally, I hope that readers may be stimulated to contribute their own ideas and energies to the sustainable development goals, in multi-stakeholder partnerships, for the benefit of peace and the succeeding generations.

Ambassador Martin Sajdik
70th President of the Economic and Social Council
Former Permanent Representative of Austria to the United Nations
in New York
Doha, Qatar/Vienna, Austria/New York, NY, USA
2015

Post Scriptum

The United Nations Post-2015 Sustainable Development Agenda and Education in a Culture of Lawfulness

When the editors of these two volumes planed this publication they did not yet fully realise the enormity of the global refugee crisis and the problems the steady stream of asylum seekers into Western Europe would present. What we experience today is not new: the first victims of violent conflicts are always the weakest groups in society—women and children. Among the refugees who have reached in the past weeks and months Western Europe are many women and children, and many of these children have been separated from their parents and are thus even more helpless and vulnerable. Given the large numbers, aid organisations are stretched to their limits and cannot always give even the basic support the refugees would need (Kurz-Adam 2015).

In armed conflicts today the majority of victims are usually women and children. Sometimes the crimes against them have a (wrongly interpreted) religious base; religious traditions may also elevate men to a privileged position. Apart from cases of severe domestic violence, the development potentialities of women are also frequently blocked through a lack of access to education and jobs. Several chapters in the two volumes provide well-documented examples of this phenomenon (see in particular the chapters by Mehrdad and Byouki or by Pakzad and Alipour). It would however be wrong to think in this context only of developing countries, even if in some of them the situation is particularly serious. Industrialized countries too have not achieved complete equality of the sexes, for instance as far as salaries are concerned, or in the treatment of men and women by political institutions (Kury 2015). The serious victimisation of children and women often leads to their life-long traumatisation. This in turn generates considerable costs for society, not to speak of the ethical implications. As Zedner (2002, p. 429) points out: "Personal crimes such as physical and sexual assault commonly entail longer-term effects",

H. Kury et al. (eds.), *Women and Children as Victims and Offenders: Background, Prevention, Reintegration*, DOI 10.1007/978-3-319-08398-8

and she adds: "General feelings of vulnerability among women, ethnic minorities, and the poor also increase the impact of crime" (ibid., p. 429ff.). Similarly, Skogan (1986) identified four key factors that increase the level of traumatisation: isolation, lack of resources, vulnerability and previous experience. Female refugees are in this context particularly vulnerable.

Compared to their victimisation rates, the role played by women and children as actual delinquents appears rather secondary. If we take Germany as an example of an industrialised society, the proportion of women suspected of having committed an offence registered by the police was 25.7 % in 2013. As far as children were concerned (under 14 years of age) their share was only 3.3 %, for youths (14 to and including 17 years old) it was 9.1 %, and for young adults (18 to below 21 years) 9.0 %. In other words, 78.6 % of all registered offences were committed by adults (21 years and older) (Bundeskriminalamt 2014). It should be added that women and children as a rule also commit less serious offences than older youth and men. Furthermore, we must keep in mind that the age of criminal responsibility is not the same in all countries, and sometimes it is lower for women than for men (see for example Pakzad and Alipour in these volumes).

A feminist criminology, dealing particularly with such questions, has only been developed in Western industrialised countries in the 1970s and 1980s (see Hartmann and Sundt 2011; Schneider 2014, p. 443ff.). Formerly, female offenders had been often considered as suffering from a personality disorder, and the "male part" of their deviant behaviour was usually overlooked (see Lombroso and Ferrero 2004). Social causes of female delinquency were rarely taken into account, but this was also the case for male delinquent behaviour. In public discussion and in media reporting the offender is often presented as he is "now" and what counts is what he has done "now" (see for instance the chapter by Hestermann in these volumes). The question why he became an offender is rarely asked. Politicians and the public tend to content themselves with the "classical" notion that all that is needed is harsher punishment to solve "the problem" (see the chapters of Hermann and Dölling or Zapatero in these volumes, also Kury and Shea 2011; Kury 2015). Collateral damages caused by incarceration for the offender and his family are rarely taken into account (see Beichner and Hagemann, Robertson et al., or Allen in these volumes). Even if alternatives to imprisonment have been rediscovered in many countries, traditional sentences are still the norm (see the chapters of Dandurand, Hamilton and Yarrow, Ehret et al. or Kury in these volumes).

Over the last few decades, criminological research has increasingly stressed the importance of (unfavourable) conditions of early socialisation for the emergence of deviant or delinquent behaviour (see Farrington, Nores und Barnett or Marshall in these volumes). The psychological damage that children and young people experience, who have to flee their home country may have a negative impact on their socialisation that may later result in deviant behaviour. Much depends on how well the host country is able to integrate them and in particular give them access to education and professional training, in order to enable them to find satisfying jobs and a sufficient income for their needs (see in particular Barberet in these volumes).

In the book "Revisiting Keynes. Economic Possibilities for our Grandchildren", one of its authors reminded us how naïvely Keynes assumed the total eradication of poverty in today's world (Baumol 2010, p. 203). When the United Nations were established in 1945 this naïve assumption still prevailed. At the time of the adoption of the UN Charter, its stipulation to promote higher standards of living, full employment, and conditions of economic and social progress and development, and the solutions of international economic, social, health, and related problems and international cultural and educational cooperation (art. 55) implied a nearly linear progression from poverty to affluence. In fact, only sixty years later, at the end of the First United Nations Decade for the Eradication of Poverty (1997–2006), according to the World Bank's analysis the total number of people in the world living on less than US$1.25 a day has begun to decrease sharply (Chen and Ravallion 2008). Not the immediate post-Second World War generation, but the likewise impoverished people succeeding it could start experiencing substantial improvements in the quality of life. If this trend continues, from the current one billion poorest people, by 2030 there may be none left—a very hopeful and inspiring vision for the United Nations post-2015 sustainable development agenda. We should however also take note that at the same time in industrialised countries, in Germany for instance, the gap between rich and poor is growing: whereas the middle class is shrinking the number of the very rich and very poor—the latter especially among the elderly—is growing.

The post-2015 agenda envisions also a substantial reduction in various forms of crime, in particular of organised crime and corruption. Here too, we should not lose sight of the fact that closer international ties, the opening of borders, for instance in the European Union, or new technologies such as the internet create new opportunities for criminal activities, many aimed at women and children, such as trafficking in persons, (child-)pornography and sexual exploitation (see e.g. the chapters by Kangaspunta et al., Howell, or Quirchmayr et al. in these volumes).

Poverty eradication is certainly an important step in the fight against crime, but it is not enough. Below are seven general suggestions for succeeding generations, suggestions, which must go beyond the confines of economic arguments.

First, because economic inequality or poverty (to use this more colloquial term) as a "root cause" of crime, even if totally eradicated will not put an end to crime. "Causes", "factors" or "motives" are by far more intricate drivers of human nature and crime than is the fixed, compelling and elaborate UN rationale to end absolute poverty by 2030. There is no society without crime, and it can therefore not be the aim to completely wipe out crime but to deal with it more effectively.

The views of two Nobel Prize winners in economics and two winners of the Stockholm Prize in Criminology (contributors to this publication) will be for us a departure point to deliver our final words in these volumes about "Women and Children as Victims and Offenders".

Gary Becker, the first of the two afore mentioned Nobel Prize winners in economics (1992) together with Luis Rayo observed that human nature is insatiable. This is because in nature there is no "absolute" of any kind, as the needs are relative. In a classically utilitarian fashion Becker argues that "as individuals strive to do better, they partly but never fully succeed since their reference points continue to rise along their earning power" (Becker and Rayo 2010, p. 181). And, indeed, the UN analysis suggests that individuals or groups are most likely to engage in crime if they perceive a gap between what they have and what they believe they were deprived of (UN Habitat 2006/2007, pp. 143–144). Here, education and public attitudes play an important role in what the media present as a desirable aim, as "success" in life.

The UN analysis outlined above inscribes itself into a broader observation about the criminogenic role of relative deprivation. It alerts us to the need for preventive education and clear policy decisions that take to a greater extent into account sustainable development goals (SDGs) than is the case now.

Moreover, material and time deprivation do condition each other. "[T]hose who are present-oriented are swept into the future that others have laid out for them" (Rifkin 1995, p. 166). Regarding children, if inattentive parents do not prepare them for mainstream culture's daily routines that ordain kids' lives, their idle time activities may involve drugs and delinquency (Levine 1997, p. 189).

As of 1987 (the year of the first UN definition of sustainable development (SD) by the World Commission on Environment and Development), SD has been understood as "development which meets the needs of the present without compromising the ability of future generations to meet their own needs" (A/42/187, Annex, para. 2). In 2002, UNESCO, in addition, defined the meaning of education in SD. It made SD "a dynamic concept that encompasses a new vision of education that seeks to empower people of all ages to assume responsibility for creating and enjoying a sustainable future" (UNESCO 2002, p. 1).

UNESCO projected into this concept of education key SD issues for teaching and learning, "for example, climate change, disaster risk reduction, biodiversity, poverty reduction, and sustainable consumption". SD "also requires participatory teaching and learning methods that motivate and empower learners to change their behaviour and take action for sustainable development. Education for Sustainable Development consequently promotes competencies like critical thinking, imagining future scenarios and making decisions in a collaborative way" (ibidem).

One author of these volumes (Mitrofanenko) documented this more advanced sense of SD as the intergenerational learning process. This is a welcome orientation that may be helpful in extending this process to other walks of life. However, among one of the complexities of sustainable development in general is that the future Environmental Justice—in societies hopefully more affluent than now, and with generations of people living even longer than now—may be confronted with a far more health-endangering environment than we have now, if it is true that affluence and environmental diseases go hand in hand (Landes 1998, p. 11). In the light of this claim, the United Nations sustainable development agenda 2016–2030 may have to be critically analysed by all concerned.

In his Presidential Address to the American Society of Criminology, Laub (2004) noted that criminology has a developmental life course with specific turning points that allow for innovations in how we understand and respond to crime. The

UN sustainable development agenda has now five such essential interlocked elements: "Planet", "People", "Prosperity", "Peace", and "Partnership" (A/69/L.85).

They may help to project into the post-2015 education (and the crime prevention education for succeeding generations relevant to these volumes) the concepts, methods, and—eventually—mandates and policies that will genuinely and effectively alter the rather superficial ways of dealing with sustainable development in general. Criminology and other disciplines may be helpful if they draw more often and more comprehensively on SD as a fundamental "unit of analysis" for charting social progress. In academic discussions the content of that unit varies more in terms of close ups than generically (Weisburd 2015). The UN generic focus on SD should motivate both academics and field practitioners to invest more in it.

Second, aware of the very energetic and recent review by the United Nations of its sustainable development agenda, we now would like to advance further the SD concept relevant to women and children as offenders and victims of crime. As pointed out in these volumes by Jan Van Dijk, winner of the Stockholm Prize in Criminology (2012), violence by intimates is most prevalent in countries where gender inequality is greatest. We therefore propose that the academic and policy-making world should more incisively and comprehensively include in it gender- and age-sensitive crime prevention as a balancing force for countering the criminogenic potential of relative deprivation.

In our view, SD includes a self-generating, creative, albeit also conflicting mechanism for renewing socio-economic and other resources. SD is geared toward their multiplication and, generally, the broadening of human intergenerational capital in any creative area of humankind, including science and education—the necessary doorway to a change in mind-set and behaviour. To live in and pursue a culture of lawfulness necessitates a change in behaviour by everyone. Citizens, companies, local and regional authorities, governments and international institutions are called to counter the threats looming over our planet (climate change, loss of biodiversity; industrial, health and security risks; excessive but preventable economic and social inequality, likewise crime and victimization levels, and so on), in the SD gender and age-sensitive crime prevention manner. This includes new paradigms, such as Restorative Justice (see the relevant chapters in volume 2), but should also include more incisively innovative anti-corruption policies.

In support of this proposal, we would like to recall what James J. Heckman, winner of the Nobel Prize in economics (2000) and David Farrington, winner of the Stockholm Prize in Criminology (2013) and many other distinguished researchers have been communicating to the world. They all emphasize that the sooner children, their parents and other educators engage in the prevention of conflict with the law, the better returns this yields for the law-abiding conduct of the children later (Heckman 2008; Farrington in these volumes). At the same time, the important role of just and visible social policies has to be stressed.

Third, the (un)successful intergenerational transmission of values is relevant to the broad interpretation of sustainable development outlined above. For instance, if one agrees that it is very difficult to alter the personal dispositions of criminals, would this not be a strong reason to modify their behaviour by changing social and situational risk factors and their perceptions of those factors (social and situational crime prevention)? Can this be done by assisting communities in developing and pursuing legitimate ownership of certain crime prevention activities, so they themselves facilitate an investment climate to prosper in the future? If such communities fail, what else can be done to prevent humanely and effectively crime?

Fourth, both questions suggest the need of a critical and multidimensional analysis of the relevance of criminological theories from their aetiological and preventive side to see whether or not they account for SD. SD is a global and universal idea of such a high rank that it breaks all intellectual clichés. It opens a path to a broader reconceptualization and verification of the suitability of criminological ideas, especially the older ones. Some of them could stand the test, others not. Basically, several sociological theories, most particularly those belonging to social learning theories, would initially qualify for their reinterpretation and verification, if and when they emphasize the importance of equal life chances in making a rational choice of behaviour ("rational choice theory", balance of chances). But also the aetiological theory of relative deprivation would retain its scientific and practical relevance at the present stage of global socio-economic development because its imbalances (sharp inequalities) undermine sustainable development.

Fifth, the concept of sustainable development may be instrumentalized and operationalized in terms of countering particular forms of crime. So far, only the sister term of "alternative development" has practically been applied to counteract one form of organized crime in developing countries—illicit drug cultivation. For the 2016–2030 SDGs, this goes not far enough.

Sixth, critical as this practical application is for countering narcotic drug addiction that "constitutes a serious evil and is fraught with social and economic danger to mankind" (Single Convention on Narcotic Drugs, 520 UNTS 151), these volumes took an interdisciplinary view of sustainable development (see also the experiences with less punitive forms of reacting to illegal drug misuse in Portugal, Kury and Quintas 2010a, b; Hughes and Stevens 2010, 2012). By if we emphasize that the treatment of women and children is even more fundamental to the future of humankind than the battle against drug addiction (i.e. SDG 3.5). This is because against the historical background of the concept of sustainable development we have to recognise a more basic evil that threatens them—slavery (Landes 1998, ch. 5; Redo 2015, p. 71).

Those deliberating universal moral values wonder whether slavery is an evil that is merely prohibited or *mala in se*. Reportedly, economists claim that the eventual prohibition of slavery was the result of its diminishing exploitation profits, and not the recognition of its inhuman nature (Landes 1998, p. 119). Rather than continuing these endless deliberations, Leszek Kołakowski (1927–2009), a Polish moral philosopher, cut them off. He pointed out that: "When one attempts to derive human rights from historical or anthropological material, these will always be the laws of particular groups, races, classes, nations that on the strength of those laws are free to eliminate or enslave other groups. Humankind is a moral concept, and if we do not accept it, we have neither a good basis to question slavery nor its ideology" (Kołakowski 1990, p. 87).

Eradication of slavery as a universally laudable moral objective is the core ideology of sustainable development, as the UN puts it (SDGs 5.2 and 16.2). To understand this objective's essential role, it must be recalled that the UN origin of sustainable development dates back to the right to self-determination of the post-colonial era. That latter right, in turn, coincides with the UN origin of human rights. It precedes the right to development of countries where that development was earlier debilitated by slavery (Landes 1998, p. 122; Redo 2012, p. 79).

The UN concept of sustainable development can thus only be understood fully when one sees that it intertwines the right to self-determination and the right to development. Internationally, the latter entails not only the compensation for earlier economic exploitation through slavery, but also the shared responsibility of countries and civil societies for the international and intercultural countering of "uncivil societies" implicated in sustainable development problems (A/51/950), whereby slavery/trafficking in people is merely one of them. "Shared responsibility" implies technical assistance in every aspect of sustainable development. For the donor countries, assisting in national capacity building in developing countries to make them more self-sustaining will be a major challenge in the years to come. If that challenge is surmountable, in 2030 sustainable development goals may be met.

Last but not least, and probably most importantly, the United Nations sustainable development agenda 2016–2030 has therefore a stimulating and transformative character. Not only are its goals progressive in the way outlined above, but they also aim at equalizing the life chances with gender mainstreaming that meets the needs of succeeding generations—all this in the name of peaceful, just and inclusive societies.

To this end the UN seeks to advance normatively the rules of our life by contributing to free societies from fear and violence. In this context, the Organization resolved "to protect human rights and promote gender equality and the empowerment of women and girls" (A/69/L.85, pp. 2/35 and 3/35). Surely, in both cases, social justice and other improvements are possible—indeed, for all children and both sexes. Therefore educationists, educators, academics, students, practitioners and others interested in gender mainstreaming, crime prevention and criminal justice reform, and all interested in any of the other sustainable development reforms according to the United Nations agenda, should begin looking into the SDGs soon.

These SDGs will advance the sustainable livelihood of succeeding generations. They also may enrich the academic science with new interdisciplinary background, facts and figures relevant to women and children. They finally can lead to the further evidence-based prevention, reintegration of women and children as offenders and victims of crime and, generally, to further social progress in the world.

A few years ago, a scholar of Polish-German Second World War history and of the difficult time of post-war reconciliation wondered:

> When you look back in history, you cannot but question, what would be today's world like, if all energy, resources and intellectual potential that were dedicated by empires and dictatorships to build ideologies against other nations were spent on universities, schools and common meeting places (Wolff-Powęska 2011).

Let us hope that our successors will find a positive response for the future we want for all.

Freiburg im Breisgau, Germany — Helmut Kury
Wien, Austria — Sławomir Redo
Zürich, Switzerland — Evelyn Shea
October 2015

References

A/42/187. (1987, August 2). Annex, The World Commission on Environment and Development, Our Common Future.

A/51/950 (1997, July 1997). Renewing the United Nations—A Programme for Reform, Report of the Secretary-General.

A/69/L.85. (2015, August 12). Draft outcome document of the United Nations summit for the adoption of the post-2015 development agenda.

Baumol, W. J. (2010). The microtheory of innovative entrepreneurship. In L. Pecchi & G Pigo, (Ed.) MIT Press: Cambridge, MA.

Becker, G. S., & Rayo, L. (2010). Why Keynes underestimated consumption and overestimated leisure for the long run. In L. Pecchi & G. Piga (Eds.), *Revisiting Keynes. Economic possibilities for our grandchildren* (pp. 179–184). Cambridge, MA/London, England: The MIT Press.

Bundeskriminalamt. (2014). *Polizeiliche Kriminalstatistik Bundesrepublik Deutschland. Berichtsjahr 2013*. Wiesbaden: Bundeskriminalamt. http://www.bka.de/DE/Publikationen/PolizeilicheKriminalstatistik/pks__node.html?__nnn=true.

Chen, S., & Ravallion, M. (2008). *The developing world is poorer than we thought, but no less successful in the fight against poverty*. Policy Research Working Paper. World Bank. http://econ.worldbank.org/docsearch

Hartmann, J. L., & Sundt, J. L. (2011) The rise of feminist criminology: Freda Adler. In F. T. Cullen, C. L. Johnson, A. J. Myer, & F. Adler (Eds.), *The origins of american criminology. Advances in criminological theory* (Vol. 16, pp. 205–220). New Brunswick, USA/London, UK.

Heckman, J. J. (2008). The case of investing in disadvantaged young children. In *Big ideas for children: Investing in our nation's future, first focus* (pp. 49–58). Washington, DC.

Hughes, C. E., & Stevens, A. (2010). What can we learn from the Portuguese decriminalization of illicit drugs? *British Journal of Criminology, 50*, 999–1022.

Hughes, C. E., & Stevens, A. (2012). A resounding success or a disastrous failure: Re-examining the interpretation of evidence on the Portuguese decriminalisation of illicit drugs. *Drug and Alcohol Review, 31*, 101–113.

Kołakowski, L. (1990). *Cywilzacja na ławie oskarżonych (Civilization on the defendant's bench)*. Warszawa: Res Publica.

Kury, H., & Quintas, J. (2010a). Zur Wirkung von Sanktionen bei Drogenabhängigen – Argumente für eine rationale Drogenpolitik. *Polizei und Wissenschaft, 1*, 32–56.

Kury, H., & Quintas, J. (2010b). Sanktionen oder Hilfe? Einstellungen zu Drogentätern – Ergebnisse aus Portugal. *Kriminalistik, 64*, 403–409.

Kury, H., & Shea, E. (Eds.). (2011). *Punitivity. international developments* (3 Vols.). Bochum/Germany: Universitätsverlag Dr. Brockmeyer.

Kury, H. (2015). *Punitivity and punishment. Results from different countries*. Bochum/Germany: Universitätsverlag Dr. Brockmeyer.

Kurz-Adam, M. (2015). Jugendhilfe ohne Grenzen? Anmerkungen zur Zukunft der Arbeit mit unbegleiteten minderjährigen Flüchtlingen in der Kinder- und Jugendhilfe. *Zeitschrift für Jugendkriminalrecht und Jugendhilfe, 26*, 272–276.

Landes, D. S. (1998). *The wealth and poverty of nations. Why some are so rich and some so poor.* New York/London: W.W. Norton & Company.

Laub, S. (2004). The life course of criminology in the United States: The American Society of Criminology 2003 presidential address. *Criminology, 42*(1), 1–26.

Levine, R. (1997). *A geography of time. The temporal misadventures of a social psychologist, or how every culture keeps time just a little bit differently*. Oxford: One World.

Lombroso, C., & Ferrero, G. (2004). *Criminal women, the prostitute, and the normal woman.* Durham/London.

Redo, S. (2012). *Blue criminology. The power of United Nations ideas to counter crime globally. A monographic study*. Helsinki: European Institute for Crime Prevention and Control, affiliated with the United Nations.

Redo, S. (2015). The UN criminal justice system in the suppression of transnational crime. In N. Boister & R. Currie (Eds.), *The Routledge handbook of transnational criminal law* (pp. 57–72). Abingdon, Oxon: Routledge.

Rifkin, J. (1995). *The end of work: The decline of the global labor force and the dawn of the post-market era*. New York: Putnam Publishing Group.

Schneider, H. J. (2014). *Kriminologie. Ein internationales Handbuch. Band 1: Grundlagen.* Berlin: De Gruyter.

Single Convention on Narcotic Drugs, 520 UNTS 151

Skogan, W. (1986). The impact of victimization on fear. *Crime and Delinquency, 33*, 135–154.

UN-Habitat. (2006). *State of the world's cities*. London: Earthscan.

UNESCO. (2002). *Education for sustainability - from Rio to Johannesburg: Lessons learnt from a decade of commitment*. Paris: UNESCO.

Weisburd, D. (2015). The 2014 Sutherland address. The law of crime concentration and the criminology of place. *Criminology, 53*(2), 133–157.

Wolff-Powęska, A. (2011, July 16). *Interview: Nienawidze, podziwiam, boje_się (I hate, admire and fear)*. Gazeta Wyborcza. http://wyborcza.pl/1,76498,9953968,Nienawidze_podziwiam_boje_sie.html?as=4&startsz=x#ixzz1Ta0zalek

Zedner, L. (2002). Victims. In M. Maguire, R. Morgan, & R. Reiner (Eds.), *The Oxford handbook of criminology* (pp. 419–456). Oxford: Oxford University Press.

Index[1]

[1] Note: Page numbers in Roman indicate volume 1 and in *Italics* indicate volume 2

H. Kury et al. (eds.), *Women and Children as Victims and Offenders: Background, Prevention, Reintegration*, DOI 10.1007/978-3-319-08398-8

D

H

N

O

MIX
Papier aus verantwortungsvollen Quellen
Paper from responsible sources
FSC® C105338

If you have any concerns about our products,
you can contact us on
ProductSafety@springernature.com

In case Publisher is established outside the EU,
the EU authorized representative is:
Springer Nature Customer Service Center GmbH
Europaplatz 3, 69115 Heidelberg, Germany

Printed by Libri Plureos GmbH
in Hamburg, Germany